MI6

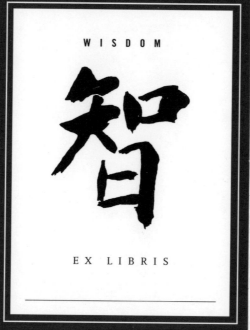

WISDOM

智

EX LIBRIS

Also by Stephen Dorril

The Silent Conspiracy
Smear

with Anthony Summers

Honey Trap

MI6

Inside the Covert World of Her Majesty's
Secret Intelligence Service

Stephen Dorril

The Free Press
NEW YORK   LONDON   TORONTO   SYDNEY   SINGAPORE

MI6 is dedicated to 'The Rodent Catcher'

THE FREE PRESS
A Division of Simon & Schuster Inc.
1230 Avenue of the Americas
New York, NY 10020

First Free Press Edition 2000
First published in Great Britain in 2000 by Fourth Estate Limited

THE FREE PRESS and colophon are trademarks
of Simon and Schuster Inc.

Manufactured in Great Britain.

10 9 8 7 6 5 4 3 2 1

Library of Congress Cataloging-in-Publication Data is available

ISBN 0-7432-0379-8

CONTENTS

LIST OF ACRONYMS

ABN	Anti-Bolshevik Bloc of Nations
ACC	Allied Control Commission
ACEN	Assembly of Captive European Nations
ACUE	American Committee for a United Europe
AIOC	Anglo-Iranian Oil Company
AIS	Anglo-Greek Information Service
AK	Armia Krajowa – Polish Home Army
AKEL	Cypriot Communist Party
AMG	Allied Military Government
ANA	Arab News Agency
ANC	African National Congress
ASIS	Australian Secret Intelligence Service
BAOR	British Army of the Rhine
BCC	Belorussian Central Council/British Control Commission
BCR	Belorussian Central Representation
BCSO	British Central Scientific Office
BFM	British Free Movement
BK	Balli Kombetar – National Front (Albania)
BLEF	British League for European Freedom
BLO	British Liaison Officer
BMEO	British Middle East Office
BND	Bundesnachrichtendienst
BNR	Belorussian National Republic
BoT	Board of Trade
BSC	British Security Co-ordination
BUF	British Union of Fascists
BW	Biological weapons
CBDE	Chemical Biological Defence Establishment
CCF	Congress for Cultural Freedom

CFEU	Conseil Français pour l'Europe Unie
CI	Counter-intelligence
CIA	Central Intelligence Agency
CIB	Central Information Bureau
CIC	Counter-Intelligence Corps
CIG	Central Intelligence Group
CIO	Czech Intelligence Office/Congress of Industrial Organisations
CIOS	Combined Intelligence Objectives Sub-Committee
CO	Constitutional Organisation (Greece)
COCOM	Co-ordinating Committee
COI	Co-ordinator of Information
COSEC	Co-ordinating Secretariat of National Union of Students
CPA	Communist Party of Albania
CPGB	Communist Party of Great Britain
CPI	Central Personality Index
CR	Central Registry
CROWCASS	Central Registry of War Crimes and Security Suspects
CRPO	Combined Research and Planning Organisation
CRW	Counter-revolutionary warfare
CSDIC	Combined Services Detailed Intelligence Centre
CW	Chemical weapons
DAD	Department of the Army Detachment
DCIS	Directorate of Counter-Intelligence and Security
DFP	Directorate of Forward Plans
DIS	Defence Intelligence Staff (Norway)
DP	Displaced Person
DSZ	Delegation of Armed Forces (Poland)
EAM/ELAS	National Liberation Front/National Liberation Popular Army (Greece)
ECA	European Co-operation Administration
EDC	European Defence Community
EDES	National Democratic Hellenic League
EEC	European Economic Community
ELD	Union of Popular Democracy (Greece)
ELEC	European League for Economic Co-operation
ELINT	Electronic intelligence
EM	European Movement
EOKA	National Organisation of Cypriot Combatants
ERP	European Recovery Programme
EUF	European Union of Federalists
EVW	European Voluntary Workers
EYC	European Youth Campaign

FANY	First Aid Nursing Yeomanry
FBI	Federal Bureau of Investigation
FHO	Fremde Heere Ost – Foreign Armies East
FIAT	Field Information Agency (Technical)
FOIA	Freedom of Information Act
FLOSY	Front for the Liberation of South Yemen
FYSA	Fund for Youth and Student Affairs (US)
GC&CS	Government Code and Cipher School
GCHQ	Government Communications Headquarters
GIS	German Intelligence Service
GNA	Greek National Army
GRU	Soviet Military Intelligence
HOP	Croatian Liberation Movement
IAEA	International Atomic Energy Agency
ICFTUE	International Centre of Free Trade Unions in Exile
ICR	International Red Cross
IDC	Imperial Defence College
IDEA	Sacred Bond of Greek Officers
IGCR	Inter-Governmental Committee on Refugees
ILP	Independent Labour Party
INA	Iraqi National Accord
IPG	Imperial Policy Group
IRD	Information Research Department
IRO	International Refugee Organisation
ISB	Information Services Branch
ISC	International Student Conference/Intelligence and Security Co-ordinator/Committee
ISLD	Inter-Services Liaison Department
ISOS	Intelligence Section, Oliver Strachey
IUS	International Union of Students
IUSY	International Union of Socialist Youth
JIB	Joint Intelligence Bureau
JIC	Joint Intelligence Committee
JICMEU	Joint International Committee of the Movement for European Unity
JIO	Joint Intelligence Organisation
JPS	Joint Planning Staff
JSTIC	Joint Scientific and Technical Intelligence Committee
KGB	Soviet Ministry of State Security
KKE	Greek Communist Party
KONR	Committee for the Liberation of the Peoples of Russia
KYP	Greek Central Intelligence Service
LAF	Lithuanian Activist Front

LCC	Latvian Central Council
LCS	London Controlling Section
LFA	Lithuanian Freedom Army
LLY	Labour League of Youth
LNC	Movement of National Liberation (Albania)
MEC	Middle East Command
MECAS	Middle East Centre for Arab Studies
MFV	Motor Fishing Vessel
MEDO	Middle East Defence Organisation
MEID	Middle East Information Department
MGB	Soviet Ministry of State Security
MI(R)	Military Intelligence (Research)
MLSF	Movement of Lithuania's Struggle for Freedom
MoD	Ministry of Defence
MVD	Ministry of Internal Affairs (USSR)
NATO	North Atlantic Treaty Organisation
NCFE	National Committee for a Free Europe (US)
NCIS	National Criminal Intelligence Service
NDFLO-AG	National Democratic Front for the Liberation of Oman and the Arab Gulf
NDH	State of Croatia
NEA	Near East Association
NEABS	Near East Broadcasting Station
NEI	Nouvelles Equipes Internationales
NID	Naval Intelligence Division/Northern Information Department
NKVD	People's Commissariat for Internal Affairs (USSR)
NLF	National Liberation Front (Aden)
NRC	National Research Council
NSA	National Security Agency/National Student Association (US)
NSC	National Security Council
NTS	National Labour Council (Russia)
NUS	National Union of Students
OAU	Organisation of African Unity
OB	Order of battle
OCB	Operation Co-ordination Board (US)
ODESSA	Organisation der ehemaligen SS-Angehörigen
OEEC	Organisation for European Economic Co-operation
OGPU	Unified State Political Directorate (USSR)
OIS	Omani Intelligence Service
OKW	Oberkommando der Wehrmacht
OMi	Nazi Ministry for the Occupied Eastern Territories

ONZA	Bureau of People's Protection (Yugoslavia)
OPC	Office of Policy Co-ordination
ORD	Oman Research Department
OSA	Official Secrets Act
OSO	Office of Special Operations
OSS	Office of Strategic Services
OUN	Organisation of Ukrainian Nationalists
PAP	People's Action Party (Singapore)
PDO	Petroleum Development (Oman)
PEU	Pan-European Union
PFLO-AG	Popular Front for the Liberation of the Occupied Arab Gulf (later Popular Front for the Liberation of Oman and the Arab Gulf)
PHP	Post-Hostilities Planning Sub-Committee
PKI	Indonesian Communist Party
POMEF	Political Office with the Middle East Forces
PoW	Prisoner of war
PPR	Polish Communist Party
PPS	Policy and Planning Staff/Parti Populaire Syrien
PRO	Public Records Office
PSIS	Permanent Secretaries' Intelligence Services
PSL	Polish Peasant Party
PUSC	Permanent Under-Secretary's Committee
PUSD	Permanent Under-Secretary's Department
PWB	Psychological Warfare Branch
PWE	Political Warfare Executive
ROC	Radiation Operations Committee
ROD	Russian Liberation Movement and Army
ROVS	White Russian Armed Services Union
RRF	Russian Revolutionary Force
RYA	Royal Yugoslav Army
SAF	Sultan's Armed Force (Oman)
SAS	Special Air Service
SB	Sluzhba Bezpeky – OUN-B secret police (Ukraine)/Stay Behind
SBS	Special Boat Squadron
SCI	Special Counter-Intelligence
SCLL	Supreme Committee for the Liberation of Lithuania
SDECE	Service de Documentation Extérieure et de Contre-Espionage
SDLP	Social Democratic and Labour Party (Northern Ireland)
SED	East German Communist Socialist Unity Party
SHAEF	Supreme Headquarters Allied Europe Forces

SIGINT	Signals intelligence
SIME	Security Intelligence Middle East
SIS	Secret Intelligence Service
SKE	Socialist Party of Greece
SLEF	Scottish League for European Freedom
SOE	Special Operations Executive
SPA	Special Political Action
SPC	Special Policy Committee
SPP	Slovene People's Party
SRS	Special Refugee Screening
SSU	Strategic Services Unit
SWG	Syria Working Group
TEA	National Defence Corp (Greece)
TUC	Trades Union Congress
UAR	United Arab Republic
UB	Urzad Bezpieczenstwa – Polish Security Service
UDBA	Administration of State Security (Yugoslavia)
UDRM	United Democratic Resistance Organisation (Lithuania)
UDI	Unilateral Declaration of Independence (Rhodesia)
UEM	United Europe Movement
UHVR	Ukrainian Supreme Liberation Council
UN	United Nations
UNRRA	United Nations Refugee and Rehabilitation Administration
UNWCC	United Nations War Crimes Commission
UPA	Ukrainian Insurgent Army
USIS	United States Information Service
WACL	World Anti-Communist League
WAY	World Assembly of Youth
WFDY	World Federation of Democratic Youth
WiN	Freedom and Independence (Poland)
WOSM	War Office Screening Mission
YAR	Yemen Arab Republic

PREFACE

This book concentrates on the postwar activities of the Secret Intelligence Service (SIS), more commonly known as MI6 – the designation of the War Office liaison section attached to its headquarters during and after the Second World War. For far too long our view of MI6 has been distorted by the Establishment's and media's obsession with the activities of traitors such as Kim Philby and George Blake, and the Security Service's (MI5's) hunt for moles, real or imagined.

The book attempts to restore some balance by focusing on what the Service was actually up to during the Cold War – namely, covert 'Special Operations' and the primary task of gathering intelligence. These operations are placed in the context of official British foreign and political policies.

Researching secret agencies – and there are few more secret than MI6 – is obviously a difficult task. Although seemingly committed to a Freedom of Information Act (FOIA), and, in opposition, one of the secret state's sternest critics, Labour Foreign Secretary Robin Cook has accepted MI6's argument that no documents should be released into the Public Records Office (PRO); indeed, MI6 is specifically excluded from any proposed FOIA. The argument goes that the Service must protect its methods and sources; though names can always be blanked out and the fact is that secret service methods have hardly changed for two thousand years. Bascially, agents are recruited through bribery, blackmail and harassment, and targets are put under surveillance and so on for the gathering of intelligence. Only the technical means change, and they are constantly being superseded by private-sector developments.

That is not to say that there are no documents available. As academic Richard J. Aldrich has successfully shown, secret material relating to MI6 can be found in the archives of related departments, while archives in the United States provide a rich and largely untapped source. But as Cold War historian John Lewis Gaddis suggests, human relations, particularly in and between secret agencies, cannot always be reconstructed from documents.

'Conversations occurring in corridors or over the telephone, or at cocktail parties,' Alex Danchev adds, 'can at times shape events more decisively than whole stacks of official memoranda that find their way into the archives.' In order to unravel the activities of MI6,

> one has to dig deep and sift carefully, in the manner of the archaeologist, but also acculturate, like some intrepid anthropologist, to a strange and secretive society whose intricate social and professional networks are familiar to their members but quite baffling to the outsider, whose currency is the informal understanding, and whose transactions consist chiefly of unwritten and sometimes unspoken agreements.

In the main, this book has been researched with the notion that there is far more in the public domain than anyone has realised – least of all the secret agencies. Indeed, a few years ago the Foreign Office's own Security Department was surprised to discover that there are numerous open sources identifying intelligence officers.

Given a work of this size, it was decided to split the book into several parts, each dealing with different areas and aspects of the Service's activities; this will enable the reader to dip into a particular area of interest. Within each part, the chapters run chronologically across a specific timeframe. The prime focus is the European continent, and some areas of the Service's operations and intelligence-gathering, principally in South-East Asia and Africa, are not dealt with in any great detail. It is intended that these areas will be covered in a separate volume on the Security Service, dealing with MI5 and MI6 involvement in counter-insurgency in the Third World. A study of MI6's worldwide stay-behind networks, popularly known as 'Gladio', will be published at a later date.

Secrecy has become an end in itself, and has more of a psychological than a practical element in its continuing hold and fascination. As George Simmel suggests, secrecy offers 'the possibility of a second world alongside the manifest world; and the latter is decisively influenced by the former' – and not always for the good.

The reality is that we are in a world that is exploding with information, even if much of it is valueless and serves only to overwhelm our ability to analyse it. This, though, is only the beginning. Up until now, MI6 has played a successful rearguard action in protecting itself, but it cannot do so for ever. The era of open-source intelligence is upon us. The reality is that secrets are increasingly difficult to protect, and it would not be a great exaggeration to suggest that there are no real secrets any more.

For encouragement and help with sources and information, I would like to thank John Hope, Richard Norton-Taylor, Peter E. Newell, Phillip Knightley,

Mark Watts, Michael Baigent, Armen Victorian, John Birks, Alan Lawrie, Stuart Brown, Kees van der Pijl, Tim Kelsey, Mark Phythian, Henrik Kabala, the Polish ex-Servicemen's Association, friends in Estonia, Morris Riley for his research on Oman, and the late John Maclaren.

There are a number of key writers to whom I owe a large debt for their previous contributions in opening up research in the intelligence field – in particular Tom Bower, whose biography of one of the Service's Chiefs, Sir Dick White, was a landmark in this area. I may not agree with a number of his conclusions and interpretations, but he certainly deserves great credit for his pioneering efforts. Similarly, the American lawyer and former State Department researcher John Loftus was largely responsible, with his fellow-writer, Australian Mark Aarons, for revealing in detail collusion between the extreme right-wing, anti-communist émigré groups and MI6. If the text deals at length with the entangled and often obscure factional and controversial politics of the émigrés, it is because they are integral to any understanding of MI6's sponsorship of these groups and their operations in eastern Europe. It was necessary to overturn a number of the oft-repeated myths and misconceptions that surround the émigrés. On Suez, the work of Keith Kyle and Scott Lucas proved essential, as did that of Mark Urban and James Adams on contemporary developments, Peter Wilkinson and Michael Smith on the Special Operations Executive, and Sir Reginald Hibbert and Nicholas Bethell on Albania.

This book could not have been completed without the sterling and greatly appreciated efforts of the staff of Huddersfield public library. They managed to make available through the British Library lending system hundreds of books from around the world, as well as many obscure articles. Institutions such as this are a precious local resource that should be nurtured and properly funded.

I was fortunate in obtaining grants from the K. Blundell Trust and the Royal Literary Fund, and I am extremely grateful for their help, which came at a crucial time. The book was long delayed partially owing to a debilitating illness. My agent, Andrew Lownie, was a welcome source of encouragement during this trying period, while my publishers were hugely sympathetic. I thank my editors, Christopher Potter and Clive Priddle, for their great patience as deadlines were missed. Partners of writers put up with a lot. Thankfully my wife, Stephanie Smith, has been immensely supportive.

Stephen Dorril
Netherthong, West Yorkshire, April 1999

PART ONE

FROM HOT TO COLD WAR

Where the Chief of the Secret Intelligence Service (MI6), Major-General Sir Stewart Menzies (pronounced 'Mingiss'), celebrated 'Victory in Europe' (VE) day is not known, but it is more than likely that he was standing at the bar of White's Club in St James's where much of the informal business of intelligence work was still undertaken. To an outsider, as Menzies drank pink gins with his friends from the upper echelons of British society, it would have appeared that little had changed since the founding of the Secret Service more than thirty years previously.

Born in 1890 to wealthy Scottish parents, Menzies went to Eton, where, with 'his good looks, fair hair and blue eyes', the 'golden boy' was 'the model of an Edwardian schoolboy hero'. When, in 1912, his father died, his mother married Sir George Holford, a lieutenant-colonel in the Life Guards, the regiment of his new stepson. Also very rich with links to the Royal Family, Holford was equerry to both Edward VII and George V. Menzies treasured the royal connection to the extent that he later helped foster the legend that he was the illegitimate son of Edward.[1]

Involved in heavy fighting at Ypres, Menzies won the DSO and in further action in 1915 was awarded the Military Cross. Transferred to general headquarters, he was assigned to Military Intelligence with responsibility for field security and counter-espionage. Along with his fellow majors in I(b), Menzies helped form a small dining club – a feature prominent throughout British Intelligence – in which they 'could exchange views more intimately than in the Mess'. Friendships made at the club endured and it continued to meet during Ascot week – racing was one of Menzies's abiding passions – and regularly at the Travellers Club.[2]

Regarding intelligence as 'high politics and a rough game to play', Menzies learned in France the valuable lesson for the future that intelligence was 'a commodity of a special kind; it not only has value in itself, but is a vital munition in the in-fighting between competing strategies and organisations'. He remained in the intelligence game after the First World War, joining the Secret Service as personal assistant to its eccentric one-legged chief, Mansfield Cumming, who was known as 'C'.[3]

The Secret Intelligence Service had been founded in October 1909 as the foreign section of the Secret Service Bureau with the task of collecting evidence of German planning for an invasion of the country. It was not long, however, before MI1c, as the foreign section became known, was concentrating its efforts on 'Red Russia'. In 1923 Cumming died 'in harness' and was succeeded by the highly professional former Director of Naval Intelligence, Rear Admiral Hugh 'Quex' Sinclair, who was known as a 'terrific anti-Bolshevik'.[4]

One observer claimed that Menzies remained in the Secret Service for 'psychological' reasons. He was 'by nature very reserved – even at times diffident' and found it more congenial 'to remain in the shadows and exert covert influence'. Officers found him 'a shy, quiet man who displayed 'an aloofness which served him well in maintaining a barrier around him'. This barrier, a junior officer, Desmond Bristow, came to believe, 'whether created purposely or not, kept the crawling members (arse lickers) of the office at bay, and there were quite a few'. One senior colleague remarked that Menzies's cover was 'superb' – 'he posed as himself'. A high Tory, a country gentleman, he spent much of his spare time hunting foxes with the prestigous Beaufort Hunt, whose social connections added to his chief asset in intelligence work – 'his network of like-minded persons throughout Whitehall and the upper reaches of society'.[5]

Menzies was appointed head of MI6's Military and German sections, reaching the rank of colonel in 1932. Seven years later, he was promoted to brigadier and soon after succeeded Sinclair, whose health had failed, in the post of Chief. In truth, Menzies would not have been the first choice of Churchill, who did his best to prevent him becoming 'C' – the unofficial title – but he was to serve the new Prime Minister loyally. During the war, Menzies hardly had a social life and rarely left his desk at Broadway Buildings – symbolically sited between Buckingham Palace and Parliament Square. He continued the tradition of allowing his senior officers unlimited access to C's office with the consequence 'that queues formed outside his room at the end of the corridor, imperfectly controlled by lights, which showed whether or not he was occupied'. The result was that he was overworked and took no leave, and his work suffered from his weariness. One of the Service's up-and-coming stars, Kim Philby, recognised the 'horrible responsibilities that world war had placed on his shoulders' with the 'ever-present threat of a summons from Churchill in one of his whimsical midnight moods'.[6]

Although he remembered him with 'enduring affection', Philby did not consider Menzies a great intelligence officer: 'His intellectual equipment was unimpressive, and his knowledge of the world, and views about it, were just what one would expect from a fairly cloistered son of the upper levels of the British Establishment.' Young officers who worked alongside Philby agreed with the assessment. Hugh Trevor Roper (Lord Dacre) later wrote that, while Menzies was 'personally considerate, patently just, patently honest ... no one could claim that he was a brilliant Chief'. Another colleague, Conservative Party historian (Lord) Robert Blake, adds that he was no 'spymaster'.[7]

While acknowledging that the successes of British Intelligence during the Second World War were 'very great' and were 'a major factor in the victory of the Western Allies', Blake recognises that 'they had nothing whatever to do with spies or espionage'. Indeed, MI6's wartime intelligence-gathering on Germany had been poor, and if it had any agents of its own there, 'the secret has been remarkably well-kept'. Its American counterpart, the Office of Strategic Services (OSS), whose 102 missions into Germany had far outstripped MI6's thirty-plus, had been concerned that much of the information MI6 shared with it was merely duplicates of material already received from other intelligence services. The few reliable Secret Intelligence Reports said to be based on 'SIS agents in Germany' turned out to be camouflaged 'Ultra' intelligence from the cryptanalytic agency, the Government Code and Cipher School (GC&CS), at Bletchley Park.[8]

Philby had recognised that Menzies's 'real strength lay in a sensitive perception of the currents of Whitehall politics, in an ability to feel his way through the mazy corridors of power'. He had been quick to claim authority over the use of Ultra – the name given to the deciphered intercepts that emerged from GC&CS – which had managed to break the German Enigma machine code ciphers. In this privileged position, he regularly presented the Prime Minister with the 'golden eggs' of the latest intelligence on German military plans. While Menzies 'bathed in the reflected glory cast upon him by the work of the boffins and eggheads at Bletchley ... the truth was that SIS could not claim exclusive responsibility for any of the major intelligence coups of the war'.[9]

Menzies, for one, realised that besides its astute control over the code-breaking successes, MI6's reputation rested on the 'significant contribution' of the Special Counter-Intelligence (SCI) units, whose function was to 'receive, record and use certain information emanating from specially secret sources' – i.e. Ultra. They were controlled by the counter-espionage Section V, which 'stood at the very intersection of these two currents, exploiting the first [Ultra] to promote the second [SCI units]'. The SCI units were also responsible for 'undertaking the penetration of enemy intelligence services and for the special exploitation of captured enemy agents'. If MI6's reputation was to survive into the postwar world, Menzies knew that it would all depend on the development of Section V – 'the brightest feather in C's cap'.[10]

Philby was also aware that for those officers engaged in the bureaucratic in-fighting to develop Section V, the previous six years, during which MI6 had concentrated its resources on the war with Germany to the total exclusion of intelligence-gathering on the Soviet Union, had been a mere interlude in the traditional battle with the Bolsheviks. The transition from 'hot' to Cold War was short. Before the war had even ended, Menzies was turning his attention to tackling the Soviet Union, though it would take until the end of the forties before the politicians would let MI6 off the leash to engage fully in Special Operations.

CHAPTER 1

THE SECOND WORLD WAR

During the war, MI6's counter-espionage Section V underwent an effective expansion. With a responsibility for the security of signals intelligence in the field, the section successfully exploited the use of what was known as ISOS (Intelligence Section, Oliver Strachey) reports – the generic term for decrypted German signals intelligence traffic. MI6 had no history of counter-espionage work and learned how to use double-cross agents and mount *'l'toxication'* or deception operations – designed to confuse the enemy as to its true intentions – from Paul Paillole, deputy of the French counter-espionage section of the pre-war Deuxième Bureau. Much had depended on the abilities of the section head, Felix Cowgill.[1]

Cowgill had been recruited in March 1939 from the Indian Police, for whom he had made a special study of communism. He brought years of counter-espionage experience to bear on his post, but had no experience of Europe, having spent the previous twelve years running penetration agents in the Comintern's network in Bengal, most recently as Deputy Commissioner of Special Branch. It had been understood that he would eventually succeed the Deputy Chief and former head of Section V, Valentine 'Ve-Ve' Vivian, as the resident MI6 expert on communism and director of a new operational department dealing with the subject. Cowgill's ablest student within the Section was the successful head of its Iberian subsection, Kim Philby.[2]

While Philby shared with his colleagues a genuine desire to defeat Nazism, he also acted as an agent for the Soviet Union's People's Commissariat for

Internal Affairs (NKVD). His Soviet handlers' main priority was to ascertain what subversive and espionage work MI6 was engaged in against the USSR. As an essentially defensive 'vigilant' organisation, primarily concerned with security and threats, both external and internal, against the USSR, the NKVD's prime objective was to root out subversion from wherever it might originate. Philby recalled that as soon as he began to work in MI6 in July 1940, his Soviet control 'began to demand information . . . But I constantly reported that MI6 was not engaged in any subversive and espionage work against the Soviet Union . . . MI6 was not permitted to engage in it then; the USSR was Great Britain's ally. But Moscow didn't believe it, it didn't believe it for a long time.' To their general incredulity, Philby could only report, correctly, that MI6 did not have a network of agents inside the Soviet Union. The NKVD then assumed that if the British were not directly involved, they must be working through the Poles and the Czechs, but, once again, Philby had to disabuse them of that idea.[3]

For a long time, Philby was viewed with deep suspicion by his Soviet handlers. It was a situation which only changed when it seemed certain that Germany would lose the war and he was able to report to Moscow what they wanted to hear. Senior MI6 officers had begun to think about the future and 'what the primary target of their activities would be after the defeat of the Axis powers'. They had come to the conclusion that MI6 'would have to deal with the secret service of the USSR and the intelligence services associated with Communist Parties in other countries – in short, with international communism, whose authority, of course, had increased a great deal due to the imminent victory over fascism'. The Service's leadership had decided on a modest start to combat the future threat and had established a small archival and non-operational records section. It was given the task of studying past records of Soviet activity, primarily related to the struggle against international communism, and the collecting and collating of current material. It was a harbinger of work which, in time, acquired great significance. Its establishment, however, had not been prompted by Soviet activities abroad but by events much closer to home.[4]

During April 1943, Security Service (MI5) watchers had tailed a long-term member of the Communist Party of Great Britain's (CPGB) Central Committee, Douglas Springhall, to a clandestine meeting with Ormond Uren. When arrested in June, Uren, a secret CPGB member who worked in the Hungarian section of the sabotage and resistance organisation, the Special Operations Executive (SOE), confessed to passing on to Springhall details of SOE communications and policy on eastern Europe to demonstrate that he was 'a sincere believer in Communism'. When another of Springhall's contacts, Olive Sheehan, a Customs and Excise clerk at the Air Ministry, was similarly arrested, she disclosed in her defence – quoting a source in the Security Service – that the British were withholding vital intelligence from the Russians.[5]

In light of the Springhall case, Vivian instigated a discreet inquiry which reported to Menzies in August 1943. Its conclusions ran counter to then current Foreign Office thinking and displayed the built-in prejudices of the security services. 'The contradictions between Great Britain and the Soviet Union', Vivian suggested,

> are as great as those between Britain and Nazi Germany ... Soviet Russia is our friend only while it can obtain benefit from this friendship. It does not trust us and will exert all efforts in espionage activities against us even in years of friendship. When it will obtain everything it can from a friendship, it will inexorably activate all the secret forces against the ideals for which Britain struggles ... In this way our most dangerous enemy after the war can turn out to be the secret aggression of Soviet Russia ... But we must not permit this error – we cannot trust the Russians in the same way we can trust, say, the Czechs and Americans or give them information which might betray an important or sensitive source or allow officers of local Soviet intelligence to study our organisation anywhere.

On 13 August, whether by coincidence or design, Menzies met with the Permanent Under-Secretary at the Foreign Office, Sir Alexander Cadogan, who had responsibility for MI6 and for harmonising its overlapping, and sometimes conflicting, functions with those of SOE and MI5. Menzies warned Cadogan that he had 'Communists in his organisation'.[6]

The Security Service wanted to take action against the Communist Party and, in particular, those working in government departments. In October, MI5's Roger Hollis, who monitored the activities of the CPGB, submitted a report to the Home Office in which he stated that the Service was 'aware that the Soviet Government was actively engaged at the present time in obtaining espionage information concerning the British Government'. The Soviet espionage organisations, Hollis revealed, 'seemed to operate through two channels: one directly through the Communist Party, utilizing the Party organisation and the Communists who are in the armed services and the Government to collect espionage data'. The second espionage group 'is apparently completely separated from the Communist Party and operates on ... a diplomatic level'. This involved the Soviet embassy and the various trade commissions which enjoyed quasi-diplomatic immunity.[7]

In a minute to Churchill on 28 October, Duff Cooper, the chair of the Security Executive, which nominally controlled the Security Service, outlined MI5's case. Churchill agreed with it in principle and, in November, the Home Secretary recommended that, in order to plug any leaks, 'all departments engaged on secret work should be advised to transfer known Communists, as notified by MI5, to other departments'. He had wanted the policy made public, but Churchill demurred, concurring with the advice of his unofficial intelligence adviser, Desmond Morton, that 'MI5 tends to see dangerous men too freely and to lack that knowledge of the world and sense of perspective which the Home Secretary rightly considers essential'. Churchill ruled that a secret panel of the Security Executive would decide what action was necessary on cases submitted by MI5. The existence of the panel was not finally notified to the secret departments until February 1944.[8]

Close to MI6 in his intelligence work, but 'a greyer eminence than Menzies's, Morton was 'certainly no friend of the left'. He was 'deeply concerned with the spectre of post-war European communism', and this included a personal interest in the various governments-in-exile and national committees in London. In early April 1944, in the pre-planning period for the invasion of Europe, Churchill expressed concern that communist members of the French National Committee were coming to London. In a secret telegram to Duff Cooper, who had left the Security Executive for a post in Algiers, Churchill warned that the French representatives would not have access to any British secrets. He added: 'I suppose that you realise that we are weeding remorselessly every single known Communist from all the secret organisations. We did this after having to sentence two quite high-grade people to long terms of penal servitude for their betrayal, in accordance with the Communist faith, of important military secrets.' On the 14th, Churchill similarly minuted Cadogan: 'We are purging all our secret establishments of Communists because we know they owe no allegiance to us or to our cause and will always betray secrets to the Soviets, even while we are working together.'[9]

While limited investigations, which consisted of little more than checking names against secret lists of known communists (negative vetting), did take place, there were no purges – at least not in the secret establishments. Dissatisfied with the Security Executive secret panel procedure, MI5 would not risk revealing its sources and only submitted one case. Cowgill later recalled that there had been one relatively low-level inquiry inside MI6 but it led only to the dismissal from Section V of a secretarial-grade assistant. Her schoolmaster husband had turned up in MI5 Registry records as a member of the Scottish Communist Party.[10]

Within MI6 there was a natural suspicion born of senior officers' anti-Bolshevism and a belief that Stalin's Russia would not be a durable peacetime ally. When SOE suggested allowing NKVD officers to operate in parts of the British Empire in order to run their agents for the war effort, MI6 refused to countenance the idea. The NKVD was regarded as a potential 'enemy organisation', and Menzies expressed 'grave concern' at the effect co-operation in Europe would have on its networks. When, in turn, MI5 suggested setting up its own liaison arrangements with Soviet security agencies in London, Menzies advised that 'it would be a waste of effort and an embarrassment'. The Russians were 'more interested in penetrating our intelligence than in helping', he added. Mindful of the MI5 reports, Menzies admitted to James Angleton of the OSS's counter-espionage division, X-2, which liaised in London with Section V: 'We've been penetrated by the communists and they're on the inside, but *we don't know exactly how*' (my italics).[11]

And that was the point. Despite the presence in its ranks of senior officers who had operated against the communists in India, MI6 lacked any precise intelligence on the modus operandi of the Russian Intelligence Service, its structure and its relationship with local communist parties. It is, therefore, more than a coincidence that in March 1944, a month before Churchill communicated his fears, Menzies had 'nominally' reconstituted the anti-communist Section IX. Its head was Jack Curry; his deputy was Harry Steptoe, recently stationed in Shanghai.[12]

Philby had a low opinion of Curry, who was 'hampered by deafness', and thought his deputy 'a near mental case'. Fellow officer Malcolm Muggeridge liked Steptoe: 'A little cocksparrow of a man with a bristling moustache, a high voice, monocle and lots of suits, ties, hats and shoes', who was 'a master-hand at letting fall the technical terms of espionage (letter-box, chicken-feed, cover, etc.) thereby giving an impression of effortless expertise'. In contrast, the about-to-retire Curry was an experienced former MI5 officer who had co-operated with MI6's Vivian and Cowgill in the 18(b) policy of interning fascists. Phillip Knightley is probably correct in his assertion that Section IX's first role was a 'counter-espionage one' before it became an 'offensive espionage operation'.[13]

Philby's Soviet controllers had immediately seen the significance of the new section and ordered him to work towards becoming its head. Luckily for Philby, the idea that in peacetime Section V would take over IX's functions caused a certain amount of friction with MI5, which had responsibility for counter-espionage. Section V thus became 'a fulcrum for the application of political leverage'. Philby exploited the feuds within the intelligence community and 'nearer home, the jealousy felt by Vivian for Cowgill'. He succeeded in ingratiating himself with the 'enfeebled' Vivian and effectively undermined Cowgill's standing with 'C'. During mid-May 1944, Philby was left in charge of Section V as Cowgill was absent in Canada and the United States, helping to negotiate a signals intelligence (SIGINT) agreement on co-operation on cryptanalytic exchanges – known as BRUSA.[14]

On the eve of the Allied invasion of France, Section V, whose staff roster had risen to 250 officers, became increasingly important to the Allied counter-espionage effort. It had already begun analysing recently captured Gestapo files and the increasing volume of Axis security records which fell into Allied hands. The files were to be used in the capture of leading Nazi agents as the Allied armies moved into occupied Europe. Much of the early work of compiling and editing of this intelligence haul was undertaken by another former

MI5 specialist on Communism, Robert Carew-Hunt. Covering a specific area, such as Spain and Portugal, the 'Purple Primers' listed 'all that was known about active members of the Abwehr and Sicherheitsdienst'. After GC&CS cryptanalysts had cracked the Abwehr ciphers, MI6's Registry overflowed with a self-updating trove of signals intelligence with names of officers, agents and safe houses. This success gave MI6 'the right to be the senior Allied counter-espionage service'.[15]

While the events on the western front remained the top priority, by the summer of 1944 British and American cryptographers had already begun to focus on the future. Bradley F. Smith speculates that besides dealing with the sharing of Axis-signals, the Brusa agreement 'embraced neutral and even Allied military SIGINT' – i.e. Soviet traffic. The question of when Britain began to target the communications of its then chief ally remains a sensitive subject. In his official history of British Intelligence during the Second World War, Professor Hinsley asserts that, in the wake of Germany's attack on the USSR in June 1941, work on Soviet communications, codes and ciphers ceased for the duration of the war. Is this true?

At Bletchley Park, GC&CS continued to read the output of German intelligence organisations which had broken Soviet codes, particularly those gathering signals on the eastern front. In particular, it was reading the cipher of the Luftwaffe, whose signals intelligence organisation was listening to Soviet communications and passing them back to Berlin. More importantly, Smith has uncovered documentary evidence that, in early 1943, Bletchley began directly intercepting Soviet traffic.[16]

This change reflected the views of officials at the highest levels of the intelligence community. A member of the Joint Intelligence Staff, Noel Annan, recalled that as early as February 1943, the chair of the Joint Intelligence Committee (JIC), Victor Cavendish-Bentinck, had written an indiscreet memorandum which had an 'off-the-cuff whiff of prescience about the postwar world'. Cavendish-Bentinck wrote that

> since Stalingrad our immediate strategic objectives had changed. Until then it had been in our interest to do all we could to take pressure off Russia. Now that the tide had turned, it was in our interest to let Germany and Russia bleed each other white. We would find it easier to effect a landing in Europe, and Russia, however sentimental the British people might be about her, was likely to be a troublesome customer at the end of the war.[17]

Cowgill told Philby that fifteen people were already working at GC&CS on Soviet ciphers and that Menzies had proposed adding more people to work on deciphering. That Bletchley had been engaged in this area was confirmed by Menzies's Foreign Office adviser, Robert Cecil. He recalled that with the dissolution by Stalin of the co-ordinating body for worldwide communist parties, the Comintern, on MI6 instructions GC&CS had been 'intercepting and decrypting the instructions that were being sent from the Kremlin to partisan groups and resistance movements under Communist control as to the tactics to be adopted as the day of liberation drew nearer'.[18]

The first steps in a Anglo-American intelligence alliance acting against the Soviet Union began in the months before D-day when order-of-battle (OB) specialists met in London. The British team, led by Col. F. Thornton and Maj. N. Ignatieff, who both 'harboured engrained hostility to the Soviets and deep suspicion of Stalin's future intentions', exchanged intelligence with their American counterparts on the ability of the Red Army to tie down German units. Liaison officers, such as Col. Firebrace, who dealt with their Russian counterparts in London on intelligence matters, held similar prejudiced views. They were unwilling to admit that the Soviets had been 'generous' in handing over material about their own forces and information on the German divisions on the eastern front. Instead, they reported 'the most negative possible view of the Soviet intelligence-sharing effort' until this was 'gradually formalized and then served as the basis for a general conclusion that the prospects for "post-hostilities" co-operation with the USSR were extremely bleak'.[19]

These negative views were taken on board by the chiefs of staff, who were also beginning to consider the nature of the postwar world. In August 1943, they had established a Post-Hostilities Planning Sub-Committee (PHP) chaired by Gladwyn Jebb, who was in immediate conflict with the chiefs' insistence on the identification of the Soviet Union as the only potential enemy after the defeat of Germany. Jebb described PHP members as 'would-be drinkers of Russian blood'.[20]

Even with 'special security treatment', Moscow was quickly informed of the PHP deliberations because one of the 'Ring of Five', Foreign Office official Donald Maclean, was passing on details of the main discussions. Soviet news agencies soon began referring to 'nests of Fascist opposition' in the West. Diplomats attacked the reports, but a deputy under-secretary, Geoffrey Wilson, observed that there was more to the Soviet complaints than officials might suppose. 'If we make the necessary allowance for Soviet terminology . . . it has an element of truth in it. The people who, whether consciously or unconsciously, are doing their best to wreck the Anglo-Soviet alliance, are by no means confined to "obscure people without honour in their own country".' In a reference to the PHP, Wilson noted that 'the suspicion and even hostility of the Service Departments towards Russia are now becoming a matter of common gossip'.[21]

Just five weeks after D-day, the PHP's 'wild acolytes' recommended that, if faced with a hostile Soviet Union, German help might prove 'essential' to

Britain's survival. On 27 July, the chief of the Imperial General Staff, Viscount Alanbrooke, wrote in his diary after meeting the Foreign Secretary, Anthony Eden: 'Should Germany be dismembered or gradually converted to an ally to meet the Russian threat of twenty years hence? I suggested the latter . . . Germany is no longer the dominating power in Europe – Russia is. She has vast resources and cannot fail to become the main threat in fifteen years from now. Therefore, foster Germany, gradually build her up, and bring her into a federation of Western Europe.' These views reached the ears of Foreign Office officials. In August, Senior Foreign Office official Orme Sargent reported that the chiefs of staff and 'certain high-placed officers' were speaking of the Soviet Union as 'enemy number one', and even of 'securing German assistance against her'.[22]

These were not isolated opinions. In Washington, the former Director of Military Intelligence and head of the British Military Mission, General F. H. N. Davidson, enquired of one of President Roosevelt's confidential advisers 'whether the United States could be counted on to march with Britain in the "next war" against Russia'. At that stage, such a view was regarded as belligerent and the response from the White House was distinctly disapproving.[23]

The chiefs of staff presented their long assessment to the Foreign Office in October, noting that 'we cannot afford to eliminate from our mind the conception of an expansionist and perhaps eventually aggressive Russia'. A British diplomat in Moscow, Frank Roberts, thought that the chiefs were 'not only crossing their bridge before they come to it, but even constructing their bridge in order to cross it'. Officials were worried that the 'simple military mind' would signal an all-out preparation for war with Russia. Despite Foreign Office objections, the chiefs sought Eden's agreement that contingency planning for a war with Russia would be allowed to continue but confined 'to a very restricted circle'. Such ideas were too sensitive for the Foreign Office, which limited the circulation of PHP texts – though Donald Maclean received copies – and ensured that hostility to the Soviet Union was downplayed. Eventually, the Foreign Office withdrew from the committee; a decision 'welcomed' by the military planners who were now free to persist with their 'anti-Russian extravagances'.[24]

Following the success of the invasion of the Continent and the realisation that the end of the war was in sight, it became evident that the control or independence of the countries of Europe ultimately rested on the strength of Russian arms. In October 1944, Churchill continued with his policy of asserting a right to be heard on Europe's future and struck his famous 'percentage' deal with Stalin. It accepted that the Soviet Union would have an almost free hand in Romania and Bulgaria in return for Stalin's recognition of British predominance in Greece and of joint Soviet and Allied influence in the future of Hungary and Yugoslavia. What set the pattern for the immediate postwar world, particularly in relation to what was about to happen in eastern Europe, was not, however, the actions of Stalin but Churchill's plan for Italy, over which he was prepared to have 'a good row' with the Russians.[25]

In a policy that undermined East–West relations, the Soviet Union was not allowed a role in the Allied military government in Italy. Churchill saw the country 'primarily as a joint Anglo-American responsibility' and did not bother to consult Moscow on the surrender terms which Stalin, quite reasonably, viewed with deep suspicion. 'Hawks' among the British diplomats, who already saw the Cold War on the horizon, ensured that they only 'informed the USSR but did not consult it' on major policy issues. Churchill lacked the foresight to see that his stance on Italy was bound to be interpreted by Stalin as a harbinger of things to come. Stalin had little alternative but to interpret Churchill's attitude as an insult, which he repaid in kind by refusing the Allies a role in eastern Europe.

A few diplomatic figures had argued for a tripartite form of control which one senior official believed would 'mean that we and the Americans would have the day-to-day possibility of cross-examining the Russians on their intentions towards the Allied countries and Eastern Europe generally'. The military rejected such a plan, a decision that suited Stalin. Historian Herbert Feis has written that 'the Soviet Government was to maintain that the Italian set up was a good and fair model for use in nations liberated by the Red Army'. In one sense, Stalin was happy to see the British and MI6 interfere in Italy's political affairs since he was, according to one writer on Italian resistance, Charles Delzell, 'quite willing to leave events to Anglo-American management as long as he could exercise similar undisputed sway over his sphere of eastern satellites'. American officials realised that the decision to minimise Moscow's role in occupied Italy 'might give the Russians a convenient excuse later on to restrict Anglo-American activities in Romania, Bulgaria and Hungary'. Which is precisely what happened: the Americans reluctantly acknowledged that, given the Italian analogy, it was 'only natural and to be expected'.[26]

MI6's Foreign Office adviser, Robert Cecil, had also turned his thoughts to the future. 'If the freedom, for which the West had fought, was to be preserved', Cecil concluded, then 'the task of keeping track of international Communist activities would soon have to be resumed.' In August 1944, Philby, who had expected to begin work on the illegal organisations of the Nazi Party and, when the war ended, to work in Berlin as chief of counter-intelligence, was informed that Vivian wanted to appoint him the *operational* chief of MI6's anti-communist work in place of Curry.[27]

Cowgill received no warning of Vivian's decision, and it was only on his return from a tour of inspection of SCI Units in liberated Europe on 23

October that he discovered that Philby had achieved his goal of heading Section IX. He had done so by stressing his willingness to collaborate with the Security Service, which was involved in an ultimately unsuccessful battle to incorporate Section V into MI5. 'At one stroke', Cecil bitterly recalled, Philby 'had got rid of a staunch anti-communist and ensured that the whole post-war effort to counter communist espionage would become known in the Kremlin. The history of espionage records few, if any, comparable master-strokes.' Ironically, Cowgill would resign from MI6 because of his 'opposition to the redirection of energies in British counter-espionage from Germany to the new Soviet threat'.[28]

The creation of Section IX had been welcomed in the 'warren of wooden-partitioned offices and frosted-glass windows' of Broadway Buildings by senior officers because 'it seemed to hold out the prospect of a continued MI6 foothold in post-war counter-espionage work'. Older officers also saw an opportunity to 'stay at their desks drawing a salary for a few more years pending retirement'. Junior officers, who thought their superiors 'lunatic in their anti-communism', were happy that Philby had been promoted and pleased that 'at least one communist should have broken through and that the social prejudices of our superiors had, on this occasion, triumphed over their politicial prejudices'.[29]

The new rapidly expanding anti-Soviet department was not yet fully operational, but Philby began to recruit staff, including Robert Carew-Hunt, head of Section V's subsection dealing with North and South America, who prepared background papers on communism, and Jane (Sissmore) Archer, a trained barrister from MI5's B Division, who was an expert on Soviet espion-age and the Comintern.[30]

Who sanctioned Menzies's expansion of the section or, for that matter, GC&CS's Soviet signals initiative is unclear. Cecil spent his last years trying to expose the inconsistencies and propaganda inherent in Philby's account while ignoring the more interesting question of why he allowed IX to expand at a time when the Foreign Office was still trying to dampen down hostility to the Soviet Union. Any official go-ahead would appear to have been the result of pressure from the military. Indeed, Menzies shared the military view on Russia and, according to future Chief Dick White, he 'ordered the resumption of operations without Churchill's knowledge because he knew that the Soviets would be a major problem'.[31]

MI6 began to make use of captured Soviet soldiers liberated by the advancing Allied armies in the West. Nazi collaborators and former members of the Baltic Waffen-SS, who had sought refuge in Sweden as the German defence collapsed, were recruited by Swedish and British Military Intelligence – 'neither of which asked too many questions about the Balts' wartime activi-ties'. The first link between MI6 and former SS men, they were used to gather intelligence on the Soviet armies as they swept across eastern and northern

Europe. By the end of the year, MI6 had made contact with resistance organisations in the Baltic states and renewed relations with anti-communist, pro-German exile groups such as the Promethean League and Intermarium, which the Service had sponsored before the war.[32]

CHAPTER 2

REORGANISATION: SPECIAL OPERATIONS

Although hostilities continued, by 1945 senior officers in 'The Firm' – as MI6 was affectionately known to its staff – knew that the end was not far off and 'an air of relaxation wafted through the narrow corridors' of head-quarters. Colleagues drank to the future in the small Seniors' Club in the basement of head office, where they talked shop about the lay-offs and cutbacks, or were already intriguing about promotion and appointments abroad. Those officers that had decided to stay initially had little to do, and a number, such as Desmond Bristow, deployed their espionage expertise in the serious endeavour of discovering which pubs had been supplied with rationed beer.[1]

All officers of whatever rank knew, however, that MI6 would soon be faced with its traditional enemy – Russia. Indeed, it seemed to Hugh Trevor Roper and other wartime entrants that the professionals, who were 'lunatic in their anti-communism', sometimes regarded the war as 'a dangerous interruption of the Service'. The younger officers were invited to the Chief's office – the 'August Presence', as it became known – where they heard Menzies declare that 'we are in a rapidly changing world, politically and economically ... Basically, it is becoming clear that Germany will slowly become our ally and the Russians our enemy.' In anticipation, the summer months were spent reading books and papers on Marxism, communism and the Soviet Union. 'A real war had just ended,' Bristow recalled, 'and something which became known as a "Cold War" was beginning.'[2]

It was also self-evident that this war would be 'in a special sense an intelligence conflict'. In looking back at the Cold War, Michael Herman, a senior intelligence official who served in the Cabinet Office, concluded that 'never before in peacetime have the relationships of competing power blocks been so influenced by intelligence assessments. Never before have the collection of intelligence and its denial to the adversary been such central features of an international rivalry. The Cold War transformed intelligence into a major element of the peacetime international security system.' Menzies had no illusions about what the policy-makers, strategists, the military, the Foreign Office and politicians would require of MI6, but as he considered the options he must have wondered whether it could deliver. Would Menzies be able to reform a service that in many ways reflected his own limited outlook? And would the 'coherent and relatively well-ordered' British Intelligence 'community' which, academic Richard Aldrich has noted, emerged only during the Second World War, retain its overall coherence beyond 1945?[3]

Trevor Roper had his doubts. When he looked around Broadway Buildings as he was about to re-enter civilian life he noticed 'flitting like shadows in the crowded wings' the same 'part-time stockbrokers and retired Indian policemen, the agreeable epicureans from the bars of Whites and Boodles, the jolly, conventional ex-naval officers and the robust adventurers from the bucket-shop'. These people realised that MI6 would have to absorb some of the new 'immigrants', but it felt to junior officers that those responsible for recruitment wanted to ensure that they took on only 'those who would sustain, not imperil, the old fabric' of the pre-war Service.[4]

Similarly, Aldrich concludes, moves to perpetuate the coherence of the intelligence community 'lost their way in the bureaucratic and political upheavals at the end of the war'. Those upheavals had a great deal to do with the intense and bitter rivalry that had developed between MI6 and the sabotage and resistance organisation, the Special Operations Executive (SOE). And behind the rivalry lay the uneasy relationship between intelligence-gathering, which was MI6's primary task, and the organisation of 'Special Operations' (SO) – psychological warfare, assassinations and paramilitary activities – which were the responsibility of SOE.[5]

There were many inside SOE for whom the war 'had become a way of life and who were convinced that the Baker Street headquarters or something like it would have an important role to play in the uncertain post-war world'. This particularly applied to the CD or Executive Director, Colin Gubbins, who was already thinking in terms of combating the postwar threat of communist domination of the Balkans and eastern Europe.[6]

Gubbins's 'deep hatred of Communism' had developed in north Russia, as ADC, in 1919, to General Ironside of the Archangel Expeditionary Force which supported the White Russian, anti-Bolshevik forces fighting under the command of Admiral Kolchak. He then served in Ireland, where he became an admirer of the IRA's Michael Collins, whom he regarded as the guerrilla fighter *par excellence*. A Russian-speaker, during the thirties Gubbins worked in the War Office's Soviet Section of the Military Intelligence Directorate. As a member of the small General Staff (Research), later Military Intelligence (R), which operated under the wing of MI6's own sabotage Section D, he researched guerrilla warfare with responsibilties for organisation and recruitment. In 1940, Gubbins was seconded to the new SOE, where 'his suspicions of Soviet motives were far better informed and far more deeply held than those of most of his colleagues'.[7]

Gubbins's desire to keep SOE as an anti-communist vehicle was, however, hindered by the rows with MI6. In February 1944, in the wake of several JIC reports that attempted to deal with SOE–MI6 controversies in Europe, Churchill had resigned himself to 'the warfare between SIS and SOE which is a lamentable, but perhaps inevitable, feature of our affairs'. SOE had become unpopular within Whitehall because of its independent attitude and its determination to 'resort to and encourage every form of terror'. Above all, MI6 was 'determined that SOE's charter should not be prolonged beyond the end of hostilities'.

It was a view shared by the Foreign Office's Orme Sargent 'who remained unhappy about SOE's intimacy with the exile governments in London', particularly those from the Balkans.[8]

Nevertheless, by the spring of 1944 senior officers had started to plan for a postwar role for Special Operations. Gubbins, in particular, pressed for a decision, as he feared losing his best men to other organisations. During April, Douglas Dodds-Parker, one of the original members of MI(R) who 'had not only an extraordinary wide acquaintance' but whose 'manipulation of the old boy network was exceptional', encouraged junior minister Harold Macmillan to lobby for future Allied control commissions in newly liberated countries to include a small element of SOE officers. Macmillan had been impressed by the SOE British Liaison Officers (BLOs) he had met in Italy but, in August, his proposal was vetoed by the Foreign Office. In contrast to the American OSS, no representatives were sent to Hungary, Romania and Bulgaria, as there was no desire to extend reciprocal arrangements to the Russians for Italy and Greece.[9]

By October, senior SOE figures were ready to consider Russia as a new enemy. They argued that the organisation should think about setting up agent networks to deal with the potential threat, and Gubbins ordered that a list of its agents in central Europe be drawn up. He minuted: 'It is considered most desirable that contact should be maintained with them to form a nucleus of tried and experienced agents capable of rapid expansion in the event of another war.' City and business figures were to be approached to provide the agents with cover as foreign representatives of British firms. He added that 'there are many people both within and outside SOE who have wide business and commercial contacts and will be willing and anxious to help in this scheme'.*[10]

A draft proposal on SOE's future by Robin Brook, a senior officer responsible for the western theatre, was redrafted by the minister in charge, Lord Selbourne, as 'The Role of SOE in the Immediate Post-Armistice Period' and submitted for discussion to the War Cabinet. Selbourne wanted SOE missions to operate in all European countries and to work against potential German stay-behind networks and subversive organisations. His plan was rebuffed by the War Cabinet deputy and Labour leader, Clement Attlee, who 'resolutely set his face against the establishment of anything in the nature of a "British Comintern" '. Selbourne once again redrafted his paper for Churchill with a more 'defensive' view of SOE, in which he suggested that it 'should not be amalgamated with [MI6] because the methods and techniques are very different'. Foreign Secretary Anthony Eden, however, was sure that 'the only sound plan in the ultimate future will be to place SO and SIS under the same controlling head'. As in the American OSS, the two tasks – intelligence-gathering and special operations – would be combined in one organisation.[11]

Gubbins tried to retrieve the situation and appealed directly to the chiefs of staff, who requested further views on the future of SOE. On 30 November, the chiefs accepted Eden's minute but agreed to Foreign Office control only as a 'temporary measure'. Like Selbourne, they preferred War Office control with SOE having its own head, who would deal directly with them on all operational matters. Throughout the winter of 1944/5, Selbourne and Gubbins continued to plan operations in the context 'of SOE's self-appointed post-hostilities role', believing that it was 'very much an SOE responsibility to prevent the outbreak of civil war' as the Germans withdrew from parts of Europe. Gubbins was able to put in place forty missions in Italy, where Churchill feared the development of a civil war similar to that in Greece.[12]

At the same time, MI6 planners staked their own claim to a future post-hostilities role. In late February 1945, Kim Philby presented the Foreign Office adviser, Robert Cecil, with 'the charter' of Section IX. Cecil, who claimed that his vision of the future was 'at once more opaque and more optimistic', was taken aback by the scale of demands which included the establishment of a substantial number of overseas Section officers under diplomatic cover. Cecil, who later acknowledged that Philby 'foresaw more plainly than I the onset of the Cold War', sent the memorandum back, suggesting that the demands be scaled down. Within hours, Ve-Ve Vivian and Philby had descended upon Cecil, 'upholding their requirements and insisting that these be transmitted to the Foreign Office. Aware of the fact that I was in any case due to be transferred in April to Washington, I gave way.' Cecil consulted with 'the

---

* This may explain a number of well-publicised arrests in the late forties and early fifties of British businessmen in eastern Europe.

Office' – he does not say with whom – on the financial implications and the increased diplomatic cover. He later reflected 'with a certain wry amusement on the hypocrisy of Philby who, supposedly working in the cause of "peace", demanded a large Cold War apparatus, when he could have settled for a smaller one'.[13]

Section IX quickly became the pre-eminent department of MI6 and the best officers, primarily the same age as Philby, who had joined the Service during the war, transferred to the Section. A worldwide empire was slowly created with a headquarters staff of sixty officers and another sixty officers overseas, equipped with personal ciphers for direct communications to Philby. Their mission was 'to keep Philby informed about Soviet, American, British and French intelligence activity in their areas of operations and to establish working relations with the local foreign counter-espionage and security systems'. It was agreed, however, that they would have little contact with their French and Italian counterparts as their services were held to be infiltrated by Soviet agents.[14]

Philby recognised that he was in 'an idiotic situation'. 'If all my operations against the Soviet Union and the Communist movement failed every time, I would soon be fired. If I achieved success every time, I could do significant damage to the Soviet Union. There was no single way out of the situation. In every case I had to make a decision.' What Philby, in his role as a NKVD agent, did not do was make a priority of penetration of the enemy intelligence services – the 'acid', as Anthony Verrier calls it, 'which eats into the enemy's vitals, causing collapse – sometimes – at a moment not always easy to predict'. This lacking factor, Verrier correctly asserts, 'enabled Philby to be a traitor secure from detection for many years'.[15]

This was not entirely Philby's doing because he was just following long-established practice. The MI6 training manual from the period includes a four-page memorandum on the recruitment and handling of agents in 'normal, not wartime, intelligence operations'. MI6 practice for recruiting agents stated that

> such persons are initially recommended to the service either by
> a friend already in the service or by particular alumni of the
> service designated for this purpose . . . Both MI6 and MI5 have
> such former officers appointed for this purpose, particularly
> those who are connected with British universities . . . By far
> the largest number of British agents are not 'agents' properly
> speaking, but voluntary informers.

It goes on to state that

> the successful intelligence service will not normally recruit
> employees and then infiltrate them into any situation. Any such

attempt will almost certainly be crude and unsuccessful. On a long-range basis the British method is to take a person who is young and newly engaged upon a career useful to British intelligence and so to pay him and otherwise assist him as increasingly to develop his usefulness over an extended period of years.

Given that the evidence suggests that the majority of political warfare operations involved the use of 'agents of influence', MI6 strategy for recruiting agents had clear advantages. However, it was only successful in building up networks of sympathetic supporters and front groups. Where MI6 singularly failed to achieve greater success was in recruiting agents to penetrate enemy and opposition organisations.[16]

A number of internal reviews into the structure of the intelligence and security community were being undertaken within Whitehall in which a variety of bureaucratic scores were settled. Perhaps acknowledging that he would lose out in this internal battle, Gubbins had already made his own arrangements to ensure that some semblance of an SO capability would be in place after the war. Considerable sums of money were put into the mass production of specialised weapons and wireless equipment which were obviously too late for Europe, or even South-East Asia, but Gubbins made no effort to halt their manufacture. Indeed, he busied himself trying to build up some kind of post-hostilities network, even in areas that the Foreign Office had deemed off limits. One of his most trusted colleagues, Harold Perkins, travelled to Prague to contact SOE's resident agents. In signals back to London, he recorded their wartime cover and stressed that 'the continuity of the stories should not be broken'. In Budapest, another officer revealed that 'the few agents we had are blown. A new organisation would have to be built up in cells initiated by our past agents and helpers. We must assume that in the event of trouble all our past collaborators would be arrested.'[17]

In order to secure a permanent role in Germany, the head of SOE's German directorate, Gerald Templer, was given the responsibility of developing contacts with the 21 Army Group. Working in parallel, Peter Wilkinson planned for the Clowder Mission for southern Austria to be attached to the 8th Army in the British Zone of Austria. Their plans, however, were frowned upon by JIC chair Cavendish-Bentinck, who did not have a very high opinion of Gubbins, and Orme Sargent, who minuted that SOE must not be allowed 'under cover of this kind of proposal to continue operations in the post-hostilities period'. On the ground, however, SOE units were integrated with the army in Germany and Austria to carry out a number of unspecified 'special assignments'.[18]

With Gubbins absent abroad, in May 1945 Selbourne commissioned a final draft paper on SOE's future. He explained that in view of the Russian menace, the situation in Italy, Central Europe and the Balkans, and the smouldering volcanoes in the Middle East, I think it would be madness to allow SOE to be stifled at this juncture. In handing it over to the Foreign Office I cannot help feeling that to ask Sir Orme Sargent to supervise SOE is like inviting an abbess to supervise a brothel! But SOE is no base instrument, it is a highly specialised weapon which will be required by HMG whenever we are threatened and whenever it is necessary to contact the common people of foreign lands.

It was regarded as an unimpressive document not least because it largely rested on the idea of a resurgent Nazi 'Fourth Reich' underground which officials soon realised would not materialise.[19]

In the twilight of the Churchill administration, Lord Lovat accepted the temporary post of Under-Secretary of State for Foreign Affairs, responsible for the functions of the Ministry of Economic Warfare, including oversight of the remnants of SOE when these were taken over by the Foreign Office. Lovat was a supreme example of the way the British intelligence community operated through the old-boy network and family ties. At the outbreak of war, he joined the Lovat Scouts, which had been raised by his father for the Boer War but now specialised in irregular warfare. Lovat then commanded the Field Craft Wing at the Inverailort Irregular Training Centre in the Western Highlands, and went on to be awarded many gallantry awards as leader of Commando Unit No. 4, which had been inspired by the paramilitary formations adopted by Gubbins at the beginning of the war. At the time of the Warsaw uprising, Lovat had been sent to Russia as a member of a parliamentary delegation intended to bolster the Soviet alliance. Quoting Byron, Churchill wrote to Stalin that he was sending him 'the mildest-mannered man that ever cut a throat'.[20]

With the support of Lovat and encouragement from Gubbins, in May the chiefs of staff set up a 'SOE Evaluation Committee' which sought 'an unbiased opinion' from regional commanders. While some of these reports spoke highly of the military value of SOE, others called for 'closer co-ordination and control at every level'. This became the central issue as the Foreign Office and the chiefs fought for effective control – which hitherto had been noticeably absent – over MI6 and SOE's tendency to play a 'semi-lone hand' and to develop its 'own foreign policy' had resulted in, Richard Aldrich suggests, 'a great deal of administrative friction both in Whitehall and at headquarters level of the major operational theatres of war'.[21]

The Foreign Office had still not turned against the Soviets, though certain individuals and particularly factions in the military, which supported SOE lobbying for a post-hostilities role, were already thinking of the next war.

Orme Sargent had been encouraged in calling for a 'showdown' with the Russians by his friend Robert Bruce Lockhart, who told him that 'the Anglo-American armies in the west could go through the Russian armies quite easily because of their enormous preponderance in armour and air power'. Throughout the spring of 1945, virtually every JIC policy discussion reflected fears of Soviet intentions and argued for 'getting tough with the Russians'. Churchill even telegraphed Field Marshal Montgomery directing him 'to be careful in collecting German arms, to stack them so that they could easily be issued again to the German soldiers whom we should have to work with if the Soviet advance continued'. Montgomery later admitted that the secret order had been issued. Churchill went as far as to ask the Joint Planning Staff (JPS), which had taken on the military's post-hostilities planning functions, for a report, known as Operation UNTHINKABLE, on the possibility of taking on Russia.[22]

It was assumed that the Third World War would start on 1 July with ten divisions of German troops joining with British and American divisions in launching an attack on the Soviets between Dresden and the Baltic. The study, which was presented to the Prime Minister on 22 May, only five days after the formal surrender by Admiral Doenitz of German forces, concluded that 'the best we could hope for was to drive the Russians back to about the same line the Germans had reached. And then what? Were we to remain mobilised indefinitely to hold them there?' On the 31st, the chiefs of staff rejected the report as unfeasible and insisted that Britain should be thinking in terms of defence.[23]

Less than a week after VE day, Churchill had lamented in a meeting with his ambassador to Moscow, Archibald Kerr, that 'the Soviets were dropping an iron screen across Europe from Lubeck to Trieste, behind which we have no knowledge of what was happening'. Churchill's fears were reflected in a 23 May JIC paper on 'Relations with the Russians', which laid particular emphasis on the exchange of intelligence and technical information. The Russians were characterised by 'suspicion' and 'an obsession with security and prestige'. The report concluded that 'no Russian request should normally be granted unless some request of ours to which we attach importance is granted in connection with it'. This distorted picture of wartime intelligence co-operation with the Soviets, which painted a dismal picture of the prospects for the future, enjoyed a wide circulation and was frequently cited by those trying to point British 'post-hostilities' policy towards the USSR into a more 'realistic' and assertive direction.[24]

Official recognition that a chill now ran through attitudes towards the Soviets was made plain on 26 June 1945, when the Air Ministry issued a general order that 'all intelligence reports, technical and otherwise, which had hitherto been sent, or made available, to the Russians, either by automatic inclusion on a distribution list or otherwise are no longer to be so disclosed except when a comparable quid pro quo is arranged'. As Bradley F. Smith notes, it marked a shift in British intelligence priorities from 'securing intelligence from the Russians about the Germans to acquiring intelligence on the Russians from the Germans'. Three days later came confirmation that British intelligence was actively compiling OB intelligence on the Soviet Red Army. The War Office's MI3 declared that the bulk of its information on the Red Army had been derived from the Germans, especially from low-level wireless 'Y' intercepts and captured documents, as well as from Japanese intercepts and material secured from the Poles, who had managed to break the Soviet Air Force ciphers. In the judgement of MI3 the time had come to interrogate British-held German PoWs in the hope of gathering intelligence on the Soviet Union.[25]

Like other services, MI6 was subjected to general but limited inquiries into reorganisation. Commissioned by Churchill, a committee headed by Sir Findlater Stewart, formerly chair of the recently disbanded Home Defence Executive, looked into the reform of the Whitehall intelligence structure in the context of the amalgamation of the three service ministries in a new Ministry of Defence. The inquiry was 'somewhat toothless' in that Cavendish-Bentinck had already persuaded the chiefs of staff that the intelligence structure should remain intact. With the approval of the military chiefs, he also set in train the creation of the Joint Intelligence Bureau after noticing that 'there were junior officers in the intelligence divisions of the Air Ministry, War Office and the Admiralty all doing the same job, writing the same things, gathering the same information, most of it not secret in any way. I thought this should be rationalized.'[26]

Meanwhile, Menzies resisted pressure from the Foreign Office to appoint Cavendish-Bentinck as his Vice-Chief, preferring to surround himself with military men whom he could trust. Instead, he appointed Major-General John Sinclair, the last wartime Director of Military Intelligence, as his deputy and successor-designate. Menzies did bring in an outsider as his Assistant Chief. A 'quiet and experienced organiser', Air Commodore James 'Jack' Easton had been the RAF's Assistant Director for Intelligence with responsibility for providing facilities for MI6 and SOE's operations. He was respected by the younger officers as a 'subtle intelligence officer who was quick to see the order out of any chaos presented to him' and whose 'intelligence was manifest as soon as he started speaking'. Philby considered him 'dangerously smart': Easton 'never raised his voice, but could kill with a word filled with irony and sarcasm'. Unfortunately, given that the Service needed a shake-up precisely in those very sections where their power was unquestioned, 'the coterie of swashbuckling old Russia hands, who disdained the notion that a man without "green thumbs", insensitive to the world spies, should exercise authority', tended to report direct to Menzies and Sinclair. These 'Robber Barons', 'safeguarding their territorial perquisites and responsible for all tasks within them', were, Anthony Verrier acknowledges, 'certainly immune from intro-spection about organisation and methods'. They ensured that 'no root or branch reorganisation was considered or attempted'.[27]

Cavendish-Bentinck, too, was called upon to look at the future organisa-tion of MI6. The committee included the JIC Secretary, Col. Denis Capel-Dunn, and two senior Foreign Office officials, Neville Bland (whose proposal that MI6 officers be given the same conditions of service as civil servants had already been accepted by Bevin) and Ivone Kirkpatrick, the latter having been considered by Menzies as his possible successor. The final report presented to the chiefs of staff on 5 June 1945 recommended that GC&CS be give extra funds, while Menzies was instructed 'to hoard all the money he could before the war ended because we knew that after the war the Treasury wouldn't give a penny if it didn't have to'. The JIC chair was later told that this had been achieved.[28]

It remains an intriguing but largely unanswered question how MI6 managed to fund its SOs in a period of great austerity – the actual amount allocated to the Secret Intelligence Service by the secret vote which went through Parliament was quite small. While a large percentage of its budget was hidden away in other departments, particularly the Armed Services, it is uncertain whether this was enough to cover expensive SOs such as the large bribes and subventions paid out to assets and agents, particularly in the Middle East. It has been alleged that US intelligence covertly used Operation SAFEHAVEN funds, which had originated with the gold hoard that the Germans had plundered from Europe, as 'black currency' for operations in Italy in the late forties, though the CIA has denied it. However, a knowledge-able insider source has suggested that a portion of this tainted gold was, indeed, used by MI6 to fund its SOs. Certainly, MI6 agents engaged in black-market operations of the kind successfully exploited by SOE in the Far East, while offshore banks and tax havens have been rumoured to have acted as channels for the Service's dirty money.[29]

In early June 1945, an ad hoc committee was set up to consider SOE's immedi-ate future. It consisted of Cavendish-Bentinck, representatives of the chiefs of staff and the Treasury, Menzies and Gubbins, who found himself heavily outnumbered. Cavendish-Bentinck recommended that 'SOE should become a wing of the SIS and that meanwhile every effort should be made in the interests of efficiency and economy to unify the activities of the SIS and SOE'. He added on the 22nd that 'we must cut our coat according to our cloth and if we produce a large establishment it will be turned down, and there will be no Special Operations organisation in peacetime'. On 16 July, under pressure from Menzies, Gubbins finally accepted the fusion of the two organisations.[30]

Increasingly, SOE operations overlapped with those of MI6. With hostilities with Germany at an end, Menzies sent Philby to Athens and then Frankfurt, where he saw the chief of Allied Intelligence in Europe, General Long. The aim was to organise operations for the gathering of military and political intelligence about the situation in the territories in Germany and eastern Europe occupied by the Red Army. War Planning soon became an integral part of MI6's activities and much thought was given to the setting up of anti-Soviet Stay Behind (SB) networks throughout Europe.[31]

When Churchill's 'caretaker' government was defeated by the Labour Party, Lord Lovat, who had responsibility for SOE, was among the ministerial casualties. It had not been a happy time for Lovat, for 'within the year the military curtain rang down on Special Service'. This was not entirely true but was believed by those on the Right who had wanted to preserve SOE, which, according to Robert Cecil, was 'liquidated with almost indecent haste'. SOE historian M. R. D. Foot claims that the new Prime Minister, Clement Attlee, ordered that SOE and its networks were 'to end immediately' and were 'closed down at 48 hours notice'. He adds that Foreign Secretary Ernest Bevin 'signed SOE's death warrant on lines laid down by Eden in 1945' and agreed that components of SOE would come under the control of MI6. It was not an arrangement that met with the approval of Cecil, who believed that 'if relations with SIS had been more cordial, one first-class organisation could have been created out of the best of two elements but the chance was missed'.[32]

The truth, Richard Aldrich discovered, was that 'on the contrary, many components of SOE marched out of the Second World War into the Cold War without breaking step'. In fact, a few SOE units – protected by the military – in Germany, Austria, Iraq, Iran and in the Far East, continued to operate without any effective Foreign Office control. On 11 September, Colin Gubbins learned that Bevin had agreed to the amalgamation of SOE with MI6. Bevin thanked Gubbins for his contribution to the war effort and disclosed that 'C' would be the common executive head. Thus elements of SO were amalgamated with other clandestine bodies and official organisations, enabling important continuities to be maintained in personnel and doctrine. It was not an ideal solution for SOE's supporters but it met 'the universal recommendation for much closer control of special operations'.[33]

'Because of its poor wartime record', Patrick Seale records that Menzies 'had to fight for the Service's existence in the face of scepticism from the new Labour government and rivalry from other agencies, such as SOE'. With the SO problem now solved to his satisfaction, and in order to make the Service more responsive to peacetime intelligence-gathering, in September Menzies appointed MI6's own Reorganisation Committee to review the workings of the Service. It was chaired by the Director of the Passport Control Department, Maurice Jeffes, 'a capable, if colourless, administrator'. It also included the

Secretary of the Planning Staff and Production Committee, Alurid Denne, who had control of the USSR region; Chief Staff Officer Christopher Arnold-Forster, a naval officer who was about to retire to rejoin a City stockbroking firm; Capt. Edward 'Eddie' Hastings, another naval officer serving on the Joint MI6/GC&CS Committee of Control at Bletchley; David Footman, the head of the Political Section; John Cordeaux, a former Naval Intelligence officer who had run the wartime Dutch Country Section and represented the 'G' sections, which administered overseas stations and supervised their operations; and finally Section IX's head, Kim Philby, representing the interests of counter-espionage.[34]

Meeting throughout October and November 1945, the committee worked against the background of the defection of Igor Gouzenko, a cipher clerk at the Soviet embassy in Ottawa who, in September, had sought asylum in Canada. He was followed by others and 'as spy after spy fell like skeletons out of the cupboard, indignation rose that the Soviet Union should have organised such networks of agents and sympathisers to steal secrets from their Allies during the war'. It came as no surprise to the anti-Bolsheviks of MI6, but the Gouzenko case had a direct effect on the security services. The committee looked at the question of how the Service could best counter Soviet Intelligence and undertake espionage work against the Soviet Union. Philby reported to his Soviet controllers that the 'Committee members expressed the thought that the priority in work against the USSR should be given to the issue of studying the achievements of the Soviet Union in its work on new secret weapons, particularly uranium bombs'. Scientific intelligence-gathering was given particular priority.[35]

The fundamental question that the committee considered was whether MI6 should be organised along geographical lines by country or by functional specialisation, focused upon subjects such as economic, political and scientific intelligence. A compromise was adopted and, henceforth, MI6 was divided into five directorates. The two most important were:

Production (II) – responsible for operational intelligence-gathering and organised on geographical lines with regional Controllers covering northern, western and eastern Europe, the Middle East and the Far East, with another for London-based operations.

Requirements (III) – responsible for analysis and distribution and organised on functional lines.

The other three directorates were Finance and Administration (I), which was administered by an SOE officer; Training and Development (IV), which addressed the growing demand for technical resources and was again run by a former SOE officer, John Munn; and what would become increasingly important, the War Planning Directorate (V).

Beneath the Controllers were the Production or 'P' officers, who supervised operations in two or three countries and were responsible for channelling intelligence gathered abroad to Broadway. Requirements was subdivided into 'R' sections, each responsible for a particular subject – Political (1), Air (2), Naval (3), Military (4), Counter-Intelligence (5), Economic (6), Financial (7), GC&CS/GCHQ (8) and Science (9), which pinpointed what information was required from the five geographical 'P' sections. This basic pattern of organisation remained unchanged for many years.

In 1948 refinements were made to the system with three Chief Controllers – Kenneth Cohen, Chief Controller Europe, John Teague, CC Mediterranean, and James Fulton, CC Pacific – overseeing the eight control areas, which often had overlapping responsibilities.

Since 1931 MI6 has been forbidden to operate within Britain's three-mile limit, and under the Controller Production Research (CP2) the UK Station's function was officially to act as a staging point for officers sent into areas where there was no MI6 station or where operatives faced particular difficulties. The station employed 'buggers and debuggers' to run arm's-length operations, including those against foreign embassies in London which, technically, were not on British territory.[36]

Under the new system Kim Philby controlled the key area of Requirements counter-intelligence (R5), which replaced Section IX and took over Section V. Philby was still responsible for supervising the worldwide collection of all anti-Soviet and anti-communist material, intelligence which, according to Philby's reports to the Soviets, was used 'to discredit individuals in Soviet embassies and communist activities in other countries, to create provocations against them, to force or encourage them to defect to the West'. A great deal of attention was paid to interrogating former Soviet PoWs and other displaced Russians. Philby discovered that the mostly low-level defectors did not know very much about the Soviet Union but were 'very eager to tell whatever they thought British intelligence officers wanted to hear'.[37]

The committee's final report concluded with a 'design of something like a Service, with enough serious inducements to tempt able young men to regard it as a career for life'. It helped that a number of older officers were pensioned off as the Service pruned sections left over from the war, and that Bevin agreed to place officers within the Civil Service pay and benefits structure, which included an allowance for school fees when stationed abroad. Unfortunately, the positive aspects were undermined by Menzies who, while accepting its broad thrust, could not bring himself to cut out more of the dead wood which the plan demanded. Old and trusted colleagues became the Controllers of the Production sections, who, with their own individual and often outdated ways of operating, which harked back to earlier battles against the Bolsheviks, had seemingly learned little from the changes that had been ushered in by the war. Basking in the glow of perceived wartime success, as the younger officers were to discover, they were to have a crucial, highly distorting and damaging effect on the effectiveness and efficiency of the Service.[38]

On 27 November, Findlater Stewart's own report was finally delivered to the Cabinet Secretary, Sir Edward Bridges. A suggestion that in order to avoid wasteful duplication MI6 and MI5 should share a combined headquarters in London was rejected. Instead, the report 'favoured MI6's continued covert life with an added limited capacity to undertake clandestine SOE-style oper-ations'. It would appear that the inquiry had little impact within MI6, though the Service did lose its prize asset, control of the cryptanalytic agency at Bletchley which reverted to Foreign Office supervision.[39]

It was also recommended that 'the time-honoured parallel system, which had so neatly divided the nation's intelligence and security responsibilities since 1909 between MI5 within the Empire and SIS elsewhere in the world, was endorsed'. This was accepted by the Prime Minister after the Colonial Office insisted that outside agencies were not welcome 'on the grounds that disclosure of such could have a disruptive effect'. Careful limits were to be put on their activities. 'Even in the colonies acceding to independence, where SIS could have expected to move in, the British government decreed that MI5 should keep its monopoly.' Known as the Attlee Doctrine, this drawing of the frontier between MI6 and MI5 operations only finally broke down 'when Commonwealth countries such as Cyprus or Ghana became involved with foreign powers – and so entered SIS territory'.[40]

Senior MI6 officers detested the Doctrine, but those officials 'who forecast that the new generation of governments were likely to be the main mischief-makers of the future were earmarked for Whitehall's dustbin of embarrassing discards'. The Doctrine also applied to the dominions of Canada, Australia and New Zealand where MI6 was, too, excluded. The Doctrine was later held responsible by MI6 officers 'for the misleading British assessments of African and Caribbean developments'.[41]

Having lost the battle to retain SOE as a separate organisation, Gubbins, with his deputy, Harry Sporborg, and Director of Finance, John Venner, who had been engaged in secret efforts to retain SOE's financial accounts, ensured that the transfer of SO technical assets and resources went smoothly. It was agreed with Menzies that Gubbins would deal with MI6 Vice-Chief John Sinclair. In a parting shot, Gubbins issued a memorandum that recommended 'the establishment of a worldwide network of dormant SOE agents, ready to spring into action on the outbreak of the third world war, backed up by an extensive production of material of a sort designed for special operations'. While the military agreed with the broad thrust of his proposals it was realised that financial restraints made full implementation impractical. A more modest appraisal was undertaken by the JPS, but even this proved too much for the Foreign Office. Sir Alexander Cadogan would only agree that, in times of tension, 'when we pass from a green light to an amber light period, SOE should then set up their organisation in approved countries abroad to meet the threat which has taken shape. Meanwhile, in our view, their preparations for such expansion should be confined to this country.' Sporborg protested to Cadogan that this would be no more than a 'study group' which would be incapable of meeting the requirements in time of war. The chiefs of staff agreed and, in December 1945, recommended acceptance of the JPS paper on the future of SOE. Thus, in essence, tentative agreement was reached on the foundation of what became a European-wide SB network, popularly known as 'Gladio'.[42]

Gubbins's appointment was terminated on 1 January 1946, but the final decision on SO was taken, according to the diary of the Chief of the Imperial General Staff, Alanbrooke, in mid-month after much informal, high-level discussion. By the time the new JIC chair, Harold Caccia, and Menzies attended a meeting of the chiefs of staff to discuss SOE, Alanbrooke had already taken the matter up with Sinclair. They had decided that 'by amalgamating the Secret Intelligence Service with SOE, we could provide a combined organisation that would function automatically in Peace and War'. The amalgamation took effect from 15 January. Two days later, the chiefs confirmed that an SOE 'liquidation party' under John Musson was carrying out the exercise, though it took several months before the process was complete. 'Liquidated' were SOE's technical facilities, including the cipher section which had been kept open until May by the 'mercurial codemaster' Leo Marks, and the supply of various 'Q' devices such as false passports and documentation, miniature cameras and microphones, specialist munitions and weapons used in assassinations and sabotage. The latter were 'asset stripped' and combined with MI6's 'Technical Aid' and 'Documents' support sections into a single Technical Section, housed at Artillery Mansions, near Westminster. Similarly, the training section based at Gosport was merged into MI6's Training and Development Directorate with input into the General Tradecraft course.[43]

During July 1946, the War Office began its own investigation into the 'Control of special units and organisations' and their relation to MI6 activities. The resultant SO directive, which was approved by the Foreign Office, contemplated two forms of SO activity, namely 'covert support to British national interests where threatened, and the maintenance of an organisation capable of quick and effective expansion in time of war'. The first were known as current and were part of the 'revamped SOE units' of the SO branch which was headed by Harold Perkins, who formally handed over all the existing SOE networks. These units would eventually be involved in operations such as detaching Albania from the Soviet bloc (or orbit, as it was known within MI6 and the Foreign Office). The second, and in Gubbins's view by far the more important, were 'prospective' and were planned in anticipation of war and enemy occupation. These came under the remit of MI6's new Directorate of War Planning which seems to have operated on the activist agenda of the chiefs of staff. Its first head was SOE's Brig. John Nicholson, who had been GSOI with the Middle East forces. Executive responsibility for the SO units lay with the Controller in London, and under him regional controllers in Cairo and Singapore. In turn, they were directly responsible to the Vice-Chief of the Service, John Sinclair. War Planning officers were attached to Area Controllerates to oversee planning for sabotage and subversion operations, and the recruitment of stay-behind networks. In addition, War Planning officers under Brian Franks helped develop SOE strategy, with the SAS taking on the role of the wartime British Liaison Officers (BLOs).[44]

Some of the older MI6 officers resented the intrusion of the SO operatives into their hallowed ranks. According to the head of the SOE mission in Greece, and later of the SO contingent inside MI6, Montague ('Monty') Wood-house, 'after SOE was disbanded, only a few ex-SOE officers were incorpor-ated in SIS, and only in junior positions. Almost all senior positions in SIS were held by war-time intelligence officers, who regarded special operations with disrespect.' David Smiley was one of the old SOE hands who 'got the impression that they regarded us as a lot of bungling amateurs'. Gubbins, however, continued to maintain close ties with Menzies, and observers recog-nised that SOE, which continued to 'lurk within' MI6, had a disproportionate influence to its size. This was particularly noticeable in Balkan and Greek affairs, where its stranglehold on operations in the last two years of the war meant that 'the post-war SIS emphasis in this area concentrated on "counter-revolutionary" activities'.[45]

New entrants to the Service, many of whom happened to have been employed by SOE, had to make few adjustments. While they 'found them-selves being trained rather haphazardly, for tasks' such as 'agent running on classic intelligence lines', they also found themselves undertaking 'an opposed [defended] river crossing' as 'so many had done in the war'. Their former head, meanwhile, did not just quietly disappear into business and retirement. Biographer and intelligence insider Peter Wilkinson intrigues with his comment that Gubbins 'no longer had any *formal* responsibility for special operations', which vanished 'into the mists of "official secrecy"'.[46]

Gubbins's heart was still with SO and a great deal of his spare time was spent setting up the Special Forces Club in Kensington. Besides acting as a social club and charity for Resistance members, it helped 'maintain a world-wide network which could be activated in the event of a future war and provide the nucleus of national resistance which experience had taught him would otherwise take years to develop'. Recruitment for later Balkan oper-ations was largely conducted through the club by Gubbins, assisted by Doug-las Dodds-Parker and Gerry Holdsworth. Likewise, in the absence of a formally sanctioned full-blown covert operations programme, 'dining clubs' and 'awards clearing houses' for former 'secret armies', specialised units, such as MI9, and even Admiral Godfrey's Naval Intelligence Directorate acted in a similar capacity, displaying the British habit of informal links and the enduring use of the old-boy network for conducting SO.

While it was true that 'clandestine services shrank rather than expanded' after 1945, many of the SO operatives remained on call. A number became entangled in numerous worldwide counter-insurgency campaigns when the British had to deal with guerrillas who had been (and the irony was not lost on those involved) trained and armed by SOE during the war. It was only natural that to counter them former SOE officers were recalled for duty, first in Palestine and then in Malaya.[47]

Despite the disbandment of SOE as an independent centre, and in the face of strong Foreign Office opposition, some regional SOE organisations still 'managed to survive until 1947, independent of and often in parallel with MI6 representation'. Increasingly, however, SO and the more aggressive intelligence-gathering, which had had a degree of autonomy under the protection of the military, would require the approval of the Foreign Office. Belatedly and gradually, the Foreign Office would impose its view of the Cold War on the Secret Intelligence Service.

Over the winter of 1945/6, MI6 reorientated itself to take on the Soviet challenge and developed, one of the new intake, George Young, thought, into 'a well-trained corps speaking every known tongue and a few unknown ones, experienced in separating fact from forgery, and with specialist qualifications in the professional crafts ancient and modern'. A leading figure in Military Intelligence, Major-General Sir Kenneth Strong, concurred, later boasting that the latter years of the Second World War and the beginning of the postwar world were 'in a sense the golden age of British Intelligence'. 'Fortunately', Young wrote, 'Menzies remained in the saddle until 1952, during the rundown of defence and military organisations. His successors benefitted for at least a decade from his methods and influence.' Others begged to differ.[48]

CHAPTER 3

CONTAINMENT

During July 1945, the Foreign Office's new Permanent Under-Secretary, Orme 'Moley' Sargent, was lunching with a colleague when they heard news of the Labour Party's decisive general election victory. Sargent descended into 'the depths of gloom, prophesying a Communist avalanche over Europe, a weak foreign policy, a private revolution at home and reduction of England [sic] to a second class power'. Shortly after, he produced a memorandum, 'Stocktaking after VE Day', which stated that 'Britain was still a Great Power' and that its main enemy was the Soviet Union. Britain, Sargent argued, had to maintain its interests in the countries of eastern Europe, though Romania and Hungary were thought to be already lost to Soviet domination. 'Further', as historian John Saville noted, 'he developed an early version of what much later came to be known as the "domino" theory'. Britain needed to take action in these countries else, if they fell to the Soviets, its position would be threatened 'further west' in Germany, Italy, Greece and Turkey.[1]

These assumptions were shared by the chiefs of staff and the Joint Intelligence Committee (JIC), which provided the military with a report to the effect that a hostile Soviet Union would be ready to launch a premeditated war by 1956. Using this report, in July 1945 the military's Joint Planning Staff (JPS) produced a digest based on a series of regional appreciations, 'The Security of the British Empire', which outlined British strategic requirements for the postwar world. With regard to MI6 and the Government Code and Cipher School (GC&CS/GCHQ), the chiefs gave a high priority to 'national'

or 'strategic' intelligence and, in particular, Soviet strategic weapons development.[2]

Most officers inside MI6's Broadway offices regretted the removal of
Churchill from Downing Street – Robert Cecil recognised him as 'a hard
taskmaster; but to consort with him was to consort with greatness' – but they
had little to fear as the election of a socialist government did not bring about
any major break in foreign, defence and intelligence policy. Indeed, Attlee
'promptly removed any threat that the secret organisations might not survive
into peacetime', while the 'permanent government' tried to ensure a seamless
continuation in all three interlinked areas.[3]

Sargent recognised that Britain was not strong enough by itself to withstand Soviet power and needed to enlist the help of an ally. 'The process of
inducing the United States to support a British resistance to Russian
penetration in Europe', he minuted, 'will be a tricky one, and we must
contrive to demonstrate to the American public that our challenge is based
on upholding the liberal idea in Europe and not upon selfish appreciations
as to our position as a Great Power.' An alliance with the United States was
thus not the overriding aim of Britain's foreign policy, but the means by
which to hang on to its imperial past by building on the rhetoric of saving
Western civilisation from the Soviet threat.[4]

John Saville has written that Foreign Office officials, aloof from the economic realities of Britain's bankrupt state, 'appeared incapable of assessing with
any degree of realism the world that was emerging from the massive blood-
letting of the Second World War'. Professor F. S. Northedge adds that they

> never doubted that Britain's old position in the Middle East and
> other such areas of the world would sooner or later be restored
> to more or less what it always had been. Arabs, Iranians and
> even Jews would get used to the idea that Britain, by reason of
> her long experience, was the natural agency to govern them, to
> define their various needs, including defence, and to guide them
> on their way to prosperity and security.

Whitehall, Saville concludes, 'lacked a sense of history, a recognition that the
balance of political forces in the world had changed and was continuing to
change'. Officials were unwilling or unable to understand the opportunities
opened up by nationalism.[5]

Harold Laski told friends that Labour would 'turn the Foreign Office upside
down', but these illusions or 'deeply ingrained beliefs', which Lord Franks later
described as 'the habit and furniture of our minds', were also generally
accepted within the higher echelons of a Labour Party that had little intention
of instigating a 'socialist' foreign policy. Outgoing Conservative Foreign Secretary Anthony Eden had been particularly keen to see the robust anti-communist
Ernest Bevin take over in the Foreign Office. Bevin's private secretary, Frank

Roberts, underlined the close postwar understanding which amounted to a bipartisan foreign policy: 'I had worked under Eden throughout the war and was often used by Bevin as an intermediary to keep Eden informed or to get his reactions.' Eden admitted that there were no important differences on foreign policy between the Conservatives and the new Labour government.[6]

Professor Alan Bullock's monumental biography of Bevin presents a picture of 'a towering Foreign Secretary who seemed to have an almost unerring sense of direction and was the inspiration and the focus of responsibility for a series of initiatives which sought to defend British interests against Soviet encroachments and threats at the beginning of the Cold War'. In reality, Bevin was a Cold War warrior *par excellence* and the dupe of far cleverer minds in the Foreign Office. He was semi-literate and his officials wrote the majority of his telegrams, which he did not always read. Control of the paper flow was easily achieved since the minister, who had a preference for broad generalisations rather than details, and who faced an enormous workload, was hardly ever in the office because of ill health. His speeches in the House of Commons, which did not always make sense, were tidied up for Hansard. Officials were content that he made few changes within the department, so ensuring that the traditional methods of formulating policy were retained. The sensitive aspects of the Cold War and views of Soviet policy continued to be 'developed outside of the Cabinet Room in ad hoc meetings with a few selected Ministers and officials'. The main points of policy were thus set by 'a relatively small group of officials in the Foreign Office who took advantage of the force of Bevin's personality'.[7]

Bevin's much-trumpeted anti-communism appealed to right-wingers. He told former senior SOE official and Conservative politician Douglas Dodds-Parker: 'Leave communism to me. I know all about it. I have been fighting it in the unions for thirty years.' He certainly had a familiarity with communist tactics as former leader of the Transport and General Workers' Union, but it was a world away from international relations, and it could, as a previous admirer, Denis Healey, admitted, 'lead him astray'; in fact, it became more of a hindrance than a help. Like his officials, Bevin was convinced that the Russians were intent on destroying the British Empire, and he shared the same blind spot in that he regarded Western motives as pure, while 'irrationally expecting the Soviets to see them in the same manner'. At the same time, he made 'no allowance for and gave no legitimacy to Soviet threat perception'. By the autumn of 1945, with the massive victories and sacrifices – as many as 27 million dead – on the eastern front still fresh in the memory, Bevin was comparing Stalin to Hitler. Eden was already having reservations, believing that Bevin was 'hysterical' in his relations with the Russians and was leaving Britain with 'few friends'.[8]

If there was a major Labour figure who had a real grasp of the emerging landscape, then it was the taciturn Prime Minister, not Bevin. Attlee opposed

Bevin's power politics and as a pre-war internationalist wished to build up the United Nations (UN) as an effective counter to aggression. It was a policy that the chiefs of staff considered 'defeatist', accusing him of 'practically preaching unilateral disarmament'; while within the Foreign Office it was 'sabotaged' by Sargent, who 'laughed' at the UN. Influenced by private briefings from 'the original and independent strategic thinker', Sir Basil Liddell Hart, Attlee threw down a challenge to British foreign policy. In October 1945, he asked rhetorically in the Cabinet 'where the danger now lay' and bluntly asserted in the Defence Committee that 'there was no one to fight'. He argued that Britain should pull out of the Middle East as it was strategically unimportant. Bevin vigorously resisted after officials filled his mind with visions of the 'domino theory': 'The Soviet Union approaches the Middle East as an artichoke whose leaves are to be eaten one by one.'[9]

Attlee questioned the prevailing orthodoxy that the Soviet Union was committed to world domination. He refused to see the Soviet Union as a major threat that required a military doctrine which he believed, correctly, was beyond Britain's manpower or resources. Innovatively, he viewed foreign policy through the eyes of the Soviets, suggesting that 'we must at all costs avoid trying to seek a cure by building up Germany or by forming blocs aimed at Russia'. He acknowledged that Egypt was 'a British satellite' and thought it unfortunate that Russia had not been invited 'to share responsibility' for the Suez Canal. 'Our claim that we occupy these positions as trustees for the rest of the world that can trust our disinterestedness is not likely to be generally accepted.'[10]

To the consternation of officials and Bevin, in early 1946 Attlee was quite willing to abandon Greece and Turkey. With the Foreign Office's Christopher Warner hovering over his shoulder, Bevin 'quite deliberately struck up images of appeasement', warning that the Soviet Union 'had decided upon an aggressive policy based upon militant communism ... and seemed to stick at nothing, short of war, to obtain her objectives'. The military added that there was 'little or no obstacle in Europe to a Russian advance to the western seaboard ... It was therefore essential to conduct an offensive from bases in the Middle East against the Soviet Union war-making potential.' Unmoved, Attlee wrote to Bevin that Soviet policy might be dictated by fear of another war: 'Fantastic as this is, it may very well be the real grounds of Russian policy. What we consider merely defence may seem to them preparations for an attack.' Attlee worried that 'if Britain adopted the proposed stategic plan, subsequent preparations and moves would ... increase suspicion and contribute to the possibility of war occurring'.[11]

We now know from the recent declassifying of eastern European and Soviet archives that Attlee's analysis was substantially correct. Two commissions appointed by Stalin and headed by senior officials from the Commissariat of Foreign Affairs, Maxim Litvinov and Ivan Maisky, to study postwar reparations and peace treaties, concluded that the main Soviet goal should be to ensure a durable peace, enough for the USSR 'to become so powerful' that 'no combination of powers . . . could even think' of threatening her. That would require 'about ten years for the healing of the wounds inflicted by war', a war that had led to material losses which surpassed 'the national wealth of England or Germany' and which constituted 'one-third of the overall national wealth of the United States'. Fearing that an anti-Soviet bloc would emerge around the Allies, Litvinov argued that 'we must seek some kind of co-operation, in order to have at least a few decades of peace'. Unaware of the 'percentage agreement' betwen Churchill and Stalin, he thought in terms of a 'maximum sphere of interests' which the Soviet Union could claim.[12]

Remarkably free of Marxist-Leninist dictates, the Maisky/Litvinov recommendations formed the basis of Stalin's strategy at Yalta and Potsdam, and his search for 'a protective territorial belt around the USSR, to neutralize the resurgence of its traditional geopolitical rivals, Germany and Japan'. Stalin wanted to be a 'partner in managing the world'. In their study of the new evidence, two Russian historians, Vladislav Zubok and Constantine Pleshakov, conclude: 'At no point did Stalin's demands and ambitions in 1945–46 exceed the maximum zone of responsibility discussed by Litvinov and Maisky. In fact, in some cases Stalin's moves in the international arena were more modest in scope.' During 1946, Stalin 'kept restraining "revolutionaries" not only in Iran, but also in Greece and other places where he did not want to provoke premature confrontation with the British and Americans'.[13]

Christopher Warner was unwilling to consider such heresy, and he continued to work behind the scenes to create a committee under Foreign Office control to counter the Soviet threat. The initial move came in January 1946 when the JIC prepared an analysis of the Soviet Union's capabilities and intentions. The report led to Frank Roberts, then diplomat in Moscow, sending to London throughout March a stream of telegrams on Anglo-Soviet relations which were to have a considerable impact within the Foreign Office.[14]

Not a Russian-speaker, Roberts was helped by 'an excellent and very sensible expert on the Soviet scene', George Bolsover, who went on to head the London School of Slavonic Studies, in which capacity he maintained close ties with MI6. There was also a pre-war Foreign Office 'Intelligence Officer', J. H. Adam Watson, later of the Information Research Department and a key figure in Washington, co-ordinating information policy and Special Operations (SO) with the Americans. The special section they established to report on the Soviet press proved to be an invaluable source for the Moscow telegrams. Roberts concluded that 'we are faced with a Soviet policy designed to advance Soviet interests at every possible opportunity, regardless of those of its allies, and it now seems regardless even of treaty obligations'. He went on to outline an 'alarming' situation in which 'Soviet security has become hard to distinguish from Soviet imperialism and it is becoming uncertain whether there is, in fact, any limit to Soviet expansion'.[15]

In receipt of the telegrams, Warner called for a counter-propaganda campaign to fight communism and backed Roberts's proposal for a body to study Soviet activities. In truth, however, Roberts had not been dogmatic in his approach and was advocating a realistic assessment which judged that 'these people were hostile but if you handle them the right way you can live with them'. Warner slapped down such views and insisted that they not only collate material but, in a mirror image of Soviet covert planning, co-ordinate Foreign Office departments in a high-level global British response. Warner concluded: 'The first essential is to treat the problem of Anglo-Soviet relations in the same way as major military problems were treated during the war. It calls for the closest co-ordination of political strategy, for a very thorough study embracing every aspect of Soviet policy – not forgetting the ubiquitous activities of the communist parties directed, if not controlled in detail, from Moscow.' At his request, in April 1946, the 'Committee on Policy Towards Russia', or 'Russia Committee', was created to analyse Soviet thinking and make policy recommendations. Composed of Foreign Office officials, during its weekly meetings it was required to plan Britain's counter-strategy with particular attention paid to what Warner described as 'the Russian campaign against this country'. The committee maintained close contact with the JIC 'with a view to co-ordinating intelligence and policy at every stage'. The intention was to mobilise world opinion in co-operation with the United States and, 'to a lesser degree', France.[16]

At the first meeting of the Russia Committee, chaired by Oliver Harvey, on 2 April, Warner rejected Soviet claims regarding the need for security as a catchword to cloak a foreign policy of aggression. On 7 May, the committee considered Warner's lengthy memorandum, 'The Soviet Campaign against This Country and our Response To It', in which he warned of the Soviet Union 'practising the most vicious power politics' in which 'the Soviet Government are carrying on an intense campaign to weaken, deprecate and harry this country in every possible way.' Warner added that 'we should be unwise not to take the Russians at their word, just as we should have been wise to take *Mein Kampf* at its face value'. He based his assessment on three points: the return to the pure doctrine of Marxism-Leninism-Stalinism; the intense concentration on building up Soviet industrial and military strength; and the revival of the bogy of external danger to the Soviet Union. In a bleak assessment, Warner dismissed Soviet claims of 'war weariness' and Soviet suspicions of western behaviour. While recognising that the Soviet Union would not get involved in another war 'for at least the next few years . . . As in the case of Hitler and Poland, they may miscalculate. The time might, indeed, come when they were actually ready to consider war as a deliberate aim, and perhaps at no distant date.' He believed it was important 'to attack and expose the myths . . . that a new Germany is to be built up for use against Russia' and that Britain had 'aggressive designs against Russia'.

Warner advocated a 'defensive-offensive policy' with a propaganda campaign backing social democrats with 'all such moral and material support as is possible, without going as far as actually to endanger their lives or organisation'. Acknowledging that this had already been undertaken 'in certain cases and on special occasions', he added 'it has not been accepted as a principle that we should do so'. But now the situation required 'exceptional methods to strengthen the hands of friends in the coming elections in France, the Social Democrats in Germany and to help the Austrian Government to resist communist infiltration and Russian intimidation'. Warner's memorandum was very influential in formulating foreign, defence and intelligence policy and, according to one historian, ranked 'as a British equivalent to the Truman Doctrine a year later'.[17]

In May, the Russia Committee drafted guidelines for a counter-offensive propaganda campaign to be planned by Ivone Kirkpatrick, who had organised similar activities while working alongside Menzies for British Intelligence during the First World War. He also drew on his Second World War experience with the Special Operations and Political Warfare Executives as wartime controller of the BBC European Services, though he had been vitriolic in his criticism of the management of both organisations. Recommending that the campaign be educative, Kirkpatrick suggested 'that the BBC Home Service be approached though the BBC's Governors; that the Royal Institute for International Affairs (RIIA) should be approached with a view to the inclusion of suitable material in their publications; and that the Foreign Office should endeavour to influence the home press and foreign correspondents in the right direction'. Abroad,

> the support of the BBC's foreign service should be enlisted; that the Central Office of Information should be requested to carry suitable material in the feature articles which it placed in large numbers of foreign newspapers and also in newsreels and documentaries; and finally that the Foreign Office arrange for visits to Britain by foreign trade union leaders, politicians and publicists who could be relied on to take the opportunity of disseminating British propaganda on their return.

Kirkpatrick drew an analogy with wartime SO: 'The V sign was emblazoned all over the world. But at the same time we acted. We parachuted men, money and arms into occupied territory . . . Propaganda on the largest possible scale was co-ordinated with our policy. The result was a success.'[18]

These proposals prefigured a 'liberation' policy and were certainly a decisive moment in the formation of the Cold War. It would be wrong, however, to assume that the Russia Committee was any kind of all-embracing co-ordinating or overseeing body in respect of the intelligence services. The strongest impetus for a counter-strategy continued to emanate not from the Foreign Office but from the military. Many of the MI6 operations that Warner hinted at, and those ranged against the Soviet Union – such as those Michael Herman has termed 'intrusive' intelligence-gathering, which ventured into Special and Political Action (psychological warfare) – had been set in train with the sanction of the chiefs of staff. The evidence suggests that, in terms of a counter-offensive, the military and MI6 were in advance of the Foreign Office by about twelve months. During this period MI6 did not have a Foreign Office liaison officer looking over the shoulder of Menzies, who to a great extent relied on the support of his friends among the military. While the Chief had access to the Prime Minister and, seemingly, met regularly with Bevin – though there appears to be no documentary record of such meetings – he did not have the close relationship with them which he had enjoyed with Churchill.[19]

It was also true that once the broad parameters of policy were set, the means of achieving results were largely left to Menzies's discretion. Oversight was minimal and often non-existent. Liaison by the JIC chair, Victor Cavendish-Bentinck, who was briefly inserted into the hierarchy as the Foreign Office representative following Robert Cecil's departure in April, was similarly disrupted in August 1945 when he was appointed an ambassador. As Cecil noted: 'These drastic changes coincided with the post-war reorganisation of MI6 and Philby's setting up of Section IX. It was a bad moment to relax Foreign Office supervision over MI6.' Indeed, the position of Foreign Office adviser was not resumed for another seven years.[20]

Gladwyn Jebb wrote that the Foreign Secretary 'welcomed the new committee and took much interest in it', though others have suggested that Bevin was 'not yet willing to authorize wholesale implementation of its recommendations . . . for tough counter-propaganda methods'. The extent of Bevin's commitment to SO remains a matter of dispute. The writer closest to MI6 thinking, Anthony Verrier, believes that Bevin was 'an enthusiastic supporter', while academic Richard Aldrich considers that he was 'never an enthusiast of covert activities'. There is a third opinion which suggests that Bevin was a relatively strong enthusiast for such operations, but was reluctant to endorse them until he had resolved the dispute with the Prime Minister. Attlee's opposition to Foreign Office strategy was not countered until the beginning of 1947; until then, Bevin had no room for manoeuvre and, in effect, it was Attlee who refused to give the Russia Committee free rein. Once released from that constraint, Bevin probably sanctioned more SO – even if only indirectly – than any other postwar Foreign Secretary.[21]

Certainly, Bevin was initially far from convinced by the Russia Committee's strategy, partly because of its expressly anti-Soviet stance, which he knew would be opposed by Attlee and the Left of the Labour Party. The Foreign Secretary wanted a more positive approach extolling the virtues of social democracy. Raymond Smith provides evidence that the hardliners, Warner and the new Permanent Under-Secretary, Sargent, remained convinced of the strategy and manoeuvred Bevin into supporting a 'counter-offensive' campaign by consciously playing on the social democratic theme. Within the space of two years, the theme had been abandoned and replaced by an explicitly anti-Soviet message.[22]

A publicity sub-committee of the Russia Committee was set up to consider propaganda measures that might be approved. Gradually, officials chipped away at Bevin's wariness as they considered action on a country-by-country basis, beginning with Iran. The Foreign Secretary eventually agreed to a propaganda campaign in Iran which 'proved to be the hammer and chisel' by which officials gathered support for their strategy. The same tactic was adopted 'for the whole of the Middle East and also in respect of certain matters in Germany'. At the same time, contacts were made with the Dominions, Colonial, India and Burma Offices and with the Control Offices for Germany and Austria, where officials were 'drawn into the Foreign Office's anti-communist stratagem'. Backed by opinion from missions overseas, the Russia Committee discreetly began to reformulate its counter-strategy in an attempt to secure Bevin's approval. This led to a call for more 'ideological' reporting from the missions in order to determine which local groups 'subscribe in reasonable measure to the fundamental thesis of social democracy and which are inspired by the pseudo-communism of Moscow'.[23]

Officials also played on the conviction that there was a 'Communist Fifth Column' whose target was 'top warmonger Ernest Bevin'. Furious, Bevin exploded: 'What have I done for them to be getting at me?' With Bevin's sanction and Attlee's go-ahead – he had no scruples about domestic security operations – Warner instructed MI6's counter-espionage department, R5, and MI5's F Branch to prevent infiltration by crypto-communists into 'innocent' international delegations from western countries. He especially emphasised Russia's 'clever trick' of establishing international federations of various kinds under the control of communists, prime examples being the World Federation of Trade Unions and the proliferation of peace congresses. According to George Young, MI6 'had no difficulty in establishing who was manipulating the whole complex, and the sources of funds'. Investigations were also ordered into the International Student Congress which met in Prague in August 1946, prompting further inquiries into the management of the British National Union of Students.[24]

By September 1946, the controller of the BBC's European Service, General Sir Ian Jacob, had been conscripted to the Russia Committee to seek 'guidance' on policy towards the Soviet Union. Sargent was subsequently able to minute that 'the BBC are over the whole foreign field extremely helpful and co-operative'. Although by then many low-key action programmes were in place, Warner and others were concerned that the Prime Minister was still unconvinced of the need for a 'defensive-offensive' policy. A more hardline approach was required. In early November, senior diplomat Sir Nigel Ronald told the Russia Committee that 'we shall without question have to have recourse to the most unusual methods: but then we are dealing with most unusual people'.[25]

On 1 December 1946, in a self-typed letter, Attlee informed Bevin that he was 'worried about Greece' and concerned about the drain on Britain's limited resources. He thought that the 'strategic importance of communications through the Mediterranean in terms of modern warfare is very much overrated by our military advisers . . . The Middle East is only an outpost position. I am beginning to doubt whether the Greek game is worth the candle.' He warned that even if America gave economic assistance to Greece and Turkey, Britain should not be expected to continue military obligations. When Foreign Office minister Hector McNeil cabled Bevin that there was considerable reluctance to continue British commitments to the two countries, the chiefs of staff hit back with a report, 'Future Policy towards Turkey and Greece', which stressed their importance and that 'American assistance was essential' in Greece to combat the 'bandits'. Still not deterred, Attlee made 'a cool and rational' – also described by John Saville as a 'socialist' – criticism of Foreign Office and the chiefs' policy which he characterised as 'a strategy of despair'. They were propping up 'essentially reactionary' governments which 'afford excellent soil for the sowing of communist seed', with the result that Britain was seen as 'supporting vested interests and reaction against reform and revolution'. He went on to question the assumptions made about the ideological basis of the Soviet Union and its apparent aggressive desire for world revolution. Finally, he called for serious negotiations with Moscow.[26]

Attlee's attitude 'stunned' Foreign Office officials. Immediately, they began to co-ordinate their response with the chiefs of staff. On 9 January 1947, they replied that negotiations were unacceptable and Bevin rebuked the Prime Minister, accusing him of 'appeasement': 'It would be Munich all over again, only on a world scale, with Greece, Turkey and Persia as the first victims in place of Czechoslovakia.' Isolated and shaken by Bevin's memorandum, Attlee was faced by the rebellious chiefs, who were asked by the Chief of the Imperial General Staff, Montgomery, 'whether they were prepared to resign rather than give way over the Middle East'. Sir Arthur Tedder and Admiral Sir John Cunningham 'agreed wholeheartedly'. When the Prime Minister was informed of their resolve, he capitulated to the overwhelming pressure. Thus was the course of the Cold War set with the militarists gaining the upper hand, though there was a twist.[27]

On 29 January, Chancellor of the Exchequer Hugh Dalton recommended to the Cabinet that 'as it is absolutely out of the question for the UK to shoulder such a burden, we should cut our losses and abandon Greece'. Six days later, the British ambassador in Washington, Lord Inverchapel, informed the Americans of the decision and, on 21 February, at three o'clock, the First Secretary at the Washington embassy, and former MI6 officer with the wartime British Security Co-ordination (BSC), Herbert Sichel, delivered a historic note on blue paper to an old friend, the head of the Near East Division of the State Department, Loy Henderson, announcing that Britain would be withdrawing aid from Greece as of 31 March.[28]

The main obstacle to the Americans taking on Britain's interventionist role in the Cold War was thought to be the prominent isolationist Senator Arthur Vandenberg. MI6, however, had prepared the ground well. In his thesis on the role of British Intelligence in wartime American politics, Thomas Mahl suggests that MI6 planted three 'social companions' close to Vandenberg. The three women were Mrs Mitzi Sims, who claimed close ties to BSC head William Stephenson; BSC agent Elizabeth Thorpe, who was better known by her *nom de plume* 'Cynthia'; and Eveline Paterson (Lady Cotter). Cynthia, whose 'loyalty to her employers', according to the secret BSC history, was 'complete', and whose importance 'it would be difficult to over-emphasize', operated by singling out top men and then seducing them. Eveline Paterson moved in diplomatic circles and was intimately involved with Vandenberg in the crucial 1945–48 period. Using this unique access, the Service helped impel the senator to put his considerable influence behind Truman and an internationalist stance that was more sympathetic towards British policies. Mrs Paterson was his companion during the drafting of the 'Vandenberg Resolution', which paved the way for the Senate to pass, on 11 June 1948, the North Atlantic Treaty. Considered by the FBI to be a British Intelligence agent, Mrs Paterson appears to have been 'run' by the American pro-British BSC/OSS veteran Donald Downes, who had run Cynthia during the war.[29]

Debate still continues about the reasons for the sudden British announcement on Greece. Was it purely a financial action following a disastrous winter for the economy? In fact, as we have seen, the decision did not arrive out of the blue, but was 'the culmination of long-term discussions within and amongst several government departments, in which strategic factors were probably as important as financial necessity, realpolitik, or political pressure'. Robert Frazier suggests that by this decision – which directly led to the launch on 12 March of the 'Truman Doctrine' and the aggressive ideological crusade against communism known as 'containment' – 'it may not be too far fetched to consider that Britain started the Cold War'.[30]

In his biography of Bevin, Francis Williams suggests that the Foreign Secretary

shrewdly assessing in his mind the current state of American
opinion and cumulative effect upon it of Russian policy decided
that the time had come to force the American administration to
a major policy decision ... It was a declaration deliberately
designed to bring America fully into the defence of Europe ...
Judging by its developing consequences Bevin's carefully timed
act must be seen as one of the most decisive strokes in the
history of diplomacy ... He had achieved his first purpose.

W. N. Medlicott accepts that Bevin had 'hatched a tricky plot', though, of
course, he had been forced into the position by Attlee's insistence on moving
out of Greece. It is entirely possible that the Prime Minister's capitulation to
the chiefs of staff was dependent on that policy being implemented, thus
forcing Bevin to turn to the Americans. John Saville has pointed out that it
is possible to see the outline of a compromise that included major reductions
of troops in Austria, Trieste, Greece and Japan, considerable reductions in
the Middle East, and evacuation of India and Burma by 31 March.[31]

Bevin and the Foreign Office still saw Britain as a world power, and any
comparative decline in economic and military strength was viewed as 'a
temporary rather than a permanent phenomenon', which could be 'rectified
by combining the resources of Western Europe with those of the British
Empire'. He held, however, extraordinary ideas on the Empire, which Ronald
Hyman has described as 'neo-Palmerstonian cosmoplastic dreams'. This was
expressed by Bevin's absurd version of the 'Third Force' in which attempts
to organise a western European Union were related to a Euro-Africa bloc
linking Europe to the Middle East and Africa. Bevin's idea was to exploit –
and that is the correct term – the 'invisible empire' of the Sterling Area, which
'included 1,000 million people', with the aim of dealing with the dollar 'area
on a basis of equality'. In practice, the Sterling Area proved to be a financial
burden that hindered economic recovery.[32]

Behind the Third Force lay the idea of Britain retaining an independent
role 'in the first rank of global powers'. It would be based on 'post-war
economic recovery and a middle democratic socialist way between the harsh
and conflicting ideologies of unfettered American capitalism and repressive
Soviet Communism'. In order to sustain its role, Foreign Office officials recognised that, in the short term, while economic recovery took place, Britain
would be dependent on the Americans for economic and political support.
It was acknowledged, however, that Britain's relationship with the United
States – built on an unprecedented degree of wartime co-operation – had
'increasingly developed into one where Britain was very much the junior
partner', and this had 'aroused concern and resentment amongst British
elites'. In the long term, the Foreign Office was confident that Britain would
regain its independence from the United States.[33]

Britain would also have to avoid being drawn into a federal European system, which would threaten relations with the Commonwealth, although there was no reason to oppose a loosely based, non-federalist western European Union. Bevin and the Foreign Office found European integration increasingly unacceptable as France, Italy and Belgium were regarded as thoroughly penetrated by Soviet communism. There was a resultant fear – and the idea of disease was never far from their minds – that dealing with communist and unstable governments might result in 'contamination'. To avoid this, the Americans would be required to help block the spread of communism and stabilise British imperial influence. United States anti-colonialism would be blunted, Bevin believed, by sharing with it the exploitation of Africa's strategic raw materials and by appeals to anti-communism.

Bevin 'appears to have had no ideas of how to proceed with his grandiose plans'. What did take place was a series of counter-insurgency campaigns, mostly conducted by MI5-backed local security forces as part of the Attlee Doctrine, against nationalist and democracy-seeking movements, which were rarely communist-backed as the propaganda alleged.[34]

These campaigns and the Bevin Cold War enterprise were kept afloat by the valuable Marshall Aid dollars which flooded into the Treasury. As economist J. M. Keynes acknowledged of an earlier American loan: 'thus it comes out in the wash that the American loan is primarily required to meet the political and military expenditure overseas'. American dollars allowed Britain to pursue the domestic and foreign policies that had brought about the balance of payments crisis. With Attlee's strikingly accurate prognosis sidelined, Britain continued to maintain a grandiose global defence structure that involved a massive military commitment to the Middle and Far East, even though the loss of Singapore during the war had openly revealed the limits of British imperial power.[35]

Britain's military presence remained, however, either too outdated or deficient in numbers to back up Bevin's dreams of world influence. Without 'the gunboats', much of the burden would have to be left to the limited resources of the intelligence services. This was recognised by the chiefs of staff who, in May 1947, as austerity began to bite, issued a definitive statement on 'Future Defence Policy'. They noted that within the Soviet Union 'the high standard of security achieved renders our collection of intelligence difficult and makes it all the more likely that Russia will have the advantage of surprise at the onset'. The chiefs concluded that 'it is also of the greatest importance that our Intelligence organisation should be able to provide us with adequate and timely warning. The smaller the armed forces the greater the need for developing our Intelligence Services in peace to enable them to fulfil this responsibility.'[36]

In turn, this would lead to an expansion of SO. As Richard Aldrich argues, during the war covert action and subversion were 'peripheral compared to the grand strategic direction of the war'; it was armies which won the battle. In the Cold War, however, 'subversion and other forms of covert action would increasingly constitute central instruments in this struggle'.[37]

CHAPTER 4

'UNCERTAIN ALLIES'

In the postwar intelligence world, Stewart Menzies had one card which he could play to advantage, namely the immense goodwill and respect that were shown by allies to the Service following victory. Dick White wrote of his predecessor in the *Dictionary of National Biography* that foreigners found in Menzies 'the personal embodiment of an intelligence mystique they believed characteristically and historically British'. This 'contributed to his international influence and it was a potent factor in establishing the Anglo-American and other Allied intelligence alliances'. The Chief – who made only one trip abroad during the entire war – must have known, however, that deep down such influence and alliances rested largely on myths and that, while a 'special relationship' with the Americans on intelligence co-operation was constructed, each side remained ambivalent about the other's motives and intentions.

At the beginning of the war the Cabinet had accepted a chiefs of staff report that Britain could only continue to fight with any chance of success if the United States provided economic and financial support. It thus became essential to move America from its policy of isolation, and a prime role in achieving this objective was tasked to MI6 and its North American station, the British Security Co-ordination (BSC).

The BSC internal history (known as 'The Bible' to former officers), which offers a fascinating insight into MI6 field craft, reveals that the Service's operations in this covert war against the isolationists in the United States – code-named '48 Land' – mostly involved 'political warfare' (or psychological warfare as the Americans called it). BSC officers recruited members of the press and radio, used the leaders of the eastern establishment to front as directors a number of groups that were secretly controlled by the British, subsidised news agencies, planted stories, manipulated opinion polls, and smeared opponents. So-called 'combat funds' were used to legally harass targets, while litigation was favoured as a means of gaining further publicity for additional disinformation. Officers rarely met with sub-agents, such as journalists and academics; instead, they operated through intermediaries or agents recruited in the host country.[1]

According to Ernest Cuneo (code-named 'Crusader'), who acted as liaison between the White House, the various US security and intelligence agencies, and British intelligence, the BSC campaign of trying to push the United States into war was a great success. Indeed, it was 'a pushover', reminding Cuneo of the Chaucer line, 'He fell upon her and would have raped her – but for her ready acquiescence.'[2]

Out of this success, which resulted in Lend-Lease and other economic and arms initiatives, grew the notion of a 'special relationship' between the United States and Britain. It has been persuasively argued by Susan Ann Bower that this special relationship was based on a myth created through British propaganda efforts to help bolster Britain's foreign policy concerns. The Americans were largely concerned, as Clive Ponting has written, with realpolitik – 'making some cool calculations about where their national interests lay'.[3]

By the beginning of 1941 Britain was 'as near to bankruptcy as it was possible to go without actual default'. At which point, the country was forced to liquidate on a massive scale its financial and commercial assets in North America, handing over in the process its entire gold reserves. It was then forced to hunt around for further scraps of gold to pay the demanding Americans, whose attitude Churchill described as like that of a 'sheriff collecting the last assets of a helpless debtor'. But that was not all; Britain also transferred all its major technical and intelligence secrets to the Americans. Britain's claim to be an independent power had collapsed to the point where the country was, in effect, Ponting suggests, 'a client of the United States'. The myth of the 'special relationship' was thus sedulously cultivated, 'in part to help support the dreams of strategic strength but also to disguise Britain's real role . . . it was both convenient and comfortable to believe in the identity of interests between the two countries, the shared heritage of the "English-speaking peoples" and American magnanimity'.[4]

There was, of course, some substance to the notion of a special relationship in the intelligence field, and the idea was promoted by MI6, 'the Friends', with their American 'Cousins'. Charles Ellis, who had been stationed in Washington as deputy to BSC's head Sir William Stephenson when the US entered the war, was credited by senior US wartime intelligence officer David Bruce with helping to set up the Office of the Co-ordinator of Information's (COI) Secret Intelligence branch. As important, but largely unrecognised, was the contribution of Walter Bell, a former barrister who had helped run the small pre-war MI6 office in New York when the United States was regarded as an 'intelligence backwater'. Bell joined Ellis in the BSC, where he played a key role in the early days of the COI's successor, the Office of Strategic Services (OSS), and when posted back to London was appointed the MI6 liaison officer with the OSS.[5]

Initially, MI6 was the senior partner in the Anglo-American intelligence relationship; a position that was reinforced by Bill Donovan's signed agreement with Menzies which barred OSS men from running operations into Europe. In addition, MI6 officers 'assessed the intelligence and passed along as much product as they felt their American juniors could profitably assimilate'. The Americans supported the arrangement because, as the head of the Secret Intelligence section, Henry Hyde, later recalled: 'OSS owed everything to the British services. Everything – even such technical matters as suitcase wireless sets, one-time pad ciphers, and all manner of devices used by secret services came to us through Menzies's generosity.'[6]

Menzies's air of superiority – another case of the Greeks teaching the Romans – owed a great deal to the spectacular success with Ultra and the breaking of the German Enigma code machine. It was, however, misplaced. As Ponting has pointed out, 'when the British fought alone . . . they were unable to take advantage of the information they were receiving because of their lack of military power'. Churchill had been well informed about German military intentions but 'could do little to counter them. Intelligence could play its full part only when British inferiority in manpower and equipment had been replaced by American superiority in both areas.'[7]

Wartime MI6 officer Malcolm Muggeridge recalled 'those Elysian days' when the first OSS officers arrived in London, but realised 'how short a time the honeymoon lasted!' The British set-up was soon 'overtaken in personnel, zest and scale of operations, above all, in expendable cash!' The change came after D-Day, when the OSS broke the accord with Menzies and began to deploy its units in large numbers in Europe. By 1945 the Americans had taken effective charge in some theatres of operations. American Intelligence officer Lawrence Huston admitted that 'our very close relations with British Intelligence remained good but not nearly as close. Our interests were growing apart in the Middle East.' Increasingly, OSS officers took a more independent line and a number viewed their relationship with MI6 with a certain cynicism, and were wary of co-operating too closely with their British 'allies'. OSS officers joked that they were fighting to 'Save England's Asiatic Colonies'.[8]

According to the official history of the CIA, the British had 'allowed American officers to observe the inter-relationships of their services and the working of their intelligence system, for reports to the OSS and benefit of the American system'. The Americans did not, however, regard this solely as an act of disinterested friendship. Aides close to President Roosevelt thought that MI6 had used this closeness to 'penetrate' the OSS and that, therefore, its usefulness after the war would be 'seriously impaired'. The OSS was seen as too dependent upon British sources for its information. Short-sighted officials in the Foreign Office hoped and believed that this dependence would continue after the war. In summing up the success of British intelligence strategy in the United States, in August 1945, J. G. Donnelly commented that 'the Americans, without necessarily knowing it, are bound to continue to see the world in large measure through the British window'. Donovan's failure to be appointed to head a postwar centralised intelligence service, primarily because of his pronounced anglophilia, was proof that that would not be the case.[9]

Collaboration between Britain and the United States seemed to change little with the ending of hostilities, but a number of joint committees, Alec Danchev observes, 'soon withered and died', while 'others eked out a precarious existence on the coat-tails of the old wartime Anglo-American aristocracy'. Danchev stresses, however, that it was not all decline: 'The organisation was moribund; but the animating spirit was never completely quenched. At American behest, co-operation went underground.' While many British Intelligence officials were willing to make it known that they had a new enemy – the Soviet Union – in their sights, it took longer for the Americans to adjust their view. With the war against Japan still raging, the Americans remained amicable towards the Russians and, unlike the British, were still willing to exchange intelligence with their partners in the Far East. Substantive collaboration with the British continued on scientific and technical information exchange, intelligence assessments and operations. In particular, this was true in the burgeoning field of electronic communications, where the British aimed for '100% co-operation' with the Americans on signals intelligence (SIGINT).[10]

The initiative in transforming the wartime collaboration into a postwar SIGINT alliance – the true heart of the special relationship – was taken by the British, who, despite an undoubted brilliance in cryptanalysis, realised that it would be they who would need partners and not the other way round. The foundations were laid during a spring 1945 world tour by the head of GC&CS at Bletchley Park, Sir Edward Travis, his assistant, Harry Hinsley, and Commander Clive Leohnis of the Admiralty Operational Centre. The aim was to transfer redundant personnel and resources from Europe and the Middle East to the Far East for the war with Japan. At the end of April, the trio began talks in Washington with representatives of the army, navy and State Department, and were encouraged to discover that the Americans were already persuaded of the need for an Anglo-American attack on Soviet codes and ciphers.[11]

Much was dependent in this field on personal relationships. A good example of this informal 'underground' was provided by MI6's scientific adviser, Professor R. V. Jones, who was responsible for establishing with the American Eric Ackerman a unit at Obernkirchen which monitored Russian radar. According to colleagues at the main US signals intelligence-gathering agency, the Army Special Branch, 'although this was almost the only British effort in the field, it made it well worthwhile for them to exchange information with us'. By June 1945, informal agreements had also been reached between officials of the British War Office and US War Department on intelligence-sharing arrangements and for collecting material – code-named RATTAN – on the Soviet Union. 'There is no other field in which it is so essential that the British and ourselves work closely together,' an American official reported, 'because when a nation begins to throw its weight around here, there and everywhere, it is a good idea to have an accurate idea of how much weight is involved.' The Americans were similarly impressed with the RAF's 'excellent' methodical early 'Ferret' flights to plot Russian radar, while the two sides' photographic reconnaissance organisations began to share their maps of various parts of the world.[12]

When the US administration began to think in terms of a peacetime central intelligence agency, officials turned to the anglophiles in the intelligence community to create its outline. OSS man and former New York lawyer William H. Jackson put forward a proposal to take advantage of the intimacy of US–UK military relations to make a thorough study of the British Intelligence system, before the 'Foreign Office got around to regarding Americans once more as foreigners'. During July 1945, Jackson spent two weeks in London, where it appears that his principal informant was the soon-to-be departed Foreign Secretary, Anthony Eden. Jackson submitted his report to Bill Donovan and James Forrestal, Secretary of the Navy and an influential voice in intelligence matters. Highly sympathetic to the British approach to the organisation of secret intelligence, the report established in government circles the idea that Jackson was an expert on British Intelligence. With Kingman Douglass, a friend of Menzies who had been the senior US Army Air Force intelligence liaison officer in the British Air Ministry in London during the war, Jackson was an influential adviser to the War Department committee, looking at the problem of unifying the intelligence services.[13]

In seeking a solution, the Americans drew on British experience. A remnant of the BSC lingered on as part of the Treasury delegation to the US dealing with the European Recovery Programme, while MI6's Walter Bell returned to Washington to provide guidance as First Secretary to the British ambassador, Lord Inverchapel. Other intelligence personnel had been seconded to the British Joint Staff Mission where MI6 liaison officer Tim O'Connor had been advising on cryptanalytic collaboration. In London, the appointment of former BSC deputy Charles Ellis (who was much admired by the Americans for his contribution to the development of their own intelligence service) as MI6 Controller for North and South America was seen as a sign of further close co-operation on intelligence matters.[14]

It became clear, however, that there would be a divergence of goals between the two countries, and in some areas, for instance South-East Asia, Britain would be heavily dependent on American willingness to share its resources. The collapse of power in that region appeared to make little or no impression on British perceptions, but it did on the Americans. Despite Charles Ellis's promotion to Controller for South-East Asia and the Far East, even the most sympathetic US Intelligence officials became increasingly wary of sustaining Britain's continuing colonial ambitions. By October 1945, when Travis, Hinsley and Group Capt. Eric Jones returned to Washington to resume negotiations on peacetime SIGINT collaboration, the JIC was reporting that problems had begun to creep into the intelligence exchanges, with clear signs of an American reversion to isolationism. Opposition to intelligence co-operation, though initially only in the SIGINT field, was overridden by a presidential edict to the US military: 'In view of the disturbed conditions of the world and the necessity of keeping informed of technical developments and possible hostile intentions of foreign nations . . . it is recommended that you authorize continuation of collaboration between the United States and the United Kingdom in the field of communications intelligence.' It gave the Joint Chiefs of Staff *carte blanche* to 'extend, modify or discontinue this collaboration, as determined to be in the best interests of the United States'.[15]

Around this time, the anglophile David Bruce visited London as part of a survey on events in Europe. After dining with Menzies, Bruce persuaded Allen Dulles, who was helping to reorganise American intelligence, of the value of a centralised service. Following an intense bureaucratic turf battle between the services, state and the White House, on 22 January 1946 the Americans established their new agency, the Central Intelligence Group (CIG), forerunner of the CIA, which was set up – unconstitutionally – as an interim intelligence-gathering co-ordinating body for the National Intelligence Authority. The CIG employed many former OSS officers sympathetic towards the British, including its chief of plans, Henry Hyde, and Acting Deputy Director Kingman Douglass. Menzies struck an intelligence-gathering agreement with Douglass in order to share material in common studies on the Soviet order of battle (OB), with the result that a permanent CIG Liaison Group was stationed in London. They attended meetings of the newly created Joint Intelligence Board, which covered a 'complete exchange of information from all sources and all subjects except commercial'.[16]

During February and March 1946, Menzies also chaired a secret Anglo-American conference in London to settle the details of a joint SIGINT agreement with the US military. Also acting on behalf of the Canadians and

Australians – the 'White Commonwealth' – Menzies reached an agreement which expanded upon the CIG–Joint Intelligence Board accord. During July and August, on behalf of the new CIG director, General Vandenberg, Jackson and Douglass were in London to further study the British intelligence system. Their subsequent report greatly 'influenced the development of the Central Intelligence Agency'. To some American intelligence officials, including the anglophiles, this proved to be a misguided influence. Ernest Cuneo later blamed the CIA's illegal covert activities on the OSS tradition which he believed had developed from the British Security Co-ordination. The British, he argued, 'should acknowlege some responsibility for starting us down the primrose path'.[17]

A visible sign that a special intelligence relationship existed was the group of British officers who were attached to the CIG in Washington. They included Peter Parker, later chair of British Rail, who had served during the war in a 33rd Corps counter-intelligence unit on the North Burma border. He had been dispatched with an American unit to Tokyo in October 1945 and was sent the following spring to Washington to head a CIG section analysing captured German and Japanese documents for information on the new enemy. Alongside Americans and Canadians, Parker 'distributed information over a wide field: military, political, technical and commercial'. The CIG, Parker recalled, was 'about as sensitive a spot as most for a young man to register the realities of peace breaking out between the Allies'.[18]

The transition from the heroic image of the Russian people to a nation from whom captured German intelligence was deliberately hidden was hard to swallow for Parker: 'It is easy now to appreciate the prompt logic of the West in squaring up to Stalin, but then I believe it puzzled some young men wretchedly: it did me.' Parker felt the 'chill of it long before I knew to call it the Cold War'. Within months of the Menzies–CIG accord, he also felt a change in the special relationship. He 'detected that key documents and analyses were not reaching us; there was an uneasiness in relationships with senior Americans [and] what had been an Allied intelligence team was coming unstuck'. Worse was to follow when loyalty checks were instigated for the flimsiest of reasons and the British were made unwelcome. It was not all one-sided, though. The head of MI6's R5 section, Kim Philby, was ordered not to inform the Americans about his work. Unless it was deeply secret, there did not appear to have been at this stage any Allied co-ordination of counter-espionage.[19]

Shortly after the formation of the Central Intelligence Agency (CIA) in June 1947, relations with the Americans were formalised by the 'CIA–SS (British Secret Service) agreement' which, building on the CIG–JIB accord, gave approval to the practice of not running operations in each other's territories. As Richard Aldrich notes: 'Like their wartime predecessors, this agreement was not always strictly observed.'[20]

In the same period, British signals intelligence-gathering was undergoing its own reorganisation. GC&CS, where by late 1945 some six thousand personnel were assigned to work on strategic cryptanalysis and SIGINT, had been transferred from Bletchley Park to Eastcote, north-west London. During June 1946, the Government Communications Headquarters (GCHQ) was offically established as its successor, although the name had been previously used as a cover. Responsibility for GCHQ was transferred from MI6 to the Foreign Office, which reflected the Service's loss of influence within White-hall. GCHQ was now tasked to take on new priorities. Alan Stripp, an Intelligence Corps officer who was monitoring Iranian diplomatic traffic from a tiny outpost at Abbottabad in north-west India, recalled that by 1946 officers had taken a crash course in Russian: 'The Cold war was already beginning to concentrate everybody's minds.'[21]

Problems, however, arose over the SIGINT negotiations which were put on hold following the controversial sale of British Rolls-Royce Nene and Derwent jet engines, and, allegedly, jet aircraft, to the Soviet Union. The British chiefs of staff and security services were angry at the sale of what were, in fact, in an era of rapidly developing technology, obsolete designs. Even more so were the Americans, with senators accusing British ministers of all kinds of treachery and threatening to curtail the flow of vital Marshall Aid dollars. Intelligence co-operation was put 'under review' while the disclosure of the 'sources of American intelligence', 'methods of acquisition' and 'information pertaining to cryptography and cryptographic devices' was stopped. Not long afterwards the Foreign Office reported that the flow of intelligence on a range of military subjects, in particular conditions in the Soviet Army, which passed through the machinery of the Combined Chiefs of Staff in Washington, was 'disappointing'. British officials were forced in April 1948 to issue a statement to the effect that 'no aircraft had been sold to Russia since the end of the war, and that no engines on the secret list had been or were going to be supplied'.[22]

The statement paved the way for the signing in June 1948 of the formal and final UKUSA Agreement, also known as the UK-USA Security Agreement or 'Secret Treaty', between the SIGINT agencies, GCHQ and the National Secur-ity Agency (NSA). It divided SIGINT collection responsibilities among the First Party (the United States) and the Second Parties (Britain, Australia, Canada and New Zealand). It has remained the most important and resilient part of British Intelligence's 'special relationship' with the United States. The prolonged negotiations were an indication that the agreement had finally been resolved very much on US terms. Britain may have had the brains – GCHQ's cryptanalysis was highly valued, and had access to sites in the Commonwealth denied to the US – but it was the Americans who provided what was most vital – finance and, eventually, the technical knowhow.[23]

The Americans were also moving into the area of Special Operations (SO) in Europe, which, at first, was welcomed by a cash-starved MI6. Britain's withdrawal from Greece and Turkey led to a reassessment of her economic position. A December 1949 CIA estimate concluded that Britain's financial difficulties would lead to a reconsideration of its overseas commitments, but it would probably make every effort to avoid taking drastic action. There was an awareness of 'inevitable post-war competition and possible confrontation between Britain and America', which would be 'focused in intelligence instead of public diplomacy'. The US viewed Britain as a declining power, and while it was 'prepared to be conciliatory to a certain degree in public', it intended to use the CIA 'to secure American objectives in private'. The CIA was not there 'to bolster a fading British presence'.[24]

In turn, MI6 officers worked to ensure that British policy-makers did not become 'over-dependent on information from foreign services', but 'kept intact and secure our potential for intelligence-gathering and independent action'. Senior officers were not impressed with the last CIG and first CIA director, Rear Admiral Roscoe Hillenkoetter, who lacked 'a cutting edge'. He believed that SO generated 'noise' which directed unwanted attention to clandestine intelligence-gathering. He opposed sponsoring the exile movements because his experience in wartime France had shown that guerrilla tactics and resistance movements 'yielded inadequate returns'. Anti-American attitudes were widely held within Broadway, which ordered its field officers not to share intelligence with their opposite numbers in the CIA. At the Madrid station, Desmond Bristow exchanged 'insignificant' information with the local CIA representative, Al Ulmer, but was aware that 'such an open rapport with our American friends' had to be kept secret from head office, since it would 'certainly not have been appreciated'.[25]

It was soon apparent to Malcolm Muggeridge, however, that in the post-war world the CIA/NSA network, 'with ramifications all over the world, came to outclass our once legendary Secret Service as a sleek Cadillac does an ancient hansom cab'. This led to a certain amount of resentment. While it was true that a 'special relationship' did develop between the British and American intelligence agencies – though more particularly between GCHQ and the NSA, where personal friendships were especially close – they remained, in George Young's phrase, 'uncertain allies'.[26]

CHAPTER 5

THE WORLD-VIEW

While it is true that today's Secret Intelligence Service (SIS) is primarily an intelligence-gathering agency which has no official role in analysis and research, this has not precluded MI6 from having its own world-view.

Within its ranks, during the late forties and early fifties, MI6 had a small intellectual circle of 'brilliant young academics' who had joined the Service at the beginning of the war. Not necessarily on the Right, and including social democrats and former communists who had turned against 'the God that had failed', they had railed against older pre-war officers – the 'old buffers', who were seen as 'laughable and inefficient', and obsessed by the 'Bolshevik Bogey'. They had, however, come out of the war profoundly anti-communist, and it was not long before these 'young turks' were promoting and reinforcing the orthodoxy of an expansionist Soviet Union with a leader bent on world revolution. Their analysis tended to be hampered by an adherence to a classical view of Marxism which they believed Lenin had adapted for world revolution and Stalin had adopted as his political creed.[1]

MI6's intellectuals were organised around the Political Section (R1), which advised the Chief on developments around the world and assessed the value of political intelligence before it was forwarded to the Foreign Office. R1's prime purpose was to supply the 'missing links in the picture presented by Foreign Office reports'. While it was true that the Service did not enjoy enough power to formulate policy, which was left to the Foreign Office, the possession of information from secret sources did, as Kim Philby discovered, give the Service 'a certain power of decision in individual cases'. It was also true that R1's officers and assets were highly capable agents of influence, and leading publicists and journalists such as Malcolm Muggeridge were allowed to read its reports.

The Section was headed by David Footman, an acknowledged expert on Soviet communism. The son of a parson, he had won a Military Cross in the First World War and after a period in the Levant Consular Service had joined the Service in 1935. Footman had written a number of scholarly works on Russian revolutionary history, but he was not highly regarded by officers, who thought him only 'competent'. Foreign Office adviser Patrick Reilly made the curious remark that 'he was emphatically not the man to commission any study of Stalinist policies'. He was regarded with a certain amount of suspicion because of his association with left-wing intellectuals, and Menzies went so far as to suggest that Footman had suppressed anti-Soviet intelligence.[2]

MI6's leading theorist was Robert Carew Hunt, who laid out his critical views on Marxism in two books – *The Theory and Practice of Communism* (1950) and *Marxism: Past and Present* (1954). These academic texts attempted to 're-examine the basic concepts of revolutionary Marxism'. Working inside the anti-communist section (R5), he developed his theories from discussions with MI6 'insiders' and 'Sovietologists', such as Isaiah Berlin, A. J. 'Freddie' Ayer and Leonard Schapiro.[3]

A pre-war lecturer in philosophy at Oxford, Berlin was a noted authority on Karl Marx. Son of a Riga timber merchant who fled the Bolshevik Revolution, Berlin served with the Ministry of Information, then in the Washington embassy's Survey Section, producing weekly political summaries, and, over the winter of 1945/6, in Moscow. Ayer had served during the war with the British Security Co-ordination (BSC), the Special Operations Executive (SOE), and as an attaché in Paris. A barrister, the austere Schapiro had been brought up in St Petersburg and was a fluent Russian-speaker. During the war, he worked for the BBC monitoring service and then with MI5, before being posted to the Intelligence Division of the Control Commission in Germany. He returned to the Bar in 1946 and later became a lecturer in Russian studies at the London School of Economics.

A less-publicised member of this loose-knit group was the established writer and close friend of Berlin, Goronwy Rees. A former communist who broke with the Party at the time of the Hitler–Stalin pact, Rees had served as an intelligence officer with the Planning Staff (Operations) of the 21st Army Group. He was then appointed senior intelligence officer to the staff of Sir William Strang, political adviser to the commander-in-chief, Field Marshal Montgomery, in the Control Commission in Germany, where he was responsible for diplomatic relations with the Russians. He left Germany in November 1945 to become part-time director of a firm of general engineers, while continuing in the afternoon to work alongside Ayer in the Political Section.[4]

Another important voice was Hugh Seton-Watson, who had served in eastern Europe until 1941. He was then transferred to the SOE Yugoslav section in Cairo and, in January 1944, moved to Istanbul, where he built up contacts with prominent Balkan refugees who flooded into the city. In late 1944, he was promoted deputy in charge of the Danubian group – the Bulgarian, Hungarian and Romanian sections of Force 133 at Bari. Bickham Sweet-Escott thought his deputy 'knew more about this part of the world than any other Anglo-Saxon I have met'. With his 'encyclopaedic knowledge', Seton-Watson helped convince London that Mihailovic's lieutenants in Yugo-slavia were collaborating with the enemy, and that Tito was a better bet for military support. When attempts to put SOE liaison officers into the newly occupied Danubian countries were stood down, Seton-Watson transferred to London, where, following a short period on loan to the intelligence division of the Control Commission in Germany, he joined MI6. Although he officially returned to academic life at Oxford in 1946, he remained close to MI6 as an adviser on communist and Balkan affairs, and during the summer of 1946 he travelled extensively through Czechoslovakia, Bulgaria, Romania and Hungary. In the following spring he revisited Czechoslovakia and Hungary, and made a study of Greece. Seton-Watson was later recruited by George Kennedy Young to an MI6 analytic team to help produce high-grade studies on Soviet intentions and policy-making.[5]

Another later recruit was the leading Soviet expert and programme organ-iser for the BBC's Overseas Service, Malcolm Mackintosh. Having served in the army during the war in the Middle East and Italy, he had seen the Red Army in action at first hand, and over the winter of 1945/46, as a member of the Allied Control Commission in Bulgaria, had witnessed the behind-the-scenes manoeuvring of Soviet commissars.[6]

Head of station in Vienna in the late forties, Young later recalled that MI6 did not go along with the thesis that the West had played a part in hardening Cold War attitudes. 'That was not how it looked to those who were involved.' Mackintosh accepted that 'the victorious march of the Soviet Army into East-ern Europe, Manchuria and Korea' had given the Soviet leaders 'an opportu-nity to resume the export of Communism'. Soviet leaders were telling their people that 'the war they had just won was by no means the end of the struggle ... their mission was the overthrow of capitalism, not merely the defeat of this or that national enemy'.[7]

Recently returned from the Moscow embassy, where he had helped formulate Frank Roberts's influential telegrams, to take up the post of Director of the London School of Slavonic Studies, George Bolsover also believed that 'Soviet statesmen approach policy from a fundamentally ideological stand-point'. In his lecture on 'Soviet Ideology and Propaganda' at Chatham House on 11 November 1947, he dismissed the argument that Stalin and his colleagues used ideology 'as an instrument for maintaining their power at home and extending their influence abroad'. He warned against this tempting theory because it 'suggests the possibility of solving fundamental problems by various international "deals" among the Big Three or at least the Bigger Two'. For Bolsover, Soviet policy could only be made 'coherent and intelligible if interpreted in terms of Marxism-Leninism', the essence of which was dialectical and historical materialism.

Mackintosh believed that the occupation of wide areas of Europe and the Far East had extended the borders of the Soviet Union, and 'provided bases from which a policy of expansion could be carried on'. While Poland, Romania and Bulgaria were being turned into Soviet satellites, the new frontiers of the Soviet base were 'being tested for soft or undefended spots where further penetration might succeed or protection zones set up'. In western Europe the situation was more confused. According to George Young, during the summer of 1946 MI6 had 'intercepted' Soviet 'instructions to Western Communist Parties, including the Communist Party of Great Britain (CPGB), to foment civil conflict'. If this is true, it has an echo of similar material which had come to the attention of Section IX over the winter of 1944–5. In the event, Mackintosh accepted that, despite communist opinion in Italy and France which rated their chances of success as high, 'nothing, however, was done, and there is excellent evidence that Stalin was against any attempt to seize power'. Instead, an attempt was made to strengthen the communist position inside the coalitions in France and Belgium based on a 'general strategic decision against attempts to seize power in countries beyond the reach of the Soviet Army'.[8]

A different state of affairs existed in East Germany, where the Russians were 'well-advanced' with their plans to create a communist state. Young was disturbed that, 'while the Western allies were faithfully and literally observing the Four Power agreements, the wretched East German Socialist stooges, who were used as a front while the Communists were put in positions of power, could only wriggle feebly'. In conversation with Young, the East German communist leader, Grotewohl, admitted: 'I have a pistol in my back.' In Czechoslovakia, where President Benes and his non-communist ministers were held in international esteem, Young thought that 'a little more discretion was required' in order 'to lull American suspicions while their forces were still at full-strength in Germany'. While assuring western visitors that there was a Czech road to socialism, the communist Prime Minister, Klement Gottwald, 'brought Ministry of Interior, police and trade union "factory guards" under strict control, seduced the Left Wing of the Socialist Party and even found some willing instruments in the People's and Nationalist Parties'.[9]

Mackintosh suggested that, in the three years to 1947, the evidence pointed to a Soviet strategy of 'territorial expansion of the Soviet heartland by gaining control of countries and provinces bordering the Soviet Union, whether allied (Poland, Yugoslavia and Greece), ex-enemy (Bulgaria, Romania and

Hungary) or neutral (Persia and Turkey), but to adopt a more cautious attitude in countries out of reach of Soviet military power (Italy, France and Belgium)'. Seton-Watson set out the Soviet blueprint in his 1950 book *The East European Revolution*. 'During the first stage the communists seized control of most of the "levers of power" – in particular the security police, the army general staff and the publicity machines.' During the 'bogus coalition' second stage, the governments still contained non-communist parties, 'but these are represented by men chosen no longer by the party membership but by the communists. The essential feature of this stage is that ... any bourgeois parties ... are driven into opposition.' In the third stage of the 'monolithic regime': 'There is a single communist-managed "front", with one hierarchy, one centralised discipline and one organisation.' All open opposition is 'suppressed, and its leaders either escape abroad or are arrested as "spies of the western imperialists" and either executed or sentenced to long prison terms'.[10]

Seton-Watson argued that secret policeman in the eastern bloc had an interest in the maintenance of international tension. 'As long as it is believed that imperialist Powers are straining every muscle to infiltrate spies, agitators and saboteurs' into their countries, 'so long will the maintenance of a huge host of secret informers, uniformed and plain-clothes policemen, concentration-camp guards, and special elite formations of political troops be justified'. Thus, unwittingly, MI6's intrusive intelligence-gathering operations in eastern Europe contributed to maintaining the repulsive system of 'ordinary people acting as spies on their friends and neighbours, of disappearances and show trials'. Seton-Watson added that 'the interests of the police and the political class require that the people of the Soviet Union and the popular democracies should live forever in the shadow of war'. Did he conversely believe that western intelligence agencies had a selfish interest in propagating the myth of a Soviet Union bent on world domination?[11]

During August 1947, the US Central Intelligence Group (CIG), which was slowly being transformed into the CIA, circulated an evaluation based on papers retrieved from the burglary of the safe of a Soviet satellite's chief of mission. The contents of the document were microfilmed before being returned to the safe. What is interesting about this document, whose authenticity was accepted by the intelligence agencies, is the different interpretations given to the contents.

For the hardliners, it outlined a Soviet strategy to prevent the expulsion of communists from western European governments as a prelude to Marshall Aid. The chief of mission had proposed 'strike movements and social agitation in Italy, France and Belgium destined to weaken the governments in these countries'. In Italy a general strike would be instigated to overthrow de Gaspari and install a communist administration, to be followed by the victorious drive of the 'Greek partisans' towards Salonika. The paper also called for the destruction of Balkan opposition to Russia – which, as Trevor Barnes suggests, was 'an important clue to a source of tension between Stalin and Tito which was to have momentous consequences a year later'. To the cautious, the document revealed a split within the Kremlin between the hawks – supporters of the Minister of Foreign Affairs, Vyacheslav Molotov, who believed in pursuing the proposals outlined above – and the doves around Minister of Foreign Trade Anastas Mikoyan, who argued that the satellites were a burden and that the Russian economy could not sustain an offensive stance. Although these were only discussions and proposals, it is likely that the find was highly regarded within intelligence circles, given the fact that MI6 had no sources in Russia.[12]

Within MI6, events in eastern Europe, about which George Young claimed the Service was 'well-informed', were viewed with confusion and growing anger; in particular, the 'nonsensical' percentages formula which Churchill had agreed with Stalin. Typically, there was frustration at the lack of action by the West. 'We were not prepared', Young recalled, 'to take the minimal risks of exploiting internal weaknesses of the Soviet Bloc by active political warfare.' He claimed that, through defectors, MI6 knew by the autumn of 1947 that the Soviets intended 'to bring to heel' Yugoslavia and Czechoslovakia. An attempt at reassertion by right-wing Czech socialists in November was quickly 'countered by a demagogic Communist campaign for punitive wealth taxes and the seizure of large estates. Socialist will collapsed as they resigned from the Prague government.' It was apparent that the communists would launch a takeover in Czechoslovakia, 'but nothing was done to bolster up the will of those Czechs who might have resisted what was in fact a skilfully conducted bluff'.[13]

Similar consolidation of Soviet political control over East Germany was carried through 'without any attempt on our side to impede or delay it. One needed to have no illusions about Pieck, Ulbricht, Grotewohl and other East German politicians. But nothing was done to exploit their internal jealousies or their resentment at the Soviet pressure on them: some of them would gladly have re-established their links with the West if the channels had existed.' In Hungary, Soviet plans for 'rigging the impending elections were allowed to go on without Western challenge'. MI6 suggestions that the British government 'use some of its considerable unorthodox skills to assist its Hungarian Social-Democratic comrades' were dismissed by the Labour Party chair, Sam Watson, on the basis that if they did so 'the Rooshians will behave like rampaging beasts'. MI6 officers came to believe that there was an unwritten assumption that 'Warsaw, Prague and Budapest had ceased to be part of Europe and nothing further should or could be done about them'.[14]

The area where all MI6's impressive expertise might have been expected to bear fruit was in the Balkans, where SOE had been intimately involved. It

was a region where Britain still sought to defend its perceived special interests. Indeed, MI6 had poured agents into the area from places such as Austria,
Italy and Turkey, from where it ran major SO and intelligence-gathering
operations. Despite their best efforts, and, in particular, Hugh Seton-Watson's
insights and the investment of financial and human resources, MI6 failed to
deliver intelligence on the major event of the period, namely the Stalin–Tito
split.

The Foreign Office had been reduced to despair about Anglo-Yugoslav
relations. In late July 1946, Churchill's former private secretary and Foreign
Office official John Colville wrote that 'secret information showed that the
Yugoslav regime was actively doing all that it could to bring about Communist world revolution, with aid to the Greek rebels as only one of its moves
and with Britain as its special target'. Robert M. Blum records that President
Tito pursued an aggressive regional policy,

> laying claim to territory in Austria and to the British and Ameri-
> can occupied port city of Trieste. He fuelled the Greek civil
> war in hopes of absorbing an expanded Macedonia. He signed
> treaties of friendship with Moscow and with other Soviet bloc
> countries, integrated his economy into the Soviet-bloc system,
> brought in Soviet military and economic advisers, and, alone
> among East European leaders, enthusiastically rejected partici-
> pation in the Marshall Plan. With rare exceptions, Tito's propa-
> ganda organs piped a chorus of praise for the Soviets and scorn
> for the West.[15]

Tito, who had been committed to establishing popular fronts under clear
communist control, was dissatisfied with the all-party coalition governments
that had been established with Stalin's consent throughout central and eastern
Europe. Tito 'favoured a communist offensive, while Stalin, aware of the
international position of the Soviet Union, favoured a more cautious
approach'. Thus, when in September 1947 Stalin summoned the first meeting
in Poland of the Communist Information Bureau (Cominform), which aimed
to co-ordinate propaganda among communist parties, and made him its *de
facto* leader, Tito 'mistakenly assumed he was to head a new international
committed to a revolutionary offensive not only in Eastern Europe but in
Greece and even Italy and France'. In his speeches Tito announced that the
time had come to resume the advance towards socialism by means of popular
fronts which would break with the 'parliamentary cretinism' of coalition
politics. Shortly after, a number of eastern European communist parties, and
those led by former resistance fighters in France and Italy, reorganised their
parties into mass populist movements.[16]

Geoffrey Swain argues that 'if support for the popular front "from below"
is taken as a touchstone, then the Cominform had become Tito's international'.

Indeed, MI6 saw its foundation as confirmation that the world had been divided into two warring camps and 'a declaration that the Soviet Government regarded itself as engaged in a major struggle against the non-Communist world in both Europe and Asia'. During 1947, the Joint Intelligence Committee (JIC) placed growing emphasis on 'political infiltration and the promotion of unrest' by the Soviets, and asserted that Stalin believed that 'the capitalist world is about to collapse'. It was largely untrue, but it suited western perceptions because battle had now been joined in the Cold War.[17]

The general view was summed up by the British ambassador in Moscow, Sir Maurice Peterson, who cabled London that it was time 'to return blow for blow and to embark on open political warfare against communism'. Christopher Warner advocated nurturing organised resistance to communist influence in the Commonwealth and to Soviet attempts to control various international federations. He wanted a 'ministerial lead to encourage and strengthen the efforts already being taken so that it could be more effectively organised'.[18]

Bevin responded by manipulating the Marshall Aid ideal. Reporting to the Cabinet on the recent meeting in Paris, the Foreign Secretary argued on 8 July that 'it is far better to have [the Soviets] definitely out than half-heartedly in'. Confrontation had replaced the idea of negotiations since 'any other tactics might have enabled the Soviets to play the Trojan horse and wreck Europe's propects of availing themselves of American assistance . . . at least the gloves are off, and we know where we stand with them.' Britain and America were now working together as an increasingly 'effective and aggressive team'.[19]

A former British Intelligence official, Michael McGwire, later concluded that

> if there were still doubts in Stalin's mind about the thrust of Western policy after the Foreign Ministers' meeting in Moscow, these would have been finally dispelled by the proposed European Recovery Programme . . . The Anglo-French stance at the Paris meeting, following as it did on the heels of the Truman declaration, the stone-walling on reparations at the Council of Foreign Ministers, and the eviction of the Communist members of the French and Italian coalition governments, appears to have finally convinced Stalin that the West was indeed on the offensive against Communism. Not only was co-operation no longer a practical option, but even the possibility of 'peaceful co-existence' was in doubt. The hard-line pessimists therefore moved into favour in Moscow.[20]

Far from being, as the West assumed, a sign of the resumption of the Soviet drive for world revolution, the creation of the Cominform, which came only a week after President Truman's speech introducing the doctrine of 'containment', indicated, as Robert Frazier suggests, Stalin's 'assumption that the Truman doctrine amounted to a declaration of war'. While Soviet policies appeared to be aggressive and to be based on an offensive strategy, Stalin was actually engaged in a defensive foreign policy which required the reining in of all the communist parties worldwide in order to retain control of their activities. When French Communist Party member Jacques Duclos told the Comintern that 'France was fast falling under the influence of the United States and that something had to be done quickly to reverse this trend', Stalin stamped on any ideas of an insurrection. Moscow 'had decided to consolidate its gains in Eastern Europe' and now was not the time for 'opportunism'.[21]

The Cominform, in Beatrice Heuser's opinion, was an attempt at centralisation, and its first meeting was designed to bring the parties, particularly in Yugoslavia, into line. This reflected a factional dispute within the Kremlin which remained largely unknown to western intelligence, though the filched documents from the safe of the Soviet satellite chief of mission gave an indication of such divisions. The ideological faction led by Andrei Zhadanov, the senior Soviet representative in the Cominform, was in favour of 'following a radical, revolutionary line to stage strikes and overthrow colonial powers', which 'found favour with the Yugoslavs'. The rival conservative, anti-western and isolationist faction led by fellow Soviet delegate Georgi Malenkov supported 'the centralisation and consolidation' demanded by Stalin, who 'had a deep dislike for coups and revolutions and personally preferred gradualism'.[22]

In retrospect, Malcolm Mackintosh refused to accept this analysis. While he agreed that Zhadanov headed a domestic faction, it was 'not certain that he was anything more than Stalin's mouthpiece in foreign affairs'. He added that there was 'no move away from Cominform policy after his [Zhadanov's] death in August 1948', and that 'it is probable that in foreign affairs the personal role of Zhadanov has been exaggerated'. The reality was that MI6 did not know. As George Young acknowledged, compared to the wealth of material from intercepts and agents about Soviet activities in Germany and Austria, MI6 had no reliable intelligence from inside the Soviet Union and lacked 'high-grade intelligence on Russian intentions and policy-making'. It was another decade before MI6 or the CIA had even a low-level mole in Moscow.[23]

'In the sense of collecting information', former senior intelligence official Michael Herman has written, 'the West picked itself off the floor in 1945.' An academic specialist in intelligence studies, Herman has also noted, however, that 'Russia was deeply secret; in the late forties we had only the sketchiest ideas about it ... we were in a continuous struggle to open windows on to the Soviet Union'. Junior Labour foreign minister Christopher Mayhew recalled that 'at that time our knowledge of the Soviet Union, and especially of the blacker elements of Soviet oppression, was extremely limited. We had few secret sources of intelligence; defectors were few and far between; the movements of western visitors were strictly controlled; and the Soviet media gave little away.'[24]

MI6 found itself in a double bind. Despite worsening relations between the USSR and the West, and Bevin's apparent dissatisfaction with the intelligence he was receiving, the Service was expected to abide by the conditions set by the government which barred direct intrusive operations inside the Soviet Union. Officially, limited arm's-length operations were allowed in the satellite countries, and Menzies interpreted this broadly to include Soviet states such as Ukraine and those in the Baltics and the Caucasus, but the intelligence take was poor. Where the West did win the intelligence battle, Herman concludes, was in collating and analysing these slithers of information. After 1945 the JIC, chaired by the head of the Foreign Office Service Liaison Department, remained the focus of strategic intelligence and an important link between the military, the diplomats and the intelligence community. Membership of the JIC included the heads of the armed service intelligence departments and of MI6 and MI5. It retained subordinate regional JICs that had developed within wartime commands in Europe, the Middle East and Asia.[25]

George Young recalled that there was no systematic study of 'the top Soviet power structure, in the armed forces and the KGB'. The practice in the Foreign Office was 'to take each intelligence report in a separate docket, comment on it and file away'. Thus, information from both overt and covert sources was 'never properly assessed'.[26]

The spark that ignited the communist split was Tito's decision in January 1948 to station Yugoslav troops on Albanian territory. This, and Tito's continuing supply of arms to the rebels in the Greek civil war, caused unwanted complications for Moscow and led to Stalin's belief that the Cominform needed to be disciplined. Given his long absences through illness, it took time for Stalin to crush the Zhadanovite faction and bring Tito down with it. But once under Stalinist control, the Cominform attacked the Yugoslav communists for their incorrect line on home affairs and, more importantly, for their foreign policy, which it equated with Trotsky's 'left slogans about world revolution'. In February, Tito was summoned to Moscow and told by Stalin to end support for the Greek communists.[27]

Given that Tito regarded himself as the communist International's most loyal agent, it was not surprising that Stalin's ejection of the Yugoslav communists in March stunned them, nor that the decision was kept secret. Basing his assessment on rumours, in mid-June British ambassador Charles Peake cited several recent developments which indicated that Tito was in trouble with Stalin. The Foreign Office's Southern Department was confident, however, that neither the 'the top Yugoslav Communists nor their colleagues in the other Orbit countries will fail to toe the line if the Kremlin gets tough'. The appearance of communist unity in the Soviet bloc was finally shattered on 28 June 1948 when a Czech newspaper, *Rude Pravo*, announced that the Cominform meeting in Bucharest had 'expelled Yugoslavia from the family of fraternal Communist parties for pursuing domestic and foreign policies hostile to the Soviet Union'. The Foreign Office and MI6 had not anticipated the action and it was to prove to be a major intelligence failure.[28]

When reports of Tito's dispute with the Comintern reached the West, the news was received with 'scepticism if not outright disbelief'. A scholar on the Soviet Union, Adam B. Ulam, stated that 'any man who, prior to June 1948, would have predicted a break between Tito and Stalin would be entitled today to be honoured as a prophet with occult powers of predicting the future but certainly not as an expert basing his prognosis upon factual evidence'. Snippets of intelligence appear to have been picked up by agents of the US 430th Counter-Intelligence Corps in Austria, and MI6's George Young later claimed to have had foreknowledge from agents within the Balkan communist parties. If there were raw intelligence reports on the subject they remain classified. There is no indication that officials dealing with Yugoslavia had any inkling of the internal disputes with Moscow. A prime problem was that the American and British embassies in Belgrade were under siege and their diplomats were 'virtually unable to function', the British faring only a little better because of 'a small residual feeling for their contribution during the war'.[29]

Proof of the lack of intelligence comes from Bevin's minister liaising with MI6, Hector McNeil; though there was no love lost between the minister and the Service. Dining shortly after the split with *New York Times* correspondent Cyrus Sulzberger, McNeil 'sneered at British and American intelligence services and diplomats for not knowing about Tito's fight with Stalin'. McNeil was never going to be a favourite of the security services. A socialist since his student days, he was a heavy drinker who explored London's seamier side with Guy Burgess, his private secretary from January 1947 until mid-1948. Burgess, who had been in MI6's Section D at the beginning of the war and had spent a period with MI5, was in a prime position from which to inform the Soviets. He had access to the yellow boxes in which MI6 sent their reports and also managed to make a copy of the key to the safe containing the secret reports to which only Bevin, McNeil and Orme Sargent had access.[30]

The Foreign Office continued to regard Tito as a Soviet puppet even after unmistakable evidence to the contrary. Bevin believed the split was a 'put up job'. A former communist and head of the Labour Party's International Department, Denis Healey, who had a deep knowledge of the socialist and communist tactics in Europe, was 'startled' by a discussion with the Foreign Office's Evelyn Shuckburgh concerning the split. Shuckburgh suggested that 'it might have been a trick to deceive the West'. Healey replied that 'no one of any political understanding could believe that governments, even when led by Communists, can conduct their affairs as if they are secret agents'. Policy towards Yugoslavia, however, remained one of 'masterly inactivity'.[31]

Beatrice Heuser concludes that 'Western diplomats overlooked the disagreements about foreign policy and if they noted them, they still failed to see their overall significance'. The British embassy did receive information via the Czech embassy which confirmed that the split was due to foreign policy differences, but diplomats assumed that Tito had yearned to break away from the Soviet Union, which was demonstratively not true. Two days after the Cominform communiqué, the British chargé-d'affaires in Belgrade, Cecil King, reported that the 'Yugoslav Party are attempting to set up their own brand of communism in opposition to the Kremlin Party line. This is one of the most important developments in the whole history of Communism. For the first time there is a chance of establishment of a heresy upon a firm territorial base.' King thought that its attractions both to other Balkan states and to the western communist parties would be 'strong indeed', and suggested that Albania would follow the lead.[32]

It would take six months before the West accepted that there had been a major split between Moscow and Belgrade. The problem was 'exacerbated by the West believing that nationalism would have a more profound effect on Tito's thinking than ideology'. Christopher Warner had been told the previous year by Charles Peake in Belgrade that there was 'no chance whatever' of splitting the communist parties along 'Muscovite-Nationalist' lines, but he refused to accept the analysis. In reality, Tito was driven by ideology and 'probably took Marxism-Leninism more seriously than did Stalin'. The Titoists' ambition 'seemed to be that Yugoslavia should be regional leader of a Communist Balkans within a wholly Communist Europe'. And if proof was needed, following the split the Yugoslavs resumed arms shipments to the Greek rebels, who acknowledged that 'Stalin showed himself to be hostile to any revolutionary struggle in any country in which his control was not assured'.[33]

MI6's Robert Carew-Hunt undertook a study of the pre-war Comintern in the belief that its postwar successor, the Cominform, would follow the same pattern. There was, however, no 'genius' such as Willi Munzenberg to spread the Marxist gospel through fronts, agents and fellow-travellers. The Cominform was not 'a hotbed for intelligence agents', nor was it 'riddled with Stalin's secret police'. A West German intelligence official, Dr Gunther Nollau, concluded that

> during the nine years of the Cominform's existence not a single Cominform agent was arrested in the free world. Not a single passport was impounded that could be shown to have been 'fixed up' by the Cominform ... Is one to assume that the

Cominform worked in such secrecy that its activities could remain undiscovered? If so, it must be the only intelligence service to have achieved this feat for so long. Between 1947 and 1956, hundreds of Soviet, Polish, Czech or Hungarian agents were caught in Western Europe, but never a Cominform agent. Why was this? The answer is because there were no Cominform agents.[34]

CHAPTER 6

PROPAGANDA

Social Democrat peer Christopher Mayhew was always proud of his role in creating the Foreign Office's semi-secret Information Research Department (IRD), which for thirty years poured out a stream of Cold War propaganda. It is regarded as one of the Labour Party's few successful interventions into the secret world. The truth, however, is that from the start Mayhew was hoodwinked.

Even a Foreign Office history of the first year of IRD admits that it 'evolved from plans drawn up in 1946', when hardliners on the Russia Committee pressed the Foreign Secretary, Ernest Bevin, to implement an anti-communist propaganda campaign. This was true, but, in fact, the Russia Committee was merely reviving elements of the wartime Political Warfare Executive (PWE), which had not been completely abolished.[1]

It was only in May 1945 that the PWE, which had had a precarious existence, achieved single ministerial control under the Foreign Secretary; at which point it went into 'liquidation', mostly because in the changeover from war to 'what was expected to be peace, political warfare was regarded as a contradiction in terms'. That view did not last long and, on 3 August 1945, when the director of the Special Operations Executive (SOE), Colin Gubbins, wrote a farewell letter to PWE's former head, Robert Bruce Lockhart, he urged the need to revive 'the Black Propaganda organisation both in Europe and the Far East', and argued that it should be combined with what remained of SOE. Lockhart took up the idea with Bevin, who, two weeks later, approved Lockhart's recommendation that PWE continue in Europe and the Far East so long as military government existed. Subsequently, a number of psychological warfare specialists 'found billets in the various information services of the Government'. PWE was officially subsumed within the Foreign Office's Political Intelligence Department, headed temporarily by Major-General Kenneth Strong, while Ivone Kirkpatrick monitored its activities. Bruce Lockhart was pleased that there was some continuity but concerned that the 'best talent' would be allowed to leave.[2]

In mid-July 1946, Bruce Lockhart met with Strong, who was now head of the new Joint Intelligence Bureau (JIB). They were eager to maintain some continuity of PWE in view of 'the serious international situation', and wanted to press the Labour government into setting up a peacetime psychological warfare unit. Aware of the divisions within the Labour Party, and the fact that there was still residual support from the war for the Soviets, Bevin vetoed their ideas.[3]

Bevin wanted to pursue a more positive option of extolling the virtues of the 'Third Force', which was intended to help Britain retain an independent role in the first rank of global powers in 'a middle democratic socialist way between the harsh and conflicting ideologies of unfettered American capitalism and repressive Soviet Communism'. The officials did not, however, give up on their plans. Indeed, Strong hoped to keep the continuity of PWE in his own JIB. Other officials cleverly manoeuvred Bevin into supporting their 'counter-offensive' campaign by consciously playing on the social democratic theme, in which they never truly believed. Gradually, the officials began to chip away at Bevin's wariness as they considered action programmes on a country-by-country basis. Agreement for a propaganda campaign in Iran 'proved to be the hammer and chisel' by which officials continued to gather support for their strategy. Despite the Foreign Secretary's apparent reluctance to pursue it, campaigns were soon evolving in other countries. At the same time, pressure was brought to bear by the chiefs of staff, who wanted to renew political warfare. Christopher Warner later admitted to Bruce Lockhart that the impetus for the IRD was the result of a paper submitted by hardline military figures, such as the RAF's Sir John Slessor, at the Imperial Defence College (IDC).[4]

In the wake of the announcement of the formation of the Cominform, which was perceived by British officials as the vehicle for subversion of western European democracies, the more hardline officials in the Foreign Office 'found an important ally' in the Parliamentary Under-Secretary, Christopher Mayhew. In effect, Mayhew, who during the war had responsibility for SOE and had served in one of the 'secret armies', the Phantoms, became their unconscious front man.

In October 1947, Bevin had come under attack from Soviet Foreign Minister Molotov at the United Nations, and had been subjected to a torrent of anti-

British propaganda. Furious at not being able to respond with well-researched information on the Soviet system, Bevin ordered Mayhew to organise something. Mayhew replied with the idea of a 'propaganda counter-offensive', with the recommendation that a small separate Foreign Office department be set up to supervise the programme, which would give specific support for the 'Third Force' position. With the approval of Attlee, a meeting was called with a trio of the Foreign Office's senior officials: Sir Orme Sargent, Ivone Kirkpatrick and Christopher Warner. The Foreign Secretary, however, was not then convinced that such tactics were necessary, and Warner's proposals remained unapproved until late in the year, after the Cominform declaration against the Marshall Plan in November and the breakdown of the Council of Foreign Ministers in December, which led to a hardening of attitudes.[5]

On 6 December, Mayhew submitted a paper on 'Third Force Propaganda' which advised the Foreign Secretary to 'proceed quietly at first, being careful to stick to the truth and to balance anti-communism with anti-capitalist arguments so as to reassure the Parliamentary Labour Party'. Bevin and Attlee agreed to Mayhew developing his low-key ideas for a 'Communist Information Department'. Officials, however, wanted something more hard-hitting, with Sargent calling for the creation of a special organisation for an 'offensive' against the Soviets, while the chiefs of staff wanted 'certain "black" secret operations'. Warner took the proposals to the Russia Committee and rejigged Mayhew's paper, drawing 'more extensively on the political arguments of his own 1946 draft than on the concept of the "Third Force", about which he had in any case expressed doubts'.[6]

Only then, in the wake of the failure of the November Moscow Council of Foreign Ministers, did Bevin – and the Cabinet – endorse the Foreign Office's memorandum, 'The First Aim of British Foreign Policy', which accepted earlier proposals from the Russia Committee. It was a belated triumph for the hardliners in the Foreign Office, and the Russia Committee, now chaired by Gladwyn Jebb, was at last free to take the offensive against communism. Bevin, however, was still not prepared to abandon the 'Third Force' concept. In his presentation of the case to the Cabinet, on 5 January 1948, he said it required 'us, as Europeans and as a Social Democratic government, not the Americans, to give a lead in the spiritual, moral and political sphere to all democratic elements in Western Europe which are anti-communist and, at the same time, genuinely progressive and reformist, believing in freedom, planning and social justice – what one might call the "Third Force"'.[7]

Three days later, the Cabinet finally accepted the need for anti-communist machinery as devised by Warner and Mayhew and set out in 'Future Foreign Publicity Policy'. Bevin told his colleagues that 'the only new machinery required will be a small section in the Foreign Office to collect information concerning communist policy, tactics and propaganda and to provide material for anti-communist publicity'. Mayhew recognised that 'since anti-communist propaganda would be anathema to much of the Labour Party, it would have to be organised secretly'. But his concern was not just with the repercussions within the Labour Party. In a minute to Bevin, he commented that 'one of the problems that constantly faces us in anti-communist publicity work is to discover publicity media which are definitely non-official so as to avoid undesirable diplomatic and political repercussions when certain issues are raised'.[8]

A taste of the anti-communist counteroffensive came to the fore six days later, on 14 January, with the surfacing of 'Protocol M'. Its text, which was published in the Berlin evening paper *Der Kurier*, appeared to be a blueprint for a campaign of communist-inspired industrial subversion and sabotage in the Ruhr, Germany's industrial heartland in the British Zone. Highly detailed, it provided names of agents involved and set out a three-stage timetable which would lead to a general strike in March 1948 as part of the Cominform's campaign to disrupt the Marshall Plan. On the 15th, *The Times* reported that British authorities in Berlin regarded the document as 'genuine', while the *Daily Herald* headlined its article with 'Plot to wreck Marshall Plan'. The following day, the *New York Times* provided the additional information that the British had been monitoring a courier service involved in the planned subversion, and that the Foreign Office had confirmed the authenticity of the document. By coincidence, or more probably by design, the document gave backing to intelligence reports received ten days previously concerning 'a Russian directed propaganda and sabotage organisation (FAST BOWLER)', which was said to be engaged in the infiltration of German trade unions, involving many of the same individuals featured in the Protocol M allegations. Within the British Zone, the British authorities distributed copies of the text widely as part of the propaganda effort backing new anti-communist regulations which they were seeking to impose.[9]

Simon Ollivant, who made a study of the Protocol M controversy, is correct in suggesting that it was probably not the work of Mayhew's new machinery, which was not yet operational. Ollivant adds, however, that 'it is most probable that it was handled by those who were in the process of setting it up'. These included Ivone Kirkpatrick, the supervising under-secretary in charge of the German Political Department, who was planning more repressive measures against the communists of the KPD. Kirkpatrick had asserted that 'we should not hesitate to hit back hard and use fairly unscrupulous methods'.[10]

The day after Protocol M was publicised, Christopher Warner, who had succeeded Kirkpatrick in charge of Information Services, outlined to the Russia Committee the responsibilities of the new department's organisation, to be known initially as the Northern Information Department (NID). First, it would have 'an offensive branch attacking and exposing Communist methods and policy and contrasting them with "Western" democracy and British methods and policy'; secondly, 'a defensive branch, which would be concerned with replying to Soviet and Communist attacks and hostile propaganda'; and finally, 'a positive branch which would deal with the "build-up" of the Western Union conception'. The Foreign Office reported that it had managed to obtain extra funds for the new propaganda department.[11]

In February, Warner had dined with Bruce Lockhart and had sought advice on how best to proceed and who to recruit. Warner had already appointed as the NID's head Ralph Murray, who had served with the PWE during the war, while Bruce Lockhart recommended Harman Grisewood for recruitment. Murray's first decision was to change the organisation's name to avoid confusion with the Naval Intelligence Department. Kirkpatrick was made responsible for recruiting 'contract' staff, including writers with wartime experience in propaganda and eastern European émigrés. Eight permanent officials were recruited, including Guy Burgess, who had been employed for a short period by Hector McNeil before the junior minister became embarrassed by his behaviour and offloaded him to the new department, where he 'showed a dazzling insight into communist methods of subversion and propaganda'. Others who supervised the work were the Kremlin-watcher Robert Conquest and Jack Brimmell, who was recruited from the Russian Secretariat, which read all the main Soviet periodicals.[12]

In the cramped offices of Carlton House Terrace, eight 'desks' were established for geographical areas such as eastern Europe, Africa, China and Latin America, as well as to cater for economic affairs. The Information Research Department's work was divided into two categories. Category A consisted of analysis of intelligence collected by other agencies and Foreign Office departments which was not to be published. Category B consisted of 'briefings' which were disseminated to the media, academics, trade unions and foreign officials for their own use. Many of the first briefings concentrated on conditions inside Soviet Russia, including the existence of gulags and slave labour. During the summer, the briefings were supplemented by the weekly production of confidential 'digests', which presented 'general news' and 'specific interests' on current relations with 'Soviet Russia, her satellites, and with the principal national and international agencies involved'.[13]

The Russia Committee authorised the IRD to develop channels to disseminate its work. Norman Reddaway, Mayhew's private secretary, who had also served in the 'Phantoms', passed Soviet material on to trade unions, the labour movement and to the International Secretary of the Labour Party, Denis Healey, who was 'an important source on European communist movements'. Others in contact included labour attachés abroad, who became the link with the Trades Union Congress (TUC) at home. An anti-communist organisation, 'Freedom First', which had been set up by leading TUC figures, was also subsidised. The link was unintentionally exposed in late 1948 during the Lynskey Tribunal into political corruption, though few noticed at the time. IRD briefings were supplied to a large number of selected MPs and journalists, including the editor of the *Daily Herald*. Material was also placed with news agencies, notably the Arab News Agency, which had been established by MI6, and the London Press Service. It developed close links with a syndication agency and various publishers leading to the establishment of a publishing company, Ampersand, to print anti-communist books.[14]

Chaired by Mayhew, the Colonial Information Policy Committee was established by the ministerial committee on anti-communist propaganda to co-ordinate programmes in Britain's colonial possessions. The IRD established its most important regional office in Singapore, with an additional office in Hong Kong, to provide material for South-East Asia. Agreement was made with French and Belgian authorities in Africa to counter nationalist movements while, from its inception, IRD began exchanging information on 'publicity' with the United States State Department and overseas missions.[15]

Mayhew had been wary of upsetting Labour's left wing and the latter exchange appears to have been undertaken by Foreign Office officials without his co-operation or knowledge. He thought that the British effort, based on social democratic values, was superior to American propaganda, which he described as being 'crude'. He was certain that there was insignificant co-operation with the infant CIA, though Tom McCoy, who acted as the Agency's liaison with the IRD throughout most of its life, revealed that there was a close relationship both at the planning stage in London and Washington, and at field stations throughout the world. In the Far East, Ralph Murray made sure that arrangements existed so that 'our respective operations complement one another', while in the Middle East there was 'full and complete co-operation', though efforts were made to ensure that there was no impression of a 'joint operation'.[16]

While officials initially paid lip-service to the Third Force idea, they were soon calling for something stronger. The chiefs of staff, always fascinated by the clandestine, had from the beginning wanted to transform the IRD into a peacetime equivalent of the PWE with a capacity for secret 'black' operations. While allowed to implement a 'defensive/offensive' programme, the department was not authorised to conduct subversive operations. Bevin was not at this stage willing to allow the propagandists free rein. This view may have been reinforced by the Protocol M episode, which was beginning to unravel to the embarrassment of the Foreign Office.

After a 'careful and exhaustive investigation' of the provenance of Protocol M, Hector McNeil was forced to backtrack in the House of Commons on 19 April 1948, stating that its authentiticity was now 'in doubt', though, he added, the plan was corroborated by recent developments and by other information 'already in our possession'. The results of the investigation revealed that the document had been obtained from 'a reliable informant' in the Social Democratic Party – the party close to the British authorities – called Kielgast. Insisting that the document might still be genuine, officials stated that it had been 'very good anti-Soviet propaganda'. Only later did officials reveal that its author had been a one-time agent of the Americans called Hahn. Released records indicate that the Foreign Office knew at an early stage that the document was a possible forgery. 'Consequently, the decision to promote it', observes Simon Ollivant, 'was not so much a simple error of judgement but a deliberate act of policy.' It was exploited to expose a perceived communist threat even though intelligence reports indicated that British fears were misplaced. Ollivant concludes that the Foreign Office's 'keen interest in audience reaction – their monitoring of the operation – was the characteristic behaviour of deceivers, whether professional magicians or aspiring propagandists. These and other features of the story indicate that the Foreign Office's handling of the Protocol was more skilful than first impressions might indicate.'[17]

In May 1948, an ad hoc ministerial committee was established by Bevin to oversee and control IRD activities, but it met only three times over the next three years. The effect was that IRD escaped ministerial scrutiny and gradually its activities became more hardline. As in so many areas of the secret world, informal arrangements for the 'day-to-day conduct of anti-Communist propaganda overseas' became the norm. At an Imperial Defence College lecture on political warfare, Bruce Lockhart privately discussed with John Slessor a scheme for the co-ordination of political warfare by a high Foreign Office official or someone with a seat on the chiefs of staff. The role fell to the secretary to the chiefs, General Leslie Hollis, who chaired the Inter-Service Committee on Propaganda Dissemination (the head of the IRD attended its meetings), which included MI6's Stewart Menzies, Christopher Warner and the JIC chair, William Hayter. From the beginning, IRD officials were thus able to interpret the guidelines in the broadest terms and, within a year, the organisation had been transformed into an aggressive anti-communist crusade engaged in 'political warfare'. The social democratic theme was, to all intents and purposes, dead, replaced by a projection of western principles and practices. Increasingly, Mayhew was sidestepped by Foreign Office officials who tended to have a poor opinion of a minister who was prone to change his views: one day he was 'like a right-wing Tory and next like a left-wing Socialist'.[18]

When Mayhew later claimed that the IRD was a 'well-kept secret' which 'did not leak', he was making reference to the domestic audience, primarily left-wing Labour MPs. In November 1948, Mayhew had ordered the transfer of Guy Burgess whose behaviour he deemed unsuitable. According to Michael Smith, not long afterwards 'a Soviet Bloc newspaper carried a remarkably accurate article on the secret organisation'. It was cruelly ironic that its exposure should happen at the very moment that Bevin gave the go-ahead for a more aggressive campaign against the Soviets.[19]

Bevin had previously ruled out anti-communist propaganda to Iron Curtain countries, 'taking the view that HM Government should not incite people to subversive activities if they were not in a position to lend active assistance in overthrowing their regimes'. By the beginning of 1949, however, 'offensive' propaganda began to be linked with subversive operations within the Soviet orbit. Ad hoc groups considered the development of more 'subversive propaganda'.[20]

The IRD maintained a strong relationship with the BBC. It supplied material, 'provided it was neither quoted directly, nor attributed to the government as being official policy'. The BBC was an ideal conduit for IRD material because it was, as one former official described it, 'in a class by itself'. The Corporation was regarded as semi-independent and an authoritative source of factual information which, of course, made the insertion of material from IRD 'briefing papers' so much more effective and productive in terms of propaganda. The IRD regarded its relationship with the BBC as perhaps its most important, and it became, according to one former IRD operative, 'the official source for Bush House's East European services'.[21]

The former head of the wartime German Service, Hugh Carlton Greene, who had worked in close collaboration with the PWE, was appointed controller of the BBC's External Services to the Soviet Union and eastern Europe. When Bruce Lockhart was asked his advice on the BBC's broadcasts to the USSR, he suggested that the IRD should be engaged in 'truthful' broadcasting. The Director of Overseas Broadcasting, General Sir Ian Jacob, formerly Military Assistant Secretary to the Cabinet, told him that, instead, Mayhew was urging the BBC to 'lambast the Russians in our Russian broadcasts'. A member of the Russia Committee, Jacob had apparently agreed to 'temper its broadcasts to accord with the national interest'. He had also agreed to consider IRD's idea to 'plant' stories 'to draw [the Soviets] out on subjects to which we would like to know the answers'.[22]

In June 1949, after a tour of Yugoslavia, Czechoslovakia, Bulgaria and Poland, the journalist and MP Vernon Bartlett, a psychological warfare veteran who had worked during the war for the PWE, met with Christopher Mayhew, Norman Reddaway, Robert Conquest and other IRD officials. Bartlett informed them that the propaganda put out by the BBC 'encouraging elements hostile to the present regimes' was premature and 'only had the effect of endangering the elements'. With the Stalin–Tito split still fresh in his mind, Mayhew, however, saw an important distinction between 'trying to overthrow satellite regimes altogether and trying to prise them away from Moscow without altering their communist complexion'. The Foreign Office agreed but wanted to go further, and felt that 'it was important to keep them in good heart by a vigorous propaganda which would show that we are alive to what was going on behind the Iron Curtain'.[23]

Ian Jacob was troubled by the tough stance demanded by Mayhew and his officials. There was a delicate balance to be struck because the relationship with the IRD clearly undermined the BBC's claim of 'complete objectivity and independence'. Hugh Greene later played down the IRD link and defined the External Services' propaganda role as being 'to get our audience to accept our view of events', with a subsidiary objective 'to shake faith in Stalin'. He did not think that 'it should be any part of our objectives to contribute to the overthrow of the Soviet regime or to "liberate" the Soviet peoples'. It was, however, Greene later recalled, 'certainly part of our aim to keep alive their links with the West and the belief that somehow, someday ... things might be better and Russian rule might be shaken off'. He believed that in broadcasts directed from Britain to eastern Europe the BBC was 'always careful to avoid any hint of encouragement to sabotage or revolt'.[24]

In December, the ad hoc ministerial committee on anti-communist propaganda agreed that all restrictions on subversive propaganda in communist countries should be removed. It endorsed the IRD, which was no longer a passive organisation, engaging in 'propaganda in other countries designed to stimulate subversive activities in the Soviet orbits'. The IRD worked closely with MI6's anti-Soviet section, R5, on these operations. Now funded from the Secret Vote, which enabled it to execute covert and semi-covert operations, the IRD began recruiting on a larger scale, using intelligence officers from some of the wartime propaganda agencies such as the PWE, and a number of émigrés from eastern Europe. The IRD would eventually have representatives in most British embassies abroad. It became a service department 'on call' to support the latest anti-Soviet projects of other agencies and departments. The 'offensive' message dominated and, whereas other information agencies contracted, the IRD's staff expanded to over three hundred people, with sixty in the Soviet section alone.[25]

Opinion within MI6 was divided on the IRD's merits. Many officers believed that it was too 'low-key' and 'defensive' for effective work, while in the recollection of one former MI6 officer, the IRD was involved in 'some of the more dubious intelligence operations which characterised the early days of the cold war'. 'Non-attributability' became the central feature of the circulation of information, as did the wartime technique of 'surfacing' rumours and disinformation – i.e. planting stories in third countries or foreign publications which could be recycled domestically. Although IRD apologists have always denied it, 'black' material such as forgeries, lies and fabrications was disseminated for use by its own outlets and by MI6-funded radio stations and news agencies. By the organisation's engagement in these 'cowboy' operations, however, the more worthwhile tasks became tainted.[26]

Christopher Mayhew believed that the IRD was extremely successful. It may have been on some levels, but a number of diplomats were turned off by its straightforward anti-communism which they found counterproductive. Mayhew is certainly to be praised for highlighting, in the late forties, the existence of slave labour and the gulags in the Soviet Union. Just as factually correct was the substance of the attacks on Stalinism. But such efforts were undermined by their origin in a covert agency; secrecy does ultimately corrupt, and the moral high ground was lost as soon as the tactics used became no different from those of the Soviet propagandists. More, perhaps, would have been achieved by openness and honesty.

The reality, which seemed to escape Mayhew, is that the members of the 'secret state' have always been extremely successful at manipulating the Labour Party. Labour MPs know, or want to know, very little about the workings of the security and intelligence services, and invariably leave matters to officials. Ironically, it was a Labour Foreign Secretary, David Owen, who in 1977 closed down the IRD because of its contacts with right-wing journalists and propagandists who were actively anti-Labour.

CHAPTER 7

ROLL-BACK

By 1948, in the absence of full-scale war, the Joint Intelligence Committee (JIC) had concluded that the Soviet Union would continue to employ Cold War methods to weaken the western powers by fostering nationalism in the European colonies and creating unrest and civil war in western countries by means of political blackmail, infiltration and subversion. Despite alarmist intelligence reports, 'nothing happened'. The same view held after Tito's defection from the Soviet sphere, but again Moscow did not move.[1]

Nevertheless, Bevin ordered the Foreign Office to review the security situation in Europe and, in particular, the Greek civil war. The 'Bastions Paper' reported that 'Soviet policy aims to control Greece'. It was seen as 'a particularly weak bastion in the defences against Communism', being 'one link in a chain of bastions along the perimeter of the Soviet sphere, where the Russians had established themselves solidly'. The paper concluded that the measures taken so far – Marshall Aid, the Brussels Treaty, the Truman Doctrine and actions to prevent a communist victory in Italy and France – were not enough. A battle remained to be fought in Germany, Austria, Trieste, Greece and Turkey, and if one of these 'bastions' was to fall then the others would follow.[2]

Despite Stalin's failure to suport the Greek insurgents, Greece 'inclined the British Government to adopt a confrontational attitude towards Soviet-directed world Communism'. The chiefs of staff's backing of 'special operations' for a 'subversive war' against the communists became the spur for a wave of covert-action operations by the intelligence services. These, however, required some form of centralised planning rather than the ad hoc arrangements then in place. Following pressure from the chiefs and the Foreign Office, discussions began on the need for a 'permanent Cold War Planning Staff'. As Richard Aldrich suggests, this 'constituted a critical turning-point in the higher direction of the British Intelligence community'. The chiefs pressed for military participation in the planning, while a 'forecast of Russian moves' from the Foreign Office was accompanied by a request for major offensive measures far beyond previous propaganda efforts.[3]

A September 1948 paper by the armed services' Directors of Intelligence reviewing communist policy concluded that 'the only method of preventing the Russian threat from ever materializing is by utterly defeating Russian Communism'. In reviewing the paper, Field Marshal Montgomery wrote in his diary that 'We could not win the "cold war" unless we carried our offensive inside Russia and the satellite states. In fact, what was required was a world-wide offensive, using every available agency. To date we had failed to unify our forces to oppose Soviet "cold war" aggression.' Besides calling for counter-action, the Directors agreed that the whole question of intelligence on Russia should be reviewed. 'Perhaps at this late hour there will be a proper set-up to control and direct this very important aspect of our national defence. It must also be hoped that the clock is not on the point of striking.' The chiefs of staff called for a body not only to oversee the direction of the conflict but also to control 'all executive action'.[4]

The JIC and chiefs' papers were considered at a conference on 9 and 10 September, chaired by the Minister of Defence, A. V. Alexander. Speaking for the chiefs, in a blistering critique aimed at Bevin, Lord Tedder deplored the present conduct of the Cold War. He said that it appeared to be based solely on the Information Research Department (IRD), which was 'completely inadequate' when the requirement was the employment of measures 'short of actual shooting'. Suggesting an interdepartmental planning body to co-ordinate the response, he qualified his criticism by adding that it 'should not be taken out of the hands of the Foreign Secretary'. For the Foreign Office, Ivone Kirkpatrick pointed out that the chiefs were 'incorrect' in presuming that IRD was the only Cold War propaganda mechanism. He added that the Russia Committee was 'in fact the Cold War Planning Staff' whose membership would now be expanded to include the chiefs. Although officials agreed on the danger of 'losing the Cold War' and the need for an accelerated response, Kirkpatrick warned that 'the Foreign Secretary was inclined to the view the covert activities would not pay a dividend'.[5]

Pressure was also applied by the Commandant of the Imperial Defence College (IDC), John Slessor, an important background figure during the Cold War who had been engaged in the wartime air drops of SOE agents. Senior strategists used the influential IDC as 'a forum for detailed discussion of the prosecution of the Cold War' and called in a report by Slessor for 'expanded machinery and a planning section for "day-to-day operations"'.[6]

The idea of destabilising eastern Europe achieved a measure of interdepartmental support when the enlarged Russia Committee, with Tedder as the chiefs of staff's representative, met for the first time in late November. Chaired by Gladwyn Jebb, it considered a paper, 'British policy towards the Soviet orbit in Europe', that advocated a policy of offensive rather than defensive containment. The paper had been written by Robin Hankey, who had opposed SOE's role at the end of the war and had taken over from Warner as head of the Northern Department. Having served in Warsaw between 1945 and 1946, and primed on Marxist-Leninist texts, Hankey had a deep suspicion of Soviet motives. Taking on board the military recommendation of a 'roll-back' stance (i.e. rolling back Soviet control of eastern Europe), the committee called for 'relatively long-term' operations to loosen the Soviet hold on its orbit countries. The planners assumed, mistakenly as it turned out, that 'the war-weary populations of Eastern Europe would require little encouragement to rise up and overthrow their totalitarian governments'. The short-term objective aimed at 'promoting civil discontent, internal confusion and possibly strife in satellite countries so that they will be a source not of strength but of weakness to Russia'. This was to be achieved through a revival of robust use of psychological warfare and Special Operations (SO) methods.[7]

This was a major step forward, but intelligence officials remained largely scornful of Foreign Office efforts. 'There was still a generation of senior Foreign Office officials', George Young recalled, 'who had an inborn dislike of any sort of action, and who had spent their wartime years trying to sabotage the SOE saboteurs.' They remained hesitant of special operations which, 'by their very nature, were difficult to control and often cut across the mainstream policies of more orthodox departments'. While he recognised that the political atmosphere within Whitehall had changed, by the time the restrictions were lifted Stewart Menzies discovered that it was one thing to advocate aggressive containment or roll-back but 'to find the resolve and resources to implement special operations against a foreign power was quite another'.[8]

As Young discovered, 'there was always a case for doing nothing'. An activist would find himself gradually 'enmeshed in a web of gentlemanly procedures and left to eat his heart out in a room at the end of a long corridor with some imposing description of his office, but in fact damned with the invisible but effective label of "difficult"'. This was 'sufficient to keep the brakes on'. And, indeed, as Richard Aldrich notes, Bevin 'wavered when faced with the challenge of taking widespread actions against Albania and Yugoslavia'. Some Russia Committee members stated 'that it was important to realise that the satellites were lost to us for the time being and that we should preserve our attack for places where the battle was actually joined, in Berlin, Greece, China and South-East Asia'.[9]

At the end of the year, Young's carefully cultivated sources among the eastern European communist parties reported that the Kremlin was calling off general revolutionary activity in Europe. 'This was particularly interesting', Young recalled, 'as the Berlin blockade was still operating, the French and Italian communists were at their most obstreperous and Molotov at his most obstructive.' Young believed that if Stalin was 'ruthless' once he acted, he 'was always cautious before he moved'. Tito's determined reaction to the Soviet attempts to undermine his position was seen as leaving 'the Russian dictator uncertain as to his next steps in consolidating his Eastern and Central European dependencies. The Western response to the Berlin blockade was unexpected.' The Soviet response was to advise the Austrian Communist Party, which Young had spent his time in Vienna trying to penetrate, 'that revolution would have to be postponed, perhaps for decades, and that it might even have to go underground'. Malcolm Mackintosh noted that 'no plans for the conquest or subversion of any major Western country were put in hand, notwithstanding the fact that in two of them, France and Italy, the local communist parties were the largest single parties.'[10]

In a more confident frame of mind, Tedder looked forward to the collapse of the Soviet regime 'in the next five years'. General agreement was given to his idea of a 'small permanent team which will consider plans' and to bringing in the Americans 'at as early a stage as possible'. At a meeting in December 1948, the head of the BBC European Services, General Ian Jacob, suggested that the Foreign Office 'like the service Ministries should have a director of plans'. In February 1949, Bevin approved the setting up of the Permanent Under Secretary's Committee (PUSC), which would be responsible for long-term planning. Working closely with the Russia Committee, the PUSC included Foreign Office officials specifically responsible for security and intelligence. It absorbed some of the important machinery of the Service Liaison Department which had been headed by Victor Cavendish-Bentinck, then Harold Caccia and, finally, William Hayter. It excluded chiefs of staff representation as Bevin resisted a larger role for the military in Cold War planning and the supervision of operations. He would not 'agree to an offensive policy involving the encouragement of subversive movements', as such activity 'would require the revival in peacetime of the PWE and SOE'. Bevin's resistance did not last long, however, and was soon ground down.[11]

The Foreign Office was influenced by Cecil King's dispatches from Belgrade and, in February 1949, noted 'the emergence of Tito as an anti-Soviet deviationist and opponent of the Soviet Union's hegemony over the Orbit'. This development, the Northern Department concluded, 'may in the long run, prove more important than the degree of consolidation so far achieved. As long as he is successful in retaining control, Tito is a reminder to the Soviet Government of the continuing dangers of defection within the camp and a source of encouragement to anti-Soviet elements within the Eastern

European countries.' In truth, the Yugoslavs still hoped for a reconciliation with Stalin, and it was months after the split before they considered developing any new doctrines. Indeed, Beatrice Heuser asserts that 'there was no such thing as "Titoism"' which, in reality, was an invention of the western press. On this misperception, the British and Americans hoped to use 'Titoism' as 'an erosive and disintegrating force within the Russian sphere', and built around it a new aspect of their liberation policy, namely that of 'encouraging' other communist governments to 'follow Tito'.[12]

While resisting a full-scale covert response, in mid-February Bevin did identify three immediate objectives: to save Greece; covert encouragement of Tito's Yugoslavia; and thirdly, 'detaching Albania from the orbit'. Bevin now accepted the policy that Fitzroy Maclean, a hawkish cold warrior who had developed a close relationship with Tito at the end of the war, had been pressuring the Cabinet to accept, namely 'keeping Tito afloat'. Once Bevin received the authority of the Prime Minister, 'special machinery' was required to implement the Albania operation. In early March, Air Chief Marshal Slessor called for a counteroffensive by 'specially qualified staff' who would make use of 'all appropriate economic and political weapons'. At the same time the new Foreign Office Permanent Under-Secretary, Sir William Strang, submitted a proposal for 'a small secret committee' which would include Gladwyn Jebb and the MoD's Maurice Dean. A permanent 'Cold War sub-committee' of the Russia Committee was thus established which became known as the 'Jebb Committee'.[13]

MI6 now had the political backing to support eastern European resistance movements through propaganda 'but also by infiltrating exiles who were trained to organise insurrections' with arms and aid. Menzies told the JIC that he intended to make good use of a captured wartime German report compiled by a Russian PoW which provided 'suggestions for political warfare against the Russians and containing plans and a map for military action in support of this policy'.[14]

The committee also had a domestic agenda. Kim Philby refers to the 'Jebb Committee' as the 'Committee to Fight Against Communism'. According to Philby, it had responsibility for planning psychological warfare operations primarily against Soviet-backed peace fronts and conferences. These included MI6's London station working against delegations to Britain from socialist countries and their representatives residing here, the recruitment of British merchant seamen, and the use of the British press and media, which was the responsibility of a special department known as BIN/KOORD. Some of the 'dirty tricks' were farcical, with MI5 agents disrupting conferences by 'impregnating lavatory paper with an itching substance at halls hired by communist organisations'. Years later, a former junior MI6 officer and *Guardian* journalist, Mark Arnold-Forster, told Labour minister Tony Benn that while MI6 'take no interest in domestic politics', there had been one occasion when 'there was to have been a peace conference in Sheffield, which was really just a cover for support for the North Koreans, and Clem Attlee ordered it to be stopped'. On that occasion, MI6 arranged 'to bug every single telephone within half-a-mile of the conference centre and had set up recording devices'. Arnold-Forster added, smiling: 'Wasn't Clem Attlee a marvellous Prime Minister?'[15]

During July the Russia Committee agreed that the objective should be 'to weaken the hold of Moscow over the countries which it at present dominates; to resist, and if possible to curtail, the influence of Communism with its proclaimed hostility to Western ideals and interests'. It was to be undertaken by 'propaganda, inducements and covert activities as may be appropriate'. Yugoslavia was to be used as a propaganda wedge that would emphasise the treatment the country had received at the hands of Moscow. A PUSC paper circulated to ministers on 'British Policy Towards Soviet Communism' cautioned that 'actions involving a serious risk of war or likely to encourage fatal resistance should be avoided'. The first step would be to establish 'a modus operandi with Yugoslavia to detach Albania from the Soviet orbit, and to encourage the emergence of "national deviationism" in other countries'.[16]

During 1949, MI6 kept a watch for any threat to Tito's position in the form of a Stalinist coup or invasion. The JIC reports were particularly alarmist, expressing fears that the Russians might resort to arms. After pressure was applied with the offer of economic assistance for curtailing arms supplies to the Greeks, Tito gave a private undertaking to Fitzroy Maclean that 'no other help would be given to the rebels'. By the summer, intelligence reports showed that Tito was keeping his word. Twelve months later telephone taps from Austria indicated that Tito's chances of survival had improved with the lessening of a Soviet military threat. There was, however, a fear that Tito might be the target of a Soviet assassination squad and, according to senior Yugoslav figures, MI6 provided intelligence to Tito on such attempts.[17]

In their studies of 'Anti-Stalinist Communism', Foreign Office officials were forced during 1949–50 to admit that the Yugoslav expulsion from the Cominform may have delayed the development of more independent tendencies in western communism. They acknowledged that they had overestimated 'the drive for independence of the communist regimes themselves' and that, far from supporting the break, the Italian and French communist parties had come out against the Yugoslavs. Despite these reservations, the roll-back policy took hold.[18]

The Foreign Office, Richard Aldrich suggests, was 'hesitant and uncomfortable when presented with the option of covert activities', though there was 'an initial desire to stay in step with the United States'. Indeed, there was reluctance to expand the programme, but it is untrue to say that Britain 'cannot be said to have a particularly activist tradition when compared with parallel intelligence communities in the United States, France or the Soviet

Union'. A French Intelligence study concluded that Bevin had a 'nonchalant attitude' towards SO with the embarrassing consequence that he 'found it necessary to lie to the House of Commons while covering up for SIS operations he had not even been consulted about'.[19]

The majority of the special operations of the late forties and early fifties were initiated by the British and then taken over by the Americans. It was primarily lack of money which accounted for the smaller scale of involvement, and the requirement that MI6 never took credit for successes. Though the KGB, which was essentially a defensive organisation, is assumed to have had a long activist tradition, in fact there is little evidence that, except for a number of assassinations and kidnappings directed against British and American SO assets in Germany and Austria, it engaged in any SO activity in western Europe. Certainly, there was nothing to compare with MI6's record, which included stay-behind nets in most European countries, the sending of agents and weapons, even if only on a limited scale, into the Soviet satellites, and the direct attempt to overthrow the communist regime in Albania. Even so, within the Foreign Office enthusiasm for SO continued to waver, and after 1949 was short-lived. It was the military which supported an aggressive policy. When MI6 was finally given the green light for SO in support of 'liberation' strategies against the Soviet bloc, it found 'its in-house capabilities inadequate and so was forced hastily to reassemble old SOE sections'.[20]

In one sense, however, it is clear that the initiative had already been lost. George Young's sources in the communist parties alleged that Stalin was now turning to the Far East. In Europe, according to Hugh Seton-Watson, the communists had been unable to achieve stage one of the takeover by way of the 'infiltration of police, army and bureaucracy' of France and Italy. Stalin realised that 'war is not a good risk for the Soviet Union until she has won control of Germany', but he recognised that prospects were much more favourable in Asia, where 'state machines are fragile and economic misery is growing'. Indeed, Young's sources told him that 'Moscow's consolatory guidance to the inner councils of European communist parties, who had obediently put the brake on direct revolutionary action, had been that hand in hand with the Chinese, the USSR would spearhead a Communist drive round South-East Asia'. This change in communist tactics was 'reflected in directives to the Asian Communist parties in 1948, probably transmitted during the Conference of "Progressive Youth of Asia" and the Congress of the Indian Communist Party, both of which were held in Calcutta early in 1948'. According to Young, after these meetings 'the tactics of the Communists in all Asian countries changed from co-operation with the non-communist nationalists to extreme and often violent opposition, sometimes culminating in armed uprisings'. The global concept was for 'an extension of Soviet power under the pretext of attacking "colonialism" in its various forms'.[21]

Behind this assessment lay an intelligence conspiracy theory of truly global proportions. Young believed that the 'Bandung Conference and Nehru's sympathetic compliance with Soviet policies indicated some progress along' what he termed 'the curve of the global outflanking movement'. By which he meant that Stalin's move to the Far East was the prelude to subversion in the Middle East and Mediterranean, which would then seep back into Europe, 'thus fulfilling one of Lenin's *obiter dicta* that World revolution would be won on the banks of the Ganges'. Even the liberal Seton-Watson was to write that 'the struggle between the West and the Soviet Union for the support of Asia and Africa will decide the future of the world'.[22]

During 1948, there did indeed occur revolutionary upheavals in Malaya, Burma and Indonesia, whose Communist Party representatives had attended the Youth Congress. This, however, only reflected the fact that explosive nationalist situations already existed in these countries. The irony – given the West's enthusiastic support of Tito against Stalin – was that the only European communist delegates to attend these conferences were members of the Yugoslav Communist Party. Under the influence of the soon to be disgraced Zhadanov, the Yugoslavs advocated to their hosts 'insurrection as opposed to compromise'. Mistakenly, the British blamed the outbreak of violence on Stalin and proceeded to pursue a policy of 'containment' in South-East Asia.[23]

Major resources were redirected by MI6 towards the region, but the first test was not encouraging. Western intelligence failed to predict the attack by the North on South Korea in the middle of the night of 25 June 1950. Despite evidence of major military assistance which has recently come to light, Korea – which was of no strategic value to Britain – was not part of a master plan nor symptomatic of a general aggressive shift by Moscow, but 'a piece of Stalinist opportunism that went badly wrong'. Looking back, Lord Franks, who was ambassador in Washington during this period, admitted that 'we got it wrong in the sense that it wasn't part of a concerted stepping-up of a Russian threat. I don't think this was there.' That, however, was not how it looked to Whitehall. Junior minister Kenneth Younger wrote in his diary that 'a North Korean army invaded South Korea, and set in motion a whole train of action of which the consequences are still largely guesswork'.[24]

The outbreak of the Korean War was followed by an update by the Joint Planning Staff on 'the spread of Communism' for the chiefs of staff's committee. The 11 July 1950 report estimated that 'war is not inevitable but that the circumstances in which war is most likely to occur will be when Soviet leaders may consider themselves strong enough to risk a major war of indefinite duration regardless of Western reactions; this may be for 1955 onwards but the estimate is based on very slender evidence'. The planners warned the chiefs, however, that 'the possibility that war may break out at any time before or after 1955 cannot be disregarded'. They outlined the four Cold War methods of extending 'Russian Communist control' used in the years since

1945 which would be deployed by Stalin: a) by supporting a coup d'état by pseudo-constitutional means as in Czechoslovakia; b) by political pressure as in Poland; c) by the support, either directly or indirectly, through satellites, of communist rebellion as in China; d) by Russian-inspired military aggression by a satellite as in Korea.

The chiefs, the Foreign Office and MI6 now all believed that the time had come for a counter-offensive as 'the present extension of Soviet control and domination has now begun to impinge directly on the Commonwealth's ability to defend its vital interests and to meet its commitments to its allies. Further expansion must be resisted.' The planners presented a checklist of important Cold War areas 'whose loss in peace would ... jeopardise our basic strategic requirements and prejudice the ability of the allies to fight a major war'. Europe remained at the top but Korea was now put second because of its potential knock-on effect. 'If the forces of the United Nations were to fail to stem the drive of militant Communism in Korea it would be a major defeat for the Western Powers, and would shatter the faith of the free countries of the Far East and South East Asia in the ability of the Western powers and the United Nations to defend them from Russian domination. Repercussions would, in fact, be felt in other parts of the world, notably Western Germany.'[25]

The main effect of the Korean War upon Britain was that it shifted the views of the American administration. In Washington, Franks reported that Britain was now regarded as 'a dependable ally'. MI6 was happy to see the promotion within the recently created Central Intelligence Agency (CIA) of covert-action-oriented operatives and the appointment, in October 1950, of a new Director, General Walter Bedell Smith, Eisenhower's wartime chief of staff. Bedell Smith had even considered appointing as deputy a Britisher, Major-General Kenneth Strong, Eisenhower's former head of the intelligence staff. MI6 was, however, happy with an avowed anglophile, William H. Jackson, in his place. The new Director was praised by George Young because he 'put the house in order, and gave the CIA a set of firm goals, so that when Allen Dulles [Deputy Director of Plans responsible for covert action] took over [in 1953] he could indulge in his passion for sudden operational sallies without worrying about the base'.[26]

Relations between MI6 and the CIA subsequently became particularly close, with joint planning on a number of special operations. Nevertheless, this was to be short-lived.

PART TWO

THE FRONT LINE

In the months leading up to the end of the Second World War, MI6 was already thinking in terms of the next conflict – its officers now had to mop up the remnants of the Third Reich and neutralise those potential Nazi stay-behind units determined to hold out to the bitter end. In the immediate aftermath, intelligence nets had to be dealt with for any signs of a Nazi revival in an effort to stamp out any such awakening in its infancy. MI6's extensive files on the Nazi Party, intelligence and SS officers were to be put to good use in dealing with the thorny problem of rooting out war criminals.

At the same time, MI6, Special Operations Executive and intelligence officers belonging to various obscure units flooded into Germany determined to retrieve the secrets of the Nazis' intelligence agencies. They also aimed to plunder the latest technological advances and seize information on nuclear, missile and biological and chemical warfare developments. Although the British were extremely well prepared and successful in gathering intelligence, it soon became apparent that they had failed to gain their share of the techno-logical prize, being outclassed by the Americans with their almost unlimited resources. It was a pattern repeated throughout the emerging Cold War.

Once established in Germany and Austria, MI6 soon turned its intelli-gence-gathering efforts towards the East and, initially, was extremely success-ful, exploiting the intelligence on the Soviet Union found in Nazi intelligence agency files. The Service was able to make good use of low-level defectors among the numerous Soviet displaced persons who found themselves trapped in Germany. This source of intelligence on the Soviet Union soon began to dry up, however, and major Soviet security operations during 1946 led to the arrest of entire chains of agents and the break-up of intelligence networks. Double-agent operations also collapsed and became totally unproductive.

Germany and Austria now emerged as the front line of the new intelligence Cold War. In order to fill the gap on Soviet military plans, MI6 increasingly turned to using Nazi intelligence officers with experience of the eastern front. Many, it turned out, were wanted war criminals with unsavoury records. They had, however, run agents in the East and, in desperation, MI6 used them to revive anti-communist networks in eastern Europe and the Soviet Union.

CHAPTER EIGHT

GERMANY AND THE '3 X 5s'

On the back of the major news stories splashed across the world's headlines during the period 1996–7, centring on the deposit of vast sums of 'Nazi Gold' in Swiss banks at the end of the Second World War, there appeared other interlinked allegations including the claim that the gold stolen from Jewish victims of the Holocaust had been used to plan and underwrite a postwar Nazi revival. Despite the orchestrated release and publicising of official documents, few, if any, of the allegations were new or even true.

Indeed, well into the postwar period, journalists had propagated the myth of the 'Fourth Reich'. The Sunday newspapers paid a great deal of money for tales of former Nazi leaders who had laundered huge quantities of Reich gold abroad in preparation for the Nazi rebirth. Writers popularised the myth of a brotherhood of former SS officers which had organised secret underground networks such as Die Spinne (Spider) and ODESSA (*Organisation der ehemaligen SS-Angehoriger*). These were said to have organised the landing of top Nazis by submarine off the coast of South America where they were destined to revive the old order. The truth was somewhat different, certainly less glamorous and a great deal more shabby.[1]

Investigating 'The Nazi Menace in Argentina', author Ronald Newton found that the historic record had been left 'booby-trapped with an extraordinary number of hoaxes, forgeries, unanswered propaganda ploys, and assorted dirty tricks'. The most successful disinformer or dupe was the American Ladislas Farago, 'a somewhat Hemingway-esque figure with a strong

Hungarian accent and a confidential manner', whose 'good connections with the CIA and secret services of several European countries enabled him to investigate and publish on a non-attributable basis' a series of half-correct tales. He spent the war years in Naval Intelligence and during the fifties worked for Radio Free Europe, exhorting eastern Europeans to revolt. Farago alleged that there had been 'a vast enterprise' involving the transfer of Nazi funds to South America in an operation code-named Land of Fire (a reference to the archipelago Tierra del Fuego). According to Farago, as late as June 1944 heavily guarded armoured trucks carried the consignments across Germany and France to ports in southern Spain where U-boats took aboard Martin Bormann's precious cargo and then sailed to Argentina. 'The submarines arrived at intervals of six to eight weeks throughout 1943 and 1944, keeping up the flow of the "treasure".' Two were supposed to have 'arrived on July 23 and 29 1945, weeks after V-E Day', with the cargoes unloaded by sailors stranded in Argentina from the scuttled pocket battleship *Graf Spee*. This 'myth', which was revived during 1997 by a local newspaper in Patagonia, appears to have surfaced first in September 1962 in a German newspaper, *Kölnische Rundschau*. An anonymous reporter detailed the transfer from Germany during 1944 or early 1945 of several hundred million pounds' worth of gold by way of Spain to Argentina, where it was used to make possible the escape of two thousand high-ranking Nazis. There is a suspicion that this story may have originated with *Express* journalist Sefton Delmer.[2]

There is a great deal of intelligence speculation but little in the way of hard fact in Farago's writings and in the 'conspiracy theory' presented to the press during 1996–7 by the World Jewish Congress. As Newton discovered, much of the 'Fourth Reich' myth had originally been perpetrated by British Intelligence, which fanned United States fears that the Nazi hierarchy would find sanctuary in Argentina, Britain's traditional 'golden market' in South America. The Foreign Office recognised that German families and companies were a 'valued if not indispensable element' which, if removed, would allow the United States to assume economic supremacy in the region. In order to influence opinion in Washington, MI6's station, the British Security Co-ordination (BSC), resorted to an extraordinary range of propaganda using the advertising agency J. Walter Thompson as consultants, and a BSC subsidiary, LatAmer Ltd, to run operations. By February 1943, based on Government Code and Cipher School (GC&CS)-deciphered German radio traffic, the BSC possessed 'almost complete information about the more important parts of the German intelligence set-up' in Argentina. This revealed that there was no 'Fifth Column' and that Nazi infiltration was virtually non-existent. Even so, by mid-1944 British propaganda efforts had convinced the United States that Argentina would become the centre of a Fourth Reich.[3]

The 'hoax' had, in fact, been born in September 1943, when the British let it be known that they had learned from 'most secret and certain sources' –

a double agent run by a Colonel Russell, though more likely through Ultra – that an Abwehr agent, Ernst Hoppe, was travelling to Argentina. Hoppe was said to be planning to meet a U-boat off the coast of Argentina, carrying a large amount of money belonging to Nazi officials to be invested in Argentine property. Other 'secret reports confirmed' the story, though none stood up to the simplest scrutiny; knowledgeable Foreign Office officials had their own suspicions. In January 1944, Evelyn Shuckburgh reported: 'That a lot of Germans are already here with a lot of their money is a constantly repeated assertion which we have been unable to confirm. The story is always being renewed by communist or refugee newspapers in Montevideo, picked up by the Moscow press, and returned here with circumstantial details attached.'

At the end of 1996 the World Jewish Congress released a previously secret letter written in February 1945 by the US Treasury Secretary in which Henry Morgenthau stated that 'Argentina is not only a likely refuge for Nazi criminals but also has been and still is the focal point of Nazi financial and economic activity in this hemisphere'. He added that the Nazis had been estimated to have invested over one billion dollars in Argentine businesses, ranches, banks and insurance companies. These estimates were, the report admitted, based on 'conjecture'. Shuckburgh had reported that 'Our Friends' (i.e. MI6) could find 'no evidence' to back up these types of claims. While on temporary secondment in early 1945 in London from the Buenos Aires embassy's intelligence unit, Gerald Warner reported that American officials had been trying for months to run down these stories and rumours. They had, however, apparently discovered the true source and had found the rumours to be baseless.[4]

The US Federal Bureau of Investigation (FBI) had investigated information alleging that 'various top ranking Nazis were escaping to Argentina or had invested money. Investigation to date has failed to disclose that the Germans have attempted to transfer their funds to Latin America for the purpose of seeking a safe haven, nor has any information been developed that Nazi officials have escaped to Latin America.' The source of the allegations, which formed the basis of numerous newspaper articles, turned out to be the reports of the 'fire-breathing' Colonel Spraggett on Radio Atlantic, a short-wave station that broadcast seemingly authentic messages from Germany to Argentina. In fact, the station was located near London and was part of Sefton Delmer's black propaganda operation to persuade ordinary German soldiers that their leaders were deserting them for South America. Apparently, the purpose had been explained to the Office of Strategic Services (OSS), but its London station chief, William Casey, had not informed his rivals in the FBI, which had jurisdiction in the region. For political reasons, the gaffe was never made public by the Americans, primarily because the idea of a Fourth Reich was useful to the US State Department, which was orchestrating the 'Safe haven' investigations that were designed to eradicate postwar German economic influence in South America.[5]

Elements of the hoax had been believed within sections of the British intelligence community or, at least, had been used to justify prolonging the existence of a 'Special Operations' capability. Lord Selbourne, the minister responsible for the Special Operations Executive (SOE), had in his final submission in May 1945 referred to the revival of Nazism as a reason for continuing SOE's remit in Germany and Austria which, he recognised, would constitute the front line of the Cold War.

A mysterious SOE unit, known as ME 42, was attached to the military intelligence component of Field Marshal Montgomery's 21 Army Group, in Germany, after Executive Director Colin Gubbins had made representations to the chiefs of staff and 'much pressure' had been applied by Harry Sporborg on the commander-in-chief of the British Army of the Rhine (BOAR), General McGreery. The chiefs of staff would give the Foreign Office no details of what they called ME 42's 'extremely useful work', though Gubbins had made it known that he wanted it to be involved in 'unattributable propaganda, clandestine counter-intelligence activities, the pursuit of enemy assets and looted property, and the building up of a long-term SOE organisation'. A number of '12 Force' personnel who had served the German and Austrian sections of SOE joined with SAS members in forming a War Crimes Investigation Unit in Germany to track down SS men involved in mass killings. While this found favour with the Foreign Office, there was concern that some of the ME 42 operations were directed against the Soviets. Robin Hankey subsequently voiced his conviction that they were of a 'dangerous political character' and resolved to restrain such activities, but he was not entirely successful.[6]

It helped that Major-General (later Field Marshal) Sir Gerald Templer, who for a time had headed SOE's unsuccessful German X Section, was put in charge of all intelligence matters in the British Zone of Occupation in Germany. Facing the Russian Zone and the divided city of Berlin, the British Zone ran from Kiel in the north to Bonn in the south, where it met the French and American zones. Templer's military intelligence staff occupied an elegant casino at Bad Oeyenhausen, a small spa town a few miles north-west of Herford in Rhine-Westphalia. From there, and at another centre at Munster, General Bill Williams, Montgomery's former principal intelligence adviser, 'began to construct an impressive empire, which extended via the regional British Control Commission (BCC) offices throughout the British Zone'. The Intelligence Division had about four thousand personnel with regional offices in each 'Land' and an advance headquarters in Berlin. As with the German section of the Foreign Office, the various branches of Military Intelligence employed former German intelligence officers for several years.[7]

MI6 operated their own large stations under cover of the Political Division of the Control Commission, the Civil Affairs administration and intelligence sections of 21 Army group. Within the British Zone, MI6's main centre of operations was established at Bad Salzuflen, headed by Harold Shergold, a former master at Cheltenham Grammar School and wartime military intelligence officer in the Middle East and Italy. It also had an outstation within the British consulate at Düsseldorf. In the 'spy swamp' city of Berlin, MI6 had its main station in offices adjoining the former Olympic building with additional offices in the BCC building at Lancaster House, where officers under 'light cover' were attached to the BCC's Intelligence Division, run by the former chief of staff of the 14th Army, Brigadier J. S. 'Tubby' Lethbridge. The Intelligence Division's main task was liaison with the numerous British intelligence and security units that operated in Germany and supplying the various denazification tribunals with relevant intelligence. Counter-espionage was run by Brigadier Dick White, who was transferred from MI5 to Supreme Headquarters Allied Europe Forces (SHAEF) after several notable catches. White discovered to his dismay, however, that there was little in the way of a co-ordinated security and intelligence plan for postwar Germany.[8]

In February 1945, as Allied armies entered Germany, a joint MI6, MI5 and OSS Counter-Intelligence (CI) G-2 War Room had been created to deal with enemy secret intelligence and subversive functions; this, however, excluded locally inspired subversive or resistance groups. It was jointly chaired by MI5's T. A. 'Tar' Robertson, fresh from his 'double-cross' successes, and Robert Blum of the American X-2. Robertson informed the French that it was an Anglo-American body and that they could not be part of its directing staff, though they were allowed arm's-length representation.

Conceived by its effective chief, Dick White, the London CI War Room tightened communications between the analysts and the Field Security sections, thus releasing the talents of the senior Special Counter-Intelligence (SCI) detachment in Germany. The SCI task was to interrogate and make use of captured German Intelligence Service (GIS) agents, transmit intelligence collected in the field from the GIS through secure channels to London, and pass on from the CI London War Room special information about the GIS which was not suitable for transmission through ordinary channels. In addition, SCI officers were to penetrate the pro-Nazi resistance and stay-behind networks that had begun to show up in the Intelligence Section, Oliver Strachey (ISOS) material, and counter any subversive or terrorist actions. German 'hit squads' had allegedly been issued with 'poisoned aspirin tablets, chocolate bars and sugar' (later developed for use by Gladio agents). They had also developed 'a cigarette lighter that could kill any smoker who used it'.[9]

A special edition of Section V's German primer had also been prepared for wider dissemination as a SHAEF document entitled 'German Intelligence Services'. The rust-red, six-inch-thick volume contained thousands of names compiled from 3 x 5-inch file cards by Robert Carew-Hunt, who prefaced it with an apt quotation from Hamlet (Act IV, sc. V): 'When sorrows come, they come not as single spies, but in battalions'. By the time counter-intelligence officers began work in Germany itself, the Central Personality Index (CPI) had over one hundred thousand cards which consisted of counter-intelligence suspects and Nazi or other German organisations that were otherwise not of CI interest. The thirty sets of CPI were widely distributed for targeting suspects for arrest by MI5 through the Civil Security Liaison Officers, including four to 21 Army Group. The CPI information was augmented by interrogation reports from Camp 030 which dealt with agents and suspect agents of the Abwehr, the Gestapo and the SD, who had been investigated and interrogated by the Field Security sections. In addition, a Commission for Criminal Organisations, headed by Colonel Airey Neave, formerly in charge of 'Room 900' of the MI6 offshoot MI9, was created to interrogate Nazi prisoners suspected of war crimes.[10]

According to research by John Loftus, the British gave the Americans their card files on the Nazi officials, so that there would be a joint Allied effort to arrest suspected war criminals after the war. In return for this valuable intelligence coup (which was to be the foundation of the OSS and Counter-Intelligence Corps (CIC)'s anti-Nazi database), 'the British demanded an unusual system for post-war interrogation of Nazis'. There were three tiers: 'low-ranking Nazis could be interrogated unilaterally by the Americans, provided that summaries were sent to the British; some Nazis would be questioned only at special centers in Germany such as Camp King, where British interrogators would be able to interview them as needed'. Camp King, near Oberusal, was formerly the Luftwaffe's primary interrogation centre for captured British and American fliers during the war. In mid-1945, it was seized by the Americans and transformed into a holding centre for the highest-ranking Nazis and intelligence personnel in captivity. About two hundred SS, SD and Abwehr men were placed on British payrolls and assigned to write 'histories' of their wartime experiences with particular emphasis placed on material about the USSR and eastern Europe. Leading Nazis in the final category were to be flown to London for debriefing. According to Loftus, 'the Americans faithfully complied', but when the British recommended that the War Room become the basis of a combined Anglo-American anti-Soviet intelligence centre, they were reluctant to co-operate.[11]

Dick White discovered that 21 Army Group 'boasted a motley collection of officers', whom he blamed for 'shallow thinking', and no counter-intelligence organisation of any note. Many of the best officers had been demobbed and the Control Commission officers often lacked experience or were of low calibre. The small staff was soon overwhelmed by the avalanche of intelligence and interrogation reports of Nazi suspects. In consequence, with staff largely ignorant of what was really going on, the British Zone became a safe haven for wanted Nazis, a fact that was soon reported in American newspapers. Even before hostilities had ceased, a number of senior Nazis had made approaches to British Intelligence, seeking 'to save their own necks and perhaps win a life of some comfort by selling the only commodity they had to bargain with: information'. They were initially rebuffed.[12]

In November 1944, Karl Marcus (alias Carlsen) had arrived in France disguised as a deserter but, in reality, on a mission for Walter Schellenberg for whom he acted as political adviser. Marcus had been sent 'to get in touch with the British, particularly Lord Vansittart', former Permanent Under-Secretary of the Foreign Office, with proposals for peace negotiations. He was brought to London for interrogation whereupon he disclosed 'valuable military and counter-espionage information regarding Sicherheitsdienst plans and intentions, German participation in [communist] activities in Greece, a new secret German weapon, the training of Polish partisans [for service against the Russians], and purported German military intentions in the West'. Despite this information, Marcus does not appear, initially at least, to have been taken very seriously.[13]

Nor, while the war was in progress, was the head of the Fremde Heere Ost (FHO), General Reinhard Gehlen, who had begun plotting his future in October 1944. He 'had no illusions about the course of the war' and 'had known for months that the game was up'. His only concern was 'what could be salvaged from the inevitable wreckage of unconditional surrender, and how it could keep him afloat as Germany and its leaders went under'. Gehlen was convinced that it would not be long before the Western powers recognised that their ultimate enemy was their present ally, the Soviet Union. They would then require his services and those of his co-conspirators in the FHO who could provide them with 'expert knowledge of the extent and real nature of the Soviet threat to the West'. Gehlen believed that the FHO files contained 'the fullest, most up-to-date information in existence on the Soviet Union's military capability, resources, performance and leadership'. Determined to exploit this valuable asset, towards the end of the war Gehlen organised a secret approach to the British through Hermann Baun, who was in charge of agents of the Frontline Reconnaissance Detachments or Walli units, who operated behind Soviet lines. In return for asylum, Gehlen offered his organisation and 'priceless files on the Soviets'. To his surprise, the British turned down the offer but did move to exploit the capture of Gehlen's officers at Flensburg.[14]

MI6 had committed some of its best officers to Germany, and those experienced counter-espionage officers in place were regarded as being particularly adept at squeezing information from interrogated Nazis. Faced with the task of recruiting informants to infiltrate the numerous self-help organisations for escaping war criminals and the neo-Nazi groups which were being revived, there was an increasing readiness to exploit the skills and knowledge of ex-SS officers and overlook what crimes they might have committed. It was a messy business in which investigators frequently cut deals – sometimes with financial incentives that could be used to advantage on the black market – in order to land more important fugitives or coerce them into betraying former colleagues who could also be recruited as informants.

The investigators' task was made easier by access to the co-ordinating CPI unit which had been established at BOAR and its store of card files on war crime suspects. Building on the CPI cards system was the Central Registry of War Crimes and Security Suspects (CROWCASS), which was established in Paris in May 1945, following a call by the Supreme Commander in Europe, General Dwight Eisenhower, for international co-operation in hunting and prosecuting war criminals – an inter-service, inter-Allied card data file used for intelligence purposes in postwar Europe. The extensive political-biographical information on mostly German nationals on the thirty-six thousand cards was compiled from British and American agents in eastern Europe, along with captured Nazi records and informant debriefings. Set up by a British officer, the CROWCASS lists cross-referenced the names of fugitive war crime suspects with the rosters of more than eight million people being held in the six hundred or more Prisoner of War (PoW) and Displaced Persons (DP) camps in Germany, Italy and Austria. An enlargement of the list was compiled by the United Nations War Crimes Commission (UNWCC), which was charged with collating evidence on war crimes. Individuals were screened by Field Security and other intelligence officers to see whether they were on the CROWCASS list or not: if so listed they were to be arrested.[15]

The majority of the postwar, pro-Nazi self-help groups existed in name only, while 'others were groups of wayward adventurers who operated briefly and spasmodically during the chaotic post-war months, then faded into oblivion, accomplishing little'. The most famous group, ODESSA, later promoted by the thriller fiction of Frederick Forsyth, did exist, but it was not 'a world-wide underground league of old Nazis financed from South America with Nazi gold, which arranged the escape of the Third Reich villains from Martin Bormann downwards and, with the secret assistance of the Vatican, smuggled them out of Europe'. In reality, as Ladislas Farago with his early privileged access to American CIC and OSS secret files acknowledged, ODESSA was 'actually little more than a shadowy consortium of a handful of freelancers and never amounted to much in the Nazi underground'. There never was a single coherent unified structure; the archives instead suggest that 'numerous little groups of old SS comrades which sprang up often used the term, with its hint of remoteness and mystery, to lend themselves more importance than they possessed'.[16]

The real purpose of these scattered groups was not to found a 'neo-Nazi international' but to serve as self-help societies, supplying forged papers to help their members stay alive and evade arrest. It would be wrong, however, to suggest that there was no hint of 'conspiracy' in the setting up of and use of escape routes. The first Nazi underground 'ratline' was founded by former Hitler Youth leaders in the winter of 1945–6 and involved German trucking companies transporting wanted fugitives to remote hideaways. The most active group was the Brunderschaft (Brotherhood), which had its beginnings in a British PoW camp at Neueundorf in 1945–6. It was started by a former staff officer, Major Helmut Beck-Broichsitter, and a former SS lieutenant-colonel, Alfred Franke-Gricksch, who began working for MI6 from 1945 and was allowed to bypass the denazification procedures. It was closely associated with the flying ace and hardline Nazi Colonel Rudel, whose own Kamerad-enwerk was well funded by his many friends among German financiers. The reality was that all these groups were under close surveillance and thoroughly infiltrated by British security and intelligence agencies which 'from time to time used nationalist groups for their own purposes, but in any case at all times securely controlled them'. In truth, they were unable to operate without British Intelligence turning a blind eye to their operations.[17]

Investigation of the neo-Nazi self-help organisations overlapped with, and was quickly supplanted by, the intelligence requirement for information on Soviet activities in Germany and eastern Europe. Many leading British military and intelligence authorities believed that the West lacked adequate organisation to take effective counter-intelligence measures against the communist threat. In Germany, there was a great deal of espionage activity by the Soviets, who set up a number of spy rings and attached so-called 'experts' to the numerous 'technical reparations commissions' which travelled throughout the Allied zones as intelligence-gathering fronts. To counter the threat, British intelligence agencies began to recruit ex-Nazis to infiltrate these organisations, other front groups and the German Communist Party. In February 1946, British intelligence officers requested authority from the Joint Intelligence Committee (JIC) 'to release at their discretion, certain categories of interned individuals connected with the German Intelligence Service'.[18]

It soon became clear, as Christopher Simpson has noted, that the 'same cross-checking capabilities that permitted the location of thousands of fugitive Nazis also created a pool from which the names of thousands of "suspects" who might be useful for intelligence work could be drawn'. It has been alleged that, in particular, CROWCASS was manipulated by the American officer in charge of its lists, Leon G. Turrou, a central European émigré and zealous anti-Bolshevik. In order to ease their recruitment, war criminals were not prosecuted and requests for information on Nazi suspects were misleadingly returned, marked 'no information'.[19]

Under the cover of Neave's war crimes unit at Flensburg, officers from MI9 and the War Office's MI14 interrogated a handful of officers who had been members of General Gehlen's FHO unit and were willing to trade information for their release. On this occasion their offers were not turned down and MI6 moved to exploit their capture. During the autumn of 1945, MI9 and MI14 officers assembled around fifty former Abwehr, OKW (Ober-kommando der Wehrmacht) and FHO officers at a 'hush-hush' camp at Ostend, administered by 21 Army Group headquarters. British interrogators began to look systematically for additional German intelligence officers who had served on the Russian front or in the eastern sections of the GIS.[20]

Gehlen's personal representative, Col. Scheibe, an 'arrogant Nazi' who had been in charge of the FHO's daily situation reports and was responsible for preserving the Gehlen papers, was the first to be interrogated. He revealed a good deal of information about Gehlen to the British, who arranged through the Americans for his name to be removed from the list of prisoners held in US custody. In the same month, the British dug up in the Flensburg area a set of the documents that Gehlen had microfilmed. These were sent to the Joint Documents Center at Hochst. Soon after, a small reconstituted FHO group was ensconced at Camp King, producing reports on the strength of the Soviet Army based on their files from which MI6 extracted the maximum intelligence. At the same time, the US Army picked up a unit of the Wehr-macht wireless interception regiment attached to the FHO which had surren-dered intact, around which the nucleus of a German external intelligence service would be built up.[21]

Early in 1947, the British moved another of Gehlen's former assistants, Lt-Col. Adolf Wicht, with a few other Abwehr and FHO officers, to the British intelligence headquarters at Munster. Wicht, who from 1943 until the end of the war had headed a FHO group that evaluated the interrogations of Soviet PoWs, had salvaged some of his personal files and was asked to put together a series of reports on his experiences for use in the espionage battle with the Soviets. Military Intelligence had the idea of developing Wicht as an alternative to Gehlen. MI6 officers who read the reports were, however, less impressed with the results. Philby had made his own study of Gehlen's reports: 'I knew about the Gehlen unit from the summer of 1943 onwards ... It seemed to be no better than the other sections of the Abwehr, which means that it was very bad indeed. No exaggeration.' He revealed that MI6 wasted eighteen months on Gehlen before dropping him – 'not because they were disillusioned in him, but because the contents of his office required enormous funds'. MI6, which felt the money was beyond its means, 'made a clever move' – they handed Gehlen over to the Americans as 'a friendly gesture'. The Americans latched on to him. Wicht was squeezed dry and then passed on to Gehlen, who recruited him with open arms to his 'Organ-isation'.[22]

MI6 and MI5 maintained a close level of co-operation with their US counterparts but 'this did not preclude them from competing with the Ameri-cans for informants and spy networks and attempting to maintain their perceived (if not actual) position at the top of the intelligence heap in the western zones of Germany'. The Americans, however, had more resources and were able to pour in a large number of intelligence officers, who swarmed across Germany looking for scientists and intelligence specialists. The British were often outgunned and outclassed by the Americans, who bought up or simply pinched some of the best agents. But tight-laced British officers did not rate the CIC. Antony Terry, a German-speaking British commando who had been taken prisoner in the ill-fated St Nazaire raid, worked as an interrogator of high-ranking Nazis at the London Cage. He 'never felt happy' dealing with the CIC officers in Germany. 'They seemed very haphazard in their job and they didn't keep their files very secure . . . They were forever posturing, glamourising themselves as spy-catchers, but in my estimation the American OSS and British Intelligence were more professional.' Many undoubtedly experienced officers left the CIC soon after the war and were replaced by raw recruits who had little aptitude for the work. Even worse, the British thought, was the French intelligence service, which was riddled with pro-Soviet communists and considered a hostile organisation second only to the USSR agencies.[23]

In Washington, Military Intelligence had asked the newly created Central Intelligence Group to take over the Gehlen Org. but it declined, while the CIC remained distinctly unfriendly. It was not until July 1949 that responsibility for the four-thousand-strong Org. was formally assumed by the CIA's Office of Special Operations, headed by Richard Helms. According to Allan Dulles's biographer, the CIA

> had neither time nor experience to build its own networks. Instead the new agency had to make do with co-operative ventures cobbled together in haste and trust: arrangements with foreign intelligence services professing similar targets and interests, as Gehlen offered. Only gradually did the dangers in such collaboration become evident: the contrasting agendas of the two services, the ease with which the communist side could penetrate and manipulate the German networks, for instance, and the destructive effects of admitting former Nazis into the American Cold War effort.[24]

As Kim Philby had predicted, and despite the propaganda to the contrary, the Gehlen Org. was to prove 'a constant irritant' to the American intelligence community. Much of it was, however, of its own making. It is not often noted but, during the war Gehlen had relied on wireless interception for much of his intelligence and did so into the late forties. It was his American handlers who persuaded Gehlen to run agent networks in eastern Europe. This proved to be a major mistake. Many of the sensitive posts were given to the old-boy Nazi network of East German refugees, who proved to be riddled with Soviet agents. The Org.'s intelligence-gathering capabilities behind the Iron Curtain, lacking proper professionalism, were judged 'poor to dismal'. Worse, 'a consummate political operator', Gehlen used the Org.'s Special Operations Unit as a vehicle for developing contacts at all levels of the West German government and state institutions. Even so, the American agencies treated his reports with respect, with the result that Gehlen's slanted intelligence was to have a distorting effect on the course of the Cold War.[25]

For reasons that remain unclear, MI6 preferred to spend their limited resources on Gehlen's great rival, the 'smooth and wily' Walter Schellenberg. A 'university-educated intellectual gangster' and skilful political manipulator, he was generally regarded as a 'sorry specimen of an intelligence officer'. Schellenberg was interrogated and debriefed by British Intelligence officer Stuart Hampshire, who was not too impressed by his wartime abilities: 'I was struck by how naive his conception of how things worked in England and how Churchill might think or behave, how ill-instructed he was.' An interrogator from the US Air Force, G. W. Harrison, wrote in his report that 'his demeanour has not produced any evidence of outstanding genius as appears to have been attributed to him. On the contrary, his incoherency and incapability of producing lucid verbal or written statements have rendered him a much more difficult subject to interrogate than other subjects of inferior education and humbler status.' A United States military court had tried and convicted Schellenberg of helping to trap and exterminate Jews in France; he was, however, quickly given clemency and, following British intervention, was freed by the US High Commissioner for Germany, John McCloy. Schellenberg subsequently became an adviser to MI6 in London and was then flown back to Germany to reconstitute an intelligence operation similar to the Gehlen Org.[26]

MI6 then began to seek out Schellenberg's former colleagues for the new unit to be based on the SS Service, the Sicherheitsdienst. One of MI6's first catches was Karl Marcus, already in British hands, whose services had been previously discarded. Marcus had been the co-ordinator of agents in Byelorussia, known as V-men, who controlled the SS networks of White Russian collaborators, and he knew the identities of SS agents throughout eastern Europe. His role was to recruit former colleagues for Kim Philby's Section IX and work in co-operation with Lord Vansittart, whose unofficial propaganda activities were co-ordinated with the Service's anti-communist operations. Those recruited included SS and SD officers with knowledge of Stefan Bandera's Ukrainian nationalist resistance movement, OUN-B. They had retained their contacts with Bandera's men, who were now scattered in DP camps throughout Germany. In order to increase his effectiveness, Marcus was appointed mayor of a small town in the British Zone of Germany, from where word spread that MI6 was recruiting intelligence specialists. Marcus was able to supply the all-important 'persil' certificates – i.e. whitewashed documents such as faked identity cards – and assistance to his old friends, including a Dr Emil Hoffman.[27]

Hoffman belonged to the inner circle of a neo-Nazi underground umbrella group, Deutsche Revolution, which had dreams of rebuilding National Socialism in Germany as part of a West European Union bulwark against the Soviet Union. Other neo-Nazi groups in the British and American zones linked up to Deutsche Revolution, including one led by a former Panzer Corps officer, Ernst Janke, and Kurt Ellersiek's Organisation Suddeutschland. Some of their members were planning for armed guerrilla 'Werewolf' resistance detachments against an anticipated Soviet attack, though a number were regarded as *agents provocateurs* employed by British Field Security. From the beginning, the northern part of the network had been penetrated by British Intelligence, and Hoffman was widely assumed by his fellow-conspirators to be working for the British, a fact from which he derived his importance within the Deutsche Revolution. Hoffman reported to a British Intelligence officer, a Major 'Kruk' (Crook), and fed him information about other SS fugitives, one of whom was Klaus Barbie.[28]

Barbie had been an early SD recruit, successfully specialising in tracking British-backed agents parachuted into the Low Countries and France. Barbie later became the Gestapo chief of Lyons, where news of his vicious activities in infiltrating and breaking resistance groups quickly filtered back to London. Barbie was marked down for future interrogation about the betrayal of British agents, while the French regarded him as a war criminal. He had featured in the first UNWCC list published in December 1944, and appeared before the war ended on a CPI card as 'a dangerous conspirator'. He also appeared on the first edition of the CROWCASS lists in July 1945 as wanted for murder and subject to 'automatic arrest'. According to one of John Loftus's sources, Barbie was 'first and foremost a British agent', and it was during his time in their employment that the records of his atrocities and brutal war crimes were sanitised. 'His status was mysteriously downgraded to security suspect', which may explain why the British have consistently refused to declassify its records on him. Tom Bower has noted that the British destroyed most of their archives concerning the occupation of Germany, which, as he points out, was a convenient means of concealing their 'own unsavoury dealings with the Nazis'.[29]

Barbie was on the run and survival was uppermost in his mind. Contrary to the image often presented, Barbie was no master spy. He had been 'reduced to the existence of a petty criminal', stealing and making small deals on the black market. On his travels around a ravaged Germany he peddled forged papers, by which route he eventually came into contact with the clandestine groups of SS men and Nazi officials found throughout the western occupation zones. In particular, he made contact with a circle of old comrades who ensured their safe asylum by selling their expertise to the Allied intelligence agencies. Through this circle Barbie came into contact with Hoffman and MI6.

The British code-named Barbie's group 'Red Lilac'. He was responsible for talent-spotting and identifying intelligence officers in hiding for Schellenberg's new British-backed service. He became particularly adept at setting up safe houses and courier systems for the growing roster of recruits for MI6's anti-communist research programmes based on leading strategists of Alfred Rosenberg's Omi Institute, which had dealt with Nazi policies for the eastern front.[30]

In March 1946, a joint British/American long-range covert counter-intelligence operation, NURSERY, penetrated a number of the National Socialist subversive groups and arrested over a thousand suspects, effectively destroying the underground organisation. It was, however, soon replaced by 'a rather nebulous but evidently effective organisation, mostly of former SS officers', which maintained an underground railroad for escaping Nazis. During the autumn, things began to go seriously wrong for the network after Marcus quarrelled with Hoffman, who quit in pique and 'promptly teamed up with MI6's rivals in Military Intelligence'. In doing so, he helped expose the Deutsche Revolution network.[31]

Based on Hoffman's information on the Deutsche Revolution network, Military Intelligence moved in on Barbie. In early November, he appeared in Hamburg, where he was involved in organising a clandestine association of former SS officers. There, he was arrested by Field Security officers who had inserted into the group a penetration agent – a former Waffen-SS cadet known as 'Mouse Acker'. He claimed that Barbie, who had access to an arsenal of buried weapons, was planning a number of murders and was intending to escape to Denmark. The arresting officer told Barbie: 'Well, my dear friend, we are not Americans. You are not going to run away from us.' Taken to a British safe house, Barbie spent two days in makeshift cells in a requisitioned villa, with two other suspects. Although locked in separate cells, Barbie and his two companions still, somehow, managed to escape.[32]

Tom Bower has speculated that 'Barbie was allowed to escape'. He had been prematurely detained on information that proved to be unreliable, and so once the action had been set in motion it was decided to allow him to escape in order to continue surveillance of his organisation, thus hopefully exposing more conspiring SS officers. Barbie never really forgave the British for his arrest and their failure to protect him: 'I lost all interest in the British, and all faith in their promises.' When, over Christmas 1946, Emil Hoffman tried to persuade him to return to the British, Barbie refused, fearing re-arrest. Given certain assurances, he was persuaded to meet Hoffman's controller, Major Crook, at Bad Godesburg on the southern edge of the British Zone but, still suspecting a trap, he failed to appear and, instead, headed for Munich and the Americans. That, at least, is one version of the story. Another suggests that British Intelligence had squeezed Barbie dry and, with his usefulness to them over, simply passed him on or 'loaned' him to American agencies; first to the highly secretive Department of Army Detachment (DAD) and then the CIC.[33]

On the night of 22/23 February 1947, dozens of British and American security officers launched the highly successful Operation SELECTION BOARD, which swooped on the illegal underground neo-Nazi political groups belonging to Deutsche Revolution. 'Bereft of its key personnel and its financial support, what was left of the Nazi underground was judged to be helpless and moribund.' There were over ninety arrests, which included all but one of the movement's major figures. The exception was the head of intelligence for the group – Barbie, who was responsible for the procurement of false papers, printing equipment and the smuggling of refugees. Barbie had been high on the arrest sheet but was protected as a valuable source and was helped to make another escape.[34]

Not long after, Barbie was introduced to Dr Emil Augsburg, a veteran of the Amt VI (Department 6) of the SS RSHA, Nazi Germany's main security headquarters. The SS's chief Soviet political expert during the war, Augsburg had been one of the leaders of the Berlin-based Wannsee Institute, the special research centre on the Soviet Union which had an extraordinarily rich collection of files on eastern Europe. Although born in Lodz and, according to official Polish sources, of Jewish parentage, this did not affect Augsburg's entry into the SS, where he was eventually attached to Adolf Eichmann's IV B4 'special tasks' department handling the Jewish question, and then as head of a mobile killing squad on the eastern front, where he obtained 'extraordinary results' in murdering Jews. He also served on Himmler's staff in Gehlen's 'Polish Section', infiltrating agents into Poland. Despite his war record in special tasks, with his wide knowledge of Slav languages and eastern European politics, Augsburg was a natural target for Allied Intelligence.[35]

Augsburg fled to Italy at the end of the war, where he sought and found assistance from circles close to the Vatican. After a year or two, he returned to Germany under the alias 'Dr Althaus' and initially worked for the British, though his first loyalty appears to have been to Gehlen. Augsburg acted as a gate-keeper for the exchange of information among groups of informants working for different Allied intelligence services, and was an important source of information for Barbie's network. According to the American CIC officer Allan Ryan, it was understood that Augsburg was working for the British during 1947.[36]

By March 1947 the US agency DAD had no further use for Barbie and in April he was passed on to the CIC, despite the fact that he was on their wanted list. The man who proposed him was an old wartime colleague, Kurt Merk, who worked for both the British and Americans, though they later dropped him when his claims of knowledge of a vast ex-Nazi intelligence network failed to materialise. The CIC agent running Barbie thought that the SD man could prove a valuable tool in the intelligence war against the Soviets in Germany, specifically against Soviet-sponsored organisations and intelligence operations in Germany, France and eastern Europe. There were, however, two conditions on his employment, namely that he sever all connections with the neo-Nazi underground and that he reveal details of British efforts to employ Selection Board personalities as intelligence sources. His first task was to produce a report on the British recruitment of SS men – 'which unsurprisingly is no longer to be found in the CIC records'. Barbie's controller, Erhard Debringhaus, has admitted that the Allies had hoped to exploit the Deutsche Revolution subgroups and that former SS and Nazi leaders were allowed to escape the denazification process and re-emerge in postwar German politics. It seems that their exposure through Selection Board may have been the result of rivalry between MI6 and Military Intelligence.[37]

In a report at the end of May to CIC headquarters in Frankfurt, Debringhaus wrote that

> Barbie impressed this agent as an honest man, both intellectually and personally, absolutely without nerves or fear. He is strongly anti-Communist and a Nazi idealist who believes that he and his believers were betrayed by the Nazis in power. Since Barbie started to work for this agent he has provided extensive connections to French intelligence agencies, to Banat German circles [refugees from the German minority in Yugoslavia], to high-ranking Romanian circles and to high Russian circles in the US Zone.

From a safe house in Augsburg, Barbie displayed some skill at penetrating local cells of the Communist Party in Bavaria. In the cold light of day the results turned out to be 'trivial', and though the reports he produced from 'scores' of his subagents in eastern Europe were taken seriously, there is no evidence that they were anything more than the product of 'paper mills' with little intelligence of relevance or veracity.[38]

In the end, the system that evolved for denazification quickly collapsed under pressures at home and problems in the field. British intelligence officers such as Eric Morgan, who interrogated senior war criminals in Germany, England and Belgium, acknowledged that the enormous displacement of people in Germany made 'screening virtually useless'. An Austrian Jew and former SOE agent who was recruited by the army, Roger Elliot, found that he had been made responsible with a Dutch colleague for the screening of twenty-five thousand internees. Despite taking the post seriously, he realised that the task was impossible and that 'the biggest war criminals could have got through our fingers'. He had only been asked to assess whether a particular German was 'a danger to security or of interest to Intelligence'.[39]

The same situation existed in Austria, where George Berman, attached to the intelligence staff of the British Army, encountered similar problems. There were also logistical problems involved in screening potential suspects. A year after the war, one million former combatants – among them 200,000 Poles, nearly as many from the Baltic states, 110,000 Ukrainians, 40,000 Yugoslavs and many Hungarians, Russians and other central and eastern Europeans – still resided in the DP camps. When exiles from eastern Europe began to seek residence in Britain and the Commonwealth, Military Intelligence shifted the burden of screening on to Home Office officials, who had no records against which to check names for war crimes. In turn, the Security Service, which concentrated on 'communists', had little interest in war criminals, who did not in their view constitute a security risk.

In hunting down quislings, collaborators and war criminals from eastern Europe, CROWCASS proved to be an inadequate tool because only 2,500 names on the consolidated list were non-German. The problem was that the Soviet Union refused to co-operate with CROWCASS because to have done so would have 'left it open to investigation of the various crimes the Soviets had themselves committed in the years of the Stalin–Hitler Pact, such as the Katyn Forest and the later forced deportation of suspect Balts and Poles'. In consequence, the CROWCASS lists did not include Soviet-derived suspects. Eastern Europeans guilty of war crimes had little to fear from Allied investigation teams which, guided by CROWCASS and the UNWCC list – which also excluded eastern Europeans, since the Russians had refused to participate in it – were almost exclusively concerned with Germans and Austrians.[40]

Even so, there was little eagerness to pursue Germans. The head of the London CI War Room, Martin Furnival-Jones, informed MI6, MI5 and the OSS's X-2 that as of 1 October 1945 no new CPI cards would be produced. By the autumn, the War Room had been reduced to just thirty staff, and within a year of VE day, it had shut down with its Registry dismantled. During April 1946, each of the participating services received a portion of its files. Subsequently, one of T. A. R. Robertson's assistants at MI5 delivered to Col. Gerar-Dubto of French Intelligence several tons of documents, including the complete order of battle of the German secret services supplemented by biographical records. The story went that the MI5 officer had discovered the haul in Frankfurt, but no one in London was interested: 'With the disappearance of the central collecting point for Allied counter-espionage went the basis for the efficient co-operation that had marked the assault against the German intelligence services.'[41]

In addition, the political climate had changed. The Cold War was emerging and the steam had gone out of war crime investigations. By the summer of 1946 the British and Americans had adopted a policy seeking Germany's favour which was followed by ending any thoughts of punitive action against the former enemy.

By this juncture CROWCASS had turned into a monster archive with over forty thousand records, and the British and Americans gave up the task of controlling it. With a requirement to find reliable anti-communist assets, they concerned themselves solely with selecting German officers and agents likely to be of interest to their intelligence agencies. Nazi-hunter Simon Wiesenthal was 'devastated' to discover from his intelligence contacts that the western allies were using former Nazis for intelligence-gathering. He was told that they needed them 'for the future, and not information on the past'.[42]

MI6 and Military Intelligence were particularly concerned with gathering intelligence on Soviet activities in their zone in Germany. At the beginning of 1946, they took charge of the Naval Intelligence Forward Intelligence Unit, which had specialised in commando-style operations against enemy shore establishments with the purpose of capturing personnel and documents of intelligence interest. It was being wound down in Hamburg, and the head of MI6's Dutch Section (P8), George Blake, was appointed its nominal commanding officer, replacing Captain Charles Wheeler, a Royal Marine who went on to become the BBC correspondent in Washington. The unit had conducted the interrogation of U-boat commanders in Kiel, and these contacts proved useful to Blake in developing agents. Using the unit as cover for secret service operations, Blake organised networks in the Soviet Zone, which would gather intelligence on the Soviet order of battle and on political and economic developments. By the spring of the following year, Blake had succeeded in building up two networks in East Germany whose members were nearly all former naval and Wehrmacht officers.[43]

Germany, according to Sheila Kerr, was 'a major base for intelligence operations. Communications between the Soviet Union and the Eastern bloc were routed through the Soviet Military Command in Germany.' She adds that British Intelligence 'used human and technical sources of information' to garner intelligence on what was happening in East Germany, where the communist-controlled Unity Party held sway. MI6 officers in Germany had wanted to help the Social Democrats, who were being bludgeoned into joining the Unity Party, 'but nothing', recalled George Young, 'was done to exploit their internal jealousies or their resentment at the Soviet pressure on them: some of them would gladly have re-established their links with the West'. In place of covert assistance, Young's colleague John Bruce-Lockhart ran a series of black propaganda campaigns in which 'forged statements of Swiss bank accounts were dispatched from Zurich to senior government officials in east Berlin in anticipation that communist censors would open and query the contents'. In addition, 'embarrassing documents' about East German officials were 'surfaced' for use as blackmail. Other forgeries were sent to West German communists 'to stimulate distrust among party members'. Young adds that 'some German Communists for a time nourished hopes that Berlin would one day again rival Moscow as the intellectual centre of Marxist thought, but the proponents of their abortive Euro-communism gradually disappeared, and the obedient [Walter] Ulbricht took over'. MI6 had good intelligence on the political deliberations and pressures from Moscow, having recruited 'one source close to Ulbricht'.[44]

MI6 anti-communist operations overlapped with the requirement to create networks to penetrate eastern Europe and gather intelligence as the Iron Curtain began rapidly to close. Even while the war was still raging and entering its final stages, MI6 officers had made secret contact with pro-fascist elements among the central and eastern European nationalist groups. British Intelligence saw the potential value of their pre-war connections with organisations such as the Promethean League, Intermarium and the Ukrainian OUN-B in again mounting anti-Soviet espionage operations. These groups had recent experience in fighting communism, having participated in brutal anti-guerrilla campaigns against popular, well-organised partisans. Western intelligence officers were attracted to those exiles who had retained contacts and supporters in their homelands. In particular, they gave backing to the more militant collaborators in the belief that their 'tight discipline, dedication and experience in conducting underground military and political activities' were qualities lacking in the more moderate groups.[45]

While the British Army was forcibly repatriating thousands of soldiers, including minor collaborators, to the Soviet Union and Yugoslavia, MI6 and Military Intelligence officers were simultaneously recruiting a number of quislings and war crime suspects for their own operations. While Allied files may have been regarded as an inadequate tool for investigating eastern European war criminals, they now came into their own as a talent-spotting tool, even though, in practice, CROWCASS had for 'administrative reasons' collapsed in May 1946. CROWCASS was moved in June to Berlin and the office was closed down during the following summer, with the lists transferred to the Berlin Document Centre. This did not, however, affect the files being used for recruitment since over two hundred uncollated separate lists and sub-lists remained in circulation while the card index, which was at the heart of the system, remained intact. When intelligence agencies wanted to request information on individuals applying for a visa, they sought information from the massive 'Central Registry (CR)' in Germany, where the 3 x 5-inch CR cards took up a space approximately ten by twenty feet. Although it was true that eastern Europeans made up only 10 per cent of the CR files, they were, according to John Loftus, 'sufficient to identify the top two or three hundred collaborators in each Eastern European country and to pinpoint their post-war residence in the Allied zones of Europe'. Each request for information was logged, which, as Loftus discovered, remains 'the best evidence for passive government assistance to Nazi immigration by ignoring incriminating data'.[46]

British Intelligence officers actively protected their recruits from the clutches of their Field Security colleagues, whose task it was to arrest and interrogate suspects before handing them over for trial. Not long after the end of hostilities in Europe, the British had already begun to provide training and logistical support to the exiles for infiltration operations into their home-lands to obtain intelligence. This quickly developed into mounting guerrilla incursions which included, according to one informed source, joint British and American targeting of Romania and Albania, using assets identified by former Nazi intelligence officers. These operations are said to have been run out of Frankfurt by a British Intelligence team under the cover of the British High Commission office in the IG Farben building, with its partner in the planning the American DAD. The chief British Intelligence officer, whose responsibilities are said to have included these émigré operations, was Leo Long, later suspected of being loyal to Moscow.[47]

The Soviet and Yugoslav authorities soon became aware of these oper-ations as communist agents had quickly penetrated the DP camps and the émigré organisations that MI6 and others were attempting to revive or construct. Soviet intelligence networks effectively uncovered the use of Nazi collaborators and alleged war criminals, but few in the West wanted to know or were willing to take on trust communist accounts, couched as they were in the language of Cold War propaganda. What was apparent fairly early on in their genesis was that the recruitment of these extremist elements, who used terror as a tactic against all who would not help them, was counterpro-ductive. The militant nationalists alienated those left in the homelands, whose support was vital, and helped push them into the embrace of the communists. As one commentator observed, 'Instead of increasing support in these coun-tries for the West, and undermining communism, the result was the opposite.'[48]

The attention paid by the Soviets to the dubious agents being run by MI6 for their eastern European exile operations quickly began to cause severe embarrassment. Once they had been squeezed of useful intelligence, MI6 wanted rid of the worst cases, and worked to help them leave Europe by means of various 'ratlines'. Similar thoughts existed within US Counter-Intelligence which watched with alarm moves by the French to extradite Klaus Barbie for war crimes. In order to escape detection, Barbie was shifted around obscure and highly secretive units. As so often was the case, they were loath to simply dump an agent who knew so much about their work. He thus, paradoxically, became a security risk who had to be protected. In turn, fearful that once in French custody he would reveal his ties to their own intelligence service, the British – acting through their intelligence liaison at the high commission – insisted that the Americans solve the problem by shipping Barbie out of Germany down one of the ratlines.[49]

In helping their comrades, the safe-help neo-Nazi networks did not have 'the enormous resources of the one agency that took care of more Nazis than all the others combined – the refugee bureau of the Vatican'. The postwar ratline to South America had partly developed out of Allied escape lines built up during the war to rescue PoWs who, following the Allied landing at Anzio in January 1944, had made their way to the neutral Vatican.[50]

An atmosphere of intrigue has always been associated with the Vatican, but it is apparent that there was no Catholic intelligence service. According to David Alvarez, 'the Holy See was usually no more informed about events than many secular powers ... The vaunted international network of priests and faithful was chimerical.' It was, however, useful for running a ratline. The British created a secret Organisation in Rome for Assisting Allied Escaped Prisoners-of-War, under the command of Sam Derry, who reported to Norman Crockett of the escape-and-evasion outfit MI9. The British minister at the Vatican, Sir d'Arcy Osborne, supported Derry's efforts and revealed its existence to Giovanni Montini, head of the Vatican's secretariat for international affairs and at the heart of Pope Pius XII's clandestine affairs. Helping to run the escape line was Osborne's assistant, Hugh Montgomery, a devout Catholic and homosexual lover of Montini, the future Pope John Paul I. It would be surprising if MI6 had not had some kind of 'handle' on Montini. At the end of the war, Derry joined MI6, taking over from Crockett as head of MI9.[51]

The Pope had asked Montini 'to supervise Vatican efforts for the resettlement of millions of refugees and displaced persons who swarmed into Germany, Austria, Italy and France'. Officials offered shelter to escaping German officials, among were war criminals who were offered a place on ratlines to evade capture. One, which led ultimately to South America, ran out of Germany through Austria into the Free Territory of Trieste and then to Italy which, fighter ace Hans Ulrich Rudel acknowledged, was the transit point for virtually all the escape routes. Those sponsored by ODESSA and travelling on to the Middle East embarked from Bari. The Brotherhood had contact with the Rome Association of Officers – former Italian and German fascists – and, in particular, with Bishop Alois Hudal of Pontificio Santa Maria dell' Anima. In the thirties, Hudal had sought areas of co-operation between the Catholic Church and Hitlerism as part of an anti-Bolshevik alliance. Former Nazis regarded him as their own 'scarlet pimpernel' who, as 'the spiritual director of a band of pro-Nazi clerics in Rome', was 'the chief impresario of the Vatican's rescue efforts'.[52]

Hudal's primary role was to supply essential travel documents which were obtained from Montini, whose Refugee Bureau issued 'identity certificates' to 'stateless and displaced persons'. During 1945, Montini's section released a number of regular Vatican state passports to a handful of important Nazis who disguised themselves as clerics. Montini also headed the Church's international welfare organisation, Caritas Internationalis, which also aided fugitive Nazis. Additional documents were obtained from the French High Commissioner for Germany, François Poncet, who, as head of the International Red Cross (ICR), furnished travel certificates to British and US Intelligence. Security contacts informed Simon Wiesenthal that those destined for the Middle East 'received their vital travel documents from the Egyptian Red Crescent which had people working with the ICR in Geneva'.[53]

Britain retained a strong interest in South America, and the Foreign Office reported that in order to protect its investments and ensure economic stability in the region – in particular Argentina, where pre-war Germany, too, had a significant financial interest – German methods and discipline would still be needed. This would require an influx of qualified German technicians and specialists; in practical terms, South America needed plumbers, mechanics, builders and electricians. In order to achieve this, each country was to have a strict quota for immigrants for these occupations. These quotas were partly filled by minor Nazis and collaborators from eastern Europe with would-be escapers fitted to each category and 'given forged papers and a crash course in Spanish or Portuguese'.[54]

During the summer of 1947, sponsorship of the ratlines was taken over by the Americans and organised by the senior officer of the 430th CIC in Vienna, Major James Milano, an intelligence officer well known to the British.

Milano had begun his intelligence career as part of Operation TORCH in North Africa, where his unit's training programme had been undertaken by MI6's Lt-Col. Charles Boyle. In late 1943, Boyle was responsible for the intelligence course at Castellamare di Stabia, near Sorrento, which prepared Allied intelligence officers for duties in occupied Italy. The course dealt with 'war criminals and what to do with them, the Nazi Party, paramilitary organisations, displaced persons, and the history of the country'. Milano was subsequently decorated by the British with an OBE for his exploits as an undercover agent in Italy. He then worked closely with British officer Col. Peter Lovegrove, who headed the planning sessions for the occupation of Austria.[55]

In Austria, Milano ordered the chief of CIC operations, Lt Paul Lyons, to 'establish a means of disposition of visitors'. Lyons's first step was a meeting with Monsignor Draganovic, who was close to Hank Bono, formerly of the 420th CIC in Italy but who was working in intelligence in Trieste, where Draganovic had an office. Lyons struck a deal with Draganovic, who used the money to fund his own ratline, on a means to move exiles and 'defectors' out of Europe, though by the time the 430th took over most senior collaborators had already made their way down the ratline. The Americans wanted them out of Europe, fearing that if they were caught by Soviet Ministry of State Security (MGB) agents they might reveal details of their interrogation by British and American intelligence agencies and their employment in Allied secret operations. Milano and Lyons claimed that they did not deal with Nazis, SS or SD men – only bona fide defectors from the Soviets. They did, however, admit that 'as time went by it sometimes became necessary to bend the rules'; which, in reality, meant including former Vlasov officers, Belorussians, Ukrainians and Baltic DPs, who had served in the German Army and in SS units. They were sent south in US trucks and clothed in American uniforms, a support group ensuring that there was no trace of the fugitives' true identities.[56]

Through CIC officer Dominic Del Greco, the Americans developed close relations with their MI6 and MI5 counterparts at the British military headquarters in Klagenfurt. Milano had worked in Italy during the war with 'Butch' Groves, a senior MI6 case officer who operated under cover of British Army Intelligence in Graz, and in Vienna in an 'unspecified capacity'. The head of the British Field Security Section dealing with counter-intelligence in Austria, Captain Archibald Moorhouse, agreed to see the American-sponsored convoys across the Austrian border into Italy, while Milano's old MI6 mentor, Charles Boyle, served on the Graz-based Austrian Quadripartite Censorship Committee, which was responsible for the censorship and monitoring of mail and telephone communciations between Austria and South America.[57]

By the end of 1947, the hunt for Nazis and war criminals had effectively ground to a halt in Rome. While there were units of the CIC which continued with impressive work, they were told to keep their hands off war criminals living in the US Zone in Austria who worked for British or French Intelligence. One such figure who did eventually go down the ratline to South America in 1950 was a 'mechanic', Klaus Altman, otherwise known as Klaus Barbie.[58]

CHAPTER 9

AUSTRIA: THE SHOOTING GALLERY

Britain's postwar relationship with Austria proved to be difficult because the country was seen as a former part of Nazi Germany. It was enemy territory and the British 'did not deviate from this position for some years after the war'. Indeed, the Austrians had to wait for a decade for a treaty of independence and genuine freedom while the Cold War was fought over their country.[1]

In the British view, despite the fact that stringent control had made opposition to the Nazis in Austria unlikely, the internal resistance had proved 'disappointingly weak and without much consequence for post-war Austria'. Official policy encouraged the resistance groups but 'without committing us to support one group or another'. When a number of resistance leaders were released by the Germans during 1942, they continued to organise as the '05' group under Dr Hans Becker. Slowly built up over the next two years, at the end of 1944 a Swiss Liaison Office was established in Zurich as a channel to the West. Its existence was made known to the Allies by Fritz Molden, who contacted the US Office of Strategic Services (OSS) in liberated Paris and provided it with intelligence about the Wehrmacht and the German war economy in Austria and northern Italy.

A Provisional Austrian National Committee was established in December, consisting of right-wing and Liberal spokesmen, but this was comprehensively destroyed by the Gestapo in February 1945. Arms were dropped in March to the few resisters remaining, but the great coup, which 05 planned, never took place – though key personnel made sure that note was taken of their own limited role. It was not until the spring that Karl Gruber, who had spent the whole of the war working for a German firm in Berlin, returned to Austria to engage in last-minute resistance action as head of the Tyrolean underground. As one account later noted, Gruber displayed a 'strong element of political ambition'.[2]

Shortly after the liberation of Vienna in April, the Soviets installed the old socialist leader Karl Renner as Chancellor of a provisional Austrian government. The British and Americans disliked his apparent popularity with Stalin, but the government had been able to ward off attempts by the Austrian communists to install their personnel in positions of power in the wake of the arrival of the Red Army. The communists were further undermined by their poor showing in the November polls, which illustrated their lack of real support.

Secret Political Warfare Executive (PWE) directives had been vague about the relationship between Austrian underground activity and the country's future, but the Allies decided that they needed young anti-communists who could be entrusted to look after a free independent Austria. Very quickly, the small number of resistance workers found themselves employed at the highest levels within government. The dynamic Gruber headed the Foreign Ministry, while Molden was appointed his senior political aide. The Ministry was particularly important to the Allies since Austria lay on the frontier between East and West and, in the immediate aftermath of war, it was feared that the country might be absorbed into the Soviet sphere of influence.[3]

Politically conservative, Gruber quickly impressed the Americans with his 'can do' attitude, providing a western-orientated counterweight to Renner. Under Gruber's stewardship, 'Austria's attachment to the West went far beyond the limits even of a formal diplomatic alliance'. It was, noted British intelligence officer and later *Telegraph* journalist Gordon (Brook) Shepherd, 'allowed to grow into an exaggerated subservience to American foreign policy which on occasions even proved embarrassing to the other members of the Western alliance'. Both Gruber and Molden retained their wartime 'clandestine links', particularly to American intelligence. Molden married the daughter of senior OSS officer and later CIA chief Allen Dulles, while Gruber continued to provide documents to the US Army Counter-Intelligence Corps (CIC) 430th Detachment, and did so until at least the early fifties. The British, however, considered these pioneer cold warriors to have too close a relationship with the Americans and resented their influence. MI6 even sought to convince the remaining resident OSS representatives that Molden had been a German spy.[4]

Austria was divided up between the Allies into four sectors with Britain being responsible for the provinces of Styria and Carinthia in the south-east, including 'a tiresome frontier with the truculent Yugoslavs'. Vienna was also partitioned into four, but the Allies were allowed to roam at will in a city that was second only to Berlin as a centre for espionage. Intelligence operations would frequently erupt into violence in what was dubbed 'the shooting gallery', where constant reports of Russian soldiers on the rampage made the atmosphere tense.

Employed by the Information Services Branch (ISB) of the Allied Control Commission (ACC) in Austria, Suzanne Fesq recalled that over the winter of 1945 'a sinister feeling of menace hung over the city, stalking the streets and pervading the air, so that you didn't even feel secure in your own home. At any time of the day or night, a great battering on the door could bring doom and disaster. People, once kidnapped, were never heard of again, so that you never knew what fate to expect, and the very few who did escape, never dared tell.' Fesq had worked for the Psychological Warfare Branch (PWB), supplying news information to the Special Operations Executive (SOE), and was then attached to the 'Queer Unit' of the news desk of Allied Information Services in Trieste. In 1947 she married the controller of the ISB, Charles Beauclerk (Duke of St Albans), who had served in Military Intelligence and Psychological Warfare.[5]

The British were strictly forbidden to enter the Russian Zone but with a special pass were allowed to travel through the territory in order to reach their own region. 'Sometimes, for no reason at all,' Fesq writes, 'passes were torn up, vehicles confiscated and travellers sent back on foot through snowed-up mountains. Every day new tales of incidents in the Russian zone came to light, and nobody undertook the journey lightly.' She was appalled at the repatriation of Russian PoWs and their treatment in the camps where there were many suicides and murders.[6]

Beauclerk and Fesq stayed at Sacher's Hotel in the Ring, which had been requisitioned for senior British officers and where the writer Graham Greene 'usually breakfasted in his room on pink champagne'. Still an active part-time MI6 agent, Greene was researching the screenplay for *The Third Man* and 'sniffed and soaked up the putrid atmosphere with the appreciation of a connoisseur'. Also staying in the hotel was Marsha Poutschine,* a former Reuters reporter covering the Russian front, who worked as a Russian interpreter for the ACC. She translated for British Intelligence and often came into contact with senior Soviet officials. A White Russian from St Petersburg – her family had escaped to Britain following the Bolshevik revolution – she was a 'Monarchist' who was dedicated to the destruction of the Soviet state. When she reached Vienna in July 1945, Miss Poutschine asked Colonel Alan Pryce-Jones, an intelligence officer attached to the staff of the deputy commander-in-chief, General Winterton, about the official attitude to the Soviets: 'Were we or were we not supposed to treat them as Allies?' Pryce-Jones replied that 'official policy remained the same, to establish good

---

* She later married the British consul in Vienna, (Sir) Alan Williams.

relations with the Russians and to make a success of our work with them here in Vienna'. She soon found, however, that this was difficult to achieve. A report by one intelligence officer noted that 'from the attitude taken up by our people here, one would think that the Austrians and not the Russians had been our Allies during the war'.[7]

Despite her antipathy towards, even hatred of, the Soviets, Marsha Poutschine came to see that many of the stories about the Russians – a number originating from Information Services – were exaggerated or simply untrue. Suspicion on both sides was high and others shared her pessimism that it was helping to divide the former allies. A combined intelligence report was sent to the War Office and the new Labour Foreign Secretary, Ernest Bevin, which concluded: 'We were not claiming to know the rights and wrongs of these attitudes; we merely wished to point out that the two sides were drifting dangerously apart, becoming enemy camps partly as a result of avoidable misunderstandings.' Unfortunately, the report was ignored.[8]

Somewhat oddly, the resident MI6 station was sympathetic to all things Russian. The passport visa officer, George Berry, had been pre-war head of station in Riga and then, during the war, in Moscow. Poutschine often dined at Berry's flat with two other officers, Colonel Gordon-Smith and 'Alec'. The evenings were 'devoted to listening to Russian music and to looking at slides of the Soviet Union, lapsing into Russian as they reminisced at length'. After warnings from Berry about the dangerous Soviets, she was persuaded by Alec to undertake 'swanning operations'. Driving with forged documentation and semi-official approval into the Soviet Zone and across the border into Czecho-slovakia, they picked up minor intelligence on the Soviet occupation forces, mostly from Red Army soldiers who became openly friendly on meeting an Englishman. Alec 'believed the more we knew about the Russians the more chance there was for peace and better relations. It was important to discover the true state of affairs. We could then avoid misunderstandings which might lead to serious trouble between us.' Rather curiously, Alec added that 'among Europeans only Russians were truly democratic at heart' – by which he meant that they were not hindered by hierarchy or class in addressing one another.[9]

Berry's successor as head of station was George Kennedy Young, who had been put in charge of supervising the liquidation of the foreign espionage sections of the German intelligence agencies and collecting evidence of their success or otherwise against British targets. A journalist, Young went back to Fleet Street after demobilisation and was sent as the British United Press correspondent to Berlin, where he engaged in unofficial intelligence-gathering on the Red Army. Young, however, had been surprised and disappointed by the general lack of interest in serious foreign news and, in 1946, had been willingly recruited into MI6 by John Bruce-Lockhart, a friend from St Andrews University. He was offered the post of head of station in Vienna, which he found to be 'a challenge and inspiration'.[10]

Young's first task was to weld into a competent team the wartime MI6 and SOE personnel who had finished up in Austria attached to the 8th Army. By July 1945 the Austrian provisional government had been in place for three months, but the local SOE station had not been disbanded along with other military-based units. Despite fears that the continued presence of SOE in Austria would lead to 'duplication and confusion' in clandestine activities – British Troops Austria had its own own military counter-intelligence and security units – SOE was allowed to retain a presence. The chiefs of staff supported its Deputy Director in London, Harry Sporborg, who argued that SOE should be permitted to stay 'so that our contacts in Austria which have been built up over the past few years should not be lost'. Against the reservations of the Foreign Office, the chiefs of staff had agreed that it would be 'unwise, with Europe in the present unsettled state, to lose these valauble SOE contacts'.[11]

On the ground, however, SOE was impeded, and its information from these high-level contacts, which 'had been hard to obtain', was reluctantly handed over to British Troops Austria. SOE was 'then diverted from its network of Austrian agents to conduct routine interrogations with prisoners in security compounds'. When in September the chiefs of staff learned what was happening they were angry that the identity of SOE officers might be compromised by the mundane security work, and that the usefulness of their Austrian contacts might 'be destroyed' and 'their lives endangered'. These contacts, the chiefs reported, 'could only be approached in special ways' and 'certainly cannot be transferred at will'. Accordingly, they 'reprimanded' British Troops Austria and instructed SOE's remaining twenty-four personnel to resume work on their 'long term role', which was discussed with the Special Operations chief of station, Edward Renton.[12]

The head of the Foreign Office's Northern Department, Robin Hankey, was dismayed by SOE's survival in Austria, and officials expressed horror at the enthusiasm of some of its officers for freelance operations of a 'somewhat dangerous political character'. Hankey warned that 'the Russians are watching us and we must be particularly careful not to allow any activities of the cloak and dagger variety to continue under our auspices'. There was a suspicion that, besides 'maintaining certain contacts', SOE might be involved in shadowy and undefined 'primary operational tasks' which could have 'the most dangerous repercussions'. As historian Richard Aldrich notes, 'Hankey's fears were well grounded'; one sensitive operation in October involved its officers 'lifting . . . most valuable' and 'essential' film of German rocket technology from the Russian Zone. MI6 slowly took the place of SOE but eight officers still remained in December 1945 and, despite Foreign Office reluctance, they continued to operate alongside MI6 into 1946.[13]

One early Cold War special operation involved releasing hydrogen balloons carrying propaganda leaflets across Soviet lines. MI6 scientists working at the training school, near Gosport, had developed the technique from Japanese specialists captured at the end of the war. They had designed and constructed the Fugo high-altitude balloons which were big and buoyant enough to carry a high-explosive bomb. SOE officer David Howarth, who had been responsible for ferrying agents on the 'Shetland Bus' to and from Norway, retained links with MI6, which called him up when 'they had a simple and ignominious job to be done'. For this operation, Howarth was sent under cover as an army captain to 'a charming provincial town', Graz, in Styria, in the south of Austria. From Graz, he drove east towards the Hungarian border, where he helped release six or eight balloons a night: 'It was all unspeakably secret, from the Russians and their allies, and from the Austrians too, and the rest of the British Army.' The operation, while regarded by Howarth as 'reasonably harmless, naughty rather than wicked', was suspended after a couple of months when one of the balloons drifted back into Austria, causing embarrassment to the authorities.[14]

With the support of his deputy, George Young put together a formidable team who were 'later to spread out into overseas stations as star performers'. Helping Young were other colleagues in the embassy and officers in the 'Int. Org.' – the intelligence organisation of the Austrian Control Commission which included a liaison officer to the embassy-based station, who was usually a representative of R5, the Service's counter-espionage section. Personnel included Young's deputy, Patrick Martin-Smith, MC, a devout Roman Catholic who had served with the Commandos before joining SOE's Special Force No. 1 missions in north-east Italy and Slovenia. He continued to work with SOE in Austria before being assimilated into MI6. Maj. Cyril Rolo had served on the General Staff in the Western Desert and East Africa (as did Young), and later with SOE in Italy and Austria. On joining MI6 in 1946, he was posted to the Allied Commission in Vienna, where he headed a sub-station at Klagenfurt. SOE officer Charles Gardiner, CBE, born Israel Gold, was the son of Austrian Jews who emigrated to Birmingham to work for a firm of silversmiths. Gardiner had worked with Martin-Smith in Slovenia and Italy. Naturalised as a British subject in 1946, 'his perfect knowledge of German and of the local Austrian scene, added to a distinct flair for Intelligence work, made him a natural choice'.[15]

Young believed there was 'little doubt as the immediate postwar Soviet aim of bringing Austria under communist control', but he was happy to discover that 'the Austrian Ministers, who nowadays do not get much credit in the British media, showed themselves tough and resolute: some of them had suffered in both Dolfuss's and Hitler's concentrations camps'. Those such as Dr Bruno Kreisky, who became Foreign Minister and then Prime Minister, were former SOE 'collaborators' in Scandinavia, where they found exile during the war. Others were close to the leading MI6 asset in Vienna, Edgeworth 'Edge' Leslie, who had adopted the country as his own, wearing lederhosen 'to the manner born'. Employed before the war in the prestigious firm of solicitors Slaughter and May, which supplied numerous recruits to the intelligence services, he also worked for Dansey's Z-network. Leslie spent the war years in Berne working for Allen Dulles and SOE's John McCaffery: 'By the end of the war many of his Austrian friends were people of influence who had not collaborated with the Nazi regime. Extraordinarily, the post-war Austrian Government was formed in his house at Igls above Innsbruck'.[16]

Young thought that there had been a time 'when we seemed prepared to let Eastern Austria go the same way' as East Germany, but it did not happen. The credit for this, he later wrote, 'must go to the Austrians themselves, who stood up to Russian bullying even though on occasion "counsels of wisdom" were being pressed on them by Western "friends"'.

Young could have been referring to Dr Kurt Waldheim, who joined the Austrian Foreign Ministry in December 1945 as personal diplomatic secretary to Karl Gruber. Fritz Molden was responsible for Waldheim's vetting, contacting the American CIC and OSS, which told him that 'there were no charges against Dr Waldheim with respect to any Nazi past'. In January 1946 the Allied Denazification Bureau's responsibilities were handed over to the new Chancellor, Leopold Figel, with instructions to carry out a thorough purge of the government's administration. Almost immediately, rumours began to surface that Waldheim was under investigation.[17]

Dr Waldheim's concealed past probably had less to do with his alleged Nazi connections than with his wartime intelligence activities. He had not been a member of the Nazi Party – though his wife had joined – but did support Party-sponsored organisations. There is little or no evidence of pro-Nazi views, and he appears to have been a bureaucrat who even expressed anti-racist views. Waldheim's disputed military record is, however, another matter.[18]

Between 1942 and 1944, Dr Waldheim served as an intelligence officer (03) in the Ic unit of Military Intelligence with General Lohr, of Army Group E. Stationed in the Balkans, Army Group E fought one of the most brutal and ferocious guerrilla wars in modern European history. The US Justice Department Report, which provided the basis for the 1987 decision to bar Waldheim from entering the United States because of his activities in the Balkans, stated that Lt Waldheim would have 'drafted orders on reprisals, made recommendations based on the interrogation of prisoners, provided intelligence data to military units arresting civilians and co-operated with the Nazi intelligence arm in its tasks of deporting and killing prisoners'. During the forty-five-day Kozara campaign against Tito's partisans in the summer of 1942, thousands of Croatian partisans and civilians died in battle or in the concentration camps as a result of *Sauberungen* ('cleansing') operations. Corpses of civilian hostages hung on makeshift wooden gallows all the way from Kostajnica to Banja Luka. When, fifty years later, reporter Robert Fisk visited Kostajnica, a transit point for thousands of child prisoners, he discovered that civilian prisoners had been routinely shot only a few hundred yards from Waldheim's office. The Jasenovac concentration camp, where prisoners had their heads cut off with saws, was only a few miles down the road. 'Yet he was to say later', Fisk reported, 'that he did not know about the murder of civilians there.'[19]

According to a colleague, Waldheim's expertise lay in his dealings with the resistance groups. With a knowledge of Serbo-Croat, he 'knew exactly what the atmosphere was like in the Serbian Chetnik camp'. It was the same with the Ustashi, whose collaboration was 'for the most part his doing'. For his services in Kozara, Waldheim was awarded a silver medal with oak leaf clusters by the fascist Ustashi leader, Ante Pavelic. After service in Greece, Waldheim returned to Yugoslavia and, in late 1944, took part in meetings with Dreza Mihailovic's chief of staff over negotiations to allow the anti-communist Chetniks to contact the Allies. During the forced retreat of Army Group E, General Lohr, who was desperate to avoid surrending to the communists, sent Waldheim – his English-speaking non-Nazi intelligence officer – west on a mission to the British Army, which was nearing Trieste. Waldheim did not get through and ended up in Klagenfurt, though 'it was during these last few weeks that Western intelligence became aware of Waldheim'.[20]

In 1988 the Ministry of Defence released a report into allegations that Waldheim had taken part in the murder of British servicemen captured in Greece. It was curiously circumspect about his past, and Robert Fisk condemned it for failing 'to address one of the most critical issues surrounding men like Dr Waldheim in post-war Europe: the suspicion that they gave their services to the British and American intelligence agencies after the war and that their wartime activities were thus "forgotten". Dr Waldheim and his colleagues had an intimate knowledge of the communist forces in the Balkans at the end of the Second World War – when many Allied leaders thought they may have to fight the Soviet Union.' British intelligence officers attached to the 8th Army in northern Italy had come across Waldheim's name during interrogations of a captured Wehrmacht intelligence officer. They then compiled a list of two hundred German intelligence officers working in the Balkans, including Waldheim, which they handed over to the OSS in April 1945.[21]

Knowledge of his intelligence activities helps explain his subsequent internment in the PoW camp near Bad Tolz, in Bavaria. This was an interrogation centre that specialised in questioning 'prisoners of interest' to US military intelligence. 'What made Waldheim interesting was his knowledge of Communist organisations and partisan tactics, which he had acquired as an Ic officer.' Waldheim was an expert on Yugoslavia – 'knowledge which would be highly prized in the post-war world'. This was particularly so because most of Army Group E's intelligence staff had been captured by the Yugoslavs. A reliable anti-communist, Waldheim had a wealth of information about a country 'which the Western allies might have to invade at any moment'.[22]

Yugoslav leader Tito had been asserting his country's right to appropriate parts of South Carinthia and Styria, including the important city of Klagenfurt, which his troops had seized at the time of the German surrender. When the British intervened, arguments over disputed territory threatened to turn violent. In the fierce propaganda battle that followed, 'not only did Belgrade accuse British forces in Carinthia of encouraging guerrilla incursions into Slovenia by Ustashi "refugees", it also claimed that the western Allies were providing notorious war criminals with safe havens in their zones in Austria. In addition, Belgrade was enraged by the increasing reluctance of the western powers to approve – or even respond to – Yugoslav attempts to extradite alleged war criminals.' A great deal of this was true, as no more than 5 per cent of Yugoslav requests were honoured. It was also a fact that anti-communist refugees were being used by MI6 in a campaign to acquire valuable intelligence about Tito's regime. Belgrade further alleged that many Wehrmacht intelligence officers, who had served in the Balkans, were now working with MI6 in Austria – 'lending their expertise to a Western effort aimed at destabilising Yugoslav border regions'.[23]

Waldheim may have been one of these former officers. Certainly, his political support of the Catholic Church's anti-communist campaigns was a major factor in his career. Besides his closeness during the late forties to representatives of the Catholic-sponsored Slovene nationalists, he also had contacts with Mitja Ribic, deputy chief of the Slovene branch of state security and future Yugoslav prime minister. There were rumours that Ribic helped Waldheim back the Alpa-Adrica movement which proposed 'a cultural union of Catholic Slovenia and Croatia with Austria, Italy and Catholic southern Germany'. This was part of the Vatican and MI6-run Intermarium project for exile operations in eastern Europe, which had the support of the Austrian government (see Chapter 11). According to one source, the Austrian liaison to Intermarium was Dr Waldheim.[24]

The intelligence-gathering priorities for George Young and MI6 were 'Soviet troop deployment down the Danube and the Kremlin's longer-term intentions, while keeping an eye on Tito'. He accomplished the first by encouraging the desertion of disillusioned young Red Army soldiers, whose low-level intelligence 'soon confirmed the steady rundown of Soviet forces and their replacement by static units of virtually untrained conscripts'. More important long-term intelligence came from the retrieval of Luftwaffe records that had been hidden following the end of hostilities in Lower Austria, now in the Soviet occupied zone. From forward airfields in the Soviet Union, the Germans had carried out a systematic photo reconnaissance of a large part of the country. The results of this were now buried close to a Red Army checkpoint. Young arranged for a Klagenfurt newsagent and bookseller – set up in business by SOE – to deliver regularly a complimentary copy of a 'girlie' magazine to the post. 'One day when the soldier was happily studying the pictures, the van halted along the road and the driver and mate – a former Luftwaffe officer who had helped bury the plates – dug furiously, retrieved the mass of material and stowed it in a specially constructed compartment.' Using the photos and incoming intelligence, MI6-recruited Luftwaffe officers were able to monitor and keep a regular check on Soviet airfields.[25]

On the frontier of the Cold War, Austria was regarded by MI6 as a key area from which to collect intelligence on Russia and the Soviet satellites, most notably Czechoslovakia, Hungary, Romania and Tito's Yugoslavia. Major sources of information were political refugees, deserters from the Red Army, Displaced Persons (DPs), anti-communist groups and Catholic organisations, and undercover agents who had worked for the British during the war but now found themselves trapped behind the Iron Curtain. British Intelligence made a priority of setting up underground routes of escape and communication, with those heading for Vienna secretly transported down a 'ratline' to the British Zone for debriefing. Attention was paid to the screening of political refugees and close liaison was maintained with Allied counter-intelligence units. Young's major success was in persuading Czech and Hungarian refugees to return home and infiltrate the Communist Party in the expectation that they would be sent on activist courses and gradually rise up the party hierarchy.[26]

As part of the military's 1947 Operation LARWOOD, MI6 created contingency plans for active resistance in the event of an invasion by Yugoslav troops. The Yugoslav/Austria border dispute was left unresolved by the January Big Four conference of foreign ministers at Lancaster House, which Waldheim attended as the Austrian delegation secretary. It was shortly after the conference that, following the execution of General Lohr for war crimes, the Yugoslavs began an investigation into Waldheim's wartime activities. The first accusations were made in a Yugoslav file submitted to the United Nations War Crimes Commission (UNWCC) in London, charging him with 'putting hostages to death' and 'murder'. Michael Palumbo has suggested that the file was prepared against Waldheim for purposes of blackmail, pointing out that despite extensive research not a single document has been uncovered implicating him in a war crime. At the same time, Yugoslav security agents sent a list of former Wehrmacht officers on the UNWCC list – Waldheim's name was prominently featured – to Colonel Gonda of the Red Army, in the knowledge that Soviet Intelligence was interested in recruiting Austrians, often by blackmail. According to a Yugoslav security agent, Anton Kolendic, the Soviets were 'particularly angry with Gruber, whom they considered to be a British agent'. He heard Gonda 'talk about an incident that could be staged to compromise Gruber. Hence their interest in Waldheim, who was Gruber's secretary.' There was also talk of 'exposing' Waldheim in order to embarrass his boss, while another agent claimed that 'the Yugoslav secret police were going to recruit him but the Soviets let them know that he was already recruited'.[27]

In the wake of a rapid rundown of British troops, Larwood's contingency plans were abandoned in mid-1947 – though communist infiltration from Yugoslavia and elsewhere was still seen as a threat. Through his agents in the eastern European communist parties and from defectors, Young claimed that he was warned in the autumn of Stalin's break with Tito – a claim that is not in the diplomatic record. Stalin's expulsion of Tito from the Cominform was reflected by the Soviets dropping support for Slovene separatists in Carinthia, which opened the way for Austria to commit itself to the West. By this stage, Foreign Office officials considered the Austrian government to be anti-communist and solidly attached to the West, though more allied to the United States than Britain. 'One did not need to be a dupe of Communist propaganda', Gordon Shepherd recalled, 'to know that, during these years, the American High Commissioner was potentially the most powerful man in Austria, or to see that Austria itself was, for all practical planning purposes, already considered part of NATO'. The West had faith in officials such as Dr Waldheim, who was appointed in 1948 to the number-two post at the Austrian mission in Paris. This was the beginning of his diplomatic rise; he was eventually to attain the post of Secretary-General of the United Nations.[28]

Tito apparently viewed Waldheim as a 'pliable' and 'Soviet' man, who had 'likely ties to the United States' and was thus an ideal person for the UN job. It was later discovered that the UNWCC held file No. 79/742, which listed Waldheim as a Class A suspect, while the June 1948 CROWCASS 'Final Consolidated Wanted List' included him as suspect No. 313622 – wanted for 'murder'.[29]

The Foreign Office and the US State Department disliked UNWCC because it was an international inter-Allied organisation which was not solely their preserve. It was difficult to control the smaller nations, who were actively seeking to prosecute alleged war criminals and took no account of the political realities of the emerging East–West conflict. The British and Americans thus attempted to shut down UNWCC as quickly as possible. 'Their first step was to choke the Commission by systematically denying it funds and personnel.' When members wanted to extend its activities, the British and US delegations blocked them. The British then tried to close it immediately, but were persuaded to let the budget run until the end of the year, when final evidence for cases had to be submitted. The Commission was subsequently wound up on 31 March 1948, when those accepted as prima facie cases were 'packed away in cardboard boxes to await a decision by the United Nations' as to what was to be done with the forty thousand files remaining in New York. The UN's assistant secretary-general in charge of its legal department, Ivan Kerno, declared that the files would remain closed 'in all but the most extraordinary circumstances'. A Slovak who had known Allen Dulles since the end of the First World War, Kerno appears to have been employed by British Intelligence when serving with the wartime Czech government-in-exile in London. He subsequently became an informant for US Intelligence and is understood to have been an agent of the CIA during his period at the UN.[30]

At the height of the Waldheim controversy in 1988, *The Times* expressed the view that his case might have been covered up by the British. The MoD report on Waldheim mentions the allegation that he 'had been of assistance to British Intelligence', but, as Robert Fisk pointed out, 'instead of stating flatly that he was not (which would go some way to dismissing claims that the British deliberately destroyed wartime records about him) the ministry reported blandly that "it has been the practice of successive governments not to comment on speculation or allegations concerning intelligence matters"'.[31]

George Young left Vienna in 1949 'with the sense of a job well done'. The new Second Secretary and head of station was Peter Lunn, a Royal Artillery officer who had been seconded to MI6 during the war and, as the hard-working head of P3, had supervised operations in Austria and Germany before taking command of the Hamburg station in 1947. The son of Sir Arnold Lunn, also intelligence-linked and head of the well-known travel agency and populariser of skiing abroad, Peter was slightly built and had a marked lisp. Before he joined the Vienna station, Lunn – who skied for England in the 1936 Olympics at Garmisch – managed to find time to train with the British Olympic team at St Moritz.[32]

A 'zealot and militant anti-communist' Roman Catholic who was regarded as a highly effective officer, Lunn conceived the idea for one of MI6's most productive postwar operations. While leafing through reports from a source in the Austrian Post, Telegraphs and Telephone Administration, he noticed that a number of telephone cables linking the Soviet Army HQs, units and airfields ran beneath the British and French sectors of Vienna. Lunn called in Peter Taylor, a former communications officer with Montgomery in North Africa and now a telephone engineer attached to the Post Office Technical Department experimental station at Dollis Hill, and asked him to study the feasibility of attaching a telephone tap to the cables. Taylor confirmed its feasibility and a Col. Balmain, an experienced private mining consultant, agreed to construct a tunnel from the basement of a police post to the main telephone cable running between the Soviet headquarters at the Imperial Hotel and their military airfield at Schwechat. Lunn obtained approval from head office in record time and money was made available for Operation CONFLICT, though the Foreign Office was not informed. Lunn received unofficial approval from the ambassador, Harold Caccia, a recent chair of the Joint Intelligence Committee (JIC), but he was only told once the project was up and running. Lunn was obviously aware that the Foreign Office would not have approved, and Caccia only did so because 'I couldn't look at myself if there'd been an invasion and I denied the chance of getting the information'.[33]

The operation was an immediate success and led two years later to the setting up of two more cable taps. SUGAR ran from a specially established imitation jewellery shop, Gablons, managed by an Austrian Jew, Mr Prior. Commercially successful, out of its profits MI6 managed to finance the running of the operation. LORD was run from a smart suburban villa in the French sector inhabited by John Wyke and his wife. Partly of Dutch origin, Wyke had been in the Dutch section during the war and was MI6's leading technical expert. A tunnel was dug from the cellar by British Post Office workers disguised as Royal Engineers, while a detachment of Royal Military Police undertook guard duties. The Dictaphone cylinders containing the interceptions were collected each day by a laundry van – a favoured cover for British Intelligence operations. An early operation whereby an MI6 officer would collect the tapes from a schoolgirl strolling in Schoenbrum Park apparently ended in near-disaster when the officer was mistakenly arrested on suspicion of child molestation.[34]

Conflict produced a mountain of material which needed to be processed. Eventually, it became too much for the Austrian station and the processing was transferred to London, where RAF planes arrived three times a week with special drums from Vienna.

MI6's transcription service had been set up after the war by Wilfred Dunderdale with a 'big crew' of about a hundred Poles and White Russians. Highly secretive, Dunderdale insisted on direct access to 'C', avoiding assistant chief Jack Easton in order, as he saw it, 'to protect his operation'. Most of the crew were old and, although it was not realised at the time, a number had been recruited by the Russians in Paris before the war. In order to deal with the enormous output of Conflict, a specially created Y Section was based at Carlton Gardens under Col. Tom Grimson. A former commanding officer of the Irish Guards, always immaculately dressed in dark pin-stripe, Grimson was one of a number of army personnel who joined MI6 after the war to supplement their pensions. His personal assistant was Pamela Peniakoff, widow of 'Colonel Popski', the legendary White Russian, wartime leader of the No. 1 Long-Range Demolition Squadron. A number of members of the wartime Polish intelligence service joined Y Section, whose administrative officer, Mr Newell, also recruited the daughters of White Russian émigrés as translators.[35]

Once transcribed, the Vienna material was passed on to a section of twelve army and RAF officers with a good knowledge of Russian. It was then collated into a regular bulletin on the Soviet armed forces in Austria for MI6 and military customers. According to a former MI6 officer: 'They were important operations and the customers became very excited about them, particularly the defence establishment. They really thought they were on to something.' Among the recipients of the 'take' was a grateful CIA, which, while unimpressed with the quality of the information, was – initially, at least – starved of alternative sources.[36]

By the end of 1951, the CIA was co-operating with MI6 on the Vienna tapping operation. Carl Nelson of the Office of Communications had conceived of a similar plan to Lunn's, unaware that MI6 were already tapping into the Soviet land-lines. Nelson's intervention forced MI6 to let the CIA into the secret, and he helped install a further five taps in and around Vienna. The original tap at Schwechat, however, proved to be the most valuable source. According to Harold Caccia, its most important scoop was 'clear proof that the Soviets had no intention of launching an attack' through the Balkans. It was to have, the CIA confirmed, 'enormous significance for the disposition of American troops during fighting in Korea'.[37]

In 1950 Lunn left Vienna to become head of the Berne station and was replaced by (Charles) Andrew King. A former member of the Communist Party, King had been a pre-war member of Dansey's Z-network and had served abroad during the war in Switzerland. His homosexuality – normally regarded as a security risk – was tolerated within the Service and had not prevented him serving as Controller of Austria. King's deputy in Vienna was Gordon Alston. A 'dark haired soldier with twinkling eyes and a strong sense of adventure', Capt. Alston had served as the intelligence officer with the Middle East Commandos before joining David Stirling's SAS unit in the original raid on German shipping in Benghazi harbour. In late 1943, Alston was employed by MI6 as part of Fitzroy Maclean's mission to Yugoslavia and Tito. Returning to Vienna as head of the visa section was George Berry, while in Graz and Klagenfurt were the two cover posts of 'civil liaison officers', occupied respectively by R. Rosslyn Penney and Anthony Goschen. The Int. Org. liaison officer to the embassy staff was Anthony Cavendish, a young officer who had been transferred from the much larger German station after falling out with Donald Prater – another former member of the Communist Party.[38]

The ending of the Vienna tunnel operation was seemingly 'hushed up' when 'a tram, passing over the tunnel where it went under a road, suddenly caused the tunnel to collapse and the tram to sink into the resulting deep depression!'. Its success, with its faint echoes of Bletchley's triumph against the German wireless traffic during the war, was to have a direct impact upon the Service. Grimson's deputy within Y Section, George Blake, recalled that there were 'senior officers in MI6, especially among those who were directly in control of "Y", who believed that the future of spying lay in the technical field and that in time the human element would become less and less important'. There lay in the future the possibility of 'clean' operations without the messy and time-consuming necessity of running and controlling agents in the field.[39]

CHAPTER 10

ROCKETS, BOMBS AND DECEPTION

At the end of the war, MI6 was tasked by the Joint Intelligence Committee (JIC) with gathering intelligence on the Soviet production of weapons of mass destruction, and specifically nuclear weapons development. The Service's internal reorganisation in the autumn of 1945, therefore, laid a particular emphasis on gathering scientific intelligence. Against such a closed and security-conscious country as the Soviet Union, however, this was to prove immensely difficult, and was to present MI6 with a major headache as for many years the Service's obsessive secrecy hindered any assessment of its true capabilities in this area.

During the war years of close co-operation with the United States on the manufacture of the atom bomb, atomic intelligence had been part of scientific intelligence, but with the end of hostilities it was decided to treat it as a separate department in a direct arrangement between the Foreign Office and the Atomic Energy Directorate in the Ministry of Supply, codenamed 'Tube Alloys'. MI6's former scientific officer attached to the Air Ministry, Dr R. V. Jones, recalled that 'it was also argued that atomic matters were too secret to be entrusted to the normal scientific intelligence organisation, and that the Americans would only share their information with us if specially secret arrangements were made'. Jones thought 'that argument was already hollow' as the McMahon Atomic Energy Act 'had all but severed exchanges with Britain in atomic matters'.[1]

Dr Jones knew that the true explanation for hiving off atomic intelligence was 'more likely to be found in the personal motives and ambitions of those who had jumped on the atomic bandwagon and who wanted to keep everybody else off. Maybe they thought that they alone were fit enough to be entrusted with the awesome responsibility of atomic developments or maybe they had less worthy motives.' His sarcasm was specifically aimed at Eric Welsh, with whom he had fought bitterly for control of postwar atomic intelligence – a battle that Jones lost.[2]

Born in 1897, Lieutenant-Commander Eric Welsh served during the First World War in Naval Intelligence, where he was provided with a cover story or 'legend'. In 1919 Welsh was placed with the Norwegian paint company, International Paints and Compositions. Recruited to MI6 for his knowledge of Norwegian, Welsh helped establish at the beginning of the Second World War a joint Anglo-Norwegian Intelligence Service whose primary objective was to monitor the movements of the German battle fleet around the Norwegian coast. Continuing his links with Norway – his wife was a niece of the composer Grieg – he was involved with the Commando raid on the heavy-water plant in Norway, but had no specialist knowledge of nuclear matters. In fact, Welsh had once remarked to MI6's Dr Jones: 'Who ever heard of heavy water?' He boasted of 'being the only regular SIS officer with a scientific degree', though in fact he had no scientific training. Despite this handicap, Menzies made Welsh responsible, in May 1942, for atomic energy and all aspects of scientific and technological intelligence. He handled the liaison with Tube Alloys, thus relegating Jones to a support role.[3]

A short, rotund ladies' man, who drank and smoked to excess, Welsh was said to be 'an excellent operational organiser' and a 'master of dirty tricks'. While he supported the efforts of Dr Jones, he revealed little about his covert work and sources, and managed to manoeuvre out of the office Jones's assistant, Charles Frank, who had quickly rumbled Welsh. In retrospect, Jones suspected that Welsh 'was beginning to use me, as he ultimately used others in more eminent positions, as a puppet'.[4]

Welsh's efforts were not entirely negative. MI6 was able to keep abreast of the progress of Anglo-American atomic relations and latest developments, 'since he had persuaded our own authorities to send their signals to America over our office link, which was especially secure'. Even so, Welsh did this by bypassing the MI6 office in Washington, the British Security Co-ordination (BSC), and relying instead on his own representative, (Sir) James Chadwick, a Nobel physicist from Cambridge who directed the British team working on the bomb in America. An influential voice on policy-making in the atomic field, Chadwick kept 'his eye open for British interests in the American Atomic project'.[5]

When the Anglo-American Intelligence Committee was formed in November 1943 to deal with atomic matters, Welsh ensured that all copies of documents went to his representative at Tube Alloys, Michael Perrin, but not to

Jones. A former ICI employee, Perrin regarded the committee as a 'trivial exercise'. In turn, Welsh, who was generous with the view that no serious German bomb programme was under way, refused to share any details with an increasingly frustrated Office of Strategic Services (OSS), which supplied technical and scientific intelligence to the 'Manhattan Engineer District' – the London-based body that co-ordinated information on atomic energy. This was probably 'nothing more complicated than the bred-in-the-bone jealousy of intelligence organisations for sources'; but, henceforth, Welsh 'held the whip hand in all nuclear intelligence matters', which, Jones concluded, was 'disastrous to Scientific Intelligence generally'.[6]

The end of the war was followed by 'a year of madness' as Scientific Intelligence was reorganised. After lobbying from the Naval Intelligence Division (NID), the JIC created a special committee chaired by Professor Patrick Blackett, which included Dr Jones, the Scientific Adviser to the War Office, Charles Ellis, and the NID's Edward Gollin. 'Many in senior posts were exhausted by the strains of war', and Dr Jones found that they were 'not interested in undertaking a fundamental appraisal of Intelligence for the post-war world'. His wartime experiences had shown 'the desirability of keeping the collecting and collating sides of the work as intimately together as possible, and it was this aspect that had given me such an advantage over all other branches of intelligence, where they had been separate'. On the basis that MI6 retained control of human (HUMINT) and signals (SIGINT) intelligence-gathering, Blackett rejected Jones's argument and recommended that the three service ministries retain their own separate Scientific and Technical Intelligence Sections, with an additional Section (R9) inside MI6. Given that there was to be no overall co-ordinating head, Dr Jones realised it would inevitably lead to confusion and duplication.[7]

Blackett's recommendations were approved by the JIC, which accepted Jones's argument that the new sections should be, at least, housed in one building. Even this, though, proved to be unsatisfactory, as the near-derelict leased premises in Bryanston Mews were distant from the services and MI6 headquarters. In one bizarre episode, when the landlord showed some prospective buyers around, 'they turned out to be members of the Russian trade delegation and they had quickly to scramble to pull down the MI6 charts on the walls'.[8]

MI6 liaison was maintained via the Joint Scientific and Technical Intelligence Committee (JSTIC), made up of thirteen representatives. Menzies disliked Blackett's unwieldy proposals and tried to persuade Dr Jones to stay, but he had had enough: 'To add to the craziness of the scheme, Blackett overlooked the fact that Atomic Intelligence was not part of it. This was going to be done by Welsh and Perrin entirely independently of the main Scientific Intelligence organisation.' The JIC had also acquiesced in 'an irregular arrangement' made with the Americans by Sir John Anderson, who supervised the Tube Alloys Directorate, whereby another authority, 'the Anglo-American Combined Tube Alloys Intelligence Organisation', would operate in parallel with the JSTIC with Welsh's representative as its head. Disliking the new arrangements, and openly unsympathetic to the new socialist government, Jones returned to Aberdeen in the autumn of 1946 to take up the post of chair of natural philosophy.

During the summer of 1945 the chiefs of staff completed a detailed report on Soviet capabilities which 'emphasised the radical scientific and technical developments that had recently taken place in the field of "weapons of mass destruction" and in associated methods of strategic delivery, particularly the guided rocket'. In comparison with Soviet strategic offensive and defensive capabilities, everything else was considered of lesser importance. The chiefs and the JIC made acquisition of technical intelligence from Germany on these areas a top priority.[9]

The chiefs had wanted and assumed continued close co-operation with the United States in the scientific field. It was a naïve belief which displayed a lack of foresight about the real power of the United States and the shape of the postwar world, where Britain would be very much the junior partner or even rival in intelligence affairs. It was true that Air Marshal Sir John Slessor had advocated on 16 June that if co-operation 'proves impractical – and for commercial reasons the Americans make it so, though I believe we have both of us more to gain commercially from co-operation than from competition – then our secret scientific intelligence organisation should be extended to cover the United States'. He was, however, embarrassingly wide of the mark when he added that the 'Americans are insecure people and I do not believe we should have any serious difficulty in finding out all they are doing if we are prepared to spend the money to do so. Conversely their secret intelligence is amateur to a degree and I do not think we should have much to fear from them.'[10]

The first evidence that American capabilities had been underestimated came with the collapse of the Third Reich, when British Military Intelligence engaged in a systematic operation to locate scientists and related personnel who had used their skills for the Nazi cause. In a forerunner of similar programmes to recruit Nazi intelligence officers and other collaborators, a specialised team concentrated on the capture of German laboratories, industrial patents and similar useful hardware. Britain and the United States jointly created a Combined Intelligence Priorities [later Objectives] Sub-Committee (CIOS) to co-ordinate efforts to seize particularly valuable targets. Delegated to co-ordinate the operation, the JIC chair, Victor Cavendish-Bentinck, did not, however, 'possess the experience to understand or assemble technical details of weapons design and manufacture', being more used to supervising the gathering of pure intelligence.[11]

Raids on behalf of CIOS were carried out by subordinate teams such as the 'Sugar Force' in Italy and the T-Force in France, Holland and Germany. These units had only minimal armed strength, but they travelled with accomplished linguists, Western scientists and police specialists, which permitted them rapidly to identify and capture knowledgeable experts and technologically useful materials. Initially, the Americans were outclassed by the professionalism of their British counterparts, but this was, as Tom Bower points out, 'deceptive'. The British had no executive powers and saw themselves as largely providers of information to the Supreme Headquarters Allied Europe Forces (SHAEF). Britain's attempts at plunder were, in fact, either too gentlemanly or else totally undisciplined. The personal assistant to Rear Admiral John Godfrey, Director of Naval Intelligence in Room 39 at the Admiralty, Ian Fleming, had created a naval team, the 30 Assault Unit, with the express purpose of locating technical intelligence, such as details of the latest submarines and torpedoes, but the unit ended up employed as 'armed and expert looters'. The T-Forces were no more effective, and British efforts were soon overwhelmed by the resources available to the much more aggressive Americans.[12]

Out of military liaison units which, with the Americans and Russians, were entitled to venture into each other's zone of occupation, grew the Field Information Agency (Technical) (FIAT) groups. One of the British subgroups, the Enemy Personnel Exploitation Section, specialised in targeting German scientists with particular reference to Nazi Germany's rocket programme.

In the three-way battle with the United States and the Soviet Union to secure German rocket secrets, Britain – against whom over a thousand rockets had been fired – had a distinct advantage in that 'British Intelligence knew more about the V-2 and the men who had developed the world's first and only long-range rocket than either the Americans or the Soviets'. As undersecretary in the Ministry of Supply and chair of the Flying Bomb Counter-Measures 'Crossbow' Committee, Duncan Sandys – Winston Churchill's son-in-law and commanding officer of the Royal Artillery's first Z anti-rocket battery – had overseen the collation of all intelligence gathered by MI6 on Germany's rocket operations. Although this was a military failure, in that it appeared far too late to affect the outcome of the war, technical experts knew that the V-2 was a weapon of the future and urged the intelligence agencies to make the tracking down of Germany's rocket specialists and their technical documents a priority.[13]

Almost inevitably, Britain came second to the Americans in the race – known as Operation OVERCAST – to garner the rocket secrets. This was primarily because British rocket experts simply handed over to US intelligence officers nearly 90 per cent of their target intelligence and received little in return. This included all the information they had gathered on the manufacture and launch site at Peenemunde during the secret weapon investigation, a remarkably detailed Target Information Sheet, complete with aerial photographs pinpointing the last V-2 site at Nordhausen, as well as the names of key personnel. Also handed over was MI6's major coup – the Osenberg List. Detailing the names and responsibilities of senior German rocket person-nel, which analysts had cross-referenced against captured SS files, the list had been discovered stuffed down a toilet at Bonn University.[14]

Armed with this priceless intelligence haul, American troops and technical specialists reached Nordhausen first and, in late May, despite an agreement that ensured that all captured war material was to be equally shared, trans-ported fourteen tons of documents into the American Zone in order to deprive the British of the booty. The haul was then sent to Camp Ritchie, Maryland. In addition, in early June, one hundred V-2s were covertly transported to the Antwerp docks, where British Intelligence officers could only stand by and watch as they were shipped off to the United States.[15]

On 13 October 1945, 21 Army Group's Field Marshal Montgomery sent a top-secret message to the secretary of the Advisory Committee on Atomic Energy, revealing that in the course of the Allied advance into Germany a special mission known as ALOS was 'sent to carry out an investigation into the progress made by the Germans into the development of nuclear energy'. General Groves's ALOS mission included an MI6 field team headed by Eric Welsh, who was determined to retain as much as possible when it came to sharing the prospective nuclear information from Germany.[16]

Leading the MI6 mission to obtain German nuclear intelligence was Sir Charles Hambro. 'Enormously tall and athletic, with broad shoulders, broad eye, and a broad smile', and from a distinguished line of Norwegian bankers from Denmark, Hambro was 'one of the most respected men in the City'. In the same house at Eton with Gladwyn Jebb, of the Foreign Office's Russia Committee and former adviser to SOE, and Stewart Menzies, Hambro knew his way around the secret world. Besides being head of SOE, he had also been in charge of its Scandinavian section, where he worked in collaboration with Welsh. When Hambro left SOE in 1944, he went to Washington as head of mission of the innocuous-sounding Combined Raw Materials Board, which had a secret role in allocating scarce and vital uranium ores. He also sat on the Combined Development Trust – aka the 'Insecticide Committee' – which had been set up in June by Britain and the United States in order to control world supplies of weapons-grade uranium. Code-named the 'Murray Hill Project', it aimed to prevent the Soviet Union from acquiring ore for its own project.[17]

In April 1945, Hambro and his assistant David Gattiker were hot on the trail of the uranium ore that the Germans had seized from Union Minière in Belgium at the beginning of the war. It had been tracked by the Americans to a German firm, near Stassfurt, deep inside the Russian Zone. In a clandestine operation, over a thousand tons of ore – the bulk of all the available uranium supplies in Europe – was eventually recovered and shipped to Britain. In addition, Britain and representatives of the Czech government-in-exile had held talks on plans to mine ore in Czechoslovakia. Unfortunately, the Czech chief of intelligence, Colonel F. Muravitz, had passed on to Soviet agents the minutes of these talks, which concluded with British interest in shipping processed ore from the Sudeten Mountains. It was the Soviet Union, therefore, which signed a secret agreement with the Czech President, Edvard Benes, to exploit the uranium mines at Jachymov, which had been the world's main source of the ore in the early part of the century.[18]

On 22 April 1945, along with an *ad hoc* American T-Force, Hambro, Perrin, Welsh, Dr Jones and the GC&CS (Government Code and Cipher School) Ultra specialist Frederick Norman descended on Horb, where Germany's principal nuclear scientists, research laboratories and their only nuclear pile were located. Dr Jones saw this as a 'heaven sent opportunity for Britain to get back into the atomic intelligence game'. Simultaneously, German's remaining stock of heavy water was recovered. Six days later, in Rheims, Hambro negotiated a deal with the Americans, who had no legal jurisdiction over the matter, for the captured leading German atomic scientists to be detained for up to six months 'at His Majesty's pleasure'.[19]

Hambro and Welsh selected the top German experts for debriefing either at a special centre at Göttingen or at RAF Tempsford, a former SOE launching site for resistance teams destined for France. As part of the operation, ten physicist members of the German 'Uranium Club' were brought back to Britain for interrogation. They were remanded into the custody of Welsh at Farm Hall, a Georgian country house near Cambridge, which had been SOE Special Training School Number 61. Not only had it been a staging post for agents going out, it had also served as an interrogation centre for returning agents and their captives. Dr Jones had subsequently persuaded Menzies to turn it over to MI6. In an operation code-named EPSILON, Welsh had the place completely wired with microphones in the bedrooms, dining room and library, which monitored the conversations of the scientists. Weekly résumés of the transcripts were circulated to Perrin, Dr Jones and his assistant, Charles Frank, offering an unparalleled source of information about Germany's nuclear effort. During 1945, dozens of German scientists, including a number who had initially been handed over by the Soviets, arrived at Tempsford in total secrecy for 'indefinite interrogation' to determine whether they should undergo further unspecified 'special treatment'.[20]

The British were also looking to acquire technical information and documents, and an overt British Enemy Publications Committee was set up in 1945 expressly to import the huge cache of German classified scientific information. It failed to function, however, because it had still not managed to set an appropriate exchange rate for the trade in journals. In an attempt to fill the vacuum, MI6 set up its own networks and fronts to develop British scientific publishing.

The first meeting in the Cabinet Office of the Scientific Advisory Board took place on 25 November 1946, chaired by Sir John Anderson, supervisor of the Tube Alloys Directorate and chair of the newly created United Kingdom Atomic Energy Committee. The secretary was Professor Robert Hutton, an authority on specialised metals, while other distinguished scientific advisers on the board included Sir Wallace Akers, Sir Charles Darwin, Sir Alfred Egerton, Sir Richard Gregory, Sir Edward Salisbury and later Sir Alexander Fleming and Sir Edward Appleton. These were largely established figure-heads for what was, in fact, an MI6 front, as evidenced by the attendance of Charles Hambro, who acted as Eric Welsh's representative. One outcome of the meeting was the forging of a relationship with the old publishing firm Butterworth.[21]

The emissary from the board to Butterworth was Count Vanden Heuvel, a shadowy MI6 officer who had been chief of station in Berne during the war. Dutch by birth, 'the epitome of a diplomat with his imperial whiskers and black homburg' and known to many as 'Fanny the fixer', his prime postwar role was in the recruitment of 'Z' agents – journalists, publishers and businessmen. One was Butterworth's joint managing director, Major John Whitlock, a former SOE officer and 'intelligence veteran' with 'a reputation as a freemason and likeable rogue'. He had been at the board meeting with fellow-director and SOE officer Hugh Quennell, who enjoyed some prestige at Butterworth, though others saw him as 'an insufferably arrogant and xeno-phobic Englishman'. A solicitor in the City, Quennell had acted for Hambros when the bank purchased a quarter of a million Butterworth shares during the war.[22]

The idea was to develop scientific publishing through a new company – Butterworth Scientific Publications – using the expertise of a talented German exile who had also been at the initial board meeting, Dr Paul Rosebaud. He was to edit a proposed journal using German scientific papers and the reports of 'correspondents' placed abroad. An Austrian scientist, Dr Rosebaud had been at the outbreak of war an editor at Springer Verlag, the leading publisher of scientific books and journals in Europe. He knew many top-level scientists working in the nuclear field throughout Europe and became a particularly important catch for Eric Welsh, for whom he obtained 'certain technical intelli-gence', which he passed on at great personal risk. Rosebaud was subsequently invited to Britain to work and, in November 1945, was smuggled out of Berlin in military uniform by Welsh. With MI6 support from Welsh, Hambro and Vanden Heuvel, Rosebaud helped to establish a Springer affiliate in London with an initial stock of a hoard of books that had been hidden in the Herb-erstein castle and retrieved by the British. Both 'novices in the world of science', Quennell and Whitlock leaned on 'the cloak and dagger man', Vanden Heuvel, for advice. It was through the MI6 man that they received the reports from Rosebaud. Though Vanden Heuvel had a 'meagre knowledge of science', it 'nevertheless elevated him to the status of expert compared to that possessed by the other laymen present' at the publishers. No doubt it was Welsh who was really behind the operation.[23]

An important player in this MI6 network was Captain Robert Maxwell, MC, later publisher of Mirror Newspapers and plunderer of the company pension fund. In November 1945, Maxwell, a Czechoslovakian émigré who spoke eight languages, including Russian – a rare skill in the British Army – was employed in the British Zone in Germany as an interrogation officer at the Intelligence Corps HQ at Bad Salzuflen, near Iserlohn. He was involved in interrogating German scientists, but whether he knew Welsh is not known. Maxwell certainly met Hugh Quennell, an officer in the Control Commission, when he moved to the Press and Publicity Branch of the British Information Service in Berlin. During 1946, he also came into contact with 'the Kaiser', Dr Ferdinand Springer, the owner of Springer Verlag, whose fortunes were then at a low ebb. While still working at the Control Commission, Maxwell became a director of a firm that later offered to distribute Springer's journals.[24]

Butterworth Scientific Publications failed to prosper and in 1948 a joint company was created with their German partners Springer Verlag – Butterworth-Springer. It was incorporated in April 1949 with Butterworth's Quennell and Whitlock as directors, while Maxwell was appointed managing director, with Dr Paul Rosebaud, on attachment to MI6 and working freelance for Butterworth, editor of its scientific journals. Rosebaud's reports on visits to Springer 'tended to reach Quennell via Vanden Heuvel, who got to know Robert Maxwell through Whitlock'. Unfortunately, the new company was not a great success and Butterworth, which felt that Springer enjoyed the most advantages from the deal, decided to withdraw. There followed protracted negotiations organised by Vanden Heuvel and, in May 1951, Butterworth agreed to sell its interest to Maxwell for £13,000. Agreeing also to a change of name to Pergamon Press, Butterworth set aside a considerable debt of £10,000.[25]

As his official biographer, Joe Haines, acknowledged, this was 'more money than Maxwell possessed at that moment, so he borrowed. He first went to Sir Charles Hambro.' Who introduced Maxwell to Hambro varies with the different accounts. Haines says it was via the Board of Trade (BoT); Maxwell said it was Whitlock; Betty Maxwell claims it was Vanden Heuvel, Hambro's business 'fixer'. Whoever it was, the meeting gave rise to a City legend that Hambro had been so impressed by the forward-looking Maxwell and sufficiently persuaded of his business acumen that he ordered the chief cashier to give Maxwell a cheque book with authority to draw cheques up to a total of £25,000. In fact, the 'legend' was no more than a cover story. The meeting certainly took place, but the matter of money had already been fixed by MI6.[26]

An *ad hoc* meeting of MI6 officers to discuss scientific publishing took place at Broadway with Desmond Bristow, recently returned from Spain, an R5 officer, Tim Milne, a wartime member of the Inshore Patrol Flotilla and Control Commission officer in Germany, Stephen Moir MacKenzie, Gerald Cruickshank and Vanden Heuvel. Along with a plan to set up Marshalls Travel Agency to organise the Service's travel arrangements, the committee also agreed to advance £25,000 to Maxwell in order to buy the shares for the new company that was to become Pergamon Press. Maxwell was at the time being run as an 'agent' by George Young, who appears to have used him during his time in Vienna for his Czech contacts. Eventually, moving into the publication of Soviet scientific journals, Pergamon quickly became the world's leading authority on Soviet bloc publishing. Some of the money invested certainly came from the 'progressive banker' Charles Hambro, who was then providing the BoT with financial advice and acting as a benefactor to MI6 good causes.[27]

The intelligence agencies in Germany required firm policy guidelines on future acquisition and recruitment operations. In December 1945, the JIC Secretary, Colonel Haddon, was informed of concerns that the 'few hundred individuals' who were to be employed in the UK and then returned would have 'an inside knowledge of our latest service secrets and the lines on which we are now working'. In considering the security aspects, the JIC concurred that the Germans would quickly discover Britain's latest scientific and technical secrets and recommended that they be employed for a maximum of one year, to 'suck them dry'. Even this proved too much for the conservative Home Office and MI5, which feared a 'Trojan horse' was being created. The intelligence agencies asked whether 'in the event of another emergency' they ought to be 'prevented from returning to Germany?'[28]

Similarly, the JIC was particularly agitated by information that the Russians were attempting to recruit large numbers of scientists and technicians. Paul Rosebaud informed MI6 that a number of the leading scientists had decided 'to collaborate as closely as possible with Russia . . . especially those who have some knowledge in secret weapons'.[29]

By the summer of 1946, MI6 estimated that there were 12,000 skilled scientists and technicians available in the western zones of which 2,800 were regarded as 'eminent'. With reliable reports that newly opened Soviet research institutes were recruiting Germans, MI6 warned that 'the result of this intake of Germans will be very greatly to speed up Russia's industrialisation plans, and to contribute substantially to Russian war potential'. MI6's proposed solution was drastic. One thousand scientists in the British Zone should be 'quarantined' for up to two years and 'rehabilitated' by compulsory training for other occupations. Turning this down as unworkable, intelligence officers in the Control Commission suggested that four hundred should be 'removed as soon as possible from Germany, whether they are willing to go or not'.[30]

Alarmed by the MI6 reports, the deputy chiefs of staff were also concerned that Britain was suffering 'an acute shortage of scientists and technicians in all fields'. They recommended that more German scientists be brought into Britain in a more efficient manner. In an effort to deny their talents to the Soviets, a list of targeted scientists employed in aviation and missile design – most of whom had already been working for more than a year for the British in Germany – was compiled by British Intelligence. The chiefs were also worried by reports from Sweden of Soviet rocket tests in the Baltic. In response, MI6 teams of exile agents were sent into the Soviet orbit tasked to look for evidence of Russian atomic energy and rocket developments. The rocket reports, however, turned out to be false, and Dr R. V. Jones was able to show that the alleged tests were, in fact, meteorites.[31]

MI6 officers in Germany were also tasked with recruiting scientists from the Russian Zone. They were convinced that 'there is an opportunity now to obtain high-grade intelligence from these men which will enable us to build up an almost complete picture of Russian scientific and technical activities in Germany and make it possible to forecast more accurately than we can at present the progress of Russian development of weapons during future years'. It was a naïve conviction, but during December 1946, as part of the effort to deny the Russians certain scientists who were listed 'on account of their scientific or technical eminence in certain warlike subjects', British Intelligence launched the highly secret Operation MATCHBOX, which planned the escape of German scientists from the Soviet Zone. The Enemy Personnel Exploitation Section of FIAT was responsible for targeting men who had worked on engines for submarines – a subject that particularly interested the British – and research chemists for IG Farben.[32]

Although the War Office's MI10 had made assessments that Germany – reliant on First World War formulae – had produced no new gases, chemical warfare investigators, headed by Commander A. K. Mills of the Ministry of Aircraft Production, discovered at the I. G. Farben complex the development of lethal new strains of nerve gases. A key figure was the company's chief chemist, Walter Reppe, who was subsequently found guilty at Nuremberg. US Army officers were able to arrange his temporary release to work on reports for the Army Chemical Corps, but American plans to send him to the United States fell through when the British stepped in and transported him to England. The British also captured General Walter Hirsch, head of Wa Pruf 9, the Wehrmacht's main chemical warfare section, and Rudolph Ulm at a chemical warfare experimental station at Spandau.

Besides using German research to further British efforts, the investigators were also looking for clues to Soviet capabilities in the chemical and biological warfare field. Sources about Soviet developments were limited to speculation based on the evidence of refugees and captured German and Japanese intelligence assessments which suggested that the Soviets had begun research in the early thirties. The interrogation of German chemist Professor Richard Kuhn revealed that all documents relating to a new nerve gas, Soman, had been buried in a disused mine shaft, but Kuhn understood that the documents had been retrieved by the Soviets and taken to the Karpov Institute in Moscow. By 1946 MI6 believed that the Russians had an entire reassembled factory on the banks of the Volga devoted to new agents. Intelligence was, however, inadequate in all areas, and MI6 and other agencies were unable to check out the reports from German files. In the end, much of the speculation was based on clues picked up from reading Soviet scientific literature, and this lack of intelligence led to alarmist reports about Soviet capabilities and willingness to use biological and gas warfare in any future conflict.[33]

The Matchbox 'evacuations' were run by 'one of the various intelligence agencies in Berlin' which operated an 'underground railway' to a secret address in the British Zone 'to which a candidate should proceed under his own arrangements'. The agency also sought to gain 'intelligence coverage of Russian sponsored research and developments in the Soviet zone and, if possible, in Russia itself'. Messages were sent by agents of exile groups to target groups deep inside the Soviet Zone. 'Candidates' then made their way to a 'transit hotel' at Bad Hermannsborn where 'special arrangements' were made for denazification.[34]

'Intelligence exploitation' of those that managed to escape was carried out by 'intelligence agencies in Berlin' or following 'evacuation to the UK' where, by mid-January 1947, forty Germans were 'in residence' for interrogation. In March, British Intelligence began dumping German scientists on Commonwealth countries, including Canada and Australia. Twenty scientists were sent to Canada, including four wartime I. G. Farben chemists. A top-secret message in early April from Brigadier 'Tubby' Lethbridge, head of the Control Commission Intelligence Division, to the commander-in-chief noted that forty-eight of the scientists on the British lists of likely 'evacuees' were working on V-2 rockets, jet engines and radar. He added that their disappearance would thus 'have a serious effect on Russian research'.[35]

Western intelligence agencies continued to systematically monitor and assess the worth of individual scientists in Germany with the most important secretly registered on an 'Objectives List' by the Anglo-American Combined Allocations Board. At the same time, British Intelligence not only monitored their movements but also scrutinised all applications for foreign travel. A 'watch list' was compiled of those employed in the Soviet Zone, noting the names of those who might be attracted by a western offer. Seeking any route to deny their services to the Russians, the British offered the Germans attractive terms of employment in Commonwealth countries. On British advice, as part of Operation PAPERCLIP, Washington reversed its previous policy and began encouraging emigration to South America and to the Commonwealth as an effective means of denying scientific expertise to the communists. More German scientists were secretly resettled in North America, but Canadian officials and Royal Canadian Mounted Police security officers 'thoroughly distrusted background checks conducted by the CIA and British Intelligence' as a number of these men could be classed as Nazi war criminals.[36]

BACKFIRE was the code-name for a British project for the complete technical analysis of those V-2s that remained in British hands. At a former German Navy artillery range near Cuxhaven, British rocket experts interrogated key Peenemunde personnel who helped in the test launch of V-2s into the North Sea. British Intelligence made an intensive effort to persuade the German V-2 experts not to sign with the Americans and instead accept employment in Britain. In the end, however, none accepted the offer, but a few were brought to London for further interrogation, including the main target, Werner von Braun. He 'thought the British might be unfriendly to me, but I found I was wrong'. There followed a 'friendly shop talk' with Sir Alwyn Crow, the man in charge of developing Britain's top-secret missile programme at the Rocket Propulsion Research Establishment at Westcott, near Aylesbury.[37]

'The entire discussions', recalled Major Robert Staver, who ran the London end of the US scientific intelligence team, 'centred on how the British might form a research group of the German scientists; would not these men who were planning to leave for the United States reconsider as the British might have more to offer them; if not, who would be left behind who would be important for such research; and would it not be possible to have the group work in a joint British-American project possibly in Canada?' The senior scientists would not be moved: 'We despise the French, we are mortally afraid of the Soviets, we do not believe that the British can afford us, so that leaves the Americans.' The discussions went on at length but, typically, there were no technical interrogations. The British were able, however, 'partly by chicanery, and partly through clever staff work ... to gain possession of many of the most important German engineers who they used on Backfire'.[38]

The retention of the engineers turned out to be a secondary success; the best rocket scientists went to Russia and America. Nevertheless, the British did manage to gather together nearly a thousand Germans at the isolated area off the Dutch coast where hundreds of Wehrmacht PoWs were employed as construction crews. Units of officers had spent months scouring France and Germany for 'enough V-2 parts to reassemble rockets' but they were discovered to be 'barely operational'. Inevitably, Backfire was something of a damp squib and, by September, 'only three rockets had been launched'. Britain had effectively lost the missile race to the Americans and to the Soviets.[39]

In an attempt to regain the initiative, in early 1948 Stewart Menzies appointed a three-man 'Defectors Committee' to collate quarterly reports on attempts to recruit Russians. Chaired by Assistant Chief Jack Easton, the other two were Robin Brook, a former senior SOE officer who had been personal assistant to Gladwyn Jebb and in charge of the organisation of resistance in France, and an officer formally attached to the War Office, James Fulton, a wartime intelligence officer attached to 21 Army Group and subsequently seconded to the Political Division of the Control Commission in Germany. Easton told Tom Bower that the results 'were not impressive'.[40]

MI6's first defector was the head of the Soviet Reparations Mission in Bremen, Colonel J. D. Tasoev, who fled to the West in early May 1948. Much to MI6's enduring embarrassment, Tasoev changed his mind almost as soon as he landed in London. While he was kept in detention in Hammersmith police station, senior MI6 officers pondered what to do next. Legend has it that Harold Perkins suggested drugging and dumping the Soviet into the North Sea from an aeroplane. Wisely, Menzies vetoed Perkins's solution and Tasoev was accompanied back safely to the Soviets in Berlin, but not before sparking off a minor diplomatic incident and a few awkward questions in Parliament.[41]

The Service had much greater success with its second major catch, Colonel Grigori Tokaty-Tokaev, chair of the Soviet State Commission on missile development, where he had had unique access to information on Soviet policy discussions in an area about which the western intelligence agencies were particularly lacking. He told MI6 about the initiation of a major programme in April 1947, backed up by a substantial cadre of Soviet scientists with lengthy experience in missile research.[42]

Tokaty-Tokaev had also been a lecturer in jet engine technology and rocket propulsion at the Zhukovsky Air Force Academy in Moscow, and had enjoyed a long career at the élite Institute of Engineers and Geodesics. At the end of the war, he had been transferred on the orders of Stalin to Berlin with instructions to help in the kidnapping of German scientists who might assist the Soviet missile research programme. As the senior scientific adviser to the Russian commandant in Berlin, General Ivan Serov, Tokaty-Tokaev was ordered to contact Professor Kurt Tank, Focke-Wulf's chief aircraft designer, and Dr Eugen Sanger, a jet propulsion expert, who, if they refused to go voluntarily to the East, were to be kidnapped. 'Nobody will interfere with you,' Serov told him. 'But remember, Comrade Stalin relies on you to produce results.' Tokaty-Tokaev, however, was unable to recruit either specialist, which displeased the Soviet dictator, who declared that the number of captured German specialists of the highest calibre was 'a very poor sum total ... The British got Busemann, and perhaps Tank, and now the French have got Dr Sanger.'[43]

Professor Tank, who had been displeased at his reception by the British in London, had been warned off by British Intelligence after he made preparations in November 1946 with twenty other aircraft designers to contact the Russians. Instead Tank, 'with microfilm of his fighter-plane designs hidden safely in his trousers', and carrying false documents, used a ratline through Denmark for Argentina. The British did manage to recruit before the Russians another Focke-Wulf jet-fighter designer, Hans Multhopp, a former Nazi Party member who worked until 1950 with other German aviation experts at Farnborough. They could not prevent, however, another Nazi Party member, supersonics engineer Otto Golling, who had been working in London, from venturing in 1947 into the Soviet Zone in Austria, where he sought residence.[44]

When Serov ordered further kidnap operations, Tokaty-Tokaev 'underwent a crisis of conscience'. During October 1946, Soviet arrest squads had systematically searched for and arrested numerous scientists and technicians during Operation OSVAKIN. Trains had taken the unwilling to Moscow, but a similar operation in the following January 'fizzled out' as many of those on the wanted list had already fled to the West. Tokaty-Tokaev was opposed to the kidnap operations and had considered defecting to the Americans, but his plans went awry when he became the target of émigrés, probably from the anti-Soviet National Labour Council (NTS), who were kidnapping Soviets on behalf of US Intelligence: 'I was hunted by émigré organisations dating from the revolution; they asked me to put them in touch with underground movements in the USSR; they also tried to persuade me to desert to the West.' Tokaty-Tokeav had joined various underground dissident nationalist groups in the thirties, in reaction against Stalin's policies, and had maintained contacts with opposition figures from his native Ossetian people in the Caucasus.[45]

The émigrés did attempt a kidnap but Tokaty-Tokeav managed to escape. Fearful, though, that the Soviet Ministry of State Security (MGB) would arrest him for contacts with the organisation, he decided, in the late summer of 1948, to defect to the British. 'He was received in Berlin by the local SIS station and flown straight to London, where he was debriefed at the Special Liaison Centre, at Section V's old offices in Ryder Street', headed by Commander Wilfred Dunderdale. One function of this 'highly-secret' sub-office, which was staffed mainly by elderly émigrés, was to process defectors. A major catch for MI6, Tokaty-Tokaev was also 'a godsend' and a test case for the handling of defectors by the Foreign Office's newly created propaganda organisation, the Information Research Department (IRD). He was that rare figure – 'a genuine ideological defector'.[46]

After a long debriefing on the state of Soviet missile development, Tokaty-Tokaev was passed on to the IRD, which had been instructed by Foreign Secretary Ernest Bevin to arrange the publication of a pamphlet based on his 'Notes on Bolshevism – Communism'. It proved, however, to be 'a less than happy experience'. The author caused considerable confusion by disclosing his existence before the pamphlet was ready. In September, the IRD circulated

Digest #5, detailing the circumstances of his break with the Soviet regime. He described how the Soviet Union, which he said was preparing for a third world war, had degenerated into a Nazi-style dictatorship, run by slave labour. This hard-hitting counter-attack was provided to information officers in British embassies, the BBC and selected journalists. On 7 September, a London press conference to announce Tokaty-Tokaev's defection undid much of the preparation when it turned into a near-brawl between British officials and Russian journalists.[47]

Although the IRD was supposed to rein in Tokaty-Tokaev, in January 1949 a series of articles by the defector appeared in the *Sunday Express* 'which were so virulently anti-Communist that their effect was questionable'. Jebb of the Russia Committee was not impressed, and Christopher Mayhew thought them 'too highly contrived or unoriginal to carry conviction'. This did not, however, prevent the IRD from publishing later in the year his views on 'Soviet warmongering' in a pamphlet entitled 'Inside the Kremlin'.

Tokaty-Tokaev went on to collaborate with one of his debriefers to write three books, *Stalin Means War* (1951), *Betrayal of an Ideal* (1954) and *Comrade X* (1956), but it was his information on missile development which proved to be the most useful. Quite what Tokaty-Tokaev told MI6 remains a matter of conjecture. He later told Nicholas Daniloff that he 'did not pass on what were regarded by the Soviets as secrets. General discussions, yes, but not details.' In the sixties, he was appointed head of the Department of Aeronautics and Space Technology at the City University, London.[48]

Tokaty-Tokaev proved to be the last major defector for many years. By 1950 the flow to the British had dribbled to only cooks, mechanics and low-ranking soldiers whose sole value was as 'talent spotters' – 'identifying those Russians and others whose defection would be valuable'. There was little further success in this area. While eighty-three Russians had come into the hands of British Intelligence during 1948, the following year the figure had dropped to twenty-eight, and by 1950 was down to a miserly seventeen. An analysis of the files on the defectors undertaken in the spring of 1951, by an officer 'who had been employed for the last five years on the interrogation of Soviet defectors', made depressing reading and called into question the extent of the 'valuable intelligence' gathered. The majority had belonged to lowly ranks in the Red Army and had fled to the West 'because of their association with German women'. Ideological defectors accounted for only 3 per cent of the total. For young, ambitious MI6 officers serving in Germany, such as John Taylor, 'the failure to attract defectors was heartbreaking'.[49]

While the flow of defectors had virtually dried up, a steady stream of German PoWs released by the Soviets made the long journey home. During the spring of 1949, the Joint Intelligence Bureau (JIB) employed eight German linguists at Bad Driburg, a small Westphalian spa town, and later at Herford, in a special unit interrogating the 'Dragon Returnees'. Fed and comfortably lodged, they were questioned on what they might have learned of intelligence value to the Allies during their captivity. The range of JIB interests was wide, covering economic, industrial and technical intelligence. One of the interrogators, Denis Hills, was 'asked to concentrate on the work of German engineers who had been involved in Soviet rocket development, based on the V-2, notably in Krassnogorsk'. A team of German specialists and draughts-men worked with the interrogators – 'without them, the quality and detail of our reports would have been immeasurably poorer'. Working under the JIB supervisor, Dr Stern, Hills's own German assistant was Dr Plessner, an expert on jet propulsion from Peenemunde.[50]

A year later, even the Dragon Returnees as a source of intelligence had become a mere trickle. More alarmingly, the exercise turned out to have been a complete waste of time and effort. When, in the mid-fifties, MI5's Peter Wright reviewed the files at the Defence Scientific Intelligence Unit in North-umberland Avenue, he discovered that no one at MI6 had bothered to process the material, which was 'stacked up in dozens and dozens of dusty volumes'.

Based on the limited intelligence at their disposal, the Allies assessed Soviet capabilities in the rocket field as being poor, but Werner von Braun warned that with the facilities available, the Russians would be able to construct a good team of experts. While the cream of the German rocket team had been recruited by the United States, and a number of key personnel had been denied to the Russians, the Soviet Union did have possession of the wartime production plant at Nordhausen which was still in reasonable condition. They had also managed to entrap into their employ a 'brilliant engineer', Helmut Grottrup, who headed the Soviet Institut Rabe – the cover name for the resumption of the Rocket Enterprise.[51]

The fact was that the prediction of capabilities and intentions in the Soviet rocket programme was full of uncertainty and continued to be so into the late fifties, when spy aircraft and later satellites made a massive advance in surveillance capabilities. MI6 'had little raw data to go on and based assump-tions on the rate and state of Britain's own missile development', and the intelligence which Col. Tokaty-Tokaev had been able to supply. A good deal of the economic intelligence on which the development of weapons was based came from overt sources, while much was still provided 'by what the Germans had accumulated in terms of maps, aerial photographs and PoW interrogations'. The detailed reports on destination, equipment and inven-tories removed from locations such as Peenemunde at the end of the war were added to the reports of interviews with 'repatriated Germans who had worked on the Soviet missile programme'. One difficulty with these sources, Peter Hofmann found, was that 'their reports were often disparate and they were usually repatriated before production of any missiles began'. The large number of such reports did, however, provide 'a foundation for other sources to build on, including information on various rocket production and development installations and the test stand at Kaputsin Yar', on the east bank of the Volga.[52]

The limited state of intelligence-gathering remained the same when, in September 1952, MI6 and the CIA held a major joint conference on 'Soviet Guided Missile Intelligence'. What was available was acknowledged as being 'based on the intelligence of early Soviet exploitation in Germany', most of which had come from Tokaty-Tokaev. The colonel informed the conference that: 'The immediate aim of the Soviets is to get a selection of reasonably effective guided missiles into service as soon as possible. They are prepared to accept relatively unsatisfactory weapons available today rather than wait several years for greatly improved designs. They will go for modifications which show some improvements and can be achieved quickly.' Hofmann notes that during the joint conference, as had been the case over the previous seven years, 'certain performance characteristics are assumed; given these characteristics, projections of various stages in the programme are made given whatever other intelligence information is available'.[53]

Throughout 1947, the JIC had repeatedly made the assertion that 'our intelligence about Soviet development of atomic weapons is very scanty'. An April 1948 JIC report, 'Sigint Intelligence Requirements', while obviously directed towards signals intelligence-gathering, had a wider focus which was also applicable to MI6. The JIC's 'Priority 1' targets, whose requirements reflected the JIC's 'future hopes rather than current capabilities', were:

1 Development in the Soviet Union of atomic, biological and chemical methods of warfare (together with associated raw materials).
2 Development in the Soviet Union of scientific principles and inventions leading to new weapons, equipment or methods of warfare.
3 Strategic and tactical doctrines, state of training, armament and aircraft of:–
  a) Soviet long-range bomber force.
  b) Soviet metropolitan fighter defence force.
4 Development in the Soviet Union of guided weapons.[54]

In the July 1948 report, 'Soviet Intentions, Interests and Capabilities', concerning atomic weapons, the JIC argued that: 'Existing estimates of the date when the Russians began their programme and their ability to overcome the technological difficulties involved suggest that they may possibly produce their first atomic bomb by January 1951 and that their stockpile of bombs in January 1953 may be of the order of 6 to 22.' This was a worst-case scenario and constituted 'the maximum possible based on the assumption that the Russian effort will progress as rapidly as the American and British projects had done'. The JIC officials did not believe that it would be capable of doing so. The Soviet Union, however, would take the same length of time as the

United States to build the atomic bomb; four years since the go-ahead was given for the all-out project in August 1945. This was a major intelligence failure and reflected MI6's inability to penetrate the Soviet government and administration at any level. In contrast, by the beginning of 1945, Soviet Intelligence 'had a clear general picture of the Manhattan project'. Klaus Fuchs had handed over all the reports prepared in the New York office of the British Diffusion Mission, while Alan Nunn May had even presented the Soviet embassy in Ottawa with microscopic amounts of uranium-235. The British never achieved such levels of success, and the JIC had to rely for its assessments on meagre scraps of intelligence.[55]

The JIC report acknowledged that

> the manufacture of atomic weapons demands not only a high standard of scientific knowledge and the application on a very large scale of difficult industrial techniques, but also the use of large quantities of Uranium. The most reliable present estimate that can be made of Russian progress indicates that the limiting factor is their supplies of Uranium. At the present time it is considered to be most misleading to attempt to forecast how much Uranium will be available to any Russian project beyond January 1952 since this depends on two unpredictable factors: a) the discovery within Russian-controlled territory of new high-grade deposits, which is believed to be unlikely, and b) the success the Russians will have in developing a practicable process for large-scale extraction of the small percentages of Uranium present in oil-shales, large deposits of which are available to them.

Earlier in 1948, the JIC received MI6 intelligence, apparently based on reports from their agents in the exile groups, that an enormous labour force was mining uranium ore at Aue in the Soviet Zone in Germany, near the Czech border. The Anglo-American 'Insecticide Committee' had been unable to stop the deal between the Czechs and the Soviets on the supply of uranium ore. The Americans, and almost certainly the British as well, sent agents recruited from the exiled Yugoslav National Committee, headed by Radovan Popvic, into Czechoslovakia to obtain information on the mines. Similarly, reports were received that in Bulgaria high-grade uranium deposits had been discovered by the Soviets using captured German documents. British and American Intelligence subsequently recruited agents from the Turkish minority in Bulgaria to penetrate the mining complex at Bukovo, in the Rodopi Mountains.[56]

Aware of the intelligence interest, the Soviet MGB used the opportunity to launch a deception operation, designed to conceal the existence of huge, newly discovered uranium deposits in the Urals. According to one of the agents involved, Pavel Sudoplatov: 'A game developed in which some of these Turkish agents were fed with carefully inflated figures of the mines production.' Based on the Bukovo figure, the intelligence assessment was that the Soviet Union would not be able to obtain enough uranium to sustain any atomic project, or at least not until the fifties. In the end, the Soviet Union was to gain most of its uranium ores from the mines in the Urals and East Germany, which were to prove more productive than those in Czechoslovakia and Bulgaria.[57]

Whether these penetration operations were co-ordinated with the Americans is not clear because nuclear matters were one area of Britain's 'special relationship' with the United States where a full and frank intelligence exchange did not exist. During February 1946, the United States had been rocked by public revelations from the Igor Gouzenko affair in Canada about the extent of Soviet espionage within the wartime atomic programme. The result was that Congress passed the McMahon Act, which imposed drastic restrictions upon the exchange of atomic intelligence, making it an offence to divulge any information to foreign states, including Britain. As Alec Danchev notes in his study of the 'Very Special Relationship': 'The British badly underestimated the McMahon Bill which was very much a pattern in British atomic diplomacy.' The man chosen to try to break this impasse was Dr Wilfred Mann, who, in October 1948, was invited by 'the Admiral', Eric Welsh, to take over as the MI6 Washington representative of the Directorate of Atomic Energy, liaising with the CIA. Responsibility for collecting intelligence on atomic energy had been transferred in February 1947 from the 'Manhattan Engineer District' to the Central Intelligence Group, as the Nuclear Energy group within the Scientific Branch of the Office of Reports and Estimates, and then to the newly created CIA.[58]

In the late thirties, Mann had worked with Niels Bohr in Copenhagen. During the war, he was employed by the Ministry of Supply in the Directorate of Tube Alloys, but did not take part in any nuclear work, being involved, instead, in the general area of Scientific Research and Development. From the end of 1941, he liaised with the Russian trade delegation and from the spring of 1943 served as a physicist with the British Central Scientific Office (BCSO), exchanging information with the Americans in Washington, where Eric Welsh's representative, the leading British scientist James Chadwick, also had an office. For his contribution to the war effort, Mann received the Medal of Freedom. After hostilities ceased, the BCSO became the British Commonwealth Scientific Office, where Mann dealt with classified matters covering a wide range of scientific issues but, again, not nuclear physics. During the autumn of 1945, he returned to teaching at Imperial College in London, and during the following April was offered the post of Principal Scientific Officer in the new Directorate of Atomic Energy, a branch of the Ministry of Supply that had taken over the responsibilities of Tube Alloys.

In July 1946, Mann was posted to the National Research Council (NRC) of the Canadian Atomic Energy Project laboratories, at Chalk River, and, within a month, became UK representative on the United Nations' Atomic Energy Commission Scientific and Technical Committee, which considered the control of atomic energy.[59]

Before taking up the liaison post, Mann consulted in London with the highly secretive 'special group' responsible for atomic intelligence within the Directorate of Atomic Energy. It was headed by Welsh, who retained his reputation for deviousness to the extent that he even excluded the Chief Scientific Adviser in the MoD, Henry Tizard, from his deliberations. In Washington, Welsh introduced Mann to the local MI6 representative, Peter Dwyer, 'a witty and congenial colleague with a good sense of humour'. An Oxford graduate from an artistic family, Dwyer had worked for Fox Films and Movietone News in the thirties before being recruited by MI6, in 1939, to work in Paris. Then, after the fall of France and a period as head of station in Panama, he was posted to Washington as a South American expert for the British Security Co-ordination (BSC), where he was regarded as 'one of its better people'. Kim Philby, who took over from Dwyer, soon discovered that he had 'a great deal more to him than just wit'. A skilled counter-espionage officer, Dwyer was responsible in 'a brilliant piece of analysis' for identifying atomic bomb spy Klaus Fuchs, after narrowing the investigation down to two scientists, Dr Rudolf Peierls and Fuchs.[60]

Dwyer warned Mann that his posting would be difficult as the previous incumbent, Gordon Baines, had been turfed out of his office in the CIA headquarters, telling colleagues that such liaison was no longer worthwhile. The special nuclear energy group in the CIA continued to be completely fettered by the restrictions of the McMahon Act and members, who took precautions not to be seen talking to him in public, warned Mann that the relationship was now cold. Although personal relations remained cordial and friendly, there was no co-operation on the American side in transferring information for fear that their own group might be disbanded. He was, however, able to broker a small intelligence exchange.

In possession of a small number of deciphered Soviet intercepts relating to their atomic bomb experiments, Mann, who was known within the British embassy as 'the atomic bomb', was able to give the 'voraciously eager' Americans raw and processed intelligence reports. In return, he received from the Atomic Energy Commission – the body responsible for all nuclear developments in the US, both military and civil – non-restricted technical information, which Mann thought 'only just made the task tenable'. The lack of real co-operation created substantial difficulties in trying to predict the timescale for the production of a Soviet bomb, which was MI6's prime concern.[61]

On 29 August 1949, to the shock of British Intelligence, the Russians exploded their atomic bomb. An American WB-29 of the long-range detection project, 'Snifden', had returned from a 'weather' flight near Kamachatka, in the Soviet far east, to its Pacific Ocean base with evidence of the bomb's detonation. As a member of a small, secret team, Mann attended the White House 'war room' where, in a hurried briefing, 'I learned that a radioactive cloud had been detected and then followed by the US Air Force from the Pacific, across America and to the eastern shores of the Atlantic'. There had been, it would appear, considerable deliberation about informing Britain because of the provisions of the McMahon Act. Although a 'Modus Vivendi' had been drafted in January 1948 whereby the Americans made concessions on the release of atomic energy information in return for Britain releasing more of its uranium stockpile and rescinding its wartime veto on use of the bomb, leading US officials in the atomic energy field ensured that information remained restricted.[62]

On 5 September, Dick White, the deputy director and head of counter-espionage at MI5, called Michael Perrin (deputy controller-general of Atomic Energy, Technical Policy, at the Ministry of Supply) to his office. Perrin, whose colleagues at Tube Alloys had thought little of his scientific ability and advice on nuclear policy, was well known in Whitehall and 'moved with perfect ease in the committee rooms and club dining rooms where so much of the business of government was done'. He had a reputation for 'efficiency and discretion, if not great flair', and if someone needed to be consulted about a delicate matter relating to atomic energy, Perrin was the natural choice. White handed Perrin a transcript and a FBI report that showed that a British scientist had leaked information to the Soviet consulate in New York about the Manhattan Project. Perrin instantly realised that the culprit was Klaus Fuchs.[63]

Such news might have stopped all Anglo-American co-operation, but five days later there was a cross-Atlantic top-secret teletype discussion with Perrin and Welsh in the American embassy in London about the 'radioactive cloud' which was now drifting towards Europe. Menzies and MI6 agreed to co-operate and quickly dispatched to Washington radioactive fall-out samples which a RAF Halifax from Aldergrove airbase, near Belfast, had managed to gather over the Atlantic.[64]

On 18 September, Menzies took Perrin to see the Prime Minister at Chequers to brief him on the latest developments. Using Peter Dwyer's secure channel to Menzies, President Truman cabled the news that they had 'ninety-five per cent proof' that the Soviets had detonated a nuclear device. On the 23rd, Truman, who remained sceptical to the last that the Soviets had the enormous capability required to construct a bomb, publicly announced there was 'evidence that within recent weeks an atomic explosion occurred in the USSR'.[65]

The former wartime liaison officer between the American agencies and the BSC, Ernest Cuneo, left a sensational claim among his personal papers.

He asserted that the former head of the BSC, Sir William Stephenson, informed him that the Soviet Union would explode its first atomic bomb 'on or about 27 September 1949'. 'When Sir William gave me this staggering information on 18 February 1948 – a year and a half in advance of the event – I asked him how good the source was. He answered: "Triple A, Triple 1". I asked the question which never should be asked: Exactly how do you know? "We have a little window," Sir William said. Moles were then called "little windows".' Cuneo claims that he transmitted the information to 'US authorities'. It seems extremely unlikely – no other such evidence has come to light – and the fact remains that MI6's inability to predict accurately the Soviet Union's possession of the bomb constituted a major intelligence failure.[66]

Hitherto, the chiefs of staff had accepted the advice of the JIC that the Soviets might achieve an atomic capability by the early fifties, probably in 1952. Overnight all the intelligence and military and political assessments by the military and politicians became redundant. Fears were exacerbated by the Klaus Fuchs atom bomb spy trial in January 1950, after which the chiefs concluded that Soviet atomic development was now 'much more advanced than it was thought to have been'. It had been assumed until that point that Russia's vast superiority in conventional forces – itself a gross overestimate and another major intelligence failure – was no longer balanced by America's sole possession of the nuclear threat. The chiefs 'reflected with discomfort upon Britain's position now that a nuclear armed adversary might quickly reach the Atlantic seaboard in a future war'.[67]

The failure led to a greater degree of co-operation between Britain and the United States on atomic intelligence and the restrictions of the McMahon Act were tentatively loosened during 1951, but fuller disclosures had to await a revision of atomic agreements in 1958. Mann, though, was involved with a series of discussions in London on joint efforts to assess Soviet nuclear production capabilities which led, at the beginning of the year, to MI6 and the CIA correlating their estimates. Nevertheless he felt that his efforts had been thwarted by the arrival in Washington, in October 1949, of the new MI6–CIA liaison officer, Kim Philby: 'My immediate reaction when I learned later of his defection was to feel that all the work I did during the eighteen months that we were together had been an almost complete waste of time.'[68]

Mann left Washington in April 1951 and returned to Shell Max House where he represented the Directorate of Atomic Energy at the fortnightly meetings of the Cabinet Advisory Committee on Atomic Energy, chaired by Sir Roger Makins. Finding the post of a temporary civil servant 'unfulfilling', he resigned to take a position with the National Bureau of Standards in Washington. Perrin also left in the summer, depleting MI6's limited expertise in the field of atomic intelligence. In Washington, Mann was replaced as attaché by Dr Robert Press, who had joined the Directorate of Atomic Energy in 1948.[69]

Until his death in 1954, MI6's atomic intelligence-gathering remained in the hands of Welsh, who, senior MI6 officers eventually concluded, was 'a complete charlatan'. For a decade he had been able to hoodwink the different departments and the Americans over the nature of his 'hush-hush' work. George Young, who undertook a review of Welsh's work, discovered that 'he did his best to impress the US Atomic Energy Authority (AEA) that his work for "C" was too delicate to be revealed, while his MI6 colleagues were told that this applied to his AEA liaison: if need be his confidential exchanges with the Americans were invoked as a further excuse . . . In fact, MI6 intelligence on Soviet nuclear development was practically nil.'[70]

CODA: DECEPTION

In parallel to the quest for scientific intelligence were operations based on 'scientific deception'. The vehicle for these activities was the London Controlling Section (LCS), a highly secret department in the offices of the War Cabinet involved in deception planning. Working in wartime on strategic matters as part of the Joint Planning Staff (JPS), its aim had been to divert enemy resources away from planned Allied operations and to direct them against imaginary operations devised by LCS officials. This had involved such famous operations as 'The Man Who Never Was' and 'Monty's Double'.

The C-in-C Middle East, Field Marshal Sir Archibald Wavell, had outlined the LCS modus operandi in a memorandum – 'Aids to surprise with particular Reference to Deceiving, Mystifying and Confusing the Enemy on the battlefield'. The ruses included 'false information or disguise', 'feigned retreat', 'encouragement of treachery' and 'weakening of the enemy's morale'. He foresaw the importance of 'signals deception' and the need for intelligence on the enemy's thinking. Essential to successful deception was secrecy, which required that participants were not always aware of the motives behind an operation. This was a 'separate war' of political and psychological warfare for 'professionals', which meant MI6.[71]

When, in September 1945, LCS controlling officer Col. John Bevan left, it seemed that the deception agencies had been disbanded. The chiefs of staff, however, decided to allow the LCS to continue in peacetime on 'a care maintenance basis', with the 'objective of maintaining a reservoir of the specialist skills and knowledge learned during the war'. Bevan's successor, Col. Ronald Wingate, a former member of SOE and JPS, kept it alive by holding dinner parties at his club for former members. He ensured that the mysteries of deception remained secret by getting LCS members 'to swear never to discuss publicly what it was they had done', since 'we might have to take on the Russian General Staff'.[72]

Situated in Churchill's former war rooms, the postwar LCS worked closely with the chiefs of staff, MI6, MI5 and a number of scientific advisers. In 1947,

John Harvey-Jones of Naval Intelligence, who had qualified as a Russian interpreter from the special course at Downing College, Cambridge, joined the LCS. He found it 'a pale shadow of past glories', consisting of just 'three of us', the victim of the 'decentralisation of British deception capabilities'. Resources were 'parcelled out' to other departments, such as MI6, 'as the need or opportunity arose'. It was not an entirely happy experience as Harvey-Jones discovered that there was no overall or central direction, but this did not 'preclude endless and bitter inter-service warfare, which seemed to take precedence over the common goal of resisting the onward march of Russian influence'. Despite this, he believed that 'the work I was doing was worthwhile'.[73]

In mid-1950, another chiefs of staff review of the LCS recommended that 'the technique of deception, suitably modified to present conditions, could play a useful role in our defence preparations'. It was put on an operational basis in a Cold War context and renamed the Directorate of Forward Plans (DFP). A centre for the study of operational physical, radio and intelligence deception techniques, the Visual Inter-Service Training and Research Establishment (in 1951 it changed its name to the Joint Concealment Centre), was set up to work under the overall direction of the DFP. Responsible for strategic deception, the DFP operated on a worldwide basis and had eight officers – five in London, one in the Middle East and two in Singapore.[74]

Key staff included John Drew, who during the war was employed by the deception 20 Committee and after in the Cabinet Office. In 1951, he took charge of intelligence issues and cover plans in the MoD, and had direct access to MI6 headquarters. Noel Wild had run black propaganda operations for the Political Warfare Executive and later headed SHAEF's own inter-Allied deception staff. Engaged postwar in 'unspecified intelligence duties', he was posted to Greece with the British Military Mission and then to the War Office, before being seconded to MI6. From 1950, Wild advised the chiefs of staff on subversion and counter-insurgency. He believed that 'Soviet activities and finance were behind many of the troubles at home and abroad' and that 'many contemporary troubles were the work of communist agitators'. Brig. Dudley Clarke was 'an expert in unorthodox warfare and clandestinity', who had founded the Middle East A-Force. An operational 'genius', he had taken charge of Gen. Eisenhower's deception section at SHAEF for the invasion of France. In the postwar years, Clarke remained 'as mysterious and impenetrable as ever, and was rarely heard or seen outside his small circle'. Head of public opinion research at Conservative Central Office, in 1952 he joined the DFP to work with MI6's own deception unit and helped advise the Australian Secret Intelligence Service on deception techniques.[75]

Harvey-Jones did not share his colleagues' views on the machinations of the Soviets. He recalled that time after time, 'we would ascribe to the Russians degrees of premeditation and intricate organisation of interrelated but disparate events, in widely disparate parts of the world, that we, with all our sophistication, would have been hard put to pull off'. No account was taken of 'the deeply ingrained patterns of behaviour and the all-embracing bureaucratic nature of the Soviet regime which made such intricacies nearly impossible'. He thought that 'their aim was to start to rebuild their homeland, ravished and devastated as it was. Given the poverty of their resources, the ineffectiveness of their organisation and the size of their task, it was obvious that they had more than enough to do for many years to come.'[76]

But what did the peacetime DFP actually do? At a low level, we know that the services were involved in the radar camouflage of equipment and the use of decoy lighting, but at a strategic level little is known. We can only speculate at what 'resisting the onward march of Russian influence' actually meant in practice. Churchill expected the DFP to 'confuse and mislead' the KGB and 'to put ourselves in a position to do this if war comes'. Wild and Harvey-Jones give the impression that the DFP used its expertise to monitor and unravel alleged Soviet deception operations. In 1945, a leading wartime operator, author Denis Wheatley, suggested that 'in peacetime, after the great reduction of our forces, military deception would be almost valueless in persuading our potential enemies that Britain was to be feared'. But it could be done, he argued, by 'scientific deception'.[77]

Wheatley envisaged creating a dummy secret base which would be visible to reconnaissance aircraft. It would subsequently be leaked that the base 'possessed a new scientific weapon of great power – perhaps one which would enable us to bombard Moscow with atom bombs – then not considered possible – or something of that kind'. The chair of the chiefs of staff committee, Dickie Dickson, thought the idea 'sound', and it may be that something similar was put into practice. When recalling MI5's use of émigrés during the fifties for deception purposes, Peter Wright revealed that 'an entire department of the Foreign Office' provided MI5 with 'chicken feed' to be given to double agents to pass on to the Russians. According to Wright, it consisted of 'wholly unbelievable faked secret documents about weapons we did not have, and policies we had no intention of pursuing'.[78]

The obvious area for using scientific deception was, as Wheatley envisaged, nuclear weapons. As Brian Cathcart, author of a history of *Britain's Struggle for the Atom Bomb*, has written, 'somebody was duped' about the true state of British weapons development. And, on Cathcart's evidence, it was the British public first, and then perhaps the Russians. It is entirely possible that deception was aimed at three particular areas – one, to hide the fact that Britain was building the atomic and then the hydrogen bomb; two, to suggest that Britain had more bombs than it actually had; and three, that its nuclear arsenal was an 'independent deterrent'.[79]

The decision to go ahead with Britain's atomic bomb was taken at the Cabinet Committee Gen 75 on 25 October 1946, when Attlee and Bevin determined that the country should have an 'independent nuclear deterrent'. The Foreign Secretary exclaimed: 'We've got to have a bloody Union Jack flying on top of it.' The determination to embark on this 'grandiose folly', which cost £100 million, was, Anthony Verrier believes, 'governed by a belief in national prestige and international status, coupled with a marked, if veiled, distrust of the United States. Britain's atom bombs were not built primarily to deter the Soviet Union, but to reinsure against an American failure to do so.'[80]

It is now known that the number of nuclear bombs that Britain possessed in the fifties was much lower than the figures bandied around. A chiefs of staff sub-committee undertook a consideration of the requirements to counter a Soviet nuclear threat which was expected to emerge by 1957. It estimated that this would require two hundred nuclear warheads, but this was never achieved. There was only enough plutonium to produce fifteen to eighteen bombs annually from 1951 onwards and, as Peter Malone discovered, this proved to be an overestimate. This makes a mockery of a 1956 estimate in the *Guardian* – which, of course, may have been the result of a deception – which suggested that Britain's stockpile was 'at least a thousand'. Similarly, the United States had very few bombs – perhaps 'five or six' – in the immediate postwar period, though a production drive may have pushed the figure up to fifty by the end of 1948, when B29s arrived in East Anglia, providing a near-permanent nuclear presence on British soil. Details of the US store were probably passed on to Moscow by Donald Maclean, who was in a perfect position to help his Soviet controllers with the tonnage of uranium bought by the Americans. In turn, the Soviet Union probably had a stockpile smaller than fifty up to mid-1953, when the first series-production bombs entered the nuclear arsenal.[81]

The Macmillan government, in particular, is revealed to have been 'extremely economical with the truth in its statements about nuclear matters'. Declassified US files from the early sixties show that the British government's claim that its nuclear deterrent was 'independent' had little basis in fact. In the immediate aftermath of the 1958 US–UK agreement on the exchange of nuclear information, British scientists at Aldermaston were handed a carbon copy of the design for the US warhead for the Polaris missile. Historians' accounts have always stressed that the Polaris warhead was British-designed, one of the key factors that made the missile 'independent'. As Mark Urban has revealed, 'few secrets of the Anglo-American special relationship were more sensitive than Britain's dependence on American help in building its atomic bombs. Washington and Whitehall conspired to keep the secret from a British public which might have questioned the "independent" status of the bomb.'[82]

We now know that the British 'H-bomb' exploded in the South Pacific in 1957 was not, in fact, a genuine hydrogen bomb but a very big A-bomb supplemented with hydrogen fuel. The first hydrogen bombs had failed to meet expectations and the tests left the scientists deeply disappointed. The government, though, had boldly declared them a great success and, in order to retrieve the situation, the so-called H-bomb test was organised as a deception. The Americans were not deceived by Macmillan's sleight of hand, suggests Professor John Bayliss, but the Russians probably were. He adds: 'If deterrence was a psychological game, Britain had its part to play in emphasising, perhaps even exaggerating, the disastrous consequences of aggression.' Which is precisely how Denis Wheatley had envisaged the role of the LCS in peacetime.[83]

In July 1951 the Cabinet Secretary, Sir Norman Brook, warned Prime Minister Clement Attlee of intelligence fears that Russian agents could arrive in London with suitcases full of kits to make an atomic bomb, which could be put together in a garage. Based on meagre intelligence, a great deal of speculation and amid fears of what the Soviets might be capable of, it was a perfect example of the problems faced by, and failures of, scientific intelligence-gathering and analysis in the late forties and early fifties. Failure was masked by disinformation and deception.

A Tube Alloys analysis stated that

> an atomic bomb might be broken down into a number of parts
> and introduced into this country in about 50 small packages of
> moderate weight. None of these packages could be detected by
> instruments as containing anything dangerous or explosive, and
> even visual inspection of the contents would not make identifi-
> cation certain. The bomb could subsequently be assembled in
> any premises with the sort of equipment usual in small garages
> provided that a small team of skilled fitters was available.

Quite rightly, Attlee appears not to have been unduly concerned. This same scenario was publicised by the intelligence services in the seventies, when stories suddenly appeared in the press about Soviet special forces, Spetznaz, and when world terrorism was at its peak. The scenario resurfaced again in the mid-nineties following stories, which proved to be untrue, about the alleged sale of weapons-grade plutonium from the states of the disintegrating former Soviet empire.[84]

PART THREE

THE SOVIET EMPIRE

For many of the pre-war officers who remained in MI6 after the war, the battle with the Nazis had been a mere interlude in the continuing struggle against the Bolsheviks. In their rush to recommence intelligence-gathering on the Soviet Union they were willing to recruit, without discrimination, agents who only months previously had actively collaborated with the Nazis and in some cases had been responsible for atrocities against Jews.

MI6 turned to their pre-war contacts in the émigré world and attempted to revive organisations they had financed in the thirties, such as the Promethean League and Intermarium. When officers discovered that they were no longer effective, MI6 resurrected the former Nazi-sponsored Anti-Bolshevik Bloc of Nations (ABN). The neo-fascist ABN, controlled by Ukrainian nationalists, was the most extreme and most important of all the exile organisations during the Cold War. A high point came in the mid-eighties when its leader was welcomed to the White House by President Reagan.

Emigré politics are factional, bitter, convoluted and always controversial. The following chapters attempt to correct some of the misconceptions found in previous accounts by writers on intelligence, and to make sense of the postwar manoeuvrings which paralleled the jockeying for position in émigré special operations by British and French Intelligence, and later the CIA.

For many years, discussion in Poland and among the émigrés in the West about the underground remained a taboo subject. Polish archives covering this area were later destroyed on the orders of the government because the conflict was seen as a 'shameful period with Poles fighting Poles'. Poland is now a free and active democracy, but for other countries that suffered under Stalin and the Soviet yoke, and collaborated with the Germans, it has proved difficult to face up to the past.

In Latvia during the spring of 1998, SS veterans marched through Riga; while in Lithuania the first trial in any of the former Soviet countries of an alleged war criminal was undertaken only following intense pressure from the West. Ukraine, the sixth largest country in Europe, continues to slide into economic ruin, still controlled by corrupt politicians and the secret police. Similarly, Belarus remains divided between extreme nationalists and the former communists still unsure of its relationship with Russia.

Little changes in the intelligence world, and today MI6 officers use the Baltic states as a staging post for missions into Russia. The former southern states of the old Soviet Union are once again an arena for the 'Great Game', while control of the Baku oilfields is a major prize for shady businessmen and oilmen, often operating under cover of the intelligence services. In the old Intermarium states MI6 has, in recent years, opened liaison offices with its counterparts in Poland, Hungary and the Czech Republic.

All the émigré groups referred to in the following chapters are either inactive or collapsed many years ago. Yet they all provided a bloody legacy, leaving deep and long-lasting wounds in both the émigré and home communities which, in many cases, have not healed. MI6 bears some responsibility for aiding the émigrés' romantic illusions. The idea of rolling back the Soviet Empire was never more than a dream and, in reality, often a nightmare.

In intelligence it is argued that necessity is the mother of invention, over-riding all ethical considerations, but in the case of the émigré groups the results did not justify the moral vacuum. The intelligence flow from behind the Iron Curtain never developed beyond a trickle, and quality was thin at best. What did arrive in the West cost the lives of many thousands of national-ist guerrillas.

CHAPTER 11

INTERMARIUM

The dream of a postwar Pan-Danubian [Con]Federation* from the Baltic to the Aegean under Habsburg rule – a sort of recreation of the Austro-Hungarian Empire – was kept alive by Austrian monarchists under the direction of pretender to the throne Archduke Otto von Habsburg. The monarchists had the enthusiastic support of Winston Churchill, who, like many of its adherents, had been a member of the Brussels-based right-wing Pan-European Union (PEU), founded in 1922 by Habsburg and Count Richard Coudenhove-Kalergi as 'the only way of guarding against an eventual world hegemony by Russia'. Churchill had laid out his support for the 'United States of Europe' in the *Saturday Evening Post* in February 1930: 'Let the British Empire, excluded in this plan, realise its own world-spread ideal. Even so, the mass of Europe once united, once federalised or partially federalised, once continentally self-conscious – Europe with its African and Asiatic possessions and plantations, would constitute an organism beyond compare.' Churchill's conception, which for a time had its supporters within the Foreign Office and MI6 – of a federal Europe but with the Empire still intact – did not change for the next twenty years.[1]

Churchill's and Coudenhove-Kalergi's conception of a federated Europe

---

* There are differences between a 'confederation' – meaning independent states in alliance – and a 'federation' – states surrendering certain powers of sovereignty and forming a common government but with individual decision-making on internal affairs.

was enthusiastically 'seconded by various Central European Federal Study Clubs' located in London, Rome and Paris. The clubs had been created by political exiles from the Russian-dominated countries who, in turn, formed the movement known as Intermarium. Meaning 'between the seas', Intermarium was founded in Paris in the mid-thirties by a former Tsarist general. An anti-communist Catholic lay organisation, it brought together an alliance of militant émigré groups from central Europe. A 'secret international organisation', it recruited as members 'people whose homes are to be found in the "intermare"' – that part of Europe between the Baltic, the Black Sea, the Aegean, the Ionian Sea and the Adriatic. The desired goal of the sixteen nations was to create a cordon sanitaire within central Europe and to liberate their territories from the Soviet Union. Proclaiming the necessity of a powerful anti-communist Pan-Danubian [Con]Federation under the name Intermarium, the aim was to hasten the overthrow of the USSR. Before the Second World War, the organisation received support and funding from MI6 and French Intelligence for its anti-communist operations. Within MI6 it came under the remit of Stewart Menzies and, in Paris, the émigrés' friends, Commander Wilfred 'Biffy' Dunderdale, his deputy Tom Greene, and Charles Ellis.[2]

Although not expressly fascist, Intermarium members shared many of the characteristics and anti-Semitism of the clerical-fascists. The depression of the early thirties had ravaged central Europe, one historian wrote, 'like some medieval epidemic ... cancerous cells, already diagnosed in the political body, throve on its depredation. In the end, it claimed the very concept of a liberal society as its victim and the soul of Europe already exposed to the ideologies of violence and inhumanity.' A number of central European leaders actively collaborated with the Nazis, employed by the Abwehr as pre-war 'agents of influence' as well as informants on other émigré groups. According to American intelligence records, when the Wehrmacht marched into eastern Europe, Intermarium became 'an instrument of German intelligence', though there is evidence that the ties to MI6 were never completely severed.[3]

Following the German *Anschluss* in 1938, MI6 was ordered to undertake operations in Austria under the control of Menzies, who began to recruit among the underground monarchist 'cells' which made contact with the West. Among the refugees was Count Coudenhove-Kalergi, who fled Austria when the PEU offices in the imperial palace were occupied by the Nazis. In London, where his ideas elicited a ready response from Catholic circles, Coudenhove-Kalergi called for the unification of Europe around a Paris–London axis which suggested, for the first time, a prominent role for Britain.[4]

In early June 1939, the British Pan-European Committee, which received the support of the banker to the exiles, Warburgs, held its inaugural meeting in the House of Commons, chaired by 'a true Empire-builder', Leo Amery, the man who had introduced Churchill to the count. Victor Cazelet, the British liaison to the head of the Polish government-in-exile, General Wladyslaw

Sikorski, took charge of the secretariat. His presence confirmed Polish interest in ideas of federation and a 'Central European solution'. With the outbreak of war, the revival of federalist ideas was, Feliks Gross and M. Kamil Dziewanowski point out, not accidental.

> The shaky independent existence of Central and East European states between the wars had ended in political catastrophe; and it had become obvious that the isolated nations of this region could survive only as long as Germany and the Soviet Union were militarily weak or genuinely peace-loving ... The future security of Central and Eastern Europe called for new answers, since a zone of small and weak states could guarantee neither political nor economic stability.

A federal solution was pushed vigorously by the Polish foreign minister in exile, Count August Zaleski, a member of the Pan-European Committee, Zaleski was also a prominent member of the Central European Federal Study Clubs, the backbone of Intermarium. More hardline than Sikorski, he resigned over a Polish accord with the Soviet Union which failed to indicate the position of Poland's eastern border with Russia.[5]

Through intermediaries, Menzies established clandestine relations with the poverty-stricken Habsburg who, with Vatican support, travelled to Paris in October 1939 to talk to French, Czech and British officials and politicians. His MI6 contact was Commander Kenneth Cohen, responsible for 'higher political tasks'. He did not rate Habsburg very highly but Menzies arranged that 'a subsidy be paid to Archduke Otto, one that was not short of £50,000 a month'. Cohen was amused by the Archduke's insistence that he walk backwards when he left 'his tawdry little bedroom'. Otto later left for the United States, where he promoted his ideas of a Catholic state called Danubia. In March 1942, the Deputy of the British Security Co-ordination in New York, MI6 officer Charles Ellis, revealed to 'Q', the head of the Office of Strategic Services (OSS), William 'Bill' Donovan, the existence of the hidden subsidy with a view to the Americans taking over the funding. Although the Americans had little faith in Habsburg, Donovan was willing to support Count Coudenhove-Kalergi, who also moved to the United States where he continued to lobby for his own Pan Europa project.[6]

Although Coudenhove-Kalergi had the support of Churchill, the Foreign Office was irritated by his activities and 'his addiction for forming Unions out of some ill-assorted partners'. They disliked the fact that, during the war, the Prime Minister continued to back the anti-communists among the central European federalists because, as senior Northern Department official Geoffrey Wilson pointed out, 'there is little evidence that the Soviet Union will be prepared to agree to federation in Eastern Europe after the war'.

During the spring of 1942 the issue of a federation was broached with the Soviet foreign minister, Vyacheslav Molotov, who rejected such ideas outright. Molotov said that 'the Soviet government had certain information to show that some federations might be directed against the Soviet Union'; which in the case of Intermarium was certainly true. When the United States swung round to the Soviet viewpoint, the fate of the federalist plans was sealed. By 1943, when the Czechs concluded an alliance with the Soviets, the idea of a Balkan federation was effectively dead. The socialists, social democrats and those in the centre abandoned the scheme – they continued, however, to support ideas of federation and played an important role in founding the postwar European Movement – leaving the right and extreme-right groups to pursue the project. But this did not discourage the Poles, whose main political parties at the core of the resistance still believed that it would be possible to create such a federation in spite of Russian opposition. Likewise, a few officials in the Foreign Office continued to support ideas of federation and sought encouragement from the Vatican, whose postwar policy, it noted, would 'favour the creation of a large Danubian federal State, if it gives promise of stability and is not controlled by Bolshevik Russia'. In pursuit of this objective, as early as February 1943 the British ambassador to the Holy See, Sir Percy Osborne, had embarked upon the task of presenting the Vatican with, in his own words, the 'anti-Bolshevist bogey dope'.[7]

In the same month, there were meetings concerning German peace proposals headed by elements in the SS which looked to the postwar world. In Berne was stationed Claude Dansey's principal lieutenant of the independent Z-network in Europe, Frederick 'Fanny' Vanden Heuvel, a director of Eno's Fruit Salts, whose status as a papal count gave MI6 an entrée to the Vatican. Vanden Heuvel met with the head of the OSS station, Allen Dulles, and a representative of the head of the SD's (Sicherheitsdienst) international department, Walter Schellenberg. Dulles is alleged to have told his friend of twenty years, Prince Max Hohenlohe, that the peace must avoid the excesses of Versailles by permitting the existence of a 'Greater Germany' which would include Austria and a section of Czechoslovakia. This 'Federal Greater Germany' would be part of 'a cordon sanitaire against Bolshevism and pan-Slavism' which, in association with a 'Danube Confederation', would be 'the best guarantee of order and progress in Central and Eastern Europe'.[8]

Although the Allied agreement on an unconditional peace scuppered the SS-proposals, Dulles planned to 'pick loose the secondary Axis allies – elements of his envisioned Danube Confederation – ahead of the advancing Red Army'. In particular, he made plans for Bulgaria, Romania and Hungary, where 'contacts with MI6 remained unbroken'. He wanted to exert 'certain subversive pressures' on these countries by establishing secret contact with 'influential members of the ruling classes who are not regarded as whole-heartedly in sympathy with the Nazis'. One such leader was Romania's Marshal Antonescu, who sought a 'Confederation of south-western and central Europe ... [in] co-operation with democratic governments of the West'. Dulles's plans had supporters within the Vatican, where British representative Sir Percy Osborne was guided by Father Krunoslav Draganovic, Secretary of the Confraternity of San Girolamo and representative of the Ustashi and Croatian Red Cross. Moving in the highest Vatican circles, from early 1944, Draganovic began to lobby the British in favour of the Pan-Danubian Con-Federation, delivering a lengthy memorandum on the subject to Osborne.[9]

Churchill, too, was still thinking in terms of a postwar Danubian confederation or even a Habsburg restoration which, he told the War Cabinet, would be centred on Vienna. In early 1944, Churchill established a Central European Committee which distilled the views and advice of a small coterie of central European experts and propagandists centred around Chatham House's Royal Institute of International Affairs. The committee promoted the creation of a Confederation of Central European Nations under London's control, which a small number of hardline anti-communist officials in the Foreign Office, notably Orme Sargent, hoped might contain Soviet power in eastern Europe. The committee's report, which found favour with Churchill, proposed a western-backed multinational Danubian state with Austria at its centre. It was envisaged that Austria would be detached from southern Germany and that Vienna 'would once again become master of the Danube region'.[10]

Churchill wrote to President Roosevelt: 'As you know the idea of Vienna becoming the capital of a large Danubian federation has always been attractive to me, though I should prefer to add Hungary, to which Uncle Joe is strongly opposed.' Nor did the emerging military and strategic landscape affect the Vatican's view. At the beginning of 1945, in a review of postwar hopes for Europe, Pope Pius XII favoured an anti-communist Central European Federation of Catholic states, 'which would stretch from the Baltic to the Black Seas'. As late as July 1945, with the Red Army occupying most of the Danubian region, the goal of a federation remained a British priority because 'any other seemed unacceptable'. The British sought to directly influence and shore up their support in central and south-eastern Europe, and the idea of a pan-Danubian 'federation' still carried weight in intelligence circles. The concept remained a general, if imprecise, objective because the planners still required the protection of Britain's most important communication routes to the eastern Mediterranean and the Middle East. This was pursued as a realistic goal, and it was naïvely hoped that the Soviets would recognise the value of a federation. The Dulles brothers, though, were not to play a part in the construction of an anti-communist league along the Danube.[11]

As the Red Army rolled across the Austrian border, MI6 unveiled its plan to launch a 'political league against Bolshevism' and to provide 'material aid for anti-Soviet counter-espionage and paramilitary operations'. British

Intelligence and, more particularly, the remnants of SOE were convinced that it would not be long before war broke out with their former Soviet allies, and they were determined to prepare for such an outcome. By the summer, a number of MI6's most experienced officers and Balkan experts were already well established in the British Zone in Austria. Officers were posted to Graz and Klagenfurt under cover of the 'Civil Liaison Office' to penetrate the émigré groups in order to recruit suitable foot-soldiers. Using a well-established tactic, masonic lodges were created to attract 'the most eminent leaders in the Balkans'. MI6 was said to be 'in a hurry and didn't want to lose any time', and its officers did not discriminate in their efforts which included giving 'succour even to Nazis and the Ustashi'. A network of émigré centres was established in Italy, Austria and Germany, as well as Paris and London, which reached into all parts of the Balkans. The vehicle for this renewed anti-Bolshevik crusade was the MI6-backed Central European Federal Study Clubs and their militant umbrella group, the revived pre-war organisation, Intermarium. The nucleus of East–Central federal thought, Intermarium was reactivated at the end of 1944 by intelligence personnel and officers and men of the Polish Second Army Corps in Italy. Its journal was immediately smuggled into Poland under German as well as Soviet occupation, and stimulated an interest in the cause of European integration.[12]

In London, a study club with support from MI6 and the Polish government-in-exile was resurrected under the presidency of August Zaleski, and its secretary, Karel Locher, who had worked in the Czech Foreign Office. With representatives from Slovakia, Latvia, Estonia, Ukraine, Romania and Yugoslavia, one of its first acts was to create, in October 1945, a refugee and propaganda organisation, the 'Scottish League for European Freedom', which would be responsible as an MI6 front group for 'rescuing' a number of the Intermarium assets (see Chapter 21).

Equally involved in Intermarium was French Intelligence, following an order from President de Gaulle – a strong advocate of a Pan-Danubian 'federation' – to adopt an aggressive campaign 'to gain the sympathy of the peoples of Eastern Europe'. The Deuxième Bureau station in Austria was tasked with creating a counterweight to British plans in the region, based on contacts made in thirties Paris with intelligence networks in Innsbruck and Freiburg. On the ground, however, from the beginning of the project, MI6 officers tentatively liaised with their French counterparts to co-ordinate operations. Within a year of the war's end, MI6 had helped to build up Intermarium into a well-developed movement which was regarded as 'the only organisation of international character . . . for combatting the Russians'. A fourteen-page 'Free Intermare' charter was published, appealing to the Estonians, Latvians, Lithuanians, Poles, Ukrainians, White Ruthenians, Czechs, Slovaks, Hungarians, Romanians, Serbs, Croats, Slovenians, Albanians and Greeks, 'to subordinate sovereignty to a higher European authority'. The problem was that the internal divisions among the national groups were all too noticeable and there was a tendency 'to deposit all these quarrels on the lap of this future authority'.[13]

While the Poles were a major influence, the top echelon of Intermarium became increasingly dominated by ex-fascist leaders and known collaborators. It organised around a core of Croatian Ustashi, Slovakian Hlinka Guard and Hungarian Arrow Cross members and a sprinkling of extremist Poles, Ukrainians, Slovenes and Latvians. Many were 'regular go-betweens for [MI6] and Abwehr agent-handlers, veterans of the Prometheus nets the British had rigged between the wars'. They included:

- Miha Krek, president and leader of the Catholic Slovene People's Party, who operated through the Assistant General of the Jesuits, Monsignor Anton Preseren, who was the leader of a powerful group of Slovenes within the Vatican which received 'help from the English'.
- Krunoslav Draganovic, the 'quasi-official' representative of the Croats to the organisation. A Catholic priest, he was wanted as a war criminal for helping to persecute Croatia's Serbian minority.
- Casimir Papee, who had been Poland's ambassador to the Vatican since 1939. His fellow-countryman, Myz-Mysin, was 'the group's counter-espionage expert in Rome'.
- Monsignor Ivan (John) Buchko, who was regarded as 'the spiritual leader of the Ukrainian resistance movement' and had extremely good Vatican connections.
- Ferdinand Durcansky, who had been the Slovak Foreign and Interior Minister and was wanted as a war criminal for helping to slaughter Slovakian Jews.
- Ference Vajta, a senior Intermarium leader and the organisation's chief propagandist in the 1946/7 period. He had been hidden by the émigré underground in one of the many monasteries in the Rome area.[14]

Vajta had been a leading anti-Semite in the Hungarian clerical-fascist Arrow Cross party. Since the early thirties as a journalist in Rome, he had operated in underground émigré politics, working on behalf of the Hungarian secret services with contacts with a number of western intelligence agencies. A 'generally unsavoury' character, Vajta was a trusted and loyal agent of the Nazis in Budapest, and during 1944 served as Consul General for the regime in Vienna. In this role he organised the escape routes for 'refugees' – fleeing Arrow Cross members – and helped save 'the great majority of Hungary's bourgeoisie and aristocracy' from the advancing Red Army. At the end of the war, Vajta had been placed on a 'Black List' of wanted war criminals and was detained by the US Counter-Intelligence Corps (CIC) and interned for a short period at Dachau. He was, however, quickly released on the orders of an anonymous British Military Intelligence officer. Vajta was soon active in attempts to revive Intermarium, and during the summer of 1945 worked for both French and British Intelligence. He had one priceless asset, namely access to the 'treasure' which became the prime source of Intermarium's funding. Known as a 'conceited adventurer true to only money', in the last months of the war Vajta had stripped Budapest of millions of pounds' worth of artefacts and industrial equipment which he shipped by rail to the Allied zones in Germany.[15]

Intermarium and its intelligence assets were intimately linked to the Vatican, which worked in close collaboration with British and French Intelligence. On 25 June 1945, representatives of the notorious Croat Ustashi had made contact with Archbishop Andreas Roharcher of Salzburg, in the American Zone in Austria, and had asked for the Pope's assistance in creating an independent Croatian state and support for a Pan-Danubian 'federation' as a bastion against the Serbian-backed Yugoslavia. Roharcher approached the Allies and offered to put the Ustashi at their disposal; a proposal the British immediately accepted.

Intermarium's most active branch was in Rome and joined with the Vatican, according to a US CIC report, under 'direct leadership of the Pope', in the battle against 'atheistic communism'. The branch campaigned amongst the Allies for permission to establish a volunteer anti-communist army for use in an imminent war against the USSR. Its leading members were deeply involved with the Vatican officials responsible for the various relief programmes, which served as cover for the smuggling to the West of fascist fugitives out of eastern Europe. These senior Vatican priests and bishops simultaneously became leading officials in Intermarium. The Vatican did not discriminate and any Catholic, including Nazis and their collaborators, was able to seek assistance from the Church. Intermarium was one of the first organisations to campaign openly for freedom for Waffen-SS PoWs.[16]

The use of the Catholic Church in the anti-communist struggle was discussed by the Foreign Office's Russia Committee in May 1946. The majority view was that it was necessary to keep a distance, but 'there were some suggestions that opportunities might occur in the future for using the influence of the Vatican on specific matters'. The committee was of the opinion that as the Catholic Church was one of the most powerful anti-communist influences 'it might be of advantage, without directly seeking the co-operation of the Vatican, to assist the Church in deploying its influence by facilitating the movements of its emissaries, or by other inconspicuous means'. It was recommended that the representative at the Vatican should be 'furnished with information regarding Communist activities for use in his contacts with members of the Papal entourage'.[17]

By mid-1946, Intermarium was sufficiently strong for an intelligence-backed 'large-scale propaganda campaign' to be launched in the Italian Displaced Persons (DP) camps. Large sums had been placed at its disposal to produce a regular bulletin in Rome and distribute its charter in the camps. By the second half of the year, the relationship between the British and French intelligence officers on the ground had developed into a high degree of co-operation in clandestine planning. This was promoted as an example of the 'Third Force'. 'Europe for the Europeans, without Russia and the Americans' became the slogan of Intermarium, which hoped to exploit what was viewed as the inevitable conflict between the United States and the Russians. The Anglo-French alliance did not survive for long because it became apparent that the British wanted total control of the project, and they gradually took the initiative away from the French.

American intelligence officials recognised that the MI6 men were 'very clever and very hard, harder even than the French and better prepared'. De Gaulle, the main architect of the French strategy, was soon out of power, and not long after 'the Vatican retired from the circle of French interest'. Declining offers to direct all émigré politics from Paris, in July 1946 many of the Intermarium leaders broke off relations with the French. They relocated to Rome under British protection, and established close contacts with the Vatican and anti-communist Italian politicians. Relations between the Vatican and MI6 over the British handling of Intermarium were, however, not always harmonious, as the Vatican wanted a more robust approach.[18]

The Poles and British could no longer afford to carry the financial burden, and funds began to dry up, forcing the Intermarium leaders, in July 1947, to seek American assistance. Vajta was in a powerful position; he was one of the few men who knew the details of the Hungarian industries that were re-established in Italy at the end of the year following his successful negotiations with the Italian government of de Gaspari. A number of Intermarium's leaders subsequently transferred their loyalties to the United States, where they found senior positions in CIA-financed and controlled fronts such as Radio Free Europe, Radio Liberation and the Assembly of Captive Nations. The existence of the National Committee for Free Europe later helped improve their situation, providing 'useful occupations' for the exiles, including 'preparing blueprints for their liberated countries'.[19]

Among those Intermarium countries which the exiles hoped to 'liberate' were Hungary, Romania and Czecho/Slovakia.

HUNGARY

Following the occupation of the country by the Germans in March 1944 and the collapse of the government led by Admiral Horthy, approaches were made in September to the West by representatives of Hungary – including one led by Archduke Otto von Habsburg and a secret mission to British headquarters in Italy – to save the country from Soviet occupation. It was not to be. The Germans seized Horthy and in October installed as prime minister the fanatical fascist Arrow Cross leader, Ferncz Szalasi, whose regime 'fed its warped and frustrated patriotism on bestial anti-semitism'. Szalasi was executed after the war. Among the million Hungarians who fled from the Soviets was a small but extremely active Arrow Cross element which maintained strong links between the exiled communities, revered executed war criminals as martyrs and supported former Nazis as reliable anti-communists. Elements of British and American Intelligence proceeded to scour the DP camps to recruit Arrow Cross members for operations into Hungary.[20]

Unlike in other eastern European states, in November 1945 a genuinely free election was held in Hungary which was won by the Smallholder's Party with 60 per cent of the vote. The Allied Control Commission under the control of the Soviet Union's representative would not, however, allow the party to take up more than 50 per cent of the seats in the cabinet. With a foothold in government, the communists then began a propaganda campaign to deni-grate the Smallholder's Party as 'a nest of reaction'. The main attack came in the early months of 1947 when the communist-dominated Interior Ministry security service (AVO – Allamvedelmi Osztaly) discovered a nationalist conspiracy by the 'Hungarian Unity Society' – 'alleged to have as its objective the re-establishment of the Horthy regime as it had existed before the German occupation of Budapest'. The ultra-rightist conspirators had, the AVO claimed, collected stores of arms and planned to set up a rival government-in-exile in the event of a communist-dominated government. The conspiracy provided the communists with an opportunity to strike at their opponents and pro-western elements in Hungary. Controlled by Gabor Peter, the AVO – housed in the old headquarters of the Arrow Cross secret police – began to investigate several parliamentary deputies, including Prime Minister Ferenc Nagy and President Tildy. While the investigations took place, Nagy was away on holiday in Switzerland and he resigned without returning to Budapest.[21]

With the deposing of the pro-western Nagy, the Soviet-aligned govern-ment launched a series of 'faked trials, political purges and an oppressive police rule'. Naïvely, members of the Smallholder's Party made contact with western intelligence agents, thus providing the communists with a propa-ganda coup that they exploited to the full. During the course of one day in 1947, over one hundred British agents disappeared from the streets, 'leaving MI6 bankrupted'. These were 'carriage-trade informers' on whom Claude Dansey's Z-network had relied since the thirties, and included 'many sophisti-cated Jewish businessmen'. Intermarium was one instrument used to create trouble for the communist regime and push the interests of the exiles. A resident MI6 officer in Vienna was responsible for recruiting refugees and Arrow Cross 'patriots' from the thousands who had sought sanctuary in the DP camps in Austria. Recruits were given money, accommodation and received basic training and instructions at an MI6 training camp at Furstenfeld.[22]

In the spring of 1947, Intermarium leader Vajta, whom Nagy had denounced as a 'Nazi', was arrested in Rome by the Allies after the Hungarian government accused him of being a 'war criminal'. He was, however, released after the intervention of the Vatican and senior Italian politicians. During September another attempt was made for his extradition, but after a meeting with British and French intelligence representatives, Vajta was able to leave with Vatican assistance for Spain with an American visa. In Madrid he set up a new organisation, the Continental Union, to attract émigré leaders away from the British-controlled Intermarium. Launching a vitriolic propaganda campaign, Vajta accused Intermarium of being 'penetrated by British free-masonry and Soviet agents'. His outburst and activities became an embarrass-ment to his new American sponsors, but despite evidence from the US European Command that identified him as a war criminal, Vajta was allowed in December to enter the United States.[23]

In September 1948, a British agent, Kavan Elliott, was arrested in Budapest by the AVO and, after interrogation, expelled from the country. Elliott had been employed before the war by MI(R). An explosives expert, he had been stationed in Sofia at the beginning of the war as a military attaché, later working for the Balkan Intelligence Service, and had developed a relationship with the charismatic leader of the Bulgarian Agrarian Party's left wing, Dr Georgi Dimitrov, who was funded with SOE gold to build a resistance network. Elliott later helped him escape to exile, firstly to Yugoslavia and then to the West. Dimitrov subsequently worked for an SOE radio station in Palestine for Free Independent Bulgaria, and was alleged to have been a conduit for funds to Serbia, which may have been true since both projects were run by SOE's resident Bohemian, Archie Lyall. The Communists later accused Dimitrov, who was close to the Serbs, of being a pawn of SOE, which had a grand strategy to bring Bulgaria and Serbia together in a new Balkan federation 'dominated by Britain'. After a period in Yugoslavia, Elliott was captured by the Germans and imprisoned as PoW in Colditz. Dr Dimitrov later became leader of the Bulgarians in exile in the United States and along with Nagy a leading member of the CIA-backed 'Green Internationale', the International Peasant Union.[24]

Immediately after the war, Elliott was posted to Germany with responsi-bilities to investigate the Nazi Labour Front (Deutsche Arbeitsfront) and stayed on as a member of a mysterious unit, Special Operation 3. He was a close friend and colleague of senior MI6 officer Archie Gibson, who was responsible for running agents behind the Iron Curtain. In late 1946 Elliott travelled to Budapest, ostensibly as a private citizen and businessman employed by Unilever. He was not an MI6 'Established Intelligence Officer' but was one of the Service's 'Unofficial Assets', and later admitted that he was 'running errands' for someone at the British legation. That was the Second Secretary, Harry Morris, a former City solicitor and banker with the National Provincial who had served with SOE in Gibraltar and then from 1943 with MI6 in Spain and Portugal.[25]

Acting as a courier for Elliott was Ted Sanders, employed by the Hungarian subsidiary of the US International Telephone and Telegraph Corporation. Born in St Petersburg, Sanders had served in the Intelligence Corps during the war and was later attached to the British Military Mission in Budapest. Also in contact with Elliott on his trips to Vienna was Antony Terry, a journalist with Ian Fleming's Mercury News Service, which organised the foreign correspondents for the *Sunday Times*. Terry, who worked part-time for the *Sunday Times*, was employed for a short while by MI6 and reported to the head of station in Vienna, George Young. Not used to trusting intelligence officers, Terry regarded Young as someone who would 'back one up to the hilt . . . and even though he stood up for his principles and had no illusions about the frailty of human nature, there was never the slipperiness one felt in the others'.[26]

In his biography *I Spy*, Geoffrey Elliott suggests that his father was collaborating on a Vatican project – i.e. Intermarium – for an anti-communist Balkan federation which was being pursued by the head of the Catholic Church in Hungary, Cardinal Mindszenty. He suggests that Elliott, who had moved from Budapest to live near the cardinal's residence at Esztergom, was responsible for 'orchestrating the lines of communication between Mindszenty and the Vatican'. A later show trial alleged that these lines ran from Mindszenty to the Budapest head of Actio Catholica, Miklos Boresztoczky, via 'an official trusted agent of the British power . . . well-versed in secret matters', to the 'correspondent' at the Vatican, Actio Catholica's director, Zsigmond Mikalovics. The plans included schemes to restore the Hungarian crown to the Habsburgs, while Actio Catholica, using funds raised in the United States, organised anti-communist propaganda in the West. Three more agents belonging to the Elliott network were hauled in by the AVO during December 1948.[27]

Inside Hungary resistance to the communists persisted. Eighteen-year-old Paul Gorka was studying architecture in Budapest and helping to guard Cardinal Mindszenty when, in the late forties, he helped organise the Catholic Resistance Movement, which linked up with MI6 in Vienna. The leader of his group was Bela Bajomi, a former naval officer who owned a textile factory in the capital. Bajomi managed to escape to Vienna underneath the carriage of one of the few trains leaving Hungary for Austria. Once in Vienna, Bajomi contacted MI6 and was asked to organise a group for resistance and intelligence-gathering activities.[28]

A number of patriotic young Hungarians were recruited for courier duties: 'Their task was to slip over the border into Hungary, contact reliable friends and organise resistance movements, sabotage and above all information gathering.' A typical low-level agent, Gorka collected information on heavy industry, mining and transport for his MI6 contact in Vienna, 'Mr Thompson'. He carefully noted the types of Russian vehicles, armour and tanks and their number plates which enabled MI6 to compile a breakdown of the Russian units stationed in Hungary or in transit through the country. The group also provided details on the construction of the largest Russian military airport in eastern Europe.

Gorka claims that the group's most important intelligence-gathering coup was sight of Russian documents that detailed contingency plans for the complete takeover of the country and government by their Hungarian puppets in the event of the further deterioration of the situation in Yugoslavia. Interestingly, Gorka reveals that once relations between Stalin and Tito had been settled to the satisfaction of the West, MI6 began using Yugoslavia as a launching pad for sending couriers and agents into Hungary. Yugoslav intelligence officers worked hand in glove with their MI6 counterparts. One Hungarian agent told Gorka about a meeting in Belgrade for an infiltration mission with a wartime SOE officer who had undertaken undercover operations into German-occupied Serbia.[29]

In addition to military information, Gorka recalled that his network was asked to provide MI6 with 'low-grade information of little or no real use . . . for example, the positions of bus terminals, vehicle registration numbers, the production of milk and butter'. The requests often baffled the group, which saw no relevance to their resistance struggle. The group put their information on 'white-carbon paper, which we used by writing between innocent sounding lines, held it up to the light of a window, and then posted it to Vienna to a Herr Johann Voessen' – an MI6 safe house. Unfortunately, the method was unsophisticated and the couriers' letters were often intercepted: 'As so often happened many were caught at the border, often with the secret police lying in wait.' In 1949, Vladimir Lieszkovszky, a former air force cadet and later student of aero mechanics, was arrested and sentenced to ten years for spying on behalf of British Intelligence. Another MI6 agent and courier, Nandi Fain – a former Hungarian Army officer who had escaped to the West in 1948 – was arrested during the summer of 1950 and received a life sentence.[30]

Bajomi was 'kidnapped' by Hungarian agents in Vienna and executed in April 1951. Soon after, Paul Gorka was arrested, tortured and imprisoned for life. He was eventually freed in October 1956 during the 'Hungarian Uprising' through the efforts of the Hungarian Freedom Fighters (HFF). He subsequently escaped to Britain and became deputy leader of the HFF movement. With good reason, Gorka remained bitter about his betrayal and the way MI6 had used the resistance, concluding that after so many security failures 'the spymasters were more agent provocateurs than secret intelligence agents'. Many of the anti-communist centres on the Austrian side were thoroughly penetrated by Soviet and Hungarian agents. The operational failures were eventually listed in a communist-produced series of White, Blue and Grey propaganda books which detailed the trials of Hungarian 'spies' who worked for western intelligence agencies.[31]

In late November 1949, a month after the trial and execution of a number of senior communist officials accused of working for British and American Intelligence, the Hungarian secret police arrested Edgar Sanders. Despite British Foreign Office and US State Department protests, he was sentenced to thirteen months' imprisonment. In December the Hungarian government nationalised all major industries and foreign-owned plant, including IT&T. There followed a number of trials directed against 'counter-revolutionary traitors and foreign agents', a number of whom were undoubtedly working for MI6.[32]

Fourteen members of the Anti-Bolshevik Guard were arrested and imprisoned in 1950. Led by General Ferenc Farkas, a former Hungarian intelligence officer who commanded Szalasi's army against the Russians, the MHBK was one of the main resistance organisers in the West working with MI6. It was in contact with 'cells' in Hungary through the courier Imre Horvath, a former army officer, who had recruited agents among members of the military police. But it, too, collapsed. In the period from 1948 to 1952 hundreds were arrested and imprisoned, while over forty-five people were executed by the Soviets for alleged spying activities.[33]

Exiles such as Paul Gorka blamed Kim Philby for the betrayal. While it was true that, as head of Section IX, Philby certainly had knowledge of the early recruitment of Hungarian exiles via Intermarium and, as station head in Washington, had overseen the transfer of former Arrow Cross assets to Canada and Australia, by the time of the major arrests he was out of the intelligence loop. The security lapses were more likely the result of low-level infiltration of the numerous and often badly organised anti-communist groups – a number of which were secret police fronts instigated by Soviet agents.

ROMANIA

During the Second World War, Romania was run by an authoritarian regime – predominantly Iron Guardist in character – which had been set up in September 1940 under the leadership of the non-Guardist and pro-British General Ion Antonescu. He had decreed that 'if Germany flourished under a Führer and Italy under a duce, then Romania should recognise him as the "Conductor"'. The Iron Guard was built around the idol worship of Captain Cornlieu Codreanu of the Legion of St Michael, who had dedicated himself to the task of 'purging Rumania of Jews, foreigners, communists and Freemasons'. Under the leadership of a known assassin and terrorist, Horia Sima, the Guard, with their distinctive green shirts and silver crucifixes, practised a unique brand of nationalist Catholicism – 'a cult of death'.[34]

The Germans used the Iron Guard as a means of controlling Romania and placed several of its officials in key government posts. Subsequent internal conflict between Antonescu and Sima led in January 1941 to the Guardists attempting to seize power. In the 'bestial pogroms' that followed, Guardists went on the rampage, killing communists, liberals and Jews. A number were skewered on meat hooks with their throats slit, others were skinned alive, while some were forced to kneel and were beheaded. Even their German sponsors were appalled, and the rebellion was eventually put down by the SS. The leaders were sent to Germany but were only put under 'protective custody' as 'Hitler kept them as a threat to be used against Antonescu's government if he should contemplate leaving the Axis'. In August 1944, when pro-British assets and the young King Michael organised a coup that was intended to oversee a return to democracy, the Nazis resurrected the Iron Guard as a 'National Government'. Before the Guardist leaders could be infiltrated across the border from Vienna, however, the Russian Army swept into the country and they were forced to flee to safety.[35]

One observer who monitored the arrival of the communists, who had been guests of Stalin in Moscow, blamed the resultant political upheaval in Bucharest on the British and American intelligence services, which continued to support and encourage the old conservative parties – the National Liberal and Peasant Parties – 'in their fight against the leftists'. Embarrassed by the failure of the left to garner widespread support among the population, the Soviets were 'forced to intervene', safe in the knowledge that with the British fighting the communists in Greece, the Allies would have no grounds on which to protest.[36]

Horia Sima and his Guardists had been able to slip away in the postwar chaos of Europe and resume their political activities. Sima (aka 'Civat') survived in an Italian DP camp where he avoided detection until October 1945, when the Iron Guard 'came out of hiding'. He was surprised to discover that his colleagues had not perished but 'had regrouped and organised committees to help the refugees in all the occupied zones'. This required protection and finance, which was secured from British, French and American intelligence agencies, desperate to discover what was happening in the newly occupied territories in central and eastern Europe. French Intelligence had placed a priest in the British Zone in Germany with the specific task of co-ordinating Iron Guard recruitment. Similarly, the British used former Nazi intelligence and SS officers, who had had contact with the Guard during the war, to earmark potential recruits in the camps. Taking on yet another identity, Sima made his way to France before finally flying to Madrid, where he established an Iron Guard headquarters. As other Guardists left the DP camps, they were helped to emigrate to Canada and the United States under the aegis of the Romanian Orthodox Church and the sponsorship of British Intelligence.[37]

Within a short space of time, Stalin's agents returned to the country to put in place the foundations for one of the more repressive regimes in eastern Europe. All of which was monitored by Leslie Nicholson, who, after a few months studying the new communist threat, was posted to Bucharest in late 1945 to set up an MI6 station. Nicholson had to create new intelligence networks after Colonel Archie Gibson had been forced to abandon a number of Polish intelligence agents in Bucharest as the NKVD closed in on his activities. The tactics of the communists under the leadership of Gheorghi-Dej, who had returned from Moscow with Stalin's approval to establish a pro-Soviet regime, were designed to hinder the new government led by the National Peasant Party. It found that its actions were severely hampered by organised bands, a number of which included Iron Guardists who had changed political allegiance to the communists. Insidiously, the communists increased their power through the internal security ministry, forcing the government to stage a series of 'show trials' which played on claims of foreign intervention and backing for anti-state forces.[38]

In May 1946 the 'Great National Betrayal Trial' opened in Bucharest with Ion Antonescu and his associates accused of treason and war crimes. Antonescu was subsequently shot, but a number of Guardists who had also been convicted were spared as the Soviet Ministry of State Security (MGB) had call on their security expertise. In March 1947 there was a bungled coup attempt organised by 'a still-active splinter' of the US Office of Strategic Services (OSS). According to Christopher Simpson, 'it was undertaken without the knowledge of the State Department which was then in negotiation over US investments in the Ploesti oil fields'. British Intelligence, which had yet to establish a significant intelligence presence, was asked to help, but Foreign Office policy deemed that it would be disastrous if genuine evidence of Anglo-American interference fell into communist hands. In July a number of pro-British politicians who had helped with the coup in 1944 were arrested and charged with plotting to overthrow the government. Others in exile, such as former minister and leading Intermarium figure Grigore Gafencu, were sentenced *in absentia*. Clever deployment of *agents provocateurs* enabled the authorities to arrest leaders of the National Peasant Party, including leader Ion Mihahlache, accused of forming a 'military group', who were attempting to flee the country: 'There is evidence that a few supporters of the party had talked rashly about armed resistance to communism with American agents. Although the leaders were not directly implicated, plans had been made to bring them out of Romania by air.' The conspirators were rounded up by Romanian security police, tried in November, and sentenced to solitary confinement for life. The trial, which came seven weeks after the execution in Sofia of the Bulgarian peasant leader Nikola Petkov, 'shocked the non-communist world which appeared powerless to do anything'.[39]

Once in power, the communists installed a well-developed political terror machine, the General Directorate of People's Security, the Securitate. With over five thousand officers, it relied on an extensive network of informers and scores of Soviet advisers. It was also a crucible of paranoia and conspiracy thinking. Communist leader Gheorghi-Dej immediately instigated a purge of the government.

In early 1948, Minister of Justice Lucretiu Patrascanu was targeted by the Soviet advisers, who claimed that he was protecting opposition National Peasant Party leaders and was thus sabotaging the country's 'march towards Communism'. At the end of April, Patrascanu was detained on Gheorghi-Dej's orders and was never seen again in public. It was later revealed that he had been taken to Securitate headquarters where he was interrogated for over a year about his alleged links with 'the British Secret Intelligence Service'. Patrascanu eventually escaped the interrogators by committing suicide, slashing his wrists with a razor blade. It was, however, a long and painful process. 'In order to prevent detection of the source of the razor blade Patrascanu broke it into small pieces and then swallowed it.' This did not end the investigation. Before he died, security officers fed him laxatives, but 'although they managed to piece together the object the gastric juices had removed any traces of fingerprints'. The Securitate never did find any evidence of a link to MI6.[40]

CZECHO/SLOVAKIA

During the thirties, the Slovak People's Party, which had evolved under the leadership of Monsignor Andrej Hlinka, had adopted an increasingly extreme pro-fascist programme. It centred on Slovak independence and the dismemberment of the Czechoslovak state, which had only been created at the end of the First World War. Hlinka died in September 1938 and was replaced by another Catholic cleric, Monsignor Jozef Tiso. In the wake of the Munich crisis, an 'independent' Slovakia, a Nazi satellite, was created in March 1939 under Tiso, who suppressed all political parties other than the Slovak National Front. Tiso's grip on the country depended on the specially recruited paramilitary organisation, the 'Hlinka Guard'. It had been formed out of the nationalist's most radical wing by Foreign Minister Dr Ferdinand Durcansky, whose stormtroopers put into practice the September 1941 anti-Jewish laws.[41]

Following the end of the war, Durcansky was condemned *in absentia* by the democratic Czechoslovakian government as a war criminal responsible for destruction of the Slovak Jews. An Intermarium fugitive, he was listed in 1946 by the United Nations as a Category A war criminal, and in the following year was 'condemned to death by the Slovak National Council'.

In exile, with help from the Vatican and British Intelligence, Durcansky continued to plot for Slovak independence through his anti-communist Slovak Liberation Movement. In June 1947 the *New York Times* reported that he was in Italy, 'where he broadcasts daily to Slovakia and is in constant touch with the underground'. The Czech government announced that leaflets proclaiming that a new government would soon seize power in Slovakia with Durcansky as premier were being distributed throughout the country.[42]

The contact between the underground in Slovakia and émigré centres in Vienna and Paris was 'Stefan Ilok', who had links to French, British and later American intelligence agencies. In 1944 Ilok began working with a branch of the French resistance known as Arc-en-Ciel or Rainbow,* protecting French officers who had escaped from German camps by supplying them with false identity papers. Leaving Slovakia with diplomatic status, Ilok headed for Italy to negotiate with the Americans for supplies for the insurgents. His group, however, was captured and imprisoned in the Mauthausen concentration camp in Austria. Liberated by Patton's Third Army, he made his way back to Slovakia and renewed contact with the guerrillas fighting the communists. Ilok eventually returned to Vienna 'to alert and arouse the West to support Slovakia's cause, to raise money for the underground and to serve as a liaison between the underground and the free world'. Much of the work was taken up with supplying the intelligence services with 'information on Soviet troop movements in Austria and in the East European satellites'.[43]

In September 1947, a Czech commission headed by General Ferjencik announced that they had uncovered a 'massive conspiracy' to overthrow the government. Durcansky's network had been thoroughly infiltrated and numerous documents were produced linking scores of Slovak politicians to it. The subsequent anti-fascist purge, which spread into every corner of the government, was followed by a communist counter-coup. It occurred so quickly that the British consul wondered if Durcansky had not staged the whole affair:

> Durcansky's subversive organisation . . . appears undoubtedly to exist, though it does have a curious aspect. The evidence collected is so complete and well-documented that it is difficult to believe in the genuineness of the movement, and Dr Frastachy believes that the participants were inveigled into it by Agents Provocateurs . . . The whole thing, I was told, smacked of elaborate stage management: But it seems to have been effective, whether or not that was its purpose, in giving a handle to the instigation of the purge.[44]

---

* These escape-and-evasion groups would later become the foundation of the French stay-behind network known as Glaive.

With the spotlight on his activities, Europe was no longer considered safe for Durcansky – by now Intermarium president – and he was sent down a ratline to exile in Argentina. MI6, in the shape of Kim Philby, had attempted to transfer Durcansky and their Slovak assets to the Americans, but they were wary of recruiting such an open Nazi collaborator. In September 1950, the CIA sent a negative report on Durcansky to the US immigration authorities, which forced the British to find him a new home. Even though the British were obliged to admit that they knew that Durcansky was a war criminal, in December MI6 helped him leave Argentina via London for Canada using a UK visa. Although officially listed as living in Ottawa, Durcansky subsequently 'spent most of his time in London and Germany' working for the MI6-sponsored ABN.[45]

Driven out of Czechoslovakia by the communist takeover in 1948, Josef Josten set up the Free Czech Information news agency in London with help from MI6 and the Foreign Office's Information Research Department. Josten had served with the Allies in the Czechoslovak Brigade on the western front, and from June 1943 was employed editing texts for the BBC in London on behalf of a military propaganda section. At the end of the war, he was posted by SHAEF to Radio Luxemburg before returning to Prague and the Ministry of Foreign Affairs. Dismissed when a communist 'Action Committee' took over the ministry, Josten was forced to flee with his wife to the West, eventually reaching the US CIC headquarters at Camp King in Germany, where other Czech politicians were installed.[46]

Another Czech forced to flee from the communists was army general staff officer Colonel Prochazka, who helped create in London the Czech Intelligence Office (CIO), staffed with former colleagues. Financed and supported by MI6, it established offices in Frankfurt, Munich, Zurich, Berlin and Vienna. Making contact with the Czech underground, the CIO provided a highly successful courier service for its intelligence operatives, who had allegedly managed to penetrate the Communist Party and government departments. In Prague, Dr Potocek, a director of the First Czechoslovak Insurance Company, ran a network of twenty paid and 'unwitting' agents. The network was eventually exposed in the spring of 1956 when an informant passed to the military attaché at the Czech embassy in London copies of reports which Potocek had passed to MI6. They included detailed information on new Soviet tanks and poison gas being manufactured for the Warsaw Pact armies. Code-named 'Light', the informant, Charles Zbytek, had served in England during the war with the Free Czech Army and had joined Col. Prochazka's staff as a poorly paid clerk.[47]

Light's information enabled the Czech security service to close down 'a lethal network within Czechoslovakia, destroy a Czech resistance movement and effectively sabotage an anti-Czech organisation located in neighbouring countries, such as West Germany'. With the enthusiastic help of the KGB, they also successfully managed to place their agents within the British spy net. It soon became apparent that the CIO's operations were failures, and in 1958 MI6 decided to withdraw financial co-operation. The CIA's East European desk was informed that the network had been compromised and, during the following year, a team of MI6 officers toured NATO countries warning their security services that 'the Czechoslovak service was so effective that at least as much attention should be given to it as was being given to the KGB'.[48]

CHAPTER 12

THE PROMETHEAN LEAGUE

In the aftermath of the Bolshevik revolution, a number of 'governments-in-exile' and 'National Committees', under the Ukrainian leadership of Dr Roma Smal-Stocky, a minister of the exiled Ukrainian Democratic Republic, organised a common front, the Promethean League of the Nations subjugated by Moscow (soon abbreviated to the Promethean League). It represented 'all the minority nationalities of the former Russian empire' – Azerbaijan, Georgia, the Don and Kuban Cossacks, North Causcasia, Yukestan, Idel-Ural, Ukraine, Crimea, Ingria, Karelia and the Komi (Zyryan) Region. Initially, the Armenians were not represented as enmity existed between them and the Georgians, whom they feared would dominate an independent Caucasus.[1]

The League was primarily an organisation for Ukrainian and Georgian aspirations. After the First World War, with eastern Ukraine controlled by the Soviet Union and the western areas part of Poland, the main centres of Ukrainian emigration were established in Warsaw and Paris, the latter becoming headquarters for the League and the State Centre of the Ukrainian Democratic Republic. Under the leadership of the 'heroic' figure of Ataman Simon Petlura, the State Centre was styled as a Ukrainian government-in-exile and often acted within the framework of the Promethean League. The State Centre and the Prometheans, who were generally known as 'Petlurans', denounced 'the absence of real autonomy in the Soviet Union and stand ultimately for a "federal state of nationalities"'. They, therefore, did not support the extreme Ukrainian nationalists known as the 'integralists'.[2]

A self-acknowledged 'conspiring underground movement', in 1925 the League had begun organising in clandestine fashion in Bucharest, Istanbul, Helsinki, Prague and Paris, where it came into contact with leading figures in MI6, such as Wilfred 'Biffy' Dunderdale and Stewart Menzies, who began to administer covert support and finance. Under the presidency of Smal-Stocky it 'planned common action for the liberation of all peoples concerned'. From the early thirties onwards, the Prometheans also had the support of the Polish government and the French secret service in 'a Franco-Polish effort to instigate an anti-communist revolution in Belorussia and Ukraine'. The League 'played a large part in Polish aspirations for the development of a bloc of states in Eastern Europe, stretching from Finland to the Caucasus, in which Poland could become a true great power by exercising her "natural" position of leadership'. According to Soviet specialist John A. Armstrong, the Ukrainian leaders of the Promethean League, who were secretly anti-Polish, were, 'of course, aware of the Polish aims, but in their overwhelming desire for liberation of their peoples from the Communist yoke they accepted the assistance of the Warsaw government'.[3]

The League developed rapidly, especially in Czechoslovakia, where Thomas Masaryk showed great sympathy for the non-Russian nations, as did Poland, which gave permission in 1936 for three hundred officers of the Polish Army to attend a Promethean Congress in Warsaw. This fed the paranoia of Stalin, who considered the Polish and Czech intelligence services to be fellow-conspirators with MI6. The Promethean concept of a dynamic revolution inside the Soviet Union drew inspiration from Count Coudenhove-Kalergi's Pan-European Union. According to one of its leading Ukrainian figures, the First World War Polish hero General Pavlo Shandruk: 'the Polish, Baltic, Turkic and Mongolian revolutionaries sympathised with these ideas as did many anti-communists in the West'. There was contact between Smal-Stocky and Coudenhove-Kalergi but this did not progress very far as the count 'did not take into consideration Eastern Europe in his plans'. France was supportive but 'Poland was the key in this new European constellation'. In the interests of the Pan-European Union, the Ukrainian government-in-exile ordered its contract officers in the Polish Army to defend the Polish republic. However, this was not always successful.[4]

British intelligence officer John H. Watson made a tour of the Polish Ukraine during the summer of 1939 and reported to the Foreign Office that 'the Poles also sometimes realise that the "Promethean policy" of setting up a Ukraine State under Polish protection would have much more chance of successful realisation if Poland could count on the loyalty of her own Ukrainian minority and if the talent which is now wasting itself in hopeless opposition could be trained into an efficient civil and military cadre, loyal to Poland and capable of filling key positions in the Russian Ukraine'. The problem, as the Foreign Office realised, was that the majority of the Promethean-backed Ukrainian Committee in Paris had emigrated from 'Greater Ukraine' many years before and, it was felt, had 'very little connection with any part of Ukraine at all'. Despite this perceived weakness, the League was a major target for Stalin's security services, and in Poland was heavily infiltrated by the People's Commissariat for Internal Affairs (NKVD). As evidence of the effectiveness of the League's propaganda campaigns, its leader, Smal-Stocky, claimed that what lay behind the 1938 Moscow trials of Bukharin and other senior communist officials was an attack on the Promethean ideology. Primarily from the non-Russian regions, the accused had been charged with 'dismembering the USSR' into the constituent nationalist parts, and of having contacts with the intelligence services of foreign states, primarily the British, though the Germans were regarded with increasing respect.[5]

Covert links between eastern European nationalists such as the League and the Wehrmacht, the Abwehr and the Nazi Party had begun in the late twenties. Members of German Military Intelligence, which developed close ties with dissident nationalists in Poland and the USSR, had hoped to make use of these groups in any struggle with the Soviet Union. Despite the fact that during the thirties the Promethean League had been attacked by some German officials as a 'Polish invention', Admiral Canaris's Abwehr took over much of the network. Gradually, the thin veneer of democratic ideals to which the League paid lip-service was replaced by a more authoritarian stance which found favour with the Nazis. The principal contact with the League and other émigré groups was through Alfred Rosenberg's Ministry for the Occupied Eastern Territories, Ostministerium (OMi), which from 1943 onwards had a substantial input from the SS.[6]

In the late thirties, a small War Office section, GS(R) (General Staff (Research), made contact with the Promethean League. In the expectation of war with Germany, Colin Gubbins undertook two secret air trips to the Continent, first to the Danube and then to the Baltic, where he looked into the possibility of organising networks of anti-Nazi guerrillas. Returning in the spring of 1939, Gubbins contacted the Warsaw branch of the League as a member of an official British Military Mission to Poland. Responsible for producing papers on guerrilla warfare under the auspices of MI6's Section D, which was beginning to plan sabotage and subversive action against Nazis, Gubbins's official task was to set up an MI(R) unit in Poland which would organise stay-behind networks. He also took the opportunity to make contact with senior Polish army officer Pavlo Shandruk and the Polish liaison to the Promethean League. Gubbins then secretly visited Belgrade, which was the centre of Section D's Balkan operations and home to many White Russians, including a large contingent of the League's adherents. With the announcement of the Nazi–Soviet Non-Aggression Pact on 23 August 1939, the use of the exile groups became an even more attractive proposition.[7]

Foreign Office co-ordinator of the MI6 and Military Intelligence-backed 'subversive action' by the exiles was Fitzroy Maclean, who had travelled extensively in the Caucasus. On the Russian desk of the Northern Department, Maclean was seen as 'the most hawkish of hawks' and had a growing reputation as a Soviet specialist. As a junior Foreign Office diplomat during the mid-thirties, Maclean had served in the Paris embassy, where he became a close friend of the MI6 head of station, Wilfred Dunderdale, who had served in the Black Sea area during the First World War. Most of Dunderdale's contacts were in the White Russian exile community, and one of his tasks was to support the many anti-communist organisations that had the backing of MI6. Maclean was introduced to these émigré circles by Dunderdale. Despite their close and enduring friendship, and the fact that he was 'quite a friend' of Stewart Menzies, Maclean always denied that he was working for MI6. While there was never any formal link, and he was broadly sceptical of espionage carried out by agents, he had, while on a trip to the Soviet Union before the war, used the opportunity to take photographs which were duly passed on to the Service. According to another friend, Douglas Dodds-Parker, Maclean was a 'doer' and remained in touch with MI6 throughout his career.[8]

The signing of the Non-Aggression Pact came as a severe shock to Britain. Maclean was subsequently asked to draw up a document detailing ways of dismembering the Soviet Union and making trouble with the Russians 'by stirring up the minorities'. In October, Maclean produced a 'Memorandum Respecting the Soviet Threat to British Interests in the Middle East', which suggested that Muslim hostility to the Russians could be exploited by British Military Intelligence agents, creating havoc in Transcaucasus and the Central Asian republics of Armenia, Azerbaijan, Kazakhstan, Uzbekistan and Tajikistan, which were occupied by the Russians. 'Appeal would have to be made to such religious feelings as still exist amongst the population, to any nationalist or any anti-Russian feelings they may have, and to the bitter hatred which the present regime is bound to have engendered in many classes of the population.' Maclean recommended that 'use could be made of the natives of the frontier regions of Afghanistan and Iran, who are practically indistinguishable from the corresponding tribes on the Soviet side of the frontier'. These could 'establish contact with disaffected elements in the Soviet Union itself, and raise the standard of revolt in as large an area as possible'. He suggested that there was a need for a forward base from which to send agents across the frontier into the Soviet Union. The likely countries were Afghanistan, Turkey and Iran, although he thought that the most promising was Sinkiang, in China. He urged that 'preparatory measures' should be taken without delay in setting up 'an organisation to foment trouble within Soviet-occupied territory'.[9]

The project centred on the oil wells of the Baku, which were of strategic importance. The British business journal *The Near East* reported that 'Baku is greater than any other oil city in the world. If oil is king, Baku is its throne!' A Caucasian uprising in 1924 was, the *New York Times* reported, 'being financed and directed from Paris' by 'powerful financiers' and 'former proprietors of the Baku oil wells'. Already, by the winter of 1938, British agents were busy in the Caucasus region 'with a view to establishing . . . a bastion for the protection of British oil interests and against potential growth in Germany's appetite to infiltrate India in the event Germany succeeded in marching into Ukraine'. According to the American State Department, MI6 'is not blind to the reported ambitions of the Nazi extremists to reach out eventually for the Caucasus and neighbouring oil fields'.[10]

The planning was entrusted to a small circle of hardline anti-communist/ Soviet intelligence officers, many of them born in the Soviet Union, who were to play a key role in the postwar exile operations. Indeed, the project was to be both a forerunner and a blueprint for later operations. Its MI6 liaison officer was Charles 'Dick' Ellis, who was able to draw on his own experience and knowledge of the exile movements and the Baku region. Born in Sydney, Australia, twenty-four-year-old Ellis fought immediately after the First World War in the Baku on the Caspian Sea's western shore alongside the British Military Mission under Major-General W. Malleson. After completing language studies at Oxford and the Sorbonne, Ellis joined the Foreign Office as a diplomat before transferring to MI6 in 1924. He was then posted as a Passport Control officer to Berlin and finally to Paris, where he operated under journalist cover within the large White Russian community. During the thirties, working alongside Dunderdale, Ellis was Menzies's main representative with the anti-communist groups and the resident expert on what Stalin called 'the nationalities question – the euphemism for unrest among non-Russians making up half the population of the USSR'.[11]

In Paris, Ellis married the sister of a White Russian, Alexander Zilenski; his brother-in-law became one of his most valuable sources. Through him, Ellis made contact with another White Russian, Waldemar von Petrov, who, in turn, was friendly with one of the best-known of the exile leaders, Prince Anton Vasilevich Turkul, who was to become one of Ellis's key agents. Turkul had been a general in the Tsar's army, and after the 1917 revolution joined the counter-revolutionaries in the White Army. Turkul and other White Russian officers were eventually evacuated from Gallipoli to Paris by the sympathetic French government which, along with the British, had financed much of the anti-Bolshevik effort. In Paris, Turkul worked with the White Russian Armed Services Union (ROVS), which supervised a secret sabotage and terrorist group – the Russian Federation of ex-Combatants – run by General Alexander Kutepov, a long-standing MI6 agent who also established a counter-intelligence service – the Inner Line. Both were supported and helped financially by Menzies. One of MI6's leading agents inside the Inner Line during the twenties was Claudius Voss, Turkul's superior in the Balkan section of ROVS. Voss and Turkul went on to help create the anti-communist but pro-Russian National Labour Council (NTS), which was supported by MI6.[12]

From this complex web of ties which reached into German, French and, seemingly, Russian intelligence services, Ellis was able to forward to London a mass of information. Unfortunately, headquarters was to discover that much of it was faked, produced by the many exile 'paper mills' that proliferated in Paris. The majority of these organisations were riddled with double agents working for either the Germans or the Russians, or had been discredited by the numerous scandals that surrounded the émigré community. Inevitably, reliance on the émigrés as a source was to lead Ellis into a world of double-dealing and blackmail.

In 1940, the Security Service's expert on Soviet espionage, Jane Sissmore Archer, received information from the Soviet defector Walter Krivitsky to the effect that Soviet Military Intelligence (GRU) had recruited a pre-war Abwehr agent, Waldemar von Petrov. When an Abwehr officer was interrogated after the war, he confirmed that von Petrov had claimed to have had an excellent source of high-grade intelligence inside MI6. He said that he had worked through an intermediary called 'Zilenski', whose source, 'Captain Ellis', had supplied documents revealing MI6's 'order of battle' and information about specific secret operations, including the tapping of the telephone of the German ambassador in London, von Ribbentrop. Disturbed by the allegations, MI5 sought permission to interrogate Ellis, but MI6 refused, contemptuously dismissing the allegations by suggesting that the German officer had faked the evidence. Years later, however, Ellis was to admit to the substance of the charges, though he denied being recruited as a German agent. He had handed over detailed organisational charts to the Germans and acknowledged that he had been a translator of decrypts from the embassy tapping operation. He excused his behaviour by claiming he had run into money difficulties because of the small salary he received from MI6. He had been forced to borrow money from his brother-in-law, who had used the opportunity to extract information from him which he then sold to the Germans. Ellis came to look on the White Russians as 'a double-crossing lot of bastards who would sell intelligence to whoever would pay them'. Which, of course, was entirely true.[13]

A number of Ellis's wartime colleagues refused to accept his confession, though Montgomery Hyde, who had been one of them, later acknowledged the evidence. Ellis was clearly not liked by some colleagues – 'a horrible little man' – and a number of attempts were later made by the 'young Turks' to publicise his treachery. Chapman Pincher, whose information 'was supplied by an MI5 officer' – clearly Peter Wright – and confirmed by MI6 officers Nicholas Elliott and Christopher Phillpotts, went so far as to suggest that, besides being a German agent, 'there are strong, but unproven, suspicions that Ellis was also a mercenary spy for the Soviets'. Which roughly translates as – there was not a shred of real evidence.[14]

Bearing in mind the Service's initial support of Ellis and the dismissal of the charges, there is a suspicion that he was later made a scapegoat in order to hide a more disturbing fact, namely that he had been trading information with the Germans on the orders of Menzies. MI6 was at its core an anti-Bolshevik organisation; indeed, 'Quex' Sinclair was known as 'a terrific anti-Bolshevik', and its late entry into gathering intelligence on Nazi Germany was half-hearted at best. This may be partially explained by Sinclair's pro-appeasement stance and the large number of MI6-linked people in appease-ment circles. Until the end of 1938, MI6 believed that Hitler's ambitions lay in the East, and that he was 'devoting special attention to the eastward drive, to securing control of the exploitable riches of the south, and possibly more, of Russia'. Such intelligence was met with indifference by Prime Minister Neville Chamberlain, who told the Cabinet that a Russo-German conflict over Ukraine was no concern of Britain.[15]

Some of the intelligence that reached the Cabinet may have originated with Ellis, who knew that Admiral Wilhelm Canaris, chief of the Abwehr, had secret plans to use the White Russians in operations in Ukraine and southern Russia. Canaris was co-operating with many of the same organisa-tions as those sponsored by the British, and there is evidence that on occasion they worked in concert. The Abwehr had apparently collaborated with the British in central Europe and the Balkans in counter-intelligence operations against 'communist agents who had begun to flood into Western Europe to provoke revolutions in support of the Kremlin'. Anthony Cave Brown's suggestion that Canaris's eventual takeover of the émigré organisations was undertaken with MI6's knowledge and encouragement is probably correct. In the meantime, MI6 was still engaged in plans to thwart Soviet expansionist claims and to deny the Germans access to oil for its war machine.[16]

British secret service officials and the chiefs of staff, in co-operation with their French counterparts, quickly began to prepare plans to damage the German–Soviet Pact by creating subversion in Russia in order to cut off the supplies of strategically important goods such as oil. An early December report for the chiefs on 'The vulnerability of Russian oil supplies' was submit-ted to the War Cabinet. At this stage, the Cabinet would only sanction contin-gency planning because ministers feared driving the Soviets, once and for all, into the German camp. There was also a fear of retaliation against Allied oil interests in Persia and Iraq. Initially it seems that it was the French who led the way, organising – on 20 January 1940 – an Anglo-French conference which was held in Beirut on the subject of stopping Germany gaining oil from the Caucasus.

Three weeks later, the Cabinet asked the chiefs to revise their plans. On 8 March, they submitted a revised study, 'Military Implications of Hostilities with Russia in 1940′, which outlined methods by which the Allies could strike at the Baku oilfields. It suggested that if the oilfields were knocked out then 90 per cent of the resources would be unavailable to Stalin's increasingly oil-thirsty customer, Nazi Germany. The plan envisaged RAF bombers taking out the oilfields in an operation which, French Intelligence suggested, would leave the Baku in a sheet of flames, with the refineries possibly out of action for years. In mid-March, MI6 entrusted its expert on aerial photography, Wing Commander F. Sidney Cotton, with organising air reconnaissance of the area by the clandestine Photographic Development Unit. Simultaneously, sixty thousand French troops stationed in the Middle East, under the command of General Maxime Weygrand, were earmarked to venture into Soviet territory in Transcaucasia. In the final part of the project, British Intelligence would use the exile groups to foment unrest in the Caucasus and Soviet Central Asia. On 17 April, General Weygrand telegraphed headquarters that preparations for bombing the oilfields were well advanced.[17]

The Maclean memorandum assumed that the Russians might use the opportunity of war to undermine the British sphere of influence in the East by invading Afghanistan and Iran. In recognition of this possibility, the chiefs and General Wavell asked MI(R), which until that point had been 'a centre of repressed frustration', to form a unit in Cairo – 'to be ready to take action against any Russian incursion from Transcaucasia across Iran towards India'. The officer in charge was Colonel Adrian Simpson, a former deputy managing director of Marconi who, during the First World War, had been ADC to the Grand Duke Nicholas in the Russian Army's Caucasus 'Savage Division'. Simpson's deputy was Douglas Roberts, a specialist on Russia's southern flank and an influential member of MI(R)'s inner Special Operational Planning and Action Group – forerunner of MI6's postwar Special Operations and Political Action Branch. Roberts was a leading figure in MI6 in the late forties. Born in the Caucasus at the turn of the century, the son of the British consul in Odessa, he had served for a period as ADC to General Peter Wrangel in the White Russian Army campaign against the Bolsheviks. During the twenties, he worked in the timber trade in Finland and Russia, where he doubled as an 'illegal' intelligence asset. Roberts was subsequently posted as a Defence Security Officer (MI5) to Istanbul, which remained for many years the centre of British Intelligence operations into the Soviet Union.[18]

Back at the Foreign Office, following the sudden collapse of the Polish forces, Fitzroy Maclean contacted the MI6-backed Promethean League. On the outbreak of war, the Paris branch had issued a manifesto which declared a pro-Allied stance and began to organise an all-Ukrainian leading political centre in the struggle against Germany and Russia. Gubbins, meanwhile, had been put in command of the Number 4 (Polish-Czech) Military Mission in Paris. The Poles had the best special services in Europe, and Gubbins learned from Maclean that MI6 was still financing the Prometheans, who were spreading ideas of 'subversion and sabotage among the oppressed peoples of the Caucasus and Soviet Central Asia'. Serious consideration was given to the establishment of an independent Ukrainian state in the Polish Ukraine area through 'determined attempts' at propaganda and subversion. With the co-operation of the Paris branch, Gubbins also began to recruit a Ukrainian legion to aid Finland.[19]

In February 1940, a Russian-speaking MI(R) officer, Captain Tamplin, and his colleague, Major Gatehouse, had travelled to Finland to interview Soviet PoWs who had been captured following the brutal Finnish-Russo 'Winter War', which had resulted in the deaths of hundreds of thousands of soldiers. Their orders were to assess the possibility of using the former Red Army soldiers in a planned Franco-British operation against the Soviet Union. A banker by profession, Guy Tamplin was an ideal choice for the operation. After service in the First World War on the Lockhart Mission in Russia, he lived for a long period in Riga, capital of Estonia, becoming a specialist on the Baltic states and on eastern Europe. On the basis of extensive interrogations, the two MI(R) officers concluded that the PoWs were so traumatised by their experience as Soviet citizens that there was little possibility of them making decent recruits. Most were barely literate, and years of NKVD-inspired propaganda and sheer terror had left them totally ignorant of the outside world. Tamplin and Gatehouse believed that the likelihood of using these prisoners as a military counter-revolutionary force was 'nil'. There was little point in appealing 'to the average citizen of the Soviet Union to take active measures against the present regime ... They have lived through terrible experiences in the present war, and do not mean to risk a repetition. This risk they would certainly not take voluntarily ... Their greatest hope is for an end to the war, so that they might creep home to their families.' The only glimmer of positive aspiration was seen amongst the sizeable Ukrainian contingent.[20]

This measured report was seemingly forgotten when the war was at an end and the West, and MI6 in particular, began to resurrect the various anti-communist organisations with a view to launching anti-Soviet operations. A not-disinterested commentator, Nikolai Tolstoy, believes that the authors were harsh in their assessment, neglecting the innate sense of patriotism of the PoWs: 'It was this spectre of counter-revolution which haunted Stalin's walking and sleeping. GULAG slaves, the Poles, the Balts, Caucasians, Ukrainian peasants ... the list was endless. The collective hatred of millions of injured people was a fearful vision to contemplate.' The West played on these fears, often in a purely cynical manner, using the various exile movements to foment non-existent revolts and, thereby, sent hundreds of émigré agents to almost certain death. The simple truth of these actions, however, is that revolutionary change only usually occurs in a period of rising expectations. The later revolts in eastern Europe took place when controls had been temporarily relaxed and the population saw an opportunity for increased freedoms. Total repression, as experienced under the yoke of totalitarian Stalinism, invariably produced a state of trauma – not the seeds of revolt.[21]

As Tamplin and Gatehouse acknowledged, an exception to the rule were the Ukrainians, though they were in a slightly different position in that Poland and Stalin had never been able to impose over western Ukraine the same degree of total control that existed in the east. A sizeable proportion of the population supported nationalist aims – a flame that had not been extinguished. Even so, the MI(R) officers concluded that 'the overthrow of the Government can only be achieved by foreign military intervention'. This was accepted by a number of senior Foreign Office officials, who concluded that Ukraine is 'so well controlled by the Soviet Government and so "atomised" by the precautions taken to prevent anything like a concerted political movement or the propagation of any political views other than their own, that there is no chance of any anti-Soviet movement developing'. Nor was there a 'chance of creating an armed uprising without military assistance from abroad'.[22]

The Paris branch of the Promethean League was something of a disappointment to Gubbins; it engaged in little activity – which ceased completely when the Germans invaded France. Its leaders were arrested and a number were to die in prison, thus enabling the League to proclaim after the war that its members had not collaborated with the Germans. Despite the fact that a number of Petlurans were, indeed, anti-German, and that the leading pro-Polish, pro-Allied Ukrainian publication *Ukrainske Slovo* was also anti-German and anti-Hitler, it was still a misleading claim. The Paris declaration of support for the Allies had received a cool response by other Ukrainians, especially those in Warsaw where the real power lay. In December 1939, the Warsaw branch had refuted the declaration and insisted that it would continue the struggle for nationalist liberation.[23]

The British and French continued to revise their plans for military action in the Caucasus, though the chances of success were slim – a fact noticed by the Abwehr, which sent Paul Leverkuehn to Tabriz, north Persia, to monitor the progress of the Allies. In his opinion, an aerial assault was unlikely to succeed, though he considered Baku highly vulnerable to a land invasion. Through poor security, a copy of Maclean's Baku plan found its way into German hands. When the Wehrmacht captured Paris in June 1940, copies of the joint Anglo-French plans were discovered in the French Foreign Ministry. The confidential files of the French General Staff were also retrieved, along with those of General Gamelin's Inter-Allied Section, which included the complete records of highly secret discussions between Allied commanders-in-chief. Among the documents was the Baku bombing plan, copies of which were sent by Hitler to Stalin as evidence of perfidious Albion. The plans were publicised in the German press on 4 July.[24]

Despite this setback, as late as May 1941 the chiefs of staff in London studied plans to bomb the Caucasus oilfields; however, the Anglo-French projects were found to be impractical due to Turkey's unwillingness to risk war with Russia. Even when Hitler struck at the Soviet Union on 22 June 1941, the British-led Promethean operation was not deemed totally irrelevant. The day before Barbarossa was launched, the Special Operations Executive (SOE), which had taken over the War Office's assets, agreed to send oil demolition experts from the Middle East into southern Russia. Two days later, as a matter of urgency, the Joint Planning Staff in London ordered SOE to make preparations for infiltrating sabotage agents into the Caucasus, an operation code-named 'G(R) 16' Mission. Bands of Kurds, Armenians and Georgians were to be flown into the Caucasus to blow up the oilfields. The Russians were not told of the planning and it was only in late November, when the Germans suffered their first setback near Rostrov, that G(R) 16 was dismantled. Air Marshal Sir John Slessor later wrote that 'the feature of these discussions which, in retrospect, really makes one's hair stand on end is the air – not perhaps of complacency, but of acceptance, with which we viewed the prospect of enlisting Russia among our active enemies'.[25]

When Soviet forces advanced into the western Galician areas of Poland and Ukraine, leading members of the League decided that 'German captivity was preferable to falling into the hands of their arch-enemies'. Led by the head of the Warsaw branch, Smal-Stocky, they reached Lvov, from where they were safely evacuated by the Germans – 'probably through special efforts of Admiral Canaris who hoped to preserve the group for future use against the Soviet Union'. The man who organised the rescue was Dr Georg Leibbrant, a 'pro-Ukrainian fanatic' from Odessa, who was head of the political department in Alfred Rosenberg's OMi. Although the Promethean League was declared illegal and a number of its leaders were imprisoned in Warsaw, it was not long before they were allowed a degree of free movement in German-occupied Poland. Friendly and close relations were maintained with the Abwehr, which assigned 'contract officers' and employed certain leaders on plans for Ukraine. Many Ukrainians had been employed as officers in the Polish Army, and they were quick to denounce their former employers; Pavlo Shandruk supplied the Germans with a list of Polish officers, who were subsequently purged and shot.[26]

Leibbrandt shipped off other League members to Prague, where Smal-Stocky later insisted that the Gestapo had interned him for the duration of the war. It was, however, an open arrest, and Leibbrandt ensured that the Prometheans received funds and research assignments. The relationship with the Germans was, in fact, so close that when Leibbrandt's private Ukrainian adviser, Alexander Sevriuk, met with Smal-Stocky in Warsaw on 9 April 1941, he tipped him off about the forthcoming invasion of the USSR. The Promethean leaders then began seriously to plan the establishment of a

Ukrainian government. At the same time, leadership of the Caucasian committees passed to Mikhail Kedia, a politician of extreme pro-German and anti-Russian convictions with many contacts in the SS and Abwehr, who campaigned for the 'joint struggle of all non-Russians against the Russians'. In the midst of this collaboration, the Soviet NKVD took the opportunity to plant its own agents among the League's ranks.[27]

The Germans now had control of the Promethean assets, and three months after the invasion of the Soviet Union, in the wake of the general Soviet confusion, there was a wide and sustained revolt of the Moslem Mountaineers in the north Caucasus. 'Though relatively little is known about this rebellion, its careful clandestine organisation, synchronised outbreak, and effective character appear to place it among the most important anti-Soviet uprisings.' The rebellion paved the way for a change of regime and, when the Germans entered the area, the Mountaineers afforded them a 'genuine welcome'.[28]

The Germans needed to gain access to the vast oil reserves of Baku, and in the spring of 1942 Rosenberg's OMi renewed its contacts with 'governments-in-exile' and 'national committees' established in Berlin, Paris and, in particular, Turkey. Pressure had come from Turkey, whose support Germany wanted to encourage, to sponsor groups from countries on its borders. The Turks took a special interest in the Triukic-Muslim areas such as the Crimea and Azerbaijan, and in the Caucasus as a whole. This was, however, a very contentious policy area, with deep divisions over orientation which enabled the émigrés to exert some influence on German policy. Within the OMi, and between it and other agencies, there was a conflict – the advocates of the 'federal' solution to conquered territories, which had the support of Rosenberg, Georgian Prince Nikuradze and the Promethean League, argued against the promoters of the extreme 'nationalists', who saw in the federalist schemes a threat to German rule. The federalists were also hostile to the pro-Turkish orientation that clashed with the idea of a Georgian-led Caucasus. The nationalist faction was led by Professor Gerhard von Mende, a young Berlin lecturer on Turkic and Muslim groups and head of an economic section in the OMi, who became, in effect, the 'master protector' of the non-Russian national groups operating under German control.[29]

Promethean leaders recruited by the OMi included Cafar Seydahmet. A representative abroad in 1919 of the Crimean Parliament, he was leader of the volunteer Tartars who were organised into six German auxiliary military units, which the extreme nationalists saw as the nucleus of a future 'Crimean Army'. In Turkey, Ayaz Ishaki led the refugees from central Asian Idel-Val, who dreamed of a state 'from Kazan to Samarkand'. An old socialist-revolutionary and leading writer, Ishaki had been sent in the late thirties on a special mission to Manchuria by the Promethean League to organise a common front in Asia.[30]

Aryan racial theories and Hitler's known hatred of the Slav peoples ensured that the idea of drawing on the discontent of the various enslaved nations of the Soviet Union was not fully implemented until the tide of war had turned against Germany. Eventually, the deteriorating situation in the East forced the Nazis to use more and more eastern nationalist-based battalions. A crippling lack of manpower obliged the Germans to lower the standards of purity necessary to enter the SS and to reverse its anti-Slav policy. Enthusiastically, the SS began to accelerate the recruitment of Ukrainians and Belorussians. Aided by the Prometheans and extremist nationalists, recruiting began in the various police groups, including those who had served with SS mobile killing units, which had murdered tens of thousands of Jews in eastern Europe.

Still unwilling to concede the idea of an independent state, in March 1943 Ukrainian nationalists of the Promethean persuasion were allowed to form a Ukrainian force to fight 'godless Bolshevism'. Sanctioned by SS-Reichsführer Heinrich Himmler, recruitment began in May, and by 3 June eighty-two thousand volunteers had reported to the enlistment offices. This was enough for eight complete SS regiments. The proposed SS Division, however, could only hold three infantry regiments; so five further regiments were formed under German Police Command. These were known as the Galizischen SS-Freiwilligen-Regimenter 4–8, and became notorious in actions against Jews, partisans and other 'sub-normals'. By October, the Ukrainian Division (or Galizien, as Himmler insisted on calling it) was officially renamed as the 14. SS-Freiwilligen Division 'Galizien' and, later, XIV Waffen-Grenadier-Division der SS (Galizien Nr.1). The majority of its personnel were Galician Ukrainians who voluntarily took the oath: 'I swear by God this holy oath, that in the struggle against Bolshevism, I will give the Commander-in-Chief of the German Armed Forces, Adolf Hitler, absolute obedience, and if it be his will, as a fearless soldier, I will always be prepared to lay down my life for this oath.' Needless to say, the British and Americans who, following the war, gave succour to the former Ukrainian soldiers of the division never published this oath of loyalty to Hitler.[31]

Ukrainian hopes and expectations were nearly extinguished when in July 1944 the eleven thousand-strong division was virtually destroyed at the Battle of Brody in western Ukraine. Those who escaped, along with other Ukrainian units, formed the core of a new Ukrainian SS infantry brigade regrouped in Silesia. By the end of the year, the division was rebuilt to the full strength of eleven thousand, with eight thousand volunteers from the SS Training and Replacement Regiment 14 and battalions from the under-deployed SS-Waffen-Grenadier Regiments. Following the Battle of Brody, the division's commander, SS-Brigadefuehrer der Waffen SS Fritz Freitag, received the Knight's Cross of the Iron Cross and issued an order of the day in which he proclaimed: 'We all vow the Führer that in our new undertakings it is our intention to fight through together until victorious over the Bolshevik hordes and their Jewish-plutocrat helpers.' In early 1945 the division was renamed the 1 Ukrainische National Armee. Under the command of Promethean General Pavlo Shandruk, the First Ukrainian Division wore standard German uniforms, sometimes with Waffen-SS-issued arm shields featuring the Galician lion. In all, seventy-five thousand Ukrainians were in uniform.[32]

There remained a few nationalist elements increasingly disillusioned with the Germans, and in the knowledge that the Soviet Red Army was beginning to close in these elements began to hedge their bets on the future. In May 1943 Russian Prince Turkul had attempted to make direct contact with the head of the US OSS in Berne, Allen Dulles. Unsuccessful, he turned to a go-between, Prince Irakly Bagration, 'the pretender to the non-existent Georgian throne and one of Turkul's inner circle'. The previous September, the Germans had promoted Bagration as chief of their collaborationist Georgian Committee but, not long after, he managed to travel to Switzerland. Later in the year, the 'Promethean Underground' in Poland succeeded in making contact with its 'old English friends'. These 'friends' are not identified but are probably Colin Gubbins and members of MI6. According to the League's own account, it then began to conduct 'a series of actions' and to make plans to transfer Promethean assets to the West.[33]

Since the autumn of 1944, a young Waffen-SS officer, Dr Fritz Arlt, had been trying to form a quisling Ukrainian National Committee, but a stumbling-block had been the terms demanded by the extreme nationalists. In late January 1945, Pavlo Shandruk met with the head of the recently created Committee for the Liberation of the Peoples of Russia (KONR), Andrei Vlasov. Although the Ukrainians formally opposed subordination of their national committee to the KONR, Shandruk agreed a modus vivendi which gave the Ukrainians a degree of independence. Eventually, Shandruk, who had actively collaborated with the Nazis in anti-Semitic campaigns, received the consent of Rosenberg to head the committee and the support of Stefan Bandera, leader of the pro-western Galician-centred Organisation of Ukrainian Nationalists (OUN-B) – though his rival, Andrei Melnyk (OUN-M), was not enthusiastic (see Chapter 14). On 17 March 1945, the Germans officially recognised the committee.[34]

Their world falling apart around them, the émigrés were living in a nightmarish existence of fantasy in which, right up to the end, they continued to fight over the minutiae of deals and alliances, believing that some miracle was at hand which might deliver their independence. There were expectations that the Allies would continue the war, enlisting their support in an attack on the Soviet Union; others were looking for a means of escape. OMi's von Mende, who 'felt more at home in the more or less unreal world based on hopes for the future than in the immediate economic or military problems of the day', assumed responsibility for creating national committees among the exile groups. He travelled extensively, making contacts with the émigré leaders, including the Promethean League in Turkey. OMi sponsorship of these national committees pandered to the almost pathetic desire of the émigrés to achieve official recognition, but also acted as a means of providing them with 'papers of state' and quasi-diplomatic documents with which to 'depart with relative immunity to Bavaria, Northern Italy or Switzerland' and from there into the hands of their former 'friends' among the Allies.[35]

One such émigré contemplating the future was General Shandruk, who announced in a proclamation from the Ukrainian National Committee that the First Ukrainian Division was officially the Ukrainian Liberation Army. Shandruk considered it good policy to retain as many Ukrainian soldiers as possible in the West – 'at least those who are the most conscious patriots among the youth because, in his opinion, events could unexpectedly create favourable conditions to employ them in the interests of Ukraine'.[36]

Instead of engaging in battle with the Russians, the First Ukrainian Division was moved by the Germans to Slovakia and found itself fighting Tito's partisans in Yugoslavia. With Tito's forces and the rapidly advancing Red Army bearing down on them, the Division began to withdraw westward in the direction of Vienna and into Carinthia. The division's SS minders, Dr Arlt and Professor von Mende, recognised that the war was lost and accepted the demand made by Shandruk to dispatch a delegation to the Allied Military High Command with the aim of persuading them that his soldiers should not be handed over to the Soviets. Roma Smal-Stocky and Shandruk hoped to present to the Allied Command 'a large united multi-national assembly of groups opposed to Russian Communism imperialism' – i.e. the assets of the Promethean League. The contacts made by the League at the time of the MI6-backed Baku project were to prove invaluable, but quite how the division finally made it into British hands remains a mystery.[37]

During the division's journey towards Allied lines, which was eased by the intervention of Dr Arlt, Shandruk linked up with Father John Hrynioch, chaplain to the Ukrainian Nachtigall battalion. Hrynioch told him in detail about the existence of a nationalist political committee in Ukraine (UHVR), and the Ukrainian Insurgent Army (UPA). Thought was given to letting the division fight its way through to the homeland to link up with the UPA, but this was regarded as being impractical. Instead, Shandruk moved on to Prague where, on 11 April 1945, he made contact with Cossack leaders and 'his old friend', Smal-Stocky, whose surveillance by the Gestapo was lifted on the orders of Dr Arlt. Despite Gestapo restrictions on his movements, Smal-Stocky had retained contact with Allied 'friends' and told Shandruk that he would get in touch with 'London'. Who his link was is not known, though Harold 'Gibby' Gibson, who had been the MI6 head of station in Prague at the outbreak of war, was now in Istanbul, where his officers had responsibility for the various national committees and governments-in-exile that belonged to the Promethean League. Another possible link, SOE's Harold

Perkins, who had a special affinity with the Polish assets, was at the time running agents into Czechoslovakia.[38]

After two days in Prague, the Division proceeded across the Alps to Graz, where Smal-Stocky had advised Shandruk to seek immediate contact, through 'neutral and Allied Intermediaries', with the British High Command as soon as Allied troops reached Austria. With the news that British forces had entered Spittal and were moving towards Klagenfurt, Shandruk sent emissaries to the Polish liaison officers belonging to General Anders, commander of the Polish 2nd Corps, requesting that he intervene with the Allies on Ukraine's behalf. Shandruk also arranged for the head of the security police of the nationalist OUN-B, Mikolai Lebed, to send envoys to the British. Two were killed on the way, but a third, with Dr Arlt acting as interpreter, did manage to get through to British forces approaching Klagenfurt, where he made contact with a Canadian-born intelligence officer of Ukrainian descent. Employed by British Intelligence, the officer was attached to SOE's Special Force No. 6, working closely with another friend of the Ukrainians and Poles, Auberon Herbert. The envoy was able to set out the national position of the Ukrainians, asserting that they should not be regarded as Soviet citizens. Dr Arlt subsequently brought back written permission for the division to march to the rear of the British troops. The chief of staff of the British division, Brigadier Toby Low, told a Ukrainian representative, Dr Makarushka, that he had been informed about the First Ukrainian Division 'from above'. This would appear to have derived from the initial contacts following Smal-Stocky's intervention from Prague.[39]

On 8 May 1945, just hours before the final ceasefire took effect, the reassembled Division started its westward march, crossing the front line near Raastadt, before marching across the border at Klagenfurt into the waiting arms of the British forces. Despite loud protests from the Soviet command, a highly disciplined unit of over eight thousand Ukrainians was held by the British 5th Corps near St Veit and Spittal, headquarters of the British occupation forces for northern Italy. Following 'political talks', Father Hrynioch rejoined the division while General Shandruk was able to persuade the Allies that the division, which contained a number of war criminals, was wholly composed of Polish Galicians – i.e. non-Soviets.[40]

A further column of 1,300 Ukrainians under the command of General Shandruk had made it through to Judenburg in the American Zone, where Dr Arlt obtained permission for them to proceed to Salzburg. The First Ukrainian Division was instructed, on 28 May, to cross over to Italy and Udine, where it reached Camp 374 at Bellaria, near Rimini, on the Adriatic coast. In late June, the 1,300 men eventually made it to Spittal and were directed to the staff of the British Corps, near Klagenfurt. They were then taken to a camp at Agathenhof to be supervised by one Major Rutter. In October, the Division was transferred to another camp nearby at Cesnatico. While the British did place the Ukrainians in a PoW cage, they were assigned as 'Separated Enemy Personnel (SEP)', 'a distinction which to the Ukrainians at least denoted their special status'. Once in the PoW camp, the Ukrainians kept to their military formation, adding the Ukrainian insignia to their German uniforms for the benefit of the British, and resumed political activities. As Mark Aarons and John Loftus point out, the SS Division was 'the only Axis unit to survive the war intact, under arms and with their own officers'. Indeed, the Division was not only not disarmed, but 'in many cases more arms were issued'.[41]

Riccione, south of Rimini, was the location for a number of vast PoW camps which, during the summer of 1945, housed thousands of Germans, Yugoslavs, Russians and Ukrainians. Their fate was to become an increasing problem for the British, reflected in the growing tension between the former allies of the West and the Soviet Union. Until June 1946 the Foreign Office had stuck doggedly by the terms of the Yalta agreement, permitting Soviet repatriation missions to scour PoW and DP camps in order to identify their citizens. The majority returned home voluntarily, but those left were regarded as collaborators or war criminals.

In July 1945, Allied Forces HQ Caserta transferred Major Denis Hills to Bellaria, a few miles north of Riccione, to report on the eight thousand soldiers of the First Ukrainian Division who were being held. Hills was a distinctive and appropriate choice, a self-acknowledged fascist at Oxford University who, although he had lost this extremist edge, was still a man of the hard right and an ardent anti-communist. He was later proudly to boast that he had shielded the eight-thousand men from forcible repatriation.

Hills admitted that with few resources 'proper screening was impossible' and that it had not been his concern to 'to winkle out "war criminals"'. He told Tom Bower in 1989 that he 'knew about the SS and I was wary, but I had to make up my own mind about these people'. Even though there may have been Ukrainians in the Division who had been employed in the concentration camps and murder squads, the army, Hills said, was 'not interested' in war crimes. Before each soldier could be grilled by a member of the Soviet mission – which regarded Hills with grave suspicion – he coached the Ukrainian camp leader, Major Yaskevycz, on what stance to take. He was moved by their expressed hatred to the mission officers of the Bolsheviks and their desire not to return to the Soviet Union. Accusations of war crimes were dismissed by Hills and the British officials as Soviet propaganda, though it is certain that a large number of the Ukrainians had served voluntarily in the Waffen-SS, while others had been drafted in from police units directly involved in massacres and deportations or were former concentration camp guards.[42]

Hills's immediate task was to establish the identity of the Ukrainians, who were regarded as 'some sort of border Poles' from Galicia. Impressed with the 'extreme national consciousness' of the First Ukrainian Division,

Hills readily accepted accounts by its soldiers of their origin, even though his Polish friends despised them as 'fascist bandits'. He acknowleged that 'legally they should have been returned' and admitted disobeying orders to detect the estimated 50 per cent who were really former Soviet citizens. 'The solution I adopted was to register the inmates as displaced civilians – which was not strictly true: there were former officers among them – and to encourage them (unofficially) to disperse.' It was claimed that many of the worst war criminals disappeared because of lax security, but Hills helped a number of Ukrainians escape down a crude ratline that had been established by a young Uniate priest who 'set up a temporary refuge for them in a building in Rome'. Hills's superior in Rome 'didn't discourage' his efforts but 'preferred to know nothing official about them'.[43]

The division's last commander, Pavlo Shandruk, eventually settled in Munich, the centre of Ukrainian nationalism in exile, where he remained in contact with the division via Bishop Ivan Buchko, a high-ranking Vatican official. Buchko watched over the affairs of the Ukrainian Church and the First Division which he regarded as 'the flower of the Ukrainian nation'. Buchko was able to inform Shandruk that the division's soldiers had been 'reclassified merely as confines'. Playing a large part in securing the freedom of the division from repatriation, Buchko worked closely with the Ukrainian leaders in the DP camps, including Promethean League leader Roma Smal-Stocky, who had pre-war links with the Allied officers in charge of the camps in Austria and Germany. Buchko was particularly active in lobbying Sir D'Arcy Osborne, the British representative at the Vatican, where there was much concern over the Division's fate.[44]

Ukrainian lobbyists conducted an aggressive propaganda campaign to secure the release of the division. The chair of the Division's Civil Administration and Military Council in Munich, A. Paliy, issued a number of memoranda about its possible fate to the exiled anti-communist groups in Britain. Of particular importance was the Ukrainian Relief Committee in Great Britain, chaired by a Canadian/Ukrainian RAF captain, Gordon Bohdan Panchuk. Other groups, such as the British and Scottish Leagues for European Freedom, pleaded the Division's case to Foreign Office officials and politicians, arguing that its personnel should be set free and not sent back to the Soviet Union. The right-wing Catholic Labour MP for Ipswich and doughty champion of anti-communists everywhere, Richard Stokes, became the Division's champion in Parliament. In early 1946, Shandruk and Paliy learned that their efforts had been successful and that the Division would not be sent back but would, eventually, be allowed to settle in Britain.[45]

In August 1945, Denis Hills returned to Riccione to take part in Operation KEELHAUL, the repatriation, by force if deemed necessary, of a number of Russians. Hills found that the mood had changed since repatriation first began in 1944. At that time there was little or no sympathy for sending back to the Soviet Union Russians who were technically deserters and traitors. The official list of a thousand Russians to be repatriated had already been halved by a Major Simcock, who was responsible in the DPs Division for dealing with the Soviet Repatriation Missions. It then became the task of Hills to grade the list by classifying the DPs into three categories: 'Black' denoting that they were war criminals who should be returned; 'Grey' denoting Nazi collaborators, which indeed was a grey area, and 'Whites' – victims of Nazi oppression.

Hills later admitted that his long-term intention had been 'to reduce the list to a bare minimum', which he did by reclassifying many and inventing new categories. With the help of the Vatican, the British authorities changed the rules so that within the total of those considered for repatriation, four hundred 'Blacks' became 'Greys'. Hills was eventually able to whittle the Russian list down from 500 to 180. In May 1947, under Operation EASTWIND, these final 180 British-held Russians were rounded up and taken under armed guard to the local railhead and put on a sealed train for surrender to the Soviets at St Valentin, on the zonal border in Austria. Acting as a Russian interpreter on the packed train was a distraught young British intelligence officer, Alexander Wainman, who heard many of the Russians say that they would rather be shot than sent back. Professor Wainman reported the distressing scenes to George Young, the MI6 station commander in Vienna. 'Appalled at the evident inhumanity of the continuation of so brutal a policy', Young passed on the damning evidence to his chief, Stewart Menzies, and handed it on personally to the political adviser in Vienna, Sir Henry Mack, 'who was equally disgusted'. A strongly worded protest was subsequently dispatched to the Foreign Office, which was under strong pressure from the Vatican and Richard Stokes, MP. Foreign Office officials informed MI6 that 'no further operations of this nature were contemplated'.[46]

While there was certainly genuine concern, MI6's approach was also pragmatic. The repatriation process was interfering with its own operations to gather intelligence on what the Soviets were up to in the newly occupied countries in eastern Europe. At the same time as British soldiers were forcing unwilling Soviet and non-Soviet citizens back into Russian hands, other British troops were helping to assist defectors to escape from the Soviet Union to the West. One of the British officers involved in Operation HIGHLAND FLING was James Scott-Hopkins, who later told Nikolai Tolstoy that his unit's activities were well known in resistance circles inside the USSR. A product of Eton and Oxford, and later a senior Conservative MP, on leaving the army in 1946 Scott-Hopkins joined Military Intelligence, undertaking a course in Russian and specialised training in interrogation. A year later, he was approached by Stewart Menzies, who wanted him to feed MI6 with the information collected from the defectors as part of Highland Fling.[47]

The main beneficiaries of the unofficial change of policy on repatriation were the eight thousand Ukrainians of the First Ukrainian or 14th Waffen-SS Galician Division. Britain would decline to return anyone who had been resident or a citizen outside of the Soviet Union's 1939 borders. In January 1947, Brigadier Fitzroy Maclean arrived in Rimini to work with the Special Refugee Screening (SRS) Commission, which had been set up the previous December. Maclean's unit had to work to a September deadline to screen the Ukrainians before the Italian government regained control of the camps, at which point any occupants were likely to be turned over to the Soviets. The aims were to check that no adverse information was held against individual refugees and to track down the 'most wanted'. There were, however, officials inside British Intelligence who were prepared, in the opening rounds of the Cold War, to countenance the use of collaborators, quislings and war criminals in the battle against a new enemy. The benefit of the doubt was to be extended to those who had actually taken up arms on behalf of the Nazis. In effect, if not by intention, anti-communism, not criminality, became the criterion by which they were judged. As it was cynically expressed at the time, and as Maclean's biographer acknowledges, 'increasing the pool of freedom fighters' meant beating the deadline of 'R-Day', when the Italian government would take over responsibility for the remaining DPs.[48]

After two weeks with the SRS Commission, Maclean moved on to Rome and reported to the Foreign Office that he had been able to screen only a small fraction of the total held. The screeners had relied on the Ukrainians themselves for the history of the division, which was obviously and notably partisan. Maclean reported that the 'Camp is organised on political-military lines under a fanatical Ukrainian nationalist leader [Captain Yaskevych] who formerly served with Skoropadski [the leader of the short-lived German puppet republic of the Ukraine in 1918]'. Maclean further reported that 'most of those interrogated have admitted freely that they volunteered to fight for the Germans'. Indeed, most had been captured in German uniforms and there were 'indications that some may have served in SS units'. Although, when interviewed in 1989, Maclean was 'fairly clear' that there was 'every probability that there were war criminals amongst them', no further action was taken to check on their wartime activities.[49]

The lack of action did not surprise those British intelligence officers in Vienna monitoring the situation, who were aware that it was unrealistic to expect any serious screening to be undertaken. Only twenty men were subjected to cursory screening out of the 8,272-strong First Ukrainian Division. The security officer, Major G. H. Redfern, stated that 'Intelligence organisations could not carry out any intelligence screening of DPs with their present resources'. In reality, officials considered screening 'undesirable' because it would delay Operation WESTWARD HO!, the DP labour recruitment scheme, which was expanded to include Ukrainians for settlement in Britain. The order of the day became to protect a valuable anti-communist resource, and security screening was subordinated to the need to speed the movement of the Ukrainians out of Italy, a country that the Foreign Office feared might be taken over by the communists.[50]

On 23 March 1947, at a late-night meeting, Foreign Office junior ministers persuaded the Prime Minister to agree to the Ukrainians entering Britain. It would seem that 'on the other side of the house', MI6 had put pressure on the Secretary of State, Hector McNeil. When, in June, the Soviets protested that the Ukrainian Division contained former policemen who had undertaken killings during bloody anti-partisan operations and should thus be treated as war criminals, McNeil responded by falsely claiming that there had been 'exhaustive' screening of the division whose soldiers were, he maintained, 'ex-Wehrmacht personnel'. When challenged in the House of Commons, McNeil was supported by Richard Stokes, who insisted that the Ukrainians desired only independence and loathed the 'Muscovites' and the Germans equally. McNeil's brief was written by Foreign Office officials who had accepted a long memorandum on the virtue of the Division from the Supreme Ukrainian Liberation Council, the offspring of the wartime collaborationist Ukrainian Liberation Committee headed by Pavlo Shandruk, the division's last commander. Officials also relied on a heavily sanitised version of the division's history by Gordon Panchuk, which had been supplied to him by the head of the Division's Military Council, A. Paliy. Panchuk headed the Central Ukrainian Relief Bureau and was founder president of the Association of Ukrainians in Great Britain. With Panchuk's help, members of the division were quickly dispersed to Canada or the British Zone in Germany, with the majority settling in Britain.[51]

According to former Conservative MP Rupert Allason (Nigel West), a number of the Ukrainians were brought to Britain at the behest of British Intelligence to work as secure language specialists. Seeking two hundred native Russian speakers as teachers for MI6 and other intelligence officers, at the end of 1947 the Joint Intelligence Committee approached Home Office departments handling aliens and immigration. A Home Office official who dealt with the Galicia Division later admitted that she knew that some of these people were of interest to the security services and, in particular, MI6. Immigration officers, who had been unable to screen any individual members of the division for suspected war crimes, subsequently located a thousand suitable candidates for the War Office, which ran the courses. According to Allason, some of the Ukrainians later 'openly boasted about the atrocities that they had committed against Jews'. Those boasts 'must have been known to the British government'.[52]

In his February 1947 report, Maclean had added one provision to his recommendations, namely that wherever the Ukrainians were sent 'their existing politico-military organisation should not be allowed to remain in existence'. The Promethean League, however, had quickly resumed its work through the energetic efforts of Pavlo Shandruk, who had helped to gather together its scattered members in the DP and PoW camps. He made contact with representatives of the different nationality groups, including the Slovaks and their representative, Dr Josef Pauco, the Belorussians and a number of Poles, with a view to re-establishing the League's authority. By the end of 1945, the Prometheans had also resumed their pre-war relationship with Menzies and MI6. This had not gone unnoticed by the Soviets or US Intelligence, who both described the League as an arm's-length operation by British Intelligence to re-arm Ukrainian neo-Nazis under cover of General Ander's Polish Army.[53]

In the immediate postwar period, the Polish government-in-exile still harboured hopes of establishing a large 'East European Federation', which would include all the nations under Soviet domination. The proposed vehicle for these fantasies was to be the Promethean League. Shandruk had established contact with Polish officers Major Ponikewski and Captain Alexander, who put him in touch with the Promethean members in London – General Tad Pelczynski, Colonel Tadeusz Schaetzel and Stanislaw Paprocki. The Polish government-in-exile in London told Shandruk that they were willing to finance the League. Until the end of the war, Polish covert activities had been secured by a British Treasury loan which was to be repaid by the postwar Polish government. However, when the communist regime in Warsaw was officially recognised by London and Washington in July 1945, the Poles were left to rely on their own meagre resources to maintain their political activities which, despite drastic reductions, could not be sustained for long. MI6 was required to make up the difference.[54]

On 20 April 1946, a congress was held in The Hague at which the organisation's name was changed to the Promethean Atlantic Charter League. Dr Smal-Stocky was again elected President, with Georgian leader Dr George Nakashidze his deputy. Financed and backed by MI6, the Prometheans were once again fully functioning, and they began to rebuild their propaganda programmes for battle with the communists. In an expensive exercise, MI6 created and sponsored a number of League-linked 'front' organisations, including the New Union for Turko-Tatar Independence, 'Idel-Urala', and the Northern Caucasian National Committee, which directed selected Promethean agents for guerrilla and spy training at a British camp at Bad Homburg in Allied Germany.[55]

League activities largely centred on Turkey, which was in the front line of the developing Cold War. It was MI6's main base for intelligence work in the Balkans and central Europe and for operations directed against the Soviet Union and its southern flank. Turkey shared a long border with the Soviet Union, which had been discontented with the former's policy during the war. Stalin objected to the German-Turkish treaty of June 1941, which had facilitated Germany's invasion of the Soviet Union, and to agitation among the pro-German 'pan-Turk' groups which campaigned for the disintegration of the USSR in the hope that regions in the Caucasus and central Asia with Turkish populations would become independent or join with Turkey. The disputes between the two countries, which largely centred on the border and revisions of treaties, continued after the war with hysterical press campaigns on both sides. Stalin claimed a slice of eastern Turkey, plus the right to put Russian bases on the Bosphorus and the Dardanelles, the main thoroughfares for Soviet shipping. To protect its independence, Turkey clamoured for military aid from the West, playing on Allied fears of losing communication links to the Middle East.[56]

Istanbul was a spies' paradise, with a British embassy building 'crammed from top to bottom with intelligence operatives engaged in various forms of skulduggery'. The Yugoslavs were looked after by Roman Sulakov, a White Russian MI6 officer of 'appealing charm and boundless energy', who had been resident in the city since 1926. Many refugees from communist countries made their way to Turkey, where they were debriefed by the efficient Turkish secret service, whose head, Colonel Peredzh, had worked for the Royal Yugoslav Intelligence. He was also employed by MI6 on a monthly retainer to supplement his meagre salary. The refugees all had 'to provide detailed documentation, including several photographs, in order to get a visa . . . the authorities were well informed as to where everyone was and, quite often, what they were doing'. Unfortunately, while this should have been an excellent source of information on what was going on inside Soviet-controlled eastern Europe, the intelligence passed on to MI6 was of 'low quality owing to poor interrogations'.[57]

The MI6 liaison officer with the Turkish secret service was the Passport Control Officer, Arthur Whittal, whose merchant family had settled in the country before the First World War. 'With their knowledge of the country and the language they gave valuable help to HMG in various ways.' The family was also related by marriage to the wartime head of station, Harold Gibson. Born in pre-Bolshevik Russia, 'Gibby' Gibson, who was replaced in 1944 by Cyril Machray, had immersed himself in anti-communist White Russian circles in order to cultivate sources. Unfortunately for MI6, while the exile groups with spy networks in eastern Europe and the southern flank of the Soviet Union supplied the local station with information, most of it turned out to be fake – again a product of the numerous 'paper mills' operating in the area. Kim Philby recalled that 'it was their only way of garnering finance to keep themselves and their dreams going'. MI6 officers had to spend much of their time 'devising means of smoking such operators into the open, so we could judge what price to put on their work'. They rarely succeeded and, in spite of the care taken, Philby admitted that 'several of the exiles made regular monkeys of us'.[58]

*   *   *

Promethean League supporters were also able to draw on the expertise of the Nazi specialists who had been recruited by Philby's Section IX and other departments of MI6. Operation APPLEPIE in western Germany, run jointly by the British and the Americans, had aimed at finding and debriefing members of the SS head office department RHSA-Amt VI, who were responsible for intelligence work relating to the USSR. One of the more successful catches was Nikolai N. Poppe, a world-renowned Russian scholar on the minority groups of the USSR, who had been born in 1897 in the Chinese province of Shantung, where his father was secretary of the Russian consulate. When the Wehrmacht took control of the region, he actively collaborated with the Nazis in the creation of a quisling government for the Karachai minority, and provided information on the passes leading across the mountains into Transcaucasia. When the Germans evacuated the Caucasus during the winter of 1942, Poppe went with them and helped set up the SS-sponsored Wannsee Institute in Berlin. Poppe later justified his actions by claiming that his objective was 'to join the Germans temporarily by retreating with them into Germany, in order to emigrate to Great Britain or the United States'.[59]

Part of the SS-run 'Geography Foundation', the Wannsee Institute think-tank was the setting, in January 1942, for the conference that agreed the 'Final Solution'. In turn, the institute was controlled by the Amt VI (Intelligence) section of the SD, whose head, Walter Schellenberg, considered the establishment of the institute as one of his most successful achievements. At the end of the war, Poppe was arrested by an American CIC officer, but managed to talk his way to freedom and fled to Herford, in Westphalia, in the British Zone in Germany. There he lived undetected until early 1946, when he managed to find a place at a United Nations Refugee and Rehabilitation Agency (UNRRA) camp for Estonians in Hamburg. In July, Poppe was warned by a British female intelligence officer to flee, as a Soviet mission was on his trail. Accused of being 'an active agent of the Gestapo', for helping the Germans gain the support of the Kalmucks, he was wanted for extradition by the Soviets.[60]

The official response of the Foreign Office and the Intelligence Division in Germany was that Poppe could not be located. In fact, the Control Office admitted that it knew where he was but 'it was never our intention to hand over Poppe'. He was already being handled by British Intelligence in the shape of a 'Captain Smith' and a South African-born officer, 'Gottlieb', to whom he handed his unpublished manuscript on Mongolia. The Foreign Office officials continued to mislead the Soviets, claiming that 'we are genuinely unable to trace him', even as Thomas Brimelow was discussing Poppe's case with F. Pickering of the Intelligence Division of the Control Commission. There were Foreign Office plans for Poppe to be 'somehow spirited into [Britain] from Berlin' and given work at a British university. Poppe had managed to forward a letter to Professor Gustav Haloun, a Sinologist who had escaped Nazi Germany and was teaching in the Chinese department at Cambridge University, seeking his help to leave Germany. Poppe did receive an invitation, backed by leading British orientalists, to teach at Cambridge – but it came to nothing when his MI6 minder informed him that the British government had refused him a visa. In the meantime, the British created a new identity for Poppe and played for time. Senior Foreign Office official Christopher Warner hoped that Poppe could 'disappear' to carry on his specialised career.[61]

Before his return to his farm in Northern Ireland, 'Captain Smith' spent many months debriefing Poppe, who was transferred to an intelligence centre for German specialists at Alswede, near Lübeck. According to Poppe, most of the other specialists of interest to MI6, who included Balts and scientists, had been 'smuggled out from the Eastern zone'. Soviet requests for his extradition were received sympathetically by British officials who knew that Poppe had lied about his background; return, however, was no longer viewed as an option since the intelligence services regarded him as a security risk. In December 1946, Major-General Shoosmith told the Control Office that 'if he returned to the Russians he would reveal under interrogation the names and possible locations of former colleagues, which would result in further demands for extradition of people who are subjects of an important investigation'. This was Operation Applepie, which intelligence officer D. E. Evans informed Thomas Brimelow at the Foreign Office 'is an attempt to collect all the information which the Germans had about the Soviet Union'.[62]

Living in the British Zone in Germany under an assumed name, Poppe was still unable to obtain a British visa so, in the spring of 1947, British Intelligence approached the Intelligence Division of the US Army at Frankfurt with a request for help. A top-secret memo to the Deputy Director of Intelligence explained that while Poppe's presence was an 'embarrassment', he was still a 'valuable intelligence source'. MI6 wanted to know 'if it is possible for the US intelligence authorities to take him off their hands and see that he is sent to the US where he can be lost'. While awaiting an American response, in the summer of 1947 Poppe was visited by 'Mr Morris', a British intelligence officer of Polish origin who took him to Wolfenbuttel near the Soviet Zone; here he was reunited with his family. In September his son was sent to Holland and then England, where he was provided with employment. Meanwhile, Poppe was transferred to a counter-intelligence centre at Brake, near Lemgo, where his language skills were used during interrogations of defecting Russians. In the following year, still under the protection of British Intelligence, which provided him with a new identity and cover story, Poppe was returned to Herford to teach Russian at an intelligence school for British officers.[63]

Poppe was by now in a bad physical and mental state and, according to one American report, looking like 'a walking skeleton', was 'contemplating suicide'. In May 1948, accompanied by a British intelligence officer, he was transferred from the British to the American Zone for a debriefing and meeting with Carmel Offie, officially the political adviser to General Lucius Clay, US Military Governor of Germany, but also representative of the secret Department of Army Detachment (DAD). Offie and DAD officers – most of whom went on to join Frank Wisner's Office of Policy Co-ordination (OPC), for whom Poppe would work – were heavily involved in transferring former Nazi anti-communist assets to the United States. Towards the end of January 1949, Poppe received an invitation from an American university and was sent to Camp King, near Oberursel, where he was again debriefed as part of the 'historical study group' project, before finally leaving for the United States, in May 1949, under the BLOODSTONE programme. Poppe was the first man to be shipped down the official US CIC ratline. The British and Americans genuinely did not believe that he was a war criminal, though they knew he was a collaborator, and used the escape line to keep him out of the clutches of the Soviets. Poppe kept up contacts with leading British Sinologists and Turcologists; his past was soon forgotten. In 1950, Poppe was elected a member of the Royal Asiatic Society and, in 1978, was received as a fellow of the British Academy.[64]

In February 1947, Kim Philby was posted to Istanbul to replace Cyril Machray as station head. Operating under cover as First Secretary: 'It was his first overseas posting and, in the light of the continuing tension between the USSR and Turkey, it was a highly appropriate one for the former head of Section IX.' Philby's priority was to recruit agents for short-term missions and, for extended periods, others who would be able to establish lines into the USSR. 'His zone of activity extended throughout the countries of the Caucasus, the Donbas and the Ukraine. He located people who had left these areas of the USSR before or during the war, and who still had relatives in Georgia, Azerbaijan and Armenia, in the regions of Stavropol, Krasnodar, Rostov-on-Don, Ukraine and the Crimea: and when he found them he suggested that they return to their countries in the services of Great Britain.' Philby was an 'energetic enthusiast' for these plans, which were 'regarded with high hopes' in London. His superiors were 'convinced that if several groups of people were sent into Georgia or Armenia, and informed locals that they were from the outside world and gave them some gold, the locals would start weaving a spy network for MI6 and prepare a rebel movement against the authorities'. In order to advance the operation, Philby established a good relationship with the head of the Istanbul office of the Security Inspectorate, whose help was essential. He also had the assistance of five fellow-officers in the embassy, including the Second Secretary, a 'capable and companionable deputy', Hereward Attlee, and a 'sturdily enthusiastic junior' Third Secretary, the Honourable John Wilson, a wartime naval officer.[65]

To prepare for the operations, Philby and his deputy undertook a survey of the rugged frontier bordering on Transcaucasia for the War Planning Director-ate. The infiltration operations were designed for the setting up of stay-behind networks in the southern areas of the Soviet Union and the Caucasus in the event of war. In early 1947, MI6 officers met with a Turkish representative in Switzerland to discuss using the various exile groups under the Promethean League umbrella. In turn, the representative contacted the groups with confirmation that MI6 was willing to back them with training and finance. The outlook for infiltration operations was, however, not as promising as it would have been 'if Stalin, immediately after the war, had not deported to central Asia and Siberia whole ethnic groups, such as Crimean Tartars, Chechens, Kalmyks and Karachai, which were accused of having collaborated with the German invaders'. Other alleged 'nations' such as Cossackia and Idel-Ural, which were members of the League, were purely artificial concepts, owing a great deal to Nazi ideas of a divided eastern Europe ruled by Germany; with the war ended they lacked the necessary support for survival.[66]

Philby's principal operation was CLIMBER, which was designed to infil-trate MI6-backed Promethean agents into Georgia. 'His plan, which was approved by MI6, was to start by sending five or six groups of five or six people in for several weeks. But it became clear quite quickly that it would not be easy to find volunteers for these missions.' An emissary was sent to Noe Jordania, president of the Georgian Menshevik government-in-exile in Paris and one-time head of the independent Republic of Georgia, which fleetingly came into existence in the confusion following the October Revol-ution. A leading figure in the Promethean League, Jordania had worked with MI6 officers 'Biffy' Dunderdale and Tom Greene before the war, and was one of the few members to adhere to the Allied cause in 1939. Unfortunately for the operation, the emissary dismissed Jordania as a 'silly old goat' and Climber was launched with 'deep mutual suspicion'.[67]

The Georgian exile movement did manage to recruit two 'climbers' in France who were trained in London in 'elementary diversionary techniques'. In co-operation with the Turks, MI6 set up a reconnaissance mission to find safe houses and a reliable means of communication. The operation itself was a disaster and was one of a number in Turkey and the Middle East that were betrayed by the Soviet agent Philby. In their early twenties, the two volunteers had been born in Paris and knew nothing of the Soviet Union. On Turkish insistence they were put over the frontier opposite a Red Army garrison: 'One was shot within minutes of crossing the border. The other was never seen again failing to make any communication.' When Philby later defected to the Soviet Union, he learned of the fate of one of the young men, Rukhadze, from the chair of the Georgian KGB.* 'It was an unpleasant story, of course

---

* Ministry of State Security, which succeeded the NKGB, People's Commissariat of State Security, in March 1946.

. . . I knew very well that they would be caught and that a tragic fate awaited them. But on the other hand, it was the only way of driving a stake through the plans of future operations.' A number of Armenians were found for another Promethean operation and induced to venture into the Soviet part of their homeland, but they, too, were 'pitilessly sacrificed to the vengeance of the MGB'.[68]

Although there was no Russian contact with Philby in Turkey, he was able to keep in touch with his handlers by the simple method of writing letters to his Foreign Office friend and fellow-traitor in London, Guy Burgess. Philby kept the MGB 'fully informed of these operations, which were usually carried out by the British, only occasionally by the Americans'. According to his control in London, he would provide names of agents and sometimes the date and place of the infiltrations. 'We knew in advance about every operation that took place by air, land or sea, even in mountainous and inaccessible regions.' The Soviets were careful, however, 'not to use his information to conduct a systematic dismantling of the networks concerned. If the operations were of major importance and could cause great damage, we took appropriate action – but otherwise we tended to do nothing, because Philby had to show results to his superiors.' The MGB did 'turn' a number of the captured spies but 'with such subtlety that Philby was able to continue his work for the British with a solid veneer of success'. Only two of the cases Philby betrayed during 1948/9 survived, though it has to be said that, even without his actions, the chances of the operations succeeding were remote indeed.[69]

In 1949 Philby returned to London, where he had a meeting with Commander Anthony Courtney of Naval Intelligence about extending the anti-Soviet operations into the Black Sea area. A Russian-speaker, Courtney had served before the war in the British legation at Bucharest, a centre for the various émigré groups, where he was pressed into service for MI6 by the head of station, Edward Boxshall. Having served in the Royal Navy during the war, in January 1946 Courtney was put in charge of the new Russian Section 16 of the Naval Intelligence Division. 'It had become clear that, with the elimination of Germany and Japan, plans concerning the "potential enemy" of the future must already be orientated towards Soviet Russia . . . which their Lordships had entrusted primarily to myself.' Courtney was one of the first exponents of the art of 'Kremlinology', and his views were carried from 1947 onwards in the *Spectator*, where he wrote articles on the Soviet Union under the pseudonym 'Richard Chancellor'. As head of the Russian Section he worked in close co-operation with MI6, and was on personal terms with Stewart Menzies. 'I had certain ideas involving the use of fast surface craft and submarines in co-operation with MI6, and I felt sure that the Royal Navy had a great deal to offer in this respect . . . It was in pursuance of these ideas of mine that discussions took place about the feasibility of obtaining information from the Black Sea area.'[70]

Philby listened to Courtney's proposals 'with interest, for he had a wide knowledge of Turkish affairs and his support was essential if Naval Intelligence was to make any contribution to the common effort in the Black Sea, where our information was deplorably scanty'. Courtney was initially disappointed that nothing appeared to come of his ideas, though he regarded it as 'typical of our more general experience of MI6 and Foreign Office resistance to any practical initiatives for the improvement of our intelligence effort'. In fact, Philby had already considered the idea while stationed in Turkey. 'After it was shown that diversionary operations on land were impossible, Philby suggested doing it by sea. The idea was to send patrol-cutters from Riza to the Soviet side somewhere between Batum and Sochi. London agreed, but asked that there be Turkish support, for without it the expedition would fail.' Turkish secret service support for the project was apparently enthusiastic.[71]

Run by MI6 Middle East specialist and another member of the Whittal family, Michael, the infiltration operations began after Philby left and were based on Prince's Island, the Mamara, in Turkey, from where agents were sent by boat across the Black Sea and landed in deserted spots in the vicinity of Sukhumi, Sochi or further north towards the Crimea. Caucasian anti-communists were recruited in Istanbul by the North Caucasian Emigration Society – another MI6 front organisation. Again, the operations were a disaster, resulting 'in yet another successful deception operation by the Russians'. In the knowledge that security had been breached, MI6 eventually mounted their own double-cross operations.[72]

According to Pavlo Shandruk, 'external circumstances' prevented the League from being fully revived. During the summer of 1947, MI6 had tried to create an exile body to co-ordinate and organise the activities of all the émigré groups that it covertly supported. Together with another international émigré organisation, Freedom International, the Poles joined the Promethean League to the Anti-Bolshevik League for the Liberation of Nations (ALONS), but it was not a success. An attempt to merge the Promethean League with the extreme nationalists of the Anti-Bolshevik Bloc of Nations (ABN) was initially abandoned because the younger, more militant members of the ABN were against the League's Polish orientation. It was still sponsored by the Polish government-in-exile and seen as too old-fashioned and cautious in its approach. The Poles, however, were running out of money, and MI6 had no choice but to force the issue. In July, MI6 fused the other main émigré grouping, Intermarium, with the ABN and then, in September, the Promethean League followed suit.[73]

Shandruk and the League blamed the Allies for failing adequately to support them. 'They had all the political centres and armed formations of the non-Russian nations for the establishment of democracy and peace in the East but no action followed.' This was not quite true, but it did take a while for the British and Americans to offer support, by which time many felt that the moment to strike had passed. Disillusioned, Prince Nakashidze left for South America and, in 1947, Smal-Stocky emigrated to the United States, where he joined the faculty of Marquette University. Before he left, Smal-Stocky had transferred the leadership of the League to Shandruk, who began working with the Americans. This was not a success, and he acknowledged that as the 'man responsible for the political and diplomatic actions of the Ukrainian government-in-exile', he had miscalculated the actions of the Allies. By 1949, Polish finance had ended, curtailing meaningful activities. Shandruk came to regard his efforts as 'idle dreams' and, in October, he took the advice of Smal-Stocky and also found refuge in the United States.[74]

The Promethean League did not, however, completely disappear. Besides the Georgians, the most important and active component of the organisation were the Belorussian émigrés who worked in close collaboration with the League's leaders. In the dying days of the Third Reich, Shandruk had met with representatives of Belorussian political groups, including President Radislaw Ostrowsky, whose views he found 'very instructive'. 'He stated openly that he would go hand and hand with me, he would use all his prestige in my support, and that if we were able to form any Ukrainian national military units under the political sponsorship of the Ukrainian National Committee, the Belorussian National Committee would have its forces join ours. He was also unequivocally opposed to German proposals of any subordination of national committees to [Vlasov's] KONR'. General Anders's Polish Army in Italy had taken under its protective wing the fugitive Belarus Division, which created a pool of anti-communist MI6-backed resistance fighters for operations in their homeland.[75]

CHAPTER 13

BELORUSSIA

Belorussia (now known as Belarus) lies in an area between the Baltic states and Poland in the west, Ukraine in the south, and Russia in the north and east. The Belorussians, also known as the 'White Russians' or 'White Ruthenians', have thus been subject to the buffeting of history as their more powerful neighbours have fought over their territory.

Following the Bolshevik suppression of the German-backed Belorussian National Republic (BNR), the 1921 Treaty of Riga cut the country in half – with the western Catholic region ceded to Poland while the eastern Orthodox part went to the Soviet Union. This effectively also divided the Belorussian nationalists into two antagonistic factions. A socialist Polish senator and former cabinet member of the BNR, Radislaw Ostrowsky, was seen as the only person capable of uniting all the warring nationalist factions, but he was a highly controversial figure – accused of receiving Bolshevik gold to fund his subversive activities. Ostrowsky's attempt at collaboration with the Poles ended in 1928 with his arrest for fraud.[1]

The French had a long history of engagement in Poland and Belorussia, and used the MI6-sponsored Promethean League to instigate a Franco/Polish-backed 'anti-communist revolution' in the region, through the 'Abramtchik Faction'. Funded under the umbrella of the League by MI6's Stewart Menzies, its head in Paris and leader of the western nationalists was Dr Mikolai Abramtchik, who also took handouts from the Vatican. Assertions by émigré historian Nicholas Vakar that Abramtchik 'undoubtedly was connected with, and inspired – perhaps led – by the Communist under-ground', have prompted accusations that the Belorussian leadership was controlled by Soviet spies. This is an oversimplification, for any ideological commitment they held was subordinated to the nationalist cause and, like all zealous converts, they became increasingly authoritarian as the fulfilment of their dream became ever more remote. By the mid-thirties, 'persecuted by the Poles and betrayed by the Russians', Ostrowsky 'turned to fascism'.[2]

The nationalists were treated as desirable anti-Polish elements by the Germans, who realised that they could act as guides for the Wehrmacht's march eastwards into Poland and, later, Soviet Russia. An attempt was made to build a Belorussian 'army of liberation', and through Georg Leibbrant, the chief of the Nazi Ministry for the Occupied Eastern Territories (OMi), Alfred Rosenberg approached V. Zacharka, head of the BNR in Prague. Soviet forces entered the Polish, western part of Belorussia in September 1939, and in the new year Stalin ordered a purge of nationalist elements. Nevertheless, many Belorussians managed to escape to Germany, where Dr Franz Six – later responsible for the mobile killing units that would sweep away thousands of Jews in the Soviet Union – recruited thirty leading nationalists for Operation Barbarossa. On the eve of the German invasion, these 'foster-children' of the SD intelligence service met secretly in Berlin to plan a new Belorussian administration, though they were regarded by the SS as anti-German 'conspirators', covertly organising for an independent state 'which would be directed as much against Germany as against Great Russia'. The SS, therefore, rooted them out and promoted those pro-Nazi nationalists with strong anti-western views, such as Ostrowsky, Franz Kushel, Stanislaw Stankievich, and Dimitri Kasmowich.[3]

Assembled with collaborators in Warsaw, Ostrowsky was entrusted with organising the puppet apparatus around the capital, Minsk, while Stankievich had responsibility for Borissov. Ostrowsky's men – taking their lead from his rants against the 'Jewish Kremlin' – took control of the region in a bloody act of slaughter carried out by Belorussian members of the Einsatzgruppe B, run by Dr Six's assistant, Friedrich Buchardt. In Smolensk, Kasmowich cleared the area of Jews and communists. During September and October 1941, Stankievich and Kushel sanctioned the massacre of men, women and children. By 26 October, Kushel's deputies had helped to liquidate over thirty-seven thousand people, raping 'girls they expected to shoot' and smashing 'in the heads of whatever infants they didn't flip alive into mass graves'. Even the SS were shocked by the savagery.[4]

Despite the brutal methods, Belorussia was increasingly plagued by Soviet partisan activity. In September 1943, Belorussian overlord Generalkommissar Wilhelm Kube was assassinated and replaced by SS Brigadeführer General Kurt von Gottberg, who ordered the deployment of nationalist units in anti-partisan operations. Minsk became an embattled fortress. Meanwhile, the Nazis dissolved a number of pro-nationalist Belorussian committees and deported their leaders to Germany but, alarmed by the military situation, they had no choice but to bring them back to bolster the regime. Mikolai Abramtchik, who had been entrusted by Zacharka with 'preserving the idea of Belorussian statehood and independence', returned, but von Gottberg decided that the person to form a 'central Belorussian authority' was Ostrowsky. On 21 December 1943, a Belorussian Central Council (BCC) was created and eventually a 'Belorussian army', whose members wore the national white-red-white insignia.[5]

On 27 June 1944 – with the 'sound of Red Army guns echoing in the distance' and 'under the watchful eye of SS officers' – a thousand BCC 'delegates' met in Minsk for an All-Belorussian Congress. An adherent of the 'Führership' principle, Ostrowsky was president. Although Belorussia was now savaged by Soviet partisans, he claimed the Belarus Legion was ready to fight Stalin's 'bandits'. German surveys had shown that Ostrowsky and his conspirators were émigrés with no following, but they were loyal and they continued to collaborate with the Nazis to the end. The BCC did not survive, and on 29 June 1944 its members were evacuated to Berlin, where they reorganised as a national committee under the supervision of Professor Gerhardt von Mende, a deputy in Rosenberg's OMi, who was regarded as 'a great friend of all non-Russian peoples enslaved by the Bolsheviks'.[6]

Stankievich was appointed Intelligence Minister, while Abramtchik was made responsible for liaison with other governments-in-exile. Belorussians who reached Germany were reorganised into the 30th Waffen-SS Grenadier Division, the Belarus Legion, under the command of General Kushel. The legion fought on the western front until the end of the war, with a number of legionnaires recruited into the Otto Skorzeny-trained 'Black Cat' guerrilla forces, which were parachuted in behind Russian lines. These stay-behind nets were supplied with weapons until the spring of 1945, but they proved to be a failure, as most were mopped up by the NKVD, which successfully planted agents among the remaining units and within the Belarus Legion.[7]

As the war closed, Belorussian envoys were dispatched to the Allies with an offer to turn over to them 'a vast espionage network behind Soviet lines' and an active anti-communist guerrilla force. It was decided that the best chance for safety lay with the Polish government-in-exile in London and, through Promethean League contacts in France and Switzerland, Abramtchik was able to conclude a deal with the Polish leader, General Wladyslaw Anders. In the spring of 1945, the legion made contact with Patton's Third Army, and its soldiers were interned as PoWs near Regensburg, in the American Zone in Germany. The presence of the Belorussians, however, soon became an embarrassment, since the camp was effectively controlled by Franz Kushel, who used his position to recruit for a guerrilla army, the White Ruthenian Veterans League. Fearing possible exposure, the Americans decided to allow legion members to 'quietly escape' to the nearby French zone. The French subsequently approved the establishment in Paris of an exiled Polish Military Mission, which served as a cover for recruiting leading Belorussians. The western Belorussians under Abramtchik, manoeuvring for independence from Ostrowsky, Kushel and Stankievich, volunteered to work with French Intelligence (Service de Documentation Extérieure et de Contre-Espionage – SDECE). His colleagues were provided with para-diplomatic status as members of the Polish Military Liaison, which helped launch covert operations on behalf of the SDECE which, between 1948 and 1954, parachuted almost one hundred French-trained émigrés into eastern Europe.[8]

Meanwhile, the eastern leaders under Ostrowsky had moved into the British Zone, where they were provided by British Military Intelligence with cover posts in the United Nations Relief and Rehabilitation Agency (UNRRA). Ostrowsky used his network to collect information which he then sold to the British and Americans. Unfortunately, the 'intelligence', which largely consisted of captured NKVD documents and manufactured information, was used to settle old scores in a reign of terror in the DP camps. The Allied Operation TOBACCO was intended to flush out Soviet agents among the DP but the information was largely disinformation originating with Soviet agents active in the camps.[9]

MI6 knew precisely who best to enlist for its Belorussian exile operations, partly from pre-war ties but also because it had recruited a major war criminal, Friedrich Buchardt, commander of one of the mobile killing units around Minsk. As chief of Emigré Affairs for the SS, Buchardt acquired an encyclopedic knowledge of the various collaborators in eastern Europe and Russia. In exchange for immunity from prosecution, Buchardt offered to trade his seminal work on political warfare on the eastern front, 'The Treatment of the Russian Problem During the Period of the National-Socialist Regime in Germany'. Laying particular stress on the role of native collaborators in SS operations, the paper was written soon after the German surrender, with additional material provided to British Intelligence by other former SS officers. Completed in 1946, the study was 'an invaluable source' whose information, when tested against later intelligence, was regarded as 'precise'. It was particularly useful as a manual for future émigré operations, illuminating, as it did, the mistakes made by the Nazis.[10]

The French and Poles worked closely with British Intelligence, which transported a number of Belorussian leaders to London, where they were provided with funds and found employment as translators. Kasmowich was recruited by MI6 and lived in England under the name 'Zarechny', while Abramtchik also became a frequent visitor to London. 'Academic centres' and 'research organisations' were set up where 'ex-Nazi diplomats and intelligence officers helped them map out new strategies for the Cold War'. According to American investigator John Loftus, Abramtchik's staff were employed at a private research institute known as the Francis Ckryvana Library, where his portrait hung prominently in the lobby. Publishers and printers poured out a stream of propaganda books and pamphlets for the émigré groups of the Promethean League, glorifying their nationalism under Nazi Germany and condemning Soviet ethnic actions against minority groups. Throughout 1945 and 1946, a team of former Nazi collaborators, issued with false papers identifying them as discharged Polish officers, toured the DP camps gathering together the dispersed members of the Belarus Legion. They were then provided with forged documentation by Father Maikalaj Lapitski, an Orthodox priest and former collaborator.[11]

Factionalism was rife among the exile groups and the battle to control the Belorussian community was bitter. Ostrowsky, who was well known for his collaboration with the Nazis, was soon engaged in reorganising his supporters into a more acceptable organisation. At the end of 1945, the Nazi-created Belorussian Central Council was transformed into the Belorussian Central Representation (BCR), but it did not end the factionalism. In November 1946 a Belorussian National Centre was set up as 'an inter-party organisation with a platform embracing all anti-Soviet trends and groups'. It failed to unite the warring parties, and the nationalists, once again, split.[12]

In an attempt to break Ostrowsky's ties to MI6, Abramtchik – another collaborator but, unlike Ostrowsky, not known to have been involved in war crimes – created his own BNR, which claimed its lineage from the First Belorussian Convention in 1918. The constitution adopted in Paris, in November 1947, stated that Abramtchik was 'the only legal supreme representative of the Belorussian people'. Primarily a Catholic grouping, it received funding from the Vatican, the Polish government-in-exile and a number of international anti-communist sponsors, which enabled Abramtchik to travel throughout western Europe and the United States, organising 'BNR Council Sections'. Abramtchik's action was viewed by other nationalists as 'undemocratic and unconstitutional'; and he was accused of 'dictatorship, sectarianism and political trickery'. In the war of words that followed, Ostrowsky's BCR was, in turn, accused of being infiltrated by communist agents and run by war criminals. 'In order to avoid any further scandal', MI6 'transferred their loyalty to Abramtchik and cut their links to Ostrowsky'.[13]

With Ostrowsky's past an increasing embarrassment, MI6 exiled him to Argentina. It gradually became apparent, however, that the Abramtchik Faction, which was racked by 'continuous inner strife and splits', was itself riddled with communist agents. To add to the suspicion, Polish communists and Soviet agents compiled a dossier on the whereabouts of a number of high-ranking Nazi collaborators within the organisation, which received widespread publicity in exile circles. On the advice of Dr Gerhard von Mende – 'the patron saint of the Belorussians', who now acted as a high-level talent-spotter and adviser to MI6 on East European exiles – MI6 decided to bring back Ostrowsky as a replacement for the increasingly discredited Abramtchik.[14]

While both groups continued to make claims about contacts with the underground in Belorussia, most testimonies agree that the anti-Soviet guerrillas had been almost entirely liquidated by 1946. Nevertheless, Ostrowsky continued to claim the support of '50,000 Belorussian partisans' under the command of guerrilla veteran General Vituska. Scattered in the forests and depths of Belorussia, these guerrillas were said to be attacking tanks and armoured police and troop patrols. Abramtchik, too, operated in a fantasy world, presenting medals to a non-existent guerrilla army. Nicholas Vakar recognised that the Belorussian nationalists seemed 'to live a diluted sense of reality' with 'an amazing capacity to believe anything they wish to believe'. Like many émigrés, they existed in 'apocalyptic expectancy of the final settlement' when their hopes would be fulfilled.[15]

Despite the evidence, or lack of it, MI6 continued to sponsor the Belorussians. In December 1947, Ostrowsky, along with several other ministers of the former quisling government, began to 'rebuild an organisation dedicated to the unity of all White Russian people in exile'. By the following March he had revived the BCR as a government-in-exile, nominating ministers and diplomats, and he had issued an appeal to Belorussian emigrants to recognise the BCR as 'the only legitimate representative of the Belorussian nation'. Appointing himself head of the Belorussian 'Liberation Movement', plans were made to send teams based in the British Zone in Germany on missions to the old country. Abramtchik's supporters continued to boycott these efforts and launched a fresh campaign to discredit Ostrowsky's men, but these men were now regarded as good anti-communist assets and had the protection of MI6, which dismissed Soviet accusations of war crimes as smears and communist propaganda. Even when Stankievich was picked up as a war criminal on the Soviet wanted list for 'aggressive questioning' by the US CIC and provided the interrogators with a partial confession, he was released on the intervention of the staff of the military governor of the American Zone in Germany, General Lucius D. Clay. British Intelligence told Clay's staff that Stankievich was a victim of Soviet vilification.[16]

There was, however, little let-up in the Soviet attacks, and this had an effect, forcing leading members to seek a safer haven. The collapse of the Promethean League and the departure of leading spokesmen to the United States encouraged a number of Belorussian members to join them. At the last conference of the Belarus network at the Backnmangg DP camp near Stuttgart, in June 1949, a motion was carried to transfer Belorussian assets to the United States, where there would be greater safety and access to new financial and material support for the nationalist cause. Franz Kushel, who had been working for the Americans since 1947, moved, in May 1950, to New York, where he ran the Abramtchik Faction. Responsibility for it was shared between MI6 and the Americans, through the Office of Policy Co-ordination (OPC)-sponsored Belorussian American Association, which consisted almost entirely of new émigrés.[17]

By the beginning of 1951 Ostrowsky's BCR was established in Washington under a new name, the Belorussian Democratic Republic in the USA, in order to appease its American hosts. Nevertheless, the factional in-fighting continued. Ostrowsky told American intelligence officials that the Abramtchik group was 'honeycombed with Soviet agents', thus confirming CIC reports that some of its senior officials had links to Soviet Intelligence. When OPC chief Frank Wisner sought confirmation of these reports from MI6, its Washington liaison officer, Kim Philby, 'dismissed the accusation with the claim that this was merely sour grapes and just part of the internal dissension expected in exile groups'. MI6 was, at the time, short of funds, and wearing the hat of the former head of Section IX, which had recruited the Belorussians immediately after the war, Philby wanted 'to unload the troublesome Abramtchik on to the OPC'. Wearing his other hat as a Soviet agent, Philby was both able to damage the exile programme by sustaining the atmosphere of distrust among the groups and betray the infiltration operations into Belorussia, which had recently been launched. Wisner chose to accept the advice of Philby, recognising that he had greater experience in this area.[18]

Philby was quite happy for the Americans to take over responsibility for the Abramtchik Faction because, by the spring of 1951, the infiltration operations using his men were near to collapse. 'The few parachutists that had been sent to Belorussia had been captured or killed. Several turned up at news conferences to exhibit the British or American equipment with which they had been supplied and to proclaim themselves as having been Soviet agents all along.' Philby's exposure at the end of the year as a possible Soviet agent led Wisner to drop the Abramtchik Faction and shift resources to Ostrowsky. 'Those that had previously been an embarrassment to the American authorities now became attractive propositions.'[19]

With the approval of MI6, Ostrowsky moved to London, where he worked on a new joint MI6/OPC operation to penetrate the Soviet Union. Co-ordinator of these paramilitary operations was Dimitri Kasmowich, whose cover post was as an accountant for the US Army in Germany. He was assigned the task of recruiting volunteers in Britain, the United States and Germany. During 1952, in order to challenge and overcome the 'chauvinistic groups which sabotage the common anti-communist action', the OPC attempted to unite the nationalists by setting up a broadly based Belorussian National Liberation Committee in Germany under the leadership of Kasmowich. It did not come to anything, primarily because of Abramtchik's anger at the loss of American funding. He retaliated by releasing the information that Kasmowich was 'a former communist official and a major Nazi collaborator', who was now employed by MI6. With his cover blown, Kasmowich 'fell into a depression and began drinking heavily'. On the orders of Ostrowsky, he was expelled from the Belorussian Liberation Movement which 'led to further factionalism'. The in-fighting within the Belorussian camp was seemingly endemic to all the exile communities in the West.[20]

With the collapse of the Promethean League, its Belorussian leaders, Ostrowsky and Stankievich, became leading lights in another MI6-backed umbrella organisation, the more extreme and militant Ukrainian-dominated Anti-Bolshevik Bloc of Nations (ABN). Smal-Stocky recognised it as 'a revolutionary underground movement which called for a common continuous revolution of all subjugated nations against Soviet Moscow', which upheld and promoted the League's ideas. A close reading of the League's own propaganda suggests that the ABN, which was controlled by Stefan Bandera's faction of the Organisation of Ukrainian Nationalists, OUN-B, acted, in effect, as the military wing of the League. Ostrowsky would eventually become vice-president of the ABN. Despite the ever-continuing in-fighting among the exiled Belorussian nationalists, and his supposed expulsion from the movement by Ostrowsky, Kasmowich remained from 1954 until his death in 1991 the representative of the Belorussian Council in the Central Committee of the ABN. He was also one of the Belorussian representatives to the World Anti-Communist League (WACL) and, in 1967, a co-founder of the European Freedom Council.[21]

With the end of the Cold War, Belarus finally achieved independence from the Soviet Union, but the vast majority of the ten million population wondered whether it had been worth the wait. Shunned by the West and neglected by Russia, the country had an economy that could not survive the shock. In turn, President Lukashenko gained power on a wave of popular support with his aim of economic reintegration with Russia. The nationalists, whose leaders found political asylum in the United States, once again found themselves in a minority, with the national flag abandoned and Russian adopted as the official language. During the election, Lukashenko linked the opposition nationalists to the wartime collaborators with the Nazis. A leading Belarus writer predicted a gloomy outcome: 'I see a despotism coming of a more fascist form. The communists were at least civilised in their fight against the national movement.'[22]

CHAPTER 14

THE ANTI-BOLSHEVIK BLOC OF NATIONS

Operational names are usually chosen at random, but the choice of the code-name INTEGRAL for the MI6-backed exile operations into mainly western Ukraine was clearly deliberate.

The thirties movement in central and eastern Europe of 'integral nationalism' did not, in the main, live by a cohesive ideology but rather propagated a set of irrational, even mystical beliefs which 'conceived of the solidarity of all individuals making up the nation'. It completely opposed the Marxian concept of class and class struggle. Totalitarian in concept, it deified the nation to the point of racism: nationalism was 'based on feelings, which are carried by the racial blood'. Historian John Armstrong observed that the nationalists 'in some respects went beyond the original Fascist doctrines'. Indeed, they had much in common with the Romanian Iron Guard, the Hungarian Arrow Cross, the Croatian Ustashi and the Latvian Thunder Cross.[1]

The young western Ukrainian nationalists of Galicia despised the way in which their elders in groups such as the Promethean League had compromised with the Poles. They put their faith in the illegal Organisation of Ukrainian Nationalists (OUN), modelled on the Bolshevik concept of party organisation and the successful guerrilla operations of Michael Collins and the Irish Republican Army (IRA). The OUN was led by 'Colonel' Eugene Konovalets, who made contact with German Military Intelligence, the Abwehr, which was regularly supplied with intelligence by the nationalists in western Ukraine. The intense interest shown by the Nazis in the Ukrainian problem aroused the anxiety of the Polish government and provoked a series of trials, banishments and executions which created in the OUN a hatred of 'the Polish orientation'. This culminated in the murder of Polish Interior Minister General Peiracki in June 1934. The Polish authorities arrested a number of OUN leaders who had conspired in attacks on Polish officials, including Stefan Bandera, Mykola Lebed and Yaroslav Stetsko. At the beginning of 1936, a Warsaw court handed down death sentences which were later commuted to life.[2]

In May 1938 Konovalets was assassinated in Rotterdam by means of a bomb disguised as a box of chocolates handed to him by an 'illegal' Soviet agent, Pavel Sudoplatov. Following Konovalets's death, the movement turned to Colonel Andrei Melnyk, a moderate of dignified military bearing. He faced, however, a strong, extremist opposition led by the younger generation of activists centred around the anti-Polish, anti-Russian Stefan Bandera, a 'folk hero' to many Ukrainian exiles, who was chair of the executive of the OUN in western Ukraine.[3]

From the mid-thirties, MI6, under its chief, Admiral Sir Hugh 'Quex' Sinclair – previously head of Naval Intelligence in the 'Intervention' years against the Bolsheviks – patronised Bandera's extremist faction, which had been condemned by the League of Nations as a 'terrorist syndicate'. Open to a variety of offers, Bandera's followers were recruited by the MI6 head of station in Finland, Harry Carr, and used as a network of informants inside the Soviet Union (since Bandera was in prison it is unlikely that Carr actually met the OUN leader as some accounts suggest). Carr, who was attracted to Bandera's brand of anti-communism, soon began to deliver funding and support for operations to infiltrate agents across the Finnish–Soviet border – although Galician Ukrainians, with their peculiar accents, would have been easily recognisable in the Soviet Union. Whether Carr knew about the German connection or indeed co-operated with the Abwehr on operations is still unresolved.[4]

Andrei Melnyk, Richard Iarii and Colonel Roman Sushko, who was head of the OUN military organisation, continued to develop close ties with the Abwehr and opened an 'excellent communications' channel to Admiral Canaris. He 'cared little about the details of the OUN's programme'; what mattered was that it was a 'nationalist fascist group'. At the end of 1938, the Abwehr used OUN activists to encourage Ukrainian nationalism in Ruthenia – a province in eastern Slovakia, renamed Carpatho/Ukraine – in a bid to undermine the Soviet Union and Poland. When the Ukrainians were ordered to submit to Hungarian rule in the area, they resolved to proclaim their own independence under an OUN supporter and priest, Monsignor Augustine Voloshyn. He created the Carpathian Sic Guard to persecute Jews, gypsies, Poles and Czechs, and to defend the Ukrainians against Magyar incursions. Declared a republic on 14 March 1939, Carpatho/Ukraine retained its independence for precisely twenty-four hours until the Hungarians moved against it. Voloshyn's ill-fated cause did, however, provide hope for the nationalist aspirations of the OUN. Subsequently, thousands of these Carpathian Ukrainians went into exile in Germany, expanding the ranks of the OUN and acting as a recruiting pool for Abwehr secret military formations.[5]

Alfred Rosenberg, whose Ministry for the Occupied Eastern Territories (Ostministerium – OMi), would be responsible for administering the conquered eastern territories, had already decided that although the OUN was 'entirely unfit to lead a political operation to seize hold of the population', the nationalist formations could be used in the expected attack on Poland to carry out intelligence duties and 'aim at the annihilation of the Jews and Poles' behind enemy lines.[6]

In the confusion that followed the German and Soviet invasions of Poland in September 1939, Bandera and Lebed were released from Warsaw's Swiety Kroyc prison and immediately began to challenge the authority of the leadership. Bandera first went to Cracow and then to Italy to meet Melnyk to discuss the differences of opinion that existed between the OUN leadership in Rome and the younger, pro-Bandera 'Home Executive Committee' in western Ukraine. Bandera's representative at a nationalist convention in Rome, Jaroslav Stetsko, called for a dynamic person to lead the nationalist cause. The reasons for the dispute are obscure but at its heart was the wish to launch a more aggressive policy in pursuit of Ukrainian independence. The conflict came to a head during the following January when Melnyk was dismissed for 'tolerating traitors among the party heads' – a forerunner of much fratricidal in-fighting. One reason for these intense and bitter disagreements was a Soviet deception operation which infiltrated NKVD agents into the Nazi Party training school with the intention of 'forcing these gangsters to annihilate each other in a struggle for power'. Another element revolved around the willingness or not of the differing OUN factions to intervene in the Russo-Finnish War which broke out in 1939. Attempts by Carr and MI6 to infiltrate Banderite OUN agents into Russia during the short war floundered and badly misfired. They did, though, set an example for a more militant policy.[7]

It would appear that MI6 gave considerable thought to using OUN assets to trigger a revolt in the Soviet eastern Ukraine, though given the logistical problems it is hard to believe that the plan was in any way a serious proposition. In March 1941 the Second OUN Congress led to a split in the nationalist ranks, breaking it into two camps – OUN-M[elnyk] and OUN-B[andera]. The latter proved to be the most effective, with its call for 'revolutionary action' for 'national liberation'. Prior to the invasion of the USSR, the Germans poured money into Bandera's group (claimed by its members to be about twenty thousand strong) with the result that OUN-B became even more closely tied to the Abwehr as key Melnyk supporters, such as Richard

Iarii, who had a direct link to Canaris, changed sides. Bandera ensured his grip on the organisation by appointing the ultra-loyal Stetsko as his first lieutenant; while Mykola Lebed entered a Gestapo training academy at Cracow, establishing the 'Ukrainian Training Unit' and creating the Sluzhba Bezpeky, the OUN-B's 'ruthless' internal security service. According to one OUN eye-witness, Mykyta Kosakivsky, Lebed led his men in torture sessions which included beating naked Jews with iron bars and burning the open wounds into which salt had been poured.[8]

In April 1941, the Abwehr gave the go-ahead to the OUN-B leadership to organise its sympathisers into two armed military formations, under Abwehr programmes code-named 'Nachtigall' and 'Roland'. The latter was formed in Austria under the unofficial command of Colonel Iraii, for reconnaissance and sabotage duties in Ukraine. Officially led by German officers, with the Abwehr's Professor Theodor Oberländer in charge of the political side, Nachtigall had an unofficial Ukrainian staff headed by Roman Shukhevych, leader of OUN-B's military section. Both units wore German uniforms with blue-and-yellow collar badges: there were never any Ukrainian uniforms. A Greek Catholic Uniate chaplain, Father John Hrynioch, who had worked for German intelligence, was appointed to Nachtigall. He helped facilitate contacts between the Italian secret service and Uniate groups in Galicia and Rome.[9]

When Operation Barbarossa was launched, on 22 June 1941, the OUN-B in Cracow formed a 'Ukrainian National Committee'. Nachtigall advanced with the Wehrmacht to Lvov, reaching the city in the morning of 30 June, while Roland was dispatched to southern Bessarabia. Three days later, Lebed arrived in Lvov with the tail-end of the Sonderkommando 4b of Einsatzgruppe B. Prior to their withdrawal, Soviet NKVD personnel had slaughtered three thousand political prisoners, mostly Ukrainian nationalists and a few Jewish Zionists. Stacked from floor to ceiling with dead bodies, the police cells were said to have been flooded in blood. Inevitably, retaliation and revenge were swift. OUN-B militiamen attacked the Jews. General Korfes recalled seeing, on 3 July, 'Banderists . . . hurling grenades down the trenches' which 'contained some 60–80 persons . . . men, women and children'. In the weeks that followed, deserters from the Nachtigall unit and the Sonderkommando murdered over seven thousand Jews and Poles – the latter's addresses supplied by OUN-B to the Gestapo lists. Andre Pestrak was an enthusiastic recruit to the Ukrainian military police who was put in charge of a unit attached to Einsatzgruppen C (it replaced 'B' on 11 July), which massacred thousands of Jews in 'cleansing operations'. After the war, Pestrak moved as a DP to Britain, where he died in 1989. The Ukrainians were used for the dirty work in the pogrom 'Action Petlura', and in the ghetto-clearing operations in Warsaw and Lublin. Sonderkommando 4a confined itself 'to shooting of adults while commanding its Ukrainian helpers to shoot children'. An estimated nine hundred thousand Jews disappeared from the Ukraine during the German occupation.[10]

Informal agreement had been reached with the Germans, particularly Canaris's Abwehr, that the Banderites could engage in political activities in Ukraine in return for military and clandestine collaboration. This loose agreement was, however, liberally interpreted by the OUN-B, which assumed that it had been given a free hand. The OUN-B wanted an independent government, allied to Hitler's Reich, which would consolidate 'the new ethnic order in Eastern Europe' through the 'destruction of the seditious Jewish-Bolshevist influence'. On behalf of Bandera, who had remained in Cracow, the OUN-B's chief political officer, Wolodymyr, wrote to Adolf Hitler asking him to 'support our ethnic struggle'. Following hard on the heels of Nachtigall, Stetsko arrived in Lvov on 30 June ready to organise a hastily summoned 'National Assembly'. The Assembly proclaimed an independent Ukrainian state in the name of Stefan Bandera, who had been recalled to Berlin by the Supreme Command of the Wehrmacht, and his lieutenant, Jaroslav Stetsko, who assumed the title 'Head of the National Assembly'. On the local radio the Uniate priest attached to Nachtigall, John Hrynioch, read out a pastoral letter that praised the Germans and recognised Stetsko as Prime Minister. The OUN-B also succeeded in obtaining a statement of support from the Uniate primate, Metropolitan Andreas Sheptytsky. These moves had the full support of the bulk of Galician youth, who defected from the Melnyk faction to the OUN-B, but disturbed the Wehrmacht officers who had helped organise Nachtigall.[11]

The announcement of an independent Ukrainian state went against Nazi policy, but German officers were initially reluctant to take countermeasures. Hitler, however, who considered Ukraine a territory for exploitation and colonisation, and thought the Slavs to be 'subhuman', was not prepared to tolerate nationalist ambitions. Professor Oberlander's personal appeal to Hitler to the effect that a great opportunity was being lost was brushed aside with crude racist language. A German Foreign Office official told the Ukrainian Foreign Affairs Minister in the National Assembly, Volodymyr Stakhiv, that the discussion regarding the liquidation of the Ukrainian government, which took place in Hitler's headquarters in the presence of Ribbentrop, Keitel, Himmler and Hitler, 'only lasted a few minutes'.[12]

The 'exhilarating days', as they were later described in OUN-B publications, were soon brought to a close. Accordingly, within a few days, the so-called nationalist government was disbanded and told to withdraw the proclamation. This the Banderites refused to do and, on 6 July, a number of its leaders were arrested by the SS and kept under house arrest in Berlin. They were, however, allowed to carry on with political activities, and Stetsko was able to consult with the ambitious security chief and Home Affairs minister in the Lvov 'government', Mikolai Lebed, who, under the *nom de guerre* 'Maxim Ruban', had escaped arrest and was delegated to take command of all OUN-B activities.[13]

Meanwhile, 'marching groups' of OUN-B (and OUN-M) personnel moved eastwards behind the German Army further into the Ukraine in an attempt to set up nationalist administrations. With the arrest of Bandera and concerned that they might rebel, the Germans withdrew the Nachtigall and Roland units from the front lines to Frankfurt-an-der-Oder, where they were later united into a single formation, Schutzmannschaftbataillon (Guard Battalion) No. 201, which in 1942 was sent to Belorussia to fight Red partisans. Many of the officers refused to accept the posting and were imprisoned in Lvov. In contrast, Melnyk's more moderate and accommodating OUN-M had zealously retained its own contacts with the Wehrmacht and, once the OUN-B administration was set aside, took over the reins. This resulted in bloody civil strife between the two factions. Lebed played a leading role in the terror that followed with his élite Sluzhba Bezpeky (SB) – which was modelled on the Gestapo – assassinating those Ukrainians who refused to join OUN-B's enforced united front. 'It was highly effective and fractious and completely without scruple.' Two OUN-M leaders were shot in the back on 30 August by an assassin who was immediately, and conveniently, killed by Ukrainian police. Eventually, the in-fighting was put down by the SS: 'The separatists, only recently privileged, promptly became pursued pariahs.'[14]

On 15 September 1941, the Gestapo arrested two thousand Ukrainian nationalists. Melnyk was put under house arrest, while Bandera, Stetsko and a number of other leading OUN-B members were transferred from Berlin and confined as 'privileged' internees within the Sachsenhausen concentration camp. Other Ukrainian nationalists were less lucky and were executed or later died in Auschwitz, including Bandera's two brothers, who had cement poured over their water-soaked bodies. Although, on 4 October, a 'Wanted' notice was put out for Lebed, he was never arrested. Lebed had friends in high places, while his deputy, Father John Hrynioch, had retained the favour of German Intelligence. Bandera and Stetsko were still permitted to continue political activities and continued to pursue the goal of an independent state. At least once during 1943 Stetsko was allowed to travel to Poland to confer with Lebed. An outstanding organiser, Lebed was soon 'secretly pulling the strings' within OUN-B, and as his own political ambitions grew, he gradually developed an intense factional rivalry with Bandera, who remained trapped in Germany. As one émigré writer noted, it is these 'facts' which gave 'full meaning to the political and personal dividing lines within the post-war Ukrainian emigration'.[15]

Any British plans for a revolt in eastern Ukraine collapsed following the German invasion, which forced the Soviet Union to align itself with Britain and its allies. In these changed circumstances, foreign policy dictated that it was in Britain's interest to preserve the integrity of the Soviet Union, whose economic wellbeing would be severely undermined by the loss of Ukraine. Any MI6 actions that might indicate British support for the Ukrainian nationalists were, therefore, curtailed. Indeed, surveillance against pro-German Ukrainian organisations was stepped up and MI6 exchanged information with its counterparts in the United States and Canada, where émigré support and funding for the nationalists were particularly strong. MI6 was of the opinion that all the nationalist groups in North America were 'directly or indirectly influenced by Berlin'. At the same time, MI6 made efforts to monitor developments inside Ukraine, though intelligence-gathering was to prove difficult.[16]

Inside the Ukraine, during the spring of 1943, OUN-B guerrillas – made up of German-trained police and military formations who had killed their German officers and abandoned their posts – assumed the title of the Ukrainian Insurgent Army (UPA). Its commander, under the *nom de guerre* of Taras Chuprynka, was senior Nachtigall officer Roman Shukhevych. To the end of the year, Galicia was subject to intense Soviet partisan activity, and OUN-B forces led by Bohdan Kruk – sometimes referred to as the Director of the UPA Red Cross – were recruited to pacify the countryside. More often than not these various formations were engaged in a civil war, sometimes fighting different nationalist factions, occasionally the Germans, often the Soviets, but mainly the Poles. Despite the execution by the Germans of a number of leading members of his organisation, Andrei Melnyk continued to support the Nazis; a stance that was to 'prevent his faction from playing a major political role' in postwar nationalist affairs.[17]

During 1943, a number of PoWs and deserters from the Red Army and from non-German SS units, including Belorussians, Georgians, Azerbaijanis, Turkestanians, Cossacks, Armenians, Uzbeks, Tartars and even Russians, went over to the UPA 'to form a national formation of enslaved peoples'. In émigré myth-making accounts of this period, Ukrainians portrayed the UPA as 'the third military and political force in Eastern Europe' which soon became 'the champion of all revolutionary forces representing not only the resistance movement of Ukraine, but all the subjugated peoples of Eastern Europe, the Caucasus and Central Asia'. Rosenberg's OMi and German Intelligence saw this as an opportunity to co-ordinate resistance activity against the Soviet Army and sponsored a committee of subjugated nations. On 21 and 22 November OUN-B nationalists in Zhitomir set up an 'Anti-Bolshevik Front' to co-ordinate the activities of the 'enslaved' Soviet ethnic minorities. Tolerated by German Intelligence, the conference was attended by thirty-nine delegates representing twelve peoples of eastern Europe and Asia with the common slogan 'Freedom of the Individual – Freedom of the Nations'. The front was a direct precursor of the postwar Anti-Bolshevik Bloc of Nations (ABN), though the nationalists continued to deny its Nazi origins.[18]

Just before the Red Army reconquered eastern Galicia in the summer of

1944, 'the supreme and only guiding organ of the Ukrainian people for the period of its revolutionary struggle', the Ukrainian Supreme Liberation Council (UHVR), was created at a meeting in the Carpathian mountains, on 12 July, by the OUN-B to unite all the factions. It was intended to garner popular support, provide a broader organisational base for the resistance and serve as an underground political guiding body for the UPA 'until the formation of the government of an independent Ukrainian state'. Shukhevych was elected secretary general, Mykola Lebed general secretary of the Foreign Representation (ZP UHVR), with Ivan Hrynioch and Bohdan Kruk on its council. Its formation went too far for the Germans, and a number of its leaders were temporarily imprisoned. The deteriorating military situation, however, forced the desperate Nazis to seek allies where they could and, in August, Himmler sanctioned a secret SS programme, Operation SUNFLOWER, designed to co-ordinate German and OUN efforts during the German retreat from the Soviet Union. The UPA insisted that the negotiations be kept secret in order to keep alive the myth that it did not co-operate with the Nazis. In October, as Ukraine finally came under Soviet control, Melnyk, Borovets, Bandera and Stetsko were released from detention to organise a final defence. According to the UHVR constitution, its centre would always be in Ukraine and only one delegation was permitted to leave Ukraine to go abroad – the ZP UHVR. Late in the year, SS favourite Lebed left Galicia for Rome, where he made contact with high-level Vatican networks.[19]

The centre of nationalism reverted to its traditional strongholds in Galicia, where the number of fighters was never to exceed fifty thousand – though nationalists optimistically claimed over eighty thousand. The final drama was played out in an atmosphere of confusion and in-fighting as the Germans tried to entice the OUN to join with the anti-communist Vlasov movement but were rebuffed as there was 'fratricidal hatred' between the pro-Russian leaders of the Vlasov army and the anti-Russian Ukrainians. During 1943 the idea had been common that Germany and the Soviet Union would exhaust themselves in battle and that, with the help of the Allies, the nationalists would be able to assume control of western Ukraine. The destruction of so many German divisions during 1944 put paid to such fantasies, though some Ukrainians did not lose hope that it would not be long before rivalry between the Allies erupted into armed hostility and, in anticipation of that event, OUN-B began to send emissaries to potential allies in the West.[20]

Despite the intense hatreds aroused, there were attempts to establish contact through the London-based Polish government-in-exile with British and American intelligence agencies. OUN leaders did not manage contact with the London Poles but low-level negotiations did take place in Lvov in November 1943 with members of the Polish underground 'Armia Krajow' (AK), and it seems that the AK radio link with London was used to pass on messages to British Intelligence about the UPA/OUN. The OUN-B next turned to Italian Army officers who were returning home, and persuaded them to take with them their emissaries disguised in Italian uniforms and help them contact British and American troops. Early in 1945, a senior OUN figure and former head of the 'Ukrainian Police' in Lvov, Yevhen Wreciona, made a covert journey from Slovakia to Switzerland, where he met with British intelligence officers at the embassy in Berne.[21]

In anticipation of the coming struggle with Soviet forces, Shukhevych broke up the UPA armed formations into underground cells and attempted to preserve a 'bridgehead' that would hold until hostilities erupted. UPA units around Volhynia and in Galicia were able to develop and equip a large and efficient underground force utilising thousands of tons of arms, ammunition and other war material left behind by the retreating German Army. This was initially a highly successful strategy, with up to two hundred thousand Red Army troops tied down and more than seven thousand officers killed. By the beginning of 1945, in south-west Ukraine and eastern Poland, UPA units – some still led by German SS officers – continued to attack the Red Army and Polish militia. The UPA – primarily a guerrilla fighting force – soon found itself isolated, which the OUN-B regarded as proof of the weakness of the military strategy. In May the nationalists were facing a Soviet Army that was at the height of its power. A conspiratorial and terrorist faction, the OUN-B believed that 'a totalitarian state could be damaged only by a totalitarian organisation striking from below'. Its conviction was that the UPA soldiers 'had chosen the fastest route to death, though one decorated with laurels'. Despite the superior Soviet forces, over the next two years a near civil war ensued with 'counter-revolutionary bandits' in effective control of many villages and rural districts.[22]

At the war's end, many leading members of the OUN fled west to avoid capture by the occupying Red Army. As they did so they forged links with the remnants of the fascist Slovak Hlinka Guard which had also continued its guerrilla war against the communists and supplied the Ukrainians with many of their weapons. After holding out with a few thousand of these troops in the wild Slovakian mountains, Bandera eventually surfaced in the British Zone of Germany, where he re-established contact with MI6, claiming with some justification that his group was organising a rebellion in Ukraine. MI6 was desperate to gather intelligence on what was happening behind the Soviet lines in the newly occupied territories and was willing to recruit agents without judgements on their past activities. Harry Carr believed that 'his single-minded purpose was to continue the interrupted struggle against communism'. It was inconceivable that Carr and his colleagues did not know about the atrocities committed in Galicia, but it mattered little. To his subordinates Carr would not have been 'in the least sympathetic to any inquiries about Bandera's past. His overriding concern was the current campaign against Stalin.'[23]

A War Office report on the 'Ukrainian Nationalist Movement and Resistance in Ukraine' – which was valid to March 1945 – is a model of its kind. Seemingly accurate and fair in its assessment, it could only have been based on OUN sources, probably backed up with Soviet intelligence, possibly German intercepts of Red Army signals and MI6 intelligence-gathering. It concluded that with 'the inevitable Sovietisation and Russification of the Western Ukraine under Soviet rule it will be seen that Ukrainian nationalism has little prospect of being anything more than a nuisance to the Soviet Union in future years of peace'. It was not what MI6 or the OUN-B wanted to hear.[24]

Bandera's second-in-command, Yaroslav Stetsko, escaped to Austria, where he managed to avoid the attentions of Allied units. Major Stephen Dattner had been sent to Klagenfurt in command of the 310th Field Security Service (denazification) unit to arrest and interrogate suspected Nazi war criminals. Using 'black lists' compiled by MI6's Section V, Dattner's task was to unearth and detain important Nazi officials, SS members and collaborators known to be in the area. Dattner was 'deeply concerned and astonished', however, to discover that Stetsko was openly engaged in organising OUN-B political activities, even though he was on the 'black list' and subject to automatic arrest for his crimes. Downplaying his murderous past, Lebed had established himself in Rome as 'foreign minister' of the Ukrainian Supreme Liberation Council (ZP UHVR) and was active in talks with Vatican Uniate Bishop Ivan Buchko. Lebed also arrived with a treasure trove of intelligence material on the Ukrainian resistance movement. Following close behind was Father John Hrynioch, who had been awarded the German Iron Cross for his work with the Nachtigall battalion. By the spring of 1945, Lebed had established contact with the US Office of Strategic Services (OSS) in Berne. In Switzerland, the former Abwehr agent and chief of the German-Ukrainian police in Lvov, Vretsonia, offered his services to American Intelligence, as did, in Munich, Volodymyr Stakhiv, minister of foreign affairs in the Stetsko 'government'.[25]

When the Soviet authorities realised that Bandera and Melnyk, who had found refuge in Switzerland, were once more organising campaigns in Ukraine, they demanded their and other anti-Soviet Ukrainian nationalists' extradition. According to his daughter, Natalia, Bandera and his family were 'constantly obliged to flee from one place to another to avoid discovery. Berlin, Innsbruck, Seefeld . . .' The Soviet Ukraine Republic delegate at the United Nations charged that Bandera and Melnyk were running special schools to train cadres in sabotage and intelligence work against the Soviet Union, and listed numerous atrocities committed by them. Although dismissed as smears and propaganda, the charges were essentially true. The western intelligence agencies responded by helping OUN leaders to go into hiding to escape the Soviet investigators. On the instructions of his British handlers, Bandera fled to Munich, in the American Zone, where he reformed his OUN-B organisation. During 1946 Soviet military officials repeatedly demanded Bandera's extradition, but US officials informed them that they had no knowledge of Bandera's whereabouts. Natalia recalled that they moved from Munich to 'Hildesheim, and finally a lonely house in the forests of Starnberg were the places in Germany and Austria where we lived'. Even though they had accurate information on his past, US CIC officers fore-warned Bandera of the Soviet moves and, in an operation code-named ANYFACE, he was kept under surveillance to protect him from Soviet assas-sination and kidnap attempts.[26]

New attempts were made to unite the different factions* and a conference of Ukrainian delegates, held in March 1946 with the aim of creating a common platform and front for the liberation of Ukraine, produced a policy that rebuked all 'totalitarian mono-party' trends and condemned all acts of terror-ism. It was clearly directed at the Banderites, and it was no surprise, therefore, when the OUN-B refused to take part in a so-called Ukrainian Co-ordinating Committee. In April, with the backing of MI6, the OUN-B created an over-arching organisation for all the former pro-fascist nationalist exile move-ments, reconstituting the Nazi-sponsored 1943 Anti-Bolshevist Front, as the Anti-Bolshevik Bloc of Nations (ABN). Well-produced leaflets and posters appeared in the occupation zones of Germany, the source of whose funding was, according to CIC reports, unknown. The true source, besides their own funding efforts from the DP camps, was a secret subvention from MI6.[27]

In June 1946 OUN-B's annual conference produced a hard-headed appraisal of the international situation with regard to the Soviet Union, correctly concluding that British power was on the decline. Even though the OUN-B was sponsored by MI6, Bandera had repeatedly warned his supporters that they would have to rely on 'our strength'. The OUN-B had wanted to send agents back into the Ukraine as quickly as possible, but these ideas 'were not immediately re-embraced by MI6 despite their repeated advances'. This resulted not in an abandonment of the links with British Intelligence but in an increase in the use of conspiratorial methods. OUN-B would take material support from where it could, while retaining an intense distrust of the Americans. Since January there had been contacts between the OUN-B and the US embassy in Warsaw. The head of OUN-B intelligence had met with the American station chief for the purpose of sending propaganda material abroad. This was received in the autumn by the assistant naval attaché, but 'there is little evidence that anything was done with it'. In fact,

---

* In the immediate postwar period, OUN-B became known as OUN-r (revolutionary) and continued to attract young nationalists who had military experience in the Waffen-SS Galician Division or the UPA. Melnyk's OUN-M, in turn, changed into the OUN-s (solidarist) and continued to enjoy centres of support, especially in Paris. To avoid confusion, I will continue to use the older terms.

OUN-B was 'more of a headache to American intelligence than a boon'. In Germany, American intelligence agencies found 'the price set by Stefan Bandera for complete co-operation involved types of political recognition and commitments to his group which no American in Germany was in a position to make'. The divide was widened following the insertion into OUN-B headquarters of a CIC agent who managed to photograph 'eleven volumes of their secret internal files' which contained proof that the majority of its members 'had worked for the Gestapo and the SS as policemen, executioners, partisan hunters and municipal officials'. The Americans simply could not understand the intense bitter and deadly rivalry between the different nationalist factions.[28]

The OUN-B gained dominance over its rivals by control of the DP camps in Germany, Austria and Italy, where the traditional enemy, the Russians, were not admitted to the MI6-backed International Committee for the DP and Political Emigrés, which had been formed just after the war in Hanau, Germany. Within the camps eastern Ukrainians lived in fear of being repatriated to the Soviet Union, and the prospect of internment in a labour camp, or death. Western Ukrainians, who were mostly followers of Bandera, were exempt because of their Polish origin. The easterners, therefore, tried to prove citizenship of the western region, but they would only be 'helped to escape the repatriation if they would accept the Bandera-Stetsko leadership'.[29]

During the summer of 1946, following the establishment of liaison with the US CIC by Roman Petrenko – a senior member of OUN-B's secret police, the Sluzhba Bezpeky (SB) – the OUN-B embarked on a reign of terror in the camps. Father Hrynioch had acted as the go-between when the CIC office in Rome made an approach to Lebed, after which Petrenko offered the SB's services in eliminating communist agents. On 22 July, the SB handed the CIC a list of alleged communist refugees, mostly, but not exclusively, in the Frankfurt am Main area. In response, the Americans arrested several hundred people who were questioned and in many instances tortured by OUN-B members dressed in US military uniforms. The torturers included Lebed. Yet out of all those arrested, only 1 per cent of the cases turned out to warrant further investigation; all were set free within a few months 'for lack of evidence'. This made the Americans more cautious and, as time went by, the OUN-B's secret police largely took over what was known as Operation OHIO.

The atmosphere of denunciation was heightened by Stetsko's accusation that Melnyk's OUN-M followers were both Gestapo and NKVD collaborators. In turn, Melnyk accused one of Bandera's closest assistants, Richard Iarii, of being a Soviet agent (Polish communist publications said he had been a Gestapo agent). Headed by Mykola Matwiyeko and Ivan Kashuba, the SB launched a killing spree in which more than one hundred Ukrainians were murdered. A few were undoubtedly Soviet agents but most appear to have been DPs who, for various reasons, opposed the OUN-B, objected to black market activities, or were members of more moderate, but still anti-communist, Ukrainian groups. Another reason why some were eliminated was that they knew too much about the Ukrainians' pro-Nazi past and partici-pation by OUN supporters in the mass murder of Jews, Poles and 'Red' Russians. Personally directing Ohio were Lebed, Stetsko, Stefan Lenkovsky, Father Hrynioch and Stefan Bandera. In Kornberg, Mittenwald, Munich and other camps in Germany and Austria, many DPs were questioned, tortured and killed. Mittenwald had an underground torture chamber which was used by the SB until the summer of 1948. A private flat in a camp near Kornberg served for interrogations during 1946 and 1947, while, in 1949, another interrogation chamber was set up at Regensberg. In the two years to 1951, a bunker in the basement of the DPs' hostel at Furnchstafe, in Munich, was the scene of SB torture. According to a former CIA employee, 'in the Mittenwald camp American intelligence used techniques borrowed from the Nazis by burning murdered bodies in large bread ovens. To compound the horror these were the very same ovens used to bake the bread for the hungry residents of the camp.' The CIC-sponsored organisation that cremated at least twenty victims in the ovens was the OUN-B.[30]

According to Fletcher Prouty, who was responsible for US Air Force air support for CIA missions overseas, a series of assassinations was undertaken by 'the best commercial hit men you have ever heard of'. Known as 'mech-anics', they were 'Ukrainians, mainly, Eastern Europeans, Greeks, and some Scotsmen. I don't know how the Scotsmen got in there, but there they were.' Prouty asserts that teams of 'mechanics' were used in cross-border infiltration operations to rescue agents and in the murders of alleged Soviet agents. During 1947, a joint British/US émigré espionage network infiltrated with agents organised by Soviet and Czech Intelligence was 'liquidated' as part of Operation RUSTY. To mask the deaths, the killings were attributed to factional violence among rival Ukrainian groups.[31]

The war inside Ukraine – which killed an estimated thirty-five thousand members of the Polish and Russian secret police and troops in the two years following the end of the war – was kept going by a campaign of terror during which OUN guerrillas cut off the arms of those peasants who assented to collectivisation. The majority of Red Army units stationed in Poland were involved in trying to rebuild the country, and it took time for the Ministry of Internal Affairs (MVD) to create the Department to Combat Bandits, which successfully began to organise a network of informers in the countryside. In a brutal campaign against the 30–40,000-strong UPA, whole forests were burned and extensive use was made of counter-gangs. Polish Brigadier-General Ignacy Blum later admitted that the UPA had succeeded in setting up ambushes, destroying militia outposts, laying waste to deserted villages and blowing up bridges. The terrain was an advantage for the insurgents, as were their treacherous fighting methods and excellent intelligence-gathering methods derived from access to captured MVD organisation and operation manuals. The man responsible for leading the anti-bandit campaign, Col. Jan Gerhard, acknowledged that 'the Banderites . . . with their conspiratorial style . . . were the best organised'. The OUN-B 'ruthlessly' controlled the Supreme Council, the UHVR, while the SB security groups attached to UPA units made them hard to penetrate.[32]

Most fighting took place in western Ukraine: there was only limited resistance in the east and very little took place in what would have been assumed to be the promising territory of Carpatho-Ukraine, where there was continuing conflict between the OUN-M and OUN-B. In many areas the hard winter of 1945/6 extinguished the UPA insurrection. The offensive by the Soviet anti-guerrilla units inflicted 'huge losses' on the Ukrainian insurgents and after 1946 morale 'declined sharply' with only small pockets of resistance. Courier links with the UPA broke down in May 1946, and to keep the illusion going fabricated reports were handed to their intelligence sponsors. Photos purporting to show military action in Ukraine were stage-managed in the Bavarian forests, while radio broadcasts from a transmitter inside Ukraine reporting on UPA successes were discovered to emanate from no further than a room next door to OUN-B headquarters.[33]

The final blow came in March 1947, when Poland's deputy defence minister, General Karol Swierczewski, was killed in a UPA ambush. This led in the following month to a pact between the Soviet Union, Czechoslovakia and Poland to co-ordinate their anti-guerrilla operations. Later that month, the Polish government launched VISTULA, a large-scale operation to wipe out the UPA and to resettle the peasants from the south-eastern sector into the former German lands of the north-western provinces. It was a brutal campaign: 'extermination battalions' and 'pseudo gangs', made up of defectors from the underground and locals pressed into the front line, fought alongside MVD units. The communist authorities ordered mass deportations and the forced recruitment of villagers to spy on the nationalists. These were quickly identified and eliminated by the SB, the OUN's security service, but there was never any certainty about whether they were genuine or not. The SB tactics eventually alienated the OUN's support among the peasants.[34]

During the spring, further attempts at contact between the UPA and the Americans were made when the US vice-consul in Warsaw and an Associated Press correspondent travelled to the UPA headquarters in Presovo, Slovakia, to 'familiarise themselves with the actual situation of the Ukrainian Nationalist Underground'. The visit did not lead to any reconciliation with the Bandera faction; instead, the Americans decided to collaborate with the known 'sadist and collaborator of the Germans', Mykola Lebed, who was beginning to distance himself from Bandera. Following a number of approaches, the Americans finally accepted Lebed as an intelligence asset and arranged to smuggle him from Rome to Munich, where his handlers helped set up a 'Liberation Council', with substantial funding from US Army Intelligence.[35]

Moves were made by a Ukrainian Co-ordinating Committee to create a governing body to co-ordinate military activity in Ukraine, but once again the Banderites refused to join. Even though they remained a destabilising factor in Ukraine émigré politics, MI6 continued to back them to the hilt. Support also came from the Vatican, which lobbied the British and Americans to render material assistance to the Ukrainian nationalists, and the Uniate Church, which 'maintained intensive contacts with guerrilla leaders and secret representatives of the Vatican'. During the summer of 1947, MI6 moved to enlarge the ABN into a body to co-ordinate and organise the activities of all the émigré groups it covertly supported. In July, MI6 joined the federalist Danubian grouping, Intermarium, with the ABN, and then, in September, added the Polish-orientated Promethean League. Not all the émigré groups joined the ABN because of the dominance of the Ukrainians and the OUN-B.[36]

By July, Vistula had reduced the UPA to a small underground force. The organisational structure had been destroyed and the Soviet government announced that 'all counter-revolutionary fascist bands under German command had been annihilated'. The guerrillas were reduced to living during the winter months in appalling conditions in underground bunkers. Isolated from the world, such conditions 'generated severe psychological effects' among the guerrillas. While there was still some fighting, UPA commander Roman Shukhevych knew that the military struggle was over, and in the autumn ordered the remaining battalions under the command of Major Bayda to escape to the West. From an assembly point near Przemysl, they managed to fight their way over the mountains, through Czechoslovakia, to the American occupation zones in Austria and Germany. During what became known as the 'Great Raid', a considerable number of guerrillas died along the 1,500-mile route.[37]

In September, a delegation of OUN-B crossed into the American Zone where, after initial thought was given to sending them back, they were interned for interrogation in order for US Intelligence to decide 'what disposition is to be made of them'. In April 1948, General Clay's representative, Carmel Offie, met with three of the leaders, who told him that their nationalist groups were 'ready to revolt'. They wanted an aggressive propaganda campaign to publicise the actions of the UPA, the 'striking arm' of the UHVR, which they claimed was 'engaged in an armed conflict with the Soviet troops in Ukraine'. In reality, the conflict was all but over. From 1948 onwards, UPA actions increasingly took the form of terrorist acts such as the assassination of prominent communist officials. Unaware of the reality, Offie tried to interest the State Department in the Banderites but was brushed off. The thinking was that 'we have to be very careful not to give too much encouragement to Ukrainian Nationalists because of the effect this might have on racial Russians'.[38]

In Germany there was no let-up in the increasingly irrelevant political manoeuvring which was becoming ever more obscure in its reasoning. The Banderites finally agreed to join the Ukrainian Co-ordinating Committee though they insisted that it recognise the UHVR as the only revolutionary body having the exclusive right to direct the UPA and formulate foreign policy. In June the Ukrainian National Council was set up in West Germany as an official provisional government. The Promethean Andrew Livitsky was made president, with the elderly social democrat Mazepa as Prime Minister and Stetsko vice-premier. The British Foreign Office thought that there was a chance that the council might prove to be 'most important' and finally resolve the factional problems. It was not to be. Because of its strength on the ground inside Galicia and other parts of western Ukraine, the OUN-B demanded majority representation on the executive committee. When this was refused, it declined to take seats on the executive and insisted that the council should be treated as only the foreign representation of the UHVR. The refusal to co-operate cloaked another spate of in-fighting and a bitter battle by the so-called 'moderate' wing of the OUN-B led by Lebed and his Vatican allies for control of the UHVR.[39]

Although an 'avid' supporter of the OUN-B, by the spring of 1948 the Vatican's Ukrainian contact for Intermarium, Bishop Buchko, had become impatient with Bandera's intransigence and Führer style of leadership. Buchko thought Bandera, who saw himself as the leader of the 'Foreign Branch' of the UVHR, had become 'an overrated extremist' whose army was 'largely dispersed and lacking all types of necessary equipment'. Lebed and Father John Hrynioch, who claimed to be in contact with the military leader of the UPA, Shukhevych, regarded themselves as the 'foreign representatives' (ZP UHVR). It was an obscure differentiation which centred on whether the government-to-be should be based in Ukraine or abroad. In August, Lebed and Hrynioch had a secret showdown with Bandera in Munich. After they had explained their plan to develop the UHVR's 'foreign representation' as a second supra-party body, Bandera furiously attacked them as 'opportunists' intent on weakening the OUN-B. Lebed retorted that the UHVR 'hoped, some day, to set up a free democratic government which is divorced from all dictatorial pressure'. Denouncing the OUN-B's 'trend toward Fascism', Lebed's group quit the session. Bandera retaliated by ordering his organisation to avoid all contact with the new American-backed Ukrainian centre in Augsburg. Increasingly, the splits within the nationalist movement mirrored differences between the British and Americans on how to pursue the struggle in Ukraine.[40]

In late 1948 a new, enlarged ABN – including the most extreme of the nationalist groups in its ranks – was formally launched with Yaroslav Stetsko assuming the presidency as the OUN-B seized supreme power. Besides funding a number of its constituent members, MI6 provided a huge amount of finance to the ABN. The source of the money was hidden by having the funding directed through Vatican intermediaries. In November, the International Press Bureau released the 'Chuprynka Plan', accredited to the head of the UPA, which envisaged the division of the USSR and eastern Europe into four distinct regions: Serbia, the Caucasus, Turkestan and the 'Scandinavian-Black Sea Unit'. As the British Foreign Office recognised, it was a restatement of the aims professed by the Federal Clubs of Central Europe and their parent body, Intermarium, which was now part of the ABN. A Foreign Office official concluded that it betrayed little real interest in federalism and, instead, 'admits the superiority of one nation [Ukraine], the most powerful, over the rest, as in the present Soviet system'.[41]

During 1949 more changes took place within the various Ukrainian associations, the result of which was their gradual takeover by the Banderites. Initially, differences between the factions were patched over with in-fighting absent from the Second Congress of the Ukrainian National Council in June. This did not, however, last long, as Bandera insisted that his group be allowed complete control over the UHVR and of all paramilitary activity in Ukraine. He, therefore, demanded that the Banderites on the executive committee be 'used as the channel through which all action should be carried out'. This was unacceptable to other political centres, such as that led by Lebed, and the short-lived coalition once again fell apart. At the end of the year, the Banderites reissued their ultimatum, but the council refused to consider such an uncompromising stance.[42]

Lebed soon fell foul of the rival Bandera faction, and the CIA – which with other US agencies had recently broken off relations with Bandera – helped smuggle him to the United States under a false name. Reaching New York in October 1949, Lebed continued to work for the Ukrainian underground on behalf of his American sponsors. Another arrival was the new MI6 liaison officer with the CIA and Frank Wisner's Office of Policy Co-ordination (OPC), Kim Philby, who tried to interest the Americans in taking over the entire British-funded Ukrainian network. During meetings with State Department officials, Philby also requested that they take over other émigré groups because of his service's lack of funds. The Americans initially balked at the suggestion because of the known fascist past of the extremists such as the Banderites. Philby did, however, persuade Frank Wisner to run joint operations with MI6 and, in time, US aversion to the extremists of the OUN-B diminished, thereby facilitating the emigration of a large number of DPs in western Europe to North America, where they constituted a substantial recruiting pool for operations.[43]

The British government had sent, on 13 July 1948, a secret telegram via the Commonwealth Relations Office to all Commonwealth governments with a proposal to end Nazi war crime trials in the British Zone of Germany. It explained that for reasons of political expediency – 'future political developments in Germany' – the time had come to 'dispose of the past as soon as possible'. No fresh trials would start after 31 August that 'would particularly affect cases of alleged war criminals, not now in custody, who might subsequently come into our hands'. The British government believed that 'punishment of war criminals is more a matter of discouraging future genera- tions than of meting out retribution to every guilty individual'. As a result of this new policy, MI6 took the opportunity to transfer large numbers of its former Nazi-sponsored émigré assets to Canada and Australia, and to the United States, where Congress passed the Displaced Persons Act in the same year.[44]

In his role as the senior British Intelligence officer in North America, Kim Philby persuaded the Canadian authorities to make an exception to the blanket exclusion of former members of the Waffen-SS. His efforts were indirectly aided by a well-known Ukrainian-Canadian leader, Gordon Bohdan Panchuk, director of Canadian postwar relief work, who informed his government that Division members had passed British security checks and that they had only joined the Wehrmacht to defend their homeland against the Russians. Backed by heavy lobbying from ultra-right-wing Cath- olics, on 31 May 1950 the Canadian Cabinet passed an order-in-council to admit several thousand men who had served in the Waffen-SS Galicia Division, including several alleged war criminals using false identities. Screening of these men was rudimentary and often undertaken by inexperi- enced officials with little knowledge of the Nazi regime. They were over- worked, with up to thirty-five interviews a day, and made no attempt at a physical search for SS tattoos. Using a simple 'negative clearance' criterion for the screening process, the system could only have worked if the screeners had had effective sources; these were absent since they 'depended almost exclusively on British Intelligence', which was primarily interested in looking for security risks – communists – not war criminals. Canadian security had had access since 1947 to the Central Registry of War Crimes and Security Suspects (CROWCASS) lists of war criminals but failed to circulate them: 'They were simply filed away and forgotten.' Even if the screening had been efficient, it is unlikely that it would have worked: 'MI6 duped the Canadian authorities, where there was no offensive intelligence agency, into admitting immigrants by supplying them with false documents.'[45]

The British Foreign Office played along with the deception. On behalf of the Foreign Secretary, L. Scopes wrote to Canada House on 4 September 1950 with respect to a Canadian inquiry on the status of the Ukrainians:

> While in Italy these men were screened by Soviet and British missions and that neither then nor subsequently has any evidence been brought to light which would suggest that any of them fought against the Western Allies [some units fought

against the Americans in France following D-Day] or engaged in crimes against humanity. Their behaviour since they came to this country has been good and they have never indicated in any way that they are infected with any trace of Nazi ideology.

When they surrendered to the Allied forces at the end of the war, they were members of the 1st Ukrainian Division of the Wehrmacht which was formed in September 1944, and which was only in action once (against the Red Army in Austria during April 1945) being employed in training and guard duties in Austria and Yugoslavia during the rest of its existence. Some of its members, however, appear to be survivors of an earlier formation known as the 14th Galician Grenadier Division. This was also a Wehrmacht unit, as an attempt by the Germans to make it into an SS Division having apparently been resisted by the Ukrainians themselves. This unit seems to have been formed about July 1943, and to have been destroyed at the Battle of Brody in June 1944.

Although Communist propaganda has constantly attempted to depict these, like so many refugees, as 'quislings' and 'war criminals' it is interesting to note that no specific charges of war crimes have been made by the Soviet or any other Government against any member of this group.[46]

Rarely have there been so many untruths in such a short statement.

In December 1952, at the request of MI6, the Canadian government set up a committee on defectors which permitted the entry into the country of 'defectors' who did not meet normal security requirements. The term 'defector' became a convenient euphemism for allowing in former Nazis posing as anti-communists. Secrecy was paramount, and a three-country agreement between Britain, the United States and Canada ensured that information about these 'defectors' could only ever be released with the joint consent of all three governments. When the Canadian authorities did eventually investigate the role of MI6 in transferring its émigré assets to their country, the inquiry was hampered by the 'disappearance in the early seventies of files relating to the subject of Nazi war criminals'. They had been replaced at some stage with a 'false docket'. Similarly, immigration records had been destroyed as a matter of course, and when a huge batch of files was found to have escaped destruction, investigators were informed that the files had been destroyed weeks before. The protection of Nazi assets went as high as the then Prime Minister's office where 'Louis St Laurent and his aides were personally involved in communicating with the alleged war criminals, their protectors, and those that would have had them expelled from the country'.[47]

*　　*　　*

During 1949 there was a debate within the Foreign Office's Northern Department regarding 'Ukraine, Ukrainian Insurgency, and Emigré Organisations', and the feasibility of an alternative to Soviet rule. Officials regarded the resultant paper considered in March as 'scarcely relevant', as there was no question of an alternative government. The idea of using the various exile groups to foment rebellion within Ukraine had already come too late. The UPA had been reduced to pockets of token resistance and, in September, the UPA commander belatedly recognised the reality of the situation and ordered the deactivation of the army and its transformation into a purely underground resistance network. Starved of accurate intelligence, MI6 knew little about the reality on the ground and went ahead with schemes to parachute agents into the region, in the expectation that they would be welcomed into the arms of a well-organised guerrilla force. The Foreign Office thought that, at best, the OUN-B and other émigré organisations could only be used for 'information and intelligence purposes' and with 'financial or other encouragement of their internecine quarrels being carefully avoided'.[48]

Run by Harry Carr, MI6's Northern Division controlled INTEGRAL – the operation to send agents into Ukraine. Ukrainians, primarily belonging to OUN-B, were trained at the Special School in Holland Park and run by officers operating from bases in Turkey and under cover of the Control Commission in Germany. The officer in charge of the operation was Colonel Harold 'Gibby' Gibson. Working with him was Hubert O'Bryan Tear ('always known as OBT'), a former SOE officer in the French RF Section and German Control Officer, who was later posted to the small station in Moscow. The first group of three was dropped from an RAF aircraft, without wing markings, in the Kiev region in July 1949, and other Banderite groups followed during the next ten months. MI6 appears to have infiltrated most of its spies into the western regions of Ukraine. Czech wartime pilots had perfected a workable but highly dangerous method of evading Soviet radar screens by flying at only two hundred feet across the Russian border and climbing at the last moment to five hundred feet, the minimum height for a safe parachute drop. Soviet ground crew monitored every flight and shot at some but the planes 'survived every flight'. While the drops were successful, nothing more was heard from the agents and they were assumed to have been captured. According to his Soviet handler, Yuri Modin, 'during his tour of duty in Istanbul, Philby had already helped us wreck several attempts to send in agents. He did the same thing from Washington.'[49]

Since August 1948, the Policy and Planning Staff of the US State Department, the controlling body for OPC operations, had been considering the issue of 'Ukrainian National Liberation'. A senior figure from the OUN-B had contacted Secretary of Defence James Forrestal directly with an offer of the services of an estimated hundred thousand Ukrainians, mostly from the 'Bandera party', in the western zones in Germany. As to making use of these 'dissident elements in combating Communism', it had been decided in Washington to give the responsibility to the CIA, but it was to be handled 'in some special manner under Frank Wisner', who was already recruiting 'shock troops' for 'roll-back' operations. The US National Security Council advocated establishing relations with the resistance groups as a means of acquiring intelligence on Soviet 'mobilization in the area'. The OPC as well as the Soviet Division of the CIA's Office of Special Operations (OSO) began parachuting émigré agents into Ukraine, infiltrating 'as many as seventy-five guerrillas into the region over a four-year period'. On 5 September 1949, two agents were landed near Lvov, in the CIA's first deep penetration of the Soviet Union, and later, four parachutists were dropped in the Carpathian area. OSO operational head Harry Rositzke realised that 'they would not survive' and blamed unrealistic operational demands by the Pentagon. According to a formal complaint placed before the United Nations by the USSR, the security police captured four US-backed exiles and former Nazi collaborators within days of the first parachute drops. The agents were interrogated and then shot.[50]

A Soviet amnesty for UPA members launched in the first week of 1950 proved to be particularly effective as eight thousand guerrillas handed in their weapons. Many had originally fled into the forests to escape conscription to the coalfields. In March, the supreme commander of the UPA, Roman Shukhevych, acknowledged by the Soviets as 'a bold man, competent in clandestine work', was killed by the MVD in a village near Lvov, after being trapped in an underground bunker. While this did not end UPA activities, and it was true that small-scale resistance went on for a number of years, the UPA was no longer able to inflict major losses on the Soviet forces or pose a serious threat to the communist administration. MI6 knew little of this and continued to parachute agents into eastern Poland, between Lvov and Bridy, near Ternopol, and between Kolomiya and Kamenets, where Ukrainian, Polish and White Ruthenian insurgents were still thought to be fighting the Soviet Army. Looking for a safer route to Ukraine, British parachute drops were switched to aircraft taking off from Cyprus or Malta, while the Americans favoured bases in Greece and West Germany.[51]

It was against this background that Harry Carr made his first trip to Washington in early 1950 to consult with his American counterparts on the Polish and Ukrainian operations. Welcomed by Philby, Carr met with the avowed anglophile Harry Rositzke, who, along with the CIA analysts, appears to have had a much more realistic view of the Ukrainian operations, having already concluded that the OUN/UPA guerrillas 'could play no serious paramilitary role' in the event of a Soviet move against the West. Instead, Rositzke's group favoured using the guerrillas as a temporary base inside the USSR for espionage. Their agenda was dominated by the failure of the initial missions and the effect on future plans. OSO planned six drops in 1950, while MI6 hoped to send in at least two more teams. 'The requirement for co-ordination concerned not only which groups were receiving Western support but also the intended dates of the missions and predominantly technical information. Their object was to avoid clashes.' All this was discussed in front of Philby, who took the notes for future reference. Unfortunately for the Americans, Carr was only willing to discuss the broad outline of his operations, which they felt was unsatisfactory. Philby recalled that the Washington talks were largely taken up with 'skirmishes' about Stefan Bandera, who was regarded by the Americans as highly disruptive. The British, however, 'put up a stubborn rearguard action'.[52]

In May 1950, the Banderites continued their spoiling tactics and finally withdrew from the National Ukrainian Council in Augsburg. The Banderites regarded the sudden emergence of various nationalist groups in Munich – such as 'the supposedly democratically inclined' Ukrainian government-in-exile, led by Mykola Liwycky, Director of Press and Information of the Ukrainian Information Bureau, and the Committee for the Liberation of the Ukraine from Bolshevism, which ran 'Radio Liberation' – as manoeuvres by the Americans and their Russian émigré advisers to create divisions between the Ukrainian nationalist groups. At some point in 1950 Bandera secretly visited Washington in an unsuccessful attempt to establish better relations with the Americans. Increasingly, the Banderites focused their energies on the ABN, which took on a more neo-fascist character. This did not worry MI6, though it was concerned about its own lack of funds for such groups as the Treasury coffers were increasingly empty for special operations. The ABN was still able, though, to collect considerable funds from its supporters in Canada, and its mood remained buoyant.[53]

Several teams of agents, their numbers ranging from four to six, parachuted into the Soviet Union during 1950. Two of these missions disappeared without a trace. The operations were, however, compromised from top to bottom. Pavel Sudoplatov of Special Tasks and Ilarion Kamazuk, an MGB operator, had planted an agent in the surviving Bandera group which had made its way to West Germany, where MI6 'picked them up and carried them to England for training'. Bandera, who was increasingly concerned about the lack of radio communications with the UPA, had decided to send his head of the security service (SB), Mynon Matwijejko, to Ukraine to restore the movement. Meanwhile the planted Soviet agent kept in contact with his handlers by mailing a coded postcard, informing them 'of the Matwijejko group's route back to Ukraine'. He revealed details of their planned landing and instructions were given to the Soviet air defence command not to attack the British plane that was flying from Malta carrying Matwijejko. 'We not only wanted to protect our own man, who was with them,' Sudoplatov recalled. 'We wanted to take them alive.'[54]

In March 1951 Philby gave his friend and Foreign Office traitor Guy

Burgess, who was leaving the Washington embassy for London, 'the names and arrival points of three groups of six men who were to be parachuted into Ukraine'. This information eventually reached MGB/KGB officer Yuri Modin, through another member of the 'Ring', former MI5 officer Anthony Blunt. Modin acknowledges that he 'made good use of it'. In the late spring, the British dropped the three parties in an area within fifty miles of the nationalist stronghold of Lvov, and others on the territories of Ternopol and Stanislaw. Again, none of the teams reported back.[55]

In April, a high-level conference was held in London between MI6 officials and a CIA team. The occasion was a European tour by Allen Dulles, recently appointed Deputy Director for Plans in the CIA, with responsibilities for Wisner's OPC and the OSO. Once again, a row broke out over the Ukraine operations and the appalling record of Bandera, which the OSO officials claimed was hindering recruitment and proving to be positively counterproductive. The Americans claimed that there was no evidence that OUN-B commanded any substantial support in Ukraine. Despite the failed operations and the continuing urging by Dulles to abandon Bandera, Carr steadfastly refused to break the relationship. The operations continued, partly because of the belief that thirty-five thousand Soviet police troops and Communist Party cadres had been eliminated by OUN-B/UPA guerrillas in Ukraine since the end of the war. If true, it was all in the past; forced collectivisation implemented during the year cut vital supplies to the underground. The resistance was simply no longer effective.[56]

In May, Bandera's representative, Mynon Matwijejko, and his team, which had been under constant surveillance since landing in Ukraine, surrendered voluntarily to the Soviet authorities. After a month of interrogations by Pavel Sudoplatov, Matwijejko 'realised that except for the names of secondary agents, there was nothing we didn't know about the Ukrainian emigrant organisations and the Bandera movement. He was taken aback by my recital to him of the biographies of all their leaders, bitter conflicts between them, and details of their lives.' Somehow, Matwijejko managed to escape his captors, but gave himself up after only three days when he discovered that the OUN-B network in Lvov was not functioning. He learned that much the same experience had faced the original two teams parachuted into Ukraine in 1949. What existed of the local movement had been inflating its intelligence reports to London and Munich. Matwijejko decided to co-operate with the debriefers and, at a press conference staged by the Ukrainian authorities, denounced the Bandera movement, using 'his authority to appeal for national reconciliation'. Further denunciations came from 'W. Kruk', whose earlier recruitment by the NKVD had been a major intelligence coup. A senior UPA commander, his arrest and 'turning' had enabled the Soviets successfully to thwart a number of operations. Pardoned by the Supreme Soviet Presidium, Kruk later became an archivist of the Academy of Sciences of the Ukrainian SSR.[57]

Carr's refusal to break with the OUN-B was partly based on his knowledge that the Americans were increasingly relying on Reinhard Gehlen and his Organisation, for whom MI6 had little time or respect. While Gehlen claimed that Bandera was 'one of our men', his American intelligence advisers had helped block Bandera's access to the Org. Gehlen was able, however, to warn the CIA that Bandera's group inside Ukraine was, in all probability, penetrated. He did have access to information on Bandera from the Ukrainian 'specialist' Theodor Oberlander, political adviser with the Nachtigall battalion which swept into Lvov in 1941 and who later became a minister in the Bonn government. After surrendering to American troops at the end of the war, Oberlander had been sent to London to an Anglo/American Intelligence Service camp for debriefing. Thereafter, he was 'handed from office to office' before returning to West Germany, where he was 'allowed' to go underground.[58]

Frank Wisner was also using Gehlen for the OPC/CIA's own Ukrainian operations. The first of three OPC/CIA missions involving five of Wisner's Gehlen-backed agents was dispatched into Moldavia, between south-east Ukraine and Romania, in mid-August 1951. A former Red Army PoW and a Soviet deserter, who had served in the Vlasov army, were instructed to make their way separately to Ukraine and the Caucasus before making their escape via Turkey. The ambitious project was terminated when, soon after they arrived, their radios went quiet. A month later, another agent was dropped into Belorussia, but only lasted a few weeks before being picked up by the Soviet secret police. Two further agents similarly disappeared. Moscow Radio later announced that the insurgents had engaged in gathering intelligence for 'imperialist intelligence' and 'ideological diversions'.[59]

Given the continuing lack of success of the Bandera agents, the MI6 hierarchy could no longer stand idly by, and so a discreet secret review of operations was undertaken. Carr was able to retain control of the Baltic operations, and the establishment of a 'Joint Centre' with the CIA in the I. G. Farben building in Frankfurt for anti-Soviet operations was agreed. The MI6 liaison officer between headquarters in Germany and the centre was Michael Lykowski, alias Mike Peters, who joined the CIA's George Belic to manage the project. Lykowski and Belic paid 'tens of thousands of dollars to Ukrainian agents who often reappeared wearing new clothes, boasting the ownership of new cars and hosting champagne parties in the nightclubs. Occasionally, they disappeared from Frankfurt for ever.' These 'special training' schools in Germany were found to be riddled with Soviet agents, and as with other unsuccessful émigré operations it was often less a case of Philby betraying the networks than of low-level Soviet agents infiltrating the émigré community at every turn.[60]

Although the infiltrations carried on throughout 1951/2 produced little intelligence feedback, the American-backed Gehlen programme was stepped up in the summer of 1952 with regular parachute drops. In August and

November American planes dropped more agents in south-west Ukraine. Sixteen agents were lost on at least five missions mounted during 1952/3. British losses in this period are unknown, as are those of the separate OSO operations. Despite the failures, 'as the flow of "intelligence" radioed to West Germany increased, MI6 confidently assured customers in Whitehall that it was running a reliable network'. It was only later that it was discovered that those few agents who did manage to radio back were acting under Soviet instructions. As in Poland, the agents had been turned and the Soviet radio deception soon bore fruit. Unlike other deception operations this one did not run for long, and the cases were publicised in the Soviet press at great length.[61]

In May 1953, the Soviet newspaper *Pravda* reported the execution of four Ukrainians alleged to have spied for the United States. A year later, Soviet radio announced the execution of V. O. Okhrymovych, who had parachuted into Ukraine from an American plane. A leading figure during the war in both the OUN and the UHVR, Okhrymovych had left for the West after 1945 on a 'special mission'. The official Soviet communiqué stated that he had revealed the identities of 'his accomplices in espionage activities in Ukraine'. Taking into account the general communist-style propaganda language in which they were couched, the communiqués issued following the executions were, in fact, remarkably accurate. One reason for subsequently publicising the cases at the United Nations was that the Soviets took the insurgent threat seriously and could not allow the risk of its revival while the deception operation was played out.[62]

It was apparent, indeed blindingly obvious, to both MI6 and the OUN-B that the Ukrainian networks were totally compromised. Bandera, who had always been ambivalent about foreign support, took the initiative and began to draw away from his British and American sponsors. In the mid-fifties he 'tried to create an even smaller, more secret network', which made him 'a target for Soviet assassination efforts'.[63]

Ukrainian guerrillas fought in numbers until at least 1948 in the western provinces of Ukraine. According to two CIA-trained radio operators, who remained to the bitter end, the last major UPA unit was crushed by Soviet security troops in regimental strength in November 1953, though small pockets of resistance continued for another three years. In truth, it took the Soviets only four years to suppress OUN/UPA. During the Second World War, the OUN/UPA believed that the Germans and Russians would exhaust themselves and that as a result they would emerge as a 'third force' which would win Ukrainian independence. Similarly, when the Cold War began, the nationalists expected a confrontation leading to war between the West and the USSR. They were wrong on both counts. The problem for the Ukrainians, who were torn by ethnic, ideological and political divisions, was that they suffered from what Alexander Buchsbajew has called 'suicidal romanticism'. There never was a chance that they would succeed.[64]

There were a number of additional reasons for the nationalist failure. Even though the OUN was extremely security-conscious, as early as 1940 the NKVD had infiltrated the organisation at a high level. Although there were contacts with counterpart organisations in the West and with British Intelligence, no material supplies were delivered to the guerrillas in Ukraine. Gradually, the war of attrition reduced the quantity of weapons and ammunition available for a sustained campaign. Christopher Simpson argues that 'what this meant in strategic terms was that the guerrillas received neither the military support they needed to survive as an insurgent movement nor the patient camouflaging that might have permitted them to exist as spies. Instead, they were used as martyrs – some of whom died bravely; some pathetically – and grist for the propaganda mills of both East and West.' This is a view shared by one senior American diplomat who described the role of the OUN in these campaigns as 'little more than puppets in the hands of back-stage agents'.[65]

The real problem – about which MI6 may have reached the correct conclusion but which it refused to impart to its émigré agents – was the same as that reported by Maj. Gatehouse and Capt. Tamplin when they interviewed Russian PoWs in Finland. 'Contrary to the widely held belief', Buchsbajew concludes in his study of guerrilla warfare, 'even the popularly backed, well-armed or highly motivated insurgents cannot succeed against a modern totalitarian state.' Harry Rositzke came to the conclusion that the Ukrainian operations were 'not worth the effort'. In retrospect, he realised that after the Czech coup in 1948 there were 'no resistance groups in Eastern Europe . . . or none that could be trusted'.[66]

The nationalists had wished to unite the whole of Ukraine into a new independent state, and in pursuit of this goal told the West's intelligence agencies that Ukrainian resistance after 1945 was spread throughout the region. In truth, resistance was mainly limited to the former Polish territories: Soviet west Ukraine and certain districts west of the Curzon Line which were left to the Poles after 1944/5. There was a deep and unbridgeable divide between the western and eastern regions of Ukraine. It is a tragic irony for the nationalists that, despite their often heroic efforts, the same division exists today. The 1994 general election split the country down the middle, with nearly 90 per cent of western Ukraine voting against the eventual victor, who came from the eastern region. The most vocal opponents of the result, who threatened the stability of the country, were the still-active Banderites. The preceding year, seven hundred former members of the Waffen-SS Galician Division, the majority now living in Canada and the United States, with a contingent of eighty from Britain, held a reunion in the nationalist stronghold of Lvov. Most remained unapologetic about the past.[67]

CHAPTER 15

POLAND

News of the Warsaw Uprising by the Polish Home Army (Armia Krajowa – AK) reached London on 1 August 1944, surprising critics of the executive director of the Special Operations Executive (SOE), Colin Gubbins, who was identified in some circles with a small group of conservative, anti-communist Polish officers who were in favour of keeping the Home Army intact for eventual use against the Russians.

The Poles, recalled Peter Wilkinson, who had travelled to Poland in July 1939, 'had cast their spell over Gubbins, appealing particularly to the romantic side of his nature'. As chief of staff of a British Military Mission that was part of a Military Intelligence (Research) operation – funded 'from another organisation' (MI6) – Gubbins had tried to set up a stay-behind network that would operate behind German lines in the event of Poland being overrun by the Nazis. As the prospect of war grew, Gubbins, who had spent time on the Polish desk, where officers nicknamed him 'Gubbski', developed close personal links with members of the Polish Mission in Paris and officers of the Polish General Staff. When the MI6 Paris station had been evacuated to London in June 1940, Commander Wilfred 'Biffy' Dunderdale (code-name 'Wilski') started a P5 section which concentrated on the many Polish groups he had cultivated in pre-war France.[1]

Polish Intelligence enjoyed a healthy respect in MI6 circles – justifiably so, because of the major role it played in the success enjoyed at Bletchley Park by the Government Code and Cipher School (GC&CS) in signals cryptanalysis. The first steps in breaking the Enigma machine code, as used by the Germans, were made in early 1933 by Marian Rejewski of the Polish Cipher Bureau, using stolen instructions from French Intelligence. The British did not manage to break the Enigma ciphers until after they had been given access to Rejewski's work at a secret meeting with the Poles and the French in the Pyry Forest, near Warsaw, in July 1939. It was Dunderdale who brought an intact Engima machine to London 'in a heavily escorted diplomatic bag and met at Victoria Station by Stewart Menzies . . . dressed in a dinner jacket with the rosette of the Legion d'honneur in his button hole'. Dunderdale was also chief liaison officer to the ultra-secret Agency Africa run by Major-General Rygor Slowikowski (*nom de guerre* 'Dr Skowronski'), who had gathered intelligence on southern Russia for the Second Bureau of the Polish General Staff, on the eve of war. The agency was the 'most extensive and efficient Allied intelligence network' operating in Vichy-governed French North Africa during 1941–2, playing a leading part in the planning of Operation TORCH, the Anglo-American invasion of Algeria and Morocco in November 1942. In Algiers, Slowikowski worked closely with Colonel Anthony Morris of MI6's Inter-Services Liaison Department.[2]

SOE created a parallel section to MI6's P5, EU/P, responsible for Polish minorities, which was taken over in July 1941 by a former Baltic shipbroker, Ronald Hazell. The Polish country section was run by Major Mike Pickles, another member of the Military Mission to Warsaw, as was SOE's overall director (MP) for Poland, Czechoslovakia and Hungary, Harold Perkins, one of Gubbins's most loyal and trusted supporters. A former proprietor of a textile factory in southern Poland, Perkins was described by Peter Wilkinson, regional controller in charge of liaison with the Poles, as 'larger than life in every dimension'. With the help of the Polish VI Bureau, Perkins helped design the cylindrical containers for arms and essential supplies that were dropped by parachute all over Europe.[3]

Gubbins had been one of a small circle of British friends in London trusted and consulted on a wide range of subjects by the head of the Polish government-in-exile, General Wladyslaw Sikorski. The circle included the liaison officer to the Poles, Conservative MP Major Victor Cazalet, a close friend of Lord Selbourne, head of the Ministry of Economic Warfare, which controlled SOE. Cazalet and Selbourne were members of the Imperial Policy Group, an anti-communist/Soviet grouping of right-wing Tories who advocated 'imperial isolationalism' for the British Commonwealth and Empire. The IPG was viewed in some quarters as favouring the defeat of Bolshevism above that of war with Germany. Its secretary, Kenneth de Courcy, was close to Menzies and his White's Club network of MI6 officers. Hostile to any body that challenged its efforts at policy co-ordination on Poland, the Foreign Office disliked these political contacts and, in particular, the role of Sikorski's closest Polish collaborator and 'eminence grise', Dr Jozef Retinger, another of Gubbins's friends.[4]

A pragmatic leader, General Sikorski had been working for a rapproche-
ment with the Soviet Union, with a view to reconstituting a new Polish state
at the expense of Germany. The announcement by Berlin Radio on 13 April
1943 that the bodies of about ten thousand Polish officers had been discovered
in mass graves in the Katyn woods dashed such hopes. While the Soviet
Information Bureau in London dismissed the discovery as a 'fabrication', the
Polish government-in-exile stated that, following the German 'categorical
statement that they were murdered by Soviet authorities in the Spring of
1940, the necessity has arisen that the mass graves discovered should be
investigated and the facts alleged verified'. From that point on, diplomatic
relations between the Poles and the Soviet Union remained in abeyance. This
had a direct effect on the British government, which was determined, in the
interests of the war effort, to preserve a good relationship with the Soviets.[5]

Sikorski's death on 4 July 1943, when the aircraft bringing him back to
London, which also included Cazaelet on the passenger list, crashed on take-
off in Gibraltar, was a devastating blow to the London Poles – one from
which they never fully recovered. Churchill 'showed little sympathy' for
Sikorski's successor as prime minister, Stanislaw Mikolajczyk, one of the
general's main allies in London who, from 1941 to 1943, had been deputy
premier and minister of internal affairs in the government-in-exile. Leader
of the Polish Peasant Party, Mikolajczyk was virtually unknown in British
circles and lacked international experience, although he was a seasoned politician who shared Sikorski's pragmatic approach to foreign policy. Churchill
repeatedly told him that the western powers were not prepared to go to war
with the Soviet Union over Poland. 'The essential fact was that control of
Poland was seen as vital by the Soviet Union, as it was not by Great Britain
or the United States.' Mikolajczyk accepted the realities of Poland's fragile
position and that he would have to make 'concessions on matters of prestige'
which the London Poles, who followed a rather romantic view of history,
would not accept.[6]

Gubbins had numerous official dealings with the Polish leader and had
a high regard for his 'courage, integrity and commonsense'. Likewise, Mikolajczyk, who had been responsible for the clandestine civilian administration
inside Poland and also for the mobilisation of Polish communities abroad,
was well disposed towards Gubbins and SOE. Supported by Lord Selbourne,
Gubbins took more seriously than most the commitment to Poland and the
resistance, particularly during 1944 when the Polish underground state
increasingly turned its attention to the problem of power in postwar Poland.
But as the chiefs of staff acknowledged in January, 'special operations in
Poland are bound up with political considerations to a greater extent than
in any other country'. Once the Warsaw uprising began, voices in the British
intelligence community were raised, accusing Gubbins of 'having encouraged
the Poles for personal ambition to embark on this desperate adventure which

ran clear counter to the directives SOE had received from the Chiefs of Staff'.[7]

Some Polish quarters had indeed expected, because of Gubbins's support, that supplies would be forthcoming at the critical moment. There had been, however, a misunderstanding in the message sent to the AK (Home Army), primarily due to the Polish VI Bureau continuing to send messages in their own ciphers, without reference to any British agency. Gubbins had, in fact, adhered strictly to the policy of the Joint Intelligence Committee (JIC), which had concluded, after consultation with SOE, that responsibility for any uprising must be left to the Poles. 'It was recognised that Polish resistance would not be of any use to the more important invasion of Europe.' The false hopes were generated by people inside Poland. While the Red Army waited on the other side of the Vistula – probably not then in a military position to help the heroic Polish fighters of the Warsaw uprising, whom Stalin regarded as a 'handful of power-hungry adventurers and criminals' – 'the flower of the Polish underground, perhaps 200,000 people, were killed by the Germans'.[8]

The uprising effectively destroyed the power of the London-controlled underground and split the pro-western politicians in Poland and abroad into two camps. Those who supported Mikolajczyk worked for a compromise with the communists in Poland in the hope of supplanting them through a formal alliance with the Soviet Union. Mikolajczyk's resignation as Prime Minister in November 1944, however, was welcomed by the Foreign Office because 'it meant the end of those silly Poles'. The opposing group, which took over power in the London government-in-exile, believed that the Polish question would be satisfactorily resolved only if confrontation, which they sought, arose between the western powers and the Soviet Union. Increasingly, the Foreign Office viewed these internal squabbles with disdain. The Home Army was no longer of strategic interest and was viewed 'as a major impediment to the establishment of good post-war relations with the Soviet Union'. Likewise, SOE's co-operation with the Polish resistance was to be 'strictly subordinated to the search for an Anglo-Soviet agreement'.[9]

Senior SOE figures did not, however, view the situation in quite the same light as the Foreign Office. In October, Harold Perkins wrote in a confidential memorandum that 'the chief threat to world peace is now the increasing divergence becoming evident between Russian aims and the policies of the western allies'. He wanted to keep SOE's Polish agents active so that they would be able to set up new intelligence networks and organise resistance cells against any Soviet-controlled regime. He added that there were

> few Englishmen who possess a first-hand knowledge of Russia,
> of Russian mentality, and of Russian methods. The Poles on
> the other hand have several thousand persons having those
> qualifications and being at the same time bitterly hostile to
> Russia, although friendly to us. In the event of war with Russia

they would be of inestimable value to us. They represent an
asset which should not lightly be discarded.[10]

While the envisaged supplies for Warsaw did not materialise, the Home
Army had not been entirely without support. Up to October 1944, SOE had
covertly dispatched for 'military and political purposes . . . at least £35,000,000
in gold and currency', using secret Polish couriers. These massive amounts
worried the chiefs of staff, who 'feared that portions of this money and the
air-drops of arms intended for sabotage operations against the retreating
Germans would be salted away to be used in a fight against the advancing
Soviet armies'. Only after pressure from Gubbins was SOE allowed to send
a Military Mission to Poland to assess what resistance was left. Led by Colonel
'Bill' Hudson, it consisted of Peter Kemp, Peter Solly-Flood, and two Poles,
Anton Popieszalski (aka Tony Currie) and Roman Rudkowski, an air force
colonel. Hudson discovered that the majority of the Polish agents dropped
into the country had failed to survive the German occupation, the Warsaw
uprising and the Soviet People's Commissariat for Internal Affairs (NKVD)
murder squads. The official files record that by the beginning of 1945 SOE
was expending little effort on Poland but, according to Peter Wilkinson,
Gubbins, who was increasingly relying on émigré sources, was spending 'a
disproportionate amount of time' on the country. Wilkinson adds cryptically:
'by no means always on SOE's business'.[11]

Large sections of the London-controlled Home Army, which had been
ordered to make themselves known to the advancing Soviet Army and to
offer to fight alongside it, were critical of the government-in-exile's moderate
policies and refused to lay down their arms. Once the fighting had finished,
the Soviets demanded that the AK units be subordinated to the Soviet-
controlled Polish Army or be disarmed and interned. Unfortunately, the Red
Army had already ambushed and destroyed some AK units, and, as the
British feared, a number instead preferred to remain underground as part of
a clandestine anti-communist network. On 19 January 1945 the Polish GHQ,
after consulting with Gubbins, formally disbanded the AK, but at the same
time activated the organisation known by the cryptonym Nie (*Niepodleglosc*
– Independence), which was intended to carry on the political struggle. The
extreme right-wing nationalists also vowed to remain as a conspiratorial
force, arguing that the underground should prepare to destroy pro-Soviet
and communist forces. It, too, based its strategy on the assumption that armed
conflict would break out between the West and the Soviet Union, and so
directed its energies to preparing for a rebellion inside Poland for when that
day came.[12]

In response the NKVD unleashed a terror campaign, intended to destroy
the underground, against the same forces with which, a few weeks earlier,
it had on occasion co-operated. By early 1945 the communists were equating

the AK with the Gestapo. In January, SOE officer Major Pickles reported to the Foreign Office that the NKVD was still the only real authority in Soviet-occupied Poland: 'The rest is fiction.' The next month SOE reported that the Russians were 'plundering the population in an alarming manner'. A March SOE report described 'the position of the Poles after the entry of the Russians' as 'far worse than before'. The 'Red Army completely devastated the countryside, looting absolutely everything moveable'. By then most Polish villages had a cell of one or two communists which, according to Pickles, comprised 'the poorest peasants who were attracted by promises of land and drawn, generally speaking, from the dregs of the population, who had everything to gain by any sort of change'. Lord Selbourne and Gubbins made regular representations to the Foreign Office on the situation in Poland but officials remained unwilling to intervene, still reluctant to damage Anglo-Soviet relations.[13]

The spring offensive weakened the underground forces – as many as fifty thousand members of the AK were arrested and transported to Siberia, as were the leaders of the new political organisation Nie – but was not completely successful. The security forces were small and heavily infiltrated by members of the underground, with many officers unwilling to kill their fellow-citizens. It took until May 1945 for the Internal Security Corps (Korpus Bezpieczentswa Wenetrznego – KBW) to be formally set up and trained. Under the control of the Supreme Political Commission to Combat Banditry, special 'agit-prop' groups attached to counter-insurgency units spread dissension and propaganda that portrayed the underground as terrorists who killed peasants and who were intent on depriving the people of the fruits of peace. The western powers failed to respond to the arrests of resistance leaders, again fearful of a confrontation with Stalin over Poland, and refused to countenance any overt support to the underground.[14]

During the summer of 1945, the Polish communists developed a twin-track strategy, allowing former opponents into government as the price to be paid for western recognition of the provisional government. In June, Moscow allowed Mikolajczyk to return to Poland as deputy prime minister, with his Peasant Party (PSL) given five out of the twenty seats in the cabinet. With Mikolajczyk's return, the London government-in-exile ceased to enjoy any significant role and the struggle for power was played out within government between the PSL and the communists (Polska Partia Robotnicza, PPR), which continued to combat the underground. Closely watching these events were the staff of the British embassy in Warsaw, which occupied most of the fourth floor of the Hotel Polonia. While not a nest of spies, it did include its fair share of intelligence and former SOE personnel.

Ambassador Victor Cavendish-Bentinck, who had recently vacated the chair of the JIC, had a long association with Poland, having served there as a junior diplomat after the First World War. Somewhat cold and austere, he was sympathetic towards the Poles, being well aware of Polish 'achievements in clandestine as well as overt warfare against the Germans', and regarded the Polish intelligence personnel as 'the best people by far'. The counsellor in the embassy, Robin Hankey, whose father, Lord Hankey, was regarded as the creator of the JIC, had also served in the embassy before the war. Press attaché Patrick Howarth had served with SOE in the Middle East and Italy, and was an old Polish hand, having run operations with the Poles in Cairo. A pre-war journalist, Howarth had replaced Denis Hills on the quarterly journal *Baltic and Scandinavian Countries*, run by the Baltic Institute in Gdynia, during the brief Anglo-Polish honeymoon. Another former journalist on the staff was Michael Winch, who, in 1939, had written an interesting eye-witness account of the short-lived Carpatho-Ukraine Republic, where the German-backed local authorities had treated him as a British spy. Vice-consul Alan Banks had served with MI6 in Dakar, West Africa, while the resident MI6 officer was a 'colourless chap', Lewis Massey. A fluent Polish speaker – his mother was Polish – Massey acted as interpreter for the ambassador.[15]

The Russians protested to the British that SOE radio networks in Poland, supposedly closed down at the end of the war, were still active. The Foreign Office, anxious to recognise the new Moscow-controlled regime, demanded that they be closed down, but Harold Perkins resisted. He knew that Menzies was, 'without doubt', 'very interested in the question of Polish communications in view of the excellent intelligence which is obtained via these channels'. Eventually, an agreement was reached for SOE to retain control of the Polish radio messages – 'in view of their bulk and the dislocation of intelligence operational importance that might be caused'. When the Russians continued to complain that the British were still supporting 'terrorist activities', Perkins simply handed his Polish networks over to MI6.[16]

Polish contacts with western intelligence agencies, particularly MI6, made in the pre-war period were not lost during the war and were carried on into the immediate postwar period. These lasted until about 1948. The head of Polish Intelligence with the Polish government-in-exile in London, Colonel Tadeusz Wasilewski, had helped MI6 recruit some of its best sources on Germany. Although officially attached to the Ministry of Defence, Colonel Stefan Mayer – an extremely important figure in Polish Intelligence (though not, as is sometimes described, its head), who had played a role in the Polish efforts to break the Engima machine code – was employed by MI6 after the war. It would seem that MI6 also had access to the files of the head of the Polish Deuxième Bureau during the war, Colonel Gano. The official view was that they had 'disappeared', but rumours persist that he handed them over to the British, who had them destroyed. It would appear, however, that they were entrusted to Mayer, who acted as a weeder of Polish documents for MI6.[17]

According to the untested sources of newspaper editor Stewart Steven,

MI6 ran another intelligence and covert operations network outside of the Warsaw station, headed by 'Captain Michael Sullivan', a former SOE officer who spoke fluent Polish. 'Sullivan's' father was a paper manufacturer whose business had been almost exclusively with the Poles. As soon as Poland was liberated, 'Sullivan', who had worked in eastern Europe during the war, went there undercover as head of a British relief agency to set up a network that became 'the hub of the huge anti-communist, anti-Russian resistance movement'. Steven gives a lurid account of 'Sullivan's' activities during 1945, which ranged from psychological warfare operations, resulting in bread riots, to helping incite anti-Semitic demonstrations. In 1946 Perkins, who was now responsible for MI6 operations in Poland and Czechoslovakia, posted to the MI6 station as assistant military attaché another former SOE officer, David Smiley, as a replacement for Major Seddon. Smiley remembered Perkins as 'a big man, full of fun', who insisted on 'joining me for the more hazardous and exciting missions'. The Polish authorities later declared Smiley *persona non grata* for spying, and he returned to Germany and his regiment, the Blues, as second-in-command. By May, many of SOE's former agents in Poland had been arrested by the NKVD. 'In many cases, we understand they are charged with being British agents,' an official noted. Perkins was frequently mentioned by the new regime in Warsaw during the subsequent show trials of alleged spies.[18]

In the immediate post-hostilities phase, Poland was in chaos, with the country in economic and physical ruin. War had left Warsaw a devastated city but not, at least for the first postwar year, a police state. There was indeed considerable freedom of expression, and the British embassy did not want for information. According to Cavendish-Bentinck, however, the Communist Party gradually asserted 'a complete grip on the administrative machine. The press is regimented.' The Russian and communist-controlled 'Security' police, manned by 'Corner boys, pimps and thimble-riggers', produced 'an atmosphere of terror'. He acknowledged in reports to London that the PSL enjoyed considerable support, and if elections were held at the end of 1945, 'this party would certainly secure over sixty per cent of the votes cast'. He added that the Polish communist clique who controlled much of the government 'have no intention of abandoning power if the elections should go against them'.[19]

As a result of the arrests in May, a new conspiratorial organisation, the Delegation of Armed Forces (Delegatura Sil Zbrojnych – DSZ), had been created under the command of Colonel Jan Rzepecki. A military formation that sought to curb uncoordinated resistance, it succeeded in gathering together the old AK network, but its organisation was far from complete when, in August, it too disbanded following the formal dissolution of the underground state. In the amnesty that followed, most of the AK/DSZ core did not, however, reveal themselves to the communists. Several underground groups established the co-ordinating commission of political parties, known as 'The Centre', to which, in September, out of the remnants of the AK/DZS, another military organisation was established, Freedom and Independence (Wolnosc i Niepodlegtnosc – WiN), which geared its tactics closely to those of the legal opposition, the Peasant Party (PSL). WiN had been conceived as an underground organisation that would provide a moderate rallying point for former members of the AK who took the view that a continuation of the armed struggle would be counterproductive. While it allowed for the liquidation of 'particularly harmful persons' and was prepared to undertake armed resistance to prevent the nation's destruction, it aimed not to provoke the Soviets. It backed co-operation with the coalition government, recognising that 'the maintenance of good political relations and economic co-operation with the Soviet Union' was 'necessary and positive'.[20]

Following his arrest in November, WiN's commander, Colonel Jan Rzepecki, publicly called for an end to underground armed activity. This was not universally accepted by the WiN rank and file, who regarded it as a straightforward military organisation. Almost alone among the Soviet satellites, the underground continued throughout 1945/6 to play a significant role in keeping alive the official opposition movement in a period when the communists knew that they were still weak. The security problem in the countryside remained serious throughout the second half of 1945, with around, according to Ministry of the Interior figures, eighty thousand activists in the underground. Special action units of the extreme nationalist National Military Union (Narodowy Zwiazek Wojskowy – NZW) carried out 'pacification' raids against pro-government villages, while the well-organised Ukrainian nationalist UPA underground army remained a major problem along the south-east border. A 'veritable no man's land', where guerrilla activity assumed the proportions of a civil war, the 'Wild Fields' were a no-go area for British Intelligence officers. One man who did manage to report back from the area was the 'mysterious' Auberon Herbert, who, David Howarth recalls, unexpectedly turned up in the area as the Polish correspondent of the *Tablet*; clearly on a low-level intelligence mission.[21]

A major reduction of Soviet troops on Polish soil took place during the winter of 1945/6, which Mikolajczyk thought provided new opportunities. In January he told Cavendish-Bentinck he 'was certain that the Communist leaders would think out other plans to remain in power when the elections go against them' but that it would be difficult for them to 'remain in office without the active support of the Russian Army ... if it came to a clash between the Army and the people the Polish soldiers would refuse to act'. In March, Cavendish-Bentinck feared that any escalation of the underground attacks might spark an uprising that would result in stern retaliatory measures by the Soviets, including the return of troops. The British ambassador contacted individuals connected to the underground, urging restraint and a dispersal of forces to avoid repression and the imposition of a permanent military dictatorship. There was a view that it was more important to keep the country together and not risk even further repression by the Soviets. MI6, which was primarily concerned with protecting its intelligence-gathering networks, took a similar view. On the other hand, the Service had been tasked with preparing for a potential East/West conflict and wanted the underground to preserve its forces and be ready for that moment. When the international situation began to look bleaker, MI6 asked the Polish underground to prepare a stay-behind network. The Poles did not, however, always believe what MI6 was telling it and viewed the Service with some suspicion. There was a great deal of bitterness, with the feeling that, having fought side by side with them during the war, the British had let them down.[22]

The communists alleged that the underground were taking their orders from the 'well-known Russophobe' General Wladyslaw Anders, a cavalry officer in the Tsarist army prior to the revolution and then in Polish units in Russia. Captured by the Soviets in 1939, Anders had organised Polish forces under Soviet command in 1941 and had then, in the following year, led Polish soldiers out of Russia. Transferred to the command of the Supreme Headquarters of Allied European Forces (SHAEF) of General Eisenhower, Anders's forces were used in several gallant campaigns against the fascists in North Africa and Italy, contributing, in particular, to the Allied conquest of Montecassino in 1944. At the end of the war, Anders's Polish Army was scattered throughout Italy, West Germany and Austria. Warsaw claimed that the Polish Corps were being kept in existence and reorganised in the western occupation zones in Germany in order to carry out subversive activities against the Polish government. Both sides believed that a new war would soon break out, and the communists were alarmed that Anders's army might receive help from the remnants of the Home Army within Poland. There was undoubtedly an element of justification in these fears.

In renewing a pre-war friendship, Harry Carr, head of MI6's Northern Division, instructed his officers to make contact with General Anders, who was encouraged to re-establish relations with his officers in Poland. Surviving members of the underground maintained contact with the Polish government-in-exile and with MI6 in London, while a number of these groups had contact by courier or wireless with Polish forces in West Germany and Britain. In addition, some of the extreme nationals had managed to move to West Germany to link up with other groups in order to carry on the fight against the communists. It was also obvious that Cold War attitudes were hardening. The Foreign Office paper of October 1946, 'Strategic Aspect of British Foreign Office Policy', advocated a state of armed preparedness against Soviet pressure, as it was vital to prevent particular countries from succumbing to communist domination. It was considered essential 'to support and encourage as far as we can our friends in those countries, and so to keep alive in them the connection with the Western democratic ideas which our policy towards them represents. The best hope of this is in Poland, since the Poles are born conspirators.'[23]

Gradually, however, the communist PPR began to nationalise the security apparatus until Soviet troops and Ministry of Internal Affairs (MVD, which succeeded the NKVD) units were no longer required to quell the underground. Political control over the internal police was tightened, which enabled the Soviets to keep a low profile during the elections. In conversation with Cavendish-Bentinck, Mikolajczyk spoke only of their role 'behind the scenes' in the top echelons of the PPR, the security apparatus and in directing the campaign against his party. The Soviets continued to be active over the winter of 1946, but their actions were well concealed. They were also helped by the fact that, while guerrilla actions had caused real anxiety, once the police and political forces had taken the upper hand, the existence of the guerrillas could be 'used as an excuse for repressive measures' against Mikolajczyk's legal PSL party. Government propaganda portrayed the PSL as 'the legal façade of a reactionary guerrilla underground movement', while Mikolajczyk was denounced as a 'British agent' and accused of secret dealings with Anders – 'on behalf of his masters, the British imperialists'. Finally, two political trials were staged to incriminate Mikolajczyk.[24]

In June 1946, a referendum on the question of abolishing the senate was opposed by Mikolajczyk's PSL. The openly fraudulent referendum proved to be a public relations disaster, and the communists directed their anger at the British ambassador, who had delivered a note to the Polish government drawing attention to the 'grave irregularities' in voting. Polish security tightened their surveillance of Cavendish-Bentinck, who had been using his private aeroplane as a 'peering machine' to ensure that he was well informed, visiting the estates of landowners whom he had known in Poland during his earlier posting in 1919. They then tried unsuccessfully to have him made *persona non grata*.[25]

A technique favoured by the security police was 'the blockade', whereby agents kept surveillance for a number of weeks on the home of 'a suspicious character' and arrested everyone who called on him. A 'blockade' was imposed on the flat of Cavendish-Bentinck's long-time family friend Count Ksawery Grocholoski, but the ambassador, who had notice of the count's imminent arrest, made the injudicious move of visiting him. According to Reuters correspondent John Peet, who later defected to East Germany: 'The Count had apparently been caught red-handed in possession of stolen secret government documents and was kept prisoner in the bathroom awaiting visitors. A distinguished-looking foreigner rang the bell and was cuffed with handcuffs. There was speculation in diplomatic circles that "Bill" had gone on a little low-level spying of his own.' A former member of the Home Army, Count Grocholoski was charged with being an underground agent, who had collaborated with the Germans and was conveying secrets to the British. Cavendish-Bentinck wrote that the real object of his arrest was 'to deter us in the future from attempting to make any contact if we should so desire with the underground movement'.[26]

In a second trial beginning on 4 January 1947, just two weeks before the Polish general election, former Home Army officer and commander of WiN Colonel Rzepecki 'confessed' that Mikolajczyk had given him advice that 'had caused him to continue armed resistance to the government with his guerrilla forces, despite the amnesty'. Five days before the election, Count Grocholoski was sentenced to death, and the following month Cavendish-Bentinck was forced to leave the country.[27]

After the trials and the fraudulent elections, the Polish government began to move against the PSL and in particular Mikolajczyk. Fortunately, the last head of the Polish underground state and a leading member of the PSL, Stefan Korbonski, had maintained contact with reliable sources inside the government. A communist official, whose life Korbonski had saved during the Warsaw uprising, tipped him off that the security police intended to arrest him along with other members of the executive committee of the PSL. Korbonski told Mikolajczyk, who initially considered staying in the country to influence world opinion. When other sources, however, informed the British and American embassies that he would almost certainly be tried and executed, Mikolajczyk made secret plans to leave. According to former SOE official Douglas Dodds-Parker, he was rescued 'with Bevin's willing help' in an MI6 exfiltration operation using former SOE personnel organised by Gubbins, who had informed Mikolajczyk that he was about to be 'liquidated'. Co-ordinating the effort was a secret unit of Allied officers in Berlin which helped smuggle out politicians, scientists and intelligence sources throughout eastern Europe via an 'underground railway'. One of its agents told the *New York Times*: 'We get some hot customers, hot with the breath of the Russian pursuers on their necks.'[28]

On 17 October 1947, Mikolajczyk sought the assistance of the First Secretary at the American embassy in Warsaw, George Andrews. After he had consulted with his opposite number in the British embassy, officials worked quickly and suggested several possible methods of escape. A plan to smuggle him out of the country in a coffin was dropped in favour of helping him to get to the Baltic port of Gdynia. Three days later, carrying only a toothbrush and a revolver, Mikolajczyk jumped into the back of a truck where he was joined, according to the official American report on the escape, by another person – probably an MI6 officer. After a long and dangerous trip through numerous checkpoints, Mikolajczyk finally reached Gdynia where, 'through the contrivance of an old SOE hand and wartime associate of his named Ronald Hazell', he boarded a British ship disguised as a British naval officer. 'A gentleman with the character of a bank manager', Hazell had been employed in shipping with the United Baltic Corporation and had occasionally worked for MI6. A member of Gubbins's circle, he was a close friend of Harold Perkins and a member of the pre-war Military Mission to Warsaw. Vice-consul at Galatz in 1940, after wartime service in SOE, Hazell was appointed vice-consul of Gdynia in March 1947, as a cover for MI6 duties.[29]

Mikolajczyk set sail for freedom on the *Baltavia*, reaching England at the end of October. In the interests of security, he had not informed his colleagues of his plans, and this led in some quarters to bitterness and accusations of 'ruthless calculation'. Korbonski and his wife also managed to escape from Gdynia on a Swedish ship for Gothenberg, but other members of the PSL were not so lucky. A number were caught on the Czechoslovakian border, and under duress revealed the connivance of the British and American embassies in the escape of Mikolajczyk.[30]

Mikolajczyk initially stayed in London, where his wife had remained after his return to Warsaw at the end of the war. His stay was marked by a propaganda campaign partly centred around the activities of the British League for European Freedom (BLEF) and the Mid-European Studies Centre, which employed exiles to undertake research on historical, cultural and political subjects in their respective countries. The BLEF was close to the Poles, who, according to the president of the Polish Ex-Servicemen's Association, respected the organisation because 'it knew about the situation in Poland better than most'. In November 1946, Mikolajczyk told a Royal Institute of International Affairs meeting that he had decided to flee to the West because he thought his death might well have led to revenge and unnecessary bloodshed from his own supporters, which would have given the communists 'the chance to drown the people's opposition in blood'. It was clear, however, that he was not wanted in London by the Polish government-in-exile and, at the end of 1947, Mikolajczyk moved to the United States, where he was destined to play 'a lone hand'. There were deep divisions within the American Polish exile community, and many disliked his attempted policy of cohabitation with the communists. Frustrated, he organised and then dismissed his own committee, eventually promoting 'his own politics in second exile'. In truth, Mikolajczyk's considerable reputation was entirely destroyed by his defeat and subsequent flight from the country, bringing to an end the opposition activity of the PSL. Patrick Howarth was to report that following his departure 'further darkness descended on Poland'.[31]

The WiN network of around sixty thousand activists and supporters retained a considerable degree of organisational coherence until late 1946. This was partly because the security police – the 'Red Gestapo' – found it difficult to break into the underground, where each cell consisted of five personnel linked to the next cell by only one person. Underground activity appears to have reached a peak in September/October, which coincided with renewed security operations, with more troops and officials killed than at any time since the end of the war. By January 1947 guerrilla activity had markedly declined. The underground had been severely weakened by the security campaigns during the election period, with heavy losses within the political and military leadership. During the previous October, the president of WiN, Franciszek Niepokolczycki, and seventeen other members of the supreme command had been arrested, while the new supreme command under Wincenty Kwiecinski was rounded up in early January. Regional networks and provincial commands were devastated by the arrests. Acknowledging that a full-scale insurrection would not succeed, the underground had hoped to sustain the spirit of the opposition, but the crushing of the PSL in the fraudulent elections had sapped its strength, resulting in a slump in morale. Another amnesty during February/March saw fifty-five thousand supporters of the ex-AK leave the underground, even though many suffered persecution.[32]

During June the British embassy reported that Poland 'seemed calmer in the past three months than at any time since 1945'. It was thus an odd time for Carr's Northern Division to launch a major covert intelligence-gathering operation, BROADWAY, which involved dropping agents and equipment into Poland to make contact with the resistance.[33]

On the back of a Soviet attempt to encourage the remaining Poles in Britain to return home, MI6 took the opportunity to recruit agents among the targeted exiles. A number of Polish Army personnel did go back, and though most returned to low-level jobs, a few were promoted into senior posts and were able to provide MI6 with valuable information, at a time when any information obtained from behind the Iron Curtain was treated like gold dust. Through these connections, MI6 retained contact with WiN and the recently established coalition of émigré Poles in London, the Polish Political Council. The information was, however, only fragmentary, as the MI6 agents sent into Poland were invariably arrested or killed. In 1950, Warsaw Radio reported the break-up of another network. Former Africa Agency head Rygot Slowikowski, known as 'the birdman' to the Polish communists, who reviled him, was mentioned in one espionage trial in Warsaw with 'insinuations that he ran a post-war network and that the accused was one of his agents'. Slowikowski's old MI6 friend Anthony Morris was at the time stationed as assistant military attaché at the embassy in Rome, from where many operations into eastern Europe were run.[34]

Since 1944 the underground had been broken up by the security forces five times, but had managed to reorganise and rebuild itself. By 1947, when a determined drive by the Polish security police wiped out the remaining cells of resistance, it was thought that WiN was finished. Just before WiN was broken up by the security police, however, the organisation sent delegates to Paris, London and Washington with the news that it was being built up again. 'Miraculously', in 1949 a Pole with 'impeccable resistance credentials',

Stefan Sienko ('Wiktor'), secretary of IV Zarzad Glowny WiN, escaped to the West and made contact in London with General Anders. The general still had over 110,000 Poles under arms in the United Kingdom, in the Polish Resettlement Corps (PKPR), 'marking time against the imminent Communist collapse'. Sienko told Anders that WiN 'still existed; with funds and equipment from the West, it might be revived' to carry out 'espionage, subversive activities and sabotage'. WiN would be able to mobilize thirty thousand guerrilla fighers. Anders informed MI6, whose officers – especially those involved in operations in the Baltic – renewed their acquaintance with the Polish delegates.[35]

Communications were established with WiN during the summer of 1950. The London WiN Centre maintained contact with the WiN Home Organisation in Poland mainly by letters from 'family' to 'friends outside', and by occasional meetings between the two sides arranged by a WiN courier to the West. This soon became too big an operation for the British to undertake by themselves. According to former CIA officer George Muslin, Operation Broadway 'got too expensive for the British and they passed it on to us'. In November, with the Korean War fresh in their minds, an agreement was reached in London between the Office of Policy Co-ordination (OPC)/MI6 and Pawlem Sapieha, Colonel Aciolek and Edward Kulikowski of 'WiN Centre Abroad'. OPC officers Walpole Davis and John Evalovsky subsequently moved to London as control officers for the operation.[36]

MI6 and the OPC were quickly engaged in an effort to build up WiN as part of the resistance network throughout eastern Europe. Soviet troops would have to pass through Poland if they advanced into western Europe, and the military planners hoped that WiN could slow them down if war came. It was even mooted that the other operations in eastern Europe would be used to 'divert and distract Soviet attention from the main target: Poland'. Agents were parachuted into the country in an operation reminiscent of SOE activities during the war. MI6 and the OPC began to pump in money – well over one million dollars of gold sovereigns with which to bribe officials – arms, sophisticated explosives, timers for sabotage targets, and radios. MI6 and the OPC marshalled virtually the entire Polish émigré movement abroad in support of the 'WiN Home Organisation', which claimed to attract enormous support. OPC chief Frank Wisner boasted it had at its command 'the loyalty of 500 activists, 20,000 partially active members and 100,000 sympathisers who were ready for service in the advent of war'. Wisner backed up his claims with 'photographs of burnt-out tanks and gun-ravaged police buildings' which had been smuggled to the West 'to prove the underground's success against the communists'. Wisner insisted that all WiN needed was anti-tank weapons 'to drive the Red Army out of Warsaw'.[37]

During 1951 WiN claimed to be steadily building towards becoming an effective fighting force capable of delaying any Soviet advance to the west.

Simultaneously, the demands of the WiN guerrillas in Poland, which MI6/ OPC and the military continued to support, grew dramatically, and special operations officers only balked, according to Tom Bower, when a request came through to send an American general so as to bolster the resistance. This did not, however, arouse any great suspicions, since WiN had begun to smuggle out reports and documents revealing the Soviet order of battle and its military capabilities in eastern Europe. 'This intelligence apparently came from WiN moles inside the Defence Ministry.'[38]

Unfortunately, the British and American efforts lacked the required professionalism. Anders and the London WiN Centre declined to provide MI6 and the OPC with any details about the Home Organisation in Poland. There were still residual feelings of distrust towards their former allies, and it was felt that security was paramount; the smaller the circle of those with knowledge of the identity of WiN agents the better. The London Poles preferred to operate in the 'quiet and dark'. The counter-intelligence staff of both agencies were naturally appalled by this potential security lapse, which broke every rule of clandestine work. The operation was thus deprived of the basic information needed to exercise control over the people involved. It was an example of professional carelessness in a general spirit of over-confidence and arrogance, characteristic of the period. When the agencies discovered that the majority of agents parachuted into Poland had quickly fallen into the hands of the authorities, they changed tactics and sent in agents in the guise of businessmen attending trade fairs. These were regarded as having a better chance of survival than dropped agents. The optimism proved to be misplaced, however.[39]

MI6 and the OPC went on with the operation regardless, and corners were cut because, in the words of Wisner's deputy and chief of the OPC's East European Division, Frank Lindsay, over whose desk all the WiN material passed, 'we were fighting a war and it was all in the short term'. The chiefs of staff on both sides of the Atlantic wanted results and were pushing their respective intelligence services to achieve them quickly. The excessive demands of WiN's Home Organisation had, however, raised doubts about its soundness, added to which were the dark suspicions about the MI6 liaison officer in Washington, Kim Philby, who had attended meetings where the WiN operation had been discussed. But when James Angleton voiced fears to his trout-fishing partner, the CIA director General Walter Bedell 'Beetle' Smith, and Allen Dulles to the effect that WiN was a Soviet deception oper-ation along the lines of the twenties' 'Trust', they preferred to bow to Wisner's conviction that WiN was a legitimate resistance organisation. Angleton continued to argue that deception had been the Russian Intelligence Service's classic tactic since Tsarist times, but he was ignored.[40]

WiN, though, was a target for a limited counter-espionage investigation when Bedell Smith asked General Lucian Truscott, retired commander of the

Fifth Army, to reassess the Agency's covert operations into eastern Europe, Truscott travelled to Germany in April 1951 to see 'what those weirdos are up to and put the lid down'. He was not impressed by WiN controller Walpole Davis, and the fact that no useful intelligence had been delivered. On viewing the training of exiles, he declared that 'these agents won't survive . . . the émigré groups are certain to be penetrated'. This accurate forecast was dismissed by MI6 and the OPC, which continued to accept WiN's credibility, preferring not to consider the possibility of a deception operation. Menzies, according to Stewart Steven's source, held the view that 'once you grant the enemy a mind so supreme that it thinks of everything, you are left with no choice but to do nothing'. 'But WiN was leaking like a sieve,' recalled a participant. 'The Polish militia were told in advance and the men were picked up as soon as they touched the ground.' By mid-1947, the Polish security forces had thoroughly penetrated WiN, and there came a point when the guerrillas did not know who to believe or trust. According to Jan Gerhard, a colonel of the General Staff in charge of operations, 'thanks to our intelligence agents, we had precise information about WiN' which was used to turn a number of its leaders. Among those arrested were infiltrators who were allowed to escape and set up false networks.[41]

The Polish security service, Urzad Bezpiecznstwa (the UB or Bezpieka), had captured the WiN leader, Sienko, who agreed to co-operate with the UB as a double agent, as he could see no possibility of continuing the struggle. The WiN Home Organisation courier to the West was kept under tight surveillance, unaware that all meetings with the London Centre representatives in Poland took place in UB-arranged safe houses. The whole WiN Home Organisation network, it turned out, was a huge, elaborate deception operation orchestrated by the MGB. The intelligence reaching them from Warsaw was Soviet disinformation. The Polish security forces had even staged mock battles to give WiN credibility, and had taken over the clandestine radios supplied by MI6 and the OPC. George Muslin subsequently discovered that 'the whole agent-running programme in Germany had been infiltrated by the communists before we took it over. We learnt this when one of the agents managed to get back out of Poland and told us we'd been had.' Muslin claims that 'we closed down the whole operation, abandoned it on the spot', but it was not quite like that.[42]

Although there was no explanation for why the Soviets chose this particular moment to expose the deception, it would appear that the MGB decided to roll up the WiN operation after the exposure of the 'Kolberg Ring' in West Germany. Colonel Gregor Kowalski, a former Polish cavalry commander who had escaped in 1939 to Britain, where he was appointed adjutant to Col. Sikorski, was one of the few officers to return to his homeland afer the war and to be trusted by the communist-dominated Polish government. At some stage he changed allegiance and, during 1948, was sent undercover to the

British Zone of Germany as the head of a Polish reparations mission to found an espionage network, the Kolberg Ring, which ran successfully for three years. Concerned mainly with the question of German rearmament, Kowalski renewed his friendship with a number of British officers, whom he began to cultivate for information. A counter-penetration operation that planted 'chicken-feed' in the ring finally closed it down in May 1952, when MI5 arrested Maria Knuth, the sexual bait in honeytrap operations run by the ring. According to author 'E. H. Cookridge', whose information was often derived from senior MI5 officer Guy Liddell, the destruction of the ring led to the uncovering of other Polish-backed spy networks. This was possibly the factor that forced the Soviets finally to reveal their own highly successful deception operation.[43]

The UB proceeded to arrest about a hundred people, most of whom were put in prison; others were tortured and a few executed in secret. Beginning on 27 December 1952, to the general disbelief of MI6 and OPC officers, Radio Warsaw broadcast a series of programmes exposing WiN, revealing that the resistance network had been a puppet of the UB since early 1948 when the commanders of the WiN Home Organisation, J. J. Kowalski (Kos) and his deputy, Stefan Sienko, 'sought out the Communist authorities in Warsaw, heartsick with the realisation that what was intended initially as a "continuation of our activity during the Nazi occupation" had degenerated into "criminal, anti-Polish activity"'. The West had been sending gold straight to the UB coffers which, in turn, funded the entire deception operation. The WiN Home Organisation leaders announced that they had not been able to reveal the structure of the organisation 'for the simple reason that it did not exist'. Besides the fabricated deception material that WiN transmitted to London, 'the only information which we sent them after repeated and insistent requests was the menu from one of the Warsaw restaurants'.[44]

The WiN débâcle had a dramatic and debilitating effect on James Angleton and other western counter-espionage officers, including a small group of his supporters in MI6. Although Philby was blamed for the betrayal, Angleton reasoned that the organisation had been compromised well before the MI6 officer was briefed on its activities. Philby's true role, Angleton argued, was to provide the necessary feedback on WiN and other underground groups to his Soviet handlers. On the basis of the information he provided, the Soviet deception planners were able to modify their information to fit in with the thinking, prejudices and desires of the MI6 and OPC officers running WiN. 'The point was not that these movements were betrayed,' Angleton claimed, 'it was that they were made credible to the CIA [and MI6].'[45]

The Radio Warsaw broadcasts coincided with the last radio messages received from western-trained operators in Ukraine and provided the communists with a major propaganda coup. The deception had served to draw out genuine Polish resisters so that they could be caught and, thereby, convince the Poles that opposition was useless. Coming soon after the election of Eisenhower, which encouraged the idea of rolling back communist control in eastern Europe, it also – very effectively – taught the West a lesson about meddling in eastern Europe, where Soviet totalitarian control remained as tight as ever.

CHAPTER 16

THE BALTIC STATES

Throughout the twenties and thirties, MI6 had used its stations in Scandinavia and the Baltic states to build up an extensive range of contacts and operatives. The head of station in Finland, from where the majority of cross-border operations to insert agents into the Soviet Union for intelligence-gathering or as couriers to the anti-Bolshevik underground took place, was Harry Carr. Teams of guerrillas from General Kutepov's Combat Corps were 'sent across the Finnish border to assassinate communist officials with the hope of creating conditions for a wider revolt; terrorist actions which only led to more repression'. An austere and dedicated anti-Bolshevik, Carr formed strong links with White Russian émigrés and members of the dissident nationalities and minorities within the Soviet Union.[1]

It helped that Carr had been born, at the end of the last century, near St Petersburg, where his father was the manager of British-owned timber mills. The family emigrated to England to escape the Bolsheviks, but Carr returned in 1919 to Murmansk as an interpreter to the head of an expedition to overthrow the new Soviet government, General Ironside (whose ADC was future Special Operations Executive (SOE) Executive Director Colin Gubbins). It was a venture which, Tom Bower believed, 'influenced Carr's whole life'. Eventually evacuated as the expedition collapsed, Carr joined MI6 and was posted, in 1921, to Finland under the traditional light cover of an Assistant Passport Officer. After five years, he was appointed head of station in Helsinki. His appointment coincided with one of the lowest points in the

Service's history, as it had just been revealed that a major anti-Bolshevik network, the Monarchist Association of Central Russia, better known as the 'Trust', had been thoroughly penetrated as part of a highly successful deception operation run by the Unified State Political Directorate (OGPU) – later absorbed into the People's Commissariat for Internal Affairs (NKVD), the forerunner of the Ministry of State Security (KGB).[2]

According to Bower, Carr had the necessary characteristics, even if they were idiosyncratic, to make him an ideal intelligence officer. In the end, however, they would also cause his downfall. 'A hypochondriac, who avoided any kind of physical discomfort', even to his own staff Carr was an 'obsessively secretive' man. A colleague claimed: 'It's said that he even slept with a handkerchief stuffed in his mouth.' His belief that 'security was an end in itself' often distorted his judgement about sources and helped cover up the fact that much of his 'secret' material either came from 'completely open sources' or had simply been 'manufactured'. As chief of operations in Helsinki, Carr relied on his 'garrulous bon viveur' assistant, Rex Bosley, who spoke the difficult Finnish language, his associate in the Latvian capital, Riga, Leslie Nicholson, and Alexander McKibben in Tallinn, Estonia. 'Sandy' McKibben had been born in Moscow of wealthy Scottish parents and spoke fluent Russian and Estonian. Established as a timber dealer in Tallinn, he was forced to abandon his business because of the Bolsheviks. MI6's anti-communist campaigns were top-heavy with senior MI6 officers such as Carr's closest friends, the Gibson brothers, Archie and Harold, who had been born in pre-Bolshevik Russia and whose families had had business interests in the Baltic or Soviet Union. The most important were the former timber merchants such as Cyril Cheshire, the half-Russian chief of station in Sweden, Brigadier Douglas Roberts, and the Sillem brothers in Riga, who had owned a brewery in Estonia on the border between Russia and Finland. Drawing on these contacts, McKibben developed a wide-ranging intelligence-gathering network among military, political and security circles in the Baltic states. A particularly rich source of information was the Director of Military Intelligence in Estonia, Colonel Villen Saarsen – 'as he was for the Germans for whom he was also providing services'. In general, MI6's pre-war intelligence-gathering and recruitment of agents was, Bower concludes, 'amateurish in the extreme'.[3]

With the signing of the German–Soviet Pact and the declaration of war, the Baltic states took on renewed significance for British intelligence-gathering, often controlled from Sweden, which became the major refuge for those Balts fleeing the Soviets and later the Nazis. One such was an anglophile and former professor of English at Estonia's Tartu University, Ants Oras, a valuable pre-war contact for the British embassy in Tallinn, where his brother had worked as a secretary. Russian tanks crossed the Baltic borders on 17 June 1940 and, despite occupation by the Red Army, Professor Oras maintained contact with MI6 via the Anglo-Estonian Friendship Society. When he was implicated in espionage activity by the NKVD, Oras managed to evade capture and escape to Stockholm, from where he helped organise a courier service to the resistance in Tallinn. When the Germans invaded the Soviet Union in June 1941, eighty young Estonians who had found refuge in Germany were recruited by the Abwehr. Using swift motor boats and then low-level air-drops, they were inserted into Estonia and linked up with the 'Forest Brotherhood' commanded by Colonel Leithammel. At the same time, the British embassy staff in Helsinki moved to Sweden, where Carr became First Secretary responsible for targeting the Germans. For many of the older MI6 officers, however, the war was merely an interruption in the battle against the Bolsheviks. As Bower notes: 'It took a long time for them to realise that the world was a different place.'[4]

It might be assumed that before the war the Baltic states were a democratic oasis, faced as they were by the totalitarian regimes of Hitler and Stalin. Their fate was often seen in tragic terms but, in reality, Estonia and Latvia had been themselves near-dictatorships, which partially explains why they endured some of the worst atrocities and mass killings of the entire Second World War. Estonia was 'cleansed' of the few Jews there, while more than two-thirds of the Jewish populations of Latvia and Lithuania were wiped out. The Germans were helped in the massacres by collaborators in the locally recruited security battalions; in Latvia many were members of the fascist Thunder Cross. The three countries were also a recruiting ground for the SS, and while Lithuania was 'largely written off as a racially inferior hotbed of discontent', Latvia and Estonia provided 'an untapped source of troops'. Many of the worst collaborators were later recruited by MI6 for anti-communist operations, with little regard to their past.[5]

The director-general of the collaborationist Latvian administration was General Oskars Dankers. Beneath him, and a key figure in the internal Latvian security apparatus, was Vilis Janums, head of the personnel department of the Home Affairs committee, responsible for all police units. Taking its name from its chief, the notorious paramilitary 'Arajs Kommando' had the task of isolating and executing Jews, gypsies and communists. During August 1941 the Arajs Kommando massacred fifteen thousand Jews and between September and December another twenty-nine thousand were deported for execution under guard of the Kommando. The mass deportations and shooting of Jews had been organised by the Latvian 'Kommando' in Riga, headed by the Director of Operations in the Ministry of Interior, Lieutenant-Colonel Robert Osis. A former Latvian Army officer, Osis had been recruited before the war by MI6's Leslie Nicholson for intelligence work. Talks in February 1942 between the SS and General Dankers resulted in an official appeal for Latvians to form 'Schutzmannschaft' police units. The recruitment was organised by the head of the Ministry of Interior's Committee of Latvian Volunteer Organisation, Gustav Celmins, and Paul Reinhards, director of the Labour Department, while the command of these 15,000-strong units was assigned to Robert Osis. They were used to guard the deportations and were responsible for herding Jews to killing sites in the Rumbula forest, and securing the perimeter while the massacres were carried out.[6]

These Baltic units also supplied men to serve in SS units that carried out executions in other states, notably in Belorussia. An outline agreement was reached with the SS for the formation of a legion commanded by Inspector General Rudolfs Bangerskis and a chief of staff, first Col. Alexander Plensners and later Arthur Silgailis. By order of SS chief Heinrich Himmler, during August 1943 a police regiment was created under the command of Lt-Col. Osis, who helped transform it into the Latvian Legion, whose volunteers were allowed to wear the Latvian 'Firecross' on their black collar patch. Osis subsequently took command of the 33rd Regiment of the 15th Waffen-SS Latvian Division, serving as its liaison officer with the Nazis. These fully fledged SS brigades and divisions – the 15th, 19th Latvian and 20th Estonian – with a total strength of over thirty thousand men, were tasked with ridding the Baltic area of Soviet partisans. Among those who served in the SS were Alfred Berzins, responsible for sending civilians to concentration camps and recipient of the German Iron Cross; Dankers's personal assistant, Col. Arvids Kripens, who 'ordered the murder of thousands of innocent civilians'; and leader of the Thunder Cross Gustav Celmins, who served as a Nazi agent inside nationalist circles throughout the war. Celmins was responsible for the well-being of the Latvian units, creating a welfare organisation, the LPK, and newsletter, *Daugavas Vanagi* (Hawks of the Daugava river).[7]

Lithuania never succumbed to the Nazis to the same extent as Latvia and Estonia, and while it provided recruits for Defence Battalions, there was no Lithuanian SS Legion. Following invasion by the Soviets, underground resistance cells of the Lithuanian Activist Front (LAF) were formed in October 1940, and contact was established with the erstwhile Lithuanian minister in Berlin, Colonel Kazys Skirpa. With the launch of Barbarossa, the Germans established the LAF as a provisional government. Soon after, indiscriminate killing and massacre of Jews was undertaken by several bands of *ad hoc* executioners. One leading LAF member was Anatas Grecevicius (Gecas), who had been in the Lithuanian Air Force before the German invasion and thereafter joined the 2nd Lithuanian Auxiliary Battalion. Fellow Auxiliary member Juozas Aleksynas was in Belorussia with the 2nd Company during October 1941, when the battalion moved south-eastward to Minsk to take part in 'actions' against the Jews. 'It was clear that our purpose in the Minsk area, although it had never been expressed as such, was the mass killing and extermination of Jewish people.' Aleksynas added that Gecas was 'in charge of all our operations during this time' and gave the order to shoot. Another member of the 2nd Battalion and participant in the 'actions', Motiejus Migonis, agreed that 'Gecas was the officer'. For his actions in Belorussia, Gecas was awarded the German Iron Cross.[8]

The end of 1941 saw the creation of the largest military political organisation of Lithuanian nationalists, the Lithuanian Freedom Army (LFA), with its guerrilla units known as Vanagai (Falcons). Originally an anti-German group, with the tacit approval of the Nazis the LFA developed into an explicitly anti-Soviet movement. In October 1943, the Supreme Committee for the Liberation of Lithuania (SCLL) was created out of seven different political parties and resistance groups to provide direction and leadership in the struggle for national independence. The SCLL issued its first statement in the following February, the same month in which negotiations between General Povilas Plechavicius and the German military command resulted in the formation of a 'Home Army' of 'Local Detachments' to fight against the Soviet Red Army. Plechavicius was a staunch nationalist and a legendary figure in Lithuania, and his call for volunteers was immediately successful. The Germans were astonished when sixteen thousand Lithuanians joined the crusade. Twenty battalions of the Territorial Defence Force (TDF) were formed, commanded by Lithuanian officers. The Germans, however, refused to meet the old general's demands for a national army, and the bulk of the recruits were contemptuously dispatched to Germany for guard duties.[9]

In Estonia and Latvia, where respectively 70,000 and 150,000 men were in the German-sponsored units, there was limited resistance to the German occupiers. In August 1943 an underground nationalist Latvian Central Council (LCC) was created which predicted that 'the end of the war would leave both Germany and the USSR weakened, allowing Latvia to regain its independence with aid of the Western powers'. Affiliated to the LCC was the 'Kurelis' group which had been raised in March 1944 by the German OKW Abwehr 11 as a camouflaged guerrilla organisation of Latvian nationalists to fight behind Russian lines. Its figurehead was former Latvian Army general Janis Kurelis, but it was commanded by Captain Kristaps Upelnieks, an ardent patriot but one with little military knowledge. The LCC had by this time made contact with Swedish, British and American Intelligence.[10]

From the summer of 1944, following a succession of German defeats which left many Balts believing that the war was lost, many Latvian Legion soldiers deserted and, along with others who were unwilling to serve outside their homeland, joined the Kurelis group. In turn, when the German Army retreated, Kurelis members did not remain behind Russian lines but moved to the forests north of Lake Usma, in Kurzeme, where the organisation increased its strength from the additional deserters and defectors. In November, however, it lost the protection of the army when Hitler transferred responsibility for activities behind the front line to the SS. The SS subsequently moved against Kurelis, executing officers, including Capt. Upelnieks, and assigning the unit to the inspector-general of the Latvian Legion, General Bangerskis. Late in the month Bangerskis managed to secure the release of three hundred former Kurelis members from a concentration camp in Prussia. With the reoccupation of the country by the Red Army, Kurelis became an anti-Soviet resistance underground. A thousand armed men established themselves in the Courland, a heavily forested area along the Baltic coast, which became a militarised no-man's-land overrun with retreating German soldiers and Latvian SS.[11]

In Lithuania – the Germans having failed to raise a full SS unit – Plechavicius resisted SS pressure to allow the use of the Defence Force outside the country's borders. Eventually, after armed clashes broke out between units on both sides, Plechavicius cut off negotiations with the SS and, in May 1944, was arrested with the staff of the Home Army for disobeying German orders. Before he was sent to the Salaspils concentration camp, near Riga, Plechavicius ordered thousands of Lithuanians in German uniform to desert and disappear into the forests with their weapons. Armed resistance began during the summer as the armies of the Soviet Third Belorussian front began to move across the border into Lithuania. Late in 1944, up to two thousand German-trained guerrilla warfare specialists and demolition experts were dropped behind Soviet lines in Lithuania by the Germans, but to little effect.[12]

Throughout the war, nationalist elements in the Baltic states had managed to maintain contact with the outside world, which enabled Harry Carr and Sandy McKibben to develop their knowledge of the anti-Nazi and anti-Soviet resistance. In early 1944, as the Red Army began to sweep across eastern and northern Europe, Carr began to consider the rebuilding of an intelligence network in the Baltic, with the intention of penetrating the Soviet Union. McKibben was sent to organise the network from Stockholm, where he was under constant pressure from representatives of the three countries to help the nationalists in the anti-communist struggle. This was initially undertaken in conjunction with Swedish Intelligence, with which Carr had developed a close working relationship. By the summer of 1944 both the military SMT (Svenska Militär Tjanst) and the civilian AS (Allmän Säkerhetsenhet) were sending agents into the Baltic states to gather intelligence in the first of more than sixty operations.[13]

The Estonian resistance, Misiunas and Taagepera write, 'was favoured by the geographical proximity of Finland and Sweden'. Traces of organised resistance formed around underground circles in Tallinn were able to maintain contact with representatives to Finland who were in contact with intelligence agencies in Sweden and London. During 1944, these circles created an underground organisation, the Republic National Committee, which resembled the LCC. By mid-June, following increased Gestapo activity, 'foreign connections were beginning to have a significant role in the activity of the Committee'. Regular contact was maintained by fast motor boat with Stockholm, where August Rei, a leading Social Democrat, was active. The committee managed to install a provisional government in September before the German retreat and the arrival of the Soviets. When the Soviets broke through Estonian defences, the provisional government decided to withdraw to Sweden.[14]

In Latvia, Dr Vladmars Ginters and Vladmars Salnai, the latter a former deputy foreign minister, had been important pre-war sources for MI6. During 1943 they fled to Sweden where, in 1944, determined to resist the Soviets, Ginters re-established contact with MI6 officers, informing them of the underground with whom Salnai was in radio contact. German agents, however, soon uncovered the existence of the Latvian National Council, and at the end of the year arrested and deported most of its leaders. The Germans continued to court the nationalists and established, on 20 February 1945, the Latvian National Committee with Latvian Legion commander Bangerskis and the chief of staff, Arthur Sigailis, attending the opening session at Potsdam. On 7 May, with Courland rapidly being occupied by the Soviets, the Latvian National Council endorsed the setting up of a provisional government led by Colonel Osis.[15]

With the help of Swedish Intelligence, MI6 was soon sending teams into Latvia to report back, particularly via the Riga network, intelligence on the Soviet-held territory. Regular contact was maintained with the Ginters network, which included pro-Germans, known as the 'Wood Cats', and members of the Arajs Kommando, who were protecting the escape corridor to Sweden. The Swedes were to give sanctuary to Balts, former SS and police officers who were wanted as collaborators and war criminals but were to be used as long-term infiltration agents. As the war ended and the Soviets consolidated their position in Latvia, forcing more of their agents to flee the country to safety, MI6 lost contact with the two principal intelligence-gathering networks.[16]

In April 1944, the Lithuanian SCLL committee sent an arms specialist to Sweden to purchase weapons. He was, however, arrested by the Gestapo in Tallinn, Estonia, and after being tortured, revealed the identities of the SCLL committee members. A majority were subsequently arrested and confined in prison in Bavaria. The committee's activities were severely restricted and, one account suggests, 'soon faded after the return of the Soviets'. The Lithuanian representative in Berlin was still able to send information on the homeland to colleagues who had fled to Sweden at the beginning of the conflict. These included, in particular, the diplomat Dr Walter Zilinskas, who, in turn, was able to keep Sandy McKibben abreast of the situation in Lithuania. Zilinskas told McKibben about the SCLL which, despite the arrests, he claimed, had the rudiments of a resistance organisation. He added that although some of its members had collaborated with the Germans, they were all committed anti-communists and nationalists. An operation was put in place to secure a link with the SCLL to discover the situation on the ground, but because MI6 lacked the money it was financed by the American Office of Strategic Services (OSS). The mission ended in failure, however, when the courier was arrested and sent to a concentration camp. The link was to remain broken until late 1945, when renewed attempts where made to re-establish contact.[17]

The surviving members of the SCLL who had collaborated with the Germans cut those links only when the end of the war was in sight. By January 1945, Soviet armies had completely overrun Lithuania, though it was some time before they could gain effective control of the country. Along with the intelligentsia, who had been advised to leave, many Lithuanians fled. Over half of those who had survived forced labour in Germany or service in the Wehrmacht stayed in the West, while 50,000 more followed as refugees. Another 150,000 emigrated to Poland, while Russian deportations and executions in the 1944/5 period accounted for the loss of 200,000 Lithuanians. What remained of the Home Army and other units became guerrillas, and by the spring of 1945 it was estimated that there were 30,000 active resistance fighters in what became known as the Forest Brotherhood. In addition, in Kurzeme, where the most powerful group was called 'Silent Forest', there were 14,000 armed Latvian soldiers in German uniform, wearing the Latvian 'Rising Sun' on their collar patch.[18]

At the time the Red Army crossed the Estonian border, the 20th Waffen-SS Division had been evacuated from the Baltic front to regroup in Silesia, in a last-ditch defence of the Third Reich against the Russians in Czechoslovakia. A battalion commander in the Division, Alphons Rebane, who won the highly prized Knights Cross, managed to fight his way through to the West with a thousand men. In April, they fled towards the British in Germany, and when the war ended went into captivity in PoW camps with a few hundred Estonians from a reserve battalion that had been stationed in Denmark. The British then transferred the Estonians to DP camps. In late April, Latvian Legion units under Colonel Janums had also made their move towards the western allies. Eventually 4,500 men were assembled in forests near Schwerin and surrendered to the approaching Americans. All Latvian military personnel in Denmark were sent to the PoW Camp at Heide in Germany, and later transferred from there to Camp 2227 at Zedelgem in Belgium.

By the beginning of 1945, Carr reported to Kim Philby of the newly created anti-communist Section IX that he and Rex Bosley were successfully gathering intelligence on the Baltic states from the thousands of refugees who passed through Sweden. He also reported that they had established a radio link with the resistance in Latvia. Carr, who had received a CMG (Companion of St Michael and St George) for his wartime work, returned to Broadway in July and was promoted to controller of MI6's Northern area, which included responsibilities for Scandinavia and the Soviet Union. Often operating outside the normal chain of command, Carr worked directly through Menzies, who 'shared his view of the world'. In effect, Carr was able 'to develop his fiefdom without any outside interference or external security surveillance'. With the backing of the chiefs of staff, who were desperate for information on the

Soviet forces which one day they might have to oppose, Menzies gave Carr the go-ahead to re-establish networks in the Baltic region and recruit agents regardless of their wartime activities and collaboration with the Germans. Sandy McKibben, who was attached to the Special Liaison Centre in Ryder Street, near Piccadilly, was given responsibility for managing and supervising the new operations and re-establishing contact with the Balts.[19]

Using captured German intelligence files, Leslie Nicholson spent the first few months following the end of hostilities in London studying the Baltic, and drawing up dossiers on key individuals who might be of use to Section IX. Many were Nazi collaborators and former members of the Baltic Waffen-SS who had sought refuge in Sweden after the German collapse and were fearful of Soviet retribution for their wartime activities. They were pounced on by the Swedish intelligence agency, SMT, for recruitment in intelligence-gathering and infiltration operations. MI6 liaison with SMT's Åke Eek, who had been regarded as a Nazi sympathiser, was undertaken by McKibben, who did not ask too many questions about the Balts' war record. Other targets for the MI6 recruiters were found among the many thousands of Balts who had ended up in the West at the end of hostilities and were dispersed in the DP camps. MI6 was helped in its task by the lenient attitude the Foreign Office took towards collaborators and alleged war criminals from the Baltic region.[20]

In March 1945 the British government had made it clear that soldiers from the Baltic states were not deemed to be Soviet citizens and, therefore, were not subject to repatriation without their own consent. This was well received by the estimated fifty thousand Balts in the British Zone of Germany, among whom were around twenty thousand who had served in the German Army. There were, in addition, a number who were considered war criminals by the Soviets and thus feared possible extradition proceedings. Their cases were taken up by the Baltic representatives in London, such as August Tomas, head of the Estonian legation, who cultivated Foreign Office officials, regularly intervening on their behalf. Tomas and the other legates were to be closely associated with the British-backed covert missions to 'free' their homeland.[21]

A large number of the fifteen thousand Latvians in the West were considered war criminals by the Soviets. A still-disciplined unit in their SS uniforms with their own officers under the command of Colonel Robert Osis, their 'very SS-minded' stance inevitably led to disturbances with other nationalities in the camps. In his camp, Osis, who had commanded a roving execution squad in Latvia and Poland and had been a pre-war intelligence source for MI6, met Feliks Rumniaks, who had deserted from the Latvian SS Legion in January 1945. At the instigation of Osis, Rumniaks made his way to Sweden, where he tried to make contact with MI6 through the exiled LCC, which had a close relationship with the Service. Although some accounts suggest that he was unsuccessful, Rumniaks later claimed that he was rescued from incarceration in a Swedish DP camp and recruited in Stockholm by veteran MI6 officer Harold Gibson. He was subsequently trained in the use of codes and ciphers by Kim Philby, who had made a special trip from London. In Germany, Osis resumed his ties with MI6 almost immediately. He too would later claim that Philby had recruited him and that MI6 had smoothed his path to Britain, where he became one of the chief links in forging a Latvian intelligence network of agents composed almost entirely of former Waffen-SS men.[22]

In Lithuania, a few leaders of the SCLL survived the war, while the linchpin of the underground, General Plechavicius, found himself in the British Zone in Germany. The organisation turned out to be in generally poor shape. Initially it had a good supply of arms and ammunition, retrieved from retreating German soldiers and occasionally from Red Army frontal units, while special care was taken to collect the arms of fallen NKVD men. There was also a certain amount of clandestine arms dealing in the Baltic region. As time went on, however, the shortage of munitions became acute. Even so, this did not prevent the exiled leaders from telling their agents in the homelands that their actions were the prelude to a general war between the West and Stalin's Soviet Union. MI6 officers, however, were much more circumspect in their opinions. Intelligence officers in the West wanted the Balts to deliver better and more precise intelligence on the state of communist control in the Soviet Union and the likelihood of an assault on the West, though they did not disabuse their charges of their inflated optimism.[23]

Largely cut off from the outside world, the underground appears to have veered from optimism to despair, only rarely touched with realism about its desperate situation. They had faith that American President Roosevelt and Britain's Prime Minister Churchill would hold true to the Atlantic Charter which they had signed in August 1941, proclaiming the sovereign right of people to seek territorial integrity. This became a benchmark for émigrés throughout Europe, though it was ignored by the Foreign Office. According to one account: 'At no time did they delude themselves into believing that they could drive the Soviets out of their nation. Their object was rather to harass, to delay, to attract the attention of the West, and above all to remind the people that they were victims of aggression, not partners in the "glorious Soviet State".' It was true, nevertheless, that when news reached Lithuania of the atomic bomb drops on Japan, 'there was a moment of intense hope'. It was thought inconceivable that the West would abandon the Baltic states. Many Lithuanians 'believed that the occupation was only temporary and that the Allies would invade'. Later it was thought that the conflict between the wartime partners would implode into a new world war which the Soviet Union would lose, leaving Lithuania independent.[24]

'Reality', however, 'methodically and pitilessly destroyed whatever hopes remained.' In September 1944, Stalin had sent 'one of the most cruel and merciless executioners', General Sergei Kruglov, deputy director of SMERSH ('Death to Spies'), which had a special responsibility for strengthening the Soviet hold over the 'liberated countries', to crush the resistance that had successfully mounted a series of attacks on Soviet units, inflicting mounting losses. Over eighty thousand troops were garrisoned in Lithuania, but the bulk of the anti-guerrilla work was undertaken by the Soviet NKVD. Kruglov created a special NKVD department for 'bandit' affairs, the OBO, which handled intelligence-gathering and the creation of local militia units. Favourite tactics included employing OBO-trained infiltrators among the resistance groups, the use of *agents provocateurs* posing as German, British and American intelligence officers, and the widespread use of pseudo and counter-gangs in an effort to prove that the guerrillas were nothing more than terrorist bandits. Jonas Luksa, who belonged to a mythical guerrilla unit known as Iron Wolf, wrote that by July 1945 there were no armed Germans to be found in Lithuania. This did not, however, prevent the NKVD from parachuting in a number of agents disguised as German soldiers armed with German weapons.[25]

There followed a policy of scorched earth and terror, with the mass deport-ation of those deemed to be opposed to the Soviet Union or sympathetic towards the guerrillas. Many insurgents were killed, while the treatment of those captured was brutal and extreme. They were usually tortured and, as an example to others, a number were left naked 'tied to trees by wire, their bodies skinned with limbs hacked off, eyes gouged and as a further marker the Lithuanian emblem of the Knight's Cross cut into their breast'. The amnesties for former guerrillas that began in the summer of 1945 became increasingly successful. This left around twenty thousand committed to the fight which they believed would be resolved by the Allies honouring the pledges made in the Atlantic Charter. By the end of the year, however, the regional organisations of the underground were 'severely crippled by arrests of leaders and the ranks thinned as a result of the ruthlessness'. All they were left with was the illusion that war was about to break out between the Allies and the Soviet Union.[26]

Little of this background was known when, in early July 1945, Sandy McKibben returned to Stockholm to meet Walter Zilinskas, who was unemployed following the closure of the Lithuanian embassy. McKibben promised financial aid to Zilinskas through his MI6 contact, Passport Control Officer George Berger. He was subsequently replaced by Maclachlan Silverwood-Cope, who operated under commercial cover as Second Secretary at the British embassy. During the war Silverwood-Cope had developed close links with Finnish and Norwegian Intelligence. MI6 officers in Scandinavia began recruiting agents for Baltic operations. Among one of the earliest was the Lithuanian intellectual and passionate nationalist Stasys Zakevicius, who had studied history at Oxford University. He had served as an adviser to the German administration during the occupation and had managed to escape from Lithuania with the Germans on one of the last trains to Denmark. Won over by agents of McKibben, Zakevicius became the nucleus of the new Lithuanian operation. Changing his name to Zymantas, he brought into the service the diplomat Stasys Lozoritis and a well-known journalist who had escaped to the West in early 1945, Jonas Deksnys. The latter quickly established links with the anti-Soviet guerrillas in Lithuania, many of whom had gone into the forests after serving the Germans in various capacities. During the autumn, MI6 – with Swedish help – sent Jonas Deksnys back to Lithuania, to assess the strength and test the claims of the SCLL.[27]

Many Allied officials believed that the Latvian Legion, almost entirely anti-Russian, would be handed over to the Soviets. In order to defend it against Soviet repatriation missions, Bangerskis set up what was ostensibly a self-help and welfare society in Germany. Gustav Clemins's LKP had moved there in late April 1945 and was located at Lübeck, where it continued relief work for Latvian refugees. Bangerskis was, however, denounced by some of his fellow-countrymen and was arrested on 21 June 1945 by British intelligence officers.

A secretive organisation, Daugavas Vanagi included many fascists who had served with the German occupation forces. As part of its 'welfare work', a leading collaborator, Dr Alfred Vladmanis, was permitted by the British to organise in their zone in Germany, among the 'ex-Wehrmacht Balts'. In the process, Daugavas Vanagi tightened its control of the German DP camps by routing out so-called Soviet stooges. It also developed international links with leading Latvian exiles such as Alfreds Berzins, secretary of its Latvian Central Committee, Bolreslavs Maikovskis and Gustav Clemins – all leading lights in the MI6-backed Intermarium émigré organisation.[28]

The Latvians set up another front organisation, the 'Latvian Red Cross', to lobby the British government against repatriation. They also had a powerful advocate in London, Charles Zarine, the Minister of the Latvian Delegation during the war, who had been authorised to exercise full authority over Latvia's resources and representatives when contact with the home country had been broken. He argued that although membership of the Latvian Legion had been voluntary, the unit had been 'forcibly' taken into the Waffen-SS. They were, therefore, not pro-Nazi but simply anti-Bolshevik. He also lobbied for the Latvians to be separated from German PoWs and the 'special SS cages', and, instead, to be put in their own DP camp. Zarine was treated sympathetically within the Foreign Office, particularly by Thomas Brimelow of the Northern Department who, before the war, had met Zarine while serving in the British consulate in Riga. Brimelow's stint in the Moscow embassy between 1942 and 1945 had left him wary of Soviet intentions.[29]

On 31 August 1945, the Foreign Office ordered that members of non-German SS formations and non-German nationals in German uniform would not be placed in automatic arrest categories (unlike their German SS comrades). They were to be dispersed and released as ordinary non-German nationals. Two weeks later, two hundred Baltic ex-Wehrmacht members were given straightforward DP status, although the Foreign Office asserted that this was 'not to be taken as a precedent'. At the end of September, following Zarine's intervention at the Foreign Office, most of the former Latvian police and Waffen-SS members were transferred to a collecting centre at Zedelghen, in Belgium. There was, however, still the matter of the presence of a number of war criminals in the camps. The Soviets had requested the extradition of Colonel Arvids Kripens, the regimental commander of the Latvian Legion, who was discovered to be at Zedelghen. British military authorities investigated the charges and decided in November that the Soviets had a prima facie case against him. Brimelow minuted that the evidence against him was 'pretty black'. But, on the day before a Soviet officer visited the camp to complete the transfer, Kripens received advance warning and attempted suicide by plunging a knife into his chest. Whether the attempt was serious or staged, Kripens survived. On the following day, Zarine, who considered Kripens to be 'an honest and good man', intervened on his behalf with the Foreign Office. In the same month, the British quietly released the Legion's commander, Bangerskis.[30]

Thomas Brimelow consulted with Colonel Isham at the War Office for clarification on the status of the Latvian formations and whether, in fact, they were all SS who had seen action on Soviet territory. Isham had damning evidence that Kripens had been a volunteer in the SS Legion, but it was not well received by Brimelow, who had toughened his stance against the Soviets. While officials recognised that there was a cast-iron case against Kripens, they refused to countenance his transfer, as it would have set a precedent for the many Balts then under suspicion. Although the International Military Tribunal at Nuremberg had declared the entire Waffen-SS a 'criminal organisation', Brimelow put forward a new defence to the effect that it was not enough that someone had volunteered for an SS formation; the Soviets would have to present a prima facie case that the individual had committed war crimes. Given the high standard of evidence required to meet the criteria, the Balts were, in effect, rendered immune from prosecution.[31]

Kripens was not repatriated, but laundered through the Allied screening system. After recovering from his suicide attempt, he was sent to another DP camp, where he worked for the military authorities before being passed on to a selection team for emigration to Australia. Forty years later, the All-Party Parliamentary War Crimes Group which examined the case concluded that the Foreign Office had 'operated a double standard' by demanding from the Soviets 'a more exhaustive case than would have been required for German SS officers'. The British authorities were 'apparently ignorant of, or wilfully avoiding, information concerning the activity of collaborationists in German-occupied Latvia'.[32]

On 21 December, Brimelow ordered that the remaining nineteen thousand non-German Wehrmacht Balts be discharged and dispersed. The German Department of the Foreign Office added that 'the sooner they are disbanded the better; there is no prospect of our ever being able to palm them off on to anyone'. Latvian Legion fears that they might be repatriated thus evaporated. When Col. Osis returned from one of his regular visits to the British HQ, he was 'in a high state of excitement, and soon word spread through the camp that all Latvians must "disappear"'. From unidentified sources, the soldiers acquired civilian clothes, papers and, by the New Year, 'the entire population of the camp had melted away'. In January 1946, around 16,500 of the Balts acquired DP status and the majority took refuge in camps where they were not screened, despite the fact that many hundreds had SS blood markings tattooed under their armpits. When the United Nations Refugee and Rehabilitation Agency (UNRRA) attempted to test their eligibility there was a storm of protest and a flurry of lobbying by their supporters in Britain.[33]

Meanwhile, MI6 began to plan for New Year operations into the Baltic. During August, it had revived its ties with the LCC, led by Dr Vladmars Ginters and Verners Tepfers. Ginters had been asked by his MI6 handlers to help send an advance team into Latvia to reactivate contact with the underground, which was still holding out in the forests. In October, MI6 recruited a team of Latvian agents from among the refugees, and in conjunction with Swedish Intelligence tried to smuggle them into Latvia. This first infiltration operation had to be abandoned when the speedboat carrying supplies and arms was overturned in a freak wind near the Courland coast. At McKibben's request, Ginters and Tepfers were asked to look for suitable candidates for future operations.[34]

In the new year, the British approached these infiltrations into the Baltic at 'arms-length'. Menzies told the Joint Intelligence Committee (JIC) that it was essential that Moscow 'should not become aware of the nature' of these operations, and one such mission was even camouflaged as being under United States sponsorship; MI6 supplied the Latvians with American weapons and equipment with the labels of origin clearly visible. Often handled through intermediaries, a number of the agents who landed in Latvia were unaware that they were financed and controlled by British Intelligence. Three such agents, who had not even been supplied with the most basic identity papers, were quickly captured, with their radio intact, by the NKVD, and were subjected to intense, brutal interrogation. The 'false flag' ploy, a favourite of MI6, failed, and the Soviets, using intelligence from their agents in London, had proof that the British were back in the game, resuming their pre-war activities.[35]

During January 1946, McKibben and Stasys Zymantas, MI6's Lithuanian expert, held the first of a series of meetings to discuss possible operations in Lithuania. At the meeting in Hamburg with Zilinskas, it was agreed to re-establish contact with the underground, which was still active, having garnered offers of practical support from the embittered rural population which opposed the Soviet decree to collectivise the farms. The Soviet response during the following month was to deport thousands of families and conduct mass arrests, with a series of reprisals designed to break the back of the armed resistance. Fearing NKVD interrogation, the guerrillas took to extreme methods to avoid arrest, preferring suicide to being taken alive. Further, in order to protect their families and friends from reprisals, 'it seems, the guerrillas blew themselves up with grenades held close to their face, so that they could not be recognised'.[36]

Soviet security agencies also began to move against centres of resistance abroad, which were being co-ordinated from the Allied zones in Germany by the SCLL. The SCLL was 'almost wholly comprised of former Nazi-collaborators, men such as Plechavicius who at the very least had worked with the Germans as long as collaboration served their purposes'. When the Soviet government presented evidence and identified individuals against whom specific allegations could be made, the British response was to stonewall. In February 1946 the Soviets demanded Plechavicius's extradition as a war criminal, but their evidence that he had presided over 'the recruitment and deployment of paramilitary units which were involved in numerous actions against Jews and Soviet partisans' was simply dismissed. The reason the Foreign Office gave was that despite the Intelligence Bureau of the Control Office being well aware that 'Plechavicius is in our Zone', and the fact that the Russians were also 'aware of this', there were 'vital intelligence reasons which preclude the possibility of our handing him over to the Russians'. Instead, the authorities decided to keep him hidden.[37]

In March, at a second conference in Lübeck, McKibben and Zymantas considered reports brought back by Jonas Deksnys from Lithuania via Poland. Deksnys was the long-time leader of the Lithuanian Freedom Fighters Association, an underground organisation established in 1940 and active during the German occupation, mainly composed of younger political activists of national-liberal orientation. He had been, for a short time, imprisoned in a German concentration camp. In a graphic account of the current situation in Lithuania, Deksnys told MI6 that despite the Soviet terror tactics, the countryside was a no-go area at night, under the control of the fearless Forest Brotherhood with thousands of Soviet officials and sympathisers being killed by the guerrillas. In addition, he claimed that the thirty thousand guerrillas distrusted the SCLL because it had collaborated with the Germans. Deksnys also reported what was later to become highly significant, namely that his companion during his stay in Lithuania had been arrested. None of the MI6 officers queried the circumstances.[38]

Taking on board Deksnys' negative report on the SCLL, and in order to help co-ordinate policy and strengthen MI6 contacts with the resistance under the direction of Zymantas, an Information and Liaison Centre was formed in the British Zone in Germany. An attempt was made to reorganise the resistance on the classic Home Army/government-in-exile pattern. Such co-ordination had not been possible previously because the Council for the Liberation of Lithuania had been broken up by arrests at the end of the war, forcing leading political leaders and resistance centres to flee to the West. In Lithunania, Deksnys had met with Dr Juozas-Albinas Markulis, who persuaded him of the necessity of collaborating with a new organisation, the United Democratic Resistance Organisation (UDRM), which was to form the basis of MI6's co-ordinating body.[39]

Presented as 'an initiative of the émigrés', the UDRM was created in June 1946 in an attempt to unite the various resistance groups that had functioned during the German occupation. A group of refugee political personalities in the West was invited to serve as a committee representing the guerrilla movement in Lithuania, whose leading UDRM members included Deksnys, Markulis and Juozas Luksa. The UDRM sought to achieve 'more adequate and effective results in the struggle for the restoration of Lithuania's independence and for the realisation of the great ideal of democracy'. More importantly, although the UDRM had its own armed wing of 'Freedom Fighters', it was working to an MI6 agenda that sought to eschew openly violent tactics and seek other means of achieving the nationalist aim. It would appear that MI6 was more interested in maintaining its intelligence-gathering capability than backing any ideas of counter-revolution through guerrilla warfare. These attempts to organise the intended committee caused dissension among the émigrés, who were unaware of the British input. Unsurprisingly, the liaison established with the guerrillas proved to be unsatisfactory as the armed freedom fighters refused to subordinate themselves to a purely political body. Instead, a body subservient to the UDRM, the Supreme Staff of Armed Partisans, was formed to direct the political programme.[40]

Unity under national command was finally achieved at the end of 1946, but it blossomed only for a brief period. During the summer, the UDRM was able to cite six major battles fought against the Soviets, involving up to one hundred of the Forest Brotherhood, who had sustained themselves without any significant support or supplies from the West. Official Soviet newspapers wrote of 'the strength of anti-government activity in Lithuania' where 'robber bands' were 'a prevalent feature of contemporary life ... using sabotage, diversions and murder'. The Soviet security troops hit back by employing 'false flag' groups whose well-publicised atrocities were designed to drive a wedge between the population and the guerrillas. In addition, the successful use of the amnesty for guerrillas was acknowledged by the UDRM as a worrying development.[41]

Unbeknown to the underground and MI6, a decision had been taken by the head of the Ministry of Internal Afffairs (MVD – it replaced the NKVD in March 1946), General Kruglov, who held an honorary British knighthood for his security services at the Allied conference at Potsdam, to sanction the mounting of a classic double-cross operation based on the techniques of the 'Trust', which had entrapped British Intelligence in the twenties. This was placed under the control of Major Janis Lukasevics of the Latvian NKGB/MGB's Second Chief Directorate, which was responsible for counter-intelligence. In receipt of top-secret reports from their agents in London concerning plans for further operations into the Baltic republics, Lukasevics began using captured infiltrators to play back radio messages to MI6. In March, August Bergmanis, a former radio operator for the wartime Kurelis resistance group, was released as a PoW by the Soviets and 'turned'. Now working for Lukasevics, Bergmanis tapped out the call sign of one of the captured MI6 agents to a receiver in Stockholm, followed by messages that all was well.[42]

In early August, a well-equipped fishing boat arranged by a Swedish pastor working for MI6 landed two more MI6-backed agents into Latvia. Lukasevics decided 'not to touch them' but 'to continue finding out what their specific tasks were'. His security police 'found out that their job was not just spying but also to prepare the way for other spies, to set up a link and new points of support and to establish contact with resistance groups'. During November one of the agents made contact with Bergmanis, who was continuing to send messages to Sweden. MI6 needed to know whether or not Bergmanis, who had contacted them only after a long silence, was under Soviet control. MGB patience paid off when the agent reported back that Bergmanis was 'clean'. As a result of this brilliant deception operation, by 1947 many of the leading figures in the Latvian underground had been identified and captured. In one notable coup, twelve guerrilla leaders had been persuaded to attend a meeting in Riga to discuss their plans and activities with a 'British officer'. Falling for the ploy, they provided detailed biographies of their comrades, enabling the local security police to round up the leading guerrillas.[43]

MI6 remained undeterred. After setting up a network of agents, Feliks Rumnieks returned to Latvia on MI6's behalf. His aim was to discover the fate of the teams previously sent and to report back. He was unable to fulfil the second part of the task, however, as he was arrested at the end of the year. Interrogated by the MGB, he admitted that he had carried out various tasks for British military intelligence and was working for MI6. Subsequently tried for treason, Rumnieks was imprisoned for many years. Inexplicably, Zarine and his supporters refused to acknowledge these setbacks and continued to maintain a steady stream of recruits for the secret operations into Latvia.[44]

In London, the Society of Latvians in Great Britain acted as a domestic pressure group advocating the immigration of Latvian DPs to Britain as part of the Labour government's European Voluntary Workers (EVW) scheme to import much-needed labour for agriculture, mining and industry. Under a Cabinet directive, Ministry of Labour recruiters sent to Germany did not allow enquiries into 'the political background of particular national groups' to obstruct them in this task. Screening was minimised by 'relaxation of existing checks' in order to avoid 'a bottleneck'. A number of Balts who did arrive in Britain under the EVW scheme were found to have the characteristic Waffen-SS tattoos under their armpits. When this became public, Zarine took the matter up with a clearly embarrassed Foreign Office which, nevertheless, dismissed the tattoos as 'perfectly innocuous'. According to Tom Bower, at least one Lithuanian revealed that he had killed 'terrorists' while serving under the Germans, but the interrogator concluded that he 'did not pose a threat to security' and so was allowed to stay. Officials drew an unwarranted distinction between members of the Waffen-SS, 'a military formation', and the 'political German SS'. When the Soviets responded with accusations of war crimes against key individuals, Zarine defended them as 'great national patriots, men of quite modest means; anti-Bolshevik, of course, but certainly not to be described as fascists'.[45]

Zarine lobbied hard both outside and inside Parliament to prevent their deportation, working closely with Conservative MP Alfred Bossom, President of the Anglo-Baltic Friendship Society, and the Duchess of Atholl, chair of the British League for European Freedom. With Catholic support, the duchess roused public opinion against their forced repatriation, portraying them as honourable anti-communists who were being persecuted by the Soviets. A number had been brought into the country by the British League's sister organisation, the Scottish League for European Freedom, which worked closely with MI6 (see Chapter 21).

In February 1947, Zilinskas, Deksnys and Zymantas attended an MI6 conference at Osnabruck, near Hamburg, where discussions focused on the covert funding and recognition of the Lithuanian UDRM. It had the support of General Plechavicius, who continued to enjoy the protection of MI6, which was still receiving reports that the resistance network inside Lithuania was intact and engaged in fighting the Soviets. MI6 and the UDRM leadership were not, however, convinced that it was leading to success. A more 'realistic line' was being pushed by Deksnys and, in London, by the chief of Lithuanian diplomats abroad, Stasys Lozoraitis. A former envoy in Rome, from where he retained close ties to the Vatican, the former foreign minister had been given plenipotentiary powers to look after Lithuanian interests in the West.[46]

At the end of May, 'two guests from abroad' – Daunoras and Loyys – made contact in Lithuania with the guerrilla leader Juozas Luksa, providing the 'first direct information we had received from the West'. Lozoraitis's communiqué laid bare the cold reality of the situation:

It is not certain that the tension arising out of the territorial and political expansion of the Soviet Union must necessarily and immediately lead to war. As long as the internal situation of the Soviet Union remains unimproved, they have no interest to attack America and England. As to the latter, at this moment they are not prepared for war materially or morally, especially for war on behalf of the freedom of states which found themselves in the Soviet sphere. From this it follows that in Lithuania it is necessary to save resources, avoiding sacrifice in the armed struggle, avoiding additional reasons for the Bolsheviks for deportation and so on ... As far as the impact of the armed struggle on the evolution of present-day international politics, pertaining to the Lithuanian question, is concerned, I feel I can confirm that the death of our best men will not accelerate development of events and its political effect, influence on propaganda for Lithuanian freedom, will be painfully disproportionate to the sacrifices and national losses.[47]

The guerrilla leaders chose to ignore these pessimistic western assessments and, indeed, refused to believe them. 'They condemned us to death at Yalta, Potsdam ... They continue to repeat the mistakes, not daring to raise a voice of protest against the annihilation of our nation, not even wishing to know that we are not yet disappointed with them, that we are continuing the struggle with their "ally" not knowing defeat.' The guerrillas believed that the West simply did not understand the communists. 'We learned that we had been abandoned to die alone ... We were loath to admit this painful reality.' A strengthening of Soviet counter-insurgency tactics resulted in a further thinning of ranks and 'a never-before experienced attitude of despair'.[48]

Dogged Lithuanian efforts to establish and maintain a unified command had few parallels in the other two countries, where there was 'no evidence of mimeographed guerrilla publications, of active contact attempts with the West, of organised officer training, of city intelligence activity, or of concerted campaigns against elections'. Soviet reports mention the destruction of an Estonian National Committee and a nationwide Latvian Guerrilla Communications Staff which appears to have operated in Riga until 1947. The Forest Brotherhood continued to fight hard in most areas of the Estonian and Latvian countryside, but its backbone had been broken, though several hundred Soviets continued to be killed annually. The UDRM continued to organise formal training courses during the summer of 1947 for specially selected officers, while, following discussions with the visitors from the West, further attempts were made to centralise the passive and active movements. Adolfas Ramanaukas was assigned the task of organising and dealing with foreign contacts, and the selection of people to go abroad. The Lithuanians had a regular courier service across Poland and East Germany, and during 1947 couriers travelled west, but only to return with further depressing news on the international situation.[49]

A national conference of guerrilla leaders opposed the strategy proposed by the UDRM for a government-in-exile. According to MI6's intermediary, Stasys Zymantas, the UDRM failed to reach an accommodation as the armed guerrillas were unwilling to assume the role of a Home Army 'without a direct influence on the future self-government of the country'. They rejected the UDRM policy, which favoured shifting the emphasis from armed to passive resistance, and smeared such advocates as 'Bolshevik agents'. The UDRM was beset by security fears that the movement had been infiltrated by Soviet agents and, in December 1947, the Presidium dispatched Luksa and Kazimieras Piplys to the West with a special mission. They eventually reached London, where Luksa gave MI6 debriefers a graphic description of the treachery of Dr Juozas Markulis, whom he insisted was a Soviet agent. Luksa also pointed the finger of suspicion at Deksnys, which further split the Lithuanians. McKibben was forced during the summer of 1948 to confront Deksnys in Stockholm. Unaware, however, that Markulis was a communist, and a serving MGB officer whose function was to penetrate the guerrilla movement 'as part of a plan to divide the resistance into factions and cause as much hostility between the two groups as possible', McKibben could discover no evidence for the charge of treachery.[50]

In practice, the UDRM was both an MI6 and an MGB front group. The interesting situation developed in which the agenda set by the NKGB coincided with that of MI6, which recognised that a liberation policy was unlikely to succeed. It wanted to preserve its intelligence-gathering capability, which would be threatened by the inevitable Soviet backlash against any fully overt guerrilla campaign. The Soviet aim was not only to cause dissension but, more subtly, to channel the Lithuanian resistance into a form that could be more easily controlled. Their agents therefore pushed the idea of 'passive resistance'. According to Thomas Remeikis, by the end of 1948 the UDRM was barely functioning.[51]

Luksa moved on to the United States, where he made 'a very thorough report' for the CIA on the guerrilla action behind the Iron Curtain. He received, however, 'little more than expressions of interest' from the Americans, but the SCLL armed guerrillas continued to cling 'to their only hope of liberation from the West to the very last'. To the men in the forest, the Allied policy of containment 'sounded like a promise of liberation. Western propaganda and Stalinist terror assured such misperception of reality.' In expectation of a global conflict, the SCLL leaders set up an exclusively guerrilla-based resistance organisation.[52]

Back in London, the head of the Latvian legation, Charles Zarine, proved to be a useful asset for MI6, talent-spotting suitable agents among the ex-collaborators. Zarine helped Sandy McKibben recruit Rudolph Silarajs, a former officer in the Latvian Air Force, who was languishing in the Sebors DP camp in Belgium. Through Silarajs, MI6 officers were introduced to several other Latvian collaborators, including Vitold Berkis, who had worked for the Nazi security police in Riga with responsibilities for political intelligence, and Andrei Gladins, a former member of the murderous Arajs Kommando. Both were transferred from Belgium to Britain for training.[53]

The recruiting pool was enlarged during 1948 when a platoon of the Lithuanian Police Battalions commanded by Anatas Gecas was brought to Britain 'almost intact'. In 1944 Gecas had fled with his battalion south to Italy, where he claimed he joined a Polish unit and fought against the Germans, gaining a Polish Iron Cross. According to one report, Gecas became 'a major asset' of MI6 and, after settling in Scotland as a mining engineer, provided intelligence that was useful in the creation of Baltic networks. During a libel trial in 1992, High Court judge Lord Milligan said that he was 'entirely satisfied' that Gecas had taken part in the execution of thousands of innocent civilians. Soviet attempts to extradite him for war crimes were obstructed by Whitehall, apparently for fear of exposing his intelligence ties.[54]

At the beginning of 1949, MI6 took over full control of the Baltic infiltration of agents from the Swedes and transferred the operation, code-named JUNGLE, to Hamburg in the British Zone in Germany. MI6 also instigated an expansion of the Special Liaison Centre, in Ryder Street, where the Baltic section was divided into three, each with a full-time émigré officer responsible for recruiting agents. Selected by McKibben and approved by Carr, along with a veteran army officer, Colonel Sutkos, who worked among the recently imported 'Westward Ho!' workers (those recruited in the DP camps to work in British mines and textile factories), Stasys Zymantas was responsible for the Lithuanian agents; Rudolph Silarajs looked after the Latvians; while Alphons Rebane, commander of the 20th SS Estonian Division, oversaw the Estonians.[55]

Rebane had been one of the former SS officers invited to Britain in 1947 as guest workers. A drinker and a gambler, he was plucked from a textile mill in Bradford, West Yorkshire, by McKibben, who agreed to take on his former SS Division General Inspector, Vaino Partel, as his adjutant. Partel knew the whereabouts of other SS members for recruitment, and the two then drew up lists of suitable candidates. There were plenty of recruits willing to risk their lives in what they believed to be an honourable attempt to liberate their homeland. 'Westward Ho!' was bringing thousands of Baltic Waffen-SS men into the country, and by 1949 no fewer than 9,706 Latvians had arrived, a large percentage of them ex-combatants, thus providing a pool of fit young men with military training and experience. MI6 recruiters tracked down men in the DP camps and EVW hostels and offered them employment on special missions connected with the 'liberation' of their homelands. More than forty Estonian volunteers, including Waffen-SS men such as Leo Audova and Mark Padek, were recruited, assembled and prepared for special operations.[56]

Working in the background were representatives of Dauvagis Vanagi – the association of Latvian ex-servicemen. In March 1949, Zarine informed the Foreign Office that Colonel Vilis Janums was in London on business for Dauvagis Vanagi. A former regimental commander of the Latvian Legion who was a war crimes suspect, Janums was also involved with former members in setting up the Latvian Restoration Committee. Zarine told officials that

> Mr Janums is a man of understanding and realises the factors that go to make up the present situation. He does not, therefore, wish to be an embarrassment. He feels, however, in view of the rather intimate knowledge he has of the ways and psychology of the Russian army – both from his having served with the Tsarist Army and fought against the Red Army – it might be of interest and value for him to have a talk with someone from military circles here if this could be arranged.[57]

Janums was passed on to the War Office's MI3, where Lt-Col. Stoney listened to his plea that his fellow-Latvians in Britain and the British Zone in Germany be given military training 'before they get too rusty'. The files on Janums are restricted, but it is known that he specifically referred to the thousand Latvians in the Mixed Service units – a paramilitary service set up by the British Army of the Rhine to guard military installations. The Latvian Legion's Arthur Sigailis was the chief liaison officer of these Baltic units, through which he kept in touch with former legionnaires. Stoney said that it was official policy not to train them in anything other than guard duties. There were, however, strong parallels with the American Labour Service Units which had acted as cover for recruitment and military training. The fact that several hundred ex-combatant Balts were being employed in auxiliary army units and receiving British Army pay suggested to the Soviets that these units were designed for a future war.[58]

In order to tighten security, the training of the émigrés was transferred from Stockholm to London. The agents lived at the 'School', a Victorian house in Chelsea which was rented from a retired British officer stationed abroad. Looked after by the Flowers family, agents were taught Morse code by George Collier, while John Crofton explained the basics of tradecraft and the type of intelligence the Service was seeking. Former SOE officers illustrated surveillance methods, organising dead-letter drops and how to survive behind enemy lines. Training in the use of small arms took place at an indoor range, while outdoor training was undertaken at the former SOE wartime training school at Fort Monkton, Gosport. The more rugged guerrilla-type training, with special forces, took place on Dartmoor and in the Scottish Highlands.

Those who successfully completed the course were issued with forged passports, identification cards and work permits. Finally, in a gesture that high-
lighted the grim reality of their situation, the agents were issued with
'L-Tablets' – cyanide suicide pills.[59]

The first six Estonians who completed the MI6 training course were
presented to the ambassador, August Torma, at Estonia House in London.
The route back to their homeland would, however, be long and difficult. The
increased security measures and tightening of control by the Soviet political
police in the Baltic ensured that it was increasingly difficult to infiltrate agents
into Estonia. It was, therefore, decided that Latvia offered the best and safest
route.

From an early date, MI6 developed the idea of infiltrating agents into the
Baltic states by sea, the method being preferable to air-drops which were
considered too 'noisy' and more likely to attract the attention of the Soviets.
Landings from boats could be made silently and, hopefully, secretly. It took
nearly eight months of protracted negotiations between MI6, the Navy and
the Foreign Office before the operations could be launched. Most of the
problems centred around finance as 'the British budget was tight, and for
covert operations especially it was spread thin'. It seems that it took the
persuasive powers of Menzies to win over the Director of Naval Intelligence,
Rear-Admiral Sir Anthony Buzzard, and his deputy, Captain D. C. Ingram, to
MI6's scheme. Chosen to oversee the landings was a close friend of Menzies,
Commander Anthony Courtney, head of the Russian Section 16 of the Naval
Intelligence Division (NID), which had taken over MI6's wartime private
navy. Section 16 liaised with MI6's R3, whose chief until the mid-fifties was
Frank Slocum. At the end of 1948, Courtney was appointed Chief of Intelli-
gence to the flag officer at Hamburg. He had 'certain ideas involving the use
of fast surface craft in co-operation with MI6, and felt sure that the Royal
Navy had a great deal to offer in this respect'.[60]

In the spring of 1949, the Navy's 'most advanced eyes and ears on the
Baltic', David Wheler, shared responsibility for setting up the sea operations
with the man who took over from Courtney at Kiel, John Harvey-Jones (later
chair of ICI). Harvey-Jones joined the NID in the summer of 1946 as a Russian
interpreter, working under Courtney in Germany. He was then appointed to
the secret deception organisation, the London Controlling Station (LCS),
before being posted back to Hamburg, where he debriefed refugees from
East Germany and Poland, and studied the rapidly expanding Soviet
merchant fleet in the Baltic.[61]

Courtney's work involved close liaison with the Lurssen brothers of Vege-
sack on the Wesser River, 'where I was struck by the potential capabilities
of stripped-down ex-Kriegsmarine E-boat hulls, powered by the incompar-
able twin Mercedes-Benz 518 diesel engines'. Harvey-Jones recalled that 'we
still possessed two of these superb craft' which were taken to Portsmouth

for refurbishment. 'We decided to strip one of them down and increase her power. With the combination of her low weight and enhanced power she would be able to show her heels to any other surface ship then afloat.' In addition, silent underwater exhausts were installed, enabling the craft to approach the enemy's shore with the minimum of noise. To serve as captain, the British had the pick of former E-boat aces, but were on the lookout for one with experience of operating in the Baltic. In May 1949, Courtney and Harvey-Jones met in Minden with an unemployed former E-boat captain, Hans Helmut Klose. Never a Nazi, Klose was a dedicated naval officer who shared their common dislike of Bolsheviks and, more importantly, had, from 1944 until the end of the war, dropped German agents behind the Russian lines for sabotage missions. Since Germany was still demilitarised, 'it was essential that she operate under a British officer', and under Harvey-Jones's responsibility a German crew, 'with a fierce detestation of the Russians', was recruited from among Klose's wartime comrades.[62]

The boat operated under cover of the Fishery Protection Service which had been formed by the British military government. It was maintained by the Royal Navy in Hamburg to protect the West German fishing fleet from interference by Soviet naval vessels, and to recover and disarm the numerous mines strewn throughout the Baltic Sea during the course of the war. On training sessions, the crew 'came to know every inch of the Baltic coast and every defence which the Russians maintained, in a particularly intimate way'. The Baltic, Harvey-Jones recalled, 'was our oyster and we roamed it at will'. During operations, Klose was to sail from Kiel under the white ensign for the five hundred-mile journey to shelter at Bornholm on the Danish coast, before hoisting the Swedish flag at Gotland, where he awaited the go-ahead from Hamburg.[63]

There were further delays while discussions were completed in London and Washington with officials of the US Office of Policy Co-ordination (OPC), which eventually agreed to fund the Baltic boat service as long as MI6 provided access to the service and shared the gathered intelligence. After protracted negotiations between the head of MI6 in Germany, John Bruce-Lockhart, and General Gehlen, it was also agreed to combine with the Americans on selected operations, and an arrangement was made whereby the Gehlen Org. would train a number of agents who would be inserted into the Baltic states via the British sea route. Gehlen also sent in teams by parachute – the American's favoured method.

The first Operation Jungle group sent into the Baltic under cover of the Fishery Protection Service was launched at the beginning of May. On board was the Latvian double agent Vidvuds Sveics, who had been planted among the British-backed émigrés by the MGB's Major Lukasevics. After a perfect landing at the Palanga beach, in Lithuania, the group made for the forest, but Sveics had managed to separate himself and raise the local militia. In the shooting that followed, two members were killed. The mission had been betrayed, but Deksnys and Kazimieras Piplys, the representative abroad of the UDRM, escaped and made their way inland. In June, Piplys was able to get a letter back to Zymantas, but was killed a few months later in a bunker in southern Lithuania. A number of officials at Broadway headquarters began to have suspicions about some of their agents, but they were not thought serious enough to jeopardise further planned operations.[64]

In reality, by 1949 the first phase of the struggle had ended in Lithuania. Whereas the period from 1944 to 1948 had been a time of relative strength for the underground groups, there followed immediate decline, with the guerrillas unable to inflict any significant losses on the Soviet forces. The majority of farms were now collectivised, which initially gave a boost to the underground but wrecked the supply system for the guerrillas. At the same time, the Lithuanian Communist Party had strengthened its grip on the country by tripling party membership. Good-quality recruits for the Forest Brotherhood, who were willing to endure the appalling conditions that now existed, were dwindling. Around twenty thousand guerrillas had been killed, and while an almost equal number of communists had died too, the security troops continued to bear down on the insurgents. One small pocket of resisters did attempt to reorganise in a more conspiratorial style. Jonas Zemaitis, who had trained in French military schools and was a former member of the Lithuanian Freedom Army, was instrumental in putting together in February 1949 an exclusively guerrilla-based central resistance organisation, the Movement of Lithuania's Struggle for Freedom (MLSF), as part of a breakaway from the UDRM. Clearly, open warfare was no longer possible, and the guerrillas could no longer paralyse the functioning of local Soviet administration. This ability had been largely lost by the end of 1946 in Latvia, where guerrilla activity was effectively crushed by 1949. The Soviet policy of deportation and scorched earth was working, and the Forest Brotherhood was forced into retreat. Estonian guerrillas continued to fight for a few more years but at an insignificant level. In all three countries, the freedom fighters were often reduced to actions that 'started to fit the "bandit" label the occupation forces tried to pin on them'.[65]

During 1949, efforts were made to weld the various resistance groups into one resistance centre. The CIA took over control of the SCLL with the aid of their new asset, Gen. Plechavicius, who had transferred his loyalty from MI6. His new sponsors immediately eased his emigration to the United States. In another attempt to resolve the convoluted differences that existed between the nationalist groupings, a meeting took place in July 1949 in Baden-Baden in West Germany, with delegates from the SCLL. In attendance were Luksa and Deksnys, the latter as a member of the UDRM Council and official delegate abroad of the nationalist underground. The delegates agreed that the SCLL would be responsible for the liberation struggle abroad and would eventually act as a government-in-exile. The liberation inside Lithuania was to be conducted by its own resistance centre with close co-operation between the two. As one observer wrote, 'it proved to be a controversial decision' which was rejected by the UDRM. A decision backed by its British sponsors and Soviet agents inside the organisation, who each feared losing control over the resistance movement.[66]

At the end of October 1949, accompanied by John Crofton, the second Jungle team was flown to Hamburg, where they were met by Anthony Cavendish, a junior MI6 officer. Cavendish was responsible for 'babysitting' the team until the naval liaison officer, Commander Courtney, received word from Klose that sailing conditions were favourable. Included in the team were a former SS member, Vitolds Berkis, and Andrei Galdins, ex-Arajs Kommando. No one probed into their backgrounds. Cavendish's philosophy was that 'if somebody was needed to do a job and if he had committed war crimes, I would use him to do the job, ones I felt essential'. The agents were landed safely and taken to the home of Father Valdis Amols. Unfortunately for the British and Latvians, the secret police had instigated a major MGB deception operation, 'Lursen-S', of which Amols was part. This also involved the creation of a phantom guerrilla group led by 'Garis', which the two Latvians eventually joined in May of the following year. The Soviets then engaged in a radio deception game, transmitting information back to Britain which MI6 analysts found to be 'bland and imprecise'. Indeed it was, as the MVD controllers were barred from using real low-grade intelligence ('chickenfeed') and, instead, had to make do with material collated from newspaper articles. Even so, the little intelligence coming out of the Baltic states from individuals and groups not known to be under the control of the Soviets was regarded by MI6 analysts as 'poor'.[67]

Recognising that it would need to develop its contacts with the western agencies, the MLSF called upon the underground forces to improve the quality of their intelligence-gathering. Information was processed by Zemaitis and eventually passed on to Deksnys as the official delegate abroad. This was an unfortunate choice. The discovery by Soviet troops of a second UDRM training camp gave rise to further accusations of betrayal. Towards the end of 1949 Luksa provided another account for the British and Americans of the destabilising role of an alleged Soviet agent on the UDRM committee, Dr Juozas Markulis.[68]

By 1950 the revolt in the woods was over. The last battle in Latvia was recorded in February, and the guerrillas in Estonia had been worn down to isolated bands. While there were still around five thousand guerrillas in Lithuania, final mopping-up operations by the militia effectively killed their resistance, and the countryside was now relatively safe. The radios had gone quiet and the only groups left were those run by the MGB – but MI6 did not read the signs. The most serious problem for MI6, about which it remained in the dark, was that Deksnys – who had returned to Lithuania – had been arrested by the Soviet secret police and had been 'forced to co-operate as a price for survival'.[69]

During the early summer of 1950, the head of MI6's Northern Division, Harry Carr, made his first trip to the United States, where he met with the head of the Soviet section of the CIA's Office of Special Operations (OSO), Harry Rositzke. It was not productive, but George Belic, chief of Soviet affairs in Munich, was allowed to meet McKibben in London to 'exchange views at desk level'. This was achieved, but McKibben continued to look down on the American new boys. Fortunately, Belic had good reason to ignore MI6's misplaced air of superiority. Juozas Luksa of the SCLL/MLSF had switched allegiance from French Intelligence to the Americans and had told the CIA of his belief that Deksnys had been 'turned'. In June, Belic informed McKibben that the CIA believed that Deksnys was now working for the MGB. Even though he knew that Deksnys had recently failed a security check, McKibben felt that he had to allay American fears and brushed aside the news as the normal result of factional exile politics between the British-sponsored UDRM and the now American-backed SCLL.[70]

In October, the Americans conducted their first parachute drop into the Baltic area, using agents trained at Gehlen's special intelligence school in West Germany. An unmarked C-47 was flown by two Czech former RAF pilots from a US Air Force base in Wiesbaden to Lithuania. Benediktas Trumpys, Klemensas Sirvys and leader Luksa – who had written a highly romanticised account of the underground's exploits during his stay with American Intelligence – were successfully parachuted into the Baltic countryside.[71]

During November, 'in a desperate bid to stop the rot', Carr was forced to undertake a second trip to Washington, where he was once again confronted by accusations that the UDRM had been penetrated. Carr was unmoved, and could only claim that 'our group is watertight'. The MI6 officer who took the notes at the fraught meeting was the liaison officer with the CIA, Kim Philby – he recalled the event in his autobiography. 'Both MI6 and the CIA had their Baltic puppets, whose rival ambitions were usually quite irreconcilable. It was with some relish that I watched the struggling factions repeatedly fight themselves to a standstill.' According to Philby, 'the visit ended disastrously, with both Carr and his opposite numbers in the CIA accusing each other, quite justifiably, of wholesale lying at the conference table'. Carr closed the meeting by dismissing the security fears of his hosts with the boast that 'the proof of our certainty is that we are stepping up our activities'.[72]

By April 1951, MI6 was ready to send another team of four agents into Latvia. One member of the team, Lodis Upans, yet another ex-Ajas Kommando enlisted by MI6, had been sent to investigate the 'Maxis' network

– a situation for which the MGB had meticulously prepared. Also in the team was a newly trained radio officer, who was, in fact, an MGB penetration agent planted at the heart of the British operation by Lukasevics. Janis Erglis had originally been recruited in a German DP camp by John Ransome, an MI6 officer attached to the 'Technical Section' of the British Control Commission. While the MGB allowed some of the British agents to reach their destination, where they were met by fictitious guerrilla groups that lived tightly controlled lives in the forests, others were captured and either turned or killed.[73]

A second American operation in April to enter Lithuania was deemed a failure. Team members were soon captured and, under threat of torture, agreed to collaborate. One radio operator sent messages back to Munich which proved to the satisfaction of the listening CIA officers that the sender was under Soviet control. Julijonas Butenas, a journalist who had been active in the anti-Nazi underground, managed to evade the MGB trap, but his mission was short-lived. In the following month, surrounded and under siege from Soviet security troops, Butenas committed suicide rather than be taken alive. It was a pattern that was to be repeated.[74]

That spring, six CIA officers led by Rositzke – who had arranged to be posted to Munich for a tour of duty – arrived in London for a conference with their MI6 counterparts to survey all Anglo-American operations in the Soviet Union and the satellite countries. The recent differences in Washington were dismissed by Carr as 'a family row', while the Americans looked forward to 'an open and frank exchange'. It was not to happen. The CIA was convinced more than ever that what remained of the guerrilla force was under Soviet control. The British failed to respond and the conference ended on another note of frustration. 'The British just humoured us. We went round in circles, rehashing the past.' The only concession was that Anthony Vaivada, an American of Lithuanian parentage on Rositzke's staff, was given a full briefing by McKibben on MI6's Lithuanian operations.[75]

In May, Philby had been recalled from Washington following the disappearance of Donald Maclean and Guy Burgess. Suspecting him of being a spy and responsible for tipping off the Foreign Office traitors, the CIA demanded his expulsion. To Rositzke and his colleagues the cause of their Soviet disasters became self-evident: 'We were betrayed by the Brits.' This was only partly true. While Philby had certainly betrayed the overall outline of the plans and, in some cases, considerable detail, Carr and McKibben had ensured that he had never been privy to the full scale of the operations, since they wanted to keep the Americans in the dark about what they were really up to. It was also an unfortunate assessment since, in reality, the deception being run in the Baltic by the NKGB – of which Philby probably had no knowledge – was the true cause of the disaster. In the event, CIA security concerns had little impact in the MI6's Northern Division, where Carr and

McKibben continued to believe in Philby's innocence. By then there was too much self-interest from the émigrés and the officers involved for doubts to be raised or for the operations to be curtailed. Besides, Carr's obsessive secrecy prevented any objective appraisal. Tom Bower believes that Carr's qualities were too limited to enable him to detect a clear deception. As he suggests, Lukasevics's deception could only flourish because 'it developed best in the very conditions which Carr believed prevented the danger'.[76]

The struggle inside Lithuania continued to be encouraged by the principal political organisation abroad – the Supreme Committee for the Liberation of Lithuania (SCLL). It was co-operating with the CIA in the mission of Luksa, who had been appointed by the commander of the Movement of Lithuania's Struggle for Freedom (MLSF) as its intelligence chief and main liaison officer with the West. In July 1951, the command of the southern region released a leaflet, 'Freedom Is Coming from the West', which stated that 'the United States has sufficently understood its mission to be the vanguard of the West ... The rush of political events of today is approaching the moment when the independence of Lithuania will manifest itself again.' It claimed that the US had promised material aid and called upon Lithuanians to 'join this holy struggle against Bolshevism with weapon in hand'. It was true that the CIA's final instruction to Luksa's group – at a meeting attended by Col. Antanas Sova, the principal military functionary abroad organising the missions – did identify with the 'liberation of all occupied countries' but, for all the rhetoric, MI6 and the CIA were primarily concerned with gathering intelligence.[77]

July's bulletin also attacked the passive tactics of the British-backed UDRM Committee and its leader, Jonas Deksnys, who was described as a 'paid active intelligence agent of foreign states'. Luksa's return resulted in a brief period of intensified guerrilla activity, boasted by promises of help from the West. At the same time, the MVD's Gen. Kruglov returned to Lithuania to take charge of the final liquidation of the resistance.[78]

At the end of September 1951, a team of three was landed in Latvia by Klose. Its leader, Bolislov Pitans, was an ex-Latvian Waffen-SS soldier who had arrived in Britain in 1947 as part of the 'Westward Ho!' scheme. Working as a baker, he was approached by MI6 in 1950 for special training for a mission with two former Estonian SS members. They were to help contact the Estonian underground with the aid of the Maxis group of guerrillas. Again, it was a disastrous operation. The leader of the Maxis group, Arvits Gailitis, who was picked up by Klose, turned out to be another Soviet penetration agent. In London, Gailitis was debriefed by MI6's Rudolph Sila-rajs, who, if he had any doubts, was unable to break his cover. Gailitis eventually fell ill from the strain of maintaining the façade and was returned to Latvia suffering from a nervous breakdown.[79]

Even though the chances of survival for the guerrillas were now slim, the western intelligence agencies continued to send agents into the Baltic states.

They demanded more in-depth information on Soviet capabilities and intentions. It soon became apparent to the guerrillas that the British and American agents were intent on intelligence-gathering and not on supporting guerrilla warfare. Estonian appeals for arms brought only a few crates of pistols and machineguns from the Gehlen Org. Zigurd Krumins, who was landed on the Estonian coast in the spring of 1952 as part of an OPC/Gehlen operation, had been ordered not to fight alongside the guerrillas or to furnish them with arms and assistance, except in the event of a future war between the superpowers. Krumins lasted only eighteen months before he was captured by Soviet security forces and sentenced in Riga to fifteen years in prison. The life of a western agent sent into the Baltic region was for many sheer hell.[80]

Although low on Secret Vote funds for the infiltration operations, MI6 was able to keep the gold flowing through its JUNK operation. Tony Divall, who had served with the Royal Marines during the war, on being demobbed in 1946 was recruited into the 'T-Force' at Bad Salzuflen, in Germany, hunting down suspected war criminals. Officially recruited into MI6, he developed a talent for running agents and was made responsible for Junk, supervising an underground railway that ran agents and consignments of Swiss gold watches into the satellite states in exchange for defectors and illegal roubles. By the early fifties, using professional smugglers, jewellers and money launderers, Divall was running five Junk networks, the money from which was used by the Stockholm station to run agents into the Baltic states.[81]

Lithuanian Zigmas Kudirka was recruited in the autumn of 1950 after arriving in Britain from a DP camp. After twelve months training as a radio officer and in short-range shooting in Chelsea, outdoor survival in Scotland, night-time parachuting in Oxford and water navigation in Portsmouth harbour, Kudirka helped land a number of agents in Latvia. In April 1952, he returned with another nervous wreck, Lodis Upans. Operating on the instructions given by Silarajs before his departure, Upans had handed over all his codes to other agents. Unfortunately, these agents were working for the Soviets. In the autumn Kudirka was sent into Lithuania with agent 'Edmundes'. For the next three years he hid in a farmhouse attic, only venturing out occasionally at night. Three years later, Kudirka moved to a town where he used his MI6 money to live in a safe house. He pleaded to be rescued from his futile existence. MI6 radioed back: 'Chin up. It's not so bad.' He later discovered that Edmundes was an MGB plant. Arrested, Kudirka soon confessed and was sentenced to fifteen years. Appealing on the basis that he had been working, unbeknown to himself, under Soviet control, he was released after two years. Kudirka remained bitter about his treatment by MI6: 'I trusted the British and I suffered every day. They put me into the web and completely abandoned me.'[82]

In October 1951, Juoas Luksa was killed in an encounter with Soviet state security troops engaged in a search-and-destroy operation. 'Mopping up operations followed and in 1952 the resistance was completely destroyed.' The fact was that 'without support from abroad a long guerrilla war against the total-war strategy of the Soviets became militarily impossible, especially under conditions of complete sovietization'. In late 1952, the American-born Aldofus Ramanaukas, who took over the leadership of the MLSF from the unwell Zemaitis, ordered the demobilisation of the guerrillas, thus formally ending the armed struggle. During the same year, the British-backed UDRM also folded. It has been estimated that the guerrilla war in the three states resulted in 75,000 direct civilian casualties, the deaths of 30,000 guerrillas and, perhaps, of up to 80,000 Russian soldiers.[83]

The end of the armed struggle was extremely bad news for the western agencies, for while they had not been willing to countenance providing material support to the guerrillas and had advised against terrorist action, the underground groups had provided cover for intelligence-gathering agents. Without their presence these agents had even less chance of survival.

By the summer of 1952, MI6 had evidence that other Special Operations against the Soviet Union had also failed. Much of this was open knowledge, as the Soviets had ensured that reports of the capture of western agents and the success of their deception campaigns had been spread across their newspapers. The infiltration operations had also been heavily publicised during debates at the United Nations. Further, the Americans were beginning to receive reports from their own agents – to which MI6 had some access – that there were no guerrillas in the forests and that the revolt had ended. The CIA became convinced that their training camps had been infiltrated by Soviet agents. Partly through arrogance and misplaced faith in the effectiveness of its security procedures, MI6 chose to ignore the signs. Senior officers Carr, McKibben and Silarajs still believed that the Baltic operations were in good shape, though Maj. John Liudzius, whose parents had emigrated from Lithuania to Britain many years previously and who spoke the language fluently, dissented – 'I told them but they would not listen' – and for his sins was shunted off to South Korea to replace George Blake.[84]

Assistant Chief James Easton had become aware that Carr was operating without official authority, and a discreet, secret review of these operations took place inside MI6, in which Carr was deeply involved. It did not, however, lead to their curtailment, merely the sharing of the burden with the CIA at a 'Joint Centre' in Frankfurt. Carr ensured that he retained direct control over the Baltic operations, which he continued to believe, against all the evidence, were highly successful – the 'Crown Jewels' of the Service's anti-Soviet operations.[85]

During the autumn of 1952, another Klose mission dropped off agents in the Baltic and picked up a senior member of the Latvian Maxis group who was, almost inevitably, yet another MGB officer. Under intense questioning and scrutiny, followed by three months of training at the Special Liaison

Centre, the double agent Janis Klimkans did not reveal any trace of treachery and was openly accepted within MI6 by both Silarajs and McKibben. The Soviets were now in a perfect position to exploit the situation – which they did to the full, expertly using Klimkans as an *agent provocateur*.

Privy to details of the operations and the names of the future provisional nationalist government of a liberated Latvia, Klimkans regularly reported his intelligence back to his controllers via the Soviet Trade Mission in London, which passed it on to Lukasevics and the MGB in the Baltic. Klimkans returned to Latvia in the autumn of 1953 with weapons, supplies and a million roubles which, in a neat twist, was used to finance the continuing and remarkably successful Soviet deception operation. By this stage the guerrilla campaign was at an end and any hope of organised resistance finished, but MI6 continued with a desperate operation that had been compromised from its very beginning. The result was that many lives were needlessly sacrificed – all for a meagre trickle of intelligence which the analysts later concluded was 'worthless'.[86]

PART FOUR

THE BALKANS AND RUSSIA

Initially, the Special Operations Executive (SOE) had openly backed 'progressive' resistance movements. Senior SOE official Bickham Sweet-Escott recalled that they were 'not necessarily the people who hoped that when the war was won things would go back to being just what they were ... They were risking their lives for war aims of their own which differed in many important respects from ours. Rarely was this elementary truth grasped by the Foreign Office.' Geoffrey Wilson was a lone voice in arguing that SOE should continue to back national liberation movements and 'to spot as early as possible those which are going to be the emergent social groups ... and to try to make them our friends. If they are friends of the Russians too, so much the better.' By 1944, however, SOE was an anti-communist organisation concerned with the spectre of postwar communism and held the view that these groups were 'mainly created by Soviet propaganda'.[1]

It was a view buttressed by intercepts from the Government Code and Cipher School (GC&CS) which had decrypted 'the instructions being sent from the Kremlin to partisan groups under Communist control'. According to MI6's Foreign Office adviser, Robert Cecil, they revealed 'Moscow's hidden hand in planning for the post-war take-over of Eastern Europe'. The decrypts were collated in a Section IX paper intended for the Prime Minister but which Kim Philby managed to obstruct. Churchill, however, already believed that Britain was 'approaching a showdown with the Russians about their Communist intrigues in Yugoslavia and Greece'.[2]

In fact, Soviet advisers instructed local movements that 'they should be flexible, and be ready to serve as junior partners in post-war coalition governments'. It was a policy opposed by Tito. Historian Geoffrey Swain argues that 'Tito had been committed to establishing a popular front "from below", i.e. under communist control'. The co-ordinating body for communist parties, the Comintern, was controlled by the Yugoslavs, who kept in radio contact with resistance groups across Europe. It was Tito who urged communists in the West and Balkans to follow the route of revolution, thus distorting western perceptions of Stalin's foreign policy.[3]

Ralph Miliband and Marcel Liebman suggest that at the core of the Cold War was 'the determination of the Western powers to contain revolutionary and even reformist movements everywhere'. Closer than 'Cold War' to the 'real nature of the confrontation' is the notion of 'international civil war', and the first test came in Greece.[4]

CHAPTER 17

GREECE AND THE CREATION OF THE PARA-STATE

In the mid-eighties an MI6 deputy station officer was expelled from Athens for his involvement with his CIA counterpart in the illegal burglary of the flat of an alleged Middle East terrorist. The burglary followed complaints from the British that the new socialist Greek government was soft on terrorism and was emasculating the Greek Central Intelligence Service (KYP) – regarded on the Left as a hotbed of political intrigue and subversion. Britain – accused by the Greek Prime Minister, Andreas Papandreou, of 'providing staunch unquestioning support' of the United States – had always had difficulty in reconciling itself to the idea of a left-wing Greek government and had preferred, albeit reluctantly, to back the authoritarian Right which controlled the Greek para-state.[1]

Since the Second World War the British had been the most formidable opponent of the Greek Communist Party (KKE) and were determined that postwar Greece would be non-communist 'in order to safeguard Britain's vital lines of communication through the eastern Mediterranean to Suez and the petroleum of the Middle East'. Regarded by the British as part of their sphere of influence and almost as a colony, the country 'was to be democratic in order to serve as a stable ally'. Ideally, this would be achieved by way of a constitutional monarchy, even though the idea was opposed by every substantial resistance organisation, all of which were founded as republican movements whether on the Left or Right. There was still widespread bitterness against King George II, who had supported the pre-war fascist Metaxas regime by suspending the constitution.[2]

The largest liberation organisation resisting the German occupiers, the National Liberation Front/National Popular Liberation Army (EAM/ELAS), had been founded on the initiative of the KKE. The 'popular front' EAM was composed of the KKE and two small socialist parties, the Socialist Party of Greece (SKE) and the Union of Popular Democracy (ELD). A large proportion of the rank and file were not communist sympathisers but joined the nationalist movement for patriotic reasons. It was also true that for the majority of EAM supporters their resistance to the Germans was part of a general liberation movement which sought Greek independence against any imperialist threat, including British interference in Greek affairs. Naturally, this philosophy found little favour with Winston Churchill, who openly voiced his loathing of the 'base and treacherous' EAM/ELAS. He could not, however, ignore ELAS's military wing, which had nearly fifty thousand men and women under arms. On the Right was the National Democratic Hellenic League (EDES), headed by General Nicholas Plastiras, with an army of 4,000 guerrillas under the command of Colonel Napolean Zervas.

While it was the responsibility of the Special Operations Executive (SOE) to direct the resistance, in addition to gathering intelligence, MI6 played a significant role in promoting the royalist cause. Support came from the Cairo office of the Inter-Services Liaison Department (ISLD), where a key officer liaising with the Greek government-in-exile was David Balfour. A brilliant linguist, he had already undertaken a mission into occupied Greece disguised as an Orthodox priest. MI6 'effectively threw in its lot with the King's supporters', who included a group of six high-ranking officers in Athens, led by Col. Spiliotopoulos, and 'another shadowy royalist organisation' in Salonika – the 'defenders of northern Greece' – headed by Col. Aryropoulos.[3]

Such support brought MI6 into conflict with SOE. During the spring of 1943, SOE mission head Brig. Eddie Myers had warned that there would be a civil war if the King returned without a plebiscite, but Churchill and the Foreign Office chose to ignore the advice and actually arranged for Myers's removal. Similarly, MI6 officers such as Balfour and another ISLD operative, Nigel Clive, who was attached to the SOE mission to EDES in Epirus under Lt-Col. Tom Barnes, believed that SOE had made 'a mess of it in Greece'. During the summer, intelligence officer and Oxford art historian Ellis Waterhouse suggested to the Foreign Office that 'Greece is a brand which can yet be plucked from the burning, and our post-war influence in the Eastern Mediterranean may depend very much on our success in doing so. But to do this we must pursue a somewhat reactionary policy.' This meant backing EDES and its commander, Col. Zervas, who pledged 'to support the return of the King, even against the will of the Greek people, if it was necessary for the interests of Britain'. MI6 officer Maj. Frank MacAskie, a former journalist and deception specialist from the Middle East 'A-Force', assured American journalist Cyrus Sulzberger that the King would return, but until that time Archbishop Damaskinos would act as Regent of Greece.[4]

It was a decision that appalled the chief of the SOE mission in the mountains, Christopher 'Monty' Woodhouse, as near civil war broke out between ELAS and EDES. He could, however, do little, as Zervas's guide, Tom Barnes, who lacked 'the political sophistication required to operate in the mystifying world of Greek resistance', was working to a different agenda. What Cairo headquarters did not know was that Zervas had 'made a secret bargain with the Germans during November 1943'. Attached to the Barnes Mission, Nigel Clive admitted that 'for Zervas, the first priority was EAM/ELAS. This conditioned his contacts with the Germans.' When the larger ELAS forces failed to score a quick victory over EDES, Col. Zervas made use of the negotiated ceasefire with the German occupation forces to turn his guerrilla army – backed with newly arrived British arms – against ELAS. After intense and bitter fighting, he succeeded in repulsing the latter's offensive and an uneasy truce between ELAS and EDES was installed by Monty Woodhouse in February 1944. After the war, Brig. Myers admitted that 'if the British Mission had not gone to Greece, ELAS might well have overcome all opposition in the mountains. EDES might have been virtually obliterated.'[5]

The Foreign Office feared that if EDES was annihilated then nothing would stand in the way of the Communist Party (KKE) imposing a Bolshevist dictatorship on Greece. The policy, therefore, was to save the right-wing forces of EDES and build it up as a counterweight to EAM/ELAS. In a few cases, British intelligence officers helped EDES-linked Security Battalions, the armed anti-communist police force operating under the joint orders of the Germans and the quisling Greek government in Athens, with funding. During the spring of 1944, Nigel Clive reported from EDES headquarters to Cairo that Barnes was trying 'to create a Zervas legend'. He added that 'it was plain to everyone in occupied Greece, and especially to both EAM/ELAS and to EDES, that the Germans would soon be on their way home'. What would happen after the occupation was already the subject of intense debate.[6]

In July, senior Foreign Office official Piers Dixon recorded in his diary his success in converting Foreign Secretary Anthony Eden to the notion that 'at all costs Greece must not become Communist'. The intention was to root out and destroy the communists: 'The plunge was taken to support [George] Papandreou [head of the provisional government in Cairo] and extirpate EAM.' A month later, Eden's personal emissary to the guerrillas, David Wallace, reported to the British ambassador to the Greek government-in-exile, Rex Leeper: 'We are committed to not wishing at any cost to see EAM establish themselves. Now that we have taken this open political stand against them, it must follow that ... militarily also we should be wise to attach increased importance to Zervas and the opportunities his position offers for development ...' Wallace admitted that Zervas was 'a British creation ... we are responsible for his continued existence ... He has been a completely loyal ally and will still do exactly what we tell him.' He concluded that 'unless Allied troops arrive in the country to take over the main centres from the Germans, or we reinforce Zervas to a point where he can take offensive action to protect the population in territory at present controlled by ELAS, there will be a most bloody slaughter ending in a Communist dictatorship ... Athens was of course the key to the situation...' Nigel Clive reported to MI6's Political Section that 'genuine collaboration [by EAM with a Greek government] never was and never can be within the furthest bounds of possibility', and that an armed clash between EAM/ELAS and the Right was 'inevitable'.[7]

Churchill wanted to cut off supplies and contact with EAM/ELAS, and thereby destroy the communists. Arriving in London for consultations, Col. Woodhouse argued that such action would be a tactical mistake and would simply strengthen the hold of the Greek Communist Party (KKE): 'Consequently a wiser strategy would be for Papandreou to continue to parley with the communists, no matter how futile the talks might be, in hope of preserving the status quo until British troops could enter Greece the moment the Germans departed. The presence of British armed forces would then provide the Greeks with a measure of stability, permitting the moderates to disentangle themselves from their alliance with the KKE.' Eden and a pessimistic Churchill reluctantly accepted Woodhouse's deception plan after seeing a Joint Planning Staff report which concluded that EAM might attempt a coup within a fortnight of the arrival of British forces. Communist control would be weak and it would probably collapse with the continued presence of the British.[8]

The PM's mood was lightened by his private talks in Moscow with Stalin on 9 October. During the meeting, Churchill scrawled out the percentages formula which foresaw that in Romania the Russians would have 90 per cent authority, the other Allies 10 per cent; in Bulgaria the Russians would have 75 per cent with the other 25 per cent going to the Allies; in Hungary and Yugoslavia the split would be fifty-fifty. In exchange, Britain would retain a 90 per cent share in Greece and the Russians only 10 per cent. Churchill, however, remained deeply suspicious of Soviet intentions and, it would seem, of American motives. American Office of Strategic Services (OSS) officers informed Washington that, to the disgust of Yugoslav militants who favoured a more revolutionary approach, the Soviet mission under Col. Gregori Popov had told EAM 'to agree to any demands of the National Government'. Civil war was not inevitable but British intransigence probably helped to ensure that it did take place.[9]

On 18 October 1944, the Germans finally left Athens, but it was not until five days later that the first British troops entered the city, during which time ELAS guerrillas took up positions. SOE and later MI6 officer Hugh Seton-Watson noted that 'had the Communists wished to seize power in

Athens at this time they could easily have done so. They chose otherwise.' Nigel Clive decided that 'this opportunity . . . was not taken for a mixture of reasons: the presence of Communists in Papandreou's government of National Unity; divided opinion in the KKE leadership; uncertainty about the size of the oncoming British forces; and a reluctance to engage in armed confrontation with the police and Security Battalions'. He did not consider the possibility that EAM was simply complying with Soviet instructions to co-operate with the provisional government. 'The issue was not if, but when, the clash would occur,' Clive went on. 'It was generally accepted that EAM/ELAS would make a bid for power and that [the British commander] Scobie would soon have a battle on his hands in which British troops would be involved.' On 11 November, Churchill advised Eden: 'I fully expect a clash with EAM and we must not shrink from it, provided the ground is well chosen.' Three days later, British Ambassador Rex Leeper received an MI6 report which warned that the KKE had made tentative plans for a coup d'état if its demands were not met. Soon after, Scobie's political adviser, Harold Caccia, appointed Clive as a liaison officer to the Greek government. He told Clive that the plethora of reports that had reached him confirmed the MI6 assessment.[10]

One reason for the failure of EAM/ELAS to act was that the leadership was correctly and deeply concerned about the actions of the Right, which was waiting in the wings for its moment to strike. During November 1944, Greece's pre-war fascist leadership was conspiring to regroup behind British power. One former minister under Metaxas, Constantine Maniadakis, predicted that the British would help Greece 'create a "Right" political life with the King at the head'. Therefore 'we must all return as soon as possible and organise ourselves, because the future belongs to us'. They were helped, as the leader of the socialist SKE, Stratis, acknowledged, by EAM/ELAS aggressiveness, which was proving counterproductive: 'The danger of a Rightist coup becomes greater by the very excesses of EAM.'[11]

The head of the Greek National Unity government, George Papandreou, thought that the prospect of a leftist coup d'état was remote but believed that the essential prerequisite for government success was the demobilisation of ELAS. This was to be accompanied by the parallel demobilisation of the feared Mountain Brigades. Hugh Seton-Watson thought that 'it is only a mild exaggeration to describe' the Rimini Brigade and the Sacred Squadron 'as a private army of the Greek Right'. Rex Leeper, who was now acting as the real power in the land, opposed Papandreou's manoeuvres and pressurised the Prime Minister to abandon the scheme. At the same time the mobilisation of the National Guard, the majority of whose commanders had participated as collaborators in the hated Security Battalions, began. This naturally disturbed the Left. Papandreou tried demobilisation again but this time he used the negotiations to try to drive a wedge between the socialist moderates and the communists in EAM/ELAS. His intrigues, however, went awry, alienating the moderate Left which chose, in the interests of unity, to side with the communists.[12]

The demobilisation issue and the fear of the return of the King polarised sides and began pushing events to an inevitable climax. When, on 3 December, EAM supporters converged on the centre of Athens, outnumbered police 'panicked' and opened fire, killing ten people and wounding over sixty. The shooting in Syntagma Square was not the only violence. In the morning, members of the Right's clandestine 'X' organisation under Col. Grivas had attacked ELAS units, which, in turn, laid siege to police stations during the afternoon. Even though EAM fury had been directed at the police and not at the British, the excuse required for military intervention was provided, and British troops subsequently intervened to protect X members.

From London, on the 5th, Churchill directed General Scobie 'to act as if you were in a conquered city where a local rebellion was in progress . . . We have to hold and dominate Athens'. Most accounts miss out the next sentence, which read: 'It would be a great thing for you to succeed in this without bloodshed if possible, but also with bloodshed if necessary.' Foreign Office official Piers Dixon advised that there would be a 'lasting stain' if British troops clashed with young Greeks who were the tools of 'Communist-trained Commissars'. The Prime Minister, however, was 'in a bloodthirsty mood and did not take kindly to suggestions that we should avoid bloodshed if possible – though I couldn't agree more that force must be used if required'. In his history of the Cold War, Victor Rothwell concludes that

> on the whole, it was probably the British, especially following a visit to Athens by [British minister Harold] Macmillan and Field Marshal Alexander early in December, who took the initiative in provoking the clashes between British troops and ELAS which then broke out and which caused a furore against the British government . . . The use of force was certainly favoured, and indeed insisted upon, by Churchill.[13]

Ronald Scobie proved to be a poor commander, so control of ground operations against the guerrillas was handed to General 'Ginger' Hawkesworth, whose plan was to drive ELAS out of Athens sector by sector. To each British battalion was attached a company of the National Guard, which was increasingly made up of X and former Security Battalions personnel. Their task was to mop up, searching houses for hidden weapons and for any ELAS fighters who had been infiltrated into the city. Aimed at flooding Athens with battle-hardened troops, Hawkesworth's tactics proved to be too much for ELAS, which soon lost the battle of Athens, thus suffering a major defeat.

There had been a miscalculation on the past of the KKE and EAM, which badly underestimated the willingness of the British, to whom considerable goodwill was still displayed, to intervene militarily. During December, EAM found it more important to use their main forces against EDES rather than against the British. EDES had earlier made clear that it regarded EAM/ELAS as the main enemy and the Germans as the lesser evil. As Heinz Richter concludes, the December events proved to be 'on the one hand an armed struggle between ELAS and the British, and on the other a civil war between the Greek Right and the Greek Left'. The KKE also overestimated the support it would receive from the Soviet Union. During the revolt, British journalist Kenneth Mathews reported that the Soviet mission head, Col. Popov, remained the 'very image of non-intervention'.[14]

During Christmas 1944, Churchill and Eden visited Athens to reinforce Britain's foothold in Greece. Archbishop Damaskinos of Athens, who impressed Churchill with his talk of the 'dark sinister hand behind EAM', was appointed Regent until a plebiscite on the King's return could be held. Churchill still saw the King as the guarantor of British interests. Having sheltered MI6 officer Frank MacAskie during the occupation, Damaskinos had been in touch with the Greek Prime Minister of the government-in-exile on the possibility of forming an anti-communist counter-bloc to EAM/ELAS. He quickly developed a working relationship with Ambassador Leeper in Athens, where British officials expressed the hope that the 'percentages' agreement with Stalin on non-intervention had given 'the majority' – i.e. the anti-communists – enough time to arm themselves.[15]

There can be little doubt that Churchill fought for the restoration of the King without reserve. Robert Frazier believes that 'he never understood the amount of opposition to the King within Greece, or the strength of the EAM. He was confident that the sight of the Union Jack and a few armoured cars would enable the Greek government to install itself in Athens without incident.' His last-minute decision to restrain the King from returning with the troops was based on 'the possible effect on public opinion of a restoration "on the point of British bayonets", rather than on the possibility of civil war'.[16]

While the fighting continued and the reinforced British forces gradually gained the advantage – by mid-December seventy-five thousand troops were stationed in Greece – EAM began negotiating a truce. On 5 January 1945, EAM/ELAS commenced a withdrawal from Athens. On the 8th, Churchill told the House of Commons that there had been a 'fairly well-organised plot or plan by which ELAS should march down upon Athens and seize it by armed force'. Two days later, a truce was agreed, and on the 12th, at the seaside resort of Varkiza, a formal agreement was signed between EAM and the Greek government. This called for a plebiscite to be followed by the election of a constituent assembly, the demobilisation of the ELAS forces and an amnesty for political crimes.

Even as this was being signed, Rex Leeper was writing that 'there can be no understanding between the Greek Government and the hard core of irreconcilable communism that is the left of EAM. . . it is a struggle to the death'. Leeper put the blame on the Soviet Union. The reality, historian and specialist on Greece Professor John O. Iatrides has explained, was very different: 'Greece's traditional political parties had essentially disappeared, their popular base destroyed by the enforced paralysis of the Metaxas dictatorship and the years of enemy occupation. What had survived was a coterie of familiar political figures whose legitimacy as a governing class was apparent only to themselves' and whose 'only common link was their fear of the growing mass populist movement activated by EAM, which now appeared to threaten to sweep all of them into the "dustbin of history"'. Academic Peter Weiler has suggested that the 'Cold War struggle' in Greece was not created by the Soviet Union but began at a much earlier date as the result of internal conflicts. 'Because of the effects of the Second World War, communist and nationalist forces were now in a stronger position than they had been earlier. It was this development, which often had little to do with the Soviet Union, that Britain sought to stifle.'[17]

Elizabeth Barker, who had served in the Political Warfare Executive (PWE) during the war, saw at first hand Soviet control of Romania and Bulgaria. Somewhat surprisingly, in her 1948 book *Truce in the Balkans* she wrote that

> in many ways, Russian occupation was far less obtrusive and all-pervading than British occupation . . . In Greece, the British occupation – or the invited presence of British troops – was far more conspicuous and outwardly irritating . . . The British, outwardly, appeared far more the conquering and dominating race than the Russians . . . British intervention and control of Greek affairs was also outwardly far more striking than Soviet intervention in Romanian and Bulgarian affairs.

Though technically an independent country, Greece had become, in reality, a form of British protectorate. From the beginning Leeper had a 'range of powers and responsibilities more akin to those of a colonial governor than a head of a normal diplomatic mission'. Leeper's power was, however, exercised behind the scenes. A number of the more enlightened British officials, such as Macmillan, had wanted to use this power to penetrate Greek state machinery in order to instigate the necessary reforms for a democratic system of government. Their advice, however, was rejected by the deeply reactionary Churchill, who instructed Leeper not to interfere in the details of internal Greek politics. He was ordered to follow traditional British policy towards Greece, which meant that 'Greece should be kept on the right line by British influence on the King or at the moment on the Regent; whilst at the same time close contact was maintained with the pro-British section of the Greek oligarchy: should there be deviations, an intervention at the highest level would be sufficent to bring Greece back into line.' The result was that 'the whole area of public administration was not even touched'. The British did organise police and gendarmerie training missions, but they only arrived when Greek security forces 'had already been almost completely re-built'. The effect of Churchill's restrictions was to put a stop to any liberalising initiatives. Observers came to regard the British embassy as 'the bulwark of conservatism and reaction', which deliberately refused the opportunity to exert pressure on the Greeks for the good.[18]

Rex Leeper was partially reliant on the intelligence delivered to him by the local MI6 head of station, Nigel Clive, who had access to MI6 officers attached to 'British Troops Greece' and the British Military Mission. Their primary task was to deliver regular reports on communist activities, focusing on party organisation, recruitment, sources of funding; activities of leaders and satellite organisations; infiltration of communists into non-communist groups; relations with foreign communists; activities in the labour unions and any anti-British activity. While MI6 officers and British Liaison Officers often worked alongside the security forces, which were thoroughly controlled by the Right, there is little evidence that they penetrated these organisations for intelligence-gathering in the same manner as they did the communist groups. MI6 remained resolutely anti-communist.

From the beginning, the British came under pressure from home and international opinion which could see only an imperialist power siding with the most reactionary elements in Greek politics. Particularly sensitive to such criticism, Leeper, who had helped run the PWE during the war, created in Athens an offshoot of the PWE, the Anglo-Greek Information Service (AIS), whose chief was a Balkans specialist, Col. Kenneth Johnstone. Another leading AIS member, Geoffrey Chandler, had served with SOE and PWE in the Middle East and Greece. In order to counter critical views, the AIS built up a small coterie of well-briefed and sympathetic journalists. The most important was the *Times* correspondent, Frank MacAskie, who was also on a 'special assignment' for MI6 and acted as a confidant to other journalists.[19]

In view of Britain's role in organising the Varkiza conference, which had negotiated an accommodation with EAM, it was, Nigel Clive recalled, 'natural for the British Embassy to think that the forces of moderation had won a victory from which the Plastiras Government would be the first beneficiary'. Plastiras, republican head of the new government, was well aware, however, that public opinion had swung well to the right. His long experience in Greek politics had 'taught him that the only way to hold power was to fill the key positions in the Army and Police with his own trusted followers and to instruct them that law and order (which might mean turning a blind eye to right-wing excesses) should take priority over strict observance of the Varkiza Agreement'. It became apparent, however, that Plastiras's virtues 'did not include political subtlety and sophistication'.[20]

In trying to remedy royalist predominance in the Greek Army, Plastiras came up against the opposition of the 'non-political' British Military Mission, which was reorganising the military. Hugh Seton-Watson realised that the Mission's official non-interventionist stance, though 'theoretically admirable', meant in practice that the Right was not restrained and retained its military influence: 'a non-political Greek officer is a very rare species'. The opposition Populists used the opportunity to defy the Varkiza Agreement and, as Clive was well aware through his contacts, 'made no secret of excusing rampant right-wing terrorism by the National Guard through much of the countryside where . . . past membership of ELAS was judged to be a crime'. The British embassy knew of the right-wing penetration of the army and National Guard by X and the conspiratorial Sacred Bond of Greek Officers (IDEA), a secret organisation of monarchist and conservative officers which took shape during the winter of 1944/5. Sadly, even though Leeper saw the dangers of the extremists' growing influence, all the embassy was prepared to do was 'to make a forlorn request on the eve of the plebiscite for restraint'.[21]

When the Foreign Office suggested to Leeper that one way to curb right-wing extremists was to induce the Greek government to take more drastic action against former collaborators, Churchill took strong exception to the instruction and minuted officials that 'the Communists are the main foe'. He added that there should be 'no question of increasing the severities against the collaborationists in order to win Communist approval'. Even the conservative and often reactionary Foreign Office found Churchill's stance 'astonishing', but there was little it could do to change it.[22]

The British embassy and MI6 pursued a traditional Foreign Office policy of trying to outflank the opposition within Greece by isolating the Left and 'building up a strong, moderate and progressive Centre, whose virtues might not have an immediate appeal to an electorate shaken by war and civil war'. Leeper believed that a republican Centre could be created and 'brushed aside the comment that there was a gap – some thought it unbridgeable – between what should and what could be done in the foreseeable future, when memories were so vivid of December 1944'. A new party, the Union of Popular Democracy/Socialist Party of Greece (ELD/SKE), splitting EAM, was founded and welcomed by the British embassy as the beginnings of a broad centre republican block. AIS, however, observed that it lacked funds and direction. Whether it received covert funding from British Intelligence, which is likely, is unknown. The party was, however, unsuccessful. Political warfare officer Geoffrey Chandler acknowledged that it was 'a sad but inescapable truth that the Centre had no more than a small voice and this fell largely on deaf ears'. Greek politics were highly idiosyncratic, largely corrupt and self-serving: 'Politicians had political ambitions – their own accession to power – but not a single economic or social thought.'[23]

While it worked to create a viable Centre – a policy that would characterise all MI6's postwar operations throughout the Empire, Commonwealth and Northern Ireland – the embassy tried to demonise EAM/ELAS as a simple tool of the Kremlin. A visit to Athens by the head of Section IX, Kim Philby, led to an expansion of MI6 and Military Intelligence intelligence-gathering on the communists, and the reporting to London of 'anything which seems to implicate either Russia, Bulgaria, or Yugoslavia in the present Greek revolt'. The British ambassador reported to London in January 1945 that while intelligence reports indicated that 'ELAS is receiving munitions, though not financial assistance from Bulgaria', he had 'absolutely nothing definite re Russia'. Two months later, despite available American-derived intelligence to the contrary, the British launched a psychological warfare campaign claiming that the KKE's policies and funds 'stem from Russian sources, probably through mediation of Bulgarian and Yugoslav "agents"'.[24]

Right-wing Greek politicians needed little persuading of these 'facts'. Seeing himself as the only person capable of saving the country, General Plastiras assumed leadership of 'national reaction', which effectively allowed the Right to engage in excessive violence in the campaign against the Left. At the same time, he vigorously fought any intervention by the British to prevent the establishment of an exclusively right-wing and republican regime. In the early spring, Leeper and Archbishop Damaskinos realised that Plastiras's regime 'had become an unmitigated disaster' and would have to be removed.[25]

Despite his support of the Right, General Plastiras did not enjoy a reciprocal admiration. The former republican Populists now eagerly embraced the royalist cause and were increasingly convinced that public opinion was moving in their direction. On 4 April 1945, when a political scandal began to break, they withdrew their support from Plastiras. On the following day, an extreme-right royalist newspaper, *Ellinikon Aima* (Greek Blood), published the text of a compromising letter that Plastiras had sent, in June 1941, to Pierre Metaxas, the Greek ambassador to Vichy France, where he had lived in exile. It indicated Plastiras's willingness to mediate through Nazi Germany for an end to the war between Italy and Greece. In addition, an MI6 report of 1 April 1944 on an attempted exfiltration of General Plastiras was uncovered, which mentioned further German efforts to recruit the general, though it appeared that he had rebuffed them. The newspaper disclosure 'shook the Greek political scene to its foundations and gave the pretext for Plastiras's overthrow'. It was also seen as part of a major Populist offensive on the part of loyalist right-wing leader Konstantinos Tsaldaris, for the earliest possible date for a plebiscite on the return of the King.

There was speculation that a copy of the letter had originated with Ionnis Rallis, the former Premier of the last government of the occupation, who had threatened if convicted of collaboration with the Axis powers to produce evidence damaging to Plastiras. Rallis had been promoting the penetration of the police and gendarmerie by followers of the secret right-wing societies, and Plastiras, it seems, had tried to stop them. Further details of Rallis's threats to implicate Plastiras in collaboration were passed on by MI6 to the embassy in Athens. During the occupation, Rallis had controlled the notorious anti-communist Security Battalions which at the end of 1944 had been incorporated into the controversial Third (Mountain) Brigade for anti-communist operations. While on trial, Rallis confirmed that he had been in contact with British Intelligence and that these ties remained unbroken. It was also revealed that other 'traitor' ministers had been in contact with British secret organisations. Rumours persisted that the British had pressurised the court to show clemency to Rallis and acquit others. SOE mission chief Monty Woodhouse wearily observed that 'in the mood of the time Communism seemed a worse crime than collaboration; and collaboration, unlike capital punishment, admitted degrees'.[26]

The American press, which was generally antagonistic to Britain's position in Greece, viewed Plastiras as a victim of British intrigues in favour of the royalists. Widespread rumours suggested that the British had leaked the letter to the newspaper. Heinz Richter suggests that the 'British Secret Service leaked the letter to *Ellinikon Aima*' and that Plastiras's fall 'was staged by British Intelligence', though Leeper was unlikely to have been informed. Interestingly, Rallis did tell the court that 'the British Intelligence Service' had suggested that he take over as Prime Minister. It was true that SOE mission member Nigel Clive had renewed contacts with a number of the younger members of the royalist Populists, including Giorgos Drossos, who was a leader writer on *Ellinikon Aima*. More intriguingly, a copy of the letter, which had been held by the Foreign Office since 1941, was requested on 7 March 1945 by the Second Secretary in the Athens Embassy, Fred Warner. The Southern Department cautioned Warner that there would be 'very grave danger' in his using it in any way against Plastiras, since the British had been involved in bringing the general to power. Warner replied that he simply required it because he had received reports from the AIS that Rallis was threatening to disclose its existence.[27]

Although the Foreign Office regarded the affair as 'a troublesome business', officials acknowledged that 'we did want to get rid of Plastiras anyway'. Indeed, his removal proved to be a watershed. 'His fall from power dashed the hopes of the republican Right to lead the national reaction. Anti-communism was now synonymous with the cause of the King.'[28]

During the spring and early summer, as British troops dispersed throughout Greece to collect the arms surrendered by ELAS, they were accompanied by the National Guard, which garrisoned its battalions in every major town. The 'rabid Royalist elements' within the Guard used the opportunity to exploit marshal law, and within a matter of weeks imprisoned nearly sixteen thousand left-wing sympathisers. Leeper told Damaskinos that 'the National

Guard were engaging, in some places, in what could only be described as terrorism'. Both claimed to be powerless to do anything about it, at least until a new Gendarmerie was in place, to be organised by Sir Charles Wickham's police mission, which had yet to arrive in Athens. Wickham had served in the British Expeditionary Force against the Bolsheviks at the end of the First World War. He acted against the IRA when divisional commander of the Royal Irish Constabulary, and as Inspector-General of the RUC was involved in the creation of the 'B' Specials.

The tense political situation had been expected to improve when the Labour Party won the British general election in July 1945. The AIS reported to London that the election had lifted the optimism of republicans and the socialist Left, but this was to be short-lived. Following the policy of Churchill, Foreign Secretary Ernest Bevin proved to be no friend of the Left, and insisted on elections being conducted as soon as possible, even though royalist terror was rampant in the countryside. It 'threw the republicans into panic but delighted the Populists'.[29]

During July and August, Monty Woodhouse undertook an extended fact-finding tour through the Peloponnese, following alarming reports that ELAS was planning an armed uprising. In fact, in discussions with the British Mission liaison officers he discovered that there was a systematic campaign against the Left. Excluding all leftist evidence, Woodhouse found that 'what remains is bad enough', with the prisons continuing 'to fill up daily' and with six thousand people being held of whom more than 90 per cent were members of EAM. Given the Right's control of the state, Woodhouse noted that 'an ex-guerrilla was as likely as not to be found in gaol, and an ex-member of the Security Battalions as likely as not to be found in the uniformed services'. In reports to Athens, he made the point that 'obviously, this makes the prospects of the left-wing at the elections hopeless'. Only in towns where British units were stationed, which were few, did the Left find any semblance of security. On 24 August, *The Times* reported that signs of a serious deterioration in security were apparent. Right-wing bands were involved in terrorism, a fact that Woodhouse, a moderate conservative but still an anti-communist, admitted – 'the blame lay primarily on right-wing forces'. Close co-operation had been established between the National Guard, the royalists and the right-wing bandit groups such as X as part of the *'parakatos'* – the clandestine para-state that was increasingly controlling events.[30]

The British Missions did little to counteract the prevailing impression that the clandestine forces enjoyed British backing in their persecution of the Left. Woodhouse reported that 'the Right take our approval for granted'. As the former chief of the Australian Relief Team in Greece, Colonel A. W. Sheppard, discovered, even when there was clear evidence of abuse and hounding of the Left, British officials failed to report accurately what was happening. When he asked the British consul in Salonika, Edward Peck, why, he was told: 'There are enough people making propaganda for the Left, why should I.' A number of British officials did complain to London about right-wing atrocities but word never came back to curb the excesses. Sheppard understood that there was collaboration between liaison officers and the Right, and reported that in every British Mission there were members of 'a special Foreign Office service', i.e. MI6, who took care that the 'right' decisions were made. Service members 'pursued their own independent policy which was not even controlled by the British Foreign Minister'.[31]

The right-wing extremists were being backed by the secret organisation, IDEA, which fought for the reintegration of the Security Battalions into the army as 'good nationalists'. It infiltrated the new divisions, putting into high positions its own men, who then weeded out liberal elements in the officer corps. IDEA opposed the process of democratisation within the army, using the pretext of the danger of communism. A part of the *parakatos*, IDEA had supporters in the Greek general staff; these were fanatical anti-communists who viewed the KKE as a 'fifth column' in league with its northern neighbours whose policies were directed against the territorial integrity of Greece. Leading members of IDEA included Staff Chief Vendiris, who controlled general staff policy and had the support of the majority of senior army officers, and the head of the Security Division, General Liosis. Leeper recognised the problem but was seemingly unable, or unwilling, to do anything about it. The consent of the British Military Mission, which functioned as a consultative authority for the Greek War Ministry and general staff, was required for major appointments, but its veto was not exercised. As a result, the purge of the army, which was central to the Varkiza Agreement, was never instigated and was effectively quashed by the head of the Military Mission, General Rawlins.[32]

Geoffrey Chandler was one of those in the AIS who saw the lack of resolve being reflected in the negative press that was aimed at the British embassy.

> British policy in Greece was continually being attacked from without and within for its positive actions . . . Such attacks were misdirected. Our policy was more reprehensible for what it failed to do rather than for what it did . . . We were therefore accused of wholesale interference but did not exercise it . . . We trained the Gendarmerie, often to see such training prostituted to the administration of injustice. British inaction was often interpreted by the right-wing as approval of their acts, at least as connivance. It inevitably helped the Right and increased the antagonism of the Left. The irresponsible actions of a few British individuals helped to give colour to the tale of British partiality. The responsibility was ours, but malice aforethought was lack-

ing. The pathetic attempt to divorce all advisory functions from politics was carried to an extreme which nullified the possibility of making that advice effective.[33]

British officials were haunted, suggests John O. Iatrides, by 'the possibility, perhaps the certainty, that the victory of the Communist-controlled Left in Greece would create conditions so favourable to the Soviet Union that Stalin would be induced to take an active interest in that Balkan country as well'. When the Greek Regent visited London in September 1945, the British government offered to cede, along with Cyprus, the Dodecanese Islands to Greece. The negotiations foundered, however, when Foreign Office Under-Secretary of State Hector McNeil received intelligence reports to the effect that 'if a coup established a Communist government then the bases would be granted to the Russians'. The political situation in Athens remained in flux and, in October, Prime Minister Voulgaris was replaced by the liberal Themistocles Sophoulis.[34]

In mid-November, McNeil, along with Southern Department head William Hayter and the Labour MP Francis Noel-Baker, visited Athens to discuss the situation with Leeper and Greek officials. It added to the impression that the government was little more than a British puppet regime. British officials, Professor Iatrides believes,

> felt compelled to take decisive action at critical moments to maintain a semblance of balance while trying to preserve the image of sovereignty in Greek hands. As a result, early post-liberation Greek governments were little more than British creations which needed London's endorsement and continuous support to survive against domestic opponents, whether of the militant Right, the Left, or a combination of both.[35]

Interpreter for the McNeil delegation was MI6 officer and Greek specialist David Balfour, who noted in his report; 'For a few weeks or months the advent of Sophoulis . . . may keep foreign criticism a little less acrimonious; arrests may become less indiscriminate, deportations rarer and trials juster . . .' The Sophoulis government considered that democratic conditions could only be created by the appointment of more reliable democrats to commanding positions in the army and civil service. 'Here, like their predecessors,' Hugh Seton-Watson observed, 'they were opposed by their British advisers, who hoped to create a "non-political" army and administration.' Indeed, there was stern opposition from the British Missions when Sophoulis tried to instigate radical changes in the security apparatus. When Foreign Minister Rendis complained directly to Bevin that the British Missions were preventing the removal of right-wing extremists from the army and the Gendarmerie, officials refused to acknowledge that there was a serious problem, and shrugged off the accusations as left-wing propaganda. Likewise, General Rawlins regarded reports of the influence of X and IDEA as exaggerated because many members had been republicans. The truth was, however, that – fanatical in their hatred of communism – they had made their peace with the King. Consequently, 'the conviction grew that the British policy makers wanted the Populists in power in order to restore the King'.[36]

When Sophoulis ordered the closing of X offices throughout the country, the Right reacted, and on 21 January 1946 X took over in Kalamata and engaged in widespread terrorism. By the spring, a War Office assessment by intelligence offshoot MI3 of the strength of the X organisation showed that the Right had built up a respectable military potential. They may have also been aware that this potential was based on the arms it indirectly received from the British. Many of the police, who had obtained new arms from the British Police Mission, passed on their older weapons to X. Col. Grivas worked in close consultation with Konstantinos Venteres, who, according to the American embassy, was leader of the 'inner cabal' of the general staff. Grivas also co-operated with the Populists. 'Thus X linked all the branches of the Right', and as the active arm of the *parakatos* was increasing its control over large tracts of the country. Leeper did not believe that the violence, which he thought was exaggerated by the Left, was serious enough to postpone the elections. His adviser, David Balfour, knew, however, that Sophoulis's 'appeasement' venture had 'as good as failed already by the mere fact that the majority of Ministers are Populists'.[37]

On 18 April 1946, a new Prime Minister, Konstantinos Tsaldaris, was sworn in with a totally right-wing, primarily Populist (royalist) government. 'It signalled that the Right had taken power for good,' Heinz Richter concludes. 'So far excesses had been mainly the work of the parakatos, which was outside the government's control. The new policy was aggressively anti-communist and the parakatos became a part of the government's repressive machinery.' Legislation reinstated the notorious pre-war Security Committees and the Gendarmerie was purged of leftist elements, transforming it into a weapon of the Right against the Left.[38]

The leader of the extreme right of the Populist Party was Petros Mavromichalis, Minister of Defence and later Minister of the Interior (1947–8), who was described by US Intelligence as a former Nazi collaborator. According to British secret sources, he was 'actively involved in financing right-wing bands and had managed to persuade Crown Prince Paul, the King's brother, to contribute funds to the cause'. By the autumn, British Intelligence estimated that the official security forces, in which IDEA played a central role, had distributed fifteen thousand arms to the irregular rightist bands. Nigel Clive reveals that the British embassy, which considered him a 'second Zervas, only worse', knew that Mavromichalis had a hand in the activities of royalist terrorists in the Peloponnese. In June, the Defence Minister chose one of the founders of IDEA to draw up a roster of officers eligible for promotion to the army's High Command. Without any sign of difficulty – British Intelligence reported that a quarter of the Greek National Army (GNA) was considered unreliable – the consent of the relevant British Missions was secured to purge liberal elements within the GNA and Gendarmerie and appoint in their place strongly politicised generals with ties to IDEA.[39]

The British had a well-deserved reputation for having the best intelligence on all groups in Greece, and most American diplomats and intelligence officers in their early days in Greece deferred to their more seasoned British colleagues and looked to them for leadership. By 1946, the Americans were more confident of their own abilities and were beginning to pursue an independent line. The Greek section of the OSS had been absorbed into the Central Intelligence Group under cover of the Information Centre of the US embassy. They were supervised by the Greek-American 'special attaché', Thomas Karamessines, who maintained a 'working liaison with all Greek and British security offices'. In commenting on an intelligence report prepared by Karamessines on the takeover by the Right and their terrorist campaign against the communists, American Ambassador MacVeigh telegraphed Washington that

> under the guise of royalism, this program actually approximates fascism at a time when, if anything has been proven by events, it is that fascism has no place in the modern world. By their policy of continually enlarging their definition of Communism to include all who do not support the return of the King, the extremists of the Mavromichalis type now conducting the government's crusade against Communism are risking the creation here, by confirming the alliance of large numbers of democrats with the extreme left, of the same sort of ideological civil war which has occurred in Spain.

MacVeigh's warnings went unheeded. The Right launched an aggressive campaign against the Left with a series of large-scale arrests which the British consul in Thessaloniki, Edward Peck, feared would provoke an 'explosion'. Alleged communist sympathisers were deported to concentration camps on isolated islands, where there was no shelter, a shortage of drinking water, poor food and no sanitary arrangements. The power of the Right and the failure to take measures to restore the economy led to a 'Third Round' of the civil war, which began in the summer of 1946.[40]

According to communist sources, it seems that the left-wing guerrillas operated independently of the KKE during the winter of 1945/6 and that it was only in mid-February that the Party decided to organise them under a central command. Even when the government's authority collapsed in northern Greece, and a 'violent reaction' nearly heralded a full-scale war, the KKE, according to British Intelligence reports of late June, was 'still unsure whether to commit itself to such a conflagration'. MI6 indicated to Hector McNeil in London that the insurrection was essentially a tactic, and that the top KKE leadership hoped that political negotiation would bring them into a Greek cabinet. It was a forlorn hope.[41]

The fact was that the chances of a negotiated solution were becoming increasingly remote – even if the British had wanted to find one. MI6 officer Nigel Clive blamed the rapidly deteriorating political situation and the paradox that 'despite this embarrassingly evident British presence, the Embassy was not in control of Greek affairs'. AIS's Geoffrey Chandler did not see the problem in quite the same way. He noted that 'the reality of Communist banditry had long been recognised and condemned, but not its counterpart' (the term guerrilla had been dropped by the psychological warfare warriors in favour of the more pejorative 'bandit'). British official representatives remained, he believed, 'too gentlemanly, too unworldly perhaps, to recognise the harsh, uncomfortable facts of discrimination and partiality which were practised on the government side and into which the name of Britain was inevitably dragged'. He rejected the official view that

> British influence – even if brought to bear – would have been too late . . . The analysis had never been correct and policy had therefore been lacking. It was clear that armed rebellion by KKE would have been certain under any circumstances; that rebellion should become civil war had never been necessary. By seeing only the possibility of the one and failing to see the germs of the other we had lost our chance of influencing events and shared the responsibility for tragedy.[42]

The Greek Civil War, Heinz Richter concludes,

> was by no means the result of a conspiracy, either from the Left or from the Right. The thesis that a democratic Greece became the victim of sinister communist aggression devilishly premeditated in Moscow is a survival of Cold War propaganda: Greece in 1945/46 was far from being a democratic state and Moscow was against civil war – Greece, after all, belonged to the British sphere of interest and Stalin had written off his Greek comrades as had been proven by his behaviour in December 1944. Similarly, there was no masterly right-wing conspiracy against the liberties of the people which was in its turn directed by the sinister forces of capitalism from abroad, as the Greek communists have asserted. The central motives on this side of the fence were revenge and anti-communism on the part of the Greek Right and an intention to restore pre-war domination and to contain communism on the part of the British.[43]

American embassy attitudes, which had been disapproving of 'the regime imposed by British bayonets', underwent a mysterious and dramatic change during the early autumn of 1946. In a reversal of his previous strongly held views, which had been backed by well-informed intelligence, MacVeigh came out in support of the British embassy and cabled the State Department that the KKE was secretly controlled by Moscow and that the Soviet government must be 'assigned responsibility for continued strife'. According to Foreign Office sources, MacVeigh became more understanding of the British position following treatment of his ailing wife by British Army doctors who had 'practically saved her life'. MacVeigh considered Rex Leeper 'suspiciously Jewish' but appears to have had a good relationship with his successor, Sir Clifford Norton. Bevin had yet to receive any evidence of direct Soviet involvement – an MI6 officer had claimed to have seen crates of Soviet arms being shipped south from Bulgaria – but Norton advised the Foreign Office that the Soviets were attempting to gain control of Greece, thereby outflanking 'Turkey's defences and the whole British position in the Middle East'. The principal villain to the British, however, was Tito, who was known to be nurturing dreams of territorial expansion into northern Greece.[44]

The plebiscite on the return of the King on 1 September 1946 took place in an atmosphere of considerable violence, intimidation and corruption, though this was not enough to invalidate what turned out to be a decisive vote, which gave the King 69 per cent of those cast. It also helped increase the power of the former head of EDES and now the National Party, Napoleon Zervas, who became *de facto* 'leader of the intransigent Right, with which', Nigel Clive suggests, 'no one in the British Embassy had any sympathy'. Thomas Karamessines subsequently reported on plans by the Greek general staff 'to neutralise the KKE completely and effectively, even if it be necessary to declare the party illegal'.[45]

In January 1947, Prime Minister Tsaldaris resigned but was appointed Minister for Foreign Affairs in a coalition government that excluded the liberals and the Left. Leeper cabled London that 'the Right is the only guarantee of a pro-British foreign policy in Greece . . . But the real problem . . . is not only that their leaders are very second-rate . . . but also that they are controlled by forces outside their party.' The British wanted to remove the Minister of Public Order, General Zervas, principally because his anti-communism 'lacks finesse'. The Americans disliked the Minister's 'dictatorial and fascist tendencies' and the backing he received from 'the British-organised Greek Gendarmerie force, which still includes many officers and men who did police duty for the Germans during the occupation . . .' The *New Statesman* noted in February that 'after one and a half year's work by the British Military and Police Missions . . . Greece remains the one country in Europe, outside Spain, whose Army contains in positions in authority a greater number of ex pro-Nazis and collaborators than those identified with the Resistance'. The Civil War continued but the chiefs of staff optimistically reported that 'the back of the bandit opposition could be broken in a period of between two and three months'.[46]

Prompted by Bevin's initiative during the previous month to withdraw troops from Greece owing to Britian's precarious economic condition, President Truman's speech to a joint session of Congress on 12 March 1947 revealed that the Greek government had asked for American assistance. Agreeing to the request, the President thus introduced the 'Truman Doctrine' which would enable successive American policy-makers to intervene on behalf of 'free peoples resisting armed minorities'. The Americans had 'great advantages' over their predecessors, recalled Monty Woodhouse. 'They came fresh to the job, without the staleness and disillusionment which characterised the British.' Yet the Greeks 'also found them harder to deal with than the British; more inflexible, less adaptable . . . more inclined to impose American methods regardless of national characteristics'.[47]

In September, a meeting of British and American intelligence officials agreed on 'the ineptness of Greek propaganda' and suggested a concerted campaign 'to arouse the people within Greece' to 'break guerrilla morale'. A co-ordinated political warfare programme was initiated which included the construction of a US-backed radio station in Salonika to cover the Balkans. Despite the chiefs of staff's assessment, the new round of the civil war did not go well for the Greek government, and guerrilla tactics had the army 'tottering', with the 'Democratic Army' holding four-fifths of Greece. It was in these circumstances that, in September, MI6's David Balfour prepared a 'possible compromise policy' to end the conflict. The proposal included granting a truce, an amnesty, dissolution of parliament, admission of KKE/EAM into a new government, complete disarmament and disbandment of the Democratic Army, acceptance by KKE/EAM of the King and of the British and American Missions, revocation of oppressive measures and new elections with proportional representation. Balfour left out 'an all-important factor: the policy of Moscow', but acknowledged that 'by coming to an arrangement with the leaders of the KKE, a Greek Government would in fact be making, to some extent, a tacit agreement with the larger forces supporting the KKE'. Inevitably, the Foreign Office rejected Balfour's proposals, partly because it regarded Soviet policy as 'the determining factor in the conflict'.[48]

The determining factor in the government's response was increasingly the attitude of the American embassy. US financial and military aid to the Greek government had reached, by the end of 1947, 'sufficient proportions to undermine what remained of British influence'. The American embassy in London was instructed by the State Department in December that while it desired the 'closest possible collaboration' with Britain over Greece, it would be on the basis of the US's 'dominant role' which would include the ability to deliver advice to the Greek government 'independently of Britain'. The chiefs of the respective military missions reached agreement on collaboration which left the British in charge of organisation and training while the Americans oversaw operations. In practice the two overlapped and there developed a 'special relationship', as there was in the intelligence field, which minimised potential 'rifts'. While there was a general agreement on sharing intelligence and secret material, officials from both sides regarded the Greeks as 'infested with communists', and so a security codeword, 'Henley', was used on papers 'not to be shown to the Greeks'. Much to the regret of the British, however, the Americans continued to gain hegemony in Greek affairs, which caused a degree of friction. At the end of the year, Bevin even contemplated sending additional British troops to Greece – which indicated that finance was not the overriding concern in British policy – with the aim of balancing the influence of the Americans.[49]

A CIA study of 9 February 1948 on the 'Possible Consequences of Communist Control in the Absence of US Counteraction' treated the issue of Soviet influence in Greece as a known fact. The British Foreign Office, too, could only see the Kremlin as the main backer of the rebellion. The Foreign Office's Robin Hankey commented: 'I feel that the Russians are really our enemies over Greece . . . Without active Soviet involvement and direction there would be no civil war.' The US State Department Office of Intelligence Research report of 27 April followed the same line. 'It is reasonable to assume that all action in support of [communist guerrilla leader] Markos takes place with prior knowledge and approval of Moscow and with the participation of Soviet co-ordinators on the spot.' Moreover, 'the immediate aim of Soviet policy toward Greece is to prevent the stabilisation of the Greek economy by keeping the country in a constant state of turmoil . . . which it hopes will frustrate the American aid programme and lead eventually to a situation in which the Communists can take over in Greece'.[50]

MI6 officers agreed with the assessment, even if the available intelligence was revealing a slightly different story. Monty Woodhouse concluded in his comprehensive study of the civil war that 'two things are certain, however; that the rebellion could not have continued without some foreign support; and that the KKE was disappointed with its scale'. It was known that Yugoslavia, Bulgaria and Albania had helped the guerrillas, but US intelligence reports in May showed that 'Markos was not getting as much support as he desired from the Soviet satellites and that present indications were that general Kremlin policy was not to push for a Communist victory'. In July, British Intelligence – unaware of changing Comintern policy towards Greece – reported that 'Bulgaria is increasingly unco-operative towards the andartes [guerrillas]'. Other reports indicated that the satellites had withdrawn support from Markos.[51]

The Americans were increasingly impressed with the role of the National

Defence Corps (Tagmata Ethnofylackha Amynhs – TEA) which had been established as a militia to protect the civil community in response to the Prime Minister's pledge to 'exterminate' the guerrillas. TEA was later described by US counter-insurgency specialists as a model of 'counter-organisation' and control of the population, and counter-guerrilla action. This was partly because it featured a high degree of political indoctrination which was 'superimposed on a political-policing role of intelligence, vigilance and repression'. The counter-guerrilla campaign incorporated aspects of British colonial doctrine, including the clearance of the population from particular areas to create a 'no-man's land'. It was regarded as a near-ideal example of effective counter-revolutionary strategy, whose development was a 'paramount requisite of the Cold War'.[52]

Despite the new security measures and the fierce government response, during the last three months of 1948 morale in Greece reached its lowest point, and both British and American Military Intelligence concluded in January 1949 that the military position had deteriorated in the previous twelve months. Yet within the space of months the situation had changed irrevocably, and the Greek National Army (GNA) became increasingly strong. The final sweeps by the GNA began in the Peloponnese in December, taking advantage of the winter weather to root out the guerrillas, with the bulk being captured or killed by February 1949. A prime reason for this success was the reorganisation of the intelligence-gathering capability. Woodhouse noted, 'both on the ground and in the air, American support was becoming increasingly active, and the theoretical line between advice, intelligence and combat was a narrow one'. The army was better disciplined, there was an improved army intelligence service, and British and American officers were no longer just involved in the supply of weapons and training but were also planning and conducting operations.[53]

To improve Greek intelligence work, Thomas Karamessines, head of the US CIG Station, organised his Greek counterparts into KYP, the Greek Central Intelligence Agency. It would develop into an integral part of the shadow Service, engaging in widespread political surveillance against all who might be associated with the Left. In order to do so, and to bypass regular laws, it was funded directly by the CIA. In the spring of 1949, Karamessines established the first CIA station, which grew into one of the biggest in Europe. The most important element in battling the guerrillas proved to be the police, whose special role was to zealously collect and file intelligence on left-wingers in the cities and larger towns. Between early 1947 and mid-1948 the police had 'largely destroyed the mass organisation of the KKE in the main cities', and in Athens they had 'caught nearly all important cadres' by April 1949. These results were achieved 'partly by skilful detective work, which earned the admiration of the police mission, and partly by intensive surveillance and intimidation of the population'. By August the control of the villages by the Gendarmerie was 'complete'.[54]

The sudden collapse of the guerrilla-based Democratic Army was also undoubtedly helped by the wish of the Cominform countries to seek an accommodation with the Greeks at the expense of the Yugoslavs. Pressed hard by the British and Americans, Tito finally fell into line in late June 1949. The communists offered a negotiated settlement but Britain and the United States had no intention of pursuing it. In October the war was finally abandoned by the KKE leaders, who acknowledged their military failure.

Since December 1944 almost 158,000 people had been killed, of whom just over a half were guerrillas and their sympathisers, the rest being Greek Army and Gendarmerie casualties, or civilians. On 31 October 1949, as the British government finally began removing its troops from Greece, the Foreign Office stated publicly that economic imperatives – the stated reason for Bevin's invitation to the Americans and the impetus for the Truman Doctrine – had never been a factor in the retention of these troops, since the cost of maintaining them in Greece had always been very low.[55]

Despite the success, the Right became increasingly frustrated at the delay in silencing the communists. Voices called for a totalitarian solution, while IDEA officers talked 'unreservedly about "traitors in the rear", about the need to "clear up the situation" and impose a new regime'. They demanded a 'Directory for the supposed salvation of the endangered country'. As Monty Woodhouse wearily noted: 'It wasn't required but they got their wish twenty years later with the generals.'[56]

CHAPTER 18

YUGOSLAVIA: THE GOLDEN PRIEST, STOLEN TREASURE AND THE CRUSADERS

In early July 1997, the go-ahead was given for the implementation of the NATO-sanctioned Operation TANGO, which involved the attempted capture of two Serbs, indicted by the war crimes tribunal in The Hague of 'ethnic cleansing' during the war in Bosnia, five years previously. Simo Drljaca, the police chief of Prijedor, had helped to set up Omarska and the other notorious 'detention' camps of north-western Bosnia, where Muslims were tortured and killed. A colleague, Dr Milan Kovacevic, a professional anaesthetist and former mayor of Prijedor, was allegedly in day-to-day management of the Omarska camp.

British Prime Minister Tony Blair gave a formal instruction to the Joint Intelligence Committee (JIC) that Drljaca and Kovacevic should be arrested and flown to The Hague for trial. In turn the JIC tasked the Chief of MI6, David Spedding, to take control of the operation. Spedding handed it over to the 'General Support Branch', which handles 'dirty' operations and uses the SAS's Counter-Revolutionary Warfare (CRW) wing as its executive arm. One of the SAS's NATO special force functions is kidnapping. Members of the undercover surveillance 14th Intelligence Company tracked the targets in Bosnia until the SAS moved in for a 'fast-ball' operation – hitting the targets when they least expected it.

A joint team of the CRW wing and SAS D Squadron were flown to Bosnia with operational control in the hands of a British liaison team at the Headquarters Multi-National Division (South). Satellite links were run direct to the SAS's 'Kremlin' war room in London and MI6's command-and-control room in the basement of its Vauxhall Bridge headquarters. Landed at their target points by American Black Hawk helicopters, the SAS snatch squad found their quarry. The operation was judged a huge success, even though one target was killed in the attempt. When challenged, Drljaca pulled out a pistol and shot one soldier in the leg before being gunned down in a hail of bullets; in contrast, at Prijedor hospital, Dr Kovacevic surrendered peacefully.[1]

The tragedy that was Yugoslavia is illustrated by the fact that Kovacevic had himself been born in a concentration camp. His mother was held during the Second World War in Jasenovac, a camp established by the Croatian fascist regime for the imprisonment, torture and killing of Serbs, Jews, gypsies and dissidents. In 1997 MI6 was in the honourable position of bringing war criminals to justice; in contrast, fifty years earlier it had recruited Serb, Croat and Slovene war criminals, collaborators and quislings for its intelligence-gathering operations in Tito's Yugoslavia.

When in 1941 the Germany and Italian armies entered the already fragmented Yugoslavia, 'the fragile kingdom' fell apart in a defeat that was 'as much political as military'. The main victors and beneficiaries when the Germans and Italians divided the country into zones of influence were the fanatical nationalist Slovenes and Croats, who seized the opportunity to impose their extremist creed on the population at the expense of the hated Serbs.[2]

A Croat Ustashi (roughly translated as 'to awaken') unit entered Zagreb with the German Army on 10 April 1941 and proclaimed a free and independent State of Croatia (NDH) (which included Bosnia). Led by Zagreb lawyer Ante Pavelic, the Ustashi movement had been formed in the late 1920s as a clandestine fascist group which, during the thirties, conducted a campaign of international terrorism, organised by Pavelic's right-hand man, Adrija Artukovic. In contact with British Intelligence since the assassination with Dido Kvaternik of Yugoslav King Alexander in Marseilles in 1934, Artukovic took refuge in England but was eventually handed over to the French for the murder of their foreign minister. He never came to trial, however, owing to the protection of the Italian government. Catholic and western-orientated, Croatia having been ruled by the Austro-Hungarian Empire for centuries, the Ustashi were provided with military and logistical support by Benito Mussolini and the Hungarian dictatorial regent, Admiral Horthy.[3]

On 16 April, the Poglavnik (Führer) Pavelic nominated himself Prime Minister of the NDH. Bolstered by the support of sections of the Catholic Church, in particular the Archbishop of Zagreb, Aloysus Stepinac, and Bishop Ivan Saric of Sarajevo, the Pavelic Nazi-puppet government received the backing of the Croat ultra-nationalists. It could, however, only rely on the backing of a few thousand Ustashi faithful, and was dependent on Italy for support and military aid. This did not prevent the Ustashi from brutally suppressing their opponents and exterminating in almost unsurpassed cruelty thousands of Serbs, gypsies and Jews. The Ustashi aimed to kill one-third of the Serbs on their territory, exile one-third, and convert one-third from orthodoxy to Catholicism. The chief of secret police, Dido Kvaternik, turned his Ustashi killers on the Jews, while the Minister of the Interior, Adrija Artukovic, established a network of concentration camps where 'Pavelic's followers slaughtered over a half-a-million people'. Italian journalist Curzio Malaparte interviewed Pavelic: 'While he spoke, I gazed at the wicker basket on the Poglavnik's desk. The lid was raised and the basket seemed to be filled with shelled oysters ... "Are they Dalmatian oysters?" I asked the Poglavnik. Pavelic removed the lid from the basket ... and he said smiling, "It is a present from my loyal Ustashi. Forty pounds of human eyes." '[4]

An ecclesiastical adviser to Pavelic and fervent Croatian nationalist, Dr Krunoslav Draganovic, was sent to Rome to help boost the status of Pavelic's murderous regime. Although the Vatican was well informed about the atrocities, these were put down to communist propaganda or the work of communists themselves. The Catholic Church was similarly fully supportive of the nationalist and predominantly clerical-orientated Slovene People's Party (SPP), whose leaders, such as Miha Krek, a former minister in the pro-British Royal Yugoslav government, and the Bishop of the Slovene capital, Ljublijana, Gregory Rozman, 'bitterly opposed both Western liberalism and Eastern Communism'. They sought the creation of an 'independent' Slovene state and in pursuit of their goal supported the Tripartite Pact with the Nazis and Italians. When the Nazis did invade, however, and the true nature of their brutality became evident, Krek and other disillusioned SPP leaders fled to London. This did not prevent Krek from establishing himself 'as a viable tool of the Germans' and backing his supporters in Slovenia, who were quickly forced to seek an accommodation with the occupying forces.[5]

Determined to keep alive the nationalist impulse, and hoping that their zone would be saved from the savagery that the Germans had inflicted on the northern zones of the former Yugoslavia, SPP members collaborated with the Italians in suppressing the rising tide of guerrilla warfare by joining the Italian-controlled Voluntary Anti-Communist Militia, known as the 'White Guard'. They helped the Germans carry out clandestine activities against the partisans, who were led by the communist Josip Broz, otherwise known as 'Tito'. With Krek now vice-premier of the exiled Yugoslav government in London, leadership of the SPP passed to the ultra-nationalist Bishop Rozman, who put 'the Catholic Church's considerable moral authority behind the White Guard, helping organise its command and intelligence structures'. A secret anti-communist security police force in Ljublijana supplied the Italians with intelligence for arrests.[6]

At the behest of the Germans, General Nedic of the Serbian Volunteer Corps had formed the Serbian Government of National Salvation and declared his support for the right of the Germans to control the semi-independent state. A First World War hero, Kosta Pecanac, placed his Yugoslav 'Chetniks' (literally a member of a Cheta – armed band) at Nedic's disposal. They were granted the status of 'legalised' Chetniks and formally incorporated by the *chef de cabinet* General Miodrag Damjanovic into a quisling force, the Serbian State Guard, 'recognised by the Germans and tolerated for their undisguised hostility towards the growing menace of the Communist-led Partisans'. Also recognised was the militant anti-communist fighting force, the Volunteer Corps, which had been established by the Serbian fascist leader Dimitrije Ljotic, from members of his Zbor movement.[7]

The main threat to the Germans and Italians was initially General Dreza Mihailovic, a Serbian nationalist whose followers were known, because of their opposition to the Germans, as 'illegal' Chetniks. Working for 'a greater Serbia', the strongly anti-communist and pro-monarchist Mihailovic wanted, however, 'to prepare and husband resources for the moment when the enemy, weakened and tottering, could be overwhelmed by a combined frontal assault from the Allied regular armies and a well-timed sabotage and guerrilla campaign in his rear'. He had the support of a pro-Serb clique within the British Foreign Office and the controlling minister of the sabotage and resistance Special Operations Executive (SOE), Lord Selbourne, a dyed-in-the-wool conservative and fervent monarchist. The general's main backing came from Cairo where SOE officer Guy Tamplin, of the Near East Arab Broadcasting station, was 'stubborn in his support', as was the officer dealing with Yugoslav propaganda, Archibald Lyall, later to join MI6. The promotion of Mihailovic by Cairo conferred on him, the SOE officer in Istanbul dealing with the Serbs, Hugh Seton-Watson, acknowledged, 'a political role' in which he saw himself as 'the legal representative of the government inside Yugoslavia'. The general saw it as his duty to combat the Croats and the communists and 'if help could be obtained from the Italians against them, it should not be rejected'; 'collaboration' being part of the accepted rule of warfare in Yugoslavia. Although there was no direct collaboration with the Germans, during 1943 fifteen thousand Chetniks fought in close co-ordination with Italian, German and Croat pro-fascist anti-partisan units, while Mihailovic's commanders co-operated in local campaigns against the communists.[8]

These informal alliances were fundamentally undermined in September 1943 by the capitulation of Italian forces, which were forced to withdraw from Yugoslavia. When the vacuum was filled by the Germans, who imposed pro-Nazi regimes, MI6 and SOE saw it as an opportunity to try to peel away some of the nationalist elements from their Nazi masters. At the end of 1943, British Intelligence tried to engineer a split between the Ustashi and the Nazis. SOE and MI6 Balkan specialist Hugh Seton-Watson was asked to interview Dr Brancko Jelic, a Croatian nationalist and right-hand man to Pavelic, who had been erroneously suspected of being party to the assassination of King Alexander. In early October 1939, Dr Jelic had been detained at Gibraltar on his way to Italy and had been interned for the duration of the war. Quite what Jelic could do from his island prison, other than provide names and contacts, is unclear. In the event, the Ustashi remained loyal to their Nazis hosts.[9]

In Nazi-occupied Slovenia, General Leon Rupnik was installed as 'Predient' with the support of Ljotic's Zbor movement. Abandoning the Italians, Bishop Rozman met in secret with Nazi officials and proposed the formation of a new quisling force, the Domobrans (Home Guard), to replace the White Guard. Swearing an oath of loyalty to Hitler, the Domobrans' 'Information Department' gathered intelligence on anti-Nazi Slovenes, while its 'Black Hand' helped organise 'cleansing' operations with the Gestapo. Knowledge of Domobran 'war crimes' reached the British Foreign Office from its delegation to the Vatican. The Vatican, too, was shocked by the excesses, but not enough for it to curtail its support of the Slovene nationalists. As the Slovene SPP supporters agonised over who would win the war, they were increasingly excluded from power and replaced in key positions in the Domobrans by the pro-German Zbor movement. The young Ljenko Urbanic, known as 'little Goebbels' for his work in the Information Department, launched a propaganda campaign against the 'clerical' faction inside the SPP. It had organised a 'secret pro-British underground network' which by 1944 was forwarding information to British Intelligence agents and Miha Krek in London. A subsequent purge by the Germans led to a number of clericals being arrested and sent to concentration camps.[10]

Meanwhile, the British had encountered difficulties in deciding which of the opposition movements within Yugoslavia to support as they contemplated opening up another front in the Balkans.

Reporting directly to Winston Churchill on the political front and General Bevil Wilson, who had been working for UNRRA, on the military side, former Foreign Office diplomat and founder member of the SAS, Fitzroy Maclean, was given the task of discovering 'who was killing the most Germans and suggest means by which we could help them kill more'. He was told that 'politics must be a secondary consideration'. Unfortunately for Maclean, politics was what it turned out to be all about.[11]

Fearing that SOE would attempt to sabotage his mission, which was to be air-dropped into Yugoslavia, Maclean went to extraordinary lengths to maintain its security. Whether his paranoia was rational or not, his efforts are testament to the intense and bitter 'secret army games' which existed between SOE and MI6 and, more particularly, the various factions within British Intelligence that operated in the Balkans. Maclean refused to accept the first parachute offered by SOE, since 'one of the things SOE did to people they wanted to get rid of was to put a blanket in their parachute'. Although he did in the end use SOE transport and communications, worried that his signals would be suppressed Maclean ensured that he had his own separate direct channel to Stewart Menzies through MI6's cover organisation, the Inter-Services Liaison Department. The intelligence officer for the mission, who also worked for MI6, Major Gordon Alston, had played a similar role for David Stirling in the Middle East with the first detachment of the SAS, with whom Maclean had also served.[12]

On 6 November 1943, Maclean finally delivered his report, which concluded that Mihailovic's forces were failing to take on the Germans and that the only significant opposition was coming from Tito's communist partisans. His report had the 'effect of a blockbuster' and 'made it much more difficult for the Foreign Office to carry on its kid-glove policy towards Mihailovic'. It was 'praised' by the chiefs of staff and backed by Cavendish Bentinck on the JIC, which had been influenced by Ultra intercepts showing that the Wehrmacht was engaged in constant battles with the partisans as distinct from the Chetniks, thus corroborating Maclean's account. Hugh Seton-Watson acknowledged that 'for three years the partisans had conducted, in complete physical isolation, a heroic struggle'. Many of Mihailovic's 'exploits' turned out to have been carried out by Tito's forces, which had captured the equipment of several surrendered Italian divisions. Mihailovic was then allowed to wither on the vine; left 'to rot and fall off the branch, rather than be pushed'. After April 1944, when the British Military Mission was withdrawn and military material was denied to Mihailovic, the supply of arms, medical stores and equipment was transferred to Tito and proved to be of great value in tying down German divisions. A postwar assessment by the US Department of the Army of the German 'order of battle' concluded that the partisans had prevented 'well over one-half million German troops' from being committed to other fronts.[13]

Maclean's report caused outrage and continued to do so for a long time on the Right, which constructed a conspiracy theory in which the unseen hands of communists had manipulated the evidence that produced the change of policy. Rightists such as the Catholic writer and member of Maclean's mission, Evelyn Waugh, exacerbated Anglo-Yugoslav relations by overt contacts with Croatia's ultra-nationalist Ustashi supporters. According to Maclean's biographer, Frank McLynn, Waugh provided the Foreign Office with violently anti-partisan reports in which he appeared to have doctored the evidence. Waugh subsequently leaked his slanted information to right-wing British Catholics, bizarrely portraying Maclean – a hardline anti-communist – as a 'Red'.[14]

Despite the release of SOE records in July 1997, and the efforts of a right-wing pro-Mihailovic faction to put the blame on the shoulders of an openly communist SOE officer in Cairo, James Klugman, as McLynn and specialists on the subject have shown, there were no grounds for the conspiracy theory. There was no alternative to the support Tito received, which only accelerated 'a process which was inevitable'. 'There was no way we could stem Tito,' former diplomat Sir Reginald Hibbert concludes,

> and the only sensible thing to do was to ride with the punch. It is a perversion of history to suggest that the Partisan movement was foisted on Yugoslavia, either by the Russians or by us. If it was foisted on them by anyone, it was by the Germans. One cannot sufficiently over-emphasise the destruction of Yugoslavia by the Germans and the terroristic edge the German Army used to consolidate its power.

Historian Mark Wheeler believes that the conspiracy theory led to a fatalistic belief that the Serbs

> didn't make their own bed – the British did it for them! This fits in with the tradition of 'perfidious Albion' in Eastern Europe – the British have a uniquely competent and uniquely evil secret service, et cetera. In the Balkans there is a constant motif that one is not responsible for one's own fate, that malign foreign influences, especially the British Secret Service, are manipulating them ... Of course, like all clichés, this one contains some truth.[15]

Maclean was, by the end of 1943, already formulating ideas about the postwar world. 'Events will show the nature of Soviet intentions towards Yugoslavia; much will also depend on Tito and whether he sees himself in his former role of Comintern agent, or as the potential ruler of an independent state.' Maclean thought that Tito might become independent of Moscow and be willing to co-operate with the West. Indeed, Churchill had agreed to severing the link with Mihailovic in the hope that Tito would be prepared to deal with Britain. Initially this was justified; British officers of the Liaison Mission in Yugoslavia observed that Tito was very much 'his own man' and that Yugoslavian nationalism would assert itself after the war. Ironically, however, given the onslaught from the Right, it turned out that Maclean and MI6 were to be very wide of the mark in their assessment; Tito was Moscow's most zealous supporter. A more realistic assessment was made by US Office of Strategic Services (OSS) officer Frank Lindsay, who in his final report wrote that

> the basic policy of the present government is the complete orientation of Yugoslavia into the Russian sphere. This policy is being implemented primarily by the Yugoslav communists and is not being directed locally by Russian representatives ... the top Yugoslav leaders are so thoroughly indoctrinated with Soviet policies and methods that there is little or no need for day-to-day directives from Moscow.

This proved to be substantially correct.[16]

By the summer of 1944 the partisans were at the threshold of Serbia, and it was clear that, unless Hitler's promised secret weapons became a reality, the Germans were facing defeat. With nowhere to go, General Nedic decided that he had no choice but to seek an agreement with Mihailovic on collaboration against the communists. The Serbian State Guard became an effective instrument of Mihailovic, while members of Ljotic's Zbor movement began to look upon him as 'a secret ally'. Nedic and General Damjanovic agreed to place all armed formations of the Serbian Government of National Salvation under the command of Mihailovic, who told them that 'I still have contact with the British and Americans. I have every reason to believe that Anglo-American forces will land on the Adriatic coast where we will assist them to maintain law and order.' His only problem was that he lacked weapons, which Nedic solved by attaching Chetnik officers to his staff in Belgrade, where the Germans agreed to supply the request for fifty thousand rifles.[17]

In October 1944, Tito installed himself in Belgrade. During the following month, Pavelic reluctantly agreed to an approach to the Allies. His envoy secretly left Zagreb for Italy to present the Supreme Allied Commander in Caserta with a memorandum admitting that, while the HND had been a child of the Axis, 'Croatia cannot exist without the support of Great Britain'. Envisaging Croatia 'as part of an anti-communist bloc of western-orientated Balkan states – Turkey, Greece and Albania – in opposition to Moscow-imposed regimes in the region', he requested a military mission be sent to Croatia, but the Ustashi representative received 'a cold reception'. Simultaneously, Slovene leader Miha Krek began lobbying western leaders. According to Mark Aarons' study of American intelligence files, Krek tried to convince MI6 that the Domobrans were 'a viable post-war political and military alternative to the communist-led partisans'. When the Royal Yugoslav government-in-exile ordered its followers to join Tito's forces, Krek stepped up his efforts, formulating a plan to transfer the Domobrans to 'Allied control for fighting against the Germans'. Support came from clerical leaders Bishop Rozman and Anton Preseren, a member of the Slovene colony in Rome and Assistant General of the Jesuits. In November, Pope Pius XII promised Krek and Preseren help for the Catholic SPP, but their request that the Allies occupy Slovene territory to avoid the 'tragic shredding of innocent blood' came to nothing.[18]

These requests were obviously naïve, particularly so when, in March 1945, many Domobrans joined forces under the command of Serbian General Damjanovic, who, acting on the advice of Zbor's Dimitrije Ljotic, unified the Yugoslav pro-German quisling forces in Slovenia. In April 'a camarilla of all-powerful Ustashi officers and scheming politicians', who had taken control of what remained of the disintegrating State of Croatia, presented Pavelic with a memorandum recommending the formation of 'an anti-Communist bloc based on some project for a federal reconstruction of Yugoslavia which would command the sympathy of the Western Allies'. Desperation also forced Mihailovic to seek an accommodation with Pavelic. In this unreal and nightmarish world, with nothing left to govern, a Slovene National Committee planned to seize control of the state from General Rupnik, when the Germans pulled out.[19]

In the spring of 1945, with the Red Army approaching 'independent' Croatia, Pavelic realised that 'they who had sowed the storm must now bow their heads before the whirlwind, save what could still be saved, go underground again in their old conspiratorial haunts in Austria and Italy'. He had faith that 'one day they would be needed again'. He sent emissaries across the border to make contact with British Intelligence and the Catholic Church. There then followed an exodus to Austria of Ustashi and senior NDH quislings, including the Minister of the Interior, Adrija Artukovic, and his co-conspirator, Dido Kvaternik. Pavelic had already entrusted one of his closest acolytes, Father Krunsolav Dragnovic (who as vice-president of the Ustashi Office for Colonisation had played a part in the extermination of Jews and Serbs during the bloody anti-partisan campaign in the Kozara mountains), with the transfer to Switzerland and Austria of truck-loads of valuables, gold and currency. They were intended to finance new Croat resistance in Yugoslavia against the communists. On 4 May 1945, the Poglavnik made his last public appearance in Zagreb. Later in the day, with an Argentine passport in the name of 'Ramirez', Pavelic, along with Max Lubric, controller of the concentration camps, the commander of the Black Legion, Boban, and 'the group of desperadoes known as the Colonel's Camarilla', also slipped across the border into Austria.[20]

On 13 May 1945 Tito sent a message to his First Army: 'A group of Ustashi and some Chetniks, a total of over 50,000 men, is reported by the Third Army in the Konjice-Sotanj area. It includes Pavelic ... and a huge number of criminals. They are attempting to cross at Dravograd and give themselves up to the British.' Tito issued the order for their 'annihilation', but some twelve thousand anti-communist Serbs, including many Chetniks in German uniforms, reached Allied headquarters. Army Intelligence officer and later Labour Cabinet minister Anthony Crosland, while recognising that many were simple peasants, met a number who 'freely and in fact proudly admitted that since 1942 they had been fighting only Tito. When one pointed out to these people that we were bound to treat them as enemies they could not see it at all. They are genuinely pro-British and seemed to think we shall help them against Tito.'[21]

Following in Pavelic's wake were a number of senior Ustashi who made it to a safe base near Salzburg. Wanted for 'war crimes' by the Yugoslav authorities, according to Mark Aarons and John Loftus, they included:

- Stejpan Hefer, regional governor-general of Baranja, where he was responsible for the slaughter of Serbs and the deportation of Jews by terror squads.
- Ljbo Milos, a senior official at the Jasenovac concentration camp, where his speciality had been the 'ritual killing' of Jews, using a knife to cut their throats and to slice open their stomachs.
- Dr Vjekoslav Vrancic, Deputy Minister of Foreign Affairs and under-secretary in the Interior Ministry; wanted for administering the camps.
- Veliko Pecnikar, head of the Poglavnik's personal bodyguard and also commander of the brutal Gendarmerie which worked in close collaboration with the Gestapo.
- Bozidar Kavran, commander of Pavelic's headquarters and a trusted aide.
- Srecko Rover, implicated in a plot to assassinate Yugoslavia's King Peter. He held a senior position in Pavelic's personal bodyguard.
- Lovro Susic, Minister of Corporations, who worked closely with the Nazis on the deportations for forced labour in Germany and later served with the SS Division Prince Eugen.
- Father Josip Bujanovic, a Croat priest party to the massacre of Orthodox peasants.[22]

The British Army in Austria, under the command of Field Marshal Alexander, initially disarmed the Ustashi and, in late May 1945, surrendered to Tito's forces, quite legitimately, around 18,500 Chetniks, Ustashi, Slovenian White Guards and Domobrans. In the near-civil war that followed in Yugoslavia, a great many atrocities were committed. The killings were, a senior member of Tito's Politburo admitted, 'sheer frenzy'. Right-wing supporters of Mihailovic have always regarded the repatriations as an act of 'sinister duplicity'. Count Tolstoy has pointed an accusing finger at SOE's Sixth Special Force and, in particular, its commanding officer, Charles Villiers, one-time chair of British Steel. Villiers claimed to have absolutely 'no connection with or knowledge of the repatriation of Royalist Yugoslavs'. This was despite a statement by his deputy, Major Edward Renton, that on behalf of the Fifth – whose General Staff, Brigadier Toby Low, was his closest friend and best man – Villiers had been involved in negotiating surrender terms with the 15th Cossack Cavalry Corps. Even so, while Villiers's silence about this period was suspicious, and it was true that unit members certainly saw the trains taking the repatriates, the evidence does not support the conspiracy theory. On the ground, a number of those who could have been returned were protected by SOE personnel and intelligence officers working on their own initiative.[23]

SOE's Sixth Special Force, initially headed by Peter Wilkinson and operating outside normal military command and Foreign Office direction, had been involved in dropping war material to the Carthinian Slovene partisans, but began to steer a more pronounced anti-communist tack in January 1945 in the face of changing international circumstances. On assuming command in May, Wilkinson's brother-in-law, Charles Villiers, had noted communist attempts to take over in Austria, where resistance had been weak, and the possibility of the Slovene partisans grabbing Carthinia. Villiers argued that this could be countered by the unit's expertise in frontier matters. MI6 outfits were operating in the same area but little is known about their activities.[24]

The Sixth's Major Renton, Patrick Martin-Smith, Lt. Finlay Lockhead and Alex Ramsay, who was the first person into Klagenfurt, were employed in Carthinia and later formed the rump of a Special Operations section in Austria which was taken over by MI6. One of their tasks was the recruitment of agents to find out what was going on inside Tito's communist state. Lockhead was soon running informants among those to be repatriated, who supplied useful information on Yugoslav troop movements. At the same time, Villiers had been 'flying in and out' of 'Tito's land' keeping the Fifth Corps informed on 'who was who'. Anti-communism and assistance to British Intelligence overrode all other considerations, with the result that while one section was busy hunting down war criminals, another was seeking suitable targets for recruitment in intelligence-gathering operations. In doing so, as Mark Aarons discovered, the British, having repatriated the small fry, went 'to astonishing lengths to protect the genuinely guilty'.[25]

Crossing British lines, Pavelic hid with Artukovic in the Convent of St Gilgin until picked up and released by British occupation forces, from which time they were 'protected by the British in British-guarded and requisitioned quarters'. For security reasons, and because of the inevitable embarrassment knowledge of his presence would bring, for the next three months Pavelic was hidden by British Intelligence at Klagenfurt in the British Occupation Zone. Pavelic brought with him more gold for safe-keeping in one of the Austrian monasteries. Most was converted on the black market, but some 2,400 kilos was secreted in Berne. A substantial quantity was designated the property of the Catholic Church in Austria, and was sent with a British Intelligence officer, Lt-Col. Jonson, to Italy. According to a US Treasury report, the Ustashi had looted gold worth 350 million Swiss francs of which 150 million was seized on the Austro-Swiss border and impounded by the British authorities.[26]

The Domobrans found sanctuary in the Displaced Persons (DP) camps, and then Trieste, which contained a large Slovene population, and finally the Eboli DP camp in Italy. British Military Intelligence Field Security Service units were soon combing the Austrian countryside and DP camps looking for war criminals. General Leon Rupnik and eighteen other Slovene collaborators were captured by Field Marshal Alexander's troops near Spittal, and their extradition was requested, in June 1945, by the Yugoslav ambassador in

London. Other sections of British Intelligence were, however, conniving with Krek and a British 'agent', Reverend Achin, to recruit elements of the Domobrans for intelligence-gathering and later, under the spiritual leadership of Bishop Rozman, for anti-Tito operations. Contacts were made with the Vatican where Anton Preseren led a powerful group of Slovenes, who received 'help from the English'.[27]

Those Ustashi remaining undetected by Tito's secret informers and Allied search teams dispersed, hiding themselves among the thousands of DPs in the network of camps in Italy and Austria. With Pavelic hiding in Austria, the task of developing the exiled Ustashi movement fell to his 'alter ego', Krunoslav Draganovic, who was Secretary of the Croatian Confraternity of San Girolamo, which was attached to the Vatican in Rome. Draganovic had transferred an estimated 400 kilos of the safe-housed Ustashi gold to Rome to finance new networks. The US Treasury report later suggested that 'the balance of approximately 200 million Swiss francs was originally held in the Vatican for safe-keeping. According to rumour, a considerable portion of this latter has been sent to Spain and Argentina though the Vatican's "pipeline", but it is quite possible this is merely a smokescreen to cover the fact that the treasure remains in its original repository.' Initially, this appears to have been the case, and through control of the looted treasure, the 'golden priest' of San Girolamo, Draganovic, held considerable sway over the activities of Pavelic's followers. He remained, however, under threat from the Yugoslav War Crimes Commission for his involvement in the forced conversion of Orthodox Serbs to Catholicism.[28]

During the summer of 1945, Draganovic undertook a tour of the DP camps of northern Italy and the regions around Klagenfurt and Villsach on the Austrian–Yugoslav border. There he established contact with the senior Ustashi leaders and their chief representatives in the camps, where the Ustashi were already developing political organisations. This led to the formation of a fully fledged intelligence service run by Pavelic's son-in-law, Veliko Pecnikar. Through the assistance of other Croat priests, a regular courier service was maintained between San Girolamo, where many of the leaders found sanctuary, and the scattered Ustashi groups. Helped by the Ustashi treasure, Draganovic created a 'ratline' using the monastery, which had territorial immunity, as a safe asylum for the émigrés most in danger of arrest by the Allies. Other funds went to support Pavelic's Krizari (Crusaders), a guerrilla force which, operating from bases in Austria, was intended to link up with the underground resistance which had supposedly been left behind in Croatia. The operation was commanded by Bozidar Kavran with assistance from Lovro Susic, Draganovic's partner in hiding the loot in Austria, and Father Josip Bujanovic. Pecnikar maintained contact between the Crusaders and other clandestine neo-fascist organisations in Austria and Italy.[29]

As head of the Croatian Clerical Party, Draganovic worked closely with its Slovene counterpart in support of efforts to create a Catholic-dominated Pan-Danubian Confederation of Catholic nations in Central Europe. On 25 June 1945, Pavelic and his close Crusader collaborators made contact in the American Zone in Austria with a papal mission, headed by Archbishop Andreas Rohracher of Salzburg. They asked for the Pope's assistance in creating, as part of the Intermarium project, an independent Croatia as a bastion against a Serbian-dominated Yugoslavia. In addition, Rohracher intervened with 'sympathetic elements of the British forces ... to create a favourable impression' in preparation for the Crusaders' offer 'to put themselves at the disposal of the Anglo-American leadership'; an offer immediately accepted by British Intelligence, which was helping reorganise the Ustashi for 'eventual use against Tito'.[30]

Not that any of this had gone unnoticed by the Yugoslavs, who had successfully infiltrated the camps in Austria. By July, they knew that Pavelic had been taken prisoner by British troops at Klagenfurt, even though the Foreign Office was unaware of this fact, insisting that he must be in the American or Russian zones in Austria. In mid-August, the Foreign Office decided that on a narrow definition the anti-communist Croats, Slovenes and Serbs, whose extradition and repatriation were demanded by Tito's regime in Belgrade, were not 'war criminals in the proper sense'. It did admit, however, that 'some of them are clearly collaborators of the blackest dye; but the Yugoslav request also covers others who may well be properly considered as political opponents of the present Yugoslav regime rather than as traitors to the Yugoslav state'. It was decided, therefore, that Yugoslavia would henceforth be a 'special case' and Allied commanders would no longer be authorised to hand over alleged traitors and renegades.[31]

Throughout the summer and autumn of 1945 there were continuous allegations from the Yugoslav authorities to the effect that the British were protecting former Nazi collaborators in Carthinia. The presence of known Slovene collaborators and the holding of regular demonstrations by the nationalists kept the issue alive. British Intelligence reported in November that trouble was brewing along the Austrian border with Yugoslavia, where the Carthinian Slovenes held strong separatist feelings. They were being subjected to 'political and intense propaganda and pressure', seemingly from both the nationalists and the communists. Peter Wilkinson, former regional SOE head and now a political adviser in Vienna, wrote a report in April 1946 on 'the Slovene minority in Carthinia' in which he stated that the activities of the Slovene nationalists were 'a source of continual nuisance'.[32]

By this time, MI6 was also mounting major and aggressive intelligence-gathering operations using Ustashi assets in a tightly knit network of cells from a 'spy centre' in the divided territory of Trieste. This had been established by Draganovic with the help of Croat priests in the monasteries and the logistical support of British Intelligence.[33]

For a few weeks following the official end of hostilities, there had been a serious possibility that the port of Trieste, which was populated by a mixture of Italians and Slovenes, would be the setting for a first armed conflict between East and West. The Yugoslavs had ethnic claims to the Istrian peninsula, and with a view to annexing the territory Tito had ordered the partisans to enter Trieste before the British Eighth Army arrived from Italy. The partisans won the neck-and-neck race, arriving on the morning of 1 May 1945, while the Germans were still defending their positions. A massive show of Allied force, and Stalin's refusal to intervene on Tito's behalf, prevented any further bloodshed and forced the withdrawal of the partisan troops. The subsequent Italian Peace Treaty established Trieste as a 'Free Territory', a solution that pleased neither Belgrade nor Rome. The treaty proposed that Trieste be governed by a representative of the United Nations Security Council, but bickering over the appointment between the Italians and Yugoslavs continued for several years. The territory was thus split into two zones, leaving the city and the surrounding area (Zone A) under joint British and American military control, and the larger south and west region (Zone B) under Yugoslav military administration.[34]

Within Zone A, which was riddled with communist agents, right-wing organisations were encouraged, while the Allied Military Government (AMG), which was commanded by General Terence Airey, who had worked with SOE during the war and then as acting deputy Supreme Military Commander Italy, sought 'the gradual liquidation of all Communist organisations'. British Military Intelligence officers established a special anti-communist security office which co-ordinated its activities with American colleagues and Italian 'Special Branch' police. Its main task was to control Yugoslav subversive activities, but Trieste became a centre for 'Anti-Bolshevist' activities with terrorists, helped by Italian fascists, smuggling weapons into Yugoslavia. Trieste, according to one Military Intelligence officer, was the 'meeting point for the resistance forces inside Yugoslavia and the forces who were financing, controlling and directing them in Italy'.[35]

In November 1945, Tito announced that 'terrorist organisations had been discovered which were led by priests and made up of Ustashi, who had changed their names to Crusaders'. His government passed on reliable intelligence that, with the collusion of the Vatican, Ustashi leaders were using a ratline from Austria to Italy. The Foreign Office feigned ignorance, but it was conclusively established that, in April 1946, disguised as a Catholic priest, Pavelic had left Austria for Rome, where he found sanctuary at San Girolamo. During the summer, Yugoslavia demanded the repatriation of Bishops Saric and Rozman. The Foreign Office, however, favoured the suggestion that the Holy See should 'arrange' Saric's escape either to Switzerland or Portugal, even though this would be 'protecting a man whom we and the Vatican know to be a war criminal of the worst type'. It was known Bishop Rozman had 'collaborated with the enemy' and was subject to 'automatic arrest', but he was allowed to live in comparative luxury in the Bishop of Klagenfurt's palace in the British Zone in Austria. There followed a 'long and ultimately successful campaign' by influential British political and Church officials to 'save the quisling bishop of Ljubljana', even though Rozman was laundering stolen gold on the Austrian black market and using the profits to finance Crusader activities. In November, he slipped away from Klagenfurt, where he had linked up with the Crusader command, and made for Salzburg in 'an American army staff car'. He made for the safety of Italy and the Vatican, but 'before the final arrangements could be made' Rozman disappeared.[36]

The main Crusader network, which was supplied with top-quality British military equipment, was centred on Villach in Austria, where a Pavelic aide, Bozidar Kavran, organised the incursions into Yugoslavia. Two-way radio contact was maintained by a former concentration camp administrator, Dr Vjekoslav Vrancic, with a courier service operated through the Catholic Church. According to Mark Aarons, a senior figure was Srecko Rover, who was arrested by the 62nd Field Security Service unit in the spring of 1946 and transferred to the Fermo DP camp. From Fermo, the centre of the postwar Ustashi revival in Italy, Draganovic organised a major intelligence and terrorist network. The camp's administrative staff were all Croats who 'deliberately' sabotaged and falsified the records of the DPs.[37]

During early 1946, there was 'increased activity among émigrés in organising and planning an anti-Tito uprising'. With Anglo-American assistance, a violently anti-Tito Slovene National Democracy party was created in Trieste as the nationalists worked to co-ordinate their activities. The former head of the Croat Peasant Party, Dr Eugen Macek, attempted to negotiate an agreement among all the anti-communist factions, especially the Crusaders. High-level co-operation by the Ustashi was maintained with their Slovene counterparts led by Franjo Lipovec, who had been recruited by MI6 in Trieste, where he was 'employed on a salary basis' by an Army Intelligence unit. The main Slovene liaison to the Crusaders, until his assassination in 1946 by communist agents, was Professor Ivan Protulipac, while Lipovec remained the contact man with the Italian government and Military Intelligence officers. Italian Prime Minister Alcide De Gaspari assured Lipovec that 'his government would unoffically do everything within its means to strengthen the Tito opposition'.[38]

Tito struck back on 13 March 1946, when the successor to the dreaded Bureau of People's Protection (ONZA), the Administration of State Security (UDBA), captured Chetnik General Mihailovic. He had been betrayed to the UDBA by one of his 'devoted' commanders, Nikolai Kolabic, a former collaborator with the Serbian Nedic government and the Germans. The Yugoslavs tried Mihailovic on 25 March and executed him shortly after.

By mid-year there was a struggle between British and American Intelligence for control of the Ustashi assets. The British went as far as to carry out an anti-American campaign among the émigrés, claiming that many US-recruited anti-communists had been betrayed in Yugoslavia. Released through the intervention of the Americans, senior Crusader figure Srecko Rover was instructed by Veliko Pecnikar to contact an American intelligence officer in Trieste, Col. Lewis Perry, who recruited him to organise a safe route for infiltrating agents into Croatia. Rover was to assume an increasingly leading role in the Ustashi network, recruiting exiles in the Allied zones in Germany, Austria and Italy. Mark Aarons and John Loftus have suggested that MI6 also used these assets 'to destabilise and, if possible, overthrow the Tito administration'. Whether MI6 officers ever seriously considered this option is unclear, though, in the interests of gathering intelligence at whatever cost, they certainly did allow the exiles to run their own political and military campaigns against Tito, their objective being the overthrow of the communist regime. This is a subtle difference which, nevertheless, does not absolve MI6 from its indirect support of terrorist acts.[39]

The British continued with sponsorship of the Crusaders, organising, in August 1946, the dropping of 'a considerable number of pamphlets in Croat territory by planes apparently from the British Zone of Austria'. Signed by Pavelic, the pamphlets declared that 'ceaseless warfare would continue until such time as either Tito or Pavelic was permanently eliminated'. It was intended that the latter would be the victor in 'this death struggle'. Through-out the winter of 1946, Rover was engaged in a new recruiting drive for the preparation of major cross-border operations. This suffered a temporary setback when Rover was arrested travelling through Austria. During February and March 1947 eight arms shipments were made to Franjo Lipovec and the Slovenes in Trieste for forwarding to guerrilla units that operated mainly in the Gorensko and Pohorje mountains, 'clothed in British and American combat dresses'. Supplied with arms by the American Army and with training at Udine, they had use of British camps in Austria 'to which they retire for periodic rests'.[40]

The British government had agreed to repatriate Ustashi and other quislings for trial. From July to October 1946, British Military Intelligence launched a series of operations, known as KEELHAUL, to arrest war criminals and quislings among the exiles in the DP camps. Keelhaul resulted in the arrest of nearly four thousand Yugoslavs, who were then to be screened and delivered to Yugoslavia as part of Operation HIGHJUMP. When the Allies realised the scale of the enterprise, and the lack of money at the War Office for proper continuous screening in the camps, they desperately sought a solution. In addition, there was deep suspicion on the Yugoslav side, where many of Tito's closest advisers and aides were obsessed with the Machiavel-lianism of the British Secret Service. In turn, Stalin repeatedly warned the Yugoslavs about British Intelligence and 'English duplicity'.

Anglo-Yugoslav relations were near breaking point over the vexed question of repatriations. Tito, who was waging an increasingly strident propaganda campaign against Britain and the United States, correctly asserted that Britain was failing to abide by agreements and was colluding, in particular, in the escape of Yugoslavia's most wanted man, Ante Pavelic. A pro-Croat clique in the Foreign Office loathed Tito, but also realised that if the two to three thousand hard-core Ustashi in the DP camps were not handed back then they would launch cross-border raids into Yugoslavia, prompting retaliation from Tito in Trieste and other disputed areas. They also knew that time was running out. The camps would soon be handed over to the Italians, who, concerned with problems of 'banditry', would want the inmates sent back.[41]

'The question was, what to do?' Junior Foreign Office minister Christopher Mayhew recalled that

> Some of these people in the camps were the worst sort of war criminal, others were merely anti-Communists who had taken a wrong turn in the war. But we were pledged by all kinds of treaties and United Nations resolutions to return anyone against whom there was a war crimes charge or a prima facie one of active and wilful collaboration with the enemy. We couldn't send them all back as they'd be executed without trial, and there had already been controversy about the Cossacks in 1945. We needed someone to sort out the sheep from the goats.

In November, a former member of the American OSS, Professor Royse, visited Yugoslavia and suggested the use of categories of white, grey and black to sort out the problem of the screening of the Ustashi. A Balkan specialist, Royse was highly regarded by the Foreign Office's Southern Department. On 22 December, Royse saw junior minister Hector McNeil, and gave a report that prompted the establishment of the War Office Screening Mission (WOSM). It was Royse who suggested to McNeil Brigadier Fitzroy Maclean as a candidate to lead the Mission. Mayhew concurred: 'Maclean, who spoke the languages, knew the political background, and could sort out a war criminal from a tough anti-Communist fighter, Croat, Ustase or whatever.'[42]

Maclean's WOSM, later called the Special Refugee Screening Commission but better known as the 'Maclean Mission', was to screen and sort out the confused political and ethnic affiliations of some twelve thousand Yugoslav prisoners held mostly in Germany, and to look for war criminals. His remit, however, conflicted with the hidden policies of some sections of the Foreign Office and MI6, which by 1947 were quite prepared to turn a blind eye and even help the Vatican smuggle the Ustashi out of Europe by reclassifying 'blacks' (known war criminals) as 'greys' (Nazi collaborators). Maclean was an obstacle to this manoeuvre, but found that he was often circumvented by higher authority. As Maclean's biographer acknowledges, the western Allies changed the rules at every turn during the screening process, while the most wanted Ustashi had already made good their escape from the British-controlled zones in Austria and Italy.[43]

The Yugoslavs were, in turn, incensed by the presence of 'anti-repatriation agitators' in the DP camps. Even before Maclean started, the situation had been inflamed when, in January 1947, a Yugoslav vice-consul visiting the Eboli camp to identify the 'most wanted' was surrounded by a hostile crowd of Chetniks and murdered. According to (Lord) Peter Carrington, who was responsible for a camp in the Rhineland, the behaviour of the Chetniks and Ustashi in the camps, which were set up and largely administered, often without guards, as their own city states, was 'appalling'. 'Murder between the factions was frequent. Atrocities against the local population if, as sometimes happened, the inmates of the camps went on unauthorized sprees in the countryside, were equally common.'[44]

The Yugoslav government had been particularly angered by the decision of the British to supplement their Army of the Rhine with four hundred troops of the Royal Yugoslav Army (RYA) in the form of a Civil Mixed Watchman's Service. Their principal task was to act as a labour unit, but to the Yugoslavs it was naturally seen as a recruiting pool and potential threat. Yugoslav protests were met with British refusals to disband the Watchman's Service. British Intelligence was also running in Germany a group of Serbs loyal to the collaborator General Damjanovic. Most had served in the Serbian quisling administration or in Chetnik formations fighting alongside the Germans; others, such as Ljenko Urbancic, were former members of the quisling Slovene Domobrans. Only a handful were handed over to the Yugoslavs, despite being automatically placed on the 'black' list, while many were simply allowed to 'escape' from custody before the proposed transfer of the camps to Italian control.[45]

The Maclean Mission's intelligence officer, David Haldane Porter, believed that the British had encouraged and protected Damjanovic's supporters. They had proclaimed themselves 'ready to take part in the Third World War under the leadership of Great Britain and the United States of America against Soviet Russia' and had been 'engaged in dissident and subversive activities since the end of hostilities', apparently with the 'blessing of the Allied authorities'. In Italy, where the Serbs had their own guards at the Eboli camp, Damjanovic had organised his fanatical supporters into military formations which Porter understood 'were formed not for disciplinary or administrative reasons, but in order to establish a new army to continue the fight against Communism in general and the present Yugoslav Government in particular'. Although, officially, they had been disarmed when they surrendered, the group had access to a hidden cache of arms and even had their own wireless transmitter which broadcast to Yugoslavia with the message 'we're coming to get you, you bastards'. When they did venture into Yugoslav territory, security troops were waiting for them. A number of Serbs in the uniform of the RYA were trapped, arrested and later executed.[46]

During February 1947, Maclean began working in Rome on the list of wanted Croats, most of whom, including Ante Pavelic, were being protected by the Vatican's 'DP Resettlement Chief', Krunoslav Draganovic, Secretary of San Girolamo. The Yugoslavs had demanded Draganovic's extradition because of his role in the 1942 summer offensive in the Kozara mountains in western Bosnia. Maclean later recalled that many people in Rome knew that Draganovic was working to transfer Croats via a ratline to Genoa and then to South America; within the intelligence community, it was 'an open secret'. Major Stephen Clissold of the Intelligence Branch of Maclean's Mission, who as a young British liaison officer had served with Evelyn Waugh in Croatia during the war, submitted a report on Draganovic to the War Office. It revealed that the priest had handed out false identity documents to some of the most notorious Ustashi war criminals who had travelled in disguise to San Girolamo, where the production of ID cards was a thriving industry. Thus, able to obtain Italian residence permits and other documents, they were allowed to receive genuine exit papers from the International Red Cross (whose Croatian representative was Draganovic) and entry visas from the South American embassies with which Draganovic had numerous contacts.[47]

Draganovic's ratline was partially funded by Pavelic's gold, but he had many paymasters and would take money from any source, playing one intelligence agency off against another. Clissold believed that funds were provided by the Vatican's charitable organisation, the Assistenza Pontifica. It was accepted by Maclean's liaison at the Foreign Office, Mark Wallinger, that the Vatican

> has permitted the encouragement, both overt and covert, of the Ustashi. This wholly undesirable organisation has not only been collectively responsible for vile atrocities on an immense scale during the war but has ever since its inception made use of murder as a normal political weapon. There is surely all the difference between shelter to, let us say, a dissident Slovene priest, and giving positive aid to a creature like Pavelic.[48]

A key figure in the Vatican – the 'scarlet pimpernel' – was the pro-fascist Bishop Alois Hudal of the Pontificio Santa Maria dell'Anima, a Slovene by birth and close to Archbishop Stepinac, the notorious prelate of Zagreb. Hudal's prime role was the supply of travel documents, 'identity certificates' to 'stateless and displaced persons'. The Collage Croatto on Pizza Colonna in Rome, a seminary for Yugolsav priests who were adherents of Pavelic, was a crucial sanctuary for wanted war criminals and collaborators. The main go-between and organiser of this particular ratline, whose success depended on access to Red Cross documents, was again Dr Draganovic. One end of the network was run by Dr Brancko Jelic, who was finally released from British detention in December 1945 and given three months to leave the country. The Foreign and Home Offices preferred to 'let sleeping dogs lie', however, and over the following two years, with the aid of his brother, who had escaped from the communists, Dr Jelic helped run the London end of an escape line to the New World for wanted Ustashi. It is unlikely that Jelic's activities could have been undertaken without the knowledge and endorsement of MI6.[49]

While the Maclean Mission intelligence section had penetrated San Giro-lamo and put the 'Balkan Grey eminence', Draganovic, under surveillance, Clissold and Maclean discovered that at the same time he was being tipped off by someone in British Intelligence, which was 'honeycombed with Ustashi sympathisers who openly co-operated with him'. Maclean later recorded his bitterness that Draganovic 'usually had advance warning of any operation to arrest war criminals; in some cases he was even provided with lists of those to be arrested'. Maclean pointed the finger at a British officer at the Military and Intelligence HQ in Rome for leaking to Draganovic 'details of every search-and-arrest operation'. Aarons and Loftus claim he had close relations with Colonel C. Findlay, Director of the Displaced Persons and Repatriation section of the occupation force in Italy, and his assistant Major Simcock. These contacts proved invaluable, for they were only too willing to assist the priest's clandestine activities. Other officers readily accepted Draganovic's pleas that his 'good patriots' were innocent victims of mistaken identity; though there was plenty of evidence to the contrary. He also played on the hardliners' fears that liberal officers were 'inevitably strengthening the position of Tito's government in a country where 90 per cent of the liberty-loving and Christian population is unanimously opposed to communism'.[50]

In one case, three days after the Yugoslav government had requested his extradition, Ljbo Milos, who had sought sanctuary at San Girolamo, mysteri-ously escaped arrest following a tip-off to Draganovic from someone in British Intelligence. Milos eventually went down the ratline to Argentina, where he became a major figure in the Ustashi's international terrorist apparatus. In March 1947, Major Clissold swooped on the port of Genoa after a reliable tip-off that several wanted war criminals would be on the Buenos Aires-bound SS *Philippa*. Clissold's men arrested sixteen prominent Ustashi, includ-ing General Vladimir Kren, formerly head of Pavelic's air force. The arrests were, however, undermined by the intervention of the Vatican and MI6 supporters in the House of Commons, who pleaded for the release of the Ustashi politicians, including Kren, who was a leading member of Intermar-ium. It was a pattern that would be repeated.[51]

Maclean's Mission did manage to reduce the full list of suspects to between five hundred and a thousand suspected 'blacks', and in February and April about forty to fifty 'quislings' were returned to Yugoslavia. Allied Military Intelligence units then carried out a series of operations in the DP camps under various code-names. In April, they launched Operation BACKHAND at the Fermo camp, with those arrested being sent to the British-run Military Prison and Detention Barracks in Rome. Professor Royse of the Inter-Governmental Committee on Refugees (IGCR) noted that a 'military oper-ation similar to that at Fermo' was necessary in order to remove about forty Ustashi from Bagnoli before the IGCR could take over the camp; an essential precondition for the return of the country to Italian rule. In May, Operation CROSSLINE resulted in the arrest of a number of key Ustashi at Bagnoli. These included Srecko Rover, who was sent to Rome where, to the dismay of the Maclean Mission, he was unconditionally released and allowed to continue his work with the Crusaders, as deputy to Bozidar Kavran, at the Trofaiach terrorist base.[52]

Another member of the Maclean Mission, Annette Street, recalled that 'my section certainly never caught anybody, and I doubt if many people were brought to book'. In practice 'greys' were released unconditionally and allowed to solicit international assistance, including emigration to other coun-tries. The British seldom arrested or consented to the handover of any Yugo-slav who had assisted them, though the United States political adviser in Rome believed that similar consideration was not shown to American agents. 'British interrogation of arrestees has centred more around American intelli-gence plans and operations than around patriotism or otherwise of the indi-vidual concerned.' Bitter feuding took place between the British and American intelligence agencies over control of the Ustashi assets and operations, but it did not last long. By the summer of 1947 they began to co-ordinate activities as the Americans started to develop their own networks in eastern Europe.[53]

During June, the British had second thoughts about the repatriations because of reports of the harsh treatment received by those that had returned. A secret policy was endorsed by the Allies, which meant that future screen-ings would be undertaken by a Joint Review Committee. This proved to be more sympathetic towards the refugees, with the result that many escaped judgement and found sanctuary with 'the Good Father', Dr Draganovic, before travelling down a ratline and taking permanent refuge in Argentina. Argentine dictator Juan Perón was keen to build up the rabidly anti-communist Croats into a praetorian guard and issued thirty-five thousand entry visas.[54]

The major runners of ratlines were fugitive war criminals and collabor-ators from the former pro-fascist Intermarium states which were now under communist control. These escape lines were ultimately controlled – since they had penetrated them so thoroughly – by the Allies, and it was known at the time that British Intelligence, helped by the Vatican at 'the highest levels', was the most active participant. The American ambassador in Belgrade, John M. Cabot, who knew a great deal about the wartime activities of the Ustashi, was 'disgusted' that the Allies appeared to be employing 'the same men we so strongly criticised the Fascists for using'. 'It is crystal clear', Cabot wrote in June 1947, 'even on the basis of material available in this embassy's files that we have flouted our own commitments and that by our attitude we are protecting not only Quislings but also [those who] have been guilty of terrible crimes committed in Yugoslavia.' He noted that 'we are apparently conniving with the Vatican and Argentina to get guilty people to haven in the latter country'. He might have been thinking of Nikola Rusinovic, a leading Ustashi ideologue and quisling, who had wartime 'special responsibilities' for organising joint counter-insurgency operations with the Italians against Tito's partisans. The Yugoslav War Crimes Liaison Detachment had requested his extradition but it was officially turned down because US Military Intelligence officials were using Rusinovic as a source of information.[55]

In June 1947 a top-secret (FAN-757) cable had been communicated through military channels to the British authorities in which the US State Department agreed in writing to using the Vatican to smuggle collaborators out of Italy to Argentina. In December, Foreign Office official Victor Perowne wrote that 'His Majesty's Government have asked the Vatican to assist in getting Greys [i.e. Nazi collaborators] to South America, although they are certainly wanted by the Yugoslav Government'. American officials noted that 'some arrangement has been worked out with the Vatican'.[56]

During June 1947, a US Counter-Intelligence Corps (CIC) officer, William Gowen, who instigated a high-level investigation, code-named Operation CIRCLE, into the murky ties between the Vatican and the fugitive collaborators, was given access to the San Girolamo files which contained the identities of twenty Croatian war criminals being sheltered by the Vatican. Gowen subsequently informed a senior US intelligence officer in the Rome headquarters, James Angleton, about the material. Angleton shared the building with members of MI6 who, unbeknown to Gowen, were working with Angleton on the second floor 'to hide the Nazis from the CIC on the first floor'. Gowen discovered that the man running the San Girolamo-based ratline, Dr Draganovic, had 'high-level connections with British Intelligence' and that his network was being funded by MI6, which had taken it over from the French. Further, the Americans had agreed to share the financial burden. He submitted his report on 6 July, and on the following day the CIC obtained permission to arrest the leaders of the Croatian ratline and to 'take Pavelic into custody on sight'. The MI6/Angleton team then 'rushed to control the damage' caused by the Gowen report.[57]

The Foreign Office did finally move against Pavelic, but bureaucratic manoeuvres, largely influenced by the fact that British Intelligence had helped to protect him, ensured that the process was painfully slow. Pavelic was able to use his close relations with the Italian police, which had existed since the thirties when they sponsored him in exile, to avoid the attentions of Yugoslav agents. Although there was reliable and accurate intelligence on his where-abouts and movements, the CIC received an official 'Hands off Pavelic' notice, and the order to arrest him was quietly sabotaged by American agents acting on behalf of British Intelligence. In September, Pavelic left Italy with a Red Cross passport, arranged by Draganovic, in the name of a Hungarian, 'Pablo Aranyos', for Argentina, where he was employed by Perón as a 'security adviser'.[58]

Among other Ustashi war criminals identified by the Maclean Mission as being spirited away by Draganovic and his acolytes, according to Aarons, were: Father Dragutin Caber, an officer in Pavelic's personal bodyguard who presided over a massacre of Serbians; Dragutin Toth, Pavelic's Minister of Finance; Lovro Susic, his Minister of National Economy; Vilko Precnikar, a general in his bodyguard; and Vjekoslav Vrancic, responsible for Croatia's concentration camps and secret police. During the last half of 1947 the ratline was temporarily transferred to Trieste and the safety of a joint British / Ameri-can intelligence team. Subsequently, William Gowen was set up, smeared and accused – wrongly as it turned out – of helping to smuggle into the United States a Hungarian fascist collaborator, Ferenc Vajta.[59]

As Pavelic's men were escaping justice in Europe, Tito's security police moved against the head of the Roman Catholic Church in Croatia, Archbishop Stepinac, who was accused of collaboration with the Ustashi. A supporter of the NDH, though a critic of Ustashi excesses, Stepinac was the first senior Church dignitary to be imprisoned by an East European communist govern-ment, and there was 'a feeling that he had been arrested less for his wartime contacts with Pavelic than for his public denunciation of the anti-Church campaign in Yugoslavia'. The result was that the British were even more reluctant to send people back to Yugoslavia, and the rules on the Joint Review Committee were tightened even further. This effectively meant that there would be no more repatriations, and by November 1947 British forces had abandoned any semblance of searching for wanted Yugoslavs. Soon after, Bishop Saric 'escaped' Yugoslav justice by crossing the border into Switzer-land, to be followed by Bishop Rozman to the American Zone in Austria and eventually to the United States.[60]

At the same time, Tito's government instigated a series of political trials which 'revealed' the hand of British Intelligence behind every setback or internal dispute. The accused were charged, 'not with opposition, which was their real crime, but with passing state secrets, or slanderous information, to foreigners. The evidence published at the trials suggested that they had done no more than talk to their British or American friends in a manner critical of the regime.' The Serbian leader of the People's Peasant Party, Dr Dragoljub Jovanovic, who had criticised the government's policies on co-operatives and over-reliance on the Soviet Union for foreign policy, was arrested, charged and imprisoned for nine years for conspiring with British agents to organise a Serbian and Croatian 'peasant block' against the government. One of the alleged British agents was Hugh Seton-Watson, who was accused of giving instructions to Jovanovic on behalf of 'the British Intelligence Service', an accusation that Seton-Watson publicly denied.[61]

The Maclean Mission eventually wound down its operation and was relocated to the British Intelligence centre at Herford, in the British Zone of Germany, where it dealt with DPs and oversaw the legal hearings into their cases. The Mission's impressive card index of wanted war criminals, based on information provided by the Yugoslavs and from their own interrogations, was combined into voluminous files on collaborators' past and present activities. These were used to track those war criminals who had disappeared, though, in fact, virtually no screening had been undertaken in Germany. In reality, the Foreign Office put legal obstacles in the way of extradition. The case against the Yugoslav traitors 'must be strong enough to justify the presumption that they would, if tried in a British court by British standards of justice, be both sentenced to death and executed'. This was not a problem for the man tasked with examining the approaches made by the Soviets and the satellite countries for the extradition of alleged war criminals. The President of the Extradition Tribunal, in Hamburg, was Archibald Lyall, an MI6 officer who was sympathetic to the Serbs.[62]

Lyall was a slightly Bohemian character, with a taste for 'tarts and prostitutes' and a definite air of mystery. 'There were, of course,' according to friends, 'a great many Archies; one doubts whether any of even his closest friends knew all of them.' He became a barrister but rarely practised. Pronationalist, Lyall went to Spain in 1937, where he reported on the war trials by the Spanish Nationalists and became a great friend of a Carlist, Peter Kemp, who would also join him in MI6. At the outbreak of war, he was employed by the War Office to write a phrase book for soldiers. During his trip through the Balkans, Lyall had worked at the Dragutin Subotic School of Slavic Studies, and had become friendly with a number of Serbs. In February 1940, he was appointed press attaché in Belgrade, and then two years later became head of the Yugoslav section of SOE in Cairo. The following year, he transferred to the Psychological Warfare Bureau in Jerusalem, creating propaganda in support of Mihailovic. He subsequently moved to SOE headquarters in Bari and served in Belgrade, the Middle East and Italy.[63]

In November 1945 Lyall transferred to the Control Commission in Vienna, where he served with the Legal Division of the British Element of the Allied Commission in Austria dealing with war crimes. Although he actually had little legal experience in court, he was appointed a judge in the military court in Klagenfurt. According to his friend, Michael Sykes, Lyall regretted that a number of DPs, 'whose only crime was anti-communism, went to their deaths. But it was not too late for Archie and his tribunal to save some of them ... he derived much satisfaction in throwing out cases lacking strong evidence.' In 1948, Lyall was posted to Trieste under a cover post as Deputy Director of the Information Services for the British Element of the Allied Military Government, and two years later was made Director of the Public Information Office.[64]

The fanatical followers of Damjanovic were among the last to be screened. Approximately one thousand suspects were dealt with by the Maclean Mission, and this figure was reduced to a select group of forty-four, including Ljenko Urbancic, whom Yugoslav authorities regarded as 'one of the most ardent propagators of collaboration with Germany in the armed struggle'. By the spring of 1948, the forty-four cases had been cut to six and, even then, four of these were reopened following the intervention of British Intelligence because one claimed to have 'three volumes of captured communist documents, hidden in Germany and Italy, which we should not be able to get, if we handed him over'. The 135 interrogated at Munster by Major Clissold were reduced to only eighteen, but fourteen managed to 'escape' before the repatriation date. According to an American report, in a similar episode a group of Dimitrije Ljotic's Zbor movement was transported towards the Yugoslav border but owing 'to careful British planning, all managed to effect escape during the course of the journey and became widely dispersed throughout the US Zone of Germany'.[65]

In March, Bozidar Kavran's deputy at the Trofaiach Crusader base in Austria, Srecko Rover, took charge of the incursion operations that were designed to rouse anti-communist Croats to revolt against Tito's government. During Kavran's absence, Rover was responsible for all aspects of the missions, overseeing the secret radio channels to men already inside Yugoslavia and guiding new groups across the border. The Crusaders boasted of having between 40,000 and 300,000 guerrillas in the Papuk mountains, but this was almost certainly a gross overestimate. In June, as an active member of the Ustashi Revolutionary Organisation and in order to seek recognition for the Ustashi's political front, the Croatian State Committee, Aarons reveals that Rover approached American CIC agents in Frankfurt to request training and communications equipment for his recruits. By the summer, however, when Rover launched the last disastrous Crusader incursion into Yugoslavia, code-named GUARDIAN, there was no effective underground, and any prospects of success had disappeared.[66]

During 1948, Yugoslavia's efficient security police effectively destroyed the Crusaders. The exile groups were thoroughly penetrated by its *agents provocateurs*, and the Yugoslavs were well aware of their plans, including their secret radio codes. In the radio deception game that followed, Ustashi guerrillas were lured to prearranged meeting points, where they were either killed or detained by Yugoslav security troops. Late in the year, there were several trials of Slovene White Guards, Croatian Crusaders and Serbian Chetniks, which revealed that many of their leaders were notorious war criminals. In August, over ninety members of the western-sponsored Crusader terrorist group were brought to trial in Zagreb, including a number who had 'escaped' from British custody.[67]

The Foreign Office had already dismissed the encouragement of anti-Tito groups and guerrilla incursions as 'undesirable', and MI6 had withdrawn its support, primarily for financial reasons. There was a recognition that Tito controlled the secret police and army, 'so that any uprising or civil war in Yugoslavia would either be crushed by the Yugoslav Communists or taken advantage of by the USSR'. The crucial reason, however, was the announcement of the Tito–Stalin split and the subsequent change of British policy during the autumn of 1948 to one of 'masterly inactivity' over Yugoslavia. As a result, the former Foreign Office Permanent Under-Secretary, Lord Vansittart, who was 'babysitting' a Ustashi group that was close to MI6's anti-communist section R5, immediately dropped the London-based Yugoslav National Committee, which was responsible for promoting the Ustashi cause.[68]

Likewise, the American President and his National Security Council had also decided against further support of guerrilla warfare in Yugoslavia, but that did not stop a faction of the Office of Policy Co-ordination (OPC)/ Central Intelligence Agency (CIA), which possibly did not believe the reality of the Tito–Stalin split, from adopting, at the end of the year, 'the highly dangerous policy of staging an anti-communist uprising to overthrow Tito and install a Western-style government'. The OPC/CIA began to infiltrate into Yugoslav right-wing exiles, mostly Serb Chetniks, who were 'conspicuously clothed in American Air Force uniforms'. The operation was a disaster. They were quickly picked up by the security police and imprisoned, but not before they were paraded through Belgrade where they were recognised as former Ustashi and Chetnik collaborators. When these secret operations were uncovered the Foreign Office angrily dismissed them as 'idiotic American behaviour' which played 'straight into the Soviet hand'.[69]

The Ustashi leadership recognised that the complete collapse of the Crusader operations had ended this phase of their paramilitary campaign. Their efforts were now geared towards helping their members migrate from Europe to safe sanctuaries in South America and the white Commonwealth countries. They were helped by the decision in July 1948 of British Foreign Secretary Ernest Bevin to stop all war crimes investigations and trials. On 26 July, his Under-Secretary of State for Foreign Affairs, Christopher Mayhew, made a statement in the House of Commons which effectively blocked further requests for repatriations and thereby closed a dishonourable episode. Most of the Ustashi, such as Ljenko Urbancic and Vjekoslav Vrancic, were allowed to escape into the protective custody of the Vatican. During their investigations, Fitzroy Maclean and his team found evidence implicating United States Intelligence in many of the successful Ustashi escapes to South America. Others, such as Branislav Ivanovic, were helped to seek new lives and pursue their political objectives in the British Commonwealth, principally Canada and Australia. A Commonwealth Investigation Service report said Ivanovic was 'very anti-communist' and that he had 'worked with the intelligence services of England and America whilst domiciled in Austria'.[70]

The man who had organised the last raids into Yugoslavia, Srecko Rover, successfully applied for International Refugee Organisation (IRO) assistance, and in September 1948 was accepted as eligible for resettlement. As Mark Aarons notes, astonishingly he was given the post of Chief of Police for the IRO, a position from which he was undoubtedly able to help his fellow-Ustashi. When Rover emigrated to Australia, the British government denied the documented claim that he had worked for their intelligence organisations.

Pavelic's right-hand man, Artukovic, eventually fled in 1949, via Ireland, to the United States, where he lived in Los Angeles as a free man. Although his true identity was discovered and deportation proceedings were instigated, Artukovic managed to resist their implementation.[71]

In Argentina, Pavelic founded, in 1956, a new Ustashi terrorist group, the Croatian Liberation Movement (known by its Croat acronym, HOP). The following year, he was wounded in an assassination attempt, believed to have been masterminded by the Yugoslav secret police. He settled secretly in Franco's Spain, where he died in Madrid in December 1959. The HOP leadership then passed to Stejpan Hefer, a Croatian lawyer who had fled his homeland to Austria in 1945. The Yugoslav government had requested his extradition in August 1946, but the British authorities claimed not to know of his whereabouts. Hefer surfaced a year later in Italy and travelled down the ratline to Argentina, where he resided until his death in 1973.[72]

Much to the consternation of western intelligence agencies, in September 1967 the architect of the ratline to South America, Krunoslav Draganovic, suddenly disappeared behind the Iron Curtain, turning up unexpectedly in Yugoslavia. HOP leaders believed that he had been set up by Yugoslav security police as part of an elaborate entrapment operation. Draganovic denied this, claiming that he had returned 'deliberately and freely'. This strange episode remained unexplained at the time of his death in June 1982.[73]

Despite their bloodstained background, the exploits of the Ustashi continue to be praised by nationalist politicians. In April 1996 the President of Independent Croatia, Franjo Tudjman, who was accused of trying to white-wash the history of the Ustashi, said that the remains of Ante Pavelic should be returned to his homeland. Disturbingly, fascist slogans from the Pavelic era were being used at medal ceremonies for police and militia. One official said that 'there's a lot of rewriting of history going on here'.[74]

CHAPTER 19

THE MUSKETEERS IN ALBANIA

Proclaimed King Zog in 1927, Ahmed Bey Zog was a member of a powerful family from the Mati region in central Albania. Three years previously, he had seized power – some accounts suggest with British Military Intelligence help – by overthrowing the Orthodox Bishop Fan Noli, who had tried to carry out social reforms, including land redistribution, that alienated the chieftains who controlled the regions. Ruling in a lavish style, which contrasted sharply with the poverty of his subjects, Zog ran what Julian Amery called a 'wonderfully liberal dictatorship', though others experienced it as authoritarian indeed. When Italy invaded Albania in April 1939, the King fled (along with a chest of gold bars looted from the national treasury) to exile in France, but with the French defeat he was forced to move to London – not, however, as a monarch driven by the Axis powers into exile from an allied country, but as a private refugee. There was no Albanian government-in-exile and no prospect of one. His influence on the Foreign Office was reliant on the pressure applied by private citizens such as Mrs Aubrey Herbert, whose husband had once been offered – as had a number of western politicians – the Albanian Crown.[1]

Nor was there any prospect of an internal revolt against the Italians. The fact was that there was a lack of intelligence on Albania, and what little did come through to MI6 tended to be unreliable – a common complaint and one that was sustained during the Cold War. The trickle of intelligence was channelled through Cairo to Margaret 'Fanny' Hasluck, who collated the slivers of information – it would appear – to no great effect. 'It was a commonly held view among those who had lived and worked in King Zog's pre-war Albania that Albania's political destiny was determined by the northern Greg highlanders rather than the southern Tosks. It followed that the key to any uprising against the Italians in Albania in 1941 was thought to lie in the north, among the Greg chieftains and tribes, stimulated from Yugoslavia.' According to Albanian specialist Sir Reginald Hibbert, who served with the Special Operations Executive (SOE) in Albania during the war and was later a Foreign Office diplomat: 'The calculation proved to be false on every count.'[2]

Elizabeth Barker, in 'British Policy in south-east Europe in the Second World War', writes that 'the tiny, remote, mountainous country' on the northwest edge of the Balkan peninsula with a population of little more than a million 'seemed just the right place' for Britain's first experiment in encouraging guerrilla warfare in the region. The scheme was run by MI6's Section D and the irregular warfare specialists led by Colin Gubbins in MI(R). Section D agents, such as Julian Amery in Belgrade, recruited exiles in Greece and Turkey, including one of Zog's strongest supporters in the north, Abas Kupi, who had forcibly resisted the invading Italians – 'for a few hours'. They then positioned arms dumps on the Greek border. On 7 April 1941, a pre-war adviser to Zog's gendarmerie and Section D officer, Dayrell Oakley-Hill, led northern chieftains Gani Kryeziu and his brother into Albania from Kosovo, on the Yugoslav border, with a force of three hundred men. They had 'no assurances of support or supply from anywhere' and the revolt quickly collapsed. Albania proved to be 'less ready or suited for it than its neighbours'. Reginald Hibbert later wrote that the problem was that the country was 'so backward politically, the nationalism was not developed and the peasants were not in a position to be used'.[3]

The only group that had a real chance of organising a cohesive resistance was the Communist Party of Albania (CPA), which had been formed with the help of two Yugoslav communist envoys in November 1941, electing as secretary-general Enver Hoxha. Having been a student in Paris, Hoxha arrived back from France in 1936 already a 'very skilful operator in the mafia-like aspects of communist politics'. In 1942 the CPA formed the Movement of National Liberation (LNC). A number of nationalists were involved, the most notable being the landowner Abas Kupi, although his hope was to rally people to the monarchist cause. The nationalists were unwilling to ditch their hostility to the communists in the interest of a resistance front. Likewise, it would seem that Hoxha was more concerned with ensuring the primacy of the CPA in the Albanian resistance than to draw the widest possible range of nationalist sentiment against the occupier.[4]

In July 1943, Mussolini's government fell, and the collapse brought about a national revolt in Albania. In response, the Germans sent a crack parachute division into the capital, Tirana. Following a crackdown, many Albanians fled to the mountains and into the arms of the LNC partisans. During the autumn, those nationalist leaders who had stayed out of the LNC formed an association of their own, the Balli Kombetar (National Front – BK). A passive organisation, it wanted to avoid useless destruction and wait for the day of national uprising when the Germans would be facing final defeat. Led by a former diplomat, Midhat Frasheri, and Aba Ermneji, the nationalist BK was anti-monarchist and anti-Italian but wished to keep for Albania the provinces annexed by the Axis powers in 1941. In November, Kupi was expelled from the LNC and founded a third movement, Legalite, which proclaimed its loyalty to King Zog.

The Germans played a clever hand in Albania. 'Unable to spare any more troops, the Germans decided to pacify Albania by political conciliation.' They allowed an elderly group of pre-war statesmen to erase the Italian institutions and appealed 'to the type of Albanian nationalist and republican represented in the Balli Kombetar'. To administer 'Greater Albania', the Germans set up a Regency Council of three men who had not collaborated with the Italians – the pre-war Prime Minister Mehdi Frasheri (brother of the Balli leader, Midhat), who was appointed Senior Regent, Lef Nosi and Anton Harapi. Among the chieftains and nationalists 'no single leader raised a voice in protest against the Germans and the make-believe government in Tirana'.[5]

The Germans formed an Albanian army commanded by General Prenk Previsi and a gendarmerie under the Minister of the Interior, Xhafer Deva, a native of Kosovo, the region annexed from Yugoslavia. In Kosovo the Germans established an association of local chieftains, the Prizren League, with Deva as president. From among the Kosovo Albanians four armed battalions were later expanded into a special SS division, named after Skanderbeg, Albania's fifteenth-century national hero. It was used in operations against the LNC and Tito's Yugoslav partisans.[6]

The first SOE liaison officers into Albania were the professional soldiers Lt-Col. David Smiley and Neil 'Billy' McLean. Entering from Greece, they eventually found Enver Hoxha's headquarters and set up a liaison link with the LNC. Strongly conservative and anti-communist in their views, their sympathies were strictly with the nationalists. With another right-winger, Julian Amery, son of Leo, Secretary of State for India and one of Winston Churchill's closest friends, they made up the group known as 'the musketeers' which supported the BK and the Abas Kupi Legalite movement. Other colleagues included Alan Hare, an old Etonian and the younger son of Lord Listowel, Tony Neel, John Hibberdine, Anthony Northrop and Peter Kemp, who all appeared to dislike anyone in SOE who had 'progressive ideas'. They held a minority though highly influential view within SOE.[7]

On 17 December 1943, SOE's Brig. E. M. 'Trotsky' Davies reported to headquarters that the BK and the Zogists 'are co-operating with Germans, who are exploiting them with arms in large quantities, setting them to guard main roads, police towns and lead patrols thus freeing the German troops'. He added that while they had promised to fight the occupiers they had consistently failed to do so. 'I consider the Allies' attitude should be made public forthwith, showing quislings, traitors and non-resisters to Germans will receive appropriate punitive treatment from the Allies in due course.' Davies recommended recognising the LNC as the sole resistance organisation. Even the musketeers were forced to concede that the nationalists 'collaborate with the Germans' and that 'we may be forced to collaborate exclusively with the Partisans' as 'the only military force worth backing in the country'. Three weeks later, Davies survived an ambush by a pro-Nazi BK group. One Albanian specialist speculated: 'Did someone on the Allied side want to get rid of this proponent of LNC support?'[8]

In early 1944 the beginnings of a nationalist coalition were put together with Mehdi Frasheri, Abas Kupi and others, as part of an attempt to crush the communists. There 'was undoubtedly indirect collaboration through the "nationalist" collaborators'. Kupi's organisation in Tirana intervened on his behalf in the collaborationist politics of the capital. According to German documents, Kupi made contact with German officials and told them that he would not fight them, even in the event of an Allied landing. The German emissary to Tirana confirmed that there had been direct collaboration with the BK, extremists who even denounced the British mission of Billy McLean for giving 'an important moral and material contribution . . . to Bolshevism'. Smiley and Amery were regarded as 'agents of the Third International in disguise'. SOE officer and actor Anthony Quayle, in a debriefing report of 30 April 1944, described the BK as 'an undisciplined agglomeration of individuals held together only by their hatred of Communism'.[9]

A July 1944 report by the American Office of Strategic Services (OSS) on Albania – 'Political and Internal Conditions' – acknowledged that 'Xhafer Deva, Rexhep Mitrovic and Midhat Frasheri are with the Germans . . . Anti-semitic measures are being adopted now.' A seized SS document revealed that Deva had been responsible for the deportation of 'Jews, Communists and partisans' to extermination camps as well as for punitive raids by the SS Skanderbeg Division. The small mountain territory had few Jews, so relatively few were captured and killed, though Christopher Simpson adds 'not for lack of trying by the Balli Kombetar organisation and the Albanian SS', which was implicated in 'a series of anti-semitic purges that rounded up about 800 people, the majority of whom were deported and murdered'. The LNC held Deva responsible for 'the Tirana massacres' of 4 February 1944, and other excesses committed by the Gestapo 'in collaboration with the Albanian gendarmerie'.[10]

Anthony Quayle concluded that the right-wing nationalists, who were regarded as 'near-quislings', are 'anxiously looking to the future . . . who will save them now from the revenge of the partisans on the day the Germans leave Albania?' The nationalist reluctance to fight was, writes Reginald Hibbert, 'in historical terms, unforgiveable, and as the war drew to a close it was not forgiven, and they reaped a terrible requital'. The LNC partisan movement had its main strength in the centre and south, and had been weak in the mountains in the north. As the war went on, however, the partisans grew in strength and they began to move northwards, threatening the nationalists.[11]

By the time the CONSENSUS 11 mission, which included McLean, Smiley, Amery and the remnants of another mission, SLENDER (Alan Hare), moved back into Albania in April 1944, the balance of forces had moved in favour of the communists. The musketeers, however, already thinking in terms of the postwar world, wanted increased support for the anti-communist Kupi and the Zogist forces, north-east of Tirana. By the summer, however, units of the BK were integrated into the German command, while Kupi's Legalite movement was regarded by the British headquarters in Cairo as 'not a military factor'. Although there was no support for the return of the King, Kupi continued to indulge in his intrigues and the Germans allowed one of his followers, the northern Greg chieftain Fiqri Dine, to organise a German-sponsored government which soon collapsed.[12]

The only nationalists in Albania to embrace wholeheartedly the idea of building the future Albania by fighting the Germans were the Kryeziu brothers, Gani, Said and Hasan. The Kryeziu movement, however, was quickly crushed, thus eliminating the only effective non-communist resistance to the Germans in the north. When it became clear that the German forces would soon evacuate the country, in late August, Kupi joined General Prenk Prevesi and Fiqri Dine to plan an attack on the Germans, but their forces, typically, 'melted away'. In the last days of the campaign, a motley crew of Zogists/BKs, Dine, Prevesi and sixty armed Albanian troops attached themselves to the Consensus mission. It is not surprising, given the pedigree of the Albanians to whom McLean/Smiley/Amery attached themselves, that Hoxha and the communists were suspicious and, indeed, hostile to the Consensus mission. The nationalist resistance had been a 'fiction'.[13]

By the autumn of 1944, the German forces were pulling out and it was clear that the communists had won the civil war. Amery, however, believed that the game was still not lost: 'I was in Albania at that critical moment. With a very small British or American intervention we could have saved Albania for the West. This is what we did in Greece, after all. British forces stamped down on the communist resistance, bringing up General Zervas and the traditionalists.' In London, the War Office recognised that it was not within Britain's power to prevent a communist government that would look to Yugoslavia and Russia for support. 'We must therefore aim at strengthening our position with partisans now in order that after the war we may be able to influence the partisan government.' The result was that Amery and

Smiley were forced to abandon Kupi. He later made his own way out with Ihsan Toptani, a rich Albanian trader. Recognising their contribution and support in the Kosovo region, Enver Hoxha offered the Kryeziu brothers a place in a provisional government but they refused. Said was eventually evacuated by the British HQ Liaison Mission to Italy.[14]

Viscount Bill Harcourt, who ran SOE operations out of Bari with Force 399 and when stationed in Tirana saw the new regime at first hand, thought Hoxha an extremely disagreeable character: 'a fat, pudgy, self-indulgent fellow with pink and white face. He speaks good French but has a nasty way about him.' Harcourt found Hoxha surrounded by 'a mixture of Communists and plain ordinary bandits'. He told American journalist Cyrus Sulzberger that 'it was decided in the end to back Hoxha because his outfit appeared to be the best of a very bad lot'. It was not long, however, before the Right, just as it would with Yugoslavia and Tito, developed its conspiracy theory. Peter Kemp put the musketeers' case forward in his book *No Colour or Crest*: 'Albania was a totally unnecessary sacrifice to Soviet imperialism. It was British initiative, British arms and money that nurtured Albanian resistance in 1943; just as it was British policy in 1944 that surrendered to a hostile power our influence, our honour and our friends.'[15]

Reginald Hibbert dismissed this as a red herring put forward by people who had failed to understand what had happened: 'The heart of the matter lies in [the] claim that it was British help which brought the partisan leaders to power in Albania – "had British aid gone the other way Albania would be a pro-western democracy today". And he [Smiley] implies that it was commies, moles, liberals, lefties and softies in SOE and among his fellow British liaison officers who were guilty of turning Albanian communists against the best efforts of himself and those of Billy McLean and Julian Amery.' Hibbert puts forward the counter-argument, and a deeply ironical one, that it was Smiley 'who armed and trained the 1st Partisan brigade in 1943, and it was this brigade which led the partisan invasion of the north in 1944, having survived the German efforts to destroy it in the winter. Smiley described the arrival of this brigade in the north as his blackest day in 1944.' The unpalatable truth was that the LNC had popular support and that 'a revolutionary force was released in Albania in 1944 and that was the primary force which swept Enver Hoxha to power'. The Soviet Union played only a minor part. It was, as Hibbert acknowledged, 'not British help but Italian and German violence and destructiveness which brought about the revolution in Albania ... Hitler's disastrous achievement of bringing communism into eastern and central Europe extended to Albania too.'[16]

There is no doubt that the majority of those who gave their support to the CPA were soon disillusioned with the new society ushered in during 1945. There was widespread terror and ruthless persecution as Hoxha cleared out the middle class, Catholics, non-communists, merchants and foreigners

– in fact anyone he thought likely to oppose him – in a series of show trials of 'major war criminals'. Torture appears to have been used against opponents. Britain, the United States and the USSR recognised the new Albania in November 1945. The following month, bogus elections were held on a single list dictated by the CPA, and the resultant assembly abolished the monarchy and declared, in January 1946, a people's republic with a Soviet-style constitution. Thereafter, 'Albanian relations with the West rapidly deteriorated' as the Allies refused to repatriate a number of leading Albanian nationalist politicians – 'war criminals' – who had fled to Allied-occupied Italy or Greece and had been granted the status of 'political refugees'. Hoxha also railed against the West for attempting to undermine and overthrow his regime. Conspiracy trials were used to accuse the western powers of 'sinister intentions towards Albania'.[17]

Behind the communist rhetoric, the twisted paranoia and the myth-making which Hoxha used to batter his people into silent obedience, there did lie elements of truth. Hoxha had reason to be vigilant. When at the end of hostilities SOE officer Squadron-Leader Tony Neel, who had served in the North among the Catholics, and his American counterpart left Albania they are alleged to have said: 'We shall be back in another way.' During the last months of the war, British and American intelligence units in Italy had indeed begun 'to pay close attention to Albania, not so much for itself – though there were many in Britain who hoped to see King Zog, who was living in exile in London, restored to the throne – as for its strategic relationship to Yugoslavia and Greece'. Civil war was about to erupt in Athens, and Yugoslavia's Tito was in the process of grabbing Kosovo with its five hundred thousand ethnic Albanians.[18]

Still commanded by Viscount Harcourt, at the end of the war SOE's Force 399 continued to focus its activities in south-east Europe from its base on Bari. The wartime centre for Italian fascist propaganda directed at the Middle East, Bari had become the Allied headquarters for propaganda warfare. According to Robin Winks, 'BBC bulletins were rebroadcast through Radio Bari and were aimed, for a time, most specifically at Albania'. In London, intelligence files had been maintained 'on the Albanian underground move-ment, as well as on the Society of Friends of Albania – a pro-Zog group – and the more liberal Anglo-Albanian Association'. The OSS Research and Analysis section had also begun updating its December 1943 'Who's Who of Albanian Guerrillas', which identified up to fifty-five guerrilla groups and a hundred different leaders. From early 1944, it was evident, Winks concludes, 'to anyone with even limited access to these files that something was intended for Albania'.[19]

Winks even suggests that in early 1945 'a few teams were parachuted into Albania to make contact with splinter groups; most simply disappeared, though some made their way to Yugoslavia to report on the confused situation'. That SOE was still operational is confirmed by the visit to Bari during the summer of 1945 of MI6 Section IX head Kim Philby. While there, he was 'instrumental in getting a pet bugbear chosen for an airdrop into Yugoslavia; but instead of breaking his neck he covered himself in glory'. Operations may have continued until the summer of the following year, when SOE was officially disbanded.[20]

Albania had come under increasing Yugoslav influence but, British Intelligence reported, it was also receiving help from a large number of Soviet 'advisers'. In March 1946, the Foreign Office detected 'a close parallel between the present penetration of all spheres of administration by the Russians and the same process carried out by the Italians prior to 1939'. The only question seemed to be whether 'Albania would remain a sub-dependency of the Soviet Union or would succeed in raising itself to vassal status proper'.[21]

In June, one of thirty-seven Albanians 'confessed' at his trial that the head of the British Military Mission in liberated Tirana, Lt-Col. Alan Palmer, had given him instructions before he left to keep in touch after the victory of the communists with nationalist leaders Fiqri Dine and Muharren Bairaktar. He added that a British liaison officer, Major Arnold, had even suggested the assassination of Hoxha. Against this backdrop of anti-British propaganda there had been talk of replacing the Mission with a legation, but it came to nothing. Relations with Britain finally ended on 22 October 1946 when two British destroyers, *Saumarez* and *Volafge*, struck mines in the three-mile-wide Corfu channel, seriously damaging the ships and killing forty-three men. In reprisal, Britain retained ten million pounds' worth of Albanian gold, lodged in the Bank of England during the war (in April 1949 the International Court of Justice at The Hague found against Albania and ordered compensation to be paid to Britain). The French minister in Tirana, Guy Menant, was now the main source of the few dismal scraps of information that reached the West.[22]

It seems that by 1946 British Intelligence was actively engaged in unofficial planning for operations in Albania, albeit on a small scale. Contacts had already been made with Albanian émigré groups. One of MI6's White Russian agents, General Turkul, was alleged to head an organisation in Belgrade that supported the return of King Zog to the Albanian throne. According to the informed sources of John Loftus, by this time the British and Americans were planning for a possible guerrilla uprising in Albania to liberate the country from communist domination. On the American side, operations were run by the secret Department of the Army Detachment (DAD) out of Frankfurt, with a British Intelligence team under cover of the British High Commissioner in Germany, which had a liaison office with DAD in the I. G. Farben building. DAD operations were overseen by the State-Navy-War Co-ordinating Committee, whose Washington liaison officer to the covert unit was Frank Wisner. A former OSS officer who had been involved in similar wartime operations in Romania, Wisner was a high-powered lawyer who happened to represent the financial interests of a group of wealthy Albanian refugees, members of the BK and the royalist movement, who were seeking redress for the loss of property confiscated by the communists. In 1947, Wisner was appointed by Dean Acheson Deputy Assistant Secretary of State for Occupied Territories, an intelligence rather than a diplomatic post.[23]

In September 1947 another staged spy trial took place in Tirana, during which the accused maintained in court that the British and American missions had encouraged them to start an armed uprising against the regime. Whether this was true or not, former CIA officer and Soviet specialist Harry Rositzke revealed that 'a few trained men', apparently royalists, 'were dropped into Albania in 1947'. The main action did not start until 1949 as a joint British-American effort. The planning, though, began in early 1948.[24]

Before his departure to Istanbul in January 1947, Kim Philby had been told that his first priority was the Soviet Union and 'not to concentrate too much attention on the Balkans'. The reason, it would appear, was that remnants of SOE were still active in the region. Rodney Dennys, who had joined MI6 in 1937 and had received an OBE for his 'double-cross' work in Section V, was operating under the cover of First Secretary of the British Middle East Office in Cairo when a full-scale operation in Albania was first mooted. He later told Nicholas Bethell that in his opinion: 'It was the dying twitches of the SOE. For a moment, years after it had been disbanded, SOE came back into its own, with agents in the field, and in the Balkans, SOE's favourite area.' It seems that members of the disbanded Long Range Desert Group, which had seen more fighting in Albania than SOE, were first approached for such a mission but were 'either indifferent or sceptical about counter-revolution'.[25]

Operation VALUABLE, as the action against Hoxha's Albania became known, was primarily an SOE or, more accurately, an MI(R) operation, mirroring the unsuccessful 1941 venture, and featuring a number of Section D veterans. Initially, the guiding hand was former SOE director Major-General Sir Colin Gubbins, whose 'unusually clear perception of communism' only reinforced his opposition to it. In January 1948, he gave a lecture at the Royal United Services Institute on the wartime successes of 'Special Operations'. MI6 Chief Sir Stewart Menzies was, apparently, 'far from enthusiastic' about launching a major paramilitary operation (such operations tended to carry 'a high noise level' and were difficult to conceal) but agreed 'as a way of keeping happy the ex-SOE "stinks and bangs people" who still enjoyed some influence in the clubland fringes of intelligence'.[26]

The Special Operations Branch, which was directed by Harold Perkins and made up of SOE personnel who still 'lurked inside MI6', had been set up precisely for this situation, but it soon became apparent that it lacked the resources to mount such a major operation. Realising that this might be the case when the war ended, Gubbins had given Gerry Holdsworth a new assignment to build an association of SOE operatives. Gubbins's 'immediate concern was to establish some method whereby people with particular qualifications could be swiftly contacted in the event of a new war or emergency'. Holdsworth, who had been a member of Section D and had ended the war running operations in Italy and the Balkans from Bari, helped found – in 1947 – the Special Forces Club in Knightsbridge. The club acted as a contact point for former SOE operatives and a recruiting pool for future operations.[27]

Although officially retired, Gubbins retained a relationship with MI6 and, in 1948, he and other 'friends' approached Julian Amery with the idea of mounting an operation in Albania. Amery, who was at that stage trying unsuccessfully to enter Parliament as a Conservative candidate, was chosen by Gubbins and Menzies 'not because of his wartime record and connections' – there were plenty of men who had fought in Albania, who had either returned to civilian life or were serving as regular soldiers – but because he was 'available, and he was committed'.[28]

Albania was at the time going through a period of political upheaval, little of which appears to have been known to the West. Contrary to western propaganda, relations between Tirana and Moscow hardly existed, and Stalin seemed content to leave Albania to be looked after by Tito, who treated it as a client state. From mid-1947, Hoxha did develop contact with Stalin, which gave him some hope of holding off Tito's embrace, but Koci Xoxe, the number-two man in the CPA and Minister of the Interior, worked willingly with the Yugoslavs. Albania's exclusion from the Cominform – the only communist regime to be so treated – was interpreted by the British embassy in Belgrade as a sign that Albania would soon be formally annexed by Tito. Albanian communist leaders visiting Belgrade were described by British officials as 'either persons of complete insignificance or else characters out of a farce'. When Xoxe forced out a number of Hoxha's supporters, it seemed that Albania's federation with Yugoslavia, and maybe with Bulgaria, was not far off. Stalin's breach with Tito and Albania's backing of the Cominform in June 1948, however, allowed Hoxha 'to turn the tables on Koci Xoxe just as Xoxe was on the point of eliminating him'. The unexpected news of the Yugoslav expulsion was received with great jubilation by Hoxha and his associates, and Albania was thus able 'to emerge from under Yugoslavia's wing'.[29]

The rift with Belgrade, however, left Albania's economy in a very precarious state and the country physically isolated. It was left friendless in the Balkans and there was no firm Soviet commitment to come to its defence after Yugoslavia repudiated its alliance with the country. An increased sense of paranoia was reflected in the publicity given to a series of spy and show trials. There was, reported the French diplomat Menant, a 'general uneasiness', and a purge of officials with any links with Yugoslavia was taking place. The Sigurimi, the Albanian secret police, controlled every aspect of daily life. During September, Menant reported that there were Yugoslav-inspired insurrections and guerrilla activity among the Shala and Hoti tribes in the north.[30]

Tito undoubtedly wanted to overthrow Hoxha in 1948 so that he could bring Albania into a Yugoslav federation. Hoxha knew this and suspected that Tito was in league with Albania's traditional 'enemy', Britain. During that year, an Albanian 'confessed' that former SAS officer Fitzroy Maclean had hired him to assassinate Hoxha. Maclean was regarded as a 'most wanted war criminal' in Albania, on the grounds that he had masterminded Tito's defection to the West in 1944 by 'turning' him. Reginald Hibbert believes that 'since Fitzroy was Tito's ally, Hoxha would have deduced that Britain was manipulating Tito in its own aim of destabilizing Albania. Hoxha put two and two together. He knew that the British were after him and that Tito was also, in a different way. What was more natural than that he should link the two and then see Fitzroy Maclean as the eminence grise.' It is also possible, Hibbert adds, that the Albanians confused Fitzroy with Billy McLean, 'so like Fitzroy in so many ways', who had actually spent time in the country.[31]

Julian Amery began 'expert lobbying' on behalf of MI6, which ensured that enough funds were available to strengthen his hand. On his return to London from a visit to Greece, Amery had 'the germ of a plan'.

> I hadn't realised how close the communists were to bringing down the Greek government. I had made some study of guerrilla movements from 1939 to 1945 and it was clear to me that the only way to defeat them is to strike at the safe harbours that they often have on the other side of frontiers, either by hot pursuit, which is more normal, or by stirring up a guerrilla movement against the government providing the harbour.

He then began feeding senior Conservative figures and his SOE friends, many of whom had transferred to MI6, the idea that 'it was time for retaliation against Stalin's aggressive activity in Europe'. An operation against the specific 'harbour' of Albania 'would also frustrate [Stalin's] scheme for controlling the Adriatic's entrance . . . he was equipping Saseno Island [off the coast of Albania] with submarines and rockets, based on the German V-2 models, capable of reaching the Italian mainland'. Despite this latter bizarre claim, which was almost certainly disinformation, Amery's lobbying 'struck a sympathetic chord with British ministers and officials'.[32]

Albania was first mentioned at a meeting of the Cold War Sub-Committee of the Russia Committee on 25 November 1948. The meeting was attended by senior Foreign Office officials, Ivone Kirkpatrick, Roger Makins, Bevin's private secretary Frank Roberts, JIC chair William Hayter, as well as Air Force chief Lord Tedder. Chaired by the Assistant Under-Secretary of State and expert on Soviet affairs Gladwyn Jebb, who during the war had supervised SOE, the committee considered a paper, 'British Policy towards the Soviet Orbit in Europe', by Robin Hankey, another assistant under-secretary. He proposed that British policy should go on the offensive but stop short of a 'hot war'. Kirkpatrick thought that, in the present state of finances and in view of public opinion, it would be best to start offensive operations in a small area, and suggested for consideration Albania. 'Would it not be possible to start a civil war behind the Iron Curtain and by careful assistance to produce a state of affairs in Albania similar to the state of affairs the Russians had produced in Greece?' Hankey wondered whether 'it would not be possible to arrange that the operation should be undertaken by the forces of resistance in Albania. We knew that there was opposition to the present regime and it should be possible to make use of it.'

Other members pointed out the difficulties of working with underground movements and that nothing should be done to jeopardise the potential for other 'developments like the Tito–Cominform dispute'. The meeting set up a sub-committee to consider Hankey's proposals in view of the dispute's implications. At the end of the meeting, Lord Tedder said that he thought 'we should aim at winning the "cold war" (by which he meant the overthrow of the Soviet regime) in five years' time'. The committee arrived at no specific conclusion about Albania but did decide 'that our main aim should certainly be to liberate the countries within the Soviet orbit by any means short of war'. The tactics would mirror SOE's wartime operations: 'promoting civil discontent, internal confusion and possible strife'.[33]

In considering an operation against Albania, the Russia Committee decided on 16 December 'that there could be no question of taking action without co-ordination with the United States government', though members worried that 'there was a lack of co-ordination of [American] subversive activities'. Retaliation was to be on a modest scale as the principal problem was Britain's declining resources. Amery's friend and former colleague, Billy McLean, who had just been recruited to the Albanian operation, was advised by a Foreign Office official that 'church mice do not start wars'.[34]

Amery's intentions were publicly laid out on 22 January 1949 in *Time and Tide*. He wrote that 'the position of the Albanian state is particularly precarious. It is desperately short of food, a number of political outlaws are still in the mountains, and news of recent purges suggests that the Albanian Communist Party is deeply divided between Stalinists and Titoists. In the face of a popular revolt the regime would be hard put to defend itself.' Anton Logoreci, a Catholic anti-communist Albanian of liberal views and leader of a small group of exiles settled in Britain since the beginning of the war, disputed Amery's analysis. The wartime head of the Albanian section of the BBC's Overseas Service, Logoreci wrote to *Time and Tide* exposing what he termed the 'naive and short-sighted' idea of destabilising the Hoxha regime. Reginald Hibbert, who 'had lived in north Albania outside of the relatively narrow

Kupi circle', found it 'impossible to believe that circumstances could have been created by 1949 favourable to a return by émigrés and a popular uprising'. He also considered 'the dirty-tricks departments of Western intelligence agencies' to have had 'a very patchy record' with a tendency 'to distort the home team's intelligence assessment and policy-making processes'. It was 'unwise to base the experiment in destabilisation on an assessment of Albania made by the musketeers'.[35]

Against the advice of his spokesman on the Russia Committee, Frank Roberts, by mid-February Foreign Secretary Ernest Bevin had decided that the time was right to support a project 'to detach Albania from the orbit'. On the 23rd, Roberts told the committee that his boss had agreed to the plan. Prime Minister Clement Attlee had been informed about the operation and had apparently given his verbal consent. Bevin 'confined knowledge of both the decision and the execution to Attlee, [Chancellor of the Exchequer] Hugh Dalton and a select few in Whitehall', primarily the Cabinet Secretary, Norman Brook. Once given the official go-ahead by Bevin and Brook, Menzies ensured that within MI6, in order to maintain the 'capacity for plausible denial', the details were entrusted to a very small group of professionals which required that a number of senior divisional heads were excluded. The operation was overseen by a specially set-up committee, chaired by the assistant chief, Air Commodore Jack Easton, with Harold Perkins as head of operations, and a deputy Jessica Aldridge.[36]

Within MI6, the philosophy of the wartime SOE-backed subversion campaigns was gaining ground, even if until this point the exiles had only been used for 'propaganda and intelligence operations'. Operation Valuable was a 'rare exception'. The SO staff believed that 'well-trained agents could organise a guerrilla-backed operation which would then be supplied by airdrops'. In time, they would be joined by local groups, which would eventually lead to a full-scale civil war. 'The trouble that this would cause the Russians would alone be sufficient justification for the operation. But what if the anti-communist revolt in Albania sparked off others throughout the Balkans? The whole basis of the Russian satellite empire could be shattered by an uprising that had its birth in one small guerrilla operation.'[37]

In his study of the Albanian operation, Nicholas Bethell argues that the go-ahead given to offensive action was

> a carefully considered act of policy based on the idea that Stalin would be impressed by a Western decision to act against him militarily, even on a small scale and in an outpost of his empire. It would make him think twice before launching further aggressive enterprises. It might also, incidentally, detach Albania from the Soviet orbit, ending Enver Hoxha's harsh rule and allowing the emergence of a kinder and less anti-Western government.

The problem was that there was no indication of any real interest in mass upheaval on the part of the Albanians. The head of the British Military Mission in Greece, Monty Woodhouse, argued that Bevin was 'misled by inaccurate reports of the strength of potential resistance to Communism within the country'. The mistaken assumption by MI6 was partly due, Beatrice Heuser suggests, 'to the absence of first-hand information about the country, as they had no British or American diplomatic mission there and had to rely on the French and dubious second-hand reports'. In addition, in dealing with Albania, Woodhouse recalled that Bevin was 'uncompromising, having never forgiven the communist government for mining British destroyers in the Corfu Strait in 1946'. He thus 'gave tacit sanction' to mounting 'a disastrously unsuccessful attempt to infiltrate anti-communist agents into Albania in the hope of undermining the Government' for which 'there was little reason to expect it to succeed'.[38]

'The British,' Richard Helms recalled, 'as usual, were short of funds, so they invited the Americans to join the operation.' William Hayter was told to square the American side and in March flew to Washington for a three-day conference. His delegation included Gladwyn Jebb, Earl Jellicoe, ex-commander of Special Air Services/Special Boat Squadron troops in Athens during the revolt, and the embassy's Balkan specialist and local MI6 representative Peter Dwyer. Sitting opposite were Robert Joyce of the State Department's Policy and Planning Staff (PPS) and the Office of Policy Co-ordination (OPC) chief, Frank Wisner. Both ambitious and devious, with ultra-right-wing views, Wisner was, unlike his rival Allen Dulles, a strong anglophile with a romantic sense of the British Empire. Albania was one item on the agenda, which included other political and psychological warfare operations in Italy and Yugoslavia. 'The immediate objective was the removal of a communist ruler ... The longer term objective was the establishment of a Western strategic presence on the Balkan flank.'[39]

The British were apparently struck 'by the enthusiasm of the Americans to catch up with MI6 and embark on covert operations, but were dismayed by the profusion of discussion which exposed the absence of any co-ordination or confident leadership in the American intelligence organisation'. Wisner, it seemed, intended to take on the mantle of leadership. The June 1948 National Security Council (NSC) directive gave the OPC *carte blanche* to fulfil its objective to counter 'the vicious and covert activities of the USSR, its satellite countries and communist groups'. The OPC was nominally controlled by the State Department's PPS, which functioned as the operational arm of the NSC and was the nucleus of America's Cold War effort. It initiated the OPC's 'political action' programmes, often thought up by Wisner, who would 'get them cleared by Bob Joyce at State'. Later, there was intense rivalry with the 'professionals' of the CIA's espionage and counter-intelligence branch, the Office of Special Operations (OSO), who regarded OPC operations as 'chaotic'. Though the head of the CIA might object to 'the recklessness of the covert operations', he would be ordered by State to co-operate.[40]

According to one version of the Washington conference, Joyce had said little when Hayter oulined the MI6 plan to topple the communist regime in Albania. 'He knew the Balkans scene' and 'disliked what he saw'. Wisner, however, was impressed by MI6's plan, as outlined by Hayter, to overthrow Hoxha. Whatever Joyce's personal feelings, he had initially endorsed the views of the army colonels on the OPC's Paramilitary Staff who had pushed the operation, even though there had been 'plenty of doubt about the feasibility of the plan'. At a meeting of the White House–State Department–Pentagon group established to oversee the operation, General John Magruder argued with Joyce that 'Albania was unimportant; a military attempt to overthrow Hoxha would only anger Yugoslavia and Greece alike. But Joyce took the position that slicing off a Russian satellite would have a propaganda impact justifying the risk.' In the end, largely because of the threat of Russian submarines – a recent agreement between Tirana and Moscow involved aid for Albania in return for a Russian right to build a naval base at Valona – the military went along with the idea. As did Wisner, who thought it was exactly the kind of covert action in which the OPC should be engaged.[41]

Albania had become an attractive target for the military planners. Harry Rositzke, across in the CIA, recalled the thinking: 'The rebels in Greece were on their last legs, Tito had isolated himself from Moscow, and the Russians were working hard to stabilize the shaky Hoxha regime in Tirana. The tide in the Balkans appeared to be running against Moscow. Albania looked soft, and a breakthrough there might unsettle the other satellites.' Wisner assured Joyce that the operation would be 'a clinical experiment to see whether large roll-back operations would be feasible elsewhere'. While it took American politicians a few more years to formally articulate the concept, Michael W. Dravis writes that 'by 1949 the action men of the OPC were already seeking counter-revolution, not merely containment'.[42]

Wisner's judgement was initially endorsed by Frank Lindsay, his OPC deputy in charge of a myriad of operations in eastern Europe whose personal and professional success depended on dispatching agents into the Soviet Union. Lindsay was, in the beginning, very 'gung-ho' about the Albanian operation and expressed the view that 'Hayter and MI6 represented the finest traditions of the Anglo-American world'. Lindsay had been OSS's senior staff officer to Tito's headquarters in Yugoslavia and, after the war, chief political adviser to General Sir Terence Airey in the disputed territory of Trieste. He knew the Balkans: 'The Communists were supplying their guerrillas in Greece out of their bases in Macedonia, Bulgaria and Albania. The requirement came essentially out of State: we have to do something to relieve the pressure on Greece by stirring up a little trouble in their own back yard.' A friend of

Fitzroy Maclean, he had long grasped that 'Tito was the man for the West to back'. By the time Lindsay went to work on the Albania operation, plans had already been made to run arms covertly to Yugoslavia, which appeared to be threatened by a Russian invasion. 'Tito told us', Lindsay recalled, 'that he wanted weapons badly, but not overtly, because this would give the Soviet Union a pretext for attacking him. We sent him five shiploads of weapons.' Lindsay, who shared his views with Maclean, would soon become wary of raising the social democrat flag in Albania but, initially, was enthusiastic about the idea.[43]

In March 1949, Julian Amery laid out his ideas on 'Resistance' in *The Nineteenth Century and After*. He suggested that MI6 might not be ready for special operations: 'Our Defence authorities are seriously neglecting this branch of warfare . . . its chief cause is the failure to think of Resistance as a distinct branch of warfare requiring the maintenance in peace as well as in war of a separate Resistance Service.' He argued that it was time to reply 'to Communist revolutions in China, Malaya and Greece by launching insurrections or sabotage campaigns in the Balkans or Turkestan . . . The vital need is to build up a powerful Resistance network behind the Iron Curtain and in threatened areas.' He added that without 'safe harbours' into which 'non-combatants can withdraw beyond reach of reprisal', the Resistance would 'confine its immediate activities to the spreading of propaganda, the collation of intelligence, and occasional acts of sabotage. It will also prepare for a general rising to deal a knock-out blow . . .' To follow through, Amery continued, would require 'a strong cadre of professional resistance agents', but 'successful Resistance cannot be improvised . . . it takes time to train the directing cadre of liasion officers and sabotage experts. It takes time to lay the foundations of local Resistance organisations. It takes time for propaganda to mould the spirit of Resistance in the required direction. It takes time to build up the apparatus of communications and supply.' Was MI6 in a position to meet Amery's requirements? Even without the benefit of hindsight, the answer should have been no. Given the drawbacks, Kim Philby thought it 'surprising that the operation ever got off the ground'.[44]

On 1 April 1949, the US PPS, chaired by George Keenan, assessed the Albanian situation 'in the light of stimulating Titoism as a disintegrating force regarding Communist movements'. Although it considered overthrowing Hoxha's pro-Moscow regime by a pro-Tito gang, 'it was agreed . . . to assist in the setting up of a new regime which would be anti-communist and therefore pro-Western'. The US would make 'full use . . . of the refugee organisations representing the various free movements within the satellite countries. Assistance and, wherever possible, support should be given to elements within the captured countries which represent a weakness in the political control within the Russian orbit.' Two weeks later, Frank Wisner flew to London to inform MI6's Chief that the Americans had agreed to back

Operation Valuable – known under its American code-name as BG/FIEND (the first two letters refer to communications cryptonyms).[45]

The US decision to effectively pay for MI6's Albanian adventures was greeted with relief inside Broadway. At Buck's Club, McLean and Amery were given the green light by Wisner and in a series of meetings with senior Foreign Office officials – Orme Sargent, Charles Bateman and Anthony Rumbold – and with SIS officers – Harold Perkins and Jessica Aldridge, and an old colleague from Albanian days, Alan Hare – they provided background information and details of contacts. Over lunch, McLean and Wisner began to draw up plans and decided that Malta would be an ideal forward operations base, while the Americans, who were supplying most of the finance and logistical support, would use Whelus Field in Libya as a rear base and supply depot. Wisner later remarked that 'whenever we want to subvert any place, we find that the British own an island within easy reach'.[46]

The operation's first American 'commander' was James McCargar, a foreign service officer on loan to the OPC. From a wealthy family with newspaper interests in London, McCargar had served during 1946/7 in Bulgaria, noting communist links with the rebels in Greece. He recalled being summoned to a conference in Washington where

> I remarked on an intricate organisational chart on the wall. One of my colleagues – I didn't even know that he was even interested in the operation – rose and then started his discourse by pointing to the chart and saying: 'I have now worked all this out, and, as you will see, you need 457 bodies for this operation.' He then spoke for forty minutes, without once mentioning the country with which we were concerned. I confined myself to remarking that I didn't think we could find 457 'bodies' and I would happily settle for six brains.

In London, McCargar observed the British approach to the same problem.

> After sitting around a table in a desultory fashion for an hour or two, one Englishman finally said, 'I say, why don't we get old Henry up here? He knows about this.' A day or two later Henry showed up from down in Sussex, and the problem was put to him, he finally agreed to take the task, although he said, 'This will wreak havoc with the garden, you know. Just getting it into trim.'

Even if they appeared amateurish, McCargar recognised that 'The expertise was 99 per cent British. They had so many people who had been there during the war, most of them young and intelligent. We only had American citizens of Albanian origin, none of them specialists in what we were trying to achieve.' The British were initially reluctant to acknowledge McCargar's ingenuity at covert action. 'I believe I'll give this back,' Gladwyn Jebb had intoned after studying a list of his recommendations. Jebb 'held it aloft between two manicured fingertips', McCargar noted, 'like a dirty dog's ear'.[47]

As Gubbins and Menzies had hoped, 'Amery went about his business, cultivating opposition politicians, engaging in just the kind of activities – totally serious in purpose, yet', Anthony Verrier remarks, 'marked by a Balkan touch of fantasy – for which his wartime experiences had fitted him all too well.' During the spring, McLean and Amery took on the role of 'special advisers', and with expenses provided by MI6 undertook a tour of the Mediterranean's exile centres. 'The secret services', Amery recalled, 'asked me to set up the organisation for an Albanian counter-revolution.' The pair had kept in touch with their former comrades and 'attention turned again to those old lists of guerrilla contacts' which British and American Intelligence had kept since the end of the war. A large number were now living in exile: Midhat Frasheri was in Turkey; Abas Ermenji in Greece; the Kryeziu brothers, Said and Gani, and Abas Kupi in Italy. They were to be told that Britain and the United States would sponsor their guerrilla bands, but at arm's length.[48]

As was the norm with exile groups, the three main political movements were at loggerheads. The royalists, notably King Zog and his military commander, Abas Kupi, who led the Legalite Movement in Exile, were opposed to the republican BK led by Frasheri, Ermenji and Hasan Dosti. In turn, both were sworn enemies of the national independents known as Independenza, whose members were mainly pro-Italian Catholic collaborators from the north-west of the country. While they were unified in their fervent opposition to communism and outside interference from neighbours, Greece and Yugoslavia, 'very little else' united them. This was not surprising because, as the US embassy in Rome reported in December 1948, 'each was originally established for the primary purpose of destroying the others'.[49]

There had been, Billy McLean recalled, 'a great panic among our Albanian friends' in late 1947 when Hoxha had put pressure on the Italian government for the forcible return of 'collaborators' and 'war criminals'. A number were arrested and imprisoned in Rome. During November, the former head of the BK, Midhat Frasheri, requested of the American ambassador in Rome that fifty of his followers be allowed to enter the United States to counter communist 'intrigues' in the Albanian exile community. On the list were Hasan Dosti, Albania's Minister of Justice during the Italian occupation; Mustafa Merlika-Kruja, Premier from 1941 to 1943; and Xhafer Deva, who had been responsible for the deportation of Jews. While the US authorities considered Frasheri's request, a number of BK supporters were interned outside Rome, fearful that they might be sacrificed in the run-up to the April 1948 Italian general election. Just after the election, McLean persuaded Foreign Office official Orme Sargent to intervene with the new Italian Christian Democrat government, which agreed to their release.[50]

The US State Department maintained a Political Biographic Section which cross-filed all the reports on the émigré leaders. The section had access to a 1948 publication by the Albanian government which identified the major fascist collaborators and war criminals; these included a number of people on the list of fifty. After checking the biographical files, the State Department replied that it did 'not believe it would be appropriate' to facilitate their entry: 'It is apparent that the politicial backgrounds of many of the Albanian exiles in Italy are somewhat checkered and that the presence of these persons in the United States in the circumstances envisioned might sooner or later occasion embarrassment to this Government.' By late 1948, American intelligence agencies were using these people in their resistance networks, and sought ways around the restrictions.[51]

The United States policy document NSC-50 pushed for 'relationships with anti-Soviet resistance groups', but the State Department had demurred at the thought of getting directly involved. The British, too, had 'already served notice that they had no intentions of again backing into the government-in-exile business'. The solution was the creation of 'private organisations' or 'fronts' with no official sanction which would provide 'plausible deniability' in the event that operations created embarrassing fall-out. Frank Wisner's OPC persuaded wealthy individuals to back the 'Free Europe Committee', which was dedicated to assisting 'political and intellectual leaders who fled Communist tyranny in Eastern Europe', and collecting them together in one body for psychological and political warfare. General Dwight Eisenhower lent his name to the money-raising arm of the projected committee, the Crusade for Freedom, whose president was the former high commissioner in Germany, General Lucius Clay. Registered in the spring of 1949, Allen Dulles's National Committee for Free Europe set up an Exile Political Operations division and resolved to openly support the 'lost abandoned people', as one of the Albanians characterised their assembly.[52]

'Collaborators' and 'war criminals' were brought into the United States as part of the State Department's covert project known as BLOODSTONE, which was initiated in June 1948 and ran through to 1950. According to James McCargar, 'it was [Carmel] Offie who was doing the arranging'. Thrown out of the foreign service for illegal currency dealing, when Offie returned to Germany in January 1949 he became Wisner's right-hand man in the OPC, responsible for all 'émigré liberation projects'. He set about recruiting émigrés, including Albanians, in the DP camps, and then directed their activities when they entered the United States. Although lacking a passport, by April 1949 Hasan Dosti was in Washington urging officials to support an Albanian National Committee in Exile. On 12 May, Robert Joyce took steps to obtain a visa for Midhat Frasheri, suggesting to the State Department's Southern European Division that the Albanian's request 'is considered in the national interest' by 'our friends'.[53]

On 1 May 1949, Perkins, Alan Hare – who 'had perhaps the most chequered and exhausting career of any British Liaison Officer in Albania' – McLean and Amery went to Athens, where the two musketeers discussed Valuable and the prospect of gaining the support of the Greek government for the project with the British ambassador, Sir Clifford Norman. They also talked with Pat Whinney, MI6's station head, who during the war had been deputy to Frank Slocum in MI6's private navy in the Mediterranean, and his deputies Eric McCloud and John Badderley, formerly of the Coldstream Guards. Amery met former Prime Minister Themistocles Sophoulis and other politicians, and argued that the main priority was to close Albania's southern border to deny it access to the Greek rebels. He said that the British intended to recruit BK insurgents in a campaign against Hoxha's regime, and were seeking help on intelligence-gathering and the setting up of arms dumps and bases near the border. It soon became apparent, however, that the Greeks were more interested in their own territorial claims on northern Epirus than in establishing an independent Albania. Amery 'tried to convince them that their territorial claim was counter-productive. They were in mortal danger from their own communist rebels and a policy of annexation just did not make sense. A policy of retaliation did make sense.'

One of Greece's richest men and a leading arms dealer, Bodosis Athenisiades, introduced Amery to the Greek National Army commander, Field Marshal Alexander Papagos, who insisted that the frontiers with Albania and Yugoslavia were closed to visitors. 'An unnamed, unknown pseudo-military mission fossicking about in the north would . . . increase rather than diminish the degree of Albanian and Yugoslav support for communist guerillas and their "Greek Democratic Army".' In essence, this was the view of Albanian exile Stavro Skendi, who wrote that Hoxha 'would exploit to the full any large-scale incursion which came across the border'. While Amery could not gain the direct approval of the Greek government, he needed its tacit support, particularly as Corfu was needed as a radio and listening post. He knew that his lobbying had been partially successful when Bodosis signalled Papagos's consent by leaving six bottles of brandy in his hotel room. As long as the operation did not originate on Greek territory, the government would turn a blind eye.[54]

McLean and Amery outlined their ideas to BK military commander Abas Ermenji. On 20 May, McLean and Ermenji were joined by Harold Perkins and the three flew to Rome for meetings with the seventy-year-old leader of the BK, Midhat Frasheri. While Frasheri was sympathetic, Ermenji raised objections to the involvement of other groups in the project. Unable to change his mind, MI6 moved him out of the way to Trieste, where he was minded by Archie Lyall, who was operating under cover as head of the British Element of the Allied Information Services. At the same time, operation planner Alan Hare was replaced by John Hibberdine, who had served with the resistance among the Catholic tribes of the North. On the 25th, McLean and Amery returned to London where they discussed ideas with Dick Brooman-White, a wartime Section V officer dealing with the Mediterranean who had recently returned from Turkey, and Tommy Last, who had served in the War Office and the army during the war. They also conferred with Foreign Office officials Anthony Rumbold and Charles Bateman, and Conservative politician Harold Macmillan, at the Turf Club. Macmillan, who had worked with Carmel Offie at the end of the war, was a senior figure in the European Movement, which included in its exile section an Albanian committee.[55]

The leading Albanian exiles were gradually being assembled in Rome to form a political committee behind which the differing factions could unite. Amery and McLean had 'a belief in the Rob Roy virtues of tribal leaders' and preferred Abas Kupi, 'a bewhiskered old rascal with a smashing reputation as a mountain raider', whom Amery found in Istanbul. Unfortunately for the British, Kupi's Legalite movement was viewed as 'unimportant' by the majority of Albanian exiles, who also had difficulty fathoming his peculiar dialect. The two musketeers were joined by a friend of the exiles, Auberon Herbert, whose family had been active in pre-war Albania, and the three made a tour of the refugee and DP camps in Italy looking for suitable recruits for guerrilla training. The thirty or so they found lacked basic military training but they were enthusiastic, fired up by nationalist propaganda. Kupi had declared to his men in the camps: 'You are not alone! In Albania there are hundreds of thousands of nationalists in the mountains; the government forces are confined to the towns and cannot go into the countryside; the government has had to proclaim a state of emergency from 10 at night until the morning; some towns are already in nationalist hands!' A proposal was made to raise 'a parachute regiment from this flotsam', but it was never a real runner.[56]

Amery was seemingly unperturbed by French Intelligence reports from its embassy in Tirana that although 'the Albanian population as a whole was largely hostile to the regime and increasingly anti-Russian, they are under complete control and no dissident or resistance movements exist except potentially'. He believed that 'clandestine operations directed at Hoxha would lead to a major uprising' whose success, however, would 'depend on the million odd Albanians living in the Yugoslav Kosovo region'. After a first phase of acquiring operational intelligence, the second phase would consist of a main effort from Yugoslavia. Kim Philby recalled that 'our experts considered – quite wrongly, in my opinion – that Marshal Tito, after his break with the socialist bloc, would adopt a hands-off policy towards any changes in Tirana'. Fitzroy Maclean was approached to act as the go-between with Tito, but advised Bevin that Yugoslavia would not provide support and opposed any such operation.[57]

Beginning in 1949, a great wave of purges hit the eastern European communist parties, the victims being mainly 'home' communists who 'had never been trained in the Moscow school of dialectic and were distrusted by Stalin'. Technically the purge began in Albania with the condemnation and execution of the 'Titoist' Minister of the Interior, Koci Xoxe, on 11 June. This was followed by show trials in Budapest with fabricated evidence of a planned Yugoslav coup. Similarly in Sofia, a number of leading communists were accused of organising a coup d'état in association with the Yugoslavs. 'For good measure a number were also accused of being British agents.' The purges corresponded, Balkan specialist Hugh Seton-Watson concluded, 'to the victory within the party leaderships of the "Muscovites" over the wartime resistance leaders'. Service in the Republican army in Spain was viewed with suspicion, as were 'non-Muscovites' who had been in wartime resistance movements that had come into contact with British missions. The particular target, however, was the Yugoslav Party, which was 'superior in quality than other East European Communist Parties. It was something of an élite.' The result of purging the Yugoslavs in Albania was 'cataclysmic', and though it added to the 'basic instability' within the regime, it 'did not mean the collapse of Hoxha'. Security was tightened once again. The internal security force was strengthened to fifteen thousand carefully selected men, while every police chief from now on had a Soviet adviser beside him. Stalin himself had insisted on the new interior minister, Mehmet Shehu. There were estimated to be a thousand Soviet officers overseeing the Albanian administration.[58]

In June 1949, the second-in command of the Royal Horse Guards in Germany, David Smiley, who had spent much of his wartime career in Albania with the SOE, started secondment number two to MI6 after being approached by the Service's representative in north-east Germany, Xan Fielding, an experienced former SOE officer in Cairo, Crete, France and South-East Asia. Smiley's close friend and contact in 'the Firm' was Harold Perkins, who at the end of the war had been responsible for SO in Poland, Czechoslovakia and Hungary, and as head of the Special Operations Branch was currently running a wide range of anti-Soviet subversive activities. Smiley received a one-sided and partial briefing from 'Perks', who told him that

> the situation in Albania was fluid, the Communists under Enver Hoxha and Mehmet Shehu had gained control of most of the country, thanks entirely to the arms sent to them by SOE and not, as their history books now show, due to Russia – though they received moral support from Tito in Yugoslavia. There were, however, still pockets of resistance where members of Balli Kombetar and the followers of Abas Kupi's Legalite movement had taken to the mountains and were fighting the Communists. If these groups could be contacted and helped with arms and money, they might have a chance of thwarting the Communist take-over.

Told that Bevin 'was very keen on the idea', Smiley realised that there was also the question of Albanian support of the 'Russian-inspired' civil war in Greece. He needed little persuading that 'it would clearly be in the interests of the West if the Albanian conduit could be blocked', but was aware, however, that it would be a difficult task. The few SOE people taken on by MI6 after the war tended to be regarded by the Service's old guard 'as a lot of bungling amateurs'.[59]

Smiley was given command of the planning staff. His friend, Julian Amery, was informed that he had been 'duly entrusted with training those Albanian volunteers who were to be infiltrated by sea into the southern part of the country. The OPC took on the training of another group to be dropped in by parachute to the Centre and North. The prospects were good. The Communist regime was hated and the Albanian people had a long tradition of Resistance.' A number of Albanian refugees who were found in the DP camps were moved to a special school in the British Zone in Germany to be trained by Colonel Brian Franks of the SAS and MI6's War Planning Department, where he had worked alongside Smiley and Perkins. The main body of men, however, was to be trained in Malta. In the meantime, Smiley went to discuss the operation with the local OPC representative in Athens and the head of the British Military Mission. 'Safe-houses' were found in Greece and enquiries were undertaken into the possibility of using Corfu as a forward communications base for the operation.[60]

Because Malta was within the Commonwealth, it came under the 'Attlee Doctrine' and security was thus the responsibility of the Security Service, MI5. Fortunately for the operation, the MI5 representative and Security Liaison Officer on the island was a former colleague of Colin Gubbins. A staff intelligence officer at Eastern Command at the beginning of the war, Maj. Major had spent much of his career in the Military Intelligence Directorate, where he had been aware of Gubbins's special interests. A descendant of Oliver Cromwell, he had been Gubbins's successor at Coleshill, running the stay-behind network in the event of a German invasion, when his friend took over command of SOE. For the Albanian operation, Major had been briefed to secure army and Colonial Office backing for a suitable out-of-the-way headquarters which could house thirty-six men for two to three months. Fort Benjimma had been built during the Napoleonic wars. Standing in wild country on the far side of Medina and away from the more populous area of Valletta, it could be approached only by a rough track. Close to secluded bays where sea landings could be practised, it was an ideal choice. Major ensured that cover was kept, and dealt with Customs over the equipment that was sent in – such as machineguns, pistols and wireless sets.[61]

The supply of equipment was the responsibility of operations quartermaster Frank Quinn, a Far East specialist who had joined the Service in 1946 and was attached to Department Q of MI6, which was tasked with obtaining 'clean' equipment – arms and explosives that were free of markings so as to distance any potential disasters from British sponsorship. Quinn had been transferred to Smiley for special duties at the beginning of 1949 as part of Valuable. He supplied the small arms, grenades and explosives, and trained the men in their use. He was involved in the 'endless discussions which took place on communications'. The station chief in Vienna, George Young, was asked to help, and 'a dreary search took place for [wireless] sets still in working order after four years in store. Finally, sheer necessity produced an expedient almost guaranteed to fail. Communication would be ground to air [the most difficult and unreliable method].'[62]

Quinn also had a role in finding a suitable boat with which to land the guerrillas. Searching the south of England without success, he finally located a boat powered by a twin diesel engine in Malta. Handing over £6,000 in cash, Quinn then removed all the fittings, which might indicate its origin, and renamed it the *Marie Angelo*. Eventually, an elderly sailor aged nearly seventy, Halliday Paterson, was found and flown by MI6 to Malta to captain the *Marie Angelo*. Unfortunately, he soon fell ill and was flown back to London, where he died a month later. Paterson's death threatened the schedule of Valuable but, fortunately, the head of station in Athens, Patrick Whinney, who had operated a secret boat service during the war, had already lined up an alternative crew and boat. The previous October, Whinney had recruited two ex-navy officers, Sam Barclay and John Leatham, to run supplies from Athens to Salonika to help government forces against the communist rebels during the Greek Civil War. He had subsequently persuaded his superiors to fund the fitting of a powerful Ruston-Hornby engine to their boat, the *Stormie Sea*, which was specially adapted with dummy fuel tanks hiding sophisticated radio equipment.[63]

In Malta, the thirty Albanians – who were provided with cover as members of the Pioneer Corps – were met by MI6's Rollo Young and Alastair Grant, an army captain on secondment to the Service. The recruits were taken to Fort Benjimma, where Smiley, under cover as the deputy chief of staff in the Castille, Valletta garrison headquarters, was already in place with his wife. A wartime cipher clerk in the First Aid Nursing Yeomanry (FANY) in Nairobi, Moy Smiley was taken on temporarily to help with the ciphering work. Smiley's radio operator from SOE days in Albania and in Thailand, Bill 'Gunner' Collins, controlled the communications with London. Among those helping train the Albanians was Robert 'Doc' Zaehner, who had served with SOE in Persia. An Oxford professor of eastern religions, Zaehner soon shed his 'mad professor' image and within three months had become fluent in Albanian and Greek.[64]

With the operation barely up and running, there were those who already feared that 'failure was stalking the operation'. Frank Lindsay, aware that Tito had no intention of helping, asked Michael Burke to accept a short-term assignment. The former football star and 'danger-loving' OSS man had served behind German lines in Italy and France during the war before finally working from Grosvenor Square in London, organising the dispatch of agents into Germany. Burke had been the model for Gary Cooper in the film *Cloak and Dagger*. 'Divided between curiosity, loyalty and scepticism', Burke agreed to serve. In July, released by Warner Brothers, he used his cover in Rome as a film executive with the fictional 'Imperial Films' to act as an intermediary between the OPC and the Committee for a Free Albania, and to investigate Italian and Greek locations for the operation, Lindsay asked him to bear in mind that he wanted a detailed report when the operation was over. The OPC also appointed John Papajani, an American of Albanian origin who had worked with Wisner during the war, to the Fort on Malta as an interpreter. Although 'charming', Papajani was regarded as 'unreliable' and 'not a good choice for a sensitive task'. As part of their financial support, the OPC arranged that MI6 would provide £10,000 worth of gold sovereigns packed in wooden cases which were flown by the RAF to Malta.[65]

In early June, OPC officer Robert Low arrived in London to be briefed on the details of the operation by Stewart Menzies. A US Army reserve officer, knowledgeable about the Balkans, having worked with the OSS in Cairo, Low had been an intelligence officer in western Europe during the last year of the war, and then a Time-Life correspondent in Prague. He recognised that 'the United States was for the moment still the junior partner'. It was entirely up to the British 'cousins' to provide local knowledge and political guidance; their men had 'served in SOE during the war and were the world's experts in this kind of thing'. He found that those MI6 officers who had served with SOE in Albania were 'bitter' at seeing their efforts turned against them, in particular the Corfu incident, and despised the Hoxha regime. They had, however, undertaken a lot of planning which Low thought was 'feasible' and made sense.[66]

On 24 June, with another American intelligence officer, Robert Minor, Low flew to Rome with the British team to conclude their talks with the exiles on an agreement for a president and executive of an Albanian committee. The only obstacle appeared to be the agreement of King Zog. According to Anthony Verrier, McLean and Amery 'were pretty sure that Zog would not do' as a figurehead. Amery, 'for all that he saw large issues in terms of right and left, was well aware that the counter-revolution must have a leader who gave lip service to social democracy'. Zog, who had moved to Egypt in 1946, was thus approached only 'as a matter of form'. Agreement was reached on 7 July 1949 between the differing groups that Midhat Frasheri would be chair of the executive of the Committee for Free Albania, which would put the nationalist's case before the world. The King's nominee, Abas Kupi, was appointed chair of the military junta, with Ermenji as deputy and the King's own secretary, Gaqi Gogo, as secretary to the junta and the executive. McLean,

Hare and Harold Perkins then flew to Cairo and joined up in Alexandria with Amery and Low. Seven days later, they met the King, who refused to accept the establishment of the Committee. He was only willing to support their effort after a diplomatic speech from Amery, who said that a referendum on His Majesty's return could take place after the operation had succeeded, while the Committee would remain only a representative body. Low thought Amery's speech masterly: 'I've never seen such diplomacy in my life. He was like Talleyrand. He convinced Zog that he would be best advised "as a firm believer in democracy" to give us his support.'[67]

The local political situation had slightly changed in late summer when the Greek ambassador in Washington put pressure on the American adminis-tration to take action against Albania. The rebels were still active, and among Greek leaders there was an increasing clamour in favour of seizing northern Epirus. The secretary-general in the Greek Foreign Office, Panayotis Pipenelis, who as a leader of the secret, conspiratorial IDEA group of right-wing nation-alists was a major influence on the Foreign Minister, Tsaldaris, warned the new US chargé d'affaires in Athens, Robert Minor, that there might be 'minor incidents' across the Albanian frontier. 'Hawkish' Foreign Office official Anthony Rumbold had no problem with that, but the State Department warned that it could do little about the incursions.[68]

In Athens, on 5 August, Greek Prime Minister Alexander Diomedes told the British ambassador, Moore Crosthwaite, that 'he knew about the proposals for the establishment of an Albanian committee'. Two days later, London advised the Athens embassy of the Committee for Free Albania's imminent formation in Paris, pointing out in all innocence that 'we have watched its development with benevolent approval'. Privately, the State Department realised that there might be problems ahead – which accounted for its demand for the Committee to be kept at arm's length. The US embassy in Athens noted that the 'British government's dislike of the Hoxha regime is well-known and, consequently, eventual elimination of Hoxha, which would arouse no regret in England, might result in the recently formed committee being considered as de facto legal government of Albania'. The Foreign Office cabled the Rome embassy on the 7th: 'We are not playing up the formation of the committee in our publicity, as we do not want to lend any substance to the belief in Yugoslavia and elsewhere that the western powers are behind it.' Dean Acheson gave similar advice to US missions, that the Albanian exile committee came under the umbrella of the Committee for a Free Europe, which was 'a private organisation'.[69]

In the hope that when the Albanian exile insurgents were sent back to their homeland they would carve out a foothold in the country, Frank Wisner sent to London his psychological warfare head, Joe Bryan, a well-born Virginian known as 'the Duke of Richmond', who had covertly funded the animated version of Orwell's *Animal Farm*; Bryan was to co-operate on drafting an announcement of the formation of the Committee. On 26 August, Midhat Frasheri, Abas Kupi and Said Kryeziu announced in Paris the formation of the Committee for Free Albania. Frasheri told the assembled press that 'the present Albanian regime of Marshal Enver Hoxha is so weak that it may collapse at any time'. Despite the request of the OPC, the French intelligence service refused to take part in the launch of the Committee because, according to a former SDECE officer, the Committee was considered to be 'an unrepresentative fabrication'.

At the end of the month, the main émigré leaders made their way to other European capitals to advertise their existence and their cause. In London, they were put under the wing of Peter Kemp, another SOE veteran who had been in Albania and had worked in Poland with Perkins. A confirmed anti-communist, he had fought with the pro-Franco Carlists in the Spanish Civil War, alongside his close friend, Archie Lyall. The Committee received little publicity while in London and was ignored by official agencies, though Hugh Carleton Greene, who was head of BBC broadcasting to eastern Europe, did meet them, and gave them a daily slot for broadcasts to Albania. Whether these were successful is debatable, as the number of radios in Albania was extremely low, with batteries and electricity in short supply.

Joe Bryan did not enjoy his time in London. It seemed a waste of airplane tickets and and space at the Ritz. 'We had a few small triumphs,' Bryan recalled, 'but I never disabused myself of the feeling that we were a bunch of amateurs.' Kupi was installed at the equally expensive Berkeley Hotel, the manager of which was a former member of SOE; here, he was questioned by MI6 minders. Expecting him to be at the forefront of the paramilitary operation, they did not find his answers encouraging. 'Kupi did not', Nicholas Bethell writes, 'intend going in with the first operations.' The roadshow then moved on to the United States.[70]

None of this had gone unnoticed in Albania. Enver Hoxha later wrote that

> We made official requests to the British and American governments for the extradition of war criminals, not only Albanians, but also Italians and Germans, who had stained their hands with blood in Albania and were now under their jurisdiction. Contrary to the declarations and the joint commitments of the allies during the war and the decisions which were taken later on this question, they turned a deaf ear and did not hand them over to us. On the contrary, they kept the chiefs in luxury hotels, while they trained their 'fighting men' in Rome, Munich, London, Athens and elsewhere.

Ignoring the inevitable rhetoric, his analysis of internal Albanian émigré politics was probably accurate.

> Each of the heads of reaction in exile defended the interests of the employer who fed him. Right from the start they began to quarrel, abuse one another and come to blows. Nevertheless, a certain unity was achieved in the so-called 'Free Albanian Committee'. The quarrels, however, continued and the contradictions became more acute. In exile, the 'crabs' were tearing one another to pieces. Quarrels existed not only between the chiefs, but also between the chiefs and the misled individuals, who were caught up in the current of betrayal and who had been promised 'paradise' by the 'fathers of the nation'.

Interestingly, Hoxha adds that 'there were some who repented and wanted to return and a few did so . . .'[71]

The exiles, however, had some reason to be optimistic. During the summer of 1949, the Albanian press and radio began reporting border clashes and other similar incidents. Run-ins were said to have taken place in August along the Greek–Albanian frontier. At about the same time an Albanian member of parliament was killed by an anti-communist guerrilla band operating in northern Albania. There were provocations along the border with Yugoslavia. News of skirmishes continued through to the autumn and, during a tour of the northern provinces, Hoxha complained about the existence of the Committee of Free Albania, 'whose aim was to bring about the overthrow of the communist regime'. A visa had been obtained by Robert Joyce for Frasheri and his colleagues, and in early September, Frasheri flew with Abas Kupi to New York. With Xhafer Deva and Hassan Dosti and several others, they established the National Committee for Free Albania, which was substantially funded by the OPC with money laundered through various foundations. They were looked after by Robert Low and the OPC-backed Committee for a Free Europe, with the State Department keeping its distance. When Kupi returned to Europe, Frasheri stayed in New York to set up a political office.[72]

On 5 September 1949, at the first meeting in Washington of the Council of the North Atlantic Treaty Organisation (NATO), British Foreign Secretary Bevin proposed to institute a counter-revolution in Albania. He was well aware that Dean Acheson shared his views and that the American Joint Chiefs of Staff 'had their eye on Valona, a natural harbour just north of the Greek frontier, as a potential forward base for their fleet in the Mediterranean'. Bevin and Acheson were also aware that this was little more than a rubber-stamping exercise, a decision 'virtually imposed on minor allies who were ignorant of the details and on a major ally who acquiesced to the principle'. Indeed, 'their arguments about ridding Albania of Enver Hoxha reflected decisions which had been taken several months earlier'. Suitably alarmed at intelligence reports of the Soviet presence in Albania – 1,500 'advisers', 4,000 'technicians' to train an army of 25,000, and plans to develop Valona as a submarine base – NATO members agreed in principle 'to weaken the position of the present Soviet-dominated regime in Albania and, in connection with a possible revolt seek, as an immediate priority objective, to eliminate Soviet control'. Even so, as Anthony Verrier has noted, this was an historic decision: 'A military alliance committed to the defence of Western Europe was about to approve an operation on the flanks, not the central front. The operations would be outside the NATO area.'[73]

By the time of the NATO Council meeting 'several hundred people were involved in planning and training for the operation'. The target date had been set for the autumn of 1949, when a succession of moonless nights would provide cover for dispatching teams. The decision was backed up by a CIA assessment on 12 September, which, while it noted that 'a purely internal Albanian uprising at this time is not indicated, and if undertaken, would have little chance of success', concluded that the Hoxha regime was weak and 'the possibility of foreign intervention . . . represents a serious threat to the regime'. A State Department briefing paper prepared for Bevin's visit stated its preference for 'a Western-orientated regime such as is desired by the Albanian National Committee', but noted that 'it could not be expected that Albania would be governed democratically'. The paper recommended 'that the US act in co-ordination with the UK and France*. . . to weaken the position of the present Soviet-dominated regime in Albania'.[74]

US policy on the satellite states was laid out on the 14th in a report to the NSC which invited the American government 'to reduce and eventually to cause the elimination of dominant Soviet influence in the satellite states of Albania, Bulgaria, Czechoslovakia, Hungary, Poland and Romania . . . The time is now ripe for us to place greater emphasis on the offensive.' On the same day, the Albanian plan was discussed formally at a meeting in Washington between the British team of Bevin and Gladwyn Jebb and the Americans, Acheson and his deputy assistant, Llewelyn Thompson. Britain's policy towards Hoxha, said Bevin, was one of 'unrelenting hostility'. He asked whether the Americans 'would basically agree that we try and bring down the Hoxha government when the occasion arises' or incite it to become a Titoist-type deviationist government. Acheson replied that a policy of eliminating Hoxha made more sense than attempting to lure him down the Titoist path.[75]

For all the co-operation there remained 'discord about operational objectives and methods' which 'bred misunderstandings between Washington and London'. Although Acheson had agreed to Bevin's proposal, he made known his concern that 'the situation must be handled with the greatest care to avoid

* The French were sympathetic to the idea and had their own operations under their MINOS exile programme.

the Greeks precipitating a crisis or the USSR intervening'. He was worried that the Greek National Army (GNA) might seize the opportunity presented by victory over the communist rebels and move into Albanian territory. If Bevin displayed any reticence at the meeting it was over the question of a successor to Hoxha. Bevin asked if he was 'thrown out', 'what government would replace Hoxha?' He was sceptical of the National Committee for Free Albania and told Acheson that what was needed was 'a person we could handle'. He enquired, 'Are there any kings around that we could put in?' As Richard Aldrich notes, 'Bevin knew full well that the available kings were more amenable to British than to American influence.' A US official responded that 'we had taken no decision with respect to a possible future government' as 'the situation was still too fluid'. With the first team of guerrillas ready to go into Albania in three weeks' time it was an unsatisfactory position.[76]

The *News Chronicle* headline on the 19th read 'The Albanian volcano is about to explode'. Indeed, under cover of a moonless night, the first British team of nine Albanians was transported by Motor Fishing Vessels (MFV) manned by men of the Royal Navy to the Adriatic. There they were switched to a Greek caique, the *Stormie Sea*. On 3 October, the nine 'pixies', each supplied with a British Army watch with a lethal cyanide pill taped to it, were dropped off by the *Stormie Sea* and rowed in rubber boats to the coast. The selected landing place was 'Seaview', the cove on the Karabaun peninsula, south of Valona, from where Billy McLean and David Smiley had been rescued in 1943. This former BK territory had recently been flown over, and Smiley had used the aerial photographs obtained to acquaint the trainees in Malta with the terrain. Smiley knew it as 'a rocky area of steep cliffs with the odd inlet where a boat could beach, from where goat tracks led inland'. Once ashore, they broke up into two groups. The men were mostly from Albania's southern region with several speaking Greek, and Smiley recalled that the idea was that 'they would then move inland to tribal areas where they had friends and relatives, and would signal back on the state of the country and the chances of further operations to help those already fighting'. Operation Valuable was up and running.[77]

On 8 October, five days after the first group went in, Kim Philby stepped off the SS *Caronia* in New York. In late August, while head of station in Istanbul, Philby had received the offer of a posting as liaison officer in Washington with the American intelligence community, an appointment he immediately accepted. Returning to London in September, he was briefed on the new post by Maurice Oldfield, deputy head of the anti-communist section, R5. He also had a meeting with the man with overall responsibility for intelligence relations with the FBI and the newly created CIA, Jack Easton, who was also chair of the executive committee overseeing Valuable. Although the many books on Philby, who had some knowledge of the Albanian operation – having made contact with Abas Kupi's Albanian Legalite Movement in Exile in Turkey – make no mention of him being briefed on Valuable during his short period at Broadway, it is inconceivable that Easton did not bring him up to date on the operation, though without the files the level of detail remains unknown. In London, during the month of September, it is claimed that Philby met every week with his KGB handler, 'Max' – though the Moscow files are said to show that he reported 'nothing substantial, no important news'. Leaving with his family for America at the end of the month, Philby officially joined the Washington embassy as First Secretary on the 10th, the same day as a second British team of eleven – five from the Korco area and six from Gjirokaster – was landed in Albania on a beach north of Valona.[78]

Once ensconced in Washington, Philby was appointed to the Anglo-American 'Special Policy Committee' (SPC), which ran Valuable/Fiend on a day-to-day basis, as joint commander with responsibility for co-ordinating the operation's two sides with his American opposite number, James McCargar. Other members included Robert Joyce and George Jellicoe, a British special forces specialist seconded to the Foreign Office, who gave 'political guidance'. According to Jellicoe, Philby 'was the one who made all the operational decisions'. Philby arrived in Washington at a time when, McCargar recalled, MI6 'was held in high regard by those who had had close association with it'.

In particular, the British worldwide communications network was one of the invaluable assets that the British War Cabinet had retained during the wartime liquidation of overseas assets. McCargar remembered that on three separate occasions, Philby, who had a great reputation among the American intelligence officers as a 'young Turk', 'came into my office with urgent reports which I had not yet received through our channels'. Philby characterised his fellow-members of the SPC as 'convivial', by which 'he seemed to imply approachable and humorous, green, and more than cold-blooded enough to keep their distance emotionally from all those poor doomed devils scrambling over Albania's scrubby beaches'.[79]

Members of the SPC were not completely happy with their remit because the Foreign Office and the State Department insisted on maintaining close supervision of the project. Philby found that 'we could never act as free agents. Headquarters never allowed me to forget SIS's commitment to Abas Kupi, and behind headquarters, there loomed the Bevin formula for veto: "I won't 'ave it."' There were also disputes over tradecraft, and despite the OPC pouring money into the project, there were problems with essential equipment which was often lacking in the field, in particular good radio transmitters. Each guerrilla group in Albania had a bulky B2 radio set which had been used by SOE during the war; it relied on pedal power for transmission. Radio security was minimal as there was no time for Morse training and the operatives, transmitting over open channels, spoke using only a rudimentary code for details. In Corfu, at the palace on the north-east of the island, overlooking the Corfu channel, David Smiley waited at the radio base run by Alan Hare for news from his charges. Nothing was heard until 12 October, when one of the agents from the first team radioed that things had gone wrong. The communist security forces had been waiting for them, with Albanian troops surrounding the whole coastal area. Three of their guerrillas had been killed, one captured, and another had simply disappeared. The five guerrillas of the second group did make it to the Kurvelesh region, where they tried to set up resistance cells among the villagers, who remained suspicious – especially as no arms were made available.[80]

Smiley moved to the Greek mainland under cover as GI (OPs & I)* with the British Military Mission. He stayed ten miles outside Athens in a safe house, waiting for news of the Albanians' return. At the end of October, four of the original nine men eventually made it back to Greece. The second team found life in the mountains, where it was already snowing, extremely tough. They did, though, make it back to Greece, from where they were exfiltrated – with some difficulty – from the clutches of the Greek authorities, who would have been quite happy to see them perish. From Greece they were escorted back to Malta by Rollo Young, for debriefing. The operation had been unsuccessful. 'Four of the twenty men put ashore were lost and the others had failed to inspire any genesis of an anti-government movement. Several Albanian civilians had also been arrested and killed.' Nicholas Bethell adds that MI6 and OPC officers knew the results were 'disappointing' but thought that the first phase of the operation had not been disastrous.[81]

The US State Department continued to support action against Albania. On 21 October, the US Joint Chiefs of Staff reported to the State Department that the Soviet Union was still training Greek guerrillas in Albania and building military works along the coast, including a submarine base in Valona Bay that could be used for guerrilla operations against Greek and Yugoslav islands. Meanwhile, back in Albania, the countryside was rife with rumours of political plots. Hoxha reported that western intelligence agencies were recruiting Albanian 'war criminals' for operations against the country. Yugoslav agents were said to be operating in the North in collaboration with Greek 'monarcho-fascists' in the South. On 24 October, the interior minister, Mehmet Shehu, spoke of 'internal reactionaries' planning to overthrow the people's power through acts of sabotage, and assassinations. He called for an intensification of the class struggle.[82]

While this may have been precisely what the émigrés had wanted to hear, their political organisation was in turmoil and unable fully to exploit the situation. In the early morning of 3 October, as the first guerrilla team was

---

* General Intelligence (Operations and Intelligence).

making its way ashore to Albania, Midhat Frasheri – 'the lynchpin of the fragile agreement [Low] and his British colleagues had spent weeks negotiating in Rome' – was 'lying on his bed, supposedly dead of a heart attack'. Frasheri's sudden mysterious death with its hint of foul play led James McCargar to a personal crisis of conscience. By then the majority of the Albanian-American community, including its leading spokespersons and the respected Greek Orthodox prelate in America, Marko Lipa, were publicly in opposition to the presence on the Committee for Free Albania of known collaborators. The big problem, with Frasheri dead, McCargar recalled, was 'Who's going to be the successor chairman of the Committee?' The problem was solved by Carmel Offie, who came forward 'very forcefully with the suggestion of Hassan Dosti'. McCargar was appalled, given Dosti's role during the Italian occupation as a leading figure in their puppet government. 'I and several others screamed bloody murder on this. I said, you can't use somebody with that background, it's a blot on everybody's escutcheon.'[83]

Offie, however, overrode the objections and, in the words of Philby, who watched the proceedings with bemused cynicism, 'railroaded a handful of Albanian refugees in New York into forming a National Committee ... Hassan Dosti was a young lawyer who, according to the OPC, had an impeccable record as a democrat.' In support of Dosti and in order to bolster the Committee, Offie brought to America another churchman, Bishop Fan Noli, to challenge Lipa for control of the Greek Orthodox Church. He was followed by 'a bevy of Hitler-era stooges' including Xhafer Deva, who used the SS Skanderbeg Division in a massacre of Albanian partisans. Despite 'voluminous files of adverse information', a US intelligence officer who debriefed Deva reported that he was a 'person of uncompromising personal honour', a 'pure patriot', and an outstanding 'operational contact and source of information'. The Committee went on to play an important role in recruiting Albanian refugees for a series of raids into their homeland sponsored by the OPC. Michael Burke was not impressed. He recognised that the Committee was 'more a rallying point than a valid base for political revolution'. He knew that one of the basic principles for the success of guerrilla movements is that they adopt a comprehensive political programme with which to indoctrinate their people. The Albanian counter-revolution, however, 'lacked such a message'.[84]

In Belgrade, on 2 November 1949, Tito told the British ambassador that 'the Albanians were all out to provoke frontier incidents and to do everything in their power to provoke Yugoslavia into some action that could be represented as aggression'. Tito was afraid that Moscow might engineer a coup in Tirana and accuse the Yugoslavs of being behind it. Stalin would then have the excuse he was looking for to order an attack on Yugoslavia. Intelligence reports indicated that Tito's agents were, in fact, operating in the north of Albania where there was, the British embassy reported, 'very considerable unrest'.[85]

A week later, journalist Cyrus Sulzberger had lunch in London with Julian Amery, who told him that 'English foreign policy is founded on two principles: that God is an Englishman, and that the road to India must be kept open. So far, God has provided Tito but England is doing very little about capitalising on this.' Amery appeared to be somewhat out of the intelligence loop. He was 'discouraged about the situation in the Balkans. He thinks England and America have not only wasted far too much time doing nothing about Albania, but that they may not do anything before spring. If such is the case, he believes it will be too late. Yugoslavia will fall and Greece will go too.' Amery was convinced, Sulzberger wrote in his diary, that

> for a small sum in gold, Albania can be saved by promoting a revolution. It would not take a great deal of time to make proper arrangements with some of the northern tribes. He believed this must be done now, before the Russians have completed their submarine base and before the Russians sign their treaty of miltiary alliance with Hoxha. Otherwise, it will be too late.

Sulzberger recorded that Amery 'has a rather high respect for the shrewdness and political ability of King Zog'.[86]

The intelligence available to the planners during November and December was sparse. The CIA was unsure of the situation in the country and could come to no firm conclusions about the stability of the regime or the existence of any opposition. A 15 December report on the resistance made gloomy reading, contrasting sharply with the OPC's optimistic belief – as recalled by McCargar – that 'we had only to shake the trees and the ripe plums would fall'. It was true that the *Telegraph* reported on 30 January 1950 that there had been a mutiny in the Albanian Army and a purge involving two hundred officers – how they came by the information is not known – but the Sigurimi, the local secret police, had been trained by their Soviet colleagues to deal with such emergencies. Any internal resistance that did exist was as yet unorganised and ineffective. The CIA concluded that

> the settlement of differences among exiled Albanians to provide leadership and co-ordination is a prerequisite for any effective Albanian resistance against the Hoxha government. Not even this turn of affairs, however, would assure the achievement of any successful resistance without material aid from an outside power. This combination of factors necessary for the overthrow of the Hoxha regime is, as yet, lacking.

In order to try to surmount the problems, 'political differences would ultimately limit recruitment to strict quotas: 40 per cent from the Balli Kombetar, 40 per cent from the Legalite, the rest from other factions'.[87]

At the same time as the Albanian operation was running, the British and

Americans were involved in a similar but unreported operation in Bulgaria. Philby was party to the discussions that took place in Washington, the details of which he passed on to Moscow. The British and Americans were, naturally, particularly interested in the situation in the Balkans: 'telegrams were filled with names like Subacic and Mikolaichik and those of anti-soviet leaders in Romania, Hungary and Bulgaria'. There could be no question of using the *Stormie Sea* for another Valuable mission as it was assumed, correctly, that it had been compromised by the failure of the first two missions. The crew of the *Stormie Sea* subsequently spent the winter of 1949/50 running 'mysterious cargoes to agents in Bulgaria through the Black Sea'. They were eventually paid off at the end of the following year and alternative arrangements were made with a new crew and boat, a fast-moving converted German E-boat, the *Henrietta*, on which the OPC had spent £80,000. It was captained by a former RAF pilot, James Blackburn.[88]

During the winter of 1949/50 the British and American SO teams re-evaluated Valuable/Fiend. In a specially secure room in the Pentagon, the SPC held post-mortem meetings on the first two incursions. Years later, Philby recalled that 'the information they brought back was almost wholly negative. It was clear, at least, that they had nowhere found arms open to welcome them.' The first two missions had been disasters but the loss of 20 per cent of the agents was judged by wartime standards to be acceptable. With more training and better radio communications, it was argued, more ambitious future landings could be successful. Properly created intelligence 'cells' would eventually be expanded into 'centres of resistance'. Acting as agent for the Soviets, Philby knew what had happened, but he also realised, as an experienced intelligence officer, that 'the operation, of course, was futile from the beginning. Our infiltrators could only achieve something by penetrating the towns under Communist control.' His private opinion was that the planners had made a grave error in assessing the state of the country. The presence of infiltrated exiles 'would have been useful only if the country was seething with revolt. That, perhaps, was the unspoken assumption behind the whole venture.'[89]

Philby's analysis was borne out by the reports of the returning missions. Once on the ground, the 'pixies' discovered that their political leadership and western handlers had grossly miscalculated the degree of counter-revolutionary fervour among the largely demoralised population. The clannish Albanians, although tough, independent and warlike, 'had a peasant's faith in numbers, and the type of warfare the agents tried to teach them – hit-and-run attacks on police posts, sabotage and terrorism – struck them as unmanly'. In addition, because Britain and the United States were determined to maintain deniability, agents found it difficult to persuade the people they met that they enjoyed the support of the West.[90]

The Italian authorities in Rome, where the OPC's Michael Burke and

MI6's John Hibberdine had taken over from an ill Peter Kemp in running that end of things, were not informed of the operation. It later emerged, however, that Italian Intelligence was well aware of the transfer of the 'pixies' to the *Stormie Sea* off the coast. From the lighthouse at Otranto, officers watched the entire transfer through telescopes. The information was then passed on to James Angleton at the CIA in Washington, with whom certain Italian intelligence officers had a particularly close relationship. As part of the ongoing professional and bureaucratic battle between the OPC and the CIA – the counter-intelligence people objected that the guerrilla activities put their own agents at risk – 'with great glee', Angleton advised McCargar that the Albanian operation was 'well and truly blown'.[91]

When the Albanians had been debriefed on Malta they hinted to Smiley that 'they might have been expected'. It was recognised that there was a leak somewhere. The senior officer in MI5 counter-intelligence at the time, Dick White, later told Nicholas Bethell that 'no doubt Philby betrayed the Albanian operation, but overshadowing this is the fact that all émigré organisations are hopelessly infiltrated from the outset'. Likewise, White's opposite number in the CIA, James Angleton, also took it as an article of faith that Russian Intelligence had penetrated all the émigré groups and 'attributed the apparent leaks to the Albanians in Rome'. It was true that Albanian agents were particularly active among the émigré community in Rome, and Christopher Andrew is correct to assert that 'security both in the SIS training camp in Malta and among rival groups of Albanian émigrés was sometimes slapdash'.[92]

In the opinion of a number of American Fiend intelligence officers, 'the recruitment of Albanian émigrés was too hurried and insecure, with the result that word of the operation quickly spread throughout the émigré community and as quickly reached Russian agents'. According to these officers, the Russians, aiding the Albanians, were able to penetrate the operation with an agent who corroborated Philby's general reports and provided more detailed information on the time and place of agent landings. It was later learned that one of the Albanians recruited by the guerrillas in the second landing had been subsequently arrested, tortured and executed, but not before he had given to the security forces full details of relevant codes and radio signals. Using such information, in time, Albanian Intelligence developed its own highly successful 'double-cross' operation.[93]

That the Albanian operation was an open secret was revealed on 27 March 1950 in a brief but specific report in the *New York Times* by Cyrus Sulzberger. It said that two groups had been landed on the Albanian coast with orders to take radios into the hinterland and build up communications with the anti-Hoxha movement. James McCargar was furious, but Sulzberger remained unrepentant: 'I can't think why they were so upset. There seemed to be plenty of people in the Balkans who knew what was happening and obviously the Russians knew about it down to the last semi-colon.'[94]

In the spring of 1950, once the groups had been accounted for, Smiley's job was over and he returned to his regiment in Germany, 'very downcast and completely mystified as to what had gone wrong'. Shortly after, he was replaced by Anthony Northrop, another SOE veteran who had been dropped into Albania twice during the war. His cover post was as a major in the Royal Ulster Rifles. James McCargar, disillusioned by the imposition of Hassan Dosti to chair the Committee for Free Albania, bowed out of the operation to a new OPC mission in Austria. He did not, however, make it to Vienna, but instead returned to the Foreign Service. In his place, Wisner appointed a tough intelligence officer, Gratian Yatsevich, as the new commander of Operation Fiend to work alongside Kim Philby. A former OSS officer with a specialised knowledge of the Balkans, though not Albania, Yatsevich had spent three years in Bulgaria from 1946 as a US military attaché.[95]

Although the smell of failure hung heavy in the air, by this time the Albanian communists had withdrawn support for the Greek rebels, which 'gave some comfort to those who planned the operation and believed, irrationally, in its feasibility'. In fact, 'it was hoped that all would be in train for a national uprising'. The surprise outbreak of the Korean War put paid to any idea of abandoning the project, and the military immediately ordered a bigger and more active response. The OPC poured in more resources with renewed vigour. The only problem was that the Americans, Greeks, Italians, Yugoslavs and British were all running operations that overlapped, causing confusion and making security increasingly difficult.[96]

American operations became more ambitious than the British, involving air drops into 'denied areas'. Because the area they had targeted was in the centre of the country and away from the coast, the OPC decided to send their small groups in by air, and parachute them into areas they knew best. They used Polish veterans of the RAF run by Roman Rudkowski, an air force colonel who had parachuted in with Peter Kemp to liaise with the Polish Home Army in late 1944. This was to be a matter of operational dispute between the OPC and their British counterparts. Rodney Dennys had taken over from Kim Philby as head of station in Istanbul, where he had some contact with Valuable, dealing with a number of Albanian refugees and exiles involved in the operation. Married to Graham Greene's sister, he was a veteran of Section V and the Middle East cover, the Inter-Services Liaison Department, having joined the Service just before the outbreak of war. Like other MI6 officers, Dennys thought that 'it was a mistake to use parachute drops. An aircraft in a deserted area sticks out a mile. Small boats were better.'[97]

The OPC's Albanian recruits were disguised by assigning them to special 'labour battalions' under American army command in Germany, where they would carry out public works in the country's ruined cities. It was Carmel Offie who set up the labour battalions with the aid of Lawrence de Neufville, a CIA 'special adviser' to the American High Commissioner, housing Company 400 in a large villa just outside Heidelberg in the American Zone. The Americans left the recruitment of the 250 Albanians to Kupi, Ermenji and Kryeziu. Assembled during June 1950, with Major Caush Ali Bashom, a Ballist, as senior officer, and Xhemal Laci, a monarchist, as his deputy, the recruits were of low quality, with a number in poor health. In addition, exile political in-fighting ensured that their training was continually interrupted.[98]

The British operation continued when, in early June 1950, Doc Zaehner flew six men to Athens for a third mission which this time would go into Albania overland. Zaehner co-operated with Patrick Whinney, whose deputy was now Frank Stallwood, a former schoolmaster who had served with the Intelligence Corps in the Middle East before joining the Service in 1946. Organising the British side in Athens was a former commander of the gendarmerie under King Zog, Dayrell Oakley-Hill, an ex-Section D and SOE officer. In 1946 he returned with the United Nations Relief and Rehabilitation Administration (UNRRA) to Tirana, where Hoxha accused him of stirring up the émigrés. In Athens, Oakley-Hill reported directly to London, while the OPC side was run by Bill Brummell and Horace 'Hod' Fuller, who was responsible for 'safe-houses'. The Athens end of the operation, however, eventually fell apart because of a lack of co-ordination with the Greek intelligence service, which resented what they saw as British interference in Greece's foreign affairs.[99]

Harold Perkins organised with Tracey Barnes, head of the OPC's newly created Psychological and Paramilitary (PP) warfare staff, an anti-communist propaganda drive. The first drop by plane of anti-Hoxha leaflets over the Korce area took place in early August 1950. The initial load had to be dumped at sea. The first successful release took place in mid-September, but Oakley-Hill discovered that the American pilot had released the leaflets over the wrong area. They caused some confusion in neighbouring countries. Yugoslav officials knew that leaflets had been dropped in Albania and the Kosovo and Metohia areas of Yugoslavia, seemingly by mistake, because they were in Bulgarian and summoned the Bulgarians to take action against the communist government. One senior Yugoslav official told Cyrus Sulzberger that they suspected the Russians, but the journalist knew that 'they originated with C. D. Jackson's "amateurish" Free Europe Committee'. Perkins also deployed balloons for releasing leaflets using technology developed by MI6 scientists which, in turn, was based on Japanese wartime experience. Barnes preferred to fill the balloon baskets with such scarce items as flour, needles, razor blades and other superior western toiletries, along with a note announcing that they were a gift from the 'Albanian National Liberation Front'. A Radio Free Albania temporarily went on the air, but there were few radio receivers in the country.[100]

The Albanian news media, meanwhile, carried reports of parachutists dropping from aircraft flying in from Italy. In July, the Albanian government sent a note of protest to the Italian government complaining that it was permitting the parachuting of agents into Albanian territory. Major trials were held in southern Albania of agents who had crossed the border from Greece, while another was held in the North of Yugoslav agents.

During August Kim Philby travelled to London with OPC director Frank Wisner and the State Department's Robert Joyce, to attend a special meeting of the Russia Committee. Joyce and Wisner were acquainted with the committee's objective of promoting civil strife in the satellite countries with the aim of weakening the Soviet Union's control. The two main items on the agenda were, firstly, to reach a consensus between the British and American intelligence communities on the likely date for the Soviet Union to launch an attack on the West, and, secondly, to co-ordinate the OPC/MI6 operations to overthrow the pro-Soviet governments of Albania, Latvia and the Ukraine. Joyce kept the record for the Americans while the British minutes were written up by Philby.[101]

In September, Oakley-Hill's aborted overland mission was revived and the first unit was put into Albania from Greece. The survivors trickled back to Malta in early November, but they were no more successful than earlier incursions. During November, James Blackburn's boat landed two more British-backed teams on the Albanian coast with instructions to contact Gani Bey Kryeziu's men, who had apparently crossed into eastern Albania from Yugoslavia. The British ambassador in Belgrade, Charles Peake, informed the American chargé d'affaires, Bob Ream, in advance that the missions were going in, but never confirmed they had been dispatched. The two teams were immediately captured by the security forces. Cyrus Sulzberger again picked up information on this 'disastrous effort'. The few survivors who made it out told their friends and colleagues in Malta that Hoxha's security men had tightened their grip on the country and free movement was virtually impossible. 'Morale', not unnaturally, 'declined alarmingly' and 'an aura of doom began to surround the fort'.[102]

During the autumn of 1950, news of Valuable/Fiend continued to leak. The counsellor at the American embassy in Belgrade let slip to Sulzberger that the 'CIA and the British are up to another plan to overthrow the regime in Albania'. After a number of false starts and failures, nine OPC-sponsored Albanian trainees from Company 400 were dropped into the country on 19 November. They were ill prepared for the operation, having been trained for only three weeks, and even then the training was regarded as being inferior to that offered by the British on Malta. Adem Gjura later said that he was 'sent into the field with no plan of action and no idea where he might find friends. His men had been selected with little regard for physical or mental aptitude they might have for such a daunting task. They were scrawny and unfit, not the "commando" type. And their training was rudimentary.' Astonishingly, they received no parachute training. In the event, the Polish pilots could not locate the arranged dropping point and the vital supplies ended up in another town. In addition, several hundred security police had flooded the area and were lying in wait for them. 'Very soon', Selim Deci recalled, 'we knew that our landing was known to the security forces.' Gjura discovered that many villagers already knew his name. Days earlier 'the security police had let it be known that "Adem Gjura" was about to fall from the skies and that they must all look for him'.[103]

Selim Deci was arrested the day after the landing. Gjura was luckier but was only saved because he landed several miles from the landing zone. Along with his colleagues, at the end of December he escaped to Yugoslavia without achieving any of the objectives. Deci was tortured and sentenced to hard labour, to be released forty years later. Furious at having missed Gjura, the Albanian secret police extracted a terrible revenge, arresting and executing more than forty members of his family.[104]

Back on Malta, the flaws in the planning were all too apparent to Anthony Northrop. He had come to the conclusion that the operation was being continued 'for political and bureaucratic reasons'. Senior officials in MI6 blamed the 'pixies' for the failures. The Service appeared to be using it as 'their showpiece of anti-Soviet retaliation' and, under pressure from the military, instead of cutting back insisted on more and bigger operations. The 'hotheads' craved the success in the field that would help their careers, and it appeared to Northrop that 'Broadway was experimenting with his young Albanian men, using them not as allies but as sacrificial lambs'. There was no longer the surgical skill that a few years earlier had made SOE the world's experts in guerrilla warfare. Northrop thought that the only tactic that might have succeeded was the assassination of Hoxha, but that had not been sanctioned by Bevin and was vetoed by Perkins as being too 'noisy'.[105]

Although the main chronicler of Valuable, Nicholas Bethell, had originally seen it as a well-thought-out operation, he appears to have altered his view – perhaps as a result of interviewing the Albanians.

> This was the secret service at its worst – patronising, inefficient, irresponsible. I could understand their ruthlessness in a ruthless conflict, but not when it was backed by such dismal lack of professionalism and disregard for the lives of the Albanians whom they were sending into the field, not to mention their families, innocents who were also condemned to endure Hoxha's revenge.

The Service, and Bethell, would later try to lay the blame for the failures on Kim Philby, but this was only part of the story. It was true that he did much to sabotage Albanian operations and had 'alerted the KGB to the seaborne landings in October 1949, to cross-border infiltration in the summer of 1950, and to the first CIA parachute drop in November 1950'. But he probably only passed on the broad outlines, and even without his help, as Christopher Andrew concludes, 'covert action in Albania was probably doomed'. Much to the chagrin of western intelligence agencies, it was later discovered that Albania had devised its own radio 'double-cross' system.[106]

In January 1951, the Albanian Ministry of the Interior reported a large and unsuccessful infiltration in the North. Forty-three guerrillas had entered the country by boat and parachute and had been defeated by the police in a gun battle lasting several days. Twenty-nine guerrillas had been killed and fourteen captured. During the following month, another group of guerrillas moved into Albania and was initially well received by the villagers it encountered. With several reports coming out of open organised resistance and uprisings, there was optimism that this mission might well succeed.[107]

In April, senior Yugoslav official Professor Milovan Djilas told Cyrus Sulzberger in Belgrade that in Albania 'things are getting worse. It is a pitiful little country, Hoxha has lost the support of all elements and merely keeps in the saddle by brutal police methods. The police are loyal because they have been established as a privileged class.' Although a committee of Albanian exiles opposed to Hoxha's regime was set up in Yugoslavia during 1951, Djilas expressed fears about outside interference in Albania. Ironically, Anglo-American actions in the country were mistakenly viewed as Russian attempts to stir up trouble as the prelude to an invasion of Yugoslavia. Yugoslav spokesperson Vlado Dedijer revealed that a bomb thrown at the Soviet embassy in Tirana had killed several Russian diplomats and military staff. Dedijer thought it the action of 'a Soviet *agent provocateur*'. It was unlikely, but this terrorist act sparked off an unprecedented reign of terror and repression.[108]

The initial success of the latest mission into Albania was short-lived as the expected men, weapons and equipment failed to materialise. They were eventually picked off one by one by the security forces and, in early May, the survivors were forced to make their way to Yugoslavia, where they were interned for a number of years. During the spring, Archie Lyall moved from Trieste to Rome, where he replaced Peter Kemp and John Hibberdine on Valuable. At the same time, a disillusioned Michael Burke left Fiend to organise equally disastrous agent drops into the Soviet Union. He was replaced by Joseph Leib, a former major in the American Army and a public relations specialist. Before he left for Germany, Burke handed Franklin Lindsay his final operational report in which he stressed that 'the political requirement could only have been met by a major military operation'. Lindsay agreed, though other senior figures in the CIA did not. Wisner apologised to Kim Philby for the failures: 'We'll get it right next time.'[109]

Frank Wisner's OPC now operated within the remit of the CIA, but as an independent section ultimately responsible to the new Director, Walter

Bedell Smith. Although professionally friendly with Philby, in the light of a series of compromised MI6/CIA operations Wisner had apparently already developed doubts about the British liaison officer. He told Bob Joyce that there was perhaps a traitor in their midst, most likely within the SPC. In an unpublished memoir, Joyce revealed that 'Wisner had arrived at Philby as the most likely culprit'. In late May 1951, following the disappearance of the British diplomats Guy Burgess and Donald Maclean, the CIA's gun-toting William Harvey put together a five-page memorandum which traced Philby's career and contacts. Harvey asserted that the MI6 man was probably a Soviet agent. His personal assistant, Hugh Montgomery, was certain that his boss had developed his suspicions as a result of the Albanian failures. Harvey handed his damning report, which is now in the CIA's collection of super-secret case files known as the 'Black Files', to the Director, who immediately sent a copy to Stewart Menzies with a warning cover letter demanding that Philby be fired or the all-important intelligence link would be severed.[110]

Among the MI6 officers who accepted the American evidence against Philby was the Assistant Chief, James Easton, who chaired the Service's internal committee on Valuable. Easton became 'an outcast for daring to believe the worst about a trusted member of the Firm' and was cut out of top-level discussions. In a private note to the director of the Joint Intelligence Bureau (JIB), Maj.-Gen. Kenneth Strong, Bedell Smith, who had personally briefed Philby, wrote: 'I hope the bastard gets his. I know a couple of Albanian tribesmen who would like to have half-an-hour apiece with him.' Soon after, Strong, who had served with Bedell Smith during the war as Eisenhower's chief intelligence officer, was temporarily posted to Washington to act as MI6 liaison to the CIA. He soon became a familiar figure, and so impressed was the CIA Director that he wanted to appoint Strong deputy in charge of the agency's intelligence operations, but the NSC balked at appointing a foreigner. In August, Strong was replaced by the official MI6 representative, Machlachlan Silverwood-Cope, who stayed until the following January, when the post was taken up by John Bruce-Lockhart; the latter being largely responsible for healing the wounds with the American 'cousins'.[111]

Despite the fact that Philby was now under strong suspicion as the 'Third Man' and was regarded by a number of CIA officers as most definitely a traitor, in mid-1951 it was decided to proceed with the Albanian operation. Indeed, the OPC began putting in substantial sums. Prompted by Burke's report and his own experience of touring the CIA stations in Europe, Franklin Lindsay was having real doubts about rolling back the Iron Curtain. 'It was peacetime, not wartime. The stuff that had worked against the Germans did not work against the Russians, who seemed impervious.' Lindsay realised that the OPC/MI6 operations were getting nowhere. He did not blame Philby for the failure, however, believing that the Soviets would not have wasted him on Albania. He thought that the operation went down because 'we couldn't maintain security in the DP camps and because the communist security apparatus was so damn strong'. The situation became worse when the OPC began to throw money around. There was a lot of careless gossip among the émigrés in Rome and Athens – and despite the worries of the counter-intelligence people monitoring the radio transmissions from the agents in Albania that the 'fist' – the individual style and pattern that distinguishes telegraph operators – was not quite right, Wisner sent in more teams.[112]

The OPC decided to transfer their loyalties to the monarchists and began to target the Zogist groups, though the switch to a pro-monarchist strategy did much to undermine the democratic claims of the operation. During the summer, ostensibly to buy real estate, King Zog visited Washington, where he discussed the situation with Gratian Yatsevich. Meanwhile, the training continued, although relations between the Albanians and MI6/OPC deteriorated. With the sanction of Greece's military leader, Alexander Papagos, the CIA established a new base in the Kalanissia island group a few miles north of Corinth. As part of Britain's policy of 'handing on the torch' in the Balkans, the CIA had taken over 'nearly all the British secret networks and installations'. Disguised as a radar station, the base accommodated teams of refugees from Albania, Bulgaria and the Soviet Union. High-powered boats dropped agents on the Albanian coast on secret missions, though the favoured means for the Americans was dropping agents by air.[113]

At midnight on 23 July, with the Philby investigation still in progress, the Americans parachuted twelve more young Albanians into the field in various locations. Once again, disaster struck, with the security police waiting for them. Four were burnt to death in a house, six were shot dead and two – Kacem Shehu and Muhamet Zeqir Hoxha – were captured. Hoxha, no relation to the dictator, had landed on Vergoi Plain: 'But instead of finding ourselves in a safe place, we were immediately surrounded by Albanian security forces aided by armed civilians.'[114]

On 10 October 1951, Shehu and Hoxha were put on trial in a Tirana cinema along with others from previous operations and those alleged to have invaded Albania under British, Greek, Italian and Yugoslav sponsorship. Muhamet Hoxha, who had been tortured and kept in appalling conditions, recalled that the trial was 'very boisterous, designed to show the defeat of the Anglo-Americans and the triumph of the security forces'. During the staged event, the defendants confessed to various crimes, revealing essential facts that proved to be true and precise with regard to names and dates. Interestingly, despite the best efforts of the Albanians to publicise the trial, little if anything appeared in the western press. While the trial continued, on 15 October the Americans dropped a further party of five in the mountains of the Dibra region. The three who survived spent their entire time dodging Albanian patrols before crossing into Greece at the end of the month.

Although most of those on trial were given prison sentences, few reappeared following the trial. A number were killed in captivity, while Muhamet Hoxha spent decades in prison being starved and beaten. A few of those captured revealed enough details of the training and operation to provide the security police with sufficient intelligence to stage a deception operation. The exile centres were easy prey for infiltration by communist agents, while the terrorising of families back in Albania provided further information. There followed bitter disillusionment, and the Albanians began to drift away from the training areas. This was not surprising given that sixty agents were parachuted in during 1951 but not a single word came back. 'Seldom', Robin Winks writes, 'had an intelligence operation proceeded so resolutely from one disaster to another.'[115]

In late October, a meeting in Rome with MI6's Harold Perkins and Anthony Northrop and the OPC's Joe Leib considered the problems. The meeting again ended in a dispute about the different methods of delivering agents into the field, with the British regarding the parachuting in of men at five hundred feet as suicidal. The Americans were all too willing to put the blame on Philby for the failures but, as Robin Winks has pointed out, 'frequently the drops did not take place where they were meant to, so any information relayed by someone inside the operation would have been wrong. Further, as the disastrous drops required low flights, followed by a supply drop well away from the men and almost square on a village, the drops themselves rather visibly could have alerted the authorities.' It seems that the drops were being detected 'simply because they were badly performed'. Philby thought that 'the general lack of attention to detail by the OPC, and a misplaced optimism about Albanian readiness for revolt, together with a disregard for the Albanian agents who were being sent in as though they were "just down from the trees", were at least as important in accounting for the disaster as any treachery on his part'.[116]

Privately, the British considered the Americans to be 'innocents'. John Bruce-Lockhart believed that Wisner's problem was that he 'failed to appreciate the toughness of his adversary' and had not seen enough of the 'hard end' of war. At the same time, Bruce-Lockhart realised that 'we were getting nowhere. Unlike World War Two, we had no SIGINT [signals intelligence], no PoWs to debrief, and no aerial reconnaissance.' The British gave up trying to infiltrate agents: 'It was pointless. They were quickly killed or turned into double agents.'[117]

The British gradually realised the futility of Valuable and quietly began to withdraw as the country's worsening economic position prevented it from engaging in full-scale operations. Abas Ermenji, unwilling to see his BK followers take 'another tumble through the meat grinder', asked them to stop going on missions. On Malta, Fort Benjimma continued briefly with a few trainees and a skeleton staff under Anthony Newman's command but was finally dismantled by MI6's new Middle East director, George Young. Small groups of Albanians were trained on Dartmoor by Anthony Northrop, but his reservations and the lack of will from the incoming Conservative government led to the British decision to end their part of the operation. They did so, Philby recalled, 'without having made any noticeable dent on the regime in Tirana'. What had started out as a British operation, then a 'joint' or, until early 1952, a 'co-ordinated' effort, now became the sole preserve of the Americans.[118]

Those guerrillas who had managed to escape through Greece were transported to Britain for a 'Welcome Home' party at Caxton Hall, in London. MI6 bullied the Home Office into allowing them into the country under the pretext that they were 'good friends of ours from Greece'. The remaining trainees were subsequently 'scattered throughout the world' with a fair proportion finding their way to the Commonwealth, while a few found employment through the Ministry of Labour in Britain with the Forestry Commission and an ordnance factory.[119]

Bob Joyce had likewise concluded that the operation was not serving any useful purpose, but Wisner shrugged off the criticism, knowing that he had the support of CIA Deputy Director Allen Dulles. Gratian Yatsevich agreed to carry the fight on with members of the Royal Guard led by the most experienced guerrilla 'pixie', Hamit Matjani. A CIA favourite, Matjani, the 'Tiger', had made fifteen incursions into Albania by the land route, which proved to be the most secure. His sixteenth mission, a parachute drop, was, however, his last. Making the best of a bad situation, Yatsevich secured Angleton's help in Rome to pick out the weaker elements of the Free Albania Committee and replace them with members of the Catholic Independenza group, a number of whom had worked with the Italians during the war. In Washington, King Zog's military commander, Nuci Kota, a founder of the Albanian National Committee and a leader of the Free Albania Committee, led a new CIA-financed Albanian Committee of the Assembly of Captive European Nations (ACEN). Wartime collaborator Hassan Dosti was especially active in the ACEN, whose pivotal Political Committee was controlled for much of the fifties by the BK organisation.[120]

In order to discover what was going wrong with the operations, on 28 April 1952 five royalists who had followed Zog into exile, including Zenal Shehu, leader of the operation, and Nalil Sufa, together with a radio operator, Tahir Prenci, were sent into Albania's Mati region. This seemingly successful operation left two agents with previously recruited resistance groups who kept in touch by radio with OPC officers in Greece. It soon became apparent to the OPC chief in Greece, Al Ulmer, however, that 'we were dropping them into a controlled situation'. Indeed, the police had lain in wait at a house owned by Shehu's cousin. They killed or arrested and tortured the guerrillas and then forced the radio operator to broadcast an all-clear signal to an MI6 base on Cyprus: 'There was a fail-safe drill which involved transmitting the signal in a way that warned it was being sent under duress ... But the militia knew the drill.' Ulmer was all for stopping the operation, particularly after 'repeated requests for arms and things, for drops, where they would shoot at the planes', but no one heeded his warnings. Especially 'that guy in Rome ... Leib had no business in intelligence'. In early August, weapons were parachuted in following another radio request. At the same time, the Albanians who were controlling the whole situation tantalisingly dangled in front of the OPC operators the prospect of sending out three guerrillas – secret policemen from the Sigurimi – for clandestine briefings.[121]

While Wisner may have believed that Fiend was back on track, Franklin Lindsay knew that it had failed and was allowed to set up a 'murder board' to shut down unsuccessful operations. During 1952 about a third of the eastern European operations were weeded out. Before he left the service for the Ford Foundation, Lindsay drafted a paper for the State Department and the NSC in which he concluded that 'in peacetime the Russians seemed to penetrate them with ease' being 'much better at handling such threats than the Germans'. In addition, the military 'did not appreciate the years of political organisation that lay behind successful resistance movements'. Lindsay had seen at first hand the 'horrifying loss of life, suffering which racks every level of society, wholesale destruction, the murder of hostages, starvation' which resistance entailed. Dulles would not be persuaded by Lindsay's paper. When told that the air-drops were getting nowhere, he replied: 'At least we're getting the experience we need for the next war.' After a brief lull the OPC, now part of the CIA's Directorate of Plans, created new exile operations which were even more reckless.[122]

Meanwhile, the radio base in Cyprus was in receipt of further requests for agents to be parachuted in for meetings with dissident elements. The CIA agreed and, on May Day 1953, as part of an outlandish scheme to liberate Albania with a force of OPC-backed émigrés based in Italy, three more Albanian guerrillas were dispatched. Reviewing the options for operations against other Soviet satellites, senior CIA official Richard Bissell came across the Paramilitary Staff project: 'It did not stop with agent drops or guerrilla warfare in the mountains, but was to escalate steadily until it culminated in a full-scale invasion of Albania with ships, aircraft, parachute drops, and thousands of men.' Bissell thought the plan preposterous: 'How did those OPC colonels think they could get away with a provocation of that magnitude?' – or conceal it. On 28 April, Cyrus Sulzberger had talked with Greece's defence minister, Panayotis Canellopoulos. 'Astonishingly indiscreet', he revealed details of the planned 'coup de main'. He said that 'American troops, if necessary, will be used to "maintain order" after a local coup. The Greeks have agreed to keep out, the Yugoslavs have been more or less warned to do so.'[123]

On New Year's Eve, Radio Tirana announced that men trained for the final part of the operation had been arrested by the Sigurimi and were awaiting trial. The show trial in April 1954 revealed for the first time the extent of the Albanian deception. The Sigurimi had rolled up the entire network. For eighteen months, advised and assisted by Soviet specialists, they manipulated the American operation by controlling the flow and content of messages transmitted to Cyprus. 'We forced the captured agents to make radio contact with their espionage centres in Italy and elsewhere, hence to play their game,' Enver Hoxha later boasted. 'The bands of criminals who were dropped in by parachute or infiltrated across the border at our request came like lambs to the slaughter ... Our famous radio game brought about the ignominious failure of the plans of the foreign enemy, not the merits of a certain Kim Philby.' The trial revealed the operation in excruciating detail with a roster of names and dates. On 12 April the court pronounced the death sentence for the leading conspirators.[124]

The trial was followed by a reign of terror throughout the country in which, it has been estimated, several thousand people out of a population of less than two million were killed. Up to two hundred agents had already been lost, while the number of Albanians killed simply for being related to them may have been as high as a thousand. When asked about the loss of life, former OPC officer James McCargar could only mouth: 'Too bad.' Abas Ermenji later lamented the futility of the exercise: 'Our "allies" wanted to make use of Albania as a guinea-pig, without caring about the human losses, for an absurd enterprise that was condemned to failure.'[125]

There was nowhere for the operation to go, and it fell to the CIA South-East Division chief, John H. Richardson, to liquidate Operation Fiend. A wartime veteran of the Counter-Intelligence Corps in Italy, Vienna and Trieste, who joined the post-war Central Intelligence Group and then the CIA, 'Jocko' Richardson visited London, where he met with senior MI6 officials. He then flew to Rome and told a tearful station chief, Joseph Leib, that Albanian activities would end immediately. During the summer of 1954, Company 400 was disbanded, along with the training facilities at Heidelberg and the CIA-controlled base on the Greek island. The final surviving Albanians were resettled in Britain, the Commonwealth and the United States.[126]

The British had cut their ties to the operation earlier than the Americans but not early enough to avoid unnecessary bloodshed. Nicholas Bethell, who was struck by the tragic story of the Albanian survivors, remains bitter about those in MI6 who allowed it to continue beyond any sensible limit. 'They should have seen how it was going wrong. They should have aborted it and saved the lives of those involved.' Bethell, however, retains a romantic regard for the musketeers who initiated the project. It is hard to see why. While acknowledging that the operation had failed its objective of liberating Albania, Lord (Julian) Amery continued to believe that it had achieved some success in that 'it certainly forced the Soviets and the Albanians to call off the civil war in Greece'. There is no evidence for that assertion. More realistic is the caustic conclusion drawn by respected defence specialist John Keegan, in his review of Bethell's book *The Great Betrayal*. 'It is a gruesome story, made all the more so by the perception, apparently denied to the masterminds of subversion, that the Albanian communists, like the Yugoslavs, were far more adept at deciding the future of their country than a bunch of meddling romantic meddlers with a public school education and a free supply of plastic explosive.'[127]

The musketeers clung to the belief, and continued to do so, that Philby was responsible for the failure, but their *bête noire*, Sir Reginald Hibbert, is surely right to claim that the Albanian operations 'could have been expected to fail even if Philby had not betrayed them'.

> The enterprise was based on the wrong appreciation of the balance of forces in Albania. The condition of the people was undoubtedly deplorable and Hoxha had enemies in his own ranks. But the revolution had swept away everyone who was capable of acting as a leader outside the control of the ruling party. In this respect Albania was similar to the satellite countries of Eastern Europe. It was a forlorn hope to suppose that exiled followers of the nationalists who had failed in 1944 would, when trained by Smiley and infiltrated into Albania, be able to raise a following against the iron rule of the Communist Party of Albania after six years of draconian social engineering. The scheme was thought up and implemented by men who had failed to understand the revolutionary forces which enabled Hoxha and the CPA to come to power in 1944. All it achieved was to make Hoxha's long-standing propaganda line about the hostility of the capitalist powers and their nefarious intentions from wartime onwards appear more plausible, and to give Hoxha another pretext for tightening 'revolutionary' controls.[128]

On a wider front, the British and Americans were thus 'guilty of all the sins of subversion and interference, disregard for national sovereignty and war-mongering, of which they always accused their Cold War enemy, the Soviet Union'. It was not until 14 December 1990, nearly forty years later, that riots finally broke out in Tirana and other large cities. Statues of Hoxha and Stalin were pulled down and the process of building democracy began.

Ironically, it was not the result of activities by guerrillas and subverters but, Bethell concludes, the influence of Italian television which had been beamed into the country.[129]

CHAPTER 20

THE NTS AND 'YOUNG RUSSIANS'

Not only was MI6 engaged after the Second World War in supporting the various émigré separatist groups opposed to the Soviet Union, it also provided aid and comfort to a number of other anti-communist organisations that were similarly antagonistic to the Soviet regime but, unlike the nationalists, wanted to keep the Russian empire intact. Divided by a variety of often bewildering ideological and philosophical views, and riven by personal animosity, these 'Greater Russia' groups rarely co-operated with each other, preferring the tradition of factional in-fighting and the launching of tirades against their émigré nationalist 'enemies' in the Anti-Bolshevik Bloc of Nations (ABN), Abramtchik Faction, Intermarium and the Promethean League. The émigré Russians worked in the midst of a complex but small network of senior security and intelligence officers in MI5 and MI6 – most of Russian origin and strongly anti-communist – their agents and a number of crucial propaganda assets working with the exile community.

Anatole Baykolov, a White Russian, had arrived in Britain in 1917, and for many years worked as a journalist in London, supplementing his income as a translator and analyst of Soviet affairs. A 'mild liberal', Baykolov was chair of the Russian émigré Social Democrats in Britain. In 1923, he joined the Labour Party and acted as adviser to the General Council of the TUC on Russian affairs. Six years later, Baykolov published *In the Land of the Communist Dictatorship* – a book based on information on persecution collected from recent defectors from the USSR. It attracted the attention of the Duchess of

Atholl, who had begun to take a keen interest in what was happening inside the Soviet Union. She was to become a key friend to the émigrés during the war and in the immediate postwar years, when they were in desperate need of sympathetic allies.[1]

Kitty Atholl had been created a Dame of the British Empire in 1918. Two years later, her husband had been offered and had turned down the Crown of Albania, after Lloyd George, 'who had the imaginative but quixotic idea that the head of a Scottish clan might make an admirable leader of the mountain tribes of Albania', had proffered it twice to Aubrey Herbert, MP. In 1923, at the age of forty-nine, Kitty became the first Scottish woman Member of Parliament and was, for the next sixteen years, an influential figure on the Conservative Right.[2]

Baykolov proved to be 'a powerful influence' on Kitty, and she, in turn, used her contacts to open doors, enabling him to act as a 'free-lance diplomatic correspondent'. By the mid-thirties, with the duchess's help, he was a source of information and an adviser on Soviet affairs to Winston Churchill and the Permanent Under-Secretary at the Foreign Office, Sir Robert Vansittart, who employed him as part of his private intelligence network. When Kitty turned her attentions towards Germany, she too became a member of the Vansittart network, and was in receipt of information from his chief informant, Malcolm Christie. From this advantageous position Baykolov was able to obtain 'visas and other favours involving the Foreign Office'.[3]

During the twenties and thirties, Baykolov obtained much of his information from the traditional base of the Russian émigrés, Paris, where he had 'a special friend in the British Embassy'. Although he would almost certainly have known the MI6 head of station, Wilfred 'Biffy' Dunderdale, his contact was probably Dick Ellis, who worked undercover as a journalist and acted as a 'special friend' to the émigrés. Baykolov also co-operated with Ellis's key agent in Paris, Prince Anton Turkul of the White Russian Armed Services Union (ROVS), which schemed to restore the Tsarist monarchy in Russia. The source of much of Baykolov's information for Kitty Atholl was the Russian émigré group, the NTS (Narodnyi Trudovoy Soyuz, meaning National Labour Council, though usually mistranslated as 'National Alliance of Solidarists'). Turkul and the head of ROVS in the Balkans, Claudius Voss, had collaborated on the creation of the NTS, which was founded in Belgrade in July 1930. A leading British intelligence agent, Voss ran ROVS' MI6-friendly counter-intelligence service, the Inner Line, which sponsored the NTS. Baykolov convinced the duchess that 'the Russian émigré organisations were working overtime through bodies such as the NTS and others to undermine the Soviet regime and to form a provisional government when the Soviets collapsed'.[4]

No detailed or reliable account of the history of the NTS exists. It originally took its membership from a younger 'New Generation' of exiles who had fled the Bolshevik wrath and had settled in Yugoslavia and Bulgaria. It attracted those exiles who favoured the restoration of the geographical borders of the Tsarist empire, including the ethnic minorities and Slavic regions of the Balkans, Ukraine and Belorussia. Initially a left-of-centre grouping, NTS soon moved to the right, promoting an anti-Marxist philosophy of national-labour solidarity, based on three components – 'idealism, nationalism and activism'. It enjoyed the support of several European intelligence services, in particular MI6, and also attracted substantial funds from businessmen with interests in pre-revolutionary Russia, including Sir Henry Deterding, chair of Royal Dutch-Shell, and the armaments manufacturer Sir Basil Zaharoff. Although largely propagandist, the NTS did send individual members undercover into Russia, though little is known about these missions.[5]

Another anti-Marxist Russian group was the Mladorossy ('Union of Young Russia'), founded in Paris around 1930 by young, well-educated émigrés. A high proportion of its membership was made up of the sons of former Tsarist officials, who believed that only a monarchical form of government could fulfil Russia's historical legacy and lead the country back to greatness. The Mladorossy regarded the 1917 revolution in an interesting light, believing that it had been responsible for purging Russia of 'negative elements', while Stalin's policies in the 1930s were supported as a revival of nationalism which signalled the end of communism. Their slogan was 'The Tsar and the Soviets!' With a strong following in France and Belgium, the Mladorossy was led by Alexander Kazem-Bek, who, opposed to democracy, was impressed with Italian fascism – appropriating its style, psychology and anti-communism. His followers were also characterised by extreme anti-Semitism.[6]

As a 'Caesarist' organisation that believed in strong leaders, the NTS, too, was impressed by fascism, which was seen as 'a powerful force for the restoration of a feeling of pride in one's country'. Moving its headquarters to Paris in 1932 and then to Frankfurt, the NTS became an openly fascist group, supportive of the Nazi Party. In 1933, Kazem-Bek travelled to Berlin and signed a friendship pact with Bermondt-Avalov's Russian National Socialist Movement (ROND), which had the support of the Gestapo, but no long-term significant collaboration emerged from the meeting. The main problem was that these groups were deeply religious and opposed the Nazis' anti-clericalism. From 1934 onwards, the NTS found it 'increasingly unhealthy to operate within the Third Reich', and after a series of Gestapo raids it closed down its German branch in August 1938.[7]

It was around this time that Claudius Voss's MI6-sponsored Inner Line uncovered evidence that the NTS was penetrated by Soviet Intelligence, the NKVD. The head of the secret service section at NTS headquarters in Belgrade was arrested by Yugoslav police as a communist spy, while, at the same time, many NTS files disappeared. As a result, the Inner Line cut off financial support to the Russians, though the shortfall was made up by the Polish and Czechoslovakian intelligence services (Voss ran Slovak counter-intelligence), which were traditionally close to MI6. Senior NTS figure Dr Georgi Okolovich, a key MI6 agent who had run operations into Russia on behalf of Harry Carr, also worked for the Polish Intelligence 2nd Bureau of the general staff, whose representative, Captain Nexbritsky, made it possible for the NTS to send around 150 people on special missions into the Soviet Union to 'liberate the Homeland'. All were captured before they achieved anything, which gave rise to concerns about security breaches. According to one émigré account, the Polish Security Service discovered that Okolovich had been working with the Soviets. He was arrested as a communist spy, and after a trial was sentenced to death. He had 'powerful friends', however, and was able to escape via Romania to NTS headquarters in Belgrade.[8]

That Anatole Baykolov was in receipt of information from the Paris-based 'Alexander Guchkov circle', a secret military-intelligence group of White Russians tied to ROVS, gave rise to questions about his true loyalties. The circle worked closely with German intelligence agencies, though other sources suggest that it was heavily infiltrated by Soviet agents. A few émigrés in Paris claimed that Baykolov was working for Soviet intelligence – his work for Prince Turkul added to the suspicions – but this had more to do with the traditional émigré rivalries that plagued the movement, rather than any basis in fact. Certainly, Baykolov had the approval of the Security Service, and he remained in contact with senior MI5 counter-espionage officer and Soviet specialist Guy Liddell, who had strong links with the White Russian community. In turn, he was a major source of information for the Foreign Office's Sir Robert Vansittart.[9]

In the late thirties, Dick Ellis, who had his own links to German intelligence agencies, had been employed in the surveillance of the German embassy in London with another MI6 officer and member of the private Vansittart network, Captain Henry 'Bob' Kerby. Of Scottish parentage, 'a huge man with a bald, cannon ball head and rubbery features usually creased with a smile for he had a lively sense of humour', Captain Kerby was born in 1914, in St Petersburg, where his father – an adviser on forestry to the Tsar – was one of Britain's first MI6 agents. The family left Russia following the Bolshevik revolution and Kerby subsequently joined the British Army before being recruited in the mid-thirties into MI6, where his knowledge of Russian made him a natural for intelligence work. Baykolov had been one of Kerby's informants and had been responsible for reporting to MI5 that Mrs Wallis Simpson, the mistress of the Prince of Wales, was a secret agent of the Germans.[10]

The operations against the German embassy would not have succeeded without Kerby's close colleague in the Vansittart network, 'Klop' Ustinov, who also used Baykolov as an informant. Father of the actor/director Peter Ustinov, Klop was a Russo-German by birth. A short, dapper man who often sported a monocle, according to his son 'he seemed to fancy himself as something he was really not, a man of mystery, at least not in the way he understood it'. He had a strongly held belief in life as 'a superficial existence' and a personality which made him an ideal candidate for a spy. A journalist by trade, Klop was press attaché at the German embassy in London from the mid-twenties until the mid-thirties, when he was required to prove he was of 'pure Aryan descent'. Introduced to Vansittart by his private secretary, Sir Clifford Norton, he was quickly employed as an informant. Klop was also well acquainted with the Director-General of MI5, Sir Vernon Kell, and kept in touch with a stream of German visitors to his home at Redcliffe Gardens, who helped supply Vansittart with information on the Nazis. In reward, Vansittart secretly helped Klop apply for British citizenship. The 'notice of intent' was published in a Welsh-language newspaper in the knowledge that German Intelligence would have few Welsh-language experts. From that point on, Klop determined to appear British and deliberately expunged his past.[11]

With his strong connections to the Russian exile community, Ustinov was recruited by MI5 as an 'agent runner' and was closely involved with Dick White, Guy Liddell and Malcolm Cumming. His great success was in obtaining high-grade intelligence from Baron Wolfgang zu Putlitz, a junior secretary at the German embassy, who was also being run by his close friend Henry Kerby. Later, when zu Putlitz was air attaché at The Hague and realised that Walter Schellenberg's SS Security Service was moving in on him, Vansittart organised an operation whereby Klop 'travelled into Holland and, at great personal risk, led zu Putlitz to safety'.[12]

In 1939, just before the declaration of war, Kerby was appointed honorary attaché in Riga, Latvia, where he worked alongside Leslie Nicholson. It was not long, however, before Kerby and Nicholson were forced to flee to London via Russia. Kerby was then made acting consul at Malmö until 1941, 'where his Russian contacts, and most especially his contacts with the NKVD, were to come in very useful'. Subsequently classed 'specially employed War Office', Kerby worked with resistance movements behind enemy lines in Denmark, where he was briefly jailed, Poland and Yugoslavia.[13]

Although not officially aligned with the Nazis, a large number of NTS individuals and groups co-operated with Wehrmacht combat units, Alfred Rosenberg's Ostministerium (OMi) and Kaminsky's Russian Nazi Party. They were attracted by the call for 'an anti-communist revolution in the USSR, assassination of Soviet leaders, disenfranchisement of Jews, and confiscation of Jewish property' and found a sympathetic controller in OMi's Georg Leibbrant, though the Russian-born chief tended to favour the Baltic Germans and

Ukrainian separatists at the expense of the NTS. When war broke out, Vladimir Poremsky and other leading members of the NTS Executive Council, such as Dr Georgi Okolovich and Dr Alexander Truchnovich, rallied to the Nazi cause with a secret agenda to make themselves the new rulers of a puppet state inside the Nazi-occupied zones of the USSR. The small NTS, whose initials were paraphrased Nosin Smet Tiranom ('we bring death to traitors'), had a disproportionate influence, and this was exploited to achieve an effective monopoly of leadership among the émigrés seeking favour from the Nazis.[14]

The Mladorossy avoided the 'solidarists' of the OMi, preferring to back the Waffen-SS-sponsored Russian liberationists. Its leader in Europe during the war was the Cossack Nicholas Dulger-Sheiken, who left Russia following the defeat of the White armies. British-educated, Sheiken lived during the thirties in Greece, where he joined the 'Young Russians'. His true loyalties are difficult to disentangle, as he worked for German Intelligence while an agent for Greek counter-intelligence. He was, however, in contact with MI6 officers, including the managing director of a shipping company, Roger Gale, and a passport control official in the Athens embassy, Albert Crawford. He also knew 'Father Dimitri', alias David Balfour, who was said to be a personal friend of the Grand Duke Dimitri Pavlovitch. Before the war, Balfour had been in Paris, working in Russian émigré circles. In 1940, Sheiken arranged the escape of the Mladorossy leader, Kasem-Bek, from occupied France via Lisbon to the United States.[15]

Hitler's invasion of Russia in June 1941 split the émigrés and some Mladorossy members refused to back the Nazis, preferring the more honourable option of fighting for the Russian national revolution in the French Army and Resistance. Inevitably, NTS relations with the Nazis turned out to be highly ambivalent.

In the aftermath of Barbarossa, in the eastern areas occupied by the Wehrmacht, the Nazis employed a host of NTS members. Many worked for Admiral Canaris's Abwehr and General Gehlen's Fremde Heere Ost (FHO – Foreign Armies East), with the military favouring the NTS to the exclusion of other émigré groups. Russian was the language used in all dealings with the exiles, and the NTS exploited the situation by placing its cadres in strategic positions. The NTS became an integral part of the Nazi propaganda, espionage and extermination apparatus in the East. Vladimir Poremsky was appointed director of education at an OMi school, where he reported to the Gestapo on émigré 'suspects'. As head of a political department of the counter-intelligence known as 'Ingwar', Georgi Okolovich was responsible for combating the partisan movement in Belorussia and in locating Jews who had escaped the mass shootings. In January 1943 the staff of the Special Service Division 'R' (Sonderstab R) was formed as a front-line military intelligence unit comprised of former members of the Red Army who had surrendered to the Germans. Staffed largely by NTS members, its commander was the German general staff officer 'Colonel von Regenau', aka Boris Smyslov-sky-Holmston, a former White Russian officer who had fought against the Bolsheviks during the civil war.[16]

NTS influence was considerable in the various psychological warfare campaigns among PoWs. The main theme of its propaganda was the 'libera-tion' of the USSR from Stalin, communism and the Jews through a mutiny by the Red Army. A Russian radio station was established to pump out NTS propaganda which represented Adolf Hitler as the liberator of 'all the peoples of Russia' whose purpose was the promotion of eternal friendship and alli-ance between 'free and united Russia' and 'the great German nation'.[17]

In December 1943, on behalf of MI6's Section V head, Kim Philby, Klop Ustinov was posted to Portugal, where he remained for the rest of the war. His brief was 'to establish contact with those German opposition circles which wanted to join the Allied side', working under the counter-intelligence resi-dent, Charles de Salis. According to his wife, he expected to be assassinated at any time and was told that Schellenberg wanted to poison him: 'He always expected a needle from a lethal syringe to pierce his skin and he stood with his back to the wall, facing and watching everybody.' Klop was subsequently to play an important role in disentangling the role of Prince Turkul in the German-backed 'Max-Klatt' intelligence network which claimed to have a spy ring inside the top levels of the Soviet military.[18]

Operation MONASTERY had originally been conceived in July 1941 by the Soviet Administration for Special Tasks and the Secret Political Depart-ment of the NKVD in close co-operation with the GRU as a counter-intelligence exercise. Its aim was to penetrate the Abwehr's exile agent networks inside the Soviet Union by creating a pro-German, anti-Soviet organisation known as 'Throne' which sought contacts with the German high command. The chosen agent was Aleksandr Demyanov, whose father had been chief of counter-intelligence for the White Army in the northern Caucasus. Code-named 'Max' by the Abwehr, Demyanov made contact with the Germans in December, but instead of backing Throne, they recruited him as a full-time agent with the task of setting up a Moscow-based spy ring. In early 1942, Max was parachuted back into the Soviet Union to set up his network but, in a direct parallel with the British double-cross operation, the Soviets created a phantom network with apparent sources of information among 'elderly ex-Tsarist officers'. This phantom network became an impor-tant channel of 'disinformation' which was passed on to another German agent, Richard Kauder (Klatt), who, in turn, communicated directly with the FHO intelligence head, General Gehlen.[19]

Much of this was known to the British. In a highly secret interception operation, Bletchley Park's Government Code and Cypher School (GC&CS) had monitored the steady stream of signals originating in Sofia which revealed the military and strategic plans of the Red Army. It showed that information was being sent by agent Klatt to Abwehr headquarters in Berlin. The Russian source of this information was pinpointed to 'a secret transmitter operating near Kuibyshey, on the Volga, where the NKVD Intelligence Centre had been evacuated when the fall of Moscow seemed imminent'. British knowledge of the operation was, in turn, known by the NKVD, which had been kept well informed by one of its agents in London, MI5 officer Anthony Blunt, who handed over the GC&CS material to his Soviet control. As the Klatt traffic continued, MI5 'reluctantly concluded that it must be part of some gigantic double-cross system which the Russians were using deliberately'. This was correct, but MI5 went on to erroneously conclude that Klatt 'was a double agent used by the Russians to feed the Abwehr with chicken feed'.[20]

A number of authors have drawn similar conclusions and asserted that Soviet agents within the émigré community in the West were responsible for establishing the bona fides of Max and, indeed, took credit for finding such an impressive source of information. According to one of the Soviet officers at the centre of the deception, however, 'these leaders were never double agents. They were simply exploiting a good opportunity to verify a name for the Abwehr and thus justify their financial support by the Germans.' Indeed, the Germans only used Max 'intensively when they were convinced he was not involved in the pre-war intelligence operations of the Russian émigrés', which they knew had been thoroughly penetrated. The other key agents in his Max–Klatt network were planted on him by the Germans and not by the Russians.[21]

At the end of 1944, Walter Schellenberg, now head of SD foreign intelligence, instituted a formal inquiry into Klatt's activities. There were two views within SD as to whether he was a genuine agent or a Soviet plant. It seems that at the beginning of 1945, the Gestapo in Vienna had decided that he was a Soviet agent, but this view changed in March when he managed to persuade an Abwehr officer that he must escape from the city before the arrival of the approaching Russians. An SD officer agreed to his request and he was allowed to move westward with an officer who had been told to let him escape on the way.[22]

During the spring of 1943 the German Army, with the NTS playing an important role, had experimented with the establishment of a Russian Liberation Movement and Army (ROD), built around a dissident Red Army lieutenant-general, Andrei Vlasov, famous for his defence of Moscow as commander of the Soviet 20th Army. For ideological reasons, Hitler had no intention of allowing a full-scale Russian army, and its nominal leader, Vlasov, was retained merely as a propaganda weapon. The idea was revived by Himmler in January 1944 and led to the emergence of several assorted units. According to Catherine Andreyev, however, ROD 'never in fact existed, it was a term coined by those Germans agitating for a change in Nazi policy towards the Soviet Union, and they created a mythical army in order that those Soviet citizens fighting in the ranks of the Wehrmacht should feel some kind of unity and have some concrete aim for which to fight'. A unified military formation 'remained a desire and not a reality'.[23]

Although Vlasov refused to endorse the organisation, the NTS had a 'very significant influence' on the proposed liberation movement. Victor Baydalakov, who had been head of the NTS since 1930, became part of the Vlasov ideological leadership, while other senior figures, such as Dr Vladimir Poremsky, General Trukhin and General Meandov, played a central role in the Army Intelligence's political warfare project around Vlasov, serving as political officers among the eastern European troops who defected to the Nazis.[24]

Even though the NTS was treated preferentially, its leaders considered themselves as 'Russian patriots' who believed in the sanctity and concept of the Russian Empire. Increasingly, they became dissatisfied with their position with regard to German ambitions in the East and especially concerning the treatment of Russian PoWs. Their support began to take on an anti-German line as they finally realised that the Nazis intended to subjugate the Russian people into a state of semi-slavery. During 1944, with the Red Army moving steadily westward, the NTS opened itself up to discussion of political matters and adopted a new draft programme which paid heed to the new Soviet realities. New Soviet members inserted a passage into the NTS manifesto to the effect that all nationalities whose territories lay within the boundaries of the Russian state were part of the nation: 'The only exception to this were foreigners and Jews.' The taking up of anti-Semitism was a new trend.[25]

In the end, Russian national interests led the NTS into conflict with the Gestapo, which did not particularly trust Dr Poremsky and the other leaders owing to their past employment by British Intelligence. Investigations by the Intelligence Section of the German Special Service Division 'R' also revealed that there was a small section of NTS members in Berlin who were in fact working for the Soviets. With their powerful backers, the NTS members were initially given the benefit of the doubt, but when, during the summer of 1944, the NTS headquarters in Warsaw was discovered to be in communication with the Soviets, the Gestapo began a round-up of senior NTS officials. More than sixty were sent to concentration camps, where twenty-eight perished. By the end of the year, a further two hundred had been arrested. This did not stop the remaining NTS leaders from co-operating with the Germans in organising stay-behind networks in the East but, as the Red Army passed by, most were mopped up by NKVD troops.[26]

On 14 November 1944, five hundred delegates assembled in Prague amid scenes of great rejoicing, to launch the manifesto of Vlasov's Committee for the Liberation of the Peoples of Russia (KONR), which called for the overthrow of the Bolsheviks. The Prague manifesto, which was carried by radio and was heard with enthusiasm by Russian PoWs in Allied camps in France, accepted 'aid from Germany, always provided that such aid is consistent with the honour and independence of our Homeland. This aid, at the moment, provides the only practical possibility of armed struggle against the Stalinist clique.' In January 1945, Vlasov was finally allowed to form two divisions which were known as the Armed Forces of the Committee for the Liberation of the Peoples of Russia (VS KONR). On 22 February, the former head of Division 'R', General Smyslovsky-Holmston, was given permission by Vlasov to create the 1st Russian National Liberation Army, which was only allowed to exist because of the bureaucratic nature of the Nazi regime. It was all in vain, however, as the war was soon over.[27]

During March 1945, those NTS leaders still alive after internment in the concentration camps were released by the Gestapo following pressure from Vlasov. By what means or through whom it is no longer known, but Dr Poremsky managed to contact his former British Intelligence sponsors before the final defeat of Germany.[28]

In July 1944, the War Cabinet had accepted the principle that if the Soviet Union demanded the return of PoWs they would have to be handed over. This all-embracing policy of compulsion was very much opposed by the man responsible for SOE, Lord Selbourne, but there had been intense and inevitable pressure from Soviet officials, who privately feared the motives of the 'English interventionists'. 'Only too easily would they suspect Britain was planning to harbour enemies of the Soviet Union to build up the nucleus of collaborators with fascism, anti-Soviet fanatics, who would be armed with British or American weapons and launched against the Motherland.' Evidence existed to back the views of both Selbourne and the Soviets.[29]

Selbourne had information from the head of SOE's Russian section – which had responsibility for persuading Soviet citizens in German ranks to desert – suggesting that Russian PoWs were being repatriated against their will. Major Len Manderstam had personally intervened to save forty members of the Russian ROD captured in France, with the intention of training them for operations behind German lines. A Latvian exile and fluent Russian-speaker who had served in the Bolshevik Army, Manderstam had turned violently anti-communist, eventually emigrating to South Africa before volunteering in 1939 for military service in SOE. Soviet NKVD liaison officers in Britain had objected to Manderstam's plan, particularly when they discovered that the Russians in camps in Surrey and Yorkshire were being courted by exiled White Russians. Georgi Knupffer, leader of the Mladorossy in Britain, was accused of spreading Tsarist propaganda among the PoWs. Born in St Petersburg, Knupffer regarded the 1917 revolution as a plot by Jewish bankers. In exile, he became heavily involved in monarchist politics, founding an Integralist organisation in Britain. He was said by fellow – but more moderate – anti-communist Geoffrey Stewart-Smith to be 'well known in Britain for his anti-Semitic views' and for playing down evidence of Nazi war crimes.[30]

To appease the Soviets, the Foreign Office tried to dismiss Manderstam, suggesting that because he was 'a Russian-speaking Balt' he was incapable of carrying out 'an objective interrogation'. The demand was successfully rebuffed by Selbourne and Colin Gubbins of SOE, and Manderstam was able to save his forty parachutists. (Where the Russians disappeared to is not known, but one suspects into the arms of British Intelligence and the NTS.)

By the middle of 1945 most of the Russian PoWs had been returned to the Soviet Union. The last major party of over three hundred, destined for almost certain liquidation at the hands of the security police, was accompanied, kicking and screaming, to the Soviet Zone in Germany by MI6 officer Captain David Crichton of the Russian Liaison Group. The handling of the Russian PoWs set a pattern to which the British government stuck, in the main, under the legal agreement signed at the inter-Allied conference held at Yalta in February 1945. The agreement obliged the British authorities to repatriate, by force if necessary, tens of thousands of 'Soviet citizens' – both PoWs and civilians – though forced repatriation was a definition left open to differing interpretations. The agreement stemmed from the concern of the western allies to secure the speedy repatriation of their own nationals who had been captured by the Germans and liberated by the advancing Red Army.[31]

In the early spring of 1945, a roving SOE unit operating in the Carpathian Alps under the command of Patrick Martin-Smith received intelligence that a large band of Cossacks, who realised that the war was lost, wished to join the Allies. The day after VE day, reports came in of continuing fighting between the Cossack Corps and Yugoslavs. A senior SOE officer, Major Charles Villiers, who had a long association with Tito's partisans, was sent to restore order and secure the surrender of the Cossacks. Hoping to find a refuge in the West, the Cossacks, proud of their anti-Bolshevism and responsible for many bloody massacres in the name of this cause, put their faith in the Allied commander-in-chief in Italy, Field Marshal Alexander, who had fought against the Bolsheviks with the Baltic *landswehr* in Courland and still 'bore proudly' a Russian Imperial Order. Their hopes were misplaced, however, and on 1 June they were repatriated amid appalling scenes of chaos. A number of Cossack officers shot themselves after killing their wives and children.[32]

A different fate awaited the White Russian Schutzkorps which, on 21 May 1945, was saved from extradition. The sole surviving unit of the old Russian Imperial Army had, after the civil war, set up a skeleton military establishment in Serbia to train a future anti-Bolshevik army. Led by an Imperial officer, Colonel Anatol Rogozhin, the German-armed Schutzkorps was saved by the intervention of Col. Walton Ling, Assistant Red Cross Commissioner for Civilian Relief in northern Italy. During 1919, Ling had served as a senior artillery liaison officer in the British Military Mission to the White Armies in South Russia. He 'saw their recent struggle against Tito's partisans as but a continuation of the war against Bolshevism'. Found a safe haven in Austria, at Klin St Veit, by August 1945 over half of Rogozhin's 3,500 troops had simply disappeared. Their disappearance had not gone unnoticed and, at Potsdam, Soviet officials handed the British a complaint that Rogozhin was heading an anti-Soviet force around Klagenfurt.[33]

On 3 May 1945 General Smolensky-Holmston and his 1st National Russian Army had crossed over the Swiss border and were eventually interned in Liechtenstein for three years. Early in the month, Dr Poremsky tried, on Vlasov's behalf, to contact the British in Hamburg, hoping to persuade them not to send back Vlasov troops captured by the western Allies. The mission failed. One who managed to escape was Wilfred Strik-Strikfelt, a Russian-speaking Balt and Vlasov's main liaison officer with the German Army. Born and educated in pre-1917 Russia, of a German merchant family, he had fought with the White Army against the Reds. Of strong 'pro-British sympathies', Strik-Strikfelt had worked with MI6 before the war. Vlasov's KONR survivors were hunted by the Red Army units in Czechoslovakia and many were quickly liquidated. Vlasov himself fell into Russian hands on 12 May 1945, west of Hanover. On 26 August 1946 Pravda announced that Vlasov and nine of his officers had been condemned to death and hanged; rumour had it by piano wire with a hook inserted at the base of the skull.[34]

Contingents of NTS stragglers and former members of Vlasov's army found their way finally to an UNRRA camp at Moenchehof, near Kassel in the western region of Germany. When the end came, several senior NTS leaders who might have been tried as collaborators were freed by the Americans. Only Dr Poremsky – 'a 200% Nazi' – was imprisoned as a war criminal, but he was released in 1946 on 'health grounds' following the intervention of MI6. Poremsky made no secret of his collaboration with the Germans but claimed that it had been with the consent of the British. MI6 needed him to renew his leadership of the organisation and relaunch its activities, which began in November 1945 with republication of the paper *Possev* (The Seed). NTS leaders made efforts to sell their intelligence networks to the Allies, and with the support of the US military government set up a 'secret operations committee' which established sections for espionage and subversion, internal security and liaison with the western intelligence agencies. The problem was, however, that NTS clandestine activities inside the USSR turned out to be greatly exaggerated, mostly untrue and largely mythical. In addition, as with the other émigrés, the NTS was hampered by leadership splits over its direction.[35]

While stationed in Rome immediately after the war, MI6 officer Kenneth Benton developed a useful informant working for UNRRA. From a Tsarist family that had escaped to England following the 1917 revolution, the inform- ant knew a number of anti-communist exiles in Rome, including a young aristocrat who had worked in the Soviet government service and whom Benton hoped to recruit as a source. In turn, the young aristocrat was being sought by the NKVD because he was a member of the NTS. When Benton telegraphed the head of the Political Section in London with his good news, he was astonished with David Footman's reply that 'we do not use Russian émigré organisations'. Benton believed that Footman was echoing Kim Philby, who had 'made no secret of his contempt for the wretched right-wing refugees from Communism who were his potential recruits'. Philby said, 'never trust a Tsarist émigré. They're all as twisty as eels.' While Footman's assessment was undoubtedly correct, other sections within MI6 were already recruiting among the Russian émigrés.[36]

Under the direction of MI6 Controller for Western Europe, Kenneth Cohen, in the newly liberated countries agents were recruited from the DP camps using MI6-sponsored 'charities' such as the Organisation for Assist- ance to Foreign Displaced Persons in Germany. The NTS organised mass escapes from the camps and protested – at times successfully with refugee groups – against the forced repatriations of former Russian citizens. The NTS initially had some success in the chaos of eastern Europe in gathering information from Russian military and civilian personnel in the occupied territories, and helped in a number of low-level defections. Senior MI6 officers stationed in Germany, including Harold Shergold and John Bruce-Lockhart, were urged by headquarters to recruit Russians for the MI6-backed NTS intelligence-gathering Operation SHRAPNEL, which 'cost a lot of money' but in the end produced 'poor results'. The broker for NTS agents interested in employment with MI6 and the other western agencies was Berlin propa- gandist Yvegniy Romanov, chair of the NTS Executive Bureau. His closest colleague, NTS chair Poremsky, also ran the Possev publishing house, in Munich, where millions of leaflets were printed at British and American expense for use in propaganda operations inside the USSR.[37]

In early 1946, a founder member and a senior figure throughout the war, Constantine Boldyrev, created elaborate plans under MI6, French and United States sponsorship for NTS-led bands of exiles to be established undercover, away from prying Soviet eyes, as construction companies based in Morocco. Meanwhile, a White Russian aristocrat émigré who had lived in Germany for many years, Prince Boloselsky, toured the DP camps looking for Russian PoWs and Vlasov veterans to work in Morocco with the promise of a 'prosper- ous life'. An ex-Soviet serviceman and PoW who joined the German Army, N. I. Yakuta, had been interned in a Munich DP camp at the end of hostilities. He soon regretted his decision in 1946 to go to Casablanca. 'Without a cent in my pocket, ignorant of the language and morally depressed, I was compelled to sell my labour for almost a song in order to keep body and soul together.' Yakuta spent five years in Morocco in back-breaking jobs. In reality, 'these were military groups, companies of the Vlasov Army, most of them soldiers together with their officers'. Boldyrev recalled that 'we kept them together in order to provide special fighting units in a war with the Soviets'. The intelligence agencies subsidised these Vlasov colonies, at the same time preserving their military potential. Groups of them were subsequently sent to the Allied zones in Germany to be trained at Bad Homburg and Bad Wiessee for operations inside Russia. MI6 ran the NTS infiltration operations from Klagenfurt under cover of its local station, the 'Co-ordination Division' of the Austrian Control Commission.[38]

Lord Vansittart had not been idle during the war years. He maintained close personal contact with Sir Stewart Menzies and Desmond Morton, Churchill's own intelligence adviser, who was haunted by the spectre of postwar communism. By August 1944, Vansittart had already voiced in public his anti-Soviet views: 'His suspicion of Russian ambitions was traditional and deep-rooted; his acceptance of the Soviet Union as a wartime ally was an act of expediency, an extreme indication of his anti-Germanism.' Following the defeat of Nazi Germany, Vansittart did not retire gracefully but instead embarked on his own semi-official anti-communist crusade. An early Cold War advocate who believed that Russia was 'possessed with the lust of world domination', he used the House of Lords to rail against the Soviet Union and what was happening in eastern Europe. 'Time and time again he inveighed against the violation of basic human rights behind the Iron Curtain, and exposed for public scrutiny the fate of political prisoners.'[39]

In the immediate post-hostilities phase, Vansittart acted as a 'babysitter' to the various exile movements, primarily the Czechs and the Yugoslavs but also the Russians, supporting and encouraging them in their political aspirations. His own pre-war anti-German intelligence network, which remained largely intact, helped him to pursue a private propaganda anti-Soviet liberation policy. He also retained links with Kitty Atholl and with leading MI5 and MI6 figures. His conduit and informant, Anatole Baykolov, ingratiated himself with various right-wing newspapers and magazines, supplying them with information about the alleged ill-treatment of Russian PoWs in Britain; information that most likely came via his friend, Dr Georgi Knupffer, the Russian Mladorossy émigré, who had been promoting Tsarist propaganda in the camps.

The Young Russians were reconstituted after the war in Munich as the Russian Revolutionary Force (RRF), an émigré resistance movement apparently running psychological warfare operations, mostly from a radio station and with extensive leafletting, in the Balkans and the southern states of the Soviet Union. Knupffer was its political officer with responsibility for fund-raising, though from where he drew his financial support is not known; other émigrés assumed that the source was the intelligence agencies. Suspicions were aroused by Knupffer's habit of castigating the efforts of all the other émigré groups. He was seen as a highly disruptive figure within the Russian émigré community.

A number of right-wing commentators have suggested that Baykolov was a Soviet 'agent of influence' but, although he may have been, no real evidence has been proffered. In fact, Baykolov continued to enjoy the support of MI5, whose Soviet expert, Guy Liddell, assured Vansittart that he was 'very reputable'. Vansittart also built up his links with the émigrés through association with the British and the Scottish Leagues for European Freedom.[40]

Behind the scenes, Vansittart was helped by Liddell, who had responsibilities through Operation POST REPORT for MI5's security files on the émigrés, and by Kim Philby and Section IX, which was recruiting among the exiles. A key figure was Karl Marcus, who, working on behalf of Walter Schellenberg, had been sent to France in November 1944 in order to establish contact with Vansittart as part of an aborted peace negotiation. Marcus had worked in Belorussia, controlling networks of Soviet collaborators, and through working with Schellenberg knew the identities of key agents in eastern Europe. After the war, he was appointed mayor in a small town in the British Zone of Germany, able to provide new identity cards and assistance to old SS comrades. Word soon spread that the British were recruiting anti-communist experts.[41]

As part of the post-hostilities assessments by MI5 and MI6 counter-intelligence of the German and Soviet intelligence services, another former member of the Vansittart private intelligence network, Klop Ustinov, made frequent trips to Germany in the uniform of a British colonel. Speaking perfect German, he was 'obviously the ideal person to be entrusted with the interrogation of suspect Nazis' and was deeply involved in the denazification process. Late in 1946 Klop was transferred to Geneva and Berne, where the head of station was Nicholas Elliott, whose family he had known since the beginning of the war. Elliott also knew Vansittart through his father, the headmaster of Eton, and 'consulted him on numerous occasions'. The Elliotts were 'devoted to Klop' and the pair spent a good deal of time attempting to piece together a picture of the postwar Soviet intelligence networks in Europe.[42]

Towards the end of the war, British counter-intelligence teams had discovered, in Brussels, a cache of German intelligence dossiers dealing with a Soviet GRU espionage network, the Rote Kapelle (Red Chapel), which revealed numerous links to an important Swiss branch. In March 1947, a former British member of the Swiss end of the ring, Allan Foote, gave himself up to the authorities in Berlin and was able to present his MI5 debriefer,

Courtney Young, with a full picture of its activities, adding greatly to the limited knowledge gathered from investigations of Soviet radio signals carried out by the Swiss Bundespolizei. Analysis of these dossiers enabled Elliott and Klop to draw up a detailed picture of GRU activities in Switzerland, which provided MI6 with a blueprint for communist activities during the Cold War. Contrary to the recollection of one of the ring's leading figures that the controllers of the Comintern had 'decided that Soviet Intelligence would no longer use Communist militants' and that there would be 'a total separation between the secret service and the Party', the Elliott/Ustinov assessment concluded that the majority of the GRU's sources 'were lifelong Communist activists'. As Nigel West has pointed out, the pair were given 'a unique opportunity to study the methodology of a Soviet network, offering several tangible clues to post-war espionage'.[43]

As part of their study of the German intelligence services, MI5 and MI6 counter-intelligence staff put together a report on the 'Max–Klatt' spy network which had supplied the Abwehr with intelligence on the Soviet military and which had aroused the suspicions of the professionals for its apparent successes. It was viewed as an 'extensive and infallible intelligence service which delivered information with equal speed from Leningrad, Kuibischev, Nororossik on the Western desert . . . suspiciously free from the administrative hitches to which most spy systems are liable'.[44]

On 3 May 1945, Klatt was released from a Gestapo prison and subsequently picked up in Austria by the United States Counter-Intelligence Corps (CIC) which, in turn, handed him over to the Office of Strategic Services (OSS). Klatt and his colleagues hoped to reconstruct an agent network in the Soviet Union which could be sold to western intelligence agencies. By November, Allen Dulles's successor to the OSS, the Strategic Services Unit (SSU), had concluded an agreement with Klatt, and he was put to work in Salzburg against the communists. What they obtained for their money, however, appears to have been little more than an expensive paper-mill, which produced no intelligence of value. The Soviets also tried to reactivate Max in Paris after the war, but the émigrés were no longer interested and the operation quickly collapsed.[45]

A leading member of the Max–Klatt network was the 'notorious professional spy' General Turkul, about whom some British intelligence and security officers were sceptical. In reviewing his activities, MI5's Peter Wright believed that Turkul had been a Soviet agent all along. Towards the end of the war Turkul had assumed control of a Vlasov unit of Chetniks and pro-fascists for use against Tito's partisans. He also established contacts with the Allies, and by the end of hostilities had managed to find refuge in Austria, where he set up a 'Russian National Central Committee'. Employed by the SSU on the 'Crown Project', Turkul looked out for communist agents among the 'defectors' and those refugees sent down the ratlines. During 1946, a joint British-American Special Counter-Intelligence Unit (SCI/A) used him to re-recruit a former anti-communist colleague and fellow-pre-war MI6 agent living in Germany, Claudius Voss.

MI6 and the SSU employed both Voss and Klatt's deputy, Ira Longin, in building 'intelligence nets', though the SCI/A had strong suspicions that Voss was a long-standing communist agent. Turkul's strident anti-Semitic and anti-communist propaganda activities also attracted the attention of the CIC, which began to investigate his past. It did not, however, have any evidence to indicate that Turkul was anything other than 'an old-time anti-Bolshevik constantly dreaming of leading again the fight against the Soviets with any available means'. The CIC thought him to be a 'vain, not-too-clever opportunist seeking always to be at the head of an organisation of power and influence'. During the spring, the CIC foiled a Soviet attempt to kidnap Klatt and, in expectation of a similar move against him, in July Turkul left Salzburg for Germany, where he tried to embark for South America. This was seen later as evidence, when he did not go east, that he was not a Soviet agent and that he had 'allowed himself to be "used" by known or suspected Soviet agents due to his own stupidity, blind vanity, or his own non-evaluation of personalities around him'. In September 1946, he was arrested by the CIC along with Klatt and Longin, who were all transported for interrogation to the 7707th European Command Intelligence Centre (Camp King) at Oberursel in the US Zone in Germany.[46]

Turkul was interrogated by a wartime MI6 officer, Professor Gilbert Ryle, and a CIC officer, Johnson. They produced a report which concluded that there was 'no doubt' that the Max–Klatt network had acted as 'a trojan horse' for Soviet intelligence. In parallel, Klatt was also interrogated by Arnold Silver, later a senior CIA officer, who realised that Turkul's 'entire so-called network for the Abwehr was a Soviet-controlled military deception operation from beginning to end'. He further suggested that Turkul was 'a useless oaf who had lent his name to the Klatt network as the man who allegedly recruited sources in the USSR'. According to Silver, Turkul 'never recruited even one source, although Klatt managed to convince the Abwehr that Turkul was one of his principal agents'.[47]

By early 1947, MI6 had concluded its investigation of Turkul and Longin, but it had a continuing interest in determining whether the Max–Klatt network had, indeed, been used for deception purposes. The officer given the task was Klop Ustinov, who was sent to Camp King to question Klatt. After intensive interrogation by Silver and Ustinov, Klatt was removed to a cell where he attempted to hang himself. Cut down, Klatt subsequently revealed that he had suspected as early as the end of 1941 that his network was being used by the Soviets. He later discovered that one of his key agents had indeed been a Soviet agent. Klatt was also able to confirm that Turkul and Longin 'had been mere figureheads to help add an air of authenticity to the network'. As Russian émigrés, 'they could plausibly have acquaintances in the USSR who could be developed into sources'. Neither, though, 'knew that the entire operation was Soviet-controlled'.[48]

By mid-year Klatt, Longin and Turkul, the latter's credentials again checked by MI5, had been released into the US Zone in Germany where they were able to resume their anti-communist crusade. A member of the League of Saint Andrew's Flag and the Russian Monarchist Organisation, Turkul resumed leadership of the 'new' NTS, which was eventually taken up by the Gehlen Organisation under the sponsorship of the Americans. Klop Ustinov remained in Switzerland until early 1948, and then returned to a 'hush-hush' job in intelligence in London.[49]

From 1948 onwards Prince Turkul tried to merge the different Russian anti-communist/Soviet groups into a workable coalition. The result was the 'Combat Union for the Liberation of the Peoples of Russia' with its own military centre called SWOD. His tactics, however, were seen by other émigré leaders and intelligence officials as divisive and disruptive. Emigré leaders such as Turkul and others in the NTS were described at the time by western intelligence officials as 'hotheads' and 'dreamers' but, since they were the only group thought to have penetrated Russia, they were supported despite the misgivings.[50]

The principal NTS Council members were the president and spiritual leader, Dr Poremsky; Georgi Okolovich, controller of secret operations, who worked for the Gehlen Org.; Roman Redlich, Okolovich's deputy; Evgeny Romanov, liaison officer with MI6 and the CIA; Michail Olskej, in charge of the internal security service and operations against other émigré groups such as the Ukrainian OUN-B; and an MI6 agent, Lev Rar, Director of the Foreign Organisations Branch (UZU). Working for the Nazis, Rar had been given a post in the secretariat of the Vlasov Committee. After the surrender of Germany, he was held in the Fussen PoW camp and later moved to Britain, where he worked for the BBC. He was regarded as an expert in running various NTS 'fronts'.[51]

Despite NTS propaganda which suggested that the organisation was engaged in a successful penetration of the Soviet Union, the reality was very different. In 1949, in what was an indirect criticism of the NTS methods, the director of psychological warfare for the US Army, Lieutenant-General Wedemeyer, admitted that 'the life of an agent in Russia today would not be worth very much. We do have a few. That is something that has to be generated very slowly, an intelligence organisation within Russia. We do not get from Russia very good intelligence reports, but they are improving.' In acknowledgement that any networks that existed were being mopped up by the secret police, in January the NTS's governing Council adopted a resolution calling for the complete reorganisation of the movement. A new strategy, the so-called 'Molecular Theory', using a decentralised cell structure of agents inside the Soviet Union, was to be implemented with cells building on other cells. While that may have been a rational response to failure, the claim that this was necessary for the preparation of a revolution with direct action inside the Soviet Union flew in the face of the facts. Separate MI6- and CIA-sponsored NTS operations in the Soviet Union were spectacularly unsuccessful.[52]

In May 1949, former SS leader Werner Ohletz, previously in charge of the section that had taken over military intelligence from Admiral Canaris, and with extensive experience of the Russian émigré organisations, warned the US War Department that it was 'dangerous to co-operate with the NTS'. He reported that German counter-intelligence had found that all the émigré organisations 'were infiltrated by the NKVD with such effectiveness that it was impossible to discover the connecting lines from top ranking people to the common follower'. Gehlen's officers in the Organisation could never be sure whether they were dealing with 'figments of their imagination of some harum-scarum intelligence peddler, or with doctored material fed to them by the Russians'. On the back of the Ohletz report, one source warned Gehlen that 'ninety per cent of all intelligence reaching the Americans is fake', while one of his investigators concluded that 'people working directly for the Soviet Union are recklessly given cover and support' in the NTS. A US Staff Intelligence Report chose the NTS as an example of the danger of employing émigré organisations as intelligence collection agencies. It concluded that the NTS was thoroughly penetrated by Russian agents, open to Soviet deception measures, unreliable and irresponsible. They did not want their own agencies to fall into the trap of the Germans, who had failed to realise that the NTS was working for the Soviets.[53]

It was against this background of entirely negative reports that MI6's Kim Philby, in Washington as liaison officer with the OPC/CIA, attempted to reach some kind of agreement on co-operation with the Americans on the émigrés and, in particular, the NTS. Under-Secretary of State Robert Lovett had recently ordered a 'careful study' of the Vlasov movement. During the subsequent meetings, which Philby viewed with a degree of amusement, there were 'many skirmishes', particularly over the reasons for a series of unsuccessful drops of NTS agents into the Soviet Union. Although MI6 put up a stubborn rearguard action in favour of the NTS with which they had long been associated, 'the story was one of general American encroachment ... The dollar was just too strong. And for financial reasons MI6 was compelled to transfer by a formal agreement responsibility for NTS operations to the CIA.'[54]

MI6 and the CIA agreed to establish a 'Joint Centre' at Frankfurt to exploit the assets of the NTS, who claimed that an active network was still operating inside the Soviet Union. They agreed to co-operate on the infiltration operations known as SHRAPNEL, with the Americans taking on the responsibility for funding. Philby was not displeased with the outcome, as one of his tasks for his Soviet intelligence masters was to aggressively stir up factional disputes between the Russians and other non-Russian émigré groups, while at the same time betraying every agent to his NKVD handlers. Then a junior officer, George Blake later recalled that though the CIA's 'methods of operating were on the whole not to the liking of most SIS officers who, both by tradition and necessity, practised a more subtle approach and favoured more discreet ways of getting-hold of intelligence, the CIA, by sheer force of numbers and money, was able to produce far more information than SIS, with all its experience and know-how, could ever hope to lay hands on'.[55]

By 1950, the espionage assignments were chosen by the CIA with logistical support from the Gehlen Org. The British role appears to have been purely one of training while partaking in psychological warfare and counter-intelligence operations in exchange for the intelligence 'take' – which was mediocre at the best of times. The CIA used the Institute for the Study of the USSR as an annex to the NTS, where recruits could be housed. At least ten NTS members at any one time were trained in Kaufbeuren and at an advanced camp at Bad Wiesee while others were trained in the British Zone. NTS operatives spent up to nine months on the British course at MI6's Holland Park facility, where they were taught to operate radio transmitters, use invisible ink and secret codes, and collect military intelligence. At Fort Monckton and at secret camps in the countryside, where there were mock-ups of Soviet border guard posts, operatives practised river crossings. MI6 'baby-sitters' 'Foster' and 'Radford' looked after the NTS recruits, who had been brought in from throughout Europe.[56]

Morale within the training groups was not always good, especially when they received reports that other NTS teams had been captured by the Soviets. A Soviet propaganda booklet, *Caught in the Act* (1963), lists twenty-three agents captured trying to penetrate the Soviet Union between 1951 and 1960. One of these, N. I. Yakuta, had been recruited into a labour unit in Casablanca and, hence, into the NTS by Georgi Okolovich. Trained by the CIA for a mission into Russia, he was given a suicide pill by his trainers, who told him that if captured he was to deny his connections with the Americans and 'say that I was connected with the French Intelligence Service'. On occasions, the Americans were blamed for poor planning, while Okolovich was held responsible for operational 'bungling'. Eventually, Radford told his charges that 'in the changed situation it had been decided to wind up the training programme and postpone the landings'. The problem, though not one immediately apparent to the intelligence agencies, was that the NTS was riddled with Soviet agents. Added to this, the NTS appeared to have no actual agents in the field.[57]

On 11 May 1951, Conservative MP John Baker-White, director of the Economic League and an acknowledged expert in psychological warfare, who had worked with MI6, told the House of Commons that 'there are broadcasts by various anti-Communist political groups. For example, from Madrid there are broadcasts directed to Russia by the Russian Revolutionary Force (RRF) ... There is a steady infiltration under the Iron Curtain of anti-Soviet leaflets emanating from various émigré groups ...' A year later, the RRF was in the news for a 'cloak-and-dagger victory in Prague', where it had ingeniously inserted black propaganda leaflets into the communist newspaper *Rude Pravo* which brought down the wrath of the secret police upon the editor. RRF leader Nicholas Sheiken denied that the movement was used for intelligence-gathering or that it received support from western intelligence agencies, primarily because the RRF, which favoured a 'Greater Russia', believed that the CIA was pursuing a 'separatist' agenda among the émigré groups. It is difficult to see how these psychological warfare operations were funded other than through external agencies, particularly since Georgi Knupffer was the man responsible for fund-raising.[58]

What was interesting about the RRF was the consistent propaganda it put out attacking the NTS, which it claimed was thoroughly infiltrated by the KGB. Within certain circles of the émigré press and aligned neo-fascist, anti-communist networks there was a fierce attack on the NTS for being little more than a Soviet 'front'. The CIA was attacked for not taking heed of its warnings and for supporting an organisation that was regarded as social democrat and even pro-Soviet. In addition, the western Allies were needlessly sending Russian agents to their deaths by parachuting them into the Soviet Union and the waiting arms of Stalin's secret police.[59]

If the CIA refused to listen, MI6 officers handling the Russians did not. They knew that the NTS was producing intelligence of little worth and by the mid-fifties decided to end the liaison with what was turning out to be a very expensive failure.

THE BRITISH AND SCOTTISH LEAGUES FOR EUROPEAN FREEDOM

The fading fingerprints of the British League for European Freedom (BLEF) and its sister organisation, the Scottish League for European Freedom (SLEF), are to be found all over the MI6-sponsored exile operations. Without their overt and behind-the-scenes political support for the exiles, it is unlikely that many of the secret operations would have been initiated, particularly since their role appears to have involved bringing to Britain and, once here, supporting and protecting a pool of solid anti-communists from which MI6 was able to recruit operatives. Their activities centred on three strong, independent-minded individuals – two Scots, the Duchess of Atholl and John Finlay Stewart, and an Englishwoman, Mrs Elma Dangerfield.

By 1930, Kitty Atholl was interviewing anti-communist refugees from the Soviet Union who told of the oppression of the people, particularly with regard to the northern timber camps where many well-to-do peasants (kulaks) had been conscripted against their will. The following year she published *The Conscription of a People*, with an acknowledgement to the White Russian émigré journalist Anatole Baykolov, who appears to have supplied much of its content. It was an interesting and accurate examination of the role of slave labour in the Soviet Five Year Plan, with particular emphasis on the timber export industry, a trade the duchess tried to curtail.[1]

During 1931, her 'great friend' and fellow-Unionist activist, John Stewart, who referred to the duchess as 'Lady Kitty', also wrote a pamphlet on 'Russian Timber'. Sixty-one-year-old Stewart had been a consulting forestry engineer, employed by the Colonial Service in India and, in the late thirties, on contracts in the Baltic states, where he had 'many intimate friends among Ministers and diplomats'. The fact that at least half a dozen senior MI6 officers who were later engaged in the anti-communist exile operations had backgrounds in the timber business in the Baltic countries is probably more than a coincidence. Stewart also worked in eastern Europe and undertook extensive travel in Soviet Russia, where he had friends among the intelligence personnel at the German embassies.[2]

Stewart dated his expressed interest in exile politics to the signing of the Russo-German pact on 24 August 1939, which he recognised as 'a much greater Russian danger to the world than a German one'. According to his daughter, it was about this time that her father became 'very interested in the plight of the Balts'. He had come into contact with British intelligence officers, and although she did not know precisely when, Dr Stewart thought it was probably in the course of his work in the Baltic.[3]

Back in Scotland, Kitty Atholl served as Honorary Secretary on the Scottish 'Invasion Committee' dealing with measures and planning to be undertaken in the event of an invasion – a post that brought her into contact with various obscure branches of the intelligence services with responsibilities in this area. While in London, the duchess 'spent much of her time giving her energies and more money than she could spare towards assisting refugees from Europe'. In 1944, she began 'to hear of atrocities and mass deportations taking place in Eastern Europe: of the sufferings of the peoples of Poland and the Baltic states at the hands of the Russians'. No doubt one source for this information was John Stewart, but the main input came from Mrs Elma Dangerfield, editor of the *Whitehall News*, which chronicled the plight of refugees and the fate of the peoples of eastern Europe as Stalin's army swept across Poland and towards the West. Mrs Dangerfield was the key figure in the founding of the BLEF, though it was Kitty Atholl whose standing gave it authority.[4]

Married to a naval officer who was killed in the war, Mrs Dangerfield was a journalist by profession who initially worked for an offshoot of the MI6-controlled MI9, helping at Beaconsfield with the construction of special gadgets such as miniaturised compasses and maps printed on silk for escaping British PoWs, and then for a time in the Admiralty. She hoped to do more for the war effort, and Duff Cooper at the Ministry of Information asked her to continue her writing, which led to a proposal for a series of articles on the 'free women of Europe'. It entailed interviewing a large number of exiles during which time she became increasingly interested in the plight of the Poles. It was during visits to the School of Slavonic Studies that she met Frederick A. Voight, the editor of *The Nineteenth Century and After* magazine. A former *Guardian* foreign correspondent, who had worked for MI6 in the thirties as part of Claude Dansey's Z-network, Voight had travelled extensively throughout eastern Europe, including to Ukraine, where he had seen at first hand the devastation inflicted by Stalin. Between 1943 and the war's end, under the pseudonym 'Quentin Valey' in the *Daily Mail*, Voight was the champion of the Serbian collaborator General Dreza Mihailovic. He then became a propagandist in the cause of the Greek government, pushing stories of communist atrocities, violations of women and so on. Thoroughly right-wing, anti-communist and anti-Russian, Voight had friends among all the exile movements in London, and through his introductions Mrs Dangerfield came to know everyone of interest.[5]

The most important contact was Rowmund Pilsudski – cousin of the famous Polish leader – who had escaped from Paris to Britain, where he joined the Polish forces as a parachutist and worked for the Polish government-in-exile's Ministry of Information. He introduced Mrs Dangerfield to Polish exile circles, where she met SOE officer Joseph Retinger, and Victor Cazelet, the British liaison officer to the Poles and their Ministry of Information. Working within the Polish ministry was a Political Warfare Executive (PWE) Polish section officer, Diana Giffard (Lady Airey of Abingdon). She married the head of the 'private army' Intelligence School No. 9, which was attached to the escape organisation MI9, and later Conservative Member of Parliament, Airey Neave. After the war she joined MI6 for a short period and was involved in Polish affairs, and was active in conservative Polish circles.

As part of a Polish initiative, and with the support of the Czech and Hungarian governments-in-exile, in 1942 Mrs Dangerfield and Voight formed the Middle Zone Association. It discussed federation plans for a postwar *cordon sanitaire* running through central Europe, designed to provide protection against Germany and the Soviet Union. With members such as writer Rebecca West and the editor of the *Tablet*, Douglas Woodruff, it was very much the forerunner of the British League, and paralleled other Polish federation initiatives such as the Promethean League and Intermarium.

One of Mrs Dangerfield's first journalistic efforts in the exile field was an account of the Katyn Forest massacre of Polish officers by Stalin's henchmen, which had been discovered by the Germans in April 1943. The murder of the Polish officers was attributed to the Germans but many knew the truth. Despite the enthusiasm for the alliance with the Soviet Union, those actually dealing with the Soviet government were less sanguine. Unofficial – but still publicly unstated – doubts about Soviet intentions in eastern Europe were greatly reinforced by the uncovering of the massacre. By January 1944, ten months after the discovery of the mass graves at Katyn, even the left-wing paper *Tribune* had become openly critical of the Soviet Union's policies. With no second front and the war not yet won, the official view, however, remained supportive of the alliance with the Soviet Union, and criticisms, however well documented, were anathema. When Mrs Dangerfield published her own account of the massacre, based on Polish sources, for *The Nineteenth Century and After*, it caused a furore and made her, like Voight, *persona non grata* at the Foreign Office.

An offshoot of the Middle Zone Association was the Deportees Committee, which Mrs Dangerfield created with Mary Melville, daughter of a former Labour Solicitor General, to publicise the deportation of thousands of people to Russia from territories occupied by the Red Army. It was supported again by Rebecca West, and included Labour MP Ellen Wilkinson, Eleanor Rathbone, who was one of the first women MPs and during the thirties a stern critic of the appeasers in the British Establishment, and the socialist writer George Orwell. It was also promoted by politicians Victor Raikes and Ivor Bulmer-Thomas. Raikes was a Conservative MP who supported numerous hard-right causes. A right-wing Labour MP, Bulmer-Thomas was a fluent Italian speaker who also worked for the Political Warfare Executive (PWE), writing a book on psychological warfare in 1942. In the PWE Bulmer-Thomas had responsibilities for feeding black propaganda into Mussolini's final fortress.[6]

With Polish money, Mrs Dangerfield bought the *Whitehall News*, which had an all-important newsprint allocation, for the Middle Zone Association. A weekly, the *News* reported on the activities of the exiles and the Resistance in Poland. In October 1944, the Poles asked Mrs Dangerfield to broadcast on the BBC External Service on the Warsaw Uprising. Feeling that she was not well known enough, Pilsudski introduced her to Kitty Atholl, who, with Foreign Office support, agreed to broadcast a message of encouragement to the Polish Resistance fighters in Warsaw shortly before their destruction by the Germans. Moving to London, the duchess and Mrs Dangerfield, noticing the establishment by the Lord Provost of Glasgow, Sir Patrick Dollan, earlier in the war of a committee to support Polish aspirations, decided to create a similar but national platform. A once fiery leader of the radical Independent Labour Party (ILP) in Glasgow, Dollan had been impressed by the Polish exiles who had moved to Scotland at the beginning of the war and, as with many other ILPers, appears to have moved to the right as a dedicated anti-communist.[7]

Mrs Dangerfield's BLEF was dedicated to giving assistance to 'all countries in which freedom was threatened', particularly so following the partition agreement signed in Tehran and Yalta. Writer Mary Stock wrote in tribute of the duchess that 'she was thus prepared to welcome the victims of Russian tyranny, of German racialism and of fascist nationalism to the glowing hearth of her indignation', earning for herself, according to the affiliations of her critics, the alternative titles of 'Red Duchess' and 'Fascist Beast'. In November 1944, the BLEF mounted its first meeting with the support of four right-wing Tory MPs – Maurice Petherwick, the Hon. John Stourton, Major Guy Lloyd and, again, Victor Raikes.[8]

Mrs Dangerfield has said that she was completely unaware that in the same year the Scottish League for European Freedom (SLEF) was set up by its chair, John Stewart, Kitty Atholl's close friend. Its first president was the Earl of Mansfield (and later Lord Field Marshal Ironside), who appears to have become friendly with Stewart through their mutual interest in forestry. Mansfield was a 'diehard' Tory, active in the British Empire Union and co-founder with Maurice Petherwick of the Imperial Policy Group (IPG), both of which had specialised before the war in cultivating East European anti-communists who happened to collaborate with the Nazis. As secretary of the pro-appeasement and anti-Bolshevik IPG, Kenneth de Courcy had campaigned to keep Britain out of any European war. The IPG collated good intelligence on Europe which was accepted by the Foreign Office and by de Courcy's friend and fellow White's habitué, Stewart Menzies. Mansfield was also associated with the Tory pro-appeasement paper *Truth*, which at the outbreak of war was openly anti-Semitic and anti-communist, maintaining close links with a right-wing faction inside the Security Service. Out of *Truth* developed another influential right-wing group, the Society for Individual Freedom, in which Mansfield was a leading member.[9]

The Scottish League advisory council contained the usual range of the worthy and the old, along with prominent members of the Borders landed gentry and aristocracy; essentially a section of the Scottish establishment with links to the Royal Family. These included a former editor of the *Scotsman*, Sir George Waters; a Governor of South Australia, Sir Malcolm Harvey; Sir David Moncrieff of that Ilk; and a chair of the Scottish National Party, Professor Andrew Gibb. Probably the most important member was Guy Lloyd, Unionist MP from 1940 to 1959, who worked with MI6 during the war. An administrator for paint manufacturers J. and P. Coats, which supplied a number of senior people for SOE, in 1940 Lloyd served with the Royal Warwickshire Regiment in France. In the same year he won a by-election and was active in Parliament on the backbenches in a self-appointed role as watchdog over the socialist members of the wartime coalition. Lloyd voted against the Yalta agreement and became a thorn in the side of the government over the forcible repatriation of Russians to the Soviet Union.[10]

One reason for the existence of two Leagues was that, although she was generally regarded as being on the right of the Conservative Party, Kitty Atholl's campaigning against the government's non-intervention policy in Spain had made her a number of enemies among Scottish Unionist MPs. Two of these MPs were to become prominent in the SLEF and were particular opponents of the duchess, partially explaining the split. These two were Vice-President Capt. John McEwen, a former diplomat and Under-Secretary of State for Scotland, and Lt-Col. Sir Thomas Moore, Unionist MP for Ayr Burghs from 1925 to 1950, who had fought with the British Army in Russia during the intervention and in Ireland against the IRA. Moore's extreme politics had caused him problems within his own party. He explained that pre-war revulsion against communism and co-operation with Germany led him to associate with the Anglo-German Fellowship and the anti-Semitic and pro-fascist Link organisation.[11]

It was also the case, however, that anti-communist fervour was easily capable of overcoming any personal emnity. Tom Burns, leading right-wing Catholic publisher of the *Tablet*, chair of publishers Burns & Coates, and director of Hollis and Carter, was one of the BLEF's supporters. Burns had played a part in the 'Friends of Nationalist Spain', whose formation had partly been the responsibility of Kenneth de Courcy. He was a friend of right-wing publisher and British intelligence officer Douglas Jerrod, who, with Secret Service help, had organised the plane that flew Franco out of Tenerife to Tangier and Seville in July 1936. Pro-Franco, like most of his Catholic colleagues, such as the 'highly conspiratorial' Douglas Woodruff and SOE and MI6 officers Peter Kemp and Archie Lyall, during the war Burns worked for MI6. He reported directly to Kim Philby as a press attaché for the Ministry of Information in Spain, where he organised Allied propaganda.[12]

The BLEF campaigned to draw attention to the fate of eastern Europe at the hands of the Red Army. Genuinely concerned about the tragedy of Poland, the organisation was soon transformed into an anti-communist grouping which had the support of a number of Labour movement figures. They included Ivor Bulmer-Thomas, whose membership is partly explained by his strong advocacy of the Catholic wing of the Anglican Church. With the election of a Labour government, he soon grew disillusioned with socialism and opposed the policy of nationalisation. He dedicated his second book, *The Socialist Tragedy*, to 'all Social Democrats in the hope that when confronted with the choice between Socialism and democracy they will choose democracy'. He defected to the Tories in 1950. The second Labour MP was George Dallas, a former TUC General Council member who had chaired the party's International Committee during the war and had been a close colleague of the first minister responsible for SOE, Hugh Dalton. It was concern at Soviet manoeuvres in eastern Europe which led Dallas into the BLEF.[13]

The most important link to the Labour government, however, was Richard Stokes, secret intriguer and 'fixer' for his friend, Cabinet minister Herbert Morrison. Labour MP for Ipswich (1937–55), Stokes was a socialist of the most idiosyncratic kind. A militant anti-communist in the thirties, he had called, in 1940, for a negotiated peace with Germany and campaigned for the release of Sir Oswald Mosley and other pro-fascist detainees, including the anti-Semitic Capt. Ramsay. Stokes's anti-Zionist views were a strong influence on Clement Attlee and Ernest Bevin, who both displayed signs of anti-Semitism. Curiously, he also had friends among the many anti-socialist groups such as the Institute of Directors, the Economic League and Aims for Industry. Through the BLEF Stokes intervened on behalf of known collaborators and alleged war criminals, a number of whom were subsequently recruited by MI6. He was in direct contact with the MI6-sponsored exile umbrella groups such as the Anti-Bolshevik Bloc of Nations (ABN), Intermarium and the Promethean League. In effect, Stokes acted as a front man for the policy that MI6 was secretly pursuing. It is almost certain that Stokes was an MI6 asset. Immediately following the end of hostilities, Stokes, Mrs Dangerfield and Kitty Atholl went to Paris where, with the support of Leon Blum and the socialists, they set up an organisation similar to the BLEF, known as the League of the Rights of Man. Duff Cooper was the British ambassador, and they were received sympathetically by Winston Churchill, who was staying at the embassy.[14]

There was a degree of support for Stokes on the Left but it did not last long. One of the important threads in postwar Labour Party thinking was the so-called 'Third Force' position – neither capitalist nor communist; neither Moscow nor Washington – but it was to prove very difficult to sustain during the developing Cold War. The problem was that those on the Left found it very difficult to be in the same boat as right-wing politicians such as Stokes; particularly so when it became clear that he was working in some very murky areas. George Orwell, who had been involved in an earlier enterprise with Mrs Dangerfield, expressed this dilemma very clearly when, in November 1945, he declined to speak for the BLEF, one of the first pressure groups to warn of what the Soviet Union was actually doing in eastern Europe: 'I cannot associate myself with an essentially Conservative body which claims to defend democracy in Europe but has nothing to say about British imperialism . . . I belong to the left and must work inside it, much as I hate Russian totalitarianism and its poisonous influence in this country.'[15]

The BLEF was devoted to 'bringing home to people the unhappy plight of the many Displaced Persons (DPs) in Germany', and the Duchess of Atholl lobbied the new Labour government to stop the forced repatriation of thousands of eastern Europeans, sending a resolution to this effect to the first meeting of the United Nations. Expressing similar concerns, on 7 June 1945 Stokes had asked in the Commons whether there were any agreements concluded at Yalta and Tehran which had not been disclosed to the public. Churchill misled Stokes by replying that 'there were no secret agreements'.

During July and August 1945, the newspapers reported scenes of violence surrounding the forced repatriation of Cossacks and Ukrainians at the Flensburg DP camp, with shootings, killings and kidnapping by NKVD officers. The original source for these reports was Colonel Laurence Shadwell, the officer commanding the 506th Military Government Relief Detachment of the British Army of the Rhine, at Kiel, with responsibilities for the DP camps. A committed Christian who was appalled at government policy, Shadwell had privately communicated information to the Duchess of Atholl. In addition to military reluctance, political pressures – largely forced by the League – were building up to end the policy. Further, from 1945 onwards Stokes made several interventions in Parliament and privately with Foreign Office officials not only to end the threat of repatriation but also to secure the release of a number of Waffen-SS and Yugoslav collaborators placed in the DP camps. This was backed by a sustained campaign to rouse public opinion through the press, principally by the duchess in *The Times* and the *Tablet*.[16]

The BLEF was initially funded on a small scale by the Polish government-in-exile through Pilsudski, but the Poles soon ran out of money. Available evidence of intelligence funding is slim, though there was certainly American interest. Mrs Dangerfield acknowledges that some of the people she was involved with had 'different objectives and mysterious backgrounds' and that they probably had intelligence ties. There is evidence that the League was being manipulated or used by British Intelligence, but this was not obvious to Mrs Dangerfield, even if she was suspicious of a number of individuals with whom she was in contact. The Edinburgh-based SLEF, however, displayed all the hallmarks of an MI6 'front'. It was officially launched in October 1945 under the auspices of the Central European Federal Club at its London address in Thurloe Street. The Federal Clubs had also been the sponsoring agency of the MI6-backed exile movement Intermarium. The latter certainly had some Polish input, but if the SLEF received any similar help it was discreet. As Robert Bruce Lockhart noticed, a deep dislike of the Poles had developed in Edinburgh, principally because of their perceived 'arrogance'.[17]

John Stewart's daughter acknowledges that her father 'was involved in getting "refugees" out of the Baltic. It was entirely secret. All sorts of people were involved including British Intelligence . . . it was all very "hush hush".' 'Well-thought of by the exiles', according to his daughter, Stewart began his work the day war ended. He was 'instrumental in bringing over a number of Poles, then Balts, Croats and finally Ukrainians'. He worked closely with a 'Ukrainian go-between who used to turn up with a different name each time' – but how they got the refugees over remains 'a dark secret'. There appeared to be no hint of American Intelligence involvement, but Stewart's daughter was well aware that her father's limited financial resources were insufficient to keep the League going.[18]

At the begining of 1946, the SLEF moved to an address in Grosvenor Place, and on 24/25 June, with the assistance of Intermarium, held a major Congress of Delegates of the Oppressed European Nations in Edinburgh's Rainy Hall, titled 'Oppressed Europe Speaks'. The meeting, which attracted delegates from across eastern Europe, was chaired by Dr Karel Locher, a former official in the Czech Foreign Office and Honorary Secretary of the Federal Clubs. Its president in London was the former Polish Foreign Secretary, August Zaleski. A telegram supporting the initiative was received from Rome from Intermarium's president, Miha Krek.[19]

In the meantime, Kitty Atholl had retained her links to Lord Vansittart, who used the House of Lords to rail against the Soviet Union and what was happening in eastern Europe. Vansittart's anti-communist crusade was helped by Anatole Baykolov, who supplied material on the ill-treatment of Russian PoWs in Britain, information that originated with the Russian émigré and head of the Mladorossy in Britain, Georgi Knupffer. Mrs Dangerfield confirms that Knupffer was also a source of information to the BLEF. This association with pro-Russian groups took place despite the antipathy between Baykolov's support for the National Labour Council (NTS) and Knupffer's championing of the Mladorossy. The pro-Russian stance was, however, completely unacceptable to Ukrainian supporters of the SLEF, who were violently opposed to the advocacy of a 'Greater Russia'; another reason why the two Leagues rarely co-operated.[20]

The Foreign Office was also supplying Baykolov – who continued to enjoy the support of MI5 and its Soviet expert, Guy Liddell – with information on the situation of refugees and PoWs in other countries. According to Cossack exiles who managed to stay in the West – partially through the efforts and support of the BLEF – the Duchess of Atholl and Mrs Dangerfield obtained much of their information from Baykolov, though a great deal appears to have come from the Polish government-in-exile's Ministry of Information. Mrs Dangerfield was provided with voluminous evidence for her 1946 book *Beyond the Urals*, which was one of the very first insider accounts of the Soviet gulags.[21]

It was Richard Stokes who, in 1947, pushed the Labour government into letting into the country eastern Europe DPs as cheap labour. BLEF members expressed 'joy' on hearing news of the decision. MI6 used the opportunity to import under cover of the European Voluntary Workers (EVW) scheme, often with the intervention of Stokes, good, reliable anti-Soviet 'assets'. The League helped the Society of Latvians, which acted as a domestic pressure group advocating the immigration of Latvian DPs to Britain, and was heavily involved in casework on behalf of the exiles. A number happened to be collaborators, quislings and even war criminals, whom the Home Office wanted either to repatriate or eject. Working closely with the Latvian ambassador in exile, Charles Zarine, Stokes and the BLEF lobbied hard both inside and outside Parliament to prevent the deportation of Balts who had entered Britain illegally.[22]

During May, Stokes pursued the matter of Ukrainian repatriations and Operation EASTWIND in the House of Commons. Considerable indignation had been aroused by sensational newspaper reports that made much play of the numerous suicides that had taken place when the DPs were placed on the trains for transport to the Soviet Union. In London, through the efforts of the Duchess of Atholl and Mrs Dangerfield, the BLEF bombarded public figures with protests, largely based on evidence supplied by Baykolov. According to Denis Hills, who was overseeing the vetting of the exiles in the major Italian camps, a great deal of what appeared in the press accounts originated from 'a Uniat priest who had access to the camp', and was thus largely the Ukrainians' own propaganda. On 21 May, Stokes rose in the Commons to enquire into the truth of such reports, thus completing the information 'loop'.[23]

Stokes was closely connected with a number of émigré groups and actively and aggressively intervened on behalf of Slovene, Ustashi and Chetnik collaborators, quislings and war criminals held by the Allies. The Slovene former deputy head of the Yugoslav government-in-exile and president of Intermarium, Miha Krek, was a particular influence on Stokes. Regarded as 'a vigorous, active and unyielding adversary of the communists', Stokes regularly took up cases with Cabinet ministers and Foreign Office officials. In June, Krek began agitating against the policy of repatriation, a cause promoted by Guy Lloyd, who asked for an investigation into the whole matter. During August, Krek, who was applying considerable pressure on the Foreign Office, persuaded Stokes to take up the case of the quisling Slovene, Bishop Rozman.[24]

When Stokes tried to clarify, in the House of Commons, the nature of the repatriation operations, the Parliamentary Under-Secretary for Foreign Affairs, Christopher Mayhew, defended the Yalta agreement and repudiated the reports of violence and attempted suicides. However, on 2 September Mayhew wrote privately to Stokes: 'I think the whole incident and the policy behind it is absolutely revolting.' Stokes continued to pursue the matter and, on 4 December, led the attack in an adjournment debate concerning the fate of anti-Tito Yugoslavs. Stokes, who had campaigned against the Nuremberg war trials, dismissed the business of finding and trying war criminals.

The wider campaign spearheaded by Stokes, involving leading churchmen and 'refugee defence' committees such as the BLEF and SLEF, had an influence on public opinion when, in July 1948, Foreign Secretary Ernest Bevin put a stop to war crime investigations and refused Soviet requests for the return of quislings. On 26 July, Mayhew effectively closed the chapter on the extradition of war criminals who had illegally entered Britain with a statement in the House.[25]

During August, Frances Blackett, daughter of the government scientist, Professor Patrick Blackett, arrived unnanounced at the League's headquarters at 61 Gloucester Place and volunteered to work for free as the BLEF Secretary. According to Mrs Dangerfield, she and Kitty Atholl remained wary of Ms Blackett's activities within the League because they thought that she might have been 'planted' on them as a 'Foreign Office spy'. The BLEF was at the time involved in a particularly controversial campaign to allow the Polish doctor Vladislav Dering to remain in the country.[26]

Dr Dering, who had worked in the Auschwitz concentration camp, came to Britain after the war and ended up in Scotland, where he took part in a Christmas mess party with some Polish officers. According to one account, a drunken Dering boasted that his suit 'belonged to a Dutch professor. He went up the chimney. Do you see my pipe wallet? I got that from a prisoner. It's made out of a prisoner's scrotum.'[27]

Dr Dering's extradition had first been requested by the Polish government two years previously, when he was accused of performing barbaric experiments on the inmates of Auschwitz. It was a charge backed by the final list of the Central War Crimes Registry in which he was listed as 'wanted for torture' by 'UK'. Evidence, including statements from witnesses claiming that he had, under a local Novocaine injection in the spine, surgically removed the ovaries from young Jewish women from Salonika aged from sixteen to eighteen, was dismissed as Jewish propaganda. Although the Home Office believed there to be a prima facie case, officials noted that they had been sent 'a mass of testimony in favour of Dering' and worried that 'there is little doubt that his case will be championed by some Members of Parliament'. Indeed, the BLEF roused its supporters and considerable weight was given in the Home Office to statements of support made by a group of Polish émigrés, who turned out to be friends of the doctor in London. In a success for the League, the case was then quietly dropped.[28]

The BLEF, which represented the international side of anti-communism, had ties to UK domestic anti-communist groups and contacts with similar organisations on the Continent and in the United States. It was particularly close to Common Cause, which was formed by a maverick leftist, Dr C. A. Smith, in 1948. Smith met Leon Trotsky in 1933 in France, was chair of the ILP from 1939 until 1941, then quit the party in 1944 to join the Common Wealth Party as its research officer. Common Wealth had grown out of the '1941 Committee', which had been set up by the publisher of the Picture Post, Edward Hulton, the writer J. B. Priestley and Richard Acland of the Forward March committee. It seems to have had two aims: to undertake long-term planning as part of a 'post-War New Deal' and to provide a platform for war aims as a loyal opposition to the National Government.[29]

Hulton, who was on the advisory board of the BLEF, had co-operated with MI6's Section D in 1939 in helping to set up a bogus news agency, Britanova, and two years later used the Post as a front for another intelligence creation, the Arab News Agency, both of which MI6 resurrected after the war. As the Cold War hotted up, Hulton, whose Russian wife exerted a strong influence on him, moved sharply to the right and became fiercely anti-Soviet. He had been deeply affected by what had happened in Poland and used his personal column and his journal, World Review – edited by a Polish exile – to promulgate his views. Memos rained down on the editor of the Picture Post, accusing him of 'reiterating Soviet propaganda'. Although the magazine had – on Hulton's instructions – supported the Labour Party in 1945, it was not long before he attacked Labour, 'appalled that the conduct of our foreign policy should be in the hands of Mr Ernest Bevin'. He regarded the Soviet government and the Communist Party as a 'relentless foe' which was 'determined upon the complete destruction of all peoples who will not obey their dictates one hundred per cent'. Hulton had also taken to acting behind the scenes, setting up 'private dinners' at the Dorchester Hotel for 'top-ranking Tories' whom he had briefed by 'intelligence personnel'.[30]

When a number of Common Wealth members left at the end of the war to join the Labour Party, Smith became its chair and, as the Cold War developed, his anti-Stalinism became more pronounced. What was left of Common Wealth failed to move with him, and along with three members of the executive, Smith resisted and formed, at Easter 1948, Common Cause, whose main stated aim was to oppose the activities of the Communist Party of Great Britain. Smith became a member of the BLEF, and the two organisations would eventually share in Elizabeth Street, London, an office donated by the wealthy sponsor of right-wing causes, the Duke of Westminster.[31]

Common Cause had a complementary organisation in the United States, Common Cause Inc., which engaged in similar work and also sought the exposure of fellow-travellers and communists. The American group was formed in January 1947 by a New York socialite widow, Mrs Natalie Paine, a friend of Clare Boothe Luce, wife of the owner of *Time* and one-time ambassador to Italy. Also on the Common Cause Inc. board were Professor of Law, Adolphe Berle Jnr, who was well known as 'a conduit for CIA funds throughout this period'; Max Eastman; US ambassador to Poland and champion of the émigrés within the Republican Party, Arthur Bliss Lane; senior editor at *Reader's Digest*, Eugene Lyons; State Department under-secretary, Sumner Welles, who was, ironically, later 'exposed' by Senator McCarthy as a 'raving homosexual'; and Hodding Carter. The organisation's 'unofficial adviser' was John Foster Dulles and its chair was Christopher Emmet, who later turned up as head of the American Friends of the Captive Nations, the domestic front group for the CIA-sponsored co-ordinating body for exile groups, the Assembly of Captive European Nations (ACEN).[32]

An MI6 'agent of influence' in the early stages of the war, Emmet had been a key figure in the United States in helping turn the country from isolationism to giving support to the British against Germany. He was 'the classic example of those who ran the British Intelligence fronts before and during World War II and who, having proven themselves faithful and competent, went on to run the CIA/MI6 fronts of the Cold War'. In January 1946, Emmet had written to a fellow-British agent that 'we got in some good blows against one form of totalitarian aggression' and now hoped to do 'likewise against the other form of the same danger'.[33]

Common Cause Inc. is known to have been linked to its British namesake with joint meetings taking place in London. Like its British counterpart, it developed ties to the émigré groups and engaged in international trades union activity. The American organisation had already made contact with the 'Russian Solidarists', better known as the NTS, and Christopher Simpson notes that it sponsored the NTS leader Constantine Boldyrev on a tour of the United States in late 1948.[34]

Significantly, many of the self-same Common Cause Inc. personnel also crop up on the board of the American National Committee for a Free Europe (NCFE), which was backed by the covert Office of Policy Co-ordination (OPC), and, later, the CIA-funded American Committee for Liberation from Bolshevism. Indeed, it seems that Common Cause Inc. was the 'sister organisation' of the NCFE, which offered thinly veiled 'private sector' cover for militant exile operations.

These groups had grown out of the Free Europe Committee, formed in Washington in 1948 by retired diplomat Joseph E. Grew at the request of George F. Kennan, who was the official in the State Department responsible for the OPC. It worked closely with the OPC, and then the CIA, to maintain contact between exile groups in the West and their underground counterparts in eastern Europe. Initial membership included Berle Jnr, Allen Dulles and ex-Office of Strategic Services (OSS) personnel such as Frederic R. Dolbeare. It was closely involved in the activities of exile groups interested in federation and European unity. During this period, the Americans began to pour millions into such groups. Head of the OPC and architect of the covert funding policy Frank Wisner 'believed in the tremendous espionage potential of its Eastern European émigré organisations, their value as propagandists and agents of influence'. These networks are important because they help to explain who was backing the BLEF and Common Cause with funds.[35]

The BLEF had gradually run out of Polish funding and sought other means of finance, with the principal target being the Americans. There is evidence of US Intelligence interest though, once again, it appears that it was at arm's length. Mrs Dangerfield recalled in 1997 that she had been in touch in the immediate postwar period with a former senior OSS officer, who had served in Switzerland working with the German anti-Hitler resistance and whom she assumed was in the CIA. He apparently visited London on a regular basis until he died suddenly. In the late forties, Mrs Dangerfield did travel to the United States on a number of occasions and reported to Lord Vansittart in a series of letters that she had been successful in obtaining funds for an East European Institute which the League had set up, and for the short-lived British Political Institute, which had been formed with Vansittart to look after the interests of the exile groups, principally the Yugoslavs. Mrs Dangerfield recalls that a particular target had been the Rockefeller family. She also met with the Dulles brothers and others involved in the NCFE, and with former OSS head Bill Donovan and his supporters of the American Committee for a United Europe (ACUE), which covertly funded the European Movement.[36]

The BLEF was, itself, closely tied to the European Movement (EM), principally through the Nouvelles Equipes Internationales (NEI), which had been created in Lucerne in March 1947 as a union of Christian Democrats. Backed by Swiss financial interests, it shared a desire to promote Christian solidarity and opposed the idea of a 'neutral' Third Force. Promoting Christian values in the light of 'national situations and international problems', it supported liberal free-market economics and had an 'unshakable determination to fight Bolshevism'. Advocating 'a free Europe', the NEI set up an exiles section of anti-communists from eastern Europe – Czechs, Hungarians, Lithuanians, Poles, Romanians and Bulgarians. For the exiles it represented 'a hope and a guarantee that their legitimate interests were being taken into consideration'. The Christian Democratic Union of Central Europe organisation of exiles from countries behind the Iron Curtain grouped together a number of socialist but mainly Christian Democrat and Catholic parties. Considering European unity as another means of opposing communism, their aim was to fight against communism by means of propaganda, to inform the West of the situation behind the Iron Curtain, and to carry on social welfare activities among refugees.[37]

The small British section of the NEI, in reality an offshoot of the BLEF, was not active domestically. The chair of the section was the Duchess of Atholl, who was also a member of the NEI executive committee. Others on the committee included Mrs Dangerfield, Tracy Phillips, a member of the Church of England's Foreign Relations Council, and Barbara Ward, deputy editor of the *Economist*. As an affiliated organisation and the principal refugee 'defence committee' working among the exile groups, the BLEF section of the NEI worked closely with the emerging EM. Major supporters of the BLEF and members of the influential EM cultural subcommittee were the poet T. S. Eliot and Douglas Woodruff, editor of the *Tablet*. The presence of such Catholics may be one reason why staunch British Protestants opposed the British committee and regarded European unity as a 'papist plot' – the 'black shadow of a newly risen Holy Roman Empire'. While this is little more than conspiracy theorising, it is true that American support for Luigi Gedda, a prominent Vatican official who ran 'Catholic Action', a significant force in the 1948 elections, increased when he began to deploy his organisation to promote the idea of 'Western Union', explaining that the Pope had agreed that 'the Church should carry the banner for a federation of European states'.[38]

East–West relations were to have a direct bearing on the project for European unification and, according to long-time pro-European federalist Count Richard Coudenhove-Kalergi, the EM regarded its prime task as 'not the securing of world peace but the defence of Europe against the imperialism of the Soviet Union and the liberation of the oppressed nations of Eastern Europe'. In consort with other moves such as Marshall Aid, the count saw the EM as 'a part of the anti-Bolshevik system of alliance'.[39]

During 1947 introductory talks among the various groups promoting

European unity indicated the desirability of bringing within the orbit of the EM the countries behind the Iron Curtain. As a result, émigré delegates from eastern European countries under Soviet control attended The Hague Conference in May 1948. Believing that the EM was an anti-communist organisation with designs 'to bring about the establishment of a European army rearming the Germans against the USSR', exile delegates agreed to attend a small meeting in London. After talks with Conservative politician Harold Macmillan and Polish fixer Joseph Retinger, the foundations were laid for a Central and Eastern European Commission of the EM. This initially included exiled personalities from Bulgaria, Czechoslovakia, Hungary, Poland, Romania and Yugoslavia, with representatives later joining from Estonia, Lithuania, Latvia and Albania. It dealt with countries inside the Iron Curtain and tended to be more moderate than the neo-fascists of the Anti-Bolshevik Bloc of Nations (ABN), which espoused the aspirations of the nationalist elements inside the borders of the old Russian Empire. The commission's objective was to uphold 'the right of individual and political freedom for the countries under Soviet domination in Eastern Europe and urge their inclusion in a future united Europe'. It was to become 'a rallying-point for focusing the political ideas of the exiles along lines on which general agreement was possible' and placed a particular emphasis on supporting refugees, which is obviously one reason why BLEF stalwarts worked so closely with it.[40]

Supporting and co-ordinating the activities of the exile groupings, the commission was chaired by Macmillan with Retinger as general secretary. While Retinger would seem an obvious choice (he was after all a Pole linked to the underground and a former wartime SOE recruit who was known to be close to MI6), Macmillan's appointment was, at first sight, an odd one. It is known, however, that since the last days of the war in Italy he had had a working relationship with Carmel Offie. A postwar US political officer in Germany, Offie was the senior OPC officer responsible for émigré affairs, working closely with the Free Europe Committee. Under Operation BLOOD-STONE, Offie had organised 'the care and feeding of émigrés who were illegally helped to emigrate to the United States'. The commission was housed in the City offices of Macmillan's 'right-hand man', Edward Beddington-Behrens, who was particularly friendly with a group of anti-communist Yugoslav émigrés and was a member of the BLEF's advisory council. It was run by an ex-SOE colleague, George Morton, who had also operated in Italy as an associate of former SOE director Colin Gubbins, who, in turn, retained 'a special interest' in the work of the commission.[41]

The commission aimed to 'study the problems of Eastern Europe and to sustain the cause of the European peoples enslaved under Soviet domination'. As usual in exile politics, there were endless discussions among 'the bandits', as Macmillan referred to them, and although not the most ideologically militant, the exiles used the commission to advocate the liberation of their countries from communist dictatorship. The basic declaration issued by the commission in December 1949, while supporting the liberation of eastern Europe, did not, however, refer to exactly how this was to be achieved. Retinger specifically ruled out the idea 'of an Eastern European fighting force formed from exiles for the defence of Europe', and did not appeal for 'volunteers to form a fifth column'. Instead, officials advocated propaganda campaigns, particularly in relation to the plight of refugees. There were some diplomatic successes and, owing to its efforts, in 1950 the Consultative Assembly of the Council of Europe created a 'special committee' to watch over the interests of countries not represented in the Council of Europe. Chaired by Macmillan, it was the first and only official body to defend the interests of the countries of central and eastern Europe.[42]

Another EM-affiliated group, the European Union of Federalists, had under its wing the Centre International des Syndicalistes Libre en Exil, which had been formed in Paris in October 1948. Better known as the International Centre of Free Trade Unions in Exile (ICFTUE), it grouped together Eastern European trade unionists from Bulgaria, Estonia, Hungary, Lithuania, Latvia, Poland, Romania, Czechoslovakia, Ukraine and Yugoslavia who favoured federalism as the only alternative to the dictatorship from which they hoped to free their countries. The ICFTUE was run out of the offices of the Confédération Générale du Travail Ouvrière, which was initially supported and partially funded by the American Federation of Labour and later by the CIA. It was headed by Sacha Volman, a Romanian exile who worked with underground anti-communist forces in eastern Europe. The Centre was a recipient of CIA largesse, laundered through United States foundations. One of its tasks was 'to assist refugees', and it co-operated with sympathetic officials in the British Foreign Office, members of Parliament and groups such as the BLEF.[43]

Also working on the fringes of the EM and affiliated to the commission was the International Federation of Free Journalists of Central and Eastern Europe. Founded in Paris in 1948, at a congress attended by writers and newspapermen from thirteen countries, it included representatives from the Baltic and Balkan countries. The federation set up regional unions and operated its own press agency, the Free European Press Service, which specialised in news from behind the Iron Curtain. A second congress of eastern and central European journalists took place in London, a year later, and for a similar one in Berlin, Malcolm Muggeridge, who was operating on behalf of MI6, nominated as its chair the former senior SOE officer and leading EM advocate, Douglas Dodds-Parker. 'From such small initiatives', Dodds-Parker later wrote, 'were to spring the broadcasting of Radio Liberty and Radio Free Europe to Russia and the occupied Eastern countries.' Given that these two radio stations were funded by the OPC-sponsored NCFE, it is probable that this was the source of the funding for the federation. The federation's Polish chair, M. Wierzbianski, admitted that it worked in consultation with the Americans.[44]

In July 1949, senior State Department official and supervisor of the OPC, George Kennan, arrived in London for talks with the chair of the Joint Intelligence Committee (JIC), William Hayter. Kennan told Hayter that while in the short term he did not envisage the incorporation of eastern Europe into a federation, in the long term he believed that European unity could only be achieved, in 'Phase Two' of unification, once an overextended Soviet Union had retreated behind her own borders. In May 1950, during the Tripartite Foreign Ministers' Conference in London, the United States secured the agreement of Britain and France in associating Eastern bloc exile groups with the Council of Europe at Strasbourg.[45]

The BLEF continued to be supported by Baykolov, Georgi Knupffer and the Russian émigré groups. Drawing on these sources, in 1950 Mrs Dangerfield convened a meeting to discuss 'the formation of an organisation to make known what was believed to be the widespread opposition in Russia to the Soviet regime'. The BLEF claimed to have helped thousands of Russian workers in this country who had managed to evade repatriation from Germany at the end of the war. The Duchess of Atholl wrote that they were 'making this opposition known to compatriots who had fled from Russia in much earlier days', which suggests the NTS and Mladorossy organisations. A British Free Movement (BFM) was set up with Lord Inverchapel, who as Sir Archibald Clark Kerr had been ambassador in Moscow during the war, as its first president. In order to focus these concerns, during the summer of 1951 the BFM helped publish a collection of statements made by Russians in Britain.[46]

In contrast, by 1950 the SLEF was helping to bring in the most extreme of the émigrés and was being supported in its efforts by MI6. John Stewart was honorary editor of the Foreign Affairs Information Service, and with the SLEF published a steady stream of well-produced pamphlets, often printed in Munich, home of the new generation of émigrés. In 1950, at eighty years of age, Stewart was still very active, penning many of the pamphlets which illustrated the organisation's range of interests, including 'Communism in Action', 'The Russian Danger', 'Will There be a Revolution in Russia?', 'The Ukrainian Liberation Movement in Modern Times' and 'UPA: Story of the Ukrainian Underground Army'.[47]

One of Stewart's most trusted lieutenants in the late forties and early fifties, and another prolific pamphleteer, was Major John Frederick Charles 'Boney' Fuller, a well-known and highly respected military strategist. Anti-Semitic and a dabbler in the occult – he had been a friend of Aleister Crowley – Fuller had joined the British Union of Fascists (BUF) in 1934, in the belief that fascism had 'come to stay'. Admitted to Oswald Mosley's inner circle, Fuller visited both Mussolini and Hitler. He was also a founding member of the pre-war Nordic League (known initially as the White Knights of Britain or the Hooded Men) which had been established by Nazi agents run by Alfred Rosenberg. Its activities, which were directed from Berlin, included providing an insider's view of the British élite. Fuller had also written intelligence reports on British organisations and individuals for Goebbels, the head of the Nazi propaganda department, and Heinrich Himmler, chief of the SS. It is said that Fuller would have been made minister of defence if Mosley had come to power, and was regarded by the Nazis as a possible 'Quisling'. Despite the fact that MI5 had him under surveillance, when war came he and his Polish wife were not among the more than seven hundred BUF supporters detained under the 18b regulations. Even Mosley was puzzled by this omission. One possible reason, which would explain a great deal, was that Fuller was an MI6 agent and thus protected.[48]

'Boney' Fuller's importance for the SLEF was that he had been active among the Ukrainian nationalists before the war and among the Ukrainian communities in both Britain and Germany after the war. In the mid-thirties, around the same time as MI6 was recruiting the Banderites in the OUN, the Ukrainian émigré community in London had been penetrated by German Intelligence. This had been undertaken with the help of Fuller to ensure Anglo-German 'understanding'. He thought that Hitler's greatest mistake during the war had been to treat the Ukrainians as subhuman, *Untermenschen*, thus ignoring the military potential of the nationalists. With the support of his good friend Richard Stokes, at the end of the war Fuller had helped assist one of the leading figures in the OUN-B, Jaroslav Stetsko, and maintained contacts with the Ukrainian nationalists in the DP camps throughout the forties. By 1950, Fuller was seventy-one, a wizened old man but still active, calling for a moral as well as a physical and economic campaign against the Bolsheviks and the Soviet Union.[49]

The Foreign Office was unhappy with the SLEF's independent activities and the regular rebukes it received from Stewart about the alleged ill-treatment of the EVWs, especially the Ukrainians from the Polish regions and the Belorussians. Officials were particularly annoyed when Stewart announced his intention of holding under the auspices of the SLEF, on 12–14 June 1950, an apparently innocuous anti-communist international conference of refugees in Edinburgh. Sponsored by MI6 and the Foreign Office propaganda unit, the Information Research Department (IRD), the Congress of Delegates of Independence Movements Anti-Bolshevik Bloc of Nations of Europe and Asia was an important meeting for a number of eastern European murderous thugs, Nazi collaborators and wanted war criminals who were working with MI6 on exile operations against the Soviet Union – the most important group being the Ukrainians.[50]

As David Cesarani notes, 'the British authorities did little to curb the activities of the formerly pro-Nazi OUN/B when it was using strong-arm tactics to establish its hegemony over the Ukrainian refugees, DPs and ex-servicemen in the British Zone in Germany'. Foreign Office files from 1950 and 1951 provide evidence of the SLEF and the ABN running joint 'front' groups and exercises, agitating among the EVWs, fomenting strikes and demonstrations in support of 'separatism' in the European DP camps, and attempting to take over the Association of Ukrainians in Great Britain. Agitation was particularly strong among the Ukrainian communities in Yorkshire, which became hotbeds of anti-Soviet politics and the power base for the ABN. Members of the Galician Division got together for annual celebrations in their Waffen-SS uniforms. Sections of the Foreign Office were alarmed by this rabidly right-wing, neo-fascist trend, and the fact that Ukrainian émigrés felt bold enough to hold public meetings and pass resolutions in support of the ABN. One of its leading members stated that 'our organisation was never a study group, and it will never be one. ABN is an organisation of fighters in the first place. Into it should come people of courage, men dedicated to the liberation of their countries, and ready for sacrifice. We have no time and no room for orators. ABN is for action.'[51]

What its spokesmen would never admit, however, was that the ABN had been created in 1943 under the control of the Nazi OMi and Alfred Rosenberg. Many of the leaders of the ABN, such as Romanian Grigore Manoilescu, Bulgarian Dimitr Waltscheff, Belorussian Radolslav Ostrovosky, and Slovak Ferdinand Durcansky, had been closely associated either with the Nazi quisling administrations or with the neo-fascist regimes of their respective states. Because of their records, many had been unable to obtain an immigration or visitor's visa to the United States or to other countries. They continued to perpetrate the myth that the ABN had been founded after the war as an independent body. It also remained secret that 'vast sums' were being paid to the ABN by MI6 through a Vatican channel, to disguise its true source. Later funding and help came from the West German government.

In attendance at Edinburgh was Stefan Bandera's deputy in the OUN-B, Yaroslav Stetsko, which showed the true character of the conference. Stetsko had accompanied Nazi formations to Lvov in 1941 and had been at the head of the short-lived Ukrainian government. Wanted by the Soviets as a war criminal, he was able to travel to and from Britain with ease. Gradually, he ensured that the 'moderate and democratic member groups' quit the ABN, which increasingly allied itself with the SLEF in 'refugee' work. Stetsko was a well-known figure at the Foreign Office, and in June 1949 felt confident enough to ask for a private meeting with Ernest Bevin. At the Edinburgh conference, Stetsko consulted on liberation policy with Lord Vansittart, who had his own back channels to the SLEF.[52]

The Ukrainians and other participants at the Edinburgh conference were supplied with passports and travel documents by MI6, and put up in hotels at the Service's expense. Others brought to the conference under the guise of the ABN by MI6 included men such as Dr Stanislaw Stankievich, president of the Belorussian National Centre and of the Council of the Nations of the ABN; council chair Alfred Berzins, leader of the Latvian Underground Movement; and a delegation of the Romanian Iron Guard which supplied its share of militants. The Croatian delegation was made up of Ustashi from the Croatian Liberation Movement of Pavelic and Hefer, and the Bulgarian chapter was represented by the Bulgarian National Front, a group of wartime fascist legionaries. From further afield came Kajum Khan, president of the National Turkestan Unity Committee.[53]

During the public session, the conference called for 'the formation of a common anti-Bolshevik front of all freedom-loving nations on both sides of the Iron Curtain for the defence of freedom, religion and culture'. Delegates sought closer co-operation between the western intelligence agencies and the resistance movements among 'the oppressed nations'. They aimed at the 'destruction of Russian imperialism' by 'splitting up the USSR and re-establishing independent nation states'. The ABN military spokesman, General Ferenc Farkas, who under the Hungarian neo-fascist Szalasi regime had headed a special court sentencing opponents of the quisling Arrow Cross government, declared that the subjugated nations were ready to fight and called for 'the synchronisation of efforts and co-operation'. Stetsko added that if war broke out the enslaved nations were in a position to 'set up an army of more than ten million soldiers'.[54]

There followed a big press conference which brought publicity in all the major newspapers. A well-organised IRD publicity operation involving a number of its front news agencies ensured that the publicity was well exploited and broadcast by radio stations to eastern Europe. This resulted in a sustained counter-propaganda campaign by the Soviet Union which attacked the conference and those in attendance. A number of other more moderate exile groups were angered by the overtly militant and military aspect of the meeting. The Poles, who were not represented, accused the participants, primarily the Ukrainians, of ignoring 'harsh reality'. A Polish exile press agency release to the *Scotsman* was bleak in its assessment. It concluded that there was no opportunity 'to shake off that hated Bolshevik yoke . . . Today any active resistance against Russia would be lunacy: it would bring only bloody repression, massacres and mass deportations, without even the slightest hope of achieving the aim so much desired.'[55]

MI6 political liaison with the ABN was undertaken through Auberon Herbert and the Scottish Conservative MP, Neil McLean. Herbert had recently taken up one of the SLEF's hobby-horses, writing to the *Daily Telegraph* about the use of slave labour in the timber areas of Siberia. 'It would do the Ministry of Supply no harm to know how Soviet timber is cut, and the British public would, no doubt, benefit by a closer knowledge of the really modern methods employed in exploiting the endless forests, and the 30 million foresters of Siberia.'[56]

McLean was irresistibly drawn to the semi-clandestine ABN organisation. 'Its very name was music to his ears', wrote his biographer, 'and its avowed intentions coincided with his own ideals.' The methods it proposed – internal subversion and covert encouragement of national aspirations in every ethnic group within the Soviet Union and in every satellite state – were those that McLean himself advocated. Herbert and McLean visited the ABN head-quarters in Munich, which was a 'hive of activity and conspiracy', for talks in early 1951. With his command of languages, McLean was able to talk with the heads of the North Caucasian Committee, the Turkestan National Unity Committee, and representatives of Azerbaijan and Georgia. He also had time to visit a small group of Kalmucks, part of the Cossack regiment that the Allies had attempted to hand back to the Soviet Union at the end of hostilities but who had managed to escape the fate of their compatriots. Herbert was principally concerned with the Belorussians and the Ukrainians, and subsequently made many trips to Canada to lecture to the tens of thousands of Ukrainians who had settled there.[57]

By the end of 1950, John Stewart was convinced that the Soviets were intent on war and had issued a military handbook entitled 'Economic and Military Strength and Weakness of Red Russia and Independence Movements in the USSR', outlining the feasibility of overthrowing the eastern European and Soviet regimes by supplying funds and arms to national liberation movements, such as the Ukrainian UPA. Shortly after, Boney Fuller – in regular contact with Stetsko – wrote a slim SLEF pamphlet, 'How to Defeat Russia', which argued against mere containment and instead recommended a psycho-logical offensive coupled with a strong military defensive posture. He argued that the offensive should be aimed at undermining communist power within the Soviet Union and its satellites, while suppressing it elsewhere. The mili-tary posture should be based on a strong West Germany, the prospect of German reunification, the use of German and Spanish troops, the creation of a hundred divisions with forty stationed in Germany, and the deployment of émigré nationalist forces. Ambitiously, in January of the new year, Stewart forwarded these ideas to the Foreign Office and the Prime Minister.[58]

The Foreign Office was well acquainted with Stewart and was increasingly irritated by his activities. He was accused of exaggerating 'the strength of the resistance movements behind the Iron Curtain', which, according to the latest intelligence, 'are, though often still active, losing rather than gaining strength'. Officials were, however, willing to recognise the worth of his argu-ment that 'in the event of war, the resistance and separatist movements could have value for us'.

John Peck, who had just returned from the The Hague to take up the post of assistant responsible for the IRD, thought that Stewart had 'swallowed the Ukrainian nationalist line whole. His violent anti-Russian, as distinct from anti-Soviet, feelings are a poor guide to the formulation of a rational foreign

policy and his obstinate insistence on the value of the near-apocryphal resistance movements behind the Iron Curtain makes his practical recommendations not merely foolish but dangerous.' Peck regarded his solution to the
problems of dealing with the Soviet states 'as useful as "Mein Kampf"'. The
ABN was not held in much higher regard, but it was acknowledged that the
British could 'not wash our hands of all national movements in case they
may be of future use to us'. Of Stewart, Peck concluded that 'it can only be
said that though his heart is in the right place it is perhaps excessively large'.[59]

Neil McLean eventually became disillusioned with the ABN as 'most of
the other national committees seemed to be at loggerheads and unable to
agree on a concerted policy or a co-ordinated line of action'. He felt, however,
that his time had not been completely wasted as 'his mere presence amongst
them had encouraged them to believe that they were not forgotten by the
free world'. MI6 was still involved, but gradually began to lessen its support.
After 1951, the ABN began to receive direct funding from the West German
government. The Foreign Office grew increasingly apprehensive about
having any relationship with the émigré groups and was content for the
Americans to take them on or for responsibility for their affairs to be managed
within a European context.[60]

In May 1951 the White House endorsed State Department plans to accelerate the association of the exile groups with the Council of Europe. Outlining
their proposals in a paper entitled 'The Concept of Europe', State Department
officials explained that their eastern propaganda efforts lacked 'the positive
qualities which are necessary to arouse nations'. The new strategy would be
based on the theme of 'European Unity' which, it was hoped, would encourage eastern Europeans to stiffen their resistance to communist domination
and 'retard the Sovietisation of their minds'. This would be coupled with an
increased emphasis on human rights, which President Truman believed to
be 'going in the right direction' and 'a good contribution toward the goal of
. . . subverting Iron Curtain countries'. Much to the annoyance of the Foreign
Office, which wanted to curtail émigré affairs, evidence of the new strategy
was seen in the new year in London.[61]

In late January 1952, the BLEF helped to organise a major conference for
eastern European exile groups at Church House, with more moderate
members than those associated with the ABN. It was sponsored by the
Central and East European Commission of the EM which, in contrast to the
ABN, dealt only with those countries outside the borders of the Soviet Union.
In line with its general disregard of the EM, the commission was 'very
unpopular' with the Foreign Office, which showed hostility to the conference
– its 'most ambitious plan so far'. Organised by the UK National Council of
the EM, the conference cost £4,000, which came from undisclosed 'private
funds'. The fact that the observers from overseas included Warren Fugitt
from the ACUE and Roger Bull, W. Griffith and John Leich from the US

NCFE is an indication that the true source of funding was the CIA. Indeed, during the conference the Hungarian delegate, P. Auer, thanked the NCFE for its efforts in supporting the exiles.[62]

Fifty-one delegates and observers from the various eastern European exile groups of the commission met over three days, the meetings chaired by Conservative imperialist Leopold Amery. British delegates included BLEF supporters, the ubiquitous Auberon Herbert and Neil McLean. The former had been introduced to the BLEF by the Pole Pilsudski, but Mrs Dangerfield remained suspicious of his motives. While he engaged in the social side, he studiously refused to get involved in their political activities. The other British delegate was Julian Amery, who noted the presence of 'so many old friends, some of whom were comrades-in-arms in the last war'.[63]

Other delegates included members of Common Cause, Bob Edwards of the Chemical Workers Union and founder of the Socialist Movement for United States of Europe, who had moved to the right and was prominent in a number of anti-communist campaigns, and Christopher Hollis, right-wing Conservative MP, who was close to Kenneth de Courcy of the conspiratorially inclined *Intelligence Digest* and brother of MI5's Roger Hollis. Among the more interesting delegates were those from the ICFTUE, such as the Romanian Sacha Volman; the International Peasant Union represented by the former Polish Prime Minister in exile, Stanislaw Mikolajczyk; a large number of Poles from the underground movement, including Stefan Korbonski; Charles Zarine of the Latvians; a young EM activist, Giscard D'Estaing, who, in a recurring theme, expressed disquiet at the 'temporary aloofness' of Britain with regard to European affairs; and Dr Ihsan Toptani representing the National Committee for Free Albania. Toptani, a wealthy Albanian with influential friends including Julian Amery and Neil McLean, had escaped from Albania in October 1944. His committee was a creation of the American OPC/CIA and came under the umbrella of the NCFE.[64]

Despite Foreign Office reservations, the conference proved to be 'a great success'. The chair of the 'Special Committee', the right-wing Tory MP Major Tufton Beamish, supported the setting up of a European Fund for Exiles, which would assist student exiles to continue their studies, and the initiative taken by the Secretariat of Exiled Intellectual Organisations for the creation of an Institute of Central and Eastern European Studies, along the lines of the NCFE-backed Research Centre for Central and Eastern Europe in New York. The bringing together of so many leading exiles also provided a propaganda coup which was spread throughout the Soviet bloc by NCFE-backed radio stations, the BBC and the exile press outlets, including those working with the IRD.

The Foreign Office was increasingly unwilling to back a liberation policy for the Soviet satellites and was embarrassed that 'for weeks and weeks the conference was denounced by the Russian radio and press, and by the puppet leaders of the countries behind the Iron Curtain'. Under the guidance of the newly elected Conservative government, policy was directed towards a more conciliatory tone in dealing with the Soviet Union. Special operations were seen as hindering that approach, and encouraging the eastern European exiles in their aspirations was discouraged. Belligerency was out; the exiles were to be left to the United States, about whom the Foreign Office was also wary. In September 1952, the chair of the commission, Major Beddington-Behrens, whom the conference delegates clearly identifed as the leading advocate of their case, was replaced by a professional politician, Conservative MP Richard Law, which, according to a Polish leader, Stefan Korbonski, marked the point when the commission began to act 'negatively and ceased in practice to function'.[65]

The Duchess of Atholl notes in her thin autobiography that the decline in the BLEF's 'purely political work' was attributable to the arrival of Common Cause, whose articles of association stated its purpose as 'to expose as a subversive conspiracy the Communist Party of Great Britain', and those 'who by their conduct or associations might reasonably be expected to be engaging in activities detrimental to the welfare of the State'. Formally launched in February 1952 (interestingly, just a month after the EM London conference), Common Cause's first official joint chair was Lord Malcolm Douglas-Hamilton, another associate of Kenneth de Courcy and part of Lord Mansfield's circle. Douglas-Hamilton, whose parliamentary seat was taken over by Neil McLean, was divorced in the same year and, in 1953, married Mrs Natalie Paine, the person who had been responsible for forming the American Common Cause Inc.[66]

John Stewart attacked the London conference, and indirectly the BLEF, as a failure because it did not recognise the imperialist ambitions of Russia. He wanted to see 'the confinement of the aggressive, predatory Russians within ethnic Russia, where no one will wish to interfere with them'. Citing 'private sources', Stewart warned the Ukrainian nationalist émigrés that the conference was part of an attempt to destroy or weaken the ABN and replace it with ineffective public figures. Although the SLEF/ABN alliance was in various paramilitary activities set up by the NCFE and the CIA, Stewart denied that his organisation had received any outside funding, though he said that he had been offered 'considerable sums' if he joined 'certain sectional organisations' – i.e. pro-Russian, anti-separatist groupings. He continued to stand by the ABN and put his support behind Yaroslav Stetsko, whom he knew from friends had considerable support from the influential Canadian émigrés.

By the early fifties, the profile of the SLEF was virtually non-existent but Stewart, despite being in ill health, kept up a steady stream of books and pamphlets, authored by leading exile figures. In 1953, the League's records show that finances took a nosedive, at a time when MI6 was rapidly pulling out of the exile game and was ceasing to fund many of the groups. The following year saw the 'withdrawal of British leadership and initiative in matters concerning Iron Curtain countries'. The Americans took the lead and now had the field to themselves.[67]

John Stewart died in August 1958; a grand, celebratory obituary featured on the front page of the ABN journal. The BLEF declined too, and would eventually become a creature of the ABN, whose leader, Stetsko, lived in quiet obscurity in Wimbledon. By the early fifties the Duchess of Atholl and Mrs Elma Dangerfield had withdrawn from the BLEF, the latter taking on a leading role in the EM. Without their input, by the sixties the BLEF had become little more than a meaningless acronym. It had, however, drifted into the hands of the extremists. Its treasurer was I. Rawluk of the Association of Ukrainians in Great Britain, and it operated as the British representative of the European Freedom Council – an ABN front. In the seventies, the BLEF was represented on the ultra-right World Anti-Communist League (WACL).[68]

PART FIVE

THE CHANGE

In his ground-breaking study of the 'secret Cold War', Trevor Barnes wrote that MI6 'was running its own operation to encourage unity' in Europe. The European Movement (EM) can be viewed from many different perspectives, but the principal interest of MI6 would have been its use as an anti-communist vehicle, binding together a number of disparate voices in western and, to a lesser extent, eastern Europe during the Cold War. This was part of an agenda to shape the postwar world along essentially conservative, anti-communist lines.[1]

It is not clear whether that entailed any direct support for the EM, which could only have been discreet given the opposition of the Labour government and the Foreign Office, but the evidence suggests that one objective may have been to blunt the edge of the federalists. Key individuals, such as Dr Joseph Retinger and Duncan Sandys, who were in contact, as the latter's correspondence shows, with Stewart Menzies, did receive covert assistance. Through the close relationship with these 'agents of influence', who may or may not have been helped with finance, MI6 was able to penetrate the major pro-unity European organisations and identify allies. It certainly provided a useful means of monitoring influential politicians and manoeuvres in Europe at a critical juncture in the Cold War.[2]

As so often was the case, MI6 relied to a great extent on the friendships of the old-boy intelligence network that had developed during the war in resistance circles, the principal contact point being the British sabotage and resistance organisation, the Special Operations Executive (SOE). The majority of the leading figures in the European unity movement had at some stage come within its orbit. A problem, though, remained the lack of funding necessary to run a full-scale operation. There was initial success in raising money from the City, but MI6, despite being masters of this type of operation in the United States during the war, never managed to put in place the arm's-length foundations – though there are hints of one or two, including film producer Sir Alexander Korda – that the Americans were so successful at exploiting in Cold War operations. It was not long, however, before the British discovered to their dismay that their American 'cousins', in the shape of the Office of Policy Co-ordination (OPC) and the Central Intelligence Agency (CIA), outstripped them in terms of finance and number of operations.

American success owed a great deal to the lessons learned in the highly successful British Intelligence campaign designed to change the United States' isolationist stance towards an internationalist and interventionist policy at the beginning of the war. The British Security Co-ordination (BSC) proved to be very adept at recruiting agents of influence and creating front groups. Senior Office of Strategic Services (OSS) officers took note and were at the forefront of the American efforts to forge an alliance for European unity out of the informal transatlantic network generated by former resistance workers. One key figure who was involved with the front groups and worked as a consultant for the State Department on a number of political warfare projects was the founder of the OSS, William Donovan. 'Wild Bill' was regarded by British Intelligence as 'our man'.[3]

MI6 had no alternative but to work in co-operation with the CIA to carry on its work among the European anti-communist networks. It would be wrong, however, to see the EM solely in the limited terms of European unity, since it was to act as the font from which a number of different joint British/American operations were to spring. This included working with eastern European exiles, students, trade unionists and propaganda outlets. Once again, these developed out of friendships from the wartime Anglo-American alliance.

The postwar alliance proved to be a rocky affair when it came to the continued sponsorship of the exile groups. Winston Churchill's return to power led to a number of disputes over relations with the Soviet Union which had a direct influence on support for the exiles. In the end, the CIA followed MI6's lead and by 1956 such operations had been abandoned, with the intelligence void being increasingly filled by technical means of intelligence-gathering. The fifties were a time of great change in the intelligence world, but it would take a decade of uncertainty before MI6 developed into a truly modern service.

THE EUROPEAN MOVEMENT AND 'THE BATTLE FOR PICASSO'S MIND'

In a lecture delivered in May 1994, Reader in Government at Oxford University Vernon Bogdanor made the point that the impulse to transcend nationalism through European union was 'kindled in the ashes of the Resistance'. Its federalist version, agreed the leading Italian Socialist Resistance spokesman Altiero Spinelli, 'had its roots in that crucible of passions and dreams which was the Resistance'.[1]

The first step had been taken in 1941 by Spinelli and Ernesto Rosi, when they formed a nucleus of Italian federalists and from their island prison issued the 'Ventotene Manifesto'. During the same year, talks took place within the Polish government-in-exile between its head, General Sikorski, his political adviser, Dr Retinger, and the British liaison officer, Victor Cazelet, a pre-war member of Count Coudenhove-Kalergi's Pan-European Union (PEU). Polish postwar planners hoped 'to establish in Europe some five or six regional federal blocks more or less equal in economic and military potentialities which, though strong enough to defend themselves against attack, would be economically viable organisations whose foremost need would be peace'. One would be based on Intermarium and another formed out of the countries supporting the Promethean League.[2]

It was Retinger, 'a compulsive intriguer and behind-the-scenes political wheeler-dealer', who suggested to Sikorski the worth of regular meetings with the foreign ministers of the governments-in-exile, such as Paul van Zeeland and Paul-Henri Spaak. At the end of 1941, they founded a Permanent

Bureau of Continental Foreign Ministers which later helped pave the way for the European Movement (EM).[3]

One man sympathetic to Polish aspirations was David Astor, who had created the Europe Study Group to examine the problems of Europe and the prospects for creating a non-nationalist order in Germany. At the core of the group were a number of émigré Germans destined to play a role in the EM, such as the future leader writer on the *Observer*, Richard 'Rix' Lowenthal. Interviewed for recruitment by MI6, Astor was turned down for a full-time post but was subsequently used by MI6 officer Lionel Loewe to establish contact with the German opposition. Employed as the press officer in Lord Mountbatten's Combined Operations Headquarters in London, Astor continued with his group, which drew on the ideas of the Cecil Rhodes-inspired Round Table Group and its belief that 'the British Empire should federate'. Astor's mentor was Philip Kerr (Lord Lothian), the 'most original thinker of the Round Table', who was 'regarded by many Europeans as one of the spiritual fathers of European federalism'. In the inter-war years, Lothian had supported the British Federal Union, a small group with wide influence which had been funded by Lord McGowan, chair of Imperial Chemical Industries (ICI).[4]

European unity was also a subject for discussion within the senior ranks of SOE. In 1943 the fifty-five-year-old Retinger joined SOE and parachuted into Poland to make contact with the underground Home Army. Within SOE, 'Salamander' formed a number of important friendships in the intelligence world, most notably with its Executive Director, Colin Gubbins, who shared ideas of European unity with a mutual 'old friend' and SOE colleague, Major Edward Beddington-Behrens. The latter had served with Gubbins on the Somme, and his war experiences had shaped his interest in European unity, as had his friendship with the leading federalist Jean Monnet, with whom he had worked in the International Labour Office of the League of Nations in Geneva. Hugely successful in the City, Beddington-Behrens had been influential in thirties anti-appeasement circles, being instrumental in establishing the Army League. Its chair was the leading Tory imperialist Leopold Amery, and members included Duncan Sandys, later prominent in the European unity campaign. Moving in the highest circles of the intelligence 'old-boy network', at the beginning of the Second World War, along with two 'old city friends', members of White's Club and senior MI6 officers Colonel Rex Benson and Kock de Gooreynd, he became one of the 'Twelve Apostles' – British military intelligence liaison officers with the French Army. After Dunkirk, Beddington-Behrens joined Gubbins in organising the stay-behind Auxiliary Units, designed to harass the Germans in the event of an invasion.[5]

In the United States, Beddington-Behrens' pre-war friend and Pan-European Union (PEU) organiser, Count Coudenhove-Kalergi, continued to pursue the goal of European union. In February 1942 the count became co-director of a research institute for a Post-War European Federation at the

University of New York. A year later, it held a Pan-European Congress attended by leaders of European governments-in-exile, including Paul van Zeeland. The count believed that the key PEU member in Britain was Leo Amery, who, with the endorsement of Churchill, wanted to encourage European integration as a means of combating Russia and curbing Germany's potential domination of Europe. Amery envisaged 'a freely co-operating Commonwealth' as the model for future European unity.[6]

In Europe, SOE-backed resistance workers actively campaigned for their post-hostilities vision of a federalist Europe. When Mussolini was overthrown in July 1943, freed prisoners founded the European Federalist Movement (EFM) in Milan, where one of the architects of European unity was the SOE-sponsored resistance leader Edgardo Sogno. Operating principally through Switzerland, the EFM clandestinely co-ordinated the different currents of federalism within European resistance via underground newspapers such as the Dutch *Het Parool* and, in France, *Combat*. Henri Frenay, who had helped form the Combat network in the South of France which became the backbone of the 'Armée Secrète', and who later became a member of General de Gaulle's National Committee in London, wrote in December that 'the governments which are in favour of national restorations ought to realise that ... the men of the European Resistance movement will be tomorrow's builders of a new Europe'. Only SOE's Gubbins and the OSS's Allen Dulles, with whom the Frenchman – busy organising a European unity conference in Algiers – was in contact, appeared to take Frenay's point seriously.[7]

Meanwhile, in the run-up to the invasion of Europe, David Astor, now transferred to a unit liaising between SOE and the resistance in France, helped the underground in London spread the word to groups throughout Europe. During the spring and summer of 1944, Ernesto Rossi and leaders of resistance movements from Denmark, France, Italy, Norway, Holland, Poland, Czechoslovakia, Yugoslavia and Germany secretly met in Geneva to produce a 'Draft Declaration of the European Resistances'. Released in October with the support of the London Socialist Vanguard group, it declared that 'anarchy can be solved only by the creation of Federal Union among the European peoples'.[8]

In March 1945, a Combat-backed Committee for European Federation called its first conference. With the war still in progress, Italian resistance members clandestinely made their way across the Alps to Paris. Those attending included Albert Camus, André Philip, Emanuel Mounier, Spinelli and François Bondy, all of whom were to play key roles in the European Movement. Also present was a British delegate close to Astor's thinking, George Orwell. Astor's *Observer* suggested that 'Britain must make sure that Europe becomes united under British leadership. Only as a spokesman and trustee of a United Europe can Britain pull her weight in the High Council of the Big Three . . . the choice for Europe lies between becoming either the Europe of Germany or Russia, or of federating under the leadership of Britain.' In the summer, as Allied troops entered Berlin, members of the German resistance presented a memorandum on European federation to Dulles.[9]

Retired from SOE but unofficially attached to MI6, at the end of hostilities Gubbins was approached by Retinger for help with his European project. Retinger was suspected by Polish colleagues of being 'in close touch not so much with British politics as with certain of its discreet institutions' – a hint at his MI6 connections. The records reveal that Gubbins, working closely with his business partner Beddington-Behrens, travelled across Europe developing contacts.[10]

Another senior SOE figure at these early postwar European assemblies was Conservative politician Douglas Dodds-Parker, who noticed that 'a high proportion' of those attending had a resistance background, 'but, as in Masonic circles, they usually kept this comradeship to themselves'. He informed Labour Foreign Secretary Ernest Bevin of his 'special employment' and suggested that there was 'considerable overseas support for Britain above party politics'. Bevin's response was to back his under-secretary, Christopher Mayhew, in setting up various 'joint activities'. According to Dodds-Parker, having previously rescued elements of the Vlasov Army in the South of France, he was invited to help rebuild the Free German Republic with PoWs and DPs. This secret recruitment of 'the few' led to others being brought into the German fold, such as Walter Hallstein and Eric Blumenfeld, who co-operated in 'so many European/Atlantic projects'.[11]

The main influence on British supporters came from Retinger, whose strongest backer, Astor, was now editor of the *Observer*. On 8 May 1946, as secretary-general of Paul van Zeeland's Independent League for European Co-operation (ILEC), Retinger gave a speech at the Royal Institute for International Affairs in which he viewed European unity as a counter to the 'Communist threat' and Soviet expansionism. It proved to be highly influential and led members of the former Permanent Bureau of Continental Foreign Ministers of the governments-in-exile to form the Benelux Customs Union.[12]

Without Winston Churchill it is unlikely that the EM would have got off the ground. In early 1946 Churchill embarked on a campaign to alert the West to the dire threat that the Soviet Union posed to Europe. He conceived European unity as a means of stemming the spread of communism, unity being directed 'not only at the Communist threat from outside national frontiers but also at the danger of subversion from the inside'. Churchill believed that a United Europe movement was essential to the revival of western Europe and, in a speech in the House of Commons in June, called for permission to be granted for the former enemy states of Germany, Austria, Hungary and Italy to take their place in the European system.[13]

Churchill hoped to work through the PEU and use the 'immense amount of pro-British sentiment' in western Europe. His son-in-law and closest colleague on the European project, Duncan Sandys, visited PEU organiser Count Coudenhove-Kalergi with the news that Churchill was working on plans for a pan-European initiative. The count's views, however, were considered far too federalist and idealist, and Sandys informed him that the British intended to sponsor an entirely new creation. Churchill did make use of other PEU supporters, including the British ambassador in Paris, Duff Cooper, who supplied him with political intelligence on the increasing stability in France: 'It looks as if the Communist virus is being decidedly corrected.' He saw European unity in terms of a French and German partnership as a balance to Soviet power.[14]

Although hampered by being in opposition, Churchill sought a major policy initiative, and his first move was to call in Tory members 'who have had some responsibility for the political side in the recent war'. He told them that 'if we are to win the future, we must set aside the past', adding that the Germans 'with their many great qualities, must be brought back into the community of free nations'.[15]

At the University of Zurich, on 19 September 1946, Churchill appealed for the creation of 'a kind of United States of Europe' from the 'Atlantic to the Black Sea'. He claimed that its structure, 'if well and truly built, will be such as to make the material strength of a single state less important. Small nations will count as much as large ones and gain their honour by their contribution to the common cause.' Hardly noticed was the specific exclusion of Britain from this enterprise. 'In all this urgent work, France and Germany must take the lead together, Great Britain, the British Commonwealth of Nations, mighty America, and I trust Soviet Russia . . . must be friends and sponsors of the new Europe and must champion its right to live and shine.' Churchill was not willing to give up the 'special relationship' with the United States, seeing it 'as an alternative to (perhaps even a refuge from) European federalism'.[16]

Many inside the Conservative Party questioned the wisdom of setting up a 'Western Bloc', while former resistance members were openly antagonistic. The speech, however, had an electrifying effect on opinion in Europe. Leo Amery declared that 'as for the Germans your speech may have been just in time to save them from going Bolshevist'. Churchill tried to create an all-party handling group, but it was frowned upon by Labour Prime Minister Clement Attlee. Instead, he set up a broad-based non-political 'Steering Committee' with Sandys, Bob Boothby and his friend Beddington-Behrens, and the ever-present Retinger.[17]

Formed in October 1946 as the result of a meeting between Beddington-Behrens and Belgium Prime Minister Paul van Zeeland, an economist of international standing, the European League for Economic Co-operation (ELEC) became a cornerstone of the EM. Designed to consider the technical problems of European economic union, ELEC was organised as a closed shop of the élite of economic liberalism. It was pro-British and anti-federalist. The British Economic League for European Co-operation was presided over by senior Conservative politicians – Sir Harold Butler (invited by Gubbins), Boothby, Harold Macmillan, David Eccles, Amery's son Julian, Beddington-Behrens; two Labour figures – Bob Edwards, chair of the Independent Labour Party and secretary-general of the Chemical Workers' Union, and Harry Hynd; and Lord Layton, a former PEU member and chair of the *News Chronicle*. Funds for ELEC were forthcoming from Astor and, on the initiative of Gubbins, Beddington-Behrens, considered by Macmillan to be 'a special kind of philanthropist'. Astor also paid Dr Retinger – appointed secretary-general and ELEC liaison officer with other committees – an annual grant of £500. When Edward Heath relaunched the European project in the early seventies it was ELEC which was the chosen vehicle for secret subsidies.[18]

In November, Churchill founded the United Europe Movement (UEM) with Duncan Sandys as general secretary. The UEM's committee of co-opted leading personalities, who regarded the idea of members as being 'dangerous', included Julian Amery, Boothby, Oliver Stanley, Lord Layton, the publisher Victor Gollancz, and Commander Stephen King-Hall, who devoted his *National News-Letter* to United Europe.[19]

In an attempt to allay fears of a German revival, Sandys urged resistance leaders to form a parallel French committee, the Conseil Français pour l'Europe Unie (CFEU). With representatives from all the major parties except the 'violently anti-European Communist Party', the CFEU was financed by the Centre d'Action Internationale, a small committee of eminent French bankers. Opposed to federalism and favouring the 'Unionist' approach, the CFEU recognised British leadership. Unfortunately for the British, they lacked the financial power to sustain the leading role for long.[20]

Attempts to gain access to American funding had been made from the beginning of the European unity campaign but, while there was sympathy for the cause, the requests were initially rebuffed because of British intransigence. In 1946, two OSS economists, Charles P. Kindleberger and Walt W. Rostow, had persuaded Jean Monnet to launch the idea of a UN-backed Economic Commission for Europe, but the British refused to support his federalist vision. This was partly owing to Monnet's preference for operating among socialists and the labour unions, which did not endear him to the Conservatives. Preferring to work with élite groups and independent experts rather than parliamentarians, in the words of his biographer, François Duchene, Monnet 'operated in the margin of the state in a system where the state was everything'. It was a strategy that brought him little success in Britain but found favour among the Europeans.

In the wake of the founding of ELEC and the UEM, at the invitation of the US ambassador in London, Averell Harriman, Retinger travelled to the

United States to meet members of the Council on Foreign Relations, especially his 'old friend' Adolf Berle Jnr, who agreed to lead an American section. While there was no official recognition, Retinger was encouraged by the response, particularly from John Foster Dulles, who was 'among those in America who helped us most'. He also met with former senior MI6 officer and leading banker Sir William Wiseman, an active behind-the-scenes figure promoting Anglo-American intelligence co-operation. The positive response to Retinger's visit had been made possible by the efforts of Coudenhove-Kalergi, who, although regarded as irrelevant in Europe, had supporters in America for his idea of a United States of Europe.[21]

Attempts to unite in Europe around Churchill's appeal foundered as it became clear that the majority of the resistance were pursuing a federalist agenda in opposition to the British. It was also apparent that no amount of goodwill left over from the war could bridge the political differences with the Socialist Movement for the United States of Europe, which promoted the 'International Third Force of socialists and social democrats' – between the 'dictatorship of Wall Street' and the 'totalitarian state of Stalin'. In December, the European Union of Federalists (EUF) was founded in Paris as the movement of former resistance activists with radical proposals for European unity. Chairs of the central committee were Holland's Professor H. Brugmans (1946–8), France's Henri Frenay (1948–50) and Germany's Eugen Kogon (1951–2). It had some support from the 'Keep Left' group in the Labour Party but was opposed by Attlee and Bevin, who rejected federalism.

Although Bevin believed in European consolidation and the need for defence against Soviet expansionism, he had set his face against a federal Europe. 'Federalism was a bugbear to the British Government which seemed to find it everywhere.' At a meeting with British pro-Europeans, Bevin told them that he was hostile to the idea of an European Assembly because he feared the communists might get a foot in it. The reality was that Bevin was not willing to support any initiative that ceded sovereignty or was not controlled by Britain. He was supported by Attlee, who told American journalist Cyrus Sulzberger that Britain was

> not strictly a European power. We are a member of the Commonwealth. We have to consider that and our responsibilities to it more than Europe . . . Furthermore, one must always remember that the nations of Europe have long traditions of individuality, and you cannot expect to scramble all these eggs either successfully. We shall make reasonable progress, but not as much as some optimists in the United States think should be done.

Bevin's response was to promote traditional inter-governmental co-operation. In March 1948 he created in Brussels the Western Union, a political association of Britain, France and the Benelux countries which aimed at organising collective defence.[22]

Churchill's vision differed little from that of the Labour government. He told a UEM meeting at the Albert Hall that Britain was not to be party to unity. 'United Europe will form one major regional entity. There is the United States, with all its dependencies; there is the Soviet Union; there is the British Empire and Commonwealth; and there is Europe. Here are the four main pillars of the world temple of peace.' Churchill added that 'it is for us to lay the foundation, to create the atmosphere and give the driving impulsion'. Profoundly anti-federalist, Bob Boothby spoke in terms of 'a league of totally independent sovereign states'.[23]

In July 1947, Duncan Sandys called together representatives of the British and French committees, the European Union of Federalists (Henri Brugmans), the Catholic-sponsored Nouvelles Equipes Internationales (NEI, Robert Bichet) and the ELEC (Paul van Zeeland) for a meeting in Paris with the object of setting up an umbrella organisation to co-ordinate their actions. Later in the year, the various groups merged into the Joint International Committee of the Movement for European Unity (JICMEU), with Sandys as chair and Retinger secretary-general.

In the United States, conscious of the 'tremendous growth of anti-Communist feeling' in the country and that European unity was seen as a means of resisting Russian aggression, Coudenhove-Kalergi threw his weight behind an initiative delivered by John Foster Dulles. In April, backed by OSS veterans Allen Dulles and Bill Donovan, he helped form the American Committee for a Free and United Europe. It soon became apparent, however, that only Churchill had the standing to launch the idea, though the count did persuade the Americans to fund a number of European initiatives.[24]

The UEM's Special Finance Committee, which was headed by ICI's Lord McGowan and included fellow-industrialists and bankers such as Lord Nuffield, Lord Balfour, Lord Camrose, Viscount Kemsley (Camrose's brother), Robert Fleming, Sir Malcolm Stewart, Sir Andrew Duncan of the Steel Federation, Sir Archibald Jamieson, George Gibson from the TUC, and the support of Lloyds Bank, Marks & Spencer and Vickers, had managed to raise £25,000 from private sources. British funding was not, however, enough to fulfil Churchill's ambitions.[25]

Covert US funding of 'voluntary' organisations began with Marshall Aid. Faced in the aftermath of the war with the economic collapse of Europe and the growing threat of the Soviet Union to US economic interests, the American Secretary of State, George Marshall, proposed in a speech at Harvard on 5 June 1947 the granting of economic aid through a joint recovery programme. Drawing on the previous year's Council on Foreign Relations' War and Peace Study Group report, 'Reconstruction in Western Europe', by lawyer Charles M. Spofford and banker David Rockefeller, Marshall introduced his European

Recovery Programme (ERP). He admitted that Churchill's call for a United Europe had influenced his belief that European states could undertake their own economic recovery with financial help from the United States. His statement received the support of Astor's *Observer*, which launched its first campaign for European integration around Marshall's plan. Liberal peer Lord Layton headed an ELEC committee whose proposals underpinned the plan for European economic regeneration.[26]

A total of eighteen countries accepted Marshall Aid, and on 16 April their representatives established the Organisation for European Economic Co-operation (OEEC) to implement the recovery programme. In the same month, Congress set up the Economic Co-operation Administration (ECA) to administer the aid. This required recipients to make substantial repayments for repatriation to the United States. Known as 'counter-part funds', the repayments accumulated under the control of the ECA's American administrators in Europe. In fact, only a portion were forwarded to Washington; the rest were siphoned off into illegal funds available for covert projects. The most powerful administrator of these covert funds was the US Military High Commissioner in Berlin, General Lucius D. Clay, who was approached by Retinger for help with the European project.[27]

As a result of JICMEU campaigning, in May 1948 Churchill convened in The Hague the first Congress of Europe. It attracted 750 'top people', with representatives from sixteen countries. Among those attending were Churchill, who was appointed President of Honour, Leon Blum, Jean Monnet, Paul Reynaud, Paul-Henri Spaak, Alcide de Gaspari, and a representative of the Vatican. Working closely with Paul Rijkens of Unilever and van Zeeland, later chair of the North Atlantic Council, Retinger was responsible for organising the Congress. P. A. Kerstens, an ELEC representative who had been minister for economic affairs in the wartime Dutch government-in-exile, officially raised the '£20,000' used to finance the Congress. In fact, Retinger had persuaded one of General Clay's key representatives, Shepard Stone, to support the Congress with a grant of £40,000 from the ECA's 'counter-part funds'. A former OSS officer, Stone had worked in psychological warfare during the war.[28]

At the final session of the Congress a communiqué was issued stating simply: 'We desire a united Europe throughout whose area the free movement of persons, ideas and goods is restored.' Later in the year, the EM was formalised as an unofficial but permanent body to promote the concept of a united Europe. Chaired by Sandys, with a general secretariat and offices in London and Paris, the EM set up a loose structure in which the constituent organisations had considerable freedom. The British had insisted on informal control and the executive committee had an over-representation of British and French 'unionist' delegates which Sandys, using 'arbitrary methods', and Retinger – the latter working hand in glove with Gubbins – used to counter the federalists. The Dutch, French and Belgians went along with Britain's leading role, partly because they feared a German revival.[29]

Britain was 'by far the richest of all the movements' and 'this wealth gave it considerable strength' within the EM. The all-important JICMEU finance subcommittee was headed by Beddington-Behrens. Over 80 per cent of the EM's finances came from the British-led UEM and, to a smaller extent, the French CFEU. The British quite brazenly used their financial monopoly to keep the movement in line with their own interests. When the European Union of Federalists (EUF), a small but badly funded group led by Spinelli and Frenay, organised a meeting in Zurich of thirty Swiss bankers in an attempt to raise funds, the British moved to ensure that any Swiss money went to the EM and not to the EUF. Adroit manoeuvring by Sandys and Beddington-Behrens, who met secretly with the bankers, led to the 'postponement' of the decision. Sandys then fought to scupper Spinelli and Frenay's concept of 'international federalism' which the unionists dismissed as 'impractical'.[30]

In July 1948, Retinger made a second trip to the United States, along with Sandys, Spaak and Beddington-Behrens. The latter recorded that Retinger's 'friendships in high places were extraordinary' and was taken aback that he was able 'to telephone direct to President Truman and General Marshall and arrange immediate appointments'. The principal contact, however, was Allen Dulles, who was persuaded to drop the 'utopian' Coudenhove-Kalergi and agree to underwrite secretly the EM. In the same month, Frank Wisner made a fact-finding trip to Europe where he visited General Clay, Averell Harriman, Marshall Aid's chief representative, and Britain's Foreign Secretary. On his return, Wisner took charge of the Office of Special Projects (soon changed to the innocuously sounding Office of Policy Co-ordination – OPC), which became Marshall Aid's 'political action' arm, with 'counter-part funds' funnelled by ECA administrators to Wisner. Financial problems within the EM were apparent after Beddington-Behrens resigned from the finance subcommittee in December in order to devote more time to business. The need for American funding had now become desperate.[31]

An American Committee for a United Europe (ACUE) was officially launched during a luncheon in honour of Winston Churchill on 29 March 1949, after Congress made European unity a central component of Marshall Aid. Modelled on the British-inspired EM and greatly influenced by Sandys and Retinger, the tightly controlled ACUE was an arm's-length intelligence affair mixing private individuals with veteran intelligence operatives. The chair and deputy were Donovan and Dulles, with a secretary, George S. Franklin, Director of the Council of Foreign Relations. Those on the board included CIA director-to-be Walter Bedell Smith; Arthur Goldberg, responsible for running the European covert operations of the labour union, the Congress of Industrial Organisations (CIO); trade unionist David Dubinsky and his deputy Jay Lovestone; General Lucius Clay and Charles M. Spofford, a director of the CIA. ACUE personnel viewed American federalism as an ideal political model which could be deployed with benefit in Europe.[32]

ACUE's creation was followed in April by twelve European countries and the USA and Canada signing the North Atlantic Treaty, which guaranteed mutual defence in the event of Soviet aggression. The EM played an important background role in the founding of NATO, with many of its adherents taking up senior posts in the organisation. One of the aims of the EM was to counter the rising tide of anti-Americanism in Europe, the rearming of Germany and the creation of an informal forum for promoting the cause of European unity. In May the EM gave birth to the Council of Europe and the Consultative Assembly in Strasbourg, which included the Brussels Treaty countries, and later Germany. The Council was, however, as far as the British wished to go in the direction of European unity, and from then on Sandys systematically opposed all attempts at developing the EM programme.[33]

The Conservative press was 'almost universally hostile' to the EM, which was divided, 'with its federalists, constitutionalists and functionalists arguing among themselves'. The political crisis was paralleled by a funding crisis which, in July 1949, became acute. Churchill appealed once again to Lord McGowan for funds, recognising that without the financial monopoly, the British section would lack the political clout to counter the federalists. Churchill wrote to Donovan that EM activities were 'severely restricted by lack of funds'. Donovan was sympathetic and over the next five years ACUE pumped nearly £3.5 million into the EM and related projects 'as part of the US efforts to create a bulwark against communism'. The majority of ACUE funds, five-sixths, came from 'State Department secret funds' – i.e. Wisner's OPC. They were specifically distributed to those groups and individuals who believed in a rapid approach to European integration. The man responsible for the funding programme was an anglophile and former senior OSS officer, Thomas W. Braden. He had worked for the US Military Government in Germany before being appointed Executive Director of ACUE and, in 1950, Dulles's assistant in the CIA.[34]

Responsibility for dispersing the funds within Europe was given to Churchill, though it was Sandys who co-operated with the ACUE in deciding where its funds would go. ACUE administration was not, however, highly regarded by EM officials, and the huge sums were largely unregulated. The Treasurer's Reports of the EM show that between 1947 and 1953, the EM spent £1,000,000, £580,000 of which was contributed by the Europeans, though that may have included Marshall Aid 'counter-part funds'. Between 1949 and 1953, £440,000 came from ACUE, most of whose money, £380,000, was from State Department secret funds. In August 1949, £25,000 was delivered to Churchill, and in the following March another £5,000. Intriguingly, Sandys was able on his own authority to hand over ACUE money to a separate unidentified 'British organisation'.[35]

Sandys assured the Americans that only an inner circle would know of the source of the funds. Thomas Braden later acknowledged that the leading figures in the EM 'knew and approved of CIA funding', though they were concerned lest details leaked. A former senior member of the EM did, in fact, publish details of the funds received from the United States in *Echer Tageblatt* (27 August 1949). He attacked the 'American intervention' because it proved that the Movement had no 'idealism'. Fortunately for the EM executive, this obscure article was ignored while similar accusations made by the Soviet Union were brushed aside.[36]

The EM financial subcommittee was subsequently dissolved and reconstituted with ICI's Paul Chambers as chair. Thus, at a time when American money was coming on-stream, funding still remained firmly in British hands. This remained so until November 1950, when Chambers was replaced by a Belgian treasurer, Baron Rene Boel.[37]

During 1950 the Movement began to splinter, with the federalist ambitions of its radical members increasingly at odds with Sandys' conservative policy. The Continentals were torn between support for the British and the 'negative attitudes' of Sandys, who was looked upon with 'increasing suspicion'. Fearing that the federalists had gone too far, he attempted to disband the Movement. One ACUE official complained that 'the British fear, above all, to be forced to give up any point of their national sovereignty, no matter how slight'. At the end of March, Sandys was asked to resign as general secretary.[38]

In June, the pro-European Harold Macmillan chided Churchill for not giving a lead on European unity, and lacking a 'clear or well-defined plan'. The European project was only active when Churchill indicated interest; as soon as that waned then so did that of its supporters. American officials in Europe remained horrified by the British tactics, which they believed were sabotaging European integration and causing a breakdown of Marshall Aid. After Braden consulted with Bedell Smith, the ACUE forced the replacement in July of Sandys by Spaak. Simultaneously, the headquarters were moved from Paris to Brussels. In August, a 'special committee' headed by Spaak presented a new structure plan. Unfortunately, it gave the Executive Committee even more draconian powers, which observers thought displayed 'how little respect' Spaak had at the time for the federalists.[39]

A large unspecified amount of the ACUE funding went to the British United Europe Movement, which had made a number of substantial loans to the EM. In August 1950, an agreement was reached in which British loans were written off as donations. Disaster loomed, however, when at the end of the year Congress refused to renew Marshall Aid. Fortunately, the 1951 Mutual Security Act stated that financial assistance to Europe could be used to 'further encourage the economic unification and political federation of

Europe'. At the same time, Dulles discovered that the CIA's sponsorship of organisations had become an 'operational junk heap' and decided to consolidate the operations into the International Organisations Division under Thomas Braden. Thus 'with the support of Allen Dulles and Frank Wisner, the CIA began its covert support of the non-Communist political left around the world – trade unions, political parties, and international organisations of students and journalists'. Braden's 'liberal' CIA faction recognised that in Europe the best opponents of the socialists and communists were the social democrats. During the year, the resources available to ACUE effectively trebled. Receipts from the Mutual Security Agency financed during 1951/2 'federalist' affiliated groups to the tune of £10,000, while in 1952/3 the EM Action Committee received £27,648. The greater part of ACUE funding, particularly after 1953, went to the EM's youth campaigns which, between 1951 and 1959, amounted to £1,342,223.[40]

When the Conservatives returned to power in 1951, Macmillan concluded that Churchill 'had now abandoned any effort to realise his European conception'. While American funding had helped the British to retain their predominant position in the EM, it was US influence which enabled the federalists to gain the upper hand and pave the way for institutions that sidelined the British. The turning point came in December 1951, when Spaak, realising that Britain was never going to co-operate with the European project, resigned from the Strasbourg Consultative Assembly. A year later, a reorganisation of the EM's international executive allowed the federalists to gain control. By that time, Churchill's eyes were firmly fixed on a new project – an international agreement with the Soviet Union.[41]

The federalists of the EUF – dismissed by the British unionists as 'impractical' – became the great pioneers of European integration. Despite being a small minority – mainly owing to lack of financial resources – they stuck to their views and by the early fifties had made significant progress. The former resistance workers of Europe saw their federalist ideas being taken seriously by the political élites of the countries that would form the emerging European Economic Community. Naturally, such success was viewed with dismay by the British.[42]

Unfortunately, as Douglas Dodds-Parker recognised, 'a golden opportunity was missed'. He believed that this had a good deal to do with the negative attitude within the Foreign Office towards SOE, if not to the resistance, which precluded more overt use being made of the goodwill towards Britain. The real problem, however, was that British politicians of all hues were still wedded to a superpower vision of the world which was no longer relevant and beyond the means of Britain's underperforming economy.[43]

According to former senior officer Montague Woodhouse, MI6 did not miss the opportunity to use their experience of the EM project to co-operate and finance with the CIA 'a few unspectacular activities'. Some of these have only been hinted at, while others, such as the funding of the magazine *Encounter*, have been revealed. Less well known is that all these operations began as the preserve of MI6, which only relinquished control when, at the end of the forties, funding began to dry up, leaving it little alternative but to co-operate – often with regret – with the Americans.[44]

THE EUROPEAN YOUTH CAMPAIGN

In 1947, the Soviet-funded international youth movement, the World Federation of Democratic Youth (WFDY), was racked by the divisions that went with the Cold War. The WFDY soon began to splinter, leaving the right wing and social democrats with no natural home. To fill the void, the British National Council of Social Service, chaired by (Sir) George Haynes, agreed to organise a preparatory committee, also chaired by Haynes, to launch a complementary international youth body. European federalists aligned with the EM had plans for a major youth campaign, but the financial means were not at hand and the realisation of the project was, initially, 'indefinitely postponed'. In a rare instance, however, substantial British government funds were made available for a conference to be held in mid-1948. Three-quarters of the £12,000 budget was covered by government departments including £3,000 from a bogus Prime Minister's 'South African Aid to Britain Fund', which appears to have been a cover for funds from the Secret Vote. Covert funding was also received from the French government.[45]

The success of the conference resulted in the creation of the World Assembly of Youth (WAY), with headquarters in Paris. Dubbed 'the cold war trojan horse', a British WAY national committee was elected with a broad membership, including non-Moscow-aligned socialists. It was not long, however, before it was dominated by career-minded potential politicians whose views were 'almost entirely in tune with those of their Foreign Office advisers'. Throughout the 1950s and 1960s the national committee remained in the hands of the Right.[46]

In 1952 WAY's president, Guthrie Moir, received 'a dire warning' that its 'very considerable grant aids' from the Foreign Office were at risk. Like Haynes, Moir was an Establishment figure who was placed on many different committees by the government. A PoW in Singapore during the war and then Chief Officer of the St John's Ambulance Brigade (1947–50), Moir had a successful career in religious and educational broadcasting. He was concerned that the threatened cuts were coming at a time when there was a possibility of building WAY into 'a really useful anti-communist influence'. It was in touch with the Foreign Office's IRD and circulated material from its monthly bulletin of *International Organisations*, and was able to do so without really looking like an official propaganda operation. Officials from the Foreign,

Colonial and Commonwealth Relations Offices were keen to use WAY, particularly by providing hospitality to overseas students as a counterweight to Communist Party special efforts to influence student visitors to Britain.[47]

The Foreign Office did eventually rally support against the Treasury cuts and a 'Friends of WAY' group was set up with prominent patrons, including the former PM, Clement Attlee, and Prime Minister Anthony Eden. The majority of funds, however, were received from the EM-backed European Youth Campaign's (EYC) Action Committee, headed by Andre Philip and responsible for 'special tasks'. Moir 'succeeded in obtaining the first batch of dollar aid for WAY from the Foundation for Youth and Student Affairs' – a CIA front organisation.[48]

To the embarrassment of the western allies, in the summer of 1951 the Soviet Union sponsored a gigantic youth rally in East Berlin, the cost of which had run into millions. When the US high commissioner for Germany, John McCloy, was supplied by MI6 with a secretly taken film of the rally, he instructed his staff to organise a counter-offensive. An aide, Shephard Stone, was sent to see Joseph Retinger and other senior officials of the EM with a request that it respond in kind with an anti-communist rally. Told that funds would be made available by ACUE, Retinger and Paul-Henri Spaak organised a 'special committee' to consider what form the campaign would take. The committee initially agreed to hold a rally, but to the dismay of ACUE leaders finally decided to conduct a continuous propaganda campaign to win the young to the idea of European unity. Thus was born the the EYC.[49]

The EM had complete control over its International Youth Campaign and its political section which, in March 1952, formed the EYC, which grouped together the non-communist youth organisations of western Europe. In October, it organised an Assembly of Political Youths at The Hague, which a year later became autonomous of the EM and reliant on bilateral agreements for 'special projects'. Until the creation of the youth campaign, propaganda had been virtually non-existent and, in effect, the EYC became the propaganda organisation of the EM. There was, however, a conflict between 'political' and 'educative' action, a division that grew sharper as time went on. Between 1951 and 1959, the EYC was by far the most active section of the EM, putting together a massive propaganda campaign of conferences and exhibitions, cinema shows, radio broadcasts and a large array of publications. In eight years £1.34 million of secret money was passed on to the EYC. According to the ACUE representative in Europe, Allan Hovey Jnr, the greater part of EYC finance came from State Department covert funds, which were forwarded to Hovey in Brussels. Those intended for the EYC were passed through a covering body in Paris – the Centre d'Action Européenne.[50]

The EM promoted WAY and labour youth groups such as the International Union of Socialist Youth (IUSY) and the Labour League of Youth (LLY), the youth secton of the Labour Party. These organisations received the bulk of the allocation of EYC money. In 1952, representatives of the Labour League queried the source of the funding and alleged that some money had come from US government sources. Dissatisfied with the response, the League decided to disaffiliate from the EYC, in the process producing a pamphlet explaining their reasons. Questions concerning EYC and WAY funding were also raised on the committee of the IUSY, which, in 1967, set up a special commission to investigate the origin of the 'private sources'. These included donations from the American Foundation for Youth and Students Abroad.[51]

Between 1951 and 1959, the secretary of the EYC's British section was Maurice Foley, later a Labour MP and minister. Although virtually every penny the campaign spent came from the US government, Foley denied any knowledge of CIA involvement. In 1975, the former head of the CIA's International Organisations Division, Thomas Braden, confirmed that the Agency had funded the EM and the EYC. When Braden heard Foley's denial, he is alleged to have replied, 'Bullshit.' Along with two other WAY colleagues, Charles Longbottom and Barney Hayhoe, the latter chair of the British National Committee during the late 1950s and early 1960s, Foley subsequently became a trustee of another front organisation, the Ariel Foundation.[52]

The exposure of the CIA's financial aid to WAY led to the international Secretariat in Paris becoming increasingly discredited and a fall-off in the organisation's affiliations. Eventually, WAY collapsed and, in 1977, the British National Committee – renamed the British Youth Council – disaffiliated.[53]

STUDENT UNIONS

Parallel to the covert funding of youth groups was the CIA's manipulation of the student movement, which, as Jonathan Block and Patrick Fitzgerald note, was 'pre-dated by similar British activity'. After the Second World War student organisers were approached by senior officials of the National Union of Students (NUS), who passed them on to a 'civil servant' acting on behalf of MI6. In addition, the Foreign Office, through its overseas missions and the British Council, compiled lists of those thought to be suitable candidates for invites to international conferences. References were specifically made to their anti-communist effectiveness. In July 1946 Foreign Office officials made specific enquiries about the management of the NUS, in particular: 'whether besides the Secretary and the Executive Committee there exists a governing body, and whether any of this personnel might be induced to work for the creation of a body of opinion within the delegation of the Union to balance the extremists'.[54]

The principal target of these moves was the creation in August, in Prague, of the World Student Congress, attended by western and eastern European national student organisations. The communists were in the majority at the Congress and a number of disputes arose as to the proper role of international student organisations. The Congress did, however, end on an amicable note, with a call for further co-operation and the building of a truly representative international student organisation. This came into existence shortly afterwards as the International Union of Students (IUS). Immediately after the Congress, the Foreign Office's Russia Committee undertook a study of the international student bodies and set in motion contact with the management of the NUS. It also tasked MI6 with developing contacts within the international student bodies. Operating under a 'false flag', MI6 officers stationed in western Europe, particularly in Scandinavia, posed as officials of other countries and began to recruit students as 'access agents' to penetrate communist countries and organisations.[55]

Friendly relations between the national factions inside the IUS did not last long and, in 1948, it splintered when it refused to condemn the communist takeover in Czechoslovakia. It did so again following the Stalin–Tito split, when Yugoslav students were expelled as 'Titoite agents'. 'Supposedly financed by jumble sales in Prague and Moscow', the IUS was widely seen in the West as a communist front organisation – 'the student section of the Cominform' – and in order to counteract its influence, MI6 and the CIA backed the more moderate efforts of the British NUS, student bodies from Scandinavia, and the American National Student Association (NSA). These moves, which opened up earlier rifts and completely shattered any hope of co-operation, resulted in the NSA breaking with the IUS in 1950 and forming the rival International Student Conference (ISC) in Stockholm. Although it was a founder member of the IUS, the NUS was won over to the ISC largely because of the generous help from the NSA and the backing of the anti-communist Labour Party grouping on the NUS, which included future Labour Party MPs Roy Hattersley, Brian Walden, John Stonehouse and Alan Lee Williams. By the early fifties, the new head of MI5's counter-subversion F Branch, Alexander Kellar, former president of the Scottish Union of Students, had begun organising the recruitment of British students. Most were long-term 'sleepers' who displayed sympathy with communism but acted as informers inside national and international organisations.[56]

The ISC, with its headquarters at Leiden, Holland, was promoted as an informal organisation without formal structure, with a brief to arrange meetings and conferences and organise co-operation with other international organisations such as WAY. The structure was necessary to attract the older conservative national unions which were disillusioned by the communist-controlled IUS. The initiative in creating the ISC had come from the Swedes, who 'carried on a very tough battle against the Americans and others who wanted to form an anti-communist organisation'. The Swedes 'gained a victory' and ISC was set up specifically as a 'non' not 'anti' communist organisation; a fine distinction, indeed, but one that had the backing of MI6. It was not long, however, before the ISC drew up a 'Bases of Co-operation' document governing admission to the Conference, which ensured that in practice it would be impossible to admit eastern European national unions.

Following a major conference in Edinburgh in January 1952, a Co-ordinating Secretariat of National Union of Students (COSEC) was created to implement Conference decisions. Without executive powers, its first general secretary (1953–7) was John Thompson, who had just relinquished his presidency of the NUS, while a key figure in promoting COSEC was his successor, Frank Copplestone, President of the NUS from 1954 to 1956. Copplestone was a conservative who joined with other moderates, including Fred Jarvis, who went on to become general secretary of the National Union of Teachers, 'in persuading the NUS to disassociate itself from the communist-dominated International Union of Students, and instead to affiliate with the International Student Conference'.[57]

Although the ISC was formally committed to discussing student problems and education, and not 'politics', it was widely seen as 'a creature of the Cold War', dedicated to fighting communism. *The Times* would later accuse the CIA and MI6 of using 'students to pressure international student organisations into taking cold war positions'. The president of the Irish students suggested that the fact that these organisations had survived for so long was proof that it 'served the interests of the CIA'. A Swedish minister of communications who had been instrumental in founding the ISC admitted that the revelations of CIA involvement were 'very depressing'. He accused the Americans and British of showing a 'false flag' and having 'undertaken secret activities of a type which we were fighting against'.[58]

During the mid-fifties, MI6's London BIN station, operating under Peter Lunn, began to recruit large numbers of NUS members, who travelled to communist countries or who had access to communist groups, as informal intelligence-gatherers. These student assets also had other uses. A secret internal MI6 document dated 17 July 1956 illustrates the extent of British and American intelligence planning and the problems of arm's-length control. It also reveals the sophistication of some intelligence operations. According to the document, the permanent COSEC staff in Holland consisted of three officials – 'Of these two are run, one by us, the other by CIA. The British official is not however conscious to SIS and would not, it is judged, react favourably if made conscious; nor is he aware that COSEC's source of funds is in fact mainly CIA.' It goes on to reveal that Operation SCHOLAR was run not from Holland but by an officer in the London BIN station, overtly by telegram and letter. This had led to 'irregular and broken communication', particularly as the official was often abroad, which meant that 'even in the most favourable circumstances there is likely to be a big time-lag between our telling COSEC we want it to act in a certain way and its so acting'.

The author was further concerned that 'it is sometimes possible for important COSEC emissaries to proceed on missions unbriefed'. Despite 'the frustrations', however, MI6 regarded 'the limitations as acceptable'. It believed

> it to be of paramount importance to maintain as far as possible the illusion of COSEC's complete independence. It seems to us that, if once we attempted to sharpen COSEC as a Cold War instrument, we might find it had ceased to have any point at all. Certainly it would be difficult to retain the allegiance of member organisations in the uncommitted countries of Asia and Africa, if they suspected that COSEC was being 'run' by the Americans and ourselves.

A further document from June 1960 reveals that MI6 had recruited ISC students in the Commonwealth countries and was receiving the help of their respective intelligence agencies in running the operation.[59]

For about fifteen years the CIA was the principal source of funds, supplying over 90 per cent of the ISC's finance. Most of the funding came via a three-layer 'pass through' operation which involved a score of 'primary' dummy foundations set up by the CIA. The official source of funds was the US NSA, which, in turn, received its finance from the CIA through laundered contributions from the Catherwood Foundation, the New York Fund for Youth and Student Affairs (FYSA) and the San Jacinto Fund. The foundations exercised considerable influence over the ISC because each project devised in Leiden had to be submitted to US representatives for budget approval. Between 1962 and 1964, the FYSA contributed $1,826,000 while the San Jacinto Fund delivered nearly half a million dollars for the ISC's magazine, *The Student*, and a further third of a million for international conferences.

When in 1967 the secret student funding scandal was uncovered in the American magazine *Ramparts*, the New York *Herald-Tribune* referred to 'a British counterpart of the dummy foundations' that channelled money to the ISC, but provided no other details. Pamphlets put out by the Radical Student Alliance noted rumours of parallel British Intelligence operations, even naming names, but convincing proof was not established at the time.[60]

The ISC expanded rapidly in the fifties and by 1962 had eighty worldwide members. The majority of these national unions were in Asia, Africa and South America, which caused some problems for the western European and American members that had founded the organisation. Control of conferences and COSEC, however, remained firmly in the hands of the western student unions which tried to keep the lid on political discussion. This was a period when MI6's Special Political Action section paid particular attention to cultivating its ties to national student unions in a bid to counter communist influences. Pressures, however, continued to build to give expression to the views of Third World delegations. In 1964, in an attempt to curtail the leftward drift, the ISC undertook a complete turnabout and, at the Christchurch Conference in New Zealand, adopted a charter with a liberal manifesto which condemned 'Imperialism, Totalitarianism, Colonialism and Racism'. The ISC was presented as an explicitly political counterforce to the Soviet-backed IUS.[61]

The manoeuvring within the ISC had been instigated by British representatives, some of whom went on to join MI6. Others became regular diplomats in the Foreign Office, and when the pro-Europe enthusiast Edward Heath was elected Prime Minister in 1970, a number were appointed to senior posts within the European Economic Community (EEC). The deputy chief of MI6, Maurice Oldfield, was also tasked by Heath with penetrating Europe, and a number of agents were inserted into the EEC, where, in reference to MI6's headquarters, they became known as the 'Century House boys'.[62]

Chair of the Christchurch Conference was a former NUS President (1964–6), T. W. 'Bill' Savage, who in 1968 joined MI6. Savage served in Dar-es-Salaam and in the early eighties in the Cabinet Office, before being promoted to a senior post inside MI6.

The mover of the new Charter was Aneurin Rhys Hughes, another former NUS President (1962–4). In 1966 Hughes joined the Foreign Office serving as a diplomat in Singapore and Rome before, in 1973, joining the EEC's General Secretariat in Brussels. He rose to become Head of Division for Internal Co-ordination and continued for many years to work inside the European Union.

Gwyn Morgan, who had been elected President of the NUS (1960–2) on an anti-communist ticket, filled the ISC's top post as Secretary-General and was in charge of finance. In this capacity 'he negotiated with the American foundations which supplied the bulk of ISC funds and supervised the expenditure of the several million dollars devoted to world-wide propaganda and organisation'. In 1964 Morgan departed to become head of the Labour Party's International Department and was eventually elected General Secretary of the party. An ardent pro-European, Morgan, too, pursued a career in the EEC, becoming head of the Welsh Information Office in 1975 and, from 1983, Representative of the Commission of the European Community on Turkey. Morgan was also a trustee of the Ariel Foundation.

The leader of the British delegation to Christchurch was Geoffrey Martin. Head of the NUS International Affairs section, he was elected President in 1966. Martin was deeply involved in the ISC and made great efforts to allay local Student Union fears about the source of ISC funding. A minority report on the ISC for the 1965 NUS Margate conference revealed that 90 per cent of its funding came from US foundations. The report was attacked by ISC adherents with references to 'the Communist conspiracy'. In 1968 Martin became director of the charity for the homeless, Shelter. In 1974 he joined the Diplomatic Staff Commonwealth Secretariat, and five years later was appointed head of the Office of the Commission of the European Community, Northern Ireland. He was another trustee of Ariel.

Margaret 'Meta' Ramsay, President of the Scottish NUS (1959–61), became in 1962 Associate Secretary of the ISC, at Leiden. From 1965 to 1967, Ramsay was Secretary of the Fund for International Student Co-operation (FISC), which was based in London to 'further co-operation among students of the free world'. Under its organiser, Scottish manager of the European Movement and future Labour MP George Foulkes, it held seminars for Third World students visiting Britain and organised weekend seminars for NUS officials. In 1967, the Radical Student Alliance issued a pamphlet, 'ISC, CIA and NUS', which speculated that FISC was a CIA front. FISC officials vigorously denied the claim and countered that it was financed by 'people and organisations who have shown an interest in students'.

FISC shared an office with the Overseas Students Trust (OST), which paid the NUS to employ a full-time overseas student officer. A trustee of OST was Dennis Grennan, who was the first Labour Party member to be elected NUS President in the fifties after years of right-wing rule. During his tenure of office, Grennan helped consolidate the anti-communist forces within the Union. Grennan was involved with WAY, and has been credited with setting up the Ariel Foundation. He had a special interest in African affairs during the sixties and seventies. An adviser on foreign affairs to the Labour Foreign Secretary, James Callaghan, Grennan visited Angola to report on the conditions of captured British mercenaries in prison, and allegedly helped reorganise the Intelligence Service of Zambia's President Kaunda.[63]

In 1969, Ramsay joined MI6, serving in Scandinavia – Stockholm and Helsinki – the site of ISC's original support.

THE CONGRESS FOR CULTURAL FREEDOM AND *ENCOUNTER*

One of the MI6/CIA co-operative operations that Monty Woodhouse acknowledges was the Congress for Cultural Freedom (CCF), which subsequently resulted in the co-founding and funding of the periodical *Encounter* 'as a vehicle for intellectual propaganda'. This was all part, Thomas Braden later admitted, of an international 'battle for Picasso's mind'.[64]

After the communist takeover of Czechoslovakia in 1948, MI6 had suggested to the Americans that 'it would be a good idea to provide a broader intellectual haven for Western writers'. During March 1949, the Americans began to consider their response to Soviet cultural initiatives, in particular a peace conference that had been held that month in New York as part of the Communist Information Bureau's (Cominform) campaign to shape western opinion. Eight hundred prominent literary and artistic figures had been invited to repudiate 'US warmongering'. The first response came from a New York professor and editor of the *New Leader* magazine for the anti-Soviet Left, Sydney Hook, who had founded at the beginning of the war the Committee for Cultural Freedom. His new group, Americans for Intellectual Freedom, was supported by the OPC, whose head, Frank Wisner, was already looking for ways to counter the next big Soviet-backed peace conference which was to be held in late April, in Paris.[65]

Wisner's aide Carmel Offie worked with trade unionist Irving Brown in organising the International Day of Resistance to Dictatorship and War in Paris, covertly underwriting the expenses of Hook's groups and delegates from Germany, Italy and the United States. The conference on 30 April proved, however, to be something of a disappointment, and Wisner pushed for a permanent committee of anti-communist intellectuals from Europe and the United States to counter Soviet-backed front groups. The idea was taken up by Hook and Melvin Lasky, a staff member of the *New Leader* and editor of *Der Monat*. Lasky, who had worked with German 'resistance' movements against the communists, had persuaded the US authorities in Berlin to support *Der Monat* as a cultural magazine that would bring German intellectuals to the free world. The first issue in October had featured a number of British writers including Bertrand Russell, Philip Toynbee and George Orwell. Offie also arranged covert funding for the proposal by Lasky and former communists Franz Borkenau and Ruth Fischer for an international conference of the non-communist Left in Berlin to be scheduled for the following year.[66]

In parallel, during the summer of 1949 officials of the British Foreign Office working with the secret propaganda arm, IRD, and junior minister Christopher Mayhew, floated similar ideas. The minister wanted to 'rally the forces of freedom and inspire a crusading spirit in all our peoples in defence of the civilisation, liberties and values which Europe has given the world and which are threatened by totalitarianism'. Officials sought a 'positive campaign – a crusade – to put over to the public of Western Europe the merit of Western democracy'. Northern Department head Christopher Warner argued that the best spokesmen for 'putting life into the Western gospel' would be people with 'big names and reputations among foreigners', since they would be able to 'clothe the familiar ideals in inspiring language'. Another official, R. L. Speight, suggested 'a body of leading figures working together on their own and without evident Government sponsorship, but with the Foreign Office in the background to give advice and guidance'. Figures suggested included Arnold Toynbee, Alan Bullock, Bertrand Russell, Harold Nicolson and Michael Oakeshott, but Mayhew wanted 'rather younger and less orthodox' names such as Arthur Koestler and Barbara Ward. Hector McNeil, the minister closest to MI6, was 'very chary; poets make bad committee men', while a meeting called to consider the proposal agreed that 'many were extremely woolly-minded about totalitarianism and true democracy'. For the time being, the meeting decided not to make any approaches.[67]

MI6 was also making plans. In early June, an MI6 officer lunched with senior *Telegraph* journalist and wartime colleague Malcolm Muggeridge, who was still working 'part-time' for the Service, and 'discussed at length a particular assignment'. On the 21st, Muggeridge had his final discussion on the 'MI6 project' and agreed to take it on, even though he thought all the Service's arrangements to be a 'combination of fantasy and incompetence'. It appears that, like the Foreign Office scheme, this particular project was dropped but revived once the Cold War became 'hot'.[68]

The Americans continued with their plans for a cultural counteroffensive and ACUE set up a cultural subcommittee run by two former OSS historians, Frederick H. Burkhardt and William L. Langer. The man behind the scheme was CIA officer Michael Josselson, the son of a former Estonian Jewish timber merchant, who served after the war with the US Psychological Warfare Division as an interrogator in Germany. During the autumn of 1949, he persuaded Lasky to change the Berlin conference into a cultural event, in the belief that it could better seize the initiative from the Soviets by reaffirming 'the fundamental ideals governing cultural (and political) action in the Western world and the repudiation of all totalitarian challenges'.[69]

In June 1950, as the Korean War broke out, Europe's 'men of letters' assembled in the Titania Palace theatre in the US Zone in Berlin before an audience of four thousand to launch the CCF – a body whose purpose was to 'defend freedom and democracy against the new tyranny sweeping the old'. It was committed to the 'cultural reconstruction' of a still weak and devastated Europe through 'information, education, orientation, agitation', and was sponsored by *Der Monat* and run by Lasky, who acted as secretary-general. The costs were met by the OPC, using 50,000 dollars of Marshall Aid 'counter-part' funds.[70]

Invited to the Congress were many who were active in the EM such as Julian Amery, Henri Frenay, Eugen Kogan, Hendryk Brugmans, Altiero Spinelli and François Bondy. They were, however, overshadowed by the two key polarising figures – Arthur Koestler, then 'a pugnacious and energetic cold warrior', and Ignazio Silone, 'a gentle socialist moralist'. Koestler, who, in the thirties, had helped the Soviet operative Willi Munzenberg to manage front groups for Moscow, had turned against the Communist Party during the time of the Hitler–Stalin pact and had written the highly influential book about the Moscow trials *Darkness at Noon*. Having worked for MI5 during the war, Koestler was opposed by two wartime MI6 officers, A. J. 'Freddie' Ayer, Professor of Philosophy at University College, London, and Hugh Trevor-Roper, who were to play a self-acknowledged 'mischievous' role at the Congress. Ayer had served with the British Security Co-ordination (BSC) in

New York and then in Algiers, with Malcolm Muggeridge, and later with SOE in France.[71]

What irritated Ayer and Trevor-Roper was 'the hysterical atmosphere in which the Congress was held, orchestrated as it was by revengeful ex-Communists'. Acting as an 'obstructive element', they raised objections to Koestler's role, attacking his 'dogmatism'. Supporting the idea of 'tolerance', they were repelled by the delirious applause that greeted speeches calling for war against the Soviet Union. Ayer's and Trevor-Roper's warnings were not heeded, and an informal steering committee was formed of the hardline Koestler, Irving Brown, described by *Reader's Digest* as a 'one-man OSS' who arranged for the American Federation of Labor to fund the interim organisation, and Lasky. Josselson had 'kept track of everything that transpired', and in the belief that Silone's subtler approach had won over Koestler's frontal assault, ensured that Silone joined the committee. In Washington, the Congress was regarded by the Defence Department representative to the OPC, James Magruder, as 'unconventional warfare at its best', being 'a subtle covert operation carried out on the highest intellectual level'. In November, the OPC's Project Review Board approved the establishment of a permanent executive committee, with covert CIA support. It was elected in Berlin with a British representative, the poet Stephen Spender, and an alternate, T. R. Fyvel.[72]

Operating on the fringes of the Congress was Malcolm Muggeridge, Washington correspondent for the *Telegraph*. With another former MI6 officer and son of a Russian timber merchant, the philosopher Isaiah Berlin, Muggeridge was a member of a small social circle that discussed with Frank Wisner ways of combating the communists. Muggeridge 'accepted American leadership for, as it were, the duration, as the only hope of containing the Soviet Gulag'. The former MI6 officers had influence on the leading figures in the State Department, George Keenan and Charles E. Bohlen, who brought a 'quiet revolution' in the US to foreign policy. They came to understand that there was 'confluence between the ideas of the non-Communist left intellectuals and that combination of Ivy League, Anglophile, liberal, can-do gentlemen, academics and idealists who constituted the new CIA'. One such élite member was Thomas Braden, who ran the International Organisations Division which was designed to combat the Soviet international front organisations which, the CIA claimed, had a $250 million annual budget.[73]

One of Braden's 'counter-organisations' was the Congress for Cultural Freedom (CCF), which set up a secretariat in Paris, with Josselson as Executive Director. He was regarded as a 'controlled and orderly man' who had his hands full 'attempting to organise a world-wide community of unruly and temperamental intellectuals'. Secret OPC/CIA funding for the CCF came via nearly forty different American trusts and charitable foundations – 'notional donors' as they were technically known by MI6 – with the principal conduit for covert funds being the Farfield Foundation. Its philanthropic president, Cincinnati multimillionaire Julius Fleischman, was a director of the Metropolitan Opera in New York and fellow of the Royal Society of the Arts in London. Members of the foundation would lunch every month with a guest from the Congress, usually Josselson or Muggeridge. Other secret funds were channelled through Jay Lovestone, an ex-communist Russian émigré, who had served in the OSS, organising labour resistance in Europe. According to Braden, the budget for the CFF and its magazine *Encounter* in the year during which he had control was 800,000 to 900,000 dollars. The heavy funding of the CCF originated in 1954 on the instigation of Allen Dulles, who assigned the head of counter-intelligence, James Angleton, as Lovestone's case officer. Angleton 'allowed his most loyal friends in British Intelligence to read items that Lovestone had culled from the United Kingdom, where he had good contacts with the TUC and Labour Party'. He tried to monitor the large sums of money that Lovestone controlled but was not always successful and a considerable number of payments went unrecorded.[74]

Alongside the CCF International Committee there was a British Society for Cultural Freedom, chaired by wartime propagandist Harman Grisewood. Muggeridge acted as its vice-chair; the secretary was Michael Goodwin, who had worked for the BBC Overseas News Service, while the treasurer was George Orwell's publisher, Frederick Warburg. When Griseman and Goodwin resigned, it was Muggeridge who reconstructed the secretariat, organising lectures and meetings on Cold War themes, and distributing Congress magazines. Muggeridge, however, was not suited to administration and soon became bored, with the result that the British Society never developed into an important cultural force.

The British magazine most sympathetic to the liberal, Atlanticist and anti-communist aims of the Congress was *The Nineteenth Century and After*, which had the support of the *Observer*'s David Astor. Between 1945 and 1952, the assistant and later editor was Michael Goodwin, who went on to work with the IRD-backed front publisher Ampersand. In January 1951, the Congress agreed to subsidise the magazine, which changed its name to *The Twentieth Century*. It was, however, not quite the magazine of political as well as literary views that Josselson wanted. He felt that there was a need for a magazine – to be edited in Paris in order to avoid 'Anglo-American provincialism' – that would appeal to the Europeans. During 1952, this caused some dissension in London, and Muggeridge, Stephen Spender, T. R. Fyvel, Michael Oakeshott and Fred Warburg 'somewhat light-heartedly founded the Anglo-American monthly magazine *Encounter*'.[75]

The key players were Muggeridge, operating on behalf of MI6, and Fyvel, who was working for the IRD. Strongly anti-communist, a writer and broadcaster prominent in the Zionist movement, Fyvel had been a close friend and colleague of Orwell. During the war, he worked with Richard Crossman in the Psychological Warfare Branch, which was attached to the headquarters of General Eisenhower in North Africa and Italy. Returning to London, Fyvel worked as a reader for the publisher F. J. Warburg and later succeeded Orwell as literary editor of the left-wing weekly *Tribune*. Employed by the BBC External Services since 1949, Fyvel had been recruited into the IRD two years later.[76]

Muggeridge and Fyvel insisted to Josselson that the magazine 'be edited in London'. It was to be 'editorially independent, both literary and political and while internationalist drawing heavily on the hinterland of British writers'. There would be a continuing battle throughout the fifties over its 'independence' from the secretariat in Paris and whether it was 'British' or 'internationalist'. The two co-editors were Stephen Spender and the American Irving Kristol, who in his bowler hat was seen as more English than the English.[77]

Within the space of a month in the thirties, Spender had joined and left the Communist Party. He was a former editor of the literary magazine *Horizon* and, in the immediate aftermath of the war, had worked for the Control Commission in Germany where he reported on the attitudes of writers and intellectuals. In the late forties, he contributed to Richard Crossman's *The God that Failed*, along with other European former communists who became major figures in the Congress. Spender was also a leading member of the international association of writers, PEN, which was itself subsidised by the CIA.[78]

The British Society won the argument but ceased to function once *Encounter* centred its operations in London. The magazine, which had no editorial board, was published by Secker and Warburg, which had published Orwell's *Animal Farm* after a number of publishers had turned it down. In the summer of 1949, Warburg published *Nineteen Eighty-Four*, with a press release which claimed that 'if there is a failure of nerve and the Labour Party breaks down in its attempt to deal with the harsh problems with which it will be faced, tougher types than the present Labour leaders will inevitably take over, drawn probably from the ranks of the Left, but not sharing the liberal aspirations of those now in power'. He challenged the 'Communists and fellow-travellers, well entrenched in the media', publishing books by ex-communists, many of whom were associated with the CCF. The first issue of *Encounter* appeared in October 1953 and was described by the *Times Literary Supplement* as a journal of 'negative liberalism', characterised by a 'hatred and fear of communism'.[79]

Encounter was officially 'sponsored' by the Congress and Spender was told that it would be funded by the Farfield Foundation, whose founder, Julius Fleischman, he had met during a trip to the United States. One of Muggeridge's last services had been to arrange for MI6 to pay the salary of any British co-editor of *Encounter*, using his friend, former MI5 officer Lord

Rothschild, as a conduit. According to American sources, Rothschild, who was certainly close to MI6, acted as 'a sort of British front foundation'. *Encounter* was not the only magazine that Rothschild funded in this period. Muggeridge left, disillusioned with the whole project. He thought that there were too many 'dead fruit' involved.[80]

The person who appears to have taken Muggeridge's place was Goronwy Rees, a recent member of MI6's Political Section, who described *Encounter* as an 'intellectual Marshall Plan'. Rees was a former communist supporter and shared his views about the Soviet Union with Melvin Lasky, who had changed his mind about communism in the late thirties with the Moscow show trials. Lasky, however, could never fathom Rees, and found him 'very secretive' and a 'shadowy' figure, especially after friends told him that he had been 'planted' on the magazine by MI6. Rees, who got his job at *Encounter* through Spender, later confided that the magazine had been founded as a result of a growing realisation that the alternative society offered by the Soviet Union and its satellites was one 'the West cannot hesitate to characterise as barbaric, both in the sense that they are hostile and alien, and in the sense that they lack those minimum guarantees of individual freedom and security in the absence of which no society can claim to be civilised'. A voice had to be found but it was impossible, Rees discovered, without the generous assistance of the CIA.[81]

CIA funding of the CCF and *Encounter* had been alleged by the Soviets from the beginning but was dismissed as communist disinformation. Then, in 1963, an editorial in the *Sunday Telegraph*, presumably based on information from Muggeridge, referred to a secret and regular subvention to *Encounter* from the 'Foreign Office'. This was supplemented by reports of CIA subsidies. Lasky consistently denied any knowledge of CIA financing, even though the CIA's Thomas Braden said that 'the man in charge' was a 'witting agent'. In the face of denials by Lasky and Spender, the *Telegraph* published an apology. Foreign Office mandarin Nicholas Henderson reported the strange goings-on to Anne Fleming, the society hostess and wife of the spy author: 'There's an awful fuss going on about *Encounter*, it appears that Stephen Spender did not know that it was financed by the CIA, very rum for everyone else did.' That included Freddie Ayer, who had been aware from the beginning that the source of the funds was the CIA. The denials did not shock him, even though he thought it impossible not to have known: 'I still do not understand how it could have deceived anyone who had anything to do with the Congress.' Fellow-thirties writer Edward Upward regarded Spender as 'unscrupulous – he had a great talent for publicity ... he must have been very simple. I told him years before, "It's just a Cold War paper".'[82]

Reports of secret funding did, however, damage *Encounter*'s standing, and Spender and Lasky were forced to look for alternative private 'angels'. Negotiations with the head of Mirror Newspapers, Cecil King, were finally successful, and by July 1964 they were able to announce that *Encounter*'s financial and business affairs would be handled by the International Publishing Corporation. Although it ceased to be sponsored by the CCF, intelligence connections were not far away, as the British representatives on the controlling trust included Sir William Hayter, a former chair of the Joint Intelligence Committee, while King had his own links to the CIA and British Intelligence.[83]

Although regarded by MI6 as an 'unspectacular' operation, in its first period during the early fifties the CCF did help to build through 'the battle for Picasso's mind' an Atlanticist intellectual community. By maintaining a number of magazines that were already launched but financially shaky, and by sponsoring new ones in England such as *Encounter*, *China Quarterly*, *Minerva* and *Censorship*, the CCF succeeded in making good Irving Kristol's expressed aim 'to create a certain kind of intellectual-cultural milieu, which would in turn have far-reaching, but indirect, effects'. With a relatively small effort MI6 and the IRD were able to play a still largely unrecognised role in shaping European and, more particularly, British social democratic politics. It is only recently that politicians – mainly on the Right of the Labour Party, and those that joined the SDP – whose political and cultural ideas were influenced by the CCF and its offshoots have left the scene.[84]

ROLLING BACK 'ROLL-BACK'

The rhetoric of the Anglo-American liberation policy of 'roll-back' proved to be a dangerous option in that it fed Stalin's obvious paranoia and, ultimately, proved to be counterproductive. Stalin was perpetually concerned about the machinations of British Intelligence, and there were many instances of him personally warning the leaders of the satellites to be vigilant against MI6 activities.

At the end of the Second World War, Stalin was furious that after the expulsion of German forces from western Ukraine and the Baltic states, guerrilla bands continued to fight the Soviet occupation. On several occasions, Stalin ordered his security chief, Lavrenti Beria, 'to finish off the outlaws but the irritant continued for five years'. Despite Moscow publicising the fact that they knew that the 'outlaws' had been supported by British and American Intelligence incursions into sovereign territory, the Soviet Union found itself isolated in the United Nations and unable to obtain redress. The announcement of the Truman Doctrine fuelled the general insecurity, while the offer of Marshall Aid to the satellite states – acknowledged as vital to these countries' recovery – was seen as a capitalist trap that would have left them, as is now known to have been the intention, under virtual US economic control. These western manoeuvres led to a 'volatile Soviet over-reaction to both British and American special operations which resulted in considerable turmoil in Eastern Europe'. Knowledge of western efforts would play a major part in Stalin's drive to purge numerous innocent eastern European protégés on imaginary charges of subversion.[1]

When Stalin launched his purges in 1948, the primary target was the Titoists, principally those people who had not been trained in Moscow and, therefore, might be disloyal. He feared the influence of the Yugoslavs, who were training and returning to their country of origin a large number of Spanish Civil War veterans from French internment camps. These insurgents soon came under suspicion because they appeared to be under the tight control of the Yugoslavs and loyal to Belgrade. Stalin also feared those communists who had worked in the resistance groups during the war; they had often been, quite legitimately, in contact with the British secret services, which made them in Moscow's view potentially unreliable and agents of the West.

Following the expulsion of Yugoslavia in November 1949, with the urging of Stalin the Cominform launched the 'Vigilance' campaign throughout eastern Europe with calls for the security forces to be on their guard against enemy agents. This took place against a background where 'all internal political opposition had been liquidated and there was no sign of the spread of Titoism'. Indeed, there was consternation in western diplomatic circles that 'Titoism' had done nothing to weaken the hold of international communism. Despite this lack of threat, hysteria soon gripped eastern Europe as elaborate plots were uncovered and hundreds of alleged western agents were arrested, convicted and finally shot. In a curious way, Richard Aldrich has argued, 'British and American efforts had perhaps scored an unintended success. In this sense Stalin may have inflicted far more damage in Eastern Europe than the CIA or the MI6 Special Operations Branch could have conceivably hoped to do.'[2]

This unintentional turn of events later gave rise to a conspiracy theory, seemingly deliberately 'surfaced' (intelligence jargon for planting stories) by the British, that MI6 – and later the CIA – had run a deception operation that exploited Stalin's paranoia by falsely linking a number of eastern European leaders and officials to the western intelligence services. The supposed vehicle for this Machiavellian plot was Noel Field – a Quaker, communist and former OSS colleague of Allen Dulles – who mysteriously disappeared in Prague in 1949. In the early 1950s, while he languished in a Soviet prison, Field became the Stalinist scapegoat in the purge trials of Rudolf Slansky and other communist leaders. Despite his mistreatment, Field chose to remain in Hungary upon his release in 1954, until his death fourteen years later. The first reference to Field's arrest suggesting that it was actually part of a British plot to split the communists was in R. Harris Smith's history of the OSS, where he suggested that the plot formed the basis of John le Carré's The Spy Who Came in from the Cold. Kim Philby later commented that he found the le Carré plots more complicated than the real thing.[3]

Although the theory is expounded at great length in Stewart Steven's mid-seventies Operation Splinter Factor, no reliable evidence has surfaced since to suggest that MI6 did construct such a conspiracy; while senior CIA officers have dismissed the idea, acknowledging that the Agency was in no position to undertake such a sophisticated operation. It may be that the plot idea can be traced back to the defection on 21 December 1953 of the Polish deputy director of the notorious Department 10 in the Ministry of Internal Affairs, Josef Swialto, whose job included the gathering of derogatory information on top government officials. Swialto had had access to the Field dossier, which included the details of his interrogation. According to the theory, Swialto had been recruited by MI6, who passed the case on to the fledgling CIA and while in exile gave details of the Field dossier to Frank Wisner.[4]

The truth was that the Field case became an opportunity for the Soviets to launch a propaganda counter-offensive throughout eastern Europe by link-ing the alleged American spy to communist officials and to émigrés in the West. In the background was a virulent anti-Semitic campaign that was tied to an 'anti-cosmopolitan' attack on intellectuals, who were alleged to have been part of a 'Zionist plot' to create subversion inside the Soviet Union. Stalin traced the plot back to meetings in Washington and supposed secret Israeli–American agreements made in 1947. Perhaps there was an element of justification in Stalin's concern. During 1948, Zionists had indeed offered the infant CIA use of their ready-made intelligence networks throughout eastern Europe and the Soviet Union. The offer was apparently turned down by US diplomats and politicians hostile to the creation of an Israeli state. The anti-Semitic campaign took off in early 1949, when Beria and Georgi Malen-kov persuaded Stalin to get rid of the revolutionary Zhadanov faction. In 1950, a number of the alleged plot's members were tortured and shot after the secret 'Leningrad case', in which the accused 'confessed' to links to western intelligence agencies.[5]

During the summer of 1951, Stalin became obsessed with identifying the high-level Czech figure who was referred to in supposed CIA documents as 'The Great Sweeper'. He began 'to drop hints to other Czech leaders that the Sweeper was none other than the Jewish Secretary-General of the Czecho-slovak Communist Party, Rudolf Slansky'. That autumn, the Czech press embarked on a virulent campaign in which Tito, the CIA and MI6 featured among the villains but in which Zionism was the most emphatic target. Observers in the West tended to dismiss the allegation against Slansky as a trumped-up charge that served a political purpose – even when, in November, Czech émigrés began to pick up rumours that Slansky was thinking of defecting to the West. These rumours eventually reached the Soviets and, in the early morning of 24 November 1951, Slansky was arrested, tortured and later tried and executed for his part in a supposed Zionist plot linked to the CIA. Slansky had indeed been approached by a Czechoslovak asset of the CIA, who hoped to recruit him as a spy or a defector. Whether he had in fact been recruited is not known, but the idea had certainly been taken seriously by the CIA and a case officer 'had procured a false set of documents for Slansky to use in an escape from Czechoslovakia'.[6]

Paranoia about eastern Europeans was not the sole preserve of Stalin. The British Home Office gave approval to the Security Service (MI5) for Operation POST REPORT (OPR), which involved the security screening of 200,000 foreign workers who, in the opinion of Deputy Director Guy Liddell, might in the event of a crisis constitute 'something of a Fifth Column'. OPR's purpose was not to spot war criminals but to seek evidence of whether the DPs had been infiltrated by Soviet Intelligence. Liddell was also anxious to establish whether any of these anti-communists with knowledge of Soviet affairs and the Russian language might be of use to MI5 and MI6. On 25 May 1951, the secretary of the Joint Intelligence Committee (JIC), Patrick Reilly, wrote to the Home Office recommending OPR on the basis that 'this census of the alien population could form a useful record of possible sources of intelligence on countries behind the Iron Curtain'.[7]

In June, MI5 began a massive sweep of the DP groups, interviewing Balts, Ukrainians, Poles, Hungarians, Romanians, Russians, Yugoslavs and Albanians. Security officers were principally interested in 'Communist activities including denunciations and circulation of Communist propaganda'; 'Contacts with the USSR or satellite embassies'; 'Service in the Red Army'; 'Service in the Vlasov army' and 'Contacts with Soviet inspired propaganda agencies'. In September, MI5 informed the Home Office that it regarded OPR as 'a valuable piece of war planning. It was revealing persons in this country with previous service in the Red Army and possible contacts behind the Iron Curtain ... It was producing information about potential Russian linguists ... only a small number so far is revealed as having come in under a false name.' What MI5 did not say was that the OPR questionnaires could have provided essential evidence in tracking down war criminals; the questionnaires were simply filed away.[8]

What may have been an acknowledgement that the policy of 'roll-back' against the Soviet Union and the satellites was having a negative effect – as evidenced by the purges and anti-Semitic campaigns – surfaced in early 1951. Disillusionment within the Foreign Office about America's aggressive operations was made plain to *New York Times* journalist Cyrus Sulzberger when he dined at the Defence College with Sir Geoffrey Thompson, who was 'very disturbed about the situation'. Thompson said that 'the United States is pursuing a terrible and foolhardy policy' and that 'many British now think there is more chance of the United States starting a war in 1951 than of Russia doing it'. The British feared an 'irrevocable hysterical act'.[9]

Even arch-Cold Warrior Winston Churchill was uneasy that an American strike against the USSR would result in a war in which Britain would be the prime target, since the US Air Force presence in East Anglia placed the country in the front line of a nuclear attack. In April, President Truman gave permission to the US Defense Department to store in Britain eighty-nine sets of non-nuclear components together with their nuclear cores, although these could not be 'mated' until a full-scale alert was announced. Up to this time, the pairs had been stored separately, and it was not, in fact, until two years later that authority for the deployment of complete warheads was granted by the President.[10]

These fears about the consequences of high-risk policies had mainly been expressed within the confines of the Foreign Office; the turning point in Anglo-American relations and the change of heart on the policy of roll-back came at the end of 1951 with the return to power of Churchill as Prime Minister and Anthony Eden as Foreign Secretary. Despite the fear of war, Churchill believed that the backing of a strong Atlantic alliance, along with the American nuclear umbrella, would enable him to negotiate with Stalin from a position of strength for an international settlement, 'for the purpose of advancing the international standing of his nation and his own reputation'. He now questioned 'whether or not a Cold War was necessary', an anxiety that drew him into conflict with the American administration. The Americans were primarily concerned with the implementation of European military integration in the context of the European Defence Community (EDC), but Churchill believed that the communist advance in Europe had been halted; he was prepared to sacrifice the EDC and accept a permanent Soviet presence in eastern and central Europe in exchange for East–West accommodations in what he regarded as an increasingly dangerous world.[11]

The American State Department's Psychological Strategy Board, which dealt with planning covert operations, was well aware of Churchill's intentions. It suggested that the return of the Conservatives had 'strengthened the nostalgia for the time when Britain was the leading global power, and hypersensitivity to playing the junior partner manifests itself in reflections on American inexperience'. A major area of contention was America's desire to wage economic war against the Soviet Union, a policy that most of the European allies refused to endorse.[12]

George Young had returned from Vienna to London to take over MI6's well-run Economic Requirements section (R6). It carried out 'Ernest Bevin's ruling that in Britain's shaky postwar situation economic information should be given a high priority'. The section was largely dependent on the Board of Trade and Bank of England for its intelligence-gathering tasks, which included material on oil supplies, banking and international agreements and commercial deals. Young found that 'it was indeed satisfying when a single report could pay for the annual Secret Vote several times over'. R6's other objective was to identify and deny to the Soviets key industrial commodities which they were attempting to buy on the world market. The section worked in close co-operation with the Joint Intelligence Bureau (JIB), which had interests in the economic field. Much had been learned in this area from MI6's economics guru, 'Colonel' L. S. Hodson, who had been seconded during the autumn of 1948 to the military's BRIXMIS in Berlin, with responsibility for finding out details of the economy in communist East Germany. He discovered that steel-making was in a poor state and was being propped up by the Russians. In addition, he instituted the 'Rail Watch', with agents keeping an eye on rail and, particularly, military traffic. This proved to be invaluable to MI6 and the military planners.[13]

Right from the beginning, the idea of economic warfare was beset by disagreement between internal ministries and, externally, with the United States. The Americans wanted a wide embargo and, likewise, the Foreign Office and Ministry of Defence wanted an embargo on anything that could 'build up Soviet war potential'. The economic ministries – regarding the USSR as one of their most promising outlets for British goods and a source of essential items such as grain and timber – wanted it confined to military equipment. When faced with the choice between economic warfare and a strategic embargo, American State Department officials opted for the former. They then divided their own controls into List 1A, containing items of primary strategic significance as part of a strategic embargo, and List 1B, items of secondary importance reflecting concerns of economic warfare. In order to secure European co-operation, the Americans used their economic muscle and threats to cut off aid.[14]

In November 1949 the Allies agreed to co-ordinate their export controls and formed the highly secretive multilateral Co-ordinating Committee (COCOM). There remained the problem of definition, and members agreed only to restrict most of the items on List 1A. The first meeting, in January 1950, officially adopted 167 items. America's major allies were reluctant to engage in a broad denial strategy; they preferred a more modest strategic embargo. The issue remained highly controversial, as Britain disliked being dictated to by what it saw as the most conservative forces in the US. Even the normally hardline Russia Committee wanted limits on East–West trade 'not to damage the Soviet economy but to slow up the growth of Soviet war potential' because it recognised Britain's need for Soviet grain and timber. The Europeans were able to resist US pressure and the record shows that Britain resisted economic warfare 'to the point where it nearly jeopardised the continued existence of COCOM'.[15]

Although in the aftermath of the outbreak of the Korean War there were siren voices in the United States wanting an extension of export controls and stiffer sanctions against Europeans who broke them, the CIA recognised that broad economic warfare was unlikely to be successful. In 1951 it reported that the Soviet economy, when integrated with that of eastern Europe, was relatively self-sufficient; therefore a trade block would have limited effectiveness. It argued that the only viable alternative was an embargo of essential items for military preparedeness, including some raw materials.[16]

There were also siren voices in the Foreign Office who supported American moves in this area, insisting that the USSR remained overwhelmingly superior in conventional arms in Europe and, therefore, any talk of a 'spheres of interest' type summit was premature. Typically, the Russia Committee remained unmoved by the thought of any possible thawing in relations with the Soviet Union, seeing 'no change in basic Soviet aims and strategy'. It was against this background that in late 1951 the Permanent Under-Secretary's Committee (PUSC), controlled by the chair of the Joint Intelligence Committee (JIC), Sir Patrick Reilly, undertook a review of Britain's long-term policy for fighting the Cold War.[17]

In January 1952, the British ambassador in Moscow, Sir Alvary Gascoigne, warned of 'the danger of war at the present time' and of 'the Americans getting too hot under the collar and taking action "off the cuff"'. Foreign Office Permanent Under-Secretary Sir William Strang acknowledged that the British were now anxious 'to avoid any action which might convince the Soviet Government that an attack from the West was inevitable'. He stressed the necessity of a policy to 'deflect the Americans from unwise and dangerous courses'. Churchill was visiting the Americans with precisely that objective in mind. In anticipation, a US interdepartmental steering committee warned of differences that were likely to arise with the Conservative government, which would probably be more optimistic in its interpretation of Soviet intentions. The committee prophesied that 'the British will tend to question the necessity or desirability of political warfare operations . . . which might even provoke the Kremlin to acts of aggression. The British believe that the immediate dangers of provocation over-balance the long-term deterrent results of political warfare carried on within Moscow's own orbit.' Indeed, Churchill warned his American hosts not to 'stir up something which we could not back' with a policy of 'liberation' in eastern Europe.[18]

Churchill had been due to meet the Director of the CIA, Walter Bedell Smith, to discuss 'operations against the satellites', but this did not happen. The Prime Minister was not prepared to support any new special operations but was willing to see an intensification of propaganda operations, and raised the topic of psychological warfare with the President. With an intensification of propaganda 'the democracies would make an intense effort to bring home to all the people behind the Iron Curtain the true facts of the world situation – by broadcasting and by dropping leaflets', and he believed 'the Kremlin would fear such a revelation of the truth'. Given that they were funding major radio stations broadcasting to eastern Europe and were already involved in extensive leaflet drops, the Americans were not impressed by Churchill's attempted intervention. They were more impressed by the Information Officer in the British embassy in Washington, Adam Watson, who had previously served in the Information Research Department (IRD). He had been appointed liaison officer to the US Psychological Strategy Board which co-ordinated CIA, State Department and Defense Department psychological warfare activities. Watson proved to be an influential figure, but co-operation with the Americans on matters of psychological warfare activities was apparently hindered by the rivalry between MI6 and the IRD; the former regarded the latter as 'amateurs'.[19]

In January 1952, the PUSC completed its paper, 'The Liberation of the Satellites'. Taking a general Foreign Office view that the country should concentrate on economic and political concerns in order to stem the tide of Britain's decline, PUSC (51) 16 concluded that although Britain should take part in a 'controlled and phased counter-attack against the Soviet empire', operations to liberate the satellites in eastern Europe must not be undertaken if they risked promoting war. They were seen as 'impractical and ... involved unacceptable risks'. The Foreign Office continued to worry about US policy towards eastern Europe, which brought closer the danger of war with 'one of the sore spots being too sore, and the Americans getting too hot under the collar and taking action "off the cuff"'.[20]

The PUSC paper was made available to the Americans and discussed with them. It was not taken well by the US State Department Policy Planning Staff, and the Joint Chiefs of Staff, in the shape of General Omar N. Bradley, were outraged by the paper and treated it with contempt, regarding the British as promoting a policy of 'appeasement'.[21]

In considering western pressure against 'sore spots', the PUSC had decided that even operations against Albania, in which MI6 had invested so much effort, were a dangerous option. The committee concluded that

> Soviet prestige is sufficiently involved to make it unlikely that the Soviet Government would remain inactive in the face of any determined attempt to detach Albania from the Orbit. If, for instance, the West organised a major rebellion with outside assistance to overthrow the Communist regime, it would probably provoke the Soviet Government into reaction e.g. the despatch of Soviet or satellite airborne troops, since there would be good prospect of keeping the resultant fighting localised.[22]

In mid-February, Strang noted in a memorandum to Eden that the Americans were planning new special operations, 'such as an Air Force wing to Libya to drop leaflets over the Balkans'. He warned that 'it is only by co-ordinating our activities with theirs that we can hope either to convince them that we mean business or to restrain what we may consider over-zealous activities on their part'. Eden agreed and wanted 'all proposals for action ... to be examined with very great care. We must not allow ourselves to be persuaded into taking steps which might bring us nearer to war.'[23]

The PUSC review was fleshed out some weeks later by another memorandum drawn up by the Russia Committee, dated 19 February. While the 'Future Policy Towards Soviet Union' still regarded the Soviet Union as fundamentally hostile to the free world, having a 'fanatical and dynamic revolutionary spirit' and a traditionally ambitious leader, it was in its way more optimistic in tone than previous papers, with its notion of an 'uneasy absence of war'. It noted the deeply ingrained fear of external attack held by the Soviet leaders and their acceptance of retreat when faced with determined opposition. The committee was, therefore, less concerned with overthrowing the present regime than moving towards 'our ultimate objective of a genuine settlement'. The principle for special operations was that the adoption of more aggressive measures 'must not materially increase the risk of war' as 'ill-advised action could easily lead to the closer cementing of the Soviet bloc and so have the exactly reverse effect to what we desire'. The memorandum acknowledged, however, that 'the process of reaching a settlement is likely to last decades'.

An Appendix B on 'Liberation of the Satellites' seemed to have learned a number of lessons from MI6's failed operations in the Soviet orbit, and displayed particular concern that such activities might provoke 'Soviet military counter-actions'. It noted that 'it is axiomatic that resistance groups, even if well-supplied with light arms and explosives, cannot obtain decisive results against regular troops unless the latter are either neutralised by a greater threat or already in a state of disintegration'. It went on: 'the creation of resistance groups for mass revolt and the provision of the necessary arms, etc., demands time: but all experience shows that, once prepared, "resistance" cannot stand still indefinitely or, indeed, for very long'. While it conceded that covert activity would 'increase Soviet nervousness about their lines of communication in war-time and so tend to discourage or delay plans for an offensive' and that 'an organised resistance movement is a useful source of agents and intelligence; and the knowledge that such a movement existed would help to maintain morale within the satellite country concerned', it recognised that 'it is doubtful whether any serious resistance movement could be started or maintained without definite assurances of Western intervention at the critical moment . . . such assurances could not be honestly given'.

There was concern that 'an unsuccessful uprising would almost certainly destroy any intelligence network which the Western Powers might have built up'. It would be dangerous 'even to plan or prepare for revolt unless and until the necessary margin of superiority had been achieved'. The committee concluded that 'operations designed to liberate the satellites are impracticable and would involve unacceptable risks'. This did mean the end of all special operations which the committee saw 'not as an end in themselves but as a function of a wide-scale psychological attack on the political structure of the Soviet orbit'. There was support for psychological warfare directed 'against known weaknesses and contradictions in the Soviet fabric' which might eventually 'lead to fundamental changes in the nature of the Soviet system'. These included 'specialist operations designed either to disrupt the machinery of government or the economic structure of satellite States, or to poison relations between the satellite Governments and the Soviet Union'. Consideration was given to the denial of strategic metals, though it was admitted that the Soviet Union had stockpiles of the essential items 'to last a war of short duration'.

Even when such operations were undertaken, an earlier draft had concluded that 'it will be the safest, as well as the most effective, course for the West to exercise pressure in gradual, successive, and unobtrusive forms. The West should particularly avoid action likely to humiliate rather than harm the Soviet Government; such action entails a risk of Soviet reaction out of all proportion to the possible profit to the West.'

Foreign Office reluctance to back a liberation policy was first evidenced by the spurning, in late January, of the setting up of a major conference for eastern European exile groups by the British League for European Freedom (BLEF). Organised at Church House in London with more moderate members than those associated with the Anti-Bolshevik Bloc of Nations (ABN), it was sponsored by the Central and East European Commission of the European Movement (EM) which, in contrast to the ABN, only dealt with those countries outside the borders of the Soviet Union. The Foreign Office was deeply embarrassed that 'for weeks and weeks the conference was denounced by the Russian radio and press, and by the puppet leaders of the countries behind the Iron Curtain'. With the Conservatives wanting a more open policy with the Soviet Union, supporting the eastern European exiles in their aspirations was to be discouraged. Belligerency was out; the exiles were to be left to the Americans.[24]

MI6 had already merged their exile groups into one organisation, the Ukrainian-based ABN, and had offloaded the cost of running the remnants of the remaining exile groups – Intermarium, the Promethean League, the International Flag of Liberty and several others – on to the Americans. Likewise, the CIA had set up the American Committee for Liberation from Bolshevism, organised by a high-ranking State Department official, Howland H. Sargeant, in an effort to combine in a single united front organisation a joint platform for representatives of all the Soviet refugee groups, Russian and non-Russian, with the exception of pro-communists, fascists and monarchists, who were regarded by the committee leaders as a liability, rather than an asset. Unfortunately for its attempt to bring together the disparate émigré groups under one umbrella organisation, the Americans failed to recognise the nationality problem. Former Promethean League president Roma Smal-

Stocky attacked the CIA-backed committee because it insisted on the integrity of the Soviet borders, which made it an anathema to the 'nationalist' groups. The committee did contain some representatives from non-Russian nationalists but, except for one weak and not very important group, was unable to entice the ABN into its fold.[25]

The 'Paris Bloc' of Ukrainians had initially supported the idea of the committee but co-operation with the 'Russian' organisation, as the nationalists dubbed it, proved fruitless – and relations soon collapsed. The presence of the pro-Russian SBONR, largely composed of former veterans of Gen. Vlasov and members of the NTS, created fierce invective as the Ukrainians regarded them – somewhat bizarrely – as an 'extreme left-wing group' and 'traitors'. The ABN remained outside the committee, along with the Ukrainian National Council, the Belorussian National Council, the Armenian Dasknak Party and national committees from Georgia, Azerbaijan and North Caucasus.[26]

These familiar factional in-fights were no doubt viewed with wry amusement and deep satisfaction in the Kremlin. Stalin had been 'much concerned with the prospects of the formation' of the American Committee, chaired by an old foe, Alexander Kerensky. It had been decided by the Security Mission that 'this initiative of the American reactionaries should be decisively severed and the leadership should be decapitated before its activities can develop'. Special tasks officer Pavel Sudoplatov was put in charge of planning action in London and Paris, but was unable to organise the necessary assets to 'liquidate' Kerensky when he attended the committee's opening meeting. In the end, the plan proved unnecessary because the Soviets learned that Ukrainian and Croat nationalist intransigence over Russian involvement had effectively sabotaged the committee's formation. The failure to unite the different factions was viewed as a turning point in Moscow, where 'concern with émigré organisations was put where it belonged, in the past'. This was also largely recognised in Washington, where British and US officials managed to temporarily bridge their differences. CIA Director Bedell Smith agreed that in the short term it made no sense to encourage 'a resistance campaign' in eastern Europe.[27]

After thirty-eight years in the secret world, Stewart Menzies announced his retirement in a signal to all overseas stations on 30 June 1952. Such was his reputation among some officials that, although past the normal retirement age of sixty, he could have remained in place. He was, however, a tired man and had a number of personal reasons for his decision. His wife, who had suffered a long illness, had died in March 1951. This was followed by the Philby débâcle, which appears to have hit him hard. His assistant chief, Jack Easton, claimed that 'Stewart slid out. He knew that a great scandal was about and he did not want to be involved.' He did not, however, escape the demons in retirement. According to his son-in-law, Captain Brian Bell,

Menzies suffered from nightmares, apparently to do with Philby. 'There was one recurrent theme in these nightmares, which were awful to hear. That was that there was a Russian defector who was taken up in a helicopter over the English Channel and given the choice – talk about Philby or be chucked out without a parachute. They chucked him out.' Menzies left for the country and the pursuits of shooting and horse-racing. Soon after, his second secretary, Miss Muriel Jones, with whom he had had a long-term affair, unsuccessfully attempted suicide from a drug overdose.[28]

On 3 July the JIC met and chair Patrick Reilly spoke of Menzies's reign being 'distinguished by an extraordinary devotion to duty'. In turn, Foreign Secretary Anthony Eden, who had worked closely with 'C' during the war, thanked Menzies for his services. 'Since 1945 you have had little respite. You have had to pursue the reconstruction of your Service, on a scale never before contemplated in peace, amid the insistent demands of a new and unprecedented world-wide conflict. You leave it full of promise for the future.' Eden and Churchill may have felt, however, that the time was ripe for a change at the top. Although Reilly recalled that in early 1951 Menzies had recommended Major-General John Sinclair as Chief, with Jack Easton as his deputy and successor when 'Sinbad' retired, the job was first offered to a Churchill favourite, Sir Ian Jacob, Controller of the BBC's European Services.[29]

Although his views appeared to fit in with the new administration's foreign policy, Jacob refused the post of 'C'. Whether he was a real candidate or whether it was just a whim on the part of Churchill is not known but, certainly, Menzies was pleased that Sinclair was appointed. Menzies's main concern was to ensure that the military bias of the Service continued, as he was opposed to civilians running intelligence and disliked the wartime influx of university-trained staff, whom he never completely trusted.[30]

The Director of Military Intelligence during the war and MI6 Vice-Chief for five years during the crucial period of the Cold War, Sinclair was, while 'not overloaded with mental gifts (he never claimed them)', according to Kim Philby, 'humane, energetic and so obviously upright that it was impossible to withhold admiration . . . it was distasteful to lie in my teeth to the honest Sinclair.' George Blake, on meeting the new Chief, saw 'a tall, lean Scot with the angular, austere features of a Presbyterian minister, blue eyes behind horn-rimmed spectacles and a soft voice gave him a kindly demeanour'. Unfortunately for MI6, the 'Robber Barons', the divisional heads who actually ran the Service, had little regard for his abilities and bypassed him whenever contentious operations were planned. It would not be an exaggeration to state that at times the Service was 'out of control'. Sinclair's tenure would later be characterised as the period of 'the Horrors'.[31]

Significantly, it appears that Eden allowed the PUSC to wither. It would be a few years before it was revived by Harold Macmillan and would displace the JIC in its role as a co-ordinating body for intelligence-gathering and subversion. In the meantime, there appears to have been a vacuum where there should have been overseeing control of the Service. During the period 1951–6, the PUSC usually met only once a month, and was then only concerned with editing briefs from various departments dealing with the Soviet Union. On taking the chair of the JIC in 1950, Patrick Reilly had recognised that there were dangers of MI6 'running potentially controversial operations without proper authority'. It took, however, another two years for the implementation of his recommendation of reinstating a Foreign Office adviser – a post he had occupied during the war and which had lain empty since Robert Cecil had left it in 1946. The first postwar adviser to 'C' was (Sir) George Clutton, latterly head of the Foreign Office's African Department. In the climate of the times, his three-year appointment, following a two-year stint in Tokyo as head of the UK's liaison mission to Japan, was not, perhaps, a wise decision. Clutton was a homosexual, who later came under suspicion of having been blackmailed by the Soviets while serving in Warsaw. A Positive Vetting Section, which might have picked up potential problems like Clutton, was put in place only in late 1951 following the Maclean/Burgess débâcle, and then with only four overworked officers.[32]

Churchill's private secretary, Anthony Montague Brown, had been responsible in the Foreign Office for distributing secret reports to the various departments and later acted as a liaison with the Americans on intelligence affairs. He soon realised that the intelligence reaching the Prime Minister was of poor quality and increasingly bland. When he told Churchill, the PM exploded: 'Send for C and I'll sack the shit.' It turned out that it was not the fault of MI6; the Foreign Office appeared to 'distrust WSC's discretion' and did not want him to be 'overinformed and thus more prone to interfere'. But interfering was Churchill's nature and, according to Eden's private secretary, Evelyn Shuckburgh, he vetoed all of MI6's special operations proposals. In practice, this appears to have applied to the anti-Soviet operations in eastern Europe; he had little difficulty in giving the green light to operations in other theatres.[33]

In the run-up to the American presidential elections, the British had become increasingly concerned with the shrill anti-communist rhetoric coming out of the Eisenhower camp. On 26 August 1952, Foster Dulles advised that America should 'try to split the satellites away from . . . Moscow' and shortly after specified the use of propaganda broadcasts and supplies to 'freedom fighters'. The militancy contributed to a rising tide of anti-Americanism even among Conservatives. Former SOE executive director Colin Gubbins and Joseph Retinger of the European Movement (EM) believed that the dispute was weakening the Atlantic alliance. Retinger recognised that the US was 'disliked, feared and sneered at with an unanimity that was remarkable'. 'This feeling threatened the solidarity of the Western world's defences against Communism', and both Retinger and Gubbins, with their unofficial links to MI6, believed that this tendency had to be 'checked'.[34]

During 1952, Retinger suggested to Belgium's Paul van Zeeland and head of Unilever, Paul Rykens, the idea of organising unofficial meetings of leading personalities from NATO countries with the purpose of 'promoting European unity and an Atlantic alliance'. Rykens subsequently arranged for Retinger to meet Prince Bernhard of the Netherlands, whose apparent apolitical standing marked him out as an ideal figurehead. A meeting was held in September, in Paris, during which an advisory committee was created. A leading member was Denis Healey, head of the Labour Party's International Department. At the same time, led by Gubbins and his former SOE colleague Peter Wilkinson, who had recently headed the IRD and was First Secretary in Washington, members of Chatham House convened with representatives of the US Council on Foreign Relations for a five-day meeting, during which the two groups set down their interpretations of the other.[35]

While British ideas remained fluid, the Foreign Office had effectively abandoned the policy of 'roll-back'. In September, the chair of the EM's Central and Eastern European Commission, Gubbins's long-standing friend, SOE colleague and leading advocate of the exiles, Major Edward Beddington-Behrens, was replaced by a professional politician, Conservative MP Richard Law. To Polish leader Stefan Korbonski, this marked the point when the commission began to act 'negatively and ceased in practice to function'. The slack was taken up by the CIA.[36]

Although the western intelligence infiltrations into Ukraine had rarely been successful, the American-backed Gehlen programme was stepped up in the summer of 1952 with regular parachute drops. Sixteen American agents were lost in at least five missions mounted during the following year. British losses in this period are unknown, as are those of the separate CIA operations of the Office of Special Operations (OSO). Despite the failures, 'as the flow of "intelligence" radioed to West Germany increased, MI6 confidently assured customers in Whitehall that it was running a reliable network'. Perhaps no one was reading the Soviet press, where the failures were reported at length.[37]

The Office of Policy Co-ordination's (OPC) Frank Lindsay certainly knew the true state of affairs because in the autumn he finally delivered his highly negative report on the paramilitary penetration missions to Allen Dulles. Stalin's tight grip on the communist states – through control of the security police, political organs and propaganda machinery – had made, Lindsay concluded, 'virtually impossible the existence of organised clandestine resistance capable within the foreseeable future of appreciably weakening the power of the state'. Evidence that the Foreign Office had reached similar conclusions was clear from a September brief for Eden commenting on an Eisenhower presidential campaign speech on US liberation policy which was 'calculated to raise false hopes among the peoples concerned'. The official added as an afterthought the comment that 'we would not at the same time wish to discourage them by the appearance of ready acquiescence in the maintenance of dominated regimes'.[38]

While the disagreements over roll-back policy and the fears of antagonising the Russian bear were at the core of the conflict with the Americans, British perceptions of the country's own place in the world determined the internal debate. In his study of the period, John W. Young notes the 'atmosphere of gloom' which surrounded the administration 'in which problems appeared insoluble'. The gloom was not lifted by news on 2 November – in the midst of the presidential campaign – that the United States had secretly detonated the first hydrogen bomb, raising fears of a first strike.

In December, Evelyn Shuckburgh wrote in his diary: 'the Americans are not backing us anywhere. In fact, having destroyed the Dutch empire, the United States are now engaged in undermining the French and British empires as hard as they can.' Shuckburgh added that Eden 'could never quite reconcile himself to its inevitable consequence . . . growing American dominance'. This, inevitably, had an effect on his relations with the new US Secretary of State for Foreign Affairs, Foster Dulles, and the State Department.[39]

Any help in halting and closing the growing divide between the Europeans and the Americans had to wait until the installation of the new Eisenhower regime. Prince Bernhard of the Netherlands, Retinger, Labour Party leader Hugh Gaitskell and Denis Healey then travelled to the United States to lobby for support and funds for a joint US/Europe forum designed to dissipate the misunderstandings that existed between the two sides. In Washington, Bernhard visited an 'old friend', General Bedell Smith, President Eisenhower's wartime chief of staff and Director of the CIA. Smith was sympathetic and turned the matter over to C. D. Jackson, president of the Committee for a Free Europe and special assistant to the President on psychological warfare.

On 27 December 1952 faith in the exile operations was shattered when, to the general disbelief of officers in MI6 and the OPC, Radio Warsaw began broadcasting a series of programmes revealing that the pro-western Polish resistance network, WiN (Freedom and Independence), had been a puppet of the UB security service (Urzad Bezpieczenstwa) since early 1948. Not only did it become clear that MI6 and the OPC were running 'false' networks, operating under Soviet instructions as part of highly successful radio deceptions, it was also apparent that a large number of the émigré intelligence sources were 'nothing but "paper mills"'. They often supplied no more than information culled from newspapers and the 'cocktail circuit' or from the debriefings of other refugees or émigrés. Large sums of money were spent on subsidising these émigré sources but, more often than not, their reports were 'worthless and unreliable and most frequently dedicated to selling a point of view' – a view that often led to a distorted picture of the situation behind the Iron Curtain.[40]

Taking on the new post of Director of Requirements, at the beginning of 1953 George Young tried to redirect MI6 efforts more effectively to priority targets. One of the first problems was to scrutinise the elaborate and expensive attempts to put agents into the Baltic states and Poland: operations 'regarded as the special pride and joy of SIS'. Controller for Europe Kenneth Cohen had raised the alarm about these operations but the warnings were ignored because of 'enormous pressure' from the chiefs of staff who, desperate for information, had provided so many facilities. The military were operating to wartime criteria with unrealistic expectations but, with their strict military backgrounds, Menzies and Sinclair had run the Service as an adjunct of the chiefs and acquiesced to their wishes. The clandestine exile operations had assumed a momentum of their own which proved difficult to stop.[41]

It is the nature of bureaucratic agencies such as the intelligence services that, after a time, operations tend to run the officers rather than the other way round. Kim Philby recognised the problem:

> After long indecision, a given country's intelligence service initiates some dubious operation. It takes the first step in the hope that if that step turns out to be unsuccessful, things can be turned back. Not on your life! After you take the first step, you fall hostage to yourself. You now have to take the second step, the third one and so on. The operation now takes on an independent existence, outside the control of the Service. Money that was allocated for it has already been partially spent, people have been recruited and continue to be recruited, equipment is being supplied. When someone suddenly realises – colleagues, we're moving to an abyss! – it's too late; the time has slipped away forever. His colleagues shrug their shoulders; so much money has been spent, so many resources have been allocated, so much effort has been put in. You can't turn back the clock – it would mean a colossal scandal.

And so it proved inside MI6. One of the officers running the Balts, John Liudzius, told his superiors that 'there was something wrong with the operations' but 'no one was willing to listen to me and they posted me to the Far East'.[42]

When Young, 'a brash, popular and outstanding intelligence officer', who was regarded 'as an intellectual because he read books', put the Baltic operation under close scrutiny, studied the radio traffic and the meagre results, 'it stuck out a mile from his own wartime experience in double-agent and deception work that the whole affair was under Soviet control'. After much dithering, Sinclair refused to accept the analysis, 'particularly as it would mean an embarrassing admission to the Foreign Office and the armed forces'. Instead, he backed the Controller in charge, Harry Carr, who continued to believe in the viability of the operations. All Young could do was to circulate the reports as 'KGB deception material'; by that time the Soviets had already 'blown' most of the western intelligence operations in eastern Europe.[43]

After the Soviet Nineteenth Party Congress in October 1952, the first for thirteen years and scene of his last speech, Stalin, by now 'old, ill and in all probability mentally deranged', unleashed the 'Vigilance' campaign which threatened a bloodbath larger than any seen before. Alleged spies among the highest echelons of the communist bloc were to be rooted out and executed on a mass scale. Even members of the Council of Ministers were accused by Stalin of being 'agents of British Intelligence'. These were ludicrous charges but were taken seriously, even when senior Politburo member Anastas Mikoyan and Foreign Secretary Molotov, whose wife was arrested and sent to Siberia, were personally accused of treachery. Throughout the winter, plans were made and the rumours flowed – while a smaller anti-Semitic terror campaign reached into the heart of the Kremlin.[44]

On 13 January 1953, Radio Moscow revealed the existence of the 'Doctors' Plot'; bizarrely alleged to be run by 'killer doctors' belonging to a terrorist group in the pay of MI6 and the CIA. This Jewish group of well-known doctors, a number of whom had been treating Stalin, was named as the 'Joint' and described as 'a federation of many conspiratorial groups financed from many sources, with world-wide ramifications, employing the weapons of subversion, terrorism, and espionage'. Seventy-one-year-old Dr Vladimir Vinogradov, one of the most respected figures in Russian medicine, was charged with being the leader of the conspiracy. Kept in chains and tortured, he was forced to confess that he had been a long-standing spy for British Intelligence. 'In this way Stalin paid his last tribute to British Intelligence, for which he had always shown a healthy respect.'[45]

Chaired by Soviet specialist Frank Roberts, the Russia Committee appeared 'quite confused' about what lay behind these developments. This was understandable, as no one was safe from the basic insecurity, paranoia and wrath of Stalin. The Ministry of State Security (KGB) was tasked with organising the assassination of Tito. One attempt envisaged an agent spraying a dose of lethal bacteria on the leader, another killing him with a specialised silent weapon during a trip to London. MI6 forewarned Tito at least twice of Soviet attempts on his life. The plans were dropped when Stalin died.[46]

At 8.00 a.m. on 4 March 1953 Moscow Radio announced that, during the night of 1–2 March, 'Comrade Stalin had suffered a cerebral haemorrhage affecting vital areas of the brain, causing him to lose consciousness'. Following his death, Stalin's successors appeared to show a willingness to negotiate on differences with the West. The Russia Committee, however, in a special study on 7 April, argued that any changes in Soviet foreign policy were purely tactical, short-term and designed to make the regime more popular – 'Friendly Soviet moves were described as "lures", whilst unfriendly moves were said to reveal the true Soviet intentions!' In contrast, Churchill welcomed the change of climate. With Eden in ill health and incapacitated by the need for a gall bladder operation, in April Churchill assumed control of the Foreign Office and took the opportunity to launch a series of new policy initiatives on eastern Europe. Though old, tired, lacking in energy and growing senile, Churchill retained an enthusiasm for cloak-and-dagger operations. He was, however, unwilling to back a liberation policy, and MI6's Soviet orbit operations began to wind down.[47]

On 20 April 1953, with the support of the Cabinet and the Foreign Office, Churchill called for high-level talks with the new Soviet leadership. Five days later, *Pravda* signalled Russian willingness for talks on Germany and German rearmament. The new Politburo head was Georgi Malenkov, 'a man of no popular appeal who climbed to the top on Stalin's coat-tails'. Beria remained in charge of internal security a little longer before being arrested on 10 July, charged with crimes against the state. Officials in London and Washington 'rang each other up to ask "Who is Malenkov?"' MI6 had no high-grade intelligence on the Soviet power structure and was not in a position to supply an answer. The only man who could was Labour MP Harold Wilson, who, through his links to East–West traders, had developed excellent 'unofficial' channels to the Soviet leaders and actually knew Malenkov. In May 1953 Wilson made the first visit to Moscow by a senior western politician since the beginning of the Cold War, when an embargo had been imposed following the Berlin crisis. He stole the headlines with an interview with Molotov, arranged by his old friend Mikoyan, who had also organised Wilson's visa for the USSR. Even though Wilson cleared the trip with the Prime Minister and was debriefed by Churchill and the Foreign Office on his return, his visit caused fury on the Tory Right. Anticipating such a reaction, Churchill had been using Julian Amery and Robert Boothby as a back channel to the Soviet embassy, bypassing the Foreign Office and Eden.[48]

George Young was concerned that MI6 'could never produce high-grade intelligence on Russian intentions and policy-making'. A complete new approach was required, and 'after a series of informal supper parties with the brightest SIS officers, a systematic study was started of the top Soviet power structure, its various personalities and cliques, and their associates in the armed forces and KGB'. Young was amazed that this had not been carried out in Whitehall, despite the fact that 'from both overt and covert sources there was a mass of information which had never been properly assessed and collated'. This pioneering work was carried out by Professor Leonard Schapiro, a Scot who had been brought up in St Petersburg and was bilingual, and who held the chair of government with particular reference to Soviet studies at the London School of Economics. With Foreign Office Soviet specialist Malcolm Mackintosh, he enlisted the help of leading Soviet studies experts from universities. According to Young, 'the results changed the whole emphasis in tackling Russian targets, produced expert briefing for potential sources and for the interrogation of deserters and defectors'. Young thought that the success of the project was underlined by Mackintosh taking over the Soviet desk in the Cabinet Office, a post he held until his retirement in 1987.[49]

Mackintosh thought Malenkov's strategy until his resignation as Premier in February 1955 was 'based upon Stalin's' and that he 'acted in the spirit of the decisions of Stalin's later years'. A year after Stalin's death, MI6's Hugh Seton-Watson considered eastern Europe and acknowledged that changes had occurred with the satellite leaders giving concessions to the peasants which were 'necessitated by internal economic troubles'. He saw no new foreign policy initiatives, though he admitted that it was 'premature to speculate on the meaning of these changes', but noted that 'the force which the East European communists and their Soviet masters most fear is nationalism'. Although he regarded the disruptive power of nationalism as strong, Seton-Watson acknowledged that 'the struggle is of course veiled from foreign eyes'.[50]

In early 1953 Desmond Bristow – recently chief of the Spanish station – was invited by George Young to become head of MI6's new Strategic Trade Section. As part of Operation SCRUM HALF, the section devised a systematic programme of intelligence-gathering in support of COCOM and the 'one hundred items which the United States and Britain had decided must be prevented from reaching the Warsaw Pact countries. Priority goods on the list were copper in any shape or form, aluminium, diamonds and a host of accessories not available behind the Iron Curtain, especially electrical goods and embryonic electronic goods.' The aim was to slow down the Soviets' war machine.[51]

The Allies had established a shipping intervention programme using what were known as 'receivers' by which strategic trade could be monitored. Each country was consigned a particular number of receiving companies, to which incoming goods on the strategic list could be dispatched. 'But, as Bristow found, without constant vigilance this method was full of holes, and goods continued to go behind the Iron Curtain.' With an assistant, Jack Sharp, Bristow set up agents in jobs to monitor sea traffic and employed the commercial staff in embassies abroad to supply information on shipping. He co-operated closely with Customs, Naval Intelligence and the CIA, while a liaison officer, Peter Bowie, kept in touch with internationally operating companies. In addition, GCHQ supplied the Section with intercepts of commercial traffic.[52]

In May, *Pravda* reported the execution of four Ukrainians alleged to have spied for the United States, while Moscow Radio announced that four NTS agents who, a month earlier, had parachuted into the Ukraine had been captured by the KGB and executed. When, in a further blow, four NTS agents, who worked under various aliases and disguises in East Germany, Poland and the Soviet Union, suddenly disappeared, a shudder ran through the MI6 station in the Olympia Stadium buildings in Berlin. It seemed that they had been betrayed, and a subsequent security investigation during September uncovered the mole's identity.

The head of the CIA's Soviet desk, Harry Rositzke, believed that the traitor was a Soviet Army deserter who had defected to the West in November 1949 for the love of a German woman. Under a new German identity, with his wife and children still in the Soviet Union, he had been tracked down by Soviet agents and pressurised into becoming their informer. Highly competent, he joined the NTS and gained rapid promotion within the organisation, becoming an instructor at an NTS espionage school and a consultant to US Army Intelligence. He then began passing on reports to his Soviet handlers at the MGB base at Karlshorst in the Berlin suburbs. A more public account identified him as Nikita Khorunzhi, a former member of the German Communist Party who defected in the spring of 1951. Joining the NTS, it was not long before he was appointed by the CIA as Soviet adviser to the G-2 department of US Army Intelligence and full-time instructor at their school at Bad Homburg.[53]

The CIA paid 80 per cent of the finances and controlled the training of a mixed group of Russians, Belorussians and Ukrainians at Holland Park. With the help of German agents, MI6 was responsible for training the NTS under a German-speaking ex-army officer, 'Mr Radford'. From the Soviet press, NTS trainees learned that the group of NTS agents headed by A. V. Lakhno – a wartime collaborator with German Intelligence – had been captured in the Soviet Union, along with 'pistols and a supply of cartridges, radio transmitters, radio beacons for directing airplanes to their targets, ciphers and codes, cryptographic means, ampoules with poison sewn into their shirt collars, equipment for forging Soviet documents and printing anti-Soviet leaflets, and considerable amounts of Soviet money and gold'. The subsequent collapse of morale could not be alleviated by the NTS leader and MI6 agent Georgi Okolovich, who was also working with the Gehlen Organisation. He blamed the CIA for failing to take his advice on where to parachute in the Lakhno group. It was a period of intense factional in-fighting and, fearful that security was lax, MI6 moved the group to new safe houses around London.[54]

The in-fighting was also evident within the American Committee for Liberation of the Peoples of Russia from Bolshevism, which was subject to repeated attacks by the Ukrainian-controlled ABN for its inability to resolve the 'nationalist' question. In Munich, a new US sponsored Co-ordinating Centre for Anti-Bolshevik Struggle was set up but was opposed by some pro-Russians for pumping out 'separatist' propaganda. During the summer of 1953 the committee split into two warring factions, both funded by the CIA. The Belorussia National Committee (BNC) joined the International Anti-Bolshevik Co-ordination Centre (MAKC), while the Belorussian Central Council (BCR) opted for the rival Co-ordination Centre for Anti-Bolshevik Action (KCAB) in which the pro-Russian NTS also participated. These rival centres continued to attack each other, often 'more bitterly than they do the Stalinists', while their activities became 'caricatures of European international conferences'.[55]

The first major test for Britain's new policy towards the Soviet Union and its relationship with the United States came on 17 June 1953. A peaceful protest march through East Berlin by several hundred construction workers turned into an uprising when tens of thousands of East Germans began rioting in sixty cities, calling for free elections and the downfall of the regime. It is now known from East German and Soviet archives that the uprising was more widespread, prolonged and violent than had been recognised at the time by the West. It is also apparent from the files of the East German Communist Socialist Unity Party (SED) that American propaganda radio stations had a significant influence on the build-up to the riots. Many workers taking part had expected radio support for the strikes to be followed up by a western invasion. It soon became apparent, however, that the United States, despite the roll-back rhetoric, had not actually prepared any realistic plans to deal with such situations. Washington had been caught unawares.[56]

There was little or no protest from the British when nearly three hundred Soviet tanks quelled the rebellion, and Churchill singularly failed to back up subsequent American protests. In correspondence with the Foreign Office, Churchill wrote that the Russians had 'acted with considerable restraint'. He added: 'Is it suggested that the Soviets should have allowed the Eastern Zone to fall into anarchy and riot?' Churchill was afraid that the uprising would dash hopes for his four-power negotiations and 'was intent on getting back to business as usual in Berlin'. He refused to endorse requests for a co-ordinated pro-rioters propaganda campaign with the Americans, who seemed to British officials to be out of control.[57]

As a reaction to the uprising, the American Psychological Strategy Board drew up an 'interim US Plan for Exploitation of Unrest in Satellite Europe' which was adopted by the National Security Council (NSC) on 29 June. It was designed to encourage 'resistance to communist oppression' by covert and psychological means 'short of mass rebellion'. The main response was to be a large-scale food programme for East Germany, designed to keep the Soviets on the defensive. The British had initially resisted the idea because they thought 'the risks were far too great'. Food was, however, made available at distribution centres in the western sectors of Berlin, which were still accessible to the East.

The programme elicited a massive response and was viewed in Washington as highly successful and an example of operations short of war that could be undertaken to advance the liberation of eastern Europe.[58]

Despite the fact that the Americans had not responded with force, the East German crisis and the rhetoric pouring from Foster Dulles and his supporters in the Republican Party created divisions within the western alliance. In Cabinet on 3 July, the Secretary of State for the Commonwealth, Lord Salisbury, who was acting in the absence of Eden as Foreign Secretary, expressed concern about the

> dangerous American tendency ... to interpret the situation behind the Iron Curtain as already very shaky and therefore to advocate new although unspecified measures to encourage and even promote the early liberation of the satellite countries. It is my intention to resist American pressure for new initiatives of this kind. The last thing we want to do is to bait the Russian and satellite governments into taking measures against them ... We must of course keep the spirit of freedom alive in Eastern Europe, but we should also counsel prudence and restraint.

In line with Churchill's wishes – Churchill felt that a meeting 'might well lead to an easement in world tension' – and with the support of the French, Salisbury hoped to persuade Dulles to accept high-level talks with the Russians.[59]

At the 10 July meeting in Washington, Salisbury did manage to discourage the American Secretary of State from initiating any new 'embarrassing initiatives' and, to the surprise of the participants, Dulles was unexpectedly moderate in his views on eastern Europe. On his return to London, Salisbury told the Cabinet that there was 'complete harmony of view on the attitude to be adopted toward the satellites' and that Dulles had been 'extremely helpful'. It was, however, a delusion. While there was, indeed, a temporary lull, President Eisenhower and Dulles were awaiting the formation of new policy initiatives due in the autumn. Discussions were taking place within the NSC about massively reinforcing the propaganda campaign against the Soviet bloc. Dulles was still determined to 'harry the Soviets wherever possible'. On 27 July the Americans began distributing food parcels in West Berlin, near the intersecting border, putting a strain on western allied unity, with the British wanting to get things 'back to normal as fast as possible'. Some officials in the Foreign Office, however, drew the conclusion that American policy in practice was more moderate than Dulles's rhetoric. One official wrote that 'this administration is decidedly less interventionist in practice than its predecessor, for all the bold talk about "liberation"'.[60]

The British and Americans had 'an unpleasant surprise' when the Russians conducted their first successful hydrogen bomb test on 12 August 1953.

'Within a few days', Dr R. V. Jones recalled, 'our monitoring system (with the Americans) established that it had a thermonuclear component'. According to Jones, there was a feeling of relief on the JIC, 'for in a strange way we felt that the world might somehow be more secure'.[61]

To a degree previously unknown, Winston Churchill had taken personal control of the Foreign Office and the sanction of special operations. According to Evelyn Shuckburgh, the Prime Minister 'had to be consulted about drafting points in the reply to the Soviets' and 'about every individual "intelligence" operation'. Churchill 'usually forbids' special operations for 'fear of upsetting the Russians', something that did not go down well with the US State Department and the CIA. The lack of support for the US strategy left the British, as the Foreign Office official responsible for overseeing special operations, Gladwyn Jebb, put it in September, 'in quite bad odour with the Americans on Cold War matters'. While agreeing that roll-back in eastern Europe was not immediately feasible, the American administration took little heed of British opinion and, instead, endorsed the secret hardline 'Solarium Project' for undermining Soviet control over the satellites.[62]

Despite the consistent failures of the roll-back operations, the NSC still did not preclude the detachment of minor satellites such as Albania. New paramilitary plans under the direction of C. D. Jackson, Eisenhower's psychological warfare specialist, OPC head Frank Wisner and Foster Dulles were not immediately implemented because of the forthcoming elections in West Germany. Until they were held, all covert operations in Europe were postponed in order to avoid any possible embarrassment. The plans were reconsidered in November, but this time as an Anglo-American project. On the 11th, Jackson met with the First Secretary at the Washington embassy, Adam Watson, to discuss 'country A'. Afterwards, Jackson reported that 'everything is back on track and operations should be launched from Greece and Yugoslavia'. The Anglo-American plans evolved rapidly in the months that followed, with a target date in the spring of 1954.[63]

At a conference in Bermuda on 8 December with President Eisenhower, Churchill hoped to persuade the Americans of his desire to hold talks with the Moscow leaders. He made little progress, however, and left Bermuda 'bitterly disappointed'. The only positive outcome was the signing of a declaration – with a passage inserted at Dulles's insistence – which stated that 'we cannot accept as justified or permanent the present division of Europe. Our hope is that in due course peaceful means will be found to enable the countries of Eastern Europe again to play their parts as free nations in a free Europe.' A number of the exiles recognised that these were mere platitudes and resigned themselves to the fact that 'Britain had effectively withdrawn from political action'.[64]

On Christmas Eve 1953 it was announced that Lavrenti Beria – had been executed, accused of spying for a foreign nation, Britain – according to Khrushchev, strangled by members of the Presidium. Those investigating Beria – the same people who had supervised the earlier proceedings against the alleged Zionist conspiracy – claimed that he had been part of a plot to contact the British Intelligence Service. This ridiculous conclusion was drawn after Beria ordered the end of the investigation of the Soviet ambassador to Great Britain, Ivan Maisky, who was accused of spying for MI6. Beria's intelligence ties were said to go back to 1919, during the Civil War, when he had clandestine contacts with British Intelligence in the Baku. Since 1946, Beria had been the target of a campaign by the Georgian Security Ministry to compromise him through his Mingrelian comrades, including plans to kidnap his wife's relatives in Paris as part of a Mingrelian secession conspiracy involving links to the MI6-sponsored Promethean League. A few days after Beria's death was announced, Kenneth de Courcy, who ran the right-wing *Intelligence Digest*, happened to see his old friend Stewart Menzies in White's Club: 'He frankly told me he had played a part in that event.'[65]

On New Year's Eve 1953, Radio Tirana announced that the CIA's agents trained for the final part of Operation FIEND against Albania had been arrested by the Sigurimi and were awaiting trial. American and, on a much smaller scale, British liberation policy was now in tatters. There was nothing to back up the false assumption that the eastern Europeans were ready to throw off the yoke of communist totalitarian oppression. MI6 and the CIA had ignored the lesson that 'even a weak regime could not be overthrown by covert paramilitary actions alone'. It also illustrated that, despite the intelligence 'special relationship', MI6/CIA rivalry 'so often seems to have got in the way of effective co-ordination'.[66]

As a consequence, plans for 'country A' began to die a slow death. When Dulles, Bedell Smith and C. D. Jackson met on 8 March 1954, the British agreed with them that the operation would have to wait 'until Trieste [was] settled'. The plan was revived by the CIA but it never got off the ground, partly owing to other problems facing Eisenhower in eastern Europe but primarily because the Albanian operation had been truly blown. Whether the British seriously contemplated joining with the Americans in a new operation against Albania is not known, but seems unlikely.

Around the same time, MI6 suspicions about the Baltic operations were aroused by another unsuccessful intelligence-gathering operation. London had signalled the 'Robets' group in Riga, Latvia, with a request for a sample of water from the River Tobol, near the Urals, where it was believed a nuclear reactor had been recently commissioned. A litre of water was obtained which was then passed on to the 'Maxis' group, one of whose members managed to bring it out when E-boat captain Hans Klose next landed MI6 agents on the Baltic coast. The flask arrived at the end of March 1954, but analysis of the water for traces of radioactivity revealed levels of such toxicity that it had to be dismissed as a plant. MI6's insistent questioning of their agents in the Baltic left little doubt in the minds of the KGB officers who had constructed the deception that the British knew that the networks were now under their control.[67]

In April, the show trial in a Tirana cinema of leading conspirators revealed for the first time the extent of the Albanian deception. The Sigurimi had rolled up the entire American network and had controlled much of the flow of information to the radio base in Cyprus. The executions were followed by a reign of terror throughout the country in which thousands died for what one exile condemned as 'an absurd enterprise'.[68]

When French Senator de la Vallée Poussin was elected chair of the EM Central and East European Commission, in April 1954, the secretariat was moved from London to Brussels and finally to Paris, where the exiles noticed a different political atmosphere. 'This was the equivalent', Polish leader Stefan Korbonski later wrote, 'to the withdrawal of British leadership and initiative in matters concerning the Iron Curtain countries, and was done with all the polite ceremony required on such occasions, in the form of the usual phrases and a smoke-screen of thanks and compliments.' The Americans now took over full control of eastern European operations, or what was left of them.[69]

In early 1954, Communist Party leader Nikita Khrushchev began his bid for power by claiming that Malenkov's softness on imperialism threatened Soviet security. With his position weakened, by the end of the year Malenkov had fallen from power and with him had gone any chance of détente. With renewed confidence, the Soviets began to roll up the remaining exile networks. Besides betraying parties of NTS agents parachuted into the Soviet Union, Nikita Khorunzhi had also supplied the KGB with information vital to the successful kidnapping in April of an NTS leader, Dr Alexander Trusah-novich, and nine days later the failed assassination attempt on Georgi Okolov-ich. Within a month, the Ukrainian operation had also finally fallen apart when Soviet radio announced the execution of the Americans' top agent and leading OUN-B figure, V. O. Okhrymovych, who was said to have revealed the identities of other agents in Ukraine.[70]

The Soviet Union publicised these cases at the United Nations, this time with more success. The Western Allies replied with their own propaganda initiative, with the full background to the Soviet campaign against the NTS finally being revealed with the defection to the West of the assassin of Russian émigrés, Capt. Nikolai Khokhlov, whose story, pumped through MI6 and IRD propaganda assets, received the full blare of publicity.[71]

It had become increasingly clear that the Europeans wanted a relaxation of East–West trade because they were less reliant on US economic assistance. By the end of 1953, the British sought a dramatic liberalisation of export controls, with a 50 per cent reduction in the Control List. Though they had no wish to see 'any traffic in military equipment ... capable of making weapons', the JIC urged that trade controls should be aimed only at 'vulnerable spots' in the Soviet economy.[72]

Desmond Bristow genuinely believed that MI6's Strategic Trade Section was 'actively achieving results', but, by April 1954, the 'work had become more or less routine, and the list of goods and companies we were watching had been whittled down to ten or twenty. The main concern was in the atomic field and in electronic components, mostly manufactured by America.' There was little left to do and Bristow decided to retire, leaving strategic trade in the hands of just one officer. In a victory for the British position, the list was slashed and, thereafter, COCOM concentrated 'more narrowly on items used mainly in military production, or items whose impact would be felt in the Soviet defence, rather than civilian sector'. Bitter arguments between the Europeans and Americans over strategic trade did not, however, cease, and soured initiatives for many years.[73]

In an effort to cement western co-operation in the midst of the Cold War, the first formal Bilderberg conference was held in May in the small Dutch town of Oosterbeekat, at the Hotel de Bilderberg, from which the meeting took its name. It was seen as an opportunity for shapers of opinion among élite groups in Europe to speak with one voice to their counterparts in the United States, who feared that differences over European integration and' eastern Europe would create misunderstandings.

Funding came courtesy of the Dutch government and the CIA, through the efforts of Shepard Stone, who had served during the war in Psychological Warfare and postwar in Berlin on the staff of the US Military Government. Denis Healey was invited to the first meeting and acted as convenor for the British component – Gubbins, Beddington-Behrens, Bob Boothby, Montgomery Hyde (Unionist MP and former MI6 officer), Sir Paul Chambers of ICI and Hugh Gaitskell, whose expenses were occasionally covered by the Foreign Office. The presence of other Europeans such as Antoine Pinay, Guy Mollet, Alcide de Gasperi and Paul van Zeeland showed a strong overlap with membership of the EM. Healey found Bilderberg to be 'most valuable', though 'the real value, as always, was in the personal contacts outside the Conference hall'.[74]

It was thus used, participants insist, to prevent divergences emerging by working through consensus rather than any formal procedure. This was particularly true concerning European perceptions of 'McCarthyism'. During the first conference 'sparks flew' between the two groups. According to the 'strictly confidential' record of the first meeting, a major concern was with 'long-term planning', with the main theme being the threat of, and vigilance against, communist infiltration. The intention was to pass on the general views of the discussions to opinion-makers without disclosing the source. It would seem that, at the prompting of Bilderberg, a number of anti-communist think-tanks and propaganda agencies were set up and funded by western intelligence services throughout Europe in the late fifties.[75]

If, as Churchill indicated, the British wanted to concentrate solely on psychological warfare with regard to the Soviet satellites, they hardly seemed to be in a position to undertake any major operations. When Harold Macmillan was appointed Minister of Defence in 1954, he was convinced that 'the first essential' in the Cold War was good intelligence. He was, however, dismayed at the lack of co-ordination, particularly since the battlefield had moved increasingly out of Europe into those former areas of the British Empire where the 'Attlee Doctrine' still held sway. George Young soon discovered that the Commonwealth Relations and Colonial Offices disliked receiving information that clashed with their preconceived notions about Africa and Asia. One official explained that it was 'too embarrassing to negoti-ate with anyone if I know that behind my back he is up to something quite different'. There was little or no co-operation between MI6 and MI5, and with the imperial security services. 'No one is wholly responsible,' Macmillan complained. 'It's partly Defence, partly Colonial Office, partly Foreign Office. There's no central anti-Communist organisation with any drive in it. "Cold War" alarms me more than "Hot War". For we are not really winning it, and the Russians have a central position . . . and a well directed effort with strong representation (through the Communist Party in every country).'[76]

Macmillan was one of the few ministers who still had the energy to do something about the situation and looked for 'some way of getting everyone to co-operate and pull together – the Cabinet, the Foreign Office, the Service chiefs, the information people'. Eden realised that 'it was no use asking the PM to undertake any administrative reforms – he simply would not take it in'. Churchill wanted 'not so much more officials everywhere collecting information to prove how necessary they are but a much smaller number of agents . . . who stay in the same places long enough to learn something about the facts'. This was no doubt based on the experience of his private secretary, Montague Brown, who had previously complained about the bland intelli-gence assessments the Prime Minister received from the Foreign Office, and was one of the key officials who 'always looked forward to the yellow dispatch box in which Young put the cream of "C"'s output'.[77]

There followed a running battle in Cabinet with confusion among minis-ters about precisely what it was they were seeking. There was a major differ-ence between intelligence-gathering, propaganda and special operations. By this time, there should have been an improvement in the collation and assess-ment of intelligence because the Permanent Under-Secretary's Department (PUSD), headed by Patrick Reilly and then Patrick Dean, had become a large and important section in the Foreign Office. It had taken over the responsibilities of the former Services Liaison Department, which involved 'Co-ordination of Intelligence, Representation on the Joint Intelligence

Committee and Joint Planning Staffs, Liaison with Ministry of Defence and Chiefs of Staff Organisation'. In addition, it provided the secretariat of the all-important PUSC, which, crucially, set the budgets of the security services. When, during 1954, a programme of economies was being imposed upon the British intelligence community, it was the PUSD that prepared an inter-departmental report for consideration not only by the PUSC but also by the chiefs of staff, a job previously undertaken by the JIC.[78]

In the area of special operations, increased Foreign Office co-ordination does not appear to have occurred. Here, there was much more haphazard and semi-official management without clear lines of control and command. In particular, Eden was quite happy to bypass the Foreign Office and deal directly with senior MI6 officers and the chiefs of staff, while Churchill wanted to oversee all planned operations. There were co-ordinating bodies in this period, but where they fit into the official structures is hard to ascertain. The 'Jebb Committee', seemingly attached to the Russia Committee, was apparently replaced by the Psychological Warfare Consultations Committee or 'Dodds-Parker Committee'. Named after its chair, Douglas Dodds-Parker – Under-Secretary of State for Foreign Affairs between November 1953 and October 1954 and again in 1956 during the Suez period – this committee appears to have been the kind of co-ordinating body that Macmillan sought. Among the members were the psychological warfare specialist Hugh Carleton Greene – recently head of the Emergency Information Services in Malaya and currently Assistant Controller of the BBC's Overseas Services – and the former head of SOE, Sir Charles Hambro. According to Kim Philby, they had responsibility for planning psychological warfare operations primarily against Soviet-backed peace fronts and conferences, including domestic organisations. MI6 was also engaged in undermining delegations to Britain from socialist countries and their representatives residing here. During the summer of 1952, the Foreign Office's Northern Department had revised its machinery for providing intelligence on visiting Soviet bloc delegations and the use of such information by MI6's special section (known as BIN/ KOORD) and the IRD in briefing the press and media. The Dodds-Parker Committee also sanctioned the exploitation of crew members on British merchant ships and other vessels.[79]

In early 1954, following the success of various special operations in the Middle East, MI6 reorganised its former SOE elements under Montague Woodhouse of the Special Operations Group and Political Action Branch into the Special Political Action (SPA) section. Acting under the authority of R1 who also became its chief, the SPA was officially engaged in what were known as 'political measures' which 'Higher Directive' C(102)56 noted was 'not an especially successful combination of words because it is very difficult to find a proper name for these many faceted and broad tasks'. The SPA ran MI6 agents 'operationally' in tasks that included 'the organisation of upheavals, organisation of clandestine radio stations, sabotage and espionage activities, publication of newspapers and magazines, the disruption of international conferences or control of them, influencing elections and many others'. The propaganda 'PROP' section of the SPA department was additionally responsible for 'not only exercising political guidance over long-term planning of all propaganda operations, but also for providing detailed guidance and control over the conduct of covert propaganda, i.e. the sort of propaganda for whose conduct Her Majesty's Government must not be accused'. PROP was also involved in 'deception actions' and acted as liaison with the IRD.[80]

While special operations were being reorganised, there was an internal crisis over the Baltic operations, and it was clear to MI6's young Turks that something was amiss with Harry Carr's operations. Suspicions were based not just on the bizarre episode with radioactive water but also on an analysis of radio traffic. Louise Bedarfas, an American of Lithuanian origin from the CIA's Baltic branch, who arrived in London in May, had concluded that all their actual agents were dead and that the remaining functioning radio in the Baltic was under KGB control. Unfortunately, a number of older, senior MI6 officers, whose reputations rested on the success or otherwise of the eastern European operations, still believed in the soundness of their networks, and so there was only a temporary crisis over agent status when Sandy McKibben ignored an order to stop sending them into the Baltic. An officer not involved in the operations, George Young, aka 'Scott', was brought in to assess their viability but was hampered by having to rely on what the officers controlling the operations told him. Carr assured Young that the British experience was different from that of the CIA and that there was no need to close down the networks. Young insisted, however, on a test of the Estonian network by way of a 'barium meal' – intelligence would be passed through and traced to see if it was used by the KGB.[81]

At the end of September, the KGB allowed a 'suitably ignorant but experienced' officer, Margers Vitolin, to travel to London to try to answer MI6 queries concerning the mystery of the radioactive water. Met at Kiel by Rudolph Silarajs, who ran the Latvian operations, Young and the resident MI6 officer in Hamburg, Vitolin was debriefed in a villa requisitioned by MI6 and then at a safe house in Sloane Street, Knightsbridge. Interrogated for two weeks by Young and MI6 lawyer Helmus Milmo, Vitolin admitted that he was a communist, confirming Young's suspicions. At the beginning of November, following a request by MI6, Alphons Rebane welcomed the arrival in London of an Estonian guerrilla, Walter Luks. As a former SS officer, Rebane had a high opinion of his ability to spot a communist, and Young and Carr relied on his opinion. Unfortunately, on this occasion, this ability deserted him and he ignored the advice of a colleague at the Estonian embassy who recognised Luks as a communist who had joined the Red Army in 1941.[82]

Once again, it seemed that MI6 had been misled, but Young now knew for certain that the KGB was manipulating the operations. It became clear that all the Soviet orbit operations had been controlled to a lesser or greater degree by the KGB and that the intelligence which MI6 had proudly supplied to its Whitehall customers had been either of such low level as to be worthless, or the product of disinformation. To avoid an embarrassing blow to its credibility, MI6 had concealed the fact from Whitehall. In order to make something of the disaster, MI6 decided to turn the operations around and mount their own deception operations. As part of the process, control of Baltic operations was wrested from the old regime and a number of officers were quietly pushed aside. The first casualty of the clear-out was McKibben, who was allowed to retire.[83]

In late November 1954, MI6 decided to test the Estonian network. MI6's Soviet 'expert', Harold Shergold, asked Tony Divall to run an important Estonian agent, Boris Nelk, with Ryder Latham, who had spent three years with the Control Commission in Germany and then in the Rome embassy under commercial cover. In Helsinki, Divall and Latham met with Alphons Rebane, later joining Shergold for a mission to drop Nelk off the coast near Juminda. Unfortunately, a trap had been set, and 'no sooner had the agent clambered into a dinghy for the final stage of his journey back into the Soviet Union than two patrol vessels arrived on the scene and opened fire'. The MI6 party just managed to escape into international waters. On his return to London, Divall was told that Nelk was 'suspected of working as a double agent for the KGB'.[84]

The exile double-cross game was not only being practised by the KGB and MI6. MI5's new counter-espionage D Division, under its head, Graham Mitchell, also got in on the act. On the back of the successful wartime double-cross operations against the Germans, MI5 and MI6 began 'recruiting as many double agents as possible, and operating extensive networks of agents in the large Russian, Polish and Czechoslovakian émigré communities'. Mitchell hoped that 'eventually one of those agents would be accepted into the heart of the Russian illegal network'. MI5 officers also recruited many émigré agents with the idea of recruiting others back in their homeland. Using the intelligence gathered during Operation Post Report's investigation into the loyalty of thousands of postwar émigrés in Britain, the émigrés were easy to recruit and 'enabled MI5 to compete directly with MI6 in the production of Iron Curtain intelligence, much to their irritation'. The IRD provided D Division with plausible intelligence 'chicken-feed' which could be passed to the Soviets to convince the KGB of their agents' credibility.[85]

MI6 knew that their infiltration operations in the Caucasus had also been thoroughly penetrated and undermined by Soviet-run deceptions, and decided, again, to turn them around as double-cross operations. The Service took considerable risks in sending back to Georgia as their own agent a disaffected Latvian patriot – in fact, a Russian agent whom they had 'turned'. After an unsuccessful attempt to put him ashore from an eleven-man, specially adapted boat on a beach not far from Sukhumi, which had been reconnoitred a month before, the agent was landed in the neighbourhood of Tuapse.

The boat was commanded by Mark Arnold-Forster, a lieutenant in the Royal Navy who had been demobbed in 1946 to work with MI6. Using the boat's sophisticated tracking technology, Arnold-Forster noticed intense 'indications of search activity' (ISA) such as increased Soviet radar trans-missions and loitering of ships in the area. He later discovered that the Latvian had 'deceived British Intelligence'. The agent had 'remained loyal to Russia and apparently transmitted disinformation back to the British'. It soon became apparent that the agent had 'informed the Soviet authorities in advance of our mission. He told them where we would be landing and when.' The KGB had intended to capture the boat and crew, but the MI6 team managed to escape by using the full power of the boat's customised engines to evade the closing net.[86]

As a result of this latest disaster, towards the end of 1954 a group of NTS agents being trained in London were told that an operation to land another group of agents on the Black Sea coast by submarine had been cancelled at the last moment. The senior instructor, 'Mr Radford', explained to them that 'in the changed situation it had been decided to wind up the training programme and postpone the landings'.[87]

As an inevitable result of factional in-fighting, by January 1955 two oppos-ing groups had developed within the NTS. One was led by Baydalakov, who was eventually expelled for 'betrayal of solidarity', and the other by Vladimir Poremsky, who succeeded in retaining most of the official structure. By this time, the NTS members were 'aware of a certain nervousness and suspicion among the British'. For four years MI6 had run the NTS project, SHRAPNEL, principally in the interests of gathering secret intelligence, and had in the process come to the conclusion that the use of 'Black Operations, Defectors, Internal cases within the USSR, Counter-Espionage dividends obtained by using the NTS as a magnet with which to attract offensive Russian Intelli-gence Service operations' had 'not proved worthwhile'. The NTS had not produced any substantial sources, and knowledge gained in the previous two years about the KGB operations against the exiles convinced MI6 that NTS intelligence-gathering was too low-level to be worth sustaining. The NTS people subsequently went to bizarre lengths to prove their worth. Among those expelled was George Klimov, who was made chair of the 'Central Union of Post-War Russian Émigrés' (ZOPE), financed by the Ameri-cans. It went so far as to secretly blow up its own headquarters in order to justify its claim that it posed a real threat to the KGB.[88]

In the meantime, Margers Vitolin returned to Latvia to an in-depth debriefing. His interrogation at Moscow Centre aroused suspicion that the KGB deception operation had been rumbled by MI6. Given also the absence of new MI6/CIA agents being landed in the Baltic – details of which would normally have been made known by a spy planted in the boat service – the KGB came to the conclusion that the British were probably now playing the game in reverse.[89]

The run-down of the eastern European operations was paralleled by a thaw in East–West relations. In late March 1955, just before Eden succeeded Churchill as Prime Minister, the PUSC referred back to its earlier study on the satellites and argued that, largely on the basis of the recent western agreement to rearm West Germany, there was now an equilibrium with the Soviets which meant that there was a place for genuine negotiations. The Foreign Office argued that from this position of strength the West could win concessions from the Soviets. The PUSC also considered a paper, 'Positive Action designed to Compress and Disrupt the Soviet Bloc', that entertained the possibility of 'squeezing Albania out of the Soviet Bloc' on the basis that the Soviet Union might regard the country as 'expendable'. Albania was seen as the only possible exception to British government strictures on supporting resistance groups in liberating the satellites. The possibility of such disruptive action was axed, as the prospect of some kind of deal with the Soviets was taken seriously. Eden agreed that the time was ripe for an East–West summit, which eventually took place in Geneva in July.[90]

In April, George Young had received more ammunition for his opinion of the Baltic operations when a returning Estonian agent revealed that the 'networks are completely penetrated by the KGB'. There remained, however, hesitancy in believing that their efforts had been in vain, and the failures were blamed on Sandy McKibben and one of the CIA's own agents, who had previously been accused of being a KGB plant. But failure hung in the air and, in turn, Harry Carr was quietly posted to Copenhagen, where he awaited his retirement, while Rudolph Silarajs was dismissed and sought a new life in Canada, where he died in the late seventies.[91]

Other projects also came under close scrutiny, and when John Bruce-Lockhart applied 'bromide tests', he found confirmation that the whole Ukraine operation 'had been under the control of Soviet intelligence since the first group had been captured after landing by parachute in 1950'. Similarly, he came to the conclusion that NTS operations in the Soviet Union 'had come almost completely under Soviet control'. In late 1955, MI6 finally decided 'to pull out, leaving the tiresome job of dealing with Russian émigrés to its American partner'. In transferring their assets, MI6 informed the Americans that in their opinion NTS supporter Prince Turkul had not been 'doubling as a Soviet Agent', despite the assumption in right-wing circles that this had been the case.[92]

The British were frustrated with the failure of the Ukrainian OUN-B and, considering the NTS an ineffective organisation, broke off relations with both groups in 1956. A joint MI6/CIA two-day conference was held in London on 28/29 February during which MI6 outlined their reasons for withdrawing their support from the NTS. MI6 officers

> made it clear to the NTS leadership that its objective in pursuing operations jointly with the NTS was to obtain secret intelligence on the USSR. In return for secret intelligence or the prospect thereof the British Service was ready to supply the NTS with extensive facilities in the field of training, supply, despatch and operational advice and support of all kinds. The Cold War propaganda and disruptive activities of the NTS have only been of minor interest to the British Service in so far as they could be viewed as providing a favourable climate for the develop-ment of secret intelligence operations and the provision of oper-atives.

They had drawn up 'a balance sheet in which every factor in the British/ NTS partnership can be given its due weight. Their conclusion is that the partnership has largely been unproductive from their point of view, i.e. that the results obtained have been in no way commensurate with the time and money invested.' MI6 told CIA representatives that it would finally cut off support on 1 April.[93]

Neither were things going well for the NTS's sternest critics, the Russian Revolutionary Force (RRF), which opposed CIA-sponsored umbrella groups such as the American Committee for Liberation. Ironically – given that the RFF had repeatedly portrayed the NTS as a KGB front – in 1956 the 'Young Russian' leader, Kazem-Beck, who had emigrated to the United States, returned to the Soviet Union, thus reviving rumours that he had always had links with the Soviet security services.[94]

MI6 now felt that it was time to clear the decks without leaving any embarrassing failures lying around. The Royal Navy withdrew its permission for German ships to use British naval ensigns, thereby removing the boat service's cover – though MI6/CIA agent teams continued to be sent by boat to the Baltic until the end of the year. The German government then absorbed the Gehlen Org. and ordered it to halt missions into Russia.

In June, Silarajs sent a final message, abandoning the eleven MI6 agents still operating in the Baltic: 'We can no longer help you. Will be sending you no physical or material help. All safe houses are blown . . . Destroy or keep radios and codes. This is our last message until better times. We will listen to you until 30 June. Thereafter, God help you.'[95]

During July, the KGB mastermind behind the Soviet deception operations, Major Janis Lukasevics, responded by sending an undercover officer, Janis Klimkans, to Sweden to attempt to renew contact with MI6. In September, he arrived in London where he was interrogated by Young. Exhausted, physically and mentally, from daily interrogation in 'the cooler', after four weeks Klimkans made a full confession which 'destroyed the last trust of MI6 in the émigrés'. Rebane closed down the remaining Estonian radio station and shortly afterwards left the Service to settle in Augsburg, Germany. The KGB mopped up the remaining Baltic agents, who were then either executed or sentenced to long terms of imprisonment. Klimkans was taken by MI6 handlers to the Soviet embassy in Sweden with a message for Lukasevics: 'Tell your masters that we're grateful for the lessons but we're not complete fools. And finally tell them to treat our people as well as we've treated you.'[96]

While the CIA took over responsibility for the NTS and other émigré groups, involvement with the refugees and émigrés was 'skeletonised', with instructions from President Eisenhower that it be terminated. In Germany, this responsibility was left to William Harvey, who bypassed the new station chief in Frankfurt, Tracey Barnes. It seems, according to MI6 European Operations head John Bruce-Lockhart, that Barnes was not entirely trusted with secrets. Most of the long-term émigré assets and handlers were deliberately 'scattered' to preclude 'blowbacks'.[97]

As this was happening, the Hungarian Uprising, which the intelligence agencies had not predicted, took place in October 1956. On the 19th popular disturbances broke out in Poland. When a hundred thousand students took to the streets in Budapest, they were joined by thousands of frustrated workers, who launched a series of demonstrations calling for the withdrawal of Soviet troops, the release of political prisoners, and the establishment of an independent communist regime. It looked as if the Soviet empire was finally crumbling. Despite the propaganda line emanating from the IRD, which in April had described the West's principal objective as 'to prise Hungary away from the Soviet Union', the uprising failed to rouse the British to action. While the old 'robber barons' might have wished to revive the émigré groups and back the Hungarian freedom fighters, the new Chief, Dick White, had no wish to see the Service held responsible for a bloodbath.[98]

White ordered John Bruce-Lockhart to monitor the uprising. He left for Budapest, where the local MI6 station had provided no intelligence on a possible Soviet invasion. An estimated fifteen thousand young men took up arms to counter the Soviets, with small bands of fighters establishing pockets of resistance and demobilising scores of Soviet tanks. Influential figures in the western clandestine services wanted to intervene, but embarrassingly they were in no position to do so. *Daily Telegraph* defence correspondent Michael Smith's source has claimed that some of the weapons used by the rebels were American and British, retrieved from arms caches buried by the CIA and MI6 in the woods around Prague and Budapest for use by 'stay-behind' parties in the event of war. MI6's Simon Preston recalled picking up agents on the Hungarian border to take them across into the British Zone in

Austria. 'We were taking them up into the mountains and giving them a sort of crash course. Graz was our staging post. Then, after we had trained them – explosives, weapons training – I used to take them back.'[99]

This operation was very small-scale and had no material effect on the inevitable outcome. The CIA reported to the National Security Council (NSC) that there were no underground groups in Hungary capable of sustained resistance. Despite the propaganda, there were no 'well-armed shock units' as said to have been provided by the West, while few if any 'émigré fascists' were caught. The reality was that President Eisenhower had no interest in aggressive action and 'instructed the CIA to maintain caution and avoid giving Moscow any reason to suppose that the United States had either instigated or would support the Hungarian rebels'. The same policy was followed by the British government, which had pulled out of the exile game. An estimated three to four thousand Hungarians died during the uprising, which Bruce-Lockhart noted meant that any idea of uprisings in eastern Europe 'could now be wiped off the SIS and CIA agenda'.[100]

By 1958, the CIA's émigré units had been disbanded, 'causing great dis-illusionment and bitterness among the members'. The only British operations taking place were MI5 double-cross ones. In 1959 D Division's Harry Wharton, who was handling Polish affairs, recruited the leading friend of the Ukrainian and Belorussian émigrés and former MI6 asset Auberon Herbert. MI5's double agent cases, however, turned out to be, according to Peter Wright, 'a time consuming charade'. The new practitioners were 'second-rate', without the requisite skills and, as Bruce-Lockhart had warned, British Intelligence lacked information from signals code-breaking which had been so essential during the war. More importantly, the networks were 'thoroughly penetrated by the KGB, or their allied Eastern European services', and, in the end, these operations 'served only to soak up our effort, and identify our agent runners'.[101]

In surveying the exile infiltrations with George Young, John Bruce-Lockhart, the Northern Area Controller, Arthur Crouchley, and his successor, Paul Paulson, Dick White told his colleagues that it was 'important to remove the Iron Curtain sentiment of sending someone over the wall for the sake of it'. The Cold War concept was, Young concluded, outdated – 'one had an uneasy feeling that this had become a game of shadows'. The requirement was hard intelligence, which the Service had so far failed to deliver.[102]

THE TECHNICAL FIX

MI6's inability during the fifties to put working agents into Russia or recruit sources in the Kremlin, Red Army or security services produced an intelligence gap which, as Scandinavian historian Ralf Tammes noted, 'nourished anxiety', contributing to 'exaggerated estimates of Soviet capabilities and potential'. Recognising the failure of human intelligence-gathering, the Americans, in particular, and, to a lesser extent, the British began 'to use more technical means to gather intelligence in an aggressive manner, resulting in significant innovations'.[1]

Tammes was thinking, in particular, about his own country, Norway, which, despite reservations about Britain's military commitment to the region, had long had a special relationship with MI6 – 'one which was totally centred on the exchange of intelligence'. As progress was made in the early fifties with highly secret defence preparations, Norwegian intelligence official Alf Martens Meyer reveals that more thought was given by the Defence Intelligence Staff (DIS) to 'stepping up their vigilance' and increasing the flow of intelligence about the Soviet Union. The Norwegians realised that the British and Americans hoped that this would provide them with useful information about Soviet capabilities in the North and 'played it for all its worth'.[2]

During the war years there had been close signals intelligence links, which continued after the end of hostilities when the British supplied technical devices to Norwegian Intelligence. Particularly valuable was information obtained on Soviet radar chains on the east coast of the Baltic and in northern

East Germany. Another important source of intelligence was the Norwegian Royal Air Force, whose photo-reconnaissance missions identifying Soviet MiG fighters based along its border were shared with the British. There was also close co-operation on deep-penetration 'ferret' missions carried out by Britain's RAF to gather intelligence on Russia's military capabilities in the Arctic regions, the Barents Sea and further eastwards. Intelligence gathered was compared by British analysts in the Photographic Interpretation Units against captured German photographs of the same areas.[3]

President Truman had banned American spy flights over Soviet territory, a decision that angered the Joint Chiefs of Staff. They subsequently sought and obtained Churchill's personal approval for a resumption and a secret unit was set up in June 1951. Nine RAF crews under Squadron-Leader John Crampton were trained by the Americans to fly the latest reconnaissance aircraft, the RB-45C Tornado, equipped with top-of-the-range radar. Flights were made from a United States Air Force (USAF) base at Sculthorpe in Norfolk. In March 1952 a flight to test Soviet reaction was successfully undertaken down the central air corridor to Berlin.[4]

During 1952/3, American aircraft repainted with RAF insignia and using British crews flew deep into Soviet airspace. The Anglo-American penetration raids suffered a setback when, in March 1953, an RAF Lincoln bomber – officially on a training flight but carrying out both photographic and signals reconnaissance – was shot down by MiG-15s, with the loss of seven crew, after straying over East Germany. The incursions angered Moscow – there were, it seems, no such flights by the Soviets over the United States – and raised superpower tension as the Soviet Union was concerned that some of the flights might have been nuclear bombing runs. Despite 'spurring the air force to greater efforts', President Eisenhower, who was 'a champion of aerial reconnaissance for collecting otherwise unattainable intelligence', imposed a temporary ban on military spy flights, but it was not long before the RAF was again asked to undertake American-backed missions. This time they were carried out in co-operation with Government Communications Headquarters (GCHQ) ground stations all over Europe. The unit navigator, Rex Sanders, recalled that the targets were 'fairly scattered over the southern part of Russia. We were zig-zagging from one to another, which might have added to our safety.'[5]

In 1952 western intelligence services learned from debriefed German scientific returnees from Russia about a new Soviet missile testing site at Kapustin Yar, near the Volga river. After being told that reconnaissance of Kapustin Yar was out of range of its aircraft, USAF under General Lewis asked the RAF's Director of Intelligence, A. V. M. Fressanges, if the British could undertake the mission. In late 1953, as part of Operation ROBIN, a RAF twin-jet Canberra bomber with an extended range – capable of flying higher than a MiG-15 – was 'dispatched on what was probably the first trans-Soviet reconnaissance flight, and one that its crew would undoubtedly long remember'. It was carrying cameras that were so powerful that during a test it was able to take clear shots of St Paul's Cathedral while flying off the coast of Dover.

Taking off from Giebelstadt in West Germany, the Canberra followed the Volga southwards, crossing over Kapustin Yar. Soviet fighters riddled it with bullet holes but the pilot managed to get the plane to its recovery base in Iran. According to the CIA's Deputy Director of Intelligence, Robert Amory, the RAF managed to obtain 'some fair pictures' but at a cost. 'The whole of Russia had been alerted to the thing, and it damned near created a major international incident.'[6]

The immediate result, claims one account, was that the British told the Americans 'to go it alone'. In fact, a flight of at least two American RB-45C Tornados with British crews overflew Moscow on the night of 29 April 1954 as part of a 'deep penetration' mission. More importantly for MI6, the Service's own plans for an unmanned high-flying photo-reconnaissance plane were scrapped for fear of creating further incidents. 'Expert specifications, plans and costing had been worked out but without Air Ministry backing,' George Young recalled. 'Sinclair would not proceed with the scheme.'[7]

In the aftermath of the outbreak of the Korean War, there was concern among the intelligence agencies about Allied PoWs who made confessions of their 'crimes'. There was a fear that maybe the Russians and Chinese had developed drugs that could turn a prisoner into a 'Manchurian Candidate'. There followed a brief period of close co-operation with the Americans, during which the CIA exchanged information with MI6 on a number of projects, including their ARTICHOKE programme, which looked at the effects of drugs on defectors and would-be agents. In June, CIA representatives met with their MI6 counterparts in a series of discussions. MI6 remained sceptical about the idea of a drug turning a man into an unwitting agent; one officer said that there 'had been nothing new in the interrogation business since the days of the Inquisition and that there was little hope of achieving valuable results through research'. After some persuasion, MI6 finally agreed to the importance of behavioural research, though the CIA officers remained unsure about their sincerity. The meeting reached a consensus that neither the western countries nor the Soviets had made any 'revolutionary progress' in the field, and described Soviet procedures as 'remarkably similar to the age-old methods'. The representatives agreed to continue investigating behaviour-control methods because of their importance to 'cold war operations'.[8]

Although co-operation with the CIA was short-lived, MI6's Technical Services did later take part in joint projects with MI5 into psycho-chemical research at the Chemical Defence Establishment at Porton Down, employing human guinea-pigs with particular reference to the use of LSD and other hallucinogens in interrogations.[9]

With the return of a Conservative government, in September 1952 Dr R. V. Jones was asked to take over from Dr B. K. Blount as Director of Scientific Intelligence in the Ministry of Defence (MoD). A distinguished chemist, Blount had parachuted into Greece with SOE and had been head of the Scientific Department of the Control Commission in Germany. He had found the Scientific Intelligence arrangement unsatisfactory, as Dr Jones had predicted, and the MoD decided to combine the Service's scientific sections into one body. Dr Jones was also appointed scientific adviser to GCHQ with a seat on the Joint Intelligence Committee (JIC).[10]

The directorate, based in the former Metropole Hotel in Northumberland Street, was tasked with gathering intelligence on scientific developments primarily as applied by the Soviet Union for potential warfare. Directing the collection of intelligence through every available channel required close collaboration with MI6, the services and research institutions. Dr Jones soon discovered, however, that the arrangements were in a mess and, despite Churchill's personal backing to put things right, was 'far from sanguine about the prospects'. Inter-service rivalry was still strong, with a confusing number of overlapping committees and organisations, while the staff seconded from the armed services were not of great quality or experience. 'Vested interests' had effectively 'crippled scientific intelligence', Jones reflected. He was able to institute a monthly meeting at the MoD of a small, informal committee that included MI6 Chief John Sinclair and Dick White, Director-General of MI5. They discussed technical problems and how these might be solved. Dr Jones also had some success in persuading the JIC to set up the Committee for the Provision of Experimental Facilities for Intelligence with an MI6 member and an MI5 officer, Malcolm Cumming.[11]

Before he resigned to become Deputy Secretary of the Department of Scientific and Industrial Research, Dr Blount acknowledged that 'it is necessary to remove the anomalous arrangements for atomic energy intelligence, which are actively harmful to good Scientific Intelligence'. At the beginning of 1953, MI6's Director of Requirements, George Young, attempted to redirect the Service's intelligence-gathering more effectively on priority targets. Young concentrated on improving the quality of reporting and briefing of agents on specific questions rather than sending general questionnaires to the field. This required the continual education of MI6's 'customers' – 'not all of whom were able to produce the clear-cut requirements of the economic ministries'. Young's attempts to improve R9's scientific intelligence reporting were, however, 'effectively blocked'. Suspecting that all was not well, Young checked with one of his St Andrew's University friends, a leading physicist at the Atomic Energy Authority, who confirmed that operations by MI6's supposed scientific expert, Eric Welsh, were 'useless and even dangerous'. On his return to Whitehall, Dr Jones had been promised that atomic energy intelligence would become part of the directorate, but it was not to be, and the position appeared to be no better than when he had resigned three years previously. Unfortunately, neither Dr Jones nor Young were able to persuade Sinclair to sack Welsh, who retained control over atomic intelligence. Relations with the Americans did, however, improve, and during 1953 Jones took part in the first substantial exchanges of atomic intelligence with the CIA.[12]

Partly because he could not arrive at a satisfactory solution to the problem of atomic intelligence, Dr Jones went back to Aberdeen University in June of the following year, and it was only after Welsh's death from a heart attack in November 1954 that MI6 was able to make progress with scientific intelligence. The thought within the Service was that 'more than ten years had been lost' due to Welsh's bungling. After Dr Jones's departure, the post of Director of Scientific Intelligence was downgraded and placed under the Director of the Joint Intelligence Bureau (JIB), so that 'once again scientific intelligence had no independent voice at the top level'. MI6 did, however, put more resources into the area, which became one of the Service's priorities – a policy clearly indicated by the interest of the Permanent Under-Secretary's Department (PUSD), which had taken on Foreign Office responsibility for atomic energy affairs.[13]

The British and Americans had 'an unpleasant surprise' when the Russians conducted their first successful hydrogen bomb test on 12 August 1953. 'Within a few days', Dr Jones recalled, 'our monitoring system (with the Americans) established that it had a thermonuclear component'. There was also an insistent demand from the JIC for intelligence on the test and Soviet missile capabilities.[14]

As the Service moved out of the first stages of the Cold War, many senior officers believed that the future of intelligence-gathering lay in the technical field 'and that in time the human element would become less and less important'. Technical operations, particularly the bugging of Soviet residencies, the tapping of telephones and mail interception, became 'very much in' and the Service invested 'vast' resources on these operations, often carried out in conjunction with the CIA. There was a big demand for material from this type of operation from the Cabinet Office, the Foreign Office and the chiefs of staff. Eventually, the Cromwell Road-based Technical Operations Section, which was responsible for obtaining this material, split its operations into two sections. Buggings and telephone taps were undertaken by Y-Section, whose deputy head was George Blake, while N-Section dealt with plundering diplomatic bags.[15]

Among the operations were CONTRARY – the placing of microphones in the office of the Polish Trade Mission and, in Brussels, the wiring of rooms at the Astoria Hotel, which was used by diplomats and trade representatives from communist countries; FANTASTIC – where operatives hid microphones in the office of the Soviet commercial attaché in Copenhagen; the tapping of the telephones of the Czechoslovak Export Agency in Cairo; the wiring of the London residence of a second secretary of the Bulgarian embassy; in Paris, obtaining secret information on the French atomic energy programme and, in Sweden, information on the defence forces and uranium deposits. Despite these efforts, according to Blake, the intelligence 'take' was often poor because of the lack of high-quality microphones which resulted in inaudible conversations.[16]

The technical intelligence-gathering operation against the Soviets with the most potential for success was the tapping into land-lines in Berlin in a follow-up to the similar operation in Vienna. At the end of 1953, an East German MI6 agent, a communications engineer whose children were helped to travel to the West by Service personnel, located a telephone cable containing 350 lines between Berlin and Soviet military bases all over the Eastern bloc. The line lay two hundred yards inside the Soviet Zone, underneath a highway running from a Soviet airbase to the city. The MI6 station head in Berlin happened to be the man who had masterminded the Vienna success, Peter Lunn, and he saw the potential of the agent's information.[17]

According to European Operations officer John Bruce-Lockhart, the CIA was not 'brought in for the money and technical know-how, as is commonly assumed, but because the [entry to the] site was in the American sector, and the British needed the United States to build a radar station as cover'. Over four days in mid-December, an MI6 team under the Director of Requirements, George Young, which included Stephen McKenzie, Ian Milne and George Blake, and others under Y-Section's Tom Grimson, including Capt. Montagnon, Col. Balmain, Taylor and Urwick, met with a CIA delegation in London; the delegation included Soviet section head Frank Rowlett. During the 'exploratory talks', they discussed processing and technical requirements for Lunn's plan, Operation STOPWATCH (known as GOLD to the Americans), which would require a six-hundred-foot tunnel to be dug into East German territory at Alt Glienicke, near Berlin. The plan had been passed as feasible by MI6 experts Col. Balmain and Taylor, who had gained considerable experience from the Vienna operation.[18]

Another meeting was arranged for 1 February 1954 at which the CIA's Rowlett and Lunn's opposite number in Berlin, Bill Harvey, agreed to the plan and offered to supply the finance and the necessary cover facilities, while the British would supply the technical equipment and the monitoring staff. A joint MI6/CIA team in London would be responsible for assessment and evaluation. Unfortunately, the operation was betrayed almost as soon as it was agreed. Minutes of the meeting were taken for the American side by Cleveland Cram, but the British entrusted the task to George Blake, who immediately passed the information on to his KGB handler, Nikolai Rodin. The KGB then asked him to draw a map of the plan, which he did on a piece of A4-sized lined paper.[19]

Of particular importance to the British was technical co-operation in monitoring the Soviet Navy. Britain used its submarines to gather intelligence in
the Barents Sea, as did the Americans, who began to patrol the area, making
increasing use of electronic intelligence (ELINT). Principal targets for MI6
and the Naval Intelligence Division (NID) were the ports of the Soviet Union,
but officers and naval attachés had great difficulty visiting these areas. Even
when they did manage to do so, they were always under heavy escort. MI6's
naval section, R3, developed its own contacts with members of the merchant
navy and, in particular, with shipping companies that regularly had vessels
visiting ports of interest in the Soviet bloc. R3 also made contact with Alf
Martens Meyer and the Norwegian DIS.[20]

In 1949 Meyer, a thirty-nine-year-old naval officer from Bergen, had been
chosen by DIS head Wilhelm Evang to spearhead Norway's offensive espionage activities. He eventually built up a network based on the Norwegian
merchant fleet, Operation DELFINIUS, the results of which were of great
importance to the western intelligence agencies. During the Korean War, the
DIS played a key role in gathering intelligence from China with a network
of agents in Shanghai. In addition, Meyer built up a Turkish network with
headquarters in Istanbul. From the early fifties until the mid-sixties, Delfinius
was jointly financed by MI6 and the CIA.[21]

A similar operation existed in Britain, where the fishing fleets of Aberdeen
and Hull were used to spy on the Soviet North Atlantic Fleet in Arctic waters.
Operation HORNBEAM was run by a senior NID officer, Commander John
G. Brookes, from the basement of the dockside premises of a fishing company
in Hull; during the mid-sixties he reported to the head of the NID, Rear
Admiral Michael Kyrle Pope, who has confirmed that Hornbeam was the
brainchild of MI6. Brookes recruited trawlermen to take photographs during
fishing trips, the results of which were forwarded to a Joint Intelligence
Section with MI6. Mason Redfearn was recruited in March 1963: 'Brookes
gave me a Robot Star camera [developed by the Nazis, it was capable of
taking up to forty-eight photographs at the press of a button], a telescope, a
supply of film and a book of silhouettes of Soviet naval ships.' After a training
course in London, 'I knew exactly what to look for, radars, radio antennae,
guided missile systems, and in general anything unusual.' A major success
was photographing the first Soviet nuclear-powered cruiser. Four-man naval
listening teams, including a civilian from the GCHQ station at Scarborough,
were also placed on trawlers, with equipment tuned in to Soviet signals. The
operations ran from 1950 until the mid-seventies.[22]

Norway had one of the world's biggest merchant navy fleets, sailing to
all the great seaports of the Soviet Union, eastern Europe and China. Meyer
was in contact with the owners of the major shipping companies; Lars Usterud
Svendsen of Fred Olsen Ltd was in charge of the civil side. MI6 also helped the
Norwegians establish a separate shipping company, Egerfangst, to undertake

operations. Frank Slocum was the MI6 officer in charge of these operations and, in 1954, was appointed to Oslo as head of station. His successor, Ted Davies, was a former Royal Naval Volunteer Reserve (RNVR) officer who had served with Pat Whinney and Christopher Phillpotts in Slocum's wartime 'private navy'. They could draw on the support of Sir Charles Hambro and his merchant bank, Hambros, which had a substantial stake in the Norwegian shipping empire, providing hundreds of millions of pounds of finance. Hambros Bank had a long-standing financial interest in Norway and Scandinavia, and Sir Charles had been Controller of SOE's Scandinavian Section with another influential Hambros director, Harry Sporborg, as its head. Hambro had also chaired the Anglo-Norwegian Collaboration Committee which co-ordinated resistance plans.[23]

Officers from Norwegian Intelligence were put on merchant ships, where they recruited Norwegian seamen as agents able to report from inside 'enemy' ports. Meyer recalled that 'it could be information about harbour works, the depth of the harbour and the like. Information which is not punishable to collect, but which the Intelligence Service finds valuable.' The merchant ships also operated as 'platforms' for official Norwegian agents and cameras fitted as 'gifts' from 'special sources' for spying on the Soviet Union. The first vessel, *Eger*, was ready for operations in 1956, mostly equipped with American electronics for monitoring signals radio and electromagnetic signals. Trawlers and small fishing boats were assisted by professional agents and fitted with advanced electronic equipment for spying on Soviet activities. At first the ships were mainly deployed in adjacent northern waters, the Barents and White Seas, but operations were later successfully extended to the Mediterranean and, at the beginning of the sixties, to the Far East. Operation Delfinius also gave the DIS a range of bases in foreign ports, while agents such as Meyer worked clandestinely as ship inspectors.[24]

British use of submarines for gathering intelligence in the Barents Sea was curtailed in 1956 for 'political reasons' following the Buster Crabb affair (see Chapter 29). Stepping into the breach by using the merchant navy for intelligence-gathering, Meyer was able to build up a stock of goodwill. In the decade after the war, Norway regarded itself as a 'Great Power' in intelligence terms. In exchange for its information, the country was given access by Britain and the United States to material and advanced technology from which it would normally be excluded. Meyer's biographer, Christian Christensen, stresses that Norwegian Intelligence was 'by no means a subsidiary to the British MI6 or the American CIA'.[25]

Despite these efforts, intelligence-gathering on the Soviet Union and the Soviet orbit was in a poor state. MI6 assets in East Germany were fading fast, and the Service had none of any worth in the Soviet Union, while the Americans were increasingly reliant on the unreliable Gehlen Organisation for its intelligence. Fortunately, the Berlin tunnel, which had been a colossal operation costing the Americans $25 million, was finished in February 1955. Three thousand tons of earth had been excavated by a secret team of diggers and then hidden away in a semi-underground warehouse by the US Corps of Engineers. The 1,476-foot tunnel was air-conditioned so as not to melt the snow above, with plastic explosive attached to the tunnel at the point where it crossed into the Soviet sector – to be detonated if the Russians discovered it. Experts from the Post Office base at Dollis Hill then attached taps to 295 lines carrying Soviet communications. The tapping of the Soviet military lines required 600 tape recorders to be operating continuously, fed by 800 reels of tape per day.[26]

During the summer and autumn, senior MI6 officers held a series of conferences to discuss the penetration of the Soviet Union and the other Russian orbit countries. George Young outlined a new strategy at a conference in Berlin, where MI6's largest station ran many of the major operations into the East. He told the other officers that it would be the task of MI6 to obtain 'political information' to gauge Soviet intentions and scientific intelligence to assess Soviet progress in armaments. With its one hundred officers, Berlin was split into four substations to meet these demands. One dealt with political intelligence and Soviet penetration, the second with the Soviet and East German armed forces, another with the collection of scientific intelligence, and the fourth with the planning and execution of technical operations of various types.[27]

During the night of 22 April 1956, a KGB party led by eavesdropping specialist Colonel Vadim Goncharov stumbled on Stopwatch/Gold and the telephone tap of the military traffic. In the event, the Americans refrained from setting off the explosives for fear of causing casualties. It is not completely clear why the Soviets waited a year before 'blowing' the existence of the tunnel by an open search, though, obviously, the protection of their prime source, George Blake, was a major consideration. In fact, the KGB had been searching for the tunnel using Blake's sketchy information but 'it took us a great deal of effort to locate the exact position of the tunnel', according to the KGB resident in Berlin, Yevgeny Petrovranov. The Russians conducted their searches at night using heat-seeking equipment, which failed to give the expected results because of the depth of the tunnel. 'It took us months to locate it.'[28]

During that year, it is unlikely that the Soviets could have controlled all the information that passed over the communications link, substituting 'chicken-feed'. The chief of the CIA's Berlin operation base, David Murphy, argued that 'the take from the tunnel was so massive – hundreds of thousands of conversations and thousands and thousands of feet daily of teletype traffic – there was no way they could have turned this into a disinformation operation without alerting everyone up and down the line'. By the same token, the three hundred analysts and translators in London were so overloaded with low-level material that it took them until September 1958 to clear the backlog. Given previous Soviet use of radio deception, it is unlikely that the KGB did not take the opportunity to manipulate some of the traffic.[29]

The thousands of hours of Soviet military conversations were analysed by Brigadier Eric Greer and Squadron-Leader Brinley Ryan. In Washington, fifty CIA officers fluent in German and Russian worked on this 'incredible source' in a prefab building known as the 'Hosiery Mill' because of the web of electronic cables sneaking through the building. The traffic revealed a great deal about the Soviet order of battle, gossip between officers, including conversations between a top Soviet military commander and his mistress, and some scientific intelligence. MI6 and the CIA also learned that the East German railways were not in a fit state for the launch of an attack on the West, which confirmed the lack of evidence in the traffic that the Soviets were preparing for an assault. The conclusion of many intelligence officers, however, was that little of worth had been revealed by the immense effort put into the tunnel operation. Officials thought that it was 'a tremendous operation', recalled an MI6 officer. 'But the truth of it is, they weren't good operations. We all thought they were. Everybody did. The Foreign Office said, "Very important, very important." And so on and so on. But the Russians knew.'[30]

If there were later major operations along the lines of the Vienna and Berlin tunnels, they have remained remarkably well hidden. The reality was that much of the technical burden was taken up by GCHQ, which was able to supply, through its worldwide network of listening stations shared with the American National Security Agency, a mountain of raw intelligence. GCHQ decrypts, which proved to be increasingly cost-effective, would become the backbone of MI6's own analysis and intelligence-gathering efforts. Much to the annoyance of MI6's old guard, the advent of satellites would further downgrade the contribution of human agents, regarded by some officials as expensive and unreliable.

PART SIX

THE MIDDLE EAST

British Intelligence has had a long history of special operations in the Middle East. The region was the playground for intelligence officers who, operating outside of normal chains of command and control, often engaged in the kind of robust methods that were denied to them in other operational theatres. MI6's use of special operations and political action reached its high point, or low point, during the fifties – the era known to practitioners as 'the Horrors'. It culminated in the disaster of Suez, which Donald Cameron Watt, Professor of International Relations at the London School of Economics, has described as 'a monumental conspiratorial cock-up – like much else in the historical record'.

Contrary to the line adopted in most histories of this period, it appears that a hardline faction of the British foreign policy establishment continued to pursue an interventionist agenda after Suez. That the 'cock-up' was followed by more 'disruptive actions' should not surprise: MI6 officers in the region were dreamers. T. E. Lawrence's lines from *The Seven Pillars of Wisdom* are apt: 'All men dream: but not equally. Those who dream by night in the dusty recesses of the minds wake in the day to find that it was vanity: but the dreamers of the day are dangerous men, for they may act their dream with open eyes, to make it possible . . .'

Even when the Chief, Dick White, made plain his distaste for special operations, MI6 was forced by a right-wing cabal – centred around the new Prime Minister, Harold Macmillan – to engage in a small-scale war in Oman and in an arm's-length operation in the Yemen. The use of the SAS as a counter-insurgency and paramilitary force for essentially mercenary operations, and the deployment of intelligence assets to avoid direct MI6 involvement and thus provide a semblance of plausible deniability, created a model for British operations for the next thirty years.

'UNBROKEN DREAMS'

With hostilities at an end in the Middle East, Deputy Commander of the Allied Air Forces in the Mediterranean John Slessor minuted that 'the intelligence set-up in Cairo is a mess'. There were, he insisted, 'far too many different agencies and organisations, all with direct access to the great, too often crossing each others' wires and cutting each others' throats'. His own solution was 'a drastic reorganisation at the top of all our Secret and Underground Services, SIS, SOE, "A" Force, and PWE, all as inter-related branches of one service under a single head who would be an associate member of the Chiefs of Staff Committee'. Other military figures, too, called for the creation of a specialist Middle East intelligence service under the chiefs' control.[1]

MI6 regional headquarters attached to the theatre commands in the Middle East were retained but were moved from military to diplomatic accommodation. In turn, the local MI6 cover organisation, the Inter-Services Liaison Department (ISLD), was abandoned for the Combined Research and Planning Organisation (CRPO – pronounced 'Creepo'), with substations in Beirut, Baghdad, Tehran, Amman, Basra, Port Said and Damascus. CRPO was headed by John Teague, an Indian Army and intelligence veteran who had served in Iraq and Palestine before taking charge of the ISLD in 1945. The Joint Intelligence Committee (JIC) acknowledged that Teague would be 'responsible directly to SIS in London', but in practice would be required to fulfil 'local intelligence requirements'.[2]

CRPO was housed in the Sharia Tolumbat compound in Cairo where it shared the facilities of the British Middle East Office (BMEO), which had been set up by Labour Foreign Secretary Ernest Bevin to stimulate regional stability and progress, and to secure Britain's long-range foreign policy interests in the Middle East. Some saw its object as 'the creation of a new informal empire for Britain' in which MI6 would play a full part.[3]

At the first Council of Foreign Ministers in October 1945, Bevin rejected Soviet demands for equality of treatment in the region. Foreign Office diplomat Sir Maurice Peterson told Stalin that the Middle East 'was our area . . . we had done and were doing great work in it, and . . . frankly, as regards the Arab countries, we knew a great deal about them while the Russians knew nothing at all'. Fresh from his posting in Moscow, Frank Roberts was sent around Middle East capitals 'to warn the new leaders of the potential threat from Stalin's Russia'. Using chiefs of staff briefs, the JIC concluded that the Soviet Union 'would exploit the twin vulnerabilities of Britain's oil and communications'. In a future war in the Middle East, a concerted Soviet air attack would threaten 'not only Turkey and Iraq but also Egypt'. In the wake of the 1946 Azerbaijan crisis on the Iranian border with the Soviet Union, JIC intelligence estimates became increasingly pessimistic, forecasting Soviet expansion 'by every means short of war'. They identified an eastward shift in Soviet emphasis away from Turkey towards Iran, and 'the domination of Persia' by the securing of 'a port and base in the Persian Gulf'.[4]

The Government Communications Headquarters (GCHQ) was tasked with monitoring Soviet activities in the region, and at the instigation of the JIC Middle East, which was chaired by the head of the BMEO, GCHQ personnel were redeployed to the Iranian border to work on Soviet communications. Despite this concern with Soviet intentions, the JIC's list of priorities for the region – 'Arab nationalism', the 'relations of Arab states with UK', and the 'Zionist movement including its intelligence services' – indicate that Soviet subversion was not regarded as a great problem. Indeed, over the next three years officials could find little evidence, beyond propaganda, of Soviet subversive activities in the region.[5]

The Foreign Office wanted to dismantle the remnants of Britain's own subversive organisation in the region, the Special Operations Executive (SOE). The only voices in favour of not disbanding SOE were local ambassadors who wished to retain particular personnel or members of the related clandestine Psychological Warfare Executive (PWE) to continue propaganda work. In May 1946, the British embassy in Iran recommended that in order to defeat the Soviet-backed Tudeh Party 'we should shortly pass over to a general counter-offensive . . . broadcasts, press, pamphlets and so on'. The ambassador in Tehran, Sir Roger Bullard, thought that 'only one of the present SOE will be required – Dr Zaehner' (see Chapter 28).

In June, the Russia Committee recognised the need to resist the growth of communist influence in Persia. Initially, Bevin had viewed the idea unfavourably, but as senior Foreign Office officials had predicted, he soon began to waver as the JIC called for more positive action. By July the Foreign Secretary was willing to go 'all out' on Iran. A former Indian Army officer with a string of intelligence appointments, Colonel Geoffrey Wheeler, who had been Director of the Publications Division in India during the war, was dispatched to Tehran to organise a 'Propaganda Department'. In collaboration with MI6's head of station, Harry Steptoe, he was asked to 'enquire into certain fields of Persian opinion'. On the back of Wheeler's activities, in October Bevin agreed to the opening of a general political warfare campaign, and General Pollock, director of the Middle East Information Department (MEID), left London to co-ordinate the campaign with regional information officers. By November, Wheeler had been able to persuade the Foreign Office Research Department, the Colonial Office, the Central Office of Information and several secret agencies to pool their information on communism and Soviet tactics for a propaganda campaign; a forerunner of later Information Research Department (IRD) operations. Dr Zaehner, meanwhile, was retained in Tehran as press attaché with the responsibility for 'bribing the Persian press'.[6]

A number of ambassadors found such activities distasteful, partly, one suspects, because it was so brazen. The Minister Resident in the Middle East, Lord Killearn, sided with the Foreign Office in resisting the continued presence of even single SOE officers. Expressing a preference for MI6, he argued that SOE was not good at propaganda, and added: 'As regards their other activities, in other words the payment of baksheesh, I'm not myself convinced that we, the Embassy, couldn't do the job adequately well . . . I have always disliked SOE playing a semi-lone hand as they have done during this war . . . As you know we already have our SS [Secret Service] arrangements here which work well.' Killearn noted that SOE proposed to spend '£10,000 a year on oral dissemination of pro-British views; £9,000 a year on the paying of patronage to selected politicians and government officials; and a further sum of approximately £12,000 on special secret payments in this country at the request of His Majesty's representatives'. The Foreign Office took a dim view of covert subventions, recognising that while 'it may produce good results for a time', the end result would only 'increase the anti-British tone, and consequent bribability of the newspapers concerned'. Despite appeals to ideology and loyalty, cash remained the main means of recruiting agents.[7]

While the remnants of SOE Cairo were closed down, other parts of its Middle East empire managed to survive for some considerable time. The task of winding up SOE operations and facilities was given to senior SOE organiser and banker Bickham Sweet-Escott. During the VJ day celebrations, word reached Sweet-Escott from SOE headquarters at Baker Street 'to report back to London and thereafter to be posted to another job in the Middle East'.

With wartime responsibilities in Jerusalem for SOE's SO2, which had control of black operations, Sweet-Escott was the ideal person to deal with the post-war reorganisation. Over the two years of this 'thankless task', while attached to MI6 for 'pay and rations', he ensured that he left 'a skeleton in the cupboard of every country of the Middle East'. Handed over to MI6, these SOE 'skeletons' included news agencies, such as the Arab News Agency (ANA), and the radio station Sharq al-Adna. Sweet-Escott had been involved during the war with SOE's radio and signals specialist Major Jerry Parker in locating the transmitter in Jerusalem that carried the overt Arabic freedom station, the Near East Broadcasting Station (NEABS), which was also known as Sharq al-Adna. Its postwar existence has been described by a former ANA journalist as 'a very dirty operation'.[8]

NEABS had been supported by the Foreign Office's Rex Leeper, an expert in organising overt and more secret forms of propaganda. During the First World War, Leeper belonged to the Intelligence Bureau of the Department of Information. In 1933, he was appointed head of the Foreign Office News Department, where he developed an interest in the use of democratic propaganda, particularly radio, as an instrument of foreign policy. It was Leeper who approved the use of a state subvention to the Reuters news agency and had been at the forefront in expanding the use of state-owned news agencies. Described by Sefton Delmer as 'tall and spare, with the thoughtful concentrated face of some old-time papal secretary', Leeper was also the main influence on setting up the British Council, which had a major influence in the Middle East.

Frances Donaldson's history of the British Council notes that 'many people believe that in the war years British Council staff were used for Intelligence work'. She concluded, however, that 'there is absolutely no evidence for this'. Her comment followed a memorandum from 'one of the great names in the history of the British Council', who admitted to headquarters that 'Military Intelligence people are frequently trying to make use of our staff for purposes of their own ... Military Intelligence have tried to pass people into Turkey with passports inscribed "British Council"'. The reality was that MI6 had burrowed deep into the organisation, which was an almost perfect cover.[9]

In December 1938, Charles 'Flux' Dundas was appointed as the first special British Council representative for the whole of the Middle East, which he controlled and serviced from Cairo. Dundas had 'an unusual degree of authority' and made sure that Council work was removed from the direct control of the embassy. An anti-communist who despised 'the faintest of intellectual pretensions', he appointed and trained his own staff, refusing to have any from Greece and the Balkans on the basis that they were 'pansies' and 'soft'. Donaldson claims that Dundas's health gave out at the end of 1942 and that he was succeeded by Professor Thomas Boase, who had been employed by GC&CS in Cairo. In fact, Dundas was appointed Oriental Secretary at Beirut, attached to MI6's front office in the Middle East, ISLD. He remained in the post until 1947, when he was made consul in Damascus, a position he retained until 1951, when he returned to the British Council. Describing him as 'A man of persuasive charm and considerable strength', Donaldson adds that Dundas 'had not merely to work for smooth relationships during the war but to prepare for a situation after the war when our influences could no longer be maintained by military power'. This was helped by the fact that British Council institutes were a meeting place for 'informal discussions and social contacts between the effective people in these countries and British officials and businessmen'.[10]

Well financed by the PWE, NEABS' first director was Squadron-Leader Alfred Marsack, a devout Muslim who had served in the Middle East before the war and who had devoted the best part of his life to Arab affairs, and had even converted to Islam. Interspersing popular music with conversational pieces as well as news, NEABS rapidly achieved a reputation for 'slick and effective programmes'. With a staff mostly made up of Arabs, it became a trusted station, capable of reaching a mass audience throughout the Middle East. The propaganda was subtle, the scripts not censored, and criticism of the British allowed. Indeed, the station employed the 'notorious (and quite charming) rabble rouser' and anti-British agitator Sheikh Muzaffar, who worked for the station on the understanding that once the Germans were defeated he would return to his anti-British activities. 'The fact that the Sheikh was broadcasting from Sharq al-Adna was, to many thousands of Arabs, a guarantee of the authentically Arab character of the station. It was surely inconceivable that the British would ever have allowed him on the air.' Also employed was the exiled Mufti of Jerusalem, Haj Amin al-Husseini, a supporter of pan-Arabism, which made him much 'too hot a potato for the BBC to hold'.[11]

Marsack left the station in 1945 to become the BBC Middle East representative in Cairo. He was replaced by Edward Hodgkin, who ran the station in the last stages of the war. Hodgkin was to maintain that the news Sharq al-Adna broadcast 'was never angled by any government department' and that it was a clean operation. He left for a job with *The Times* and the post was taken over in 1946 by the 'controversial' Frank Benton. In the light of Bickham Sweet-Escott's report, the structure of NEABS was changed – with MI6 retaining a secret interest. Working with MI6 in Iran was Norman Darbyshire, one of SOE's remnants, who shared a house with another SOE officer, the Oxford academic Robin Zaehner. In 1947, they travelled from Tehran to Jerusalem to set up a free independent radio station to broadcast to Iran, using the facilities of Sharq al-Adna. They managed to get it up and running but had to move on when fighting broke out in the city.[12]

Parallel to Bickham Sweet-Escott's mission, Stewart Menzies's wartime personal assistant and stockbroker, David 'Archie' Boyle, who had responsibilities in Section N for the plundering of diplomatic bags, also undertook a leisurely tour of the Middle East. In December 1945, he had been asked by the Foreign Office's Sir Alexander Cadogan to review and reorganise communications in the area, most of which had been abandoned during the war. Boyle's unintentionally amusing autobiography, which on first reading appears to be little more than a compendium of travel experiences and name-dropping, provides abundant evidence of why he would have been so valuable an asset to his Chief. Although he admitted that he knew nothing about finance, Boyle had held a good post in the City with stockbrokers Dawnay, Day & Co. A colourful, eccentric Scotsman, who was close to the Royal Family, Boyle travelled extensively and had a wide range of contacts, getting to know anyone who was deemed of consequence. An indication of his importance is the knowledge that he had accompanied President Roosevelt's special envoy and future head of the Office of Strategic Service (OSS), Col. William Donovan, around Britain at the beginning of the war, and was involved in peace feelers to Germany.[13]

During the course of 1946, Boyle met with old British friends in the embassies, governments and MI6 stations of the Middle East. He writes that he brought messages to Egypt from 'English friends' to King Farouk's *chef de cabinet*, Hassanein Pasha. MI6 policy had long been to recruit those advisers who were close to the centres of power, and in Hassanein they had a priceless intelligence asset. Boyle's old friend, however, died in a car accident soon after his arrival: 'This was the first of many unfortunate events which from then on seemed to dog our footsteps in our relations with Egypt, for Hassanein was the one cool and experienced adviser to the young King Farouk.' Even if Boyle was nostalgic for the reign of kings and was an imperialist at heart, he sensed the

> murmuring resurgence of Moslem renaissance which as in 1919
> was again in 1946 commencing to affect the Middle-East coun-
> tries as a whole. This time it was to be coupled with the race for
> oil, and the jealousies this apparently unending, unworked-for
> wealth would arouse until the whole life of those lucky enough
> to possess it within their boundaries was changed. The world
> was being reshaped under our eyes; the old friendships and
> allegiances were soon to wither away in the rush for wealth.[14]

Unfortunately, set in old imperialist ways, the chiefs of staff failed to recognise the changes generated by the race for oil, and pressurised the Foreign Secretary to reorganise the BMEO to give it political responsibilities. The military demands were 'occasioned by the need for co-ordinated political intelligence on the part of the Commanders-in-Chief in the Middle East'. This shifted the balance of the BMEO's functions 'away from development diplomacy and towards regional political intelligence work'. By 1947, having won its battle with the Prime Minister over the direction of policy in the region, the chiefs still believed that the Middle East was 'the base from which British forces can attack the Soviet flank. Its significance as a focal point of imperial communications has been vindicated by the war and is still of great value as a half-way house between the United Kingdom and the Far East. Oil from the Persian Gulf area is rendered secure by control of the Suez Canal. The Middle East also protects Africa from Soviet penetrations.' The only way this policy could succeed was by means of old-fashioned garrisons, which Britain could no longer afford. The military appeared to learn nothing from their experience in Palestine.[15]

Palestine was no longer safe for secret operations and, just before the end of the Mandate, in the spring of 1948, Sharq al-Adna was hastily transferred to Limassol. Within months of the station moving to Cyprus, the secret was out. Left-wing Labour backbencher Richard Crossman had been concerned about anti-Zionist propaganda broadcasts, which included a statement by Azzam 'Pasha', who urged the Palestinians to leave their homes and make way for 'our advancing Arab armies'. Given his depth of knowledge of psychological warfare, Crossman probably guessed the true identity of the station's sponsors and decided to refrain from asking direct questions.[16]

In June, Communist MP Philip Piratin asked Ernest Bevin 'whether he is aware that the radio station in Cyprus run by the Foreign Office Information Department has been encouraging the Arabs in their invasion of Palestine'. A source has suggested that it was Crossman who had given him the lead, though Piratin certainly received information from communist friends in Cyprus. Bevin, who specifically referred to NEABS, told Piratin that the broadcast was only 'speculating on possible Arab military activity' and that 'this station is not run by the Foreign Office Information Department nor has the Government of Cyprus any responsibility for it'. Though technically correct, this was an example of Foreign Office evasion. As the government of a colonial possession, the Cyprus administration had been told to keep its hands off the station. This may have been helped by the fact that the Director of Broadcasting for the government of Cyprus was Rex Keating, who had worked for NEABS during the war. When pressed about who did run it, Bevin answered: 'It is operated by a body of people connected with the Arabs.'[17]

The 'body of people' was the Near East Association (NEA), which was set up 'to promote the exchange of cultural and general information through-out the Near East'. According to one inside critic of its activities, it disseminated 'anti-American material and did much to keep the Arab-Israel pot boiling' by use of disinformation. The Cyprus Sunday Mail reported that it was 'the first and only association registered under the Companies Limited by Guarantee Law' in Cyprus. This 'front' company included on its board the 'great and the good' – all members of the Athenaeum – including Sir

Kinahan Cornwallis, former head of the Arab Bureau (1916–20), ambassador in Baghdad during the war and director of the Bank of the Middle East; a First World War intelligence officer, high commissioner and commander-in-chief for Palestine (1938–44), Sir Harold McMichael; and the former Director of the British School of Archaeology, John Crowfoot. There was also journalist Aidan Philip, who had worked in the thirties for the Anglo-Iranian Oil Company and then MI6's Section D, before joining SOE in Baghdad. Station manager Frank Benton appears to have had no real influence over its policies and operations. The NEA was an 'arm's-length' operation financed by 'an off-shoot of the Foreign Office' (MI6) from an office in London, and staffed by a man and a secretary who knew little about their true employers.[18]

During the late forties, Sharq al-Adna acted as the 'Light Programme' to the BBC's Arabic Home Service. Audience surveys showed that it enjoyed 'a very high rating indeed in the listening habits of the Middle East area'. The BBC was never quite sure of the position of the NEA. The BBC Eastern Service Director, Gordon Waterfield, noted that it was 'an expensive oper-ation'. Sharq al-Adna had a studio in Beirut and another in Cairo (until 1951), employing the best Egyptian entertainers and musicians. Its personnel were predominantly Palestinian. This was reflected in the news policy, which was 'explicitly pro-Arab and anti-Zionist in a way that the BBC was not. It also concentrated much more than the BBC on news from the Arab World, and carried less world news.' Its news was supplied by another MI6 front, the ANA, which was much used by Middle East journalists. Despite efforts to disguise the 'slightly' propagandist angle which only became overt in times of crisis, 'few people who listened to the station were in much doubt that there was a British hand in its control, though no one, naturally, knew what official body was responsible'.[19]

Lawrie Valls-Russell had joined the NEABS station as a security officer: 'full of patriot zeal, eager to demonstrate the enlightenment of post-imperialist Britain'. He was shocked to find that his job entailed 'political mischief-making, supporting military dictatorships and feudal deadbeats, and sniping at reform movements'. When he protested at MI6's Broadway headquarters about the radical output which he felt was using propaganda 'to discredit democratic parties that sought a middle way between disintegrating traditionalism and Leftist extremism', Valls-Russell was told: 'But it's marvel-lous cover!' When, later, 'a directive came from London ordering the station to pander less to Arab nationalists and to urge the Arabs to be realistic about Israel', he wrote 'a commentary in accordance with the new line and – after approval by the station's director, also an Englishman and an SIS appointee – it was broadcast. But most of the station's Arab employees didn't know who their real bosses were and the extremists among them protested and demanded a head.' Valls-Russell was asked by Frank Benton to take personal responsibility for protecting the cover of the station, but the 'Arab ultras were convinced that he was a traitor to the cause they thought the radio station was serving'. Valls-Russell left and was later employed by the *Economist*.[20]

Sharq al-Adna continued to be a highly successful, though controversial, enterprise whose advertisements generated substantial profits. It was successful enough to ensure that it sidestepped any political problems. Prime Minister Attlee is alleged to have remarked after one such problem, 'we'll leave it alone. It's the only secret service that earns money.'[21]

In April 1949, the Permanent Under-Secretary's Committee (PUSC) made a new assessment of the Middle East. Besides recognising that the area was a key centre of land and sea communications, it stressed the economic aspects, in particular the oil-producing countries which were seen as vital to Britain's recovery. Egypt was viewed by the military as being strategically important as an offensive airbase in the event of war with the Soviet Union. The JIC did not believe that there was a direct military threat to the region but was concerned about the effects of communist propaganda and subversion. During the summer, the head of the PUSC, William Strang, toured the area, reporting back to Bevin that the Arab states were weak, divided and faced the challenge of Russian communism on their borders without the benefit of strong leaders with which to face the threat (ironic given that Nasser would soon achieve power in Egypt). In November, the chiefs of staff restated their case that 'we must find a way of holding the Middle East at the beginning of a war with our own resources and of developing offensive action against Russia from that area. We believe this can be done. It must be done.'[22]

Bevin claimed that Britain's influence in the Middle East was 'greater than that of any foreign Power'. Technically that was correct, but as F. S. Northedge has noted, 'that influence hung by a thread; it had not been strengthened by the war'. The Foreign Secretary and other Labour ministers 'never doubted that its old position in the Middle East would sooner or later be restored to more or less what it had always been', but the country's virtual bankruptcy at the end of the war had left massive debts in the region, including £400 million to Egypt. The only way that its goals could be achieved was through the generous aid of the Americans, on whom Britain was to become increasingly dependent. It was recognised by the JIC that Britain's position in the Middle East could not be maintained without the help of the United States.[23]

By October 1950, a British embassy official in Washington was liaising with his State Department counterpart on covert propaganda operations in the Middle East. Bevin also proposed that American officials be attached to the British Middle East Office (BMEO). The BMEO head in Cairo, Sir John Troutback, objected that their presence 'would hinder the political and military work of the Office (the supply of intelligence and guidance to the Middle East Commanders-in-Chief) and would compromise the activities of the Secret Intelligence Service, which shared the Toulumbat compound'.

Troutback's outlook was, and remained, like that of many British officials, distinctly anti-American. There was considerable distrust of American policy concerning oil.[24]

The domestic demand for oil led a 'socialist' government into condoning the worst forms of exploitation and imperialism. The interests of Arabs were barely considered as it was 'not supposed that people of this kind' – invariably referred to by British officials and MI6 officers as 'wogs' – 'could run their own affairs'. Inevitably, 'the strongest political emotion which moved these people was the desire to run their own affairs and to lever the foreigner from their soil'. The problem was that the British refused to go. Often without the military strength to settle disputes in their favour, throughout the fifties the British relied on MI6 and the exercise of special operations to ensure not only their guaranteed presence but also the right to return when they wished. In the process, MI6, tied inextricably to the financial interests of the City of London, undermined every progressive movement that managed to rear its head in the region. It is possible that Britain might have dealt better with the nationalists 'had her pockets been full, but they were empty, and this was painfully obvious'.[25]

CHAPTER 26

PALESTINE

The very first example of Bevin's support for MI6 special operations came with activity directed, surprisingly, not against the Soviet Union but against Jewish emigration to Palestine. This was, however, underpinned by deliberately exaggerating the communist threat in an attempt to secure American support.

In the last year of the war, MI6 officers in Istanbul, Col. Harold Gibson and Maj. Arthur Whittal, had maintained professional ties with Mossad Le Aliyah Beth (Institute B for Intelligence Special Services – forerunner of the intelligence service Mossad), the Jewish agency that set up a network of agents who co-ordinated illegal immigration, and the Joint – an overt relief organisation. Helping with visas, Gibson and Whittal went to 'astonishing lengths to assist many clandestine undertakings, and, when necessary, to warn Jewish operatives of impending dangers'. The idea of a Jewish state, however, upset Ernest Bevin's grand strategic vision for the Middle East, and he soon reversed previous Labour policy by imposing a ceiling on Jewish immigration to the country. It was not long before the problem of dealing with 'illegal' immigration developed into a logistical nightmare, and the Foreign Secretary was forced to turn to the intelligence and security services for assistance to stem the tide of refugees seeking a homeland. For the first time, Bevin directly sanctioned the use of special operations by MI6.[1]

Palestine was not a primary MI6 concern because under the 'Attlee Doctrine' it was the responsibility of MI5 – though because of recruitment problems a number of Defence Security officers stationed in Jerusalem included MI6 officers on cross-posting. Indeed, the chief Defence Security Officer, Sir Gyles Isham, who reported to MI5's E2 (Overseas) Division in London, joined MI6 in late 1946. MI6 did, in its foreign intelligence service role, play an important part in countering the activities of Jewish intelligence agencies abroad. Despite the picture painted by fiction writers, in contrast to its largely behind-the-scenes battle with the Soviets and their acolytes, MI6 was engaged in a real war of attrition with the Zionists, and it paid a heavy price.[2]

On 9 September 1946, a grenade thrown onto the balcony of his house killed the Area Security Officer and senior MI6 officer in Tel Aviv, Maj. Desmond Doran, while two colleagues managed to escape injury. According to Nigel West, 'his death is thought to be the only "active service" casualty MI6 has suffered in the post-war era'.* Doran had served at the end of the war in MI6's Middle East cover organisation, the Inter-Services Liaison Department (ISLD), in Cairo, where he may have become known to Jewish guerrilla fighters. Doran certainly had the reputation among the Stern Gang as 'a skilled interrogator'. Seven weeks later in Rome, Irgun agents placed two suitcase bombs against the front door of the British embassy, which had become a symbol of opposition to Jewish emigration, causing extensive damage. The MI6 officer in the embassy, Kenneth Benton, felt the blast but escaped uninjured. The irony was that Benton had at the beginning of the war received a commendation from the Jewish Agency in Riga for his assistance to Jewish emigrants.[3]

The Jewish Agency's technically illegal military wing, the Haganah, many of whose members had been trained during the war either by MI6 or the Special Operations Executive (SOE), organised through its shadowy 'Brichah' escape organisation a series of underground railroads or ratlines, via Austria, to ports in Italy and Yugoslavia. In Austria, the British Army's Jewish Brigade (all of whose men secretly belonged to the Haganah) co-ordinated the shipment of Jews, under the noses of its British commanders, down the ratline into Italy, where a network of Jewish DP camps was used to channel refugees through Genoa for regular convoys to Palestine. 'To his surprise' Nazi-hunter Simon Wiesenthal discovered that some of the routes used coincided with those run by the Nazi self-help organisations. 'On occasions Jews and Nazis may even have been lodged in the same inn, without knowing each other's presence.'[4]

Relations were cordial between the Haganah's intelligence service, Mossad Institute B, and the political police in Yugoslavia, where no visas were required. In the period from the end of the war to the summer of 1946, more than 73,000 'illegals' were shipped in an assortment of barely seaworthy

---

* This would appear to be true and runs counter to the public perception that intelligence work is dangerous and violent.

craft and steamers to Palestine and its beaches, where they were secretly landed. The British argued that the Jewish Agency had deliberately chartered ancient ships so that if they made it to Palestine they would not be able to put to sea again. The vessels were crammed with illegal immigrants who, once intercepted by the Royal Navy blockade, were interned on Cyprus. In retaliation, the Haganah sabotaged the ships used by the British to deport Jews from Palestine.[5]

The intelligence available for monitoring the immigration was poor and often of low quality, and the flow of human cargo continued unabated. The signals intelligence-gathering agency, GCHQ, however, did have some success in monitoring the telephone calls of the lower ranks who were less security-conscious than the leaders of Mossad, with their grudging respect for British Intelligence. Through its liaison with the American National Security Agency (NSA), which had set up a secret code-breaking unit, codenamed 'Gold', in 1945 or 1946, it appears that GCHQ monitored the activities of Jewish Joint agents in the United States and elsewhere who were involved in financing the immigration and suppliers of arms.[6]

The British government's policy in Palestine of 'interception and detention' of illegal immigrants was nullified by sheer weight of numbers. It was a serious problem for the Attlee government, whose response may have been conditioned by the Prime Minister's personal prejudice. It is still a matter of conjecture whether Attlee and Bevin were anti-Semitic but it is true that 'even with memories of the Holocaust so fresh, there remained an unhealthy awareness in Britain of who was a Jew and who was not'. Peter Hennessy has noted that 'Attlee was no exception', while Gladwyn Jebb, one of the Foreign Secretary's closest advisers, later admitted that Bevin 'had all kinds of awful prejudices'. That his enemies made much of these is confirmed by a former editor of the *Jewish Chronicle*, Joseph Finklestone, who remembers Herbert Morrison telling him that Bevin's strange behaviour 'could be attributed to him being a secret, resentful Jew'. There were strong rumours in the Cabinet that the illegitimate Bevin had been fathered by a Jew. The Foreign Secretary is remembered in Israel as the man who 'bent his mighty will to frustrating its birth'. In part this involved giving the go-ahead for co-ordinating counter-measures with the armed services which included using MI6 for intelligence-gathering and propaganda operations against Mossad's underground, and sabotage against the shipping.[7]

Help came from the interrogation of Jewish suspects and prisoners. An officer who headed the Jewish Affairs Section of the Political Branch of the Palestine Police and went on to a senior position in MI6, John Briance, emphasised that police interrogations involved 'patience and preparation'. The Combined Services Detailed Interrogation Centre (CSDIC), which had been established in 1940 for in-depth interrogation and was run by Maj. W. B. Sedgwick, had only three other officers and was overworked. The GOC

Middle East intelligence headquarters at Fayid, on the Suez Canal, created a special section to combat illegal Jewish immigration by co-ordinating intelligence-gathering and running special operations. It used techniques for interrogation of Jewish suspects – 'snipcocks' in the words of one senior officer – which could be rough and brutal. Maurice Oldfield, who went on to become Chief of MI6, 'talked cheerfully about beating them and pushing people's heads under buckets of water'.[8]

In Germany, British Intelligence was responsible for penetrating the Jewish groups and apprehending the leaders of 'the far-flung underground organisation'. It found the task particularly hard; the little intelligence gathered in Germany and from agents in Austria and Italy along the Jewish ratline and the transit stations was collated by a special operations room in the War Office. In addition, anti-immigration stations were set up along the Mediterranean at Genoa, Trieste and Athens to prevent refugees from reaching the embarkation points and the ships sailing to Palestine. The headquarters was at Portovenere, at the tip of the bay of Spezia, from where most of the Italian sailings took place. Operating against the British in Italy was Yehuda Arazi, who had led a special Haganah sabotage squad during the war which operated in conjunction with SOE in the Balkans. He led MI6 'a song and dance for nearly two years' during which time he managed to plant one of his agents on the staff at Portovenere.[9]

During the summer of 1947, former SOE officer Maj. Gordon Lett caused alarm in London when he reported from Portovenere that Mossad Institute B intended to utilise larger four-thousand-ton ships, in order to send tens of thousands of immigrants to Palestine. Mustering all their resources, the British managed to block the ship, *Exodus*, and forcibly return its cargo of 4,500 persons to refugee camps in the British Zone in Germany. The move proved to be a public relations disaster, reviving recent memories of the Holocaust. In the United States, newspapers thundered that the British government 'had either gone mad or turned viciously anti-semitic'. Naval Intelligence officers reported that Mossad Institute B, buoyed by the publicity, had taken a decision to try to send twenty thousand refugees in one go in an attempt to flood the Cyprus camps, thus forcing the British to allow them to travel on to Palestine. In pursuance of the new policy, Mossad Institute B purchased two 4,500-ton Panamanian-flagged banana boats in the United States from the United Fruit Company, the *Pan York* and *Pan Crescent*.[10]

These ships, it was realised, would make or break British policy, and the government decided that more extreme direct action had to be sanctioned. Menzies turned to Col. Harold Perkins in MI6's biggest station in Europe, in Rome, where he collated information on the Jewish underground collected from stations in Vienna, Paris, Milan and Trieste. Perkins had 'devised a scheme to disrupt the flow of weapons and refugees: limpet mines were to be attached to the refugee ships so as to prevent them reaching Palestine'.

Sabotage or any operation that involved the possibility of death needed the approval of the Prime Minister and, according to his Assistant Chief, Jack Easton, Menzies 'sought Attlee's approval for the destruction of Jewish refugee ships sailing from Italy'.[11]

This would appear to be the first use of the new Special Operations Branch, though it was building on similar operations employing former SOE assets which had already been launched from Palestine. An Arab-speaker and junior member of the British Mandatory Government working in political intelligence, Cathal O'Connor had been chosen during the run-up to the invasion of Syria, in 1941, to train with SOE in sabotage techniques, including the blowing up of ships. At the end of the war, this SOE team, now under the control of MI6, was renamed the 'Kent Corps Specials' and 'switched to doing all we could to prevent ships chartered by the Agency from coming to Palestine'. According to O'Connor: 'It was very interesting but very harrowing. We had to deal with the poor Jews from the holocaust while the Palestinians were being hounded out of their homes and villages, as the Jews took them over.' He absolved Bevin, 'a brave and courageous man', from responsibility for these illegal acts with the bizarre excuse that by authorising the sabotage of the ships before they set sail from Europe, the Foreign Secretary had saved thousands of Jewish lives that might have been lost in unseaworthy vessels.[12]

The man chosen to oversee these sensitive operations in Italy was Count Frederick Vanden Heuvel, a papal count and director of Eno's Fruit Salts, and until recently the long-serving head of station in Berne. 'Fanny' replaced Kenneth Benton. He had secret instructions to launch an anti-Haganah campaign which would be implemented with the help of Perkins and his assistants, Wing Commander Derek Verschoyle and Col. David Smiley. The Anglo-Irish Verschoyle had been literary editor of the *Spectator* until 1940, when he was succeeded briefly in that position by Graham Greene, who was soon to join MI6. Verschoyle served with Bomber Command in the Mediterranean Allied Forces until he transferred to MI6. Smiley, who had served with SOE in Albania, had been seconded to MI6 at Perkins's request from his regiment, the Blues, which was stationed in Germany.[13]

Vanden Heuvel planned to infiltrate agents into the Haganah network using the MI6 representatives in Milan, Lancelot de Garston, who had served in Lugano and Locarno, and 'Teddy' de Haan, another former SOE officer who had served in North Africa and Italy. Their remit was to discover which Adriatic ports had been selected for the shipment of illegals. In addition, MI6 had suborned a Greek shipbroker from whom they obtained details of ships bought – largely with funds from US supporters. 'Once identified, Perkins's task was to procure the necessary equipment and then plant the explosives on the side of the vessel well below the waterline.' With a small boat, Smiley and Verschoyle posed as Adriatic cigarette smugglers and were responsible for attaching the mines, which had timers 'to ensure that the ship was sunk away from port in international waters' and to give them enough time to leave Yugoslav or Italian territorial waters. On at least one occasion, it is claimed that the timers malfunctioned: 'Those involved insisted afterwards they did not risk refugees' lives, since there were only "caretakers" on the ships in harbour.' Almost a dozen ships, including the *Struma*, were blown up, while there have been persistent rumours that one unidentified ship packed with illegals 'may have been blown up at sea, whether by accident or design'.[14]

In the summer of 1947, the *York* arrived in Marseilles and the *Crescent* docked in Venice. While Italian workmen were putting the finishing touches to the ship, the *Crescent* was rocked by an explosion. An underwater plate was blown out and water poured into the hold, causing the ship to list badly; luckily the pumps saved the severely damaged vessel. Mossad's investigation into the source of the explosion at first attributed it to an Arab terrorist group but later enquiries 'followed a trail which led Mossad leaders to the conviction that it had been a "British made" explosion'. They realised that 'the organisation to counter illegal immmigration was resorting to more direct preventative measures' and increased security around their ships. British agents prevented the sale of fuel to the ships but Mossad worked overtime to ensure that the *York* and *Crescent* would be seaworthy and, in September, both ships left for the Romanian port of Constanza, on the Black Sea.[15]

Britain was angry that a number of private American organisations were transporting Jewish immigrants to Palestine from the Balkans with the use of US military vehicles with US Army insignia and operatives wearing American uniforms. In October, the British protested, but the US administration ignored the official note. Changing tack, the British decided to play on American sensitivity to communist designs and announced a new wave of political warfare by labelling the illegal Jewish immigration railroad as a 'Red Plot'. The security services alleged that the thousands of illegal immigrants who were streaming into Palestine from countries under Soviet influence were being 'actively aided by the Soviet occupation authorities'. In order to try to win over the Americans, the British ambassador in Washington, Sir Oliver Wright, provided the State Department with 'convincing evidence' that the 'Romanian Government, with the approval of the Soviet authorities, was sending 10,000 hand-picked Communists to Palestine in the two Pan ships'.[16]

MI6 had swallowed the conspiracy theory that the Kremlin was behind the problems facing Britain's disintegrating empire. The station head in Vienna, George Young, later wrote that among the 'disciples and proxies' picked up and dropped as they suited the needs of the Soviets were 'Jewish terrorists'. While it is now known that the Soviets did, indeed, take the opportunity to insert a few agents among the refugees destined for Palestine, there was no evidence of '10,000 Communists' or of Soviet backing for the terrorists. While Mossad Institute B may have dealt with the communists of Yugoslavia, Czechoslovakia and Romania, it was a pragmatic, businesslike relationship that had everything to do with securing the release of refugees and the purchase of arms, and nothing to do with ideology. Within a year, Stalin launched a purge of Eastern bloc Jews, whom he considered to be agents of the American and British intelligence services.[17]

The British government was unable to persuade the Romanians to end support for the shipment, but Royal Navy vessels did blockade their passage. On 1 January 1948, the *York* and *Crescent* were taken to Cyprus, where they discharged fifteen thousand passengers. At Famagusta, crack units of the 6th Airborne Division searched the ships from top to bottom: 'But, owing to an unfortunate mishap, the Foreign Office released the results of this thorough search two days before the ships had reached port and before the search had actually started.' Two days earlier, the *New York Times* had carried 'official reports' that the two Pan ships were full of potential communist 'fifth columnists' associated with the terrorist Stern Gang. A further report claimed that the British had discovered 'hundreds of abandoned Romanian Communist Party membership cards on the two ships'. The Palestine Arab Higher Command backed the British charge, claiming that 'Zionism was the secret ally of communism'.[18]

There were, as far as is known, no further MI6 sabotage operations against Jewish ships. One retired officer involved described them as 'the blackest page in MI6's post-war history'. They appear to have been quickly curtailed when the Haganah threatened retaliation. Bevin's announcement of formal withdrawal from Palestine on 14 May 1948 was a declaration that the British 'would no longer fight to the finish' and was seen as a retreat from empire 'without glory'. It was also a sign to the leader of the terrorist group Irgun, Menachem Begin, that British Intelligence was 'neither omniscient nor infallible'.[19]

Following independence, it seems that there was no official liaison between Mossad and MI6, and both MI6's Nigel Clive and his deputy had their cover 'blown' almost as soon as they opened their office in Jerusalem, and had to be evacuated. In their stead, David Balfour, who had taught at Athens University until the German invasion and had spent part of the war as an agent disguised as Father Dimitri, a Greek Orthodox monk, was appointed head of station under Oriental Secretary cover at the embassy in Tel Aviv. There he remained under constant and hostile surveillance until his transfer to Smyrna in 1951.[20]

It was not until four years later, with the arrival of a major threat to Israel's existence in the shape of the Egyptian leader, President Gamal Nasser, who was equally hated by Britain's Prime Minister, Anthony Eden, that MI6 was able to establish effective liaison with Mossad.[21]

CHAPTER 27

CYPRUS

In July 1952, Archbishop Makarios, leader of the Greek Orthodox Church in Cyprus, secretly met in Athens Col. George Grivas, who during the war had organised the Greek right-wing resistance movement known as 'X', with the aim of achieving *Enosis* – political union with Greece. Three months later, Grivas made a brief visit to Cyprus in preparation for a guerrilla warfare campaign against the British occupiers. This stance had been boosted when the Colonial Minister, Henry Hopkinson, confirmed that Cyprus 'could never expect to be fully independent'.[1]

Indeed, in response to financial problems and difficulties within the Arab countries, later in the year, as part of the redeployment of UK military forces, Cyprus was chosen by the chiefs of staff to be Britain's forward base for land and air forces in the Middle East. The chiefs assigned to Cyprus, which was outside the area covered by the North Atlantic Treaty, the role of standard-bearer of Britain's prestige and standing in the Middle East, and made it the seat of the joint headquarters of the British forces and the planned Middle East Defence Organisation (MEDO). Despite these moves, Hopkinson commented: 'I do not see any reason to expect any difficulties in Cyprus as a result of this statement.'

The standard justification for the British presence on the island was given to the founder of the *Times of Cyprus*, Charles Foley, by the writer Lawrence Durrell, author of the novel *Bitter Lemons*, which covered his appointment as Director of Public Relations for the Government of Cyprus. Durrell said:

No nation was more devoted to the principle of self-determination than our own but in Cyprus it was simply 'not on'. The long chain of British withdrawals ... must end; the island could not be allowed to pass into the hands of an unstable Greek Government. That might undermine the Eastern bastion of NATO. There was also the Turkish-speaking minority to consider, eighteen per cent of the population, who were against any change. We had a duty to them; besides, Turkey played a vital part in NATO ...[2]

MI6's John Bruce-Lockhart later wrote that 'quick accurate intelligence influenced decisions at governmental level' in Cyprus, and that any British success against the rebellion or 'small war' that followed was largely 'supplied by two-legged spies', though it took a long time to set up an effective intelligence-gathering machine. According to Nigel West, the key during 1953–7 lay 'in the brilliant work done behind the scenes in Athens' by the head of station, Christopher Phillpotts, and his CIA colleague, Al Ulmer. Phillpotts used 'characteristic initiative' in organising a number of 'highly productive operations', while Ulmer and his staff 'bought influence by adding senior members of the Greek administration to the payroll'. MI6 technical sources of information from the Government Communication Headquarters (GCHQ) radar and tracking devices more than compensated for the loss of so many individual agents to the CIA, which could afford to pay more. Phillpotts's control of the technical sources helped ensure that the Royal Navy maintained an effective blockade to prevent the guerrillas on Cyprus from receiving supplies by sea. He was a good choice for this type of operation, having served in the Royal Navy since 1932 and during the war with 9th Motor Torpedo Boat Flotilla before joining MI6 and working with its 'private' navy.[3]

Off the coast of Kholorakas in January 1955, with the help of information from a secret MI6 source, HMS *Comet* intercepted a caique, *Ayios Georgios*, laden with ten thousand sticks of dynamite. One of those detained in connection with the seizure was a Grivas co-conspirator and Athens-based lawyer, Socrates Loizides, who provided the security services with a document 'testifying to the existence of a well-armed and organised secret revolutionary organisation which was plotting the overthrow of the Cyprus government'. The organisation was said to be led by 'Dighenis', which security officials believed did not refer to a specific person but was a name adopted collectively by the underground committee. Rather than alerting the Cyprus administration to potential danger, the discovery of this plot 'seems to have induced premature complacency, and a belief that revolt had been nipped in the bud – when in fact it had not yet begun'. During the spring, the National Organisation of Cypriot Combatants (EOKA) launched a series of bombings across the island. It was not until November 1955 that the local MI5-controlled

Special Branch discovered that the mysterious 'Leader' of EOKA was Col. Grivas.[4]

Confidential appraisals during the autumn by the Cyprus Intelligence Committee showed that intelligence on EOKA was poor. The committee knew nothing of Grivas's communications with Cyprus, Makarios and the nationalist leaders, or with Greece. It did, however, acknowledge that EOKA's terrorist propaganda campaign was principally designed to influence world opinion, and that the use of violence was central to the search for publicity: Grivas's tactic was to force the authorities into overreaction. The committee rejected any notion that EOKA was part of a legitimate resistance movement that sought *Enosis*. Field Marshal Sir John Harding and his hard-line security and military advisers viewed EOKA in terms of a conspiracy rather than an expression of popular discontent.[5]

American opinion and reaction in the United Nations were of paramount importance to Britain and the Colonial Office. Some of the best propagandists were sent to Cyprus to organise a counter-campaign. Director-General of Information was Leslie Glass, who had been head of psychological warfare in the Far East during the war and then of the Information Division of the BMEO before being seconded to the staff of the Governor in 1955. Handling the public relations side was Derek Lyne, a former journalist who had been in the wartime Intelligence Corps in the Middle East and Africa. In London, PR was handled by Derek Chudleigh, a man with a background identical to that of Lyne, having previously worked with the Near East Broadcasting Station (NEABS).

As Charles Foley discovered, no effort was spared by information officers in attempting to win over the foreign press with 'titillating stories'. Operation TEA-PARTY was an authentic black propaganda operation run by the Information Research Department (IRD). A handout given to journalists declared that schoolgirls had been 'required to prostitute themselves with fellow-members of EOKA'. A later pamphlet 'described the sexual relations of such girls with members of the killer groups . . . alleging that one of them had her first lover at the age of twelve'. The IRD became 'a thorn in the flesh' of the Colonial Office, for its insistence on presenting the Cyprus problem in terms of communism. 'Secret intelligence reports' were dangled before American correspondents, who were told that 'captured documents' – which they never actually saw – confirmed that EOKA was in league with the communists. This was a totally distorted view; the Cypriot Communist Party (AKEL) link to EOKA was tenuous at best. EOKA was, in fact, anti-communist and became engaged in a feud with AKEL, which eventually denounced the use of terrorism.[6]

There followed a tough counter-insurgency campaign known as Operation PEPPERPOT, which had some success during the spring of 1956 when Grivas was forced underground in the Troodos Mountains. During the operation, by way of an informer who was paid handsomely, Special Branch came into possession of Grivas's secret diary. A compulsive diarist, Grivas had incriminated in his guerrilla campaign not only Archbishop Makarios but also the archbishop's deputy, 'Bishop Anthimos, and Marshal Papagos, the former Greek Premier, as well as several other senior figures in Cyprus and Greece'. The diaries gave a full account of Grivas's secret landing in Cyprus and his meetings with Makarios. They revealed that 'the Archbishop had controlled EOKA's finances and supplies, and even named the date on which the revolt would begin. They chronicled the campaign from its beginnings to the army searches a few months before, when Grivas had been chased from the mountains. They gave away hiding places, codes and lists of EOKA weapons.'[7]

Based on this information, the British government decided in March to deport Makarios to the Seychelles Islands in the Indian Ocean. At about this time, Grivas had offered to stop all terrorist activity and order a ceasefire to allow progress with negotiations. 'Instead of seizing on this opportunity to bring Makarios back to Cyprus and to pin him down to further talks about a settlement in an atmosphere no longer permeated with terrorism', junior foreign affairs minister Anthony Nutting recalled that Eden 'hailed the Grivas offer as an indication that EOKA were cracking under the strain imposed by British security measures, and responded accordingly. EOKA was offered the alternative of laying down their arms and being deported or facing extermination at the hands of the British forces. This offer was, of course, rejected.' When Britain launched the Suez invasion, Grivas took the opportunity to initiate a new guerrilla campaign with renewed and bitter factional violence. When parachutists who had occupied Port Said returned to Cyprus, a number of the more embittered gave their weapons to EOKA, which also made an effort to persuade French soldiers to assist their campaign.[8]

The Cyprus Emergency was formally declared in November 1956, and over the next few months 'EOKA was to show that, far from being on the run, it could excel in violence anything that had been done since the rebellion began'. The Foreign Office adviser to MI6, Geoffrey McDermott, had no great regard for the man responsible for the security forces, Maj.-Gen. Kendrew. 'A brave man but not a modern-minded commander', Kendrew 'deployed thirty thousand troops without first procuring adequate intelligence on where they should winkle out the insurgents. They presented a beautifully broad and vulnerable backside for the terrorists to pepper.' Information was vital, but despite the large rewards offered the results were meagre, primarily because EOKA was 'ruthless'; 'already fifty informers had been shot'. The security forces simply did not know where to look for the insurgents. Increasingly, intelligence was extracted from interrogations, which degenerated into torture, with prisoners thrashed with a metal chain. Even the *Daily Express*, which published every piece of disinformation the information and IRD officers offered it to counter the international protests, noted in passing that 'every known method had been tried except electric shock'. The security situation improved during the first weeks of 1957 when more than sixty hard-core members of EOKA, which was a small movement, were captured. That did not, however, bring a halt to the violence, which became increasingly fierce.[9]

On 9 October 1957 it was announced that Harding had asked to be relieved of his position as Governor. His place was taken in December by Sir Hugh Foot, a self-proclaimed liberal. Although he was intensively disliked by the hardliners in the security force, in MI5 and MI6, particularly because he 'avoided the hackneyed and purposeless abuse of "terrorists"', the new Governor handled public relations with 'aplomb'. He made his own changes in the information machine, replacing Glass with a wartime special operations officer, Peter Storrs, who had held various senior information posts in Europe and Washington. The *Times of Cyprus* named Foot 'The Man of the Year – a Challenge to the Cynics'.[10]

By 1958 the level of violence in Cyprus had reached a peak. The British response was to reorganise the security apparatus with John Prendergast being brought in from Kenya, where he had been Director of Intelligence and Security, to take over a co-ordinating role in the new post of Chief of Intelligence. At the same time, with the support of Prime Minister Macmillan, the Colonial Minister Julian Amery persuaded George Young and John Bruce-Lockhart that MI6 should join in the fight against EOKA. After a period in Paris, late in 1958, Stephen Hastings was posted as First Secretary at the Political Office of the Middle East Forces, Cyprus, where he discovered an island 'locked in the bitter and, in the end, disastrous struggle with EOKA'. The terrorist movement, Hastings found, 'still simmered audibly, the long habit of murder and violence bubbling just below the surface while the ancient antipathy between Greek and Turk had increased to the point of combustion'.[11]

Hastings was responsible for foreign intelligence, a role that brought some frustration, caused in particular 'by the childish rivalry between our various security services'. He was disheartened to discover that 'in the midst of this cauldron good British intelligence was critically needed and woefully lacking. Because of the Emergency, the Special Branch had been reinforced by MI5, MI6 and, of course, Army Intelligence. An intelligence committee met weekly, and not even the amiable chairmanship of the Deputy Governor, Sir George Sinclair, could disguise the suspicion and mistrust that pervaded it. It was left to Prendergast to "rapidly establish effective control over this diverse and notoriously jealous combination of forces".'[12]

Hugh Foot had been made Governor with the aim of conducting a negotiated settlement and, with that in mind, Makarios had been released from detention in the Seychelles and allowed to return to Athens in readiness for diplomatic moves. MI5 – principally the Director of E Branch (Colonial Affairs), Bill Magan, a veteran of the North-West Frontier and Persia – and MI6 believed that if political negotiations were to stand a chance then 'Grivas needed to be located, isolated and *neutralised*'. Unfortunately, although the army 'launched massive searches, they failed to find him'. As the situation deteriorated, Foot agreed to call in the security services to track him down.[13]

Magan consulted the Service's technical officer, Peter Wright, who believed that with the help of the Defence Liaison officer, Col. Philip Kirby-Green, Grivas could be located by tracing his communications. A former Special Branch officer and member of Security Intelligence Middle East (SIME) during the war, 'KG' was also a painter who happened to exhibit his paintings in his overseas postings, including Cyprus. Wright, who arrived in Cyprus in January 1959, later commented that 'it would be too crude to say that SUNSHINE was an assassination operation . . . but it amounted to the same thing'. He was joined by John Wyke, MI6's best technical operator, to help place the taps on Makarios's telephones. The operation had two objectives: firstly to locate the radio receivers, which they were sure Grivas must use, and then to plant on EOKA a radio receiver containing a radio beacon. This was put inside a consignment of receivers that was purchased in Egypt from a Greek Cypriot arms dealer, who had been recruited by MI6.[14]

'Things started to happen,' Hastings recalled. Grivas had eluded the British for years, moving among his hideouts in the Troodos Mountains. 'Now because of the machinations of his ally Makarios he moved into Nicosia.' It had been estimated that it would take six months to complete Sunshine. 'Our security forces had learned much during the years of EOKA terrorism.' Very soon Prendergast 'had him nailed. His safe house was under constant surveillance.' Hastings was convinced that 'if he had been done away with or at least arrested and tried much subsequent trouble might have been avoided'. In particular, the 'subsequent negotiations for the island's future would have been a deal easier'. However, before Sunshine could be fully executed it was scrapped because, against all the odds, the politicians began to make progress. Geoffrey McDermott arrived in Cyprus shortly before Christmas 1958, as the Foreign Office representative at Episkopi, where he found the atmosphere 'electric'. Foot had exercised his prerogative of mercy in favour of two EOKA terrorists convicted of murder. 'This led to an early end of terrorism, as the terrorists were on the run anyway.'[15]

This unexpected turn of events appalled those involved in Sunshine. Hastings was not keen on Hugh Foot, and found him to be miscast as a colonial governor: '[His] act was excellent. But his true reactions seemed to me conditioned more by the radical left-wing thinking of his family than ever they were by a dispassionate assessment of his country's interests. To rise effectively to the top in what was the colonial service one surely had to believe, at least to some extent, in the mission which gave rise to it, not simply in the need to dismantle it.' While admitting that Foot's 'talent as conciliator was certainly invaluable at this juncture', Hastings believed that it was only with the arrival of fellow-imperialist Julian Amery that 'the business of the island's disposal began to reflect British interest'.[16]

Christopher Phillpotts had been brought in for quiet, undercover diplomacy, conveying to the Greeks a straightforward message that 'if they pressed for Enosis, it would mean war with Turkey and the possible breakdown of NATO'. It was only when the advisers to the Greek Prime Minister, Constantine Karamanlis, were shown convincing evidence of Turkish determination and military superiority that a solution appeared possible. Secret negotiations began between Greek and Turkish foreign ministers in late 1958 and continued into February of the following year at a Lancaster House constitutional conference. At the same time, Macmillan made Amery responsible for conducting talks with Makarios's chief aide, Glafkos Clerides.[17]

Hastings thought Amery had the measure of the Greek Cypriot leader, who in 'true Byzantine tradition . . . was ruthless, trusted no one, not even his closest collaborators and manipulated his opponents with a beatific charm'. The minister's constant informant and adviser was John Prendergast, whose 'effective penetration of Makarios' inner conclave was masterly'. As part of Operation Sunshine, Hastings had been running an agent from inside Makarios's immediate entourage. MI6 'knew practically everything he said to his aides and advisors, yet never throughout the interminable negotiation for the sovereign bases did we learn with any certainty what Makarios' next move would be'. Peter Wright was also involved in bugging and wiretapping the delegation.[18]

When Makarios threatened violence unless his conditions were met, Amery told him that British troops would be withdrawn and then the Turks would 'cut Greek throats'. Makarios backed down. When Makarios tried to gamble on the British losing patience and withdrew from the talks, Amery kept his nerve, despite Foot wanting to send a telegram to London 'making his view clear that Julian should give in and grant Makarios' current conditions'. Then, when the two sides thought that an agreement had been reached, Makarios intervened at the signing ceremony in London, and withheld his signature. Overnight, however, he changed his mind. The reason for the reversal was the blackmail material MI6 had accumulated during Operation Sunshine on the archbishop's 'rather unusual homosexual proclivities'.[19]

On 10 February 1959 the Greek and Turkish premiers met in Zurich and announced an agreement on Cyprus. The island gained independence with a guaranteed role for the Turkish minority in the political framework, but no *Enosis*. The Greek Makarios was elected President in December 1959 and Dr Fazil Kutchuk, the Turkish Cypriot leader, was appointed Vice-President. The agreement achieved a temporary end to the bloodshed. Much to the relief of the chiefs of staff, in his successful negotiation of an independence agreement, 'by a combination of patience, determination and above all good intelligence, Amery achieved a military base at Episkopi'. This certainly pleased Hastings: 'The sovereign base at Episkopi played a vitally important part not only in the defence of the British interest but also that of the West ever since.'[20]

Despite Amery's skill, the 'hurried agreement' did not go down well with the 'hawks'. MI5's Magan had 'a strained meeting' with Foot. He was 'furious, particularly when Grivas emerged from the precise area we had foreseen and was flown to Greece, ready to continue to exert a baleful influence on the island'. Hastings, too, blamed Foot for granting an amnesty to EOKA supporters and allowing 'this murderous character' to be 'flown to a hero's welcome in Athens'. For all his ability in gathering intelligence that proved vital to the success of the negotiations, Hastings was removed from his post by the Commonwealth Relations Office which invoked the 'Attlee Doctrine', on the basis that 'gentlemen do not spy on one another'. An MI5 officer was substituted to work with the Cyprus government, which meant providing 'tittle-tattle of very little use to the British representatives in the performance of his diplomatic duties'.[21]

Britain's interest in Cyprus had been officially defined as being purely strategic – treating the island as a solid base from which to defend its interests in the Middle East. In reality, as the 1958 Cabinet minutes reveal, privately it was admitted that the island was not strategically vital. The British, however, were not willing to lose face and for reasons of 'prestige' would not quit. During the rebellion, forty thousand British troops were held down by a few hundred Grivas guerrillas. Nearly four hundred deaths on all sides was a heavy price to pay for 'prestige'.[22]

CHAPTER 28

IRAN: 'UNEQUAL DREAMS'

In July 1949, representatives of the Anglo-Iranian Oil Company (AIOC) and the Iranian* government signed a prepared document known as the 'Supplementary Oil Agreement' which affirmed and augmented the oil concession of 1933. British Foreign Office officials hoped that this agreement would legitimise the oil industry in the minds of the Iranian people and provide the revenues necessary for the economic and social development of the country. Without the revenues, members of the Eastern Department of the Foreign Office felt, the country would slide into communist revolution.

No agreement was likely to be ratified, however, while the political climate in Iran remained unstable. The attempted assassination of the Shah the previous February had ushered in an era in which 'the cult of bullets and knives had entered Iranian politics with a vengeance'. What followed was a period of economic depression and ideological ferment of which the British despaired, and which the Iranian government proved incapable of breaking. The vicious circle offered little hope of social progress.

Popular discontent fed calls by supporters of the leading nationalist politician, Dr Mohammed Mossadeq, for the nationalisation of the AIOC, but

---

* I refer to Iran throughout, though the British were still calling the country Persia.

this potential immediate solution to Iran's problems had less to do with the economy than with the emotional pull of nationalism. At another time, and in another country, Mossadeq might well have found favour with the British; they had in the past and would in the future 'do business with' many other popular nationalists. Indeed, Mossadeq – regarded as honest and genuinely concerned for social issues – had been promoted as a bulwark against communism, but his theatrical behaviour – incomprehensible oratory and hysterical outbursts – did not endear him either to the oil company or to Foreign Office officials. In contrast, American journalist Kenneth Love found him to be 'vigorous, mentally alert, charming, witty, a very intelligent man'.[1]

As the nationalisation campaign and, specifically, anti-British feeling grew, without strong leadership the chances of the Iranian Parliament, the Majlis, ratifying the Supplementary Oil Agreement became remote. Hitherto, the Shah had appointed weak prime ministers who posed little threat to his exercise of power. It was somewhat surprising, then, that he promoted General Hadj Ali Razmara to the post in June 1950. A career soldier, small but physically powerful, Razmara had the reputation of being unscrupulous and cruel. He was also immensely ambitious. British hopes rose with his appointment in the belief that he offered a genuine possibility of political stability under which the nationalisation crisis might be allowed to subside. The British ambassador in Tehran, Sir Francis Shephard, believed in the general 'on the old yet rarely helpful precept that soldiers carry out orders'. The MI6 head of station, Ian Milne, who ran numerous agents in the Majlis, was not so sure.[2]

Razmara had originally received the backing of the American embassy in Tehran, but the State Department in Washington became progressively less enthusiastic about his actions, and he gradually turned his attentions to the British, with whom he developed warm relations. Razmara, though, was no British stooge. He was well aware that any suspicion of British meddling and influence could spell political suicide. A paradoxical situation soon developed, however, in the guise of the AIOC advancing money to the Iranian government to help solve its economic troubles. 'But the Government, afraid to be called a paid tool of the British, insisted that the payments be kept secret. Mossadeq continued to denounce the company for withholding money and no one was allowed to say publicly that it was not doing so.'[3]

The AIOC's position was hindered by the knowledge that the Americans had negotiated a deal with Saudi Arabia – the so-called '50–50 agreement' – which overnight transformed oil politics in the Middle East. The company learned of the deal during the autumn of 1950 and, accordingly, tried to make amendments to their Supplementary Oil Agreement in order to satisfy Iranian demands. In 1950 alone, AIOC made a £170 million profit, a sizable chunk of which went to the British government in taxes, but the Iranian government received only 10 to 12 per cent of the *net* proceeds. The AIOC's offer was too little, too late. Razmara, as Milne expected, had 'little choice but to withdraw the bill to sanction the oil agreement'.

On 19 February 1951, Mossadeq presented to a special Majlis oil committee a formal resolution for the nationalisation of the Iranian oil industry. Razmara responded by attempting to set up a new oil committee, with a tightly drawn membership, which would consider the nationalisation question. On 3 March, Razmara ordered a paper to be read in the Majlis which explained the technical, financial and legal implications involved in such a move. Tehran Radio broadcast the full text, which was then reprinted in the daily newspapers. This effectively served to cool the public's demand for nationalisation; the problem remained, though, that 'the technical arguments and the style of the declaration although written in Persian led to a belief that it had been prepared by the AIOC'. Conscious of this, Mossadeq used the opportunity to press the case for nationalisation.[4]

Unfortunately for the British, who had begun to believe that opinion was moving their way, on 7 March Razmara was assassinated. According to a former Special Operations Executive (SOE) and MI6 officer resident in Tehran, Norman Darbyshire, Razmara 'had in his pocket at the time, the first 50–50 agreement and he was waiting to choose his moment to present it. That would have changed our whole dealings in the Middle East.' Eight days later, the Majlis passed a bill with just one article which nationalised the AIOC. Shortly after, Mossadeq became Prime Minister, and the Shah finally approved the bill on 2 May. Mossadeq now became the idol of those large sections of the Iranian populace that admired his resolute determination to rid the country of what was regarded as corrupting foreign influence.

With both parties unwilling to compromise, a clash between Mossadeq and the British was inevitable. Mossadeq enthused his supporters with dreams of an Iran free of foreign influence, but he soon became a prisoner of the crowd – the primary factor in Iranian politics – and each success only brought forth new demands. In turn, the AIOC operated as if it were still in the nineteenth century, regarding Iranians as 'merely wogs'. For the British government, with economic collapse at home always a possibility, the oil revenues from taxes on the AIOC were desperately sought, and it was unwilling to see them given away to the Iranians. From now on, intrigue and 'the assassin's gun were to be used more often than the ballot box'. Mossadeq's dream would not be allowed to live; instead, 'dangerous men' would intervene to settle the country's future.[5]

The origins of the August 1953 coup can be partially traced back to an anonymous article that appeared in The Times on 22 March 1951. It called attention to the inner conflict of Iranian society which had come to a head in the oil controversy.

According to the article, 'For many years Persian society had been in a state of disequilibrium.' Iranian instability could partly be attributed to great power rivalry, but more fundamentally the disequilibrium originated with 'the stupidity, greed and lack of judgement of the ruling classes of Persia'. Nepotism was rife. The government was parasitic. The huge civil service was underpaid and corrupt. The uneven distribution of wealth was concentrated in the hands of the landowning class: merchants, the upper section of the bureaucracy, and high ranks of the army. Those who wished to reform Iranian society 'were faced with a choice between revolutionary catastrophe or a Royal enlightened despotism'. The article explained that the tension between the rich and the corrupt and other segments of the Iranian population had been sublimated into the drive against external domination. The AIOC had become the scapegoat. *The Times* article received wide circulation within the Foreign Office as an 'excellent' analysis of the 'internal' issues behind the oil demands.[6]

The anonymous author was Professor Ann Katherine Swynford Lambton. Reader in Persian at the School of Oriental and African Studies, she had spent long periods of time in Iran and knew 'the language [Farsi] and mentality of its people better than anyone else in the country'. During the war she had been press attaché at the British embassy – often a cover post for MI6 – 'in the dual capacity of intelligence and public relations in Tehran and Isfahan'.[7]

When the Iranians nationalised the oil industry and took physical control of the oil installations, expelling AIOC officials, the clash between the British and Americans over their differing policies towards the Middle East came to the fore. In 1951, 'after ten years of Anglo-American partnership, the wind that was blowing from Washington was felt as chilling. Disappointment, even surprise, could still be aroused in London when even the "special relationship" came under strain.'[8]

In May, Foreign Secretary Herbert Morrison, Defence Secretary Emmanuel Shinwell and the Foreign Office's Russia Committee concluded that intervention by British troops to protect the installations and the massive new refinery at Abadan was a realistic option, and that this would not increase the risk of war with the Soviet Union. A small planning team was subsequently sent to Fayid to join an already impressive array of committees, including Joint Intelligence Committee (JIC) members, to co-ordinate the proposed action. Operating under cover as consul at Meshed, Norman Darbyshire suborned the commander-in-chief of the Iranian forces at Khorramshahr and told him that he did not want to see any bloodshed. Surprisingly, the commander agreed to offer 'no more than token resistance' and stand back. At the same time, HMS *Urius* stationed off Abadan was busy reading Iranian Army signals traffic which was then cracked by the Government Communications Headquarters (GCHQ).[9]

As it turned out, the British had badly miscalculated. From 10 May onwards, repeated diplomatic communications made painfully clear the opposition of the United States to any British use of force. The chill wind continued, and culminated in a personal message on 31 May from President Truman to the Prime Minister urging him to negotiate with the Iranian government. When Attlee informed Truman of the military contingency plan, under American pressure the Cabinet was forced to back down and shelve Operation BUCCANEER.[10]

MI6 officers were angry at the lack of resolve by the Labour government and its failure to stand up to the Americans. For George Young it was a time 'of the tragic decline of Bevin and Cripps and the shrinkage of Attlee into a sphinx without a riddle'. He found it a depressing experience 'to work among lost men who can only say: "We can't have this", "Proceed with caution" (at which point all civil servants put the file in their pending tray), or just plain "No".' Young thought that the Abadan crisis 'presented the classic instance of what can happen when men do not know their own minds. There were a number of possible solutions, some conciliatory and some "tough", which might have worked; but in the last crucial days there was nobody at the helm. This could be justified as realism or empiricism.'[11]

In June, in the light of the American rebuff, Professor Lambton met with Eric Berthoud, an assistant under-secretary who supervised economic affairs in the Foreign Office who had previously spent eight years with the AIOC, to discuss the crisis in Iran. According to his minute of the meeting: 'Miss Lambton was of the decided opinion that it was not possible to do business with Mossadeq. She thought it important not to make concessions to him except to the extent necessary to maintain order in Southern Iran' – where the oilfields were situated. Miss Lambton believed that it would be possible to undermine Mossadeq's position by 'covert means'. One way in which this could be undertaken, she suggested, would be to give heart to the substantial body of Iranians who feared the risk of being denounced as traitors but whose idea of Iranian national interest coincided with the British conception. She thought that it might be possible through a 'PR officer' at the British embassy in Tehran to gradually change the public mood and thus give an opportunity to intelligent Iranians who were well disposed to the British to speak out against Mossadeq. According to Berthoud's minute, 'Miss Lambton feels that without a campaign on the above lines it is not possible to create the sort of climate in Tehran which is necessary to change the regime.'[12]

The Foreign Office accepted the strategy as outlined by Professor Lambton: Mossadeq was to be opposed; compromise was out. She also made one specific proposal that was of significance. According to Berthoud, she suggested that Robin Zaehner, lecturer in Persian (later Professor of Eastern Religions) at Oxford, would be 'the ideal man' to conduct the undercover pro-British campaign. Zaehner had worked in Tehran during 1943–7 as assistant press attaché, alongside Lambton and the press counsellor, MI6's Lt-Col. Geoffrey Wheeler. Berthoud added that 'Dr Z, was apparently extremely successful in covert propaganda in 1944 at the time that there was a serious threat that the Russians would take over Azerbaijan. He knows almost everyone who matters in Tehran and is a man of great subtlety. The line then was, of course, to mobilise public opinion from the Bazaar upwards, about the dangers of Russian penetration.'[13]

With his 'pebble glasses, squeaky voice and "mad professor" eccentricities', Zaehner, a scholar and a linguist, was an unlikely intelligence operative. He had been involved in the Albanian operation of 1949–51 as an interpreter, and in early summer took on the post of acting counsellor in Tehran, reporting not to MI6 but to Foreign Secretary Morrison.[14]

'Doc' Zaehner was already busy at work 'cultivating afresh' the excellent contacts he had acquired while in Tehran during the war. These included Ernest Perron, the most important influence on the Shah. Unlike most of his school friendships, the Shah's relationship with Perron continued into adult life. The Shah had his friend come to Iran, where Perron remained his confidant up to the day he returned to Switzerland to die in 1961. As his personal secretary, Perron visited the Shah each morning for a discussion. The Shah's wife, Empress Soraya, considered that, although he posed as a 'poet and philosopher', he was as 'slippery as an eel' and played a 'sinister role in the Shah's court'. MI6 officer Norman Darbyshire, who knew the Shah on a social basis – both were then young men – was also in touch with Perron, 'that terrible man'.[15]

Perron was open about his homosexual proclivities, including his continuing relationship with the commercial attaché at the Swiss embassy in Tehran. A freemason belonging to the high-level Pahlavi lodge, which included ministers, officials and military figures, Perron was also close to a number of the high-ranking families in Iran about whom he used to gather information which he then passed on to Zaehner. According to General Hossein Fardust, the Shah's closest personal friend, who had also been a classmate in Switzerland, Perron was privy to secrets about the Shah, including his affair with a woman called Divsaller which appears to have been monitored by MI6.[16]

Another of Zaehner's contacts was (Sir) Shapour Reporter, a young Zoroastrian Parsee from Bombay who held dual Iranian and British citizenship. A school-friend of the Shah, from 1948 Reporter served as counsellor to Seyyed Ali Zaheer, India's first ambassador to Iran. Although useful as a source, Reporter did not, as has been suggested, play a role in any operations. Undoubtedly the most important contacts and the 'keystone' of MI6 plans were the Rashidian brothers – Seyfollah, the eldest, Qodratollah, a cinema-owner, banker and merchant, and the 'political' Asadollah, who was a close friend of the Shah and acted as go-between. One of Asadollah's allies was the Mayor of Tehran, Fatouah Foroud.[17]

The Rashidians, who had been brought up by their father to believe that the British were 'very good', had helped Zaehner during the war with Majlis support for Britain. Anglophiles, they were regular visitors to London, where they had commercial concessions with British firms operating in Iran. They sent their children to English private schools and kept a family suite at the Grosvenor Hotel, managed at the time by a former SOE officer. Strongly anticommunist, they invested their own money in buying votes in the Majlis, a standard practice in Iranian politics. They also received the considerable sum of £10,000 a month from the British. Norman Darbyshire, who had lived in the same house as Zaehner during 1943–7, when he also acted as paymaster, 'used to carry biscuit tins with damn great notes', which he handed over to Zaehner. According to Darbyshire, the Rashidians received 'well over £1.5 million'.[18]

The Rashidians, with an increasing number of anti-Mossadeq allies among the bazaar merchants, were widely known to be British agents and attracted more supporters, who were supplied with British funds. 'The money was going via the Rashidian brothers to people to keep them sweet and see what they could do.' They backed former Prime Minister Sayyed Zia Ad-Din, whom the British had persuaded the Shah to allow to return from exile in 1943 and who, with covert and financial encouragement from Zaehner, had formed a new party, the National Will. With the support of the ulema, merchants, landlords and major tribes, it became the focus of right-wing politicians and opposition to the Tudeh Party, which had been founded the year before by a small group of socialists and an active branch of professional communists. Clandestine agents of the National Will had proved useful in destroying the regional headquarters of the Tudeh in several southern cities. Sayyed's supporters were a key conservative influence in the Majlis and the Rashidians encouraged them at the behest of Zaehner, during 1951–3, to oppose oil nationalisation. Sayyed also proved useful in that he was able to see the Shah two or three times a week to discuss contemporary political events.[19]

Zaehner reported to the Foreign Office's Eastern Department. It was here, under its head Geoffrey Furlong, that much of the anti-Mossadeq policy was formulated. During the summer of 1951, the department organised propaganda efforts by the BBC, which 'doubled and trebled' its Iranian transmissions. The propaganda attempted 'to whitewash Britain's record' in Iran by 'plugging the work of the British scholars in the Persian language, and particularly of Professor E. G. Browne of Cambridge'.[20]

The AIOC had its own intelligence network run by its Central Information Bureau (CIB), which had been opened in Tehran following the severe shock of the general strike in the oil-producing areas in July 1946. Using the British embassy's daily news bulletin, which was circulated in Farsi to the whole of the Iranian press, as well as certain British-backed newspapers, the CIB poured out a stream of propaganda material. This was not seen to be very effective but, later, the CIB's brief was extended to more covert activities such as intelligence-gathering, bribing officials and political intrigue. The company often acted as 'a law unto itself', and it would appear that the British embassy had little control or knowledge of its activities. The bribery included paying a portion of the royalties due to the government directly to

the leaders of the tribes, the most important being the Baktitiar, which dominated the area of the country where most of the oilfields were situated. One
leading British agent was Timour Bakhtiar, a relative of Empress Soraya, and
son of a leading figure of the Bakhtiari tribes. When Mossadeq nationalised
the AIOC, the recipients of company largesse had to go without, which went
very much against the grain of Iranian politics. So 'when emissaries of the
company began to hint that a way of removing Mossadeq and [the virulently
anti-British religious leader] Ayatollah Kashani and all their works might be
found, they were ready to listen'. These emissaries included a well-known
orientalist and director of the CIB, Dr Lawrence Lockard, and Richard
Seddon, the AIOC's executive in Tehran.[21]

On 1 July 1951, Mossadeq's security police searched Seddon's house and
impounded his files. The Iranian government subsequently alleged that the
files, some of which were distributed to the press and publicly displayed at
a United Nations meeting, proved that the AIOC had engaged in illegal
activities, including the corruption of members of the Majlis. It was claimed
that Seddon had kept 'a list, scrupulously up-to-date, of gifts made by AIOC
to a number of deputies, ministers and other politicians'. More interestingly,
not only was the CIB supporting pro-British representatives, it was also
'aiding the Tudeh press to render their opposition more effective'. Also
covertly supported was the Peace Club, 'a Tudeh front organisation which
was largely led by members of the conservative establishment'. While this
may seem bizarre, there was a certain logic to it. The Tudeh opposed Mossadeq's oil nationalisation policy on the basis that it was 'an American
conspiracy' intended to replace the British presence with US companies. To
the Soviet-backed Tudeh, 'this was a far greater sin than complicity with
Britain'. Whether or not MI6 knew about this covert support of the communists and whether its officers were actually involved is not known.[22]

The State Prosecutor issued an indictment charging Seddon with 'illegal
activities', including the destruction of documents wanted by the government.
In a curious episode, Seddon's resident's permit was at first revoked and
then, for some reason, returned.[23]

The Zaehner mission also kept in touch with Professor Lambton. Eric
Berthoud reported that 'our unofficial efforts to undermine Dr Mossadeq
are making good progress', though in reality Zaehner had run into some
unexpected problems, one such being American covert support for Mossadeq
and the Ayatollah Kashani. Professor Lambton noted that 'Kashani has
received large sums of money from somewhere. There is no evidence that it
comes from the Russians. It is not impossible that there is an American source,
not of course State Department, but perhaps the US brand of SOE who may
have for some time been supporting Dr Mossadeq and Mr Kashani as their
answer to communism.'[24]

*   *   *

The American Central Intelligence Group (CIG) had set up a station in Tehran in 1947 to take on covert operations previously carried out by the military attachés. During the next year, a large covert action programme known as (BE)DAMN had been initiated, designed to weaken Tudeh influence in Iran. Damn appears to have become a 'rogue elephant' CIA operation without official clearance. A propaganda and political action programme run through a network headed by two Iranians code-named 'Nerren' and 'Ciley', it cost the agency one million dollars annually and relied on the extensive use of disinformation. Mossadeq was portrayed as corrupt and, in one instance, as a Jew. Religious leaders were encouraged with funding to adopt a more fundamentalist line and break with Mossadeq, while mobs and *agents provocateurs* were financed to disrupt Tudeh rallies.[25]

The American plan for Iran effectively began in 1948 when Overseas Consultants, an association of US oil men represented by Allen Dulles, devised 'a comprehensive development programme', which intended to bring Iran into the modern world through 'the formation of a government petroleum company to develop the oil resources in areas outside the Anglo-Iranian Oil Company concession'. For assistance, Overseas Consultants turned to the newly created Office of Policy Co-ordination (OPC), whose leading agent, Kermit Roosevelt, was 'called upon to make things right in Iran'.[26]

The grandson of the 'rough rider' President, Theodore Roosevelt, Kermit was dubbed 'the Quiet American' by Kim Philby. He had directed OSS intelligence in the Arab world during the war and was left by Frank Wisner and Dulles to run things in his own way. During 1948, Roosevelt travelled throughout the Middle East, stopping off to renew his acquaintance with the Shah, from whom he learned of Russian efforts 'to create, by spreading chaos and violence, a power vacuum which only the Soviet Union could fill'. Although pro-British, Kermit was critical of Britain's oil dealings with Iran.[27]

Roosevelt thought that there were two different types of relationship between the West and the Middle East. The first was 'imperialist' in which the West, particularly Britain and Russia, 'sought political domination and economic exploitation'. The British had been party to 'some shoddy cynical intrigues' and had 'used their position to support ... the most corrupt groups'. The politicians whom the British controlled were 'a sorry, shaky lot, hardly worth owning'. The other relationship was based 'on common interests' and involved 'business undertakings in which the motivation is reasonable profit for both parties'. Roosevelt believed that 'the United States, alone among the major powers, has entered the Middle East only in this second relationship'. He concluded that the British had been 'doing all in their power to knife their American opposite numbers and make Anglo-American collaboration in the area a strictly one-way proposition'.[28]

Having received a briefing on the Overseas Consultants project from the head of the Iranian National Bank, Roosevelt concluded that for the country to withstand the communist challenge it would require 'drastic social reforms'. Interestingly, he 'could see no group in Iran which combined the incentive, the strength, the programme and the persistence to make a successful revolution – without foreign support'. He commented that 'Soviet observers may well have reached the same conclusion'. In opposing the communists, Roosevelt was willing to co-operate with the British and make use of their expertise on Iran but 'without having to accept it on blind faith'. He had already made contact with the leaders of the Qashqai tribe, the brothers Mohammed and Malik Khan, who placed 'their hopes on America'.[29]

Like most American officials, Roosevelt believed that 'anti-British and nationalist feeling is basic to Iran', and that these feelings were understandable. Naturally, the British disagreed. Embassy official George Middleton minuted that 'the American view is that Persian nationalism is a potent and spontaneous force which will be an overriding force on its own account regardless of the wishes and actions of any future government. Our view is that Iranian nationalism certainly exists but that its effectiveness as a political force is largely a matter of manipulation.' Nationalism, the British argued, would inevitably lead to communism. The Americans believed, wrongly in the British view, that Mossadeq was a bulwark against communism. In contrast, MI6 regarded him as a weak character who would eventually be pushed out by the highly trained Tudeh Party. They argued that the necessity was 'to get rid of Mossadeq to solve the problem'.[30]

While they could be persuaded about the communist threat, the Americans did not believe that the solution was quite so simple. According to academic Sallie Pisani, they recognised that the situation in Iran was deteriorating, but were concerned that their modernisation plans were not being implemented because of 'the crisis between the Shah and Mossadeq'. In American eyes, this crisis was 'aided and abetted by British truculence' and was responsible for delivering 'a knock-out punch to the modernisation scheme'. The Americans judged that the British were 'clearly slipping from ally to albatross status in the Middle East', and 'not only would Mossadeq have to go but so would the British'.[31]

Mossadeq received encouragement from the efforts of the American oil companies which, the British noted, 'seemed to be circling like vultures over Iran'. They were right to be concerned because the Americans, for all their anti-imperialist rhetoric, were far more practical and cynical than their British counterparts. Overseas Consultants' Max Thornberg advised the Iranian government to 'hold out for greatly increased royalties, although he informed the AIOC that he was exerting a moderating influence'. The US stance on imperialism, which had become fully developed during the war, masked a simple strategy to replace Britain as the leading economic force in the Middle East. Their bribes were bigger and their grasp of political realities sharper.[32]

Successful oilman and Assistant Secretary of State for the Near East George McGhee stated quite boldly: 'If it were not for the Cold War there is no reason why we shouldn't let the British and the Iranians fight it out' – no doubt with a view to opening up the area for American oil companies to step in. But the Americans could not quite leave them to fight it out because they learned, with some disquiet, that the British 'Stokes Mission' to Iran during July 1951 was suggesting that the AIOC could go beyond the sacred 50–50 Saudi arrangement.[33]

Lord Privy Seal Richard Stokes was a wealthy businessman – a millionaire – whose family firm had extensive connections in the Middle East. He had his own eclectic brand of socialism that, 'in effect, amounted to a personal creed', and had ties to British Intelligence. In Tehran, Stokes was accompanied by MI6's Col. Geoffrey Wheeler, then counsellor at the embassy, who left when Woodhouse's mission took over. Stokes thought that since Iranian crude was so cheap to produce, the company could breach the 50–50 arrangement without fear for its profits. Stoke's mission broke off relations with Mossadeq in August 1951 at a time when an agreement seemed close. Mossadeq's intransigence, based on Thornberg's advice and on the hope of American support (the Americans made it known that they had earlier turned down the British request for direct action), sank any possibility of a deal. In any case, the Foreign Office slapped Stokes down. The negotiations that had taken place during the summer turned out to have been a sham. There was to be no agreement with Mossadeq: he was to be removed.[34]

As the new MI6 head of station, the Hon. Christopher Montague Woodhouse, recognised: 'It was an anomaly that the idea of organising the downfall of Mossadeq was first formulated by the Foreign Office itself rather than entrusted to its so-called "friends".' MI6 had plans for its own separate mission.[35]

Woodhouse was another recruit from SOE into the Service's War Planning Directorate and Special Operations Branch. He had worked extensively in Greece during and immediately after the war, and was regarded as 'the shining but rare example of someone who had a sophisticated under-standing of the political requirements of his mission'. Woodhouse had been involved in setting up stay-behind missions in the Middle East, but had also been thinking long and hard about Iran. 'Since the communists' efforts had so far been directed at expansion in Europe and the Far East, it was not hard to guess that the next probe would be in the Middle East where they had scarcely yet scratched the periphery. The weakest spot seemed to be Iran.'[36]

In 1951, George Kennedy Young was unexpectedly promoted by the Chief to take charge of the Middle East desk. 'Menzies had seen that the era of British ascendancy, with its garrisons at key points and police and security agencies largely run by British or British-trained officers, was over.' Young had a foretaste of the change when the car in which he was being driven from Cairo airport to the Canal Zone by fellow MI6 officer Lt-Col. Brian Montgomery was stoned by mobs. On his travels in the area, Young found that 'a general complacency characterised much of the intelligence effort'.[37]

Young was an obvious choice because of his renowned abilities as an intelligence officer, but his personal views on the Middle East mind, particularly that of the Arab, left much to be desired. He was certainly no liberal and, under the influence of his Dutch wife, his views were to become more and more extreme, indeed racist, though he denied that term. He discovered 'patterns of minds so different that I would have to abandon completely the verbal descriptions we use automatically in European discourse'. He believed that the Arabs suffered from that 'perpetual neurosis . . . which makes words like "truth", "falsehood", "sincerity" and "treachery" such inadequate descriptions when our ambassadors report on their dealings with Middle-Eastern rulers'. He wrote that men in the Arab lands had not evolved 'from a tool-making animal' into one conveying meaning 'by conceptualised systems of symbols', and thought that no matter 'whatever wealth or material welfare they may acquire, either by their own acute intelligence or by the fruits of Western development and commerce, a point will always come when the discrepancy between their dreams and the reality becomes too great to bear, and there will be a desperate effort to find relief in a new focus of hate'. Young later told his officers that the Arab's chief characteristic 'is a simple joy in destruction which has to be experienced to be believed . . . There is no gladder sound to the Arab ear than the crunch of glass, and his favourite spectacle is that of human suffering . . . While the European has been building, the Arab has looted and torn down.'[38]

The immediate problem facing the new Middle East Director and his staff officer, John Stephen Longrigg, was Mossadeq. Young sent to Tehran Monty Woodhouse, who 'spent a few weeks in other parts of the Middle East, Egypt, Cyprus, Lebanon and Turkey – to acclimatise myself afresh'. Woodhouse arrived in mid-August at the British embassy in Tehran, a gigantic compound covering sixteen city blocks of landscaped gardens which was separated from the Russian embassy by one street.

> My own assets when I took up a nominal post in our embassy were considerable, but demoralised by the setbacks of the past year. Three or four young men in the embassy specialised in intelligence on Iran and the Communists. Another cultivated leading Iranians who were hostile to Mossadeq. Another conducted a useful liaison, approved by the Shah, with the Chief of the Security Police, who was well informed about the Tudeh Party.[39]

The assets, who became known as 'Monty's Army', included: the aforementioned Norman Darbyshire, the Third Secretary who was a fluent Farsi speaker; John Briance, who had come to MI6 from the Colonial Police in Palestine, where he had been a senior officer, and had been posted to Tehran the year before; Christopher Woods, formerly in SOE; Alexis Fforter, a former RAF officer of White Russian extraction, who was appointed Third Secretary in Tehran in 1951 and opened a substation at Basra; possibly the market officer, Major R. Jackson, MBE, who was later denounced by Mossadeq as an MI6 officer, though the Foreign Office issued a denial. There were also two Foreign Office diplomats who proved useful – the assistant secretary, John Fearnley, who spoke Farsi, and Sam Falle, a junior official in the embassy, whose job was to keep in touch with the younger political elements in Iran. And 'the most striking figure of all', Dr Robin Zaehner.[40]

At the beginning of October 1951, AOIC staff left Iran. On the 26th, the Labour government fell and Churchill became Prime Minister once again. For MI6 officers such as Young, it meant that 'the pall of negation was lifted'. He added that it was, however, 'only momentarily' raised.[41]

Churchill berated his predecessors, 'who had scuttled and run from Abadan when a splutter of musketry would have ended the matter'. Returning to London, Col. Wheeler explained that 'combined Anglo-American action could, of course, have removed Mossadeq at any time during the past six months ... Given a united Anglo-American front, a change of government could almost certainly be effected without difficulty or disturbance.' Foreign Secretary Anthony Eden agreed. He observed that 'without United States' encouragement he doubted whether Mossadeq would have survived so long'. Eden did not agree with the Americans that Mossadeq was a nationalist they could work with or the belief that the only alternative was 'communism, and to save Persia from communism they are ready to sacrifice the interests of the Anglo-Iranian Oil Company and those of Her Majesty's Government'. Eden 'thought that if Mossadeq fell his place might well be taken by a more reasonable government with which it would be possible to conclude a satisfactory agreement'.[42]

The new Foreign Secretary supported the 'unofficial efforts' to undermine Mossadeq, which Foreign Office official Berthoud reported were 'making good progress'. In November, Professor Lambton wrote to Berthoud: 'If only we keep steady Dr Mossadeq will fall. There may be a period of chaos, but ultimately a government with which we can deal will come back.' Eden took note of Miss Lambton's assessment: 'I agree with Miss Lambton. She has a remarkable first-hand knowledge of Persians and their mentality.' Eden sanctioned these unoffical efforts without consulting the relevant permanent under-secretaries in the Foreign Office, such as Sir William Strang. He did, though, have the support of officials such as (Sir) Donald Logan, who had served in the British embassy in Tehran during 1947–51, and was now head of the Oil Department. 'Our policy was to get rid of Mossadeq as soon as possible. We didn't think he would do any good to Iran. The two years he was there were too long for our thinking. He did nothing for Iran.'[43]

Zaehner's brief continued to be to secure the overthrow of Mossadeq by legal or quasi-legal means. Money was to be provided by MI6, but Ambassador Shephard was not to be informed. Coups d'état were not yet on the agenda, but Eden was becoming a sick man and it would take Churchill to respond with a 'whiff of grapeshot'.

The Foreign Office, however, had become embarrassed by the activities of the Zaehner mission and wanted to terminate it. Eden overruled them, but the Rashidians were now run as an MI6 operation. 'The Rashidians were the British net that was most controlled by MI6. They were true agents in the sense that they worked for the British government ... and what made them distinctive and very important for their type of operation was that everyone in Iran knew this, and therefore when someone wanted to run for Parliament and wanted British help ... everyone knew where to go.'[44]

Taking his instructions from Darbyshire, Sam Falle continued to keep in touch with the brothers for the Foreign Office. 'I started seeing the Rashidians in March 1952 and this was the policy of our government and embassy in order to have a contingency plan in case the negotiations didn't succeed.' Zaehner informed headquarters that the Rashidians had been important in fomenting the tension between Mossadeq and the religious supporters of the National Front such as Hossein Makki and Ayatollah Kashani. Darbyshire was kept informed in general terms on the political situation not only by the Rashidians but by dozens of other agents. Woodhouse had recruited an important new agent, 'Omar', who was the director-general of a government department and was convinced that Mossadeq was ruining the country. Omar attended the Council of Ministers and reported intimate details of the Iranian administration and Mossadeq's rulings. He was a member of the professional classes that Woodhouse met socially, others being 'bankers, doctors, engineers, lawyers and journalists, almost all of them critical of Mossadeq but hesitant about going too far in friendliness with the British'. In Woodhouse's view, Omar's 'objective and evidently accurate reports' confirmed that the longer Mossadeq was in office the more probable 'that Iran would pass under Soviet control'.[45]

MI6 not only ran agents for intelligence-gathering but also for 'black' operations. The Lankarani brothers were agents inside the Tudeh Party and were involved in pseudo-gang-style operations – 'organising attacks on mosques and public figures in the name of the Tudeh'. MI6 planned the opening of a propaganda radio station in Cyprus as an offshoot of the NEABS to target broadcasts to Iran. According to an officer working with NEABS, American pressure forced MI6 to abort the operation.[46]

Luck came Britain's way in July 1952 when Mossadeq overreached himself. He sought to appoint himself War Minister but the Shah refused to endorse the move and so, in a calculated ploy, Mossadeq resigned. MI6 apparently played little part in the manoeuvrings that followed, but others did.

Julian Amery, an important backbench Conservative MP and former MI6 operative, recalled: 'The question was whether we could overturn the Mossadeq government. I had a long association with Iran because of my father. Iranians who were opposed to Mossadeq kept getting in touch with me. One of these was their greatest elder statesman, Qavam Saltaneh.' Qavam came from one of the old aristocratic families which, as the Shah well knew, 'despised him and his father as upstarts'. Amery met with Qavam in March in Paris. 'He got in touch with me several times and said that he was prepared to do something about it if only the British Government would give their blessing. He came and talked about it at my house in Eaton Square. But even Churchill's Government [was] a bit slow at first.'[47]

The British were happy when the Shah appointed Qavam Prime Minister. The chargé d'affaires in Tehran, George Middleton, thought Qavam 'a very wily politician and an operator far more likely than anyone else to manipulate the various parties in the Majlis. He was a professional and I won't say devious but an elastic politician: the man to get a majority together.' The attitude of the Soviets to the change of events was interesting. Contrary to reports that suggested the closeness of the communists to Mossadeq, they had, in fact, 'remained cool, bordering on the hostile, right from the start' towards Mossadeq, and so the Tudeh's reaction to the Qavam premiership was somewhat 'predictable'. The 'American agent Mossadeq had been replaced by the British agent Qavam. The latter was preferable, especially as he had a tradition of good relations with the Russians . . . The Tudeh press therefore responded to Qavam's premiership by attacking Mossadeq.' The party had been outlawed since 1949, but by early 1952 it was estimated to have thirteen thousand hard-core, well-disciplined members and, perhaps, another forty thousand supporters. While their policies had some parallels with those of Mossadeq's National Front, there were also irreconcilable differences which led to clashes. This was recognised in some quarters in the Foreign Office which saw communism as a threat in the Middle East only because 'it could feed off nationalism'. Earlier in the year, the Eastern Department had concluded that communism had 'only limited success in exploiting nationalist sentiment'. The priority was 'to tackle nationalism head on'.[48]

Unfortunately for Eden, who placed a lot of trust in Amery, Qavam was in office for only a few days. Mass rioting in Tehran forced Qavam to send in the troops, and while a number of the officers refused to fire on the crowd, twenty-nine people were killed, with hundreds injured. Darbyshire thought that 'Amery failed miserably. We had misunderstood the Mossadeq support and so had the Shah.' Middleton viewed the result with despair, sensing that henceforth it might be impossible to stop 'the drift towards communism' and that 'the consent of the mob is now the decisive factor' in Iranian politics.[49]

Mossadeq returned to power with increased support and a claimed mandate for greater powers. Talk, for the British, was no longer of replacing Mossadeq constitutionally. The Permanent Under-Secretary at the Foreign Office called for a 'behind the scenes' effort to remove Mossadeq. Middleton concluded in a cable to the Cabinet: 'Mossadeq's megalomania is now verging on mental instability ... it looks as though the only thing to stop Persia falling into communist hands is a coup d'état.' According to MI6 Middle East Director George Young, 'HMG came hesitatingly and reluctantly to the conclusion that Mossadeq's removal would have to be engineered from the outside.' Drawn up by Woodhouse, the initial plan involved caching arms and explosives for use by the plotters, but permission to bring these in was turned down, first by the Foreign Secretary, and then by the Prime Minister. Young and Woodhouse decided, nevertheless, to go ahead, following which Young offered his resignation. He was talked out of this by the new 'C', John Sinclair, who increasingly left the planning entirely in the hands of his Middle East Director. According to Darbyshire, Sinclair 'knew about as much of the Middle East as a ten-year-old. In any case, he preferred cricket.'[50]

The course was now set, and MI6 was busy making preparations. In the summer, headquarters ordered Woodhouse to arm those tribal leaders in northern Iran who could be relied on to oppose a possible Soviet invasion. He was in touch with the leaders, 'who would do their best, but they lacked weapons'. He sought help from the air attaché, Beverley Barnard, who had a small plane at his disposal. They flew to Habbaniyah in Iraq, the chief RAF base in the Middle East. 'I collected the arms and eventually landed at Tehran after losing our way over the Zagros mountains. They were mostly rifles and Sten guns. We drove north in a truck, avoiding check-points by using by-roads. Getting stopped was the sort of thing one never thinks about. We buried the weapons – I think my underlings dug the holes.' They had also brought in some small arms and gold sovereigns. The sovereigns were exchanged for Iranian riyals, which were handed over at a secret rendezvous in the Tehran suburbs to one of the Rashidian brothers to help finance the plans for the overthrow of Mossadeq. The Rashidians were financing a prominent group of pro-British politicians including Sayyid Zia, whom they wanted to install as Prime Minister, and Jamal Emami, who headed the pro-British faction in the Majlis. 'And for all we know,' Woodhouse recalled in 1997, 'those buried weapons are still hidden somewhere in northern Iran. It was all predicated on the assumption that war would break out with the Soviet Union.'[51]

Despite their disappointment, and at times anger, at the lack of US support for their policies in the Middle East, even in opposition Churchill and Eden had backed the idea of an Anglo-American approach to oust Mossadeq.

According to Monty Woodhouse, the appointment of another friend of Kermit Roosevelt as the new US ambassador to Iran changed the atmosphere in the US embassy to one of sympathy with the British position. Loy Henderson 'knew the Russians well and distrusted them profoundly'. Indeed, for Henderson, 'all roads led from Moscow and back'. As a senior State Department official, he had been trying to raise the consciousness of the Truman administration to the Soviet threat to the Middle East. Like the British, Henderson saw 'the threat as international Communism searching to create situations which weakened the ability of countries to resist communist pressure and penetration from without'. Henderson's view made some leeway in the State Department, where colleague Charles Bohlen observed that 'if Persia went Communist, Iraq and probably the rest of the Middle East would also . . . We ought therefore to concentrate on saving Persia from communism at all costs.'[52]

One embassy official in Tehran had already anticipated the change and was working closely with the British. The head of the mission and the principal Area Director of the CIA, Roger Goiran, was a second-generation American of French descent, who was 'both bilingual and quick to grasp a European viewpoint'. According to colleagues, Goiran was a person of great charm and cultivated wit who was an old hand at the intelligence game, having been a major in the Counter-Intelligence Corps (CIC) during the war, concentrating on counter-espionage. He moved from Istanbul to Tehran, where his deputy was John Waller, a vice-consul in Iran since 1946.[53]

Among the agents that Goiran controlled were two brothers, code-named the 'Boscoes'. They had originally approached an American professor in Tehran whom they believed was working for the CIA. He wasn't, but as an old OSS colleague he had supplied Goiran with the odd titbit of gossip from the campus. Kermit Roosevelt on one of his many trips to Iran met the brothers at a safe house in Tehran in 1950. Businesslike and impressive, the eldest was a lawyer with interests in Germany, while his brother, in his late twenties, was a journalist. What Roosevelt found surprising was that they had had some kind of clandestine training, but he never discovered from whom. The brothers subsequently travelled to Washington, where they were interviewed and eventually cleared by Allen Dulles and the head of the Agency, Walter Bedell Smith. Roosevelt then used them as *agents provocateurs*. When Averell Harriman and his interpreter, Col. Vernon Walters – mystery man and later Deputy Director of the CIA – visited Tehran as part of the AIOC/Iranian negotiations, anti-American demonstrations took place, during which many people were injured or killed. The rioting had been provoked by the Boscoe brothers using their strong links with the bazaar.

The British were now looking for someone to replace Mossadeq as Prime Minister. Middleton suggested the man he had been secretly grooming for the task, Gen. Faziollah Zahedi. 'I went to see him at his country estate for some shooting ... having swopped cars three times. He seemed tough, he wanted though to be sure that the Shah was with him and also, the Americans. But he was very ill-disposed towards Mossadeq who was leading the country to hell on a wheelbarrow ... and he obviously liked the idea of power and all its trappings.'[54]

When Zahedi consented to Middleton's proposal, the British talked quite openly to him about the possibility of a line of credit of ten to twenty million pounds for the Treasury on taking power. At first glance Zahedi was something of an odd choice. He had been arrested by the British military authorities in December 1942 in Isfahan for pro-Axis activities. He was held prisoner in Palestine for the rest of the war. Although 'half swash-buckler and half-Don Juan', Zahedi was then anti-British; he was also passionately anti-communist. 'He was, in fact, just the man one would choose to set up a coup – he was ruthless and manipulative and had twice been chief of police in Tehran.' He was also totally loyal to the Shah, having served under the Shah's father in the Cossack Brigade. Almost as important for the success of the proposed coup was his son, Ardeshir, who would act as liaison between his father and the British and American intelligence services. He had strong American connections, having gone to college in Salt Lake City and returned to Iran to work under the head of the US Technical Assistance programme ('Point Four' as it was known), which was promoted by the US Information Service (USIS). The US embassy personnel had 'complete faith in him. He is brave and absolutely loyal, not only to his father but to the Shah as well. He will be an invaluable, completely reliable contact with the General.'[55]

Despite British propaganda, the Mossadeq government was generally democratic, moderate, and seemed likely to succeed in establishing a middle-class hold over the state. It was officially viewed by the Truman administration as popular, nationalist and anti-communist. Mossadeq believed that fear of a communist takeover in Iran would lead the Americans to support his government despite British pressure. This conviction was reinforced during 1952 when a number of American oilmen appeared on the scene, offering to take the place of the AIOC. 'To this end, he or some of his supporters would occasionally invoke the communist threat.' It turned out to be, however, 'clearly a counter-productive tactic' – the implications of which Mossadeq 'did not at that time fully appreciate'. The British embassy continued to spread reports that the United States would be backing Britain to the hilt and that there existed no possibility of breaking the Anglo-American alliance.[56]

The British realised that at some appropriate moment they would have to let the Americans into their plans. Indeed, as early as May a British specialist on Iran had guardedly spoken with American officials in Washington about the possibility of a coup and possible candidates for Prime Minister, including Qavam and Sayyid Zia. In August, Sam Falle wrote that in proposing the overthrow of Mossadeq to the Americans 'we could say that, although we naturally wish to reach an oil settlement eventually, we appreciate that the first and most important objective is to prevent Persia going communist'. On the 6th, Falle met with Zahedi and reported that 'he is increasing his activity and has the courage to put himself up as a candidate for the premiership in these dangerous times . . . I understand that he has contacts, probably indirect, with the Americans and I suggested to him that there would be no harm in making his claims further known to the Americans.' Falle concluded that Zahedi 'does seem to offer some alternative to Mossadeq'.[57]

On his return to government, Mossadeq had little difficulty in increasing his powers, principally by appointing himself Minister of Defence and retiring a number of officers. Practically, he had taken away the Shah's authority as commander-in-chief of the Iranian armed forces, restricting him to signing military orders. Mohammed Reza's friend, Gen. Fardust, noted that Mossadeq's policies 'did not concur with the Shah's way of thinking or his psychology. Mossadeq had succeeded to prove himself in the international political arena as the number one force to be reckoned with in Iran.' Personally and politically insecure, the Shah was angry at this blatant usurping of his role.[58]

A group of disgruntled military men who supported the Shah, meeting in the officers' club in Tehran, decided to form a secret 'Committee to Save the Fatherland'. The committee's charter declared that it was the patriotic duty of the officers to 'fight for the monarchy and the armed forces; combat extremism, and save the country from social dissolution'. Its leading figure was Zahedi, though it included many other prominent military figures: Gen. Moqadam, a member of a wealthy Azerbaijani family and head of the gendarmerie following Mossadeq's return to power; Gen. Arfa, leader of the pro-British clique in the army and the arch-conservative former Chief of the General Staff; Gen. Hejai, a close friend of Arfa since their days in the Cossack Brigade; and Gen. Hedayat, the aristocratic staff officer who had worked closely with the Shah since the end of the war. They were soon in contact with MI6, principally by way of the Rashidians. Zahedi was also able to bring on board the religious leaders, Makki, Baqai and Kashani.[59]

Britain's open strategy towards Iran was to support a series of legal manoeuvres and to attempt to undermine Mossadeq's base of support by imposing economic sanctions. The chiefs of staff had earlier forecast that depriving the Iranian government of oil revenues, its main source of income, 'might bankrupt Persia thus possibly leading to revolution'. By the end of July this had evolved into a full economic blockade. British efforts were helped by the recruitment of a number of directors of Iran's National Bank.[60]

On several occasions either the Governor of the bank, Dr Mohammed Nassirir, or the bank's representative in New York, former Governor Abal Hassan Ebtehaj, gave detailed reports of the government's fiscal predicament to MI6 officers abroad. On his way to the International Monetary Fund in

Washington, the Governor stopped off in London, where he supplied British officials with data on the state of the country's gold and other reserves, the amount of currency bills printed against these reserves, and how much longer the government could meet its payroll obligations now that it had no income from the AIOC. In short, through these agents the Foreign Office had accurate knowledge of the economic power base of the Mossadeq government.[61]

The plotters were evidently building towards a coup d'état, but Mossadeq was not unaware of British intrigue. His security police learned of Zahedi's plans and, on 13 October, issued warrants for his arrest and that of three businessmen for plotting with a 'foreign embassy' against the government. The Rashidians were arrested but Seyfollah managed to escape by jumping over the back wall of his house. He stayed at large right up to the coup. The others had to spend a few months in prison. Gen. Zahedi also escaped and took sanctuary in the Majlis before disappearing underground.[62]

Earlier in the month, Woodhouse had learned from Omar that Mossadeq planned to cut off diplomatic relations with Britain. This was announced on the 17th, just four days after the arrests. The next few days were an extremely busy time for the MI6 officers. 'With the help of the few remaining British nationals,' Woodhouse recalled, 'I was able to ensure that all our useful contacts were preserved. I arrived in London in the last week of October, while the rest of the Embassy staff set out to drive in convoy through Iraq and Syria to Beirut.'[63]

About ten days after leaving Tehran, Falle and Darbyshire flew from Baghdad to Beirut with the outline of a plan for implementation. They had a joint, unofficial meeting with the Americans – inviting their co-operation – but after much discussion they were turned down. Their plan involved the seizure of key points in the city by units loyal to the Shah, and a takeover of the main radio station – in essence, classic coup tactics.

The MI6 team met up in Beirut and then crossed to Cyprus, where they set up a new office to keep in touch with their agents in Tehran. Woodhouse recalled that the CIA head of station, Roger Goiran, proved to be 'an invaluable ally to me when Mossadeq was throwing us out because I was able to hand on to him the contacts I had'. Cyprus had been chosen by the Churchill government to become the stronghold of the British presence in the Middle East as part of the redeployment of UK military forces in response to financial pressures and difficulties in Arab countries. Radio communications were run under cover of the military headquarters, while the MI6 officers were seconded to the British Middle East Office (BMEO) on Cyprus. One of the MI6 officers transferred to the BMEO for the coup planning was Arthur 'Dick' Franks, a former SOE officer who had joined MI6 in 1949 and went on to become a Chief of the Service. An MI6 station under cover of the BMEO was a collection of huts in a small forest at Athalassa, in an area 'generally known as the "stud farm". Unlike most stud farms, however, it appears to have had radio masts, underground installations, and a very heavy security guard.'[64]

Darbyshire took over the running of the Iranian station-in-exile from Monty Woodhouse and would control the MI6 part of the coup. Although communications from Cyprus were found to be difficult because of the mountains, Darbyshire discovered that 'none of our important contacts failed to keep in touch'. The Rashidians, presumably Seyfollah, were provided with radio equipment before MI6 left Tehran. Unable to pay the brothers direct, MI6 deposited money into secret bank accounts in Zurich and New York. Soon after, leading Iranians – including deputies in the Majlis – began to slip across the border, where they were quick to get in touch with the British.[65]

Woodhouse, who had returned to London, briefed Eden on the situation at a meeting with George Young and Robin Zaehner. The latter had left Tehran shortly after the Qavam failure. To Woodhouse's surprise, Zaehner gave a very defeatist account of the Rashidian brothers' capabilities. Unfortunately for Woodhouse, Zaehner 'had no stomach for the more sinister side of intelligence operations' and had become disillusioned during his time in Tehran. To those who wished to learn about Iranian politics, Zaehner recommended *Alice through the Looking Glass*. He may have been influenced by 'his habit of smoking opium with members of the embassy staff', while his heavy drinking probably resulted from the security fears that surrounded his intelligence career. In late 1945, a KGB officer, Konstantin Volkov, had attempted to defect in Istanbul, where he provided the embassy with clues to the identities of Soviet agents alleged to be working inside the British security services. Zaehner was one of those who came under suspicion, but when confronted with the evidence and further accusations from the former communist, Goronwy Rees, he vigorously denied the allegations.[66]

Though the Foreign Office believed that the project was now dead, Eden, Woodhouse realised, had 'left one loophole open'. The Foreign Secretary had remarked in passing that an operation such as was contemplated 'would have no chance of success without American support'. Woodhouse had long understood this and knew that any coup attempt would require a joint Anglo-American effort. He also understood that American support would be more forthcoming if they saw the problem as one of containing communism rather than confronting nationalism and restoring the position of the AIOC. With that in mind, in November Woodhouse travelled with Sam Falle to Washington with an MI6 plan code-named Operation BOOT.[67]

Woodhouse had consulted Iranian experts in London before preparing the plan. He had seen Ann Lambton, though not Zaehner, who had been withdrawn and had returned to academic life at Oxford. Similar to the scheme outlined to the Americans in Beirut, this plan had two resources. Firstly, the urban organisation run by the Rashidian brothers, which consisted of senior officers in the army and police, deputies and senators, merchants, newspaper editors, and elder statesmen, as well as mob leaders. Secondly, tribal leaders in the South, who were to make a show of force and, if the Tudeh resisted, occupy towns such as Isfahan and Abadan. Both would be activated simultaneously – probably in April or September 1953. British pay-offs had already secured the co-operation of the former group. 'These forces', explained Woodhouse, 'were to seize control of Tehran, preferably with the support of the Shah but if necessary without it, and to arrest Mossadeq and his ministers.'

On 2 December, Woodhouse and Falle met members of the State Department. Falle recalled that 'we went to persuade the Americans that we weren't going to get anywhere with Mossadeq and his remaining in power was very dangerous to both our interests, also to tell them a little bit about the means we had at our disposal for changing the government'. According to Woodhouse's account, they found the State Department initially unsympathetic and received a 'chilling reception'. Falle felt, though, that 'after we had been talking for some time, they accepted that Mossadeq, remaining in power, would eventually lead to a communist take-over'.[68]

The reaction at the CIA, after some initial hesitancy, turned out to be more positive. There was still some fallout and suspicions arising out of the Philby débâcle. According to the resident MI6 officer in Washington, John Bruce-Lockhart, the CIA was initially 'reluctant' to conspire with the British in Iran. After some diplomatic massaging, officials came to realise that Iran was 'a strategic prize'. According to Woodhouse, the CIA turned out to be 'very interested'. Wisner proved to be a 'powerful ally', while Dulles was 'receptive' and went so far as to enlist the help of a young academic expert on Iran to examine the situation with the British. Woodhouse found the expert to be 'shrewd and practical, and he greatly helped in convincing the CIA that between us we could carry out an effective operation'.[69]

Professor Richard Frye of Harvard University was 'a man with a profound grasp of Iran's history, culture and language', according to Richard Cottam, who had been introduced by Frye to Iran. Cottam was in Tehran during 1951/2, undertaking research at Tehran University under a Fulbright scholarship, and subsequently advised the State Department on policy towards Iran and worked with the CIA. While in Tehran, Cottam had been introduced to Princeton professor and consultant to the CIA Theodore Cuyler Young, an academic member of the OSS whose knowledge of Iran was 'unsurpassed'. Cottam compared the situation in Iran to the French Revolution, interesting in itself as CIA officers involved in planning on Iran reportedly used *The Anatomy of a Revolution* by Harvard historian Crane Brinton as a blueprint. Brinton had served in the Research Branch of the OSS during the war.[70]

Recalling the meeting, Cottam realised that MI6 were professional operators: 'It was my feeling then that the British understood the extent of paranoia in the United States concerning communism. Those were the days of Senator Joseph McCarthy's Un-American Activities Committee, and the British consummately played on that fear in order to help persuade us to involve ourselves in the coup.' This was perfectly true, as Woodhouse willingly admitted. 'When we knew what the prejudices were, we played all the more on these prejudices.'[71]

Woodhouse decided 'to emphasise the Communist threat to Iran rather than the need to recover control of the oil industry. I argued that even if a settlement of the oil dispute could be negotiated with Mossadeq, which was doubtful [Woodhouse put much of the blame for the failure on the AIOC, which he regarded as 'stupid, boring, pigheaded and tiresome'], he was still incapable of resisting a coup by the Tudeh Party if it were backed by Soviet support. Therefore he must be removed.' It was claimed that Moscow had a new strategy towards Mossadeq: he would be 'supported by the Tudeh in his bid to eliminate British influence from Iran so that pro-communist officers could, at the first opportunity, stage a coup d'état and, in turn, get rid of the old man'. The Tudeh had apparently successfully infiltrated the military and 'with its control of the oilfields through Tudeh-led trade unions and its assets within the army, Moscow could, when the time came, seize power in Tehran'. This was a timely piece of disinformation from the British which was believed, despite a State Department assessment in January 1953 that 'an open Tudeh move for power . . . would probably unite independents and non-communists of all political leanings and would result . . . in energetic efforts to destroy the Tudeh by force'.[72]

At the same time, while on his way home from Tehran, the head of the CIA's Middle East Department, Kermit Roosevelt, was invited to meet with representatives of MI6, including John Sinclair, who put to him the proposal that they jointly topple Mossadeq. There followed a series of meetings with Woodhouse, Darbyshire and the Foreign Office's adviser to 'C', George Clutton. While others joined later discussions, it was essentially these four who oversaw Boot. Roosevelt discovered that MI6 'already had sketched out a plan of battle and, while they recognised that we might have a political problem, they could see no other reason for delay'. The American had been thinking along similar lines, but said that nothing could be done until a Republican President was in office. The Cold War warriors were about to take command in Washington.[73]

US support for Boot illustrated the difference between the Truman and Eisenhower administrations in the Cold War consensus. Whereas Truman had often tried to foster non-communist nationalist governments, feeling that some degree of social change was inevitable and that it could be channelled to America's advantage – to which roster Mossadeq could be added – the new administration tended to see reform movements as disruptive and likely to fall prey to the communists. It was also true that members of the Eisenhower administration were much more explicit in their espousal of the big business interests that lay behind the anti-communist rhetoric. In particular, the new Secretary of State, John Foster Dulles, liked to mix big business with international politics, while his brother, Allen, as Director of Plans in the CIA, made sure that intelligence operations supported commercial interests.

The Dulles brothers were partners in the law firm of Sullivan and Cromwell, the legal counsel for the AIOC. Allen Dulles had also been, for years, a director of J. Henry Schroeder – part of the huge partnership put together to organise the Industrial Bank of Persia, the financing agent for the AIOC. One of Dulles's fellow-directors in Schroeder's was Frank C. Tiaks, who was also a director of the AIOC.[74]

With the blessing of Foster Dulles, the president of Chase Manhattan bank, John McCloy, toured the Middle East, encouraging oil companies, with the aid of the bank's cheap loans, to drill new wells. As a result, the oil companies became the effective instrument of US policy in the region, and while the State Department dealt with the problem of Israel, the oil companies – in league with American Intelligence – dealt with the Arabs and Iran. The architect of this policy was a former oil geologist, Herbert Hoover Jnr, Foster Dulles's special adviser on oil policy, who, like Dulles, saw big business and anti-communism as connected. Hoover knew Iran, having been commissioned by the Iranian government at the end of the war to advise on the extension of oil concessions, and was a close friend of Kermit Roosevelt. Strongly anti-British, Hoover tended to see British plots behind any moves in the Middle East. As chair of the Operations Co-ordination Board (OCB), an arm of the National Security Council (NSC), Hoover had responsibility for monitoring the implementation of NSC policies and, most importantly, for approval of covert action funds. The high-powered board also included the CIA's Allen Dulles, Director of Foreign Operations, Harold Strassen, Executive Secretary of the Permanent Staff, Elmer Steads, and Nelson Rockefeller – of innumerable oil connections – representing the President.[75]

The Eisenhower administration became more aggressive in its anti-communism, and US ambassador Loy Henderson was in a position to evoke the new policy. The British were pleased that he quickly established himself as the 'point man' for policy on Iran. Intriguingly, Henderson had the ear of Mossadeq, and several sensitive documents were translated by the ambassador on the Prime Minister's behalf.

In February 1953 the British plans for Boot were called to a halt by the deputy under-secretary in the Foreign Office, Piers Dixon, who 'wished above all to avoid the compromise of Britain's good name by underhand action of uncertain effectiveness and doubtful morality'. He wanted the British and Americans to sit tight and allow the Mossadeq regime to fall of its own accord. His decision on 21 February was not countered by the Foreign Secretary, who had had second thoughts and wanted the Rashidians' operation closed. Apparently, Eden went as far as having MI6 radio communications in Cyprus monitored to make sure that the order to terminate was carried out. Fortunately for MI6, the radio on that day failed, and by the next day Eden had changed his mind and agreed to the re-establishment of contact with the brothers.[76]

The operation was resurrected by the Boot team in Washington, where on the 18th, at a meeting of the NSC, Foster Dulles had remarked that Mossadeq 'could not afford to reach any agreement with the British lest it cost him his political life'. Two Anglo-American meetings at CIA headquarters and the State Department were for 'operating elements' and included Allen Dulles for the CIA and, on the British side, John Sinclair and George Clutton. Sinclair gave a detailed account of the British plan and proposed that Kermit Roosevelt be the field commander of the operation. Both sides accepted General Zahedi as the successor to Mossadeq.[77]

In mid-February, Zahedi had been reported as promising that if he came to power he would establish a 'Free South in Iran', where the Bakhtiari would be given autonomy. A group of Bakhtiari tribesmen and members of the Retired Officers' Association attacked an army column in Khuzestan province causing many casualties. Mossadeq immediately retaliated by arresting Zahedi and his co-conspirators. In the confusion that followed, the Shah panicked and announced that he was taking a vacation abroad. On the 27th, rioting broke out and a large crowd of pro-Zahedi supporters attacked Mossadeq's residence, calling for his blood. The leader of the mob was the most notorious of the 'knife drawer chiefs', Shaaban Jaafari, nicknamed 'Brainless'. It was obvious that the mob had been purchased by Ayatollah Kashani – and Mossadeq believed, correctly, that the attack had been undertaken in collaboration with British agents. In the event, Mossadeq managed to flee and, after further rioting, army units were eventually able to restore order. Politics had moved back onto the street.[78]

By 1953 the alliance that supported Mossadeq was crumbling, with clashes between the various factions increasingly common. When Mossadeq took it upon himself to claim emergency powers, militant clerics opposed him. They had expected a share of power but were to be disappointed, and became increasingly incensed by the westernising legislation put forward by Mossadeq's leftist allies. The break came when Mossadeq's finance minister advocated opening new bakeries, thus threatening the traditional guilds of the bazaar from where the clerics drew their support. Mossadeq came through the political crisis remarkably well, tightening his grip with new powers and scoring an easy victory over his main rivals, Makki, Baqai and Kashani. The most important of these clerics was Kashani, who had long espoused a hatred of the British and had on numerous occasions claimed to have barely escaped the 'executioners of the British Intelligence Service'. Kashani's activities were generally regarded as being 'out of control' and the Americans had made the suggestion to MI6 that the Rashidians be used 'to discredit' him. This proved, however, to be unnecessary as Kashani was primarily concerned with personal power and supported anyone who aided his ambitions.[79]

Mossadeq's appeal remained particularly strong, though there was clearly a feeling of unease that despite the apparent recovery in the economy and the lowering of unemployment, the country could still not succeed without the oil revenues. The irony, of course, was that Mossadeq was showing every sign of turning the country into just the kind of liberal democracy that the western plotters were pledged to uphold.

On 18 March MI6 received a message from Wisner to the effect that the CIA was ready to discuss in detail tactics for the overthrow of Mossadeq. The go-ahead was confirmed in mid-April by a further message from Washington on the authority of Bedell Smith. It seems that American and British oil interests similarly reached an agreement and that 'in exchange for American support in overthrowing the Mossadeq government, the British grudgingly permitted US companies a 40 per cent interest in Iranian oil'. Final confirmation from the US State Department arrived on 27 April with the news that Zahedi would be an acceptable joint candidate. Zahedi had been suggested to the CIA station chief by a veteran politician and part-time psychiatrist, Ebrahim Kajehnuri, in the belief that only an alliance with the Americans would end British domination of Iran. Eden vacillated, but with strong American support the Foreign Office, in the shape of its liaison officer with MI6, George Clutton, decided that the Rashidian brothers should go ahead. The coup was up and running.[80]

During the spring, Eden's health problems became 'acute' and he was hospitalised for a gall bladder operation. A second operation on 29 April was not a success. A third operation for a complete cure was impossible because a bile duct damaged in the first operation could not be repaired. Eden was able to return to active politics only after months of recuperation. The reins of foreign policy were taken up by Churchill, who 'enjoyed dramatic operations and had no high regard for timid diplomats'. The Prime Minister, however, was already 'fed up with Dulles's obsession with Communism in Persia and elsewhere' while he ignored Britain's real interests. His aide, John Colville, wrote that 'we have been out of Abadan for 18 months now; Mossadeq had done all he could to ruin his country; but there were no signs that Persia was nearer Communism now, in spite of our refusal to give away everything, than she was 18 months ago'. The Foreign Office assessment was that there was 'little Soviet activity in the Middle East recently'.[81]

That was not the view within CIA headquarters, where a 'Special Iran Task Force' was created, headed by Roosevelt with assistance from the academic Donald Wilbur, and political action specialist Miles Copeland.

An intelligence veteran and Iranian specialist in the OSS, Wilbur had been with Col. Norman Schwarzkopf a founder member of the wartime Persian American Relations Society, whose meetings were held in the office of the director of the National Bank, A. Ebtahaj. After teaching at the Asia Institute, Wilbur returned to intelligence work in 1947 with the Central Intelligence Group (CIG) and then as a consultant in the Near East Division of the OPC, engaged in planning psychological warfare and political action. Posted to Tehran, he served there until July 1952, employed by the CIA in anticommunist operations – primarily against Soviet front groups. In Tehran, Copeland talked to Roger Goiran and his deputy, John Waller, but found that the most helpful source for coup planning was Catherine, the 'Cat Lady', who was employed in a small unit in the embassy known as 'the CIA within the CIA'. She had numerous contacts among the American contractors of Iranian ancestry who had come to work in Tehran, and among the 'Zirkaneh Giants', the weight-lifters who could be hired to direct and control the mobs.[82]

In the months that followed, Roosevelt travelled to Iran on several occasions to prepare for the coup. He met frequently with Zahedi and provided financial assistance. In Beirut, there were planning meetings with Goiran. It soon became clear, however, that Goiran was not suited to political action and he returned to Washington, where he was appointed chief of the CIA's Near East Divisions which, as part of the Directorate of Plans, had responsibilities for covert action in the Middle East. His Near East deputy was Archie Roosevelt, Kermit's cousin.[83]

In the middle levels of the CIA and State Department many officials were less than enthusiastic about the project. Even Goiran became opposed to the idea as he viewed it as 'putting US support behind Anglo-French colonialism'. At least two Iranian analysts, who would have expected to have been consulted, were deliberately excluded from discussions. When eventually told of the plans, 'they predicted imminent failure'. Events during the spring, however, made the task force more optimistic. Mossadeq began talks with the Soviet Union as part of his policy of 'negative equilibrium'. The move not only antagonised the clerics and enabled the pro-British to regroup, it also backfired by giving the impression that the Prime Minister was moving towards the communists. In response, Mossadeq made a broadcast on 6 April 1953, accusing the royal court of supporting plots against his life, which was mostly true.[84]

Once the American and British plans had been agreed in principle, the Committee to Save the Fatherland and the Patriotic League, aided by funds from the Rashidians and Roosevelt, won over officers in senior positions within the armed forces. These included the commander of the Imperial Guard, Col. Nasiri; chief of the air force Gen. Gilnashah; commander of the armoured division in Kermansha Gen. Timour Bakhtiar; chief of the gendarmerie Col. Ardmbadi; head of the secret police Capt. M'utazeo; commander of the motorised division in Rasht Maj. 'Q'; and, most important, the tank commanders in the Tehran garrison – Cols. Ghulam Reza Oveissi and Muhammed Kajteh-Nouri.[85]

Having extended the secret network, royal officers then supplied weapons to the rebellious tribes, especially the Sahsavens, Bakhtiaris, Afshars and Turkomans. Through the Rashidians, they established contact with conservative clerics such as Ayatollahs Boroujerdi and Behbehani, who feared that Mossadeq's 'leftist advances were endangering national security'; and dissident mullahs from the National Front, Kashani and Makki, who claimed that the ministries were full of 'Kremlin-controlled atheists', and Baqai, who compared Mossadeq to Hitler. There was also contact with Shaaban, the 'Brainless'.[86]

During April, a new plan was set in motion to force Mossadeq's resignation. It had been decided to cause chaos and insecurity by kidnapping key officials and politicians. The first signs of resistance came towards the end of the month in a typically sinister form – 'some of Mossadeq's more powerful supporters were quickly spirited away, their throats slit, their bodies burned in the Elburz mountains'. On 20 April, the tough and loyal chief of police, Gen. Afshartus, disappeared after telling Mossadeq of a mysterious rendezvous he was about to attend. A former instructor at the Military Academy with a reputation for brutality, the general had been appointed by the Prime Minister four days earlier with instructions to purge the force of foreign elements sympathetic to the US and the British. When his body was discovered a few days later in an ice storage cave, it was 'obvious that slow retaliation had been taken for his former cruelties'. Those directly involved included Baqai and his close personal friend Hussain Khatibi, from whose house Afshartus had been kidnapped on 19 April. Royalist army officers, operating for the Rashidian brothers, had been responsible for the kidnapping.[87]

Although Monty Woodhouse later suggested that the murder may have been 'due to personal motives', according to Norman Darbyshire the kidnapping was part of Boot. Its purpose was to boost the morale of the opposition and show Mossadeq's supporters that they could not have it all their own way. 'He was kidnapped and held in a cave. Feelings ran high and Afshartus was unwise enough to make derogatory remarks about the Shah. He was under guard by a young army officer and the young officer pulled out a gun and shot. That man was never part of the programme at all but that's how it happened.' Another version has it that when Khatibi fell under suspicion the conspirators had Afshartus murdered in order to destroy the key witness against them.[88]

According to the investigations and resultant confessions that were published during the year, Brig. Muzayyeni was in charge of the murder mission and Maj. Baluch-Qarai executed the order. Investigators soon implicated Baqai, Gen. Zahedi and his associates, including a number of retired generals, and a son of Ayatollah Kashani. In signed confessions, four officers accused of the plot admitted to the kidnap and the decision to kill Afshartus. Despite Darbyshire's claim that the kidnapping had got out of hand and that murder had not been a part of the plan, it is hard to see how Mossadeq's supporters could have received the right message – that they could not have all their own way – without Afshartus being murdered. American journalist Kenneth Love, who was in Tehran and worked closely with the CIA, claimed that Afshartus was strangled. According to one account, when Mossadeq appointed a new police chief, 'his candidate bragged on his first day that he had a list of British spies on the force. By the next morning the man had been gunned down.'[89]

During mid-May, CIA academic Donald Wilbur had a series of exhaustive meetings with MI6 officers in Nicosia before flying on to Beirut where he showed a plan he had developed – known as AJAX – to Roosevelt. On 15 June the pair flew on to London for meetings with MI6 officers. Eden is supposed to have read the final draft of Ajax 'very carefully making notations in the margin in his own handwriting'. Also involved was Patrick Dean, who had been appointed chair of the Joint Intelligence Committee (JIC) in April. Although responsible for intelligence and security matters in the Foreign Office, Dean played down his secret leading role, though he 'once delighted a Washington luncheon audience' with his opening remarks: ' "Mr Chairman, gentlemen" – and with a nod at Allen Dulles – "fellow conspirators" '.[90]

Serving in London at the time was Ray Clines, a CIA staff officer from the Office of National Estimates, who exchanged US intelligence estimates for JIC assessments. Up to eighteen CIA analysts were busy in London comparing economic, scientific and general strategic intelligence. Cline found that

> the wartime partnership was still paying off handsomely. The British, recognising the importance of keeping the United States actively engaged in an effort to contain Soviet disruptive thrusts, were extraordinarily open and co-operative with Americans in intelligence matters. They provided not only most of their high-est-level joint intelligence estimates but also provided the station chief in London with most of their clandestine intelligence MI6 reports.[91]

Donald Wilbur was willing to claim sole credit for the Ajax plan even though most observers have suggested that it was a 'rewrite of the much more detailed plan left by SIS Chief Sinclair and George Young'. The plan aimed to create 'a situation and an atmosphere in Tehran that forced the people to choose between an established institution, the monarchy, and the unknown future offered by Mossadeq. If such a choice had to be made, it would be for the monarchy.' The plan also envisaged pressure being applied to the Shah to secure the issuing of an imperial decree to dismiss Mossadeq, and another naming Gen. Zahedi as Prime Minister.[92]

On 25 June 1953, with CIA officers opposed to the plan excluded, the

Americans finally gave the go-ahead for Operation Ajax at a meeting chaired by Secretary of State Foster Dulles. Attending were his brother Allen; CIA Director Bedell Smith, who 'was personally inclined to favour clandestine operations'; his deputy, H. Freeman 'Doc' Mathews, 'a dark figure'; Robert Bourne, Director of the State Department's Planning Staff, later Deputy Director of the CIA; Secretary of Defense Charles Wilson; Henry 'Hank' Byroade, Assistant Secretary of State in charge of the Near East; and US ambassador in Tehran Loy Henderson, who proved to be the key person at the meeting. His argument that the Iranian Prime Minister was 'now completely in the hands of his advisers' weighed heavily in the administration's decision to support Mossadeq's overthrow. The twenty-two-page paper was passed with little comment following Foster Dulles's approval. Henderson was told that since Roosevelt had 'few details to give him', the specifics 'would have to be worked out on the spot'.[93]

At the end of July, Woodhouse was given new responsibilities by Sinclair, but before he left for a tour of the Far East he wrote a review of a book on Iran for *The Twentieth Century*. He later noted that anyone who read 'between the lines would have seen that it was written in the knowledge of an impending revolution'. Woodhouse thought that Russia had 'good reason to think Persia ripe to mark the next step in its imperial expansion'. In terms of social and political conditions, Persia offers 'a close approximation to a "revolutionary situation"', coupled with the benefit of one of the half dozen most efficiently organised Communist Parties in the world outside the Soviet Orbit'. He concluded that 'from the narrowest view-point of national interest, Persia is a legacy which we cannot afford to neglect. If we do, there is little doubt who will claim it.'[94]

In Cabinet, Lord Salisbury, who had temporarily taken on foreign affairs in Eden's absence, warned ministers that it would be 'disastrous' to give Washington the impression that 'we are only concerned with our oil to the exclusion of any consideration of the necessity of keeping Persia in the anti-Communist camp', in which case 'we may lose all control over American actions'. By July, Churchill had decided that the time had come for firm action and finally 'gave the authority for Operation Boot to proceed'.[95]

Using the pseudonym 'James F. Lochridge', Kermit Roosevelt crossed the border into Iran from Iraq on 19 July 1953. Ordered to keep his presence a secret, he stayed with a CIA officer in a safe house in the mountains. There remained, as Woodhouse recognised, 'the problem of persuading the nervous Shah to play his role which would consist simply of signing two decrees (*firmans*), one dismissing Mossadeq and the other appointing Zahedi in his place'. The problem for the conspirators was that the Shah was weak and totally unsure of what to do or whom to trust. Without his support, however, the operation could not succeed.[96]

The CIA station was augmented for Ajax. Goiran, the former station chief who opposed the coup, had been replaced by former journalist Joe Goodwin, who had covered the Azerbaijan crisis during 1946/47 for a press syndicate and knew many prominent Iranians. Other CIA officers involved in the coup, in planning and action, included Howard E. 'Rocky' Stone, a 'legend in the CIA's clandestine services', and George Carroll, a six-foot-four-inch, two-hundred-pound paramilitary specialist, who had arrived from Korea. He was described by a colleague as 'too unrestrained' but useful when 'they really don't give a damn'. He was the principal contact with the military in Tehran. Ted Hotchkiss, too, had been in Korea before being recruited in 1952 as a CIA operative.[97]

Back in Washington, Wilbur oversaw the preparation of propaganda material directed against Mossadeq. Richard Cottam wrote articles alleging communist support for Mossadeq, while right-wing writer James Burnham was also employed by Roosevelt to write propaganda. During the summer, the Damn propaganda campaign was engaged in an 'all-out effort', an 'orchestrated programme of destabilisation', which became clear when six new newspapers suddenly appeared in Tehran. The material compiled in Washington was rushed to Tehran, where it was stored for distribution at the appropriate moment. It was then passed on to the Rashidian brothers, who had contacts in four-fifths of the Iranian press. 'Any article I would write', Cottam recalled, 'would appear almost instantly in the next day's Iranian press.'[98]

In order to protect them the Shah had sent members of his family, including his twin sister Ashraf, into exile in Switzerland. He blamed the need for this on Mossadeq, who had accused Ashraf of siphoning off five million riyals from the Agriculture Bank. It was recognised by western intelligence agencies that Ashraf was the only person to whom the Shah would listen. Roosevelt told Zahedi that the five million riyals was 'no problem'. Ashraf could, he said, once there 'sell off some property to pay off her debts'. She was telephoned by Asadollah Rashidian, who told her that the British and Americans were concerned about the current situation in Iran and that they had devised a plan to solve the problem and benefit the Shah. She agreed to listen to two representatives, Lt-Col. Stephen Meade, a regular army officer on loan to the CIA who acted on behalf of Foster Dulles, and Norman Darbyshire, speaking for Winston Churchill.[99]

Princess Ashraf was persuaded to go back to Tehran to convince her brother that the plans put before him by Asadollah had the support of both London and Washington. According to Darbyshire, when he produced a great wad of notes 'her eyes lit up'. Meade and Darbyshire told her, 'here is your first-class ticket and you are booked for the day after tomorrow'. Using her married name, Madame Chafik, she arrived secretly in Tehran on 25 July and met with the Shah with the aim of 'encouraging him to act'. The meeting, however, was 'stormy', and people outside recalled hearing the two rowing. Woodhouse reports that 'they were not alone, so that it was doubtful whether she succeeded in conveying any kind of message to him'. Five days later, she left for Geneva, feeling that she had managed to bring her brother around.[100]

On 1 August, Col. H. Norman Schwarzkopf, former US adviser to the gendarmerie, openly flew into Tehran, 'stayed for two days, and was gone again'. A week later, the *New York Times* reported that he had visited Iran 'to see a few friends', one of whom turned out to be the Shah, the other Gen. Zahedi – in hiding from Mossadeq's possible revenge and assassination. Schwarzkopf managed to see the Shah, who again refused to commit himself. Col. Schwarzkopf suggested the need for Roosevelt to see the Shah personally, and a meeting was arranged by the Rashidians. The Shah finally agreed to support the plan only 'after official US and British involvement had been confirmed through a special radio broadcast'. President Eisenhower had given the final go-ahead for Ajax on 8 August after Mossadeq opened trade talks with the Soviet Union. It had been arranged that the routine BBC Persian-language news broadcast would not begin with the usual 'It is now midnight in London' but instead 'It is now *exactly* midnight'. The President departed from his prepared speech to add that the situation in Iran was 'very ominous', that the Soviet drive 'must be blocked' and 'that's what we are trying to do'. On hearing the broadcasts, the Shah and his wife left for their hunting lodge on the Caspian Sea, where he signed two blank decrees to be filled in at the right time: one was for Mossadeq's dismissal and the other for Zahedi's appointment to the post of Prime Minister.[101]

Darbyshire had wanted to direct the final stages of the operation on the spot, and had planned to fly into Tehran in an American plane. Once in place, he knew that it would not be a problem organising the operation. His request, however, was turned down by the Foreign Office and the politicians, who thought 'it would have been embarrassing if anything had gone wrong'. Because he spoke Farsi, Darbyshire was given the job of co-ordinating the operations – from Cyprus. 'In the intelligence world you play your cards pretty close to the chest,' the MI6 officer later recalled. 'We handled the money, we didn't let the CIA touch it . . . and even if you have an ally, you always go to any lengths to protect your own sources of information. We, on instruction, were more forthcoming than the CIA was with us. But on the other hand knowing the thing well, we could read between the lines and could see who the CIA were using.'

On 13 August, the original day set for the operation, rumours of an impending coup rose to their highest pitch. These were echoed the following day in a newspaper article which stated that 'the suspicious activities in Tehran of foreign agents during the past two weeks together with their internal counter-parts show that a secret organisation is hopelessly working against Dr Mossadeq's government, and the Americans and British imperialists have not yet lost faith in the use of their last card'. As the date of the operation passed, American ambassador Loy Henderson, who had not been given full details by the CIA but was told 'only that something was to be done', grew restless and flew to Beirut for a break.[102]

A new date of 15 August was set, the day on which the Foreign Minister, Fatemi, and Chief of Staff, Riyahi, were to be kidnapped in the hope of forestalling civil and military resistance. Fatemi was taken and threatened with execution, but the conspirators failed to grab Gen. Riyahi. On the same day, Mossadeq was warned of an impending move against him by two young officers of the Royal Guard. A retired civil servant from the Ministry of Finance, Mohammad Hussain Ashtiyani, whose relatives were close to the royal court, also telephoned him with details of the plan. Forewarned, the military moved tanks to surround Mossadeq's home. At 10 a.m. on the following morning, when the commander of the Imperial Guard in Tehran, Col. Nemotollah Nassiri, arrived with the royal decree to arrest the Prime Minister, Mossadeq was ready for him. It was Nassiri who was arrested by Gen. Riyahi.[103]

Shortly after, the head of the US Military Mission to the Iranian Army, Brig.-Gen. Robert McClure, informed President Eisenhower's adviser on psychological warfare, C. D. Jackson, that the

> first abortive start for a change of Government smacked very much of cloak and dagger. The delivery of his Majesty's decree backed up by armed troops was open to serious question. It was unrealistic to expect major commanders to accept the statement of comparatively junior officers that the Shah had issued a decree for delivery in this manner. The unsupported statements were supposed to have been convincing enough to cause a revolt in the Army. You know of course what happened. The following day I talked with the Acting Minister of Defence and the Chief of Staff, both of whom cited the manner of delivery, and stated it was so unusual as to cause them to doubt the existence of an authentic decree. They cited how easy it would be for a forgery to have been used.

The government had been decisive in its actions and the public received the news of the unsuccessful coup with anger, followed by jubilation – especially when a large public meeting was addressed by the released Fatemi.[104]

Ernest Perron told the Shah about Col. Nassiri's arrest and advised him to leave the country. The Shah was not a man for a crisis or making difficult decisions: 'his natural instinct was to leave, allowing events to unfold without him'. With the Empress, the Shah fled in a single-engined plane to the resort of Ramssar, from where they were flown on to Baghdad by Lt. Mohammad

Khatami (later married to the Shah's sister and appointed head of the air force). The British embassy in Baghdad cabled the Foreign Office that the Shah was wobbling. He wanted advice from both the British and the Americans on whether 'he should oppose Mossadeq openly or not, and what he should do'. A private British plane was chartered in Baghdad and the couple were flown to Rome, where they kept in touch with MI6 and CIA representatives. Perron hid in the house of his Swiss friend for the duration of the coup.[105]

The hunt was now on for those connected to Nassiri, and a massive search was made for Zahedi, with a reward of a hundred thousand riyals offered for his arrest. Shapour Dowlatshahi had been charged with hiding Roosevelt and other CIA agents in Tehran, and Zahedi had been transferred to the basement of another CIA man (Fred Zimmerman), who had been out of action with hepatitis.[106]

According to Donald Wilbur, at this point 'key figures in the military phases of the plan got cold feet and stayed home instead of carrying out the instructions they had sworn to execute'. The 'brains' behind one grouping, Maj.-Gen. Hassin Akhavi, feigned illness and confined himself to bed in the army's hospital in Tehran. He was 'worried for the failure of the coup and this was a good alibi to avoid suspicion' (he was later awarded a ministerial post by the Shah).[107]

In Washington, Wisner and Dulles assumed that the plot had failed, while Wilbur attended meetings where 'decisions were taken to call off the operations'. CIA headquarters was in 'depression and despair'. Under-Secretary of State and former CIA Director Walter Bedell Smith decided to transmit a cable to Roosevelt telling him to flee Tehran 'at the earliest moment'. The cable was to be transmitted to the CIA station in Tehran via MI6's communications link on Cyprus. When MI6's Middle East Director, George Young, saw the cable, however, he declined to pass it on immediately, thus allowing the conspirators enough time to regain the initiative. When the cable finally did reach Tehran, Roosevelt chose to ignore it, as he considered that the tide had turned. Roosevelt later admitted that 'had the message arrived earlier – when, in fact, [Bedell Smith] sent it – I should have had a real problem'.[108]

Fearing that the coup had been unsuccessful, on 16 August Henderson flew from Switzerland to Beirut, and then on to Tehran, where he contacted Roosevelt to enquire what was happening. Roosevelt remained optimistic, telling Henderson, 'We've run into some complications.' However, he added, 'I think we have things under control. Two or three days should see things developing our way.' Henderson subsequently saw Mossadeq for 'frank, hot exchanges', cabling Dulles that the Prime Minister suspected that the Americans had conspired with the British in the bid to oust him. Mossadeq had been adamant that 'the national movement was determined to remain in power in Iran and that it would continue to hold on to the last man, even though all its members would be run over by British and American tanks'.[109]

The next move was to bring out the psychological warfare assets. 'In a lurid effort to totally discredit the Left', Ayatollah Bihbihani, who received money from the Americans, sent out letters bearing the insignia of the Tudeh Party, and containing 'grisly threats' written in red ink 'to hang all the mullahs from the lampposts of various Iranian cities'. On the 16th, CIA officers made copies of the decrees signed by the Shah and had their two principal agents, Nerren and Cilley, and two American journalists, Kenneth Love of the *New York Times* and Don Schwind of Associated Press, distribute them throughout Tehran. 'Our propaganda material flooded Tehran,' Wilbur recalled. 'Clandestine papers appeared, raids were mounted on Tudeh Party offices and presses.' According to one participant, Nerren and Cilley had wanted to end their involvement but 'were persuaded to remain by Roosevelt, who threatened to have them killed'.[110]

The political officer attached to the US embassy, Goodwin, served as a communications channel for Love and Schwind. On the 17th, Goodwin took the two reporters to meet Gen. Zahedi's son, Ardeshir (who later became the Shah's ambassador to the US) at the home of the CIA officer Howard Stone, who later recalled 'his young wife sitting in a rocking chair, hiding a pistol under her knitting as she guarded the life of Ardeshir'. He told Love and Schwind that his father had been legally appointed Prime Minister and that Mossadeq's action was illegal. After the decrees were distributed, CIA assets tried to generate support for Zahedi within the armed forces.[111]

When things had gone wrong on 'Black Sunday', Darbyshire had heard the bad news from Roosevelt and the Rashidians via the radio link. MI6 had then decided 'to bring the boys out onto the streets'. John Sinclair had left the details of the operation to George Young, who 'had the wit to realise that the mobs who had cheered for Mossadeq could be induced to shout for his Monarch'. MI6 ensured that Seyfollah and Asadollah Rashidian helped coach Roosevelt through the coup. In radio contact with Darbyshire, who was controlling their actions, they were to play a crucial role in calling onto the streets the mobs from south Tehran, along with military officers. One hundred thousand dollars was put at the disposal of four plotters: the two Rashidian brothers, Mrs Malekeh Etezadi, who supervised some of the southern Tehran houses of ill repute, and Ayatollah Qanatabadi.[112]

Demonstrations continued on the 17th, and the mobs came out onto the streets. Mossadeq's response was to ask the party leaders to keep their people off the streets and to declare a ban on demonstrations. A key aspect of the plot was to portray the mobs as supporters of the Tudeh Party in order to provide a suitable pretext for the coup and the resumption of control by the Shah. Darbyshire was of the opinion that the Rashidians 'saved the day' by providing people to infiltrate the demonstrations. This had been a contingency plan – MI6 had told them not to rely on Mossadeq folding. Nerren and Cilley hired a fake Tudeh crowd, comprising an unusual mixture of pan-Iranians and Tudeh members, paid for with fifty thousand dollars given to them by a CIA officer. Richard Cottam observed that agents working on behalf of the British 'saw the opportunity and sent the people we had under our control into the streets to act as if they were Tudeh. They were more than just provocateurs, they were shock troops, who acted as if they were Tudeh people throwing rocks at mosques and priests.' 'The purpose', Brian Lapping explains, 'was to frighten the majority of Iranians into believing that a victory for Mossadeq would be a victory for the Tudeh, the Soviet Union and irreligion.'[113]

Despite Mossadeq's call for an end to demonstrations, they continued, the Prime Minister's problems mounting with the refusal of the prefect of police, Brig. Mudabbir, and the martial law administrator, Col. Ashrafi, to act on the 19th. Oddly, Mossadeq proceeded to appoint Gen. Daftary, an ally of Zahedi, to deal with the riots. Daftary promptly committed the security forces to the rebels.[114]

In order to trigger the uprising against Mossadeq, the CIA used the Rashidians to contact Ayatollah Kashani. A Rashidian ally, Ahmad Aramesh, was visited by two CIA officers, one of them George Carroll, and provided with ten thousand dollars to pass on to the mullah, which he did on the 19th. Kashani then played a minor role in mobilising an anti-Mossadeq crowd of Somak fascists and pan-Iranists to march from the bazaar into the modern quarter of central Tehran, where they swept along soldiers and officers. The larger part was played by other mullahs, especially Ayatollah Muhammad Bihbihani, who was the key person in inviting onto the streets the bands of 'knife drawers' who, buttressed with the 'Bihbihani dollars', carried out Carroll's dirty work.[115]

Other agents organised similar 'loyalist' crowds. One of the myths of the coup was that the demonstrators, carrying pictures of the Shah, were led by Shaaban Jaafari, the 'Brainless'. Jaafari was, in fact, in prison at the time, and was released only after Mossadeq had fallen. The 'tough guys' or 'ignorant ones' who took part in the march of the poor on Tehran were led by one Tayyeb Hsaj-Reza'i, who was hanged a decade later for his support of Ayatollah Khomeini.[116]

Loy Henderson later wrote that he thought Mossadeq had been ousted by an essentially popular movement which had been 'disgusted at the bad taste exhibited by the anti-Shah elements supporting Mossadeq'. Given our knowledge of who actually made up these 'Tudeh' mobs, this was disingenuous to say the least. When the mobs began pulling down statues of the Shah, it proved to be a psychological turning point. It 'snowballed', as it was intended to. When the Tudeh realised that the crowd was fake, the party pulled its own people off, leaving Carroll's bands with the streets largely to themselves. By this time, around three hundred civilians had died, trampled underfoot when the mob rioted.[117]

During this time, Ardeshir travelled to Kermanshah to elicit the support of the local commander, whom he knew. Co-conspirator Farzaniega went to Isfahan to seek the support of the military commander – though he failed in the task. An important strategy of the rebels was to seize the radio station. Stone recalled 'buttoning the uniform of Gen. Faziollah Zahedi on the day the General was to announce over Radio Tehran that the Shah had designated him the new prime minister'. Zahedi was 'too nervous to dress himself'. The general had emerged from hiding and had been transported by tank to the radio station, where leading government opponents such as Sayyed Mir-Ashrafi and Sayyed Pirasteh broadcast statements indicating that the government had already fallen. This was untrue. Zahedi gave a press conference at which he declared himself Prime Minister, and to support his claim distributed copies of the Shah's decree of appointment. The tide had turned.[118]

By late afternoon, Mossadeq's residence had been surrounded by rebel troops. Gen. Riyahi was subsequently arrested, while his deputy, Gen. Kiyani, had been met on the outskirts of the city by Gen. Daftary's men, and disarmed. Mossadeq was persuaded to leave his residence, which fell at 8 p.m. to the rebels, who proceeded to loot and ransack the house. Early next morning, Mossadeq was picked up and put under arrest at the Army Officers' Club.

When the Shah flew back into Tehran on 22 August in triumph, Henderson visited the palace and found him a 'changed man' – more confident and optimistic. The Shah offered Roosevelt a toast: 'I owe my throne to God, my people, my army, to you and, of course, to that undercover assistant of yours whom I shall not name.' It was implied that the undercover assistant was Miles Copeland. Uncharacteristically, Copeland wrote that the reference was undeserved and that the success was entirely due to Roosevelt. Copeland's role had, indeed, been a small one. On his way back to Washington, Roosevelt stopped off in London and gave a full account to Churchill. At the White House, the President pinned the National Security Medal on Kermit. Eisenhower wrote of Roosevelt that 'he worked intelligently, courageously and tirelessly. I listened to his detailed report and it seemed more like a dime novel than a historical fact.'[119]

The cost remains a matter of debate. Around a hundred thousand dollars paid for the mob in the final days, and the nine hundred thousand dollars that remained unspent from the originally appointed funds were handed over to the Zahedi regime. According to a British account, the coup cost seven hundred thousand pounds, though a more recent estimate with access to the participants and CIA accounts has put it at as much as ten to twenty million dollars. Whether Mossadeq would have survived without the coup also remains in dispute.[120]

One view holds that the regime would probably have endured without the intervention of the CIA and MI6, since the economy was heading towards recovery. Amir Taheri also argues that the reasons for outside intervention did not hold water. 'There is no evidence that Moscow and its local agents in Iran were in any position to attempt a direct take-over of the country at that time ... more importantly, the religious leaders could have ordered the massacre of Tudeh activists and leaders by declaring jihad (holy war) on communism.' Richard Cottam, however, believes that 'Mossadeq could not have been overthrown if significant elements of the population had not lost faith in his leadership'. Woodhouse held a similar view: 'There may be reasons for not being dogmatic in claiming that the revolution of August 1953 was planned and executed by our Anglo-American team. Still, I think it was. We may have done no more than mobilise forces which were already there, but that was precisely what needed to be done, and it was enough.'[121]

And to whom do the laurels go for the enterprise? Taheri concludes that the CIA was 'a junior partner in what was a British plot against Mossadeq'. This concurs with the MI6 view as expressed by Christopher Andrew: 'Roosevelt really did little more than show up in Iran with CIA funds to encourage agents the British had organised and then released to American control.' The failure of the Americans to acknowledge MI6's greater role continued to rankle for many years, as did the fact that the CIA took part only 'after Washington had decided that a policy of working with Britain to restore the Shah's powers and against Britain to increase America's stake in Middle East oil was, indeed, a sound combination of diplomacy and commerce'.[122]

After the coup a victory party at the CIA station was attended by the new Prime Minister and his son. They approached Howard Stone and asked: 'We are in ... We are in ... What do we do now?' The first step was to settle the oil dispute, and the CIA ensured that the major project of the Damn propaganda operation, which continued into 1954, was the renegotiation of the oil agreement. Herbert Hoover Jnr was the first official into Tehran after the coup, with the responsibility – while the British waited on the sidelines – for drawing up and negotiating the new consortium agreement which let in the US oil companies. As the Shah crisply pointed out to him: 'Any favour the CIA had done him would be adequately paid for in oil.'[123]

The Dulles law firm, Sullivan and Cromwell, helped negotiate the redivision of Iran's reserves, to the advantage of the American companies. The four parent companies (Jersey, Socony, Texas and Socal) involved in the Iranian consortium deal (along with Gulf) had also cut the Armco-Saudi 50–50 agreement. In the new consortium, AIOC, which changed its name to British Petroleum, held a 40 per cent share and received £34,500,000 in compensation plus 10 per cent a barrel on all exports until a sum of £510 million was reached. The scheme had been devised by Sir William Fraser and 'it was largely by his efforts that it was brought to a successful conclusion'. To further compensate their old client, Sullivan and Cromwell 'helped it on to the North Slope of Alaska, arranged a takeover of Standard Oil of Ohio, and protected it from anti-trust legislation in American courts'. Fraser, who was also chair of the Iraq Petroleum Company and the Kuwait Oil Company, did very well by the deal. Despite the investment at Abadan and the plotting of MI6 and the British government, the Iran oilfields were no longer required by British Petroleum, as vast new, more productive fields were opening up in Iraq and Kuwait.[124]

When Monty Woodhouse visited Washington, Allen Dulles congratulated him on the coup with the comment that 'that was a nice little egg you laid when you were here last time!' There was a feeling that there might be a new era of Anglo-American co-operation over the Middle East. In September, Allen's brother, US Secretary of State Foster Dulles, telegraphed acting Foreign Secretary Lord Salisbury, describing the new opportunity 'to change to our advantage the course of events in the Middle East ... I think if we can in co-ordination move quickly and effectively in Iran we could close the most dangerous gap in the line from Europe to South Asia.'[125]

There were, however, already fissures developing in Tehran. While admiring the work of 'Wisner's boys', the head of the US Military Mission, Robert McClure, told C. D. Jackson that 'it is about time for the non-military to get out of the military picture and leave that to me'. It never happened. In September, the CIA's Col. Stephen Meade was made responsible for training Iran's intelligence and security services, as part of a clampdown on any communist threat, which included a purge of the army. In November, George Carroll, 'a buddy' of Gen. Farhat Dadsetat, Zahedi's first military governor of Tehran, worked on 'the very efficient smothering' of 'a potentially dangerous dissident movement emanating from the bazaar area and the Tudeh'. The CIA was well ensconced by the time diplomatic relations were restored with Britain in December and MI6 was allowed to reopen a station with Dickie Franks in charge.[126]

MI6 judged that the Shah was 'uncertain of the extent of outside influence and intrigue among his subjects, and faced by strong tribal chiefs, by generals of uncertain loyalty, and by cross-streams of popular and religious resentment'. The Shah, MI6 concluded, 'was now willing to rule'. In early 1954, with a recently elected and compliant Majlis, the Shah began to crack down hard on demonstrators. By the time of the anniversary of the coup, the crackdown had spread to security units and the military, with a series of 'sensational arrests' during which alleged Tudeh spies and Kremlin-controlled agents were uncovered. Many lost their lives when, in October, the death penalty was imposed on those convicted of agitating for the overthrow of the government.[127]

Meade remained until 1955, when he was replaced by a permanent five-man CIA team to train the new National Intelligence and Security Organisation (SAVAK), which became feared for its ruthlessness and use of torture. Ted Hotchkiss's work in helping to set up SAVAK left him disillusioned with the CIA: 'I fought the fascists and Nazis ... my lesson was that we were becoming just like them.'[128]

Donald Wilbur had initially welcomed the change in the Shah and his increasing assertiveness. He now recognised that the new air of self-confidence 'in time developed into a type of megalomania. He gradually found frank criticism from Persians close to him no longer acceptable, although he might listen to foreigners whom he felt were honest.' One such foreigner was George Young, who had his first private audience with the Shah during 1955. The Shah told a friend that in times of crisis Young 'is a man who can take decisions and throw caution to the winds. Young is a man who believes that friendship cuts two ways and that Britain should stand by her friends even at the risk of offending others.'[129]

While the successful coup had paved the way for the stability that the West had wanted, it had brought unforeseen consequences. Once the Shah was secure, the plan drawn up by Overseas Consultants was implemented largely through the work of Roosevelt and American aid, which over the next two and a half years reached three hundred million dollars. Roosevelt travelled to Tehran five or six times a year. His line to the Shah was through the Rashidians, whose commercial interests in America were looked after by his public relations firm. He went through the commander of the Imperial Guard, Gen. Muhsin Hashimi-Nijhad, to the monarch himself. Back in Washington, Roosevelt had personal connections that led directly to the White House. The thinking of Roosevelt and his colleagues was that 'if you give a "backward" country a top flight modernisation plan, the money to fund it, an adequate and stable chief of state, and internal political stability, that country will evolve toward democracy'. Although the plan had been the product of 'optimistic idealism', it proved to be, as Sallie Pisani notes, 'an immense failure'. The bitter irony, she continues, was that Roosevelt, 'despite his extensive research, ignored political and religious movements in Iran's history'. Roosevelt believed that 'the mullah, the official clerical class in Iran, would fade away as modernisation took place'. However, by its actions the United States 'guaranteed the unremitting future opposition of the nationalist extremism of the religious right while at the same time effectively undercutting the strength and credibility of the liberal, nationalist centre'.[130]

The problem was that while Mossadeq may have been 'an incompetent and muddled prime minister', who 'knew how to demolish but not how to construct', he had represented a number of legitimate interests that were essential to the country's viability. While he did not divide the Iranian people as a whole, the urban Left 'was to remain permanently divided over his record and the reasons for his fall'. That division, argues Amir Taheri, 'benefited the reactionary religious forces, who saw Mossadeq and the Shah as two sides of the same coin'. The coup went for immediate results and ignored the long-term implications. 'Seen in that light Operation Ajax was a disaster; it created a slur nothing could whitewash.' In 1979, the long-term failure of

Boot/Ajax came back to haunt the West when the Shah was swept from power and replaced by a medieval theocracy under Ayatollah Khomeini.[131]

Roosevelt later felt sorry for Mossadeq and arranged for him to receive a pension after he had served three years of his sentence. The former Prime Minister died, aged eighty-four, in March 1967.

According to Tom Bower's sources, George Young and other senior MI6 officers drew four lessons from the apparent success of Boot/Ajax. Firstly, 'despite Philby, the CIA still trusted and respected the British for joint operations'. While there was some trust and respect, this is, in reality, a distortion of Young's more hard-headed view. Anthony Verrier's assessment is closer to the mark when he writes that 'SIS as a whole was never to be the same in American eyes'. Even at the best of times, 'suspicions and misconceptions were never far below the surface in Anglo-American relations', asserts Nigel Ashton in his study of Anglo-American relations in the Middle East. It was 'only the even greater fear of the advance of Communism in the region which held it in check'. The relationship had a 'specialness in both conflict and co-operation'. Telling is Monty Woodhouse's remark that 'so far as I know, Operation Boot was the first such operation successfully carried out with the Americans, and probably the last by the British. It was also the only one they ever carried out together.'[132]

Secondly, 'senior CIA officers appeared more sympathetic to British foreign policy than the State Department'. This is undoubtedly true but needs qualification. Contrary to Bower's view that Allen Dulles was an 'Anglophile', he was, in fact, an anglophobe and had been since his schooldays when he wrote an essay in support of the Boers. As a young man, Dulles had travelled to India, where he taught English. His opinion of the British Empire was formed by his time there, and he came to distrust the British. Like his brother, he believed that an independent British imperial policy was 'impossible where this conflicted with American political and commercial interests'. He did not, however, 'have to like the people he had to work with, and this was his view of Britain'.[133]

Young was well aware of the American view of the British, and while Bower's third and fourth points are undoubtedly true – Young's belief that MI6's clandestine operations in peacetime were of proven benefit, and that MI6 could promote British interests in the Middle East – the 'robber barons' around Young were nevertheless prepared to carry out their agenda, if necessary without the support of and often in opposition to the Americans. The one concrete result was that, flush with the success of the operation in Iran, MI6 created in 1954 the Special Political Action (SPA) section with a specific remit for undertaking similar 'disruptive' operations.

Bower finally concludes that 'Eden and Young were obsessed by MI6's desire to reverse Britain's deteriorating status in the world, and in particular in Egypt'. Up to a point; despite the myths, Egypt was of secondary concern. What they wanted to protect was Britain's role in Iraq and, latterly, Kuwait, where British-controlled oilfields lay in abundance.[134]

CHAPTER 29

SUEZ: ASSASSINS AND THUGGERY

Despite success in Iran, the Foreign Office and the government's handling of Middle East affairs was, according to MI6's George Young, a 'tale of blunder and disaster'. 'We seemed to be blissfully unaware of the extent to which the Arabs had come to resent the physical presence of British troops, and how far the rulers and politicians, who were our close associates, had become discredited in the eyes of the younger generation.' Young considered that 'the hard truth is that in the majority of cases, a course of action was forced on us as a consequence of failure to make positive decisions at an earlier stage, for a stubborn refusal to face reality can hardly be called a decision'. He later despaired of the 'complete paralysis of will which seemed to settle on us. How did the British Government get into this fix in the first place? Why didn't it sort out its Middle East policy long before Suez? Why didn't the British make up their own minds instead of waiting for the Americans?'[1]

Young did not seem to think that MI6 had been at fault, despite the fact that it had been putting more of its resources into the Middle East than it devoted to the Soviet bloc. Even so, the Service's intelligence-gathering on Egypt, in particular, was regarded as poor.

The MI6 element of the British Middle East Office (BMEO) in Egypt operated under the cover name of the 'Co-ordination Division', and was headed by H. John Collins and his deputy, a former Special Operations Executive (SOE) officer, Teddy de Haan. It moved to Cyprus during 1954, where it remained under the control of Collins until its functions were transferred to the Political Office with the Middle East Forces (POMEF), which was sited within the British Military Hospital compound at Episkopi on Cyprus. Collins liked to drink and live life to the full, a lifestyle underwritten by his French wife, the daughter of successful businessman, Antonin Besse, who had his head office in the City of London. Besse was responsible for funding the spooks' college, St Antony's, at Oxford.[2]

The MI6 station in Egypt was headed by Geoffrey Hinton, a friend of Kim Philby who had transferred at the end of the war from the Ministry of Information to work in MI6's Section V. His deputy was a former SAS officer who worked with Young in Austria, G. M. F. Alston. The local station was regarded as 'incompetent'. Its political intelligence was inadequate, while operational intelligence supplied to the services was often inaccurate or out of date. The station was also complacent, relying on the fact that the ruling Wafd Party seemed secure and the Prime Minister, Hilali Pasha, honestly co-operative. When Julian Amery informed Foreign Secretary Anthony Eden that a British instructor of the Egyptian General Staff had informed him that a group of officers was ready to seize power, MI6 assured him that 'the Army was loyal to the King'. The local station's knowledge of what the CIA was up to in Egypt was just as lacking.[3]

US Secretary of State Dean Acheson had 'borrowed' Kermit Roosevelt from the CIA to head a special committee to study the Arab world. The committee favoured the establishment of regimes that would carry out social and political reform which in turn would complement American economic aid. The National Security Council's (NSC) aim was to 'support or develop those leadership groups in the areas which offered the greatest prospect of establishing political stability orientated toward the free world'. The chosen vehicle for these ideas was Egypt, where clandestine channels were established between the local CIA station under James Eichelberger and a group of young Free Officers in the military.

On 22 July 1952, with three thousand troops and two hundred officers, General Mohammed Neguib seized power in Cairo. Not long after, King Farouk left for exile in Naples on the royal yacht, accompanied by most of the country's gold reserves. MI6 had been caught unawares and had no intelligence on the coup, and what it had on the ruling junta was mostly ill informed.

The young army officers running the country were led by Neguib, but it became increasingly obvious that the real power lay with the small group of largely anti-British Free Officers, led by the ultra-nationalist Gamal Nasser, who had inspired the revolution. Nasser had in his youth demonstrated against the British and had gone to prison for his efforts. 'The young officers', John de Courcy Hamilton in the Cairo embassy noted in March 1953, 'think we are on the decline as a Great Power; they have a real hatred politically of us in their hearts. No amount of concession or evacuation on our part will evoke the slightest gratitude in return. Whoever Egypt may want in the future as an ally, it will not be us.' The US State Department concurred, declaring that Britain was engaged in the same mistaken Middle East policy as it had pursued in Iran. Nor did it help that there were clear indications that Britain had been working towards the goal of an 'Iraq–Jordan' axis, which meant that the chances of the Egyptians becoming 'our friends are slight'.[4]

During December 1953 Eden considered a coup and, perhaps, even more drastic action against the Neguib government, but was dissuaded from taking this route by Ambassador Ralph Stevenson, a former chair of the Joint Intelligence Staff. 'There is no alternative for Egypt: assassination of Neguib would lead to one of Neguib's lieutenants, presumably Nasser [assuming power].' The CIA was the main influence upon the new Egyptian leaders and was particularly interested in Nasser. Initial contact with him was made through Mohammed Heikal, a journalist with the newspaper *Akkhbar el-Yom*, owned by a CIA agent, Mustafa Amin. Late in February 1954, Neguib was manoeuvred into resigning and was, indeed, replaced by Nasser, Roosevelt's protégé. Nasser was seen by the CIA as a strong leader, capable of taking unpopular decisions, and the CIA team of Roosevelt and Miles Copeland worked to shore up his hold in the interests of creating a viable Middle East regime which might come to an accommodation with Israel.[5]

In March 1954 Nasser asked Roosevelt to contact the British with the aim of concluding a quick and decisive settlement. The agreement, concluded in October, envisaged British troops pulling out in stages, a policy to be completed by June 1956. Embassy reports indicated that British attitudes within the Foreign Office had changed, and there was hope that the new revolutionary government would become a potential ally of the West. The Joint Intelligence Committee (JIC) was increasingly unconvinced of the requirement for troops and a military base in Egypt. Part of the agreement was that until the base was relinquished, it would be under civilian control.

The local MI6 station did not agree with these assessments, particularly those coming from the embassy. The station was run on independent lines – both in its intelligence-gathering and operations – by an ally of Young's, Freddie Stockwell, officially the consul in Alexandria – and later a leading figure in the right-wing Tory Monday Club, and his deputy, Ian Critchett. The vice-consul at Alexandria, Ralph Stockbridge, a former member of the wartime MI6 cover post, the Inter-Services Liaison Department (ISLD), in Cairo, was succeeded by the 'ace agent-runner' fresh from Tehran, Alexis Fforter, who was replaced in turn by David Crichton and, in his first posting abroad, Craig Smellie. The station rejected the suggestion that Nasser represented a new voice in Arab politics, likely to have an enduring appeal in the region. He was not seen as an aberration nor an intransigent figure, as was Mossadeq in Iran. Instead, it was reported that Nasser was unlikely to last long. Eden preferred to hear the Secret Service's wish fulfilments, and so MI6 in 'Cairo continued to send back reports which only Eden wanted to read'.[6]

Additional pressure was put on the Foreign Secretary by the backbench 'Suez Group', formed in 1953 to unite opposition to any proposed changes in the relationship with Egypt. Composed of 'a hotchpotch collection of embittered ex-Ministers and young, newly elected back-benchers anxious to cut a figure in Parliament by attacking the Government for selling out British imperial interests', it was chaired by an ex-minister, Captain Charles Waterhouse, and included Ralph Assheton, Julian Amery, Fitzroy Maclean, Enoch Powell, Viscount Hinchinbrooke and Lord Hankey, father of the modern central intelligence machinery and a director of the Suez Canal Company. It was encouraged behind the scenes by senior ministers and helped by MI6. The words 'wogs' and 'wog-bashing', 'long beloved by sound Tories and particularly those of a military bent, were much heard', recalled Foreign Office official Geoffrey McDermott, who had responsibilities on the intelligence side, 'in the corridors when President Nasser and his fellow Egyptians were being discussed'. As McDermott noted, half a dozen of the top MI6 officers went in for 'extreme right-wing politics'. There was, Amery admitted, 'a great deal of resentment about American policies' and the group held that Britain 'could only remain a world power through its presence on the Suez Canal, which was held to be vital to world and Empire shipping communications'. Group members were informed that Eden did not want a compromise, and Churchill privately encouraged them.[7]

Indeed, almost as soon as the Naguib–Nasser group seized power, MI6 had begun to conspire to bring it down. John Farmer, who was stationed in Rome, was introduced by a Cairo-based Yugoslav agent to two leading Egyptians. Prince Abdu Monheim was the son of the Khedive of Egypt and a former rector of the al-Azhar University, while Ahmed Mortada al-Maraghi was a leading theologian and former interior minister. Backing them was an anti-Nasser group of senior army figures intent on promoting al-Maraghi as Prime Minister in a post-Nasser government.[8]

At the end of 1954 Eden took two new policy initiatives on the Middle East. The first, in deepest secrecy, was a typically British solution to security, as the Foreign Secretary 'coaxed and cajoled' several Middle East governments – Iran was eventually amongst them – into a treaty of mutual defence known as the Baghdad Pact of Britain's allies in the region. The pact was concerned with the direct threat believed to be posed by the Red Army across the Soviet southern border. It was designed with political considerations, 'since a state could equally well be subverted from within by the establishment of a regime inimical to Western interests'. Britain was enthusiastic about the pact as part of the process of creating an Iraq–Jordan axis, though it would soon come to promote solely the interests of Iraq. The British had clearly hoped to involve Egypt, but the Foreign Secretary's visit to Cairo in

February 1955 was not a success, especially given the manner in which Eden – with his patrician ways – talked down to Nasser.

When the pact was established under British leadership on 4 April 1955, the day before Eden became Prime Minister, America – and Egypt – were conspicuously absent. Iraq and Turkey signed, and Britain entered several weeks later, while Pakistan and Iran joined in September and October respectively. Formally a defence alliance for deterring Soviet aggression through joint military planning and exercises, and pledges of non-intervention, the pact also included a special committee dealing with counter-subversion. Its main function appears to have been the dissemination and co-ordination of intelligence on Soviet activities in the region, and the planning of stay-behind networks and guerrilla warfare in the unlikely event of a Soviet invasion.

Eden's second policy initiative was, in practical terms, as Keith Kyle notes, 'the enemy of the other'. Left to smoulder, Eden thought that the Palestine/ Israel problem would allow the Soviets, 'the Bear', to slip into the Middle East. Following discussions with Nasser, the Foreign Office proposed a permanent solution. The few officials besides US Secretary of State Foster Dulles and Eden who knew about the initiative referred to the project as 'Alpha'. As officials considered solutions, the Egyptian General Staff Intelligence Branch set up a special operations organisation in the Gaza Strip, the *'fedayen'*, to carry out sabotage and terrorism inside Israel.[9]

Incensed at Baghdad's decision to join the pro-western alliance, Nasser began to foment unrest in Iraq, and took steps to isolate its government in the Arab world. The British and Americans sought co-operation on Syria, in particular with regard to the August 1955 presidential elections in which they hoped to back a candidate who would unite the right-wing elements, notably the Nationalist and People's Party. They wanted to prevent the election of a pro-French, anti-British and anti-Iraqi Minister for Foreign Affairs, Khalid el-Azm, who opposed the British-backed Baghdad Pact. Dissident elements on the Right tried to interest the British in an Iraqi-backed coup d'état, but at that stage officials refused to endorse it. All that was achieved was the election of a weak alternative to el-Azm, President Shukri el-Quwwatli. Better from a British viewpoint was the result of the September elections in Iraq which brought to power the anglophile Nuri Said, who was fanatical in his anti-communism and about the threat from the Soviet Union. Britain was, therefore, hopeful that some kind of accommodation could be reached on the Anglo-Iraqi defence agreement which was due to expire in 1957.[10]

Eden believed that the Baghdad Pact would bring stability to the area, but as Geoffrey McDermott noted: 'On the contrary it nettled Nasser into his first arms deal with the Communists, specifically Czechoslovakia.' The deal broke the international embargo designed to avoid upsetting the balance of power in the region. Egypt was still largely dependent on the British and French for its arms supplies, but Nasser regarded these as infuriatingly slim as they were supplied in small instalments. In May 1955, following advice from Tito, Nasser had secretly been contacted by the Soviets with an offer to supply arms. A month later, the British refused to increase the small quantity of arms that it sold to Egypt, in particular ammunition for Centurion tanks. It was a decision that Field Marshal Sir Richard Hall described as driving Nasser 'straight into the arms of Moscow'. Indeed, Nasser told the State Department that a mission was to depart immediately for Moscow. On 26 July secret deliveries of arms began to leave Prague for Cairo.[11]

London was informed of the conclusion of the arms deal on 21 September. 'The shock effect in the Foreign Office, as the incoming reports made clear that Nasser had passed the point of no-return, produced a series of high-level official memoranda.' On the evening of 26 September, the new British ambassador, Humphrey Trevelyan, saw Nasser, who told him that a deal had been concluded with Israel's old supplier, Czechoslovakia. Unbeknown to the British, during the period of the arms deal the Egyptian President was being briefed by Miles Copeland and Kermit Roosevelt, and it was they who later advised Nasser to say that the arms were coming from the Czechs and not the Soviet Union. Nasser stressed to Trevelyan that after being dominated by the British for seventy years, Egypt was not about to let the Russians do the same. As Steven Frieberger suggests, 'Why would Arab nationalists, fighting so hard to end Western colonial domination, exchange it for domination by the Soviets?' Unfortunately, the British were unwilling to take at face value what Nasser was telling them, even though the Soviet Union was never a real threat to British interests in the Middle East; particularly since 'the devotion of the Arab world to a fervent Islamic faith pointed to a vehement anti-communist stance'.[12]

On the 27th, notification of the arms deal was released by the Foreign Office's news department. The Government Communications Headquarters (GCHQ) was already busy monitoring the diplomatic traffic between Prague and Cairo for evidence of the massive deal. In what appears to have been an example of MI6 briefing, the *Economist* described the unloading of '133 huge cases of Czech arms' only ten days after the announcement of the arms deal. The Soviets were to supply arms worth over $400 million, with 80 MiG-15 fighters, 45 Ilyushin-28 bombers and 150 tanks, which would take a year to come into active service. Most of the details on the shipments were obtained by MI6 from its agent in the commercial section of the Egyptian embassy in Prague. Aged nearly sixty, and something of a playboy spy, Mohamud Hamdi was run by a woman officer in the MI6 station in Vienna. He was eventually betrayed by an agent named 'Light'. Using a prostitute who had been employed previously by the intelligence service for a similar undertaking, the Czechs launched a 'honeytrap' operation against the Egyptian diplomat. Successfully ensnared, Hamdi was pulled out of Prague by the Vienna station – run by Maurice Firth and Geoffrey MacBride, and then Nicholas Elliott and

Cyril Rolo – before the Czechs were able to effect the denouement.[13]

Views within the Foreign Office were beginning to harden. Former head of the JIC Harold Caccia minuted that if Nasser became committed to the arms deal then 'we may have to get rid of Nasser'. Through September, the options – including trying 'to frighten Nasser, then to bribe him, and, if neither works, get rid of him' – were discussed by officials, who wanted to 'stop the rot, since once the Russian technicians are in Egypt, there is no knowing how far the damage may extend'. Eventually, the Foreign Office settled on a more long-term solution, because it could see 'no outstanding military figure or group' on the horizon who could 'consolidate the loyalty of the armed forces'. The former Prime Minister, Ali Maher, who had been dismissed by the junta and had made contact with the British, was considered but was thought to be too old. The Foreign Office was still willing to return to the negotiating table over the military base but pressure from the increasingly vocal Suez Group and MI6 assessments, which suggested that the Egyptian government would soon collapse, ensured that the negotiations were undermined. On 2 October 1955 there were calls for 'no further attempts to compromise with the Egyptians'.[14]

Meanwhile, the Foreign Office continued to worry about other events in the Middle East, in particular Syria, which it regarded as 'the nearest thing in the Middle East to a Soviet satellite'. Syria was viewed as strategically important because the Iraqi Petroleum Company's pipelines ran through the country on their way to Mediterranean terminals. The British and Americans wanted to ensure a pro-Iraqi regime in Damascus through the use of overt and covert measures. The Permanent Under-Secretary, Ivone Kirkpatrick, minuted on 31 October 1955 that these measures should be limited for the time being to encouraging their 'friends' inside and outside Iraq, though 'in the event that Syria falls under Soviet domination or seems likely to do so, we should encourage the liquidation of the country and its incorporation into Iraq'. At the first meeting of the Baghdad Pact, Iraqi leader Nuri es-Sa'id raised fears about a 'major Soviet offensive in the Middle East, assisted by Saudi money and Egyptian propaganda'. Officials talked of backing Iraqi proposals to purchase Syrian newspapers, develop effective radio propaganda and promote Syrian politicians, officials and students. Potential action appears to have included the use of the Foreign Office's Information Research Department (IRD).[15]

MI6 continued to ensure that its pessimistic reports on Soviet penetration of the Middle East went directly to a receptive Prime Minister. Towards the end of November, Eden received the first of a stream of intelligence reports, known as 'Lucky Break', from a 'highly reliable source' reputedly positioned within Nasser's immediate entourage. MI6 assessed that Nasser was 'far more under Soviet influence than had been supposed and that, in return for Soviet support for his ambitions, he was prepared to allow the Russians to play any role in the area that they chose'. Senior Foreign Office official Evelyn Shuckburgh was initially sceptical of the reports and did not 'quite believe' that Nasser was thinking of 'consciously handing over his country to Communism. I think he thinks himself supremely clever and is playing East off against West to the last moment.'[16]

Despite Foreign Office scepticism, Shuckburgh realised that the West had to regain the initiative in case Egypt was permanently lost to the Soviets. Shuckburgh had been the architect of the Alpha plan, which envisaged the trading of concessions by Israel, in the form of territory and compensation, to the Palestinian refugees in exchange for recognition from the neighbouring Arab states and guarantees of security from the western powers. During October and November, the CIA attempted to broker a deal, known as Operation CHAMELEON, in which Israel would for the first time have been given official arms and aid from the US in return for accepting a lasting peace with Egypt. Allen Dulles, Kermit Roosevelt and James Angleton heard from a CIA officer who had visited Nasser that the Egyptian leader was 'willing to negotiate in principle'. The officer, however, 'expressed his doubts and does not believe in Israel's sincere desire for peace'. During December, the British pushed the Alpha plan hard but diplomats suffered a setback when Jordan failed to join the Baghdad Pact. The real problem that doomed Alpha was that Nasser would only contemplate a solution that involved the cession of a 'corridor' of desert to Jordan, which Israel would not cede. Unbeknown to the CIA, Israel was itself contemplating asking the Soviets for arms if they did not receive satisfaction from the US.[17]

The Lucky Break reports had an immediate impact within Number Ten. On 26 November, Eden passed the intelligence material on to Washington with the comment to President Eisenhower that if the Americans did not accede to Egyptian demands for finance for the Aswan Dam project, 'I fear the Russians are certain to get the contract.' The material did make an impression on the Eisenhower administration, which suggested that it would be better 'to find an alternative to Nasser . . . If he really was lost to the West, the Dam should be a present for a successor.' Even Shuckburgh acknowledged on 28 November that if Nasser was indeed a communist puppet, then 'the right course would be to overthrow him rather than to offer him an immense and burdensome bribe'. He went on, 'it looks very much as if the only possible ways of disrupting the present course of the Egyptian regime are: (i) the death of Nasser; (ii) a free hand to the Israelis'. On 14 December the British and Americans finally made an offer to finance the Aswan Dam under World Bank supervision.[18]

By January 1956 the Middle East was viewed as being in an explosive state. Eden 'attributed this mainly to Moscow's increasing determination to intrude in Middle East affairs', but Geoffrey McDermott, who saw the British and American intelligence reports, thought the Prime Minister's analysis 'inaccurate and inadequate'. Soviet policy towards the region was character-ised, McDermott concluded, by extreme caution, and any problems in Jordan and Iraq centred on the family quarrels between their Hashemite rulers which reflected 'the legacies of British imperialism, a struggle for power between the legatees and their radical nationalist rivals'. Such views were treated with contempt inside MI6.[19]

MI6 was relieved when, in the new year, with Eden firmly in the saddle, a new Cabinet brought Selwyn Lloyd to the post of Foreign Secretary, replacing Harold Macmillan, who went to the Treasury. Although a first-class staff officer during the war and a man known for straightforward honesty, Lloyd had not been regarded as a backbencher of achievement and, as he admitted, he had no experience of foreign affairs nor of foreign countries. 'He owed everything to Eden.' While the Foreign Office was not impressed by his pedestrian manner, MI6 held him in high regard – perhaps on the basis that the Foreign Office did not. George Young thought that it was not until Lloyd toured the Middle East and 'tried to bring some ordering principles into the haphazard and unco-ordinated actions and attitudes, that something like a sense of direction appeared'. One of his first actions was to ask the Israelis 'if they could invade Egypt and reach the canal within five days and return to her borders after the invasion'. The answer Lloyd received was apparently positive. As Operation Chameleon faded, the French moved in to supply arms to Israel. The French were increasingly opposed to Nasser, principally because of Egypt's support for the nationalists in North Africa.[20]

Young still felt that 'the greater part of 1956 was spent in an endeavour, futile as it turned out, to persuade the Americans to collaborate with us on some form of agreed policy'. The British and American governments both believed that something had to be done about Nasser, but misinterpretations, opposing policies and clashing personalities undermined any attempts at effective action. The US Secretary of State was clear on the need for inter-national action but would not sanction the use of force, even though the British came to believe that he had. Foster Dulles's style clashed with that of his British counterpart, while Eden came to regard President Eisenhower as 'a stupid man' and 'internationally inept'. There was little chance of the Americans joining in a general strategy on the Middle East while Britain refused to compromise on Buraimi.[21]

Since the 1930s there had been a dispute over the ownership of the Buraimi oasis, which lay between Saudi Arabia, which wanted it as a bridge to the sea, and the Trucial Sheikhdoms of Abu Dhabi, Muscat and Oman, which, with the support of Britain, wanted the area to consolidate the position of the states. A truce had collapsed in August 1952, and following arbitration by an international tribunal had been abandoned when intelligence suggested that US oil giant ARAMCO and CIA representatives were collaborating with the Saudis to subvert the area. British advisers subsequently led Trucial troops in occupying the oasis; the effect was to drive Nasser and the Saudis closer together, with the Egyptians supplying arms, financed by ARAMCO.[22]

Foreign Secretary Macmillan suggested to Dulles that if Britain retreated from the Buraimi, then the Trucial states might turn to the Russians. On 16 January 1956, Eden warned Eisenhower that 'it is increasingly clear that the Saudis, the Russians, the Egyptians and the Syrians are working together . . . if we don't want to see the whole Middle East fall into Communist hands, we must back our friends in Jordan and in Iraq. If the Saudis have their way, there will be nothing left for anybody but the Bear.' Coincidentally, an assassination plot against Iraq's Prime Minister was uncovered which implicated the Egyptian military attaché. The British subsequently tried to develop Iraq–Jordan links. Rather conveniently, MI6 furnished reports which indicated that Israel might take 'provocative action on or about 1st March' against Jordan. Fearing such an attack, Jordan requested British assistance, to which the Cabinet gave guarded support on 28 February.[23]

Around the turn of the new year, George Young issued a circular in which he presented his views on the role of the spy in the modern world.

> The nuclear stalemate is matched by a moral stalemate. It is the spy who has been called upon to remedy the situation created by deficiencies of ministers, diplomats, generals and priests. Men's minds are shaped, of course, by their environment and we spies, although we have our professional mystique, do perhaps live closer to the realities and hard facts of international relations than other practitioners of government. We are relatively free of the problems of status, precedence, departmental attitudes and evasions of personal responsibility, which create the official cast of mind. We do not have to develop, like the Parliamentarians conditioned by a lifetime, the ability to produce the ready phrase, the smart reply and the flashing smile. And so it is not surprising these days that the spy finds himself the main guardian of intellectual integrity.[24]

It was an intellectual integrity, however, that appeared to shun questions of morality. In a 1985 television interview on the BBC's *Heart of the Matter* about the morality of assassinations, and on a Radio Four series on the 'Profession of Intelligence', Young denied that Nasser's murder was ordered or considered justified. He did, however, admit that he had few qualms about ordering the death of someone in peacetime if he felt it was in the national interest; though he would not be drawn on whether or not he had, in fact, done so. Young acknowledged that the internal overthrow of Nasser was considered and, with an effective opposition, 'it was easy to see that Nasser might have been killed'. Shunning morality, Young preferred to hide behind the notion of intellectual integrity. He was never going to acknowledge the existence of an operation of a type that Foreign Secretary Douglas Hurd admitted, during the debate on the 'avowal' of the Secret Intelligence Service, was 'illegal', despite supposed protection under the royal prerogative.

As early as February 1956, MI6 had been considering a plan to assassinate President Nasser. In the Arab edition of his book *Cutting the Lion's Tail*, Egyptian journalist and one of Nasser's closest associates Mohammed Heikel published the text of a telegram from a CIA officer in London, James Eichelberger, to Allen Dulles in Washington. This contained details of a meeting towards the end of February, during which MI6 raised with Eichelberger the idea of killing Nasser. George Young spoke with a frankness that horrified the American. 'He talked openly of assassinating Nasser, instead of using a polite euphemism like liquidating. He said his people had been in contact with suitable elements in Egypt and in the rest of the Arab world, and ... with the French, who were thinking along the same lines.' Indeed, the French intelligence service, SDECE, already had a special operations action branch in Egypt, code-named RAP 700, supervised by Captain Paul Leger. As early as 1954 a paid 'hit man' from the action branch had organised an attempt on Nasser with an agent, Jean-Marie Pellay, who just missed his target.[25]

The CIA liaison officer in London, Chester Cooper, was also aware that Young was 'determined to remove and even murder Nasser' and that he was 'supported by some CIA officers'. Eichelberger, though, was apparently so alarmed by what he was hearing that he leaked much of it back to Nasser. For Nasser, this was an early confirmation of his suspicion that the Americans were playing their own game in Egypt and the rest of the region.[26]

The modern conception of the world of the secret intelligence services and assassinations derives partly from the fictionalised activities of James Bond. The licensed-to-kill operative is the model for the secret service agent of the public's imagination. While this is fantasy, the former Naval Intelligence and one-time MI6 asset Ian Fleming based the plots and details for his 007 books on incidents in his own life and information he picked up during his career in the secret world. However fantastic the story, there is always an element of truth in Bond.

In *Casino Royale*, Bond earns his double-O designation – his licence to kill – by shooting a Japanese cipher expert at the Rockefeller Center in New York. In June 1941, Fleming had visited the United States to see how an offshoot of MI6, the British Security Co-ordination (BSC), operated in the Americas. Fleming was shown around the intelligence complex by the 'Quiet Canadian', Sir William Stephenson, head of the BSC. Below Stephenson's spacious office was the Japanese consular office, occupied by a cipher expert who was transmitting coded messages back to Tokyo. He was not assassinated, but Fleming did witness the burglary of the office and out of this adventure grew the idea that would find its way into *Casino Royale*.[27]

It may be that Fleming was let into the secret that Stephenson was running an assassination squad. Just before the CIA's William Harvey, who had been presented to President Kennedy as the Agency's own 'James Bond', began recruiting members of the Mafia to help organise assassination plots against Fidel Castro, Harvey queried MI5's technical officer, Peter Wright, on ideas. 'Have you thought of approaching Stephenson?' Wright enquired. 'A lot of the old-timers say he ran this kind of thing in New York during the war. Used some Italian, apparently, when there was no other way of sorting a German spy. Probably the Mafia.' It turns out that Wright was correct. Before he died in 1990, former BSC officer H. Montgomery Hyde revealed on Channel Four's *After Dark* programme that the BSC had assassinated a German seaman who was operating as a spy in New York. This was an extremely dangerous act because the United States was neutral at the time, and there were many isolationists and anti-British politicians who would gleefully have jumped on this indiscretion, had it been made public.[28]

The BSC case illustrates a philosophy that is central to such operations and was a particular hallmark of MI6 planning – plausible deniability. The use of third parties lessens the threat of any operation unravelling to reveal the hand of the sponsoring organisation. Obviously, in times of war, constraints on such operations are not so tight and are more easily justified. Chapman Pincher acknowledges that during the war MI6 had 'no qualms about handing over a captive to a third party intent on killing him. Mikal Trinsky, who had betrayed escaping Polish Jews to the Nazis, was kidnapped by MI6 and handed over to Jewish partisans.' According to a former MI6 officer: 'Trinsky's head was eventually used as a football.'[29]

The other covert service, the Special Operations Executive (SOE), had an assassination capability that to some extent did correspond with a James Bond world. According to historian M. R. D. Foot, 'SOE was the only body competent enough to fake an accident'. SOE operational head Colin Gubbins appears to 'have seen no particular objection to SOE being implicated in a political assassination', the sort of operation that, at the time, Eden stigmatised as 'war crimes business'. When SOE proposed assassinating an important German figure in the Middle East, Gubbins told the minister controlling SOE that there was 'really no need for him to know about such things'. Czech agents trained by SOE were part of Operation ANTHROPOID, which resulted in the lingering death, in May 1942, of the ruthless head of the Sicherheitsdienst (SD), Reinhard Heydrich. What was interesting about this particular assassination was the claim of the head of the highly secret biological warfare team at Porton Down, Paul Fildes, that he 'had a hand' in the operation – most probably through coating the hand anti-tank grenades used in the ambush with botulin toxins which entered Heydrich's wounds. In the run-up to the invasion of Europe, Gubbins had proposed 'Ratweek', a grand scheme to assassinate SD officers in France, but was 'opposed by

"C" on the grounds that it would lead to reprisals throughout France'.[30]

According to Kenneth Younger, a minister of state for foreign affairs under Ernest Bevin in the late forties and a senior MI5 officer during the war, serious thought was given to the assassination of the Mufti of Jerusalem, the Indian nationalist leader, Chandra Bose, and an unnamed Balkan monarch. These thoughts never proceeded beyond the planning stage because it was concluded that 'nothing would be gained by making martyrs of such people'.[31]

SOE's assassination capability was, apparently, officially closed down at the end of hostilities, but since elements of SOE were later subsumed within MI6 into the Special Operations Branch it is clearly possible that the relevant expertise did not go to waste. Assassination as a policy was openly discussed in the postwar years. Sponsored murder gangs operated among the exiles in the DP camps in Germany and Austria. Many of these operatives, known as 'mechanics', were sponsored by the Allied intelligence services but their activities were always arm's-length operations. By 1950, the idea of assassination as a serious policy had been shelved, though within MI6 – which was involved in a number of 'comic-book' operations – the concept was not dead. It was in the Middle East that MI6 seriously considered using it as an option. As we have already seen, in April 1953 the chief of the Iranian National Police, General Afshartus, was murdered by a group of army officers operating on behalf of MI6.[32]

The dismissal on 1 March of the British commander of the Arab Legion in Jordan, John Glubb 'Pasha', by the young King Hussein, tipped British Prime Minister Anthony Eden into 'a form of obsessive madness'. The dismissal, which won back for the King 'much of the popularity which Nasser had so dangerously acquired in Jordan', was regarded as being perfectly understandable by Foreign Office officials – Hussein wanted the army commanded by a Jordanian – but Eden irrationally blamed this insult against Britain on Nasser. He raged that Glubb had been dismissed 'suddenly, like a pilfering servant'. His reaction was 'violent'. He declared a personal war on Nasser, whom he regarded as a new Hitler who must be removed. Foreign Office officials around Eden were referring to 'appeasement' and it seems that it was Ivone Kirkpatrick who was responsible for Eden's references to Nasser as a Hitler or Mussolini. On 12 March, Eden told Shuckburgh 'it is either him or us, don't forget that'.[33]

The Prime Minister was at this stage suffering from 'what the layman would call brain fever'. Part of Chester Cooper's job for the CIA while liaising with the British in London was to keep himself informed about the state of Eden's health. 'By then he was quite ill, a nervous person anyway, he was taking some sort of drug which was affecting his nervous system.' Surgery on his bile duct had not been completely successful and poison was seeping into his bloodstream and eating away at his whole system. He was taking increasing doses of benzedrine to disguise the condition. The Prime Minister was accompanied everywhere by 'a great chest of pills and at times required injections'. He was highly emotional and often worked in an atmosphere of frenzied hysteria. His private secretary, Frederick Bishop, admitted that Eden was subject to fits of temper which led to 'throwing things across the room'. Eden 'compensated for his personal ailments and political frustrations by dreaming of his enemy's destruction'.[34]

On the Monday following the parliamentary debate on Glubb's removal, Minister of State for Foreign Affairs Anthony Nutting was hosting a dinner for Harold Stassen, an American colleague on the United Nations (UN) Disarmament Commission. Earlier in the day, Nutting had sent the Prime Minister a memorandum on the Middle East proposing that the UN take on some of the responsibility for keeping the peace between Israel and her Arab neighbours, and making suggestions for neutralising Nasser's attacks on British interests as a means of softening Eden's declaration of war. Eden was not impressed. In the middle of the dinner, the Prime Minister used an open line to telephone Nutting. 'What's all this poppycock you've sent me? . . . What's all this nonsense about isolating Nasser or "neutralising" him, as you call it? I want him destroyed, can't you understand? I want him murdered, and if you and the Foreign Office don't agree, then you'd better come to the Cabinet and explain why.'[35]

A shocked Nutting tried to reason with the Prime Minister and suggested that it would be wise to look firstly for an alternative figurehead 'who would not be still more hostile to us. At the moment there did not appear to be any alternative, hostile or friendly.' Eden would not be deflected. 'But I don't want an alternative,' he shouted at Nutting. 'And I don't give a damn if there's anarchy and chaos in Egypt.' Nutting felt 'as if I had had a nightmare, only the nightmare was real'. A few days after his telephone call to Nutting, Eden said much the same to Sir Ivone Kirkpatrick, Permanent Under-Secretary at the Foreign Office. 'I don't think we have a department for that sort of thing, Prime Minister,' Kirkpatrick replied. 'But if we do, it certainly is not under my control.'[36]

Writer and former intelligence officer Gordon Brook-Shepherd claimed that the assassination of Nasser 'would have been a tall order professionally in 1956, for those so-called "wet jobs" had been abandoned by our intelligence services soon after the end of the war'. He went on to suggest that even if Eden, in the manner of King Henry in referring to Thomas à Becket, had in exasperation exclaimed 'Who will rid me of this turbulent priest?', 'Eden's knights would have said "No"'. This is a defence that apologists for MI6 have attempted to put on record. Anthony Verrier has written that 'thuggery was on the agenda. But the Prime Ministerial order was disobeyed. SIS was not living in a James Bond world . . . an elaborate assassination plan was made, carefully arranged to fail.' Is this credible?[37]

Eden appears to have bypassed his Foreign Office officials and his new Foreign Secretary, Selwyn Lloyd – although it has been said that Lloyd ordered the removal of a file from his office concerning Nasser's murder – and gone direct to MI6 through Patrick Dean, who 'had long worked in intelligence' and was chair of the JIC. Dean shared the Prime Minister's assessment of Nasser that he 'had to be removed from the scene, and by any method which came to hand'. It would appear that Eden and Dean, in turn, did not seek the approval of the Chief of MI6, 'Sinbad' Sinclair, who was seen as a weak figure by senior officers. Instead, decisions on priorities in the Middle East, and on Egypt in particular, and those concerning any assassination attempts, were left to George Young, a man on a high after the success of the 1953 coup against Mossadeq in Iran.[38]

While MI6 did not have a specific department to deal with assassinations it did have access to the necessary expertise through its 'Q' Ops section of the Technical Services Division, and to qualified personnel in the Special Political Action (SPA) section. It could also call upon the SAS, whose NATO remit included undertaking special operations and assassinations. As to the idea that the attempts were deliberately meant to fail, this is unlikely given the range and number of operations undertaken.

In 'a most secret note', Eden wrote to Eisenhower on 15 March 1956 with 'absolutely reliable information' that Nasser aimed to establish a 'United Arab States' by means of 'unseating' the Iraqi Prime Minister and frustrating the Baghdad Pact by 'the overthrow of the Hashemite families in Iraq and Jordan' and 'the monarchy in Libya, and the establishment of purely Arab republics in Tunisia, Algeria and Morocco'. Nasser intended to encourage Saudi Arabia in these moves while at the same time working to remove its monarchy. This vast conspiracy was to be achieved by dispatching intelligence agents in the guise of educational missions to all the Arab states. This was followed six days later by further information from MI6's Lucky Break to the effect that Nasser had 'already decided to engage in hostilities with Israel and has even decided that June would be the best time', when British troops would be out of the Canal Zone.[39]

Based on this intelligence, which in retrospect appears highly dubious, on 21 March the Cabinet agreed to a proposal from the Foreign Secretary that Britain 'should seek to establish in Syria a Government more friendly to the West'. Three days later in Washington, an *ad hoc* committee of State Department and CIA officials including Allen Dulles, James Angleton and Kermit Roosevelt considered whether Nasser would rally Arab support behind him for war with Israel, and what the consequences would be in terms of oil and the prospects for communism. The committee agreed a set of proposals which was put to the Foreign Office. Following a meeting at the White House on the 28th, a joint Anglo-American accord known as OMEGA was agreed, the primary purpose of which was to make Nasser aware that 'he would not enjoy most favoured nation status with the United States while he co-operated with the Soviet Union. There was to be no overriding priority to Alpha and the main burden of peace-keeping the area would be given over to the United Nations.' Keith Kyle correctly inferred that 'covert action against Nasser was discussed'. A series of 'more drastic actions' against Nasser, which Professor Donald Cameron Watt characterised as 'an Anglo-American plot to "destabilise" Nasser's regime', included the 'study of Syrian assets' for a possible coup if Damascus continued to follow Nasser in what was known as Operation STRAGGLE.[40]

On 31 March, MI6's George Young and the head of the SPA section, Nigel Clive, met with Major Wilbur C. Eveland, who had been seconded from the US Department of Defense to the CIA, and the CIA station chief in Cairo, James Eichelberger, for a series of meetings in London. The MI6 pair argued for an all-out operation against Nasser. The Service now regarded him as in the pay of the Soviet Union and prepared to follow Soviet instructions on policy in the Middle East. This involved the 'total destruction of Israel, the domination of all the Arab governments and the elimination of Western influence in the Arab area; material extension of Egyptian influence in North Africa, particularly Libya ... Egypt must therefore be regarded as an out and out Soviet instrument.' Young bellowed that it was now time that the Americans came off the fence and stated decisively whether they regarded the Lucky Break reports, which MI6 had been forwarding to Washington over the previous months, as true or 'phoney'. If they were not prepared to accept MI6's appraisal of Nasser then the CIA's 'intelligence coverage in Egypt must be regarded as poor'. Indeed, recent CIA reports were dismissed as 'rubbish'. Eveland understood that 'Iraq was the central point of British support and stability'. MI6 arguments were 'directed at proving Syria was the key to the area and the fate of Jordan and the Lebanon were dependent upon events in Syria'.

On 1 April, as Eveland drafted his cable to Allen Dulles, Young actually stood over him to ensure that he reported his comments correctly. 'Britain is now prepared to fight its last battle. No matter what the cost we will win.' MI6 was not prepared to hand over details of the covert operations it planned to instigate, but Young mapped out the outline. Young and Clive proposed a three-point programme with the first phase being 'a complete change in the government of Syria'. Syria would not be annexed by Iraq but 'a firm pro-Iraqi government' would emerge in an 'extension of Hashemite influence'. Secondly, MI6 was interested, with Iraqi help, in exploiting splits in the Saudi royal family to hasten the fall of King Saud. The Americans believed that the British had discussed joint plans with Iraq, Turkey and possibly Israel.

> Our best guess would be that the British Government is considering use of some or all of the following schemes: use of Iraqi funds to support pro-Iraqi political parties and counter Saudi-Egyptian press campaign; active support to split ASRP [the socialist Ba'ath party] through Michel Aflag and Jallal Sayed; tribal disturbances in Jazerah; border disturbances with Turkey and Israel requiring Iraqi assistance to restore Syrian stability; use of PPS [the fascist-orientated Parti Populaire Syrien] for infiltration from the Lebanon.

While Eveland ridiculed the plans and discounted the ability of the Iraqis to carry them through, Kermit Roosevelt continued to talk to the British about them.

Eveland reported that the British expected that Nasser would react violently once he became aware of these initiatives and that their response would be proportionate, ranging from sanctions intended to isolate him to 'the use of force to tumble the Egyptian Government'. The CIA text hints that MI6 expected the Israelis to undertake 'special operations' against Egypt's newly acquired Soviet planes, tanks and ammunition, as well as an 'outright attack' on Gaza; these were contemplated as 'extreme possibilities'. The Israelis were also mentioned in connection with Syria, though Young stipulated that only tentative discussions had taken place. This was misleading, as Israeli Premier David Ben-Gurion had already made an indirect proposal to Eden for a joint military operation against Nasser, thus initiating the all-important collusion. During the spring, leading Suez Group supporter Julian Amery, who was experienced at the kind of behind-the-scenes role that suited Eden and MI6, found himself suddenly welcome at the Foreign Office. He had already been in contact with the Israeli Defence Minister, Shimon Peres, and had visited the French Foreign Minister, Christian Pineau, in Paris.[41]

David Ben-Gurion had been attempting, since 1951, to establish full relations with MI6, but he had been brushed off by John Sinclair, 'whose prejudices born during the brutalities of the Palestine era were unassailable'. Although Young gave every impression of being racist and anti-Semitic, he was willing to work alongside Jews because he believed that they were 'first and foremost Europeans'. He argued that 'the treasure which the European Jews bring to Israel and which alone will ensure her survival against Arab hostility, is that quality of priceless value – the European structure of mind'. According to Anthony Verrier, the Israeli intelligence service, Mossad, 'owed much to SIS', and informal liaison was 'soon established' after its foundation. From 1948 onwards the MI6 station in Tel Aviv, usually manned by 'one of the few women officers, ensured a two-way flow of intelligence during years when overt relations between the governments varied from cool to frigid'. Young admired Mossad's ability in action and the fact that Israel had 'slipped into the role at one time played by the British forces – that of armed watcher ready to strike – the best guarantee of Egyptian, Syrian and Jordanian conduct'.[42]

The informal links with the Israelis proved particularly useful when Mossad tipped off Young that they had detected 'very high-flying planes taking off from Turkish airfields and disappearing into the blue'. Mossad watchers had spotted the CIA's 'Detachment B' of U-2s from the US airbase at Incirlik. In April 1956, as part of a new 'Detachment A', the CIA delivered two U-2s to RAF Lakenheath, under cover of the 1st Weather Reconnaissance Squadron (Provisional). Rumours quickly spread and stories appeared in the local newspaper about the hush-hush aircraft which was officially described as a new high-altitude weather research aeroplane undergoing tests. These jet-engined gliders, which had a wingspan of 80 feet, a speed of 500 miles per hour, a range of 2,600 miles and a ceiling of 70,000 feet, would revolutionise intelligence-gathering. Their high-resolution cameras could distinguish two men standing ten feet apart on the ground. Under AQUATONE the CIA promised 'all the intelligence-gathering resulting from the operation would be shared with the British authorities'.[43]

After a few practice flights disguised as weather tests over eastern Europe, Eden abruptly withdrew permission for the black spy planes to operate from British soil. Selwyn Lloyd had warned him that while 'the intelligence product would be extremely valuable', Soviet radar was able to detect the U-2s and there should be no embarrassments with a visit from Soviet leaders Marshal Bulganin and Nikita Khrushchev pending.[44]

MI6 plans were almost permanently derailed by what was a relatively minor incident, but one than illustrated the Service's ability to evade proper scrutiny.

Eden set great store by a mid-April goodwill visit to Britain of Soviet leaders for the improvement of East–West relations. They had chosen to arrive by the cruiser *Ordzhonikidze* – a warship of particular interest to MI6 and the Naval Intelligence sections that shadowed Soviet vessels and specialised in the field of electronic countermeasures.

During October 1955, Naval Intelligence had made full use of a visit by the *Ordzhonikidze*'s sister ship, *Sverdlov*, to examine the new technology believed to have been incorporated in this new class of warship. As the *Sverdlov* passed Dover, radar equipment set up in a secret nuclear bunker built into the white cliffs recorded the cruiser's 'radar image', while a submerged submarine took sound, pressure and echo recordings and, above, RAF planes took hundreds of photographs. The most intensive investigation, however, was undertaken by Commander Lionel 'Buster' Crabb, OBE, GM.

An eccentric, bisexual and alcoholic professional diver, during the war Crabb had pioneered methods for clearing limpet mines from merchant vessels and had won the George Medal for underwater bomb disposal and salvage work. His last job for the Navy before leaving in 1948 was searching ships in Haifa harbour for limpet mines placed by Jewish terrorists. He was then employed by the Director of the MoD's Boom Defence and Marine Salvage on the development of underwater cameras, and as a technical adviser to the Admiralty Research Establishment. His last appointment was at the headquarters of the Admiralty's Underwater Counter-Measures and Weapons Research Establishment in Portsmouth. Throughout this period, the outstandingly accomplished diver maintained informal contacts with the security services.[45]

Crabb had been recruited to the operation by MI6's Ted Davies, a former RNVR officer who had served in Frank Slocum's wartime private navy. Davies, who headed Section R3, MI6's naval liaison unit, worked out of the London station in Vauxhall Bridge Road run by Nicholas Elliott, and co-operated closely with the Director of Naval Intelligence, Rear-Admiral Sir John Inglis. Crabb had been asked to examine the hull of the *Sverdlov* for 'blisters' to see whether the ship housed sonar equipment and was fitted with a device code-named 'Agouti', which reduced the effect of 'cavitation', the noise made by the ship's propellers which increases the chance of long-range detection by sonar. He was also required to measure the pitch of the propellers.[46]

Before the *Ordzhonikidze* arrived, Eden had forbidden any operations that might prove politically embarrassing. Macmillan recorded in his diary that the

> PM was asked by the Admiralty about such an undertaking a good few weeks before the visit. Next, he wrote a clear and precise minute, expressly forbidding anything of the kind. After that, you would have thought everything would have been all right. Not at all. The Secret Service (without proper liaison) and in touch with minor Admiralty officers, arranged this with Crabb (a retired officer, who has specialised in 'frogman' work). The Admiralty agreed – the PM's order had either been over-ridden, evaded, or merely not passed down the line.

The *Sverdlov* appears to have been a dry run, and Davies forwarded to Nicholas Elliott a similar plan for the visit of the *Ordzhonikidze* which was to dock in Portsmouth on 18 April. Elliott referred Davies's scheme to Michael Williams, the Foreign Office adviser, on 7 April, which happened to be the day on which his father died. With his mind on this personal tragedy, Williams had given the plan, which appears to have been buried at the bottom of other proposals, only a cursory glance and had not referred it on to the Permanent Under-Secretary or the chair of the JIC. It was therefore assumed by Elliott and John Inglis that the operation had been cleared.[47]

More cock-ups followed when, after checking into a Portsmouth hotel with Crabb, Davies suffered a heart attack on the 18th. Davies, however, decided to carry on. The next day, Crabb undertook a successful dive in the harbour but failed to return from the second. Nicholas Elliott recalled that Crabb 'did one run under the ship and came back because he needed more weight. He did not come back from his second run . . . He might have gone too deep.' He suggested that he died 'from respiratory trouble, being a heavy smoker and not in the best of health, or conceivably because some fault had developed in his equipment'. Observers later suggested that Crabb, who was long past his best, should not have been asked to undertake the operation, though Elliott insisted that Crabb, 'an unhappy man' whose private life 'had gone to pieces', 'begged to be allowed to do the job for patriotic as well as personal reasons'.[48]

There the matter might have rested. However, as Macmillan records:

> He is either killed by the Russians, or drowned by misadventure
> – we don't know for certain. Then the Russians complain. The
> Admiral at Portsmouth (knowing nothing about it) denies the
> charge. Then the Commander's relations ask questions. The
> Press begin. The Admiralty issues a denial (the most idiotic
> thing possible, since otherwise we could have refused to know
> anything about it, as is always the rule with Secret Service
> work). Then the fat is in the fire. What makes it worse is that
> . . . nothing was said by officials to Ministers until the Press
> story broke . . .

Macmillan advised Eden to 'say nothing'.

Macmillan viewed the episode as a 'boy-scout' blunder. Elliott thought that the 'incompetence lay on the shoulders of the politicians, notably Eden, for the way the matter was handled. A storm in a teacup was blown up by ineptitude into a major diplomatic incident which reflected unjustifiable discredit on MI6.' He thought that Eden 'could simply have kept his head down and refused to comment "in the national interest". Instead, he flew into a tantrum because he had not been consulted and a series of misleading statements were put out which simply had the effect of stimulating public speculation.'

To a barrage of questions in the House of Commons on 4 May, the PM hid behind the Official Secrets Act and simply replied that 'appropriate disciplinary measures' were being taken. Eden then asked the Cabinet Secretary, Norman Brook, to investigate the matter. After taking an account from Sinclair, who had been on leave, Brook commissioned the head of the Treasury, Edward Bridges, to carry out a fuller enquiry, the results of which he reported to the Prime Minister on 18 May. It was not a probing investigation. Elliott escaped all criticism, while Davies was retired on health grounds and, with compensation, emigrated to the United States. Bridges did, however, suggest that the time was ripe for major changes inside MI6.[49]

Crabb's body was recovered on 10 June 1957 by fishermen on a sandbank in the mouth of Chichester harbour. He was identified by the wetsuit, though there was little left of his body and his head was missing, which gave rise to numerous and often crazy conspiracy theories. MI6 continued to carry out operations against the *Ordzhonikidze*. In 1959, the MI6 station chief in Sweden arranged liaison for a Radiation Operations Committee (ROC) operation between GCHQ and the Swedish Signals Intelligence Service. MI5's Peter Wright, with four technicians from the two SIGINT organisations, attempted to monitor the ship's cipher machines. They were unable to break the codes but the MI6 representative at ROC, Pat O'Hanlon, deemed the operation a success. 'Just like the Mounties,' he told Wright, 'we always get our man.' Not quite. The *Ordzhonikidze* was later sold to Indonesia, and when it was looked over was found to have had no technical innovations.[50]

Foreign Secretary Selwyn Lloyd had been largely unperturbed by the Crabb fiasco, for which he blamed MI6. He was, however, concerned that Eden might use it as an excuse to continue to veto the U-2 spy flights, which had been given 'the most careful thought and preparation in order to eliminate all possible risks'. The Air Ministry added that despite the veto, the CIA 'have passed to us a great deal of useful intelligence'. The U-2s were eventually moved to Wiesbaden, in West Germany. Lloyd told Eden: 'Should the active operations in Germany ever become the subject of an inquiry, the British Government could plausibly deny all knowledge of them.'[51]

After a senior Treasury representative, Frederick Milner, had visited Cairo, British ambassador Trevelyan reported to the Foreign Office that 'high officials in the Treasury particularly seem to have been free with their proposals on what to do with Nasser, which included the most extreme solutions'. These views were not made known to the Americans, who were, however, still taken aback by the British proposals they did hear to do away with Nasser. Eichelberger reported that 'if our British cousins had their way, that would be just the plan'. The Foreign Office, too, was concerned, and moved to negate MI6's threat to the diplomatic initiatives of Omega. On 3 May, Lloyd met with Foster Dulles at the NATO foreign ministers' conference in Paris, where they reviewed Omega and agreed upon a co-ordinated programme. They also discussed STRAGGLE, the operation to intervene in the elections or sponsor a pro-Western coup in Syria, which they agreed was 'already practically under Communist control'. The CIA assessed their Syrian contacts while the Foreign Office pondered what action to take. By the spring of 1956, the choices for the British and Americans came down to the long-term isolation of Nasser or MI6's demand for quick decisive action. Eden chose the latter strategy, even though the intelligence from MI6 could produce no evidence of effective, local opposition to Nasser.[52]

Eden had given MI6 'carte blanche, despite the possible impact of the intelligence service's plans upon the Foreign Office's more cautious approach'. It seems that the Foreign Secretary did not exercise any controlling interest over MI6, while Kirkpatrick, who was 'sympathetic to its activities did not interfere with its functions'.[53]

The Foreign Office's principal contact with MI6 was through the JIC chair, Patrick Dean, who also had responsibility for the Permanent Under-Secretary's Department (PUSD), which as an adjunct to MI6 had long-term planning functions and acted as liaison with the Ministry of Defence (MoD) and the chiefs of staff. Deputy Under-Secretary Geoffrey McDermott headed the PUSD, while Dean's deputy, Michael Williams, served as the adviser to MI6 Chief Sir John Sinclair. 'C' left the planning and execution of MI6's campaign against Nasser to the Controller Middle East, George Young, who was to operate from Cyprus, and his assistants on the Middle East desk in London, Cyril Rolo, with whom he had worked in Austria, and Nigel Clive, who had worked in Iraq until 1953. Despite the official chain of command, McDermott recognised that MI6 officers in the field 'would be saints rather than human beings if, in the occasional burst of inspiration or exasperation with officials, they did not employ a little private enterprise'.[54]

In opening its campaign, MI6 'dripped' information into the British press. On 5 May, the *Daily Telegraph* published a front-page article by its diplomatic correspondent headed 'Czech arms for Syria reported (deliveries said to have begun already)'. The article concerned alleged daily shipments of Soviet arms to Syria and an arms pact with the Czechs. US intelligence officer Wilbur Eveland knew that it was untrue as he had visited Syria's ports without seeing any sign of Russian activity. Eveland remembered that he had been told that 'the *Telegraph*'s man in Beirut was almost certainly a deep-cover agent of the British SIS'. He believed that this all fitted in with the attitude he encountered in meetings with MI6 officers: 'According to British intelligence, of course, Syria was headed irreversibly toward becoming a Soviet satellite.'[55]

On 15 May, Eden forwarded to Eisenhower 'the cream of the cake' of MI6's Lucky Break material. Treated by MI6 as 'authentic', the intelligence 'portrayed the Egyptians plotting the overthrow of every single Arab monarchy by means of intelligence agents disguised as educators with the ultimate aim of forming a United Arab States'.[56]

Three days later, the Treasury Permanent Secretary, Edward Bridges, delivered his report on the Crabb affair in which he recommended changes to MI6. Eden responded by agreeing that Sinclair should take early retirement – he was fifty-nine years old on the 29th – and the transfer of Foreign Office adviser Michael Williams to Bonn. According to Service tradition, Sinclair's natural successor was a naval man, his deputy, Jack Easton, but, as Nigel West suggests, he was considered at the age of forty-eight too young. Instead, Bridges pushed for an outsider, the Director-General of MI5, Dick White, who turned out to be only eighteen months older.[57]

White had read history at Oxford and had studied abroad in the United States. Returning to England, he was recruited into the Security Service in 1936 while working as an assistant teacher. He soon developed into one of the Service's outstanding officers, beginning at the start of the war as assistant director of the Counter-Espionage Branch. He became Director of B Branch in 1949. When an outsider, Sir Percy Sillitoe, retired in 1953, forty-seven-year-old White took over as Director-General, leapfrogging his former boss in counter-espionage, Guy Liddell, who had been damaged by his relationship with Guy Burgess. Thus began a period of modernisation and reorganisation within the Security Service, replacing the previous élitist amateurism with a new professionalism. Unfortunately, the process was not complete when White was approached to take over MI6, and he was initially reluctant to leave. The new Chief was regarded as honest and straightforward, and his task upon arrival at Broadway was 'to prevent the "Friends" from embarrassing the Prime Minister again and to restructure the organisation so as to minimise the damage caused by Philby'. White had been convinced of Philby's duplicity, whereas most officers in MI6 thought that Philby had been badly done by.

During June, the resignation of the government left Syria in political turmoil. The British ambassador in Damascus, John Gardener, was alarmed that the head of the new government, Nationalist Party politician Sabri el-Asali, under pressure from Ba'ath and left-wing army officers led by Col. Mustafa Hamdun and the head of security, Capt. Abdel Hamid Sarraj, wanted to create an Egyptian–Syrian union. Gardener intended to stifle it and stiffen the pro-Iraqi elements by providing funds to officers of the anti-left Arab Liberation Party, so that they could co-operate with the politicians Michel Ilyan and Jallal ul Sayid, an MI6 agent working in the Ba'ath Party. Support was also sought from tribes on the Syrian–Iraqi border and from the Muslim Brotherhood, which had been founded before the war by the writer, traveller and member of MI6's pre-war Section D Freya Stark.[58] Former President Hashim Atassi returned from Rome to build a right-wing coalition, but when a left-wing backlash was unleashed against Ilyan and the conspirators, he was forced to flee the country to the Lebanon. Subsequently, the Iraqi Chief of the General Staff, Gen. Ghazi el-Daghestani, met in Geneva with Col. Adib Shishakli, the former Syrian dictator who had been removed from power in February 1954. Shishakli also met MI6 agents in Beirut, where the local station was run by Donald Prater, and with the Parti Populaire Syrien (PPS) and military figures, who were preparing 'hit squads' to assassinate left-wing officers. Allen Dulles was wary of British plans for direct action, but allowed work to begin on the planning for a coup.[59]

By the summer, GCHQ was forwarding a considerable volume of transcribed signals traffic relating to the Middle East to the Foreign Secretary. Former GCHQ personnel who had served in the Middle East were recalled to reactivate old stations. It proved convenient that the states in the region often relied on old coding technology, refurbished Enigma machines from the war, which proved easy for the cipher-breakers. Egypt's embassy in London was using a Swiss Hagelin cipher machine whose codes could be broken because the American National Security Agency (NSA) had a back-door arrangement with the chair of the company. It also helped that the American agent for the Hagelin happened to be Inspector General of the CIA during 1952/3. GCHQ had mastered this particular machine during the war, when the Italians relied upon it, and it remained particularly vulnerable. MI5's technical officer, Peter Wright, was able, with the help of GCHQ's planning staff member Ray Frawley, to set up ultra-sensitive microphones in the London embassy, in an operation known as ENGULF. The microphones picked up enough of the sounds of the cipher wheels being set for them to be transferred by special line to Hugh Denham at GCHQ's H Division. GCHQ was thus able to read signals traffic throughout the Suez crisis. MI6 also mounted operations against Egyptian embassies abroad, and GCHQ was able to break into most of their channels. Some of the transcripts, particularly telegrams from the Egyptian embassy in Moscow, were shown to State Department officials, in exchange for intelligence from the electronic surveillance of Egypt by specially adapted aircraft.[60]

In mid-July the western offer of a loan for the Aswan High Dam was withdrawn. As a response, Nasser had already considered the possibility of nationalising the Suez Canal Company and, as part of the planning, sent out Military Intelligence Free Officers to Malta and Cyprus under cover of the Egyptian consulates to assess the likelihood of a British military attack. Nasser calculated that 'the longer the lack of response went on the less likely was a military invasion'.[61]

On 26 July in Alexandria, in a calm speech, but one that was described by London as hysterical, Nasser made his nationalisation announcement, which from a strictly legal point of view was no more 'than a decision to buy out the shareholders'. That night in Downing Street, Eden's bitterness at the decision was not concealed from his guests, King Faisal of Iraq and his veteran Prime Minister, Nuri es-Said. The Iraqi PM's advice was 'You have only one course of action open and that is to hit, hit hard and hit now. Otherwise it will be too late.' Once his guests had left, Eden summoned a council of war, which continued until 4 a.m. An emotional Prime Minister told his colleagues that Nasser could not be allowed, in Eden's phrase, 'to have his hand on our windpipe'. The 'muslim Mussolini' must be 'destroyed'. Eden added: 'I want him removed and I don't give a damn if there's anarchy and chaos in Egypt.' (Eden had by now considerably increased the dosage of the drugs he was taking and had, in turn, to increase the dosage of benzedrine necessary to counteract the drugs.)[62]

Eden immediately established the 'Egypt Committee' to supervise a response that, if necessary, would involve 'going it alone' without the

Americans and other allies. Chaired by the Cabinet Secretary, Norman Brook, it was composed of a select group of ministers and civil servants. Officially, the committee hoped that a combination of a swift diplomatic response and a decisive show of military strength might be enough to bring down Nasser. A select group of military officers drafted operations to meet the demands of the committee. Information on the military operation, code-named Operation MUSKETEER, was put on a specially restricted circulation list designated Terrapin, with many civil servants and officials who would normally have been made aware of what was being undertaken by Her Majesty's Government deliberately excluded. The Americans, usually the closest of allies, were also excluded from access to documents invariably marked 'UK Eyes Only'. Similar restrictions on American access were worked out by Patrick Dean with his French counterparts, despite British Intelligence's traditional reluctance in sharing sensitive information with Paris.

It was agreed that the more formidable the response, the better the chance that Nasser could be overthrown or even murdered by his own countrymen if his nerve broke. The committee, however, was working to 'an agenda within an agenda' which involved officially undisclosed covert action. On 3 July 1956, Eden and the chiefs of staff reached a consensus that 'we can no longer rely solely on the threat of military force to attain political stability, and we must therefore devote much more of our non-military resources to this end'. This had also been agreed to by the 'Dodds-Parker Committee' which worked closely with MI6. A former senior figure in SOE, Conservative MP Douglas Dodds-Parker, who was the Joint Parliamentary Under-Secretary of State for Foreign Affairs and regarded as an expert on the Middle East, was asked for 'suggestions for action against Egypt and Nasser personally'. Created in June, the Dodds-Parker Advisory Committee, which considered non-military measures and was responsible for much of the co-ordination in this area, included his old SOE boss, Sir Charles Hambro, and a propaganda specialist, the Controller of the BBC's Overseas Services, Hugh Greene, whose brother-in-law, Rodney Dennys, was the MI6 station head in Paris.[63]

The committee, tasked with countering Egyptian propaganda in the Middle East, proposed a large increase in capital expenditure on transmitters in Aden, Libya and Cyprus. During the spring of 1956, at the request of Eden, the IRD had stepped up its propaganda efforts in the Middle East with a special emphasis given to radio broadcasting and attempts to counteract the influence of Radio Cairo. The IRD's head, John Rennie, and his deputy, Norman Reddaway, had arranged for more 'black' propaganda, while senior IRD official Sydney Hebblethwaite asked Regional Information Officers to report on efforts to 'penetrate local broadcast stations', with a view to reducing criticisms of Britain's role in the region. Even the BBC was asked to be 'more aggressive' in its broadcasting to the area. The IRD also planted 'disinformation' about Nasser with newspapers, the BBC, the London Press

Service and with outlets in the Arab world through the Arab News Agency (ANA). In addition, forged pamphlets were produced bearing the imprint of the 'government of Egypt Information Department' which suggested that Cairo intended to control the whole Middle East oil trade. Another project was the 'exposure' of the existence of Egyptian concentration camps run by ex-Nazis. Stories began to appear in the press in late August.[64]

One of the black radio stations set up in Aden, masquerading as the 'Voice of Free Egypt', began broadcasting on 28 July. It announced itself with the opening bars of Beethoven's 5th Symphony, with its echo of the Morse code signal 'V', which had been used by the British during the war – a touch redolent of Ivone Kirkpatrick. An Iraqi announcer made vituperative attacks on Nasser, called for his assassination, and gave out a series of cryptic messages to alleged agents inside Egypt. It also attacked Israel and Zionism, even describing Pasha Glubb, the recently dismissed commander of the Arab Legion in Jordan, as a 'dangerous Zionist'. Its over-the-top manner, which suited its listeners, initially suggested that it might be an Israeli operation, or run by Nasser's enemies, but when the Egyptians publicised the idea that it was a French-backed station, operating from 'a secret place in France', the IRD mischievously corroborated the story.[65]

Dodds-Parker went to see Ivone Kirkpatrick to lay down guidelines for the committee and its specific target – 'Egypt in general or Nasser in person?' The only published account of the proceedings by Dodds-Parker is ambiguous, but there is a hint that the issue of assassination was being broached. Kirkpatrick said that Nasser was a 'Mussolini'. He suggested aiming at Nasser alone, pointing out that Mossadeq had been removed without anyone being hurt. Based on his experience in SOE, Dodds-Parker had come to the conclusion that Eden's plans would not work, principally because 'in the conditions of total war which had continued for the past twenty-five years, the Geneva Convention was outmoded, inadequate to counteract methods of subversion, political assassination and sabotage. No actions were barred by a man like Nasser who was inimical, far beyond any justification of normal anti-imperialism, to all British and free world interests and attempts to evolve reasonable progress.' The implication of these thoughts was that fire had to be fought with fire. He added that 'two of my three colleagues in the Commons did not accept capital punishment in Britain and were unlikely to agree to action which might run any risk of physical injury to Nasser'. Kirkpatrick responded: 'Yet they are prepared to risk an assault which could injure, even kill women and children, not to mention our own troops?'[66]

On the morning following his arrival at Broadway, MI6's new Chief, Dick White, was warned by Jack Easton that he had 'had to stop a lot of operations in the Middle East. Too many are suspiciously unsafe.' According to Tom Bower, White ignored Easton and 'excluded him from further discussion of the Middle East operations' and, instead, chose to be briefed by George

Young, who informed him that he and the SPA branch had been personally chosen by the Prime Minister to 'bump Nasser off'. Nigel West claims that one of the first issues facing White on his appointment was a directive from Eden who, in the face of the Crabb affair, 'imposed a permanent ban on all politically risky covert operations without a written ministerial sanction'. Is this credible? MI6 was about to embark on some of the riskiest special operations of its existence. Did, for instance, Eden issue a written order for Nasser's assassination? More likely is that Eden issued verbal instructions, which, given the circumstances of his appointment, White was in no position to ignore. It seems that White's conscience was troubled by what he heard from Young, and the realisation that he had inherited a service full of 'patriotic officers, Establishment cowboys' who were 'steeped in self-deluding mystery, convinced that SIS operations could influence the course of history'. Only a few days in the post, and regarded with some distrust within the Service, White did not question MI6's participation in the assassination plot against Nasser. While he theoretically retained overall control of Middle East affairs, all operational activity by the SPA section was left in the hands of Young.[67]

Even within Broadway, a number of senior MI6 personnel were kept in the dark about what was going on and were excluded from the circulation list of telegrams. According to Nigel Clive, it was Young who arranged collusion with Mossad, with the consent of the Israeli government but bypassing the British ambassador, who was not sympathetic towards the Israelis, and even some of his own officers inside Broadway. Nicholas Elliott was sent to Tel Aviv as the secret liaison officer and to establish a secure communications link. Eden used MI6's radio link and ciphers to contact the Israeli Prime Minister, David Ben-Gurion, and Israeli military intelligence. Similar secure and ultra-secret links were used to bypass the Foreign Office for communicating with the French.[68]

Although the Queen did see all the 'special bulletins', only a few senior Cabinet ministers and Foreign Office officials were let into the inner ring of secrecy. On 27 July, Geoffrey McDermott was called back to the Foreign Office to become head of the Permanent Under-Secretary's Department (PUSD), in effect Dean's deputy in all matters including chairing the Deputy Directors' JIC. He was part of a three-man team with Dean and Kirkpatrick in receipt of 'clear and unusual' orders from Eden, involved in intelligence and military contingency planning for Egypt. The first plan was called HAMILCAR and was based on a landing at Alexandria which McDermott saw as clear proof that the real intention was to topple Nasser.[69]

The CIA became aware that MI6 had 'crawled into a shell' and that its officers were unwilling to share information with their American counterparts. McDermott recalled that 'while we continued in the JIC to collaborate with our US friends we had to take great care that no whiff of our planning activities reached them'. Although he had all the hard intelligence at his disposal and was aware that matters were coming to a head between Israel and Egypt, that the French were supplying Israel with large quantities of arms and that the British were in very close touch with them, McDermott did not know all that was happening behind the scenes, though people felt that 'some funny business was going on'. In fact, McDermott discovered that he was being bypassed, and only Dean and Kirkpatrick were privy to the full intelligence planning. Dean would 'occasionally disappear in a mysterious manner' and, although McDermott worked closely with him, he did not discover where he was going.[70]

According to McDermott, Foreign Office officials were 'suspicious of intelligence', doubtful whether 'it was either reliable or gentlemanly'. There was 'disdain' for MI6, whose 'credibility was low' because 'the often ridiculous secrecy given to material produced a certain cynicism'. Similarly, ministers 'treated it lightly', though during the Suez affair they treated intelligence with more respect than they accorded the sober reports from the diplomats. During August, Eden's view was buttressed by MI6 reports which indicated that Nasser was facing serious internal problems. The Prime Minister had decided it was too late to negotiate.[71]

An angry Eden told Conservative MP Robert Boothby that 'we must crush this man at all costs'. Shortly after, Boothby bumped into Kirkpatrick at the Foreign Office and told him: 'I believe our Prime Minister is mad.' Kirkpatrick replied, 'I could have told you that weeks ago.' According to one Cabinet colleague, Eden was now 'intoxicated with drugs'. While Macmillan may not have been imbibing drugs, he too appeared to be living in a fantasy world, dreaming of the overthrow of Nasser and taking control of the canal as the precursor of a wide-ranging conference on the region which would redraw the boundaries of the various countries and provide a 'final solution' to the Israel problem. At a meeting of the Egypt Committee on 2 August, Macmillan pushed the idea of the Israelis invading Egypt as part of the British military operation. Macmillan, Lord Salisbury and other 'hawks' wanted to create a 'provocation' which would 'exasperate Nasser to such an extent that he does something to give us an excuse for marching in'.[72]

MI6's main task was to 'support any armed forces intervention with internal action against Nasser'. Young recognised that this would be more easily achieved if, as in Iran, the Americans co-operated. During the summer of 1956, Young travelled three times to Washington 'in a vain attempt to persuade the Dulles brothers that Nasser was not a good progressive democrat but Khrushchev's door opener to the Middle East'. He thought that the American plans for providing financial support for pro-western figures and creating a friendly grouping in the region were 'too cautious'. In early August, CIA liaison officer Chester Cooper had a meeting with Young at Geoffrey McDermott's Mayfair flat, at which the MI6 director had a go at the Americans for knocking down 'every proposal for bashing the Gyppos'. He warned

Cooper that 'your friends at home had better come up with something constructive pretty soon'. At another meeting, Young told Eveland that Britain and Iraq would proceed with plans for a coup in Syria. The CIA did come round to MI6's view and insisted that Operation Straggle, the plan for a coup, would be implemented. Michel Ilyan asked Eveland and the officer supervising operations against Syria, Archie Roosevelt, for a 'half-million and at least thirty days' to install a new regime. The target date was set for the end of August.[73]

Under the general mandate given by Eden, MI6 began to construct a 'shadow government' for Egypt without consulting the Foreign Office, despite reports from Military Intelligence and the ambassador in Cairo that there was no alternative waiting to emerge once Nasser had been overthrown. Since the spring, contacts had been opened up with figures from the old Wafd Party and with the entourage of Gen. Neguib, who had been displaced by Nasser. Besides their own contacts, MI6 also relied on members of the Suez Group.[74]

'As the old wartime basements in Whitehall were opened up for the task-force planners', Young wearily recalled that

> they all flocked in – the Lawrences of Groppi – either too puffy of face and corpulent of body to play wistful roles ... The phoney brigadiers who had once run phoney outfits in Cairo were there too, trying to find excuses for upping their rank to major-general. Julian Amery came round with news of plots and conspiracies and Colonel Neil McLean hurried from the Commons to ask to be sent on a delicate, difficult, or dangerous mission: he was offered one and to his credit carried it out admirably.

Young added that 'McLean prowls about the wilder shores in search of wars and uprisings occasionally emerging in Kurdistan, Muscat, or Eritrea with tommy gun under his arm and looking puzzled rather than wistful'. Recently elected to Parliament, McLean had used his maiden speech to put forward an imperialist defence of British policy in the Middle East. He was subsequently invited by the Royal Institute of International Affairs at Chatham House to become a member of a study group examining British interests in the area. He spent the summer on 'a fact-finding tour of Syria and Iraq', which confirmed his belief that 'Nasser was planning, with Russian help, to bring the whole of the Middle East under Egyptian domination'.[75]

McLean and the Secretary of the Suez Group, Julian Amery, who appeared to be better connected than either the Foreign Office or MI6 with Egyptian personages who might make up an alternative government to Nasser, 'had been busy behind the scenes. They were in touch with a clandestine Egyptian opposition composed of monarchists and other anti-Nasserites.' McLean and Amery were involved 'in the sort of conspiratorial activity which they both enjoyed and at which they excelled'. At their own expense, and under their own responsibility, from 27 August, in the company of two MI6 officers, they 'held several meetings in the South of France with some highly placed Egyptians they had known during and just after the war; representatives of the Wafd, colleagues of the former premier Nahas Pasha'. They also went so far as to make contact in Geneva, where the MI6 head of station was Norman Darbyshire, 'with members of the Muslim Brotherhood, informing only MI6 of this démarche which they kept secret from the rest of the Suez Group'. Amery forwarded various names to Lloyd.[76]

It was said that Gen. Mohammed Neguib would emerge from house arrest to take the presidency and that dissident officers were conferring with civilians about the assassination of Nasser and his ministers, and the installation of a government headed by Saleh ed-Din, the Egyptian Foreign Minister from 1950 to 1952. The name of the former PM Ali Mahwer was also bandied about with the claim that he had the names of Cabinet members who were ready to form a government 'in his pocket'. Another conspiratorial group within the Egyptian Army originated with Lt-Col. Hassan Siyyam, commanding officer of an artillery regiment, who had apparently recruited two other officers, who proceeded to form a group of retired and serving army officers, 'The Partisans of Right'. Although there is no evidence of MI6 involvement, the modus operandi is similar to that preceding the Iran coup and, as Keith Kyle notes, its programme of improved relations with Britain and the cancellation of trade agreements with the Soviet bloc is suggestive of British plotting.[77]

Almost inevitably, Amery's most favoured candidate was the most presentable of the former royal family, Prince Abdul Monheim, the son of Khedive Abbas Hilmi II, who had been deposed by the British in 1914. The Prime Minister under the new King would be Ahmed Mortada al-Maraghi, the former Minister of the Interior, who had left Egypt in June and eventually settled in Beirut. The conspirators told Amery that they would not move until Britain and France were advancing on Cairo. They stressed that the allies should not make any attempt to occupy Cairo.

The most important recruit to the plot was a senior Egyptian intelligence officer, Squadron-Leader Isameddine Mahmoud Khalil, Deputy Chief of Air Force Intelligence, who was approached while on a trip to Rome by a young member of the Egyptian royal family, Mehmed Hussein Khairi, grandson of the Sultan who ruled Egypt from 1914 to 1917. A few weeks later, in Beirut, Khalil was introduced to John Farmer, a representative of the SPA section who was working independently of the local station, by Hussein Khayri, a relative of the royal family. A former army officer, Khayri had served as Deputy Head of Military Intelligence until a few months after the July 1952 revolution; he was transferred to the military reserves and left Egypt.[78]

At a second meeting in Beirut, Farmer made a deal with his Egyptian counterpart. Khalil would be given valuable intelligence about Israel, which he would collect from abroad, thereby justifying frequent travel, in return for which he would establish a secret organisation of army officers in Egypt. Khalil stipulated that he should be the sole channel between the British and the conspirators, and that he should have substantial sums for expenses. As the Deputy Chief of Mossad, Yaacov Caroz, would later comment: 'Harming Israel's security by handing over secret information about her did not apparently trouble the conscience of the British.'[79]

Farmer took Ahmed al-Maraghi to see the British Foreign Secretary, Selwyn Lloyd, who assured him that Farmer had full powers to act on behalf of the British government and that the government would give the al-Maraghi group its full political and financial support. In an extensive briefing from Young, White was given details of SIS's plans concerning Nasser. White did not openly voice his opposition to the discussions at that stage. He accepted the credibility of the plot, including the recruitment of Khalil to organise a group of officers to mount the coup against Nasser. At a meeting with the Deputy Under-Secretary at the Foreign Office, Patrick Reilly, White confided, 'We've got a group of dissident military officers who will go against Nasser.' He further explained that the MI6 plan was for that group to murder the Egyptian leader. When Reilly voiced his suspicions about their reliability, White appeared unperturbed.[80]

Nevertheless, in the short term the idea of a coup and of using Khalil's assets appears to have been dropped or pursued through other channels. The Foreign Office, in particular, was not supportive of these plans, believing there was no credible evidence that an alternative was in sight. The population was viewed as being 'largely apathetic', with Nasser exercising a strong grip over them and the military. MI6 did not believe, however, that it was absolutely necessary to have an alternative in place. The Service was confident that once Nasser was overthrown suitable candidates would emerge.[81]

There was little the Foreign Office could do to control events, since MI6 was working via back channels to Eden. Evidence that something odd was going on came at the end of August, when Dean was 'sensationally promoted' to Deputy Under-Secretary and became 'unprecedentedly' the number two in the Foreign Office, directly under Kirkpatrick. 'A good few noses were put out of joint,' recalled McDermott. Following the Crabb débâcle, the post of Foreign Office adviser to the new Chief had been left vacant, as Ivone Kirkpatrick had allowed Michael Williams to go on extended leave during August before taking up the new post of minister in October. White, therefore, found himself without an adviser, while his deputy, Jack Easton, was 'preoccupied with his anti-Soviet activities', which meant that, because of a set of extraordinarily unusual circumstances, MI6 was 'virtually rudderless' and in the hands of 'a single shadowy, but influential, Whitehall figure', Patrick Dean. Patrick Reilly nominally took over Williams's role but 'he was not part of the secret cabal around Eden and knew nothing of the collusion which was taking place'. Geoffrey McDermott took over in October as the adviser, with Robin Hooper assuming his previous post in running the PUSD. It was the wrong time to leave such an important supervisory role vacant.[82]

In late August, MI6 suffered a setback when the Egyptian secret police, the Mukhabarat, raided the offices of its front, the ANA. On the 27th the Egyptians announced at a press conference that a British espionage ring had been rolled up and a former teacher who had spent twenty-five years in Egypt, James Swinburn, the business manager of the ANA, had been arrested and had promptly confessed to being in charge of the ring. Also arrested were Charles Pittuck, a local employee of Marconi, who was Swinburn's stand-in when the ANA man went abroad, and James Zarb, the thirty-seven-year-old Maltese owner of a porcelain factory.

While the anti-western output of ANA confused some British observers who knew the identity of the real owners of the news agency, it was regarded by MI6 headquarters as 'marvellous cover'. The Egyptians, however, were fully aware of the activities of ANA and that its head, Tom Little, a correspondent for the *Economist* and *The Times*, was 'a senior MI6 agent'. The propaganda minister, Col. Abd-el-Qadar, remarked to *Telegraph* journalist Eric Downton: 'We know perfectly well what Mr Little is up to.' Egyptian cabinet ministers considered arresting Little as a spy but were persuaded that he would be more useful as a free agent. It seems that the Free Officers fed Little, who believed that he had established a good relationship with Nasser, with disinformation in the knowledge that it would find its way back to MI6.[83]

Swinburn and Zarb were subjected to lengthy interrogations in Cairo's Barage prison. Long-time Service policy was that arrested agents were expected to hold out for a day or so to allow emergency measures to ensure the survival of other agents. After that it was presumed that they would talk. The Egyptians claimed that the ring had passed on to London details of military dispositions, secret political developments, and purchase missions to communist countries. Documents retrieved from Swinburn's home included reports on 'the location of Egyptian army units, the arrival of new Soviet-built tank transporters, details of a new radar station outside Cairo, the delivery of anti-tank equipment to the paramilitary national guard'.[84]

Other Britons accused and tried *in absentia* included the local representative of the Prudential Assurance Company, John Stanley, Alexander Reynolds, George Sweet, and George Rose. Reynolds, who had returned to Britain, was later sentenced to ten years' imprisonment, while John McGlashan was acquitted at the subsequent trial. The Mukhabarat never discovered the chain of command of the network and the agent to whom Swinburn reported, whom Tom Bower suggests was a British businessman handled as an 'unofficial agent' by the head of station, Freddie Stockwell.[85]

Eleven Egyptians were accused of espionage, including a headmaster, Swinburn's principal agent, Sayed Amin Mahmoud, who was later executed, and his naval officer son, Capt. Ahmed Amin Mahmoud, who for a period had been naval attaché to former President Gen. Neguib. There were reports that Neguib had been compromised and that references to him were deleted from the trial. Swinburn had been in possession of naval papers including an assessment of naval defences around Alexandria and the movements of a tank-landing ship, *Akka*, which was to be used as a block-ship in the canal, while another ship, the *Sudan*, 'was said to have been filled with explosives in order to block the entrance to Alexandria's harbour'. Most of Mahmoud's intelligence from his ten notional subagents turned out to be 'fictitious', 'webs of falsehood and imagination' constructed from newspapers. Another of Swinburn's agents, Yousseff Megali Hanna, described how 'a team of twelve East German rocket scientists had recently been recruited to aid an Egyptian missile programme' and revealed that the Syrians had asked for help in the building of aircraft repair facilities outside Damascus.[86]

A number of agents working under the journalistic cover of the ANA were reported as having written reports on communist activities for MI6. The most important source of this material had been recruited by MI6 during the war and subsequently used in operations against Soviet bloc embassies. A royalist and militantly anti-communist Yugoslav, Col. Milovan Gregorovic, the nephew of a wartime prime minister-in-exile, Slobodan Yovanovitch, was singled out for forwarding reports that portrayed Egypt as 'heading towards Communism' and thus 'inciting' Britain against the country. During June, Gregorovic was said to have reported that, on Russian advice, the Arabs had proposed forming a united front that would not only oppose the Baghdad Pact but would draw up plans to nationalise Middle Eastern oil. The effect of these reports, it was alleged, 'was to drive the British mad to the extent of interfering militarily against Egypt'. Oddly, Gregorovic was acquitted and allowed to leave the country.[87]

Two British diplomats involved in intelligence-gathering were expelled: J. G. Glove, head of the visa section, and J. B. Flux, a First Secretary in the commercial section who had worked in Cairo since 1919 and had been in contact with 'student elements of a religious inclination' with the idea of 'encouraging fundamentalist riots that could provide an excuse for military intervention to protect European lives'. On 29 August, the English-language newspaper *Egyptian Gazette* revealed more details of the espionage ring: 'Very important instructions were to be delivered to the British network in Cairo, that a special plane was due to fly from Cyprus and that meetings had already been held with some well-known Egyptian personalities . . . But what is more important is that Swinburn confessed that they were planning a coup d'état on the lines of the Zahedi coup in Iran.'[88]

The CIA station liaison officer with MI6 in London, Dan Debardeleben, had warned Major Eveland that in the wake of the Crabb affair 'we should be even more aware of the possibility that SIS might try to salvage its repu-tation by coming up with some coup'. On 30 August, CIA director Allen Dulles reported to his brother at the State Department on his talks with MI6 officers, who were persisting in their plans to overthrow Nasser. In turn, Foster Dulles told the CIA's Deputy Director of Operations, Frank Wisner, that MI6 'were more determined than ever to proceed along a certain line'. Wisner, who was generally a 'hawk', replied that the CIA knew that MI6 and the French were 'still pulling the throttle open, undoubtedly connecting it with other matters'.[89]

With no assets left in the country, MI6 had to use outside agents for its assassination plans. James Mossman, a well-known correspondent for the BBC's *Panorama* programme who had worked for MI6 during the war, was posted to Egypt as the *Daily Telegraph* correspondent in 1956. In Cairo he was approached by an MI6 officer in the local embassy, with a request to help the Service. Although Mossman said he had finished with intelligence work, the officer appealed to his patriotism, telling him that 'you must do this because we are just about to go to war with Egypt'. Agreeing to co-operate, Mossman was asked to drop off a package from the boot of his Morris Minor at the twelve-mile post outside Cairo. Given a telephone number on which to confirm safe delivery, Mossman discovered that he had contacted the wrong man. 'The package had contained £20,000 in English banknotes which was intended as a bribe to Nasser's doctor to poison Nasser.'[90]

The poison was organised by the head of the Service's 'Q' Ops Depart-ment, Major Frank Quinn, OBE, MC. On one occasion Quinn was asked to inject lethal poison into some popular Egyptian Kropje chocolates. A dozen boxes were obtained from Cairo and Quinn began, but 'the difficulty was in opening the base of the chocolate to insert the poison since the markings on the base became damaged, necessitating re-marking. One had to find the exact temperature of heat in the plate otherwise the process was ruined.' After trial and error, in which six boxes were destroyed, Quinn found the correct formula. He then worried, however, about the ethics. 'The recipient could hand one of these to innocents in his immediate vicinity. I voiced my apprehensions to the operational Section head, but was assured that there would be no danger of this in the planned precise arrangements for donation and subsequent removal of the evidence.' The chocolates were handed over, though it appears they never reached their intended destination.[91]

One plan was drawn up by John Henry and Peter Dixon, technical service officers at MI6's London station. They discussed the details with MI5 boffin Peter Wright, who told them that 'nerve gas obviously presented the best possibility, since it was easily administered'. Henry and Dixon told Wright that they 'had an agent in Egypt with limited access to one of Nasser's headquarters'. Their plan was 'to place canisters of nerve gas inside the ventilation system, but I pointed out that this would require large quantities of the gas, and would result in massive loss of life'. Wright dismissed it as 'the usual MI6 operation – hopelessly unrealistic – and it did not remotely surprise me when Henry told me later that Eden had backed away from the operation'. This account was confirmed by later Chief Maurice Oldfield, who shortly before his death in 1981 told friends about the scheme. Eden person-ally disliked the idea of poison gas. During the Second World War, he had been against what he termed the 'war crimes business', but by 1956 he seems to have had no qualms about other bizarre methods of assassination which MI6 dreamed up.[92]

The Ministry of Defence's Explosives Research and Development Estab-lishment had designed a modified cigarette packet which fired a poisoned dart. This was tested on a sheep at Porton Down by Dr Ladell, who personally dealt with MI5 and MI6's specialist requests. When the dart was fired at the sheep its 'knees began to buckle, and it started rolling its eyes and frothing at the mouth. Slowly the animal sank to the ground, life draining away.' Even Peter Wright was sickened by the spectacle. It would appear that since 1953 there had been 'close co-operation' between the British and the Ameri-cans at the Fort Detrick Special Operations Division on producing poisons such as shellfish toxin. Porton Down scientists were particularly adept at refining poisons already discovered.[93]

The French and Israelis, too, organised a number of assassination plots. The head of the SDECE and former socialist resister Pierre Boursicot, who supervised the various meetings that worked out the plan for the Suez expedition, Musketeer, was an important go-between with the British and Israeli secret services. SDECE had a special operations Action Branch in Egypt which scheduled one attempt for 1 September, the original date for Musketeer. A French commando team was to cross to the west bank of the Nile from the French embassy, in rubber boats, and destroy Nasser's Revolutionary Command Council building at the northern tip of Gezira Island. When the date was changed, the plan was aborted.[94]

An Israeli assassination attempt employed a Greek waiter from one of the famous catering companies, who was to slip a poisoned pill into Nasser's coffee. It probably would have succeeded 'but his hand shook so much when it came to the point that he gave up and confessed'. CIA operative Miles Copeland claimed to have knowledge of the MI6 assassination plans. He joked with Nasser: 'Turn your head, Gamal, and let me see if I can put this poison in your coffee.' Nasser, pointing to the nearby bodyguards, said that it would not work.[95]

On 7 September the military plan was changed to Musketeer Revise after it was decided that any assault on Alexandria would result in substantial civilian losses. Military action would now centre on occupying the Suez Canal Zone, a decision that pleased the French, who had been concerned about fighting an urban guerrilla war. General Keightley insisted that the opening phase of the new operation would require a period of undermining of Egyptian resistance by way of psychological warfare measures. It was envisaged that in phase one of the operation, Allied bombing would destroy the Egyptian air force on the ground. Phase two would see an offensive upon key military and economic targets in tandem with propaganda designed to turn the population against Nasser. In the third phase, British and French troops would land at Port Said to take control of the Canal Zone. MI6 and the advocates of psychological warfare convinced the military planners in the small team of mainly air force personnel that developed Revise that the operation was feasible. The psychological warfare campaign was to be devised by the Information Co-ordination Executive, which took on the wartime role of the Political Warfare Executive (PWE).

Cairo Radio would need to be eliminated and replaced on the same wavelength by MI6's Sharq al-Adna, the NEABS on Cyprus. Keightley 'endeavoured to get a really high grade man to head psychological warfare from among those who had experience of the 1939–45 war' but for a variety of reasons the only man he could get was 'a serving Brigadier with imagination, initiative and orginality'. Brig. Bernard Fergusson may have had those qualities, but he had no real experience of psychological warfare.[96]

In order to stiffen their resolve against negotiations, MI6 had been dripfeeding material to the 'hawks', suggesting that various Middle East governments were threatened by 'Egyptian and Soviet inspired subversion'. Officials in the IRD believed that a different propaganda line was required. Leonard Figg suggested that 'examples of Soviet-Israeli relationship are played up, but for the sake of Anglo-Israeli relations this line has to be done unattributably'. Sharq al-Adna's propaganda output angered the Israelis, who denounced it as being more aggressive than the combined radio services of Egypt, Jordan and Syria. 'And so it goes on day by day, preaching hate and war against the Jew and trying to tar Nasser with the Zionist brush,' complained Jon Kimiche, of the *Jewish Observer* and *Middle Eastern Review*. The Voice of Zion broadcast that 'the British owned NEABS on Cyprus today continued its incitement of the Arab countries against Israel, calling on them to unite and launch an attack on Israel ... This agitation was started soon after the Egyptian seizure of the Suez Canal and continued ever since.' Official relations between Britain and Israel fell to a new low.[97]

MI6 also pushed out a continuous stream of anti-Nasser propaganda through the 'black' SCANT radio station, which promoted a 'national freedom group'. It was supplied with 'useful information about the consequences for the United Arab Republic economy of Nasser's actions' by the IRD's Dick Langardge.[98]

On 20 September 1956, Eden and Foster Dulles discussed setting up 'a secret working party in London' to consider means of weakening Nasser's regime. The CIA had already begun planning such a move. UN Secretary-General Dag Hammarskjöld wanted the UN to arbitrate Arab–Israeli issues, and on the 26th the Security Council met to try to settle the Egyptian problem. Following discussions between French Prime Minister Christian Pineau and the Egyptian Foreign Minister, Mahmoud Fawzi, Hammarskjöld produced a list of six principles worked out with Selywn Lloyd which were unanimously passed by the Council on 14 October. The agreement on free and open passage through the canal and arbitration between the operating company and the Egyptian government appeared to offer a solution. MI6, however, advised Eden that Fawzi could not be trusted to stick by the principles since he was 'too close a friend of Hammarskjöld'.[99]

In the meantime, MI6 continued to make way with their plans for Straggle, though they did not put the CIA fully in the picture. Their own candidate for the coup, the former dictator Adib Shishakli, who had been forced from the Lebanon because of his drinking, was not highly regarded by the Americans, who believed he lacked popular support. By October, the military attaché in Beirut, Lt-Col. A. G. Graham, was discussing with the Iraqi Deputy Chief of Staff, General Daghestani, details of the new plan. 'A PPS paramilitary force would seize Homs, and Salha Shishakli, the former dictator's brother, would lead his men against Hama. Other PPS troops would occupy key positions in Damascus and assassinate left-wing officers. Tribes, such as the Druze in the south and the Alawites in the west, supplied with Iraqi arms, would simultaneously rebel.' Politicians involved in the plot included 'Adnan Atassi, a former Ambassador to France; his cousin Fayid Atassi, a former minister of foreign affairs; former minister of justice Mounir Ajlani; and former minister of state Hassan Atrash, a Druze leader'.[100]

In early October, as part of an official trip to Washington, JIC chair Patrick Dean discussed Operation OMEGA with State and CIA officials, including the Roosevelts. In 'utmost secrecy', the British and Americans attempted to put together 'a means of bringing Nasser down'. On 2 October President Eisenhower told Foster Dulles that the canal issue was not the one on which to undermine Nasser. Dulles mentioned the MI6 plans for his overthrow, but Eisenhower repeated that 'we should have nothing to do with any project for a covert operation against Nasser personally'. As George Young feared, the Americans would not join. A CIA note attached to the official State Department secret history of Suez concluded that estrangement between the two allies 'was becoming dangerously acute'. Despite the profound differences over Egypt, the CIA still remained in close touch with MI6 and Iraqi plans for Syria. Officials agreed that Operation Straggle could be implemented at the end of October, with the CIA passing $165,000 to its chief contact, Michel Ilyan, to carry out the coup.[101]

On 5 October, Lloyd and Pineau continued to put pressure on the Americans and, at a meeting with the US Secretary of State, informed him that 'the Egyptians were planning a coup in Libya; they had arms ready there for use and there was a plot to kill the King. King Saud was also threatened. In Iraq, Nuri was now in control but there was dissatisfaction amongst some of the younger officers and this was likely to grow if we continued to do nothing. Jordan was already penetrated and Syria was virtually under Egyptian control.' Three days later, Kermit Roosevelt dropped in on some British friends at the United Nations, where he picked up hints that things were moving towards a climax and that a military operation was in the offing. Back at CIA headquarters he predicted that at the end of the month Britain would dispatch an expeditionary force to reclaim the Suez Canal. No one appears to have taken the prediction seriously. In London, Allen Dulles and Richard Helms had dinner with Dick White and George Young about joint operations in the Middle East and, in particular, the imminent coup in Syria. Nothing was resolved, and the two senior MI6 men did not let the Americans into the secret military planning on Egypt, other than Young's comment that 'something would happen'.[102]

A Middle East specialist in the Foreign Office, Geoffrey Arthur, proposed on the 10th a long-term 'Machiavellian scheme' for an Iraqi–Syrian union, to be co-ordinated with the Americans and Iraqis. This was to be achieved by means of 'propaganda and bribery within Syria', 'the rapid build up of Iraqi forces', and 'overt and covert measures to counter Saudi influence in Syria'. British and Iraqi planning continued with Col. Muhammad Safa taking over leadership of the military committee, which was working with the prominent Nationalist Party politician in Syria, Michel Ilyan. The PPS and military conspirators had developed a plan for a co-ordinated rising against the Syrian government in which a paramilitary force would seize key cities and strategic posts in Damascus. Supplied with arms from Iraq, tribes would rebel in the south and west. Col. Umar Kabbani, who was to lead the new government, was said to be an MI6 asset.[103]

Meanwhile, the capture in mid-month by units of the French Navy of the Sudanese yacht *Athos*, which was carrying a large consignment of Egyptian arms, off the coast of Algeria, provoked French anger. On the 14th, French acting Prime Minister Albert Grazier and the Chief of the Air Staff, General Challe, flew secretly to RAF Northolt for a meeting with Eden at Chequers, where a combined move against Egypt was suggested.[104]

In the second week of October, the Foreign Office's Harold Beeley and MI6 officers met with State Department officials and Kermit Roosevelt to discuss Straggle and to set a date for its execution at the end of the month. The deadline for the operation was postponed several times. On the 18th, Eveland learned that the date of the coup had been changed from 25 to 29 October because the conspirators around MI6's agent, Kabbani, were not in place. Eveland came to suspect that MI6 'used the Iraqis to set this up, leaving the United States and Ilyan as the scapegoats in the event the coup failed'. As Andrew Gorst and Scott Lucas note, 'the co-incidence of the new coup date with the Israeli invasion of Egypt fatally undermined the attempt to overthrow the Syrian government ... After learning of the invasion, Ilyan requested an indefinite postponement of the operation.'[105]

In the midst of all this planning, George Young had chosen to go on holiday. He was suddenly recalled in early October to be told that the Service's plans for Egypt were in turmoil. Young's strategy had assumed that there would be 'a rapid descent on the Canal by a small crack British force while the main Egyptian forces in Sinai were otherwise engaged'. He was, however, appalled to discover from the Chief of the Imperial General Staff, Gerald Templer, the real nature of the military plan. 'Surely this is a deception scheme,' Young protested. 'I'm afraid not,' answered Templer. 'It's all been taken out of my hands.' Young did his best to improvise.[106]

The military plan depended to a large extent on the intelligence fed to the planners by MI6 and Military Intelligence. Although Tom Bower states that MI6 was 'unable to advise the [chiefs of staff] about the state of Egypt's armed forces', and indicates that it 'widely overestimated Egypt's ability to resist the landings', a number of officers suggest otherwise, claiming that the Service's intelligence was ignored and that the military preferred its own estimates given to the JIC. Military Intelligence appears to have grossly over-inflated its estimate of Egyptian armed strength on the ground, while MI6 officers claim that its estimates, which correctly foresaw little sustained opposition, were ignored. George Young, who remained bitter at the lack of will and indecision over Suez, complained that 'every planner covered himself with wide margins for timing and supply, and generously overestimated enemy capabilities (information to the contrary being ignored)'.[107]

Under cover as a brigadier, Paul Paulson was dispatched to the Combined Middle East Force HQ at Episkopi on Cyprus to mastermind the landing of MI6's team, which would go in with the first wave of troops on the beaches. One unit would install the puppet government in Cairo once Nasser was toppled. Another unit was responsible for sabotaging a small number of installations. As during wartime, MI6 also formed a uniformed special counter-intelligence unit whose job was to report on any Egyptain stay-behind networks operating behind Allied lines and to interrogate 'vigorously' any prisoners. Led by a Defence Security officer formerly attached to the Intelligence HQ at Ismailia, Gerald Savage, it was also expected to report on any Soviet diplomatic activity in the area and to seek out any intelligence-related documents and ciphers – for which purpose an experienced safe-cracker had been recruited.[108]

As the MI6 representative, George Young also attended, along with the Prime Minister, a meeting of the chiefs of staff's committee, where Nasser's 'contrived death' was hypothetically discussed. Eden had a 'toothy grin' when Young laughingly said that 'thuggery is not on the agenda'. Dick White claimed that he expressly told the Prime Minister that he would not sanction MI6's further involvement in Nasser's assassination. He 'made it clear that [MI6] was a hostile service, but not a collection of hit men'. Officers of the time smile at the denial. Everyone, it appears, was knowingly playing the deniability game.[109]

By then MI6 no longer had any assets in Cairo and it was decided that a three-man hit-team would be sent by the SPA group from London as 'a Special Service to assassinate Nasser'. They apparently did enter Egypt but got 'cold feet and left'. At the same time, the Egyptian security service had been tipped off about the presence in Cairo of a German mercenary who had been hired by MI6 for a 'wet job'. He disappeared before the security net was closed and was believed to have been smuggled out of the country under diplomatic cover. There was also a British plan to use SAS troops in the run-up to the invasion to kill or capture Nasser. Senior SAS officers gave an assurance that 'any evidence of their involvement would be removed so smartly as to be deniable'. The French tried frogmen, but did not know enough about the degree of protection around the President for the plot to succeed. In November there was a second French attempt ordered by the Action Branch based on Cyprus. This failed because the French networks, too, had been wiped out by arrests.[110]

In what appears to have been some kind of bizarre and still mysterious deception operation, the 'highest ranking Arab employee' in the British embassy in Beirut 'offered to sell Jordan a bundle of British Embassy documents which proved the existence of plans to invade Suez, clear instructions to the embassy of what was to be done the moment hostilities commenced and an indication of when and how they would begin'. The employee asked $100,000 for the documents, and King Hussein is alleged to have paid out a first instalment of $25,000 from 'special funds'. The documents were then passed on to Nasser, who had them examined by his own intelligence chiefs but 'decided they were fakes, aimed at frightening Egypt into making concessions in the face of British and French threats'. Nasser insisted that the documents were 'too good to be true'. The employee was thrown into solitary confinement in a Jordanian prison and subjected to intense interrogation.[111]

After his quick release following the Suez invasion, which appeared to confirm the authenticity of the documents, the British-employed Arab returned to Beirut, where the newspaper *Al Youm* ran a story about the odd goings-on at the embassy, where Lebanese employees had been fired and a huge reward had been posted for the return of the documents. The strange thing was that the man who had handed them over was never fired or investigated. He did not retire from the British embassy staff until the late sixties, and then with a pension. According to Tom Bower, the focus of the

Beirut embassy's information-gathering from the local bars, newspaper offices and journalists was the Oriental Counsellor, the Lebanese Maroun Arab.[112]

As within Whitehall, there was a divide inside MI6 headquarters at Broadway between those who thought the invasion was 'a lunatic idea' and were dismayed by the possible repercussions in the Middle East and those who supported Eden and thought that this was Britain's defining moment and could be fudged. The latter were in command, and sections of MI6 were now 'out of control'; the era of the 'horrors' was still in progress. Operations were carefully concealed from Whitehall and were being run at the Middle East area office in Cyprus, away from London's strictures.

As the planning for the Suez intervention reached a peak, intelligence officials had to turn their attention to events in eastern Europe. When a hundred thousand students took to the streets in Budapest, they were joined by thousands of frustrated workers, who launched a series of demonstrations calling for the withdrawal of Soviet troops, the release of political prisoners and the establishment of an independent communist regime. Dick White ordered John Bruce-Lockhart to Hungary to monitor the uprising.

SDECE's Pierre Boursicot arranged a secret meeting on 22 October at a private house near Sèvres, where Lloyd and Dean met Israeli Minister of Defence Shimon Peres, David Ben-Gurion and Chief of Staff General Moshe Dayan. From 7 p.m. to midnight they negotiated with the French Prime Minister, Christian Pineau, and Foreign Minister Guy Mollet. The result was a French-Israeli alliance, whereby France sold jets to the Israelis and technical information on nuclear research and development, while Mossad supplied intelligence on nationalist movements in North Africa. That night, the American NSA noticed an enormous increase in the volume of signals traffic between Paris and Tel Aviv, providing 'indications intelligence' that something important was taking place. It would appear that the NSA was unable to break the British, French and Israeli codes, though in the House of Commons a few weeks after the fiasco, in one of the few public references to GCHQ, Labour MP George Wigg, who was generally well informed, stated that the United States had indeed 'cracked' the codes. Whether or not it had, the 'special relationship' between the NSA and GCHQ continued almost uninterrupted during the Suez period. As the final touches were being put into place on the invasion plan, the director of GCHQ, Eric Jones, met with senior NSA officials in Washington in what was described as 'a profitable' exchange.[113]

The State Department and the CIA believed that the 'something' was a planned Israeli attack on Jordan. This was partly because, since mid-month, Israeli Intelligence had been pumping out what turned out to be disinformation which suggested that the Iraqi Army was about to enter Jordan. This seemed inevitable when, following the success of the anti-western parties in the election in Jordan on 21 October, the government formerly joined the

Egyptian-Syrian military alliance on the 24th. On that day, the CIA's Frank Wisner dined in London with Patrick Dean and MI6's John Bruce-Lockhart, with a view to a 'good gossip'. Unexpectedly, Dean was called away and did not return. Wisner thought that he had been snubbed and left London the following afternoon feeling, according to Bruce-Lockhart, 'angry, frustrated and insulted'. Dean had been called to brief Eden on his recent meetings in Paris and the joint plan of action that had been agreed. Israel would launch an attack on Egypt and try to reach the canal within twenty-four hours. Britain and France would then issue an ultimatum that Egypt accept temporary occupation of the canal's key points, to be followed by a full-scale Anglo-French invasion within twelve hours if no reply was received. Dean had put his signature to the protocol typewritten in French which all participants agreed to keep secret in perpetuity. Eden subsequently burned Dean's carbon copy, though the French, to Eden's regret, kept their copy of the 'collusion' intact.[114]

Douglas Dodds-Parker, who knew that liaison officers were on Cyprus with Israeli badges, was let into the secret about the collusion and thought hard about his position but decided that, since the country was 'at war', he would continue 'on the convention that actions carried out through certain secret means are "unacknowledgeable"'. In the end, the Dodds Committee appears to have achieved little because it was deliberately excluded from vital intelligence. Charles Hambro thought that Dodds-Parker had intentionally deceived him, but the secretary to the committee, Geoffrey McDermott, who in turn had been kept in the dark, later admitted that he had been instructed to provide 'as little information as possible'. Dick White learned about the collusion from the Cabinet Secretary, Norman Brook, after taking a secret oath not to reveal its existence. White was seemingly sickened by the deceit – especially of the Americans, on whom British Intelligence, White knew, relied. However, he went along with it, having little choice in the matter, having been suggested for the post of Chief only a few weeks before at the express behest of Brook. He must also have felt vulnerable, given that George Young obviously knew but had not informed his Chief. Even more amazing was that General Keightley was not informed of the collusion, and knew only from MI6 intelligence that an imminent Israeli attack was expected that would provide the excuse for the Anglo-French invasion. Naturally, he expressed surprise and indignation when he discovered that Israeli officers were operating under French auspices.[115]

In London, CIA officer Al Ulmer recalled that Bruce-Lockhart strained 'to let us know, if obliquely' what was about to happen. 'I'm going to have to get in my uniform,' he told Ulmer. 'We can't let Suez go, you realise it's the lifeline of our Empire.' On the 28th, Patrick Dean spent the afternoon with the CIA liaison officer, Chester Cooper. Like the senior MI6 officers who had given nods and winks, Dean hinted that they were in for trouble.

In Washington later in the day, the CIA's Watch Committee considered the NSA intercepts and 'highly sensitive information' from U-2 photographs of the build-up of military forces on Cyprus, the sailing of British and French ships through the Mediterranean and the arrival of French fighters in Israel, which was mobilising its forces. The committee predicted that an 'attack will be launched against Egypt in the very near future'. It was fairly sure that the French were colluding with the Israeli military, but despite 'the deliberate British purpose of keeping us completely in the dark' it did not want to believe that the British were involved in the conspiracy. Indeed, even six weeks later the CIA was still able to report that 'the evidence is not persuasive that the British did in fact connive directly with Israel, but is conclusive that the French did'.[116]

On 29 October Israel launched Operation KADESH, attacking and swiftly rolling up the Egyptian forces in the Gaza Strip, with minimal losses. The invasion, however, led to the collapse of the CIA-sponsored coup in Syria which had been rescheduled for the same day. As W. Scott Lucas discovered, 'some American officials even suspected that Michel Ilyan, the chief CIA contact, postponed the coup from 25 to 29 October at the instigation of the British and the Iraqis, who would use the disorder created by the Israeli invasion of Egypt to control the coup and foster Iraqi-Syrian union'. An American official admitted that 'we didn't know any of it, and we suspected that the British had betrayed us'.[117]

On the 30th, Foster Dulles called his brother at the CIA regarding Straggle. The CIA was still of the view that 'if the assets can be held together for a few days more without taking action we would much prefer it . . . The British are pressing us to go ahead.' Allen said that he 'was suspicious of our cousins [the British] and if they want a thing, they [the CIA] should look at it hard. Not before Nov. 1.' However, on the same day, while the CIA-backed conspiracy remained undetected, the Syrian Deuxième Bureau uncovered the Anglo-Iraqi plot when they 'intercepted two Druze leaders with hundreds of rifles and machine-guns, allegedly given to them by Iraq'. They then arrested a number of the conspirators, including leaders of the PPS, and forced others, including Ilyan, to flee to the Lebanon. He subsequently made his way to Britain.[118]

U-2 cameras were over the Sinai as Israeli forces pressed their attack on the Mitla Pass on 30 October. Even though they were still seventy miles away from the Suez Canal, after two days the French and British issued their ultimatum as planned. As expected, Nasser declined the invitation, and at dusk on 31 October British and French bombers blasted nine Egyptian airfields and attacked communications facilities, including Radio Cairo's transmitters. In the days before the invasion, Chester Cooper had found himself unaccountably excluded from meetings of the JIC, and as the bombing began he and the CIA liaison officer in London, Bronson Tweedy, were ordered to break off relations with MI6 on Middle East matters, leaving the British to 'boil in their own oil'.[119]

As the first bombs were dropped, Bernard Fergusson received an urgent cable from the Foreign Office. Did he realise that his station 'was at present broadcasting a short and frequently repeated message to the effect that the staff were heart and soul in sympathy with their fellow Arabs and that they dissociated themselves with what had been broadcast the night before'? Fergusson had arrived on Cyprus on 22 October to take up responsibilities for psychological warfare, which seemed to be in a sorry state. The main target was the softening up of the Egyptian armed forces and their will to resist, with encouragement of any elements in Egypt that might be willing to assist the British. Officials recognised that since the beginning of the Suez dispute NEABS had ceased to be an effective propaganda weapon because the Arab staff refused to accept a critical line on Nasser. As an 'Arab' station it was 'prevented from outright support of Britain'.[120]

NEABS's director, Ralph Posten, had begun to receive 'guidance telegrams via SIS making it sufficiently clear that his broadcasts . . . "were to be shaded from grey through to black"'. Posten knew that two MI6 officers were on his staff but claimed to be unaware of the station's use for 'psychological warfare'. He was 'infuriated' by some of the black propaganda he was expected to endorse. In the last week of October he went on the air 'to tell his audience that they would shortly be hearing lies and might experience bombing. They were not to believe the lies and must endure the bombs. These acts were not those of Englishmen who knew Arabia and cared for the Arab people.'[121]

At an emergency meeting of ministers on the 29th, presided over by Eden, the Governor of Cyprus was ordered to requisition the station. In anticipation, MI6's Paul Paulson seized formal control, with the result that the production team was broken up. A number resigned, including Posten. There were 'four reported sabotage attempts' while 'the remaining Arab staff conspired to put out a repeated announcement that they were not responsible for the content'. As a result, 'three known ringleaders were served with restriction orders under the Cyprus Defence Regulation confining them to their homes'. Feelings were so tense that a Royal Corps of Signals major, escorted by a small party of infantrymen, was sent to remind the staff which side they were on. The authorities at one time 'would have served Posten with the same order if they had been legally able to do so'. Posten, who was said to be given to 'emotional outbursts', was eventually flown back to London on 'medical grounds'. The Director of the Middle East Centre for Arab Studies (MECAS) was then asked 'to render assistance in getting over the message in Arabic'.[122]

Cairo Radio was eventually put out of action on 1 November. NEABS was closed and reappeared as the 'Voice of Britain'. The head of the IRD,

Jack Rennie, was responsible with assistance from a former head, Ralph Murray, who acted as psychological warfare adviser to Keightley, for putting the Voice of Britain on air within twenty-four hours, while the department's Sidney Hebblethwaite was appointed the day-to-day director. Dodds-Parker regarded it as a 'major achievement' but few others were convinced about the output. A former member of SOE, the regional MI6 officer, who was 'not easily moved by examples of political, or any other, human folly – saw with dismayed clarity that their Prime Minister expected them to launch a campaign against Nasser which could well have been conceived by Dr Goebbels'. Another problem was that the only Arabs who could be cajoled into broadcasting anti-Nasser sentiments were 'a miscellaneous bunch of Palestinians whose accents were such that Egyptians unhappily mistook them for Jews'.[123]

Fergusson admitted that 'our sequence of set-backs was farcical'. What was worse was that Fergusson discovered that there was 'no overt opposition and no indications of any covert opposition of any strength' to which to broadcast. Britain was losing the psychological war and without 'a potential opposition leader' would fail. In the House of Lords, Lord Glyn, who had worked for MI6 and SOE in the thirties and during the war, later described the broadcasts as 'amateur attempts at propaganda which were absolutely laughable and brought this country into contempt . . . that action did irreparable damage and it will take a long time to get over them'. Broadcasts from the Voice of Britain ceased at the end of the following year because its hardline stance did not withstand public scrutiny. Eventually, the entertainment music output was increased.[124]

The 2nd was a signal for Nasser's opponents to proffer initiatives. Col. Hassan Siyyam, the principal military conspirator among 'The Partisans of Right', met with the ex-minister Abdul Fattah Hassan to discuss what they could do, with each urging the other to make the first move. Meanwhile, Mortada al-Masraghi and Hussein Khairi crossed over from Beirut to Cyprus. A former member of the Revolutionary Command Council is alleged to have asked Nasser to resign to the British ambassador just before the British bombing began. George Young claimed that Nasser lost his nerve and that when the Egyptians with whom MI6 were in contact telephoned the President and told him that he had better resign before the Anglo-French forces reached Cairo, he panicked and announced his resignation. Young adds that 'the American and Soviet ambassadors then rushed round to persuade him to withdraw it'. Reassured that his position was not really threatened, Nasser withdrew the resignation.[125]

Hassan Siyyam apparently asked his civilian co-conspirators to demand a meeting with Nasser, but they would not act until the military had deposed the President. An MI6 officer later recalled that 'the assistance of some young Egyptian officers, who were strongly opposed to Nasser, had been secured and how special weapons had been buried at a convenient spot near Cairo. They were never used because certain circumstances essential to the operation did not materialise.' Peter Wright adds that it was 'principally because the cache weapons which were hidden on the outskirts of Cairo' – James Swinburn had been the MI6 representative responsible for the stay-behind units – were 'found to be defective'. Applauded by the crowds who responded enthusiastically to his call not to surrender, Nasser ordered that plans for guerrilla warfare preparations be put on alert, and an order be given for the assassination of any politicians willing to serve in a collaborationist government.[126]

Appalled by the break in the special relationship, Dick White sought urgently to repair the damage with the Americans, and through Chester Cooper was able to obtain reconnaissance photographs of Egypt. A U-2 spy plane happened to make two passes over the Cairo West airbase – one before and one immediately after the invasion. Eisenhower viewed the photographs and was struck by the scene of destruction – 'the most dramatic intelligence ever placed before him'. When the RAF bombed Egypt, a U-2 from the base in Adana, Turkey was flying over the area. The CIA passed the photographs on to their friends in MI6 and the RAF, who cabled back: 'Warm thanks for the pix: quickest bomb damage assessment we've ever had.'[127]

The State Department's Robert Amory best expressed the ambivalence of the Americans to the British action. On 3 November, he told Chester Cooper over the telephone: 'Tell your friends to comply with the goddam ceasefire or go ahead with the goddam invasion. Either way we'll back them up if they do it fast. What we can't stand is their goddam hesitation, waltzing while Hungary is burning.' Cooper immediately informed the JIC of the instruction, adding: 'I'm not speaking without instructions.' The first British and French paratroopers landed near Port Said in the early morning of 5 November. A hundred thousand men then began to disembark around Alexandria. The invasion force easily quelled the Egyptian forces facing it, but there were heavy civilian casualties. Nearly a thousand Egyptians were killed and the same number wounded in what was officially a policing action.[128]

On the 5th, MI6 began to have 'considerable anxiety' about the Soviet Union's potential response to events in the Middle East. The head of station in Moscow, Daphne Park, and the military attaché, were 'sent off on a long trip to particular areas of Russia, as near as we could get, in order to see whether we could see anything unusual'. MI6 reported that the 'Soviet military attaché in Beirut is reported to have told a Joint Arab Command that Russia has decided to help Egypt and was examining the most efficient and least dangerous way of doing this'. Syrian Radio reported that the Russians were on the way. 'Unconfirmed and probably exaggerated' intelligence briefings added that 'jet aircraft have been overflying Turkish territory. These aircraft are assumed to be Russian reinforcements for Syria and Egypt.' These reports turned out to be deliberate CIA disinformation, designed to restrain Britain and frighten its NATO partners. Nerves were jangled when a report came in that a British reconnaissance plane had been downed over Syria at a height that could only mean the use of Soviet missiles. This, too, proved to be false.[129]

MI6's Chief made an urgent request to the CIA on 5 November for an intelligence assessment of Soviet capabilities, and information as to whether or not the Soviet threat was realistic or a bluff. Allen Dulles subsequently ordered a flight by a U-2 over Syria and Israel to see if there were any signs of Soviet aircraft. 'For the British, the Soviet threat at least restored a modicum of Anglo-American co-operation between the intelligence services.' The only special relationship, as Eden later acknowledged, was this thin strand between MI6 and the CIA. Chester Cooper reported to headquarters that he would not discuss the Soviet threat with the JIC unless the American embargo on intelligence to Britain was lifted. Last-minute instructions from Washington satisfied Cooper's demand and, on the 6th, Washington forwarded to the JIC an assessment that the Soviet threat was a bluff.[130]

When Anglo-French success seemed imminent, after less than a day, the forces were compelled to stop their advance and give way to a UN peace-keeping contingent. On the 6th, the Chancellor of the Exchequer, Harold Macmillan, who had been one of the sternest hawks, had received a telephone call from Foster Dulles, applying pressure for a ceasefire. The closure of the canal, which Nasser had blocked with forty-seven ships, had a dramatic effect on the British economy. The country would rapidly run out of oil from the Middle East and would be forced to buy from alternative sources. This would have severe consequences on the reserves, which had fallen by 15 per cent. Deliberately conspiring to remove the British from Suez, the United States refused to countenance a temporary loan, forcing the Chancellor to intervene heavily on the world financial markets. With sterling collapsing, Macmillan told Eden that they could not go on.

The British propaganda agencies continued to make 'the maximum use of stories of Russian penetration in the Middle East'. On the 9th, it was reported that 'a large party of Russians had been caught trying to cross the frontier into the Sudan' and that Russian officers had been 'captured by the Israelis in Sinai'. Both reports turned out to be untrue, but this did not stop efforts to place in the press reports from Egypt that 'British intelligence estimates over the last two to three months that the flow of Russian arms into the Middle East were not only confirmed but exceeded'. These latest revelations were portrayed as a Soviet plot to dominate the West's oil and were spread around the Tory-dominated press in order to justify the use of force against Nasser.[131]

Dulles was still suggesting on the 9th that Straggle 'might be carried forward, but when British and French troops are out of Egypt'. A week later the possibility of joint covert operations in Syria was discussed at the White House, where Eisenhower allowed Allen Dulles to talk over the operation with a British official who was arriving 'incognito' – probably Selwyn Lloyd. 'The Iraqis and perhaps the Turks would be involved and the partition of Jordan seemed probable,' according to a note of the meeting. The lack of Anglo-American co-operation in the immediate aftermath of Suez, however, precluded such ideas.[132]

When fears of Russian intervention were raised by the French, the CIA assessment that the Soviets would not act was confirmed by intelligence obtained by GCHQ. A new cipher-breaking technique known as Engulf was in use against the Egyptian embassy in London, which was in receipt of relays from the embassy in Moscow. Selwyn Lloyd later wrote to GCHQ director Eric Jones, congratulating him on the signals intelligence effort which apparently proved its worth following the seizure of the canal. In the new year, Jones was rewarded with a knighthood which had been 'won by a lot of hard work by very many people within the circle and on the fringes of it, and has been partly won by friendly co-operation from people such as customers' – MI6 and Military Intelligence. The Engulf material was used to expose Egyptian claims that the Russians were offering military support and that the Soviets were 'prepared to go all the way, risking a Third World War'. On the 7th, the British embassy in Syria dismissed the alarmist reports, cabling London that 'no fresh Soviet material or volunteers have yet arrived in either Syria or Egypt'.[133]

On the 9th the Cabinet received the news that 'Russian Black Sea Fleet activities are back to normal, and the Turkish Ministry of Foreign Affairs have confirmed that the Russians have not sought their permission for the passage of Russian ships through the Bosphorus'. Five days later, the JIC concluded that 'although the Soviet Union will probably seek to win Arab sympathies by propaganda, economic assistance, strong diplomatic support, offers of arms, and possible volunteers, they themselves will not wish to become involved in fighting outside the UN framework'. British photo-reconnaissance showed that there was no Soviet build-up, which was confirmed by a U-2 flight on the 15th and the latest GCHQ decrypts.[134]

There was anger and despair when word of the ceasefire reached MI6's headquarters. Nicholas Elliott, who had been sent to Tel Aviv on a secret mission, felt 'shame'. He had, like others in the Service, an 'abysmal opinion of Eden', because 'having attacked you should have the guts, no matter what the United States attitude was, to go ahead with it. In a way it made it worse that my Israeli friends were the soul of tact.' George Young agreed and told White that 'we should have gone on and taken Nasser's scalp'. 'It all ended in shambles', however, Young recalled. 'I became an old man overnight.' He thought, 'the expedition meant the end of British power and influence in the region'; he saw the political significance as being 'the last self-conscious fling of the old British style. Its failure may even have been mainly due to this style having become over self-conscious: the play and not the reality was the thing.'[135]

Eisenhower was deeply wounded by the deception practised by its closest ally. Diplomatic relationships within the western alliance were 'mired in a fundamental deception', with the result that for a time the President would have nothing to do with Eden and there was no communication between the two. Frank Wisner took it personally and felt betrayed by his old friends, and angry that the CIA had not foreseen the invasion. Officially, the Americans claimed that they had not been caught by surprise by an intelligence failure. The reality was that while they had had plenty of informants on the events leading up to the invasion, they had totally failed to foresee the final move.[136]

Like other senior MI6 officers, George Young was bitter about the United States' lack of support: 'When the moment came it was not prepared to lift a finger. When its own Allies acted in pursuance of what they believed to be their national interests, the United States Government took the lead in preventing them ... In practice the Americans went their own way.' Suez produced a highly charged atmosphere of anti-Americanism which took a great deal of effort and time to dissipate. In November, the former chair of the JIC, Harold Caccia, wrote to Patrick Reilly that the Foreign Office should regard the 'special relationship' as purely a 'business relationship'. Regarding it as 'phoney' and an outdated example of 'old-boyism', Caccia thought that it was at an end. Around the 20th, Eden complained to his Foreign Secretary that it was only on the level of the intelligence services that the Americans co-operated. Even this was put in jeopardy, though to what extent remains a matter of dispute. In one of his last acts as the Permanent Under-Secretary, Ivone Kirkpatrick is alleged to have broken off relations with the United States and forbidden MI6 to have any contact with their CIA counterparts. According to Geoffrey McDermott, it was the US government which 'withheld co-operation at any level until we had purged our guilt'.[137]

The CIA station chief, Chester Cooper, however, has said that Anglo-American intelligence contacts were 'never completely severed' and were 'quickly resumed'. Kermit Roosevelt was sent to London to re-establish an official relationship, but Kirkpatrick ordered that no one from the Service was to see him. Instead, White tried to use unofficial channels, and one of those asked by MI6 to repair relations was Labour MP Denis Healey: 'I was the only person my friend could think of who might be prepared to see Roosevelt and make his journey worthwhile!' While he regarded the American as 'a good choice' who was 'exceptionally well regarded in Whitehall', Healey wondered 'whether my talk with Roosevelt really met his needs'. More successful was Tracey Barnes, who moved to London in December as the CIA's 'special representative'. Barnes was adept at making friends with

Tory peers and Labour MPs, and formed a particularly warm friendship with Maurice Oldfield, the rising star within the Service. Barnes, who was regarded as 'a tough operator with the brief that he should keep a closer watch on us in future', was, however, 'struck by the deep cynicism and world weariness of the British, shorn of Empire and humiliated by Suez'. A senior MI6 officer, Leslie Mitchell, told him: 'All this is a lot of shit. We're just playing games.'[138]

One of those games was Prime Minister Eden's order to MI6 on or about 23 November to proceed with renewed assassination attempts. It was Eden's last act before he left for Jamaica to recuperate at the home of James Bond's creator, Ian Fleming. The MI6 station chief in Beirut, Donald Prater, packed up immediately and left for London: 'Thuggery was on the agenda.' Eden gave his backing for a plan that involved the use of pro-British Egyptian army officers to be controlled by a 'Colonel Yarrow', using special arms that had been buried at a convenient spot near Cairo.

In 1975, the Senate Church Committee investigating CIA abuses looked into rumours that Nasser had also been targeted for assassination by the Agency. Allen Dulles had allegedly made a threat against Nasser: 'You tell that colonel of yours that if he pushes too hard we'll break him in half.' An official in the CIA's Directorate of Plans, the Agency's clandestine branch, told Brian Freemantle that 'Eden was paranoid about Nasser. At the briefing it was made clear that the assassination request was a direct, personal one from Eden to Eisenhower.' After Suez the CIA had better assets in Cairo than MI6, which makes the proposition possible, though the committee could find no hard evidence to back the claim. The notorious disinformer Miles Copeland did claim, however, that he had been selected to give the Egyptian President a pack of Kent cigarettes, Nasser's favourite brand, inpregnated by Dr Sidney Gottlieb, the head of the Technical Services Division, with a deadly botulism, guaranteed to kill within one or two hours.[139]

Eden returned to London and Parliament on 17 December and approved the suggestion of Cabinet Secretary Edward Bridges that Dean, 'in his personal capacity, undertake an inquiry into the question of balance between military intelligence on the one hand, and civilian intelligence and political risks on the other'. His recovery was only temporary, however. As George Young recognised 'the desire to play a perpetual juvenile lead seemed to take him further and further away from the orbit of reality, so that in the end the act had to be taken off'. Harold Macmillan and Rab Butler had intrigued with the US ambassador, Winthrop Aldrich, 'to give assurances that Eden would not remain Prime Minister'. Indeed, the White House conspired to ensure that Macmillan was the next PM as part of a plan to prevent the emergence of a Labour government as a consequence of the crisis. Before he resigned in January 1957, Eden put down his thoughts – his 'last will and testament' – in the aftermath of the Suez débâcle. The lesson of Suez, he wrote, was that 'if we are to play an independent part in the world . . .

we must ensure our financial and economic independence'. This, he believed, could be achieved only by excelling in 'technical knowledge' and by cutting drastically the defence budget. There was an urgent need for Britain to work closely with Europe, though he warned that the European Community might not welcome a British approach.[140]

These ideas appear to have had some input from MI6, in particular from George Young, who undertook a similar service for Eden's successor, Harold Macmillan. Young thought that the answers to questions historians would ask would not be found in the documents – questions such as 'Why didn't they go into EDC and Common Market in the beginning?' The desire for some form of integration in Europe was 'patent'. Young was a federalist with a belief in European unity in economic, political and foreign affairs. 'Equally clear was Western European emotional rejection of the United States as a dependable ally and a growing belief that the British could be increasingly written off as Europeans. To the Continental States, we appeared to have abandoned any semblance of an independent thinking over policy and rightly or wrongly were regarded as tagging along behind the United States.' By the end of the fifties, as MI6 deputy chief, Young recognised that there was 'a definite current of vigour in Europe'. Unfortunately, as far as Young was concerned, the government had 'misinterpreted the currents and we had trapped ourselves in a minor eddy'. He despaired that the country had deserted European allies and allowed the French and Germans to take the lead in Europe and had failed to grasp the significance of the emotional shift that had taken place on the Continent.[141]

'The sad thing', Young recalled, 'is that in the late fifties and early sixties Britain's power and influence vis-à-vis Western Europe were still sufficient to enable us to choose independent and constructive lines of policy had we wanted.' With particular reference to intelligence matters at the time, he felt that 'it was essential that Britain should maintain an adequate independent intelligence effort given United States policies in the Middle East'. This was despite his acknowledgement that the Americans with 'their vastly superior resources' were beginning to dominate intelligence-gathering, particularly in the technical field where GCHQ had been reduced 'to an ancillary branch of the National Security Agency'. Young's views were also made in the face of a change of US policy. On 5 January 1957, Eisenhower announced his new Middle East doctrine, which stated that 'international communism is the greatest danger to the Middle East' and that the US now intended to confront it.[142]

Young was simply reflecting the wave of anti-American feeling that swept through Britain. 'We are rapidly reaching the point', US ambassador Winthrop Aldrich cabled Foster Dulles, 'where we are thought of by the British public as enemies of Britain working against them with the Russians and the Arabs.' When the influential Bilderberg group met in February 1957 at St Simon, to discuss the agenda simply called the 'Middle East', 'sparks flew'. Intended to heal the transatlantic rift in the wake of the recent débâcle, which was threatening the West's position in the Middle East, the British and French 'almost came to blows over Suez' with the American participants. The rift was not completely healed, though Dick White and his assistant, John Briance, tried to mend fences in the intelligence field with a trip to Washington. Their talks with Allen Dulles, the new liaison officer in London, Cleveland Cram, and the chief of operations, Richard Helms, largely centred on the Middle East, where the Americans wanted the British to keep their bases as an assistance to future Anglo-American partnership.[143]

CHAPTER 30

THE MACMILLAN DOCTRINE

One of the enduring myths of Suez is that, with recognition of the immense failure, British policy on the Middle East changed, and that with the resignation of the Prime Minister, Anthony Eden, MI6 was swiftly brought under control by its Chief, Dick White, and the Foreign Office. The reality was that Harold Macmillan was just as obsessed with the idea of getting rid of Nasser as Eden had been. Indeed, it appeared that 'a tenet which transcended the Suez débâcle' was that Nasser remained 'Britain's principal enemy'. Certainly, there appears to have been no attempt to stop the reactivation of MI6's 'Restoration Plot' to overthrow Nasser.[1]

In February 1957, much to his surprise and after a break of four months from contact with the Service, MI6's key conspirator in Cairo, head of Egyptian Air Force intelligence, Mahmoud Khalil, was called to a meeting in Rome with a relative of King Farouk, Husayn Khayri, and his British contact, John Farmer. Khayri revealed the involvement in the plotting of Mortada el-Maraji Pasha, who had served as Minister of the Interior until the coup in 1952. Working within royalist circles, Khayri subsequently travelled to Munich for further meetings with another MI6 officer, David Crichton.[2]

At the same time, assassination planning meetings were taking place in Athens, where Farmer met with two MI6 officers from the Special Political Action (SPA) section. Meanwhile, the Pentagon's liaison officer with the CIA in the Middle East, Wilbur Eveland, attended a meeting in Beirut with a number of area intelligence officers. 'George Young's man', Frank Stallwood, who had worked on the Albanian operation, Valuable, and had served as head of station in Beirut in 1952/3, 'reeled into the room, as drunk as a lord. Apologizing for neither his lateness nor his condition, he took over the meeting. Teams had been fielded to assassinate Nasser, he informed us, and then rambled on about the bloody Egyptians, who'd planned to turn the Middle East over to the commies. His voice trailing off, he finally sank into his chair and passed out.' Eveland departed in disgust, leaving the MI6 officers to plot among themselves.[3]

Mahmoud Khalil returned to Egypt, where a courier contact was maintained with MI6 via his brother-in-law, Farid Sharif Shaker, who regularly travelled to Beirut between May and November 1957. It was from Khalil that John Farmer established the means by which Nasser was to be killed in what was known as Operation UNFASTEN. The Egyptian leader had a very heavy beard, which he shaved frequently. Farmer's plan was to give him a new Remington Rand which had been filled with plastic explosive and which would be detonated when Nasser switched on the razor. On his death, the al-Maraghi group would seize power and establish a new government. The CIA was made privy to the operation when, on instructions from headquarters, Farmer briefed Kermit Roosevelt, the chief of the Near Eastern Division, who was visiting London. According to Farmer, Roosevelt was rather dismissive – a stance that characterised post-Suez relations in the Middle East between Britain and the United States.[4]

In contrast to Eden, the new Prime Minister 'now laid much greater emphasis on the need to enlist American support to achieve British aims'. Despite Macmillan's development of a close working relationship with Foster Dulles, the reality was that the Americans continued to refuse to join British schemes for subversion in Egypt against Nasser. At an April 1957 meeting the Americans declined to back a proposal for the two countries to plan 'a programme of support for an alternative government' or agree 'upon the psychological moment and the means for making the existence of such a programme appropriately known in Egypt'.[5]

MI6's Middle East Director, George Young, wearily recalled that 'there was at the time little opportunity for reflection . . . but on looking round in the spring of 1957 one could sense that a new stage had been reached and passed and that fresh perspectives in history had opened up'. In particular, Young realised that the Hungarian Uprising and its suppression by the Russians had 'finally killed the appeal of international communism as a dynamic and dangerous subversive force'.[6]

Young subsequently carried out a fresh assessment of MI6's role in the Middle East which failed to bury the game of shadows; not surprising given the views he held. Young believed that the Arab world 'had lost its basic balance and would be increasingly one of violence and anarchy'. This opinion was part of his hypothesis that 'ever-heightening consciousness – the one still active element in human evolution – would lead to ever greater ethnic assertion and divergence, and not to convergence. Modern technology would only hasten this development. An Arab with a Kalashnikov and a Mercedes will be even more aggressive than one with a ball musket and a camel.' In his lectures in intelligence courses, Young 'would remind the students that Arab verbs decline in moods and not in tenses, commenting: "When the British Council premises go up in flames the odour of roasting pansy is incense in the nostrils of Allah."' Young's extreme views partly explain why he was willing to co-operate so closely with Mossad and why MI6 intelligence on the Middle East could be so poor. CIA officer Archie Roosevelt found that the Israelis viewed Arabs as 'alien, threatening, hateful and inferior . . . a people with whom they have nothing in common. Hence their intelligence failure.'[7]

Young saw MI6's primary role as countering the major Soviet effort to establish sympathetic regimes and subvert pro-western rulers. This meant close co-operation with Israeli Intelligence, and aiding the Shah of Iran to build up the notorious SAVAK, while making use of MI6 Arabic-speaking officers to alert Gulf rulers to the dangers of Soviet activities. In the fifties, the Shah turned to MI6 rather than the CIA to reorganise SAVAK. 'It was then', according to Norman Darbyshire, who had overseen the British end of Operation Ajax, 'that the special relationship began and developed.' MI6 was in personal touch with the leading SAVAK officials and its recommendations led to the appointment of regional commanders, who helped to implement British policy. Young had a personal friendship with the Shah, although 'however tactfully I tried, I could not persuade him to keep SAVAK's intelligence role separate from that of a domestic police force – a factor, as it turned out, in the estrangement of the Monarch from his people'. The CIA team training SAVAK remained in Iran until 1961, when it was replaced by a Mossad team. Under the direction of General Hussein Fardust, who helped train the 'Special Bureau' with MI6, SAVAK developed its own training programme. It would seem that it was Mossad which was responsible for training the SAVAK officers in techniques of torture and the interrogation of political prisoners.[8]

The ground for the British had been prepared by Shapour Reporter, who held a high rank as an MI6 agent. Reporter was always present when the Shah had his annual meeting with the MI6 Chief, held during the winter sports season in Switzerland. According to Fardust, at the large unofficial banquets that the Shah gave during the fifties and sixties, the only foreigner invited was the resident MI6 officer. The Shah asked Young that MI6 station heads in Tehran, such as Teddy de Haan, Alexis Fforter and Norman Darbyshire, report to him regularly. Anthony Cavendish claims that 'the more competent of the MI6 representatives in Tehran soon had more influence with the Shah than the British Ambassadors, which proved an irritant to most ambassadors!' Young recalled that the Shah made sure that 'the generals were played off against each other and thrown out. The tribes were quietened, the foreign oil interests totally without political influence . . . the whole Iranian people were advancing in terms of material welfare.' Young added that 'so far he remains on top'.[9]

Events in the Middle East during the spring and summer of 1957 appeared to endorse MI6's analysis of the region. On 17 March, the left-wing Syrian government approved, an approval based 'primarily on anti-western politics', a contract with a Czechoslovakian firm to build an oil refinery. This led to a clash with the conservatives and moves within the army against the head of Syrian Intelligence, Colonel Abd al-Hamid Sarraj. One potential cabal of army officers was the 'Damascene Group', led by Colonel Umar Kabbani. The behind-the-scenes struggle failed primarily because of, as Allen Dulles noted, 'the lack of a sufficient provocation for a decisive showdown'. In April, left-wing army officers backed by Syria and Egypt attempted a coup against King Hussein's unpopular regime in Jordan. Or at least, that was what the newspapers reported. In the event, Hussein's security advisers working with CIA officers used the opportunity to purge the army of pro-Nasser elements, while right-wing factions were encouraged inside the Syrian Army. On 7 May, the Dulles brothers agreed to resurrect Straggle/Wakeful as Operation WAPPEN. On the same day, *New York Times* journalist Cyrus Sulzberger learned from MI6 sources that the CIA was indeed scheming to depose 'the pro-Communist neutralists' with the aim of achieving 'a political change in Syria'. The CIA was working with MI6 in Beirut, co-ordinating a covert working group 'composed of representatives of SIS plus Iraqi, Jordanian, and Lebanese intelligence services'. On 8 June, the Syrian government announced that it had uncovered an espionage ring backed by MI6, with the intent of overthrowing the regime. If this was true, no details were forthcoming.[10]

In early June, Nuri es-Said resigned as Iraqi Prime Minister, and two months later a crisis developed in Syria. On 1 July, the government announced the existence of an American plot, apparently part of the Beirut-directed Wappen operation. At the same time, it seems that the CIA station chief in Damascus had organised his own version of Wakeful. Political action specialist Howard 'Rocky' Stone, who had worked with Kermit Roosevelt in Iran and had recently been involved in operations in Sudan, was brought in to plan a coup with dissidents inside the Syrian Army. Former President Adib Shishkali, who had been considered unacceptable as an ally during the Straggle planning, arrived in Beirut, where he assured Roosevelt that he was ready to assume power with the Populist Party placed in control of Parliament. The problem was that this was 'a particularly clumsy plot' and was penetrated by 'Syrian intelligence'. Syrian officers who had been recruited, 'simply walked into the office of Colonel Sarraj, named the CIA officers, and turned in the money they had been given'. On 12 August, Sarraj reacted swiftly, rolling up the network and expelling Stone and his two accomplices, vice-consul Francis Jetton and the military attaché, Lt-Col. Robert Molloy. Despite their being caught red-handed, western newspapers dismissed the reports of a CIA-sponsored coup as Soviet propaganda.[11]

On 20 August, the British ambassador in Baghdad, Michael Wright, cabled that recent events in Syria marked 'the consolidation of real power in the hands of left-wing elements in the Army'. He warned that it was 'extremely improbable' that any forces in Syria could reverse the trend towards deeper involvement with the Soviet Union. It seemed to the British that the Soviet Union, acting in conjunction with Nasser, was fomenting an anti-western coup in Damascus with the object of establishing a Soviet satellite state that would straddle oil supply routes, handling upwards of 25 million tons of Iraqi oil and a further 12 million tons from Saudi Arabia. When the United States expressed concern at the Syrian situation, Macmillan saw an opportunity 'to consider broader plans to alter the situation in the region'. Capitalising on Foster Dulles's fears, he instigated a secret correspondence with the aim of exploring the possibility of MI6 subverting the Syrian regime. What followed was the setting up of the 'Syria Working Group' (SWG) with responsibilities for the exchange of intelligence, military and diplomatic information. It also discussed covert operations against Syria.[12]

Macmillan's drive for increased Anglo-American co-operation was strengthened by the launch of the Soviet Sputnik satellite on 4 October, which caused a crisis of self-confidence in the West. Four days later, at a meeting of the Cabinet, Foreign Secretary Selwyn Lloyd reported that the Syrians were gaining an advantage because they had Russian help. He believed that in the light of Sputnik it was now more important than ever to strengthen Britain's special relationship with the United States. On the same day, at the request of the chiefs of staff, the Joint Intelligence Committee (JIC) was asked to look into the implications of the Russian launch. On the 9th, the JIC produced a top-secret one-and-a-half-page report which said that besides the scientific achievement, the Sputnik launch was proof that Russian military potential was outstripping Western expectations.[13]

Macmillan saw this as an opportunity to renegotiate Britain's position with the US on nuclear matters, but was badly shaken by news that reached him on the 9th. A fire destroyed Windscale's Pile No. 1 reactor, contaminating milk across a two-hundred-mile radius. Macmillan decided to censor reports of the disaster in the interests of keeping at bay any obstacle to the revision of the McMahon Act, which precluded the US from sharing its nuclear technology with its closest ally. Nor did the event prevent Macmillan, in the wake of the success of the Syria Working Group, from writing on the following day to Eisenhower in 'what seems to have been a bid to capitalize on the new American sense of vulnerability in order to promote still further the Anglo-American relationship'. This was to be achieved, Macmillan hoped, by 'pooling our efforts' in the field of nuclear weapons research and 'counter-propaganda of all kinds', particularly in the Middle East against Nasser's nationalism. On 13 October, Egyptian troops landed to take up positions in northern Syria alongside units of the Syrian Army. Nasser thus emerged as 'the unrivalled champion of Arab rights'. To the Americans, Nasser's intervention forestalled the possibility of a communist-backed coup, and the crisis petered out. The British, however, saw Nasser and his communist allies gaining control of the Middle East. They were already concerned that the new Iraqi Prime Minister had refused to align his forces against Arab nationalism.[14]

In Cabinet on 21 October, Macmillan sought the repeal of the McMahon Act to facilitate the sharing of nuclear weapons technology and to 'endeavour to establish, unobtrusively and without provoking the suspicion of existing international organisations, a basis on which joint Anglo-American machinery might be created for the implementation of an agreed policy towards the political, military and economic issues which confronted both governments, particularly in the Middle East'. The details were concluded two days later at the British Embassy in Washington at a meeting on 'Closer US–UK Relations and World Co-operation' attended by Foster Dulles, Selywn Lloyd, Macmillan and the British ambassador, Harold Caccia. At the subsequent Cabinet meeting of 28 October, Lloyd reported that 'largely as a result of the personal friendship between the Prime Minister and President Eisenhower, we had now succeeded in regaining the special relationship with the United States we had previously enjoyed'. The US ambassador in London, Jock Whitney, cabled Eisenhower to reassure him that the British attitude was 'best summed up by the statement, Suez taught them they have no future except in close association with us and they believe Sputniks have taught us we have no future except in close association with the free world, especially in the West, and have thus provided the opportunity to make close association a reality'.[15]

Following Macmillan's successful visit to Washington, the SWG became the model for other working groups. Without referring to any allies, and in Macmillan's case to members of his own Cabinet, nine ultra-secret working groups were set up, mainly in Washington, dealing with a wide range of issues 'to concert policy for countering Soviet encroachment'. Three committees dealt with nuclear matters, three directly with Syria, and eventually with the Middle East as a whole, Algeria and Hong Kong, and three covered Cold War countermeasures – one studying psychological warfare, another covering strategic controls on trade with the Soviet Union, and one studying economic warfare measures. On the British side Harold Caccia, a former chair of the JIC, was responsible for overall co-ordination of the committees.[16]

The Cabinet was told only that the Americans had agreed to amend the McMahon Act, which would lead to a pooling of resources in the field of nuclear weapons research and development. Ministers were made aware of new institutional arrangements with committees for weapons and nuclear matters but were given no details. They were told that in exchange, Britain would not press for any change in the representation of China at the United Nations without the consent of the Americans, who had agreed to regard Hong Kong as a joint defence problem. The exclusion of the Cabinet became a normal pattern following dissatisfaction with the input from the ministries. With the strong support of Cabinet Secretary Norman Brook, the Prime Minister set up his own working group under Patrick Dean, to consider Britain's future policies. In an echo of the way Eden ran affairs during Suez, Macmillan turned to trusted officials rather than ministers for advice and backing on policy, particularly in the Middle East. The 'hawks' were back in control.[17]

The long-standing portrayal of Macmillan as showing a distaste for intelligence and covert operations appears to be a misrepresentation. He ensured that the JIC chair, Patrick Dean, shared his ambitions for the Persian Gulf and on a continuing East of Suez role, and, in particular, in recognising that the real prize 'in respect of British strategy in the Middle East' was Iraq. Nigel Ashton suggests that Macmillan envisaged 'the possibility at this stage of some broader Middle Eastern war, in which the US, as the result of the combined planning for operations against Syria, might be drawn into backing Iraq alongside Britain against Egypt and Syria'. In early December 1957, the SWG discussed operational plans for 'possible US–UK military intervention in the event of an imminent or actual coup d'état in the Lebanon and/or Jordan'. Due to the ultra-secret classification given the committee, MI6 and CIA representatives were excluded; nor did vital logistics information appear to have played any part in its deliberations. The American Joint Chiefs of Staff Committee was alarmed by the plans for 'a military campaign with political overtones comparable in many respects to the United Kingdom–France–Israeli débâcle of 1956'.[18]

The hawks were still pursuing Nasser, and in October the courier with the Egyptian plotters in MI6's Unfasten assassination operation, Farid Sharif Shaker, met with Mortada el-Maraji, who told him that the new government would be made up of himself as Prime Minister, Husayn Khayri as Minister of War and Mahmoud Khalil as Minister of the Interior. John Farmer arranged the delivery of tranches of money to the value of £166,000 to finance a coup and restore the monarchy. He also gave the shaver MI6 technicians had packed with explosive to Khalil for delivery to Nasser. Farmer claimed to feel that there was 'an illusory element in Unfasten' in that the 'full power of the Service was not engaged in it'. Anthony Verrier records that the 'elaborate assassination plot' was 'carefully arranged to fail'. These are rather odd statements given that the shaver was actually delivered, though not handed on to Nasser. It is more likely that these views were *post hoc* accretions, particularly given what happened next.[19]

On 23 December 1957, Nasser proclaimed the existence of the 'Restoration

Plot' at a rally celebrating the first anniversary of the Anglo-French withdrawal from Suez. Khalil, it turned out, was never really working with the British and had followed the orders of his Egyptian superiors throughout. Nasser announced that MI6 had plotted his assassination, that it had financed the undertaking to the tune of £166,000, that the money had been paid to Khalil, who had been loyal to Nasser all along, and that the money had been handed over to the mayor of Port Said to help the relief of those Egyptians whose property had been damaged by the British naval bombardment of the city during the invasion. Immediately after the announcement, Farmer returned to England. In April 1958, a military tribunal sentenced – in their absence – el-Maraji and Khayri to life imprisonment.[20]

A sign of the new co-operation between the British and the Americans was the revival of the U-2 programme.

It was believed that President Eisenhower was reluctant to allow spy flights over the USSR. In fact, Eisenhower, who had pushed for aerial reconnaissance during the war, continued to allow flights organised by the Defense Department but was wary of the CIA-backed programme, except where it was tasked for specific targets – at which point he became an enthusiastic supporter. During 1957, the CIA U-2 programme was in limbo; the Soviets regarded the programme as provocative, claiming that 'reactionary circles' in the United States were responsible for aggravating relations with the West.

The man in charge of the CIA programme, Richard Bissell, initially wanted to bypass White House control. 'I therefore conceived the scheme of involving the Royal Air Force in the operation on a completely equal basis in the hope that we could contrive an arrangement whereby either the British or US government could approve an overflight independent of the other. It would be a system that didn't require two signatures to initiate an overflight.' Bissell had meetings in London with Dick White and M. L. McDonald, the assistant to the Chief of Air Staff Command for British Intelligence. White enthusiastically lobbied for the scheme in Whitehall.[21]

In May 1958, an RAF wing commander joined the U-2 project headquarters to act as a liaison officer, while in July the RAF selected five of its best pilots for the programme, Squadron Leaders Robert Robinson and Christopher Walker, Flight Lieutenants Michael Bradley, David Dowling and John MacArthur, who officially resigned their commissions, although they remained on British payrolls. Working under cover of the Meteorological Office in London and paid through a secret MI6 bank account, they were sent to the United States, where they trained on the U-2; Walker was killed in a crash during training. Robert Robinson later commented that 'in 1958 this was the most secret operation in the world and the British involvement was most secret of all'.[22]

In January 1959, the British U-2 team was sent to supplement the CIA's 'Detachment B' squadron based at Incirlik, near Adana, Turkey. Because of strained relations with the Turks, the Turkish government was not informed that RAF officers were living at the base. Robert Robinson was commander until May 1960. Allen Dulles and Richard Bissell had worked out the details of the joint mission agreement, allowing flights over the USSR upon approval of either the President or the Prime Minister. In practice, 'permission to overfly proved almost as difficult to obtain from Whitehall as from Washington'. In the end, Macmillan approved flights for British pilots to fly U-2 missions over the USSR on only two occasions (although there are hints from pilots of two others). Robinson was the first Briton to fly a U-2 high over the Soviet Union, principally over two rocket-testing sites. Most of the missions were 'bread and butter' flights over the Middle East, though there were also some peripheral SIGINT missions along the Soviet border.[23]

As a convenience to the RAF, the mile-long film taken by the U-2 was processed in New York and then returned to the British. Bissell recalled that the 'intent was for these missions to be conducted as if they were operations initiated by the RAF with approvals within the British government and results going to UK intelligence'. Dick White had been happy to agree to the scheme in the knowledge that MI6 would 'receive invaluable intelligence at neither cost nor risk'. He proved to be very clever at exploiting the Service's hold on CIA intelligence and its distribution within Whitehall.[24]

To the disappointment of the RAF pilots, who were being paid at three to four times the normal pay scale because of CIA paranoia that they might be bribed into revealing the secret, the programme lasted just over a year. Within minutes of the news of the shooting down of American pilot Gary Powers in 1960, and the revelation that he had been captured alive, the RAF unit was closed down. Robinson flew to London to see George Ward, the Air Minister, who 'told me he was prepared to lie to Parliament if he could get away with it'. In the end, 'he chose to be evasive rather than tell straight lies'.[25]

Twenty years after Suez, MI6 officer Hamilton McMillan was overheard in conversation with a senior officer talking about the period of 'the horrors'. The senior officer said that MI6 had been cleaned up by Prime Minister Harold Macmillan because 'half of them were trying to assassinate Nasser'. In a second review of the Crabb affair, and in light of the Suez débâcle, a secret report by Cabinet Secretary, Edward Bridges, imposed further restrictions on MI6 operations.[26]

It was decided that the Prime Minister had to be informed in advance of any risky undertakings formally approved by the Foreign Office adviser. This was reinforced by a significant reform in the intelligence machinery, with the Cabinet Secretary wresting control of the JIC from the Foreign Office and placing it under the control of the Cabinet Office and the Cabinet Secretary, 'who allowed an Assessment Staff to develop so that the JIC could take the initiative and prepare papers of interest'. The Foreign Office, in particular, had been concerned by the cavalier way the Service was allowed to set its own agenda in the Middle East. The Foreign Office might have hoped to have strengthened its own control over the Service, but this centralisation of intelligence formally tied the Service to the interests of foreign policy, as developed by Cabinet Office and ministerial committees. Used to the byways of Whitehall, Dick White appears to have been happy with the arrangement, in that ministers were expected to provide political direction, albeit through the Cabinet Office. He soon developed a close working relationship with the Foreign Office, which resurrected its supervisory role and direction in foreign affairs. The JIC now controlled all the requirements of intelligence consumers, and MI6 Requirement Section officers were officially tasked with interpreting JIC requirements as 'disinterested evaluators'. This relationship, however, inevitably downgraded MI6's traditional ties to the armed services.[27]

White opposed the robust operations of the Special Political Action (SPA) section and tried to clean up the Service, issuing a number of edicts that banned the more unstable special operations, in particular assassinations. Training for special operations was also curtailed. White further concentrated on internal reforms and set about the recruitment of a genuine postwar generation. The 'old-boy network' still played a part but the Service's new Recruitment Section, under the head of the Directorate of Personnel and Administration, began to recruit, direct from university, young orientalists – while a small number of the more experienced officers were sent to study Arabic at the Middle East Centre for Arab Studies (MECAS) with a view to taking up some of the senior posts in the region. White also replaced the area and regional Controller system with four regional Directors of Production (DPs 1–4) covering Europe, the Middle East, the Far East and the Americas, and Research, including Y Section, with regional responsibilities related to functions, basing his approach partly on his experience of the Malayan Emergency where MI6 and MI5 had worked together reasonably well. The 'longstop' controlling station on Cyprus was dismantled, Singapore was downgraded to a field station, and the regional JICs were abolished as Britain began to withdraw from former regions of the Empire.[28]

Again betraying his background, White put increased emphasis on counter-intelligence and counter-espionage, with the head of R5 made a junior Director. The Head of Counter-Intelligence (HCI) was made for the first time a member of MI6's Board of Directors, attending the weekly meeting. Experience had shown that officers could not be expected both to recruit and run agents, so it was decided to create three 'Targetting Sections' for eastern Europe, the Soviet Union and China which would focus on 'third country' targets, such as students, diplomats and nationals abroad. Developing working relationships with the relevant directorates, the T Sections built up files on potential targets and liaised with MI5's D Section and national security services.

This modernising process was long overdue, but an indication that White did not have complete control in the Service came in March 1958 when Jack Easton finally realised that he was not going to become Chief and reluctantly took early retirement. In a surprise decision, his replacement as Vice-Chief was George Young, admittedly one of the most senior officers but also the most controversial. The decision appears to have reflected White's insecurity, since Young had been chosen to appease the hardliners within the Service. Curiously, White was attracted to Young for his diplomatic skills within Whitehall, though the Scot had a poor opinion of most civil servants and held the majority of politicians in contempt. The reality was that those barons left in place tended to ignore White and his changes, and despite a close relationship with Macmillan, the Prime Minister often overruled the Chief's objections to 'disruptive actions'.[29]

There was still anger over Suez, and the Prime Minister was determined on revenge. He preferred to surround himself with relatives and the remnants of the Suez Group, such as Duncan Sandys, Churchill's son-in-law, the Secretary of State for the Commonwealth and later Defence, and Julian Amery, Macmillan's son-in-law and Aviation Minister. Despite the changes and the criticisms, Patrick Dean was allowed to stay on as chair of the JIC until 1960. Amery in particular saw a chance to renew the battle and remove Nasser and his influence from the Middle East. His ally was George Young. At this stage, White did not have enough influence within the Service, in Whitehall or with the Prime Minister to resist the demand for an interventionist agenda of political action. In truth, Young came to believe that Macmillan became 'little more than a posturing clown, selling out what had remained of British freedom of action to the Americans', but he had a good deal of respect for Amery. It helped that Young's friend, John Bruce-Lockhart, was appointed Director of Production Middle East with a new Middle East liaison officer replacing the former Controller, ensuring that few changes took place in operational activity in the region.[30]

Muscat and Oman was an oil-rich sheikhdom, largely controlled by Shell, with a Sultan who accepted from the British an 'annual subsidy' of £371,000 and twenty-three British officers for the army. It was one of the oil interests that the British government regarded as 'essential' and in an attempt to further them sponsored the search for oil in the Oman interior. British forces occupied the area, driving out the forces of the Imam's rebel brother, Talib bin Ali, who went into exile in Saudi Arabia, which was hoping to acquire concessions in the area. The Saudis, who had broken off diplomatic relations with Britain, withdrew from the Buraimi region bordering Oman in 1957: 'defeated in action, their resentment against Britain smouldered'.[31]

An unusual alliance of King Saud of Saudi Arabia, the US oil company ARAMCO and Nasser backed the Omani Liberation Army in its revolt against the Sultan. In July 1957, the interior rose against its occupation and Talib bin Ali's forces routed the Oman Regiment of the Sultan, providing the British with further evidence of Nasser's ability to incite trouble in the region. Macmillan believed that the Americans were involved in backing Talib and were supporting the Saudis. American intelligence reports to the US Secretary of State, however, indicated that there was 'no evidence of official support of the present uprising, and arms smuggling into Oman may have been done by Talib and his group rather than by the Saudis directly'.[32]

Macmillan was also aware that the Americans were concerned about Britain's willingness to intervene in support of the Sultan, particularly so when, after claims that only air support would be given, the British committed ground forces. On 23 July 1957, Foreign Secretary Selwyn Lloyd told the House of Commons that there was 'no question of large scale operations by British troops on the ground'. Indeed, he announced that he regarded such an operation as futile. Macmillan was to spend a considerable amount of time reassuring Eisenhower that any military operation in the Oman was justified by the common interest of defeating communism and Nasser.[33]

In January 1958, the Under-Secretary for War, Julian Amery, visited Muscat, with heavy backing from MI6, to advise on and discuss a fresh assault on the rebels holed up in the mountains, and lay down the foundations for an exchange of letters with the Sultan. The problem in combating the rebels was laid out in a secret February report from the chiefs of staff, who lamented that 'the difficulty has been to reconcile a sensible military plan with the need to avoid publicity'. Shelling and psychological warfare were not working. A British counter-attack including RAF air assaults had reduced the rebel force to six hundred men, but they continued to occupy the 'Green Mountain', where they repeatedly beat off British assaults and RAF bombing missions. In need of a new initiative, Amery turned to an old colleague and fellow 'musketeer', David Smiley, who was on leave from Stockholm.[34]

Macmillan told the Defence Chiefs that they could proceed with 'discreet military preparations' for a major assault on the rebel mountain stronghold of Jebel Akhdar, in an operation known as DERMOT. A Whitehall working party consulted Smiley and Amery and put to the Prime Minister a possible solution: if British troop landings would 'raise an international storm' and upset the US, why not secretly send in the SAS instead as a 'special operation'? The aim was 'to kill the rebel leaders' after getting intelligence on their location. The Foreign Office was anxious about the risk of exposure for the SAS, 'the success of whose operations depends on secrecy'. But 'there was a reasonable chance it would not attract publicity . . . it would not be necessary, at least initially, to inform the US of our plans'. The cover story would be that the hundred strong SAS squadron was training the Sultan's army.[35]

Throughout the whole of 1958 the insurgents were kept supplied with weapons by Saudi Arabia, most of which originated in the United States. British requests to Washington for restrictions on the use of military hardware were met with statements that the US could not tell the Saudis how to dispose of their weapons. 'No other answer could have been expected, for, as was later to emerge, the rebels were at this time in regular wireless communication with both the Saudis and the Central Intelligence Agency.'[36]

The British insisted that Sultan Sa'id create an intelligence unit within his military in return for support in suppressing the rebellion. In July, Major Malcolm Dennison returned to Oman from an MI6 training course in London. A 'quiet young man of gentle but persuasive charm and tireless persistence who spoke fluent Arabic', Maj. Dennison had served during the war with the RAF's 3 Group, supplying resistance movements in Europe with stores and munitions. Posted to the Middle East, he spent 1947/8 at MECAS in the Lebanon. Thereafter he held RAF intelligence appointments in Egypt and Aden before joining, in 1953, the Bahrein Petroleum Company. Disenchanted with the oil industry, Dennison then joined the Muscat and Oman Field Force as a political intelligence officer, rising to become a key member of the Sultan's Armed Forces Intelligence.[37]

During the year, the loosely organised military groups were consolidated into the Sultan's Armed Forces (SAF). This was made possible by military assistance and a subsidy granted by the British government, arranged by an exchange of letters in August between the Secretary of State for Foreign Affairs and the Sultan. Col. Smiley was seconded as commander of the SAF, with Col. Colin Maxwell, a contract officer with considerable experience of counter-insurgency in the Palestine police, as his deputy. In exchange, the British extended their RAF rights on al-Masira Island, where a subsidiary of the British Commonwealth Shipping Company, the mysterious Airwork Services, subcontracted work from the Ministry of Defence and the Air Ministry to help organise an air force. Airwork was used during the fifties to transport troops to trouble spots such as Malaya and to train air crew and pilots. Already, by 1949, 'press reports had begun to comment on the strangeness of Airwork's anonymous charter flights and use of different names and uniforms'.[38]

During the last week of October, Lt-Col. Tony Deane-Drummond, an SAS veteran commanding 22 SAS in Malaya, arrived in Oman to assess the situation and to see if conditions were suitable for the SAS. The British government then took the decisive decision to withdraw an SAS squadron from Malaya and fly it to Oman. In November, eighty officers and men from D Squadron arrived under the command of Maj. John Watts. The following month, Macmillan and the Defence Committee authorised a second SAS squadron: 'There was a reasonable chance its move to Oman would be unnoticed.' On 12 January 1959, Maj. John Cooper and further men from 22 SAS in Malaya arrived in Oman.[39]

MI6 operated in the area through its liaison with Oman's first European-style military intelligence G2 Int. co-ordinator and in close co-operation with the internal security service, which was staffed with contract or seconded British officers from Military Intelligence, the SAS and MI6. These officers often resumed careers in their respective parent services without loss of seniority or benefits after their period of 'secondment'. Liaison was maintained with the MI6 head of station in Bahrein, firstly John Christie and then Norman Darbyshire. MI6 was also closely involved with the British military contingent in organising the defence strategy.[40]

After a period of further bloodshed and stalemate, with the assistance of MI6 the revolt was eventually defeated at the end of 1959 with the SAS squadron taking the previously impregnable Akhdar or Green Mountain, where the rebels had hitherto withstood every assault. 'It was', Tony Geraghty considers, 'a risky, lucky operation and one that was to have prolonged effects on British defence policy generally. The tide of independence movements in the Third World was already beginning to run counter to the traditional, imperial idea of big overseas garrisons of British forces.'[41]

The new regional centre for MI6 operations was Beirut, which Said K. Aburish, a former Radio Free Europe representative, recalled that

> as a commercial centre and a home for the Middle East's political exiles, became a natural base for spies and newsmen to monitor other Arab countries, oil agreements, the Arab–Israeli conflict and the manoeuvres of the superpowers. Its very make-up facilitated the gathering and transmission of information of all kinds. For spies it was Switzerland, Tangiers and Casablanca all rolled into one: a sophisticated, extremely pleasant, neutral country complete with seedy fleshpots full of whores, pimps, smugglers, drug dealers and mercenary assassins.[42]

The British embassy hosted more intelligence officers (eight) than diplomats. The chief of station, Paul Paulson, was not an Arabist but he did speak French, a considerable advantage in the Lebanon, especially as he moved among the top echelons of Beirut society. Frank Steele worked mainly through the local security service. The head of the Lebanese security and intelligence service was Farid Chehab, who often met in the St George bar with Maurice Oldfield, who tasked him with recruiting agents. Chehab's officers were supplied with money for information which was used for recruitment. Once targeted, sources were recruited via intermediary 'cut-outs', usually local agents, or via 'unofficial assistants, resident British middlemen'. Denis Rowley worked the expensive restaurants and nightclubs, which cost a great deal of money. MI6's Security Directorate, however, discovered that his sources often turned out to be expensive failures, providing useless intelligence.[43]

Considerable sums were spent by MI6 supporting pro-western and anti-Nasser politicians in the Lebanon, such as Camille Chamoun, leader of the Maronite Christians. To the leading essayist on Middle East affairs, Robert Fisk, Chamoun was 'less a Francophile than an Anglophile' – France had created the Lebanon in 1920 – 'and his contempt for Nasser bore a strange similarity to the equally irrational hatred expressed for the Egyptian leader by Anthony Eden at the time of Suez'. Chamoun was leader of his own National Liberal Party, which included a number of conservative Shia and Sunni political leaders. Fisk recalled that he 'treated the democracy about which he boasted to foreign journalists with near contempt when it stood in the way of his domestic ambitions'. In the 1957 parliamentary elections, Chamoun's supporters put out propaganda to the effect that the opposition were in reality Nasser's candidates. In the weeks before the elections, Chamoun received suitcases of cash from Harry Hale, who had served with the British Middle East Office (BMEO) in Cairo and Cyprus before being transferred to Beirut between 1955 and 1957. Political constituencies were gerrymandered to ensure that the most prominent Sunni leader, Saeb Salam, and the Druze leader, Kamal Jumblatt, were defeated. More cash was given to returning officers to rig the ballot and ensure the election of a pro-western government under President Chamoun, who regarded the Nasser message of Arab unity as a dangerous obsession. The violent street demonstrations that followed were in protest at these transparent electoral violations.[44]

In February 1958, Nasser's United Arab Republic (UAR) of Syria and Egypt was proclaimed as a nationalist opposition to the Hashemite regimes in Jordan and Iraq. It was seen as evidence that Egypt had outflanked Iraq in the struggle for Syria, and helped consolidate the ascendancy of Nasser over the Arab world. The rise of Nasser's pan-Arabism excited the Muslims of Lebanon, especially the Sunnis, and indirectly led in the spring to a crisis as tension grew between the Christian and Muslim sects. It was seen as a reawakening of the old dispute between pro-Arab nationalism and the pro-western elements. In the following months, Lebanon increasingly became fragmented into autonomous provinces of pro-government and opposition communal leaders.

Iraq and Jordan formed the rival Arab Federation to Nasser's UAR, which proved too much for nationalist and anti-western Arab circles. The failure in the previous year of Operation Straggle had cost Britain most of what little influence it had retained in the region, but it had to face yet further losses. With the exposure of the CIA coup attempt, Syria moved to the left, and the position of the Iraqi monarchy became increasingly untenable. More money and weapons were channelled by Paulson's officers through intermediaries to various Syrian groups ambitious to overthrow successive governments in Damascus. The Syrian conspirators, used by MI6 as sources of information rather than candidates for a post-coup government, were often arrested, tortured and executed. Most of these arm's-length operations, in which those arrested had no direct contact with MI6 officers and therefore could not be traced to the British government, were unsuccessful. The officers involved, however, were protected from investigation of these failures because head office, despite the reforms, had little idea of what was going on.[45]

Concerned at the continuing instability in the region, planning by the British and American chiefs of staff for joint military intervention in Jordan and Lebanon had begun in the winter of the previous year. In the spring of 1958, joint planning was resumed, particularly on an Anglo-American military operation in Lebanon known as BLUEBAT, though the British enthusiasm for such projects to shore up their waning influence worried the Americans. Events during the summer initially eased such worries.

The coup d'état in Iraq in the early morning of 14 July 1958, which swept away the Hashemite royal family and replaced it with a cadre of officers led by Brig. Abdel Karim Qassem, was a shock to the British. The embassy was looted and burned. Prime Minister Nuri es-Said, King Faisal and numerous supporters were murdered. The crowd, according to the British Council representative in Baghdad, Norman Daniel, 'angered by British imperialism and ardent for Nasser's pan-Arab nationalism rather than enthusiastic about any of the individuals or institutions in Iraq', had caught and killed es-Said as he fled dressed in women's clothing. After burial he was disinterred, 'dragged through the streets, strung up, torn to pieces, and finally burnt'. The truth was that, despite his immense popularity, Nasser and his agents appear to have played no role in the coup. The Oriental Counsellor, Sam Falle, had seen 'unemployment, widespread poverty and actual hunger' throughout the country. Despite the oil wealth, economic progress was too slow and the feudal tribal leaders retained their influence. An acute observer was a member of the Iraq Development Board and former director of the Iraqi Petroleum Company, Michael Ionides, a wartime MI6 counter-espionage officer who had run deception operations in Syria and Lebanon. He had concluded after Suez that 'the gap between Nuri and his people has been growing fast and when he goes, it will not be just Nuri going out of power; it will be the end, or the near end of a phase when British influence, formerly dominant but steadily declining, clung on the last solid pro-British rock, Nuri Pasha, while the tide of affairs went on, beyond his control and beyond British control'. For too long, the British had supported 'client' states in which the people were alienated from decision-making.[46]

MI6's regional Director had in a general way expected the Iraq revolution, but the chief of station in Baghdad, Alexis Fforter, had failed to predict when it would take place or who would be involved in the overthrow of Britain's closest ally in the Middle East. His men on the ground had no idea of the identity of the conspirators and that the coup would be led by an obscure brigadier. They had failed to gather any intelligence on the Iraqi Free Officers movement which paralleled that in Egypt. MI6 had 'committed a classic intelligence blunder by recruiting agents among its allies and not its opponents'. General Daghestani, for instance, was arrested during the coup 'not because he was an MI6 agent, which he was, but because he was a leading figure in the government'.[47]

In contrast, MI6 knew in advance of a supposed plot against Jordan's King Hussein, intended to take place on the morning of 17 July 1958. Macmillan deliberately misled the House of Commons about the circumstances leading up to the King's request for the intervention of British forces. He claimed this had been based on intelligence that the Jordanians had supplied to the British government and which was corroborated by 'various sources'. In truth, MI6 had informed the King that a Lt-Col. Mahmud Rusan, supported by Syria, was behind a coup plot. The intelligence indicated that 'UAR agents had penetrated not only the West Bank refugee camps but also a considerable portion of East Jordan', and that they had 'responsive groups within the security forces including the Army who in all probability would not "fire on their brothers" once mob action began'. On the 16th, the embassy gave Hussein an MI6 intelligence digest which was confirmed by a 'reliable source' in Israel. According to Foreign Office adviser Geoffrey McDermott, MI6 had produced 'plenty of intelligence pointing towards this violence and indeed towards the assassination of King Hussein. Unfortunately, we had no precise information on dates.' As Nigel John Ashton suggests, this whole affair was 'suspicious'.[48]

A British parachute brigade landed at Amman airport on 20 July in response to Hussein's request for support. In the same month, President Chamoun invoked the Eisenhower Doctrine, despite State Department and CIA reports that the 'Communist Party has not sought to subvert or overturn the Lebanese government' and that 'none of the opposition parties or religious groups have seriously entertained offers of communist collaboration'. Soon Marines were driving noisily into the centre of Beirut, which in fact 'alarmed rather than reassured' Chamoun, who within days revoked the invitation. Thought had been given to sending British land and air forces to the Lebanon from bases in Cyprus, but Dulles decided that they needed to 'cool down the British on their enthusiasm for immediate action', principally because the UK wanted to push the Americans into 'clearing up the whole mid-East situation' by extending military operations far beyond Lebanon.[49]

The British and American troops finally departed three months later, after spending their time in Beirut sitting around the airport. Geoffrey McDermott thought that the British and Americans were able 'to forestall a clean sweep of the board by Nasser thanks to our immediate intervention in Lebanon and Jordan'. The reality was that Nasser, because such a move would invite an instant Israeli reprisal, had no interest in overthrowing Hussein and occupying the West Bank. The newspapers instead insisted on the existence of a sinister Nasser-led conspiracy to dethrone Hussein. The subsequent move against anti-Hussein, pro-Nasser Jordanians was organised by Brig. Gen. Radi Abdallah, the King's aide-de-camp and Minister of the Interior, who 'typified the third-world intelligence officer, even in the use of dark glasses'. Tall, charming and charismatic, with 'a weakness for women and money', Abdallah had been trained by MI6 and was in contact with Maurice Oldfield.[50]

In the end, the American intervention in Lebanon proved to be counterproductive and had the effect of removing from power those who had called the United States to their aid. According to Kim Philby, who was working from Beirut as a correspondent for the *Economist* and the *Observer* as well as operating as an unofficial MI6 agent, the Service organised 'through its agents in the SPA group several armed groups for acts of terror against unwanted activists in Lebanon'. Under its chief of station, Paul Paulson, and his deputy, Reginald Temple, MI6 established 'direct contact with the ultra-rightist party leaders and prepared the overthrow of the lawful government of Lebanon and helped strengthen the military'. Philby added that from Beirut the SPA group directed 'a psychological warfare campaign using anti-government brochures in Iraq, and undermining activities in Egypt and Syria'.[51]

The Eisenhower administration had limited American involvement in Jordan to providing air cover and transport. Privately, Dulles admitted that he 'had not wanted the British to go in' and the 'special relationship' proved to be a 'fragile thing'. Within Whitehall, George Young found that 'frank discussion of American factors was forbidden', producing 'drift, indifference and cynicism'. Young believed that

> Britain's power and influence vis-à-vis Western Europe and the Middle East were still sufficient to enable us to choose independent and constructive lines of policy had we wanted. Vis-à-vis the United States and Russia they were minimal: There could thus be nothing "special" about our relations with the Americans and we could no more be a mediator between them and the Soviet Bloc than could Liechtenstein.[52]

At a Cabinet meeting on 22 July 1958 it was decided that military intervention was not a long-term solution to problems in the Middle East and that Britain would have to come to terms with Arab nationalism. Macmillan, however, remained 'obsessed with the idea of getting rid of Nasser and ensured that Dean shared his ambitions in the Persian Gulf and on a continuing East of Suez role'. The Prime Minister preferred the company of those 'whose views, however unrelated to what Britain could do, and could not do, provided him with the romantic gloss on events which his essentially cautious Scottish soul required'. When Julian Amery warned of Nasserite and communist subversion in Arabia, 'these were the words which Macmillan heeded, not because of what was said, but because of who said them'. Amery said what others felt. MI6 was still required to gather intelligence on Egypt and stay in contact with Nasser's domestic opponents. Brook's recommendations to the Defence and Overseas Policy Committee, which had some of the same functions as the American National Security Council (NSC) with regard to intelligence, were ignored by Macmillan, but the Prime Minister agreed that the main requirement, as argued by the Cabinet Secretary, was 'to get the oil out of each of these territories for as long as the inhabitants remain fairly primitive'.[53]

In October 1959, a paper by the Working Group on US/UK Co-operation on the 'Future of Anglo-American Relations' noted that there were 'potential differences' between the two countries over the Middle East. The United States was 'overwhelmingly absorbed in the Communist threat' and regarded 'everything else as of subordinate importance', while for the British two other problems loomed large – 'radical nationalism and the security of our oil supplies which is threatened both by Communist penetration and by radical nationalism'. It concluded that these differences were 'reflected in our attitude towards Nasser and towards the new Iraq as it was to the old'.[54]

With Prime Minister Nuri es-Said's disappearance, the Baghdad Pact (later turned into the Central Treaty Organisation), the bastion of British military and political influence in the Middle East, disintegrated. Although the British might have been expected, like the Americans, to be hostile to the new regime, the government gradually altered its attitude. The fact was that economic priorities overrode all other considerations with the need to protect oil supplies. If the new Iraqi leader, Brigadier Kassem, was friendly towards the British then he would not pose a threat to British interests, particularly in Kuwait and the Gulf States. The government advised British Petroleum to restore relations with the Iraqis. Macmillan cabled Lloyd that there was 'quite a chance from the character of the men and some of their first statements that they may turn out to be more Iraqi nationalist than Nasserite'.[55]

By 1960, the assertion of British rights in the Persian Gulf had been given a higher priority in London than their defence against a real or supposed threat from Kassem's pro-Soviet Iraq. The Middle East Director, John Bruce-Lockhart, not an Arabist but well respected by the Americans, which was an advantage, was ordered to penetrate the Nasserite movement, which was alleged to be threatening British interests in the region. During the summer of 1960, a conference of the leading heads of station in the Middle East, Alex Fforter from Tehran, Paul Paulson from Beirut, Norman Darbyshire from Bahrein, John Christie from Kuwait and Ryder Latham from Turkey, met at Fort Gosport to discuss how to achieve the objective. This included working closely with Mossad and SAVAK. Against the wishes of the Foreign Office, which disliked these kinds of contacts, Nicholas Elliott had helped broker a deal with the director of Mossad, Isser Harel, for the exchange of intelligence on the Middle East. The CIA's back channel to the Israelis, James Angleton, was livid when he heard of the deal, but Dick White persisted with the relationship, agreeing to the posting of a liaison officer to Tel Aviv.[56]

The MI6 Chief did not attend the conference, which reflected the extent to which Middle East operations were still controlled by the hawks. Since they had the full backing of Macmillan, White had no choice but to go along with their decisions. In the new year, the chiefs of staff decided that Britain 'must be increasingly prepared to intervene'. Basing their views on the successful SAS intervention in Oman, the 'major military role over the next decade', the chiefs suggested, was strategic mobility – the 'fire brigade' approach to power projection.[57]

The first test came in Kuwait, where Britain feared Iraq might intervene. British Petroleum executives had urged MI6's Controller Middle East to defend their interests, not least from their American rivals, in Kuwait – 'a magic name' and 'one of our last really big economic interests abroad', which produced 40 per cent of Britain's imported crude oil, while the Emir invested £300 million in British banks in London. In late 1958, John Christie, the MI6 officer in Bahrein and one of the few Arabists in the Service, was dispatched to Kuwait to open an MI6 station with the task of convincing the Emir of Kuwait, Abdullah, and the two-hundred-odd members of the ruling family, the Al-Sabahs, that their nation's security and their personal wealth depended upon MI6 creating a counter-intelligence service out of the more or less useless special branch to infiltrate Kuwaiti society, penetrating opposition to the regime, especially potential agents in the inefficient Kuwaiti Army.[58]

The royal family was informed of MI6's presence and day-to-day liaison was undertaken with one of the officials, 'a minister with a deserved reputation for negotiating flair'. Many Arab leaders preferred to deal through MI6 officers rather than the traditional Foreign Office diplomats: 'The "back channel" permitted conversations to be discreet and honest, and MI6 could destabilise mutual enemies.' With no overseas diplomats nor any intelligence agency, Kuwait depended on the British for its intelligence, and apart from the British intelligence reports, which he trusted as the 'best information he could get', the Kuwaiti Emir received no reports from any other sources. For unofficial assistants, Christie relied on staff seconded to the Kuwait Oil Company from British Petroleum. In November 1960, military strategists at the Middle East Command (MEC) Aden produced a 'reinforced theatre plan' for the defence of Kuwait, known as 'Vantage' and later revised as 'Bellringer'. It utilised part of the considerable resources of the British-owned Kuwait Oil Company for military use by British forces in the protectorate. Typically, the Kuwaiti government was kept unaware of the existence of Vantage. With the territory having little defence against external attack, MI6 organised the visit of Commander Derek Horsford and his staff from 24 Infantry Brigade in

Kenya, who arrived under cover of a party of 'civil engineers' to help organise the defences.[59]

Defence correspondent Anthony Verrier believed that the British promoted the idea of Kuwaiti independence solely in order 'to reveal the dangers which it brought'. By doing so, independence in the Gulf became associated with insecurity. Dick White and Christie, through 'quiet and informal' conversations, were given the task of persuading the Emir that Kuwaiti independence without British protection, faced with the threat from Iraq, the continued influence of Nasser and the increased role of Russia, was a prescription for disaster. MI6 'persuaded, or coerced' Abdullah into signing an agreement that British troops could be 'invited' to defend Kuwait 'in circumstances vague enough to justify intervention'. In an informal 'understanding' with the commander-in-chief of the Kuwaiti Army, Sheikh Abdullah al-Mubarak, it was agreed that the Kuwaitis would provide logistical support for a British task force. Some Foreign Office officials regarded contingency planning for a military operation by British forces as 'no longer politically or militarily practical'. They, however, were overruled because of opinion in the City of London, which argued that 'Britain should, at all costs, take no chances with the oil supply represented by Kuwait', whose oil and investments were worth at least £100 million per annum to the British economy.[60]

In reality, the threat to Kuwait from Iraq was remote, as MI6 well knew. David Lee, the Air Office Commanding Middle East in 1961, later wrote in an official account of 'the Flight from the Middle East' that the British government 'did not contemplate aggression by Iraq very seriously'. Similarly, the threat from the Soviets was largely non-existent, while relations between Baghdad and the KGB had collapsed. Malcolm Mackintosh, the leading authority on the Soviets and the liaison between the Cabinet Office and MI6, circulated within restricted circles in Whitehall an appreciation of the situation in the Middle East, which noted: 'For reasons of prestige, or fear, the Soviet Government felt obliged to intervene as each Middle East crisis occurred, but her part was always that of an alarmed, puzzled, or even exasperated protector, who would have preferred a period of political stability in which long-term plans could gradually mature.'[61]

Things came to a head when rumours surfaced that Kuwait wanted to join the Commonwealth with the aim of replacing the 1899 protectorate treaty with independent status. On 30 April 1961, Iraqi leader General Kassem attacked 'the plot of British imperialists to draw Kuwait into the Commonwealth'. The Cabinet recommended recognising Kuwait's independence but, in a move designed 'to provoke the Iraqis to stir up trouble', the news was announced only when Iraq's Foreign Minister, who was known to have a moderating influence on Kassem, was abroad. On 19 June, Kuwait declared itself a sovereign nation and six days later, to the surprise of embassy staff, the 'unbalanced' and 'hallucinating' Kassem 'verbally' annexed it as Iraq's thirteenth province.[62]

MI6 and Military Intelligence accounts of the situation differ. The head of station in Iraq, Henry Coombe-Tennant, relying on a network of senior police and military figures recruited during the war, 'predicted that Kassem was minded to invade Kuwait'. This was confirmed by the MoD in London, which reported troop movements towards the border. Baghdad and Kuwait stations, however, reported that no specific threat could be identified. In the event, the MI6 officer took on the traditional role of 'watching trains'. On the 27th the military attaché in Baghdad signalled that an Iraqi armoured brigade 'intended' to move to Basra.[63]

Macmillan and the 'hawks' were buoyed by the success in Oman and wanted to intervene. The United States was too absorbed with the Berlin crisis in June to be much concerned about Kuwait. The Cabinet was split over a new military adventure, some fearing a 'Second Suez', while others wondered whether Britain could afford such an action. In the event, the Cabinet left the decisions to Macmillan and an 'inner cabinet' of Foreign Secretary Lord Home and Defence Secretary Harold Watkinson. The PM's foreign policy adviser, Phillip de Zulueta, argued that 'if we let Kuwait go without a fight the other oil Sheikhdoms (which are getting richer) will not rely on us any longer'.[64]

Less than twenty-four hours after the Iraqi leader had announced his claim on Kuwait, Kuwaiti police began clamping down on an alleged Iraqi 'fifth column'. On the same day, London received its first reports from the British ambassador in Baghdad, Humphrey Trevelyan, and Col. J. Bowden, the military attaché, indicating that Kassem intended to move tanks south for an attack on Kuwait. John Christie passed on the intelligence with a threat assessment to the Emir, even though MI6 never received any information to indicate that tanks had in fact been moved south. Significantly, RAF photo-reconnaissance planes based in Bahrein were not used to gather intelligence on the Iraq–Kuwait border, though they were to carry out missions on a daily basis from 1 July. On the night of 28/29 June, Bowden stated that the Iraqis intended 'a crash action'. The next day, alarmed by the rumours and the lack of warning, Lord Home asked the Emir to make a formal request for British assistance. In fact, Kassem had ordered the reduction of military activities to a minimum as he was 'determined not to initiate a military action in support of the claim over Kuwait and this order would help to prevent any misinterpretation of Iraqi intentions'. Not a single tank was moved south.[65]

The crucial decision was made on the afternoon of 29 June at the Cabinet Overseas and Defence Committee based on intelligence from Baghdad which 'at the moment seemed valid' (my italics). Further intelligence was received on the following afternoon 'which indicated that the movement of tanks from Baghdad to Basra had probably begun, and that certain naval preparations were in hand'. The US embassy in Iraq reported that it had 'no direct evidence that Iraqi armour had been moved south from the Baghdad area'. One account claims that Intelligence had lost track of a squadron of Iraqi tanks and that 'Iraqi forces currently present in the Basra area would be sufficient to invade Kuwait in the absence of any British strength on the ground'. The Foreign Office issued instructions to the British Political Agency in the Gulf and the MI6 station in Kuwait to work to secure a formal request for British military assistance and an invitation for British forces to defend Kuwait. The Political Agent, John Richmond, an Arabist and idealist, reacted unfavourably to the request that he 'encourage' the Emir to a correct decision. He thought that the British intelligence reports were 'too shallow and unclear' and took no account of the fact that 'the Iraqis might verbally threaten Kuwait but they will not invade'. John Christie believed that 'in politics, what matters is interests' and said Richmond's 'personal views were irrelevant ... Our job was simply to carry out the Foreign Office's instructions.' Richmond was 'rebuked' and told to 'keep quiet' by the Foreign Office, while the rest of the agency staff and MI6 thought that military action would 'enhance Britain's position in the region'.[66]

The lack of an immediate response from the Emir led Lord Home to dispatch another telegram on the 30th requesting assent to 'counter-measures'. Attached were alarmist reports of Iraqi intentions, designed to frighten the Emir into action. The military adviser to the Kuwaiti government, Col. John Pierce, later asserted that 'the Ruler was prodded into accepting the proffered British aid' and that the intelligence reports were the 'decisive factor' in the crisis. Christie denied the accusation, claiming that MI6 'never dressed up evidence, and never produced false evidence'. He claimed that it was 'strong advice' from London which 'tipped him over' into agreeing to military intervention. As Anthony Verrier noted: 'It had been a damn'd close run thing.'[67]

On 1 July Commander Horsford was on the spot and the 24 Infantry Brigade Strategic Reserve was in the air – secret night airlifts over Turkey had been agreed only at the last minute – even before Emir Abdullah had signed the piece of paper asking for British protection. In the morning the Kuwait Supreme Council claimed that an Iraqi invasion was an 'unquestionable fact' and that some units of the Iraqi Army were 'concentrated on the border ... in preparation'. In one highly successful operation MI6 leaked, then used, a planted story to justify the landing of the Reserve. An MI6 officer operating under cover as an oil executive leaked the story that Iraq's army was heading for Kuwait with 'the names of the units involved and their strength' to a correspondent for a leading daily newspaper who was also closely connected to the Service. The result was a scoop for the correspondent and a lead story that 'helped generate the atmosphere and the pretext necessary for the British to land'. In fact, there was no military danger to Kuwait and the British government knew it.[68]

Shortly after the landing of troops, Richmond was recalled and sent 'on leave'. John Christie regarded him as 'not sufficiently a strong character to ensure that British views and interests were sufficiently represented'. On 2 July the *Observer* reported that the Foreign Ministry in Baghdad had given assurances that the Iraqi claim to sovereignty would not be pressed by armed force. The British, however, had chosen to ignore these assurances as it was felt unwise to take chances on the unpredictability of Kassem. Planted stories in the British press throughout August suggested that the Iraqi invasion had not taken place because local commanders had refused to obey Kassem's orders. The claims, however, were unfounded. In his memoirs, Ambassador Trevelyan stated that 'when the British forces appeared in Kuwait, General Kassem quickly went into reverse, withdrew his tanks from Basra, hid them some way inland and denied that he had ever moved them'. This was also totally untrue. Iraqi Army units had moved out of Baghdad, but 'they headed north to fight Kurdish rebels, not south to invade Kuwait'. Kassem launched the attack on the Kurds in September, after accusing them of being sponsored by British agents.[69]

British troops did not leave Kuwait until October 1961, by which time they were thoroughly weary from the intense heat. The occupation had been something of a 'shambles' and had shown that British forces lacked the equipment and resources to sustain such an operation. The same criticisms were levelled thirty years later during 'Desert Storm'.[70]

When the Americans woke up to what was happening in Kuwait, it prompted a protest to Dick White from Carlton Swift, the CIA's deputy liaison officer in London, who told 'C' that 'what you're doing is not in America's interests. The State Department is unhappy with the Foreign Office. Will you let us see the raw intelligence on which you're basing the policy?' White provided the intelligence but it seems that the Kennedy administration was not impressed and, indeed, rejected 'London's overtures for discussions on joint planning of the region's defence', as Britain's strategy came increasingly to concentrate on the defence of her interests in the Gulf.[71]

Equally unimpressed by the Kuwaiti operation was the Cabinet Secretary. Expressing the view of what Anthony Verrier has termed the 'permanent government', Norman Brook wrote to the Prime Minister on 4 September that 'we are fighting a losing battle propping up these reactionary regimes. Our policy takes no account of the rising tide of nationalism in these countries. We are bound to find ourselves in the end on the losing side. We cannot win the propaganda battle against nationalism and it is idle to spend money in trying to shout down Radio Cairo.' He added: 'The forces of liberalism will eventually come to the top and when they do, we shall certainly be unable to keep the Ruler in his place by military means.'

Later in the year, in what seemed evidence of a more realistic policy towards Nasser, diplomatic relations were re-established with Egypt and the

MI6 station was reopened. 'What is less well known,' comments Professor Donald Cameron Watt, is that the British agents arrested by Nasser were released 'as part of a deal in which Egypt returned to the London capital markets'. Unfortunately, such realism did not last long. The apparent success of the gamble in Kuwait 'bred a new set of illusions about British power and influence in Arabia which were not dispelled until Aden became the scene for full-scale urban guerrilla war'; causing, in November 1967, as Brook had warned, 'an ignominious evacuation'.[72]

As part of the increasingly influential pro-Atlanticist faction that made up the permanent government of senior civil servants, Dick White agreed with the Cabinet Secretary's analysis. George Young and his acolytes, however, continued to rail against Britain's 'infection by a moralising bug'. Young cited Mossad as an exemplary service and urged 'a return to ruthlessness and a cessation of cowardice and surrender masquerading as morality'. The Chief had had to reject a proposal during the Kuwait operation to kidnap a known terrorist responsible for bomb outrages, and had been shocked at Young's approval, contrary to his orders, of a 'wet job' in Iran. Admitting that promoting Young had been his biggest mistake, White persuaded his vice-chief to retire, though, as we have seen, realising that he would not become Chief, Young already 'wanted out'.[73]

'Just as I experienced how the pre-war MI6 officers had been hopelessly out of their depth in the post-war world,' Young recalled, 'I saw my own experience becoming less relevant as younger men faced new problems and new techniques.'[74]

THE MUSKETEERS
IN YEMEN

Following the disastrous invasion of Suez, British foreign and defence policy in the Middle East was revised and found expression in the 1957 Defence White Paper, which laid emphasis on bases east of Suez. In that year, Macmillan transformed the insignificant base in Aden – the site of a massive British Petroleum refinery which dealt with the oil production from Kuwait – into the region's bastion of military power, with the Royal Navy and RAF commanding the approach to the Red Sea and the Suez Canal. The British intervention in Kuwait helped reinforce the strategy.

Parallel to this decision, in order to secure Aden's future, Macmillan organised the six tribal chiefs of the Western Protectorate bordering the colony – others joined two years later – into the Federation of South Arabia. Two factors undermined its chances of success. 'It was', Fred Halliday notes, 'an overtly British fabrication', financially dependent for its existence on Britain, with a million pounds paid out in bribes. The weakness was the 'nationalist movement' which 'ultimately destroyed it'. The establishment of the Middle East Command (MEC) headquarters in Aden in 1960 helped fuel the fires of revolution.[1]

The 1962 Defence White Paper, 'The Next Five Years', stated that Britain would continue to back the local sultans in South Yemen and the Gulf, and that the Aden base would be the permanent headquarters of this strategy. With the United Kingdom itself and Singapore in the Far East, Aden was to be one of the three key points in Britain's global military deployment.

* * *

On 26 September 1962 the Aden Assembly voted through the deal uniting Aden to the hinterland in the Federation. What no one in Aden knew was that in North Yemen on the very same night a line of tanks was rumbling into the capital Sana'a to depose the Imam. Had they arrived a day earlier, the vote would not have taken place.

The medieval kingdom of North Yemen lay in the south-west of the Arabian peninsula, with Saudi Arabia to the north and British-occupied Aden and the colony of South Yemen to the south and east. Relations in North Yemen between the warring tribes and the centre were never secure, while the Imam controlled the country, where over 80 per cent of the population were peasants, through bribery, an arbitrary and coercive tax system, and a policy of 'divide and rule'.[2]

In 1958, the Imam joined the north to the United Arab Republic (UAR) on a federal basis, but disillusion followed, and when Syria seceded from the UAR in September 1961, the Imam broke with Egypt. His son, Muhammed Al-Badr – 'an amiable idealist' – was able, however, to introduce a limited number of reforms when the Imam left for Rome for a health cure. On his return, subject to fits of insanity and reliant on morphine, the Imam never regained control. Opposition came from nationalist elements in the army which, with the help of Egyptian Intelligence, made strenuous efforts to assassinate the Imam. CIA officials 'still smile happily at the memory of the intercepted telephone call between the palace and a cleaning woman recruited to place a bomb under the Imam's bed, and her Egyptian case officer. She had some difficulty in reading the instructions, and the panic-stricken officer was attempting to talk her through the exercise.'[3]

The plot failed, and the Imam passed away peacefully on 19 September 1962. Al-Badr took over but his reign lasted only one week. He lacked the ability to move decisively and, through his friendship towards Egypt and progressive ideas, was thought unsuitable for succession by the traditionalist leaders of the Shi'ite Zaydi sect. 'He was considered unsound in canon law, had a slight limp which rendered him physically imperfect, and his personal conduct, particularly his drinking, did not meet the required standard of piety.'[4]

On the evening of 26 September tanks surrounded the Imam's palace, headed by Col. Abdullah al-Sallal, whom al-Badr had released from prison and appointed the new chief of army staff. Al-Sallal became first President of the Yemen Arab Republic (YAR). The Nasserite group that executed the coup came from a cabal of eighty left-wing army officers within the four-hundred-strong officers' corps, who had been 'formed by Arab nationalism'. Although carried out by an obscure grouping, the coup seems to have been popular. Inspired by promises of Soviet aid in establishing Yemen as a people's republic, al-Sallal was confident of support from Aden and the Federation of South Arabia.[5]

Overnight, Britain's secure base in Aden was put in peril. The CIA assessed that the Egyptians would land twelve thousand troops and that there would be a stable government within seven to ten days. Egyptian troops did indeed pour into Sana'a, the Yemeni capital, and with Cairo Radio urging nationalism and revolution in Aden, began to call for vengeance against the South Arabian tribal chiefs, who immediately sought British protection. The Foreign Office wanted intelligence on the area, but MI6, whose P17 section dealt with Aden, had none, being totally reliant on inadequate Colonial Office reports. The Service's officer in Aden, Terence O'Bryan Tear, was not well informed about the situation, having been surprised by the coup, and knew little about Egyptian activities. Intelligence-gathering in the area had been the responsibility of MI5 and the Aden Intelligence Centre, which was badly served by the local Special Branch.[6]

The first westerners into Yemen were a group of journalists, including the *Telegraph*'s Eric Downton. He recalled that an MI6 agent in Aden, using the familiar cover of press liaison official, 'tried to scare us off by saying our lives would be in danger'. The journalists managed to obtain an interview with President al-Sallal – who told them that al-Badr was dead – and 'to the astonishment of the British authorities' arrived back in Aden in a Soviet aircraft flown by a Russian pilot. The reports of the Imam's death turned out to be premature. In fact, he had escaped his ruined palace dressed as a woman and had made for the mountains, where he began organising a royalist counter-force. In the royalists' favour was the impregnability of the mountains and the ease with which passes could be dominated, but their troops were untrained and badly equipped. Shortly after the coup, King Hussein of Jordan visited London, where he met with Air Minister Julian Amery. He urged: 'Don't let your government recognise the Republicans. Nasser just wants to grab Saudi Arabia's oil but the Royalists are tough.' Hussein and Amery agreed that MI6 asset and serving Conservative MP Neil 'Billy' McLean should tour the area to deliver informed reports to the Prime Minister.[7]

A decision had to be made about whether to recognise the new republic, but 'many of us in the Government,' Amery recalled, 'had doubts whether this was good advice'. McLean, who came to be known by his constituents as 'our MP for Yemen', also had the gravest doubts. 'There were reports, but they were not well confirmed, of resistance in the Yemen.' McLean decided to go to the region himself to make an assessment. He 'did not have to dig too deeply into his pocket if at all because he flew by RAF plane from Northolt to Jordan where he saw an "old friend", King Hussein'.[8]

By 5 October, a royalist radio station was already operating from Saudi territory. Three days later *The Times* reported that three Egyptian warships were discharging tanks and troops were guarding airfields. On the same day came reports of arms reaching the royalist tribesmen through the Minister of the Interior, Sharif Saleh Ibn Hussein of Beihan, one of the small emirates belonging to the Federation of South Arabia. 'Clever, adventurous and loyal', the Sharif had been an impoverished tribal leader dependent upon British subsidies, but in late 1962 he became the sudden recipient of considerable supplies of money and arms – Saudi funds, channelled through the Aden branch of the National and Grindlays bank. It also became apparent that 'he was a front man for a British Intelligence operation'.[9]

MI6's former Vice-Chief, George Young, who was now a banker with Kleinwort Benson, was approached by Mossad to find an Englishman acceptable to the Saudis to run a guerrilla war against the republicans and their Egyptian backers. 'I can find you a Scotsman,' replied Young. He then introduced McLean to Brigadier Dan Hiram, the Israeli defence attaché, who promised to supply weapons, funds and instructors who could pass themselves off as Arabs; a strategy that the Saudis eagerly grasped. They had few pilots of their own and the whole air force was grounded in late 1962 when a number of fliers defected to Egypt.[10]

On 23 October, McLean saw King Saud, who told him that Nasser's intervention in Yemen was part of a broader plot, in league with the Russians, to undermine the security of the Arabian peninsula. He wanted Britain's support, secretly if necessary. When the British agent in Aden, Kennedy Trevaskis, who had known McLean in Eritrea early in the war, visited London for discussions, he found that

> memories of Suez seemed to lurk everywhere and there was a
> pervasive anxiety lest we should judge the situation wrongly
> and end up in splendid isolation at the side of a discredited
> reactionary regime against progressive Arab socialism. There
> was little disposition in official circles to regard revolutionary
> regimes as automatically representing the wave of the future,
> though in the early days of the Yemeni revolution it was argu-
> able that the Republican regime had come to stay and would
> have to be recognised in the long run.

Trevaskis brought with him proposals for urgent reform so that the Arabs could work towards an independent South Arabian government. He warned that 'subversion, sabotage and terrorism were just around the corner', but his proposals 'disappeared quietly into the distant mists of Whitehall'.[11]

McLean arrived in Aden, where following the proclamation of the Yemen Republic riots broke out. He met with the Governor and Commander-in-Chief, Sir Charles Johnston, and his aide-de-camp, Flt-Lt Antony Boyle, who wanted Aden 'to protect its back'. McLean told them that he was 'sceptical about the current newspaper reports, which tended to discount Royalist opposition . . . and was anxious to learn the facts'. With the permission of Sharif Hussein, McLean crossed the border into Yemen 'to see the situation for himself'. He discovered that the whole of the east of Yemen was held by the tribes, with heavy fighting in the west led by relatives of al-Badr. The main problem was the Egyptian aircraft, which were strafing the poorly equipped tribesmen.[12]

On 23 October, the British Cabinet decided in principle to recognise the republic. At the beginning of November, McLean again talked with King Saud and cabled Foreign Secretary Alec Douglas-Home (formerly Lord Home), who was under strong US pressure to recognise the new regime, urging him to delay the decision. In an effort to put further pressure on the British government, McLean arranged for a group of journalists to be flown to Amman to meet with King Hussein, and then on to Riyadh to see Crown Prince Faisal. Included in the small group taken by Jeep into the Yemen mountains of north-west Yemen were Eric Downton and Kim Philby, on his last assignment for the *Economist* and the *Observer*. Downton later suggested that 'it would be fascinating to be able to compare the reports Philby wrote on his Yemen excursion for MI6 (which was backing the royalists) and the KGB (which was backing the republicans)'.[13]

Relations between Saudi Arabia and Egypt were broken off altogether on 6 November and 'Saudi guns and gold began to flow over the border to the Yemeni Royalists'. On the same day, Prince Abdurrahman, the Imam's youngest uncle and roving ambassador, arrived in London, warning that 'Cairo and Moscow are plotting the future of my country' and 'of the very serious consequences for the entire Arabian peninsula should they succeed in their schemes'. A week later in the Commons McLean reported that Nasser 'believes that the Yemen could give him an excellent base from which to extend the Arab socialist revolution into Saudi Arabia, perhaps through a military coup d'état there, and then perhaps later into Jordan and the Persian Gulf. Also he would be in a position to turn the heat on us in Aden.'[14]

The lobbying had an effect. Macmillan recorded in his diary (14 November) that he urged President Kennedy to delay recognition. Kennedy, with 'his usual charming frankness', replied: 'I don't even know where it is.' He felt, however, that Saudi Arabia was endangered by its involvement and that recognition could be traded for a withdrawal of Egyptian troops. At the end of the month, the director of the CIA's Middle East Division, James Critch-field, was in London *en route* to Beirut for a regional conference on Soviet activities in the region. He told Dick White: 'The Russians are waging war across Arabia. We've got to stop them. Their influence is everywhere and it's spreading down to the Gulf.' White was pleased that the Americans were now against Nasser but was wary of being pressured, particularly by McLean's para-diplomacy, into taking action, as he believed that the Service should not get dragged into the conflict.[15]

On 4 December, after visiting King Hussein and Prince Faisal – the Saudi Minister of Defence and real power behind the throne – McLean again crossed into the Yemen. He met with the Imam and the director of the royalist armed forces, Prince Mohammed Hussein, who informed him of the desperate need for arms, ammunition and anti-aircraft guns. Back in Aden, he sent a telegram to Amery, reporting that 'at least half the country was in Royalist hands and that it would be a disaster if the Government recognised the Republic'. McLean concluded that the royalists could defeat the fifteen thousand Egyptian troops. In London, he reported to the Foreign Secretary, 'advocating immediate British aid'. McLean then began to canvass the Cabinet for support.[16]

In a blow to Britain, on 19 December the US formally recognised the republican regime. The CIA had attempted to persuade Faisal to offer Nasser a deal, whereby Russian aid would be replaced by Saudi money. Faisal, however, refused, regarding Nasser as the 'devil incarnate' and his revolutionary creed as 'a sinister carrier of Marxist plague'. Officially, the Americans viewed the Gulf as a British concern, but Aden and South Arabia were 'another matter'. Commenting in 1966 in the light of his experiences as commander of the United Nations observer force in Yemen, Maj.-Gen. Carl von Horn observed that

> beneath this apparently logical decision by the Americans to recognise the Republican regime lay a baser policy aimed at embarrassing the British in southern Arabia, linked with a desire to further their own oil interests in the Arabian peninsula ... under a cloak of a benefactor and supporter of national aspirations in the Middle East, there was a desire to cut the throat of British influence in the Persian Gulf.[17]

Also on the 19th, Macmillan was visited by McLean with his report.

Armed with Saudi intelligence which suggested that the royalist tribes were effectively harassing the Egyptians, Amery persuaded the Prime Minister that the Americans had exaggerated the threat of Egyptian tanks against the tribesmen. He argued that Nasser's subversion could be halted. The tribes needed 'our help' and they 'will win the war'. According to Tom Bower, Macmillan became increasingly sceptical about MI6's intelligence-gathering capabilities and its reliance on the Americans. 'Intercepts from GCHQ of messages between Egyptian commanders in the field vindicated Amery's stance', though the only source on the spot, Christopher Gandy in Ta'izz, dismissed the threat of the royalists. He thought that the hawks such as Amery were 'moved by nostalgia for lost causes'. Supported by his officials, Alec Douglas-Home was initially against backing the royalists and rejected the Saudi report, arguing that the tribes could only organise minor skirmishes. On 28 December, he suggested recognising the republicans so as not to antagonise the Egyptians, with whom relations had recently been normalised, and in order to stop Nasser's attack on Aden. When Douglas-Home stated that 'the Royalists have no hope', Amery and his friends in MI6 saw it as another example of his appeasement.[18]

On 7 January 1963, three days before the crucial Cabinet meeting on recognition of the new regime, McLean's 'intelligence report' was assessed by the Cabinet Overseas and Defence Committee, attended by the Prime Minister, the Foreign Secretary, Minister of Defence Peter Thorneycroft, Amery, Duncan Sandys and Hugh Fraser. The committee decided to advise the Cabinet not to recognise the new regime, arguing that Britain could not allow Egypt to have its way in the Yemen, as it could not lose control of the Gulf to the Americans. In order to avoid a split with the US, Britain could not give direct support to the royalists and any operation would have to be at arm's length. The Cabinet's endorsement of the decision was 'not liked by the American Government'. Kennedy cabled Macmillan that Nasser 'could not afford to pull out' of Yemen, and to allow the war to continue 'will increase violence and endanger Saudi Arabia'. Nor was it welcomed by White, who had banked on the support of the Foreign Secretary, but Amery and several senior MI6 officers regarded White as weak and in no position to decline a Cabinet decision.[19]

During January fighting broke out between the Saudis and the Egyptians, whose planes bombed Saudi border posts and dropped arms to resistance groups operating against Saudi Arabia. As veteran opponents of British interests, the Saudis had broken off diplomatic relations with Britain following Suez, but thanks to McLean's rapport with King Saud, relations were restored following the threats from Nasser. MI6 did not have a station in the capital, Riyadh, but its officers were on intimate terms with several advisers to the royal family and 'attempted to persuade them of the logic of Macmillan's counter-revolution in the Gulf'. Egyptian intelligence officers were said to be recruiting Yemeni tribesmen and providing money and rifles. The ambassador reported that the Saudis intended to support a royalist counter-offensive against Nasser.[20]

'The American thesis is that the one way of getting Nasser out of the Yemen is to give him his victory,' Sir Charles Johnson, the Governor-General of Aden, complained when he cabled Macmillan on 8 February. This was no longer seen as an option by the Cabinet, particularly after the outbreak of agitation by pro-republican campaigners following Aden's decision to join the Federation. The British were forced to bring in colonial specialists to quell the disorder. The appointment of a Special Branch Malaya specialist and the current Deputy Inspector-General of the Colonial Police, Nigel Morris, was followed by a new high commissioner, Richard Turnbull, who had led the anti-guerrilla campaign in Kenya. On the 23rd, British positions in the Federation were attacked by Yemeni tribesmen. At the same time, five thousand Egyptian troops began the 'Ramadan Offensive' into the royalist-held mountains. Two days later, Cabinet members railed that 'American policy is a menace ... The State Department wishes to save Nasser from the consequences of his adventures.'[21]

Duncan Sandys and Julian Amery urged retaliation. Various intelligence personnel, including senior MI6 figure Nicholas Elliott, began 'dropping hints' to people such as the founder of the SAS, David Stirling, that 'something needed to be done'. Washington, however, complained that British policy endangered the stability of Saudi Arabia, but Macmillan was not to be deflected. He 'allowed his cronies to plan an Arabian counter-revolution' and appointed Amery his minister for Aden, with a remit to covertly organise British support for the royalists. Working from his office at the Ministry of Aviation, Amery urged a reluctant White to undertake operations in the region. The Chief argued that the Service's priority was to supply intelligence, not to indulge in 'dubious special actions'.[22]

McLean went out to Yemen for the third time on 1 March 1963 and heard that the Jordanians and Saudis were under pressure from the Americans to discontinue support of the royalists. Once in the Yemen he found that morale among the guerrillas was high, even though Prince al-Hussan's situation was poor, with his lines of communication and supply cut. A royalist delegation visited Israel and shortly afterwards 'unmarked Israeli planes made about fifteen flights from Djibouti to drop arms over royalist areas'. In mid-April, McLean flew to Aden, from where he cabled the Foreign Secretary, stressing the need for immediate support. The Saudis quickly stepped in with a small supply of arms and ammunition, releasing stocks obtained in the form of aid from the United States. Several million pounds' worth of light weapons, including fifty thousand Lee Enfield rifles, were secretly flown out from an RAF station in Wiltshire. In order to mask their true origin, they were landed in Jordan for onward transportation via Beihan. By the end of the month, the royalists had regained some of the lost territory.[23]

A meeting was held at the end of the month at White's, with McLean, David Stirling and Amery. Also present were Col. Brian Franks, the driving force behind the reformation of the postwar SAS Regiment who worked closely with MI6, and Alec Douglas-Home. The 'unofficial minister of foreign affairs', McLean, said that 'with a little bit of help, the tribes now fighting under the Imam could easily hold off the Egyptians'. Stirling thought that it was clear that Amery, McLean and Douglas-Home (the latter had made an about-turn in his views) had already decided that what was required was an unofficial operation. The Foreign Secretary had been told that 'it would take MI6 six months to put agents into the Yemen and even then they might not have the required talent for the operation'. Informed that there could be no official SAS involvement, Stirling and Franks were there to recommend someone who could organise a mercenary operation. They approached Col. Jim Johnson, a commodity broker at Lloyd's with the firm Thomas Nelson, who had recently retired from command of the 21 SAS (TA). Stirling also brought in Lt-Col. John Woodhouse, commander of 22 SAS.[24]

McLean, Johnson and Stirling were introduced by Amery to the royalist

Foreign Minister, Ahmed al-Shami, who wrote out a cheque for £5,000 made out to the Hyde Park Hotel, whose managing director was Brian Franks. Cash for the operation was kept in one of the hotel's safe-deposit boxes. Franks invited Johnson to undertake an operation to destroy the Egyptian MiG aircraft which were strafing the poorly armed tribesmen. The royalist Minister of the Interior, Abdel Kerim el-Wazir, said that the priority was to destroy the MiGs on the ground at Sana'a airport.[25]

The SAS men operated through Stirling's Television International Enterprises (TIE) company, which set up a cover organisation, Rally Films, and sometimes under cover of a locust control unit. Johnson worked from the basement of Stirling's office in Sloane Street (next to an MI6 safe house), with a secretary, Fiona Fraser, daughter of Lord Lovat. The Saudi Prince Sultan financed the project with gold bullion. There was an absurd scenario in which the organisation was almost penniless, while thousands of pounds of gold were stacked up in the office.

On 12 April 1963, Stirling flew out to Aden as the guest of an old friend, Sir Charles Johnson, another member of the White's mafia. He discussed the situation with the deputy high commissioner, Kennedy Trevaskis, and told Tony Boyle that he intended to send support to the royalist forces. Son of Marshal of the RAF Sir Dermot Boyle, Tony was in Aden on a ground tour in the middle of his RAF career. He agreed to co-operate by helping Stirling's people as they passed through Aden.[26]

During May, McLean recruited David Smiley, fresh from command of the Sultan of Oman's armed forces which had suppressed the revolt during the Green Mountain campaign. Simultaneously, Stirling brought in Johnny Cooper, who had been under a private contract in Oman as second-in-command of the Muscat Regiment during the assault against the Saudi-backed rebels on Jebel Akhdar. Cooper had been Stirling's driver during commando operations behind German lines in the desert war, and after the war commanded A Squadron SAS in Malaya. Cooper met with Stirling, Phillip Horniblow, medical officer to 21 SAS Regiment (TA), and Tony Boyle in Bahrein.[27]

In early June, Stirling and Cooper moved on to Paris for a meeting with a French friend, Pierre de Bourbon-Parma, in order to make contact with former French members of the SAS and officials of the Deuxième Bureau. They were seeking Arabic-speaking recruits, principally mercenaries who had served in Algeria (unfortunately it was later discovered that the Algerian dialect was not fully understood in Yemen). Two brutal mercenary commanders who had served in the international forces in Katanga and the Congo (Amery and McLean had been active in the right-wing Katanga Lobby, supporting British interests in uranium in the area) were recruited to run separate operations. Col. Roger Falques was an enigmatic ex-legionnaire, who had survived a Vietminh prison camp, while Bob Denard had served in

Indochina and Algeria. Falques set up an office in Paris to recruit mercenaries, who were to be under Denard's command. At another meeting with Falques, McLean, Johnson and Cooper hammered out the details of an in-depth reconnaissance mission. The French were willing to take an active part in the Yemen operation, since they opposed American policies in the Gulf. They helped route aid through their African enclave in Djibouti.[28]

Cooper's brief was to lead a party of four French and four British soldiers into the mountains of North Yemen to establish contact with the royalist army with the aim of destroying the Egyptian aircraft at Sana'a. Back in London, Cooper contacted John Woodhouse, commanding officer of 22 SAS, who arranged for three volunteers – Sergeant Geordie Dorman, a mortar expert, Corporal Chigley, a medical orderly, and Trooper Richardson, a firearms expert – to be granted a month's leave to join the expedition. Although this was an unofficial operation, when Cooper was about to leave for the Yemen, the Commonwealth Secretary, Duncan Sandys, telephoned Stirling to stop it. Under pressure following rumours surrounding the Duchess of Argyll's divorce and the Profumo affair, Sandys was worried lest the operation prove embarrassing to the Conservative government. Stirling ignored him and Cooper left for Libya, where he met up with the French contingent before flying on to Aden. In fact, Sandys' intervention appears to have been a public relations exercise designed to hide government support.[29]

The office of the adjutant of 21 SAS Volunteers (TA) in London, Capt. Richard Pirie, was used as a 'clearing ground' for the British mercenaries. According to Pirie, the mercenaries were paid £250 per month through the Foreign Office and Ministry of Defence (which, naturally, denied it). In Aden, Tony Boyle evolved a system for passing mercenaries through Customs, while Sharif Hussein organised a network of safe houses in Beihan from which operations into the Yemen could be launched. As the traffic increased, SAS personnel such as John Woodhouse were seconded to the staff of the Federal Regular Army with others, including Peter de la Billière, employed in undercover roles. A junior intelligence officer, de la Billière attended the daily intelligence meeting chaired by the senior Political Officer, George Henderson, along with Ralph Daly, Robin Young, Bill Heber-Percy, James Nash and Michael Crouch.[30]

It was around this time, June 1963, that serious opposition first appeared in Aden with the formation of the National Liberation Front (NLF), a loose alliance of pro-republican tribal leaders and nationalists who organised in the northern capital of Sana'a. De la Billière felt that the British had done little to create a unified state and that, in consequence, the Arabs 'never developed any particular loyalty to us'. Intelligence on the NLF was lacking, and 'the only effective way we had of keeping the rulers on our side was by bribing them with arms, ammunition and money'. MI6 had one permanent officer in the Governor's office, with others drafted in as required. A colonial administrator who acted as liaison with MI6 recalled that he gave them 'a general idea of what results I wanted', which could include getting 'someone killed'. Mainly, the operations consisted of 'discrediting people, we would find out those people who were in the pay of Nasser, receiving money from organisations in Egypt, and the rulers might kick them out of the country'. Those deported were sent over the border to the YAR.[31]

On 14 June, using journalistic cover arranged by an MI6 asset, the foreign editor of the *Daily Telegraph*, S. R. 'Pop' Pawley, Smiley flew out with McLean to Jeddah where Amery introduced him to Prince Faisal and the Minister of Defence, Prince Sultan. Smiley's task was to tour royalist areas and write a report on the military situation, with an assessment of how the Saudis could help. After spending three months there, Smiley called for a training and supply operation, and the use of European mercenaries. He summarised the royalists' main failings as being, firstly, their tactics, which were 'a waste of men and effort' – instead of concentrating on the towns they should be attacking vulnerable lines of communication; secondly, 'the lack of co-ordination', which would be solved by the use of wireless; thirdly, the inadequate supply system. With a bounty of £5,000 on his head, Johnny Cooper, who had tried to blow up Egyptian aircraft but had been restrained by Yemenis who feared reprisals, had completed his own reconnaissance. It determined that the republicans could not win as long as the royalists continued to fight. Smiley presented his recommendations to Faisal and Sultan, who both agreed to cover the costs of the project. The Israelis, as well as the Iranians, also showed a willingness to help.[32]

Details soon reached Dick White, who was receiving intelligence that 'everyone is free-booting', including 'the ADC to the governor-general in Aden'. One ex-MI6 man recalled that the proposed Yemen operation was the focus of fierce debate: many senior officers wanted the government to call a halt to it, but they lost the argument. 'In those days, there were just too many people in SIS who were a law unto themselves.' White was reluctant to help, but the Prime Minister instructed the Service to aid the royalists, while the Director Middle East, Paul Paulson, was told to assist Amery. An MI6 task-force was headed by the Assistant Political Adviser to the Middle East Command in Aden (the MI6 cover post), Hubert O'Bryan Tear, an experienced intelligence officer but with no knowledge of the Arabs. He was aided in London by Desmond Harney and Dennis Womersley, a recent head of station in Baghdad. P17 co-ordinated the supply of weapons and personnel to the royalists, while MI6 reports were sent to the Aviation Ministry. John da Silva, formerly head of station in Bahrein and responsible for the Service's involvement in the Oman operation, organised MI6's commitment. He supported Amery as 'a legitimate interest'. To strengthen liaison with the Saudis, John Christie, fresh from his success in Kuwait, opened a new station in Jeddah, where he developed a back channel to the monarch and Kamal Adhan, the Saudi chief of intelligence.[33]

In July, the Egyptians launched a general offensive on all fronts with the aim of destroying the royalists as an effective fighting force. Cooper's team undertook basic training and engaged in a firefight which indicated that the Egyptians were running the campaign. Returning home, Cooper briefed Stirling and Johnson, and various members of MI6. They concluded that Nasser's objective was to destabilise Saudi Arabia to the north, with an eye on the oilfields. McLean, too, returned to London at the beginning of August and delivered a report to the government, urging an increase in the flow of Saudi arms, more British supplies to be parachuted in by unattributable aircraft, and the dispatch of western mercenaries, particularly experts in the use of mortars, artillery and explosives. In Aden, Amery met covertly with the new high commissioner, Trevaskis, to discuss plans for the secret war. Not long after, Tony Boyle resigned from the RAF and promptly joined Jim Johnson's operation in London.[34]

The Egyptian-backed republican offensive failed, despite the use of gas. Smiley had learned that the Egyptians had used gas on 8 June 1963 against the village of Al Kawma. On his return to London, McLean delivered a report on the deployment of gas. During his first tour Smiley had discovered fragments of a bomb casing which were sent to the Chemical Warfare Centre at Porton Down. Fragments were also passed on to the Israelis, who were keen to discover what type of gas was being deployed. Smiley appeared on television and published articles on the gas bombs, which some dismissed as royalist propaganda. There were allegations that the bombs contained phosgene that had been left in the country by British troops during the Second World War. Some 1,400 royalist troops were said to have been killed and a further 90 seriously wounded. Johnny Cooper made a special trip to Kent to collect up-to-date radio equipment from KW Electronics and a cine camera in order to provide proof of the Egyptian bombing of villages with napalm and poison gas.[35]

Within Whitehall there was conflict over the gas bomb reports. Colonial Office officials believed the evidence and called for retaliation, but the Foreign Office disputed it. Saudi Arabia tried to persuade the UN to mount an investigation, but no action took place. Smiley regarded this as 'sinister'. 'No one, it seemed – certainly not the United States – wanted to know about chemical warfare.' Three years later, nine aircraft armed with gas bombed the royalist village of Kitaf, and it was claimed that 'several hundred people' had been killed. Villagers responded by mutilating Egyptian soldiers who fell into their hands. It was Labour Prime Minister Harold Wilson who on 31 January 1967 'felt sufficiently confident of the claims to inform the House of Commons that gas had been used'. In truth, Smiley found the released Porton Down report 'disappointing'. 'Traces of tear gas' had been found but the bombs were 'unlikely to have contained a poison gas'. The Israelis had apparently found 'traces of mustard gas', but once Porton Down reported that the bombs only contained tear gas, the matter was allowed to die a natural death.[36]

White was concerned by a visit from CIA officer Jim Critchfield, who argued that the West could not afford to lose Yemen and, therefore, that the CIA should fight Nasser regardless of his President's policies. He added that NSA intercepts had shown that Russian pilots were flying Tu-16s with Egyptian insignia from Cairo to Yemen. Critchfield suggested bypassing the Foreign Office and the State Department in order to develop closer liaison between MI6 and the CIA. According to Tom Bower, White wanted to spurn the offer but he was under pressure fom Macmillan. It was difficult to resist closer relations after James Fees, a CIA officer posted under cover of a humanitarian aid agency to Ta'izz, provided MI6 with a copy of the republican army's field dispositions. White's change of heart was evident by early November when the CIA's Deputy Chief for Plans, Richard Helms, visited London and was asked for assistance in supporting the royalists and in softening State Department opposition to British policy. Shortly after, a CIA National Estimate identified the existence of a Soviet threat in the region.[37]

MI6 lobbying seemed to have little effect. On 21 November President Kennedy telephoned Alec Douglas-Home and asked for his personal assurance that British mercenaries would be withdrawn. The Foreign Secretary denied that Britain was involved but promised to make enquiries. The following day Kennedy was assassinated. Smiley recalled that the tribesmen heard the news of Kennedy's death on the radio and reacted with cheers, as they regarded him as the architect of American support for Nasser. 'But if they imagined his death would change that policy they were in for a disappointment.'[38]

The resignation of Macmillan in October had temporarily put all plans on hold as the new Foreign Secretary, Rab Butler, was opposed to covert support for the royalists. Interestingly, it was MI6 intelligence which saved the situation. Ministers were told that the position in Yemen and the security situation in Aden had deteriorated, with terrorism beginning to take a hold. On 10 December, a grenade was thrown at Kennedy Trevaskis while he waited to board a flight to London. He was saved by the actions of Political Officer George Henderson, who threw himself in front of the high commissioner, taking the full blast of the explosion. Henderson died ten days later. In an about-turn that remains unexplained, White now called for an aggressive policy against Nasser and, in what has been described as 'a brilliant performance', won over the new Prime Minister to supporting a clandestine mercenary operation. Under pressure from Sandys and Thorneycroft, Douglas-Home was asked to arbitrate in the dispute with the Foreign Secretary. The go-ahead for full support for the royalists was sanctioned in summer of 1964.[39]

During his second term in Yemen, Cooper was engaged in intelligence-gathering and built up 'a complete intelligence picture of the Egyptian order of battle', which he passed on to an appreciative John da Silva. At MI6's request, Cooper captured up-to-date Russian equipment including an advanced radio which had not previously been seen in the West. His team also trained the army and set up a medical team with supplies from the Yemen Relief Fund, which had been instituted by would-be 'Scarlet Pimpernels' Mark Lennox-Boyd, son of a Tory minister, and Lady Birdwood, who operated out of Aden with the help of Tony Boyle. Cooper recalled Lady Birdwood, who was chair of the anti-communist Foreign Affairs Circle with Rowly Winn, 'doling out medical supplies like a latter-day Florence Nightingale'.[40]

The first hints that the British government was helping the royalist cause came in January 1964. Labour MP Richard Marsh asked the Prime Minister about allegations that twenty thousand British Lee Enfield rifles had reached the Yemen from Saudi Arabia. Douglas-Home denied the claims but a Jersey-based arms consultant, Major Robert Turp, a director of Intor (International Ordnance), who had worked with MI6 when military attaché in Paris after the war, informed *The Times* that 'we received an order from Sheikh Ibrahim Zahid, the accredited agent of the Saudi Arabian Government. This was subcontracted to a Belgian company which applied for an export licence to supply the weapons. An export licence was granted against a certificate from the Saudi Arabian Government, certifying that the weapons were for the use of their forces and would not be re-exported.' This was correct up to a point, but Turp's conclusion was misleading. 'The rifles were not destined for the Yemen, and to the best of our knowledge they are still in use by the Saudi Arabian forces.'[41]

In February, Cooper and his men prepared for their first clandestine night air-drop of supplies, codenamed MANGO, with the discreet backing of MI6 and the CIA. Arms and ammunition were parachuted into drop zones manned by Cooper's team, who guided the planes in by radio. Meanwhile, French organisers convinced contacts in Bulgaria 'that arms should be sent to the Red Sea area, ostensibly for an African nationalist group fighting French colonialism'. The first successful drop included German Schmeisser submachine-guns whose source had been 'brilliantly concealed' with every seal number scored out, while the parachutes were of Italian origin. The supplies helped the royalist forces take on a more aggressive role. On the other side, the republicans were aided by the Egyptians and to a lesser extent by the Soviet Union and China.[42]

Using his extensive interests in Africa, Stirling recruited Jack Mulloch of the Rhodesian Air Services to fly arms into Yemen. Another colleague, Eric Bennett, worked with the Jordanian Air Force. Stirling, using his contacts through his TIE company, also negotiated with the Iranians, whose air force worked closely with the Saudis on the project. It helped that the Shah of Iran had visited MI6 headquarters in May 1962. Six years later, the story of the covert assistance was leaked to the *Sunday Times*, forcing Stirling to seek an injunction. Through a senior journalist friend he placed a series of articles in the *Telegraph* which scooped the *Sunday Times* and kept the existence of MI6 support secret.[43]

In an interesting illustration of how the 'musketeers' had access to the highest levels, in early 1964 David Smiley talked with Alec Douglas-Home and found a 'much greater interest in the war, particularly among Government circles'. There were also indications that President Johnson might abandon the stance of the previous administration. In Saudi, Smiley was asked by Ahmed el Shami and the Minister of Defence, Prince Sultan, to take command of the mercenaries. This was agreed by Jim Johnson. MI6 gathered the latest intelligence from Johnny Cooper, who travelled to Aden where he was debriefed by Ralph Daly and Bill Heber-Percy and had discussions with John da Silva. At the beginning of March, Smiley flew to Yemen, where he advised the guerrillas to 'concentrate on the Egyptian supply lines' and 'forget about frontal assaults on Republican-held towns'.[44]

Initially the campaign went well, and by early 1964 the royalists had regained nearly all the territory lost to the republicans in the Ramadan offensive. It was a major blow to the Egyptians, who had lost around fifteen thousand men since the coup in 1962. Nasser increased the number of Egyptian soldiers to thirty thousand in order that lines of communication and airfields remained protected, and, in April, travelled to Yemen in preparation for a new offensive. Smiley's advice, however, was 'ignored by the Royalists which did not enhance their chances of a military victory'. There was, Tony Geraghty concludes, 'never much hope that the Royalists would produce anything more than a military and political stalemate'.[45]

Forty-eight ex-servicemen were now employed as mercenaries, including a dozen former SAS men, under the command of Smiley, who liaised directly with the Saudis, while Mike Gooley took command on the ground in the Yemen. It was an operation that 'could never have been carried out without official support'. Indeed, it was striking for the 'degree of official connivance and co-operation it managed to acquire'. MI6 officers John da Silva, John Christie and the head of station in Bahrein, Jeff Douglas, provided intelligence and logistical support, while the Government Communications Headquarters (GCHQ) pinpointed the location of republican units.

Intelligence operatives helped with 'radio monitoring problems' and co-ordinated the crossing of tribesmen over the border from the Federation into Yemen, where they tracked Egyptian army officers. In what turned out to be a dirty war, MI6 officers 'manipulated' the tribesmen and helped 'direct the planting of bombs' at Egyptian military outposts along the frontier, while garrison towns were 'shot up' and political figures 'murdered'.[46]

When two SAS patrols from 'A' Detachment made a recce across the Aden Protectorate's border into North Yemen during late April 1964, they were ambushed, resulting in the deaths of Capt. Robin Edwards and Sapper Nick Warburton. A patrol later discovered that 'the Arabs, in their frustration, had taken a grisly revenge on the bodies of our dead comrades'. According to a US diplomat in Ta'izz, their heads had been impaled on stakes hammered into the ground in the main square. The republican government denied the report, denouncing it as a British lie, but another army patrol apparently collected the two headless corpses. Questions were asked in the Commons, including one that demanded to know what 'A' Squadron was doing in Aden since, officially, it was supposed to be on exercises on Salisbury Plain.[47]

According to the CIA officer James Fees, White took 'a lively interest in the war. After all, we were spending lots of money', particularly on the British side, where astronomical sums were being wasted. A number of senior MI6 officers opposed the project because, according to Anthony Verrier's sources, 'it degenerated into a matter of bribes to the wrong people – £30 million, to be exact, laundered through the Colonial Development and Welfare Acts, ostensibly paid into the South Arabian Federal Treasury, then handed out to tribal rulers on both sides of the border'. Corruption was endemic among the royalist tribes.[48]

The Times reported that 'stories circulate of tribesmen pledging themselves to the Royalists, receiving rifles and selling them to Republicans; and soldiers have been heard joking that they are "royalist" by day and "republican" by night'. In 1962, in the Khawlan area, Sheikh Naji bin Ali al-Gadr had had only 120 men at his disposal. He subsequently accepted arms and money from the British agent, the Sharif of Beihan, through whom the British and Saudis channelled supplies. Al-Gadr, however, was also willing to accept arms and money from the Egyptians and from any foreign source willing to support him. By 1964, the sheikh was rich enough to send his family to London for private medical treatment. The chief of the Bakil federation had over twelve thousand men under his command, twice the number of the Yemen regular army.[49]

The Yemen operation was more or less blown away on 1 May 1964, when the Cairo newspaper *Al-Ahram* published five letters – including some dated December of the previous year from Tony Boyle to Cooper. The letters, which had never reached Cooper, talked of his 'experience in demolition and small arms and the dropping of weapons by parachute and other operational matters'. Copies had reached the *Sunday Times'* newly established 'Insight' team but nearly did not see the light of day. Initial problems surfaced when it was discovered that the Stirling operation was being run through TIE, in which the newspaper's owner, Lord Thomson, had interests. In the event the editor, Denis Hamilton, backed his journalists.[50]

On 5 July, the *Sunday Times* reproduced all five letters. The British government denied all knowledge of Cooper's mission. The Americans were mightily displeased when Richard Marsh raised in the Commons the matter of the Prime Minister's 'expressed policy of British non-interference in the Yemen'. He also queried the role of Boyle. Douglas-Home replied that 'no one gave any such authorisation. Both the present High Commissioner and his predecessor have assured my Right Hon. Friend that they were not aware that the person in question was involved in any way.' Marsh dismissed the idea that Stirling, Cooper and Boyle 'could, in an area as dangerous as this, engage in activities on this scale without anyone noticing'. The PM replied that 'I must take their word for it – and I do'. His reply was 'widely disbelieved, especially as Boyle later appeared in the Imam's camp as a military adviser . . .'[51]

Although a series of successful parachute drops, carried out by unmarked aircraft operating from 'somewhere in Africa', had raised morale, when McLean returned during the summer of 1964 he found the royalists were 'once more in a precarious position owing to an acute shortage of ammunition'. On 6 September, Stirling, Boyle and royalist Foreign Minister Ahmed al-Shami met in Aden, where they were joined by an MI6 officer who, against the instincts of White, told them that the Service was willing to back robust methods. They drew up plans for establishing a 'regular supply of arms and ammunition to the Royalist forces' which would be undertaken either by parachute or overland from Saudi Arabia and Beihan, or via the Yemen coast. It was hoped that Egyptian communication and supply lines could be cut, while the royalists would be helped with 'skilled advice and practical assistance'.[52]

Jim Johnson and his team subsequently moved their headquarters from Aden to Saudi Arabia, where Johnson said to the Saudi head of intelligence that 'we can win – what do you want to do – go ahead or withdraw?' It soon became apparent, however, that the Saudis feared reprisals from the Egyptians, who had already made dummy air runs across Jeddah. The Egyptian ambassador had warned the government not to go any further in backing the war. It was rumoured that, as a means of finding a way out of the situation, the Saudis had offered Nasser a million dollars to withdraw from Yemen. In November 1964, King Saud was deposed in a peaceful coup by the ruling Saudi family, who appointed Prince Faisal in his place. The Americans then brokered an agreement whereby Faisal promised not to supply arms to the royalists, and Nasser would withdraw his troops as soon as possible and stop bombing the villages in Yemen.[53]

MI6, too, had been preparing the ground for political negotiations. During January 1965, while on yet another trip to Yemen, McLean, who had recently lost his parliamentary seat, learned that 'at Erkwit, on the Red Sea coast of the Sudan, under Faisal's auspices, a Yemeni Royalist delegation, headed by Ahmed al-Shamy, and a similarly representative group of Republicans, had met in secret and agreed to a ceasefire, which would come into effect on 8

November 1964'. Secret RAF bombing in retaliation for Egyptian attacks on camel trains carrying weapons to French and British mercenaries had helped force the first of many Egyptian retreats and their appearance at the negotiating table. Officially, the Saudis kept to their word and did not send any more supplies to the guerrillas, but, despite this, hostilities soon resumed.[54]

A routine intercept on Middle East embassies in London revealed that British plans for the region had been leaked. Staff Sergeant Percy Allen of the War Office Land/Air Directorate was arrested on 16 March 1965 in the act of handing over a bundle of classified documents to the Iraqi military attaché. Allen had had access to western intelligence assessments of the Egyptian armed forces, and some documents had already been sold to the Cairo newspaper *Al-Ahram*, which revealed that the British government had not ruled out direct military intervention in the Middle East. The documents outlined a strategy for the reinforcement of the Central Treaty Organisation (successor to the Baghdad Pact) and the regimes of King Idris in Libya and King Hussein in Jordan. Contingency plans had been made for intervention 'in co-operation with the United States . . . in the event of internal disturbances or intervention in the Lebanon and Sudan'. Central to the plans was the role of the military base in Aden, itself far from stable as civil war continued in the North.[55]

In order to ease his relations with the Saudi government, Stirling worked closely with Kemel Adham, the chief of the Saudi intelligence service and brother-in-law of Faisal, who was regarded as the King's *éminence grise*. Stirling also co-operated with the well-connected Jersey arms dealer Geoffrey Edwards, who was trying to clinch a multimillion-pound arms deal. His contacts helped Stirling gain a Saudi contract to run a radio station in Aden, which employed Tony Boyle.[56]

When the Saudi government decided to build up its air force, the Foreign Office believed that the planes would be supplied by the United States, which regarded the country as its preserve. The election of a Labour government in October 1964 changed that perception, and Edwards was party to the successful conclusion of a British arms deal worth £186 million. This included a £26 million contract to British and Commonwealth Shipping's Airwork Services to provide personnel for the training of Saudi pilots and ground crew. 'Equally important . . . Airwork also recruited former RAF pilots as mercenaries to fly operational missions against Egyptian and Republican targets along the Yemeni border', from a secret base at Khamis Mishyat.[57]

According to David Smiley, by 1965 the musketeers were chartering aircraft with 'discreet pilots', and had obtained the agreement of Israel to use its territory for mounting operations. Dick White and the CIA's Richard Helms had also helped broker an agreement between the Saudis and the head of Mossad, Meir Amit, while Stirling arranged for Israel, which had an intelligence as well as a religious interest in Yemen, to take the place of Saudi

Arabia in organising the supply of arms. A large Jewish community had existed in Yemen since biblical times, and during the 1948–50 period around fifty thousand Jews had been airlifted to Israel in an operation known as 'Magic Carpet'. The CIA helped the Israelis infiltrate back into Yemen some of these Jews to train the guerrillas in the use of modern weapons. 'The trainers, naturally, took care to disguise their true nationality.'[58]

An intelligence relationship between Israel and Iran had existed since 1960/61, when a team of Mossad officers replaced the CIA team training SAVAK personnel. It remained in Iran with CIA and MI6 encouragement until 1965, when Mossad and SAVAK 'began to run joint covert operations against radical Arab states and organisations'. In the mid-1960s, Israel provided Iran with western and captured Soviet-made arms, which were repackaged so as to disguise their true country of origin for use by the royalist forces.[59]

When asked about the Israeli connection, Stirling would say only that 'it would have been very sensitive had it been known that any Arab country had received assistance from Israel'. Indeed, King Faisal was 'a committed anti-Semite' and, therefore, the CIA and MI6 relied on other 'practical-minded members of the Saudi royal family' to develop a covert alliance between Israel, Saudi Arabia, Iran and Jordan. Although the CIA's main channel to Mossad, James Angleton, disliked these covert ties, he was pressured into creating greater liaison with Agency heads of station in the Arab countries.[60]

These secret alliances had been working well but nearly fell apart during the autumn of 1965. It seems that a leak of sensitive proposals made to Jordan created a rift with Israel, resulting in the loss of long-established contacts. The affair centred around a 'young buccaneer', Dominic Elwes, McLean's son-in-law, who had passed on to Stirling from an RAF officer, John Curtis, military secrets concerning bombing raids to be carried out in Yemen. Curtis was subsequently court-martialled. The facts of the case remain somewhat obscure.[61]

By mid-1965, Egyptian strength was estimated at around fifty-two thousand, but it soon became clear that Nasser's troops were not making any headway into the royalist mountain strongholds. Indeed, the year proved to be a turning point as the royalist forces gained control of 50 per cent of the territory. Egyptian commanders found the mountainous conditions intolerable, with their garrison troops forced to retreat to their fortified bases. During July, Stirling organised guerrilla action around Sana'a with the aim of forcing the Egyptians to abandon their airfields. It soon became apparent to Nasser that the war was draining Egypt's resources – foreign exchange reserves were depleted. More specifically, he realised that 'my Vietnam' was unlikely to result in the overthrow of the Saudi regime. Swallowing his pride, Nasser decided to fly to Jeddah to meet with Faisal in an attempt to reach a peaceful settlement. A ceasefire was declared on 24 August with an undertaking that Egyptian troops would be withdrawn within ten months.[62]

At a lecture on 20 October 1965 to the Royal United Services Institute, McLean pondered 'whether Nasser will keep his word and leave the Yemen, or whether he will use the time he has gained to try to find another way out of his predicament'. The British-backed mercenaries had reverted to providing medical aid and maintaining communications, but when, in March 1966, Smiley returned to the Yemen, he discovered that the Egyptians had already breached the ceasefire and had resumed bombing. The Jeddah agreement had broken down because of the unacceptable demands of the royalists, though 'the true cause was the inability of the various Yemeni factions to reconcile their differences in the interests of sharing power'. In response, King Faisal toured the Middle East countries to try to establish an Islamic Pact. Just to make sure that his intention was clear, 'he escalated the Royalist campaign, forcing Egypt to send more troops which Faisal could then point to as agents of communist aggression'. Nasser reinforced his troops to nearly sixty thousand men.[63]

In the face of escalating violence, in February 1966 the British government announced in a Defence White Paper that they were to abandon Aden as a base, and South Arabia would become independent in 1968. Now in opposition, Conservative politician Duncan Sandys led the ultras, who were outraged by the decision, as were MI6 officers such as John da Silva who feared the creation of a 'vacuum' in the region. Dick White, however, was happy to get out of a 'worthless fight'. At a conference of regional Directors in March, Tim Milne, responsible for the Middle East, reported on the continuing use of 'disruptive actions' such as bribes, covert funding, buggings and telephone taps, and the use of 'pencil bombs' in dirty-tricks operations. In the Gulf states, MI6 was helping to train local security services to detect threats to their regimes, and arranging where required their 'neutralisation' by 'surrogates'. Milne's survey of operations confirmed that the strategic policies revealed in the leaks from the Sgt Allen official secrets case of the previous year were still in place.[64]

In the meantime, Britain had to station in Aden seventeen thousand soldiers, who were a sitting target as urban guerrilla war gripped the town. Nasser's intelligence officers had drawn up a well-thought-out plan for the terrorists in which the first essential was the destruction of the local Special Branch. This was 'so successful that five officers were murdered in six months; others were frightened by threats to kill all who collaborated with the British and were not too zealous in their duty'. Intelligence-gathering became dependent on the Joint Interrogation Centre in the military complex at Fort Morbut, where torture was used to extract confessions from 'suspects'. Torture is an unreliable source of information and the result was a lack of intelligence on the guerrillas and their political organisations.[65]

Following a series of setbacks, Nasser had become disillusioned by the war, and his support for the NLF in Aden waned. In a power struggle between the Nasserites and a new group of more radical elements, part of the nationalist leadership split off early in the year to form the militant Front for the Liberation of South Yemen (FLOSY). On 20 June 1966, the British agreed that they would maintain air and naval backing for South Yemen for at least six months after independence. By this time, however, the revolutionary wave had taken a hold in the hinterland, with guerrillas attacking not only the British but also the sultans. Also on the 20th, the NLF and FLOSY guerrillas launched an offensive in the Radfan mountains which led to a collapse of support for the sultans, 'who were discredited for their subservience to the British'. By September, British troops had been driven back into Aden.[66]

The fighting had reached a stalemate, but the British were still running an extensive mercenary operation in Yemen with those recruited said to be paid '£10,000 per annum' by 'a mysterious centre in London' called the 'Organisation', run by Stirling and Maj. Brooke. Cooper had left in early 1966 and Stirling had been joined by Col. John Woodhouse, who had retired from long and active service with the SAS to become a part-time adviser to the British government on counter-coup measures in parts of the Commonwealth. He was also a partner in Stirling's Watchguard International mercenary operation, which was formally incorporated in the Channel Islands. In June, another of Stirling's former colleagues in the SAS in the Western Desert, explorer Wilfred Thesiger, ran into Billy McLean, whom he had known since the early stages of the Second World War in Abyssinia. He was invited to join the royalist forces and visit the commander-in-chief in the North, Prince Hasanbin Hasan, a cousin of al-Badr, at his headquarters at Qarra. A close friend of Frank Steele, who was currently serving as MI6 head of station in Amman, Thesiger was employed until November in intelligence-gathering and propaganda work.[67]

In June 1967, Egypt suffered an overwhelming defeat at the hands of the Israelis in the Six Day War. It had been anticipated by MI6 which had access to GCHQ intercepts from Cyprus. With the war in Yemen not going well, and with his country increasingly dependent on subsidies from Saudi Arabia, Nasser decided to abandon the republicans and pull out his troops, whose morale had been badly shaken. MI6 regarded their supply and mercenary operation a 'success', but the CIA's James Fees thought this was illusory. Egyptian soldiers had, in fact, avoided the British. Their real fear was the Yemenis of whom they were 'terrified'. The royalists decapitated some of the victims and had a habit of 'sending back captured troops with their lips cut off in a ghastly grin'.[68]

In November, Thesiger travelled to the headquarters near Sana'a of Prince al Hussain, commander-in-chief of the southern front, where he found

McLean and Mark Lennox-Boyd embroiled in a siege of the city. Their position soon came under attack by MiG fighters and a shell burst near by causing a splinter to nick Thesiger's head. 'A little later I heard McLean say in an irritated voice, "Damn it, look what you've done, Wilfred." Blood from my head had soaked the box of cigars he had brought with him for safe-keeping.' After two days, they managed to shoot down a MiG; Thesiger found the pilot 'an unidentifiable mess, but his map and various notes were in Russian. The Egyptians had gone but the Russians had arrived.' NSA radio intercepts had picked up something similar earlier. Soviet bombers with Egyptian markings had allegedly 'one Egyptian on board to talk on the radio, but discipline wasn't that good and in moments of stress they would start chattering in Russian'. Contrary to the accepted western view of long-term Russian involvement in Yemen, the republican leaders discovered that the Egyptians had been blocking direct communication with Moscow and had prevented the supply of Russian arms. When Nasser eventually pulled out in November and the republicans were under siege at Sana'a, the Russians 'mounted a vital airlift'.[69]

In the same month, British troops pulled out of South Yemen and vacated Aden. After a period of in-fighting and political manoeuvrings, the NLF came out on top and created the People's Democratic Republic of Yemen. In January 1968 it was announced that Britain would withdraw all forces east of Suez by the end of 1971. The decision caused a great deal of concern in the Foreign Office, which was alarmed by 'the security situation'.

Despite the Egyptian withdrawal, the civil war in Yemen continued. In 1969 two Watchguard mercenaries, former SAS personnel 'Knocker' Parsons and 'Falcon' Wilson, were killed while leading a band of royalist guerrillas in the North. When they were positively identified by the republican government as British soldiers, the British government, still officially opposed to any intervention, came under pressure at the United Nations to explain their presence. According to SAS volunteer Peter Stiff, 'the British lied their way out of it ... They insisted the men were soldiers who had been killed in action within a normal operational area in the Aden protectorate. The North Yemen people, they said, had flown their bodies to a sensitive area just to stir up a row.'[70]

In March, the Saudis finally cut off supplies to the royalists. Imam al-Badr was already tired and had become a mere figurehead. A year later, King Faisal arranged a meeting between the Republic's Prime Minister and senior royalist leaders – excluding the royal family, who were doomed to permanent exile. Al-Badr fled to England, where he lived in quiet obscurity on the south coast until his death in August 1996. In 1970 a treaty was signed ending hostilities, with the republican forces victorious; the royalists never captured Sana'a. The outcome was a coalition government with the country reborn as the Yemen Arab Republic, North Yemen. Saudi Arabia recognised the

Republic in July, and Britain and France, who had supported the covert war for eight years, during which two hundred thousand people – 4 per cent of the Yemeni population – had died, swiftly followed suit.[71]

PART SEVEN

MODERN TIMES

CHAPTER 32

THE SECRET INTELLIGENCE SERVICE

For MI6, the early sixties proved to be the best and the worst of times as its 'special' relationship with the CIA went through highs and lows. There were the occasional outstanding intelligence-gathering successes which drew the admiration of the Americans, who were awash with money and technical advances, but these were largely overshadowed by security lapses which fed the almost continual molehunts that ripped into the heart of the Service, colouring relations with the Americans and undermining operations.

A complete breach of trust was probably avoided only as a result of the high-quality intelligence that the Service was able to supply from the few sources it developed behind the Iron Curtain; though, in truth, MI6 had had no hand in the recruitment of these sources as they were 'walk-ins', volunteering their services.

From late 1958, MI6 had been running three agents – the principal one code-named Noddy – inside the Polish security intelligence service, the Urzad Bezpieczenstwa (UB), controlled by the former chief of station in Berlin, Robert Dawson, 'a solid fatherly figure with the air of a countryman' who was responsible for eastern Europe as head of the Directorate of Production 4, and run through the Warsaw embassy where John Quine and a future chief of the Service, Colin Figures, were stationed. The UB officers proved to be MI6's first major sources in the Soviet orbit of the postwar period.[1]

Close liaison between the Poles and the KGB meant that the intelligence handed over included unprecedented information about the Russian service, and profiles of military and political personalities in Moscow. There was also information on operations against French and American citizens and diplomats living in Warsaw. Realising the value of the intelligence, Dick White made sure that it was quickly passed on to a grateful CIA, which assessed it as 'the best we've ever had'. According to Soviet sources, which were probably based on revelations from George Blake, who was then in the Russian section of DP4, the Americans undertook to finance some of MI6's operations; in particular, they offered $20 million for espionage in Poland. The paradox was that the operation's success exposed the extent to which MI6 was reliant on the Americans for support.[2]

Around the same time, a lieutenant-colonel of Polish State Security, Michal Goleniewski, code-named Sniper, who had volunteered information to the CIA, finally defected on 4 January 1961. He subsequently identified two spies in Britain – Lambda 1 and 2. The Security Service (MI5) quickly discovered that the second was Harry Houghton, an employee at the Underwater Establishment at Portland. To find the first, MI6's head of counter-intelligence, Terence Lecky, and his deputy, Geoffrey Hinton, launched a molehunt. Progress proved slow, and it took the Service's best Soviet specialist, Harold Shergold, to identify the spy inside MI6 as George Blake, a middle-ranking officer who had been posted to the Middle East Centre for Arab Studies (MECAS), where he was studying Arabic.[3]

Given that for many officers memories of Kim Philby and the 'Third Man' episode had not dimmed, the prospect of another major spy inside its closest ally's intelligence service caused consternation throughout the CIA. This was somewhat lightened by the visit to Washington of Harold Shergold on 25 January 1961. He told the CIA officer running SR-9, responsible for operations inside the Soviet Union, Joe Bulik, that during the previous December MI6 had been contacted via a British businessman, Greville Wynne, by a serving GRU officer, Col. Oleg Penkovsky. Wynne, who had been introduced to East–West trade by the Conservative politician and former intelligence officer Airey Neave, had been asked by Dickie Franks, head of the Directorate of Production Research which was responsible for running the 'frequent travellers' programme, to make contact with the State Committee for the Co-ordination of Scientific Research Work, which acted as a cover for KGB and GRU agents spying on western technology. In turn, Bulik informed Shergold that Penkovsky had in fact made contact with two American students five months earlier. When Bulik showed Shergold the information Penkovsky had initially handed over, MI6 offered to help run the GRU officer, code-named Hero, as a joint operation. Despite understandable fears about MI6's security, at a follow-up meeting in early February in London the CIA agreed to the proposal, mainly because the Agency had no agents or officers in Moscow to run such an operation.[4]

Blake returned on 6 April to MI6's headquarters at Broadway Buildings, where he was interrogated by Shergold, Lecky and a former policeman, Ben Johnson. They listened in 'amazed silence' when, following a series of unproductive interrogations, Blake eventually burst out: 'Nobody tortured me! No, nobody blackmailed me! I myself approached the Soviets and offered my services to them of my own accord!' Given that he was an ideological traitor, Blake's explanation brought out the Service's worst prejudices. Nicholas Elliott considered that there were three types of treachery – 'political conviction (or misplaced idealism), venality and blackmail'. Blake, in Elliott's opinion, however, fell into another category – 'victims of a form of inferiority complex'. Blake 'wanted to prove to himself that an insignificant individual of mixed origins could become a person of consequence in world affairs'. Blake's father was Jewish.[5]

Blake had blown hundreds of western agents, including the entire MI6 OB, and had provided the KGB with details of a number of highly secret technical operations being run in conjunction with the CIA. Realising how potentially embarrassing a trial could be, initially Dick White did not want to see a prosecution of Blake. However, the need to consider the US reaction was paramount, and the MI6 Chief reluctantly agreed to a prosecution. It turned out to be a political trial, conducted *in camera*, in which the sentence was cooked up between Prime Minister Harold Macmillan, the Attorney-General, Sir Reginald Manningham-Buller, and the Lord Chief Justice, Lord Parker. Even White expressed 'shock' at the sentence of forty-two years which Parker imposed at the Old Bailey in early May 1961. Some Americans were initially sympathetic to White's plight and were willing to support his plea that the necessary security changes had been made within the Service. The CIA's counter-intelligence chief, James Angleton, however, was already suggesting to the horror of MI6 officers that the two services should pool their counter-espionage capabilities in London.[6]

After Blake's arrest the Americans feared for the security of the Penkovsky operation but were reassured by Shergold's 'professionalism'. Arriving in London on 20 April as head of a Soviet purchasing delegation, the GRU man was secretly debriefed for the first time by two CIA officers fluent in Russian, Bulik and George Kisvalter, and MI6 officers Shergold and Michael Stokes. The team noted that the most salient factor that lay behind Penkovsky's decision to help the West was 'his lifelong legend that his father had died of typhus in 1919'. In reality, he had been killed 'while fighting with the White Army against the Reds as a first lieutenant in the city of Rostov. The significance of the fact lies in a KGB accusation that Subject had deliberately concealed the true circumstances and this accusation was a matter of record on his GRU file.' His desire 'for recognition, acceptance, and honor from the West were a constant theme that emerged in the debriefing sessions . . . His enormous ego and his desire to be the best spy in history left the team limp with fatigue at the end of each of their sessions.' They then had to process the 'take'.[7]

From 20 April to 6 May 1961, there were seventeen meetings with the intelligence officers which lasted a total of fifty-two hours. These were followed on a second visit between 18 July and 7 August by another thirteen meetings which produced 1,200 pages of transcript. Penkovsky would also eventually supply 111 exposed rolls of film and 10,000 pages of intelligence reports which MI6 designated ARNIKA. The material, including seventy-eight pages of secret documents Penkovsky had brought with him, primarily on missiles, about which little was known in the West, broke new ground. He was also able to identify around four to five hundred GRU officers and another two to three hundred KGB officers, and report on personalities. From this latter information, and the addition of a Kremlin telephone directory, an MI6 Sovietologist was able to produce the first chain-of-command organisational chart for the Soviet hierarchy, thus lifting the veil of secrecy that surrounded western views of the Kremlin.[8]

Penkovsky's information was of an extraordinarily high quality which White was determined to exploit to the full through the Joint Intelligence Committee (JIC) system, with the explicit aim of elevating the Service's reputation within Whitehall. The Cabinet Office, increasingly the heart of the intelligence community, was, however, unaware of the true provenance of the source and was initially less than impressed with the substance of the reports. In fact, many officials simply dismissed the intelligence White was touting on the basis that MI6 was incapable of producing reliable, high-grade reports. Tom Bower quotes a senior Cabinet Office official who went on to become Cabinet Secretary, Sir John Hunt, as saying that a significant minority judged MI6's intelligence to be 'rubbish, given credibility because it was believed by the intelligence services themselves'. The Ministry of Defence specialists who assessed Penkovsky's material were of a different mind, and MI6 cabled Washington that his bona fides had been established 'beyond any reasonable doubt'. The liaison officer who passed on the good news was Maurice Oldfield. He recognised that Penkovsky 'had been the answer to a prayer. What he provided seemed like a miracle, too. That is why for so long he was mistrusted on both sides of the Atlantic. It seemed incredible that he could take such risks – not merely photographing Top Secret documents, but actually giving us the original documents in some instances.' Oldfield also passed on details of new arrangements made by MI6 for contact in Moscow with Penkovsky. Anne, the wife of an officer, Roderick 'Ruari' Chisholm, and formerly Shergold's secretary, was to pick up the batch of documents that Penkovsky would leave in a Moscow park.[9]

Perhaps the most surprising advocate of Penkovsky in Washington, given the later controversies, was the arch-disciple of the view that all Soviet defectors were double agents, James Angleton. On 30 June, Angleton agreed that 'this was undoubtedly the most important case we had for years'. He added that he felt it was 'terribly important that the President, who was now faced with crucial problems regarding Berlin, should have the benefit of the full story'. On 13 July, President Kennedy was provided with a full briefing on the joint operation by the Director of the CIA, Allen Dulles. On the same day, in an effort to stop the flood of refugees to the West which rose to 150,000 in the first six months of 1961, the East Germans, backed by Russian troops, erected the Berlin Wall. Geoffrey McDermott, a Foreign Office official who had had responsibilities for the intelligence services, recognised that 'permission was only given by Khrushchev at the last minute' and consequently thought that 'our intelligence was not to blame for not reporting the decision. But it is extraordinary that with our massive combined resources – and not least our numerous German agents – no reports had reached us of the movement and stockpiling of hundreds of tons of material required for the Wall.' The allies were in some considerable disarray over Berlin.[10]

One major piece of information from Penkovsky which surprised the British and Americans was his statement that 'early warning was the prime Soviet intelligence objective'. With the Berlin crisis, the possibility of early warning of Soviet moves in turn became a prime issue with MI6 and the CIA. When Penkovsky visited Paris the rudiments of a signalling system known as DISTANT were worked out for use on occasions when he had top-priority information to pass on. Discord arose between the two services on the details of Distant, but the matter was resolved in London at a meeting on 31 October attended by White, Allen Dulles and his successor, John McCone, London station chief Frank Wisner and his deputy Carleton B. Swift, chair of the JIC Sir Hugh Stephenson and MI6 officers – Charles Ransom, who had recently returned from being head of station in Rome, John Taylor and Norman Darbyshire. White explained that MI6 was basically a collector of intelligence whose task was to turn over such material to the JIC assessors who would evaluate the material before forwarding it to ministers and the Cabinet. The Americans said that they would have no alternative but to pass such intelligence direct to the President. It was a curious exchange, given the often-quoted line that MI6 Chiefs had right of direct access to the Prime Minister.[11]

On 22 December, Anatoli Golitsin, a KGB officer serving in the First Chief Directorate employed in operations against Britain and America, defected in Helsinki to the CIA. Over the following weeks he revealed to debriefers the identities of a series of KGB agents employed by western intelligence agencies. During the spring of 1962, MI5's chief spycatcher, Arthur Martin, and the head of R5 – MI6's counter-intelligence section – Terence Lecky, were allowed to met Golitsin. Although he provided no new information on the subject, his brief and vague talk of the 'Ring of Five' led to the launch of molehunts that included refocusing on the evidence on Kim Philby. White apparently became an early and enthusiastic supporter of Angleton and his investigations.

Despite the depth and range of the Penkovsky intelligence, the quality of which had never been surpassed, in January 1962 disagreements surfaced over tradecraft problems with the joint HERO operation during a meeting in London between Shergold and the chief of operations for the CIA's Soviet Division, Quentin Johnson. The American felt that it would be prudent and in the interests of security for Penkovsky to curtail his activities for six months or a year, to ease the pressure on the master spy. Shergold argued that it would be a psychological blow to Penkovsky's pride. When Johnson reported back, his boss Bulik thought that the British were less concerned about protecting Penkovsky than keeping the flow of intelligence going, and were putting him at risk. The Americans, in fact, were kept in the dark about Greville Wynne's alcohol problems and his inability to keep his mouth shut. Shergold did inform them that he intended to replace the Chisholms with another couple, Gervase Cowell and his wife Pamela, in order to service the 'dead-letter drops'.[12]

When Macmillan visited President Kennedy in Washington in May 1962, he was briefed by White on the Penkovsky material. The Prime Minister noticed that the US administration had changed its attitude to the Soviet Union; in particular, Kennedy now recognised that the 'missile gap' which had been a major issue during the presidential election was, in fact, working in America's favour, and not as previously expressed in favour of the Soviets. Penkovsky demolished the myth which Khrushchev had propagated that the Soviets had more intercontinental ballistic missiles than the US and that these were capable of precision attacks. Penkovsky said that the Soviet ICBMs 'couldn't hit a bull in the backside with a balalaika'. It was a rare example of one man's spying having a direct effect on policy. Inevitably, for one so rash, during August it seems that the West's star spy came under suspicion – though the KGB investigation would prove to be poorly managed. In the following month, Pamela Cowell arrived in Moscow to act as the new contact for Penkovsky.[13]

Soon after the Cuban Missile Crisis began, on 19 October, using photographs that had been taken by a U-2 spy plane and compared with material provided by Penkovsky, the CIA prepared a detailed memorandum on the Soviet SS-4 missile which had been identified as being on Cuba. The next day, the KGB entered Penkovsky's apartment and discovered his Minox camera. Two days later he was arrested outside GRU headquarters. The CIA considered, as did the KGB, that the pressure on Penkovsky to produce had led to his arrest. It was not until 2 November that MI6 and the CIA became aware that their prize agent had been arrested.[14]

The impression given by Macmillan's official biographer, Alistair Horne, is that Britain played a significant role in the Cuban crisis, with the elder statesman prudently counselling the young President. In truth, it was all deception. Kennedy's close confidant, McGeorge Bundy, was correct when he stated that Macmillan's advice was 'not very important'. Horne was also a friend of Maurice Oldfield, who during this period confided in his former colleague, Anthony Cavendish. According to Cavendish, Oldfield gave personal briefings to President Kennedy, while his biographer, 'Richard Deacon', states that 'he not only obtained personal access to the President to stress the value of Penkovsky's evidence, but ensured that Kennedy had an independent scientific opinion and interpretation from the British side'. Deacon claims that Oldfield's intervention was 'absolutely vital'. Is this credible? There are no accounts from CIA officers or Kennedy administration officials noting such unprecedented access and the historical record suggests that this period was the nadir of the 'special relationship'. The Americans put on the appearance of consulting the British, but only feigned interest when views coincided.[15]

An important lesson was to come out of the Cuba crisis for British Intelligence, a lesson that illustrated its increasingly second-rank status. During mid-October, the Cabinet Secretary, Burke Trend, head of the Joint Intelligence Bureau (JIB) Maj.-Gen. Sir Kenneth Strong, and MI6 liaison officer Maurice Oldfield were in Washington for a Defense Department intelligence conference hosted by the CIA's Deputy Director, Ray Cline. Unable to fill them in on details of the unfolding crisis, Cline

> misled them all week into thinking my obvious preoccupation with business was about Berlin not Cuba ... My exercise in deception was totally successful because these British friends took several occasions during the week to argue with me that the Russians would never put missiles in Cuba because of the risk to their interests in Europe. When I refused to dismiss this as an outside possibility (knowing full well they were there!), Ken Strong in particular chided me for making the American error of overrating the importance of Cuba because it was so close.

On the morning of 22 October the US ambassador, David Bruce, and the CIA chief of station in London, went to Downing Street to show the Prime Minister the latest U-2 surveillance photographs of Cuba, which contained sufficient detail to identify Soviet missile carriers. Macmillan was suitably impressed: 'Now the Americans will realise what we in England have lived through for this past many years.'[16]

Coupled with Penkovsky's purloined Soviet missile manuals, the photographs enabled the CIA 'to follow the progress of Soviet missile emplacement in Cuba by the hour'. In addition, Penkovsky's documents complemented new photographs from the Discoverer satellite programme run jointly by the CIA and the US Air Force which, after a series of failures, had begun to produce pictures by August 1960. For the first time it 'provided detailed pictures confirming the offensive capability of the Soviet missile launching site at Plesetsk, south of Archangel near the Barents Sea'. Though the early satellite photographs lacked the definition of those taken by the U-2s, aerial reconnaissance, increasingly in use for signals interception as well as for photographs, would quickly develop into 'the most important form of intelligence gathering'.[17]

Without access to its own spy planes and satellites, as Geoffrey McDermott admitted, MI6's importance was 'declining now that so much crucial intelligence is obtained either by satellites hundreds of miles up in the air or by electronic devices concealed in the fly-button'. As the intelligence historian Christopher Andrew notes, 'the primacy of the spy satellite gave the two superpowers, as the only satellite-owners, an unassailable intelligence lead over all other states for more than two decades. In the process it inevitably confirmed the relegation of the United Kingdom to the status of junior partner in the intelligence alliance with the United States.' According to Ray Cline, 'It was only because of our tradition of close collaboration with British Intelligence in cryptanalysis, espionage and general exchange of finished intelligence that we felt we should share with the British in the U-2 and satellite processes.' By the 1960s, Britain's secret intelligence-gathering had come to depend substantially on the co-operation of the US 'cousins' – which goes some way to explaining the comment made in the mid-seventies by the right-wing journalist with intelligence sources, Chapman Pincher, that 'dependence is so great and co-operation so close that I am convinced that the security and intelligence chiefs would go to any lengths to protect the linkup, and they would be right to do so'.[18]

An August 1963 evaluation of Penkovsky concluded that it was 'the most productive classic clandestine operation ever conducted by the CIA or MI6 against the Soviet target'. Dick White was able to pass on to his assembled staff the thanks of the CIA for MI6 help on the joint operation. It went some way to lifting the gloom that had existed inside the Service since Nicholas Elliott had flown to Beirut on 11 January 1963 to try to extract a confession from his friend Kim Philby. CIA officers had been appalled that MI6 had allowed Philby to escape and defect to the USSR. One result was that MI6's unrestricted access to CIA officers was 'sharply curtailed'. The Director of Plans, Richard Helms, ordered that 'there was no carte blanche'. Meetings with Oldfield needed prior approval, 'the content to be reported in writing afterwards'. To compensate for the professional snub and lack of access to Langley, Oldfield regularly met socially with the head of counter-espionage, James Angleton. With his unlimited access to Helms and CIA Director John McCone, Angleton's 'unique position in western intelligence and continuing anglophilia' attracted particular respect from a cabal of senior British security and intelligence officers. George Young thought the American was 'a gullible soul who saw himself as a Machiavelli'. The problem was that he 'had been completely under Philby's influence and sought to whitewash himself by finding KGB agents in every British department and agency'. Despite Young's observation that he 'tactfully coped with this', it seems that Oldfield became MI6's 'most ardent convert to Angleton's theories'.[19]

In South-East Asia there were formal MI6–CIA liaison meetings, but as senior CIA officer in the region Joseph B. Smith discovered, there were two schools of thought on their effectiveness. 'One was that it was a rare and beautiful thing to be nurtured with every care, because the British were the most sagacious spies in the business, with a long and remarkable tradition of success. The other was that it was a waste of time, the British officers were a bunch of supercilious snobs toward whom we should show an equivalent disdain.' A colleague warned him that the MI6 'guys are really nuts about security and won't even tell each other what they're doing, much less us'. CIA officers such as the head of the Psychological and Paramilitary Warfare Staff, Desmond FitzGerald, looked upon the 'Colonel Blimps of the Colonial Office' as 'clumsy racists', but recognised that the better MI6 officers were 'sophisticated about native cultures'. They could, though, show 'a willingness to be uncompromising – brutal if necessary – when it came down to combating terrorists and native insurrectionists'. Drawing on the British experience in Malaya and Burma, the Americans learned that the key to counter-insurgency was 'penetration and control' with the aim of 'getting inside the local insurgencies with their agents and then subverting them'. From MI6 they also learned such devious 'disruptive' tactics as 'false flag' recruitment and the creation of fake communist groups and fronts.[20]

During the early fifties, MI6's view on South-East Asia had been essentially conspiratorial – there was a 'communist threat which was a co-ordinated one and required a co-ordinated response'. The Soviets were believed to be 'increasing their efforts' throughout the region with the Sino-Soviet alliance being the key. The large Chinese communist presence was seen as a potential 'fifth column'. MI6 worked out of the Phoenix Park compound in Singapore as part of the staff of the Office of Commissioner for South-East Asia. The leading figure was Maurice Oldfield, who served two terms in the region. His work was closely integrated with that of the chair of the region's sub-branch of the JIC, Denis Greenhill, whose wife, Angela McCulloch, had worked for the intelligence services in the Middle East during the war, and the Commissioner General, Sir Robert Scott, a pre-war intelligence officer and wartime propagandist, who was highly regarded by his Foreign Office colleagues. Oldfield and Scott were largely responsible for changing Foreign Office and government perceptions of the communist threat in the region.[21]

Friend and former MI6 colleague Anthony Cavendish thought Oldfield's main achievement had been to keep in perspective 'the fluid and turbulent situation in SE Asia after the French withdrawal and stressing that personal ambitions and tribal loyalties lay behind the upsets, coups and intrigues and not the hand of either Moscow or Peking'. MI6 officers were 'quicker than the Americans to realise that there was nothing sinister about Cambodian desires merely to be Cambodians and that this was something which might stand in the way of Russian or Chinese plans'. Reading Oldfield's assessments, George Young had become increasingly aware that communism had 'ceased to be the most likely bidder for local nationalist emotion and may even be regarded with more hostility than "imperialism"'.[22]

Although he was essentially a desk man, Oldfield's 'forte was assessing and collating information supplied by others', and 'encouraging field officers to get on with the job'. A key field officer was Michael Wrigley, who had known Oldfield since serving with him in the wartime SIME organisation in Cairo, where he 'learned the arts of intelligence from his life-long friend'. As an accomplished SIS station chief in Bangkok, Wrigley 'gained international recognition for his expertise in understanding and defeating Communist subversion'. Although he had a good relationship with his CIA counterparts, he was often frustrated by Foreign Office officials who 'didn't want to believe the intelligence I produced'. Much of that intelligence came from a network of penetration agents and former officers who had been placed in key positions.[23]

A local vice-consul in Saigon in the early fifties, Donald Lancaster had exchanged snippets of information with Reuters journalist Brian Crozier. With a distinguished wartime record in Motor Torpedo Boats, 'Butch' Lancaster was one of the Service's well-known homosexuals who once tried unsuccessfully to recruit the journalist Neal Ascherson. When Ascherson felt Lancaster's hand on his thigh, 'I got up and decided not to become a spy . . .' An authority on Indo-China affairs, Lancaster officially resigned from MI6 in the mid-fifties and, in 1961, published *The Emancipation of French Indo-China*. The following year, he was appointed as secretary to Cambodia's Prince Norodom Sihanouk.[24]

A highly decorated naval pilot, Myles 'Woozle' Osborn, who served as a district officer during the Malayan Emergency, where he gained valuable experience in combating communist infiltration, was employed in 1963 under the Colombo Plan, promoting development in Asia, and as a 'hill tribes adviser' in Laos. He also reported to MI6 and gave 'valuable service' to the Laotian government.[25]

During the mid-fifties the CIA monitored the movements of freelance journalist Alex Josey, who travelled throughout the Far East attending left-wing meetings. He was constantly seen in the company of Singapore's Lee Kuan Yew, leader of the People's Action Party (PAP), who was known to associate with communists. Fellow CIA officer Al Ulmer told Joseph B. Smith that he recognised Josey. 'We were in the composite OSS–SOE unit in Cairo during the war.' A psychological warfare specialist, in 1950 Josey had been seconded to the post of Staff Officer (Emergency Information) in Malaya, helping to establish the Joint Information and Propaganda Committee. Ulmer told Smith: 'I don't think you have to worry too much about Mr Lee anymore. MI6 has a damned good case officer working on him. Josey's always been great at the vagabond leftist act.' Josey went on to become Lee's adviser and press spokesperson, and wrote two highly flattering biographies of him.[26]

A man of action, after he had 'pinpointed the leader of a terrorist link between Malaysia and Thailand', Michael Wrigley had proposed to London that he 'offer an assassin £10,000 and a British passport to dispose of the troublesome intermediary'. Head office rejected the proposal, much to Wrigley's disgust: 'They had no balls.' He had little time for the Foreign Office, which initially ignored his impressive intelligence-gathering efforts demonstrating that 'the unrest spreading across South East Asia, leading eventually to the inferno in Vietnam, was not directed from Moscow or Peking but inspired by nationalism'. Not to be beaten, he went on to produce evidence that 'contradicted the official doctrine in London and Washington that the Communist guerrillas infiltrating from Thailand into Malaysia and Vietnam were Chinese'. In fact, Wrigley 'proved that many of them were Thais, a critical distinction in an era when the Domino theory, beloved of Washington strategists, suggested that the whole region would fall under centralised Communist control'.[27]

It is generally assumed that such assessments were undertaken solely by the Foreign Office, but in the early sixties MI6 had its own analysts who had influence on both sides of the Atlantic. The 'brilliant eccentric' Frank Rendle, who took part in the debriefing of Oleg Penkovsky, was at the centre of 'a major clash of opinion between MI6 and the CIA over the Sino-Soviet split'. The dispute horrified officials and was to colour policy on South-East Asia. At issue 'was the correct interpretation of events in China. Was the split real or was it a deception to confuse Western intelligence services?' With Kremlinologist David Peck, Rendle was MI6's leading intelligence analyst on communism, rivalling James Angleton for the title 'mad Genius'. He had 'a phenomenal capacity for correlating obscure names, dates and circumstances to draw inferences which invariably made sense'. Under the name 'David A. Charles', in 1961 he made his views known in the CIA-sponsored *China Quarterly*. In discussing 'The Dismissal of Marshal P'eng Teh-huai', he argued that a rift had developed at the heart of the Sino-Soviet relationship following Peng's criticism of Mao's theories of peasant warfare. Peng had wanted a modern, professional army and nuclear status, which required continuing close friendship with the Soviets. Rendle regarded Peng's dismissal in September 1959, for leading an 'anti-party' group within the Politburo and 'intriguing' with Soviet leader Khrushchev, as evidence of a major 'power-struggle' which 'precipitated the actual phase of the Sino-Soviet dispute'.[28]

A similar 'intensive search into the Sino-Soviet relationship' was undertaken within the CIA. As head of the Office of Current Intelligence in the late fifties, Ray Cline had designated a 'few analysts with detailed familiarity with Soviet political leaders, doctrines, and daily policy pronouncements to work alongside others who were equally knowledgeable about Mao's China'. Against furious internal opposition, Cline's 'special staff' compiled data that enabled the CIA 'to lead the way in charting the strategic conflict between the Soviet and Chinese styles of dictatorship and doctrine that was basic to the definitive split in 1960'. The capture in Tibet during the spring of 1961 of a batch of 1,600 Chinese documents enabled CIA analysts to confirm that the split was for real and the serious divisions between China and the Soviet Union could be exploited.[29]

Unfortunately, operating under the influence of the deranged Soviet defector, Anatoli Golitsin, James Angleton was able to convince the Agency's management that the Sino-Soviet split was 'simply a clever ruse to tempt the United States into commitments and aid to China, which would then be used to weaken and exploit the United States'. The result was that the findings of the China specialists were undermined and delayed both inside and outside the CIA. According to Nigel Clive, who headed the MI6 department that dealt with questions arising from Rendle's analysis, Angleton's suspicions were taken on board by Maurice Oldfield, who refused to accept the reality of the Sino-Soviet split. Another Angleton devotee was Leonard Schapiro, a Russian-speaking academic 'with an encyclopedic memory and a superb command of Soviet and communist history', who acted as an adviser to Dick White. A friend of the Chief since the war, having served in MI5 and later in the Intelligence Division of the Control Commission in Germany, Schapiro enjoyed unusual influence over White, who seems to have taken seriously his conspiratorial viewpoint. Schapiro agreed that 'the antagonism between Peking and Moscow was deliberate disinformation to destabilise the West's war against Communism'. Rendle's analysis was similarly sidelined.[30]

It took another couple of years before Clive's department was allowed to state officially that the split was genuine and announce the decision, in an oblique way, to the world. Working for the Economist Intelligence Unit, Brian Crozier, who was now regarded by MI6 as a 'long-insider', was allowed access to the Service's analytic staff and, as a consultant to the Information Research Department (IRD) to secret briefing papers. After comments from various specialists inside MI6 and the IRD, a report was produced which Crozier published in 1966 as an MI6-sponsored 'Background Book', *The Struggle for the Third World*.[31]

Although Prime Minister Macmillan had been one of the first to put faith in the domino theory of communist expansion throughout South-East Asia, by the early sixties he had taken on board the MI6 analysis that had been developed by Wrigley and Oldfield. He now believed that, though the Chinese 'would take advantage of troubles in any adjacent area, they would not themselves embark on a policy of adventure'. Macmillan was highly critical of Washington, where it was believed that Chinese 'expansionist policies were responsible for all the troubles' in the region. 'It was this fundamental mistake', he subsequently recorded, 'which later led America into so many troubles ...' From the beginning, Macmillan had been against American entanglement in South Vietnam, and by 1963 was shocked to discover that the number of US military 'advisers' had risen to fifteen thousand. The British Prime Minister remained 'gloomy' about the chances of the South defending itself against the North and privately warned President Kennedy against getting bogged down in Indochina.[32]

'If Britain did not get dragged into that costly and bloody intervention', George Young believed it was 'in no small part due to the effect of Oldfield's balanced assessments, worked out with Sir Robert Scott'. Young made sure that Oldfield's reports on South-East Asia were 'the regular lead-in items in the weekly summary sent in the famous yellow box to the Prime Minister'. Young knew that Oldfield's views on Vietnam were highly respected by CIA officers in the region and by some State Department officials in Washington, where Denis Greenhill, who had come to know several senior CIA officers when chair of the JIC (Far East) in Singapore, was also stationed. In 1959, Greenhill had been appointed the Foreign Office liaison officer to MI6, and during his Washington tour worked closely with Oldfield and senior CIA officers. An important visitor to the British embassy was Robert Scott, who was now Permanent Secretary in the MoD. Given the respect accorded to this intelligence trio, Young thought it 'one of the tragedies of history that their views were overruled in Washington', where academic 'hawks' acquired 'a complete ascendancy over the naive Kennedy'.[33]

This is, in fact, misleading. It was certainly the case that occasionally – and with good reason – the Kennedy administration took a contrary view to CIA assessments on South-East Asia. On Laos, for instance, the CIA concluded that the communists' long-term political objective was absolute control of the government and country. Kennedy's policy goal, however, 'was to secure a free and independent Laos via a neutralist arrangement that included communist participation in the government'. The CIA did, however, influence the President in his belief that the only way forward in South Vietnam was a limited commitment of American special forces and small-scale covert action programmes. We also now know from recently released classified documents that during 1963 Kennedy had begun the process of withdrawing from Vietnam. The dramatic escalation of the US commitment to the region was instigated immediately after Kennedy's death by President Johnson. It was with Johnson that the hawks gained ascendancy.[34]

The Conservative government privately opposed the United States' increasing military involvement in Vietnam. The public support and token military backing Britain was willing to provide were in return for US backing of British interests in Malaya. Conservative Foreign Secretary Rab Butler told the Cabinet that it was a straightforward quid pro quo for 'the support of the US government in seeking to maintain our position in South-East Asia'. British support was on the basis that American policy was defensive. In late May, Butler told the US Assistant Secretary of State, McGeorge Bundy, that 'an incursion into North Vietnamese territory would . . . create difficulties for us'. Indeed, he regarded the failure of the Americans to suspend such plans as 'sinister', fearing that any escalation would 'probably provoke the Soviet Union and China into action'.[35]

Throughout 1964 Labour leader Harold Wilson and shadow Chancellor James Callaghan were in negotiation with American bankers for US help with the expected balance of payments problem – forecast at £800 million. A secret understanding was reached with the New York Federal Reserve Bank to the effect that if the new Labour government did not devalue, in return the Americans would promise massive support for sterling, but expected in exchange support for US diplomatic and strategic objectives. In private, George Brown revealed that the deal involved 'trading financial support for the pound against military support on SE Asia'.[36]

After his first visit to Washington as Prime Minister, in early December 1964, Wilson told his Cabinet colleagues that President Johnson had shown deep concern over Britain's economic position and 'virtually promised us all aid short of war'. Wilson said that Johnson wanted public support on Vietnam. The stakes were high and, unbeknown to Wilson, the CIA's Richard Helms had sent Bundy a summary of smears against the British Prime Minister based on material collected from the Agency's agents in London. Trying to avoid 'a liability' in the region, Wilson resisted US demands for a limited British military presence. He told a surprised President that Britain had 54,000 troops in the region, a number of which were employed to thwart Indonesian encroachments in Borneo. The non-aligned nationalist Indonesian government of Sukarno was, in a policy of military 'confrontation', claiming parts of Malaya, a British ally that had recently become independent. The Americans were unable to secure an overt military commitment. Cabinet minister Richard Crossman noted in his diaries that they wanted 'not so much the presence of British soldiers as the presence of the British flag' as a fig-leaf of international cover for US intervention in the region.[37]

Using his secret-world sources, in January 1965 Brian Crozier published the pro-MI6 view of the Vietnam War in his book *South-East Asia in Turmoil*, which demonstrated that the war in South Vietnam was totally controlled by Hanoi and the North Vietnamese Army. He added that 'for all Peking's calls for revolutionary action in South East Asia, there is remarkably little evidence of direct Chinese Communist involvement in the so-called "liberation" movements in the area'. Crozier then went on to list the instances where MI6 had discovered that the Chinese were 'quite content to let other

Communists – such as the Vietnamese, Burmese, or Sarawak Chinese – pull chestnuts out of the fire for them'. He suggested that 'the Chinese have probably been expending at least as much energy lately countering Soviet influences as they have in fighting Western "imperialism"'. He pointed out that the Americans had 'failed to grasp a disconcerting and indeed disturbing fact: that the same man can sometimes be both a Communist and a national-ist'. He attacked the Americans for relying on local despotic 'strong men' whose only credential was being anti-communist.[38]

On the ground, MI6 officers got on well with their CIA counterparts, particularly the chiefs of station in Saigon, John Richardson and Peer de Silva, who shared the essentials of the MI6 analysis. In Washington, the CIA's Richard Helms staunchly opposed President Johnson's support of the domino theory, regarding it as just a phase. He argued that the US could withdraw from Vietnam without losing the whole of South-East Asia or risking much in the Cold War. His views were not welcomed in the Oval Office, and in March 1965 the US began its non-retaliatory bombing of North Vietnam – Rolling Thunder – and landed its first combat troops in the South.

Labour's Defence Secretary, Denis Healey, who claims he did not receive any MI6 intelligence or assessments on avoiding commitments in Vietnam, recalled the American pressure on Britain to aid their war effort. 'The United States, after trying for thirty years to get Britain out of Asia ... was now trying desperately to keep us in; during the Vietnam war it did not want to be the only country killing coloured people on their own soil.'[39]

In July, while Cabinet Secretary Burke Trend was in Washington to discuss sterling, the US National Security Council (NSC) reported that 'anything which could be regarded as even a partial British withdrawal from overseas responsibilities is bound to lead to an agonizing reappraisal here . . . of Anglo-American relations'. Vietnam was 'the paramount problem'. NSC adviser McGeorge Bundy minuted that the British have 'to get it into their heads that it makes no sense for us to rescue the pound in a situation in which there is no British flag in Vietnam, and a threatened British thin-out . . . east of Suez'. Bundy told the President that 'what I would like to say to Trend . . . is that a British brigade in Vietnam would be worth a billion dollars at the moment of truth for Sterling'. Wilson knew, however, that the Americans had no desire to see sterling devalued as it would have a knock-on effect on the dollar. The war in Vietnam was beginning to cost the US billions. Wilson did agree, however, to Johnson's demand that MI6 provide help to the CIA in South-East Asia. As Tom Bower notes, it was made clear to the Foreign Office and to White, in particular, that 'nothing could be permitted to irritate that relationship'. One result was that James Angleton was let off the leash and allowed to spread his poisonous conspiracy views among MI6's counter-espionage specialists in London.[40]

The molehunts that followed produced an atmosphere of fear and paranoia inside MI6 headquarters which took years to dispel. Knowledge of their existence was confined in Whitehall to the Cabinet Secretary, who 'sympathised with White's ambition to save the beleaguered service'. By the time Oldfield returned to London and turned against Angleton, telling White that the American was a 'disaster', the molehunts were in full swing with a momentum that proved impossible to halt.[41]

In South-East Asia MI6 was working hand in glove with the CIA to 'liquidate' Indonesia's President Sukarno. In co-operation with their colleagues from the Australian Secret Intelligence Service (ASIS), MI6's Special Political Action group launched up to six different disruptive actions, including the use of forgeries designed to sow dissension within the ranks of the powerful Indonesian Communist Party (PKI) and the recruitment of 'moderate' elements within the army.[42]

On 30 September 1965 a group of left-wing army officers loyal to President Sukarno assassinated several generals who were thought to be planning a coup. The subsequent political chaos provided an opportunity for another military faction led by General Suharto, who was to install himself as President, to move against the PKI. The British ambassador in Jakarta, Sir Andrew Gilchrist, a former SOE officer and chair of the Far East JIC, telegraphed to the Foreign Office on 5 October his belief that 'a little shooting in Indonesia would be an essential preliminary to change'. The Foreign Office decided to tacitly back Suharto's generals, preferring 'an Army to a Communist regime'. MI6 and the IRD were instructed to 'blacken the PKI in the eyes of the army and the people', using such propaganda themes as 'Chinese interference in particular arms shipments; PKI subverting Indonesia as agents of foreign communists . . .' The CIA covert operation supplied the generals with arms, disguised as shipments of 'medicines'. In late October, the generals swiftly moved against the PKI and within a few months a hundred thousand supporters had been tortured and executed. The targets had been taken from lists drawn up by CIA officers in the Jakarta embassy, which was co-operating closely with the resident MI6 officers.[43]

MI6 covert help to the Americans over Vietnam took various forms, including the forwarding of intelligence reports from its station heads in Hanoi, such as Daphne Park. Headed by Sir Robert Thompson, British counter-insurgency experts with experience in Malaya and close to MI6 were seconded to Saigon as part of a British Advisory Mission. MI6 had earlier assisted the Malayan government of Tengku Abdul Rahman to 'secretly transfer to South Vietnam the bulk of the arms and war material that had been used against the defeated Malayan Communist Party'. Richard Noone, an anthropologist and special action expert, led an MI6 team of Malays and tribesmen from Borneo on a tour of duty among the ethnically similar Montagnards in South Vietnam.[44]

The Malaya experience, however, proved to be of little value to the Americans, who never really mastered counter-insurgency campaigning in Vietnam. Malaya had required substantial numbers of troops and a large intelligence and security investment. Even then, it had been a close-run thing, with favourable economic and political factors largely saving British efforts. Conveniently rising rubber prices had paid for the tremendously expensive hearts-and-minds campaign. Peer de Silva later admitted that the CIA was too impatient and never developed the kind of jungle experience essential for success.[45]

'More sensitive operations' were 'refuted by sleight of hand'. Some defence 'experts' have denied that the SAS operated in Vietnam but a photograph in the regiment's normally discreet magazine, *Mars and Minerva*, in June 1969 showed Sergeant Dick Meadows receiving the US Silver Star for his service in Vietnam. A number of US Special Forces personnel were trained by the SAS in Borneo in the techniques of jungle warfare, while, in turn, SAS men found their way to a training school in Saigon where they instructed South Vietnamese troops, who also trained in Malaya. Individual SAS soldiers, such as Captain Robin Letts, who had been awarded the Military Cross for an operation in Borneo, were transferred via the British military attaché in Saigon, Col. John Waddy, to Australian and New Zealand SAS units, as an auxiliary force for the US expedition.[46]

In the late sixties, after a spell training the Kenyan police, SAS veteran Peter Stiff was a member of an SAS team dispatched to Thailand to train Thai special forces with the co-operation of the US Green Berets. The training, however, was a cover for a more covert role which included hitting the Ho Chi Minh trail from the west through Laos.

> We were given sectors across the border in Laos to work in, and patrols of three or four of us would cross the border, seek out the locals and gather intelligence. We would not be identifiably British or American and we would wear nondescript military clothing, without insignia . . . and neither would we wear dog tags for identification. Our major task was reconnaissance.

Stiff was in Thailand for eleven months, 'but politically as far as Britain was concerned, it is certain that few knew I was there and those who did, turned a blind eye'. As he admits, his was not the only SAS presence in that theatre of operations. There were 'quite a few unofficial ones'.[47]

Secret air flights also took place from Hong Kong – the centre of Britain's contribution to the Vietnam War – with clandestine deliveries of British arms, particularly napalm and five-hundred-pound bombs. In the end, the most significant British contribution came from the GCHQ monitoring station at Little Sai Wan in Hong Kong (UKC 201 in the then international Sigint network). Working overtime to provide the US with intelligence, its intercepts of North Vietnamese military traffic were used by the American military command to target bombing strikes over the North. Together with NSA stations in Thailand and the Philippines, UKC 201 also monitored diplomatic traffic and North Vietnamese surface-to-air missile sites, enabling early warnings to be relayed to bomber crews in mid-flight. British help was explained away by referring to it as an Australian operation.[48]

The molehunts, which had been one of the by-products of the dispute over South-East Asia, had effectively crippled operations inside the Soviet Union through fear of penetration. Operations and intelligence-gathering had more success outside the Soviet orbit.

Following Suez, George Young had made the first unofficial investigation of Soviet penetration of Africa by sending Frank Steele to survey the scene. Steele received a distinctly frosty reception from colonial administrators and little happened. While he liked White personally and respected his judgement in security matters, Young, who 'foresaw the New Commonwealth countries as the main trouble makers of the next decade', felt that the Chief was too deferential to Whitehall over operations in Africa. MI6's Chief did not attempt to challenge the Attlee Doctrine until the Middle East Director, John Bruce-Lockhart, undertook a second survey in late 1959. During his trip, on 3 February 1960, as Nelson Mandela with 155 other members of the African National Congress (ANC) went on trial for treason, Prime Minister Macmillan told the all-white South African parliament in Cape Town that

> the most striking of all the impressions I have formed since I left London is of this African national consciousness. In different places it takes different forms, but it is happening everywhere. The wind of change is blowing through this continent . . . The great issue in this second part of the twentieth century is whether the uncommitted people of Asia and Africa will swing to the East or the West.

Bruce-Lockhart's report to White in the spring of 1960 warned that with deepening poverty, growing corruption and nascent nationalism, the continent looked ripe for exploitation by Soviet cadres. Basing his approach on his experience of the Malayan Emergency, where SIS and MI5 had worked reasonably well together, White began to focus on Africa. In Nigeria, both agencies, with MI6 officers moving in from Sudan, had already played a role in the 'rigging' of the 1959 federal elections which led to independence.[49]

The JIC had not expressed much interest in Africa, and the tasks entrusted to MI6 included the normal acquisition of intelligence and liaison. Most MI6 efforts in Africa were stymied by inter-agency demarcation disputes and internal Whitehall political battles. MI6 was unable to open stations where the Service felt they were needed. It did, however, occasionally conduct robust – or what the Service called 'disruptive' – operations. Including Africa as part of his remit, Bruce-Lockhart concentrated his efforts on Northern

Rhodesia and the former Belgian Congo, which had valuable uranium deposits.

George Young believed that the first test for opposing Soviet support for national revolutionary movements 'resulted initially in misjudgements and poor execution'. The chaos in the Congo immediately after independence had provided the test of revolution by proxy – 'an Egyptian detachment, ostensibly part of the United Nations' peace-keeping force; a squadron of Soviet transport planes with crews in civilian clothes; the assurance of Pandit Nehru that his officials would block any counter-action by the West while Dag Hammarskjöld looked the other way'. In the Congo, Daphne Park, who had trained wartime OSS officers, co-operated with her opposite number in the CIA in trying to overthrow Prime Minister Patrice Lumumba, who was believed to be aligning the country with the Soviet Union against the West. On 14 September 1960 Lumumba was deposed by Joseph Mobutu with the help of the CIA and MI6. Lumumba was to die in mysterious circumstances following unsuccessful CIA plans, to which Park was privy, to assassinate him. According to Young: 'The murder of Lumumba, the collapse of the Antoine Gizenga regime in Stanleyville, President Abboud's denial of Khartoum Airport for the passage of supplies, and some deft behind-the-scenes initiatives by CIA officers, put paid to the Russian ploy.'[50]

This conspiracy view of Soviet penetration of Africa was shared by Young's right-wing 'friends', who took an extreme and racist view of Africa and Africans. The official line, however, was that 'Communism (amongst African political movements) has made no great impact' and that the idea of 'pan-Africanism' could be discounted. In practice, MI6 concentrated on counter-intelligence, including the penetration of actual or potentially subversive organisations. As Anthony Verrier notes, because this was often conducted with 'skill and imagination', the aims of nationalist politicians were 'known with some precision'. Whitehall was well aware of the fact that 'men of this calibre and potential leadership would only respond to overtures on behalf of their movements, not for their own benefit'. Verrier adds that 'these prospective politicians and one-party "successor state" leaders in place (even if sometimes in gaol) were not going to blow the whistle on their paymasters (for their parties, be it stressed, not for themselves) by telling their followers "patience, time and Her Majesty's Government are on our side"'. Many of these leaders had been close to the London-based Africa Bureau, which supplied the British government with background intelligence on the nationalist movements. As evidence of its usefulness the Bureau was not put under surveillance by Special Branch and MI5.[51]

Verrier refers to the 'virtual recruitment' of Tom Mboya, leader of the moderate Kenyan African National Union; Tanganyika African National Union's Julius Nyerere, regarded by MI6 as 'an outstanding African leader', who won the 1960 election; Nyasaland's Hastings Banda, whose Malawi

Congress Party swept the board in the 1964 elections; Northern Rhodesia's Kenneth Kaunda and Southern Rhodesia's Joshua Nkomo. These 'agents of influence' were provided by MI6 with covert funds, 'establishing a pattern which has changed little over the years'. The leader of the National Union for the Total Independence of Angola (UNITA), Jonas Savimbi, who was a close contact of Mboya's, is also said to have been recruited. In 1963, Savimbi had been made chair of a group of liberation movement representatives of the Organisation of African Unity (OAU), advising on the formation of a committee that would co-ordinate fund-raising to support nationalist movements. Among his committee colleagues were Kaunda and Nkomo. Savimbi became particularly linked to the multinational company Lonhro, whose management included senior MI6 officers such as Nicholas Elliott and Paul Paulson, who happened to succeed Bruce-Lockhart on the Africa desk.[52]

Another MI6 catch was ANC leader Nelson Mandela. Whether Mandela was recruited in London before he was imprisoned in South Africa is not clear, but it is understood that on a recent trip to London he made a secret visit to MI6's training section to thank the Service for its help in foiling two assassination attempts directed against him soon after he became President. MI6 was particularly successful in placing its people as advisers to African leaders. As chief of station in Lusaka in the mid-sixties, Daphne Park helped finance Kaunda's successful election campaign and became his 'right-hand [wo]man'. In 1965, Denis Grennan, a trustee of the Ariel Foundation, which was long believed to be an intelligence 'front' organisation designed to help future African leaders, was seconded to the staff of President Kaunda allegedly to help create an intelligence service. White settler and wheeler-dealer Bruce McKenzie had been an MI6 agent since at least 1963 and after independence became the 'most important white man in Kenya', retaining an active role in military and security affairs.[53]

Around the world the Americans wanted ever more robust operations but, as head of counter-intelligence, Oldfield argued against aggressive recruitment strategies. In a formal paper, he stated that 'encouraging active recruitment would expose SIS officers in foreign countries to expulsion and would mean that SIS was more vulnerable to a rigorous value-for-money analysis. It might be hard to prove that SIS provided better intelligence than GCHQ.' Indeed, it was increasingly recognised that technical means of intelligence-gathering were both superior to agents on the ground and cost-efficient. Senior MI6 colleague Nigel Clive remarked of GCHQ that 'it's a veritable industry'. He added with relish: 'That's the stuff that really gives you an intellectual erection.'[54]

The fact was that western intelligence agencies were singularly unsuccessful at recruiting KGB officers. The only successes were among those who had decided on their own initiative to spy or defect. Tom Bower records that the only compensation was the development of new technical methods, including the monitoring from embassies abroad of KGB radio traffic which provided new openings. Overriding all MI6 operations in this period was the need to avoid further embarrassing scandals and the fear of interference by Whitehall. Morale slumped among officers with a lack of confidence being shown in senior ranks.

The reaction in Whitehall to the Blake and Philby espisodes was, naturally, one of extreme dissatisfaction with MI6 and with White, who had been put in place to clean up the Service. The reality was that few officials and even fewer ministers and politicians knew how senior or how significant Philby's position had been. Such typical ignorance had allowed the Service to escape any effective scrutiny. In other countries the disasters might have led to abolition. At the top, there was a general cynicism and weariness which stifled any major reforms. The situation was best summed up by Macmillan's private secretary, John Wyndham (later Lord Egremont), who opined a few years later that it would be 'much better if the Russians saw the Cabinet minutes twice a week. Prevent all that dangerous guesswork.'[55]

The first sign of Whitehall displeasure was the decision in 1964 to move MI6 from Broadway Buildings to a new office block, Century House, on Westminster Bridge Road. As it was now denied access to the traditional haunts of the clubs, and sidelined from the centres of power, this was an indication that MI6 was expected to operate like any other department. Increasingly MI6 was being brought under the control of the Foreign Office with its traditional ties to the armed services being downgraded. In the same year, the services were amalgamated under the MoD, with the service intelligence directorates combined with the JIB as the Defence Intelligence Staff (DIS). Cost-cutting at the MoD resulted in cutbacks for the DIS and the loss of its officers seconded to MI6. Internally, the Service Requirements Sections were separated from the rest of the Requirement machinery as MoD Advisers for the Army, Air and Navy. The other R sections were reorganised along geographical lines and more closely integrated with the Production side, where DP1 covered western Europe and the Soviet bloc; DP2 the Middle East and Africa; DP3 the Far East; and DP4 the Americas, including Latin America, and also the UK station.[56]

As a response to the Philby and Blake scandals, White oversaw the creation of a Directorate of Counter-Intelligence and Security (DCIS). This absorbed the Inspectorate of Security, the Positive Vetting Section, out of which developed the Security Branches for Vetting and Personnel (SVB and SVP), and R5, whose responsibilities for monitoring foreign communist parties were taken up by the Controllerates. The Security branches worked closely with MI5's C Division, which was responsible for Protective Security. The DCIS was subdivided into Counter-Intelligence (CI) sections covering areas such as eastern Europe, China and the USSR. These were eventually amalgamated into three Targeting and Counter-Intelligence Sections (TCI) under the DCIS, whose head was Maurice Oldfield. Against his better judgement, but aware that he had to go along with Angleton as part of the deal for US support of sterling and British aid to the Americans in Vietnam, White also agreed to the setting up of the joint MI6/MI5 Fluency Committee to investigate penetration of the services.[57]

This was not the end. The Cabinet Office, in the shape of Burke Trend, had decided that the time had come for further change. Backed up by John Briance, who had recently returned from South-East Asia, and Oldfield, who became Assistant Chief in November 1965, White took the hint and began to put in place the foundations of the modern Secret Intelligence Service (SIS). In January 1966, he initiated a comprehensive organisational redesign which returned to the first postwar model. The Director of Production was reinstated, along with Requirements, Counter-Intelligence and Security, Operational Support for specialist and technical skills, Personnel and Administration, and later a new Training section. In addition, the Labour government instituted 'a new era of strict financial control', which resulted in staff reductions on both the Production and Requirements side, and the 'first of a series of station amalgamations which served to eliminate certain stations judged to be relatively unproductive'. MI6 had had a string of officers throughout the Caribbean who had supplied good intelligence but had been superseded by the CIA. The process left MI6 with just one station in South America, Buenos Aires, leaving the Service to rely on American intelligence to fill the gap. Seven Controllers covered Europe, Soviet Bloc, Western Hemisphere, Far East, Middle East, UK, and a new department for Africa. With the collapse of the Attlee Doctrine, the Service took over responsibility for some of the former colonies that had been the preserve of MI5's E Branch, which had by convention posted Security Liaison Officers. The leaner profile was to test the Service's ability to mount operations abroad.[58]

The cost-cutting led to a proposal by the Soviet Bloc Controller, Harold Shergold, for joint MI6/MI5 sections. MI6 and MI5 scientific staff were already working under a joint head with a new research and development section. MI6 officers began working with MI5's counter-espionage K Branch on joint targeting and operations against Soviet, eastern European and, later, Chinese targets in the UK. The UK Controller also set up a joint section.[59]

Not all these changes were welcomed, and for a time there was a 'terrible atmosphere'. Naturally, there still existed the old-boy network inside the Service which regarded White's approach as 'too gentlemanly' and continuing to 'inhibit the tougher form of security which was desirable'. In March 1966, White organised a conference at Gosport to consider the changes and to assess where the Service was going. New recruitment procedures and employment conditions were put in place and, in an attempt to clear out the dead wood, the retirement age was dropped to fifty-five. Geoffrey McDermott noticed that 'all the dozen top members of the Service, and several who have recently retired – some of them into the Diplomatic Service – were personal friends of Philby ... And, curiously, half-a-dozen others have gone in for extreme right-wing politics.' Viewed by CIA officers as another example of British incompetence, the escape of George Blake from Wormwood Scrubs on 22 October 1966 once more put a strain on Anglo-American relations.[60]

The Service's inability to obtain high-grade intelligence on Ian Smith's rebellious regime in Rhodesia also put a strain on relations with the politicians. MI6 intelligence reports failed to predict Smith's Unilateral Declaration of Independence (UDI).[61]

Earlier in January, at an emergency summit in Lagos, Nigeria, an exasperated Harold Wilson had encountered fierce criticism from African and Commonwealth leaders of the government's failure to take military action after UDI. Wilson countered that 'it was all very well to speak of military intervention and of gunboat diplomacy, but this was not the 19th century and Rhodesia was a land-locked state'. Britain argued that logistical problems, Zambia's vulnerability and the kith-and-kin factor prevented a military solution. Extensive contingency planning by the MoD on the practicalities of intervention convinced many in the Ministry that such an operation, despite the success of the limited support sent to East Africa in early 1964, was beyond Britain's capabilities. In truth, there was no intention of mounting a military operation. MI6 planners sympathised too closely with the Rhodesian whites and provided only negative intelligence. Defence Secretary Denis Healey later admitted that the Chief of the Defence Staff had threatened 'resignation or military action if we ever considered doing anything there'.[62]

Wilson later said that he had been misled over his statement that oil sanctions would bring down the regime in 'weeks rather than months'. The head of Rhodesia's Central Intelligence Organisation (CIO), Ken Flowers, who offered advice to MI6, thought that the British Prime Minister had been 'deliberately misadvised'. He knew that MI6 had the 'right answers', but the intelligence had been lost in the assessment system. In fact, it is now apparent that the Foreign Office and the JIC put no pressure on Dick White to mount extensive intelligence-gathering operations. Whether this was deliberate or the result of the general poor opinion of the Service is not clear.[63]

In either case, the reforms to MI6 proceeded. Perhaps the key figure in the changes was Denis Greenhill, who returned in 1966 from Washington to London as Deputy Under-Secretary in charge of defence and intelligence at the Foreign Office. It was Greenhill who was responsible for the decision on the successor to White, who was due to retire in 1968. Oldfield had assumed that the post would be his but White, as had Greenhill, had lost confidence in his deputy. Whilst in Washington, Greenhill had cautioned Oldfield about the presence of young male lodgers in his apartment, though he did not directly question his sexuality. CIA officers thought Oldfield to be homosexual but said nothing, assuming that he had passed his positive vetting when, in fact, he had lied during the process.[64]

The other internal candidate was molehunter Christopher Phillpotts who, while he had supporters among the young turks, was gravely distrusted by some senior figures. With no strong recommendation from White, Greenhill told Foreign Secretary George Brown that there was no suitable internal candidate. Brown offered the job to Greenhill, who turned it down, and after a search for an outsider the post finally went to John Rennie, an assistant under-secretary at the Foreign Office responsible for defence matters and for chairing a number of Cabinet committees.[65]

Rennie was a true Establishment figure – Balliol College, Oxford – with a distinguished career in the Diplomatic Service. His appointment was greeted with suspicion by MI6 officers, who pointed out his lack of intelligence experience. This was true, but what Rennie did have was experience of the covert world – having been head of the IRD for five years in the mid-fifties, when use of IRD propaganda tactics was at its height in the Middle and Far East. Nigel Clive, who in an unusual appointment was made head of the IRD in 1968, thought that Oldfield 'had every reason to feel aggrieved' when he was passed over in favour of Rennie. Clive states that Rennie was appointed

> to his surprise, and no less to the surprise of the senior echelons of SIS. The case could have been made that for an outsider, his past service should have provided him with some parallel understanding of what to expect in the new role. But in fact he found it difficult to adjust to his changed responsibilities and, from first to last, he was always overshadowed by his deputy and ultimate successor (Sir) Maurice Oldfield. At no period did he feel at home in SIS.[66]

In a long tradition of Foreign Office appointments, Greenhill had been promoted to chair the JIC, but found the situation less than satisfactory. 'Initially the committee dealt primarily with intelligence gathered by covert means and forecasts on a very restricted distribution were based on this.' Greenhill discussed the problem with Trend, and 'eventually an assessment staff was established in the Cabinet Office'. The Joint Intelligence Organisation's (JIO) responsibility was 'to make forecasts and assessments on foreign affairs using all the information, covert and overt, at the Government's disposal' for consideration by the JIC and circulation to ministers and officials. This tended to tighten the Foreign Office grip on intelligence assessment since 'it was inevitable that the biggest input came from the Foreign Office'. The first head was another Foreign Office official, John Thompson, who had been with Greenhill in Washington. After initial hesitation, the Treasury co-operated thanks to Frank Figgures – 'an unusual Treasury official'. The Bank of England had a considerable intelligence staff of its own and was ready to use Thompson's information but was 'unwilling to pool its own'. The JIO also had a co-ordinating role in respect of the work of the security and intelligence agencies.[67]

Consideration of the assessment problem by Greenhill and Trend also led, on 1 April 1968, to the appointment of White to the new post of Intelligence and Security Co-ordinator. Located in the Cabinet Office, the ISC was intended to co-ordinate all information and deliver an authoritative intelligence assessment unclouded by departmental prejudices. It soon developed its own staff and was designed to improve MI6's status in Whitehall and among ministers by better targeting and intelligence-gathering, and through increased budgets and better conditions for the Service.[68]

The honeymoon did not last long. David Owen recalled that before leaving the MoD on the evening of 21 August 1968, he read highly classified reports on Czechoslovakia which stated that 'there would be no invasion. I was then woken up to be told that the Russians were invading.' Who was to blame? Christopher Andrew's source claims that SIS concluded 'from intelligence on the movement of Soviet armed forces that the Russians intended to invade'. The JIC and White had forwarded authoritative assessments to the Cabinet Office to the effect that the Soviets would not invade, sharing the Foreign Office belief that there would be no invasion 'because of the international repercussions for the USSR'. It was evident that the arrangements for assessment had failed, a scenario that Denis Healey had predicted. Healey believed that 'inevitably, once part of the Foreign Office has taken a view on an issue, it tries to interpret intelligence so as to confirm that view and tends to discount intelligence which disagrees with it'. Policy-making and assessment need to be kept separate. Greenhill later admitted that the assessment problem was never completely solved and that input from outside the Foreign Office/ MoD circle, such as that of academics, was not integrated into the process.[69]

As a result of the Penkovsky operation, MI6 had introduced elaborate plans for early warning of military action by the Warsaw Pact; the problem was that the Service had no human sources to set them in motion. Despite the vast array of intelligence sources, principally from satellite technology, and improved eavesdropping on military movements, MI6 had been unable to recruit high-level sources behind the Iron Curtain. The sorry state of MI6's intelligence-gathering was kept quiet within the Cabinet Office, but the results were widely known throughout Whitehall, where its product was not highly rated. A similar fate awaited White in his co-ordinating role, with his authority gradually being diminished. A greater reliance began to be placed within Whitehall on the intelligence gathered by GCHQ – subsidised to a large extent by the Americans as the only significant part of the 'special relationship' – which proved to be abundant, often reliable and to provide value for money. Indeed, much of the Service's own intelligence would eventually be found to be based on GCHQ intercepts. More weight was given by officials and ministers to the output from Cheltenham, with the result that MI6 became devalued.

When the Labour government won an increased majority in the 1966 general election, Harold Wilson began backing out of the deal with the Americans over sterling and Vietnam, and set in motion Britain's disengagement from South-East Asia. It seems that Healey had intended from the beginning to pull out east of Suez and from the Far Eastern bases. Intense pressure was applied by the Americans, but Wilson resisted and agreed to the devaluation of sterling.

When Wilson undertook another visit to the United States in February 1968, the State Department minuted that Britain had 'never cut a less impressive figure in Washington's eyes'. Its retreat from east of Suez signalled that Britain had conceded 'its ability to remain a world power'. In the face of these trenchant and widely held criticisms, a report by the US Bureau of Intelligence and Research, which analysed the future of the 'special relationship', was able to conclude that despite a good deal of 'sentimentality, rhetoric and cant', there remained certain important features of the alliance between Britain and the United States which were 'quite special'. That Britain was a favoured partner of the United States was almost entirely due to co-operation in the fields of nuclear weapons and intelligence. Britain's 'far-flung dependencies and Commonwealth affiliates' – its 'residual empire' – continued to give the US access to an 'unrivalled network of . . . facilities that served US foreign policy interests' and 'provided valuable – in some cases indispensable – contributions to US security arrangements'.[70]

The report went on to note that

> in the intelligence field, the US and UK give each other a greater volume and wider variety of information than either does to any of its allies. The arrangements provide for exchange of information gathered both from overt and covert sources; for the swapping of estimates; and for the preparation of joint estimates. There is a division of labor in certain geographic and functional fields, and on some areas and subjects, each nation is dependent for its intelligence mainly on the other . . . In the intelligence field, the UK gets more than it gives, but what it gives is not insubstantial.

Although the report noted that the special relationship had been declared dead every few months, it concluded that it was still very much 'alive'. This permanent relationship, which was run by a select band of unelected officials, remained secret, underground and almost entirely unknown to politicians.[71]

THE LAST OF THE COLONIAL WARS

By the late sixties, the Special Air Service (SAS) had become the overt/covert special operations arm of MI6 and the Foreign Office, taking over the paramilitary role of the Special Operations Branch of the old War Planning Directorate which, in turn, had temporarily filled the gap left by the disbandment of the Special Operations Executive (SOE).

There were senior officers within the SAS who were seriously concerned about the lack of military action and of a theatre where they could rehearse 'training operations'. Fortuitously, the regiment's interest was aroused when MI6 sources reported that 'an Iraqi-trained guerrilla training team had started work among the primitive tribesmen of the sensitive Musandam Peninsula' in Muscat and Oman. As a result of the intelligence, an SAS squadron was landed on the peninsula, while six hundred miles away at the other end of Oman, a second guerrilla force was beginning to cause serious trouble. This was the beginning of the SAS's involvement 'in one of Britain's least publicised victories of the post-war period'.[1]

The rebellion started in the mid-sixties largely as an indigenous one against the reactionary rule of Sultan Said bin Taimur. Serious guerrilla warfare broke out in the southern province of Dhofar and the rebellion became a classic revolutionary struggle, supported from South Yemen by the USSR and China. The British, with a long-standing defence commitment to Oman, 'intervened to protect the flow of oil through the Straits of Hormuz, by ensuring that a friendly government remained in power'. British money made up half of Said's income, which was used to preserve his rule. In 1964 oil had been discovered in Oman and by 1967 the Shell-owned Petroleum Development (Oman) (PDO) oil company was producing commercial quantities. Most of the royalties from the PDO were put away in a Swiss bank with little being spent on the country, where conditions for the Omani people were generally appalling.

Despite the oil wealth, there remained a lack of economic progress, a near-total absence of schools – considered by Said as 'centres of communism' – neglect of public health – resulting in rampant dysentery, tuberculosis, malaria and syphilis – and a corrupt civil regime, which fuelled sympathy among ordinary Omanis for the rebels. A feudal justice system existed within which opponents were imprisoned in barbaric conditions, subjected to starvation and repeated beatings, while British advisers stood by. The Sultan's advisers included his secretary of defence, 'Pat' Waterfield, Maj. Dennison, chief of intelligence, and his chief adviser, Maj. F. C. L. Chauncy. The Sultan's regime of 'tyranny and sadism' could never have survived 'without the active and consistent backing of the British government'. Fearing another Vietnam, the United States encouraged Britain in its role of principal supporter.[2]

The counter-insurgency campaign did not go well, however, and by 1969 the Popular Front for the Liberation of the Occupied Arab Gulf (PFLO-AG), which had evolved from the Dhofar Liberation Front, controlled all of Dhofar except for the small coastal enclave of Salalah, where the British had a military and RAF base. Within Dhofar, the PFLO-AG introduced healthcare and education facilities. The guerrillas were confident enough to shell the RAF base and Said bin Taimur's palace. Oman was the transition area between Dhofar and the Gulf, and by March 1970 the military situation had become desperate and of major concern to the British government. On 12 June, allies of the guerrillas in Dhofar, the National Democratic Front for the Liberation of Oman and the Arab Gulf (NDFLO-AG), attacked the Green Mountain area, thus extending the war into the interior, 'threatening the oil-fields, the Sultanate of Oman and ultimately, the whole of the Gulf'. Although intelligence on these guerrilla fronts was scanty, the British realised that they faced a well-organised threat. Initial attempts to persuade the Sultan to change his policies to meet the new situation were a failure. This forced Britain into 'some rather unorthodox covert actions'. The first of these was the removal of the Sultan 'in a virtually bloodless and highly popular coup that placed his progressive, Western-educated son on the throne'.[3]

The British prepared the ground with a press rumour in early 1970 that Said was willing to resign. A Foreign Office official, in referring to what had happened a few years before in Abu Dhabi, was quoted as saying that 'we need an Omani Zaid to Said's Shakhbut'. The Omani figure turned out to be the Sultan's son, Qaboos, who, following his return to Oman in 1966 after education in England and military service in Germany, was put under virtual house arrest in the palace. Although the Sultan distrusted the intelligence service and often blocked the efforts of its officers, the director of intelligence, Maj. Dennison, was able to forge a link with the experienced exiles who fled abroad to escape Sultan Said's oppressions. Although Dennison apparently played no part in the coup, his 'presence at the heart of the country's intelligence network helped to ease the transition'. He saw Qaboos and suggested that following a coup, the Sultan's strongest challenger abroad, Said's brother, Tariq bin Taimur, be made Prime Minister. With the endorsement of Qaboos, in May Dennison travelled secretly to Dubai, where he obtained the co-operation of Tariq, who was in contact with other dissident groups and had called for the Sultan's removal.[4]

Qaboos's visitors were carefully screened to exclude those who might influence him, but contact was covertly maintained with a number of officials and with selected Sultan's Armed Force (SAF) intelligence officers. A pivotal figure in the coup was Capt. Timothy Landon, who had trained with Qaboos at Sandhurst. A former lieutenant in the 10th Royal Hussars, Landon had been seconded to Oman in 1965 as a reconnaissance officer. Subsequently trained in London by MI6 in intelligence work, he returned two years later to Oman, where he represented Foreign Office interests and was 'deeply involved with British Intelligence'. By July 1969, Landon had taken over responsibility for intelligence in Dhofar and used the post to secretly meet with Qaboos in a private house near the palace. At the same time, he had meetings with the son of the Wali (Governor) of Salalah, Bareik bin Hamud al-Chafiri, who disliked the old Sultan, and the secretary to the Sultan, Hamad bin Hamud Al Bu Said, a close friend from Sandhurst.[5]

With the backing of Whitehall, the Landon–Qaboos–Bareik axis looked for further sympathisers within the country using the managing director of the PDO oil company, F. Hughes, as a means of communication. Hughes had the confidence of the Sultan and was regarded as 'the most powerful man in the country after the Sultan' and viewed as someone of 'considerable force of character and ability'. He was an ideal secret go-between. Using his own plane, Hughes frequently visited the Sultan in his palace at Salalah and was employed to pass on messages from Said to the Minister of the Interior, Ahmed bin Ibrahim, and to the Governor of Muscat, Shihab bin Faysal.[6]

The date for the coup was continually postponed. Prime Minister Harold Wilson had sanctioned it but was probably reluctant to give the go-ahead during an election period. The PDO and its northern oil installations had been unaffected by the guerrilla activity, but the situation changed when members of the SAF were attacked on 12 June by guerrillas at the military camp near Izki, close to the PDO pipeline collection point.

Following the attack at Izki, Shell representatives urged the British government to take action. Whitehall's sympathetic attitude led to the co-operation of the consul general in Muscat and noted Arabist, David Crawford, the political resident in the Persian Gulf at Bahrain, Geoffrey Arthur, who between 1963 and 1966 had been the Foreign Office adviser to MI6, and Brig. John Graham, the SAF commander in Muscat. In January, a former SAF commander, the hawkish Col. Hugh Oldman, had replaced one of the Sultan's old advisers, Pat Waterfield, as secretary of defence, thus removing an obstacle to the coup planning. Oldman, who acted as liaison and a channel of communication between Said and the SAF, was responsible for a small engineering unit which controlled the security of the Salalah palace. His assistance was, therefore, necessary for the success of any coup, and he was to play a highly important role in its planning and execution. Graham and Oldman were party to meetings with Qaboos which also included Landon and Bareik. Brig. Graham and Oldman also met with the British envoy, Sir William Luce.[7]

On 20 June 1970, the Labour government fell at the general election. The Conservatives took power and at the end of June gave the green light for the Sultan's removal. Galvanised by the attack on Izki, Qaboos and his supporters moved into action on 23 July.

During the afternoon, while Said rested in his apartments, a detachment of the SAF was told to surround the palace in the belief that this was a training exercise. A group of ten Omani soldiers, including some SAS men, was led by Bareik and Landon through the cordon and approached the palace. One of the guards at the gate had been bribed and had arranged for the other guards to be absent. Said, however, was prepared and the conspirators were met by a fusillade fired by the Sultan and loyal guards within the palace. Bareik was wounded and taken away for treatment by an SAF officer. Landon immediately radioed for air support and a British-crewed aircraft from the Sultan's Air Force dropped tear-gas bombs, providing cover for the attack. The second charge was successful and, after being wounded twice, Said surrendered to Landon.[8]

Said agreed to leave the palace only with the commander of his bodyguard, Col. Turnhill, who had prearranged to be sightseeing during the actual coup on the coast with Hugh Oldman and Brig. Graham. When news of the coup came, they quickly returned, and Said was flown to Bahrain and then on to London and exile. The Sultan took up residence in a private suite at the Dorchester Hotel, where he died on 19 October 1972. Geoffrey Arthur similarly claimed to have been far away in hospital when the coup occurred, though others disputed this and cited his central role in the coup planning.[9]

Qaboos became Sultan, and one of the first to send him a telegram of congratulations on this 'historical event' was the chair of the Shell Trading Company, whose subsidiary was the PDO. The British-officered security forces deliberately suppressed news of the coup d'état, ostensibly for internal security reasons. Officially, the coup had been an internal affair about which Whitehall supposedly learned only a few days after the event. It was not until the 27th – four days after it occurred – that it was reported in the British newspapers. In the manner of much of the disinformation that followed coverage of events in Oman, the coup was presented as a nationalist uprising, modelled on the early-fifties Nasser coup. Britain recognised the new regime on 29 July with Whitehall expressing 'amazement' at suggestions in the *Guardian* that the British forces there might have had anything to do with the coup. No questions were asked in the House of Commons, and as late as December the British government steadfastly maintained the fiction that the SAS was in Dhofar for training purposes only.[10]

The new Sultan 'knew personally very few Omanis and not one who could be a trusted friend'. Around him were British advisers and officers, 'alternately fawning and patronising'. He was well aware that he 'owed his position to them, and that he could make no positive policy decision without their support, and, indeed, without their strength to ensure its implementation'. The Sultan's uncle, Tariq, took up the post of PM, though his power was diminished by a damaging power struggle when he aroused the enmity of several individuals in the local British establishment.[11]

One of the first changes was the renaming of the country from Muscat and Oman to Oman. Jettisoning a number of the older advisers, who were packed off to retirement, the palace office, which handled all external affairs, quickly established relations with other Gulf states and all of the Arab states, except Iraq: a particularly close relationship was formed with Iran. The palace office also oversaw the operations of a special four-man SAS unit, trained by the regiment's counter-revolutionary warfare wing, which was entrusted with the Sultan's security. The British immediately began to expand their military presence, making use of seconded personnel and privately recruited mercenaries. Airwork Services was primarily used to build up the Omani Air Force through training and technical support, while also serving as the contracting agency for those military personnel not lent under normal secondment arrangements. As part of Operation STORM, an SAS team was seconded under the thin cover of a 'British Army Training Team' to operate in the 'Dhofar Campaign'. Finally, under Maj. Dennison, British officers, including a number of former MI6 officers, staffed and ran the Omani Intelligence Service (OIS), which was shaped by the coup and created following the transition. The OIS was thoroughly British and operated in English with recruitment undertaken solely through British officers. Remaining as part of the army until early 1973, the OIS built up a successful intelligence system with a network of District Intelligence Officers at every military post.

In early August, the British press was full of stories of 'Chinese officers' being involved in directing the guerrillas. This myth was a product of the British Army Information Teams, which played a significant role in military psychological warfare and deception operations and contributed, with the Foreign Office's Information Research Department (IRD), to the larger political warfare and information programme 'to which the BBC also lent unofficial assistance'. In December the guerrillas in Dhofar merged with the NDFLO-AG in a common front, the Popular Front for the Liberation of Oman and the Arab Gulf (PFLO-AG).[12]

In June of the following year the palace office made contact with the CIA in London, through Ghassan Shakir, a Libyan with close connections with the US, who, along with another businessman, Yahya Umar, had established business interests in the Sultanate. Soon after, the CIA began to route counter-insurgency aid through Saudi Arabia. In October, the British launched Operation JAGUAR, a campaign against guerrillas in the eastern section, which produced poor results. In the spring of 1972 a new offensive, Operation SIMBA, began, with the aim of throttling PFLO-AG supply lines from South Yemen. It was not successful and was abandoned in May, leaving the SAF on the defensive.[13]

Up to sixty SAS troops on four- to five-month tours of duty were transferred to Oman to work alongside the Sultan's armed forces, and between them the SAS and SAF gradually brought the insurrection under control. The intelligence set-up was revamped and a new director of intelligence was appointed in 1972. The no-nonsense former deputy, Ray Nightingale, a former Rhodesian staff officer who had been attached to the SAS, had allegedly been previously responsible for helping to organise the notorious Ugandan State Research Bureau. In December 1972 the OIS played a crucial role in Operation JASON, thwarting an alleged plot against the newly formed government. In 1974, the OIS was transformed into the Oman Research Department (ORD), with a major increase in personnel, though all key roles continued to be held by seconded British intelligence officers. By 1975 the last groups of rebels had surrendered or decamped to Yemen. With the end of the rebellion, the ORD concentrated on government corruption, economic intelligence assessments and the monitoring of religious activism. In 1979, a former senior MI6 officer who had recently retired, Reginald Temple, was appointed head of the ORD. A former stockbroker and parachute regiment officer, Temple had joined the Service in 1951 and served in Singapore during the fifties and then in Beirut, Algiers and Paris. He was succeeded by John Ault, a Far East specialist who had run the Service's training school at Fort Monkton. These appointments were a clear indication that the ORD served as MI6's Middle East office and that Oman was of some importance as Britain's last imperial outpost in the region.[14]

British involvement in the Dhofar campaign, while significant in political and military terms, was 'for public consumption in Britain – distinctly low profile. News media coverage was not prevented, but neither was it encouraged.' It was not until 1976 that the British public was told that the SAS had aided the Sultan. The public did not know, however, that the campaign had degenerated into corruption as scores of SAS troops had lined their pockets with hundreds of thousands of pounds by illegally pocketing the wages of non-existent agents they claimed to have recruited. The fraud had been uncovered by Maj. Mike Kealy, but the Colonel Commandant of the SAS, Viscount Head, ensured that it was all kept in-house.[15]

What became known as the 'Hilton Assignment' was one of MI6's last attempts at a major special operation designed to overthrow a regime opposed to British interests. The details of this episode are hard to disentangle, principally because the first and only major account was almost totally based on an explanation by a former MI6 officer with, it appears, the deliberate aim of muddying the waters. In a jumble of dates and anonymous characters, MI6's undoubted involvement is obscured as the emphasis is placed directly on a private exile operation.[16]

On 1 September 1969, a twenty-eight-year-old army lieutenant, Muammar al-Gaddafi, led a group of young Free Unionist Officers in a successful, bloodless coup against King Idris of Libya, who was on holiday in Turkey. Gaddafi put his signals training with the British Army to good use, seizing control of communications. He had taken over a sparsely populated country – half the size of India – with what appeared to be almost limitless oil reserves. Naturally, Britain – which had sustained King Idris – was appalled by the coup.

In February 1970, a counter-coup was launched from Chad by a member of the royal family, Abdullah bin Abid – the 'Black Prince' – and a group of active émigrés. It was embarrassingly unsuccessful and the conspirators were soon rounded up by Gaddafi's security service, the General Investigation Division (GID). Not long after, the British began to plot their own operation.

On 18 May an unidentified 'retired high-ranking British official' who had previously served in Libya attended a meeting at 21 Sloane Street, the headquarters of David Stirling's small film distribution company, Television International Enterprises, and contact point for Watchguard International, which offered a 'sophisticated counter-coup capability'. Also present with Stirling at the discussion on the political situation in the Middle East was a former MI6 officer, Denys Rowley, alias 'James Kent', who was not on the Watchguard payroll but operated independently, from an office next door (this also appears to have been used as an MI6 'safe house'). Rowley had left the army in the early fifties to join MI6, serving mainly in the Middle East as a 'political action' specialist, before resigning after the thousands of pounds spent on one of his networks were found to have been a complete waste of money.[17]

The trio discussed Libya, with the official stressing the point that something needed to be done. All British and American bases had been closed down, while British Petroleum oilfields had been nationalised without compensation. Gaddafi also made an ally of the Prime Minister of Malta, Dom Mintoff, then in dispute with Britain. During the discussions, and at further meetings at their respective clubs, Rowley and the official talked about the prospects of mounting an insurrection against Gaddafi. They then set about combing the ranks of Libyan exiles 'for someone rich, prominent and motivated enough to lead the movement. A short-list of six was prepared.' In exile was a powerful and influential group of Libyans, immediately ready to set up a government under the former king to replace the Gaddafi regime, once he was deposed. The key figure was Umar al-Shahli, an adviser to Idris, who had amassed a fortune of around $25 million. Al-Shahli and his brothers soon established a secret war fund in Switzerland.

According to the key Watchguard figure – senior SAS man Maj. the Honourable George Campbell-Johnson, known as 'The Pack Rat' – who took the place of Stirling while the latter recovered from a road accident, the planned uprising to bring down Gaddafi had originally been a joint MI6/CIA affair which, without warning, had been cancelled by the Americans. They had concluded that 'although Gaddafi was anti-West, he was also anti-Soviet, which meant there could be someone a lot worse running Libya'. The British disagreed, Campbell-Johnson continued, 'but the Yanks were adamant. After that we decided to go it alone with French assistance.' The British agreed at a 'high level' that it was in the country's interest for the coup to go ahead, and a 'senior British official' gave the word to Stirling to proceed.[18]

At the end of July, it was agreed between Stirling and Rowley to set up an office separate from Watchguard to plan the operation. A team of two former SAS men was employed to help with recruitment. 'Taffy B', an ex-warrant officer, had served with the SAS in Aden and the Far East, and had worked for Watchguard in Kenya. His SAS colleague, Sgt-Maj. 'Woody', was, Taffy discovered, a full-time operative for MI6, working with the Firm in 'a quartermaster cum odd job capacity'. Stirling was told by 'someone very senior indeed' in MI6, probably Oldfield, and the Parliamentary Under-Secretary for Foreign Affairs, Anthony Royle, a former Territorial Army SAS officer, that British nationals were not to be used as the trail would inevitably lead back to the British government. The situation was further complicated by the massive BAC air defence deal that had been struck with King Idris. The new Libyan government wanted the return of nearly £32 million and threatened to pull Libyan money out of the City of London unless it was repaid. Even so, Stirling 'got the impression that there would be great satisfaction if the operation was successful even though the use of British personnel was out of the question'. He thought that 'such an operation would have been remarkably easy; mostly a matter of logistics. I gave a hand in introductions to the French circle, but took a back seat from then on, though I was kept in the picture. The whole thing took much longer to put together than it ought to have done.'[19]

Just as in the Yemen, in another arm's-length operation, the Watchguard recruiters went to Paris to enlist French mercenaries. Intensive training began in August, and in the following month Taffy and Woody travelled in the guise of businessmen to Tripoli to undertake reconnaissance. The objective was Tripoli prison, dubbed 'the Hilton', where the 150 incarcerated political prisoners, mostly former army officers, were, quite naturally, all anti-Gaddafi. They were to be freed with the Franco-Belgian team of twenty to thirty mercenaries, making their escape by sea. It had been decided to mount the operation to topple Gaddafi when the Libyan leader was in residence at the palace in Tripoli. It was unresolved whether or not the mercenaries 'should actually fire the shot that killed him'. The idea was to capture the radio station with one of King Idris's aides announcing that Gaddafi had been overthrown and the King had returned.[20]

Woody was then sent to Belgium to purchase weapons with 'fake end-user certificates provided by MI6'. The main consignment of weapons and plastic explosive, however, was to be purchased from Omnipol, the Czechoslovakian arms company which was willing to supply anyone with access to foreign currency. The MI6 contact for this venture was Harry Briggs (Frank Higgins), 'an entrepreneur on the fringes of the arms business' who had been 'looking after this affair'. Previously involved in the sale of aircraft to Biafra, Briggs was contacted in August to handle the arms from the Czechs, and had formed a company with two eastern Europeans, George Strakaty (Gregor Jirasek) and his partner, Mirko Melich (Stefan Vlcek).[21]

The 'Hilton Assignment' team was due to meet in Bari ready for action in November, but the operation fell through when the Yugoslav authorities impounded the entire consignment of arms and explosives. On the 8th, Rowley met with Umar al-Shahli to relaunch the operation and, in December, the former MI6 officer travelled to Vienna to see the other MI6 contacts in the arms business to obtain new supplies of hardware. The equipment was communist in origin, with two hundred machine-guns of Czech manufacture and a large quantity of plastic explosive which was required to breach the prison walls. Playing a discreet role was another former MI6 employee, Anthony Divall, who continued as an MI6 agent in the arms business. His MI6 handler was Donald Gurrey, a long-serving officer with postings in Berlin, Paris, Warsaw, Singapore and San Domingo. Elaborate preparations had been made for the procurement, with an end-user certificate made out to a dealer in Chad and arrangements for transport by sea to Doula in Cameroon. Twenty-five French mercenaries had been hired in Toulon and a German-built coastal patrol boat, *Conquistador XIII*, had been purchased to land an assault team near Tripoli.[22]

According to Campbell-Johnson: 'The Americans found out what we were up to and learned we had an assault party ready to go in from Italy. They issued an ultimatum, saying that if we didn't get out of Italy in twenty-four hours, they would tell both the Italian and Libyan authorities. There is a great deal of bad feeling in Whitehall about the Americans at the moment.' The operation was reorganised for the following February, but on 29 December MI6 pulled the plug and warned off Taffy. Stirling's colleague Jim Johnson was 'approached by MI6 who knew that David was launching the operation. They knew it was going to be done by French mercenaries and they knew the name of the boat. They were horrified by the lack of security and the general talk going the rounds.' Stirling was telling all and sundry at White's about the progress of the operation. Despite claims that he had left the project some months previously, all interested agencies considered him to be still party to the planning. MI6 asked Johnson to go to France, where he met mercenary leader Roger Falques, who warned him that 'everyone knew about the Libyan job; that it was going to be a complete fiasco and that the French did not want to be associated with it'. MI6's request was 'to lay off'. Johnson's Mossad contact also advised him that security was lax.[23]

To Stirling's chagrin, it seems that MI6 'blew the operation' to the Italians and requested containing action. In March 1971, as an assault craft was about to leave Trieste, the Italian authorities impounded *Conquistador* before the weapons could be collected. According to one account, two boats had already sailed but were wrecked off the coast of Algeria in a storm. Stirling was apparently engaged in 'prolonged negotiations before the men involved were set free'. Not long after, he withdrew from the business of freelance soldiering.[24]

Most media attention at this time was focused on the escalating conflict in Ireland.

With the army and MI5 failing to make any headway, in 1971 Prime Minister Edward Heath decided that SIS should start to operate in Northern Ireland. Government policy on the conflict was formulated by the secret Cabinet Committee GEN 42, whose Co-ordinator of Intelligence was Dick White. From the outset, thought was given to exploiting the growing division of the IRA and Sinn Fein into militant and conciliatory camps, with Whitehall officials believing that 'a political solution required, indeed largely depended on, political intelligence in both broad and technical senses'. John Rennie was regarded as being unsuited to carrying out the task, and the Chief left it to his deputy. Maurice Oldfield, however, 'presented a reasoned case to his Prime Minister that SIS should not operate in Northern Ireland, part of a United Kingdom which was the preserve of MI5. He said with some point that SIS did not operate in England, Scotland or Wales. A bad precedent would be established if it began to operate in Northern Ireland.' Heath was unimpressed by this argument and ordered a reluctant Oldfield to establish a station in the province. Oldfield and his men soon came to realise that Northern Ireland was 'a place apart'.[25]

By the spring, SIS was on the ground, working covertly and overtly within the UK Representative structure. The UK Representative was Howard Smith, a Foreign Office diplomat and former ambassador to Moscow, who invited a senior MI6 officer, Frank Steele, to be his deputy. A very large pipe-smoking Arabist, a veteran of Suez and the Sudan, who had recently been in Nairobi, Steele knew little about Northern Ireland, but Smith considered that he could bring a fresh approach to the post. According to Steele, he was precluded from running agents 'but was expected to use his experience of conflict situations in the Middle East and Africa'. Anthony Verrier, whose main source was also Steele, claims that this included 'covert counter-intelligence operations' which, it was argued, were required to fulfil the need to find a political solution. Steele later said that he concentrated on establishing contacts with the two communities, though he had not been sent to Belfast by Heath specifically to communicate with the IRA.[26]

As regards the intelligence and security situation, Steele found the place 'a shambles'. 'There was very little co-ordination of whatever intelligence was being produced by the RUC, the Army and MI5.' With ministerial support, the army had been carrying out numerous intelligence and covert operations based on their counter-insurgency experience in other parts of the Empire, but with little imagination and negligible success. Using outdated and fairly inaccurate intelligence, on 9 August the army rounded up IRA suspects for internment but, according to Steele, this operation proved to be 'a disaster' which led to increased violence, the escape of many of the IRA's leading members, and a major boost to the movement's recruitment efforts. It is debatable whether or not much usable intelligence was provided by those interrogated afterwards by methods barely short of torture. Heath put a stop to the torture. It seems that White 'misled' the other members of GEN 42 by failing to provide them with details of the special interrogation techniques employed, which included the use of 'white noise' and sleep deprivation. This crude operation had the distinction of uniting the nationalist population and indirectly creating a new, younger, more militant leadership.[27]

By the beginning of 1972 SIS had made little headway and had produced little worthwhile intelligence. The government, however, was under increasing pressure – apparently from politicians in Northern Ireland – 'to talk to the Provisionals'. Steele thought that 'since it was not proving possible to defeat the Provisional IRA militarily, they would at some point have to be talked to'. A previous posting of his had been in Kenya, and he recalled that 'the Mau Mau's operational techniques and their obscene rituals made the IRA look like a Sunday-school choir'. Steele thought that if the British were willing to talk to someone like Jomo Kenyatta, with 'leading members of the royal family willingly shaking his hand, to people like me it seemed just pragmatic to talk to the IRA'. The army and members of MI5 remained hostile to this view, preferring the military option of defeating the terrorists before negotiation.[28]

By the summer of 1971 SIS had concluded that the Provisionals were not in a position to wage an effective guerrilla war and that this should be exposed. Steele quoted Chairman Mao – 'the fish had to be taken out of the water'. Contact was made with Catholic individuals and groups and with the nationalist Social Democratic and Labour Party (SDLP). After a series of clandestine meetings, on 22 June a ceasefire was negotiated to be followed by a meeting with the Secretary of State for Northern Ireland, William Whitelaw, on 7 July 1972, at the home of junior minister Paul Channon. The meeting was attended by Steele, who realised that it was premature. 'The difference between what HMG wanted – peace – and the unrealistic demands of the IRA was too great to be bridged.' The IRA, in the shape of Sean MacStiofain, wanted a British withdrawal within three years. Steele concluded that neither community 'had suffered enough to want peace, to make peace an absolute imperative'.[29]

These initial contacts did, however, give rise to the Sunningdale Agreement of 1 December 1973, which provided a sensible basis for a settlement in the province but which was to fall at the hands of the loyalist extremists responsible for the Ulster Workers' Strike of May 1974. Unfortunately, Whitelaw's officials never gave the same consideration to the loyalists as they did to the republicans. MI6 was never ordered to penetrate their ranks. As Anthony Verrier relates: 'The possibility of converting such men to moderate ways never arose because their place in the scheme of things was never considered. Their organisations and unions, their para-military forces and cabals remained immune from penetration, yet another irony when one considers the zeal with which MI5 and the Special Branch elsewhere in the United Kingdom seek intelligence of allegedly subversive activities.' The reality was that Whitelaw's officials brought to Northern Ireland's issues much of the old imperial outlook. 'The Provisionals were enemies with whom one could fight or negotiate. Belfast's Protestants were beyond the pale.' Steele lamented: 'We entered into something I don't think anyone expected: twenty-five wasted years of killing, maiming and destruction. We may have got fed-up but, contrary to IRA expectations, we have not gone away.'[30]

One of those specially released from internment in Long Kesh and invited to the talks with Whitelaw was Gerry Adams, commander of the Provisionals' Ballymurphy battalion and architect, with Martin McGuinness, the young Provisional commander in Derry, of the strategy of the Armalite and the ballot box. Steele found Adams to be 'a very personable, intelligent, articulate and self-disciplined man' who was 'dangerously effective'. He realised that he had a 'terrific future ahead of him'.

It took another twenty years for MI6 to regain the intiative in exploring the political option. An African specialist, Michael Oatley, who had taken part in the ceasefire arrangements in 1975 and later headed the Service's counter-terrorism desk, met secretly in 1992 with McGuinness to revive the peace process. Although, when the retiring Oatley passed on the mantle to an MI5 officer, he had the support of the MI5 Co-ordinator of Intelligence in Northern Ireland, John Deverell, the process faced near-collapse following the death of Deverell in a helicopter crash. MI5 Director-General Stella Rimington was a hardliner who briefed Prime Minister John Major that McGuinness and Adams were IRA members and could not be trusted. Privately, senior MI6 officers accused their MI5 counterparts of being 'a bunch of idiots' whose efforts had sabotaged the process.[31]

MI6's reluctance to operate in Northern Ireland was partially due to the ministerial constraint on the type of operations it could organise inside a province of the UK. No such constraint, however, appears to have been involved in its operations in the South – a foreign country. Frank Steele left Northern Ireland in 1973 to be Director Middle East. He was replaced by Craig Smellie, recently desk officer for operations in Nigeria. For contacts in the South, Smellie employed a Military Intelligence officer, Maj. Fred Holroyd, who was reminded of Robert Morley when he met the MI6 officer – 'dressed in tweeds with a yellow waistcoat, with a monocle hanging over his lapel, his manner was charming, expansive'.[32]

Although Oldfield was later to disown them, MI6 had been undertaking operations against the Official IRA in the South and had been busy recruiting agents and subagents. The Littlejohn brothers had been recruited to garner not only intelligence about the Officials but also to act as *agents provocateurs* by carrying out bank robberies in their name. The idea had been to provoke the Irish government into taking tough action against the IRA. In October 1972, the brothers were arrested and tried *in camera* in Dublin for a series of bank robberies (Smellie had also asked Holroyd, without success, to take part in bank robberies). Embarrassingly for MI6, Kenneth Littlejohn subsequently escaped from prison and talked to the media about his intelligence connections.

The explosion of two bombs in Dublin on 1 December 1972 aided the passage of an anti-terrorism bill. Although the explosions were initially attributed to the IRA, the Irish Gardai Special Branch presented fragmentary evidence that the bombers had been loyalists aided by British Intelligence in planting the devices. On 19 December, the Irish rounded up an MI6 intelligence network. This included John Wyman, who had recruited an agent within the Gardai, and Andrew Johnstone, First Secretary at the Dublin embassy. Johnstone had seen service in Aden, Syria and, more recently, Cambodia.[33]

The exposure of its operations in the South was a factor in the decision in 1973 to replace MI6 with MI5 in overall charge of the intelligence effort in Northern Ireland. In the handover, MI6 instructed its agents not to divulge their activities to members of MI5. The local station was kept in place, but by the end of the decade there were few MI6 officers in the province. It would take a decade for the intelligence effort to bear fruit through increased use of new technical surveillance equipment, greater penetration of terrorist organisations and better targeting of terrorist operations. MI6 were probably glad to be out of it.[34]

Already close to retirement, in 1973 Sir John Rennie left the Service after his identity was exposed in the German magazine *Stern*, following the widely publicised jailing of his son, Charles, and his daugher-in-law on drugs charges. Rennie was replaced by the natural successor, Maurice Oldfield. 'Moulders', as he was known to his small circle of friends, was the first of the postwar intake to make it to the top. According to Nigel Clive, 'under his leadership, SIS benefited from the good relations he cultivated with both Conservative and Labour ministers at home and from its improved standing with friendly intelligence services with which he kept in personal touch'.[35]

Following the Littlejohn fiasco and a few other well-publicised cases, the new Chief conducted an inquiry into the employment of subagents and 'cut-outs'. Finding that recruitment and control were lax, with subagents used indiscriminately and without any proper risk assessment, Oldfield curtailed many operations, largely to ensure that no further embarrassments would hinder relations with the Foreign Office. Under his stewardship, MI6 closed down the Special Political Action (SPA) section and discarded the paramilitary mission. During his time in Washington, Oldfield had had numerous opportunities to observe the CIA's paramilitary efforts and had not been impressed by such activity. As Chief of MI6, he 'insisted that if an intelligence service was to be respected, it should never confuse the collection of information with sabotage and assassination'. 'Disruptive actions' were continued, but more at arm's length under the umbrella of a 'General Support Branch' which liaised closely with the SAS. A Defence Intelligence Staff (DIS) officer as part of the Defence Liaison Staff with the MoD stationed at Century House arranged the employment and deployment of members of the SAS and Special Boat Squadron (SBS) as 'contract labourers'.[36]

The new Chief's desire for the Service to base its reputation on its ability to gather high-quality intelligence was given a major boost in 1974 when the head of station in Copenhagen recruited Col. Oleg Gordievsky, a PR (political intelligence) officer in the KGB's First Chief Directorate. Gordievsky, who was able to forward information for a period of eleven years, turned out to be MI6's most important catch after Oleg Penkovsky. Importantly for the British intelligence community, the Russian was able to provide the different agencies with a clean bill of health with his confirmation that the KGB had been unable to recruit anyone of any worth within Britain's secret state.

Gordievsky's information was not always well received as it did not fit in with the well-ingrained prejudices of the Service. He was 'often puzzled by SIS's preoccupation with the KGB's modest operational successes' and was concerned that so much time was wasted by his MI6 handlers 'asking questions about agents and penetrations and so on. They didn't ask me elementary questions about politics. I assumed that it was because they knew about these issues, but they didn't.' MI6 had always exaggerated the role of the KGB, and Gordievsky's briefings that 'the Party was the boss. The KGB was the servant, particularly in foreign affairs' were often rejected. His reports, however, were welcomed by Foreign Office officials and the assessment staff, who had long believed that MI6 was 'obsessed with fighting the opposing intelligence service rather than putting more effort into finding out more about the wider world'. The problem was that so much was invested in 'Sovbloc' operations which were regarded by the élite Intelligence Branch officers as 'the route to the top'.

Oldfield had not served in any of the Soviet bloc stations but as a counter-espionage specialist he was not about to upset the balance of the Service's intelligence-gathering targeting. He did, however, have his own agenda, and was determined to streamline the Service. The Requirements Directorate, which was the first point of contact with the Joint Intelligence Committee (JIC), was reorganised along geographical lines, while staff reductions were instigated in the Economic/Industrial and Scientific sections. Surprisingly, the JIC was demanding less general economic intelligence, which suited the Service as few officers had the necessary expertise. At the same time, counter-terrorism became increasingly important and a new joint section with MI5 was created as part of the UK Controller's growing empire.[37]

David Owen, Labour Foreign Secretary from 1976 to 1979, regarded Oldfield as 'a remarkable man' who was 'modest, quiet, unassuming, with a great sense of humour'. When Owen ordered a review of operations and cases referred to him by SIS over a six-month period, he found,

> I must confess, that they were scrupulous and that they had referred the right ones to me and they had been very good in sorting out what was technical detail and what was something which involved political content and required the authorisation of the democratic political leadership . . . I didn't get the feeling that I was dealing with a reactionary bunch of people at all. Dealing with things like South Africa and race, I found them very broad-minded and not by any means the sort of archetypal right-wing figure.[38]

Although Owen thought Oldfield 'an absolute model democrat', the reality was that the SIS Chief had allowed former senior figures and close friends such as George Young to embroil the Service in domestic affairs. While Oldfield assured Prime Minister James Callaghan that the Service 'had not been involved in any nefarious activities', he had privately been using MI6 agents as conduits for damaging anti-Labour stories and insider gossip about the rival Security Service to right-wing journalists. On the back of the alleged MI5 and MI6-backed plots against Harold Wilson, a discreet Cabinet Office inquiry was set in motion during the late summmer of 1976 in an attempt to institute greater control and to change the general ethos of the Service through a reform of the recruitment procedures. Once again, thought was given to combining MI5 and MI6 into one service, with a Director overlording a centralised intelligence group. The proposals, however, were successfully opposed and the promotion of another insider, the 'hawk' Arthur Temple Franks, as the new 'C' in late 1978 was 'recognised as a major defeat for the Whitehall establishment'. Franks did, however, undertake some reforms so that staff meetings became genuine board meetings. He also merged Production and Requirements into a combined Directorate of Requirements and Production, whose head doubled as Deputy Chief. The changes did not, however, prevent one major intelligence failure.[39]

Iran remained for the British an important symbol in the Middle East, and the Foreign Office was careful to veto all political actions that might hinder the flow of oil and disrupt economic relations with one of Britain's major markets for its arms industry. The former chair of the JIC and Permanent Under-Secretary at the Foreign Office, Denis Greenhill, visited Iran in the early seventies and had what he regarded as a 'useful and encouraging' audience with the Shah. He soon realised, however, that there had been 'an appalling failure of Western Intelligence . . . No signs of impending revolution were being identified which would soon sweep away the Shah and change the whole character of the country.'[40]

Like the majority of Iranians, the Shah believed that Britain was behind most of the country's problems, and in an attempt to placate the paranoid autocratic ruler, in the late sixties, the Foreign Office decided to downgrade the MI6 station. The Service was left to rely on SAVAK, Iran's security service, for intelligence, with only a minimal presence within the British embassy in Tehran. The last ambassador before the Shah's fall, Sir Anthony Parsons, would not even permit the limited MI6 presence to use the embassy for spying. In a repeat of the mistake that the Service had committed in Iraq in the late fifties, MI6 recruited among its friends but failed to penetrate or monitor the opposition. It was true that Oldfield saw the Shah regularly when Chief, often meeting in Zurich. His friend Anthony Cavendish reveals that 'Maurice promised the Shah that while he was Chief, SIS would not conduct any internal espionage against Iran or have any direct contact with the Armed Forces' officers or negotiate with the Mullahs', Oldfield later regretted the decision, which he said had been made against his better judgement.[41]

The only sources were people such as former MI6 officer Desmond Harney, who had been the desk officer for the Yemen operation in the early sixties and was now 'an unusually well-informed banker and businessman living in Tehran'. Harney's diary for September 1978 records his view that 'the Iranian establishment can sort out things for themselves . . . and . . . will only dispense with the Shah if they have no alternative'. While he recognised the weakness of the Shah's position and the ending of his modernisation programme, and the formidable nature of Ayatollah Khomeini and his religious class, Harney still allowed himself to hope that 'the good men of the centre would somehow get their act together, or that the half-way house of [Shapour] Bakhtiar might succeed'. By December, he realised that 'the greatest weakness is the defection and flight of the very middle class the Shah built up'. Harney now recognised that he had been 'wrong' and that the chances of stopping a revolution had disappeared.[42]

The irony was that it had been MI6's actions in undermining the nationalist Prime Minister Mossadeq and its role in the 1953 coup – in which Dickie Franks had played a minor part – which had helped to destroy the centre ground in Iranian politics. The Service's reliance in the fifties on special and political operations during the period of the 'horrors' had produced short-term gains but had long-term negative consequences. All too often in the Middle East, MI6 found itself propping up undemocratic, reactionary and authoritarian regimes while finding it increasingly difficult to gather intelligence, particularly in Iran and Iraq. In an indirect way, it turned out that the Service's problems were largely of its own making.

THE SLOW DEATH OF THE COLD WAR

The aftermath of the surprise invasion by Argentina of the Falkland Islands on 2 April 1982 naturally focused attention on the role of the intelligence services. The successive Treasury reviews of the intelligence community had led to a reduction in MI6's global role. There had been two stations in Latin America – one dealing with Portuguese-speaking territories and another with Spanish-speaking ones – but, during the late seventies, they had been consolidated into one station based in Buenos Aires. In 1982 Argentina was regarded as a 'priority for intelligence collection but in a low category', with not many resources available to the local station for the recruitment of agents. As a result much of its reporting consisted of little more than what was in the local press.

As station commander, the experienced Mark Heathcote was 'massively overworked'. The heir to a baronetcy, Heathcote had been recruited in 1970 from the P&O shipping line. Posted to Argentina in 1980, he had previously served in Northern Ireland and Greece. He had a number of high-level sources in Buenos Aires but none was privy to the innermost thinking of the ruling junta. Indeed, intelligence from these sources 'consistently encouraged under-estimation of the Argentine ambitions in the immediate crisis'. In the end, however, MI6 could have done little to rectify the intelligence deficit. The plans to invade the Falkland Islands were made by a secret cell with the majority of politicians, diplomats and even military chiefs unaware of them until the last moment. The December Falkland Islands Review by Lord Franks rebuked MI6 with the patrician criticism that 'changes in the Argentine position were, we believe, more evident on the diplomatic front and in the associated press campaign than in the intelligence reports'.

'A classic Establishment job', in the words of columnist Hugo Young, the Review was completed by Franks with the objective of 'ensuring that Mrs Thatcher's reputation should not be damaged'. But despite the 'bucket of white-wash' that former Labour Prime Minister James Callaghan suggested Franks had chucked at it, the Review did contain significant criticisms of the central intelligence machinery of assessment and requirements which it described as 'too passive in operation to respond quickly and critically to a rapidly changing situation which demanded urgent attention'. In the intelligence world it was difficult to overturn received wisdom which had been established over time, namely that Argentina would not invade until it had exhausted all diplomatic options. It is in the nature of these things that warning indicators tend to be ambiguous. One reform instigated was that the Joint Intelligence Committee (JIC) was removed from the remit of the Foreign and Commonwealth Office and placed under the control of the Cabinet Office.[1]

MI6 Chief Colin McColl later admitted that 'after the Falklands War, when we were quite clearly seen to be too thin – not just there but in other areas as well – we increased our numbers'. South America was immediately given three stations and the number of officers sent abroad and deployed on specific operations was also dramatically increased. In a confidential internal memorandum, a director of the Government Communications Headquarters (GCHQ), Sir John Adye, noted that the Treasury had 'pointed out that spend-ing on intelligence since 1979 had grown faster in real terms than most other areas in public service'. Mrs Thatcher supported the intelligence community more strongly than had any other postwar prime minister, and when the Permanent Secretaries' Intelligence Services (PSIS) committee argued for an increase in budgets she 'passed it on the nod'. During her time in office, spending on the intelligence community more than doubled.[2]

If the impression given was that the Service was expanding its operations throughout the world, the reality was that the Soviet Union was still the focus of its activities. The guiding principle was best summed up by Mrs Thatcher's foreign policy adviser and the new chair of the JIC in early 1985, Percy Cradock, who believed the Cold War 'would go on forever' and who subscribed to the view that Moscow was still intent on 'world domination'.[3]

As BBC journalist and author Mark Urban suggested, intelligence was one of Cradock's driving passions. A China specialist who had served with the JIC during 1971–5 as chief of assessments, Cradock did not suffer fools gladly and used his undoubted intelligence to 'intimidate' analysts. An éminence grise with a classic patrician manner, he did not allow movement in the political atmosphere to alter his view that nothing had changed in the Soviet Union with the election of Mikhail Gorbachev. At their most extreme, his views embraced the theory that the so-called Gorbachev reforms were a deliberate deception, a view shared by Harry Burke, the deeply sceptical chair of the most influential of the JIC offshoots, the Current Intelligence Group (CIG) on the Soviet Bloc. Despite the relatively small size of MI6 (as compared to the CIA) and the British intelligence community in general; Cradock was able to use his powerful domestic position to make an impression on the Americans with his conservative estimates and, in turn, managed to exert indirectly a degree of political influence on President Reagan. Despite the public-relations initiatives conceived to portray MI6 as a thoroughly modern service that had shed its conservative image, the general impression of American diplomats who dealt with the Soviets was that, with MI6, 'you can never be to the right of them'.[4]

Cradock relied on the twenty-five Assessment Staff from a variety of government departments who fed the JIC empire with material. These were CIGs for the Middle East, Far East, Western Europe, Northern Ireland, South and Central America, Sub-Saharan Africa, and the Soviet Bloc, which remained the most important, with functional Groups covering Terrorism, Proliferation, and an Economic Section. Attended by representatives of the intelligence services, each CIG was chaired by a Deputy Chief of Assessments. The Weekly Survey of Intelligence, known as the Red Book, consisted of sanitised assessments that protected MI6 methods and agents. While some ministers avidly read the Red Book, most found its bland style off-putting and the contents disappointing. Responsible for 'ensuring that the Committee's warning and monitoring role is discharged effectively', Cradock's assessments presented one point of view which did not allow for dissenting opinions. These assessments were based on 'facts', Cradock claimed, but British Intelligence had little information on the inner workings of the Kremlin. There was no access to Soviet diplomatic traffic. While GCHQ had managed to break some high-level military communications, that particular stream dried up in the early eighties following the arrest of KGB agent Geoffrey Prime at Cheltenham. There were no successes with major targets such as Soviet missile development and strategic placement.[5]

The assessment system relied to a great extent on the Americans. Mark Urban concludes that 'more than anything else, British intelligence is a system for repackaging information gathered by the USA. Most intelligence relates to foreign or defence policy, most of that intelligence is sigint [signals intelligence], and the vast majority of sigint processed at Cheltenham had been obtained from the USA.' Urban estimates that between 80 and 90 per cent of material flowing to the JIC is derived from the NSA–GCHQ axis. A similar situation applies to much of MI6's own information, which relies to a great extent on signals intelligence-gathering. This explains why so much effort is devoted to trying to impress the Americans, though, as Urban notes, they are increasingly uninterested. Similarly, ministers who bothered to read smudged reports on fax-like paper from MI6's Weekly Summary of Intelligence, the CX Book, were rarely impressed. David Mellor, minister of state at the Foreign Office, described them as 'humdrum'.[6]

With around 2,400 staff in 1985, MI6 divided its officers into a General Service and an Intelligence Branch. Those serving in the Soviet Bloc section of the Intelligence Branch regarded themselves as the élite, even though, with the exception of Oleg Gordievsky, the Service had failed to recruit high-quality agents. Gordievsky was a star prize, but being the KGB '*rezident*' in London was not as productive as being in place in Moscow. Even so, 'with Gordievsky it meant that MI6', according to David Boorman, Chief of the Defence Intelligence Staff (DIS), 'was able to exploit everything that he meant in terms of exerting sensible leverage with the CIA'. Foreign Secretary Geoffrey Howe found Gordievsky's material 'an important part in shaping our own strategy'.[7]

In November 1981, as part of Operation RYAN (Nuclear Missile Attack), a joint KGB–GRU initiative, amid Kremlin fears that President Reagan and the West were preparing a surprise nuclear attack, the KGB issued a telegram to all its stations in NATO countries with a requirement that they look out for any signs of preparation for a first-strike nuclear attack. Based in London, Gordievsky kept MI6 informed on Ryan and supplied many documents to his controller. On 17 May 1985, however, the Soviet First Secretary was summoned back to Moscow. The telegram was viewed as suspicious, but Gordievsky's MI6 controller did not believe that he had been betrayed by a mole inside the Service. In fact, the KGB had a senior agent in the CIA, Aldrich Ames, who, as Chief of Soviet Operations, was providing the Soviets with the names of the West's star agents. Ames is regarded as the prime source, though he has denied being responsible for Gordievsky's betrayal.[8]

Ames later stated that by the early 1980s

> I was really beginning to change how I perceived the Agency and intelligence. We were getting really good – I mean first-class – political information about the Soviets. We also had our spy satellites sending us back intelligence. What the data kept telling us was that we were disproportionately stronger than the Soviet Union and the Warsaw Pact, that Soviet forces couldn't compete with us. The bottom line was that, with only the minor exceptions, we were consistently superior militarily. It didn't matter whether we were talking about our bombers, our nuclear warheads, our megatonnage, our missiles, we were light years ahead of them. The Soviets' only military advantage was more men. We consistently drew a picture of a Soviet Union that never would decide to fight a war against us. And yet, decade after decade, the political leadership in both parties ignored that

intelligence. They were committed to running around screaming, 'The Russians are coming! The Russians are coming!'. I
knew that much of what I was doing was for nothing and I
began to realise it was just part of a silly game.

Ames concluded that the illusion was sustained because it was the easiest
way for the Agency to justify its existence to the public and politicians.

Writing under the *nom de plume* 'Alan Judd', novelist and former MI6
officer Alan Petty, in reviewing Peter Earley's book on Ames, *Confessions of
a Spy*, dismissed the American traitor as a social inadequate. 'He was an
incompetent and slipshod spy and would have been caught long before had
the CIA not been equally slipshod in its approach to personnel security. It
had all the right rules and procedures but did not apply them, which meant
that Ames walked unheeded from his office with carrier bags of documents,
avoided serious questioning of his new-found wealth and was never properly
called to account for his drunkenness.' The Ames affair left deep wounds
with its echoes of Philby. The Commons oversight committee on Intelligence
and Security later found that 'it is unacceptable that two years after a major
betrayal, the Americans have still not provided the UK agencies with a
detailed read-out of the damage Ames did to UK assets and agents'. The
report went on to express concern that some information from other sources
was probably 'tainted' and that MI6 had not started considering the matter
until November 1995. 'Judd' balanced his criticisms of MI6's American
'Cousins' with an acknowledgement that during the eighties the CIA had
indeed penetrated the Soviet system high and low.[9]

In July 1985, Mrs Thatcher ordered MI6 to arrange Gordievsky's 'exfiltration' from Moscow. On the 19th he left his wife and children and secretly
took a train towards the Finnish border, where he was met by MI6 operatives.
In the boot of a car, the Russian traitor was smuggled into Finland, then
flown via Norway to London. Gordievsky was debriefed over a number of
weeks at Fort Monkton by MI6's leading 'Sovbloc' analyst, Gordon Barrass.
Using information gathered from Gordievsky, during September the Service
distributed among British and American policy-makers a fifty-page briefing,
'Soviet Perceptions of Nuclear Warfare'. A copy was read by President
Reagan, who immediately responded by toning down his 'Evil Empire' rhetoric, thereby helping to lessen Soviet paranoia and fears of a Western first
strike.[10]

Eight months later, Gordievsky was proudly paraded at an MI6 conference on developments in the Soviet Union held at Century House and
attended by senior Foreign Office officials and officers from the other security
and intelligence services. Gordievsky was indifferent towards the political
shift that appeared to be taking place inside the Soviet Union, and suggested
that President Gorbachev could not be expected to deliver radical change.

At a similar event at the Fort, Gordievsky met the chiefs of staff and helped sell MI6's interpretation, which shared Cradock's vision of what was happening inside the Kremlin. It was an important example of where the Service was more than a mere collector of intelligence, as it is often portrayed. Here it performed a major analytical role. Nevertheless, this was a time when intelligence had to take second place to political interpretation and personal intuition. Charles Powell, who, as Mrs Thatcher's private secretary, was influential on foreign affairs, later remarked: 'I don't think intelligence as such played a big role in our view of Gorbachev.' While Mrs Thatcher subscribed to the evil empire interpretation of Soviet affairs, she also famously believed that the Soviet President was someone with whom she could do business.[11]

Mark Urban rightly points out that while the 1989 Defence White Paper, in considering the Gorbachev reforms, took account of 'fundamental and irreversible' change in the Soviet Union, the intelligence chiefs continued to protect their own territory. The MI6 mindset prevented it from viewing events in eastern Europe and the Soviet Union objectively, and the Service was caught unawares when, on 10 November 1989, East German border guards began dismantling the Berlin Wall, the symbolic end of the Soviet empire.

What became apparent even to narrow-minded officials was that western intelligence had grossly overestimated the size of the Soviet economy and its defence expenditure. MI6 recognised that the military took the biggest slice of the country's research and development budget but, according to an MI6 officer, 'we had no idea just how wide the gap was between the military and civilian sectors'. In May 1988, Michael Herman, a former head of GCHQ's J Division, which was responsible for the Soviet bloc, who was attached to the JIC in the mid-seventies, told the US Army War College: 'It will be surprising if history does not point to more overestimates than underestimates . . . it is more satisfying, safer professionally, and easier to live with oneself and one's colleagues as a hawk than a wimp.' He added that 'Western intelligence has claimed a special responsibility to lead thinking rather than to follow it. It can hardly duck responsibility if its worst-case conclusions have been propagated and used.' This was particularly so since the overestimate of Soviet military spending had a direct effect on the levels of British defence budgets. What was worse for MI6's reputation was that journalists reporting from Moscow had accurately predicted that Gorbachev was on a collision course with his military.[12]

Throughout the eighties it became increasingly evident that the British contribution to the 'special relationship' was meagre. As a world-class organisation capable of delivering up-to-date intelligence, the Secret Intelligence Service was increasingly reliant on American willingness to share its raw assessments. Such generosity was, however, dependent on Britain's ability to share the burden in policing the world. Almost since the beginning of the Soviet occupation of Afghanistan in December 1979, MI6 and the CIA had been supporting the mujahedin. Mrs Thatcher had authorised MI6 to undertake 'Disruptive Actions'.

MI6 supported one of the hardline Islamic groups commanded by Ahmed Shah Massoud, a young commander in the Panjsher valley, close to the main road from Kabul to the Soviet frontier, where he helped run operations against Soviet supply lines. MI6 sent an annual mission to the rebels consisting of two MI6 officers and military instructors. The most important contribution was help with organisation and communications through the supply during 1982 of several tactical radios made by Racal. Former senior MI6 officer Daphne Park later revealed that MI6 helped to retrieve crashed Soviet helicopters from Afghanistan.[13]

Under Project 279, Short's of Belfast were commissioned in the spring of 1986 to supply the CIA with three hundred Blowpipe missiles and later a further three hundred when the US began shipping the more modern Stinger. The missiles were used by the anti-Soviet Afghan rebels to shoot down a number of passenger planes and later became an acute embarrassment, as they presented a potential terrorist threat to the West. In 1996 it was reported that the CIA had spent more that £70 million in a belated and often bungled operation to buy back the remaining missiles, which had proved to be a lucrative commodity for the rebels on the black market.[14]

There was close co-operation between Britain and America over the invasion of Kuwait by Iraq, but the episode served only to emphasise the gulf between the capabilities of the two nations' intelligence services and the subservience of MI6 to its Atlantic partner.

In an echo of events thirty years previously, a JIC report of 26 July 1990 indicated that there was cause for concern over intelligence that Iraqi tanks were being unloaded around Basra. This was amended by Cradock the following day in a report to the Prime Minister, in which he put the argument that the Iraqi leader, Saddam Hussein, was possibly preparing for limited aggression after diplomatic moves had been exhausted. This did not, however, include the view that he was preparing to invade Kuwait, and certainly did not indicate that things might escalate so quickly. It was made clear, however, that if the Iraqis did invade then the Kuwaiti army would not be able to hold its position. While the assessors had excellent intelligence on the movement of Iraqi tanks, there was no intelligence on Saddam's thinking. Hostilities were foreseen, but not an invasion. Mrs Thatcher considered the Iraqi manoeuvres to be mere 'sabre-rattling'.[15]

Despite its long history of involvement in the Middle East, MI6 had neglected the area, preferring to concentrate its resources on the Soviet bloc, with the result that it had few high-class officers in the region and even fewer sources and agents. There were no agents-in-place in Baghdad. With a 'rising star', David Spedding, on the regional CIG (Middle East), following the invasion scores of MI6 officers were tasked with gathering intelligence on the Iraqi leadership. The effort was a dismal failure, and those in receipt of the morsels gathered often 'preferred to read the newspapers which proved to be quicker and more in-depth'.[16]

According to Mark Urban, more as a 'political gesture' than a real objective, MI6 planned Disruptive Actions aimed at supporting the Kuwaitis and destabilising Saddam. A training camp was set up in Saudi Arabia for Kuwaiti volunteers, with weapons training from members of the SAS. This was planned as a small-scale operation, but it soon became apparent that the volunteers were not qualified for guerrilla warfare and were unprepared for intelligence-gathering in Iraqi-occupied territory. More successful was the Defence Advisory Group, a joint MI6–MoD committee which co-ordinated psychological warfare operations. Videos and cassettes were smuggled into Iraq, while a radio station, Free Iraq, incited the population to revolt. These efforts were largely unsuccessful partly because of ill-defined political objectives and the lack of experienced psy-war specialists. More distressing was that no material aid was delivered to the Iraqis and Kurds who had been encouraged to revolt. As a result, thousands died while Saddam was able to consolidate his grip on the country.[17]

The intelligence generated for Desert Storm by the Americans through their vast array of technical means – signals, satellite and photographic facilities – was immense, but it proved difficult to manage. Commanders at the top had access to good intelligence but little of it found its way down to the field. In addition, the need for security and the existence of long-standing agreements ensured that vital intelligence was often not shared with coalition partners. Britain's contribution was small, and it was made abundantly clear by American officials that the US ran the intelligence show.

Christopher Curwen, a South-East Asia specialist who had followed the traditional route to the top through postings to Geneva and Washington, had been regarded as a 'safe pair of hands' as a Chief, while his successor, Colin McColl, who took over in November 1988, was chosen to give a more dynamic lead as someone prepared to instigate change. McColl needed to sell the Service to a sceptical Whitehall, knowing that MI6 had to reconsider changing its priorities with new tasks. He set in motion a review of the Service's activities which continued throughout 1989. While the need for change was recognised, there was the traditional degree of resistance, since a number of senior officers, such as Barrie Gane, who as Director of Requirements and Production was McColl's effective deputy, and Gerry Warner in the key post of Director of Counter-Intelligence and Security, belonged to the old Sovbloc élite who agreed with Cradock's assessment of the continuing Soviet threat.

Cradock, like the other intelligence chiefs, refused to believe that the Cold War had ended and propagated the idea that the Communist Party was still in charge and capable of imposing a hardline communist doctrine. Such fantasies were only finally consigned to history following the 1991 Moscow coup and the outlawing in late August of the Communist Party. Despite the collapse of communism, Cold War attitudes refused to die, and MI6 continued to devote disproportionate resources – nearly 37 per cent of its budget had been targeted on the Soviet threat – to undermining the Russian intelligence service. In the summer of 1990, Gerry Warner had been appointed the Co-ordinator of Intelligence Security in the Cabinet Office, and the officer taking over his role of Director of Counter-Intelligence and Security had been tasked with recruiting with renewed vigour key members of the former KGB, now known as the Sluzhba Vneshnie Razvedaki (SVR). By exploiting defections and offering cash incentives, Mark Urban notes, the Service was eventually swamped with 'walk-ins'. With Controller Sovbloc becoming Controller Central and Eastern Europe, MI6 played a central part in rolling up a number of Russian intelligence networks in western Europe. As a result of the economic collapse and the greater freedom of movement available, new opportunities opened up, and increased attention was paid to inserting 'deep-cover' officers into the disintegrating Soviet Union.[18]

In December 1990, in the first visit to the intelligence headquarters of a former enemy in eastern Europe, two MI6 officers accompanied by an MI5 officer travelled to Budapest. This was quickly followed by visits to other former communist states where tentative agreements were reached on liaison and training. A number of MI6 stations in eastern Europe, beginning with Poland and Czechoslovakia, were subsequently transformed from espionage bases into liaison centres with reduced personnel, while the station chief was declared to the host country's security service.

An August 1992 study by the Institute for the Study of Democracy at Georgetown University in Washington, *The Foreign Service in 2001*, noted that 'the traditional rule of thumb in intelligence gathering was that 90 per cent of the information policy makers needed was openly available. Diplomatic reporting was charged with gathering and analysing this "overt" intelligence. The remaining ten per cent, it was argued, could only be obtained covertly by the intelligence community.' The study found, however, that 'the dramatic softening of hard intelligence targets and the willingness, even eagerness, of former adversaries to share once jealously guarded information has changed that rule-of-thumb ratio. Information on munitions factories and oil fields once obtainable only with expensive satellites or eavesdropping equipment might now be had for the price of a train ticket for an embassy officer or for a lunch with a Western businessman.' It concluded that 'the recent "Open Skies" agreement dramatically simplifies photographic intelligence collection, while the demise of the Warsaw Pact reduced the frequency with which photos need to be taken. The abolition of the East German and Czech intelligence agencies and the retrenchment in the KGB and others eliminates whole sets of targets and threats.' In the Baltics, where the SVR had no intelligence agreements with the new governments, MI6 used the opportunity to construct a 'bridgehead', recruiting new sources and agents for operations in Russia and also installing listening stations covering Russia and Ukraine.[19]

In October 1992 attempts were made to set up with the SVR similar arrangements to those pertaining in central and eastern Europe. Two Russian working groups visited London to discuss agreements on co-operation on areas of mutual concern but, according to MI6 sources, while the meetings were 'long on atmosphere' they were 'short on substance'. It took another two years before the two services openly discussed joint operations against organised crime and for there to be formal liaison with the station head in Moscow openly declaring his presence. In the meantime, much to the anger of their hosts, MI6 continued to run operations in Russia to recruit sources and agents.[20]

In 1992, the Russians expelled chief of station John Scarlett, who had a reputation in western intelligence of being one of the best of the 'Russia men'. Four years later, Scarlett's successor, Norman McSween, was also expelled following his exposure on Russian television, in which he was shown waiting to meet an agent. His expulsion led to four junior personnel leaving Moscow, including two MI6 officers. McSween had been the handler for a junior Foreign Ministry clerk, Platon Obukhov, who was arrested in April 1996. Leaks from MI6 in the British press suggested that Obukhov had been a valuable agent, but he turned out to have been less than reliable. A fantasist who penned lurid crime novels, he had been in constant trouble with his superiors. His parents said that their son was psychologically disturbed and suffered from psychopathic tendencies, with paranoic and epileptic symptoms. At the same time, Vadim Sintsov, who worked in the arms industry and was recruited by British Intelligence, confessed to being paid more than £8,000 for feeding MI6 with information about Middle East arms sales. Most of his contacts with his controllers had taken place outside Russia, confirming standard MI6 operating practice.[21]

Though there were undoubted successes, MI6 also had a reputation for abandoning without adequate psychological support those agents it had squeezed dry. Victor Markarov had been a KGB lieutenant working in Directorate 16, which analysed the codes of foreign embassies. In 1985, he volunteered his services to MI6, providing information on the deciphering of Canadian, Greek and German telegrams containing information on NATO and the European Union. MI6 promised to 'extricate' him and his wife from the Soviet Union, but before he could escape, in July 1987 he was denounced by a friend and arrested. Markarov was subsequently sentenced to ten years' imprisonment in a labour camp in the Urals. Released in 1992, he made his way to Latvia, where at the British embassy he met two MI6 officers, 'Sean' and 'James Cantwell', who arranged his passage to Britain. Unfortunately, life in the West proved a distinctly unhappy experience. Incarceration had left him suffering from 'serious depression and psychological problems'. Markarov received a Service pension of £11,000, but he was isolated and unable to cope, and in 1997 was still requesting support from MI6.[22]

Following the fall of the Berlin Wall, British, US and German intelligence officers organised a joint operation to take advantage of Soviet confusion and to steal Russian military secrets. As the 340,000 Soviet troops and 9,000 tanks stationed in East Germany trudged back home, at least 600 Red Army officers defected, hoping to trade their specialised knowledge for a life in the West. Set up in May 1991, the clandestine German-American Operation GIRAFFE involved bribing dozens of Soviet army officers, sometimes with consumer durables, which included second-hand Ladas. There were separate interrogation rooms for German, US and British military intelligence personnel. A retired intelligence officer who took part in the debriefing recalled that 'many had very valuable information to pass on, things that none of our counter-intelligence people knew anything about. We were very grateful. We made them promises. We looked at them, smiled at them, gave them a cup of coffee and a cigarette, and lied to them.' He admitted that these people had been 'deceived and misled. They were squeezed dry of everything they knew and then discarded.' But not before they had handed over military plans, codebooks, aircraft technology and even a T-80 tank. According to German reports, the operation soon descended into anarchy, with independent operations running outside of central control.[23]

The British had been invited to take part but did not have access to all the material gathered. They therefore decided to buy their way in. MI6 paid three German agents involved in Giraffe more than £20,000 for their share of 'Sovmat' secrets. Discovering what was going on, the Germans became angry that MI6 was sanctioning 'James Bond'-style operations in Bavaria. A contact from the German BND intelligence agency, code-named 'Haescher', had been assigned to buy Soviet weaponry from disaffected Russian soldiers and was passing information on to the MI6 Berlin station chief, Rosemary Sharpe. An experienced officer who had previously served in London, New Delhi and Brussels, Sharpe was monitored in October 1995 meeting with 'Haescher' at a Munich hotel. Further allegations followed that three BND officers, led by the agent code-named 'Assinger', embezzled money from a joint BND–MI6 slush fund and transferred the money to accounts in the Cayman Islands. Bonn remains irritated by the refusal of MI6 and the CIA to keep it informed of their operations on German soil.[24]

Senior MI6 officers were jubilant with their success against their former adversaries and made sure that their rivals were aware of it. Based on information extracted from eastern European archives, from 1993 MI6 began supplying the French DST security service with the names of more than three hundred Foreign Ministry employees suspected of working for the former communist bloc. While this present was superficially impressive, it seems rather irrelevant and could be deemed a waste of resources. With the collapse of communism such activities had become something of a game taking place in an enclosed, rarefied world with little relevance to real life: an expensive game paid for by the taxpayer, who saw little benefit.

Having completely dominated the intelligence community, Cradock, who had stood down as chair of the JIC in June 1992, remained smugly proud of its perceived achievements. MI6, however, had not foreseen the end of communism and Mrs Thatcher's foreign policy adviser, Charles Powell, viewed this as a major intelligence failure. 'It caught us completely on the hop. All that intelligence about their war-fighting capabilities was all very well, but it didn't tell us the one thing we needed to know, that it was all about to collapse. It was a colossal failure of the whole Western system of intelligence assessment and political judgement.'[25]

THE NEW AGENDA

In contrast to the enthusiasm shown by Mrs Thatcher, Prime Minister John Major was less inclined to use intelligence, while Foreign Secretary Douglas Hurd rarely based his judgements on it.

During Major's time a formal Cabinet Intelligence Services Committee was created with responsibility 'to keep under review policy on the security and intelligence services', but ministers continued to have little time or say in the overview, being, in the main, ignorant of the intelligence world. Most decisions were left to officials, with the result that the Cabinet Secretary, the Joint Intelligence Committee (JIC) chair, Roderick Braithwaite, and Intelligence and Security co-ordinator Christopher Curwen 'had greater discretion over matters affecting the agencies'. Major was, however, more willing to let a little light into the proceedings, and on 6 May 1992 he officially admitted for the first time to the House of Commons the existence of the Secret Intelligence Service (SIS). Later that week, the MI6 station chief in Washington rather absurdly announced his position to the bemused senior staff at the embassy. The Intelligence Services Bill, published on 24 November 1993, also set up a very limited oversight committee under the chair of former Secretary of Defence Tom King, a loyal if stolid Tory MP. Conducted within the Whitehall ring of secrecy, its activities proved to be an embarrassing failure compared to the efforts of its American counterparts. Its independence is not helped by the fact that one member, Baroness 'Meta' Ramsay, is a former senior MI6 officer.[1]

Throughout the nineties the JIC saw a quick changeover in its chairs. A former ambassador to Moscow, Braithwaite had no great regard for MI6 analysis or 'soft intelligence', believing that much of its political reporting was the preserve of the Foreign Office. Peter Lever was 'a tough Whitehall operator' who was expected to restore intellectual rigour to the JIC. With staff numbers of around twenty, and Foreign Office and MoD personnel on four-year secondments, the JIC continued to suffer from a lack of in-depth specialist knowledge. Lever was seen as 'a powerful figurehead with the political muscle to ensure that the JIC remains independent of the warring factions in the different branches of the intelligence community'. His successor, a high-flier from the Foreign Office, Pauline Neville-Jones, who was viewed as 'shrewd, quick and vivacious, with a penetrating analytical intelligence', was in the chair for an appointment even shorter than Lever's.[2]

MI6 Chief Sir Colin McColl was loath to go down the same route of oversight as the Americans, and in his only public statement observed that

> secrecy is our absolute stock in trade, it is our most precious asset. People come and work for us, risk their lives for us some-times, risk their jobs often, because they believe SIS is a secret service . . . It is also very important for the people who help us abroad – and there is a difference here, I think, between us and the Security Service because our most important constituency is abroad . . . I am anxious that I should be able to send some sort of signal to these people that we are not going to open up everything, we are not going to open up our files, we are not going to allow ourselves to be undressed in public with their name as part of our baggage.

Despite these words, McColl did try to sell the Service, and took to meeting newspaper editors at Century House for lunch and opening channels to the media through his assistant Alan Petty. In addition, McColl used a new unit, Information Operations (I/OPs), consisting of twenty officers, to brief 'friendly' press contacts and especially defence correspondents.

The truth is that the Service has been willing to release information when this suits it and has put its own spin on stories, which rather undermines its claim to secrecy and that it is responsible only for intelligence-gathering and does not indulge in analysis.

McColl had been expected to retire in September 1992 and be succeeded by Barrie Gane, but the Chief reluctantly agreed to stay on and oversee changes, particularly the move into a new headquarters, and to fight for the Service's corner in the expected expenditure cuts following the end of the Cold War. McColl decided that the Service needed radical surgery. In May 1992, he proposed a plan to ministers which was agreed in July. In what became known as 'the Christmas Massacre', senior officers were told of their fate a month before the changes took effect in January 1993. Older directors and a whole layer of management were replaced or offered early retirement. With most directors now in their forties, the Service had 'the youngest senior management of any intelligence organisation in the world'. Around twenty officers or 5 per cent of the Service's Intelligence Branch were also cut. A non-Sovbloc officer, David Spedding, took over from Gane as Director of Requirements and Production. The idea was that this influx of young turks would 'make MI6 more capable of dealing with a changed environment and more flexible to cope with the challenges of the future', its priority now being the provision of intelligence, with 90 per cent of its resources devoted to intelligence-gathering. The initial result was a high turnover of directors, which produced unsettling change.[3]

Changes included closer co-operation with the Service's traditional rival, the Security Service (MI5), including the establishment of joint sections to cover the Middle East and Russia, particularly in the area of terrorism, and a shared research and development department so that 'for each piece of offensive equipment designed by the scientists for MI6, a defensive system is made at the same time for MI5'. Changes to the internal budget allocation indicated that besides traditional concerns and administration up to 15 per cent was now spent on Russia, 15 per cent on the Middle East, including aspects of the proliferation of weapons of mass destruction, 5 per cent on China and Hong Kong, 4 per cent on Argentina, 10 per cent on counter-terrorism, 10 per cent on proliferation generally, 10 per cent on the former Yugoslavia, 5 per cent on southern Africa, 5 per cent on counter-narcotics, and 5 per cent on money laundering.

By 1993, Iran had become the Service's number-two target, though there was little or no success in recruiting intelligence personnel or senior government figures. MI6 had had to rely on a number of dubious agents for its intelligence, and in the process had been willing to see them flout the law. In the mid-eighties, MI6 asked an Iranian-born arms dealer, Jasmed Hashemi, to arrange contracts with Tehran in order to monitor arms sales to Iran and, in particular, details of weapons that were threatening western shipping in the Gulf. The Service even transferred £250,000 into his account as a down payment on a false end-user certificate, in direct violation of the government's guidelines banning weapons exports to Iran and Iraq, for the purchase of £350 million worth of Chinese Silkworm missiles. The missiles were shipped to Iran in 1987, with other deals for heavily armed motor boats and 155mm ammunition sanctioned by MI6. Hashemi had broken off relations with MI6 in 1993 and was eventually arrested on fraud charges in August 1997. He was finally released from prison in February 1999 after, as the *Guardian* revealed, a deal was agreed which prevented information on MI6 operations from being disclosed in court. The judge stated that Hashemi would have been jailed for longer had it not been for the 'valuable information' he had supplied to British Intelligence.[4]

India and Pakistan were particular targets, of some importance for the American allies, but, similarly, proved difficult to penetrate. Indeed, MI6's coverage of these two adversaries was reliant on satellite-derived intelligence from the Americans, but even this failed to predict the series of nuclear tests that took place in May 1998. The Service had its sixty stations abroad reduced within a year to fifty-one, reporting to six controllers in London. According to *Sunday Times* journalist and author James Adams, within the Service the 'buzz' word was 'capacity' rather than 'presence'. MI6 wanted to be able to insert people into any country at short notice rather than retain expensive, permanent assets on the ground. A more flexible Service was desired which could respond to crisis and new threats. Treasury-led cuts in late 1993 put the Service back to the pre-Falklands era with a small cut from 2,400 personnel to 2,303 in 1994.[5]

During the first reading of the Intelligence Services Bill, the Lord Chancellor, Lord MacKay, revealed that MI6 is involved in protecting the economic wellbeing of the country by keeping 'a particular eye on Britain's access to key commodities, like oil or metals ... the profits of Britain's myriad of international business interests ... and the jobs of a great many British people, are dependent on the ability to plan, to invest, and to trade effectively without worry and danger'. The Service had formed an Economic Section within the Requirements department in the late eighties, though it suffered, despite MI6's historical closeness to the City, from a lack of suitably qualified personnel, as officers still regarded the Soviet threat as the centre of action and the way to promotion.[6]

Useful commercial intelligence collected and collated by MI6 is passed on to Britain's major companies, including City banks, defence exporters such as British Aerospace (BAe), the oil companies BP and Shell, and other global companies such as British Airways, code-named 'Bucks Fizz'. MI6 supplies 'CX' reports to corporate 'liaison officers' who rewrite them as memos for restricted internal distribution. Defence companies are among the most important recipients of CX reports. Former MI6 officer Richard Tomlinson told *Sunday Business* that in 1993 MI6 helped BAe win the controversial £500 million deal to sell twenty-four Hawk training jets to Indonesia by supplying details of a competing bid from French aircraft manufacturer Dassault. Similar intelligence was passed to BAe to help it win orders for Tornado fighters and Hawks as part of the £1.7 billion Malaysian defence package, which was linked to the Pergau Dam affair and the £234 million worth of aid sanctioned for a huge hydroelectric project. Former special forces operative and MI6 and MI5 agent Stephan Kock, who was a consultant to the Midland Bank's secretive defence finance arm, was at the centre of the defence package.[7]

There was, and it seems is, little or no incentive to target Japanese business, which has had an active interest in gathering technical and economic intelligence. The Japanese Ministry of International Trade and Industry and the

External Trade Organisation regularly use Japanese diplomats, trade organisations and intelligence services to assemble vast amounts of foreign information, nearly all of it from open sources, for translation and distribution to
Japanese companies. MI6 is too concerned with dealing in 'secret' information, neglecting what is sometimes called the 'Mossad rule', which states
that taxpayers' money should not be wasted on intelligence that could just
as well be found in a newspaper or official reports.

MI6 had developed a new agenda, known as Global Tasks. It combined the
desks dealing with terrorism, major crime such as drugs trafficking and
money laundering, and counter-proliferation of weapons of mass destruction
such as chemical, biological and nuclear weapons. Increasingly, there was
co-operation with GCHQ, which provided much of the intelligence.

In late 1989 increased attention began to be paid to the proliferation of
weapons of mass destruction, but it was not a high priority, with only two
officers working exclusively on the subject. The desk mostly kept a 'watching'
but not an active brief on proliferation, aided when necessary by experts
from the MoD, with resources committed only when tasked by the JIC.

With a wide range of agents and assets in the arms industry and among
weapons dealers – though it was all too ready to jettison its informants at
the first hint of trouble – in the period immediately before the Gulf War,
MI6 gained substantial intelligence on Iraq's production of weapons of mass
destruction. Indeed, the small number of officers dealing with Iraq reported
that they were 'swamped' by the flow of intelligence. Prime Minister John
Major believed that this created its own problems when the analysed reports
were passed on to ministers. He later informed the Scott Inquiry that

> the total number of intelligence reports is indeed huge. The
> amount of intelligence reports reaching the Foreign and
> Commonwealth Office, for example, would be around 40,000 a
> year ... Split down, about two-thirds GCHQ and one-third
> SIS, they would be of varying grades. Some of that intelligence
> would be extremely valuable, others not so. Quite a strong
> filtering process is needed. It is clearly absurd that ministers
> should read 40,000 pieces of intelligence, but it would be filtered
> through the appropriate machinery and, where intelligence was
> thought to be relevant, validated and reliable – reliable being a
> key point – the officials would endeavour to put that before
> ministers.

While it was undoubtedly true that ministers were expected to read a
considerable amount of paperwork, assessment staff argued that MI6 had
used this as an excuse for its own intelligence failures over Iraq. The Service
had failed to push the intelligence and sell it to ministers.[8]

Richard Norton-Taylor, one of the few journalists to attend the hearings of the Scott Inquiry, reported that

> witness after witness described how crucial intelligence reports were ignored, forgotten about, mislaid, withheld from ministers, or misinterpreted. It was difficult to know whether or not civil servants responsible for distributing intelligence reports to decision-makers in Whitehall were incompetent buffoons or devious manipulators. Whitehall, it seemed, learned nothing from the last inquiry into intelligence failings – the Franks Report.

The Scott Report later criticised the way MI6 had handled the 'Supergun' affair, aka Operation BABYLON. Scott said that in drafting an explanation in November 1990 to the JIC chair, Percy Cradock, on whether or not the Service had had intelligence on the Supergun, McColl had 'misled' Cradock by claiming that there had been confusing reports on its military application when, in fact, 1988 briefing notes 'lent no support to the view that there had been any confusion'. MI6 had been 'the principal hound in the hunt to uncover details of the Iraqi long-range project'. The Service had information on the 'monster' barrels by October 1989 but had not told the Foreign Secretary. The Chief had tried to cover up his organisation's failure to pass on vital intelligence.[9]

In Britain, James Adams suggests, 'intelligence is equated with secrecy, and a secret is only to be revealed to those in government with a need to know'. This often means that specialists are denied access to reports with the result that analysis is weakened and provides what the Scott Inquiry saw as 'tunnel vision'. Scott demonstrated that, time and time again, officials who needed to know most were denied access to intelligence reports because they had not been cleared by Whitehall's cumbersome vetting procedures. Even when the required intelligence did reach ministers it often failed to impress. Foreign Secretary Geoffrey Howe recalled that the intelligence reports may, 'at first sight', look 'to be important and interesting, and significant', but when 'we check them, they are not even straws in the wind. They are cornflakes in the wind.' Foreign Office minister David Mellor added that intelligence reports did not contain 'shattering information . . . They were significantly less riveting than the novels would have you believe. They weren't as interesting the metal boxes marked, "Eat after reading". They didn't tell you all you wanted to know about life.' Those dealing with Iraq often thought that they were better informed by journalists' accounts than the secret reports they received from the JIC and MI6, which lacked qualified technical and scientific input, and grossly underestimated military spending and weapons development in the Middle East.[10]

It became almost a mantra that intelligence analysis was bedevilled by poor co-operation and lack of communication between departments and other services. Another foreign minister, William Waldegrave, admitted that the conflicting evidence had been 'a constant problem with intelligence over the years'. He knew that information 'had gone into the state machinery' but 'did not come out in the right place'. Alan Clarke blamed the problems upon the 'obsessive possessiveness' of the intelligence services. Former senior Foreign Office officials responsible for liaising with MI6 warned of the risk 'in ministers and leaders and top officials becoming absorbed into a culture where secrecy comes to be confused with truth and where, after a time, contact is lost with earthly awkwardness'.[11]

After the Gulf War, counter-proliferation was seen by the Permanent Secretaries' Intelligence Services committee as a major target, and the Cabinet agreed to MI6 committing resources to it, with intelligence on the subject being collated by a special Current Intelligence Group within the JIC empire. The Service set up a new unit with a small staff – fewer than ten people, mostly recruited on permanent secondment from the MoD and the Defence Intelligence Staff (DIS). MI6 took on particular expertise from the DIS, though it had difficulty assigning suitably qualified technical officers from within its own ranks, with few having any knowledge of nuclear physics. The unit's targets corresponded to the Foreign Office Non-Proliferation Department's 'countries of concern' – Cuba, Egypt, India, Iran, Iraq, Israel, Libya, North Korea, Pakistan and Syria – which had refused to sign the nuclear non-proliferation treaties. Ballistic missiles were also a particular target. In 1994, the MoD assessed that there could be a direct missile threat to Britain from a Third World country within ten years. Critics claimed that the threat had been deliberately exaggerated to justify the continuation of defence programmes made redundant by the end of the Cold War.[12]

The Service's record in this area is not particularly impressive. Despite the presence of a large station in Pretoria, MI6 had no knowledge of South Africa's nuclear weapons programme. This is astonishing given that intelligence liaison owed a great deal to the British requirement for South African uranium. Likewise, the Service knew nothing about Israel's nuclear programme (nor its missile and chemical (CW) and biological (BW) weapons research), largely because it was reliant for intelligence on the Americans, who were secretive about dealings with their client state.[13]

There has certainly been an element of the intelligence services using proliferation as a means of filling the gaps in their tasking. Science writer Tom Wilke's assertion rings true: 'What could be more attractive to intelligence agencies hungry for new business after the end of the Cold War than to reactivate their networks in the former USSR in the cause of non-proliferation?' What is really required to tackle proliferation, Wilke suggested, is 'patient diplomacy, negotiating international agreements to control the spread of nuclear material. It is politically unsexy business, which would involve compiling inventories of all the plutonium ever produced and ensuring that it is properly accounted for.' He concluded that 'if we do not want plutonium to bring about the end of civilisation, then we must look not to the spy but to the nuclear accountant as the guardian of our future'.[14]

That similar proffered advice had been partially absorbed by the agencies was suggested by their concern over plutonium smuggling, which led MI6 to join with the American, French and German intelligence services in giving teeth to investigations by the International Atomic Energy Agency (IAEA). Links with the IAEA were strengthened following the Gulf War when the agency was criticised for failing to monitor Iraq's nuclear weapons programme. Co-operation was formalised in March 1994 when, as a clearing house for intelligence used in the fight against smugglers, an international database was set up, paid for by the Americans. In truth, of a thousand reported incidents over a four-year period, only six warranted in-depth investigation. The most publicised incident occurred during the summer of 1994 when German police in Munich arrested three men from Moscow with thirteen ounces of plutonium. It was only later that this success was exposed as a Bundesnachrichtendienst (BND)-inspired intelligence sting, known as Operation HADES. Ironically, the only country known to have lost weapons-grade uranium is the United States, which 'lost' a large quantity in the sixties. It is believed to have ended up in Israel. While it is true that terrorists with a degree in physics would probably have little difficulty in designing a workable nuclear bomb, the practicalities would be beyond any known group as it would require large, expensive and highly sophisticated facilities to engineer to the necessary high specifications.[15]

When MPs on the Foreign Affairs Select Committee tried at the beginning of 1995 to discuss nuclear proliferation, they were denied a briefing from MI6, despite having received information from the CIA and the Russian Federal Counter-Intelligence Service. All that the then Foreign Secretary could admit was that the work of MI6 was 'very sensitive stuff'. Douglas Hurd tried to fill in any gaps in the MPs' knowledge and acknowledged that Iran was regarded as the greatest danger and that an assessment agreed with the Americans suggested that it would take Iran from seven to fifteen years to construct a nuclear weapon.[16]

MI6 had also targeted Iran, along with Iraq, Syria and Egypt, for information on their chemical (CW) and biological (BW) weapons programmes, though, again, not always successfully. MI6 did not have the necessary specialists to study the problem of CW and BW, and this led to a gross overestimate of Soviet stocks and the erroneous belief that such weapons had been stockpiled in eastern Europe. The Russian Federation stated that it held 32,300 tonnes of chemical weapons, but the Service refused to accept a figure that was later officially recognised as accurate. The Service did gain accurate information on the Soviet biological programme when, in autumn 1989, the

Director of the Research Institute for Especially Pure Biological Preparations in Leningrad, Vladimir Pasechnik, defected to the West. He revealed that in contravention of the 1972 Biological Weapons Convention, to which the USSR was a signatory, a biological weapons programme had been developed under cover of the Ministry of Health, as Biopreparat.

The South African biological weapons programme remained a well-guarded secret which proved difficult to penetrate. With the election of Nelson Mandela, the British and American governments applied pressure to shut down the programme, but the need to support the new President meant that full disclosure was not allowed. Efforts were made to stem the possible recruitment of South African scientists by the Libyans, who offered huge salaries to help initiate a Libyan biological weapons programme which increasingly became the target of MI6 and CIA covert operations.[17]

The intelligence agencies claimed that Tripoli was a centre for CW and BW research, with Iraqi scientists working on weapons production. They admit, though, that they had no hard intelligence to back up the claim. Using rather dubious sources and often unreliable intelligence information, politicians and journalists have a tendency to overplay fears of CW/BW, creating unnecessary panic reactions. As MI6 knew through its well-placed sources on the Soviet biological programme, for all the millions spent and the huge resources placed at the disposal of Biopreparat, the problem of developing biological agents as weapons had never been solved. Having such biological agents is one thing; having a delivery system in which the agent is effective is another. Unfortunately, this aspect always appears to have been of limited interest to MI6. Despite the rhetoric, there is little real evidence that Iraq has solved the problem either.[18]

A former MI6 officer has alleged that the 'bread-and-butter work' of the Service's psychological warfare I/Ops section is in 'massaging public opinion into accepting controversial foreign policy decisions'. In particular, he cited 'the plethora of media stories about Saddam Hussein's chemical and biological weapons capability' – the 'ante was upped so that there would be less of a public outcry when the bombs started to fall'. In early 1998, when British and American forces were preparing to attack Iraq if Saddam did not fulfil pledges on UN inspection of presidential sites, MI6 received or invented intelligence that there were Iraqi plans to smuggle anthrax into Britain in bottles of duty-free perfume and spirits. A CX report to that effect was passed to the JIC. It was nonsense but fitted into a pattern of disinformation. While intelligence officers spread details of Iraqi weapons of mass destruction – 'Iraq could produce up to 350 litres of weapons grade anthrax per week – enough to fill missile warheads ... a long-range missile in a year and a nuclear weapon in five years' – American intelligence briefings to US staff and diplomats abroad indicated that Iraq's biological and chemical warheads, if they existed, were 'very ineffective'. The duty-free story followed on from a series of similar MI6-inspired yarns which were released into the public domain – including one by Foreign Secretary Robin Cook about a sixteen-year-old boy who had been imprisoned by Saddam's regime since the age of five for throwing stones at a mural portrait of the Iraqi President – in an attempt to justify Britain's support for the December bombing of Iraq.[19]

It became apparent only in early 1999 that Iraqi concerns about 'western spies' were largely justified. MI6 officers operating under cover had been concealed within the UN Weapons Inspectorate teams monitoring chemical and biological weapons development within Iraq. MI6 first infiltrated the Inspectorate soon after it was formed in 1991, with officers rotated through the teams. The Foreign Office was initially against the idea, believing that it would compromise the integrity of the Inspectorate. However, help from the American, British and Israeli intelligence communities was provided after the inspectors found the Iraqi concealment of its research far more elaborate than anticipated.[20]

Such compromises are not unique. In the early nineties, a Cambridge-based housewife, Joy Kiddie, who had acquired an international reputation as a 'fixer', was asked to set up a deal to supply Iran with what she believed to be medical chemicals. MI6 believed that Kiddie offered a unique opportunity to infiltrate Iran's chemical weapons programme and, in 1994, merchant banker 'Alex Huntley', aka MI6 officer Richard Tomlinson, was assigned to the counter-proliferation department and tasked with infiltrating Kiddie's circle of business friends. According to Tomlinson, 'Mossad, German intelligence, Polish intelligence and the CIA were also involved'.[21]

Through the connections of Michael Palmer, a senior London solicitor with offices in the Middle East and close links with MI6, Tomlinson was 'placed' in a trading company in Mayfair which employed a Kiddie associate suspected of trading with Iran. He was subsequently told about Kiddie's friend, a flamboyant wheeler-dealer, Nahoum Manbar, regarded by Israel's Prime Minister Binyamin Netanyahu as the greatest traitor in his country's history. The former Mossad agent, whose company, Mana International, had an office in Warsaw, was accused of supplying via false end-user certificates the technology and material that could help Iran to produce mustard and nerve gas. At his trial in 1998 on charges of 'collusion with an enemy', Manbar insisted that he had been operating with the full knowledge of Israeli and British Intelligence. Israeli companies with the sanction of the Defence Ministry had, indeed, sold military equipment to Iran during the 1980s and 1990s. Manbar, who had formally stopped trading with Iran in 1993, following American pressure, was sentenced to sixteen years' imprisonment.

It was revealed that Manbar had been using his Iranian contacts to discover the whereabouts of Ron Arad, an Israeli pilot taken prisoner in southern Lebanon in 1986, whose fate had become a *cause célèbre*. Kiddie had been asked by Manbar to help trace Arad and, as part of the deal, find supplies of chemicals for Iran, which would then release the Israeli. Sixty tons of chemicals were shipped from China to Iran, but MI6, which according to Tomlinson knew about the shipments, did nothing to stop them, even though documents indicated that Iran was planning a weapons plant. Aware that this was part of an Israeli deal to release Arad, instead of exposing a scam potentially as big as 'Iran-Contra', Tomlinson claims that in April 1995, with the approval of a senior Cabinet minister, MI6 planned to co-operate with the Iranian project. It would continue to supply materials, even though it risked giving Iran a chemical weapons capability. MI6 argued that the risk was outweighed by the possibility of discovering what the Iranians were up to 'on numerous other subjects'.[22]

Proliferation is now regarded as one of the principal reasons for the continued existence of agencies such as MI6, though insiders acknowledged to James Adams that little can be done to prevent developing countries from acquiring a nuclear capability and building chemical and biological weapons. This is particularly so when they are helped or a blind eye is turned by the agencies themselves.[23]

MI6 had set up an international counter-terrorism section in the mid-seventies and began to co-operate closely with its rival, the Security Service (MI5), in targeting the IRA abroad. When, in the mid-eighties, the Service moved into the criminal justice system by providing help and information on terrorism to the police, observers had warned of the dangers of unaccountable and secret intelligence officers being involved in the process. The warnings were not heeded, and it took until 1999 and a case at the Court of Appeal for the full danger to become apparent.

In February 1989, a Conservative foreign minister had approved a scheme by MI6 to stage-manage the unlawful deportation from Zimbabwe of leading IRA 'fixer' Nicholas Mullen. An MI6 officer told the Zimbabwean intelligence service that Britain wished to avoid 'becoming involved in complicated extradition proceedings'. MI6 officers stated that 'the ideal would be for Mullen to be arrested shortly before the departure of a direct flight and put aboard it. A stage-manager's skills would be essential here . . .' Officers also ensured that Mullen was denied access to a lawyer, to avoid the risk that the Zimbabwe authorities 'would be pressured into deporting him elsewhere'. In February 1999, after serving nearly ten years in prison for his role in an IRA bomb-making factory in London, Mullen was freed by the Appeal Court because of the failure to use the correct procedure of extradition which had rendered his conviction unlawful. Information about Mullen's deportation had been deliberately kept hidden from the original trial, while a meeting of intelligence, Foreign and Home Office personnel and police had agreed to stonewall questions from MPs. Lord Justice Rose said: 'The conduct of the security services and police in procuring the unlawful deportation of the appellant represents, in the view of this court, a blatant and extremely serious failure to adhere to the rule of law.'[24]

It was not until the aftermath of the Gulf War that there was a concerted effort by MI6 to counter global terrorism with a new era of international co-operation, oddly when Middle East terrorism as a threat to Britain has all but disappeared. Official figures show that incidents of terrorism continue to fall, while casualties in the West are lower than at any time since the early seventies. Despite this, risk and terrorism forecasting and analysis are a growth business, with the debate dominated by conspiracy theories, often generated by elements of the intelligence services.

During the Cold War, an influential group of right-wing ideologues in the intelligence world believed that terrorism was ultimately controlled by the Soviet Union; a view expounded at length by Claire Sterling in her 1981 book *The Terror Network*. The book was widely publicised by right-wing think-tanks and taken on board by politicians such as Al Haig and Reagan. In reality, there was no intelligence to back up this assertion, and MI6 and the CIA knew that when the Soviets did sponsor terrorism it was always 'opportunistic'. Such dissenting views from MI6 never officially surfaced. Today western intelligence specialists argue that the Iranians have taken the place of the Soviets. According to one such American specialist: 'What Tehran is doing today is no different from what Moscow was doing twenty years ago, and we should see the problem in those terms.'[25]

There is a temptation to fall into the same trap that snared the West in the seventies – the belief that there is an all-embracing Islamic fundamentalist conspiracy behind Middle East terrorism. The official view is that such a conspiracy does not exist. During the summer of 1993 British Intelligence prepared for the Foreign Office a paper, 'Islamic Fundamentalism in the Middle East', which looked at the reasons for the proliferation of fundamentalist political groupings, some with an international following, and the idea that there is a possibility of 'contagion', with their leaders meeting in Europe, South-East Asia, Khartoum and Tehran. The anonymous author reported that 'the coincidental rise of fundamentalism across North Africa and the Levant has certain common factors. But the main causes are internal. It breeds on failure to resolve economic and social problems, corruption in government and the bankruptcy of political ideologies – Communism, Nasserism, Baathism, etc. It is prevalent in overcrowded cities plagued by poverty and unemployment.'

He noted that

> the Iranians are peddling mischief throughout the region. Private Saudi and Gulf money donated for Islamic causes is a common factor in much of the region. The absence in Islam of a clear divide between the spiritual and the secular and between

state and religion enhances Islam's potential as a focus of opposition, offering a ready-made ideology emphasising social
justice. Fundamentalist groups can offer effective welfare
services to the poor which the state cannot match. Endemic
problems (limited resources, economic growth rates unable to
keep pace with demographic pressures) will continue to provide
a fertile breeding ground for fundamentalism.

It was recognised that

fundamentalism is not necessarily synonymous with political
radicalism or anti-Western policies. The fundamentalist groups
advocating violence and revolution are in a minority. Nevertheless, there is a strong anti-Western streak in all main political
fundamentalist movements in the region. Western, particularly
American, culture and materialism are seen as a threat to Islamic
values. The fundamentalists' wider objectives are more or less
incompatible with Western liberal principles – they are opposed
to political pluralism, religious tolerance and women's rights.
They will continue to oppose an Arab/Israeli settlement. They
are prepared to use the ballot box to gain power. But there is
every doubt that these 'parties of God' would subject their political authority, once achieved, to further the democratic process.

The author concluded that

fundamentalism does not present a coherent and monolithic
threat to Western interests in the way that Communism once
did. It is not supported by a superpower. Its appeal in Western
countries is confined to Muslim minorities and the threat of
subversion is, in the UK at least, minimal. Dealings with
extreme fundamentalist regimes would be highly unpredictable
but not necessarily unmanageable. Some countries which are
vulnerable to fundamentalism would have out of economic
necessity to maintain working relations with Europe (e.g.
Algeria which depends totally on exporting oil and gas to
Europe).

The essential message is that the West has to deal with the underlying problems rather than fundamentalism itself. Unfortunately, this message continually gets lost in the mix of poor intelligence, political spin and disinformation
which finds its way into the media.[26]

With the end of the Cold War, the threat of terrorism has declined and
the main 'terrorist states' – Libya, Iraq, Syria and Iran – have in recent years
curtailed their sponsorship of terrorism. Iran remains, in American eyes,

the funding body and power behind many terror organisations, the State Department believing that Tehran funds groups to the tune of $100 million a year. There is little evidence to back up the claim, but foreign policy concerns have ensured that the JIC has fallen into line and targeted Iran as the main threat to the West. Naturally, relations with Iran have been at a low level since 1989, when Ayatollah Khomeini called for the death of author Salman Rushdie following the publication of *The Satanic Verses*, which was condemned as blasphemous. There was also a concern that the Iranian Ministry of Intelligence had been supplying weapons to the IRA, though no evidence of delivery was proven.[27]

The Americans and British were reluctant to share intelligence on international terrorism with Germany because of its links with Iran. Iran has proved to be a lucrative market for Germany, with trade links dating back to the turn of the century; Bonn is also owed a considerable sum by Tehran for unpaid imports. The Americans have been increasingly 'irritated' by the European attitude to Iran and Germany's intention of pursuing a separate agenda of 'critical dialogue', which appears to have borne some fruit. It was known that in 1993 the head of Iranian Intelligence had visited BND headquarters in Munich. There followed leaks about an Iranian Europe-wide terrorist network which was alleged to be run from the third floor of the Iranian embassy in Bonn. Other stories in 1996 claimed that terrorist camps had been built in Afghanistan and were full of Europeans ready to launch a wave of terrorist attacks throughout Europe using purpose-built 'supermortars' specially developed for terrorist operations. Fifteen of these weapons were said to have been dispatched to terrorist groups, including the IRA. Fears were roused that Iran had built up an arsenal of biological and chemical weapons – even that 'stockpiles could already be in place in western capitals'. During the summer there were reports that the Iranians were 'prepared to use them'. In 1997, western intelligence agencies suggested that Iran's intelligence service was about to export the Islamic revolution to Africa. It was building up a terrorist network in order to attack 'soft' western targets in Africa.[28]

Newspaper reports smacked more of disinformation than any recourse to reliable information. The Germans insist that there is no direct evidence of Iranian involvement in international terrorism. Iran does attack its opponents and the campaign, using hit squads, has been bloody, leading to the murder of a number of dissidents exiled in the West. Iran does not, however, appear to target western Europe for terrorist attacks. While isolated actions by private individuals and groups are entirely possible, even Salman Rushdie is now safe from state-sponsored action. Today's terrorist groups are disparate, with different motives and ideologies, and share no central control. The majority are resolutely national, even local, often small and provide only a domestic security problem, with few transnational groups worthy of MI6's attention. Many western countries have recognised the change and have downgraded their counter-terrorism capabilities. Ironically, co-operation between national intelligence agencies is better than ever.

The reality is that the minimal terrorist threats to Britain arise out of a slavish devotion to a deeply reactionary American foreign policy on the Middle East and, in particular, its role as Washington's only military ally in the Desert Fox attacks on Iraq. British Intelligence had paid little attention to the activities and followers of Osama bin Laden, but following the terrorist bombing of the American embassies in Dar es Salaam and Nairobi in August 1998, the Saudi extremist has become a priority for MI6. It is, however, all too easy to demonise a target – 'The Global Terrorist', as the *Sunday Times* dubbed him – who is, after all, a creation of the CIA and MI6. They were perfectly happy to secure his support and train and arm his supporters during the covert war to drive the Soviet Union out of Afghanistan. Inevitably, there followed a 'disposal problem' – what to do with thousands of highly trained guerrilla fighters. As one British official admitted: 'We did worry then about these wild bearded men. But there was a lot of naivety around.'[29]

When the late terrorism expert Richard Clutterbuck was asked in 1994 to address a conference entitled 'Terrorism in Europe', he advised the organisers: 'Frankly, there is hardly any terrorism left in Europe. I suggest you change the subject of your seminar to drug trafficking.' They did.[30]

Following government concern, in 1988 MI6 had set up a Counter-Narcotics Section positioned within Requirements and Production. It was primarily responsible for tracking heroin shipments originating from Pakistan, Afghanistan and Iran, and cocaine from Colombia. MI6 officers do not gather intelligence with a view to prosecution, but to assist other agencies such as Customs and Excise and the Serious Fraud Office – not always in harmonious co-operation. There are many competing agencies in the counter-narcotics field, with intense rivalries producing confusion about roles and missions. A series of leaked stories on successes in this area cannot hide the fact that, as most specialists agree, there is little likelihood of stemming the tide of drug imports.

Colin McColl persuaded Whitehall mandarins that the Service should extend its counter-narcotics work into the area of serious crime, including money laundering or 'funny money'. At a press conference in 1993, McColl said that 'individual law-enforcement agencies can sometimes benefit from the wider look and the further reach that a foreign intelligence service has when it comes to uncovering illegal networks which operate across frontiers'. Primarily, he argued, because 'there is a tendency, I think, for bad men to operate where they think they are safe, and if we can help to reach out into some of those places we can help the law enforcement agencies in not only this country, but other countries as well'.

MI6 funds are said to have been allocated to 'fighting drug trafficking in the eastern Mediterranean and a new policy of direct action, including the use of special forces to intercept shipments, has been agreed'. John Major had sanctioned the deployment of the Special Boat Squadron (SBS) for this express purpose. MI6 had also begun working closely with GCHQ on the project, using new software designed to track money from one country to another and to delve into bank accounts. The in-house lawyer to MI5 and MI6, David Bickford, claimed that London had become the money-laundering capital of the world, with up to £200 billion in drug receipts flowing through the City as a result of the decision by President Clinton to freeze the assets of the Colombian drug cartels. The introduction of sanctions against countries that tolerate money laundering was expected to cause 'chaos in financial markets'.[31]

With regard to Russia, MI6 had been principally concerned with her weapons of mass destruction and arms sales. There was, however, now increasing concern about organised crime, and the JIC tasked the Service with monitoring the activities of the 'increasingly powerful Russian crime syndicates', commonly referred to as the Russian 'Mafia' (*Vory v zakone* – 'thieves within the code'). Gangsters, a number of whom were former KGB officers, were said to be laundering dirty money, acquired through drug trafficking, prostitution and extortion and fraud operations, on a 'grand scale in London'. Computer scientists who were once privileged members of the élite Soviet military-industrial complex were developing software devices known as 'sniffers' or 'trojan horses', which are capable of breaking through 'triple electronic firewalls' to access global networks. Such huge sums of money were involved that, 'within a few years, it could threaten the stability of the Western banking system and the integrity of our financial institutions'. One estimate from the Bank of England claimed that £2.4 billion was being laundered annually through Britain's financial system. These intelligence-generated figures are hard to reconcile with the sober assessment of the City's Joint Money Laundering Steering Group, which has stated that London has 'one of the strongest anti-money laundering systems in the world'. The amounts laundered were considered to be relatively small and described by City banks as 'chickenfeed'.[32]

That is not to suggest that money laundering is not a serious problem. It is, but it is becoming increasingly difficult to differentiate between disinformation and hard fact, and the intelligence and security services are quite happy to blur that distinction in the interest of retaining and developing their own little empires.

In 1995 the police National Criminal Intelligence Service (NCIS) produced a report on the Russian mafia in Britain, 'Ivan 1', which concluded that the lurid tales of racketeering, drug trafficking, prostitution and gunrunning had no real substance and did not pose a significant threat. A second NCIS report, 'Ivan 2', also concluded that while there was some evidence of Russian activity, it was not enough to justify the headlines. In the spring of 1996, the NCIS changed its tune. Following a meeting in London of European criminal intelligence officers, the NCIS claimed that Russian and eastern European crime organisations were linking up with major British criminals in money-laundering operations and illegal drugs.[33]

The head of Interpol, former senior Special Branch officer Raymond Kendall, said in June 1996 that 'The Cold War is over: the most dangerous threat to a nation's security comes from organised crime. Europe is now one vast criminal space, from the Atlantic to the Urals. We must fill that space with effective policing to fight the modern criminal. We are saturated by drugs and the money involved is staggering.' David Bickford has suggested that organised crime gangs be treated like rogue states: 'Many transnational criminal organisations have a formal governing structure and are economi-cally stronger than most UN states. There is every reason, therefore, to treat criminal gangs as organisations, not as individuals.' Tony White, responsible at the UN in Vienna for targeting the international drugs trade, and former head of the drugs branch of the NCIS's International Unit, acknowledged that criminals could be prosecuted for drugs trafficking but not for mafia activity, which hindered operations. 'There is no offence under UK statute of "being engaged in organised crime", or of "being an organised criminal". The emphasis then should be on offences for which we may hope to appre-hend, charge and convict those involved.'[34]

In the end, White concluded, drug trafficking could only be stopped by using draconian measures that no democratic state would be willing to impose. The reality was that the public were willing to accept 'tolerable' levels of drug abuse. White added in early 1997 that the fashionability of the term 'organised crime' had been essentially driven by dogma and political expediency.

Whatever the facts are concerning the Russian mafia, and whether or not these assessments are justified or manipulated for political purposes, MI6 was increasingly talking of the 'growing complexity and economic strength of organised crime'. The Service was supporting the NCIS with covert attempts to penetrate groups to gain insight into their modus operandi. It had also developed a counteroffensive and was said to be involved in 'direct action' – 'infiltrating mafias, hunting down gang bosses overseas and even breaking into bank accounts in foreign countries to recover millions of pounds in "dirty money"'. Britain is said to be a key player in this 'war' co-ordinated by a series of international intelligence committees established in the wake of the G7 summit of western leaders in Lyon, in July 1996, which put forward a plan to deal with transnational crime.[35]

MI6 has not been the only service attempting to carve out a new role based on organised crime. In early 1997, the MoD's Defence Research Agency produced a secret study, 'BA 2000', which looked at the idea of using special forces to help in customs operations, particularly those requiring pursuit of suspects. It considered the possibility of expanding the special forces' role into organised crime, the drugs trade and international terrorism, and foresaw them being involved in 'operations with obscure goals, not necessarily between nation states, armies or soldiers'. This may be entirely laudable, but as one intelligence official noted, an unusually cavalier attitude appears to surround this new era of covert action: 'We are one of the very few countries in the world to have legislation that allows us to work aggressively overseas.' He added: 'We take the view that stealing money from a crook is a good thing and if it's from an account in a foreign country, who cares? We are hardly likely to be sued, and anyway there are no fingerprints to lead back to us.'[36]

Based on his own experience with the NCIS, Tony White admitted that attempts to defeat drug traffickers by confiscating their assets have not lived up to expectations. 'The total amount of cash actually confiscated has been of nothing like the order envisaged and is only a tiny percentage of the profits calculated to accrue from the illicit drugs trade in the UK.' He added that rivalries remain between the different agencies and called for the creation of a multi-agency national financial investigation and intelligence service. What is required, he argued, is a police-based agency that links into transnational agencies such as Europol rather than *ad hoc* arrangements engineered by secret intelligence agencies.[37]

Despite these warnings from professionals in the field, in late August 1997, while on a trip to Malaysia, Labour Foreign Secretary Robin Cook launched a new all-out war on the 'scourge' of drugs. He stated that substantial resources would be made available and that MI6, MI5 and GCHQ would spearhead the operation, which would concentrate on intelligence-gathering. A senior Foreign Office diplomat had already been appointed in London to co-ordinate the anti-drugs drive while £42 million had been spent during the year on countering drug trafficking. A 'refocused' MI6 would use more officers from its Global Issues Controllerate for deep-cover operations to monitor trafficking routes from Afghanistan, where opium production had soared from 40 tons in 1980 to 2,800 tons in 1996, and the 'golden triangle' of Burma, Laos and Thailand, which produces the bulk of the world's heroin. Officers would also mount long-term penetration operations against Turkish, Russian and Colombian criminal organisations, but only in support of the NCIS and Customs. This was a curious initiative given reports in late 1997 which revealed that cuts to the budget of the NCIS were said to be reducing its effectiveness. Officers complained that the intelligence and security services were able to spend large amounts on the drugs problem, unscrutinised. They were increasingly forced to seek the help of MI6 and MI5, with combined anti-drug budgets of £63 million, because they were starved of funds.[38]

The police complain that giving MI6 a greater policing role places areas such as drugs trafficking off limits to democratic accountability. The Police Foundation's Barrie Irving has argued that such policies are 'short-sighted'. MI6 contends that it needs 'to operate in secret. But once you change the role to criminal justice you blur the distinction between state security and criminal justice. It seems unconstitutional to conduct policing in this way.' The break in tradition with the appointment of a senior MI5 officer, John Alpass, to the key role of Intelligence and Security Co-ordinator in the Cabinet Office was a sign that – following vigorous lobbying from the former head of MI5, Mrs Stella Rimington – the crime agenda for the intelligence and security services had taken hold within Whitehall.[39]

Robin Cook appeared to have learned little from the American experience. Having spent billions of dollars on attempting to control the supply of drugs, the State Department has admitted that the number of addicts is increasing. The drugs war has already been lost and the emphasis has to be on prevention and treatment programmes.[40]

The Secret Intelligence Service, which had previously lived in the shadows with few people aware of its physical presence, suddenly emerged into the light on 14 July 1994 when its new headquarters at Vauxhall Bridge was officially opened by the Queen. Designed by architect Terry Farrell, who had no idea of its intended occupants, the slightly weird-looking but highly prominent building cost more than £240 million and required another £86 million for substantial modifications to suit the Service's needs. The expenditure and high annual running costs have been criticised by the Commons Foreign Affairs Committee, while the Foreign Office resented having to shoulder the financial burden of the move from its own budget. For *Guardian* columnist Hugo Young, the new headquarters was a sign that MI6 still had clout in Whitehall.

> The arrival of the secret world on the banks of the Thames ... has very little to do with greater openness. It pretends to demystify their world, and make us more comfortable about them ... But we are not ... These agencies' emergence into the high-rent district signifies not their waning sense of self-protection but their growing power. They are not afraid to announce their central role in government.[41]

Evidence that, despite Britain's uncertain role in the world, MI6 is still viewed as a major national asset by Whitehall mandarins was provided by Sir Michael Quinlan's unpublished study on Britain's 'foreign intelligence requirements and capability', and financial systems and administration, for the Permanent Secretaries' Intelligence Services Committee. A former permanent under-secretary at the MoD, and director of the government's conference centre at

Ditchley Park, Quinlan found his report, which was neither wide-ranging nor in-depth, generally dismissed as a 'bland report' which eschewed the radical options most observers had expected. It left things as they were and went little beyond praising MI6 as a national asset 'tasked' by ministers and the JIC to 'further' Britain's foreign and defence policies.[42]

From September 1994 changes to the internal structure were considered by MI6's management under its new Chief, David Spedding, the first to come from outside the Sovblock empire. During 1995, major reorganisation took place, with the Controllerates for the Western Hemisphere and Far East merged into one, as were Africa and the Middle East, reverting to the situation that existed in the late fifties. Iran and Iraq remained top priorities for information on weapons of mass destruction, though the Service relied on one officer in Israel, which actually has a large stockpile of such weapons, for liaison duties. Global Tasks became a Controllerate in itself, while Operational Support became a department tasked mainly with assisting officers in overseas deep-cover operations.

Quinlan's report had acknowledged that officially GCHQ could not be regarded as a 'British' national asset since it is so reliant on the US for its input (and, no doubt, indirectly its funding). His report was followed in January 1995 by a study of GCHQ on behalf of the Prime Minister, undertaken by the chair of Smith Industries, Roger Hurn, with representatives from MI6, MI5 and the MoD, with a remit to study the role, mission and management of the agency. Cuts of 30 per cent were proposed in the 6,500 staff and in the £500 million budget. The Hurn study called for much more specific targeting of intelligence-gathering, with GCHQ being forced to develop closer ties with MI6 – responding to requirements set by the Service. It was noted that the DIS was the largest centre for analysis of the raw information gathered by GCHQ and MI6. In June, led by anglophile Les Aspin, a US commission undertaking a similar exercise on the National Security Agency (NSA) travelled to London to meet with the heads of the British intelligence community and learn what changes the various services had undertaken since the end of the Cold War. The British explained that changes in methods of operating would improve GCHQ's product, with better and more cost-effective production of intelligence. The reality is that technological advances and cheap cryptography mean that it is becoming increasingly difficult to obtain the type of intelligence that GCHQ spent most of the Cold War gathering.[43]

It was unintended but the report, and later proposals for rationalising GCHQ stations into a new headquarters and closing most stations abroad, provided more evidence for those who argue that MI6 and GCHQ, now led by Francis Richards, a former Foreign Office director for Defence and Intelligence (the main liaison post with MI6), should be amalgamated into one intelligence-gathering agency. The Foreign Office, in particular, was concerned that this would entail a loss of influence with the Americans. The promotion of Richards after the unprecedented change of two new directors in a year – David Omand became Permanent Secretary at the Home Office, and Kevin Tebbit, also a key liaison figure with MI6, is now Permanent Secretary at the MoD – is an obvious sign of Foreign Office sensitivity on this issue, particularly as senior US intelligence officials have been scathing about the British contribution. Britain does not have the funding to compete at the level at which the Americans operate, with much of GCHQ's budget needed to update its expensive computers and other essential equipment.

The British could not afford to build and operate an independent satellite, Zircon, and, instead, had to negotiate an agreement whereby Britain contributes £500 million to the NSA to keep it in the intelligence club through access to information from the second-generation Magnum satellite, launched in 1995. The decision to continue with the American programme was taken despite French efforts to involve fellow Europeans in their own spy satellite project. With its expertise in the Ariana rocket programme, France committed itself to building and launching an expensive photographic satellite code-named Helios II, a radar image craft known as Osiris, and the sigint project Zenon, designed to loosen Europe's dependence on US technology. France wanted EU countries to develop the satellites as a 'necessary precondition for achieving strategic autonomy' in the intelligence field. Outdated ideas of national security prevented co-operation and participation by Britain. Initially supportive, Germany has not offered full co-operation owing to budget restrictions, but has said that it will rejoin the project when conditions allow.[44]

The Americans were upset by the German overtures to the French, which were regarded as a snub since the NSA was sharing its satellite intelligence. The German authorities, however, had become incensed during 1996/7 by the increasingly active role of MI6 and CIA agents in their country, in particular the CIA's blunt attempts at economic espionage. German anger increased because the British and Americans often refused to share with them non-military intelligence, with – to Germany's fury – MI6 and the CIA still regarding German Intelligence as 'leaky'. The aggressive tactics of the American agencies have also provoked the French. Even though it is not a full participant in the satellite project, Germany is being given access to French political and economic secrets – France is systematically eavesdropping on US and other countries' telephone and cable traffic via a network of listening stations – as part of a joint intelligence exchange agreement aimed at rivalling the Anglo-American alliance. In late 1998, the new overseer of Germany's intelligence services, Ernst Uhrlau, called for the 'harmonisation' of Europe's intelligence agencies as part of the 'logical development' of the EU.[45]

It is a maxim of intelligence that there are no friendly intelligence services, and MI6 has been known to target its European partners. Ten officers in the UKB Unit at MI6 headquarters had been running Operation JETSTREAM which directs economic espionage against France, Germany, Spain, Italy and Switzerland. Former MI6 officer Richard Tomlinson, who revealed the details of the operation, said: 'When I saw the requirements, I was astounded. Many of the countries in the list are supposed to be allies, especially our European partners.' In Switzerland, MI6 targeted the big private banks, including UBS, by paying staff to supply information from bank accounts, particularly of overseas clients.

As part of Jetstream, in 1995 a network of bogus companies was set up throughout Europe purporting to publish technical journals, with officers posing as journalists and businessmen offering consultancy advice. MI6 used one front company as a cover for penetrating French naval bases and gathering intelligence on France's capability for tracing nuclear submarines. Officials and defence specialists were duped into providing open source information for which they were generously paid. The idea was that they would then talk about their area of expertise to consultants who were, in fact, undercover MI6 officers. The Service's interest in Europe has not been all one-way, though. One EU official in Brussels admitted that researchers spent many hours tracking down information on the US defence budget from behind an 'iron curtain' of secrecy. At the same time, it had access to other information from its 'friends', a traditional euphemism for MI6.[46]

According to Tomlinson, another Jetstream operation involved the recruitment in 1986 of a British spy, code-named Orcada, in Germany's central bank, the Bundesbank. The agent's handler during 1993–6 was Andrew Mitchell, who operated under commercial cover at the British embassy in Bonn. In a letter posted on the Internet, Tomlinson wrote that Orcada 'is a German national . . . His motive is entirely financial and he is paid very substantially. Indeed, he is among the best paid and most important of any of MI6's agents. He provided regular and detailed information on the German position during the Maastricht Treaty negotiations.' He also handed over inside information on Germany's proposed interest-rate movements. MI6 passes on such sensitive intelligence to several clearing and merchant banks, including the Midland, alleged by Tomlinson to be 'a complete MI6 bank', the Royal Bank of Scotland and Kleinwort Benson. Tomlinson adds that 'the primary intelligence requirement against Germany . . . is economic intelligence', and such spying is 'accorded the same level of secrecy and need-to-know indoctrination as highly sensitive Russian casework'. MI6 officers were 'aware that this work would be deemed illegal under European law and has not been authorised by parliament'. Following Tomlinson's disclosures, the German authorities launched an official investigation.[47]

Generally, for domestic political reasons, British politicians have been unable or unwilling to conduct inquiries into the funding and relevance of MI6 on the basis of a realistic assessment of Britain's position in the world and as

part of the EU. Questions concerning these major foreign policy issues and
the status of an intelligence service in what is a medium-ranking state are
carefully avoided. British policy circles are still obsessed with the country – as
Douglas Hurd put it – 'punching above its weight', which requires extensive
intelligence-gathering capabilities. They have never shaken off the all-too-
accurate jibe of former US Secretary of State Dean Acheson that Britain had
lost an empire but had not found a new role. Whether or not a New Labour
government which pursues an overtly conservative foreign policy is capable
of undertaking such a task is debatable; though present evidence suggests it
can not. Such a reformulation would require the downgrading and, perhaps,
jettisoning of the 'special relationship' and the recognition that the EU means
more than a mere economic alliance. Politicians have usually circumvented
such issues by holding limited internal enquiries which rarely raise
fundamental questions. The Treasury review remains the only politically
acceptable substitute for a proper enquiry into the functioning of MI6. In
1996, Treasury-initiated cuts led to a reduction in MI6's staffing levels to
about 2,150.

Those expecting the Commons Intelligence and Security Committee (ISC)
to provide any vision of the future were quickly disillusioned by its first
report in 1996, which was received as a 'profound disappointment'. As James
Adams noted: 'If the American oversight committee had produced such an
anodyne document, they would have been ridiculed. Instead, the silence has
been deafening.' Responsible for examining 'the expenditure and administration and policy', the ISC, which meets within Whitehall's 'ring of secrecy',
in Room 130 in the Cabinet Office, is regarded as 'toothless'. It is not allowed
to investigate pre-nineties operations or scandals because, in the words of
the then Foreign Secretary Douglas Hurd, 'the past is a different country'.
As a senior minister recognised, the ISC is a 'cosmetic exercise' ultimately
controlled by Cabinet Office officials. By the time of its heavily censored
second report, the committee recognised the limitations. Labour member
Yvette Cooper asked: 'How can we have proper oversight if the people you
are overseeing are the very people who are determining the information
that you get?' Given this inability to independently check the information,
chairperson Tom King admitted that 'the result is that we cannot then put
our hands on our hearts and tell the public . . . that all is well . . . because
we are not in a position to know'. Members called for greater powers in
order to properly exercise their oversight role. Inevitably, the government
vetoed the request to set up a fully fledged Commons select committee.[48]

Interestingly, despite the changes, MI6's new agenda contains strong
elements of the old. In March 1996, former senior MI6 officer Baroness Park,
a member of the Thatcher Foundation and a former BBC governor who was
involved in the suppression of a programme on Zircon, revealed in the House
of Lords during a debate on security and intelligence that Russia was still a

priority. MI6 and GCHQ have their eyes on the southern states of the former Soviet Union, which are rich in oil and natural gas resources. She told peers that 'Russia is building a new generation of nuclear submarines to replace obsolete vessels. It launched its first last year. It is building new strategic missiles and new fighter aircraft ... Russia has repeatedly lied in the past few years about her continuing research into biological warfare and she has still not disposed of her 40,000 tonnes of chemical weapons.' Clearly well briefed, Park then went on to reveal the figures on increased defence spending and burgeoning arms exports. She said: 'We need surely to know what is happening, not only in Russia but in the *client* states, which include Libya and Iraq.' She warned of Russia's foreign policy, whose main plank is 'to neutralise NATO'. She questioned whether or not this amounted to 'a stable, safe world where we can afford not to have strong and effective intelligence services, if only through early warning of the undisclosed intentions of *our enemies* [my emphasis] to buy us time to reconstitute our defences should that prove necessary'. She reminded the House that MI6 had to be active because 'the IRA has always had an international dimension (Semtex from Czechoslovakia, arms from Libya and, curiously enough, arms from Estonia) and the IRA is still with us'.

Diplomatic sources dismissed the Estonian connection as fiction. David McDuff, an affiliate of the School of Slavonic and East European Studies and an expert in Estonian and Russian affairs, said: 'This is crude Boy's Own stuff. But some of the media have been swallowing it.' The last few years have seen an unprecedented number of private briefings by MI6 officers, the purpose being to justify their new agenda. The press reports read like thrillers, and while some of them have no doubt been true, even liberal newspapers such as the *Observer* have willingly published a number of these quite obviously planted stories.[49]

Although MI6 now presents a modern 'Cool Britannia' image to the politicians and public, the long tradition of special operations has not been completely curtailed. In 1996, MI6 co-operated with the CIA's station chief in London, Thomas Twetten, in a botched operation in northern Iraq. Attempts by members of the opposition Iraqi National Accord (INA) to overthrow President Saddam Hussein resulted in the deaths of three hundred Iraqis. The conspirators had been responsible for a bombing campaign against civilian targets in Baghdad which had killed a hundred people. A meeting in January 1996 of CIA and MI6 officers and intelligence officers from Jordan and Saudi Arabia agreed to back the INA as the vehicle to overthrow Saddam. The CIA and MI6 invested millions of dollars in the London-based INA – whose leader, Dr Iyad Mohamed Alawi, once a member of the ruling Ba'ath Party, had fled to London in 1971 – which ran the operation from lavish offices in Amman. The conspirators were supplied with weapons and explosives, and were provided with a powerful radio transmitter taken from

Croatia. Unfortunately for MI6, the INA was riddled with informers and double agents.

During late June and July there were a spate of arrests of senior army officers, including a number from the élite Special Republican Guard which protects the Iraqi leader, who were said to be party to a plot to start a mutiny. It is not known how deeply implicated MI6 officers were, but a number of CIA officers were deemed to be 'out of control'. Organising the opposition from Kurdistan, they planned without authorisation the assassination of Saddam. Their plans were discovered only because the NSA intercepted Iranian intelligence communications which detailed the plotting. The failure proved to be a turning point. On 31 August, Saddam sent his tanks back into Kurdistan, crushing the opposition and destroying the headquarters of the Iraqi National Congress. One intelligence source described it as the worst disaster the CIA had suffered in its history.[50]

Despite this disaster, the appetite of the West for backing hopeless causes continues. In November 1998, following another stand-off between the Americans and Saddam Hussein over weapons inspections, attempts were being made by the CIA and MI6 to construct an Iraqi opposition out of a number of disparate and bitterly divided exile groups. One gains the impression that intelligence specialists were not entirely happy at being pushed into action by politicians when there were no clear goals and plans for a post-coup Iraq. Special operations veterans, however, were eagerly gearing up for another go at toppling the Iraqi leader.

ON HER MAJESTY'S SECRET SERVICE

Agent D/813317 Richard Tomlinson joined MI6 in 1991. Born in New Zealand, he read aeronautical engineering at Cambridge and was a Kennedy memorial scholar at the Massachusetts Institute of Technology. Fluent in French, German and Spanish, Tomlinson was approached at university where he gained a first. A lecturer had asked him if he wanted to do 'something stimulating' in the foreign service. Despite modern recruiting methods, the trusted old-boy network is still a favoured option at Oxbridge, and a number of other key universities, such as Durham and Exeter, still have a contact group of lecturers on the lookout for 'firsts' as suitable recruits.

Historian Andrew Roberts has written about his own experience of being approached in 1987 to join the 'FCO Co-ordinating Staff', as MI6 is known: the 'chat with a Cambridge contact', tea at the John Nash-designed Carlton House which overlooks St James's Park, 'a discreet lunch a fortnight later and then a delightfully absurd mini-exam, in which one of the questions was "Put the following in order of social precedence: earl, duke, viscount, baron, marquis"'. At Century House, Roberts recognised 'several of the young Miss Moneypennys from the secretarial schools' parties at university'. The questions continued in a farcical vein: 'If I had been a communist, a fascist or a homosexual . . . Where do Britain's best long-term interests lie? Washington, Brussels or Moscow?' During the medical examination, he was told that 'with Oxford it's the drugs thing, with Cambridge it's the boys'. Attitudes have changed, and by 1997 MI6 was prepared to post a 'gay couple' – 'counsellor' and chief of station Christopher Hurran and his long-time Venezuelan lover – to the British embassy in Czechoslovakia. A few years earlier, the Service had recruited a member of CND. Finally, Roberts went through the process of positive vetting (known since 1990 as EPV). It is generally conducted by a semi-retired officer with a false name, who interviews referees and other contacts, and undertakes checks on credit-worthiness.

Suitable candidates are put through the fast-stream Civil Service Selection Board. Roberts, however, decided not to join, and Tomlinson did so only after spending a number of years travelling and working in the City, during which time he had also signed up for the SAS territorial regiment. Over the last decade the Service has recruited a number of personnel from the special forces, though their gung-ho philosophy seems at odds with the image that MI6 has projected of the modern spy. Tomlinson eventually joined MI6 for old-fashioned 'patriotic reasons' and sat the standard Foreign Office entry examination before being accepted on to the intelligence service training course.

New recruits are introduced to the traditional 'tradecraft' of the world of spying and gain a broad range of knowledge from recruiting and running agents to developing agents of influence and organising and servicing 'dead letter' drops. Because of the smaller numbers, MI6 officers indulge in less specialisation than their American counterparts, though the techniques are essentially little different from those used at the beginning of the century. The infamous Dreyfus affair began when a cleaning woman, Marie Bastian, working in the German embassy but employed by the French secret service, handed over to her French controller the contents of the wastepaper baskets she emptied. MI6 recruiters still look out for 'the life-and-soul-of-the-party types who could persuade the Turkish ambassador's secretary to go through her boss's wastepaper basket'. These days, however, the spy is armed with a hand-held digital scanner which can hold the filched material in its memory and can also be used in emergencies to transmit the stolen secrets by burst transmissions via a satellite.

Such gadgets are developed for the Directorate of Special Support – responsible for providing technical assistance to operations – staffed by MoD locksmiths, video and audio technicians and scientists in sections devoted to chemicals and electronics, forensic services, electronic support measures, electronic surveillance and explosive systems. While the gadgets continue to provide the modern spy with a James Bond-like image – for instance, identification transmitters that can be hidden in an agent's shoes to enable the monitoring by satellite of their precise location – the reality is that most of the work is mundane and office-bound. Trainees still receive small-arms training at Fort Monkton, but much of the training is taken up with learning to use the computer system and writing reports in the house style. As part of the Service's obsession with security, a great deal of time is spent on being indoctrinated in cipher and communications work.

Trainee officers are instructed in how to encrypt messages for transmission and how to use the manual B***† cipher which is regarded as particularly secure. Used at stations abroad to transmit details of operations, potential sources and defectors, B*** is sent either via the diplomatic bag or by special SIS courier. Diplomatic bags are not totally secure as the success of the Service's own N-Section testified. It employed up to thirty people in Palmer Street rifling the opened bags which were then expertly resealed. The work petered out in the mid-sixties as other means of communication took over.

Officers learn about 'off-line' systems for the encryption of messages such as N***** – used prior to transmission by cipher machines – and 'on-line' systems for the protection of telegrams during transmission, code-named H*** and T********. They are indoctrinated into the use of certain cryptonyms for forwarding telegrams to particular organisations and offices such as SIS headquarters, which is designated A****. They also learn about code words with which sensitive messages are headlined, indicating to whom they may be shown. UK EYES ALPHA warns that the contents are not to be shown to any foreigners and are intended only for the home intelligence and security services, armed forces and Whitehall recipients. UK EYES B includes the above categories, the Northern Ireland Office, LIST X firms engaged in the manufacture of sensitive equipment, and certain US, Australian, New Zealand and Canadian intelligence personnel liaising with the Joint Intelligence Committee (JIC) in London. Additional code words mark specific exclusions and inclusions. E****** material cannot be shown to the Americans, while L***** deprives local intelligence officials and agencies of its content. Material for named individual officers, sometimes at specified times, is headed D**** or D****, while particularly sensitive material about a fellow officer or operation is known as D******.

The protection of files and their secure handling is a top priority, with officers taught to keep a classified record of their use and location. Photocopiers have the ability to mark and check the origin of non-authorised copies of classified material. Following the development by MoD scientists of a means of reading a computer disk without a computer, all disks are protected in transit. All correspondence by letter is secured by specially developed red security tape which leaves detectable signs if tampered with, though near-undetectable photographic and laser techniques exist to read the inside of mail and to open envelopes. Each officer has his own safe with dual-combination locking, while the filing cabinets with false tumbler locks, as an added precaution, are protected from penetration by X-rays. Since no lock is secure from picking, they collapse internally if anything more than the slightest force is used. In the event of drilling, a glass plate inside the door shatters, releasing a spring-loaded bolt to prevent opening. Frequent random checks

---

† Some code words in this chapter have had to be disguised on legal advice.

take place on the number settings to see if the safe has been opened illegally.

These bureaucratic procedures and attention to minute security rules are not merely technical; failure to carry out security precautions can lead to points deduction in the security breach points system. If an officer racks up 160 points over three years (breach of Top Secret counts as 80 points), this may lead to security clearance being withdrawn and instant dismissal.

New officers will initially be based at the exotic Vauxhall Bridge head-quarters, about which many Service personnel are sensitive, almost embar-rassed. Access to 'Ceausescu Towers', as some officers have dubbed it, is gained by use of a swipe card and PIN number. The interior comprises a hive of bare, unmarked air-conditioned corridors. The only visible signs of occupancy are the acronyms on the doors, with nothing on the walls except floor plans and exit signs. As with major stations abroad, such as Moscow and Beijing, Vauxhall Cross is classified as a Category A post, with a high potential physical threat from terrorism (HPT) and sophisticated hostile intel-ligence services (HIS). Operatives from the Technical Security Department (TSD) based at Hanslope Park, Milton Keynes, and from MI6's own technical department ensure that the building is protected from high-tech attack (HTA). There is triple glazing installed on all windows as a safeguard against laser and radio frequency (RF) flooding techniques, and the mainframe computer, cipher and communications areas are housed in secure, modular-shielded rooms. A secure command-and-control room runs major operations such as those in Bosnia, where 'war criminals' were tracked and arrested by SAS personnel.

Off the corridors are open-plan offices which give the impression of infor-mality, though security overrides such considerations. A new officer will find that since 1996 more women than men have been recruited to the Service, but males remain predominant, particularly in senior positions. As in many modern offices, officers will be seen working at computers, processing infor-mation, collating files, planning operations, liaising with foreign intelligence agencies and networks, and, most importantly, supporting the three to five hundred officers in the field, though only half that number will be stationed abroad at any one time. MI6 has been at the forefront of updating its infor-mation technology and, in 1995, installed at a cost of £200 million an ambitious desktop network known as the Automatic Telegram Handling System (ATHS/OATS), which provides access to all reports and databases. Staff are officially not allowed to discuss their work with colleagues, not even when they relax in the staff bar with its spectacular views over the River Thames, though, as Richard Tomlinson discovered, gossip is in fact rife.

All officers will spend time in the field attached to embassies, though they will have little choice as to the location. Turning down a post will jeopardise future promotions and can lead to dismissal. Stations abroad are classed from the high-risk Category A, such as Yugoslavia and Algeria, to the lesser B, such as Washington and New York, C, the European countries, and D, often the Commonwealth, where there is little or no threat. New officers might find themselves among the additional personnel sent to Malaysia, Thailand and South Korea, following the Service's boost to its presence in South-East Asia, or involved in operations into China following the transfer of Hong Kong and the winding up of its espionage operations in the former colony. In a large station such as Washington, operating under 'light' diplomatic cover will be a head of station (often a Counsellor), a deputy and two or three officers (First and Second Secretaries). There will also be back-up staff consisting of three or four secretaries, a registry clerk to handle files and documents, and communications and cipher officers. Easily identified by the trained eye in the Foreign and Commonwealth Office 'Diplomatic List' – the number of Counsellor and First Secretary posts is limited and there tend to be too many for the positions available – an MI6 officer's presence will be known to the host intelligence and security agency. In some cases, a senior officer will make his presence known to draw attention away from his colleagues.

Before postings and missions abroad, officers receive a briefing from the Information Operations (I/OPs) unit, which provides them with a list of sympathetic journalists who can be trusted to give them help and information. These contacts have become increasingly important in trouble spots such as the Balkans.

I/OPs also has a more covert role in planning psychological operations along the lines of the old Special Political Action (SPA) section and the Information Research Department (IRD). I/OPs may also, according to a former MI6 officer, 'attempt to influence events in another country or organisation in a direction favourable to Britain'. One example is MI6's determined effort to 'plant stories in the American press about Boutros Ghali, whom they regarded as dangerously Francophile, in the run up to the 1992 elections for UN secretary-general'. Foreign operations of this sort do not require ministerial sanction.[1]

I/OPs also expends considerable energy behind the scenes in 'surfacing' damaging stories designed to discredit critics of the Service. They will use off-the-record briefings of sympathetic journalists; the planting of rumours and disinformation, which through 'double-sourcing' are confirmed by a proactive agent; and the overt recruitment of journalist agents. Journalists paid to provide information or to 'keep their eyes open' are known as an 'asset' or an 'assistant' or just 'on side'. According to Richard Tomlinson, paid agents included in the nineties one and perhaps two national newspaper editors. An editor is unlikely to be directly recruited as the Service would require the permission of the Foreign Secretary and would not like to be put in the position of being refused. Such high-fliers are more likely to have been recruited early in their careers. In this case, the journalist was apparently recruited at least three years before becoming an editor and remained an asset until at least 1998. Tomlinson has said that the editor was paid a retainer of £100,000, with access to the money via an offshore bank in an accessible tax haven. The editor was given a false passport to gain entry to the bank, which he regularly visited.[2]

In trying to identify the editor 'agent', media interest centred on Dominic Lawson, son of the former Tory Chancellor of the Exchequer, who became editor of the *Spectator* in 1990 and had been editor of the *Sunday Telegraph* since 1995. Lawson denied that he had ever been 'an agent, either paid or unpaid, of MI6 or of any other government agency'. On the other hand, the youngest brother of Lawson's second wife, Rosa Monckton, had joined MI6 in 1987. In 1996, Anthony Monckton was appointed First Secretary (Political) in the Croatian capital Zagreb.

Quite separately, one of Rosa's closest friends and a godparent to the Lawsons' daughter, the late Princess of Wales had clearly been under some kind of surveillance, as evidenced by the 1,050-page dossier held by the US National Security Agency (NSA) in its archive, detailing private telephone conversations between Diana and American friends intercepted at MI6's request. While all stories linking MI6 to the Princess's death in the car accident in France have been complete nonsense, it has been alleged that working closely with I/Ops in an attempt to deflect enquiries away from the security services had been a chief of staff to 'C', Richard Spearman, temporarily posted to the Paris embassy with his assistant, Nicholas Langman.[3]

Operational officers can be casually spotted by the '*******' roller-ball pens in their top pocket (it was discovered by accident that they have the ability to create invisible ink), the Psion organiser and the specially adapted 'Walkman' they carry to record conversations for up to ten minutes on the middle band of an ordinary commercial music cassette tape. They also use laptop computers for writing reports. If that seems like a recipe for disaster, the secret hard disk contains a protected back-up.

The station is usually sited in a part of the embassy regularly swept by technical staff for bugs and other electronic attack. It is entered using special door codes with an inner strongroom-type door for greater security. Following all the procedures learned during training, officers handling material up to the 'Secret' level work on secure overseas Unix terminals (S****) and use a messaging system known as ARRAMIS. Conversations by secure telephone masked by white noise are undertaken via a special SIS version of the BRAHMS system. A special chip developed by GCHQ apparently makes it impossible even for the US NSA to decipher such conversations. Secure Speech System (H*******) handset units are used by SIS officers within a telephone speech enclosure. The most important room is electronically shielded and lined with up to a foot of lead for secure cipher and communications transmissions. From the comms room, an officer can send and receive secure faxes up to SECRET level via the C****** fax system and S***** encrypted communications with the Ministry of Defence (MoD), Cabinet Office, MI5 (codename SNUFFBOX), GCHQ and 22 SAS. An encrypted electronic messaging system working through fibre optics, known as the UK Intelligence Messaging Network, was installed in early 1997 and enables MI6 to flash intelligence scoops to special terminals in the MoD, the Foreign Office and the Department of Trade and Industry. Manned twenty-four hours a day, 365 days a year, and secured behind a heavy thick door, the cipher machines have secure 'integral protection', known as TEMPEST. MI6 officers abroad also work alongside GCHQ personnel, monitoring foreign missions and organisations.

Officers in the field may include not only those officially classed as diplomats but also others operating under 'deep' cover. Increasingly MI6 officers abroad act as 'illegals'. It is known that Service officers are sometimes employed during the day in conventional jobs such as accountancy, and provided with false identities. British banks – the Royal Bank of Scotland is particularly helpful, and to a lesser extent the Midland – help supply credit cards to officers working under cover. At the end of each month, officers have to pay off their aliases' credit cards. Banks also help transmit money overseas for covert operations. During the Cold War, banks in the Channel Islands and other offshore locations acted as a conduit for secret funding.[4]

Recruiting or running agents and gathering intelligence are the prime objectives of these deep-cover operatives, and their real work, some claim, starts at six in the evening when the conventional diplomats begin their round of cocktail parties. Such social events can be very useful for gathering intelligence and spreading disinformation. Baroness Park recalled that one of MI6's more successful ploys was 'to set people very discreetly against one another. They destroy each other. You don't destroy them.' Officers would offer the odd hint that it was 'a pity that so-and-so is so indiscreet. Not much more.' Officers will also deal with paid 'support agents' – those who supply MI6 with facilities including safe houses and bank accounts, as well as intelligence. There are also 'long insiders' – agents of influence with access to MI6 assessments and sanitised intelligence. The Service's deep-cover agents have burst transmitters with the ability to transmit a flash signal to MI6 via a satellite when they are in danger.[5]

Officers abroad may also be asked to aid more sophisticated operations designed to build up the Service's psychological profiles of political leaders. A special department within MI6 has tried in the past to procure the urine and excrement of foreign leaders. A specially modified condom was used to catch the urine of Romanian leader Nicolae Ceausescu, while the 'product' of Presidents Fidel Castro and Leonid Brezhnev was 'analysed' by medical specialists for signs of their true health.

Tomlinson's duties included recruiting agents to inform on foreign politicians. His most important task was to infiltrate in 1992 a Middle Eastern weapons procurement programme network – the BMP3 – with the object of locating and disabling a chemical weapons facility. Authorised by an unnamed senior Cabinet minister, the sabotage plan – one account suggests the planting of a bomb – aimed to intercept a shipment of machinery and interfere with its extractor fan equipment, despite warnings of the possible risk to the lives of dozens of civilian workers at the plant. In November 1992, using the name 'Andrew Huntley' and the pretext of assisting at a conference run by the *Financial Times*, Tomlinson went under cover to Moscow. His very sensitive mission was to obtain Russian military secrets on ballistic missiles and effect the defection of a Russian colonel who specialised in this area. Although, strangely, he was not given the usual 'immersion' language training in Serbo-Croat, Tomlinson soon found himself in the former Yugoslavia, whose break-up had taken the Service by surprise.[6]

When the country fractured in January 1991 into Croatia, Bosnia and Serbia, EU recognition of independent Croatia proved to be a critical and disastrous policy, eventually paving the way for Serb aggression which the Foreign Office interpreted as civil war. MI6 had been running a few federal sources in the old Yugoslavia, but they provided little worthwhile intelligence. The Service lacked appropriate linguists and had to start more or less from scratch. The JIC established a Current Intelligence Group (CIG) on the Balkans, and within eighteen months MI6's Controllerate dealing with the area had recruited a number of sources at a high level from among the ethnic military and political protagonists.

During 1993, as a 'targeting officer' within the Balkans Controllerate, whose job was to identify potential informants, Tomlinson spent a harrowing and dangerous six months travelling as a journalist to Belgrade, Skopje, Zagreb and Ljubljana, in the process recruiting a Serb journalist – journalists of every nationality were a particular MI6 target in the Balkans, as they proved to be more productive than most other sources – and a leader of the Albanian opposition in Macedonia. In 1993, UN blue-helmeted troops started patrolling the borders of the Former Yugoslav Republic of Macedonia. According to sources, MI6 used air-drops in an operation to set up arms dumps on the border of Macedonia as part of a stay-behind network.[7]

Another operation included running as an agent a Tory MP, who gave information about foreign donations to the Conservative Party. Parliamentary Private Secretary to the Northern Ireland minister, Harold Elleston was an old Etonian who studied Russian at Exeter University and subsequently became a trade consultant specialising in the former eastern bloc countries, during which time he was recruited by MI6. He worked for them in eastern Europe, the former Soviet Union and during the conflict in former Yugoslavia. After visiting former Yugoslavia in 1992, Elleston, who was employed by a lobbying firm with Conservative candidate John Kennedy (aka Gvozdenovic), notified his MI6 handlers that donations were reaching the Conservative

Party from Serbia. Despite Harold Wilson's ruling in the sixties that the intelligence services would not use MPs as agents, the Service received special sanction from Prime Minister John Major to continue Elleston's secret role. Sir Colin McColl warned Major that the party was possibly accepting tainted money via Kennedy, a key figure in arranging payments from the Serb regime.[8]

MI6 was itself seen as being pro-Serb in its reporting. In 1994, two articles arguing against western policy in the Balkans conflict appeared in the *Spectator* (the right-wing magazine unknowingly served as 'cover' for three MI6 officers working in Bosnia, Belgrade and Moldova), written under a Sarajevo dateline by a 'Kenneth Roberts', who had apparently worked for more than a year with the United Nations in Bosnia as an 'adviser'. Written by MI6 officer Keith Robert Craig, who was attached to the MoD's Balkan Secretariat, the first on 5 February rehearsed arguments for a UN withdrawal from the area, pointing out that all sides committed atrocities. The second, on 5 March, complained baselessly about 'warped' and inaccurate reports by, in particular, the BBC's Kate Adie of an atrocity against the Bosnian Serbs. *Guardian* correspondent Ed Vulliamy recalled being invited to a briefing by MI6 which was 'peddling an ill-disguised agenda: the Foreign Office's determination that there be no intervention against Serbia's genocidal pogrom'. Without the slightest evidence, the carnage that took place in Sarajevo's marketplace was described as the work of the Muslim-led government, which was alleged to be 'massacring its own people to win sympathy and ultimately help from outside'. As Vulliamy knew, Sarajevo's defenders were 'dumb with disbelief'. Despite UN Protection Force reports which found that it was Serb mortars which were killing Muslims, the MI6 scheme 'worked – beautifully', as the allegations found their way into the world's press. Vulliamy noted that 'it was quickly relished by the only man who stood to gain from this – the Serbian leader Radovan Karadzic'.[9]

Perhaps it was only an intelligence/Foreign Office faction which was pro-Serb. From March 1992 until September 1993, Tomlinson worked in the East European Controllerate under the staff designation UKA/7. He has claimed that in the summer of 1992 he discovered an internal document that detailed plans to assassinate President Slobodan Milosevic. During a conversation, an ambitious and serious colleague who was responsible for developing and targeting operations in the Balkans (P4/OPS), Nick Fishwick, had pulled out a file and handed it to Tomlinson to read. 'It was approximately two pages long, and had a yellow card attached to it which signified that it was an accountable document rather than a draft proposal.' It was entitled 'The need to assassinate President Milosevic of Serbia' and was distributed to senior MI6 officers, including the head of Balkan operations (P4), Maurice Kenwrick-Piercy, the Controller of East European Operations (C/CEE), Richard Fletcher, and later Andrew Fulton, the Security Officer responsible for eastern European operations (SBO1/T), John Ridd, the private secretary to the Chief (H/SECT), Alan Petty ('Alan Judd'), and the Service's SAS liaison officer (MODA/SO), Maj. Glynne Evans. According to Tomlinson, Fishwick justified assassinating Milosevic on the grounds that there was evidence that the 'Butcher of Belgrade' was supplying weapons to Karadzic, who was wanted for war crimes, including genocide. US and French intelligence agencies were alleged to be already contemplating assassinating Karadzic.

There were three possible scenarios put forward by MI6. Firstly, to train a Serbian paramilitary opposition group to carry out the assassination. This, Fishwick argued, had the advantage of deniability but the disadvantage that control of the operation would be low and the chances of success unpredictable. Secondly, to use the small INCREMENT cell of SAS/SBS personnel, which is especially selected and trained to carry out operations exclusively for MI6/MI5, to send in a team that would assassinate the President with a bomb or by a sniper ambush. Fishwick said that this would be the most reliable option, but would be undeniable if the operation went wrong. Thirdly, to kill Milosevic in a road crash which would be staged during one of his visits to the international conferences on former Yugoslavia in Geneva. Fishwick suggested that a stun device could be used to dazzle the driver of Milosevic's car as it passed through one of Geneva's motorway tunnels.[10]

A year later, Tomlinson acted as a counsellor to the commander of the British forces in Bosnia and worked at manipulating the sources in the entourage of Karadzic. One participant to these operations suggests that these sources 'produced a very detailed intelligence picture which included not just the military plans and capabilities of the different factions but also early warning of political intentions'. There appears to have been little evidence of this intelligence coup in the Foreign Office decisions that followed, and its value is contradicted by another source which, while admitting that several significant agents were recruited, concludes that they did not 'produce substantial intelligence of quality'.[11]

The intelligence deficit was worsened by the United States' unwillingness to provide its Atlantic partner with all its intelligence on the Serbs. General Sir Michael Rose, a former head of the SAS and commander-in-chief of the UN Protection Force, realised that during 1994 all his communications were being electronically intercepted and his headquarters in Sarajevo was 'bugged' by the Americans because Washington, which wanted to use Nato air strikes to bomb the Serbs to the negotiating table, thought the British were too supportive of the Bosnian Serbs. The Americans also monitored the communications of SAS scouts deep in Bosnian territory and discovered that they were deliberately failing to identify Serb artillery positions. This lack of trust caused friction and led to a backstage confrontation between the secret services, and reminded some observers that the special relationship existed only on the basis that the US saw Britain as a chance to extend its reach into Europe.[12]

The plans for Milosevic were not the only assassination plot in which MI6 became entangled. Renegade MI5 officer David Shayler, who was released by a French court in November 1998 on 'political grounds' following his detention in prison as part of extradition proceedings to England, first heard of a plot to kill the Libyan leader, Colonel Gaddafi, in November 1995.

Shayler had been posted to MI5's counter-terrorist G9A section with responsibilities for issues relating to Lockerbie and Libya. A higher executive officer, earning £28,000 per year, Shayler headed up the Libyan desk for over two years and was held in high esteem, undertaking presentations to senior civil servants on all matters relating to Libya. For this work he received a performance-related bonus. An MI6 officer, referred to as PT16B, with whom Shayler had developed a close working relationship, informed him during a liaison meeting on Libya that the Service was running an important Arab agent. A former Libyan government official code-named 'Tunworth', the agent was a go-between with Libyan opposition groups, including a little-known band of extremists called Al Jamaa Al Islamiya Al Muqatila (Islamic Fighting Force). Tunworth had apparently approached MI6 in late 1995, outlining plans to overthrow Gaddafi by the Islamic Fighting Force, and later met with an MI6 officer in a Mediterranean country where he asked for funding. Shayler was told that more than £100,000 had been handed over in three or four instalments beginning in December. PT16B and his colleagues wrote a three- to four-page CX report for Whitehall circulation to other agencies, which stated that MI6 was merely in receipt of intelligence from agent Tunworth on the militants' coup plotting and the group's efforts to obtain weapons and Jeeps. It seems that no mention was made of any MI6 involvement in an assassination attempt.[13]

Shayler later heard that there had been a bomb attack on Gaddafi's motorcade near a town called Sirte, but the device was detonated under the wrong car. In fact, it seems that the dissidents launched an attack with Kalashnikovs and rocket grenades on the wrong car. In a communiqué to Arab newspapers on 6 March 1996, the Islamic Fighting Force stated that its men had tried to attack Gaddafi as he attended the Libyan General People's Congress. The attempt went wrong when Gaddafi did not show up in person, and the terrorists were forced to cancel the attack. 'But as our heroes were withdrawing they collided with the security forces and in the ensuing battle there were casualties on both sides.' Three fighters were killed but the leader of the hit team, Abd al-Muhaymeen, a veteran of the Afghan resistance who was possibly trained by MI6 or the CIA, 'escaped unhurt'. Following a crackdown by Gaddafi's secret police, his family home in the town of Ejdabiya was burnt down. The back of the Fighting Force was broken and its leaders retreated to Afghanistan.[14]

When Shayler subsequently met PT16B, the MI6 officer mentioned the attack with 'a kind of note of triumph, saying, yes, we'd done it'. Shayler's reaction was 'one of total shock. This was not what I thought I was doing in the intelligence service.' He told BBC's *Panorama* programme: 'I was absolutely astounded . . . Suddenly we were talking about tens of thousands of pounds of taxpayers' money being used to attempt to assassinate a foreign head of state.' He concluded that 'no matter who is funding this, it's still international terrorism. The Brits might say we're the good guys, but it's a very difficult road to go down.'

Government officials dismissed Shayler's claims as 'completely and utterly nutty'. A Foreign Office spokesperson said that it was 'inconceivable that in a non-wartime situation the Government would authorise the SIS to bump off a foreign leader. In theory, SIS can carry out assassinations but only at the express request of the Foreign Secretary.' The 1994 Intelligence Services Act refers to MI6 being able to perform 'other tasks' and protects officers from prosecution for criminal acts outside Britain. Indeed, a clause was especially inserted into the 1998 Criminal Justice Bill – which outlaws organisations in Britain conspiring to commit offences abroad – giving all Crown agents immunity from prosecution under the legislation, including possibly the assassination of foreign leaders. It was clear to Shayler, however, and confirmed by BBC sources, that MI6 had not sought ministerial clearance for backing the attempt on Gaddafi. MI6, Shayler believed, was 'operating out of control and illegally'.[15]

Whatever the truth is surrounding Shayler's accusations, the public and politicians will not discover the full facts. Unlike in the United States, where similar, but less detailed, revelations led to a major Senate enquiry into alleged assassination plotting in the mid-seventies, there will be no House of Commons investigation. As Tomlinson explains, 'there is a deep-rooted belief that, should a policy or operation go wrong, nobody will be held ultimately responsible. The Service will always be able to hide behind the catch-all veil of secrecy provided by the Official Secrets Act or, if the heat really builds up, a Public Interest Immunity Certificate.'[16]

Given his operational experience, as a Grade 5 officer Tomlinson might have expected steady promotion through the ranks and a long career in the secret service, perhaps ending as head of a Controllerate. Senior officers, who are easily spotted in the honours lists with their OBEs, retire at fifty-five. Their attachment to the Service does not end there, however. A number are found appointments as non-executive directors with companies or subsidiaries that have dealt with MI6, or employed as security or corporate liaison officers. 'It is part of their retirement package,' Tomlinson has revealed. 'They are effectively MI6 liaison officers, just like MI6 liaison officers in Whitehall departments.'[17]

Since MI6 helped establish Diversified Corporate Services in Rome, New York and London in the late sixties, there has been an increasing trend for setting up consultancies, with the tacit approval or encouragement of the Service. Among the consultants to Ciex, which has 'cornered a lucrative market' in providing a restricted 'confidential service' in 'strategic advice and intelligence' for 'a small group of very substantial customers', are Hamilton McMillan, who retired from the Service's counter-terrorist section in 1996, and former head of the Middle East department Michael Oatley, who previously worked for another intelligence-linked consultancy, Kroll Associates. Set up in 1995 by the late Sir Fitzroy Maclean, with a board that includes a former Royal Dutch Shell managing director and a former BP deputy chair, the Hakluyt Foundation provides leading British businesses with information that clients 'will not receive by the usual government, media and commercial routes'. Hakluyt's managing director, Christopher James, was until 1998 in charge of MI6's liaison with commerce, while a fellow-director, Mike Reynolds, was regarded as one of the Service's brightest stars.[18]

Tomlinson's career in the secret world turned out to be short-lived. He returned home from the Balkans exhausted and traumatised by the atrocities he had witnessed, but, fearing that the Service's personnel managers might regard this as a sign of weakness, he did not tell them of his emotional state.* At one point he had been depressed following the death of his girlfriend. Since he had no one to whom to unburden himself – as is standard practice, his parents were unaware of his secret life – his personal problems mounted. Despite the claims of improved personnel management within the Service, Tomlinson received little or no support. It seems that the Service has not put in place any counselling provision as a result of Tomlinson's (and others') experience, but, instead, has decided that officers be vetted by clinical psychologists in order to 'identify actual or potential personality disorders', particularly those being appointed to sensitive posts. Harold Macmillan once said that anyone who spent more than ten years in the secret service must be either weird or mad.[19]

Tomlinson's personnel manager claimed that he was not a team player, lacked judgement and was not committed to the Service because he was prone to going on 'frolics of his own'. In early 1995, Tomlinson turned up for work and discovered that his swipe card would not gain him entry to MI6 headquarters. Security guards informed him that it had been cancelled. His security clearance had been stopped after he complained to his superiors that a number of MI6's operations and tactics were unethical. Tomlinson was also privy to much sensitive information, as gossip was prevalent inside

---

* Recalcitrant officers and agents under suspicion are sometimes interrogated at the 'cooler' facilities in Chelsea and in a special soundproofed 'rubber' room situated beneath a hotel in west London.

headquarters. For instance, he was aware that a British businessman had threatened to go public with allegations that intelligence officers had destroyed his company. MI6 was said to have mounted a covert operation, including telephone tapping, against the businessman to ensure that he did not contact the press. Tomlinson was formally dismissed from the Service in August 1995. He did not believe that MI6 was properly accountable to the law. This lack of accountability at the top 'cascades downwards to even the lowest levels' and provides 'a fertile breeding ground for corruption'.[20]

One MI6 officer paid for his divorce by pocketing the expenses of a fictitious agent whose fake intelligence had been taken from the pages of the *Economist*. Another senior officer sold false passports to Middle Eastern businessmen and possibly drug traffickers, and diverted taxpayers' money intended for defectors and informants – up to £400,000 – into his offshore bank account. 'Agent J' was allowed to retire on a full pension with no police investigation or prosecution because 'he knew where the bodies were buried'. The scandal was uncovered by the US authorities, who were investigating drugs in the Caribbean and came across an offshore bank account opened with a British passport issued in a false name. Senior MI6 officers are allowed to open new bank accounts and transfer cash.[21]

Tomlinson blamed his dismissal on a personality clash with a personnel manager. Other officers, including his immediate superior, protested that the personnel officer's accusations were unsubstantiated. Tomlinson was allowed to appeal to the intelligence services' tribunal, set up in 1994 and chaired by Lord Justice Brown, but, following the rejection of his appeal, he dismissed it as a 'star chamber'. 'I was denied the basic natural justice. I had no legal representation or access to papers which were said to give reasons for my dismissal. I could not cross-examine key witnesses.'* When he then told the head of the Personnel Department that he would pursue his claim for unfair dismissal at an industrial tribunal, he was informed: 'There's no point in doing that because nobody can tell the Chief what to do.'[22]

MI6 refused to co-operate with the tribunal, which led to Tomlinson's decision to write a book about his experiences. Investigated by Special Branch officers, Tomlinson was subsequently jailed for twelve months on 18 December 1997 under the Official Secrets Act in order 'to deter others from pursuing the course you chose to pursue'. He spent six months in Belmarsh prison, courtesy of Her Majesty, and was released in April 1998.[23]

Publicity concerning Tomlinson's case led to considerable anxiety in Whitehall and is said to have caused turmoil inside MI6. The Service feared

---

* In February 1999 Foreign Secretary Robin Cook accepted that MI6 staff should 'as much as possible, enjoy the same rights as other employees'. A special investigator with access to all intelligence files would be appointed to look into allegations of malpractice. Home Secretary Jack Straw, however, said that the Official Secrets Act would not be amended to allow 'whistleblowing' because the security services were now 'accountable'.

that the publicity would expose poor management and lead to calls for changes and reform. It became the task of the Director of Security and Public Affairs, and effectively C's number two, John Gerson, to 'deal' with Tomlinson. A Far East specialist with close ties with the Americans, Gerson, who is an associate member of the Centre for the Study of Socialist Legal Systems at London University, is the model of the well-versed and evasive civil servant as portrayed in *Yes, Minister*. His hobby is the classic spy's pastime of birdwatching. Rewarded with a CMG in the 1999 New Year's Honours, Gerson has been ably assisted by the main contact with the press, Iain Mathewson, a former official in the DHSS and Customs and Excise, who joined MI6 in 1980.

The Cold War was easy for the intelligence agencies, to the extent that they had clear, identifiable targets. It also provided a curtain behind which they could hide their failures. Without an all-embracing enemy to counter, the Secret Intelligence Service has developed a bits-and-pieces target list, known as the 'Mother Load' agenda, which lacks coherence. This is sometimes explained as being due to the fact that the world has become more unstable. This is nonsense. There is no danger of a world conflagration such as there was during Berlin in 1961, Cuba in 1962, the Middle East in 1967 and 1973, or at other crisis points when nuclear bombers took to the air. Threats from so-called rogue states such as Iran and Iraq are altogether of a different magnitude. Even then, it is apparent that many of the 'scares' – suitcase nuclear bombs, missiles with nuclear and biological warheads, nuclear terrorists, etc. – are either grossly exaggerated or simply manufactured by the intelligence services.

It is true that there are significant trouble spots in the world and Britain rightly has to take measures to monitor them, but what this so-called instability has exposed is the inability of agencies designed for the Cold War to tackle the problems of today. In the United States, where a much more open, democratic debate has taken place, the CIA's director from 1977 to 1981, Stansfield Turner, has suggested that the solution is to build a new intelligence service from scratch. Others talk of open-source intelligence agencies that would exploit the explosion of information and do away with the mystique that surrounds secret sources.

The most trenchant criticism of the changes that MI6 has undertaken since the end of the Cold War has come from insiders. David Bickford, former lawyer to the security services, argued in November 1997 that the British intelligence community – MI6, MI5, whose Director-General, Stephen Lander, is not regarded as an inspired choice, and GCHQ – 'is not doing its job properly'. He said that the cost was completely unjustified as there was 'triplication of management, triplication of bureaucracy and triplication of turf battles'. SIS appears to be top heavy with management, with resources being shifted away from operations to administration, such as employing lawyers to deal with the new crime agenda, as well as public relations officers, accountants, etc. There would appear, then, to be room for cuts.

Officials claim that MI6 currently costs about £140 million. This is hardly a credible figure for an organisation employing two thousand staff. Indeed, sources who were privy to the figures as presented to the Permanent Secretaries' Committee on the Intelligence Services in the mid-eighties were then quoting £150 million. What few people are aware of is that the budget only covers MI6's operations: everything else is excluded. It does not take a specialist to appreciate that a realistic budget would be considerably higher if all the running costs of maintenance, pensions, travel, overseas stations, computers, equipment, communications, and the full building costs of the new headquarters (the National Audit Office report on the £90 million overspend is to remain secret) are taken into account. The Treasury insists that costs which were previously hidden away in the budgets of other departments, such as the MoD, are now included in the Secret Vote figure for MI6. This cannot be true. Staff costs are met by the Foreign Office, while the MoD pays for Fort Monkton and the Hercules transport plane and Puma helicopter that are kept on permanent stand-by for the Service's use. It is unlikely that ministers are aware of the network of 'front' companies that MI6 set up in the early nineties, nor of the numerous bank accounts, such as the one at the Drummonds branch of the Royal Bank of Scotland, which the Service operates.

It can now be revealed that the real budget figure – intelligence sources with access to the budget call it MI6's biggest secret – is at least double the official figure. One source with access to the internal accounts puts it as high as five times this figure. Ministers and MPs are being misled. So is the Commons Intelligence Security Committee. The American experience is that it is budgetary control which provides the only means of real leverage and represents a move towards genuine oversight.

Intelligence chiefs have argued successfully that a detailed audit of MI6 expenditure would 'prejudice their operational security'. The result is, Tomlinson argues, 'a management and budgetary structure which would provide a theme park for management consultancies'. It is not surprising to learn that MI6 officers have 'little idea how to manage a budget, and even less incentive to manage it well'. Tomlinson discovered many cases of profligate waste. It was common at the end of the financial year for departments to feverishly spend the remaining budget on planning expensive operations – which, in reality, had little chance of success – in order to prevent cuts to the following year's allocation.[24]

Bickford had his own agenda, believing that British Intelligence was turning 'a blind eye to the fact that economic crime – organised racketeering in narcotics, kidnap extortion, product contamination and fraud – now poses the greatest threat to the security of the international community'. During

1995 the intelligence agencies had apparently tried to persuade the Major government to allow them to develop closer links with large companies so as to provide them with 'protective business intelligence'. The initiative failed because, Bickford claimed, the different agencies bickered between themselves on how to finance and run the new scheme. Tomlinson agrees that there is 'often bitter fighting between the two agencies over who should have primacy over a particular target or operation'. Although arbitrary ground rules are sometimes brokered between warring departments, communication between MI6 and MI5 remains 'desperately poor'. There is 'remarkably little cross-fertilisation of ideas or operational co-ordination'.[25]

Besides economic crime, the main threat to Britain, Bickford believed, was 'super-terrorism', involving weapons of mass destruction, and because of the 'common international nature of these threats', the case for having three different agencies 'falls at the first hurdle'. These threats and the many others that the intelligence services have warned us about often do not stand up to close scrutiny – indeed, the modern intelligence service's prime purpose appears to be to generate fears – but Bickford's argument that a merger between the three services would save 'tens of millions of pounds' and provide the necessary 'focused direction, integration and analysis of electronic and human intelligence' deserves to be taken seriously. Tomlinson argues that such a streamlined organisation should be accountable to a parliamentary committee so that 'intelligence targets, priorities and budgets are all controlled through the normal democratic process'.[26]

A new Treasury-led interdepartmental committee inquiry was instigated in 1998 to put the security and intelligence services under what was said to be an unprecedented 'root-and-branch' scrutiny, the aim being to expose the intelligence agencies to zero-based budgeting, a Treasury discipline that asks the agency concerned to explain from first principles the value of everything it does. As *Independent* political correspondent Donald Macintyre suggested, 'Ministers will have to be tough; when an effort was made from within the Treasury to do the same thing in the 1980s, it foundered when the security services, almost certainly with Margaret Thatcher's backing, put the shutters up.'[27]

Although the official budget for MI6, MI5 and GCHQ is claimed to be £713 million, rising to £776 million in 1999/2000 (not including a Treasury supply estimate for the capital budget of £144 million) and up to £1 billion for all agencies, Sir Gerald Warner, who as former deputy head of MI6 and Intelligence and Security Co-ordinator at the Cabinet Office (1991–6) should be in a position to know, put a figure of £2.5 billion on the entire cost of Britain's intelligence community. The reality is that the intelligence budget has increased in a period when defence spending has gone down from 5 per cent to around 3.5 per cent of GDP. Defence intelligence, the international arms trade and nuclear proliferation absorb about 35 per cent; intelligence on foreign states and their internal politics about 10 per cent; intelligence operations, including supplying diplomats and ministers in negotiations with secrets and economic espionage, about 20 per cent; counter-terrorism another 20 per cent; with counter-intelligence, counter-espionage, drugs and international crime the rest.

An inquiry conducted by the Cabinet Office in 1998, with wide terms of reference, including ensuring that the agencies' objectives are properly 'focused' on providing relevant intelligence to other Whitehall departments, asked them to justify their activities as well as their usefulness. It was acknowledged that the scrutiny team would probably recommend some 'down-sizing' of MI6, which had 'run out of things to do', though no clues were forthcoming from the politicians. The intelligence chiefs have themselves complained that New Labour has had no policy on the intelligence services, and it is true that all efforts to elicit a pre-election policy statement from the future Prime Minister, Foreign Secretary and Home Secretary met with failure. MI6 Chief Sir David Spedding, however, had no need to worry.

Foreign Secretary Robin Cook, the former left-winger who in opposition regularly criticised the intelligence and security services for their threat to civil liberties, lack of accountability and waste of taxpayers' money, had, one intelligence source told Richard Norton-Taylor, 'further to travel than his predecessors' in coming to terms with his responsibilities for the Secret Intelligence Service. It did not take long. Labour politicians who, in the main, have had little contact with the intelligence world, or much interest in its activities, have been and continue to be easily seduced by the magic of secrecy and privileged access to special sources. MI6 senior staffers knew what to do, having for so long, as Tomlinson warned, 'carefully and successfully cultivated an air of mystique and importance to their work'. Knowing that the reality is very different, SIS continues to devote considerable time and resources to lobbying for its position in Whitehall.

Cook made the short trip across the Thames to the Service's palatial Vauxhall Cross headquarters, where Spedding and his successor, Richard Dearlove, avoiding discussion of MI6's real budget, briefed him on their latest 'successes': a 'crucial role' in revealing Saddam Hussein's continuing chemical, biological and nuclear weapons programme; uncovering Iranian attempts to procure British technology; and tracking drug smugglers and countering money laundering in the City of London. And then, in April 1998, dressed in the traditional white tie and tails for the Mansion House Easter dinner for diplomats and City businessmen, Cook went out of his way – indeed, further than any previous Labour Foreign Secretary – to praise SIS, noting that they 'cannot speak for themselves' because 'the nature of what they do means that we cannot shout about their achievements if we want them to remain effective. But let me say I have been struck by the range and quality of the work.' It seems that some things in the British state never change.

NOTES

KEY

BAOR	British Army of the Rhine	L	Listener
BoT	Board of Trade	NA	National Archives
CAB	Cabinet	NS	New Statesman
CCA	Churchill College Archives,	NSC	National Security Council
	Cambridge	NUS	National Union of Students
CoS	Chiefs of Staff	NYT	New York Times
CUP	Cambridge University Press	O	Observer
DM	Daily Mail	PE	Private Eye
DNB	Dictionary of National Biography	PRO	Public Records Office
DT	Daily Telegraph	RUSI	Royal United Services Institute
E	Economist	S	Spectator
ES	Evening Standard	SB	Sunday Business
FCO	Foreign and Commonwealth Office	SE	Sunday Express
FO	Foreign Office	SLEF	Scottish League for European
FRUS	Foreign Relations of the United		Freedom
	States	ST	Sunday Times
FT	Financial Times	STel	Sunday Telegraph
G	Guardian	SUS	Scottish Union of Students
HoC	House of Commons	T	The Times
HoL	House of Lords	THJ	The History Journal
I	Independent	TLS	Times Literary Supplement
INS	Intelligence and National Security	TO	Time Out
IoS	Independent on Sunday	WO	War Office
JCH	Journal of Contemporary History	WP	Washington Post

Place of publication is London unless otherwise stated.

PART ONE: FROM HOT TO COLD WAR

1. Anthony Cave Brown, *The Secret Servant: The Life of Sir Stewart Menzies, Churchill's Spymaster*, Michael Joseph, 1988, and *Treason in the Blood*, Michael Joseph, 1996, p. 228.
2 & 3. Robert Cecil, 'C's War, Intelligence and National Security, INS, Vol. 1, No. 2, May 1986.

4. Christopher Andrew, *Secret Service: The Making of the British Intelligence Community*, Heinemann, 1985.
5. Desmond Bristow, *A Game of Moles: The Deceptions of an MI6 Officer*, Little, Brown, p. 183; Brown, *Secret Servant*, p. 229.
6. Cecil; Kim Philby, *My Silent War*, Grove Press (pbk), US, 1968, p. 124.
7. Philby, p. 124; Robert Blake review of *The Secret Servant* in the *London Review*; Hugh

Trevor-Roper, *The Philby Affair: Espionage, Treason, and the Secret Services*, Kimber, 1968.
8. M.R.D. Foot and J.M. Langley, *MI9*, Bodley Head, 1979, p. 176; Patrick Seale and Maureen McConville, *Philby: The Long Road to Moscow*, Hamish Hamilton, 1973, p. 174; Cecil.
9. Philby, p. 124; Blake review.
10. Brown, *Secret Servant*, p. 607; Douglas Botting and Ian Sayer, *America's Secret Army*, Fontana (pbk), 1989, p. 159.

CHAPTER ONE: THE SECOND WORLD WAR

1 & 2. Timothy J. Naftall, 'De Gaulle's Pique and the Allied Counter-Espionage Triangle in World War II', in Hayden B. Peake and Samuel Halpern (eds), *In the Name of Intelligence: Essays in Honour of Walter L. Pforzheimer*, NIBC Press, US, 1994.
3 & 4. Cowgill died in 1991. Cecil; Genrikh Borovik (Phillip Knightley, ed.), *The Philby Files: The Secret Life of the Master Spy – KGB Archives Revealed*, Little, Brown, 1994, pp. 193 & 230–1; Philby, p. 52.
5. John Costello, *Mask of Treachery*, Collins, 1988, p. 414; Nigel West, *MI5: British Security Service Operations 1909–1945*, Triad Panther (pbk), 1983, p. 356.
6. Borovik, p. 231; Cadogan Diaries, 13.8.43, ACAD 1/111, CCA.
7 & 8. The MI5 brief was delivered to the London FBI representative who reported to Washington: as cited in Brown, *Secret Servant*, pp. 473–4; F.H. Hinsley & C.A.G. Simkins, *British Intelligence in the Second World War*, Vol. 4, 'Security and Counter-Intelligence', HMSO, 1990, pp. 56 & 288.
9. Anthony Verrier, *Through the Looking Glass: British Foreign Policy in an Age of Illusions*, Cape, 1983, p. 37; David Stafford, *Britain and European Resistance, 1940–45: A Survey of the Special Operations Executive*, Macmillan, 1980, p. 208; Martin Gilbert, *Winston Churchill, 1941–1945*, Vol. 3, 'The Road to Victory', Heinemann, 1986, p. 729, citing PM's Personal Telegram, T 730/4, 6.4.44, 'Personal and Most Secret', No. 324 to Algiers; Churchill Papers, 20/161, CCA; Winston Churchill, *The Second World War*, Vol. 5, 'Closing the Ring', Cassell, 1952, p. 542.
10. Hinsley & Simkins, p. 288; Costello, p. 431.
11. Bradley F. Smith, *The Ultra-Magic Deals: And the Most Secret Special Relationship 1940–* 46, Airlife, Shrewsbury, 1993, pp. 60 & 198; Hinsley & Simkins, pp. 187–8; Tom Bower, *The Perfect English Spy: Sir Dick White and the Secret War 1935–90*, Heinemann, 1995, p. 66, quoting Pearson Holmes diary, Beinecke Library, Yale University; Michael Smith, *New Cloak, Old Dagger: How Britain's Spies Came in from the Cold*, Gollancz, 1996; PRO HS 4/144, 327, 334.
12. Robert Cecil, *Five of Six at War: Section V of MI6*, INS, Vol. 9, No. 2, April 1994.
13. A.W. Simpson, *In the Highest Degree Odious: Detention without Trial in Wartime Britain*, Oxford University Press (OUP) (pbk), 1994, pp. 187 & 270–1; Phillip Knightley, *The Second Oldest Profession: The Spy as Bureaucrat, Patriot, Fantasist and Whore*, Deutsch, 1986, p. 207.
14. Cecil; Richard J. Aldrich (ed.), *British Intelligence, Strategy and the Cold War, 1945–51*, Routledge, 1992, p. 17.
15. At Guy Liddell's (MI5) instigation, Section V created personality cards which were collated through a centralised SHAEF unit. The Evaluation and Dissemination Section of Section G-2 (Counter Intelligence Sub-Division) dealt mainly with Nazi paramilitary and party organisations. Headed by MI5's Maj. E. Martin Furnival-Jones, it was charged with the distribution of the CPI cards through 'doctrinated' SCI units which provided British FSS and US CIC detachments with information gleaned from 'special sources' – i.e. ISOS decrypts. The SCI units also advised on the interrogation of Italian and German intelligence officials and the recovery of secret documents. Bob de Graaff, 'What Happened to the Central Personality Index?', INS, Vol. 7, No. 3, July 1992.
16. Smith, *Ultra-Magic*, pp. 135, 144, 155, 175 & 197–8; M. Smith, pp. 179 & 300.
17. The JIC was created in July 1939 as an armed services chiefs of staff sub-committee chaired by a Foreign Office official (Victor Cavendish-Bentinck), with instructions to 'improve the efficient working of the intelligence organisation of the country as a whole' through the central analysis of intelligence produced from various sources, including MI6. The JIC advised the chiefs while the Foreign Office retained its monopoly on political intelligence, MI6 representative Philby found his MI5 counterparts 'reasonable', but the army men were 'absolutely crazy' and seething with

'wild passions'. Noel Annan, *Changing Enemies: The Defeat and Regeneration of Germany*, HarperCollins, 1995, pp. 61–2.

18. The Soviets supplied 'a large volume' of low-level German code material to the British 'Y' (interception) representative in Moscow, Edward Crankshaw. By November 1942 the British Military Mission in Moscow believed that a new era in East–West co-operation had begun. It was not to last as the Soviet military command rejected a closer Anglo-Soviet cryptanalytic relationship. Cecil, *Five of Six*; Borovik, pp. 235 & 245.

19. The British had a special security classification – 'Nonesuch' or 'Guard' – 'to indicate information which was not to be revealed to the Americans'. Smith, *Ultra-Magic*, pp. 60, 155, 175 & 197–9.

Head of Military Intelligence liaison, Col. Firebrace, a veteran of the 1919 'White' campaign with 'strong Czarist connections', drew up a report on 'our military intelligence relations with the USSR'. In February, a JIC sub-committee accepted Firebrace's negative conclusion that Soviet non-cooperation was the result of a 'deliberate political policy' to grab everything possible from the western powers and to give nothing in return.

20. Anthony Gorst, 'We must cut our coat according to our cloth: The making of British defence policy, 1945–8', in Aldrich; 'British Military Planning for Postwar Defence, 1943–45', in Anne Deighton (ed.), *Britian and the First Cold War*, Macmillan, 1990.

21. PRO FO N5 598/183/38.

22. Victor Rothwell, *Britain and the Cold War 1941–1947*, 1983, p. 115. Richard J. Aldrich & John Zametica, 'The rise and decline of a strategic concept: the Middle East, 1945–51', in Aldrich; A. Bryant, *Triumph in the West, 1943–46*, Collins, 1959, p. 242; Bradley F. Smith, *Sharing Secrets with Stalin: How the Allies Traded Intelligence 1941–45*, University of Kansas, 1996, p. 240.

23. Julian Lewis, *Changing Direction: British Military Planning for Post-War Strategic Defence, 1942–1947*, Sherwood Press, 1988, pp. 35–53; Smith, *Ultra-Magic*, pp. 155, 175 & 197–8.

24. Rothwell, pp. 118–23.

25 & 26. David W. Ellwood, *Italy 1943–1945*, Leicester University Press, 1985, pp. 29, 46 & 89; Gregory Dale Black, *The United States and Italy, 1943–46; The Drift towards Containment*,

PhD thesis, University of Kansas; Charles Delzell, *Mussolini's Enemies: The Italian Anti-Fascist Resistance*, Princeton, US, 1961. ·

27. Cecil, *'C''s War*; Borovik, p. 235; Bower, p. 66.

28. Dissatisfaction with liaison between MI6 and the Foreign Office led to the appointment of a Foreign Office official, Patrick Reilly, as personal assistant to the MI6 Chief. In September 1943, Reilly was succeeded by Robert Cecil, who was able to see the manoeuvring at close quarters. Cecil, *'C''s War*, T, 21.10.68.

29. Philby, p. 129.

30. William Stevenson, *Intrepid's Last Case*, Sphere (pbk), 1984, p. 123. Jane Sissmore was married to Wing Commander John Archer, who was MI5's wartime liaison officer with the RAF.

31. Bower, pp. 202–3.

32. Tom Bower, *The Red Web: MI6 and the KGB Master Coup*, Aurum Press, 1989, pp. 38–40; David Cesarani, *Justice Delayed*, Heinemann, 1992, p. 140.

CHAPTER TWO: REORGANISATION: SPECIAL OPERATIONS

1, 2 & 4. Bristow, pp. 170–1 & 176. Trevor-Roper, pp. 29 & 39–42.

3. Michael Herman, *The Role of Military Intelligence since 1945*, paper delivered at the Twentieth-Century British Politics and Administration Seminar, Institute of Historical Research, London University, 24.5.89.

5. Aldrich, p. 15.

6, 7, 9, 11 & 12. The exception was the minister in charge, Lord Selbourne, who 'exceeded Gubbins in his abhorrence of communism in all its forms'. Staunchly monarchist, Selbourne displayed a dislike of the leftist EAM/ELAS guerrillas in Greece that was 'only slightly less than his antipathy for Marshal Tito's partisans'. Peter Wilkinson and Joan Bright Astley, *Gubbins and SOE*, Leo Cooper, 1993, pp. 25, 133–7, 144 & 217–25.

8. Ibid., p. 197; Churchill to Ismay, 10.2.44, PRO D41/4, CAB 120/827; Aldrich, p. 42.

10. M. Smith, p. 110.

13. Philby's schoolboy friend, Ian 'Tim' Milne, was appointed head of Section V and shortly after, seeing no future in MI6, Felix Cowgill submitted his resignation and

became a lowly Service Liaison Officer in occupied Germany. Cecil, *'C''s War*.
14. Brown, *Treason*, p. 334.
15. Verrier, pp. 62–3; Borovik, p. 237.
16. The MI6 memorandum can be found in the Donovan papers, quoted in Thomas Earl Mahl, *'48 Land': The United States, British Intelligence and World War II*, PhD thesis, Kent State University, 1994.
17–19. Wilkinson/Astley, pp. 228–32; M. Smith, p. 110; PRO HS 4/51, 52, 127 & 291.
20. Lovat's family ties included his brother, Hugh Fraser, a member of the MI6-linked Intelligence School No. 9 and cousin to the Stirlings of the SAS. Also acquaintances made during special forces training at Inverailort: Mike Calvert taught demolition; Maj. John Munn instructed in map reading; 'Billy' McLean and Fitzroy Maclean, who after the war married Lovat's sister, Veronica. Out of Inverailort developed the SOE Special Training Schools, commanded by Munn, from where emerged a select group of right-wing SOE personnel, who went on to serve postwar in MI6. They included David Smiley, Peter Kemp and Archie Lyall, who, like Kemp, had served in Spain on the nationalist side. Lyall designed a coat of arms for SOE. 'Surrounded by an unexploded bomb; a cloak and rubber dagger, casually left in a bar sinister. The arms are supported by two double agents. The motto *nihil quod tetigit non* (made a balls of it).' Lord Lovat, *March Past: A Memoir*, Weidenfeld, 1978, pp. 9, 159–64, 179 & 359.
21. Aldrich, pp. 196–8; Wilkinson/Astley, pp. 233–4; Patrick Howarth, *Intelligence Chief Extraordinary: The Life of the Ninth Duke of Portland*, Bodley Head, 1986, p. 203.
22. Howarth, pp. 194–5; Brown, *Secret Servant*, p. 964, and *Treason*, p. 344; Viscount Alanbrooke, *Notes on My Life*, Vol. XIV, Liddell Hart Centre, King's College, London, cited in Smith/Deighton, pp. 35 & 50.
23. Reports on Operation UNTHINKABLE – DT, 1.10.98; letter, Julian Lewis, G, 2.10.98.
24. M. Smith, p. 61; Bradley F. Smith, 'Anglo-Soviet Intelligence and the Cold War', in Aldrich, and *Sharing Secrets*, p. 245.
25. PRO AIR 20/2610, 26.6.45; MI3 minute, WO 208/1862, 29.6.45.
26. Aldrich, p. 198; Howarth, p. 199.
27. Brown, *Secret Servant*, p. 684; Bower, *Spy*, p. 50; Borovik, p. 257; Verrier, p. 62.
28. Howarth, pp. 199–200; Brown, *Secret Servant*, p. 578; Nigel West and Oleg Tsarev,

The Crown Jewels: The British Secrets at the Heart of the KGB Archives, HarperCollins, 1998, p. 325.
29. As a result of the UN Monetary and Financial Conference at Bretton Woods in July 1944, SAFEHAVEN aimed to deprive Germany of its assets, including gold stolen from occupied countries and Jews. A Safehaven department within the Ministry of Economic Warfare (MEW) gathered intelligence and pooled it with the Americans, while MI6 units followed up leads. A Reparation Conference held in Paris, in late 1945, dealt with gold transferred to Switzerland. Gold recovered from Germany, unless clearly identifiable, was put into a pool to be distributed by the Tripartite Gold Commission, established in 1946.

Britain's delegate was Desmond Morton, a former MI6 officer who in the thirties directed the Industrial Intelligence Centre (IIC), which gathered industrial and arms-related intelligence on Nazi Germany. It was serviced by MI6's Commercial Section. A close friend of Menzies, Morton was subsequently seconded to the MEW (Intelligence Centre) and became Churchill's trusted personal assistant dealing with intelligence. ('Nazi Gold: Information from the British Archives', *History Notes*, No. 11, Sept. 1996, Historians, Library and Records Department, FCO. MI6 also set up a special unit to recover stolen art treasures located in Germany. Heading it was the Rev. David Caskie (OBE), a PoW in France who joined MI6 in late 1944, leaving a year later. Staying in France, he died in 1983.)

In 1947 250 million Swiss francs were paid out of the German gold deposits in Switzerland and placed with the Federal Reserve Bank in New York. The German and Austrian haul was transferred to the Fed and the Bank of England, to be administered by the Tripartite Gold Commission. Millions from this looted gold were loaned to the US Treasury's Exchange Stabilisation Fund 'to serve as a bankers' tool to dampen the effects of currency speculation'. It has been alleged that this fund became 'a secret source of financing for US clandestine operations' with, in late 1947, nearly $10 million laundered through front organisations and secret accounts to finance covert operations. This 'black currency' was used to thwart the ambitions of the Communist Party in Italy's general election, being channelled through the Vatican to the Christian Democrat Party. The CIA has issued a denial, though this particular operation was carried out by other agencies. William R. Corson, *The Armies of Ignorance: The Rise of the American Intelligence Empire*, Dial Press, US, 1977, pp. 299–300; Christopher Simpson, *Blowback: America's Recruitment of Nazis and Its Effects on the Cold War*, Weidenfeld, 1988, pp. 98–9 & 309; 'US and Allied Efforts to Recover and Restore Gold and Other Assets Stolen or Hidden by Germany During World War II', co-ordinated by Stuart E. Eizenstat, Department of State, May 1997, p. 98.

30. Wilkinson/Astley, pp. 233–4.

31. Borovik, pp. 241–2.

32 & 33. Lovat, pp. 9 & 359; Cecil, *'C''s War*; M.R.D. Foot, *SOE: The Special Operations Executive, 1940–1946*, BBC, 1984, p. 245, and *SOE in France: An Account of the Work of the Special Operations Executive, 1940–44*, HMSO, 1966, p. 443; Richard Aldrich, 'Unquiet in Death: The post-war survival of the "Special Operations Executive", 1945–51', in A. Gorst & W.S. Lucas (eds), *Politics and the Limits of Policy*, Pinter, 1991, pp. 193–5 & 198.

34. Seale/McConville, p. 184; Philby, pp. 129–30; Nigel West, *The Friends: Britain's Post-War Secret Intelligence Operations*, Weidenfeld, 1988, pp. 12–13.

35 & 37. Annan, p. 230; Borovik, pp. 239, 243 & 247.

36. Philip H.J. Davies, *The British Secret Services*, Intelligence Organisations Series, ABC-Clio, Oxford, 1996, p. xxii.

38. Philby, p. 132.

39. West, *Friends*, p. 10; Smith, *Ultra-Magic*, p. 181.

40. Seale/McConville, p. 184, Bower, *Spy*, p. 220.

41. G.K. Young, *Subversion and the British Riposte*, Osian, Glasgow, 1984, p. 113.

42, 44 & 46. Wilkinson/Astley, pp. 236–7; Aldrich, pp. 198–9; letter, Montague Woodhouse, 15.9.94; Davies.

43. Aldrich, p. 199; Verrier, pp. 51–77; Davies; PRO CoS (46) 11.4.46. CAB 79/47.

45. Woodhouse; David Smiley, *Albanian Assignment*, Chatto, 1984, pp. 162–8; Verrier, p. 63.

47. Wilkinson/Astley, p. 239; Aldrich, 'Unquiet in Death', p. 194, quoting PRO CoS (45) 254th mtg (2), 18.10.45; CAB 79/40, discussing JIC (45) 263 (Final), 'Manpower requirements for future intelligence organisations', 13.10.45.

48. While recognising the wartime successes, Menzies's Foreign Office adviser, Robert Cecil, thought the postwar years were 'not his best'. Bristow, pp. 171 & 183–4; Sir K. Strong, *Men of Intelligence*, Cassell, 1970, p. 111; Young, *Subversion*, p. 113; Cecil, *'C''s War*.

CHAPTER THREE: CONTAINMENT

1. Piers Dixon, *Double Diplomacy: The Life of Sir Pierson Dixon, Don and Diplomat*, 1968, p. 166.

2. Gorst.

3. Cecil, *'C''s War*.

4 & 5. John Saville, *The Politics of Continuity: British Foreign Policy and the Labour Government, 1945–46*, Verso, 1993, pp. 25 & 31; Prof. Northedge, cited in Ritchie Ovendale (ed.), *The Foreign Policy of the British Labour Governments, 1945–51*, Leicester University Press, 1984, p. 11.

6. Harold Laski told friends that Labour would 'turn the Foreign Office upside down'. Initially, Hugh Dalton, a critic of the Foreign Office, was to be appointed Foreign Secretary. Saville, p. 86; Frank Roberts, 'Ernest Bevin as Foreign Secretary', in Ovendale; Kenneth Young (ed.), *The Diaries of Sir Robert Bruce Lockhart*, Vol. 2, 1939–1965, Macmillan, 1980, p. 475; Lord Avon, *A Prime Minister Remembers*, Cassell, 1965, pp. 550–1.

7. Despite its great qualities, Prof. Bullock's book (*Ernest Bevin: Foreign Secretary 1945–1951*, OUP (pbk), 1985) is deeply flawed. It is hardly possible today to write about a Foreign Secretary, particularly one at the height of the Cold War, without mentioning the intelligence services, but Bullock effortlessly achieves this feat. Raymond Smith, 'Ernest Bevin, British Officials and British Soviet Policy, 1945–47', in Deighton, pp. 312–13; Saville, pp. 104–5.

8. Douglas Dodds-Parker, *Political Eunuch*, Springwood, 1986, p. 43; Denis Healey, *The Time of My Life*, Michael Joseph, 1989, pp. 103–4; J. Harvey (ed.), *The War Diaries of Oliver Harvey*, 1978, pp. 62–3; Rothwell, p. 252; Melvyn P. Leffler, *A Preponderance of Power: National Security, The Truman Administration, and the Cold War*, Stanford University Press, US, 1992, p. 135; Lockhart Diaries, p. 576.

9. Smith in Deighton, p. 39; Bullock, p. 117; PRO FO No. 1092, 20.3.46; Peter Hennessy,

Never Again: British 1945–1951, Vintage (pbk), 1993, p. 262.

10. R. Butler & M.E. Pelly (eds), *Documents on British Policy Overseas*, Series 1, Vol. 1, HMSO, 1984, pp. 573–4; Bullock, p. 117.

11. Bullock, p. 234; Rothwell, pp. 255–9; PRO FO 800/475, ME/46/22. 12.1.46.

12 & 13. Vladislav Zubok and Constantine Pleshakov, *Inside the Kremlin's Cold War: From Stalin to Khrushchev*, Harvard University Press, US, 1996, pp. 28–38 & 45.

14. Roberts had seen 'The Long Telegram' written by his counterpart in the American embassy, George Kennan, whose views became equally influential in shaping US policy against the Soviet Union. PRO JIC (46)38(O), final review 14.6.46, DO 35/1604; Smith in Deighton, p. 37; Rothwell, p. 248; Aldrich, p. 18.

15. Frank Roberts, *Dealing with Dictators: The Destruction and Revival of Europe 1930–70*, Weidenfeld, 1991, pp. 80–1; PRO FO 371/56763 N4065/97/38, 14.3.46, & 371/56763 N4156/97/38, 17.3.46.

16. PRO FO 371/56832 N5572/605/38G, 18.3.46; 371/56763 N4157/97/38, 18.3.46; 371/56885 N5170/5169/38; Ray Merrick, 'The Russia Committee of the British Foreign Office and the Cold War, 1946–47', JCH, Vol. 20, 1985.

17. Foreign Office officials paid little heed to Churchill's observation that the West provided the 'outside enemy' which 'communist power' needed to keep itself stable. Deputy Soviet Foreign Minister Vyshinsky argued that the extent of the Soviet propaganda campaign against Britain was exaggerated. The Soviets were genuinely concerned about 'the incomplete repatriation of war prisoners' and the 'White Russian and reactionary elements' in Germany, Austria and Italy – the source 'of a lot of trouble and irritation', made worse by MI6 subjecting them to 'anti-Soviet propaganda'. Warner blithely dismissed Vyshinsky's performance as 'special pleading'. PRO FO 371/56832 N6344/605/38, 2.4.46; Saville, p. 51; Healey, p. 101; Rothwell, p. 254.

18. PRO FO 371/56885 N6092/5169/38, 7.5.46, & 930/488, 22.5.46; Smith in Deighton, pp. 41–2.

19. Cecil, *'C''s War*.

20. Robert Cecil, 'The Cambridge Comintern', in Christopher Andrew and David Dilks (eds), *The Missing Dimension: Governments and Intelligence Communities in the Twentieth*

Century, Macmillan, 1984; Michael Herman, *Intelligence Power in Peace and War*, CUP, 1996, p. 292.

21. Merrick; Aldrich, pp. 19 & 43.

22. Saville, p. 16.

23. W. Scott Lucas and C.J. Morris, 'A very British crusade: the Information Research Department and the beginning of the Cold War', in Aldrich.

24. Smith, in Deighton, p. 43; PRO FO 371/56887 N14732/5169/38; 371/56887 N15843/5169/38, 15.11.46; 371/66370 N8114/271/38, 28.7.47; Young, *Subversion*, p. 11.

25. PRO FO 371/56887 N14732/5169/38.

26. Saville, pp. 138 & 140; Robert Frazier, *Anglo-American Relations with Greece: The Coming of the Cold War, 1942–47*, Macmillan, 1991, p. 120.

27. Smith, in Deighton, p. 47; Bevan to Attlee, PRO P.M./47/8, ME/47/4; FO 800/476, 9.1.47; Aldrich/ Zametica, p. 252.

28. H.W. Brand, *Inside the Cold War: Loy Henderson and the Rise of the American Empire 1918–61*, OUP, 1991, p. 155. Wine merchants H. Sichel and Sons had been used by Claude Dansey as part of his 1930s Z-network.

29. Mahl.

30 & 31. Frazier, pp. 147 & 159; Saville, citing Francis Williams on Bevin, p. 45.

32. R. Hyam, 'Africa and the Labour Government 1945–51', *Journal of Imperial and Commonwealth History*, Vol. XVI, 1988.

33. John Kent and John W. Young, 'The "Third Force" and NATO', in Beatrice Heuser and Robert O'Neill (eds), *Securing Peace in Europe, 1945–62: Thoughts for the Post-Cold War Era*, Macmillan, 1992; Correlli Barnett, *The Lost Victory: British Dreams, British Realities, 1945–1950*, Macmillan, 1995.

34. Bevin told Colonial Secretary Arthur Creech Jones that 'you develop Africa by putting Africans in lorries and letting them drive into the bush', Hennessy, p. 216.

35. Saville, p. 152.

36. PRO DO (47) 44, 22.5.47; CAB 21/1800.

37. Aldrich, p. 18.

CHAPTER FOUR: 'UNCERTAIN ALLIES'

1. British Security Co-Ordination (BSC): 'An Account of Secret Activities in the Western Hemisphere, 1940–45', known as 'the Bible' by its former agents, cited in Mahl; Davies, p. xxiii.

2. David Ignatius, 'Britain's War in America:

How Churchill's Agents Secretly Manipulated the US Before Pearl Harbor', WP, 17.9.89.

3, 4 & 7. Susan Ann Bower, *Creating the 'Special Relationship': British Propaganda in the United States during the Second World War*, PhD thesis, Cornell University, 1991; Clive Ponting, *1940: Myth and Reality*, Hamish Hamilton, 1990, pp. 197, 214–15, 223 & 235.

5 & 8. Nelson D. Lankford, *The Last American Aristocrat: The Biography of David K.E. Bruce, 1898–1977*, Little, Brown, 1996, pp. 130 & 186; John Ranelagh, *The Agency: The Rise and Decline of the CIA*, Sceptre (pbk), 1988, p. 68.

6. Obit. of Henry Hyde, DT, 16.5.97.

9. Arthur B. Darling, *The Central Intelligence Agency: An Instrument of Government to 1950*, Pennsylvania State University Press, 1990, p. 26; PRO FO 371/44557 AN 2560/22/45; Ranelagh, p. 235.

10. Alex Danchev, *Very Special Relationship*, Brasseys, 1986, p. 221.

11. Leohnis was later Director-General of GCHQ (1960–4).

12. Right up to the end of the war Ultra material made its way to Moscow as a 'Most Reliable Occasional source', though by April the Soviets had been told for certain that the origin was from 'interception'. Smith, *Ultra-Magic*, pp. 199–203 & 223; R.V. Jones, *Reflections on Intelligence*, Mandarin (pbk), 1990, p. 15; M. Smith, p. 24.

13. W.H. Jackson, *Co-ordination of Intelligence Functions and the Organisation of Secret Intelligence in the British Intelligence System (Top Secret)*, OSS, July 1945; Ludwell Lee Montague, *General Walter Bedell Smith as Director of Central Intelligence, Oct. 1950– Feb. 1953*, Pennsylvania State University Press, US, 1996, pp. 11, 57 & 159; Darling, pp. 18–19, 59–60 & 120.

14. Michael F. Hopkins, 'The Washington Embassy: The Role of an Institution in Anglo-American Relations, 1945–55', in Richard J. Aldrich and Michael F. Hopkins (eds), *Intelligence, Defence and Diplomacy: British Policy in the Post-War World*, Frank Cass, 1994, p. 88; John Bright-Holmes (ed.), *Like It Was: The Diaries of Malcolm Muggeridge*, Collins, 1981, p. 227.

15. Eric Jones was Director-General of GCHQ (1952–60). Smith, *Ultra-Magic*, p. 220; M. Smith, p. 27; PRO CAB 81/92 & 81/93; Harry S. Truman Library, Independence, Missouri, Naval Aide files, Box 10, File 1; Andrew, *SIGINT*.

16. David Bruce made another trip to Europe to assess the requirement for combating communist subversion. Douglass later became the CIA Assistant Director of the Special Services. Lankford, pp. 184–5; Ranelagh, pp. 102, 106, 748, 754 & 767; Smith, *Ultra-Magic*, p. 225.

17. Jackson took up a seat on the National Security Council. In 1948, Secretary of Defense Forrestal asked Jackson to participate with Dulles in an investigation of the CIA on behalf of the NSC. Jackson became a Deputy Director at the CIA under Bedell Smith and was responsible for internal reorganisation. Mahl and Andrew, *SIGINT*.

18. The chief of the CIG Soviet division was Harry Rositzke, a former OSS desk officer in London and a specialist on Soviet affairs, whose primary source was an old MI6 Section IX compendium describing the Russian Intelligence Service.

19. Peter Parker, *For Starters: The Business of Life*, Cape, 1989, pp. 36–7; Bower, *Red Web*, pp. 85–6; Borovik, p. 247.

20. Richard J. Aldrich, 'The Value of Residual Empire: Anglo-American Co-operation in Asia after 1945', in Aldrich/Hopkins, p. 237.

21. GCHQ moved to Cheltenham in 1952. This was pushed through by Wing Commander Claude Daubeny, wartime head of signals intelligence on the Air Staff and for all the services in the immediate postwar period. He wanted to combine his visits with his interest in horse-racing. Smith, *Ultra-Magic*, p. 181; Alan Stripp, *Codebreaker in the Far East*, Frank Cass, 1989.

22. Smith, *Ultra-Magic*, pp. 220 & 226; Stephen Dorril and Robin Ramsay, *Smear!: Wilson and the Secret State*, Fourth Estate, 1991, pp. 7–8; David Leigh, *Wilson Plot: The Intelligence Services and the Discrediting of a Prime Minister 1945–76*, Heinemann, 1988, pp. 47–51; Hugh Thomas, *Armed Truce: The Beginnings of the Cold War 1945–46*, Sceptre (pbk), 1988, p. 298; Historians, LRD of the FCO, 'IRD: Origins and Establishment of the Foreign Office Information Research Department, 1946–48', *History Notes*, No. 9, Aug. 1995.

23. Jeffrey T. Richelson and Desmond Ball, *The Ties that Bind: Intelligence Co-operation between the UKUSA Countries – the United Kingdom, the United States of America, Canada, Australia and New Zealand* (2nd ed., pbk), Unwin Hyman, 1990, p. 5.

24. CIA, 'The Possibility of Britain's Abandonment of Overseas Military Commitments', ORE 93–94, 23.12.49; Ranelagh, p. 235.

25. Darling, p. 128; Bristow, p. 202.

26. Peter Grose, *Gentleman Spy: The Life of Allen Dulles*, Deutsch, 1993, p. 317; Young, *Subversion*, pp. 137–8.

CHAPTER FIVE: THE WORLD-VIEW

1 & 2. Anthony Glees, *Secrets of the Service: British Intelligence and Communist Subversion 1939–51*, Cape, 1987, pp. 163 & 264; West/ Tsarev, pp. 310–12; Nigel West (ed.), *The Faber Book of Espionage*, Faber, 1993, p. 233; West, *Friends*, pp. 10–11; Brown, *Secret Servant*, p. 474; Bright-Holmes, p. 350.

3. R.N. Carew Hunt, *The Theory and Practice of Marxism*, Geoffrey Bles, 1950, and *Marxism: Past and Present*, Geoffrey Bles, 1954.

4. Jenny Rees, *Looking for Mr Nobody: The Secret Life of Goronwy Rees*, Weidenfeld, 1994.

5. In 1951, Hugh Seton-Watson was appointed Professor of Russian History at the spooks' favourite academic institution, the School of Slavonic and East European Studies. Hugh Seton-Watson, *The East European Revolution*, Methuen, 1950, p. x; Bickham Sweet-Escott, *Baker Street Irregular*, Methuen, 1965, pp. 191 & 203; West, *Friends*, pp. 11 & 23.

6. Engaged in the sixties by the Foreign Office on research, J.M. Mackintosh published *Strategy and Tactics of Soviet Foreign Policy* (OUP, 1962) and took over the influential Soviet desk in the Cabinet Office, which he held until his retirement in 1987. Malcolm Mackintosh on his time in Bulgaria in T.L. Hammond (ed.), *The Anatomy of Communist Takeovers*, New Haven, US, 1975, pp. 239–40; 'The final testimony of George Kennedy Young', in *Lobster*, No. 19, May 1990.

7–11. Young, *Subversion*, p. 10; Mackintosh, pp. 3–19; Seton-Watson, pp. 171 & 381.

12. Trevor Barnes, 'The Secret Cold War: The CIA and American Foreign Policy in Europe, 1946–1956', Part 1, THJ, 24.2.81; Rhodri Jeffreys-Jones, *The CIA and American Democracy*, Yale University Press (pbk), 1989, p. 47.

13 & 14. Young, *Subversion*, pp. 10 & 97; George K. Young, *Masters of Indecision: An Inquiry into the Political Process*, Methuen, 1962, p. 26.

15. Rothwell, pp. 391–2; Robert M. Blum, 'Surprised by Tito: The Anatomy of an Intelligence Failure', in *Diplomatic History*, Vol. XII, No. 1, winter 1988.

16 & 17. Geoffrey Swain, 'The Cominform: Tito's International?', THJ, Vol. 35, No. 3, 1992; Mackintosh, p. 21.

18. PRO FO 371/66369 N7458/271/38; 371/ 66370 N7458/271/38, 25.6.47.

19. Dixon diary, 2.7.47; PRO CAB 128/10, 8.7.47.

20. Michael McGwire, *The Genesis of Soviet Threat Perception*, Brookings Institute, Washington (where he was an analyst in the late eighties), 1987, pp. 33–4.

21. Douglas Porch, *The French Secret Services: From the Dreyfus Affair to the Gulf War*, Farrar, Straus & Giroux, NY, 1995, p. 284.

22. Frazier, p. 160; Beatrice Heuser, *Western Containment Policies in the Cold War: The Yugoslav Case 1948–53*, 1990, pp. 25–7; Caroline Kennedy-Pipe, *Stalin's Cold War: Soviet Strategies in Europe, 1943 to 1956*, Manchester University Press, 1995, pp. 95 & 152–3.

23. Mackintosh, p. 20; *Lobster*, No. 19, May 1990.

24. Interview with Michael Herman reprinted in *Lobster* No. 30, February 1996. Herman was a senior figure at GCHQ and was seconded to the JIC in the early seventies. Christopher Mayhew, *Time to Explain*, Hutchinson, 1987, pp. 107–8.

25. *Lobster* No. 30; Aldrich, pp. 16–17; Alex Craig, *The Joint Intelligence Committee and the Outbreak of the Cold War*, MPhil thesis, Cambridge University, 1997.

26. *Lobster* Nos 19 & 30; Zubok/Pleshakov, pp. 26–8; Heuser, pp. 19–23, 29 & 49–52.

27–29. Blum; Adam B. Ulam, *Titoism and the Cominform*, CUP, 1952, p. 106.

30. Philip Noel-Baker, as Bevin's Minister of State before McNeil, was presumably responsible for liaison with MI6. A pacifist Labour MP, he appointed to his private office 'a number of brilliant and attractive intellectuals' who had been in Victor Rothschild's circle. They included Stuart Hampshire, Tessa Mayor, who later married Rothschild, and Pat Llewelyn-Davies. C.L. Sulzberger, *A Long Row of Candles: Memories and Diaries, 1934–54*, Macmillan, 1969, p. 412; Young, *Subversion*, p. 11.

31 & 33. Heuser, pp. 35, 41–52 & 71; Healey, p. 107; Rothwell, p. 393.

32. In London, the head of the Far Eastern

Department, Robin Scott, saw 'the possibility of China developing in the way Yugoslavia did'. This was to be of some significance in that Scott was later to have a profound influence on policy and MI6 activities in that region. He had been, in turn, influenced by another official in the department, Guy Burgess, who briefly overlapped with a young George Blake, who was undertaking an orientation course before assuming his first MI6 posting abroad as vice-consul in Seoul, South Korea. Officials noticed that Burgess drew 'a fine distinction between Soviet Leninism and the agrarian populism which he detected emerging in Red China'. He attacked the American view that the USSR and China 'constituted a Marxist-Leninist monolith'.

34. R.N. Carew-Hunt, 'Willi Munzenberg', in David Footman (ed.), *International Communism*, St Antony's Papers IX, Oxford: Chatto & Windus, 1960; Gunther Nollau, *International Communism and World Revolution*, Hollis & Carter, 1961; Sanche de Gramont, *The Secret War: The Story of International Espionage since 1945*, Deutsch, 1962, p. 30.

CHAPTER SIX: PROPAGANDA

1 & 2. 'IRD: Origins and Establishment of the Foreign Office Information Research Department, 1946–48.'
3. Aldrich, p. 15; Lockhart Diaries, pp. 480, 490 & 492; Robert Bruce Lockhart, 'Political Warfare', RUSI lecture, 25.1.50.
4. Lucas/Morris; Lockhart Diaries, p. 648.
5. Lynn Smith, 'Covert British propaganda: The Information Research Department: 1947–77', in *Millennium: Journal of International Studies*, Vol. 9, No. 1; Ray Merrick, 'The Russia Committee of the British Foreign Office and the Cold War, 1946–47', in JCH, Vol. 20, 1985, pp. 453–68; Hugh Wilford, 'The Information Research Department: Britain's secret Cold War weapon revealed', in *Review of International Studies*, Vol. 24, No. 3, 1998; Paul Lashmar and James Oliver, *Britain's Secret Propaganda War, 1948–1977*, Sutton, Stroud, 1998.
6–8, 12 & 13. Lucas/Morris; Lynn Smith; Historians, LRD of the FCO; PRO CAB 129/23 (CP(48)8); Mayhew, pp. 108–9; M. Smith, p. 139.

9 & 10. The English translation of Protocol M is in Otto Heilbrunn, *The Soviet Secret Services*, Allen & Unwin, 1956. Simon Ollivant, Protocol 'M', in David A. Charters and Maurice A.J. Tugwell (eds), *Deception Operations: Studies in the East–West Context*, Brassey's, 1990; PRO FO 371/70477 (C163/1/18).
11. PRO FO 371/7168/N765/38G, 15.1.48; Lockhart Diaries, p. 648.
14 & 15. Lucas/Morris; LRD; Mayhew, pp. 111–12; PRO FO 371/71632A N13368/1/38G, 27.12.48.
16. PRO FO 1110/11, Warner to Gascoigne, Nov. 1948.
17. Ollivant.
18. Lucas/Morris, LRD; PRO CAB 130/37, GEN 231/2, 4.5.48; 371/70478 C2182/1/18, 23.2.48; Lockhart Diaries, pp. 686 & 632–3.
19. M. Smith, p. 139.
20. LRD.
21 & 24. Gary D. Rawnsley, *Radio Diplomacy and Propaganda: The BBC and VOA in International Politics, 1956–64*, Macmillan, 1996, pp. 23, 166 & 186; Hugh Greene, *The Third Floor Front*, Bodley Head, 1969, p. 32.
22. Lockhart Diaries, pp. 648 & 686.
23. PRO FO 371/77389 N6550/1053/63, 24.6.49.
25. PRO CAB 130/37, GEN231, 3rd meeting, 19.12.49; Lynn Smith; Jonathan Bloch and Patrick Fitzgerald, *British Intelligence and Covert Action, Africa, Middle East and Europe since 1945*, Junction, 1983, p. 90.
26. Verrier, p. 155; Young, *Subversion*, p. 12; LRD (FCO).

CHAPTER SEVEN: ROLL-BACK

1 & 2. Beatrice Heuser, 'Stalin as Hitler's Successor', in Heuser/O'Neill; Beatrice Heuser, 'Covert Action within British and American Concepts of Containment, 1948–51', in Aldrich.
3. Young, *Subversion*, p. 11; Aldrich, pp. 15 & 18; Tom Bower, *Blind Eye to Murder*, Deutsch, 1982, p. 410.
4, 5 & 6. Montgomery Diary, BLM/1/186/1, June–Sept. 1948, Section D, 'The Cold War', Imperial War Museum; Aldrich, pp. 13 & 21–2.
7. Aldrich review of Heuser in INS.
8. Young, *Subversion*, p. 11.
9. Young, *Masters*, p. 9; Aldrich, p. 209; Bower, *Red Web*, p. 85; Heuser, p. 56.

10. Frazier, p. 160; *Lobster*, No. 19; Bower, *Spy*, p. 186; Young, *Subversion*, p. 10; Mackintosh, p. 30.

11. Aldrich, pp. 22–3; PRO FO 371/77623 N171/1052/38G, 17.12.48.

12 & 13. Heuser, pp. 49, 51, 56–7 & 66, and 'Covert Action'; Russia Committee meetings, 3 & 17.2.49, PRO FO 371/77617 N3355/1051/38G, 7.3.49; 371/77616 N3356/1051/38G, 22.3.49; 371/77617 N3413/1051/38G, 4.4.49.

14. M. Smith, p. 114; PRO CAB 81/94.

15. Interview with Kim Philby, *Kodumma*, Estonia, 13.10.71; Bower, *Spy*, p. 145; Tony Benn, *The End of an Era: Diaries 1980–90*, Arrow (pbk), 1994, p. 62.

16–18. Heuser, pp. 45, 51, 66–7, 89, 109 & 123; PRO FO 371/77622 N11007/1051/38, 28.7.49.

19 & 20. Aldrich, 'Unquiet in Death', p. 195; E, 27.11.82.

21 & 22. Young, *Subversion*, pp. 12–13; Seton-Watson, pp. 387–8; *Lobster*, No. 19; Mackintosh, p. 55.

23. Heuser, p. 25, and 'Hitler's Successor'.

24. Hennessy, pp. 407 & 413.

25. PRO DEFE 6/14, JP(50)90 (Final), 'The Spread of Russian Communism', 11.7.50.

26. Hennessy, pp. 407 & 413; Grose, p. 315; Young, *Subversion*, p. 138.

PART TWO: THE FRONT LINE

CHAPTER EIGHT: GERMANY AND THE 3×5s

1 & 3–5. Ronald C. Newton, *The 'Nazi Menace' in Argentina, 1931–47*, Stanford University Press, 1992, pp. xiv, xvii, 225, 279, 310, 349–55, 422, 433 & 468–9; PRO FO 371/44708, 3.1.44, & 371/46766, 20.4.45; Annual Report, 1944–45, Special Intelligence Service, FBI, 37, FBI Archives, 64–4104-684X. Cols. Brian Mountain (later chair of Eagle Star) and Kenneth Keith (Rolls-Royce) had wanted MI6 units, especially in Switzerland, to seize German assets, including gold: 'The scent is now hot and it will belong to the person who gets his hands on it first.' The efforts of Brig. Michael Waring, intelligence officer and SHAEF liaison officer tracing Reichsbank gold, soon foundered. Despite MI6 retrieval of documents, the Mountain/Keith proposal was blocked by (Sir) Mark Turner, Under-Secretary at the Control Office for Germany, possibly because of collaboration with the Nazis by European banks. An influential banker with Robert Benson (partner Rex Benson was an MI6 officer and Menzies's cousin), Turner served with the Ministry of Economic Warfare. Leaving the Commission in 1947, he was appointed deputy chair of Rio Tinto Zinc and a director of Kleinwort Benson. Tom Bower, *The Paperclip Conspiracy: The Battle for the Spoils and Secrets of Nazi Germany*, Paladin (pbk), 1988, pp. 92–3; PRO FO 942/81. G, 24.5.96; Ian Sayer and Douglas Botting, *Nazi Gold: The Story of the World's Greatest Robbery – and its Aftermath*, Grafton (pbk), 1985, pp. 149–50.

2. Robin Dennison, *Publishing the Memoirs of Intelligence People*, INS, Vol. 7, No. 2, April 1992; Ladislas Farago, *Aftermath: Martin Bormann and the Fourth Reich*, Hodder, 1974, pp. 204–9; Kurt Tauber, *Beyond Eagle and Swastika: German Nationalism Since 1945*, Vol. 11, Wesleyan University Press, US, 1967, pp. 113 & 1108.

6. Wilkinson/Astley, p. 234; Richard Aldrich (ed.), *British Intelligence, Strategy and the Cold War, 1945–51*, 1992, pp. 200 & 212; Anthony Kemp, *The Secret Hunters*, O'Mara, 1986, p. 81; ST, 28.12.97.

7 & 8. West, *The Friends*, pp. 20–2.

9. The Direction des Services de Renseignements et des Services de Sécurité Militaire (DSM), whose head, Paul Pailloe, was well regarded by Menzies. A DSM representative was posted to the Joint X-2/Section V war room, but he resigned in November 1944. Douglas Botting and Ian Sayer, *America's Secret Army*, 1989, p. 205; M. Smith, *New Cloak, Old Dagger*, p. 179; PRO CAB 81/124.

10. Graaf; PRO WO 219(5276).

11. John Loftus, *The Belarus Secret*, Penguin (pbk), 1983, p. 167; Christopher Simpson, *Blowback*, 1988, p. 72; Naftali.

12. Bower, *Spy*, pp. 71–2, and *Blind Eye*, pp. 219–26; Mary Ellen Reese, *General Reinhard Gehlen: The CIA Connection*, George Mason University Press, US, 1990, p. 215.

The 2nd SAS Regiment War Crimes Investigation Team was led by intelligence officers Maj. Eric Barkworth and Capt. Yuri Galitzine, who seconded to the Department of the Judge Advocate-General. A naturalised Russian prince, Galitzine had been a member of an Allied Combat Propaganda Team in southern France with SHAEF's Psychological Warfare Department and a T-Force unit searching for captured Nazi documents. SOE veteran Vera Atkins was searching for F-Section survivors and attached at Bad Oeynhausen to the SAS investigation team which was still operating as late as 1948. Thirteen bilingual ex-SOE officers were sent to Germany as part of the War Crimes Group but had no investigative experience. Anthony Kemp, *The SAS Savage Wars of Peace*, Signet (pbk), 1995, pp. 3–5, and *Secret Hunters*, pp. 36, 51 & 74.

13. Brown, *Secret Servant*, p. 652.

14. Reese, pp. 8–9.

15. Simpson, p. 67; John Loftus, General Accounting Office Report GAO/GGD-85-86 entitled 'Nazis and Axis Collaborators Were Used to Further US Anti-Communist Objectives in Europe – Some Immigrated to the United States', oversight hearing before the House Sub-Committee on Immigration, Refugees and International Law, 17.10.85, p. 90.

16. Farago, p. 168; Magnus Linklater, Isabel Hilton and Neal Ascherson, *Klaus Barbie: The Fourth Reich and the Neo-Fascist Connection*, Coronet (pbk), 1985, pp. 174–5.

17. Tauber, Vol. 1, pp. 112–13 & 239–40, & Vol. 2, pp. 983 & 1054.

18. Linklater, pp. 169; E.H. Cookridge: *Gehlen: Spy of the Century*, Corgi (pbk), 1972, pp. 179–80; PRO CAB 81/124; M. Smith, p. 179.

19. Simpson, pp. 57 & 67; Knightley, *Second Oldest Profession*, p. 236.

20. Cookridge, pp. 191–2; Reese, p. 9.

21. Reese, pp. 42–3 & 47–9; G.K. Young, *Subversion and the British Riposte*, 1983, p. 132.

22. Borovik, pp. 245–6. Philby letter to Mosley (7.4.77) in Leonard Mosley, *Dulles: A Biography of Eleanor, Allen and John Foster Dulles and their Family Network*, Dial Press, NY, 1978, pp. 493–6; Cookridge, p. 192.

23. Botting/Sayer, *Secret Army*, pp. 278 & 328.

24. Grose, pp. 314–15.

25. Reese, pp. 106–8, 118–23 & 211.

26. Ibid., p. 15; BBC2, *Timewatch*, 'Chanel', 29.1.95; Simpson, p. 93; Loftus, p. 186; Brown, *Secret Servant*, p. 567. Interrogation of Walter Schellenberg in National Archives, Washington, DC, Modern Records Branch, Captured Enemy Documents Section in Record Group 165 (Records of the War Department General and Special Staffs), July 1945.

27. Linklater *et al.*, p. 186; Loftus, p. 232;

Mark Aarons and John Loftus, *Ratlines: How the Vatican's Nazi Networks Betrayed Western Intelligence to the Soviets*, Heinemann, 1991, p. 232; Mark Aarons, *Sanctuary!: Nazi Fugitives in Australia*, Heinemann, Sydney, 1989, pp. 124–5.

28. Perry Biddiscombe, 'Operation Selection Board: The Growth and Suppression of the Neo-Nazi "Deutsche Revolution" 1945–47', INS, Vol. 11, No. 1, January 1996.

29–30 & 32–33. Tom Bower, *Klaus Barbie: Butcher of Lyons*, Corgi (pbk), 1985, pp. 147–8 & 290, and *Paperclip*, pp. 155 & 290. Loftus, pp. 173, 186 & 232–3; Linklater *et al.*, pp. 173–7 & 180–6; Botting/Sayer, *Secret Army*, p. 329.

31. Part of Deutsche Revolution's strategy was to co-ordinate its activities with the British. At the end of 1946, Kurt Ellersiek was contacted, via a CIC-sponsored German agent, by a British officer who 'expressed secret sympathies with the National Socialist cause'. The officer offered to arrange a meeting with a 'British Foreign Office expert', who favoured proposals to form a conservative youth movement to work with groups abroad. In mid-January 1947, Ellersiek exchanged information with the 'expert'. At the same time, the private International Committee for the Study of European Questions published a damning report on the failure of denazification in Germany. Headed by Lord Vansittart, former Cabinet minister Lord Brabazon, Professor D.W. Brogan, and leading French and Belgian statesmen, the committee had access to an agent infiltrated into European collaborationist circles. It claimed that a new neo-Nazi underground had developed across Germany which had access to funds hidden in Switzerland. Swiss bankers denied the allegation, but it now appears more plausible following recent revelations on Nazi gold.

34. Intelligence Division 'Summary' No. 21, 15.7.47, Special Annex: 'Right Wing Movements Curtailed by Operation Selection Board', State Department Decimal File 1945–49, 740.00119 Control (Germany), RG 59, NA; NYT, 24.2.47; Botting/Sayer, *Secret Army*, p. 299; Linklater *et al.*, p. 183; Simpson, p. 187.

35 & 36. Linklater *et al.*, p. 187; Bower, *Paperclip*, p. 158; Simpson, pp. 46–51 & 302; Cookridge, pp. 243 & 295.

37. Loftus, p. 186; Linklater *et al.*, pp. 190–1; Erhard Debringhaus, *Klaus Barbie*, US, 1984, p. 130.

38. Linklater *et al.*, pp. 193–5 & 209; statement of Earl S. Browning Jr (Col. USA, retired), 'My Involvement with Klaus Barbie', 15.6.88, published as Appendix in Botting/ Sayer, *Secret Army*.
39. Graaf & Naftali; Aarons, p. 121; Bower, *Blind Eye* (rev. ed., 1995), p. 134.
40. Simpson, p. 77.
41. Naftali; Roger Faligot and Pascal Krop, *La Piscine: The French Secret Services 1944–1984*, Blackwell, Oxford, 1990, pp. 33–4.
42. Ibid., p. 299; Cesarani, p. 91; Graaf; Hella Pick, *Simon Wiesenthal: A Life in Search of Justice*, Weidenfeld, 1996, p. 133.
43. George Blake, *No Other Choice: An Autobiography*, Cape, 1990, pp. 100–2.
44. PRO FO 371/70501, 10.7.48; Appendix B, Report from HQ Intelligence Division BAOR, 371/70648, 371/70504, 29.7.48; Sheila Kerr, 'Secret Hotline to Moscow: Donald Maclean and the Berlin Crisis of 1948', in Anne Deighton (ed.), *Britain and the First Cold War*, Macmillan, 1990, p. 72; Young, *Subversion*, p. 97, and *Masters of Indecision*, 1992, p. 26; Bower, *Spy*, p. 210.
45. Aarons, p. 77.
46. The Suspects Lists are still not available for scrutiny though a copy of a March 1947 CROWCASS list is held by the MoD. Loftus; William R. Corson, *Armies of Ignorance*, 1977.
47–50. A ratline is 'the rope ladder reaching to the top of the mast, the last place of safety when the ship is going down'. Aarons/ Loftus, p. 240; Loftus, pp. 174 & 187; Aarons, pp. 77–8; Botting/Sayer, *Secret Army*, p. 329.
51. David Alvarez, 'Vatican Intelligence Capabilities in the Second World War', INS, Vol. 6, No. 3, July 1986; Owen Chadwick, *Britain and the Vatican During the Second World War*, CUP, 1986, pp. 55, 127, 297–300 & 313; Sam Derry, *The Rome Escape Line, the Story of the British Organisation in Rome for Assisting Escaped Prisoners-of-War 1943–44*, Harrap, 1960, pp. 43 & 238; M.R.D. Foot & J.M. Langley, *MI9*, 1970, pp. 165–70 & 305; Aarons/Loftus, pp. 18–19. Hugh Montgomery's brother Peter was an intelligence officer and gay partner of MI5 officer Anthony Blunt.
52–53. Farago, pp. 169–71; Tauber, Vol. 1, pp. 122–3 & 240, & Vol. 2, pp. 1054 & 1109; Loftus; Pick, pp. 126–7.
54. Linklater *et al.*, pp. 235–6.
55–58. George Neagoy, who was responsible for shipping Barbie out of Bolivia, joined the CIA in 1951. The records of the ratline were consigned to the flames by Milano, Lyons and Del Greco. Col. James Milano and Patrick Brogan, *Soldiers, Spies and the Rat Line: America's Undeclared War against the Soviets*, Brassey's, 1995, pp. 46, 61, 117–20, 144 & 220–1; Aarons/Loftus, p. 242; Simpson, p. 186; Linklater *et al.* pp. 248–50.

CHAPTER NINE: AUSTRIA: THE SHOOTING GALLERY

1–3. Robert H. Keyerslingk, *Austria in World War II: An Anglo-American Dilemma*, McGill-Queen's University Press, Canada, 1988, pp. 163 & 183; Gordon Shepherd, *The Austrian Odyssey*, Macmillan, 1957, pp. 158–9 & 169; Young, *Subversion*, p. 96.
4. Robert Edwin Herzstein, *Waldheim: The Missing Years*, Grafton, 1988, pp. 168 & 284; Michael Palumbo, *The Waldheim Files: Myth and Reality*, Faber (pbk), 1988, pp. 27 & 100; Shepherd, pp. 269–70; Hersh, p. 140.
5 & 6. Suzanne Fesq, *The Duchess of St Albans*, W.H. Allen, 1975, pp. 182–3 & 192–7.
7–9. Marsha Williams, *White among the Reds*, Shepheard-Walwyn, 1988, pp. 48, 156 & 209– 10. A journalist and author, Pryce-Jones became editor of the *Times Literary Supplement* in 1948. From 1961 he worked for the Ford Foundation in New York.
10. *Lobster*, No. 19, May 1990; Bower, *Spy*, p. 186.
11–13. Aldrich, *British Intelligence*, pp. 199 & 212; Hugh Thomas, *Armed Truce*, 1988, p. 565; M. Smith, p. 111; PRO FO 371/46604; WO 193/637a.
14. David Howarth, *Pursued by a Bear: A Biography*, Collins, 1986, pp. 162–4 & 166; Nicholas Bethell, *The Great Betrayal: The Untold Story of Kim Philby's Biggest Coup*, Hodder, 1984, p. 140.
15. *Lobster*, No. 19; Bower, *Spy*, p. 186; T obit., 21.2.95. Martin-Smith later served in Warsaw, Istanbul, Kinshasa and Tel Aviv. He recounted his wartime experiences in 'Friuli 44' (Italy, 1991). After leaving Austria, Gardiner worked in Frankfurt and then for two frustrating years in Seoul. In 1958, he was posted to the British consulate-general in West Berlin. West, *Friends*, p. 23; G, 23.2.81.
16. *Lobster*, No. 19; Ewan Butler, *Amateur Agent*, Harrap, 1963, p. 102; Nicholas Elliott, *Never Judge a Man by His Umbrella*, Michael Russell, Norwich, 1992, pp. 160–1; Young,

Masters, p. 26. Returning to Zurich as vice-consul in 1950, Edge Leslie later served undercover as a visa officer in Vienna in the mid-fifties.

17 & 18. Palumbo, pp. 30–1 & 102; Herzstein, pp. 169 & 173.

19 & 20. I, 2.11.89 & 14.3.94; Jack Saltman, *Kurt Waldheim: A Case to Answer?*, Channel Four/Robson, 1988, pp. 18–21 & 129; Herzstein, pp. 282–3.

21–23. MoD review of results of investigation and involvement of Lieutenant Waldheim, HMSO, October 1989; I, 2.11.94. The British refused access to the report which was found in the CIA archives. T, 24.5.88; Herzstein, pp. 156 & 189–93; Palumbo, pp. 52 & 99.

24. Palumbo, pp. 108 & 134; Aarons/Loftus, p. 266.

25 & 26. *Lobster*, No. 19.

27. Robert Knight, *British Policy toward Occupied Austria, 1945–50*, PhD thesis, London University, 1986; Herzstein, p. 193; WP, 30.10.86; Palumbo, pp. 52, 83 & 103–7.

28. Shepherd, pp. 269–70.

29. WP, 30.10.86; *Searchlight*, No. 140, February 1987.

30. Christopher Simpson, *The Splendid Blonde Beast: Money, Law and Genocide in the Twentieth Century*, Grove Press, NY, 1993, pp. 256 & 274–7.

31. T, 31.3.88; I, 2.11.89.

32. Blake, p. 7; Nicholas Elliott, *With My Little Eye: Observations on the Way*, Michael Russell, Norwich, 1993, p. 41.

33 & 34. Blake, p. 9; Bower, *Spy*, p. 180; Peter Wright, *Spycatcher*, Heinemann, Australia, 1987, p. 156; statement by Peter Stanswood, RMP, given to John MacLaren, 23.6.88; David C. Martin, *Wilderness of Mirrors*, Ballantine (pbk), NY, 1981, p. 75.

35 & 36. Bower, *Spy*, p. 178; Blake, p. 14; T, 24.11.95.

37. The official CIA history of the project contained within 'Berlin Tunnel' was declassified in 1977. The claim that Nelson failed to inform the British of a major technical advance which enabled messages to be monitored not only in their encoded form but as a 'clear' text is untrue. Bower, *Spy*, p. 180; Blake, p. 6; Martin, pp. 74–6; Grose, pp. 396–7; M. Smith, p. 116.

38. Vienna was a choice posting during the fifties. Experienced staff stationed there included Maurice Firth (1955–6), who headed R6 and was a close friend of the CIA's James Angleton, his deputy, Geoffrey MacBride, from the Control Commission in Germany, and third secretary Hamilton 'Ham' White. Regarded as 'too unconventional for his own good', Whyte lived 'dangerously', believing that 'calculated indiscretion is the indispensable secret of success in the information field'. Rejoining the Foreign Office, he had a successful career in the Information Services (obits: I, 23 & 27.7.90). Nicholas Elliott took over the station in late 1957 with Cyril Rolo as deputy and Donald Prater as head of the visa section. Elliott relied on his friend Edge Leslie, who had returned to the City as Second Secretary, for advice on the Austrians, as he found 'it difficult, most especially during negotiations or discussions with the Viennese, to get down to practicalities. There were delays everywhere and the bureaucratic machinery as a whole was frustrating at all levels.' Alston was listed in 1958 as 'Civil Assistant at the War Office', i.e. MI5. Virginia Cowles, *The Phantom Major: The Story of David Stirling and the SAS Regiment*, Fontana (pbk), 1960, pp. 114–15 & 309; Anthony Cavendish, *Inside Intelligence*, Palau Publishing (priv. pub.), 1987, pp. 64–71; West, *Faber Book of Espionage*, pp. 547–8; G, 23.2.81; Elliott, *Umbrella*, p. 161.

39. Blake, p. 13.

CHAPTER TEN: ROCKETS, BOMBS AND DECEPTION

1 & 2. R.V. Jones, *Reflections on Intelligence*, 1990, p. 17; Alec Danchev, *Very Special Relationship*, 1986, pp. 99–108; Danchev in Aldrich, p. 235; Arnold Kramish, *The Griffin*, Macmillan, 1986, p. 251.

3–8. Kramish, pp. 91–2, 103 & 182; West, *Friends*, p. 23; R.V. Jones, *Most Secret War: British Scientific Intelligence 1939–1945*, Coronet (pbk), 1979, pp. 269, 394, 595, 603, 621–5 & 648; Thomas Powers, *Heisenberg's War: The Secret History of the German Bomb*, Cape, 1993, pp. 283, 364, 524 & 543.

9. Richard Aldrich and Michael Coleman, 'The Cold War, JIC and British Signals Intelligence, 1948', INS, Vol. 4, No. 3, July 1989.

10. PRO AIR 2/12027, 16.6.45.

11 & 12. The British Intelligence Objectives Sub-Committee replaced CIOS in the British Zone in Germany when SHAEF was disbanded, but it 'was little more than a token gesture'. Chronically underfunded, it remained controlled by the War Office and JIC with the result that its industrial reports were bizarrely classed as official secrets. The CIOS representative on the American Field Information Agency (Technical) (FIAT) was Brig. Raymond Maunsell, former MI5 officer and head of Security Intelligence Middle East (SIME) before moving in 1944 to counter-intelligence duties at SHAEF. Maunsell put obstacles in the way of British industrialists who wanted to study German technology. Even though the head of the Federation of British Industries was Sir George Nelson, a former MI6 member of the Z-Network and director of SOE, obstacles remained, and industrialists failed to take seriously German advances in so many fields. After Germany, Maunsell directed Unilever's Information Division (1948–63). Bower, *Paperclip*, pp. 76, 86–8 & 214–17; Cesarani, p. 149; Simpson, *Blowback*, pp. 25–6.

13–15. James McGovern, *Crossbow and Overcast*, William Morrow (pbk), US, 1964, pp. 13, 100–1 & 152–4.

16. PRO FO 1032/565.

17. Kramish, p. 166; West, *Friends*, p. 23; Leslie Groves, *Now It Can Be Told: The Story of the Manhattan Project*, Da Capo, NY, 1983, pp. 170–1.

18. Powers, pp. 416–17; David Holloway, *Stalin and the Bomb: The Soviet Union and Atomic Energy 1939–1945*, Yale University Press, 1994, pp. 108–11 & 174.

19 & 20. Powers, pp. 419–20, 428 & 435; Jones, *War*, pp. 600–1; Glees; Kramish, p. 168; Bower, *Paperclip*, pp. 148–9. For the transcripts see *Operation Epsilon: The Farm House Transcripts*, University of California Press, 1993.

21–26. H. Kay Jones, *Butterworth: History of a Publishing House*, Butterworth, 1980, pp. 84, 119–22 & 130–2; Tom Bower, *Maxwell: The Outsider*, Aurum, 1988, pp. 41–2; ST, 5.10.69; *Izvestiya*, 22.12.68; Betty Maxwell, *A Mind of My Own: My Life with Robert Maxwell*, Pan (pbk), 1995, pp. 319 & 343; Joe Haines, *Maxwell*, Futura (pbk), 1988, pp. 134–8; Kramish, p. 250; Peter Thompson and Anthony Delano, *Maxwell: A Portrait of Power*, Bantam, 1988.

27. Kay Jones, p. 133; information from Desmond Bristow; Tom Bower, *Maxwell: The Final Verdict*, HarperCollins, 1996, pp. 170–4. Until the mid-fifties, Rosebaud and Maxwell remained close. Rosebaud died in January

1963; the Dutchman van den Heuvel died in April 1963, aged seventy-eight. It seems that as he lay dying in August 1963, Hambro ordered his secretary to burn all his secret papers.

Sir Charles Hambro was joint head with the former chiefs of the BSC, Sir William Stephenson, and the OSS, 'Bill' Donovan, of the World Commerce Corp (WCC). Set up in 1946, the Panama-based WCC was intended as a 'bridge over the breakdown in foreign exchange and to provide the tools, machinery, and "know how" to develop untapped resources in different parts of the world', particularly re-equipping German industrial plant. A director claimed that 'if there were several WCCs, there would be no need for a Marshall Plan'. There was also an intelligence role. Stephenson's BSC deputy, John Pepper, succeeded him as Chair, while on the board were OSS officers Richard Sicre and William Horrigan. Sister corporations included the Transamerica Corp. under James F. Cavagnaro and the British-American-Canadian Corp., chaired by Hambro with former MI6 officer Sir Rex Benson and former US Secretary of State Edward Stettinus. Under its vice-president, Satiris 'Sonny' Fasboulis, who was linked to a number of Mafia-related scandals, Commerce International (China) sponsored military assistance to Taiwan.

28. Glees.

29 & 30. Bower, *Paperclip*, pp. 151, 179 & 192; Holloway, pp. 110–11.

31. The illusory rockets may indicate the beginnings of UFO stories. In the late forties, US Project MOGUL used high-altitude balloons to monitor possible fall-out from Soviet atomic explosions. Debris from one crashed balloon was said to be the basis for the infamous 'Roswell incident' in July 1947, which led to allegations of a cover-up. Interestingly, the US Air Force admitted that it had made up stories as part of deception operations to hide the fact that their secret spy planes had been spotted. T, 29.7.95; I, 4.8.97; Bower, *Paperclip*, pp. 113 & 194; PRO BoT 211/60 (DCOS 46) 27, 11.9.46.

32. M. Smith, p. 111; PRO CAB 81/93, 81/134, FO 1032/1271A & 1032/1231B.

33. After the war the Committee on Chemical Warfare focused on nerve agents as future weapons. There was no mass production, but 71,000 captured German bombs containing the agent Tabun were brought to Britain for experimentation and used as weapons. In 1951 approval was given for the production of 10,000 devices and the Nancekuke facility at Portreath opened for pilot production of nerve agents, though stocks for offensive use were destroyed by 1957. British 'Declaration of Past Activities Relating to Its Former Offensive Chemical Weapons Programme' for the Organisation for the Prohibition of Chemical Weapons (OPCW), May 1997; Linda Hunt, *Secret Agenda: The United States Government, Nazi Scientists and Project Paperclip, 1945–1990*, St Martin's Press, NY, 1991, pp. 13, 163 & 177; Robert Harris and Jeremy Paxman, *A Higher Former of Killing: The Secret Story of Gas and Germ Warfare*, Triad/Paladin (pbk), 1983, pp. 139–44.

34–36. Glees; Hunt, pp. 35 & 127; Bower, *Paperclip*, pp. 341–2.

37 & 38. McGovern, pp. 187–9 & 201; West, *Friends*, p. 24.

39. Hunt, pp. 28–9.

40 & 41. Bower, *Spy*, pp. 210–11; West, *Friends*, p. 25.

42. Lawrence Freedman, *US Intelligence and the Soviet Strategic Threat*, Macmillan (pbk, 2nd ed.), 1988, p. 68.

43. G.A. Tokaty-Tokaev, *Stalin Means War*, Harvill, 1951, p. 149; Bower, *Paperclip*, pp. 149 & 171–2; Nicholas Daniloff, *The Kremlin and the Cosmos*, Knopf, NY, 1972, p. 50.

44. Heinz Conradis, *Design for Flight: The Kurt Tank Story*, Macdonald, 1960; Hunt, pp. 14, 149, 156 & 178.

45. Bower, *Paperclip*, pp. 269–71; G.A. Tokaty-Tokaev, *Comrade X*, 1956, p. 357.

46. West, *Friends*, p. 25; Wesley K. Wark, 'Coming in from the Cold: British Propaganda and the Red Army Defectors, 1945–1952', *The International History Review*, IX, 1, Feb. 1987.

47. 'IRD: Origins and Establishment of the Foreign Office's Information Research Department, 1946–48', p. 10; PRO FO 371/71713; IRD Digest #5, 4.9.48.

48. W. Scott Lucas and C.J. Morris, 'A very British crusade: the Information Research Department and the beginning of the Cold War', in Aldrich; PRO FO 371/77609 N135/1024/38 & N553/1024/38; SE, 2, 9 & 16.1.49. Daniloff, pp. 52 & 228, has an interview with Tokaty-Tokaev.

49. Wark; PRO WO 216/731; BAOR, 8.5.51; Bower, *Spy*, p. 211.

50. Denis Hills, *Tyrants and Mountains: A Reckless Life*, John Murray, 1992, pp. 146–7; Wright, pp. 115–16.

51. McGovern, pp. 101–2.

52 & 53. Peter A. Hofmann, 'Making National Estimates During the "Missile Gap"', INS, Vol. 1, No. 3, Sept. 1986, citing CIA document, 'A Summary of Soviet Guided Missile Intelligence', US/UK GM4–52, 20.7.53 (DDRS (75)5–I).

54. Aldrich/Coleman.

55. JIC (48) 9 (0), 'Russian Interests, Intentions and Capabilities', 23.7.48, L/WS/1/1173, India Office Library and Records; Holloway, pp. 104–5. Fuchs's self-same notes which he handed over to his Soviet controller were also presented to his colleagues in his adopted country, Britain, to provide vital early assistance to the British atomic bomb programme.

56. Jiri Kasparek, 'Soviet Russia and Czechoslovakia's Uranium', *The Russian Review*, No. 2, 1952; Linklater *et al.*, p. 211; Aarons, p. 145; Holloway, p. 111.

57. Pavel Sudoplotov, *Special Tasks*, 1994, pp. 198–9.

58. Arthur B. Darling, *The Central Intelligence Agency*, 1990, pp. 161–5.

59 & 60. Dwyer retired to Ottawa, where he became head of reporting of the secret Canadian Communications Branch, which as an undercover arm of the National Research Council was responsible for signals intelligence, in particular monitoring Soviet signals. In 1952 he was made Chair of the Security Panel Sub-Committee of the Privy Council, which looked at security cases in the civil service. He retired in 1958. John Sawatsky, *Men in the Shadows: The RCMP Security Service*, Totem (pbk), Toronto, 1983, pp. 120–1; David Stafford, *Camp X*, Mead, Dodd, NY, 1987, pp. 261–2; Wilfred Basil Mann, *Was There a Fifth Man?: Quintessential Recollections*, Pergamon Press, 1982, pp. 60–3.

61. Baines emigrated to Canada, where he took up an administrative post with the NRC at Chalk Farm. Mann, pp. 63–4; Brown, *Treason*, p. 399.

62 & 63. Mann, p. 67; Aldrich/Coleman; Brian Cathcart, *Test of Greatness: Britain's Struggle for the Atom Bomb*, John Murray, 1994, pp. 98–9 & 109; Paul Lashmar, *Spy Flights of the Cold War*, Sutton, Stroud, 1996, p. 38.

64. H. Montgomery Hyde, *The Atom Spies*, Sphere (pbk), 1982, pp. 143–4; Mann, p. 68.

From the end of the war until the Soviets exploded their first atomic bomb, British RAF reconnaissance pilots 'had been flying missions along the borders of all the Eastern bloc countries, systematically violating their airspace with a fast-dash foray whenever they thought they could get away'. During 1947–8 the RAF's 192 Squadron flew a series of experimental SIGINT missions over the Middle East, the Baltic and East Germany. In September 1948 Lancaster and Lincolns flew from Hibbaniya, in Iraq, along the Soviet border. Anthony Verrier claims that while stationed in Turkey, 'Philby served his Russian masters with his usual obtrusive skill', with the RAF losing 'at least one aircraft on the Turkish–Russian border in consequence'.

65. Holloway, p. 265.

66. Thomas Earl Mahl, '48 Land', PhD thesis, Kent State University, Aug. 1994.

67. Bower, *Spy*, p. 105. Aldrich/Zametica, pp. 362–3.

68 & 69. During the sixties, Dr Robert Press was appointed Assistant Chief Scientific Adviser to the MoD on nuclear matters. Mann, pp. 70, 74, 87.

70. *Lobster*, No. 19.

71. Anthony Cave Brown, *Bodyguard of Lies*, Star (pbk), 1977, pp. 46–7, 344 & 804–7; CoS (45)564(0), 220th Mtg (6) & 233rd Mtg (7); Julian Lewis, *Changing Directions*, 1988, pp. 238–9.

Brown writes that 'the spirit and methodology of the LCS would live on . . . and return to haunt the western Allies. The British had been extremely careful to reveal to the Russians only as much of the deception machinery as was necessary.' In July 1944, the LCS representative in Moscow told John Bevan that the Russians 'distrusted and hated the whole thing . . . We know from their treatment of [D-Day deception] that they have no special organisation comparable with yours.' He added that 'their machinery for the execution of global deceptions was slow and cumbersome' and was unlikely 'to divert brain-power to this specialised form of warfare' (Overlord file of the US Military Mission to Moscow, Bolton to Bevan, 19.7.44, MMR, NR). Brown claims, however, that the Russians 'soon established a massive deception organisation of their own'. Defector Anatoli Golitsyn did make such claims in the early sixties with regard to the Sino-Soviet split, but his testimony has

largely been discredited. Soviet security agencies, basing their techniques on the success of the twenties 'Trust' and using exile groups, did develop masterly localised deceptions operations in the Baltic, the Ukraine and Poland against western intelligence agencies. Collectively, however, 'they can be viewed as survival exercises – operations to pre-empt possible threats to the young Bolshevik state'. That remained the case after the war and there is little evidence that they engaged in LCS-type strategic operations. David A. Charters and Maurice A.J. Tugwell, *Deception Operations*, 1990, p. 16.

72. Richard Aldrich (ed.), *Espionage, Security and Intelligence in Britain 1945–1970*, Manchester University Press, 1998, p. 226.

73 & 78. John Harvey-Jones, *Getting It Together*, Mandarin (pbk), 1992, pp. 146, 149 & 155–6; Richard J. Aldrich, 'Recent Western Studies of Soviet Intelligence', INS, Vol. 11, No. 3, July 1996; Anthony Courtney, *Sailor in a Russian Frame*, Johnson, 1968, p. 52; Charters/Tugwell, p. 268.

74. PRO Minutes of 'Inter-Service Meeting on the Future of VISTRE', 79/Mob/9914 (SWVI), 24.8.51, AIR 20/11420; PREM 11/257, Churchill to Minister of Defence, M457/52, 26.8.52, and reply, 2.9.52.

75. Chapman Pincher, *Inside Story: A Documentary of the Pursuit of Power*, NEL (pbk), 1979, p. 288; Brown, *Treason*, pp. 434–5; Wild obit., DT, 14.6.95; Denis Wheatley, *The Deception Planner: My Secret War*, Hutchinson, 1980, p. 220; Brown, *Bodyguard*, pp. 49, 116 & 806; David Mure, *Practise to Deceive*, Kimber, 1977, pp. 27 & 251; B. Toohey and B. Pinwill, *Oyster: The Story of the Australian Intelligence Service*, Heinemann, Sydney, 1989, p. 44.

76–77. Charters/Tugwell, p. 273; Wheatley, pp. 227–8; Wright, pp. 120–1.

79. See Cathcart.

80. Peter Hennessy, *Never Again*, 1993, pp. 268–9; Anthony Verrier, *The Road to Zimbabwe 1890–1980*, Cape, 1986, p. 8.

81. Peter Malone, *The British Nuclear Deterrent*, Croom Helm, 1984, pp. 4–12; Holloway, pp. 153 & 322.

82. I, 12.9.94; IoS, 11.3.90; G, 5.8.95; 'Moscow Criterion: The Secret History of British Nuclear Weapons', BBC2, 6.8.95.

83. John Baylis, Professor of International Politics at the University of Wales, in *Contemporary Record*, Aug. 1994.

84. I, 14.2.95.

PART THREE: THE SOVIET EMPIRE

CHAPTER ELEVEN: INTERMARIUM

1. Count Coudenhove-Kalergi, *An Idea Conquers the World*, Hutchinson, 1953, p. 214; Gordon Shepherd, *The Austrian Odyssey*, 1957, pp. 110–12.
2. Zygmunt Nagorski, 'Liberation Movements in Exile', *Journal of Central European Affairs*, July 1950; Brown, *Secret Servant*, p. 143; Aarons/Loftus, pp. 51 & 156; Simpson, p. 181.
3. Alan Palmer, *The Lands Between: A History of East-Central Europe since the Congress of Vienna*, Weidenfeld, 1970, p. 207; Simpson, p. 181; Aarons, p. 74; Aarons/Loftus, p. 63.
4. A small group of right-wing Catholic Austrians began in March 1938 to organise resistance groups. The Legitimist students' association was recognised by Archduke Otto 'as the authorized underground monarchist movement in Austria', while the Austrian Freedom Movement joined forces with a monarchist group led by Viennese lawyer Dr Jakob Kastelic and sought a Pan-Danubian federation. These 'cells' soon made contact with MI6. Brown, *Secret Servant*, p. 189; Shepherd, pp. 155–6.
5. Coudenhove-Kalergi, pp. 116 & 214–19; Hugh Seton-Watson, *The East European Revolution*, 1952, p. 150; Feliks Gross & M. Kamil Diziewanowski, 'Plans by Exiles from East European Countries', in Walter Lipgens (ed.), *Documents on the History of European Integration*, Vol. 2: 'Plans for European Union in Great Britain and in Exile 1939–1945', Walter de Gruyter, 1986.
6. Kenneth Cohen joined MI6 in 1935 from the navy, in which he claimed to have been the only Jew. He was chief of staff to Claude Dansey, whose Z-network was independent of, though parallel to, the MI6 sections. Brown, *Secret Servant*, pp. 19, 189–95 & 801. Brown interviewed Cohen, April 1983. Information from author Michael Baigent, letter 7.5.94, who interviewed Cohen, 6.8.82, and holds OSS file, 6.4.42; William J. Donovan papers, US Army War College, Fort Carlisle, Penn.: telegram to 'Q' from the British Security Co-ordination, New York, 26.3.42; PRO FO 371/25031, R3851; Shepherd,

p. 156; Coudenhove-Kalergi, p. 214; West, *Friends*, p. 13; Robert H. Keyerslingk, *Austria in World War II*, 1988, p. 63; Richard J. Aldrich, 'European Integration: An American Intelligence Connection', in A. Deighton (ed.), *Elites and European Integration, 1945–63*, Macmillan, 1996.

MI6's operations in Austria were plagued by security fears. During 1940 the resistance groups were exposed by an agent working for the Nazi SD. Those who escaped to London and Canada were funded by MI6 to rebuild a pro-Habsburg, anti-communist Free Austria Movement. Its London leader, the last foreign minister of the Austro-Hungarian monarchy, Ferdinand Czerin, joined with Hungarian exiles and the Romanian ambassador, V. V. Tilea, and foreign minister in exile and MI6 agent Grigore Gafencu, in promoting federalism through the Fabian Society-backed Danubian Club.
7. PRO FO 371/24392, C 10407; Foreign Office Research and Press Service report, 'The Policy of the Catholic Church in the Danube Valley', 21.10.42, 371/33434; Chadwick, p. 303; Michael M. Boll, *Cold War in the Balkans: American Foreign Policy and the Emergency of Communist Bulgaria, 1943–1947*, University of Kentucky, 1984, p. 14.
8. Peter Grose (*Gentleman Spy*, p. 157) dismisses Hohenlohe's reports of these meetings, claiming that he embroidered his account. Burton Hersh (*The Old Boys*, 1992, pp. 78 & 103–4), however, suggests that much of the controversy is because 'SS summations of the exchanges appear to have passed through Russian hands on their way to the archives, after which the USSR News Services waited until 1948 and the upheavals of the Cold War to put them out as despatches'. He adds that 'their thrust is borne out' by related intelligence files.
9. Hersh, pp. 110–15; PRO WO 218 25,5; 43 CAB 66/37; War Cabinet (43) 16.6.43 CAB 65/34; Aarons/Loftus, pp. 57 & 181.
10. Anthony Eden's private secretary, Oliver Harvey, noted in his diary (26.4.44) Churchill's hankering for fallen kings: 'I am only afraid the P.M. may rush to their rescue . . . Habsburg, Hohenzollern or Glucksburg'. Also hankering was SOE controller Lord Selbourne, who embraced continental royalists and saw himself as 'fighting a rearguard action for Empire'. Keyerslingk, pp. 96–100, 137 & 230–4. Rothwell, p. 96;

David Weigall, 'British ideas of European unity and regional confederation in the context of Anglo-Soviet relations, 1941–45', in M.L. Smith and Peter M.R. Stirk (eds), *Making the New Europe: European Unity and the Second World War*, Pinter, 1990.

Chatham House operated as 'a semi-independent, confidential information and intelligence gathering office for the Foreign Office'. At the beginning of the war, Philip Toynbee established at Balliol College, Oxford, the Foreign Research and Press Service (FRPS). In charge of its South-Eastern Europe section was Prof. Robert Seton-Watson, who had served during the First World War with Toynbee in the Intelligence Bureau of the Department of Information. A powerful voice during the First War in favour of breaking up the Austro-Hungarian Empire, by the thirties Seton-Watson was a supporter of economic and political union. A separate unit for the 'Danubian Countries' headed by Seton-Watson's assistant, the Romanian-born Prof. D. Mitrany, influenced postwar planning, with members appointed to the FO's own Research Department.

11. According to Vojtech Mastny ('Europe in US–USSR Relations: A Topical Legacy', *Problems of Communism*, XXXVII, Jan. 1988), Moscow policy was 'to hinder anything that might enable the smaller states to pool their resources and gain strength'. Their 'permanent weakness and fragmentation were a prerequisite for Soviet security'. Soviet intentions in eastern Europe, however, did little to alter British aspirations – as laid out in an October 1944 Post-War Reconstruction Committee policy paper.

12–13 & 18–19. Aarons/Loftus, pp. 37–8 & 53–6; Nagorski.

14–16. Hersh, p. 182; CIC reports on Intermarium from CIC sub-detachments in Salzburg and Rome, 23.6.46, 21.8.46 & 11.4.50. R.G. 47 (Suitland), Adjutant-General's Office, 1917 forward; Aarons, p. 74; Aarons/Loftus, pp. 52–9 & 62–4; Simpson, pp. 180–3.

17. John Saville, *The Politics of Continuity*, 1993, p. 53.

20. In London, Arrow Cross members wanted for war crimes poured out a stream of violently anti-Semitic and Holocaust revisionist literature. Josef Sueli published *The True War Criminals*, which claimed that accounts of the gas chambers were faked.

Hidfo (*Bridgehead*) exposed 'the Jewish conspiracy'. Palmer, pp. 285–6. See Chapter 11, 'Hungary', in Denis Eisenberg, *The Re-emergence of Fascism*, McGibbon & Kee, 1967.

21. Gabor Peter was allegedly the lover in Vienna in the 1930s of Philby's wife-to-be Litzi Friedman. Paul V. Gorka, *Budapest Betrayed: A Prisoner's Story of the Betrayal of the Hungarian Resistance Movement to the Russians*, Oak-Tree Books, 1986, p. 17; Palmer, p. 304.

The military plot leader was Gen. Lajos Veress, and among civilian conspirators were members of the Smallholder's Party who were accused of espionage against Red Army installations. Veress was condemned to death, reprieved and deported to Siberia. He was not freed until the 1956 uprising. Stanley M. Max, *The United States, Great Britain and the Sovietisation of Hungary, 1945–1948*, East European Monographs, Boulder, NY: Columbia University Press, 1985, p. 95.

22. Simpson, p. 182; Hersh, p. 233; Gorka, p. 4.

23. It was not until a 1950 request for his extradition that Vajta was finally thrown out of the United States. The Vatican arranged his employment at a small Catholic college in Colombia.

24–27. Geoffrey Elliott, *I Spy: The Secret Life of a British Agent*, St Ermin's Press/Little, Brown, 1998; Stefan Korbonski, *Warsaw in Exile*, Allen & Unwin, pp. 28, 158, 194–7 & 232–4; Aarons/Loftus, pp. 60–5.

28–31. Gorka, pp. iv, xii, 4, 42–8, 63, 77, 95, 107 & 119–121.

32 & 33. Ibid., p. 136; E.H. Cookridge, *Spy Trade*, Frewin, 1976, pp. 32–3, and Gehlen, p. 364.

34–36. Palmer, p. 248; Scott Anderson and Jon Lee Anderson, *Inside the League: The Shocking Exposé of How Terrorists, Nazis and Latin American Death Squads Have Infiltrated the World Anti-Communist League*, Dodd, Mead, NY, 1986, pp. 14–20; Hersh, p. 209.

37. Aarons/Loftus, p. 232; Anderson, p. 34.

38. 'John Whitwell' (aka Leslie Nicholson), *British Agent*, Kimber, 1966, p. 220; Hersh, pp. 203 & 209.

39. Simpson, pp. 96–7; Palmer, p. 300; Eduard Mark, 'The OSS in Romania, 1944–45: An Intelligence Operation of the Early Cold War', INS, Vol. 9, Nos. 2, April 1994; Rothwell, p. 379.

40. Denis Deletant, 'The Securitate and the

Police State in Rumania: 1948–64', INS, Vol. 8, No. 4, Oct. 1993.

41. Durcansky was editor of the nationalist *Nastup* around which gravitated 'Young Generation' Hlinka Guardists, who were placed by Durcansky (Minister of Home and Foreign Affairs) in key state and party posts. Palmer, p. 235; Seton-Watson, pp. 146–7; Aarons, pp. 65–6; Yeshayahu Jelinek, 'Storm-troopers in Slovakia: the Rodobrana and the Hlinka Guard', JCH, Vol. 16, No. 3, 1971.

42, 44 & 45. Aarons/Loftus, pp. 218–22.

43. Stefan Ilok with Lester Tanzer, *Brotherhood of Silence: The Story of an Anti-Communist Underground*, Robert B. Luce, US, 1963, pp. ix–x & 235.

46. Josef Frolik, *The Frolik Defection: The Memoirs of an Intelligence Agent*, Corgi (pbk), 1976, p. 86; Josef Josten, *Oh, My Country*, Latimer House, 1949.

47 & 48. Frolik, pp. 66–9, 70 & 76. Bower, *Spy*, p. 257; Arnold M. Silver, 'Questions, Questions, Questions: Memories of Oberursel', INS, Vol. 8, No. 2, April 1993. 'Light' lived in semi-retirement in Folkestone until his death in 1962.

CHAPTER TWELVE: THE PROMETHEAN LEAGUE

1. Dr Roma Smal-Stocky, 'The Struggle of the Subjugated Nations in the Soviet Union for Freedom: Sketch of the History of the Promethean Movement', *Ukrainian Quarterly*, No. III, autumn 1947, and *The Captive Nations: Nationalism of the Non-Russian Nations in the Soviet Union*, Bookman, NY, 1950, p. 159; W.E.D. Allen, *The Ukraine: A History*, CUP, 1940, p. 342; Alexander Dallin, *German Rule in Russia 1941–45: A Study in Occupation Policies* (2nd ed.), Macmillan, 1981, p. 228; Alain Desrohes, *Le Problème Ukrainian et Simon Petlura*, Nouvelles Editions Latines, Paris, 1962.

2. St J. Paprocki, 'Political Organisation of the Ukrainian Exiles after the Second World War', *Eastern Quarterly*, Vol. V, June 1952. Paprocki was a member of the Promethean League in London after the Second World War. Allen, p. 342.

3. Smal-Stocky, 'The Struggle', and *Captive Nations*, p. 159; Brown, *Secret Servant*, p. 143; Loftus, p. 54; Armstrong, p. 31.

4. Smal-Stocky, *Captive Nations*, pp. 61 & 106, and *The Nationality Problem of the Soviet Union and Russian Communist Imperialism*, Bruce Publishing, US, 1952, p. 209; Pavlo Shandruk, *Arms of Valor*, Robert Speller, NY, 1959, pp. xviii & xx; J.H. Watson report made of tour of the Ukraine, June & July 1939, reprinted in Lubomyr Y. Luciuk & Bohdan S. Kordan, *Anglo-American Perspectives on the Ukrainian Question 1938–1951: A Documentary Record*, Limestone, NY, 1987, pp. 51–60.

5. E.S. Charlton, Political Intelligence Department, 5.3.40, memorandum on Polish-Ukrainian Problem, in Luciuk/Kordan, pp. 75–77; PRO FO 371/24473; Smal-Stocky, *Captive Nations*, p. 202.

6. Rosenberg's views on the Caucasus had been influenced by Alexander Nikuradze, a Georgian physicist. An avid populariser of the geopolitics of Dr Albrecht Haushofer and his theories of 'large spaces', he masterminded Rosenberg's scheme for German lordship in a Caucasus confederation, in which Georgia would play the leading role in an anti-Russian *cordon sanitaire*. Nikuradze's dreams relied on the support of the Paris-based Promethean League. Dallin, pp. 89 & 228; Allen, p. 385; Aarons, p. 73.

7. David Lampe, *The Last Ditch*, Cassell, 1968, p. 63; Wilkinson/Astley, pp. 34–5 & 36; information from John Hope; John Armstrong, *Ukrainian Nationalism* (2nd ed.), Ukrainian Academic Press, US, 1966, p. 31.

8 & 9. Frank McLynn, *Fitzroy Maclean*, John Murray, 1992, pp. 19–20, 52, 63, 136 & 181. The *Independent* article on this project (26.2.90) was based on a document (File Number N 5736/G) which had originally been released in 1970 but was withdrawn and reclassed as unavailable until 2015.

10. J. Drexel Biddle, Jr, report to State Department, 15.12.38, US National Archives M1286, Reel 3.

11. In the post-WW1 period, when British forces occupied the strategically important oil port of Baku, twenty-six Soviet commissars were executed on what Stalin erroneously believed were British orders. Teague-Jones, alias Ronald Sinclair, was the intelligence officer suspected by Stalin of ordering the execution. He went on to serve in the United States during WW2 under Ellis as consul general in New York. In October 1920, Stalin inspected Baku in Georgia, which was seen as the base for British operations, and launched a murderous campaign; a model for later excesses. Stalin remained perpetually concerned about MI6 machinations and often warned communist leaders to be vigilant. Ellis later wrote about his experiences in *The Transcaspian Episode*, Hutchinson, 1963. Reginald Teague-Jones, *The Spy Who Disappeared: Diary of a Secret Mission to Central Asia in 1918*, Gollancz (pbk), 1991.

12–14. Chapman Pincher, *Their Trade Is Treachery*, Sidgwick & Jackson, 1981, pp. 195–202: 'The Ellis Case', Chapter 45; *Too Secret, Too Soon*, 1984, pp. 52 & 452, and *Traitors*, 1987, pp. 86, 160–3 & 317–21; John Costello, *Mask of Treachery*, 1988 p. 143; Aarons/Loftus, pp. 153 & 227. See Hugo Dewar, *Assassins at Large*, 1951, pp. 1–12.

15. Andrew, *Secret Service*, pp. 412 & 422.

16. Brown, *Secret Servant*, p. 144; Aarons/Loftus, pp. 157–8.

17. Ronald C. Cooke & Roy Conyers Nesbit, *Target: Hitler's Oil: Allied Attacks on German Oil Supplies 1939–1945*, Kimber, 1985, pp. 23–31; Douglas Dodds-Parker, *Setting Europe Ablaze: Some Accounts of Ungentlemanly Warfare*, Springwood, 1983, pp. 38–9; Nikolai Tolstoy, *Stalin's Secret War*, Cape, 1981, pp. 166–7; William Stevenson, *Intrepid's Last Case*, 1984, p. 261.

18. Dodds-Parker, p. 39; Fitzroy Maclean, *Eastern Approaches*, Cape, 1951, p. 350; Richard Deacon, *'C': A Biography of Sir Maurice Oldfield*, Macdonald, 1985, p. 53; Brown, *Secret Servant*, p. 143. From the old school of Russian generals, Wrangel later created the Russian Armed Service Union with headquarters in Yugoslavia.

19–22. McLynn, p. 63; Tolstoy, *Stalin's Secret War*, pp. 157, 160–4, 171 & 183; Paprocki; Smal-Stocky, 'The Struggle'; Armstrong, pp. 33 & 55; Dodds-Parker, pp. 37 & 49; Stevenson, p. 262; Luciuk/Kordan, pp. 40–1; West, *Secret War*, p. 221.

23. Paprocki; Smal-Stocky, 'The Struggle'.

24. Stevenson (p. 265) suggests that the RAF plan to bomb Baku was given to the Soviets by the national organiser of the Communist Party, Douglas Springhall, who was sentenced to seven years' imprisonment under the OSA in July 1943 for obtaining information from an Air Ministry clerk.

25. MI6's monitoring of oil supplies to Germany was run by the only senior woman officer, Miranda Gwyer, a former secretary to Admiral Sinclair. Her brother, John Gwyer,

an officer in MI5's B1 (B) Division, played a key role in the wartime deception operation, MINCEMEAT. Raymond Challinor, *The Struggle for Hearts and Minds: Essays on the Second World War*, Bewick, 1995, p. 29; McLynn, p. 63; Sir John Slessor, *The Central Blue*, Cassell, 1956, p. 270; Paul Leverkuehn, *German Military Intelligence*, Weidenfeld, 1954, pp. 5–8; Bradley F. Smith, *Sharing Secrets with Stalin*, 1996, pp. 18–20.

26–7, 29 & 30. Dallin, pp. 11–12, 88, 117–18, 135, 235–6, 258–9, 272–3, 541, 559 & 610–11. Smal-Stocky, *Captive Nations*, pp. 11 & 162, and 'The Struggle'; Armstrong, p. 32.

28. Hitler railed against the exile groups on racial grounds – attacking Rosenberg's romantic attachment to his 'political underworld shop' – deriding them for their failure to make a revolution. 'The émigrés have accomplished nothing at all.' There was also the fear that they had been penetrated by Soviet Intelligence; the charge was correct but at the end of 1941, in the 'peculiar twilight of illegality' which existed, the Abwehr sponsored various military formations such as the Georgian Tamara Legion and the Cossack Corps, who later transferred their allegiance to the SS – 'not because of ideological proclivities but to obtain more and better arms'. Armstrong, pp. 300–1.

31. Richard Landwehr, *Fighting for Freedom: The Ukrainian Volunteer Division of the Waffen-SS*, Bibliophile Legion Books, US, 1984, pp. 19–29 & 45; Lt-Gen. Wladyslaw Anders, *Hitler's Defeat in Russia*, Natraj Publishers, India, 1975, pp. 173–204.

32. Dallin, p. 599; Landwehr, pp. 57–85 & 132–40; Basil Dmytryshyn, 'Nazis and the SS Volunteer Division Galicia', *American Slavic and East European Review*, Feb. 1956.

33. With the consent of the Polish underground, a Promethean-led Caucasian Committee under Dr George Nakashidz was created in occupied Poland. Mark Aarons and John Loftus, *The Secret War against the Jews*, Heinemann, 1995, p. 137; Smal-Stocky, 'The Struggle'.

34. On Fritz Arlt see Jurgen Thorwald, *The Illusion: Soviet Soldiers in Hitler's Armies*, Harcourt Brace Jovanovich, NY, 1975, pp. 188–91 & 312–13.

35. Dallin, pp. 558–9, 611, 625, 646 & 654–6; Nikolai Tolstoy, *Victims of Yalta*, Hutchinson, 1988, pp. 355–7; Shandruk, pp. 204–5; Cesarani, pp. 10 & 23; Aarons/Loftus,

Ratlines, pp. 180–1; Simpson, p. 170; Armstrong, pp. 171 & 180–6.

36–40. Shandruk, pp. 197–206, 227–36, 260–3 & 279–81; Aarons/Loftus, *Ratlines*, p. 186; Walter Dushnyck, 'Archbishop Buchko – Arch-Shepherd of Ukrainian Refugees', *Ukrainian Quarterly*, spring 1975; information from John Hope.

41. Disappearing from view is Dr Arlt. He was well treated by the British Army and, given our knowledge of what happened to his colleagues, it would be unsurprising to discover that he too was recruited by MI6. Shandruk, p. 289. A St Vladimir's Trident metal cap badge was manufactured in Prague towards the end of the war, replacing the SS death's-head and other German emblems. Landwehr, p. 218; Tolstoy, *Yalta*, p. 320; Aarons/Loftus, *Ratlines*, pp. 186 & 192.

42–3 & 49. Denis Hills, pp. 110–14 & 129–30; Cesarani, pp. 5 & 113; BBC2 *Newsnight*, 11.12.89; S, 23.12.89; PRO FO 371/66605; report on Ukrainians in SEP camp No. 374, 21.2.47.

44 & 45. Dushnyck; Cesarani, p. 103; Shandruk, pp. 291–3.

46. Hills, pp. 126–7; Tolstoy, *Yalta*, pp. 454–6, 461 & 468.

47. Scott-Hopkins stayed in Military Intelligence until 1950 and remained an 'intermittent' MI6 agent until 1973, during which time he became friendly with senior officers such as Oldfield and Stephen de Mowbray. Tolstoy, *Yalta*, pp. 469 & 610; Leigh, p. 116.

48. McLynn, p. 290.

50. In order to appease his critics, Maclean employed known anti-Soviets who were not unhappy at the turn of events. Ex-SOE officer Michael Lees admitted that he gave 'the benefit of every doubt' to the Ukrainians. Cesarani, pp. 87–8 & 128–9; minutes of meeting of Allied Commission for Austria, 3.3.47: PRO, FO 371/66710; ACA, Vienna to Control Office, London, 9.3.47; 371/66709; Aarons/Loftus, *Ratlines*, p. 196; McLynn, p. 285.

51. Cesarani, pp. 106, 121 & 130–1; Bower, *Blind Eye* (rev. ed.), p. 411.

52. Cesarani, p. 159; Hansard HoC, War Crimes Bill, Vol. 169, Cols 950–1, 19.3.90; Anthony Glees, 'War Crimes: The Security and Intelligence Dimensions', INS, Vol. 7, No. 3, July 1992; PRO ALG 254/1/78.

53. PRO Maclean to FO, 26.2.47, FO 371/66605, 26.2.47; Shandruk, p. 299; Aarons/Loftus, *Ratlines*, p. 204.

54 & 55. Nicholas P. Vakar, *Belorussia: The Making of a Nation*, Harvard University Press, US, 1956, p. 279; Shandruk, p. 204; Nagorski; Bower, *Spy*, pp. 205–6.

56–58. Philby, 1969, pp. 143–50; Elliott, pp. 118–25 & 135; West, *MI6*, Panther (pbk), 1985, pp. 21 & 214, and *Friends*, p. 151; Borovik, p. 255.

59–63. Designed to gather long-term strategic intelligence on the USSR, the Wansee Institute provided ethnic and Jewish surveys, and had 'one of the best Russian-language libraries' on the political, scientific, economic and military aspects of the USSR. During 1943–4, the institute furnished intelligence for the German Army to recruit exile movements. Shortly after, Poppe transferred to the SS-headed East Asia Institute – part of OMi – where he wrote reports on Mongolia. Nicholas Poppe, *Reminiscences*, Western Washington University Centre for East Asian Studies, US, 1983, pp. 154, 164, 170–5, 186–7 & 190–6; Cesarani, pp. 150–4; Simpson, pp. 48, 118–19 & 194; John Loftus, *The Belarus Secret*, 1983, pp. 168–9.

64. Hersh, p. 251; Roger Hutchinson, *Crimes of War: The Antanas Gecas Affair*, Mainstream, Edinburgh, p. 55.

65. According to an MI6 officer, Philby and his officers also 'trailed their coats . . . in the hope that the Russians would bite. The object: to obtain some knowledge of the Russians' capabilities and intentions and to obtain foreknowledge if the Russians issued war orders' (Brown, *Treason*, p. 383). Yuri Modin with Jean-Charles Deniau and Agnieszka Ziarek, *My Five Cambridge Friends*, Headline, 1995; Borovik, p. 251; Philby, p. 147. Machray was transferred to the Foreign Office's security department.

66. John Hope information & CIC files; Robert Cecil, 'The Cambridge Comintern', in Christopher Andrew and David Dilks, *The Missing Dimension*, 1984; Aarons, p. 79; Smal-Stocky, *Nationality*, p. 211.

67 & 68. See Firuz Kazemzadeh, *The Struggle for Transcaucasia (1917–1921)*, Philosophical Library, Oxford, 1968, for more on Jordania, who is the only Promethean that Philby names, perhaps because he and his Soviet handlers knew that Jordania's niece, Nina Gegichkori, was the wife of Beria, a Mingrelian from western Georgia. The Paris-based Georgian émigrés were penetrated by the NKVD, through one of its officers and Beria's secretary, Vardo Maximalishvili. When in 1951 Beria fell from favour, Stalin fabricated the 'Mingrelian Affair', which linked Beria to a Promethean conspiracy to secede Georgia from the Soviet Union as an ally of Turkey. A number of Mingrelians were arrested and 'special tasks' carried out sabotage operations in Turkey and Paris, including kidnapping relatives of Beria's wife. Smal-Stocky, 'The Struggle'; Philby, pp. 150 & 153–8; Borovik, pp. 251–2; Knightley, *Masterspy*, pp. 146–7; Cecil in Andrew/Dilks; Sudoplatov, pp. 103 & 320–3.

69. Gordon Brook-Shepherd, *The Storm Birds*, Weidenfeld, 1988, p. 51. Rodney Dennys became head of station in 1951 (Harold Perkins in 1953), with Halsey Colchester Second Secretary and Alan Banks vice-consul, Istanbul.

70 & 71. Courtney, pp. 19, 48, 51 & 53; Borovik, pp. 252–3.

72. Turkey also became a centre for guerrilla warfare programmes against eastern Europe run by the US, which had bases there controlled by the Office of Policy Co-ordination station chief. Loftus, p. 184; Bower, *Blind Eye*, p. 79, and *Spy*, p. 207.

73. MI6 attempted to establish a workable 'Ukrainian Council'; given the wide divergence in political views, it was bound to fail. At the end of the war, most of the Ukrainian 'social democrats' made their way to London, where they formed the Ukrainian Socialist Party. They were heavily involved in the republic's postwar successor, the Ukrainian National Council in Exile, under the 'presidency' of Andrew Livitsky, a Nazi collaborator. Associated with the Socialist International, they were a highly secretive group – their source of funding, which appeared to be substanial, remains unknown, though the Soviets claimed that they were MI6-sponsored. Information from Peter E. Newell & John Hope, and CIC documents; Sudoplatov, p. 252.

74 & 75. Shandruk, pp. xxii–xxiii, 205–6 & 299. Simpson, p. 170; Nagorski.

CHAPTER THIRTEEN: BELORUSSIA

1 & 2. Loftus, pp. 20–1, 54, 202 & 207; Vakar, p. 252. Vakar had access to primary and classified documents from the influential Russian Research Centre at Harvard University. Brown, *Secret Servant*, p. 143. In 1937 a small White Russian Nazi Party was founded with subsidies from Berlin.

3. Zacharka later claimed that he rejected German offcers of co-operation with the BNR. Vakar's conclusion that 'a myth is being built up by the supporters of the BNR' is closer to the truth. Vakar, pp. 165, 177 & 263; A. Rossi, *The Russo-German Alliance: August 1939–June 1941*, Chapman & Hall, 1950, pp. 26–71 & 119–24; Dallin, pp. 213–16 & 222–4.

4. Vakar, pp. 266 & 271; Loftus, p. 31; Anderson, pp. 43–4; *The Einsatzgruppen Reports*, Holocaust Library, NY, 1989, pp. 177–82; Gerald Reitlinger, *The Final Solution*, Vallentine-Mitchell, 1953, pp. 220–7; Hersh, p. 276.

5. Soviet spies took the opportunity to infiltrate the German administration, posing as collaborationists with instructions to turn the local population against the occupiers through a series of brutal reprisals. Vakar, pp. 185–6, 190–3, 202 & 263; Aarons, pp. 69–70; Dallin, pp. 221–2.

6. The number of 'delegates' to the 'Belorussian Congress in Minsk', on 27 June 1944, was, according to Niko Makashidze (*The Truth about ABN*, ABN Press and Information Bureau, Munich, 1960, p. 54) 1,039, 'from all parts of the country, representing all classes of the people'. It was not 'a German invention, but a direct product of the struggle of the Belorussian people for the liberation of their country from occupants and mainly from the Russians and the Poles'. But not, of course, from the Nazis. Vakar, pp. 202–5; Loftus, pp. 48, 167, 200 & 218; Dallin, pp. 224 & 620–1.

7. Ostrowsky edited a fascist magazine, *Ranitsa*. Chief of the Smolensk region Dimitri Kasmowich commanded one of Skorzeny's special intelligence units, while his cousin led a Black Cat unit.

8. The 29th and 30th Waffen Grenadier Division der SS (russiche Nr 1 & Nr 2), from which the Belarus Legion emerged, included both Belorussians and Ukrainians. Members of the Legion had committed atrocities in Poland, especially during the Warsaw Uprising. Vakar, p. 278; Loftus, pp. 45–56, 81, 97–105, 200 & 218; Anderson, pp. 43–4; John Keegan, *Waffen-SS: The Asphalt Soldiers*, Pan/Ballantine (pbk), 1979, pp. 139 & 158.

9. Loftus, pp. 54–5; Botting/Sayer, *Secret Army*, p. 341; Faligot/Krop, pp. 73–5.

10. 'Die Behandlung des Russichen Problems

Wahrend der Zeit des National Sozialistischen Regimes in Deutschland', Top Secret, ACSI – Sensitive Document File, Suitland, Maryland. The document was handed to American intelligence agencies which protected the author, providing him with a university teaching post. Loftus, pp. 67–8 & 203; Dallin, pp. 553 & 658; Simpson, p. 295.

11. Anderson, p. 44; Loftus, pp. 57, 97 & 165–7.

12. The Belorussian Central Representation (BCR) was also referred to as the Belorussian Council and, still later, the Belorussian Liberation Front, by the Anti-Bolshevik Bloc of Nations. ABN Correspondence, Vol. XLI, May–June 1991.

13–20. Vakar, pp. 22, 203, 220–2 & 278–80; Loftus, pp. 57–8, 68–71, 82–6, 109–18, 152, 166 & 206; Anderson, p. 44; Botting/Sayer, *Secret Army*, p. 341; Philby, pp. 180–8.

21. Smal-Stocky, 'Secret Struggle', and *Nationality*, p. 336; ABN Correspondence; Loftus, p. 166.

22. G, 10.9.96.

CHAPTER FOURTEEN: THE ANTI-BOLSHEVIK BLOC OF NATIONS

1, 2 & 4. Armstrong, pp. 19–23 & 37–8; V. Cherednychenko, *Anatomy of Treason*, Politvidav Ukraini, Kiev, 1984, pp. 12–19 & 30–40; Tomas Rezac and Valentin Tsurkan, *Wanted*, Progress, Moscow, 1988, pp. 36–9 & 76–85; Orest Subtelny, *Ukraine: A History*, University of Toronto Press, Canada, 1989, pp. 441–3; Dmytro Shtykalo, *Russian Oppression in Ukraine: Reports and Documents*, Ukraine Publishers, 1962, pp. 227–8; Danylo Chaykovsky, 'Stepan Bandera, His Life and Struggle', in *Murdered by Moscow: Petlura-Konovalets-Bandera*, Ukrainian Publishers, 1962, pp. 41–4; Sudoplatov, pp. 12–16; Allen, pp. 340–1; Simpson, p. 161; Dallin, p. 114; Paprocki. On early history see Alexander J. Motyl, *The Turn to the Right: The ideological origins and developments of Ukrainian nationalism, 1919–1929*, East European Monograph series, No. 65, Columbia University Press, NY, 1980.

By 1934 the Soviet Unified State Political Directorate (OGPU) had penetrated the OUN. Konovalets's deputy, Vassili Lebed, and his delegate in Finland were Soviet agents. Lebed met with German Intelligence in Berlin and learned that Konovalets 'had twice met with [Goering], who offered to train several of his followers in the Nazi Party school in Leipzig'. An 'illegal' Soviet agent, Pavel Sudoplatov positioned himself close to the Ukrainian leader and learned that by 1936 2,000 men were being trained in Galicia as part of an international terrorist network which was funded by the Abwehr.

3. Col. Melnyk was allied to Mussolini who, in 1938, posted a '100 per cent strong anti-German fascist' as consul to Lvov. Shtykalo, pp. 489–90; *Murdered by Moscow*, p. 35; Sudoplatov, pp. 26–9; Armstrong, pp. 23 & 36; Paprocki; Allen, p. 341; Luciuk/ Kordan, pp. 76 & 82–3.

5. Bower, *Red Web*, pp. 54, 121 & 133; Cookridge/Gehlen, p. 307; Simpson, p. 161; Armstrong, pp. 25, 33 & 42; Dallin, pp. 115–16; Yaroslav Bilinsky, *The Second Soviet Republic: The Ukraine after World War II*, Rutgers University Press, US, 1964, p. 5. Bilinsky was appointed an Associate of the Russian Research Centre at Harvard University (1956–8) which collected material for the book. Palmer, pp. 235 & 241. Voloshyn was killed by the communists in 1946.

6 & 8. Dallin, pp. 115–18; Simpson, pp. 161–3; *Village Voice*, 11.2.86.

7. Chaykovsky, p. 44; Armstrong, p. 55; Paprocki; Sudoplatov, pp. 23–4; Cookridge, *Gehlen*, p. 307.

9. The Banderites jettisoned their anti-clericalism to join cause with the Greek Catholic (Uniate) Church – 'anti-Muscovite but linked to the Vatican, pro-German but not trusted by the Germans'. Its head, Andrew Sheptytsky, a Polish count and former high-ranking officer of the Austrian Army, aimed to convert the East through the Uniate Church. Myroslav Yurkevich, *Ukraine During World War II*, p. 71; Allen, p. 390; Armstrong, p. 63; Simpson, p. 161; Committee for German Unity, *The Truth about Oberländer*, East Berlin, 1960, p. 89; Leverkuehn, pp. 164–5; Dallin, p. 485; Bilinsky, p. 96; Armstrong, pp. 74–5; Sudoplatov, p. 251; Aarons/Loftus, *Ratlines*, p. 247; Rezac/Tsurkan, pp. 15–33·

10. Dr Philip Friedman ('Ukrainian Jewish Relations during the Nazi Occupation', YIVO *Annual of Jewish Social Science*, NY YIVO Institute for Jewish Research, Vol. XII 1958–9) has documented the participation of Ukrainians in the pogroms. 'The pro-Nazi elements consciously exploited the "Jewish problem" in order to attract the largest possible number of adherents and fellow-travellers.' OUN-B adopted a virulently anti-Semitic, pro-Nazi programme at the Second Congress in Cracow. An OUN-B letter sent to the German Secret Service declared: 'Long live greater independent Ukraine without Jews ... Jews to the gallows.' Bandera's second-in-command approved of 'the German methods of exterminating the Jews' and it was only in late 1943 that the Banderites dropped the anti-Jewish line. Raul Hilburg, *The Destruction of European Jewry*, Quadrangle Books, NY, 1961, pp. 205 & 329–30; IoS, 5.5.91. See also *The Einsatzgruppen Reports*; B.F. Sabrin, *Alliance for Murder: The Nazi–Ukrainian Nationalist Partnership in Genocide*, Sarpedon, NY, 1991; Aarons, p. 54; Armstrong, p. 77; Cesarani, p. 26; Simpson, p. 164; Dallin, p. 119.

11. The proclamation is published in Roman Rakhmanny, *In Defense of the Ukrainian Cause*, Christopher, US, 1979, p. 42. Simpson, pp. 161–2; Dallin, p. 119; Nicholas D. Czubatjy, 'The Ukrainian Underground', *Ukrainian Quarterly*, 11, winter 1946; Hermann Raschhoffer, *Political Assassination: The Legal Background of the Oberländer and Stashinsky Cases*, Fritz Schlichtenmayer, Tübingen, 1964, p. 10.

12. Chaykovsky, p. 255; Leverkuehn, p. 166.

13 & 14. Armstrong, pp. 83 & 98; Simpson, pp. 16–22 & 165; Paprocki; Wolodymyr Kosyk, *l'Allemagne National-Socialiste et l'Ukraine*, Publications de l'Est Européen, Paris, 1986, pp. 112, 290 & 426–8; Dallin, p. 121; Aarons/Loftus, *Ratlines*, p. 247; Sabrin, pp. 4–5.

15. In October, Melnyk established a Ukrainian National Council in Kiev headed by Prof. M. Velychivsky. Armstrong, p. 83; Simpson, pp. 161–2 & 165; Yurkevich, pp. 72–3; Chaykovsky, pp. 500–1; Petro R. Sodol, *UPA: They Fought Hitler and Stalin*, Committee for the World Convention and Reunion of Soldiers in the Ukrainian Insurgent Army, NY, 1987, p. 105; Paprocki.

16. Luciuk/Kordan, pp. 8 & 153; A.J. Halpern, British Security Co-ordination, to G. de T. Glazebrook, Canadian Department of External Affairs, enclosing an OSS report on Ukrainians in North America, 16.8.44.

17. Despite OUN-B propaganda that it created the Ukrainian Insurgent Army (UPA), it was Borovets who in June 1940 formed 'small insurgent detachments'. His Polesskaya Sich or UPA began operations against the Soviets in 1942. Adopting the name 'Taras Bulba', he agreed to head an 'auxiliary Wehrmacht company' known as the Ukrainian Liberation Army. Two hundred volunteers joined, taking an 'oath of loyalty to the Führer'. Peter J. Boshyk (ed.), *Ukraine in World War II: History and Its Aftermath*, Canadian Institute of Ukrainian Studies, 1986, pp. 64–5; Sodol, pp. 19–20; Oleh R. Martoyvch, 'Ukrainian Liberation Movement in Modern Times', *Today's World*, No. 5, Edinburgh: Scottish League for European Freedom (SLEF), 1952, p. 102; Cherednychenko, pp. 89–91 & 182–3; Simpson, p. 162; Bilinsky, p. 342; Buch; Aarons, p. 5; Anderson, p. 24; Armstrong, pp. 98–9 & 153; Yuriy Tys-Krokhmaliuk, *UPA Warfare in Ukraine*, Society of Veterans of Ukrainian Insurgent Army of the United States and Canada, NY, 1972, pp. 257–8, 282–3 & 360; Taras Hunczk, 'Between Two Leviathans: Ukraine during the Second World War', in Bohdan Krawchenko (ed.), *Ukrainian Past, Ukrainian Present*, St Martin's Press, NY, 1993.

18 & 19. Azerbaijan sent six delegates, the Baskhirs one, White Ruthenians two, Armenia four, Georgia six, Kabardinia one, Ukraine five, the Turkestanians six (Uzbeks five, the Kazaks one), the Ossetins two, the Tartars four, the Cherkes one, and the Chuvashes one. Martovych, pp. 103–8 & 118–21; Buch, Hunczak & Czubatyj; Rakhmanny, pp. 19 & 44; Bilinsky, pp. 123–4; Simpson, p. 162; Aarons/Loftus, *Ratlines*, p. 186; Dallin, pp. 622 & 623; Luciuk/Kordan, p. 175; Armstrong, pp. 157–61 & 179; Chaykovsky, p. 502; Peter Potichnyj and Yevhen Shendera (eds), *Political Thought of the Underground, 1943–1951*, Canadian Institute of Ukrainian Studies, 1986, pp. 373–5.

20. The Melnyk faction, running SS auxiliary police units, denounced Canaris' Banderites to the Gestapo as traitors. It was also apparent that the OUN-B had been infiltrated by Soviet agents, adding to the confusion. Czubatyj; Cookridge, *Gehlen*, p. 308; Aarons/Loftus, *Ratlines*, p. 176.

21. Cherednychencko, pp. 127–8; Rezac/Tsurkan, p. 156–7.

22. Czubatyj; Armstrong, pp. 291–2; Simpson, p. 163; Cookridge, *Gehlen*, p. 189;

Martovych, p. 155; Bilinsky, pp. 125 & 130–1; Loftus, p. 107.

23. Maintaining links with the Hlinka Guard, UPA propaganda raids reached Slovakia during the summers of 1945 and 1946. Aarons, p. 73; Bilinsky, p. 116; Bower, *Red Web*, p. 121; Cookridge, *Gehlen*, p. 307.

24. War Office report on Ukrainian Nationalist Movement and Resistance in Ukraine, 13.12.45; minutes by T. Brimelow and B. Miller, PRO FO 371/47957.

25. Aarons, pp. 80–1; Aarons/Loftus, *Ratlines*, p. 247; Simpson, p. 166; Botting/Sayer, *Secret Army*, pp. 351–2; Cherednychenko, pp. 166–7; *The Restoration of the Ukrainian State in World War II*, Ukrainian Central Information Service, Toronto, n/d.

26. Dallin, p. 659; Loftus, p. 106; John Prados, *Presidents' Secret Wars: CIA and Pentagon Covert Operations from World War II through Iranscam*, NY, 1995, p. 53; Botting/Sayer, *Secret Army*, p. 355; *The Shelepin Files: Documents and Reports*, Ukrainian Information Service, London, 1975, p. 54.

27. ABN literature claimed direct descent from the 1943 committee of subjugated nations and ignored the fact that it was organised by Rosenberg's OMi. On the alliance with Nazi Germany, the ABN stated: 'The fact that some of us fought on the German side against Russia can be justified from the national political and moral point of view.' Nakashidze, Russ Bellant, *Old Nazis, the New Right and the Reagan Administration: The Role of Domestic Fascist Networks in the Republican Party and the Effect on US Cold War Politics* (2nd ed.), Political Research Associates, US, 1989, p. 77; Paprocki; Rakhmanny, p. 19.

28. Bilinsky, p. 345; Bower, *Spy*, p. 205; Loftus, pp. 106–8; Buch.

29. Anderson, p. 294.

30 & 31. Maris Cakars and Barton Osborn, 'Operation Ohio', *WIN* magazine, 18.9.75. Maris Cakars personally informed Peter E. Newell (letter, 6.9.88) that, following the WiN report, he received documentation from the Soviets much in line with his own findings. Cherednychenko, pp. 151–3.

32. There was low-level co-operation between the OUN/UPA and anti-communist Polish groups such as WiN and the extremist NSZ in attacks on Polish communist and Soviet centres but it ceased after the summer of 1946. Ethnic 'cleansing' continued with WiN and OUN/UPA groups massacring each other's villages, with the result that the Poles came to hate the Banderites. Brig.-Gen. Ignacy Blum, 'The Share of the Polish Army in the Struggle for the Stabilisation of People's Government: Actions against the UPA Bands', *Review of Military History*, Warsaw, Vol. IV, No. 1, Jan./Mar. 1959, and Col. of the General Staff Jan Gerhard, 'Further Details on Actions against the Bands of the UPA and WiN in the Southeastern Area of Poland', Vol. IV, No. 4, Oct./Dec. 1959; Bilinsky, pp. 114–18; Simpson, p. 171.

33. Armstrong, pp. 294–5; Buch; Prados, p. 53; Botting/Sayer, *Secret Army*, p. 349.

34. NYT, 13.5.47; Bilinsky, pp. 112–13 & 133–4.

35. Buch; Simpson, pp. 166–8; Aarons/Loftus, *Ratlines*, p. 248.

36. John Hope and CIC documents; Sudoplatov, p. 252.

37. It is known that the OUN took the opportunity to inflate the figures by letting DPs cross the border and return to the West as 'guerrillas'. When UPA Company 95 reached Germany, it claimed the armed strength in Ukraine to be from 50,000 to 200,000 – clearly a gross overestimate. James K. Anderson, 'Unknown Soldiers of an Unknown Army', *Army* magazine, May 1968.

38. Bilinsky, pp. 15 & 420; Hersh, pp. 248–9.

39. PRO FO 371/77586; memorandum by N.W.A. Jones, March 1949.

40 & 42. Armstrong, p. 316; Simpson, p. 168; Aarons/Loftus, *Ratlines*, pp. 248 & 256; Paprocki.

41. Aarons, pp. 75–6; Luciuk/Kordan, pp. 226–7; John F. Stewart, 'The Struggle of Ukraine for Freedom', SLEF, No. 7, 1950.

43. Botting/Sayer, *Secret Army*, pp. 352 & 355; Simpson, p. 168; Loftus, *Nazis and Axis Collaborators*, p. 90.

44–6. David Matas and Susan Charendoff, *Justice Delayed: Nazi War Criminals in Canada*, Summerhill Press, Toronto, 1987, pp. 24–7, 45 & 57: based on the report of the Commission of Inquiry on War Criminals before the Honourable Justice Jules Deschenes, 1985–6. Besides the public hearings it also includes the report prepared by Alti Rodal, *The Nazi War Criminals in Canada: The Historical and Political Setting from the 1940s to the Present*. Harold Troper and Morton Weinfeld, *Old Wounds: Jews, Ukrainians and the Hunt for Nazi War*

Criminals in Canada, University of Carolina Press, 1990, pp. 66–8, 184 & 194.

47 & 48. PRO FO 371/87433 & 371/77586; Matas/Charendorff, pp. 38, 57–9 & 84–5; Anderson.

49. Bower, *Spy*, pp. 125 & 181; Cavendish, p. 52; Cookridge, *Gehlen*, p. 308; Cherednychenko, pp. 176–8. Harry Rositzke, *The CIA's Secret Operations: Espionage, Counterespionage and Covert Action*, Westview Press, 1988, p. 23.

50. In September, the State section for émigré affairs proposed the 'rapid expansion' of an 'illegally organised military movement', the Ukrainian National Guard, 'which will form a large reserve potential in case of an armed conflict between the United States and the Soviet Union'. Hersh, pp. 249 & 275–6; Simpson, p. 173; Luciuk/Kordan, p. 209; Rositzke, pp. 18–19.

51. Sudoplatov, pp. 254–6; Cookridge, *Gehlen*, p. 308; Yuriy Tys-Krokhmaliuk, *UPA Warfare in Ukraine: Strategy and Tactics and Organisational Problems of Ukrainian Resistance in World War II*, Society of Veterans of Ukrainian Insurgent Army, NY, 1972, p. 311.

52 & 55. SImpson, pp. 149 & 172–3; Bower, *Spy*, pp. 120 & 133; Prados, p. 57.

53. Paprocki; Armstrong, pp. 317–20; Richard Deacon with Nigel West, *SPY!*, BBC, 1980, p. 150.

54 & 57. Sudoplatov, pp. 24–5 & 257; Botting/Sayer, *Secret Army*, p. 350; Rezac/Tsurkan, p. 170; Prados, p. 57; Alexander Buchsbajew, *Toward a Theory of Guerrilla Warfare: A Case Study of the Ukrainian Nationalists, 1944–48*, PhD thesis, Ann Arbor University, 1984; Cherednychenko, pp. 176–83.

56. Rositzke, p. 23.

58. Oberlander was later forced to resign as minister and later became associated with the ABN and the European Freedom Council, an ABN/OUN 'front' group. *Truth about Oberlander*, p. 175; *Der Spiegel*, 21.4.54.

59–61. Bower, *Red Web*, p. 165, and *Spy*, pp. 133 & 206; Cookridge, *Gehlen*, pp. 299–301; Hersh, p. 494; Bilinsky, pp. 115–16; Loftus, pp. 113–14.

62. NYT, 27.5.53 & 21.5.54; Bilinsky, p. 132.

63. Prados, p. 58.

64 & 66. Buchsbajew; Rositzke, pp. 37, 44 & 169.

65. Simpson, p. 173; Buchsbajew; Aarons, p. 54.

67. Bilinsky, p. 11; G, 16.8.93.

CHAPTER FIFTEEN: POLAND

1. Wilkinson/Astley, pp. 128 & 136; Lampe, p. 63.

2. Gordon Welchman, 'From Polish Bomba to British Bombe: The Birth of Ultra', INS, Vol. 1, No. 1, Jan. 1986. Maj.-Gen. M.Z. Rygot Slowikowski, *In the Secret Service: The Light of the Torch*, Windrush, 1988; John Herman, 'Agency Africa', JCH, Oct. 1987; Brooks Richards, *Secret Flotillas: The clandestine sea lines to France and French North Africa 1940–44*, HMSO, 1996, pp. 22–3.

3 & 4. West, *Secret War*, pp. 29–30, 312 & 329; Wilkinson/Astley, pp. 81 & 128; PRO FO 371/26722 C/188; minute, 1.1.41.

5 & 6. John Coutouvdis and Jaime Reynolds, *Poland 1939–47*, Leicester University Press, 1986, pp. 87–9 & 109. There has been much speculation on Sikorski's death though there is little evidence that he was assassinated. There had been a number of threats against his life from disgruntled Polish émigrés, but these were not taken seriously. The pronouncements exasperated British Foreign Office officials. One was reported in 1940 to have suggested of another leading Pole that 'we shall never have any peace until we have him bumped off'. PRO FO 371/24474 C/8090; David Irving, *The Death of General Sikorski*, 1967; A. Polonsky (ed.), *The Great Powers and the Polish Question 1941–45*, 1976.

7–14. Wilkinson/Astley, pp. 129, 179, 206 & 226–7; David Stafford, *Britain and European Resistance 1940–45*, 1983, pp. 183–5; Thomas, pp. 350 & 360; Coutouvdis/Reynolds, pp. 108, 149, 189 & 219; M. Smith, p. 110; Bethell, p. 154; West, *Secret War*, p. 311; PRO Chiefs of Staff report, Jan. 1945 CoS (44)84(0) in CAB 80/78; HS4/51, 52, 127 & 292; FO 371/47709 NI 002/265/G55 & N3354/265/G55.

15. The publication aimed to assert the Polish voice in Baltic affairs and counter German claims to the 'historically Polish' Free City of Danzig. Also interesting was the *Baltic Times*, whose editor was Arnold Smith, a Rhodes scholar and later Canadian diplomat. This was (obit. G, 26.2.94) an 'improbable' appointment 'which may well have been the cover for an intelligence assignment'. When Russian troops took over the Baltic states, Smith made his way through the Soviet Union to Cairo, where the British embassy gave him an attaché's job. He was soon involved in local propaganda work with Freya Stark, working for MI6's Section D. The *Baltic Review* was published from 1953 under the direction of the CIA-sponsored Free Europe Committee. Hills, p. 58. Howarth later joined the Home Civil Service 1948–53 as a town and country planner (telephone conversations, 20 & 31.3.94). Howarth, pp. 200–5 & 213; Vardys, p. 287; Michael Winch, *Republic for a Day: An Eye-Witness Account of the Carpatho-Ukraine Incident*, Hale, 1939.

16 & 18. PRO HS 4/45, 139, 140, 204 & 327; M. Smith, pp. 112 & 291–2. Information on 'Sullivan' was given to Steven by a former CIA officer. 'Sullivan' worked in the Middle East in the fifties and apparently died of a heart attack in Beirut in 1967. Steven, pp. 35–7, 56 & 234; Smiley, p. 162; West, *Friends*, p. 60.

17. Bower, *Spy*, p. 209.

19. Howarth, p. 211; PRO FO 371/47707 NI 486/211/55, 24.10.45.

20, 21 & 22. Coutouvdis/Reynolds, pp. 20, 219–20, 353 & 368; Stefan Korbonski, *Warsaw in Exile*, 1966, p. 232; Richard C. Lukas, *Bitter Legacy: Polish–American Relations in the Wake of World War II*, University of Kentucky, US, 1982, p. 31; Howarth telephone conversation, 31.3.94.

A pious Catholic, Herbert enrolled at the beginning of the war in a Polish unit at the special forces training centre at Inverailort. Lord Lovat knew him as 'a charming romantic' and remembered 'his tempestuous Poles departed cheering, to die with conspicuous gallantry in the liberation of Europe. They looked upon the loveable, flat-footed and wholly unmilitary Auberon as their father.' After the war, he lived at Portofina, Liguria – built by his grandfather, the fourth Earl of Caernarvon – where he was visited by various intelligence-connected friends, including Isaiah Berlin, Stuart Hampshire, Patrick Leigh-Fermor and Malcolm Muggeridge. Herbert made 'many trips up and down the Iron Curtain', working on behalf of the Polish, Ukrainian and Belorussian exiles. When he died in 1974 he was, his obituary recorded, 'much missed . . . in the somewhat eclectic circles he frequented'.

23. Hundreds of thousands of Poles had elected to remain in the West after 1945 rather than return to communist-controlled Poland. The thousands who emigrated or fled to the West after 1945 brought with them information about conditions in the country and the state of the anti-communist underground. PRO CoS (46)239(0), 15.10.46, quoted in Lewis, p. 288; Bower, *Red Web*, p. 54.

24–25 & 27. Coutouvdis/Reynolds, p. 277; Seton-Watson, pp. 174–7; Thomas, p. 347; Howarth, pp. 212 & 219, and telephone conversation, 31.3.94.

26. John Peet, *The Long Engagement: Memories of a Cold War Legend*, Fourth Estate, 1989, p. 176.

28–30. Lukas, pp. 92–4; Korbonski, pp. xi & 265–75; Dodds-Parker, *Political Eunuch*, p. 49; NYT, 4.11.47; memo by Andrews, 17.11.47, in FRUS IV, 1947, pp. 460–4; Howarth, p. 221, and telephone conversation, 31.3.94.

31 & 32. Mikolajczyk was supported by the assistant editor of *Time and Tide*, which published a long justification of his policy, and Polish specialist, Freda Bruce Lockhart ('The Polish Pantomime' and 'Meeting with Mikolajczyk', *Nineteenth Century and After*, CXLII, Feb. 1946 & CXLIII, Jan. 1947), who had visited him in Warsaw during the summer of 1946. By 1949 the Mid-European Studies Centre was being funded by the OPC-backed Free Europe Committee. Interview with Mr Hawrot of the Polish Ex-Servicemen's Association; Coutouvdis/Reynolds, pp. 216–20 & 295–301; Lukas, pp. 92 & 133; Howarth, p. 221;

33. A character in Trevor Barnes's *roman à clef*, *A Midsummer Killing*, recalls that 'it was doomed to failure. Poland was divided against itself to begin with: the communists and the WiN anti-communists hated each other. And after the horrors and destruction of the war, people were tired out. They had had enough of fighting, no matter against whom. And of course, the Soviet security police were so efficient.' Trevor Barnes, *A Midsummer Killing*, NEL (pbk), 1989, pp. 125–6; Coutouvdis/Reynolds, p. 301; PRO FO 371 66092/N/2923; Phillip Knightley, *Philby: KGB Masterspy*, 1988, p. 163.

34. Thomas Powers, *The Man Who Kept the Secrets: Richard Helms and the CIA*, Washington Square Press (pbk), US, 1981, p. 49; John Herman, 'Afterword', in Slowikowski, p. 251.

35 & 36. Zygmunt Wozniczka, *Zrzeszenie 'Wolnosc i Niezawislosc', 1945–1952*, Novum

Semex, Warsaw, 1992, p. 119; Stanislaw Kulz, *W Potrzasku Dziejowym: WiN na Szlaku AK*, Veritas, 1978; Powers, p. 49; Hersh, p. 279; Rositzke, pp. 169–71.

37, 38 & 40. Bower, *Spy*, p. 164; Hersh, p. 279; Edward Jay Epstein, *Deception: The Invisible War between the KGB and the CIA*, W.H. Allen, 1989, pp. 34–9.

39. Knightley, *Masterspy*, p. 163; Powers, pp. 48–50.

41. Rositzke, p. 170; Bower, *Spy*, p. 158; Steven, p. 35; Barnes, p. 127.

42. Buchardt; Knightley, *Masterspy*, p. 163; Rositzke, p. 171; Epstein, p. 39.

43. Cookridge, *Gehlen*, pp. 245–6.

44. Ranelagh, pp. 227–8; Hersh, pp. 280–1.

45. Epstein, p. 42.

CHAPTER SIXTEEN: THE BALTIC STATES

1–3. Cesarani, p. 138; Bower, *Red Web*, pp. 3, 20–3, 29–30 & 40–1; Kramish, p. 190. On the MI6 station in Riga, see Peggie Benton, *Baltic Countdown*, Centaur, 1984. Peggie was the wife of Frank Benton, who served under cover as the vice-consul. She helped out in the Passport Control Office. C. Leonard Lundin, 'Nazification of Baltic German Minorities', *Journal of Central European Affairs*, Vol. 7, No. 1, April 1947; L, 31.8.89.

4. Cesarani, pp. 138–9; Leverkuehn, pp. 167–71; Romuald J. Misiunas and Rein Taagepera, *The Baltic States: Years of Dependence 1940–1990* (rev. ed.), Hurst, 1993, p. 57; Armstrong, p. 597; Efraim Zumoff, *Occupation: Nazi-Hunter, the continuing search for the perpetrators of the Holocaust*, Ktav, 1994, p. 28.

5. Cesarani, p. 17; Aarons, pp. 98–9; I, 8.8.95.

6. One officer was Harry Svikeris, in charge of the 1st and 2nd Companies, which were alleged to have burnt down the villages of Sanniki and Malinova, shooting all 300 inhabitants in the process. In 1948 he moved to Britain from the British Zone in Germany as part of the labour recruitment programme. In 1949 Victor Arajs was released from internment by the British. Twenty-six years later, a West German court imprisoned Arajs for life for his crimes, which involved his units 'shooting upwards of 500 people a day'. After the war, Reinhards became a prominent member of the Latvian community in London. Aarons, p. 195; ITV

London programme, 27.6.88; 6, 28.6.88; *Searchlight*, No. 142, Apr. 1987, and No. 148, Oct. 1987; Arthur Silgailis, *Latvian Legion*, R. James Bender, 1986, pp. 15, 20, 48–9 & 198–9. Osis was wounded in December.

7 & 8. According to Aba Gefen, who in Lithuania had kept a diary of the war years, the massacres 'began on 22 June 1941 when the Germans bombed Kaunas. In a radio broadcast the commander of LAF announced that Jews were shooting at the German troops and warned that for every German soldier shot, 100 Jews would be put to death. That triggered off a wave of violence against the Jewish population.' Cesarani, pp. 93, 138–9 & 145; Anderson, pp. 35–6; Aarons, p. 195; Simpson, p. 184; Bower, *Blind Eye* (rev. ed.), pp. 254 & 478; Misiunas/Taagepera, pp. 44–7, 56–61 & 66; Hutchinson, pp. 73, 151 & 169–70.

9–11. V. Stanley Vardys (ed.), *Lithuania under the Soviets: Portrait of a Nation, 1940–65*, Frederick A. Praeger, 1965, p. 61; 'The Partisan Movement in Post-War Lithuania', *Slavic Review*, XXII, No. 3, Sept. 1963; Thomas Remeikis, *Opposition to Soviet Rule in Lithuania 1945–1980*, Institute of Lithuanian Studies Press, US, 1980, pp. 61 & 180; Sigailis, pp. 134 & 233; Cesarani, p. 141.

12–16. Bower, *Red Web*, pp. 30–1, 40–7 & 59; Misiunas/Taagepera, pp. 66–9; Vardys, pp. 82–3.

17. Juozas Daumantas, *Fighters for Freedom: Lithuanian Partisans versus the USSR, 1944–1947*, Maryland, NY, 1975, p. 68. First-hand account of the guerrilla activities during 1944–7 written by Daumantas (aka Juozas Luksa) during his time in the West. The author's true identity was revealed by the Soviets in a series of articles in the summer of 1959 and published in book form in 1960 – M. Chienas, K. Smigelskis and E. Uldukis, *Vanagi is Anapus*. Prados, p. 37; Remeikis, p. 60.

18–21. Bower, *Red Web*, pp. 38–40, 50–3 & 79; Whitwell, p. 75; Cesarani, pp. 140–4; Aarons/Loftus, *Ratlines*, p. 261; G, 28.6.68.

22 & 23. K.V. Tauras, *Guerrilla Warfare on the Amber Coast*, Voyages Press, NY, 1962, p. 37, also based on the experiences of Luksa, was almost certainly sponsored by the CIA. Powers, pp. 3, 93 & 315; Prados, pp. 37–9.

24 & 25. Vardys, pp. 103–5; Daumantas, pp. 79–80; Misiunas/Taagepera, p. 91; Thomas Remeikis, 'The Armed Struggle against the Sovietisation of Lithuania after 1944', *Lituanus*, VIII/1–2, 1962.

26. Cesarani, p. 140; Bower, *Red Web*, pp. 54–9 & 78.

27 & 30. Sigailis, pp. 225 & 234; Aarons, pp. 195–6; Bower, *Red Web*, p. 71, and *Blind Eye* (rev. ed.), p. 254.

28–29, 31–32 & 34. Cesarani, pp. 47, 60 & 142–6; Aarons, pp. 195–9; Simpson, p. 184; Anderson, pp. 35–6; Misiunas/Taagepera, p. 17; Bower, *Red Web*, pp. 59 & 64.

33. PRO FO 371/57519, 371/47053 & 371/47053; Tolstoy, p. 422.

35. M. Smith, p. 110; PRO CAB 81/9 & 81/92; Bower, *Red Web*, pp. 60–1.

36 & 38. Bower, *Red Web*, pp. 72–3 & 81; Vardys, pp. 90–6.

37. Cesarani, pp. 57 & 141; Intelligence Bureau to Political Division, Lübeck, 28.2.46; PRO FO 1049/414.

39. Bower, *Red Web*, p. 82; Remeikis, p. 214; Stasys Zymantas, 'Twenty Years of Resistance', *Lituanus*, Vol. 1/2, 1960. Zymantas had been assistant law professor at Vilnius University, Secretary of the Liberal International and London Committee of Free Representatives of the Central and Eastern European Countries, and vice-chair of the European Committee of the Lithuanian Resistance Alliance.

40–44. Remeikis, p. 54; Vardys, pp. 96 & 100–2; Prados, p. 38; Bower, *Red Web*, pp. 60–2, 72–3, 95–7 & 172; M. Smith, p. 114; Cesarani, pp. 142–3; G, 28.6.88.

45. PRO FO 371/65754, Zarine to Hankey, 21.1.47; Cesarani, pp. 54 & 98; T, 25.5.46; *The Tablet*, 15.6.46; Bower, *Blind Eye* (rev. ed.), pp. 256 & 262.

46–52. Remeikis, pp. 46–56; Vardys, p. 106; Daumantas, pp. 132 & 239; Misiunis/Taagapera, pp. 89–90; Prados, pp. 39–40; Bower, *Red Web*, p. 95.

53 & 55–59. Bower, *Red Web*, pp. 98, 110–12, 129 & 147; Cesarani, pp. 143–7.

54. DE, 3.2.94; Zumoff, p. 306.

60 & 61. Courtney, pp. 54–5; Harvey-Jones, pp. 149, 161, 173–4 & 179–80. Joshua Steward was a member of Field Service Security and the Intelligence Corps during the war and postwar in Germany, where his German and Russian skills proved useful to MI6 during interrogation sessions. He worked alongside John Harvey-Jones in gathering intelligence on Soviet plans, order-of-battle and servicing agents. He returned with Harvey-Jones to England, where he became something of a polymath (obit. G, 3.2.97). Bower, *Red Web*, pp. 101–2; West, *Friends*, p. 80.

62 & 63. Prados, pp. 41–2; Harvey-Jones, p. 180; Cookridge, p. 312; Cesarani, p. 141; Bower, *Red Web*, p. 122.

64. The Soviets published full versions of these missions in Vilnius (1960–8). J. Jakaitis, *Isdavystes Keliu* (Vilnius, 1976) is a Soviet exposé of western subversion and also includes an account of training of Lithuanian, Estonian, Latvian, Ukrainian and Polish operatives in West Germany, France and Britain in the period 1949–52. The series *Faktai Kaltina* (*Facts Accuse*, Vilnius, 1962–70) ran to ten volumes with testimony of witnesses and transcripts of interrogations of guerrillas. In referring to Soviet booklets published on the guerrilla war, in particular M. Chienas, K. Smigelkis and E. Uldukis, 'Hawks from the Other Side' (Vilnius, 1960), Thomas Remeikis admitted that 'it is reasonable to believe that the Soviet versions are correct as far as facts, dates, names and places are concerned' (*Lituanus*, Nos 1–2, 1962, and Remeikis, pp. 192–5).

65–70. Deskny's 'confessions' were published in Vilnius (1960–2), detailing the guerrillas' relationship with the West. Prados, pp. 38–9; Misiunas/Taagapera, p. 93; Vardys, pp. 85, 107 & 268; Remeikis, pp. 46, 56 & 189–94; Bower, *Red Web*, pp. 11 & 114–18; Cesarani, p. 144.

71 & 72. Chair of the Council of Nations was Alfreds Berzins, who with Bolreslavs Maikovskis ended up on the payroll of a number of CIA-backed organisations. In 1950, Gustav Celmins entered America to work with US Intelligence before eventually fleeing to Mexico after a newspaper exposed his anti-Semitic past. Bower, *Red Web*, pp. 121–5; Aarons, p. 195; Simpson, p. 184; Remeikis, pp. 47 & 195.

73–79. Harvey-Jones took charge of the naval operations at Hamburg. Courtney returned to the UK that spring, where he was offered a position by C's deputy, but decided to return to the NID and early retirement in 1953.

That western intelligence encouraged resistance beyond the pure necessities of information-gathering is implied by Luksa's first report to the guerrillas. One émigré wrote: 'sending such missions could easily be interpreted by the guerrillas as a signal of Western support for their cause and the imminence of liberation'. The CIA was

engaged in 'positive intervention' and Luksa was tasked 'to carry out covert actions designed to weaken Soviet control over its own population and the peoples of Eastern Europe; to weaken pro-Soviet regimes and Communist parties throughout Europe'. Courtney, p. 55; Bower, *Red Web*, pp. 127–43; Remeikis, pp. 48–52; Vardys, pp. 10 & 107–8.
80. Klose went on to become Admiral Commanding the German Fleet. Harvey-Jones, p. 180; Bower, *Red Web*, pp. 145 & 152–3.
81. In 1960, when CIA U-2 pilot Francis Gary powers went down in the Soviet Union, he was sent to a prison in Valdimir where he shared a cell for seventeen months with Krumins. As Prados suggests, this 'stretches credulity too far'. Krumins 'may have been working for Soviet security in 1960, and perhaps was all along'. See Gary Powers with Curt Gentry, *Operation Overflight*, Holt, Rinehart, US, 1970, pp. 206–78; Prados, p. 42.
82. West, *Secret War*, pp. 157–8.
83 & 85–86. *I* magazine, 22.9.92; Bower, *Red Web*, pp. 153–5 & 166–8; L, 31.8.89.
84. Zemaitis was caught by the Soviet security forces in the spring of 1953 and executed in 1954. A transcript of his interrogation was published in *Facts Accuse*, pp. 203–30. In 1956, Ramanaukas was apprehended and executed by the Soviets. Remeikis, pp. 47, 190 & 241–52; Prados, p. 43.

PART FOUR: THE BALKANS AND RUSSIA

1. B. Sweet-Escott, 'SOE in the Balkans', in P. Auty and R. Clogg (eds), *British Policy towards Wartime Resistance in Yugoslavia and Greece*, 1975, pp. 15–16; PRO FO N499/499/38.
2. By late 1944, counter-espionage head Felix Cowgill was recruiting into Sections V & IX experienced Bletchley officers to monitor Soviet international traffic. Malcolm Kennedy was a Japanese specialist seconded in 1918 to units of the Imperial Japanese Army. In 1920, he returned to London and the East Asian Section of Military Intelligence and was Tokyo representative of Reuter's (1925–34), and during the war served in GC&CS's Japanese Section. Because of the bureaucratic manoeuvres over the headship of Section IX, he did not join MI6 until October 1945. John

Ferris, 'From Broadway House to Bletchley Park: The Diaries of Captain Malcolm Kennedy, 1943–46', INS, Vol. 4, No. 3, July 1989; Cecil; Borovik, p. 245; Brook-Shepherd, p. 52; Brown, *Secret Servant*, pp. 616–17.
3. Vojtech Mastny, 'Europe in US–USSR Relations: A Topical Legacy', *Problems of Communism*, XXXVII, Jan. 1988; Geoffrey Swain, 'The Cominform: Tito's International?', THJ, Vol. 35, No. 3, 1992.
4. Ralph Miliband and Marcel Liebman, 'Reflections on Anti-Communism', in Ralph Miliband, John Saville and Marcel Liebman (eds), *Socialist Register*, 1984.

CHAPTER SEVENTEEN: GREECE AND THE CREATION OF THE PARA-STATE

1. Stephen Dorril, *The Silent Conspiracy*, Heinemann, 1993, p. 294.
2. G.M. Alexander, *The Prelude to the Truman Doctrine: British Policy in Greece 1944–1947*, Clarendon, Oxford, 1982, pp. 8–9.
3. Clive joined MI6 in 1941 and spent eighteen months lodging in Baghdad with Freya Stark, before joining ISLD. Nigel Clive, *A Greek Experience 1943–1948*, Michael Russell, Norwich, 1985, pp. 19, 28–9 & 129; West, *Secret War*, p. 320.
4. Rothwell, p. 202; Sulzberger, p. 220; Mary Henderson, *Xenia – A Memoir: Greece 1919–1949*, Weidenfeld, 1988, pp. 99–100; Rothwell, p. 200; Thanasis Hajis, 'EAM-ELAS: Resistance or National Liberation', in Marion Sarafis (ed.), *Greece from Resistance to Civil War*, Spokesman, Nottingham, 1980.
5. C.M. Woodhouse, *Something Ventured*, Granada, 1983, p. 73; Heinze Richter, 'Lanz, Zervas and the British Liaison Officers', *South Slav Journal*, Vol. 12, Nos. 43/4, 1989; Clive, p. 77; Sarafis, p. 113.
6. Heinze Richter, *British Intervention in Greece: From Varkiza to Civil War February 1945 to August 1946*, Merlin, 1986, pp. 170–1; Clive, pp. 85–6; Nigel Clive, 'British Policy Alternatives 1945–46', in Lars Baerenzen, John O. Iatrides and Ole L. Smith (eds), *Studies in the History of the Greek Civil War 1945–1949*, Museum Tusculanum, Copenhagen, 1987.
7. Heinze Richter, 'The Battle for Athens and the Role of the British', in Sarafis; Rothwell, p. 219; Lars Baerentzen (ed.), J.M. Stevens, C.M. Woodhouse and D.J. Wallace, *British*

Reports on Greece 1943–44, Museum Tusculanum, Copenhagen, 1982, pp. 119–59; Clive, p. 113; Lawrence S. Wittner, *American Intervention in Greece, 1943–1949*, Columbia University Press, NY, 1982, pp. 8–9.
8. Alexander, pp. 38–9.
9. An outline of the percentages deal had already been leaked in the summer to NYT journalist Cyrus Sulzberger by the American ambassador in Cairo, Lincoln MacVeigh, who was a strong opponent of British imperialism. Relations with OSS were generally bad; MI6 regarded its role in Greece as particularly 'mischievous', alleging that its officers were behind a whispering campaign against the Greek government-in-exile. Woodhouse complained that OSS neutrality over the resistance cloaked 'a benevolent bias in favour of EAM'. C.M. Woodhouse, *Apple of Discord*, W.B. O'Neill, 1985, p. 218; Charles Moran, *Churchill from the Diary of Lord Moran*, p. 185; Robert Frazier, *Anglo-American Relations with Greece: The Coming of the Cold War, 1942–47*, Macmillan, 1991, p. 59; Sulzberger, pp. 238–9; Wittner, p. 15.
10 & 12. Seton-Watson, pp. 139 & 318; Clive, pp. 144, 147 & 149–50; Nigel Clive, *Reflections on British Policy in Greece: 1945–1947* (unpub.); Alexander, pp. 66 & 71–3; PRO R 17961 FO 371/43695; 371/43704, 15.11.44.
11. Maniadakis became a minister in the 1950s. On 14 November, MI6's ISLD received information from the leader of the socialist SKE, Stratis, who believed that the communists aspired to democracy and saw their militant actions as purely defensive to prevent a coup d'état by the Right. Wittner, p. 326; PRO WO 204/8862, 14.11.44.
13. PRO Churchill to Leeper, R 199933 FO 371/43736, 5.12.44; Rothwell, pp. 219–20.
14. Ole H. Smith, ' "The First Round" – Civil War During the Occupation', in David H. Close (ed.), *The Greek Civil War, 1943–1950: Studies of Polarization*, Routledge, 1993; Richter, *British Intervention*, p. 9.
15. Alexander, p. 86; Clive, p. 165; Rothwell, p. 221; Richter, *British Intervention*, p. xi.
16. Frazier, p. 73.
17. John O. Iatrides, *Greece in the Cold War*, pp. 25–6; Peter Weiler, *British Labour and the Cold War*, Stanford University Press, 1988, pp. 11–12; PRO FO 371/48247/R 936.
18. Richter, *British Intervention*, pp. 119–20.
19. Geoffrey Chandler, *The Divided Land: An Anglo-Greek Tragedy*, Macmillan, 1959, p. 4. AIS was disbanded at the end of 1945.
20. Clive, *Reflections, A Greek Experience*, p. 153, and 'British Policy'; Richter, *British Intervention*, pp. 30 & 45; Weiler, pp. 137 & 334.
21. Seton-Watson, p. 322; Clive, 'British Policy'.
22. Churchill to Orme Sargeant, M. 383/5, 22.4.45, R7423 FO 371/48267.
23 & 25. Alexander, pp. 98–9 & 110; Chandler, pp. 106–7.
24. John O. Iatrides, 'Perceptions of Soviet Involvement in the Greek Civil War 1945–1947', in Baerenzen *et al.*
26. Alexander, pp. 106–7; Richter, *British Intervention*, pp. 97–9 & 140–2; PRO FO 6174/745/19, 1.4.44; Woodhouse, *Apple*, p. 241.
27. Richter, *British Intervention*, pp. 99, 107 & 114; Clive, *Reflections*, p. 170; PRO R4563 FO 371/482259, 7 & 14.3.45.
28–30. Richter, *British Intervention*, pp. 107 & 151; Alexander, pp. 108 & 125; report of Col. C.M. Woodhouse, 'Situation in the Peloponnese', 11.8.45, to British Embassy Athens, FO 14973/4/19; Woodhouse, *Something Ventured*, pp. 160 & 256–7. David H. Close, 'The Reconstruction of a Right-Wing State', in Close (ed.).
31 & 32. The left-wing League which reported on Greece included dramatist and Labour MP Ben Levy, who had served with the British Security Co-ordination, and the author Compton Mackenzie, former MI6 officer and director of the Aegean Intelligence Service at the end of the First World War. Richter, *British Intervention*, pp. 86, 155–7 & 324–5; A.W. Sheppard, *Britain in Greece*, League for Democracy in Greece, 1947, p. 11.
33. Chandler, pp. 160–1.
34 & 35. John O. Iatrides, 'Britain, the United States and Greece, 1945–9', in Close (ed.); Sulzberger, pp. 290–1.
36. Seton-Watson, p. 323; Richter, *British Intervention*, pp. 379 & 537–8; Henderson, p. 130.
37 & 38. Richter, *British Intervention*, pp. 378 & 521; Close, 'The Reconstruction of the Right-Wing State', in Close (ed.); Wittner, p. 114.
39. Alexander, pp. 209 & 275–7; Clive, *Reflections*, p. 177; Wittner, pp. 114 & 224–5.
40. Iatrides in Baerenzen *et al.*, State Department R 868.00/8-1046. Karamessines

was head of CIG in Athens (1947–8) and CIA station chief (1951–3). Wittner, p. 142.

41. Alexander, pp. 170 & 206–7; Chandler, p. 187; Edgar O'Ballance, *The Greek Civil War 1944–1949*, Faber, 1966, p. 121; Richter, *British Intervention*, pp. 509 & 511; Woodhouse, *Something Ventured*, p. 160.

42. Chandler returned to Greece in 1949 for the *Economist* and the Royal Institute of International Affairs, and subsequently for the BBC foreign news service and the *Financial Times*. Clive, *Reflections*, p. 178; Chandler, pp. 188–9.

43. Richter, *British Intervention*, p. 536.

44 & 45. FRUS 1946, VII, pp. 226–7; Wittner, pp. 148 & 319; PRO FO 371/58953/R16822; Thomas, *Armed Truce*, p. 887; Clive, *Reflections*, p. 177.

46. Wittner, pp. 129 & 149; Kati Marton, *The Polk Conspiracy: Murder and Cover-up in the Case of the US Correspondent George Polk*, Farrar, Strauss, US, 1990, pp. 119 & 169; NS, 1.2.47; Frazier, p. 117.

47 & 48. Wittner, pp. 104, 160–1 & 231; PRO FO 71/72238 R 757/31/19; 371/72238 R 757/31/19.

49–51. Wittner, pp. 239–40, 255 & 267. Robert Frazier, 'The Bevin–Marshall Dispute, & SDR', OIR Report 4664, 24.4.48, quoted in Iatrides, 'Perceptions of Soviet Involvement', in Baerenzen *et al.*; CIA, National Archives, ORE 69; 9.2.48; PRO FO 800/468/GRE/48/2, 11.2.48, Alexander to Bevin; FO 371/72243.

52. McLintock, pp. 14–17.

53. Wittner, p. 242; David H. Close and Thanos Veremis, 'The Military Struggle, 1945–9', in Close (ed.).

54. Wittner, p. 150. Close, 'Reconstruction', in Close (ed.).

55. HoC Hansard, cols 38–40, 31.10.49.

56. Woodhouse, *Apple*, p. 267.

CHAPTER EIGHTEEN: YUGOSLAVIA: THE GOLDEN PRIEST, STOLEN TREASURE AND THE CRUSADERS

1. G, 11.7.97; ST & STel, 13.7.97.

2. Palmer, p. 254; Aarons, p. 58.

3. Aarons/Loftus, *Ratlines*, 1991, p. 71.

4. David Martin, *The Web of Disinformation: Churchill's Yugoslav Blunder*, Harcourt Brace, US, 1990, p. 45.

5–7. Aarons, pp. 4–5 & 60–3; Stephen Clissold, *Whirlwind: An Account of Marshal*

Tito's Rise to Power, Cresset, 1949, pp. 9, 56–7 & 204.

8. Clissold, p. 57; Seton-Watson, pp. 126–30; McLynn, p. 125.

9. A.W. Brian Simpson, *In the Highest Degree Odious: Detention without Trial in Wartime Britain*, Clarendon (pbk), Oxford, 1994, pp. 84–5; information from John Hope.

10. Nora Beloff, *Tito's Flawed Legacy: Yugoslavia and the West 1939–84*, Gollancz, 1989, p. 118; PRO FO 371/44263, R1411/8/92; 371/48825, R2044/6/92; Aarons, pp. 7 & 12.

11–13. McLynn, pp. 120, 125, 136–7 & 160; 'German Anti-Guerrilla Operations in the Balkans (1941–1944)', Department of the Army Pamphlet 20–243, Washington, Aug. 1954.

14–16. McLynn, pp. 183, 243–4, 259 & 274–5. Sykes, p. 278. On release of SOE records see I, 28.6.97.

17–20. Clissold, pp. 22–3, 204–5 & 220–6; Aarons, pp. 18–20.

21. Beloff, pp. 117–20.

22. Anderson, pp. 27 & 38; Aarons, p. 219; Aarons/Loftus, *Ratlines*, pp. 70, 93, 101–2 & 124–5.

23. Six to seven thousand White Guards were shot, though around five thousand escaped the massacre. A witness was George Waddams, who had served with the partisans in Slovenia and became consul at Ljubljana at the end of the war: 'The most unpleasant feature of life in Yugoslavia today is the existence of the all-powerful OZNA [Bureau of People's Protection], the political police. This body is responsible for the murder of thousands of Yugoslavs, for the maltreatment in concentration camps of thousands more and for the permanent terror in which the vast bulk of the population lives.' Waddam published details in an anonymous information sheet, 'Today in Yugoslavia' (14.5.46). Thomas M. Barker, *Social Revolutionaries and Secret Agents: The Carinthian Slovene Partisans and Britain's Special Operations Executive*, East European Monographs, Columbia University, NY, 1990, pp. 228–32; Beloff, pp. 125 & 133; Nikolai Tolstoy, *The Minister and the Massacres*, Century Hutchinson, 1986, pp. 205, 393–4; Brig. Anthony Cowgill, Christopher Booker, Lord Thomas Brimelow and Brig. Teddy Tyron-Wilson, 'Interim Report on an Enquiry into the Repatriation of Surrendered Enemy Personnel to the Soviet Union and

Yugoslavia from Austria in May 1945 and the Alleged "Klagenfurt Conspiracy" ', Royal United Service Institute for Defence Studies, 1988. This privately funded volume based on PRO files, some supplied by the MoD, clears Macmillan of culpability.

24. Barker, pp. 39 & 209.

25. Tolstoy, pp. 395–7; Aarons, p. 34.

26. An interesting roman-à-clef is by Lawrence Durrell (*White Eagles over Serbia*, Faber, 1957), who served in the Belgrade embassy as press attaché and was clearly cognisant of certain intelligence matters. It concerns the disappearance of the gold reserves belonging to the National Bank of Yugoslavia. 'What if the White Eagles had located the treasures, what would they be likely to do . . . The Royalists would be rich enough to found their own movement on something stronger than faith. One could buy arms and agents . . . All sorts of diplomatic repercussions might be expected if the Royalist movement abroad were suddenly to come into large funds. Policy might have to be altered to meet this new contingency' (pp. 134–5). Anderson, pp. 38–9; Aarons/Loftus, *Ratlines*, pp. 77, 84 & 98; G, 23.7.97.

27–30. Slovene Gen. Leon Rupnik was eventually returned to Yugoslavia in January 1946, tried and executed in September. Aarons/Loftus, *Ratlines*, pp. 58, 79, 96–8 & 123–9; Aarons, pp. 20, 51, 126–7 & 214; McLynn interview with Maclean, 26.11.90. Linklater *et al.*, p. 242.

31. Simpson, p. 209.

32. Consolidated Intelligence Report PRO FO 371/46651 C7747, 24.10.45; 371/ 55114 C4187, 11.4.46.

33. Aarons/Loftus, *Ratlines*, pp. 78 & 122.

34. Agreement on Trieste was not reached until 1954 when the Anglo-American Zone was handed back to the Italians while the Southern Zone was incorporated into Yugoslav Slovenia. Ann Jocelyn Lane, *Coming to Terms with Tito: The Policy of the British Foreign Office towards Yugoslavia 1945–49*, PhD thesis, London School of Economics, June 1988; Roberto G. Rabel, *Between East and West: Trieste, the United States and the Cold War, 1941–1954*, Centre for International Studies, Duke University Press, US, 1988, p. 107; Beloff, p. 122. Palmer, p. 294.

35. Advisers to the AMG included Prof. Srecko Barraga, of the wartime White Guard, sentenced by the Ljubljana People's Court in his absence as a war criminal. Elizabeth

Barker, *Truce in the Balkans*, Percival Marshall, 1948, p. 221; Aarons/Loftus, *Ratlines*, pp. 124 & 133–5.

36 & 37. McLynn, p. 287; PRO FO 371/ 673380, Vivian Street to FO, 5.6.47; Aarons, pp. 27–9, 221 & 243; Aarons/Loftus, *Ratlines*, pp. 123, 127 & 129–32.

38. Hersh, p. 183; E. Barker, p. 237.

39 & 40. Thomas, pp. 722 & 910; Aarons, pp. 214 & 221–2; Aarons/Loftus, *Ratlines*, pp. 119, 126–8 & 135–5.

41 & 42. McLynn, pp. 278–80; Lane.

43. Hills, pp. 129–30.

44. Carrington, pp. 64–5; McLynn, p. 291.

45 & 46. Lane; Aarons, pp. 39–40.

47. PRO FO 371/67380, 26.7.47; Maclean to Wallinger, 17.10.47, 371/67398; McLynn, p. 287; Aarons/Loftus, *Ratlines*, pp. 99, 107 & 113–16.

48. McLynn, pp. 288–9; Linklater *et al.*, p. 243; Wallinger to Perowne, 12.47 FO 371/ 67402; Aarons/Loftus, *Ratlines*, p. 77.

49. Linklater *et al.*, pp. 237–9; Bower, *Perfect English Spy*, pp. 215–22; Simpson, pp. 84–5.

50–54. McLynn, pp. 287–90; PRO Maclean to Wallinger, FO 371/67398, 17.10.47; Aarons/ Loftus, *Ratlines*, pp. 82, 90, 102 & 109–11; Aarons, pp. 35, 215–17 & 244–6.

55. Herzstein, p. 287; Simpson, p. 210; Cabot to Secretary of State, 12.6.47, 740.00116EW/6-1147, Box 3623, RG 59, NA, Washington.

56–59. Aarons, pp. 246 & 281; Aarons/ Loftus, *Ratlines*, pp. 80–3.

60 & 61. Palmer, p. 312; Seton-Watson, pp. 223 & 291; T, 25.10.47.

62. Aarons, p. 43.

63 & 64. In the early thirties Lyall toured south-east Europe and then Russia and wrote up the encounters as gentle satires of ardent communist sympathisers – *The Balkan Road* (1930) and *Russian Roundabout* (1933). A language expert, his '25 languages of Europe' was a great success with tourists. Patricia Clarke and David Footman (eds), *In Memoriam Archie 1904–1964: A Symposium on Archibald Lyall by His Friends* (priv. print), 1966, p. 37.

65–67, 70 & 71. Aarons, pp. 32–45, 76, 134 & 223–5. Aarons/Loftus, *Ratlines*, pp. 101, 120, 128 & 138–9; PRO FO 371/72563 E, memorandum 10.9.48.

68 & 69. Heuser, pp. 45–7.

72. Anderson, pp. 38–9 & 296.

73. Aarons/Loftus, *Ratlines*, pp. 143–4.

74. I, 24.4.96; G, 16.5.97.

CHAPTER NINETEEN: THE MUSKETEERS IN ALBANIA

1 & 7. Bethell, *Betrayal*, pp. 12–16.

2–4 & 8. Reginald Hibbert, *Albania's National Liberation Struggle: The Bitter Victory*, Pinter, 1991, pp. 15, 31, 46, 64, 77 & 130–1; review article by Barry Baldwin, INS, 1992.

5 & 6. Seton-Watson, p. 142; Hibbert, pp. 64 & 145.

9, 11 & 12. Hibbert, pp. 101, 107, 139, 150 & 179; Bernard J. Fischer, *Abaz Kupi and British Intelligence in Albania, 1943–4*, nd.

10. OSS R&A report L38836, 'Albania: Political and Internal Conditions', 10.7.44 (secret), RG 226, NA; Simpson, *Blowback*, pp. 123 & 317; NYT, 20.6.82.

13. Hibbert, pp. 58 & 204–5; Seton-Watson, p. 145; David Smiley, *Albanian Assignment*, Sphere (pbk), 1985, p. 149.

14. Bethell, pp. 22–5; PRO WO 204/9535, 2.10.44.

15. Viscount Harcourt later became chair of Morgan Grenfell and served on the International Bank for Reconstruction and Development, and the International Monetary Fund. He was also a fellow of St Antony's College, Oxford. Kemp, p. 231.

16. Hibbert, p. 239; Sulzberger, p. 421.

17, 19 & 22. Robin Winks, *Cloak and Gown: Scholars in America's Secret Wars*, Collins Harvill, 1987, pp. 394–5; RG 226, Entry 115, Box 35, London Field Files and Folder 3, Mazzarine Report from London, 'Who's Who of Albanian Guerrillas'; Seton-Watson, p. 226.

18 & 20. Jon Halliday (ed.), *The Artful Albanian: The Memoirs of Enver Hoxha*, Chatto (pbk), 1986, p. 81; Winks, pp. 393–5; Philby, p. 116.

21. Rothwell, p. 359.

23 & 24. Rositzke, p. 172; Richard Deacon, *A History of the Russian Secret Service*, NEL (pbk), 1975, p. 279; Aarons/Loftus, *Ratlines*, pp. 230–1; Loftus, pp. 174 & 190; Anton Logoreci, *The Albanians: Europe's Forgotten Survivors*, Gollancz, 1977, p. 85.

25. Philby, p. 142. Bethell, *Spies and Other Secrets*, p. 299; Verrier, p. 68.

26. Verrier, p. 67; Maj.-Gen. Sir Colin Gubbins, 'Resistance Movements in the War', *Royal United Services Institute Journal*, Vol. 93, Jan. 1948; Seale/McConville, p. 202.

27. Verrier, p. 62; Patrick Howarth: *The Men and Women of the Special Operations Executive*, Routledge, 1980, p. 193.

28. BBC1, *The Cost of Treachery*, 30.11.84; Morris Riley, *Philby: The Hidden Years*, United Writers, Cornwall, 1990, p. 56; Verrier, p. 68.

29. Hibbert, pp. 221 & 234–5; Rothwell, p. 359.

30. PRO FO 371/72117.

31. McLynn, pp. 301–2.

32–34. Bethell, *Betrayal*, pp. 33–5, 37 & 38–9; Verrier, p. 68; West, *Friends*, ch. 5: 'Kim Philby and VALUABLE'; PRO FO 371/71687.

35. Logoreci obit.: I, 29.9.90; Hibbert review of Bethell and Smiley books, *International Affairs*, Vol. 61, No. 2, Spring 1985.

36. PRO FO 371/77623; Heuser, p. 77; Bethell, *Betrayal*, p. 83; Bower, *Red Web*, 1989, p. 105; Verrier, pp. 67–8.

37. Bruce Page, David Leitch and Phillip Knightley, *Philby: The Spy Who Betrayed a Generation*, Penguin, 1969, p. 212; letter from Woodhouse, 15.9.94.

38. Bethell, *Betrayal*, p. 5; Woodhouse, *Apple*, pp. 234–5; Heuser, p. 80.

39–41. Powers, pp. 40, 42 & 53–4; Verrier, pp. 57 & 74; Bower, *Red Web*, p. 104.

42. Rositzke, p. 172; Dravis.

43. Bower, *Red Web*, p. 105; Hersh, p. 273; Franklin Lindsay, *Beacons in the Night: With the OSS and Tito's Partisans in Wartime Yugoslavia*, Stanford University Press, US, 1994, p. 334; Bethell, *Betrayal*, p. 119; Verrier, p. 74.

44. Julian Amery, 'Of Resistance', *The Nineteenth Century and After*, Vol. CXLV, No. 865, Mar. 1949; Philby, p. 169.

45. Heuser, p. 78.

46. Bower, *Red Web*, p. 105; Bethell, *Betrayal*, p. 42; Philby, p. 168.

47. 'Christopher Felix' (James McCargar), *A Short Course in the Secret War*, 1963 & (rev. ed.), Lanham, NY, 1992, pp. 55–6. Bethell, *Betrayal*, p. 41; Hersh, p. 264.

48–50. Bethell, *Betrayal*, pp. 42 & 49–50; Winks, p. 395; SD 875.00/12–948; Simpson, *Blowback*, p. 123.

51. Top Secret State Department Decimal File for Albania, declassified Diplomatic Branch of the National Archives, 1948–9; Loftus, p. 89; NYT, 20.6.82.

52. Hersh, pp. 256–7 & 270.

53. Offie had worked for the Political Adviser to the American High Commissioner for Germany, as the State Department's link to the secret agency DAD, a number of whose personnel joined the OPC leadership. Simpson, *Blowback*, pp. 99–101 & 124; Hersh, p. 270; NYT, 20.6.82; Robert Joyce to Walworth Barbour, 12.5.49, 875.00/5–1249, RG, NA; Prados, p. 48.

54. Bethell, *Betrayal*, pp. 51–3; Stavro Skendi, 'Albania within the Slav Orbit: Advent to Power of the Communist Party', *Political Science Quarterly*, LXIII, June 1948.

55. Hibbert, p. 230; Bethell, *Betrayal*, pp. 53 & 57. In 1951 Lyall moved to Rome and then Spain.

56. Hersh, p. 265; Skendi; Bill Bland, 'The 1950 "Invasion" of Albania', The Albanian Society, Ilford, 1984; Roger Faligot, *Les Services Spéciaux de Sa Majesté*, Temps Actuels, Paris, 1982, p. 164, partly derived from 'Procès des espions parachutés en Albanie (compte rendu sténographique des débats du procès de Tirana), 29 mai–6 juin 1950', Sociales, Paris, 1950; Verrier, p. 73.

57. Verrier, p. 71; Philby, p. 167.

58. Seton-Watson, pp. 312–14; Palmer, p. 132; Bethell, *Betrayal*, p. 117.

59. Smiley, *Albanian Assignment*, pp. 158–9, and *Irregular Soldier*, Michael Russell, Norwich, 1994, p. 188.

60. Julian Amery, review article, 'Albanian Assignment', RUSI Journal, Mar. 1985; Riley, p. 59.

61. Major was in Kenya during the Mau Mau period for MI5 where he was responsible for 'secret intelligence'. Phillip Knightley, 'The Man Who was Q', ST magazine, 4.11.73.

62–67. ST magazine, 4.1.73; Verrier, pp. 69 & 76–7; Bethell, *Betrayal*, pp. 1, 41, 55–9, 62–5 & 71.

68. Wittner, p. 279; Verrier, p. 72; FRUS 1949, Vol. VI, p. 386.

69. PRO FO 371/78443 & 371/78213; Bland.

70. Hersh, p. 272; Bethell, *Betrayal*, p. 101.

71. Halliday, p. 81.

72 & 75. Logoreci, p. 106; Heuser, p. 78; Faligot, pp. 75–8.

73. Verrier, pp. 60 & 66–7.

74. CIA memo 218, 'Strength and Weakness of the Hoxha Regime in Albania', 12.9.49. Truman's Papers: President's Secretary File; Intelligence File, Box 249, folder: Central Intelligence memos 1949.

76. 13–15.9.49, PSF General File (A–Ato) 112, Harry S. Truman Memorial Library, Missouri; Aldrich, pp. 206–7; memorandum of a conversation between Acheson, Bevin and officials, 14.9.48, FRUS, The Near East,

South Asia and Africa, Col. VI, 1977, p. 417; State Department 875.00/8-2649.

77. Smiley, *Albanian Assignment*, p. 163, and *Irregular Soldier*, p. 191.

78. Borovik, p. 262; Deacon, 'C', p. 279.

79. Brown, *Treason*, pp. 426–7; Bethell, *Betrayal*, pp. 96–7; Hersh, p. 264.

80 & 81. Philby, p. 169; Dravis; Bethell, *Betrayal*, pp. 82–90.

82. Bethell, *Betrayal*, pp. 120–1; Bland; Joint Chiefs of Staff, 1654/4, 21.10.49.

83. Bethell, *Betrayal*, p. 108; Hersh, p. 270.

84. Philby, p. 168; Simpson, *Blowback*, p. 124; Tipton Report issued by the Comptroller General of the United States, General Accounting Office, 28.6.85.

85. PRO FO 371/78223 & 371/78211.

86. Sulzberger, p. 418.

87. Central Intelligence Agency, ORE 71-49, 'Current Situation in Albania', 15.12.49, Truman Papers, President's Secretary File: Intelligence File, Box 256, 'ORE Reports 1949 (60–74)'; Bethell, *Betrayal*, pp. 117–18; Prados, p. 50.

88. Borovik, pp. 272–3; Bethell, *Betrayal*, pp. 140–3.

89. Philby, pp. 169–70; Heuser, p. 79.

90. Page *et al.*, p. 212.

91. Bethell, *Betrayal*, pp. 75–6 & 96; Hersh, p. 273.

92. Smiley, *Albanian Assignment*, p. 163; Bethell, *Spies*, p. 299; Winks, p. 398; Andrew, *Secret Service*, p. 493.

93–95. Powers, p. 54; Bethell, *Betrayal*, pp. 90, 100–1 & 151; Smiley, *Albanian Assignment*, p. 163.

96. One report suggests sabotage attempts on the Kucova oilfields and the Rubik copper mines, but it is unclear whether they did take place and who was responsible. Almost certainly a fantasy is the claim by Leonard Mosley (*Dulles*, 1978) that in April 1950 'an army of five hundred Albanian émigrés was recruited, armed and trained in Greece, and sent across into Albania ... The émigrés and their CIA and SIS advisers had been assured that they would achieve complete surprise, and little or no resistance would be encountered. It was a wrong assessment ... Not only did the invaders meet troops armed with machine guns, mortars, and artillery, but they were ambushed at exactly those points where they had been assured they would have a free passage. Two hundred men were slaughtered; 120 were captured and subsequently executed; only

180 men struggled back to Greece . . . There was convincing evidence that the Soviet government had flown in its own troops into Albania just before the Anglo-American invasion began, and had positioned them along the exact routes the invaders followed – routes which only the planners at the top knew about until sealed orders were broken at H-Hour.' Page *et al.*, p. 212; Verrier, pp. 68 & 76–7.

97. Bethell, *Spies*, p. 300.

98. EUCOM Annual Narrative Report, Labor Services Division, 1950, European Command Labor Services Division Classified Decimal File, 1950–51 (secret), p. 22, RG 338, NA, Suitland, Md. Loftus, p. 184; Bethell, *Betrayal*, p. 129; Hersh, p. 270; Simpson, *Blowback*, p. 145; Thomas, p. 368.

99. Halliday, p. 356; Bethell, *Betrayal*, p. 143.

100. Bethell, *Betrayal*, pp. 140–3; Sulzberger, pp. 544–5; Thomas, p. 84; E. Howard Hunt, *Undercover: Memories of an American Secret Agent*, 1975, p. 93; Hersh, p. 27.

101. Brown, *Treason*, p. 419.

102–6. Sulzberger, pp. 435 & 517; Bethell, *Betrayal*, pp. 145–8, 156–7 & 164–6; Bethell, *Spies*, pp. 299–300; I, 6.9.94; Andrew, p. 493.

107. Page *et al.*, p. 214; NYT, 31.3 & 9.4.51.

108. The Soviets apparently sent a small number of fighter planes to Albania in the hope that they could shoot down foreign aircraft making the drops (NYT, 9.4.51). Djilas added that Stalin had told him in 1947 that Albania was 'the weak point' in the communist structure. 'Moscow never signed an alliance with Albania for two reasons: (1) because it wished to keep its hands free for the possibility of trading Albania off to the West in exchange for something else; (2) because it wanted to be free to provoke an insurrection there as an excuse to invade Yugoslavia.' Sulzberger, pp. 542–5.

109. Verrier, p. 77.

110. Evan Thomas (*The Very Best Men: Four Who Dared: The Early Years of the CIA*, Simon & Schuster, 1995, pp. 68–70) claims that 'in his basement of his house on Nebraska Avenue in Northwest Washington was encoding equipment that Philby used to transmit America's secrets back to the Kremlin'. This appears to be untrue. Hersh, p. 321; Brown, *Treason*, p. 422.

111. Bower, *Red Web*, p. 137; Mosley, p. 285. Ranelagh, p. 157; West, *Friends*, p. 119.

112. E. Thomas, pp. 71–2.

113–16. Bethell, *Betrayal*, pp. 180–5; Winks, pp. 390–400; I, 6.9.94.

117. E. Thomas, pp. 11 & 66–7.

118. Bethell, *Betrayal*, pp. 182–3; Philby, p. 162.

119. Page *et al.*, p. 215.

120. Prados, p. 50.

121. Hersh, pp. 32 & 273; Simpson, *Blowback*, pp. 124 & 269; Page *et al.*, p. 215.

122. During 1953, E. Howard Hunt was working in the CIA's South-East Europe Division looking for turncoats who might have betrayed the Albanian operation. Hunt suspected a bodyguard employed by King Zog and asked Tracey Barnes for advice on how to 'dispose' of him. He saw Col. Boris Pash, a White Russian who had run the Army Intelligence Alsos mission and who was in charge of Programme Branch-7 which had been set up to handle 'wet affairs' – kidnappings and assassinations. Pash served as the army's representative on Bloodstone, whose activities included 'assassination'. OPC superiors acknowledged that the 'one and only remedy' for communist double agents was assassination, though in Germany their deaths were never directly traced back to the OPC. US Senate Select Committee to Study Government Operations with Respect to Intelligence Activities. 'Supplementary Detailed Staff Reports on Foreign and Military Intelligence', Book IV, 94th Congress, 2nd Session, Report No. 94–755. US Government Printing Office, 1976, pp. 128–33; Hunt testimony, Church Committee, JFK Records, NA, Box 25, Folder 5; Corson, pp. 362–5; Simpson, *Blowback*, pp. 153–5; E. Thomas, p. 85; Powers, pp. 54–5; Rositzke, p. 37.

123. British security officers were still trying to discover the source of the story Sulzberger (pp. 730–1) had written about Albania in 1950. 'Occasionally, somebody still drops an idle question at a cocktail party on that line.' E. Thomas, p. 88; Powers, p. 57.

124. Enver Hoxha, *The Anglo-American Threat to Albania; Memories of the National Liberation War*, 8 Nentori, Tirana, 1982, p. 426; Bethell, *Betrayal*, pp. 191–2.

125. Bethell, *Betrayal*, pp. 193–4; Winks, p. 40. BBC1, *The Cost of Treachery*, 30.10.84.

126. Prados, p. 245.

127. Bethell, *Spies*, p. 302; ST, 4.11.84.

128. Hibbert review of Bethell and Smiley books, *International Affairs*, Vol. 61, No. 2, spring 1985. Hibbert, p. 235.

129. History returned as farce with the election of Sali Berisha as President of Albania. The musketeers, still having an influence on British policy on Albania, hitched their ideological bandwagon to Berisha's star, believing that he was the man able to cleanse the country of its communist past. Sir Reginald Hibbert, however, regarded him as vicious a dictator as Hoxha. His corrupt regime was eventually overthrown by a general election in July 1997 which saw the victory of the Socialist Party. The return of King Zog's son, Prince Leka, did not see a restoration of the monarchy, as the pro-monarchy referendum vote was only 35 per cent. ST, 23.3.97; IoS, 11.5.97; G, 9.7.97; Heuser, p. 79.

CHAPTER TWENTY: THE NTS AND THE 'YOUNG RUSSIANS'

1. Richard Deacon, *The Greatest Treason*, Century, 1988, p. 82, and *British Connection*, Hamish Hamilton, 1979, pp. 104–8; Costello, *Mask*, pp. 311 & 665.
2 & 3. S. J. Hetherington, *Katharine Atholl, 1874–1960; Against the Tide*, Aberdeen University Press, 1989, pp. 89 & 159–60.
4. Cookridge, p. 297; Deacon, *Treason*, p. 83. John J. Stephan, *The Russian Fascists: Tragedy and Farce in Exile, 1925–1945*, Hamish Hamilton, 1978, pp. 29–30; Aarons/Loftus, *Ratlines*, pp. 153–4.
5. Cookridge, p. 297; Faligot, pp. 165–9; Catherine Andreyev, *Vlasov and the Russian Liberation Movement: Soviet reality and émigré theories*, Cambridge University Press, 1987, p. 185.
6 & 7. Stephan, pp. 29–30; Nicholas Hayes, 'Kazem-Bek and the Young Russians' revolution', *Slavic Review*, June 1980; Andreyev, p. 182.
8. P.J. Huxley-Blythe, *Betrayal: The Story of Russian Anti-Communism*, The Friends of National Russia, 1957, pp. 16–17.
9. When the Nazis invaded the Soviet Union Turkel's name as a representative of the pro-Hitler Russian National Union was put forward as a member of a National Government to be formed on liberated Russian soil. Stephan, p. 261; Deacon, *British Connection*, pp. 106–7; Costello, *Mask*, pp. 311 & 665; Aarons/Loftus, *Ratlines*, pp. 210–11 & 213; Pincher, *Treachery*, p. 193.
10. Deacon, *British Connection*, pp. 108 & 111,

and *Treason*, p. 84. Kerby spoke to Deacon shortly before his death in 1971. NS, 28.11.86.
11. Christopher Warwick, *The Universal Ustinov*, Sidgwick, 1990, pp. 21 & 51; Peter Ustinov, *Dear Me*, Heinemann, 1977, pp. 31–3, 60 & 77.
12. This was Klop's second brush with Schellenberg. He had met with MI6's Maj. Richard Stevens just before his ill-fated trip to Holland and his capture by the SD at Venlo, near the German border. After the war, Stevens was employed by Lord Weidenfeld in London as advertising manager of *Contact* magazine, which employed a number of émigrés. He was also responsible for the translation of a number of German books dealing with intelligence matters. George Weidenfeld, *Remembering My Good Friends*, HarperCollins, 1994, p. 152; Pincher, *Treachery*, pp. 246–7; Wright, pp. 67–9; Costello, *Mask*, p. 309.
13. ST, 31.2.7; Pincher, *Treachery*, p. 246. Whitwell. Kerby persuaded Nicholson to write the book and contributed an introduction. Deacon, *British Connection*, pp. 197 & 204, and *Russian*, p. 341; NS, 28.11.86.
14. For a history of the NTS see US Department of State, External Research Paper, Series 3, No. 76, 'NTS: The Russian Solidarist Movement', Washington, 1951. For a Soviet view which is propagandist but in its essentials correct, see Konstantin Cherezov, *NTS: A Spy Ring Unmasked*, Soviet Committee for Cultural Relations with Russians Abroad, Moscow, 1963. Simpson, *Blowback*, p. 220; Cookridge, p. 296; Bower, *Spy*, p. 205; Aarons/Loftus, *Ratlines*, pp. 186 & 227; Stephan, pp. 29–30, 184 & 375; Andreyev, pp. 187–8.
15. Hayes. On Sheiken see Peter Blythe, *The Man Who Was Uncle: The Biography of a Master Spy*, Arthur Barker, 1975.
16 & 17. Cookridge, p. 297; Vakar, pp. 187–8; Simpson, *Blowback*, p. 221; Cherezov, p. 43.
18. Nadia Benois Ustinov, *Klop and the Ustinov Family*, Sidgwick, 1973, p. 215; Borovik, pp. 227–8; Aarons/Loftus, *Ratlines*, pp. 154–9.
19–21. Sudoplatov, pp. 152–7; Aarons/Loftus, *Ratlines*, pp. 168–9; Pincher, *Treachery*, pp. 125–8.
22. Leverkuehn, pp. 173–4.
23–5 & 28. Andreyev, pp. 2, 170 & 190–1; Gordon Young, *The House of Secrets*, Duell, Sloan & Pearce, NY, 1959, pp. 14–15 & 110

(an obviously CIA-sponsored book). Young was ex-Reuters and after the war opened a bureau in Stockholm for the study of Soviet affairs on behalf of the *Daily Mail*.

26 & 27. Dallin, pp. 526 & 645–7; Hagen, p. 164; Cherezov, p. 48; Cookridge, p. 297; Simpson, *Blowback*, pp. 170 & 223; Tolstoy, *Stalin*, pp. 355–7; Cesarani, pp. 10 & 23; Aarons/Loftus, *Ratlines*, pp. 180–1.

29–33. Bethell, *Betrayal*, pp. 25–33; Cesarani, pp. 158–9; Tolstoy, *Stalin*, pp. 69–70, 143, 185–97, 265, 286–7, 321–4 & 595; PRO FO 934/5(42), 92; Geoffrey Stewart-Smith, unpublished manuscript on the World Anti-Communist League, p. 59; Wiener Library Bulletin, winter 1965–6 & autumn 1966.

34. Norman Rose, *Vansittart: Study of a Diplomat*, Heinemann, 1978, pp. 278–82. He eventually moved to Argentina where his 'Suvorov Union' was subsidised by General Peron. Andreyev, p. 79; Dallin, p. 509; Wilfred Strik-Strikfelt, *Against Stalin and Hitler*, trans. David Footman (former MI6 officer), 1970.

35 & 37. Young, p. 110; Cherezov, p. 39; Cookridge, p. 297; Simpson, *Blowback*, pp. 224–5; Hagen, pp. 164–5; Blake, p. 23; Bower, *Spy*, pp. 203 & 205.

36. Kenneth Benton, 'The ISOS Years', JCH, Vol. 3, No. 3, Jul. 1995; Seale/McConville, p. 187.

38. Cookridge, p. 304; Simpson, *Blowback*, p. 224; *Caught in the Act*, Moscow, pp. 65–6; M. Smith, p. 114.

39. Rose, pp. 278–82.

40. During the war, Knupffer's friend, Capt. Henry Kerby, had been with his MI5 counterpart, Guy Liddell, an MI6 liaison officer to the Russian Intelligence Service representative in London, Captain Soldatenkov. Few details have emerged about Kerby's postwar MI6 role, though his previous intelligence experience suggests that it almost certainly had something to do with the exile operations. A radical reactionary and free trade Liberal, Kerby became a Conservative MP in 1954 (until 1971) – it has been said by his friends as a reward from MI6. Part of the imperial Right, his 'right-wing clowning' was, one observer believed, a front for a 'deeply serious and patriotic intelligent man in his political operations'. NS, 28.11.86. Anthony Cave Brown (*Treason*, pp. 266–7) suggests that Philby may also have been engaged in liaison with the Soviets, in London, during the war, which may explain Kerby's postwar knowledge of his activities. On Baykolov see Tolstoy, *Victims*, pp. 467 & 567; Deacon, *British Connection*, p. 204, and *Treason*, p. 82; Costello, *Mask*, pp. 597 & 665. Knupffer was a source of information to the BLEF. Interview with Mrs Elma Dangerfield, 6.3.96; ST, 13.2.77.

41. Brown, pp. 651–4; Aarons/Loftus, *Ratlines*, pp. 214 & 232–3.

42. Ustinov, pp. 217 & 219; Warwick, p. 53; Elliott, pp. 89 & 148–9.

43. West, *Illegals*, pp. 74–7.

44–45. Aarons/Loftus, *Ratlines*, pp. 187 & 224–30; Sudoplatov, p. 170.

46. Pincher, *Treachery*, p. 126. 'Camp King', formerly known as Dulag Luft (Transit Camp Air), had been used by the Germans for the successful interrogation of RAF and USAF officers.

47–50. In reference to the 'Ryle-Johnson Report' on 'The Turkul Organisation' – in fact, the Klatt network – on different occasions Aarons and Loftus refer to 'Ryle', 'Professor Ryle' and 'Gilbert Riles' (sic), suggesting that he worked for American Intelligence, though it is clear that this is, in fact, Prof. Gilbert Ryle of MI6 (Arnold M. Silver, 'Questions, Questions, Questions: Memories of Oberursel', INS, Vol. 8, No. 2, Apr. 1993). The claim by Aarons/Loftus, (*Ratlines*, pp. 150, 220–1, 230–1, 244 & 256) that Turkul was 'arguably the greatest professional spy of the twentieth century' has no basis in fact. Turkul died in 1959. Klop retained his London post until 1957. Mystery surrounds much of his life. His wife wrote that 'he served the cause of freedom with devotion and courage'. Klop died in 1962, one day before his seventieth birthday.

51. Hagen, pp. 167–8; Cherezov, p. 46.

52. De Gramont, p. 184.

53. Aarons/Loftus, *Ratlines*, pp. 257–8; Heinz Hohne and Hermann Zolling, *Network: The Truth about General Gehlen and His Spy Ring*, Secker 1972, p. 147.

54. The best treatment of the NTS is in a State Department paper by the external research staff, Office of Intelligence Research Series 3, No. 76, 10.12.51. Philby, pp. 165–6; Hersh, p. 275.

55. Blake, p. 23; Bower, *Spy*, pp. 133 & 165.

56 & 57. Cherezov, pp. 8–19.

58 & 59. Interview with Peter Huxley-Blythe, 7.5.97.

CHAPTER TWENTY-ONE: THE BRITISH AND SCOTTISH LEAGUES FOR EUROPEAN FREEDOM

1. Hetherington, p. 151, also telephone conversation with the author; The Duchess of Atholl, *The Conscription of a People*, Philip Allan, 1931, pp. 74–6.
2. Stewart details based on interview and conversations (22.6.94) with his daughter, Dr Janet Stewart, and research by Alan Lawrie. Also see John F. Stewart, 'Tortured but Unconquerable Ukraine', SLEF, Apr. 1953.
3. John Stewart letter to the ABN, 12.2.54.
4–6. Atholl, p. 243; interview with Mrs Dangerfield, 6.3.96; Mary Melville obit. DT, 16.2.96. Eleanor Rathbone died in 1946.
7 & 8. Atholl, pp. 243–4; Dangerfield interview; *Lockhart Diaries*, Vol. 2, p. 240.
9. R.B. Cockett, *Twilight of Truth: Chamberlain, Appeasement and the Manipulation of the Press*, Weidenfeld, 1989, and 'Communication: Ball, Chamberlain and Truth', THJ, 33, 1, 1990. Other members of Mansfield's circle were Lord Malcolm Douglas-Hamilton (whose seat was taken over by Billy McLean) and Sir Victor Raikes. *Covert Action*, No. 25, 1986.
10. Lloyd obit. T. 24.9.87.
11. Deacon, *Treason*, p. 83 and *British Connection*, p. 106; Hetherington, p. 192.
12. Hollis was Christopher Hollis, brother of senior MI5 officer, Roger. Jerrold was the chair of publishers Eyre & Spottiswoode where another MI6 man, writer Graham Greene, worked. Obits DT & I, 9.12.95; Tom Burns, *The Use of Memory: Publishing and Further Pursuits*, Sheed & Ward, 1993, pp. 58–61.
13. Stephen Dorril and Robin Ramsay, 'In a Common Cause: The Anti-Communist Crusade in Britain 1945–60', *Lobster*, No. 19; Bulmer-Thomas obits T & I, 7.10.93.
14. Information from John Hope; *Lobster*, No. 19; Dangerfield interview.
15. George Orwell, *Collected Works*, Vol. 4, p. 49.
16. Tolstoy, *Stalin*, p. 431; T, 25.5.46 and *The Tablet*, 15.6.46.
17. I am indebted to Alan Lawrie for research in this area. Zygmunt Nagorski Jr, 'Liberation Movements in Exile', *Journal of Central European Affairs*, Jul. 1950; Dangerfield interview; Lockhart Diaries, p. 240.
18. Dr Janet Stewart interview.
19. SLEF pamphlets and documents are to be found in the Scottish National Library in Edinburgh. Delegates at the June meeting included Leopol Podhvagy (Austria); General Lev Prchala (Czech lands) – leader of the London group of Czech exiles which strongly opposed President Eduard Benes's policy of appeasement towards the Soviet Union during and after the war; Professor Oras (Estonia); Reverend Robert Slokenbers (Latvia); Julius Kukasiewicz (Poland); Peter Pridavok (Slovak National Council) – 'Czechoslovakia is not a nation. It is, or rather it was, a profession'; Voldymyr Solowij (Ukraine); Miss Savafin (Lithuania); and Lt Triclav (officer in the underground army in Yugoslavia).
20, 21 & 23. Dangerfield interview; Tolstoy, *Victims*, pp. 467 & 567; Deacon, *British Connection*, p. 204, and *Treason*, p. 82; Costello, *Mask*, pp. 597 & 665.
22 & 25. Cesarani, pp. 54 & 173; Nicholas Bethell, *The Last Secret*, Futura (pbk), 1978, p. 264.
24. Aarons, p. 29; Aarons/Loftus, *Ratlines*, pp. 130–1.
26 & 31. Atholl, pp. 50 & 252; Dangerfield interview.
27 & 28. Hutchinson, pp. 45–9; *Searchlight*, No. 142, Apr. 1987.
29. *Lobster*, No. 19; letter from J.C. Banks, editor of the *Common Wealth Journal*; C.A. Smith obit. *The Liberation*, No. 25, summer 1985.
30. Tom Hopkinson, *Of This Our Times: A Journalist's Story, 1905–50*, Hutchinson, 1982, pp. 191 & 261; 'Britanova: Richard Fletcher', *Tribune*, 2 & 9.9.83; Robin Maugham, *Escape from the Shadows*, Hodder, 1972, p. 171.
32. Alden Hatch, *Clare Booth Luce*, Heinemann, 1956, p. 187; Simpson, *Blowback*, p. 222.
33. Emmet had been chair in 1940 of the Committee to Aid Britain by Reciprocal Trade, and with two other British agents had helped form 'France Forever', an MI6 front designed to promote the French exile leader, Charles de Gaulle. He also played a major role in another influential MI6 front, Fight for Freedom. Tom Mahl, *'48 Land'*, PhD thesis, Kent State University, 1994, p. 198.
34. *Lobster*, No. 19.
35. Larry Collins, *The Free Europe Committee: American Weapon of the Cold War*, PhD thesis, Carlton University, 1975; Simpson, *Blowback*,

pp. 8 & 222; Wilson D. Miscamble, *George F. Kennan and the Making of American Foreign Policy, 1947–1950*, US, 1992, pp. 203–5.

36. Dangerfield interview; information from John Hope based on the Vansittart archives.

37 & 38. ACUE commissioned American academics to undertake research projects on the problems of federalism. In 1952 the project was managed by leading European historian and propaganda expert Carl Friedrich, who was deeply committed to federalism. He was also a consultant to the Free Europe Committee on the Soviet Zone in Germany. Two historians who had served in the OSS, Frederick H. Buckhardt and William L. Langer, headed a new ACUE cultural section which funded EM projects. Richard J. Aldrich, 'OSS, CIA and European Unity: The American Committee on United Europe, 1948–60', *International History Review*, Vol. 18, No. 4, Nov. 1995.

39. Richard Coudenhove-Kalergi, *From War to Peace*, Jonathan Cape, 1959, p. 134; F.X. Rebattet, *'The European Movement', 1945–53: A Study in National and International Non-Governmental Organisations Working for European Unity*, PhD thesis, St Antony's College, Oxford, 1962, pp. 123–7 & 177.

40. Korbonski, p. 47; Edward Beddington-Behrens, *Look Back – Look Forward*, Macmillan, 1963, p. 183.

41 & 42. Offie mentioned in Harold Macmillan, *War Diaries: Politics and War in the Mediterranean, Jan. 1943–May 1945*, Macmillan, pp. 517 & 753; Aarons/Loftus, *Ratlines*, p. 269; Simpson, *Blowback*, p. 121; Beddington-Behrens, pp. 183–4.

43. Rabattet, p. 46; NYT, 3.9.64. Thanks to Scott Van Wynsberghe for drawing my attention to this article. See article seeking information on the ICFTUE by Peter E. Newell in *Lobster*, No. 28, Dec. 1994, correspondence, 14.10.95, and CIA Labour Front: 'The International Confederation of Free Trade Unions in Exile'.

44. Nagorski; Dodds-Parker, p. 46.

45. Aldrich, quoting PRO FO 371/76383.

46. Atholl, pp. 251–2.

47–49. Anthony John Trythall, *'Boney' Fuller: The Intellectual General 1878–1966*, Cassell, 1977, pp. 181–3, 216–17 & 253; *Searchlight*, Nos 171 & 172; additional information and letter, 25.5.87, John Hope; Fuller appointment diaries, King's College, London.

50–52. IRD files on the conference are closed. Foreign Office files on the SLEF/ABN either

retained or destroyed include PRO PR/916, N1073/1-2, N1073/70 & C6300/9/18, 1949. Loftus, p. 204; Cesarani, pp. 131 & 156–7; Dr C.J. Untaru, ABN official, London, 1968, quoted in Anderson, pp. 30–5; letter, John Hope, 27.4.86.

53. The participants at the 1950 ABN conference were taken on a bus trip to the home of Lady Culme-Symour. Mark Culme-Seymour was a good friend of Guy Burgess.

54 & 55. *The Scotsman*, 13/14.6.50; Aarons, p. 75.

56. Leigh, p. 196.

57 & 60. Fielding, pp. 85–8; CIC documents, John Hope. Later in 1951, McLean renewed his contact with the Turkestanis. Aarons, pp. 75–6.

58. J.F.C. Fuller, *How to Defeat Russia*, Eyre & Spottiswoode, 1951.

59. PRO FO 371/94964.

61. FRUS, 1950, III, p. 1081.

62–64. The Central and Eastern Commission of the European Movement, Full Report of the Central and Eastern European Conference, European Movement, London, Jan. 1952. Beddington-Behrens, p. 185; Bethell, *Betrayal*, p. 118; Dangerfield interview.

65. Beddington-Behrens, p. 187; Korbonski, p. 50.

66 & 67. *Lobster*, No. 19; T, 25.2.52; Hatch, p. 187.

68. Geoffrey Stewart-Smith, privately published dossier on the World Anti-Communist League, p. 49. Mrs Dangerfield remains active in the European Movement and is an executive director of the *European-Atlantic Journal*.

PART FIVE: THE CHANGE

1. Trevor Barnes, 'The Secret Cold War: The CIA and American Foreign Policy in Europe 1946–56', Part II, THJ, Vol. 25, No. 3, 1982.

2. Richard Aldrich for information on Sandys/Menzies.

3. British Security Co-ordination (BSC): 'An Account of Secret Activities in the Western Hemisphere, 1940–45', cited in Thomas Earl Mahl, '*48 Land*', PhD thesis, Kent State University, Aug. 1994.

CHAPTER TWENTY-TWO: THE EUROPEAN MOVEMENT AND 'THE BATTLE FOR PICASSO'S MIND'

1. T, 1.8.94; Altiero Spinelli, 'European Union in the Resistance', *Government and Opposition*, Vol. 11, No. 3, Apr.–Jul. 1967; Walter Lipgrens, 'European Federation in the Political Thought of Resistance Movements during World War II', *Central European History*, Vol. 1, 1968.
2. Dr J.H. Retinger, *The European Continent*, William Hodge & Chiver, 1946.
3. Chair of the FU was R.W.G. Mackay, the key MP in Labour backbench European union planning. His successor was Miss F.L. Josephy, Liberal Party and Liberal International member. Healey, pp. 195–6; Robert Eringer, *The Global Manipulators: The Bilderberg Group, The Trilateral Commission – Covert Power Groups of the West*, Pentacle Books, Bristol, 1980, p. 16.
4. Richard Crockett, *David Astor and the Observer*, Deutsch, 1991, pp. 17 & 60–4; Walter Lipgrens and Wilfried Loth (eds), *Documents on the History of European Integration*, Vol. 3: 'The Struggle for European Union by Political Parties and Pressure Groups in Western European Countries 1945–1950', Walter de Gruyter, 1988, and Lipgrens, *A History of European Integration*, Vol. 1, 1945–1947: 'The Formation of the European Unity Movement', Clarendon, Oxford, 1982.
5. Beddington-Behrens was the City's highest-paid stockbroker with Ocean Trust. Col. Peter 'Gerry' Koch de Gooreynd was personal assistant to Menzies during the war. He was a senior figure in stockbrokers Panmure Gordon, of which his father had been chair. Gerry was the younger brother of the father of Peregrine Worsthorne, one-time editor of the *Sunday Telegraph*. 'An enormously popular social figure with a house on the Ditchley estate and a famous mistress, [Countess] Laura Dudley, to whom he left his money, a case of coals to Newcastle.' Koch de Gooreynd served at Paris, 1947–50. Peregrine Worsthorne, *Tricks of Memory: An Autobiography*, Weidenfeld, 1993, p. 82. Lt-Col. Sir Rex Benson was military attaché, Washington, 1941–4. Beddington-Behrens, pp. 16, 40, 116 & 124;

G.C. Webber, *The Ideology of the British Right 1918–1939*, Croom Helm, pp. 123–5 & 142; Wilkinson/Astley, p. 71.
6. Amery, p. 16; Count Coudenhove-Kalergi, *An Idea Conquers the World*, Hutchinson, 1953, p. 116; Arnold J. Zurcher, *The Struggle to Unite Europe 1940–1958*, New York University Press, 1958. With Coudenhove-Kalergi, Zucher set up a seminar group on European federalism at New York University. During the war, Countess Coudenhove-Kalergi stayed at the home of the émigrés' friend, Auberon Herbert.
7. Frenay, who, while he eventually accepted de Gaulle as leader, was 'evidence of the persistence of loyalty to Pétain amongst army officers who were in the Resistance'. Obit. of Frenay's Resistance colleague Gen. Maurice Chevance-Bertin, I, 8.7.96; Michel, p. 353.
8. Charles F. Delzell, 'The European Federalist Movement in Italy: First Phase, 1918–1947', *The Journal of Modern History*, Sept. 1960; Lipgrens, *A History*, p. 58.
9. Crockett, pp. 108–12; Delzell; Lipgrens, *A History*, p. 243.
10. Korbonski, p. 20; Wilkinson/Astley, p. 239.
11. Dodds-Parker, *Political Eunuch*, p. 42, and *Set Europe Ablaze*, pp. 214–17.
12. Peter Thompson, 'Bilderberg and the West', in Holly Sklar (ed.), *Trilateralism: The Trilateral Commission and Elite Planning for World Management*, South End Press, US, 1980, p. 160.
13. F.X. Rebattet, *The 'European Movement'*, p. 459. His father, G. Rebattet, was former EM deputy and Secretary-General, 1948–55. Unfortunately many of the archives of the various organisations for European unity were destroyed in the fifties. Hansard, HoC, 7 & 5.6.46.
14. Letters from Churchill to Viscount Cecil of Chelwood, 9 & 20.6.46; Cecil to Churchill, 19.6.46, in Gilbert, pp. 241–3; Coudenhove-Kalergi, p. 267.
15. Dodds-Parker, *Politics*, pp. 45–6, and *Europe*, p. 214.
16. Randolph S. Churchill (ed.), *W.S. Churchill, The Sinews of Peace, Post-War Speeches*, pp. 198–202; Robert Rhodes James, *Bob Boothby: A Portrait*, Headline (pbk), 1992, p. 337; Richard J. Aldrich, 'OSS, CIA and European Unity: The American Committee on United Europe, 1948–60', *International History Review*, Vol. 18, No. 4, Nov. 1995, and

'European Integration: An American Intelligence Connection', in Anne Deighton (ed.), *Building Postwar Europe: National Decision-Makers and European Institutions, 1948–63*, Macmillan, 1995.

17. T, 20.9.46; letter, Amery to Churchill, 20.9.46, in Gilbert, pp. 279–81.

18. Lord Layton set up the British Trust before the war to help Czechs flee their country after the German invasion. By the late forties it had evolved in the minds of eastern European secret police into a front for MI6. Stevens, pp. 89 & 154. Boothby had strong links with the Czechs, giving them 'outstanding' support in the period. James, p. 184; John Pomain, *Joseph Retinger: Memoirs of an Eminence Grise*, University of Sussex Press, 1972, pp. 208–9. Pomain was personal assistant to Retinger from 1948 until the death of the Polish éminence grise in 1960. Korbonski, p. 49; Beddington-Behrens, p. 178. Labour MP Niall McDermot had worked in counter-intelligence and MI5 during the war, and belonged to the 'New Britain Group' which flourished in the 1930s with ideas of European federalism, inspired by the 'integral' Serb philosopher Dimitrije Mitrinovic. Leigh, p. 137; Lipgrens, *A History*, p. 162.

19 & 20. James, p. 337; Gilbert, pp. 283 & 290–1; Rebattet, pp. 25–30.

21. John Bruce-Lockhart (former Deputy Chief of MI6), 'Sir William Wiseman Bart – Agent of Influence', RUSI Journal, summer 1989; Pomain, p. 212.

22. Rebattet, p. 371; Sulzberger, pp. 418–19.

23. When, in June, Victor Gollancz considered resigning from the UEM, Boothby invoked the conspiracy theory: 'It is quite clear that the Russians are operating a Master Plan designed to give them complete control over Central Europe (including Austria and Czechoslavakia, and, it is hoped, Italy) by the end of the year. The way will then be ready for a debouchement from the Elbe line next year which will bring them to the Channel and the Bay of Biscay . . . This is not the moment for opponents of appeasement to separate.' Meeting at Albert Hall, 21 April 1947. Robert Boothby, *What Do You Think about Western Union?*, Conservative Political Centre, 1949, p. 7; Gilbert, pp. 399–400; Lipgrens/Loth, p. 695.

24. Coudenhove-Kalergi, p. 276.

25. Gilbert, p. 406; François Duchene, *Jean*

Monnet: First Statesman of Independence, Norton, NY, 1994.

26. Gilbert, pp. 337 & 400; Laurence Shoup and William Minter, *Imperial Brain Trust*, Monthly Review Trust, 1977, p. 117.

27 & 28. Richard Fletcher, 'Who Were They Travelling With?', in *The CIA and the Labour Movement*, Spokesman, Nottingham, 1977, pp. 58 & 69, and 'How CIA Money Took the Teeth out of British Socialism', in Philip Agee and Louis Wolf (eds), *Dirty Work: The CIA in Western Europe*, Zed (pbk), 1981.

29 & 30. Rebattet, pp. 25, 49, 60 & 183.

31. Coudenhove-Kalergi created the European Parliamentary Union (EPU) of federalist parliamentarians throughout Europe. British MPs left in February 1949 because of the overt federalism. Prone to 'autocratic tendencies', Coudenhove-Kalergi was a bad organiser who quarrelled with Sandys about the over-representation of hostile British 'unionists' in key positions in the EM. At the end of 1949, the EM created its own International Parliamentary Group. T, 29.9.48; Rebattet, p. 162; Sallie Pisani, *The CIA and the Marshall Plan*, Edinburgh University Press, 1991, pp. 67–71; Beddington-Behrens, p. 194.

32. Dorril/Ramsay, 'In a Common Cause', *Lobster*, No. 19.

33. In 1950, Astor and 'his mentor of Eton days' – and another MI6 asset, Robert Birley – helped found that 'lasting institution to post-war Anglo-German friendship, the Konigswater Conference, which provided a forum for British MPs, businessmen and journalists to meet their German counterparts and discuss subjects of mutual interest'. Dodds-Parker invited Karl Carstens and Heinrich von Brentano to the first gathering – 'The result of such friendships made possible through Konigswater can never be exaggerated.' Crockett, p. 67; Dodds-Parker, *Politics*, p. 46, and *Europe*, p. 215; Rebattet, pp. 371 & 479.

34 & 35. If successful, the funds were used in the 1950 Tory general election campaign and not in the EM. James, p. 347; STel, 3.10.93; Smith, *OSS*, p. 368; Aldrich, 'European Unity'.

36. ST, 25.5.75.

37 & 43. Dodds-Parker, *Europe*, p. 215.

38 & 40. In May 1949 the Labour Party's International Department came close to proscribing the EM. ACUE supported dissenters in the Labour Party including

R.W. Mackay, MP, delegate to Strasbourg, who sought with Spaak a compromise route to federalism known as the 'Mackay Plan'. During 1950 he was dependent on ACUE funds. Aldrich, 'European Unity'; STel, 3.10.93.

39. Though a pro-European, Macmillan was not in any way a federalist. Though recognising that Britain could not isolate itself from Europe, he had written (11.10.49): 'The Empire must always have first preference for us: Europe must come second in a specially favoured position.' James, p. 346; Alistair Horne, *Macmillan 1894–1956*, Vol. 1, Macmillan, 1988, pp. 321 & 323.

41. Horne, pp. 348–51; Fletcher, p. 69.

42. Rebattet, pp. 60–1.

44. C.M. Woodhouse, *Something Ventured*, 1982, p. 135.

45–48. Bloch/Fitzgerald, pp. 101–3; Aldrich, 'European Unity'; Joel Kotek, *Students and the Cold War*, Macmillan, 1996.

49 & 50. TO, 23.5.75; Fletcher, p. 71.

51. 'NATO, Washington and Labour's Right-Wing', in *CIA Infiltration of the Labour Movement*, Militant, 1982.

52. ST, 25.5.75.

53 & 54. Bloch/Fitzgerald, pp. 101 & 106; Aldrich, *British Intelligence*, p. 2.

55. Bower, *Spy*, p. 213.

56. Ibid, p. 145; David Triesman, 'The CIA and Student Politics', in Alexander Cockburn and Robin Blackburn (eds), *Student Power: Problems, Diagnosis, Action*, Penguin (pbk), 1969, p. 148; SUS report, Dep. 224/2/1; *The Leveller*, pilot issue, Feb. 1976.

57. Report of the Investigation Commission Concerning Recent Charges against the International Student Conference, Supervision Committee of the ISC, 16.10.67, p. A34; Triesman, p. 148; SUS reports, Dep 224/2/1; Frank Copplestone, 'A Study of International Student Relations 1945–1957', in NUS archives, Warwick University, Modern Records Centre; Copplestone obit. T, 21.5.96, and notice of memorial service, 10.9.96, which most of the names mentioned in this section, including MI6 intelligence officers, attended.

58. T, 15.2.68; SUS reports, Dep 224/2/1.

59. The MI6 documents were mysteriously sent by anonymous Austrian students to the NUS and ISC investigating committees in 1967. They were never taken seriously partly because of the possibility of forgery but also because of sheer embarrassment. I do not believe, however, that there is any doubt that they are genuine, primarily because the codes and acronyms are those used for these operations. Appendix 2, ISC Supervision Committee, 16.10.67; Bower, *Spy*, p. 214.

60. Report of the Executive Sub-Committee, Investigating possible Central Intelligence Agency subversion of the International Student Conference, Oct. 1967, NUS archives, MSS 280; Fletcher, p. 65. E, 25.2.68; Triesman, pp. 143–4 & 153; NY *Herald Tribune*, 15.8.67; *The Leveller*, Feb. 1976.

61 & 62. Triesman, pp. 147–50; Fletcher, p. 64.

63. Trustees of FISC were Sir Berkeley Everard Foley Gage, former ambassador to Siam and Peru, Gerald Woods, Midlands banker, and John Butterworth, Vice-Chancellor of Warwick University, *The Leveller*; PE, 31.3.67; Faligot, p. 193.

64. Woodhouse, p. 135; Bloch/Fitzgerald, p. 68; TO, 7.3.75; 'The Rise and Fall of the CIA, Part One', *World in Action*, Granada, ITV, 1975.

65 & 66. Michael Warner, 'Origins of the Congress for Cultural Freedom', *Studies in Intelligence*; Brian Crozier, *Free Agent*, HarperCollins, 1996, p. 64. See Pierre Gremion, *Intelligence de l'Anticommunisme: Le Congrès pour la liberté de la culture à Paris (1950–1975)*, Fayard, Paris, 1996; Peter Coleman, *The Liberal Conspiracy: The Congress for Cultural Freedom and the Struggle for the Mind of Postwar Europe*, Collier Macmillan, 1989, p. 19.

67. PRO FO 953/479 P5486, Christopher Warner, minute, 8.6.49; FO 953/482 P5758, minute, 11.6.49, Mayhew to McNeil, 27.6.49; NS, 27.2.81; Peter Weiler, *British Labour and the Cold War*, 1988, pp. 210–11.

68. In a profile in his book *Brief Lives* (Hamish Hamilton, 1982), Alan Watkins reports that Muggeridge continued to work part time for MI6. Not unnaturally, some of Muggeridge's friends in this period were former colleagues in Section V, MI6 officers such as Richard Comyns-Carr and Graham Greene. His regular contact with the Service was Dick Brooman-White, 'an acute, gentle soul' and former MI5 officer who transferred to Section V during the war. He served as an attaché in Turkey during 1946–7 and was elected to Parliament as a Conservative MP in 1951, ending his political career as a junior minister for Scotland. They lunched on a regular basis and Muggeridge picked up

political briefings – 'nothing in the reports I saw from behind the iron curtain countries which I could not have got from the newspapers' – and the latest gossip on the Service. 'I asked him how things were in the way of intelligence, and he said, in his characteristically dry way, that very good intelligence was coming from places where it was easy to get and none at all from places where it was difficult to get.' Brooman-White also debriefed Muggeridge on his travels abroad. While he was more than willing to help the Service, giving lectures to their intelligence courses at Oxford, Muggeridge lambasted its inadequacies: 'I was amused to learn [26.8.48.] that the worst dead-beats were still firmly entrenched.' Bright-Holmes, pp. 286, 295, 339–43 & 350–4.
69. Warner.
70, 73 & 77. Coleman, pp. 34, 46, 61 & 145.
71 & 72. Ibid, pp. 28–31 & 34–5; Bower, *Spy*, p. 46; A.J. Ayer, *More of My Life*, OUP (pbk), 1985, pp. 63 & 138; Warner.
74. Coleman, pp. 16, 41 & 49; interview with Braden, *World in Action*; Ranelagh, p. 250; Tom Mangold, *Angleton*, Simon & Schuster, 1991, pp. 293 & 384.
75, 76 & 79. T.R. Fyvel, *And There My Trouble Began: Uncollected Writings 1945–1985*, Weidenfeld, 1986, pp. xi–xii, 83–94 & 99.
78. Hugh David, *Stephen Spender: A Portrait with Background*, Heinemann, 1992, pp. 143 & 188; WP, 15.5.67.
80. Coleman, p. 146; David, pp. 258–9; Bright-Holmes, p. 460.
81. Jenny Rees, *Looking for MR NOBODY: The Secret Life of Goronwy Rees*, Weidenfeld, 1994.
82. STel, 27.10.63; Trevor Barnes, 'Democratic Deception: American Covert Operations in Post-War Europe', in Charters/Tugwell; Mark Amory (ed.), *The Letters of Anne Fleming*, Collins Harvill, 1985, pp. 384–5; Ayer, pp. 63–4; I, 20.7.95.
83 & 84. Coleman, pp. 73 & 186. In September 1966, King visited CIA Director Richard Helms in Washington. *The Cecil King Diary 1965–1970*, Cape, 1972, pp. 86–7 & 92–3. The CIA denied a request under the Freedom of Information Act for documents relating to King.

CHAPTER TWENTY-THREE: ROLLING BACK 'ROLL-BACK'

1. Dmitri Volkogonov, *Stalin: Triumph and Tragedy*, Weidenfeld, 1991, p. 531; Aldrich, 'Unquiet in Death', p. 195.
2. John Yurechko, *From Containment to Counter Offensive: Soviet Vulnerabilities and American Policy Planning, 1946–1953*, PhD thesis, University of Berkeley, 1980; Mastny, pp. 27–9; Aldrich, 'Unquiet', p. 207.
3. R. Harris Smith, *OSS: The Secret History of America's First Central Intelligence Agency*, University of California Press, 1972, p. 238.
4. Steven, p. 39. Unfortunately, Steven's original notes were 'lost' during a house move and he no longer recalls the names and details of his MI6 and CIA sources.
5. Grose, p. 303.
6. Robert Conquest, *Stalin: Breaker of Nations*, Weidenfeld, 1991, p. 251; David Corn, *Blond Ghost: Ted Shackley and the CIA's Crusades*, Simon & Schuster, 1994, p. 42. Steven (pp. 193–6) refers to the Slansky episode as being part of the Splinter Factor deception operation; however, Corn, who spoke to a CIA officer involved, says that it was a real operation.
7 & 8. Anthony Glees, 'War Crimes: The Security and Intelligence Dimension', INS, Vol. 7, No. 3, Jul. 1992. In the summer of 1988 Glees was appointed adviser to the War Crimes Inquiry under Sir Thomas Hetherington. He wrote a 30,000-word report, designated 'secret', using MI6 and MI5 material. A sanitised version appeared as Chapters 3 and 4 of the War Crimes Inquiry Report (HMSO, Cmn. 744, 1989). Glees had been asked to produce the report by the Home Office based on his knowledge of contemporary German history and his book *The Secrets of the Service: British Intelligence and Communist Subversion, 1919–51*, Cape, 1987. Cesarani, p. 132; O, 5.5.91.
9. Sulzberger, p. 523.
10. *History of the Strategic Arms Competition, 1945–72*, Pentagon, 1993.
11. M. Steven Fish, 'After Stalin's Death: The Anglo-American Debate over a New Cold War', *Diplomatic History*, No. 10, fall 1986.
12. Peter Boyle, 'The "Special Relationship" with Washington', in John W. Young (ed.), *The Foreign Policy of Churchill's Peacetime*

Administration 1951–55, Leicester University Press, 1988.

13. *Lobster*, No. 19; M. Smith, p. 251; Tony Geraghty, *Beyond the Frontline: The Untold Exploits of Britain's Most Daring Cold War Spy Mission*, HarperCollins, 1996, pp. 23–4.

14. Michael Mastanduno, 'Trade as a strategic weapon: American and alliance export control policy in the early post-war period', *International Organisation* 42, 1, winter 1988. Frank M. Cain, 'Exporting the Cold War: British Responses to the USA's Establishment of COCOM, 1947–51', JCH, Vol. 29, 1994.

15. Vibeke Sorensen, 'Economic Recovery versus Containment: The Anglo-American Controversy over East–West Trade, 1947–51', *Cooperation and Conflict*, XXIV, 1989; PRO FO 371/94845/38, 18.9.50.

16. CIA, 'Vulnerability of the Soviet bloc to Economic Warfare', National Intelligence Estimate No. 22, 19.2.51, FRUS, Vol. 1, 1951.

17. PRO FO 371/125006/5.

18. Heuser, p. 141; John W. Young, *Winston Churchill's Last Campaign: Britain and the Cold War, 1951–5*, Clarendon Press, Oxford, 1996, p. 37.

19. Young, pp. 70 & 85.

20. John W. Young, 'The British Foreign Office and Cold War Fighting in the Early 1950s: PUSC (51)16 and the "Sore Spots" Memorandum', *Discussion Papers in Politics*, No. P95/2, University of Leicester, Apr. 1995; PRO FO 371/10085, 31.1.52.

21. Reference and information from Richard J. Aldrich.

22. 'Soviet Reactions to Western Pressure on "Sore Spots"', 5.2.52.

23. PRO FO 371/100825, 19.2.52. The paper was challenged by staff in the Moscow embassy who argued that the West should avoid negotiations and, instead, instigate 'disruptive actions' and pursue a damaging 'arms race' with the USSR. The call for tougher measures rather than retreat was propagated in a pamphlet, 'Britain and the Cold War', by the Oxford Radical Association, which stimulated the right-wing *Economist* (26 April) to talk of 'Containment Plus'.

24. Beddington-Behrens, p. 187.

25. Aarons/Loftus, *Ratlines*, p. 223. A. Tchilingarian, 'The American Committee and the Struggle against Bolshevism', *Armenian Review*, Vol. 8, No. 1–29, Mar. 1955.

26. Kurt Glaser, 'Psychological Warfare's Policy Feedback', *Ukrainian Quarterly*, spring 1953.

27. Sudoplatov, pp. 330–1; PRO FO 371/100825/9 & 371/97591/1.

28 & 29. Brown, *Secret Servant*, pp. 703 & 720, and *Treason*, pp. 448–9; Howarth, p. 169.

30. General Sir Charles Richardson, *From Churchill's Secret Circle to the BBC: The Biography of Lieutenant General Sir Ian Jacob*, Brassey's, 1991.

31. Blake, p. 157.

32. A. Faughnan, *The Politics of Influence: Churchill, Eden and Soviet Communism, 1951–7*, PhD thesis, Cambridge University, 1993; Aldrich, *British Intelligence*, p. 23; West, *Friends*, p. 83.

33. Anthony Montague Browne, *Long Sunset: Memoirs of Winston Churchill's Last Private Secretary*, Cassell, 1995, pp. 133–4.

34. Wilkinson/Astley, p. 240; Peter Thompson, 'Bilderberg and the West', in Sklar, p. 163.

35. Alan Hatch, *H.R.H. Prince Bernhard of the Netherlands*, Harrap, 1962, pp. 212–13.

36. Korbonski, p. 50.

37. Cookridge, p. 301; Bower, *Spy*, p. 206.

38. Grose, p. 356; Heuser, p. 142.

39. Young (ed.), pp. 12–13.

40. Lyman Kirkpatrick, *The Real CIA*, Macmillan, NY, 1968, p. 153.

41 & 43. *Lobster*, No. 19; Bower, *Spy*, pp. 170 & 208.

42. Borovik, p. 172; *I* magazine, 22.9.92.

44. Payne, pp. 679–80.

45. Ibid, p. 688; Rapaport, *The Doctor's Plot: Stalin's Last Crime*, Fourth Estate, 1991, pp. 74–5; Sudoplatov, pp. 298–301; H. Montgomery Hyde, *Stalin: The History of a Dictator*, Hart-Davis, 1971; Walter Laqueur, *Stalin: The Glasnost Revelations*, Unwin Hyman, 1990.

46 & 47. PRO FO 371/125030/6-9, 4.2.53; Sudoplatov, pp. 336–9; J.W. Young, p. 148.

48. J.W. Young, p. 237; Payne, p. 710; G. Young, p. 111; Dorril/Ramsay, *Smear!*, p. 18; Harold Wilson, *Memoirs: The Making of a Prime Minister 1916–64*, Weidenfeld, pp. 143–4.

49. *Lobster*, No. 19.

50. Mackintosh, p. 87; Hugh Seton-Watson, 'Eastern Europe since Stalin', *Problems of Communism*, Mar./Apr. 1954.

51 & 52. Bristol, pp. 234–47.

53. Harry Rositzke, *The KGB: The Eyes of Russia*, Sidgwick (pbk), p. 134; Hagen, pp. 151–62.

54. Konstantin Cherezov, *NTS: A Spy Ring Unmasked*, Soviet Committee for Cultural Relations with Russians Abroad, 1963, p. 17; *Caught in the Act*, Moscow, pp. 53–4.

55. Vakar, p. 280; William Henry Chamberlain, 'Emigré Anti-Soviet Enterprises and Splits', *Russian Review*, Apr. 1954; Huxley-Blythe, 1958.

56–58. Christian F. Ostermann, 'The United States, the East German Uprising of 1953, and the Limits of Rollback', Cold War International History Project, Woodrow Wilson Centre for Scholars, Working Paper No. 11, Dec. 1994. Powers, pp. 55–6; PRO FO 371/103842 CS1016/124, 19.6.53.

59. PRO CAB 129/61/C(53)187, 3.7.53, CAB 129/61/C(53)194, 7.7.53, Policy towards the Soviet Union and Germany, memorandum; Anthony Seldon, *Churchill's Indian Summer*, Hodder, 1981, pp. 396–409.

60. PRO CAB 128/26/CC44(53)4, 21.7.53; Fish; Boyle in Young (ed.).

61. R.V. Jones, *Reflections*, pp. 23–4.

62. NSC 174/608, which called for an intensified reliance on covert action. Gilbert, p. 880; Shuckburgh diary, 27.8.53; Ostermann; FRUS, 1952–3; VIII, 85, 1.10.53.

63. NSC 174 on 'United States Policy toward the Soviet Satellites in Eastern Europe'; Heuser, p. 79; C.D. Jackson Papers, 1934–67, Box 56, cited in J.D. Marchio, *Rhetoric and Reality: The Eisenhower Administration and Unrest in Eastern Europe, 1953–59*, PhD thesis, American University, 1991; Jim Marchio, 'Resistance Potential and Rollback: US Intelligence and the Eisenhower Administration's Policies towards Eastern Europe 1953–56', INS, Vol. 10, No. 2, Apr. 1995.

64 & 69. Korbonski, pp. 50–1.

65. Sudoplatov, pp. 325–31 & 373–4; Hyde, p. 62, quoting from a memorandum written in 1967 by De Courcy, who was in Wormwood Scrubs for fraud, which was smuggled out when he was released from prison. Now deposited in the Hoover Institution of War, Revolution and Peace archives, Stanford University, California.

66. Rositzke, *KGB*, p. 173; Heuser, p. 79.

67 & 68. Bower, *Red Web*, pp. 50–1 & 170–6.

70. Khorunzhi was finally released in 1959 after five years in prison. Fish.

71. Ronald Seth, *The Executioners: The Story of SMERSH*, Grosset & Dunlap (pbk), NY, 1967. NTS leader Georgi Okolovich told journalist David Tutaev in a series of articles in *John*

Bull (11/18/25.9.54) that he was suspicious of Khokhlov.

72. Young, *Subversion*, p. 249; G, 2.1.94; Mastanduno; CAB 21/3220.

73. Bristow, pp. 245–7.

74. Healey, pp. 195–6.

75. Eringer.

76. Harold Macmillan, *Tides of Fortune 1945–1955*, Macmillan, p. 572; *Lobster*, No. 19.

77. Anthony Adamthwaite, 'The Foreign Office and Policy-Making', in Young (ed.), pp. 22–4; *Lobster*, No. 19.

78. Aldrich, *British Intelligence*, p. 23.

79 & 80. Interview with Philby in *Kodumma*, Estonia, 13.10.71; Philby was out of the Service by the time these committees were created. Perhaps he had been given details by his friends still in MI6. The most likely explanation is that he was dealing in the KGB with documents filched by George Blake. PRO FO 371/100894, 17.9.52; *The Current Digest of the Soviet Press*, Vol. XX, No. 17, 1968.

81–83. Bower, *Red Web*, pp. 173–5 & 180–2, and *Spy*, p. 205.

84. Nigel West, *The Secret War for the Falklands*, 1997, p. 160.

85. Wright, pp. 119–21.

86. Arnold-Forster went on to become a journalist working on the *Observer* and the *Guardian*. His account appeared in only the first edition of the *Guardian* and was quickly removed. Stockbroker and Assistant Director of Naval Intelligence Commander Christopher Arnold-Forster retired from MI6 after serving in the war as its Chief Staff Officer. G, 4.2.80; Prados, p. 43.

87 & 88. Cherezov, pp. 18–19 & 54.

89, 91 & 95. Bower, *Red Web*, pp. 183–5 & 190; Prados, p. 43.

90. J.W. Young, 'Foreign Office'.

92. E.H. Cookridge, *George Blake: Double Agent*, Hodder (pbk), 1970, p. 145; Blake, p. 23; Aarons/Loftus, *Ratlines*, p. 261.

93. The withdrawal of support by the British did not prevent the KGB from pursuing Ukrainian nationalist leaders. Lev Rebet was assassinated in 1957. The following October, Bandera was killed outside his Munich apartment building with a dose of cyanide fired from an ingeniously constructed gun. Stetsko managed to avoid Soviet assassins and lived in quiet obscurity in Wimbledon. Cherezov, p. 61.

94. Huxley-Blythe, pp. 219–20; Nicholas Hayes, 'Kazem-bek and the Young Russians'

Revolution', *Slavic Review*, Vol. 39, No. 2, 1980.

96. Rebane received an SS pension until his death in 1966 from alcoholism. Stasys Zymantas emigrated to Los Angeles, where he worked as a grave-digger. Between 1953 and 1958 he wrote about the partisan campaign in *Santarve* (Alliance), a London-based journal published by the Alliance of Lithuanian Resistance. He died in 1973, disillusioned by his role in the Baltic operations. Lukasevics was promoted to general, and worked in Moscow Centre during the sixties. In 1972 he was posted, under the name Yakov Konstantinovich Bukashev, to London as First Secretary at the Soviet embassy. According to Soviet defector Oleg Gordievsky, during his six years in London Lukasevics was singularly unsuccessful in building an intelligence network; at the same time MI6 seemed unaware that the Service's *bête noire* was operating under their noses. Bower, *Red Web*, pp. 187–90; Vardys, p. 288.

97 & 98. A number of authors have referred to the CIA émigré armies as being part of the REDSOX operation. This is mistaken, as the title refers to another unrelated operation. According to John Mapother, a CIA case officer in the Vienna station, the CIA had no such assets. Hersh, p. 410; E. Thomas, pp. 130 & 375; Grose, p. 437; Verrier, p. 157.

99. I, 22.10.96; DT, 21.10.96.

100. Bower, *Spy*, p. 198; Daniel F. Calhoun, *Hungary and Suez, 1956: An Exploration of Who Makes History*, University Press of America, US, 1991, pp. 320–1.

101. Herbert, who had worked in intelligence in the Middle East during the war, had a number of relatives who were also intelligence practitioners. His uncle, writer Alec, had worked for MI6. His other uncle, Evelyn Waugh, had knowledge of the intelligence world, and his family moved in intelligence circles which included Tom Driberg, a regular informant for MI5, and Roger Fulford, an ex-colleague of another relative, Roger Hollis. Nephew Auberon Waugh's first job on the editorial staff of the *Daily Telegraph* was rather like an internal posting for MI6. Waugh: 'perhaps I should explain that I tried to join the Foreign Service soon after coming down from Oxford in 1960 and was firmly rebuffed, despite a recommendation from Sir Roger Hollis, of

the rival Security Service, MI5' (I, 16.5.87). Waugh was close to the Hollis family – Roger's brother, Christopher, was his godfather, and the two lunched together (S, 22.10.88). Marcus Hollis was also an MI6 officer. Leigh, pp. 113–14 & 196; Wright, pp. 119–21.

102. Bower, *Spy*, p. 207.

CHAPTER TWENTY-FOUR: THE TECHNICAL FIX

1–3. Ralf Tammes, *The United States and the Cold War in the High North*, Dartmouth Press, Aldershot, 1991, pp. 51–2 & 76–9.

4 & 6. DT, 7.2.94; BBC2, *Timewatch*, 'Spies in the Sky', 9.2.94; Lashmar, pp. 76–82; Robert S. Hopkins III, 'An Expanded Understanding of Eisenhower, American Policy and Overflights', INS, Vol. 11, No. 2, Apr. 1996.

5. Grose, p. 402.

7. William E. Burrows, *Deep Black: The Secrets of Space Espionage*, Bantam, 1988, pp. 66–7; *Lobster*, No. 19.

8 & 9. John Marks, *The Search for the 'Manchurian Candidate': The CIA and Mind Control*, Allen Lane, 1979, p. 30; P. Wright, *Spycatcher*, p. 160, and *Secret Agenda*, pp. 166–7; Harris/Paxman, p. 205.

10. Jones, *War*, pp. 658–9.

11. Jones, *Reflections*, pp. 7–10 & 21; Bower, *Spy*, p. 149.

12. *Lobster*, No. 19; Jones, *War*, p. 659, and *Reflections*, p. 18.

13 & 14. Jones, *Reflections*, pp. 23–8 & 661; *Lobster*, No. 19.

15. Blake, p. 13.

16. 'Operation "Gold" and Others' – interview with George Blake by V. Lyadov & V. Rozin, *Izvestia*, 15/17.2.70; Cookridge, *Blake*, pp. 14–15 & 107–8; H. Montgomery Hyde, *George Blake: Superspy*, Futura (pbk), 1988, pp. 43 & 176.

17. E. Thomas, p. 128; Hersh, p. 378.

18. E. Thomas, p. 371; Blake, pp. 20–2. Blake's account is also featured in *Pravda* (International) 2, No. 11/12, 1988, and *Moscow Magazine*, Oct./Nov. 1991. Blake's map was finally released by the KGB in Feb. 1997. STel, 23.2.97.

19. See Appendix 9, 'Operation Gold', and 8, 'Was It Worth It?', in David E. Murphy, Sergei A. Kondrashev and George Bailey, *Battleground Berlin: CIA vs KGB in the Cold War*, Yale University Press, 1997.

20. West, *Friends*, p. 80.

21. Tammes, pp. 12, 118 & 121.
22. G, 27.9.88 & 21.4.95; *Operation Hornbeam*, Edit V, Yorkshire Television, 20.4.95; *Close Up North*, BBC2, 11.1.96; O, 25.1.98; DT, 18.7.98.
23 & 25. Christian Christensen, *Vår Hemmelige Beredskap, Historien om MM*, J.M. Cappelens Forlag, Oslo, 1988, pp. 143 & 148; West, *Friends*, p. 80. In the late seventies, Hambros was accused of being party to a tax avoidance scandal by the top shipping lines through the formation of shell companies in tax havens. NS, 17.8.79 & 21.9.79; Cruickshank, pp. 1–3.
24. Tammes, p. 121; Christensen, pp. 143 & 148. See Alf R. Jacobsen, *Moldvarpene* (Moles), Oslo, 1985.
26. Hersh, p. 366; CIA, 'The Berlin Tunnel Operation', CS Historical Paper No. 1, 25.8.67.
27. Blake, pp. 167–9.
28. STel, 23.2.97.
29. By the late fifties the group of émigrés originally employed in Regent's Park to process MI6's Berlin Tunnel material was transferred to GCHQ's control, working from a building in the City of London as the London Processing Group, transcribing Russian-language intercepts. M. Smith, p. 187.
30. Grose, pp. 398–9; Thomas, pp. 128–9; David Martin, *Wilderness of Mirrors*, Ballantine (pbk), NY, 1981, pp. 74–90; M. Smith, p. 117; Corn, p. 54.

PART SIX: THE MIDDLE EAST

CHAPTER TWENTY-FIVE: 'UNBROKEN DREAMS'

1 & 2. Richard J. Aldrich, *Intelligence*, pp. 25–6 & 197; West, *Friends*, pp. 17 & 101.
3. Wesley K. Wark, 'Development diplomacy: Sir John Troutback and the British Middle East Office, 1947–50', in John Zametica (ed.), *British Officials and British Foreign Policy 1945–50*, Leicester University Press, 1990; Frank K. Roberts, 'Ernest Bevin as Foreign Secretary', in R. Ovendale, *The Foreign Policy of the British Labour Governments, 1945–51*, 1984.
4 & 5. Richard J. Aldrich & John Zametica, 'The rise and decline of a strategic concept; the Middle East, 1945–51', in Aldrich;

Richard J. Aldrich, 'The Fate of Alexander Rado: Soviet Intelligence, British Security and the end of Red Orchestra', INS, Vol. 6, No. 1, Jan. 1991.
6. Ray Merrick, 'The Russia Committee of the British Foreign Office and the Cold War, 1946–7', JCH, Vol. 20, 1985; Raymond Smith, 'British Soviet Policy', in A. Deighton, *Britain and the First Cold War*, 1990; PRO FO 930/488 P449/1/907, 26.5.46; 371 56885 N7816/5169/ 38, 11.6.46; 371/56784 N7199/140/38G, 29.7.46; W. Scott Lucas & C.J. Morris, 'A very British crusade', in Aldrich.
7. Aldrich, pp. 201 & 213, and 'The Fate'; PRO E4569/1630/65, FO 371/45272.
8. Employed pre-war by the British Overseas Bank, Sweet-Escott worked for MI6's Section D before joining SOE as assistant to its head, Sir Charles Hambro. He was posted to Cairo, with responsibilities for propaganda (SO2), meeting a number of 'charming and intelligent people' such as Charles de Salis (who became Deputy Governor of Rome when the city was taken), Christopher Sykes and Ewan Butler. In late 1944, he took charge of the Bulgarian, Hungarian and Romanian sections of Force 133 at Bari and then moved to 136 in South-East Asia. At the end of the war, Parker helped establish communications in Germany and later worked for the Control Commission. Obit. DT, 27.8.92.
   In 1941, SOE's infant propaganda broadcasting to the Balkans was upgraded using a seven-and-a-half-kilowatt transmitter built by RCA and ordered by Iran's Reza Shah, who had been recently deposed. Richard Fletcher, 'How the Secret Service shaped the news', G, 18.12.81; Sweet-Escott, pp. 77, 87–94 & 264; Ewan Butler, *Amateur Agent*, Harrap, 1963, pp. 54–5.
9 & 10. Boase was a fellow and tutor of Hertford College, Oxford, and the Courtauld Institute of Art. Frances Donaldson, *The British Council: The First Fifty Years*, Cape, 1984, pp. 51, 91–102 & 110. A thinly veiled reference is made to Dundas by deception specialist David Mure in his roman à clef *The Last Temptation* (Buchan & Enright, 1984), which depicts wartime events in the Middle East. Mure refers to 'Fergie' attending parties with Guy Burgess and the 'whipmaster', Lord 'Bill' Astor, a Naval Intelligence officer in the region. Before retiring in 1966, Dundas worked for the British Council in Hong Kong, India, Germany and Australia.
11. Working for the Palestine Broadcasting

Service was Ewan Butler, in charge of black propaganda with responsibilities for the Balkans and central Europe. A former *Times* chief correspondent in Berlin, Butler worked on the station in Jerusalem with writer Christopher Sykes and operations officer Guy Tamplin, who had worked pre-war with Sweet-Escott with Baltic banks controlled by the British Overseas Bank. A friend of Douglas Dodds-Parker, Tamplin ran the SOE Balkan country sections in Cairo, and was known to NEABS staff for being 'stubborn in his support of Mihailovic in Yugoslavia'. NEABS propaganda led to confusion as each targeted country had 'a right-wing (sometimes monarchist) group and an extreme left-wing group'. In addition there was little control over the eastern European émigré staff. The Greek, Serbo-Croat and Romanian output was controlled by Archibald Lyall, later an MI6 officer. The Free Voice of Greece, which contrived to be located in the Soviet Union, attacked the Greek government-in-exile. Its politics were officially regarded as 'beneath contempt', as it urged its listeners to ignore the pro-monarchist 'For King and Country' station. Occasional staged 'Gestapo' raids on the station would add to its authenticity. In 1943, the station was forced to surrender control to the PWE. Butler, pp. 10–17, 32 & 53–67; Dodds-Parker, p. 49; West, *Secret War*, pp. 204 & 221; Sweet-Escott, p. 79; M. Senton, *British Propaganda and Political Warfare, 1940–44*, PhD thesis, Cambridge University, 1979; Peter Partner, *Arab Voices: The BBC Arabic Service 1938–1988*, BBC, 1988, pp. 29 & 53.

12 & 19. Partner, pp. 54 & 91–2.

13 & 14. David Boyle, *With Ardours Manifold*, Hutchinson, 1959, pp. 299–304. The existence of Section N remains something of a state secret, with Robert Cecil being refused permission to mention its existence in his contribution on wartime MI6 to *The Oxford Companion to the Second World War* (ed. I.C.B. Dear, OUP, 1995). M. Smith, p. 288.

15. Wark.

16. Bickham Sweet-Escott returned to the City and produced several economic and financial surveys of Greece and the Balkans.

17. HoC, 'Radio Station: Cyprus', *Propaganda*, Cols 409–10, 16.6.48; information from Morris Riley.

18. Riley, pp. 85–7; *Sunday Mail* (Cyprus), 23.4.50.

20 & 21. Ray Alan, *The Beirut Pipeline*, Collins, 1980, pp. 1 & 234–5; Laurie Valls-Russell, writing as 'Ray Alan', in the *New Leader*, 1.6.81.

22. Ritchie Ovendale, 'William Strang and the Permanent Under-Secretary's Committee', in Zametica, pp. 217–19.

23 & 25. F.S. Northedge, 'Britain and the Middle East', in Ovendale.

24. Wark.

CHAPTER TWENTY-SIX: PALESTINE

1. Tad Szulc, *The Secret Alliance: The Extraordinary Story of the Rescue of the Jews since World War II*, Macmillan, 1991, pp. 48–50.

2. David A. Charters, 'British Intelligence in the Palestine Campaign, 1945–47', INS, Vol. 6, No. 1, Jan. 1991.

3. West, *Friends*, p. 120.

4. Hella Pick, *Simon Wiesenthal: A Life in Search of Justice*, Weidenfeld, 1996, pp. 126–7.

5. Richard Deacon, *The Israeli Secret Service*, Hamish Hamilton, 1977, p. 29.

6. Jon and David Kimche, *The Secret Roads: The 'Illegal' Migration of a People 1938–1948*, Secker, 1954, p. 161; Andrew and Leslie Cockburn, *Dangerous Liaisons*, HarperCollins, 1991, p. 36; Aarons/Loftus, *Secret War*, pp. 192–3.

7. Hennessy, p. 239; Bullock, ch. 3; Kimche, p. 97; G, 30.9.94.

8. Charters; O, 26.4.87; Yaacov Eliav (trans. Mordecai Schreiber), *Wanted*, Shengold Publishers, NY, 1984, pp. 85–94.

9–11 & 15. Kimche, pp. 98, 107–8, 160–1, 176–7 & 194–6; Brian Lapping, *End of Empire*, Granada, 1985, p. 13; Szulc, pp. 48–50 & 185.

12. Letter from Cathal O'Connor to the O, 26.6.88, and telephone conversation, 30.4.96.

13. Ibid; West, *Friends*, pp. 33–4. On Verschoyle, see Anthony Mockler, *Graham Greene: Three Lives*, Hunter Mackay, 1993.

14. West, *Friends*, pp. 33–4; O, 12.6.88; G, 30.9.94.

16 & 18. Aarons/Loftus, *Secret War*, pp. 149 & 198–9; Kimche, pp. 203 & 210–11; Szulc, pp. 46 & 186; Robert John and Sami Hadawi, *The Palestine Diary, 1945–48*, Vol. 2, New World Press, NY, 1971, pp. 53 & 309.

17. G.K. Young, *Subversion and the British Riposte*, 1983, p. 12.

19. O, 12.6.88; James Morris, *Farewell the Trumpets: An Imperial Retreat*, Penguin (pbk),

1979, pp. 511–12; Menachem Begin, *The Revolt*, W.H. Allen, 1979, p. 97.
20. West, *Friends*, p. 39.

CHAPTER TWENTY-SEVEN: CYPRUS

1. West, *Friends*, pp. 69–70.
2. Charles Foley, *Legacy of Strife: Cyprus from Rebellion to Civil War*, Penguin, 1964, p. 17; Lawrence Durrell, *Bitter Lemons*, Faber, 1959.
3. John Bruce-Lockhart, 'Intelligence: A British View', RUSI, 1987, p. 41; West, *Friends*, p. 77.
4–7. Susan L. Carruthers, *Winning Hearts and Minds: British Governments, the Media and Colonial Counter-Insurgency 1944–1960*, Leicester University Press, 1995, pp. 196–8 & 209–11; West, *Friends*, p. 70; Foley, pp. 43, 72 & 103.
8. Anthony Nutting, *No End of a Lesson: The Story of Suez*, Constable, 1967, p. 56; A.J. Barker, *Suez: The Seven Days War*, Faber, 1964, p. 55; Hugh Thomas, *Suez*, 1966, p. 168.
9 & 10. Nutting, p. 56; Geoffrey McDermott, *The Eden Legacy*, Leslie Frewin, 1969, p. 131; Foley, p. 59.
11, 12, 15, 16 & 21. In 1957, Phillpotts was rewarded with a CMG and posted to Paris. His place in Athens was taken by Alan Hare, who retired in 1961 and joined the *Financial Times*, eventually becoming its chair. Stephen Hastings, *The Drums of Memory: An Autobiography*, Leo Cooper, 1994, pp. 185–6 & 192. Hastings obit. of Sir John Prendergast I, 30.9.93; McDermott, pp. 174–6.
13 & 14. Wright, pp. 145–57.
17–20. West, *Friends*, pp. 75–7; I, 30.9.93; Hastings, pp. 186–7; Bower, *Spy*, p. 231.
22. Cabinet records release, O, 1.1.89.

CHAPTER TWENTY-EIGHT: IRAN: 'UNEQUAL DREAMS'

1. Interview with Kenneth Love by Joseph Pennington, Aug. 1980.
2. Verrier, p. 105. The Milne brothers were both in MI6 and friends of Kim Philby. The elder, Ian, was born in 1912 and was Second Secretary in Tehran 1948–51, and between periods in London served in Berne and Tokyo. He left in 1968 to become a House of Commons clerk. His brother was one of those present at the wedding of Philby in 1958 and would serve in Beirut.
3. Lapping, p. 207.

4. Hassan Arfa, *Under Five Shahs*, John Murray, 1964, p. 393.
5. Ramesh Sanghvi Anyamehr, *The Shah of Iran*, Transorient, 1968, p. 154.
6. W. Roger Louis, *The British Empire in the Middle East*, OUP, 1984, pp. 648–9.
7. Sepehr Zabih, *The Mossadegh Era*, Lake View Press, US, 1982, p. 139.
8–10. James Cable, *Intervention at Abadan: Plan Buccaneer*, Macmillan, 1990, pp. 7, 23, 45 & 102; Woodhouse, 1982, p. 111.
11. G. Young, p. 15.
12 & 13. PRO FO 371/91548 EP 1531/674 & 371/91550 EP 15331/713.
14. Bethell, p. 71.
15. Margaret Laing, *The Shah*, Sidgwick, 1977, p. 110.
16. General Fardust, *The Rise and Fall of the Pahlavi Dynasty*, Iranian Institute for Research and Political Studies, Tehran, 1990.
17. Letters from Kermit Roosevelt, 28.11.84, and Woodhouse, 3.9.85; O, 26.5.85; M. Zonis, *The Political Elite of Iran*, Princeton University Press, 1971, p. 73.
18. Lapping, p. 215.
19. O, 26.5.85; Nikki R. Keddie, *Roots of Revolution*, Yale University Press, 1981, p. 118.
20 & 21. L.P. Elwell-Sutton, *Persian Oil: A Study in Power Politics*, Greenwood Press, US, 1979, pp. 150 & 241–2; Mohamed Heikal, *The Return of the Ayatollah*, Deutsch, 1981, p. 62. Zabih, p. 140.
22. Gerard de Villiers, *The Imperial Shah*, Weidenfeld, 1976, p. 164; Homa Katouzian, *Mussaddiq and the Struggle for Power in Iran*, I.B. Tauris, 1990, p. 11.
23. Allan W. Ford, *The Anglo-Iranian Oil Dispute of 1951–52*, University of California, US, 1954, pp. 95–7.
24. Louis, p. 685.
25. Mark J. Gasiorowski, 'The 1953 Coup d'Etat in Iran', *International Journal of Middle East Studies*, 19, 1987, and *US Foreign Policy and the Shah: Building a Client State in Iran*, Cornell University Press, US, 1991, pp. 54 & 69–70.
26. Pisani, pp. 122–3.
27–29. Kermit Roosevelt, *Arabs, Oil and History: The Story of the Middle East*, Gollancz, 1949, pp. 5–7, 26, 101–3, 203–11 & 258.
30. T.E. Tisdale, *The US and Iran, 1951–3: The Cold War Interaction of American Security Policy, Alliance Politics and Popular Nationalism*, PhD thesis, University of Arizona, 1989; H.W. Brand, *Inside the Cold*

War: *Loy Henderson and the Rise of the
American Empire 1918–61*, 1991, p. 243.
31. A September 1943 US State Department
memorandum made plain that the Iranian
oilfields 'were taking on great importance in
the eyes of the US government'. American
support for Mossadeq began in 1946 when
US ambassador George V. Allen contacted
the nationalist groups that combined to form
the National Front Party. Allen saw in
Mossadeq's NF leadership and nationalist
aims the possible nucleus of resistance to
Soviet infiltration. Pisani, p. 123.
32. Woodhouse, p. 110; Ronald W. Ferrier,
'The Anglo-American oil dispute: a
triangular relationship', in James A. Bill and
W.M. Roger Louis (eds), *Musaddiq, Iranian
Nationalism, and Oil*, I.B. Tauris, 1988, p. 173.
33. Dean Acheson papers, Princeton
seminars, 15/16.5.54, p. 1691; Elwell-Sutton,
p. 249.
34. Study of events in this area was carried
out by the Central Asian Research Centre,
which had been set up in 1953 in co-
operation with St Antony's College, Oxford.
It had been incorporated in the same way as
the MI6 news agencies by solicitor Victor
Cannon Brookes, who had worked with SOE
during the war. Its director was intelligence
officer and propaganda specialist Lt-Col.
Geoffrey Wheeler, who had served in India
and Iraq during the war and had recently
returned from Iran, where he had been
posted as press secretary during the
campaign against Mossadeq. During the
fifties, Wheeler was employed in 'a civil
service post in London'. His fellow director
was Prof. Ann Lambton, who had also
served as a press attaché in Iran during the
war and had played an important role in the
run-up to the Iran coup. Wheeler wrote
various IRD-sponsored 'Background Books' –
Racial Problems in Soviet Muslim Asia (1962),
The Modern History of Soviet Central Asia
(1964) and *The Peoples of Soviet Central Asia*
(Bodley Head, 1966). Louis, p. 678;
PRO FO 371/91575, memo by Peter
Ramsbotham, 30.7.51; CAB 123/20 56(51),
30.7.51.
35 & 36. Woodhouse, pp. 105 & 111;
Stafford, p. 210; Cabinet papers: G, 2.1.84
and T, 4.1.84.
37. *Lobster*, No. 19.
38 & 41. Young, *Masters of Indecision*, pp. 15,
95 & 106; Bower, *Spy*, p. 192.
39. Son of the famous Stephen Longrigg,

Longrigg joined MI6 in 1948 and served in
Paris, Baghdad, Berlin, Dakar, Johannesburg,
Washington, Bahrain and Hong Kong. He
retired in 1982 as Counsellor FCO (head of a
division) and became an administrator of the
Common Law Institute of Intellectual
Property. Woodhouse, pp. 107–11.
40. Roosevelt: 'Montague' is Woodhouse and
Darbyshire 'Gordon Somerset'. Darbyshire
returned to Tehran as station chief (1963–7)
and would also serve in Beirut, Cairo and
Bahrain. Briance would rise to be a
counsellor in Washington and Singapore
before retiring as a divisional head in 1970.
Born in 1923, Woods served in Cairo, Milan,
Warsaw and Rome, ending as a divisional
head, and was re-employed in retirement
with responsibility in the Foreign Office for
the SOE archive. According to Lord
Greenhill, a consolidated account on the
Mussadeq affair is held by the Foreign
Office, though Woodhouse has said that he
did not contribute to it. Darbyshire did,
however, write up a full account for MI6's
files. Roger Louis ('The dilemmas of British
imperialism', in Bill/Louis, p. 249) notes that
'until this time [1953] British intelligence
operations, if impinging on foreign policy,
were discussed fully and candidly within the
secret counsels of the Foreign Office. During
the Mussadiq period the records were
suppressed . . . now it had a deeper
subterranean stream that is much more
difficult to fish for historical detail.' T, 7.4.77;
Woodhouse, pp. 112 & 135; G, 28.7.80;
Lapping, p. 214.
42 & 43. Lapping, pp. 212–14 & 264;
PRO FO 371/91464; 371/91608; 371/91609
EP 1531/2095; 371/91609.
44. Richard Cottam in transcript of *End of
Empire* series, Channel 4, 1985.
45. Woodhouse, pp. 113–14.
46. Gasiorowski, p. 70; Riley, p. 78.
47–50. Lapping, pp. 214–15; Amir Taheri,
*Nest of Spies: America's Journey to Disaster in
Iran*, Hutchinson, 1988, p. 29; Katouzian,
p. 125; PRO FO 371/98254, May 1952; 371/
98239, 22.1.52; FO 371/98638, 12.9.52; *Lobster*,
No. 19.
51. I, 15.3.97; Woodhouse, p. 115; Barnard
would subsequently work in the late sixties
for MI6 in the Sudan, helping to set up a
front airline, Southern Air Motive.
52. Brand, p. 192; Louis in Bill/Louis, p. 243.
53. Wilbur Crane Eveland, *Ropes of Sand*,
Norton, NY, 1980, p. 118; Julius Mader,

Who's Who in the CIA, East Berlin, 1968, p. 201.

54. Transcript of *End of Empire*.

55. Laing, p. 132; Roosevelt, p. 13.

56. Makhreddin Amizi, 'The Political Career of Muhammad Musaddiq', in Bill/Louis, p. 57.

57. Gasiorowski; PRO FO 248/1531.

58. Fardust.

59. 'The Secret Events of the Uprising', *Ittalia 'at*, Tehran, 4.9.53; Ervand Abrahamian, *Iran between Two Revolutions*, Princeton University, US, p. 278.

60. PRO FO 371/91460.

61. Zabih, pp. 141–2. Ebtehaj, who was known as Iran's leading economist and first of the technocrats, was later arrested in 1961 along with one of the Rashidian brothers following more intrigue, this time against the Shah. He was released following British pressure (obit. I, 10.3.99).

62 & 65. Dilip Hiro, *Iran under the Ayatollahs*, Routledge, 1985, pp. 34 & 62; Elwell-Sutton, p. 310.

63 & 67. Woodhouse, pp. 116–17.

64. I, 15.3.97; Page *et al.*, pp. 284–5.

66. Louis in Bill/Louis, p. 236; Nigel West, *Molehunt: The Full Story of the Soviet Spy in MI5*, Weidenfeld, 1987, p. 31, and *Friends*, p. 148.

68. Transcript of *End of Empire*.

69. E. Thomas, p. 108; Woodhouse, pp. 118–19.

70. Smith, *OSS*, p. 193; Richard W. Cottam, 'Nationalism is a phenomenon of mass politics in the era of the nation state'. During 1956–8, Cottam was CIA political officer in the US embassy in Tehran.

71 & 72. Lapping, p. 218; I, 15.3.97; Taheri, p. 29; Blum, p. 70.

73. Kermit Roosevelt, *Countercoup: The Struggle for Control of Iran*, McGraw-Hill, US, 1979, p. 107. Sir George Clutton was a homosexual whose posting to Warsaw as ambassador made him a vulnerable target for blackmail. He later came under suspicion though MI5 investigations did not get very far as Clutton died not long after the investigations had begun. West, *Friends*, p. 149.

74. Senate investigations in the seventies into ties between the CIA and Schroeders were quickly terminated (Tully, *CIA*, p. 81).

75. John McCloy, President of Chase Manhattan, negotiated the most important aspect of the Saudi 50-50 oil agreement which turned out to be the special tax arrangements. Eveland, pp. 90–1 & 141–2; Mosley, p. 339; Roosevelt, *Countercoup*, p. 48.

76. PRO FO 371/104613; 371/104257, 22.5.53; 371/104528, 15.6.53.

77. Bill/Louis, p. 9; Roosevelt, *Countercoup*, p. 123.

78. Gasiorowski, pp. 72–3; Rubin, p. 280; transcript of *End of Empire*.

79. Hiro, p. 53; Villiers, p. 151; Woodhouse, p. 121.

80. Taheri, p. 34; James A. Bill, 'The politics of intervention', in Bill/Louis, p. 275.

81. David Carlton, *Anthony Eden: A Biography*, Allen Lane, 1981, pp. 327–8.

82. Donald N. Wilbur, *Adventures in the Middle East: Excursions and Incursions*, Darwin, US, 1986, pp. 115, 149–50 & 185. Miles Copeland, *The Game Player: Confessions of the CIA's Original Political Operative*, Aurum Press, 1989, pp. 187–90.

83. Gasiorowski, p. 74; Eveland, p. 118; Mader, p. 201.

84. James A. Bill, *The Eagle and the Lion: The Tragedy of American/Iranian Relations*, Yale University Press, US, 1988, p. 87; Gasiorowski, p. 72.

85. I. Davrupania, 'The 1953 Coup', *Ittalia 'at*, 19.8.79.

86. *Ittalia 'at*, 29.7.53.

87. Laing, p. 128; Bloch/Fitzgerald, p. 111; Mosley, p. 327; Cottam, p. 282; Katuzian, pp. 183–4.

88. The role of MI6 in the Afshartus murder is described in the *Iran Times*, 31.5.85; Pennington interview with Love.

89. Taheri, p. 34; Bill in Bill/Louis, p. 275; Prados, p. 96.

90. Wilbur, p. 188; Roosevelt, *Countercoup*, p. 135; David Wise and Thomas B. Ross, *The Espionage Establishment*, Bantam (pbk), US, 1967, p. 81; G, 28.7.80.

91. Dr Ray S. Cline, *The CIA under Reagan, Bush and Casey*, Acropolis, US, 1981, pp. 146–7.

92. Wilbur, pp. 9 & 189; Prados, p. 95.

93. Roosevelt, *Countercoup*, p. 4; Bill/Louis, p. 190; Brands, p. 280; Prados, p. 95.

94–96. *Twentieth Century*, Aug. 1953; Woodhouse, pp. 125–6; G, 2.1.84.

97. *Different Drummer*, BBC2, 5.8.91.

98. Presumably the same procedure held for IRD material. Wilbur, pp. 188–9; Gasiorowski; transcript of *End of Empire*.

99 & 100. Nicknamed 'the Whistler', Meade had previously worked for the Office of

Special Operations' Near East Division on a number of missions, including the ousting of Syria's President Shukri Quwatli in 1948. Villiers, pp. 178–9; Princess Soraya, *My Autobiography*, Arthur Barker, 1963, p. 134; Miles Copeland, *The Real Spy World*, Sphere (pbk), 1980, pp. 126 & 242–3; O, 26.5.85.

101. Laing, p. 131; Gasiorowski.

102 & 103. *Niru-yi Sevvum*, Tehran, 14.8.53; Katouzian, p. 189.

104. McClure to Jackson, 14.9.53, Robert McClure folder, Eisenhower Library.

105 & 106. Taheri, pp. 34 & 279; Laing, pp. 133–4; Fred Halliday, *Arabia without Sultans*, Penguin, 1974, p. 70; Villiers, p. 188.

107 & 108. Wilbur, p. 189; Fardust; E. Thomas, p. 109, quoting 'Clandestine Services History 208: Overthrow of Premier Mossadeq of Iran, Nov 1952–Aug 1953' (CIA). A consolidated account of the coup, *The Battle for Iran*, was written by Donald Wilbur. The main section, part three, dealing with the coup, is blacked out in the version available under the Freedom of Information Act. Roosevelt, *Countercoup*, p. 120.

109. Brands, pp. 283–7.

110. Gasiorowski, p. 77; Wilbur, p. 189; Shahrough Akhavi, 'The role of the clergy', in Bill/Louis, p. 113.

111. Kenneth Love, 'The American Role in the Pahlevi Restoration on 19 August 1953', presented to Prof. T.C. Young, spring 1960. He claimed that he, unwittingly, helped the CIA during the coup (NYT, 26.9.80). The document shows that he knew a great deal about CIA activities in Iran which he failed to report, the result, he said, of 'misguided patriotism'. *Counterspy*, Vol. 4, No. 4, Sept./Oct. 1980.

112. Verrier, p. 108; Taheri, p. 36.

113. William Blum, *The CIA: A Forgotten History*, Zed Press, 1986, p. 72; Lapping, p. 268; Gasiorowski, p. 78.

114. Katouzian, p. 191.

115. Shahrough Akhavi, *Religion and Politics in Contemporary Iran*, University of New York, NY, 1980, p. 69.

116. Gasiorowski, p. 79; Taheri, p. 35.

117. Brands, p. 287; Gasiorowski; Katouzian, p. 193.

118. Wilbur, p. 189.

119. Brands, p. 288; Copeland, *Game Player*, pp. 190–1; Stephen Ambrose, *Eisenhower: The President 1952–69*, Allen & Unwin, 1984, p. 129.

120. Prados, p. 97.

121. Taheri, p. 40; Cottam, p. 229.

122. Taheri, p. 36; Verrier, p. 108; Andrew, *Secret Service*, p. 494.

123. BEDAMN's principal agents Nerren and Ciley emigrated to the US. *Wall Street Journal*, 6.11.79; Gasiorowski, p. 128; Mosley, p. 327.

124. Obit. T, 2.4.70; Grose, pp. 501–2.

125. I, 15.3.97; G, 2.1.84.

126. McClure.

127. Zahedi's security forces 'discovered' a large Tudeh network of '458 officers' who reported to an intelligence officer in the Soviet embassy. They were uncovered following a routine traffic accident involving a Tudeh courier, who was carrying coded documents listing the names of all the network members. An Iranian intelligence unit was able to decode these documents without the aid of CIA code-breakers. It seems an unlikely explanation. Brands, p. 292; Gasiorowski, pp. 89–92.

128. Peter Avery, *Modern Iran*, Ernest Benn, 1967, p. 447.

129. Wilbur, p. 190; Anthony Cavendish, *Inside Intelligence*, 1990, p. 130.

130. Roosevelt left official government service in 1958 to become vice-president responsible for government relations at Gulf Oil, but retained his ties to the CIA. The Rashidian business deals involving military sales later came under the scrutiny of US Senate hearings during 1976. Brands, p. 292; Pisani, p. 125; Bill/Louis, pp. 95 & 473.

131. Taheri, pp. 40–1; Mosley, p. 327.

132. Verrier, p. 99; Woodhouse, p. 122; Nigel John Ashton, *Eisenhower, Macmillan and the Problem of Nasser: Anglo-American Relations and Arab Nationalism, 1955–59*, Macmillan, 1996, p. 25.

133 & 134. Bower, *Spy*, pp. 184 & 188; Verrier, p. 100; Ranelagh, p. 236.

CHAPTER TWENTY-NINE: SUEZ: ASSASSINS AND THUGGERY

1. Young, *Masters*, pp. 16–17 & 29.

2. Elliott, p. 54.

3. Verrier, p. 124; W. Scott Lucas, *Divided We Stand: Britain, the US and the Suez Crisis*, Hodder, 1991, p. 15.

4. PRO FO 371/102764; Keith Kyle, *Suez*, Weidenfeld, 1991, pp. 48–9; Ashton, p. 61.

5. Lucas, p. 31.

6. Verrier, pp. 124 & 125.

7. Kyle, pp. 42–3. Julian Amery, 'The Suez

Group', in Troen and Shesh (eds), *The Suez-Sinai Crisis in 1956: Retrospective and Reappraisal*, Frank Cass, 1988; McDermott, pp. 146–7 & 213; *The Suez Crisis*, BBC1, 22.10.96; Nutting, p. 22.

8. Brown, *Secret Servant*, p. 472.

9. Kyle, p. 56.

10. Anthony Gorst and W. Scott Lucas, 'The Other Collusion: Operation Straggle and Anglo-American Intervention in Syria, 1955–56', INS, Jul. 1989; Ashton, p. 37.

11. McDermott, p. 123; Roy Fullick and Geoffrey Powell, *Suez: The Double War*, Hamish Hamilton, 1979, p. 6.

12. Kyle, pp. 74–5; Steven Z. Freiberger, *The Rise of American Power in the Middle East, 1953–57*, 1992, p. 126.

13. Joseph Frolick, *The Frolick Defection*, Corgi (pbk), 1976, pp. 72–5; West, *Friends*, p. 102; E, 3.11.55.

14. Lucas, pp. 59 & 62–5; Freiberger, p. 69.

15. Kyle, p. 78; PRO FO 371/115469 V1023/19G.

16. Kyle, p. 84; Eveland, pp. 169–72; Evelyn Shuckburgh, *Descent to Suez*, Weidenfeld, 1986, p. 305.

17. Ashton, p. 59; Cockburn, p. 125.

18. William Clark unpublished diary, 29.11.55, quoted in Kyle, p. 84; PRO FO 371/113738 & 371/113739.

19. McDermott, p. 123; Verrier, p. 128.

20 & 21. Young, *Masters*, p. 29; Lucas, p. 158; Kyle, p. 78; *The Suez Crisis*, BBC1, 22.10.96.

22 & 23. Lucas pp. 70–1, 79–80 & 91; PRO FO 371/12180 V1077/1G.

24. Blake, p. 168.

25. G, 2.5.87; Heikal, pp. 117–18; Faligot/Krop, pp. 114–17.

26. Bower, *Spy*, p. 192.

27. John Pearson, *The Life of Ian Fleming*, Cape, 1966, p. 134.

28. Wright, p. 161.

29 & 32. Pincher, *Trade Is Treachery*, pp. 203–6, and *Inside Story*, p. 90.

30. Dalton Papers, 1941 file; Foot, *Resistance*, p. 224; Wilkinson/Astley, pp. 107–8; Amery, *Approach March*, pp. 240–1; Harris/Paxman, pp. 88–94; Brown, *Secret Servant*, p. 558.

31. Prof. Donald Cameron Watt, DT, 29.7.97.

33. Lapping, p. 261; McDermott, p. 128; DT, 4.6.85; Kyle, p. 96; Shuckburgh diary, 12.3.56.

34. Thomas, pp. 42–4; *The Suez Crisis*, BBC1, 22.10.96; Kyle, p. 69; Verrier, p. 127.

35. Nutting, pp. 34–5. In his book on Suez, Nutting used the word 'removal' but he confirmed in 1985 that the word used by

Eden was 'murdered'. DT, 24.5.85; *End of Empire*, Channel 4, Jun. 1985.

36. Nutting, pp. 33–5; DT, 24 & 25.5.85; Bower, *Spy*, p. 185; M. Smith, p. 121.

37 & 38. DT, 4.6.85; Verrier, pp. 143 & 159; Bower, *Spy*, p. 195.

39–41. Lucas, pp. 12, 109 & 116–17; Kyle, pp. 99–103; Gorst/Lucas in Aldrich; CIA London station to Director CIA, Cable LOND 7064, 1.4.56 (quoted by Lucas); Thomas, p. 28.

42. Bower, *Spy*, p. 139; Young, *Master*, pp. 29 & 127; Verrier, p. 97.

43. *Lobster*, No. 19.

44. DT, 3.9.95; William E. Burrows, *Deep Black: The Secrets of Space Espionage*, Random House, 1988, p. 79.

45. Tom Waldron and James Gleeson, *The Frogmen: The Story of the War-time Underwater Operators*, Pan (pbk), 1950; Marshall Pugh, *Commander Crabb*, Macmillan, 1956.

46. Chapman Pincher, 'Buster Crabb's Last Dive', *UNSOLVED*, No. 24, 1984.

47 & 49. West, *Friends*, pp. 82–5.

48. Elliott, pp. 24–6.

50. Wright, pp. 113–14.

51. G, 7.3.98.

52 & 53. PRO FO 371/118861; Lucas, pp. 102, 118 & 126–7; Verrier, p. 130.

54. Geoffrey McDermott, *The New Diplomacy and Its Apparatus*, Plume, 1973, pp. 141–2.

55. Riley, p. 97; Eveland, p. 177.

56. FRUS XV, Doc. 197, Eden to Eisenhower, 15.5.56.

57. West, *Friends*, pp. 85–6 & 116.

58 & 59. Lucas, pp. 130–1.

60. Nigel West, *GCHQ: The Secret Wireless War 1900–86*, Weidenfeld, 1986, p. 230; James Bamford, *The Puzzle Palace*, Sidgwick, 1983, p. 324; Wright, pp. 82–4, and *The Spycatcher's Encyclopedia of Espionage*, Heinemann, Australia, 1991, pp. 77–8; Lucas, p. 193.

61. Kyle, p. 132.

62. Bower, *Spy*, p. 185; Lucas, p. 142.

63 & 64. Lucas, pp. 132–3 & 143; Tony Shaw, *Eden, Suez and the Mass Media: Propaganda and persuasion during the Suez crisis*, I.B. Tauris, 1996, pp. 59, 119, 129 & 217.

65. Rawnsley; PRO FO 953/169 PB 1045/99A, 21.8.56; 371/125610 JE1681/12, 29.12.56; O, 27.10.96.

66. Dodds-Parker, pp. 102–3 & 115.

67 & 68. Bower, *Spy*, pp. 185–6, 191 & 196; West, *Friends*, p. 86; Kyle, p. 346.

69. Peter Hennessy, 'What the Queen Knew', I, 21.12.94; McDermott, *Eden*, p. 133.

70 & 71. Grose, p. 434; McDermott, *Eden*, pp. 35, 137 & 144–5; Kyle, p. 191.

72. DT, 27.5.85; Verrier, p. 147; Macmillan, *Riding the Storm*, p. 112; Lucas, pp. 158 & 174.

73. *Lobster*, No. 19; Chester Cooper, *The Lion's Last Roar*, 1978, p. 128; Bower, *Spy*, p. 193; Lucas, p. 140.

74. O, 27.10.96.

75. George K. Young, *Who Is My Liege?: A Study of Loyalty and Betrayal in Our Times*, Gentry Books, 1972, pp. 79–81; Xan Fielding, *One Man in His Time: The Life of Lieutenant-Colonel N.L.D. ('Billy') McLean, DSO*, Macmillan, 1990, pp. 104–5.

76. Fielding, pp. 104–5; Kyle, pp. 148–9 & 211.

77. Lucas, pp. 193–5; Kyle, pp. 149–50.

78 & 79. BBC Summary of World Broadcasts, Part IV, No. 435, 24.12.57; Yaacov Caroz (formerly Mossad deputy chief), *The Arab Secret Services*, Corgi (pbk), 1978, pp. 20–2.

80. Brown, p. 473; Bower, *Spy*, pp. 191–2.

81. Lucas, p. 194.

82. McDermott, *Eden*, p. 137; West, *Friends*, pp. 107 & 116.

83. Riley, p. 89; Eric Downton, *Wars without End*, Stoddart, Toronto, 1987, pp. 229 & 341.

84. Swinburn and Zarb were released under amnesty in 1959. Heikal, p. 154; West, *Friends*, p. 103.

85. The Second Secretary at the embassy in Baghdad was also a John McGlashan. Capt. Mohammed Hefex of the Mukhabarat claimed in court that 'the British Embassy's intelligence officer, Oliver St John' had been MI6's mastermind behind the ANA network. Swinburn had been 'running it . . . in permanent contact with St John', who had been a colonial civil servant before joining MI6 in 1948 and had become First Secretary in Cairo in 1953, when the Mukhabarat claimed it had first learned of the network's existence. West, *Friends*, pp. 113–14; Keesings Contemporary Archive, Col. 15679, 1957; O, 12.5.57; Nigel West, *Seven Spies Who Changed the World*, Mandarin (pbk), 1992, p. 206; Riley, p. 94; Bower, *Spy*, p. 189.

86–88. Kyle, pp. 218–19; West, *Friends*, pp. 103–4 & 114. Sayed Amin Mahmoud was sentenced to death; his naval son (and Youseff Hanna) received twenty-five years.

89. Andrew Weir, Jonathan Bloch and Patrick Fitzgerald, 'Sun sets over the other Empire', *The Middle East*, Oct. 1981; Lucas, p. 181.

90. Robin Day, *The Grand Inquisitor*, 1989.

91. Statement made in 1973 in author's possession.

92. Wright, *Spycatcher*, pp. 160–1; DT, 29.5.85; T, 16.3.85.

93. Verrier, p. 159; Wright, *Spycatcher*, pp. 161–2; Harris/Paxman, pp. 213–14 & 260.

94. Faligot/Krop, pp. 114–17.

95. Pincher, *Inside Story*, p. 90, and *Trade Is Treachery*, 205–6: *The Suez Crisis*, BBC1, 22.10.96; Lucas, p. 193.

96–8. Kyle, pp. 238 & 292; Lucas, p. 214; PRO FO 953/1633 P1041/33 & 953/166 P104/75, 10.9.56; Gary D. Rawnsley, 'Overt and Covert: The Voice of Britain and Black Radio Broadcasting in the Suez Crisis, 1956', INS, Vol. 11, No. 3, Jul. 1996.

99 & 100. Lucas, pp. 217–18; Thomas, pp. 106–7; PRO FO 371/128220 VY1015/File.

101. Copeland, *Game Player*, pp. 165–6 & 200–5; Kyle, pp. 103 & 275–8; Eveland, p. 229; Lucas, p. 218.

102. Lucas, p. 219; Grose, p. 433; Bower, *Spy*, pp. 196–7.

103 & 105. PRO FO 371/115954 VY10393/7G; Gorst/Lucas.

104. Baker, *Suez*, p. 67.

106. *Lobster*, No. 19.

107. Bower, *Spy*, pp. 197–8; Young, *Masters*, p. 46.

108. West, *Friends*, p. 111; Verrier, p. 152; Bower, *Spy*, p. 198.

109. Verrier, p. 147; M. Smith, p. 121; Bower, *Spy*, p. 196.

110. Heikal, pp. 169 & 231; G, 2.5.87; Faligot/Krop, pp. 114–17.

112. Said K. Aburish, *Beirut Spy: The St George Hotel Bar*, Bloomsbury, 1990, pp. 155–8.

111. Bower, *Spy*, p. 233.

113. Grose, p. 435; Freiberger, p. 185.

114. Lucas, pp. 241 & 253–4; E. Thomas, p. 143.

115. Dodds-Parker, *Political Eunuch*, pp. 102 & 106–7; McDermott, *Eden*, p. 146; Bower, *Spy*, pp. 194–5; Lucas, pp. 252 & 272.

116. Cooper, p. 159; Kyle, pp. 344–5 & 411; Hersh, p. 395.

117. Lucas, p. 277; Ashton, p. 83.

118. Eisenhower Library, John F. Dulles Paper, Box 5; Lucas, p. 277.

119. Kyle, p. 386; Bower, *Spy*, p. 199.

120. Fullick/Powell, p. 118; Bernard Furgusson, *Trumpet in the Hall, 1930–1958*, Collins, 1971, p. 262.

121. Verrier, pp. 150–4.

122. Kyle, p. 416.

123. Grose, p. 435; Freiberger, p. 185.

124. PRO FO 953/171/P1011/1, 31/12/56; Verrier, p. 124; Fullick/Powell, p. 59.

125. Furgusson, p. 264; Kyle, pp. 239–40; HoL, Vol. 201, Col. 571, 6.2.57; Rawnsley.

126. Kyle, pp. 417–19; *Lobster*, No. 19.

127. Lucas, p. 273; Pincher, *Inside Story*, p. 90; Wright, *Spycatcher*, p. 160.

128. Bower, *Spy*, p. 199; Grose, p. 439; Mosley, p. 417; Chris Pocock, *Dragon Lady: The History of the U-2 Spyplane*, Airlife, 1989, p. 34.

129. I, 21.12.94; *What Has Become of Us*, Channel 4, Dec. 1994.

130. Cooper, p. 197; Bower, *Spy*, pp. 199–200.

131. Kyle, p. 496.

132. Shaw, pp. 83 & 87.

133. Wright, *Spycatcher*, pp. 82–6; Kyle, pp. 455–60 & 486; PRO FO 371/121789.

134. I, 21.12.94; Lucas, p. 305.

135. Elliott, p. 84; *Lobster*, No. 19; Bower, *Spy*, p. 200; Young, *Liege?*, p. 79.

136. Thomas, p. 443; CIA, DCI-2, Vol. 5, pp. 1–38 contains material on the role of American Intelligence in the Suez crisis, made available May 1994 to Evan Thomas.

137 & 138. Ibid, pp. 172–3; Young, *Masters*, pp. 17 & 21; Lucas, p. 312; Healey, p. 173; McDermott, *Eden*, p. 159.

139. E. Thomas, p. 209; Brian Freemantle, *CIA*, Futura (pbk), 1984, pp. 11–12; Miles Copeland, *The Game of Nations*, Simon & Schuster, 1969, p. 202.

140. O, 27.10.96; Lucas, p. 103; Young, *Masters*, p. 39; PRO PREM 11/1138; IoS, 21.11.93.

141. Young, *Masters*, pp. 17–22, 34, 47 & 149.

142. Young, *Liege?*, p. 81; *Lobster*, No. 19.

143. Jeffrey Robinson, *The End of the American Century: Hidden Agendas of the Cold War*, Hutchinson, 1992, p. 113; Alden Hatch, *H.R.H. Prince Bernhard of the Netherlands*, 1962, p. 222; Robert Eringer, *The Global Manipulators: Covert Power Groups of the West*, 1980.

CHAPTER THIRTY: THE MACMILLAN DOCTRINE

1. Nigel John Ashton, *Eisenhower, Macmillan and the Problem of Nasser: Anglo-American Relations and Arab Nationalism, 1955–59*, Macmillan, 1996, pp. 73 & 100–1.

2. Verrier, p. 159; Pincher, *Inside Story*, p. 90; Bloch/Fitzgerald, pp. 125–6; Yaacov Caroz, *The Arab Secret Services*, Corgi (pbk), 1978, pp. 22–3; DT obit., 4.2.97.

3. Eveland, p. 247; Stallwood, OBE, died in 1978. In 1957 the French tried again with the Action Branch landing two agents with a bomb by boat. It was soon realised that they were being followed and the attempt was abandoned. Faligot/Krop, pp. 114–17.

4. Brown, *Treason*, p. 474.

5. Ashton, pp. 73 & 100–1.

6. Young, *Masters*, pp. 21–2; Bower, *Spy*, p. 207.

7 & 8. *Lobster*, No. 19; Archie Roosevelt, *For Lust of Knowing*, Little, Brown, 1988, p. 448; Gasiorowski, pp. 91 & 116–24. GCHQ built a monitoring station near Meshed, close to the Soviet border. SAS personnel were later entrusted with its protection while other personnel 'on loan' to the Iranian military helped train the special forces. Bloch/Fitzgerald, p. 113.

9. Fardust; Cavendish, p. 143; Young, *Liege?*, p. 9.

10. Douglas Little, 'Cold War and Covert Action: The United States and Syria, 1945–1958', *Middle East Journal*, Vol. 44, No. 1, winter 1990; Sulzberger, pp. 410–12; David W. Lesch, *Syria and the United States: Eisenhower's Cold War in the Middle East*, Westview Press, 1992, pp. 109–10 & 125; NS, 6.7.57.

11. Little; Prados, pp. 129–30; Lesch, pp. 138 & 165.

12–18. Ashton, pp. 122–37 & 151–3; Robinson, pp. 233–7, 246 & 257.

19. Caroz, p. 24; Brown, *Secret Servant*, p. 474.

20. Bloch/Fitzgerald, p. 126; Brown, *Treason*, p. 475.

21. Richard M. Bissell, Jr (with Jonathan E. Lewis and Frances T. Pudlo), *Reflections of a Cold Warrior: From Yalta to the Bay of Pigs*, Yale University Press, 1996, p. 116; Bower, *Spy*, pp. 224–5.

22. IoS, 26.1.97; Paul Lashmar, ch. 14, 'The U-2 – The British Story'; Nick Cook, 'How the CIA and RAF Teamed Up to Spy on the Soviet Union', *Jane's Defence Weekly*, 7.8.93.

23. Robinson, pp. 298–9; Pocock, p. 45.

24. Bissell, p. 117.

25. DT, 3.5.90.

26. David Leigh, *High Time: The Life of Howard Marks*, 1986, p. 96.

27. Nigel West, *Falklands*, p. 26.

28. Robin Maugham, who was attached to the Middle East Intelligence Centre during the war, 'lobbied high and low in order to get the authorities to approve the setting up of a centre for teaching Arabic for British personnel'. With the help of Albert Hourani – a long-term MI6 agent – approval was given in mid-1943 for the setting up of MECAS. Bower, *Spy*, p. 219; Verrier, p. 174; Blake, p. 189.

29 & 30. *Lobster*, No. 19.

31. Verrier, p. 170.

32. Halliday, pp. 282–3; Ashton, pp. 123 & 249.

33. Macmillan to Eisenhower, 19.7.57, FRUS, 1955–57, Vol. XIII, pp. 226–7; Macmillan, *Riding the Storm*, pp. 270–7.

34 & 35. David Smiley (with Peter Kemp), *Arabian Assignment*, Leo Cooper, 1979; O, 1.2.89.

36. J.B. Kelly, *Arabia, the Gulf and the West*, Weidenfeld, 1980, p. 117.

37. Smiley, p. 23; obit. of Brig. Dennison T, 17.9.96.

38. Bloch/Fitzgerald, pp. 51 & 135.

39. J.E. Peterson, *Oman in the 20th Century*, Croom Helm, 1978; Col. David de C. Smiley, 'Muscat and Oman', RUSI Journal, Feb. 1960.

40. Dale F. Eickelman and M.G. Dennison, 'Arabizing the Omani Intelligence Services: Clash of Cultures?', *International Journal of Intelligence and Counterintelligence*, Vol. 7, No. 1.

41. Bower, *Spy*, p. 235; Smiley; Tony Geraghty, *Who Dares Wins: The Story of the SAS 1950–1982*, Fontana (pbk), 1981, p. 149.

42 & 43. Auburish, pp. 7 & 192; Bower, *Spy*, p. 234.

44. Robert Fisk, *Pity the Nation: Lebanon at War*, OUP, 1991, pp. 70–1; Erika G. Alin, *The United States and the 1958 Lebanon Crisis: American Intervention in the Middle East*, University Press of America, 1993, pp. 55–9.

45. Bower, *Spy*, pp. 234–5.

46. Robert A. Fernea and W. Roger Louis (eds), *The Iraqi Revolution of 1958: The Old Classes Revisited*, I.B. Tauris, 1991, pp. xv, xvii, 55–7 & 61; Michael Ionides, *Divide and Lose: The Arab Revolt of 1955–1958*, 1966, pp. 188–9.

47. Ashton, p. 165; Verrier, pp. 184–5; *The Middle East*, Oct. 1981; Alin, p. 46.

48. Ashton, pp. 174–5; McDermott, *Eden*, p. 170.

49. Verrier, pp. 175–6.

50. McDermott, *Eden*, pp. 170–1; Aburish, pp. 89–90.

51. Kim Philby in *Kodumma*, Estonia, 13.10.71.

52. Young, *Liege?*, p. 81.

53–55. Verrier, pp. 167, 181 & 186; Ashton, pp. 108–9 & 223–30; Mustafa M. Alani, 'Operation Vantage: British Military Intervention in Kuwait 1961', LAAM, 1990, p. 91.

56 & 57. Bower, *Spy*, p. 236; Verrier, p. 181; Geraghty, *SAS*, p. 150.

58, 59 & 63. Alani, pp. 88–9, 97, 138, 210 & 281. John Christie is referred to in Alani as an unidentified 'senior diplomat'. However, his name is slipped into the notes on p. 267. Identity confirmed by Alani, telephone conversation, July 1997. Verrier, pp. 172–3 & 180–6; Bower, *Spy*, pp. 230 & 235–6.

60. Verrier, pp. 181 & 186; Ashton, pp. 223–9; Alani, p. 91.

61. David Lee, 'The Flight from the Middle East', HMSO, 1981, p. 173; Malcolm Mackintosh, *Strategy and Tactics of Soviet Foreign Policy*, 1962, p. 232.

62. Cabinet papers revealed in I, 2.1.92; Verrier, p. 189.

64. Cabinet papers G, 2.1.92; Alani, pp. 44–5; Harold Macmillan, *Pointing the Way*, Macmillan, 1972, p. 354.

65–67. Alani, pp. 101–9, 179–84, 208 & 228–9; Ashton, pp. 225–6; DT, 28.6.61.

68–70. Alani, pp. 98, 104–6, 159, 173–4, 185 & 223–4; Aburish, pp. 47–8.

71–73. Bower, *Spy*, pp. 235–9, quoting PREM 11/3430; O, 27.10.96; Verrier, p. 171.

74. *Lobster*, No. 19.

CHAPTER THIRTY-ONE: THE MUSKETEERS IN YEMEN

1 & 5. Halliday, pp. 102 & 174.

2. Fred Halliday, 'Counter-Revolution in the Yemen', *New Left Review*, No. 63, Sept./Oct. 1970.

3. Cockburn, p. 127.

4. DT obit. 22.8.96.

6. Alan Hoe, *David Stirling: The Authorised Biography of the Founder of the SAS*, Little, Brown, 1992, p. 358.

7. Around McLean had formed what his biographer, Xan Fielding, also a former SOE and MI6 officer, has called 'an alternative shadow cabinet' of right-wing and pro-imperialist politicians – an incestuous mixture of former intelligence and special forces personnel who conducted their planning in the drawing room of Amery's flat and their favourite watering hole, White's Club. They included Macmillan's son, Maurice, Secretary to the Treasury and ex-Intelligence School No. 9. Maurice's sister married Amery; he married Catherine Ormsby-Gore, whose brother, Lord Harlech, was the ambassador in Washington. Hugh Fraser, ex-I.S. No. 9, was Secretary of State for Air. Another ex-SOE colleague in the circle was Rowly Winn (Baron St Oswald), junior minister, vice-chair of the Central and Eastern European Commission of the European Movement, and chair of the Foreign Affairs Circle. In addition, there were the Hares and the Lennox-Boyds. Bower, *Spy*, pp. 244–5; Downton, pp. 249–53.

8. Julian Amery remarks at the lecture, 'The War in the Yemen', given at RUSI by Col. Neil McLean, 20.10.65; Morris Riley, 'Smiley's People: The SAS Men Return', *Anarchy* magazine, No. 37, winter 1983/4.

9. Halliday, 'Counter-Revolution'; Robin Bidwell, *The Two Yemens*, Longman/ Westview Press, 1983, p. 198.

10. *Lobster*, No. 19.

11. Fielding, p. 131; Kennedy Trevaskis, *Shades of Amber*, Hutchinson, 1968, pp. 186–9.

12. Halliday, *Arabia*, p. 18; Riley, p. 108; Trevaskis, p. 187.

13. E, 27.10.62; Fielding, pp. 132–4; Downton, pp. 331–3.

14. Fielding, pp. 133–5.

15. Bidwell, p. 210; Bower, *Spy*, p. 229.

16. Fielding, pp. 136–9; RUSI, 20.10.65.

17. Cockburn, p. 128; Kelly, pp. 255 & 261.

18 & 19. Bower, *Spy*, pp. 244–7; Riley; PRO PREM 11/4356 & CAB 129/112, 10.1.63.

20. Halliday, *Arabia*, p. 67; Bower, *Spy*, p. 243; Verrier, p. 177.

21. PREM 11/4356, 8.2.63 & 11/4357, 25.2.63.

22. Riley.

23. Halliday, *Arabia*, p. 140; Hoe, p. 367; Fielding, pp. 141–4; Bower, *Spy*, p. 253.

24–28. All three had been party to plans for SAS and SOE operations in Chungking at the end of the war. Hoe, pp. 356–60; General Sir Peter de la Billière, *Looking for Trouble: An Autobiography – from the SAS to the Gulf*, HarperCollins, 1994, pp. 202–3; TO, 21.7.78.

29. Johnny Cooper with Peter Kemp, *One of the Originals: The Story of a Founder Member of the SAS*, Pan (pbk), 1991, pp. 157–9; DT, 4.2.70.

30. Geraghty, *SAS*, p. 116, quoting the *People*,

Aug. 1967; de la Billière, p. 193; Hoe, p. 361.

31. De la Billière, p. 192; Bloch/Fitzgerald, p. 132.

32. A British military mission began training the crack White Army, drawn from pro-Saudi tribes and used for internal repression, which was deployed along the North Yemen border. Hoe, pp. 361–2; Smiley, *Arabian Assignment*, p. 150.

33–35. NS, 28.7.78; Bower, *Spy*, pp. 248–52; Cooper, pp. 166–7; Fielding, p. 145.

36. David Smiley, 'Chemical Clouds Over Yemen', S, 8.9.90; Harris/Paxman, pp. 257 & 263; PRO FO 371/168809, 16.10.63.

37 & 39. Bower, *Spy*, pp. 250–2; de la Billière, p. 209.

38. Smiley, *Arabian Assignment*, p. 161.

40. Cooper, pp. 171–3: de la Billière left in January 1964.

41. T, 25.1.64.

42. Cooper, pp. 171–8; DT, 4.2.70.

43. Riley, 'Smiley's People'; Geraghty, *SAS*, p. 115; Hoe, p. 367; 'Second "Lawrence" Foiled Nasser's Army in Yemen', DT, 4, 5 & 6.2.70.

44 & 45. Smiley, *Arabian Assignment*, p. 166; Cooper, p. 178; Geraghty, *SAS*, pp. 114–15.

46. Hoe, p. 368; TO, 28.7.78; Bower, *Spy*, p. 254.

47. Peter Stiff, *See You in November*, Galago, South Africa, 1985, pp. 37–8.

48. Bower, *Spy*, p. 254; Verrier, p. 255.

49. Halliday, *Arabia*, pp. 116–17; T, 1.2.66.

50. NS, 28.7.78; obit. of Sir Denis Hamilton by Insight writer Bruce Page, I, 14.4.88.

51. HoC, Vol. 699, 20–31.7.64, p. 267; Col. Edgar O'Balance, *The War in the Yemen*, Faber, 1971, p. 127.

52. Fielding, p. 147; DT, 4.2.70.

53. Neil McLean, 'The War in the Yemen', *Journal of the Royal Central Asian Society*, Vol. 51, Part 2, 1964, pp. 102–11; Riley, 'Smiley's People'.

54. Fielding, p. 148.

55. Nigel West, *A Matter of Trust: MI5 1945–72*, Coronet (pbk), 1983, pp. 167–8; Bloch/ Fitzgerald, p. 126.

56. Hoe, p. 367.

57. Bloch/Fitzgerald, p. 130; Halliday, *Arabia*, pp. 60–1.

58. Geraghty, *SAS*, pp. 115–16; Cockburn, p. 129.

59. Gasiorowski, pp. 124–5; Bower, *Spy*, pp. 348–9.

60. Riley, 'Smiley's People'; Cockburn, pp. 130 & 133.

61. Dorril/Ramsay, p. 366.
62. Hoe, pp. 365 & 372.
63. Smiley, *Arabian Assignment*, p. 203;
Halliday, *Arabia*, p. 70.
64. Bower, *Spy*, pp. 348–9.
65. Bidwell, p. 159. Bidwell served in Field
Security in Egypt and Germany and then
(1955–9) as a Political Officer in the Western
Aden Protectorate. Later Secretary/Librarian
of the Middle East Centre, Cambridge
University. Halliday, *Arabia*, pp. 203–7.
66. Halliday, *Arabia*, p. 175; Bloch/Fitzgerald,
p. 133.
67. *Le Monde*, 16.5.67; Michael Asher,
Thesiger: A Biography, Viking, 1994, pp. 474–
5; Wilfred Thesiger, *Desert, Marsh and
Mountain: The World of the Nomad*, Collins,
1979, p. 270.
68. Bower, *Spy*, pp. 254 & 349; *Lobster*,
No. 19.
69. Thesiger, p. 274; Cockburn, p. 128;
Halliday, *Arabia*, p. 143.
70. Stiff, p. 57.
71. Fielding, p. 155.

PART SEVEN: MODERN TIMES

CHAPTER THIRTY-TWO: THE SECRET INTELLIGENCE SERVICE

1. Blake, p. 182.
2 & 3. Bower, *Spy*, pp. 258–9.
4. Jerrold L. Schecter and Peter S. Deriabin,
*The Spy Who Saved the World: How a Soviet
Colonel Changed the Course of the Cold War*,
Scribner, NY, 1992, pp. 35–6; Bower, *Spy*,
p. 273; Blake, p. 184; David Wise, *Molehunt:
The Secret Search for Traitors that Shattered the
CIA*, Random House, NY, 1992, p. 55.
5. Blake, pp. 194–205; Elliott, p. 13.
6. Bower, *Spy*, pp. 266–71.
7 & 8. Jerrold/Deriabin, pp. 44–6, 59, 93,
264–5 & 351–4; Wise, p. 117.
9. Bower, *Spy*, pp. 277–8; Jerrold/Deriabin,
p. 193; Deacon, 'C', p. 131.
10. Jerrold/Deriabin, p. 204; McDermott,
Eden, pp. 179–80.
11. Jerrold/Deriabin, pp. 196, 262 & 286–7.
In Paris, MI6 officer Roger King was used as
contact. King had served in Bucharest in the
late forties and then Paris, retiring in 1972 as
an international security consultant and
adviser on security at airports (DM, 25.5.78).

12 & 14. Jerrold/Deriabin, pp. 294–5, 334 &
347.
13. Bower, *Spy*, p. 280.
15. Richard Lamb, *The Macmillan Years 1957–
63: The Emerging Truth*, John Murray (pbk),
1995, p. 356, quoting Bundy Oral History
interview in JFK Library; Alastair Horne,
Macmillan 1957–86, Macmillan, 1989,
pp. 382–3; Cavendish, pp. 117–18; telephone
conversation with Cavendish, 7.1.98; Deacon,
'C', p. 134.
16. Deacon, 'C', p. 135; Michael R. Beschloss,
*Kennedy v. Khrushchev: The Crisis Years 1960–
63*, Faber, 1991, p. 477.
17. Powers, p. 101; Burrows, pp. 100–7.
18. Andrew, *Secret Service*, p. 497;
McDermott, *Eden*, p. 213; *The Profession of
Intelligence*, Part 4, Radio 4, 23.8.81; Pincher,
Inside Story, p. 38.
19. Jerrold/Deriabin, p. 352; Andrew, *Secret
Service*, p. 497; Joseph B. Smith, *Portrait of a
Cold Warrior*, Ballantine (pbk), US, 1981,
pp. 148–9; Bower, *Spy*, pp. 311 & 317–18;
Cavendish, p. 8.
20. Smith, pp. 139 & 157; E. Thomas, p. 156.
21. PRO FO 371/100839 & 100847; Greenhill,
pp. 84, 88–9.
22. Cavendish, p. 7; Young, *Masters*, pp. 30 &
71.
23. Obit. of Michael Wrigley, DT, 17.1.95.
24 & 25. Crozier, p. 20; O, 26.4.87; obits of
Lancaster and Lt Cmndr Myles Osborn, DT,
23.1.92 & 22.5.97.
26. Smith, p. 199; Susan L. Carruthers,
*Winning Hearts and Minds: British
Governments, the Media and Colonial Counter-
Insurgency 1944–1960*, 1995, pp. 93 & 102–3.
27. Obit. of Wrigley, DT, 17.1.95.
28. Crozier, pp. 20, 44 & 46; David A.
Charles, 'The Dismissal of Marshal P'eng
Teh-huai', China Quarterly, No. 8, 1961.
29. Ray Cline, *The CIA under Reagan, Bush
and Casey*, Acropolis Books, US, 1981, p. 173;
E. Thomas, pp. 277–8.
30. Ranelagh, 1992, p. 802; TLS, 5.4.85;
Bower, *Spy*, p. 314.
31. Crozier, pp. 55–6 & 59.
32. Horne, pp. 291 & 417–18.
33. Cavendish, p. 7.
34. Peter S. Lisowski, 'Intelligence Estimates
and US Policy Toward Laos, 1960–63', INS,
Vol. 6, No. 2, Apr. 1991.
35–37. Cabinet papers release, ST, 1.1.95 &
G, 2.1.95; Dorril/Ramsay, pp. 56, 80–3 & 110.
38. Brian Crozier, *South-East Asia in Turmoil*,
Penguin (pbk), 1965, p. 91.

39. Healey telephone call, 31.3.94. Karl Peiragostini, *Britain, Aden and South Arabia: Abandoning Empire*, Macmillan, 1991, p. 13.
40. Peiragostini, p. 135; Bower, *Spy*, p. 340.
41. Bower, *Spy*, pp. 329 & 355.
42. Brian Toohey and William Pinwill, *Oyster: The Story of the Australian Secret Intelligence Service*, 1989, pp. 96–7; Christopher Andrew, 'The Growth of the Australian Intelligence Community and the Anglo-American Connection', INS, Vol. 4, No. 2, Apr. 1989.
43. *The Ecologist*, Vol. 26, No. 5, Sept./Oct. 1996; O, 28.7.96; Mark Curtis, *The Ambiguities of Power; British Foreign Policy since 1945*, Zed Books (pbk), 1996.
44. Toohey/Pinwill, pp. 89–90; Barry Petersen (with John Cribbin), *Tiger Men: An Australian Soldier's Secret War in Vietnam*, Macmillan, Melbourne, 1988, pp. 167–8.
45. Peer de Silva, *Sub Rosa: The CIA and the Uses of Intelligence*, NYT Books, US, 1978, p. 225; Richard Stubbs, *Hearts and Minds in Guerrilla Warfare: The Malayan Emergency 1948–1960*, OUP, 1989.
46. Terence Strong, *Whisper Who Dares*, Coronet (pbk), 1982; Peter Dickens, *SAS: The Jungle Frontier*, Arms & Armour, 1983; Roger Faligot, *The Kitson Experiment*, Zed (pbk), 1983, references to the SAS and Vietnam.
47. Stiff, p. 54; Adrian Weale, *Secret Warfare: Special Operations Forces from the Great Game to the SAS*, Hodder, 1995, pp. 199–200.
48. Stephen Merret, 'British help to US in Vietnam', *Red Camden*, Apr./May 1969; *Lobster*, No. 4, 1984.
49 & 50. Verrier, pp. 114 & 174; Bower, *Spy*, pp. 220–3; *Lobster*, Nos 19 & 27; Young, *Subversion*, p. 102; Stephen R. Weissman, *American Foreign Policy in the Congo 1960–1964*, Cornell University Press, US, 1974.
51 & 52. Anthony Verrier, *The Road to Zimbabwe 1890–1980*, Cape, 1986, pp. 85–7, 112–13 & 335; *Covert Action*, No. 4, Apr./May 1979; Fred Bridgland, *Jonas Savimbi: A Key to Africa*, Coronet (pbk), 1988, pp. 70–1.
53. Bower, *Spy*, pp. 346–7; Bloch/Fitzgerald, pp. 151–5.
54. Bower, *Spy*, pp. 336–7; Crozier, *Free Agent*, p. 56; Lord Egremont, *Women and Children First*, Macmillan, 1968.
55–57 & 59. Philip H.J. Davies, 'Organizational Politics and the Development of Britain's Intelligence Producer/Consumer Interface', INS, 1997.
58. West, *Friends*, p. 167.

60 & 61. Bower, *Spy*, pp. 344–7; McDermott, *Eden*, p. 213.
62. Release of Cabinet documents, G. 17.4.97; Peiragostini, pp. 162 & 170.
63. Dorril/Ramsay, p. 98.
64, 65 & 68. Bower, *Spy*, pp. 317 & 358–61.
66. DNB 1981–5.
67 & 69. Greenhill, p. 127; David Owen, *Time to Declare*, Penguin, 1992, p. 132; Andrew, *Secret Service*, p. 498; Bower, *Spy*, p. 363; *File on Four*, BBC Radio 4, 11.8.82.
70 & 71. Richard J. Aldrich, ' "The Value of Residual Empire": Anglo-American Intelligence Co-operation in Asia after 1945', in Richard J. Aldrich and Michael F. Hopkins (eds), *Intelligence, Defence and Diplomacy: British Policy in the Post-War World*, 1994, pp. 226–8.

CHAPTER THIRTY-THREE: THE LAST OF THE COLONIAL WARS

1. David Charters, 'The Role of Intelligence Services in the Direction of Covert Paramilitary Operations', in Alfred C. Maurer, Mario D. Tunstall and James M. Keagle (eds), *Intelligence: Policy and Process*, Westview Press, US, 1985; Geraghty, *SAS*, pp. 150–1; information to Morris Riley from Brig. Akehurst, summer 1985, and Capt. Sir Ranulph Twisleton-Wykeham-Fiennes, 1976.
2 & 3. Charters; Halliday, *Arabia*, p. 287.
4. T, 17.9.96; Ranulph Fiennes, *Where Soldiers Fear to Tread*, 1979, p. 240, refers to 'Tom Greening' instead of Landon. *New Africa*, Oct. 1979.
5 & 6. John Townsend, *Oman: The Making of a Modern State*, Croom Helm, 1977, pp. 74–5. Townsend was (1972–5) economic adviser to the Oman government. DT, 24.4.70; E, 18.7.70. Information on MD from Shell House, London, to Riley. J.E. Peterson, *Oman in the 20th Century*, Croom Helm, 1978, pp. 201–2; TO, 5.10.75.
7. Bloch/Fitzgerald, p. 137; Morris Riley, 'The Secret 1970 British Intelligence Coup in Oman' (unpub.), 1997.
8. Halliday, *Arabia*, p. 288.
9. G, 27 & 28.7.70; FT, 12.12.70.
10. Peterson, p. 78.
11. Two interesting books on the later period in Oman are by Maj.-Gen. Ken Perkins, who was seconded to Oman to command the SAF in 1975. *A Fortunate Soldier* (Brassey's, 1988) was censored by the MoD. *Khalida* (Quartet,

1993) is a fictionalised account of the censored bits, including MI6 involvement in the war against the guerrillas – sending planes across the border into South Yemen to bomb artillery without the consent of Whitehall – and secret arms sales to Iran. T, 3.8.70; O News Service, 12.8.70; Maurice Tugwell, *Revolutionary Propaganda and Possible Countermeasures*, PhD thesis, Department of War Studies, University of London, 1979.

12. Patrick Seale and Maureen McConville, *The Hilton Assignment*, Temple Smith, 1973; Halliday, *Arabia*, p. 297.

13. Finkelstein.

14. Hastings's friend, Penelope Tremayne, an *Observer* correspondent living in Lawrence Durrell's house in Cyprus in the fifties, was a freelance journalist for the RUSI Journal and Brassey's Annual in the mid-seventies and wrote a series of articles on the Oman campaign. David Lynn Price, Conflict Studies No. 53, 'Oman Insurgency and Development', Institute for the Study of Conflict, 1975. Former Army Intelligence officer and IRD officer with Forum World Features, Price was later an analyst on Middle East Affairs and editor of *Arab Oil*. Barry Davies, *The Complete Encyclopedia of the SAS*, Virgin, 1998; O, 25.10.98.

15 & 16. Seale admitted (telephone conversation, 2.12.97) that a former MI6 officer, Denis Rowley, whom he had known in the late fifties and early sixties in Beirut, had been the source. Rowley went on to set up a tourist postcard company in Portugal during the period of the coup. West, *Falklands*, 1996, p. 253.

17–24. Stiff, pp. 67, 73 & 81; Seale/McConville, pp. 65 & 122; Hoe, pp. 410–12; West, *Falklands*, pp. 162–3 & 253; Geraghty, *SAS*, pp. 124–5.

25 & 27. Martin Dillon, *25 Years of Terror: The IRA's War against the British*, Bantam (pbk), 1996, pp. 137 & 140; Verrier, *Looking Glass*, pp. 300–3.

26 & 28–31. Peter Taylor, *Provos: The IRA and Sinn Fein*, Bloomsbury, 1997, pp. 128–9, 137–9 & 146–7; Verrier, *Looking Glass*, pp. 302–9 & 318.

32. Obit. G, 5.1.98; Fred Holroyd (with Nick Burbridge), *War without Honour*, Medium, Hull, 1989, p. 40.

33. Murray, pp. 75–91; Bloch/Fitzgerald, pp. 218–20; Dillon, p. 161.

34. Dillon, pp. 180–1.

35. DNB 1981–5.

36. Deacon, 'C', p. 170; David A. Charters, 'Sir Maurice Oldfield and British Intelligence; Some Lessons for Canada', *Conflict Quarterly*, Vol. 2, No. 3, winter 1982; Davies.

37. Mark Urban, *UK Eyes Alpha: The Inside Story of British Intelligence*, Faber (pbk), 1997, pp. 13–17.

38. *The Profession of Intelligence*, Part Five, BBC Radio 4, 30.8.81.

39. See 'Whitehall Games', Dorril/Ramsay; Davies.

40. Greenhill, p. 181.

41. Cavendish, p. 131.

42. Desmond Harney, *The Priest and the King*, I.B. Tauris, 1997.

CHAPTER THIRTY-FOUR: THE SLOW DEATH OF THE COLD WAR

1. Lawrence Freedman and Virginia Gamba-Stonehouse, *Signals of War: The Falklands Conflict of 1982*, Faber, 1990, pp. 85–6; Lawrence Freedman, 'Intelligence Operations in the Falklands', INS, Vol. 1, No. 3, Sept. 1986; David E. King, 'Intelligence Failures and the Falklands War: A Reassessment', INS, Vol. 2, No. 2, Apr. 1987; Alex Danchev, *Oliver Franks: Founding Father*, Clarendon, Oxford, 1993.

2. G, 23.11.94; press conference to launch the Intelligence Services Bill, Nov. 1993; Urban, pp. 10–11.

3–7. Urban, pp. 4–7, 24, 31, 41, 73 & 288.

8–12. Ibid, pp. 14, 30–1 & 140; Peter Early, *Confessions of a Spy: The Real Story of Aldrich Ames*, Hodder, 1997, pp. 180–5; DT, 15.2.97; James Adams, *The New Spies: Exploring the Frontiers of Espionage*, Pimlico (pbk), 1995, pp. 34–5 & 40.

13 & 14. Urban, pp. 35–7; BBC 1, *Panorama*, 22.11.93; STel, 3.11.96.

15–18. Foreign Secretary Douglas Hurd later suggested that information from MI6 in a Third World country enabled the thwarting of an Iraqi-backed terrorist attack on a Coalition ambassador in Europe. Though, as Mark Urban points out, countries that did not undertake high-profile measures against Arabs did not experience any outbreaks of terrorism either. Urban, pp. 136, 147–50, 157, 163–8, 179 & 223.

19 & 20. Ibid, p. 135; Adams, pp. xvii & 79–84.

21 & 22. S, 19.10.96; O, 30.3.97 & 1.9.96; DT, 17.8.96; ST, 4.8.96; STel, 12.5.96.

23. *Focus*, Jan. 1996; *Der Spiegel*, Nov. 1997; STel, 30.11.97; O, 12.1.97.
24. G, 31.1.96.
25. Urban, p. 198.

CHAPTER THIRTY-FIVE: THE NEW AGENDA

1–3, 5 & 6. Adams, pp. 42, 89, 99–100, 106 & 138–9; Urban, pp. 183, 211, 235 & 259; Peter Gill, 'Reasserting Control: Recent Changes in the Oversight of the UK Intelligence Community', INS, Vol. 11, No. 2, Apr. 1996; T, 23.9.96.
4. G, 6.2.99.
7. SB, 10.11.98.
8–10. Richard Norton-Taylor, *Truth Is a Difficult Concept: Inside the Scott Inquiry*, Fourth Estate (pbk), 1995, pp. 99–107; Richard Norton-Taylor, Mark Lloyd and Stephen Cook, *Knee Deep in Dishonour: The Scott Report and Its Aftermath*, Gollancz (pbk), p. 105; Urban, pp. 121 & 127–8; Adams, p. 139.
11. Norton-Taylor.
12. Adams, pp. 268–9; I, 31.8.94.
13. Urban, p. 119.
14. I, 19.8.94.
15. O, 18.9.94; IoS, 21.4.96.
16. G, 19.1.95.
17 & 18. Urban, pp. 129–32; Adams, p. xiv; G, 8.1.98.
19. ST, 29.3.98; G, 25.3.98; ES, 4.4.98; I, 7.3.98.
20. SB, 10.1.99; I, 25.1.99.
21 & 22. G, 22.1.99; *Jerusalem Post*, 12.9.97; *South News*, 22.8.97; ST, 31.1.99.
23, 25 & 26. Adams, pp. 158–9, 189–90, 237 & 294.
24. G, T & I, 5.2.99.
27. STel, 1.5.94.
28. G, 24.8.96; STel, 21.4.96 & 9.3.97; O, 19.1.97; ST, 11.8.96.
29 & 30. G, 6.2.95 & 13.5.95.
31. ST, 17.11.96.
32. Urban, p. 225; T, 10.1.98; ST, 19.11.95; O, 15.15.96; I, 14.11.98.
33. O, 26.3.95; G, 22.5.96.
34. STel, 2.6.96; ST, 17.11.96; I, 24.3.97.
35 & 36. ST, 17.11.96 & 9.2.97.
37. I, 24.3.97.
38 & 39. O, 2.11.97.
40. Phillip Knightley, 'What Went Wrong:

The Drugs World War, Parts 1–3', IoS, 24.1.98, 1 & 7.2.98.
41. Foreign Affairs Committee, 'Expenditure Plans of the Foreign and Commonwealth Office and the Overseas Development Administration', HMSO, Jul. 1994; G, 21.12.94.
42 & 43. G, 16.7.94; Adams, pp. xi–xii.
44. Urban, pp. 63 & 65; I, 4.12.96; T, 27.1.97.
45. G, 26.3.97; T, quoting Le Point, 17.6.98; ST, 22.11.98.
46. ST, 16.6.96, 20 & 27.9.98; I, 18.3.93.
47. SB, 10.11.98.
48. ST, 14.4.96; G, 15.12.94 & 3.11.98; DT, 2.11.98.
49. I, 14.5.96.
50. O, 2.11.97.

CHAPTER THIRTY-SIX: ON HER MAJESTY'S SECRET SERVICE

1. *Punch*, No. 71, 2.1.99.
2 & 3. SB, 20.12.98 & 24.1.99. Family friend and former Conservative defence procurement minister, Jonathan Aitken, who was an MI6 agent, providing insights into the Saudi royal family and their defence spending plans.
4. SB, 11.10.98.
5. O, 21.11.93; BBC1 *Panorama*, 22.12.93.
6 & 7. ST, 22.9.96, 21.12.97 & 2.8.98.
8. O, 22.12.96.
9 & 10. G, 25.3.98 & 7.10.98; ST, 30.8.98; I, 2.9.98.
11. Adams, p. 101; Urban, pp. 215–16; ST, 22.9.96, 21.12.97 & 2.8.98.
12. G, 20.12.94; T, 10.11.98.
13 & 14. G, 10.8.98; ST & O, 9.8.98.
15 & 16. G, 8.8.98.
17 & 18. SB, 11.10.98; T, 15.11.98.
19. G, 19.12.97; ST, 17.11.96 & 9.1.97; O, 25.10.98.
20 & 21. G, 21.9.96, 20.5 & 8.8.98; O, 16.8.98; *Punch*, 2.1.99.
22. Foreign Secretary Robin Cook has indicated that in future the tribunal route might be allowed. DT, 3.11.98; G, 15.8.98.
23. ST, 31.3.97.
24–26. G, 27.11.97 & 8.8.98.
27. I, 29.8.97.

INDEX